WEST'S
BUSINESS LAW

Text & Cases • Second Edition

WEST'S BUSINESS LAW
Text & Cases   Second Edition

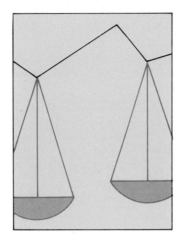

KENNETH W. CLARKSON
Director
Law and Economics Center
and
School of Law
University of Miami

ROGER LeROY MILLER
Law and Economics Center
and
School of Business
University of Miami

GAYLORD A. JENTZ
Herbert D. Kelleher
Professor of Business Law
Chairman, Department of General Business
University of Texas at Austin

WEST PUBLISHING COMPANY
St. Paul   New York   Los Angeles   San Francisco

Library of Congress Cataloging in Publication Data

Clarkson, Kenneth W.
    West's business law.

    Includes index.
    1. Commercial law—United States—Cases.
    2. Business law—United States.
    I. Miller, Roger LeRoy.
    II. Jentz, Gaylord A.
    III. West Publishing Company. IV. Title.
    KF888.C55 1983   346.73'07   82-13542
    ISBN 0-314-69641-5   347.3067

    3rd Reprint—1984

A study guide has been developed to assist you in mastering the concepts presented in the text. The study guide includes a "Things to Keep in Mind" section, an outline of each chapter, a set of fill-in questions (a type of programmed learning device), a set of multiple choice questions, the answers to the fill-in and multiple choice questions, and a new section entitled Uniform CPA Business Law Examination information. This workbook is available from your local bookstore under the title *Study Guide to Accompany West's Business Law: Text and Cases, Second Edition* prepared by Barbara Behr of Bloomsburg University of Pennsylvania.

PREFACE

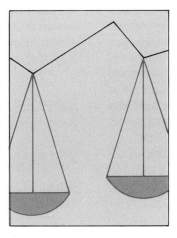

Now, more than ever before, the average business man or woman is practically inundated with possible legal problems. So, too, is the average consumer. We are clearly witnessing a trend in American society in which the law is taking on more importance. It is with this underlying fact in mind that we have written this text. Familiarity with the legal process and specific laws can only benefit today's business student whether or not the student actively pursues a career in the world of commerce. Our purpose in writing this text is to present with maximum accuracy the legal realities facing business men and women of today.

While we cannot dictate how business law should be taught, we can and have attempted to present a text that allows maximum flexibility to the instructor. To that end, you will find this text to be extremely comprehensive. Instructors can choose those areas of the law that they wish to emphasize rather than depending on the authors' personal preferences.

OTHER SPECIAL FEATURES OF THIS TEXT

In addition to being comprehensive and, we believe, accurate, our text provides some unique features for the students and the instructor.

1. *Cases fully integrated:* Cases follow the legal point that they either substantiate or illustrate rather than appearing at the back of each chapter.
2. *Cases have a unique format:* The case cite is fully presented in the margin. *Background and Facts* are first given in italics and then the actual case excerpts are presented in roman face to differentiate them. Following the excerpts is a *Judgment and Remedy* section, again in italics. Finally, in some cases, a *Comments* section follows.
3. *Vocabulary stressed:* Each time a new important term is introduced, it is presented in bold-faced. A further explanation of bold-faced terms

is given in the glossary at the end of the text. The glossary has been expanded by 50 percent in the second edition.

4. *Easy to read and learn from:* The text is written in an easy-to-read manner and is separated into sections by appropriate subheadings of four different levels. This greatly eases the learning process and allows for easier outlining by the student reader.

5. *Case questions and problems:* At the end of each chapter, there are approximately ten questions and case problems. The first five questions are usually hypothetical in nature, centering explicitly on specific areas of law treated in the chapter. The remainder of the questions are actual case problems taken from important cases, for which full and correct cites are given. Complete answers to these end-of-chapter hypothetical problems and case questions are presented in a separately bound booklet. The answers to these end-of-chapter problems and questions constitute a complete review of the law.

NEW CHAPTERS IN THE SECOND EDITION

The first edition of this text included a number of unique chapters that, at that time, were necessary to keep pace with trends in today's law. These chapters covered special partnerships (including limited partnerships), private franchises, trusts, wills, and estates, and others. In this edition, we have added four new chapters.

- Chapter 4   Torts Related to Business
- Chapter 45   Corporations — Financial Regulation and Investor Protection
- Chapter 51   Antitrust: Enforcement and Trends
- Chapter 52   Employment and Labor Relations Law

LEGAL ENVIRONMENT OF BUSINESS

The legal environment unit has been expanded to include torts related to business. New materials have been added to already existing chapters in this unit. Additionally, the unit on government regulation has been expanded and now includes the following:

- Regulation and Administrative Agencies
- Consumer Protection
- Environmental Protection
- Antitrust: Statutes and Exemptions
- Antitrust: Enforcement and Trends
- Employment and Labor Relations Law

THE QUESTION OF ETHICS

The teaching of ethics as an integral part of the introductory courses in business law is becoming common practice throughout the United States. Additionally, accreditation committees now usually require inclusion of a minimum of ethical considerations in an introductory business law course. To satisfy this requirement and the increased interest in the question of ethics, we have added nine separate sections on ethics. These specially prepared sections are found at the end of each of the nine units in the text. Not intended as a course in ethics, these sections are designed to elicit comment and discussion from the student reader. We end each of these sections with a set of sample discussion questions.

APPENDICES

Since most students keep their business law text as a future reference source, we decided to include a full set of appendices. They are as follows:

A   How to Brief a Case
B   The United States Constitution
C   The Uniform Commercial Code, fully updated
D   The Uniform Partnership Act
E   The Uniform Limited Partnership Act
F   The Revised Uniform Limited Partnership Act
G   The Model Business Corporation Act

Appendices A & B are new to this edition. Where appropriate, references to these various appendices, including the new ones, are given throughout the text.

SUPPLEMENTAL MATERIALS

We realize that most business law teachers face a difficult task in finding the time to teach all of the materials they are required to teach during each term. Therefore, we have developed, with several colleagues, supplementary materials which will ease both the students' and instructors' jobs.

Study Guide to Accompany WEST'S BUSINESS LAW, Second Edition

Professor Barbara Behr of Bloomsburg University of Pennsylvania has put together what we believe to be the most comprehensive, informative, and helpful Study Guide for business law students that exists. It is directly aimed at allowing the student to comprehend not only "black letter" law, but also some of the subtleties behind the legal process. Basically, though, it is designed to allow the student to comprehend each chapter in such a way that exam time will not be a moment of panic. The Study Guide contains:

1. A "things to keep in mind" section.
2. An outline of the chapter.
3. A set of fill-in questions (a type of programmed learning device).
4. A set of multiple choice questions.
5. The answers to the fill-in and multiple choice questions.
6. A new section entitled Uniform CPA Business Law Examination Information.

Instructor's Manual and Test Bank

In this edition, there is a fully revised Instructor's Manual prepared by Professor Frank Forbes of the University of Nebraska, Omaha. The Instructor's Manual contains the following materials:

1. Major chapter concepts with notes for classroom lectures.

2. Practical teaching suggestions.
3. Questions for the student designed to stimulate classroom discussion.
4. Full notes on all cases excerpted within each chapter, including potential classroom discussion questions.
5. A full set of test questions, including approximately 1,000 multiple choice questions with answers and approximately the same number of true/false questions with answers.
6. Additional information to help students who are taking the course in preparation for the CPA examination.

Legal Business Forms

A separate booklet of approximately forty often-used sample forms is also available.

ACKNOWLEDGMENTS FOR THE FIRST EDITION

Barbara Behr, Bloomsburg University of Pennsylvania; Robert Staaf, Daniel E. Murray, Richard A. Hausler, Irwin Stotzky, Patrick O. Gudridge, all of the University of Miami School of Law; William Auslen, San Francisco City College; Donald Cantwell, University of Texas at Arlington; Frank Forbes, University of Nebraska; Bob Garrett, American River College-California; Thomas Gossman, Western Michigan University; Charles Hartman, Wright State University-Ohio; Telford Hollman, University of Northern Iowa; Robert Jesperson, University of Houston; Susan Liebeler, Loyola University; Robert D. McNutt, California State University-Northridge; Roger E. Meiners, Texas A & M University; Gerald S. Meisel, Bergen Community College-New Jersey; James E. Moon, Meyer, Johnson & Moon-Minneapolis; Bob Morgan, Eastern Michigan University; Arthur Southwick, University of Michigan; Raymond Mason Taylor, North Carolina State; Edwin Tucker, University of Connecticut; Gary Victor, Eastern Michigan University; Gary Watson, California State University, Los Angeles.

ACKNOWLEDGMENTS FOR THE SECOND EDITION

Numerous individuals throughout the country offered help and criticism on both the first edition text and the numerous drafts of the second edition prepared throughout the last several years. In particular, we had help from the following individuals at the University of Miami: Robert Staaf, Kenneth Burns, Judith Kenney, Thomas Crane; and from the University of Texas at Austin: Sylvia A. Spade, David A. Escamilla, Peyton J. Paxson, and JoAnn W. Hammer.

Frank S. Forbes of the University of Nebraska-Omaha, the author of the Instructor's Manual and Test Bank, offered numerous comments and criticisms throughout the entire production of the second edition. To him we owe a special note of thanks.

We also received comments from the following professors: Jeffrey E. Allen, University of Miami; Raymond August, Washington State University; David L. Baumer, North Carolina State; Barbara E. Behr, Bloomsburg University of Pennsylvania; William J. Burke, University of Lowell-Massachusetts; Robert Chatov, State University of New York-Buffalo; Larry R. Curtis, Iowa State University; Gerard Halpern, University of Arkansas; June A. Horrigan, California State University-Sacramento; John P. Huggard, North Carolina State; John W. McGee, Southwest Texas State University; Robert D. McNutt, California State University-Northridge; Thomas E. Maher, California State University-Fullerton; David Minars, Brooklyn College-New York; Joan Ann Mrava, Los Angeles Southwest College; Thomas L. Palmer, Northern Arizona University; Charles M. Patten, University of Wisconsin-Oshkosh; Arthur D. Wolfe, Michigan State University.

Finally, a special note of thanks is in order to Mary Gilmore for typing, editing, and managing the monumental task of keeping all of the work in order throughout the entire production process of this book.

As always, any remaining errors in the text are solely our responsibility. We welcome comments from all users of this text, for it is by incorporating such comments that we can make it an even better one in future editions.

CONTENTS IN BRIEF

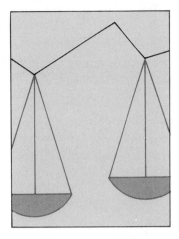

CONTENTS

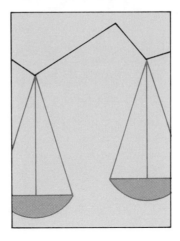

UNIT II
Contracts

UNIT III
Personal Property and Bailments

UNIT V
Creditors' Rights and Bankruptcy

UNIT VI
Agency and Employment

UNIT VII
Business Organizations

TABLE OF CASES

The principal cases are in italic type. Cases cited or discussed are in roman type.

xix

WEST'S BUSINESS LAW

Test & Cases • Second Edition

UNIT I

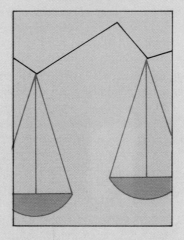

THE LEGAL ENVIRONMENT OF BUSINESS

CHAPTER 1

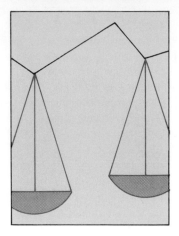

Introduction to the
Study of Law

Law has developed because individuals and society need certain standards that govern relationships among individuals and between people and their government. Law works within a social order containing numerous activities, among which are business activities. Thus, the study of law includes the impact of law on business activities. The rules, or laws, to be described exist as an expression of the standards set by society.

WHAT IS LAW?

Oliver Wendell Holmes contended that law was a set of rules that allowed one to predict how a court would resolve a particular dispute—"the prophecies of what the courts will do in fact, and nothing more pretentious, are what I mean by the law." Aristotle saw law as a rule of conduct. Plato believed law was a form of social control.

Cicero contended that law was the agreement of reason and nature, the distinction between the just and the unjust. The British jurist Sir William Blackstone described law as "a rule of civil conduct prescribed by the supreme power in a state, commanding what is right, and prohibiting what is wrong."

There have been and will continue to be different definitions of law. We can begin to understand something about the nature of law by looking at two approaches to the study of it. The *traditional approach* sees law as a body of principles and rules that courts apply in deciding disputes. The study of law is the study of these rules and the general principles of right and wrong on which the rules are based. Reason and logic tell how the rules should be applied in specific cases. The traditional approach is based on the idea that the principles of right and wrong change, if at all, less rapidly than society changes. This approach fulfills one of the important functions of law—to provide stability, predictability, and continuity so that people can be sure of how to order their affairs.

The *environmental approach* sees law as only one part of the total environment of society. Law is the institution that specializes in social control, and other parts of society act upon and influence it. Studying the process by which the broader society shapes the rules to govern itself is part of the study of law. In the legal world this approach is known as sociological jurisprudence. The environmentalist emphasizes how social change is accomplished by using the legal system and how law functions to provide an orderly process for social change. The environmentalist believes that if law fails to adapt to changes in technology, attitude, and organization, social change may become violent.

Most of the material in this book takes the traditional approach. It presents the rules of law that apply to the business world and the principles on which they are based. Remember, however, that outside forces in the environment *do* shape the rules. The interplay between logic and social pressure and the tension between stability and change act on law and the courts.

SCHOOLS OF LEGAL, OR JURISPRUDENTIAL, THOUGHT

The court opinions in this book show that judges often refer to custom, logic, history, or a philosophy of what is right in making a decision. Sometimes, however, they may seem to ignore custom and history, to stretch their logic to the breaking point, and to depart from previous notions of what is right. Law is often shaped by "legal reasoning"—reasoning that is employed by a judge to achieve justice in an individual case but that is apparently inconsistent with prior decisions. It would be easy to shrug one's shoulders, say "that's legal reasoning," and dismiss the majority of judges as illogical or dishonest. However, there are reasons for deciding a case one way as opposed to another. Part of the study of law, or **jurisprudence,** is discovering what these reasons are.

All legal philosophers agree that custom, history, logic, and ideals have influenced the de-

velopment of law in some way. They disagree, however, on the importance that each of these influences should have in shaping law, and their disagreements have produced different schools, or philosophies, of jurisprudence.

The Natural Law School

The natural law philosopher assumes that there is an ideal state of being, either inherent in the nature of humanity or derived from a divine source. This ideal state, or *natural law,* presupposes a definite right and wrong. The purpose of a legal system is to help society approach the ideal of natural law. People do not create this natural law; they discover it through the use of reason and the knowledge of good and evil. The natural law school emphasizes ethics as the source of law's authority. It uses basic philosophical values to make legal decisions. Documents such as the Magna Carta, the Declaration of Independence, the U.S. Constitution, and the U.N. Declaration of Human Rights reflect natural law ideals in phrases like: "We hold these truths to be self-evident, that all men are created equal, that they are endowed by their Creator with certain inalienable Rights *   *   *."

The Historical School

The historical school emphasizes the evolutionary process of law. It concentrates on the origin and history of the legal system and looks to the past to discover what the principles of contemporary law should be. The legal principles that have withstood the passage of time—those that have worked in the past—are deemed best suited for shaping present laws. Thus, law develops in and with the social environment. Law's legitimacy and authority come from adhering to the principles that historical development has shown to be workable. Followers, or adherents, of the historical school are more likely than those of other schools to strictly follow decisions that have been presented in past cases.

The Analytical School

The analytical school uses logic to shape law. A legal analyst examines the structure and subject matter of a legal code and uses logical analysis to extract the principles that underlie it. By analyzing cases and rules, analysts formulate general principles, and these principles become the starting points for legal reasoning. Individual laws are judged on the basis of whether they are in logical agreement with these starting points.

The Legal Realists

Legal realism is based on the idea that law is shaped by social forces and is an instrument of social control. It stresses the pragmatic and empirical sides of law. Legal realists see law as a means to a social end, and they desire to predict and influence lawmaking. They believe that despite moral law, historical development, and logical analysis, the same conclusion will not always follow from the same set of facts. A reviewing court may view facts differently than a lower court. For the legal realist, the legitimacy of law and of legal institutions is measured by how well they serve the needs of society.

HISTORY AND SOURCES OF AMERICAN LAW

Because of our colonial heritage, much of American law is based on the English legal system. Without a knowledge of this heritage, one cannot understand the nature of our legal system today.

The Establishment of Courts of Law

In 1066 the Normans conquered England, and William the Conqueror and his successors began the process of unifying the country under their rule. One of the means they used to this end was the establishment of the king's court. Before the Conquest, disputes had been settled locally according to local custom. The king's court sought to establish a common or uniform set of customs for the whole country. The body of rules that evolved under the king's court, called *Curia Regis*, was the beginning of the *common law*. As the number of courts and cases increased, the more important decisions of each year were gathered together and recorded in year books.

Judges, settling disputes similar to ones that had been decided before, used the year books as the basis for their decisions. If a case was unique, judges had to create new laws, but they based their decisions on the general principles suggested by earlier cases. The body of judge-made law that developed under this system is still used today and is known as the **common law**.

Stare Decisis

The practice of deciding new cases with reference to former decisions eventually became a cornerstone of the English and American judicial systems. It forms a doctrine called ***stare decisis*** ("to stand on decided cases"). It means that judges attempt to follow the *precedent* established by the decisions of the past.

The rule of *stare decisis* performs many useful functions. First, it helps the courts to be more efficient. It would be very time-consuming if each judge had to reason out the policies for deciding what the law should be for each case brought before the court. If other courts have confronted the same issue and reasoned through the case carefully, their opinions can serve as guides.

Second, *stare decisis* makes for a more just and uniform system. All courts try to follow precedent, and thus different courts will often use the same rule of law. (However, some variations occur because of different states and regions following different precedents.) Also, the rule of precedent tends to neutralize the personal prejudices of individual judges. If they feel pressure to use precedent as the basis for their decisions, they will be less influenced by any prejudices.

Third, the rule makes the law more stable and predictable. If the law on that subject is well settled, someone bringing a case to court can usually rely on the court to make a decision based on what the law has been.

Finally, *stare decisis* reflects the experience of the past and is based on the wisdom of the past.

Sometimes a court will depart from the rule of precedent because it has decided that the precedent is incorrect. For example, if changes in technology, business practice, or society's attitudes necessitate a change in the law, courts might depart from precedent. Judges are reluctant to overthrow precedent, and whether they do will depend on the subject of the case, the number and prestige of prior decisions, the degree of social change that has occurred, and the identity of the deciding court. (The Supreme Court of the United States, when deciding a constitutional question, is the highest authority in the land and is therefore freer to reverse the direction of the law than a lower court.)

Sometimes there is no precedent on which to base a decision, or there are conflicting precedents. In these situations, a court will: (1) refer to past decisions that may be similar to the current case and decide the case by reasoning through analogy; (2) look at social factors—changes in the status of women, for example—that might influence the issues involved; and (3) consider what the fairest result would be.

Cases that overturn precedent often receive a lot of publicity, and it might seem that they are fairly common. In reality, the majority of cases are decided according to precedent by the rule of *stare decisis*.

MORE RECENT SOURCES OF LAW

Much law has been made since the officials of the king's court made decisions with reference to the year books. Today, courts have sources other than precedent to consider when making their decisions.

Constitutions

The federal government and the states have constitutions that set forth the general organization, powers, and limits of government. The U.S. Constitution[1] is the supreme law of the land. A law in violation of the Constitution, no matter what its source, will be declared unconstitutional and thus cannot be enforced. Similarly, the state constitutions are supreme within their respective borders (unless they conflict with the U.S. Constitution).

The U.S. Constitution defines the powers and limitations of the federal government. All powers not retained by the federal government reside in the states or the people. For example, the Constitution gives the federal government the power to regulate *interstate* commerce. The states retain the power to regulate *intrastate* commerce. The citizens of the United States are guaranteed various individual freedoms by the Constitution, particularly the Bill of Rights; acts by the government may not infringe these freedoms. The Constitution also delineates how federal powers are divided among the three governmental branches, establishing a system of checks and balances. Thus, the legislative power (power to make laws) is vested in the Congress; the executive power (power to see that laws are carried out) is vested in the president; and the judicial power (power to determine what the law is and whether laws are valid) is vested in the courts.[2]

The process for deciding whether or not a law is contrary to the mandates of the Constitution is known as **judicial review.** The judicial branch of government has the authority and the power to make such a determination. This is part of the system of **checks and balances.** The power of judicial review was first established in the famous case of *Marbury v. Madison*, which determined that the Supreme Court had the power to decide that a law passed by Congress violated the Constitution:

> It is emphatically the province and duty of the Judicial Department to say what the law is. Those who apply the rule to a particular case, must of necessity expound and interpret that rule. If two laws conflict with each other, the courts must decide on the operation of each.
>
> So if the law be in opposition to the Constitution, if both the law and the Constitution apply to a particular case, so that the court must either decide that case conformably to the law, disregarding the Constitution; or conformably to the Constitution, disregarding the law; the court must determine which of these conflicting rules governs the case. This is of the very essence of judicial duty.

---

1. See Appendix B for complete text.

2. State governments are generally established and organized the same way as the federal government.

If, then, the courts were to regard the Constitution and the Constitution is superior to any ordinary Act of the Legislature, the Constitution, and not such ordinary Act, must govern the case to which they both apply.[3]

In another famous case, *United States v. Nixon*, the Court established its power over actions of the president. In 1974 a grand jury indicted seven individuals for obstruction of justice and conspiracy to defraud (among other things). President Nixon was ordered by the special prosecutor to produce tapes, memoranda, papers, and transcripts. The president attempted to avoid the subpoena on the ground of "executive privilege," but this ground was denied him by the district court.

"Executive privilege" is the right of the members of the executive branch to keep certain communications private because decisions could not be made properly without frank discussions of delicate matters. The president's view of the privilege was broad, and he claimed the courts lacked power to demand the records sought. The Supreme Court eventually heard the case, denied the claim of executive privilege that was the heart of the controversy, and affirmed the order of the district court. Among other things, the Court balanced the president's claim against the needs of the defendant and the courts to have the records:

> *   *   * The Sixth Amendment explicitly confers upon every defendant in a criminal trial the right "to be confronted with the witnesses against him" and "to have compulsory process for obtaining witnesses in his favor *   *   * " It is the manifest duty of the courts to vindicate those guarantees and to accomplish that it is essential that all relevant and admissible evidence be produced.
> *   *   * [T]he allowance of the privilege to withhold evidence that is demonstrably relevant in a criminal trial would cut deeply into the guarantee of due process of law and gravely impair the basic function of the courts. *   *   *[4]

The other branches of government exert checks on the judiciary as well. The president appoints federal judges, with the Senate's approval. Congress controls the budget, possesses the power of impeachment, and can even control the jurisdiction of the lower federal courts.

Codified Law: Statutes and Ordinances

Another source of law in the United States is the statutes enacted by the Congress and the various state legislative bodies (statutory law). In addition, cities and counties pass ordinances, none of which can violate the U.S. Constitution or the relevant state constitution. Because the states retain many powers, Congress can pass only the legislation that falls within the range of power granted to it by the U.S. Constitution.[5] Today, legislative bodies and regulatory agencies have assumed an ever-increasing share of lawmaking. A large part of the work of modern courts is interpreting what the rulemakers meant when the law was passed and applying it to a present set of facts. In large part, statutory law has replaced the common law.

Case Law and Common Law

Case law comprises the rules of law announced in court decisions. It is the aggregate of reported cases. It is sometimes called judge-made law. Generally, case law is an interpretation of the other sources of law that have been described here. Once a court has interpreted a statute, a regulation, or a constitution, the interpretation becomes part of the authoritative law on the subject.

Case law can be viewed as a subset of common law. Common law comprises those principles and rules of action that relate to the government and to the security of persons and property

---

3.   5 U.S. (1 Cranch) 137, 2 L.Ed. 60 (1803). How to read case citations is explained at the end of Chapter 2. How to brief a case is presented in Appendix A.
4.   318 U.S. 683, 94 S.Ct. 3090 (1974).

---

5.   Given in Article I, Section VIII; there are eighteen specific powers given to Congress. Amendment X reserves all other powers to the states or to the people.

and that derive their authority solely from the usages and customs of a society. It also comprises the judgments and decrees of the courts recognizing, affirming, and enforcing such usages and customs (that is, case law). Common law began as the ancient unwritten law of England, but what we mean by common law today includes the statutory and case law background of England and of the American colonies prior to the American Revolution. Common law should be contrasted with present statutory law just described, which is law enacted by state and federal legislatures. Where it does not conflict with a statute, common law has the same force as statutory law in most states because the states have adopted common law by legislative decree. For example, the California Civil Code, Section 22.1, states that the "common law of England, so far as it is not repugnant to or inconsistent with the Constitution of the United States, or the Constitution or laws of this State, is the rule of decision in all the courts of this State."

Thus, in areas where legislation has not covered the relevant issue, courts still refer to the common law. The history and circumstances of the various states differ, and this has given rise to differences in the common law in each state. Even where legislation has been substituted for common law, courts often rely on common law to interpret the legislation on the theory that the people who drafted the statute intended to codify a previous common-law rule. Further, the judicial methodology used in making decisions has its origins in common law.

Administrative Agency Regulations

An administrative agency is created when the executive or legislative branch of the government delegates some of its authority to an appropriate group of persons. Administrative agencies exercise legislative, executive, and judicial power—in their rulemaking, they are using legislative power; in their regulation and supervision, they are using executive power; and in their adjudication procedures, they are using judicial power. Unlike legislators, presidents, governors, and many judges, administrative agency person-

nel are rarely chosen by popular elections, and many do not serve fixed terms. As a result, great power is given to people who may not be responsive to the public.

Since the New Deal days, government agencies have proliferated in the United States. Federal agencies include the Federal Communications Commission, the Civil Aeronautics Board, the Federal Aviation Administration, the National Labor Relations Board, the Consumer Product Safety Commission, the Environmental Protection Agency, the National Highway Safety Transportation Administration, the Internal Revenue Service, the Food and Drug Administration, and the Interstate Commerce Commission. There are also state and local boards and agencies—for example, environmental agencies and state labor agencies.

Administrative law is the branch of public law concerned with the executive power and actions of administrative agencies, their officials, and their workers. When an individual has a dispute with such an agency, administrative law comes into play. The scope of administrative law has expanded enormously in recent years, and the scope of administrative agencies has increased so much that their activities have come to be called administrative process, in contrast to judicial process. *Administrative process* involves the administration of law by nonjudicial agencies, whereas *judicial process* is the administration of law by judicial bodies (the courts). Because administrative bodies are only "quasi-judicial," appeals from their rulings can be taken directly to the courts after administrative remedies have been exhausted. The proper court for such appeals varies according to the agency's governing statute and the type of action in question.

Federal administrative agencies have expanded the number of their rulings at what appears to be an exponential rate. Some observers and citizens believe that the United States is in danger of having an overly bureaucratic government, and devices such as "sunset laws" and legislative veto of agency rules have gained support as methods for keeping administrative agencies under control.

SOURCES OF COMMERCIAL (OR BUSINESS) LAW

The body of law that pertains to commercial dealings is commonly referred to as commercial, or business, law. It includes most of the topics in this text—contracts, partnerships, corporations, and agencies, for example. Many of the principles of business law were developed centuries ago from what was known as the *law merchant*.

The Law Merchant

A system of mercantile courts existed in England well before the advent of the common law courts. These courts administered the law merchant, derived from uniform customs of the merchants, many of whom traveled from place to place to do business. The law merchant was important during the Middle Ages when the fair, or market, was an important commercial event. In fact, the Magna Carta made special provisions for merchants. Section 41, for example, states that all merchants should "have safe and secure conduct, to go out of, and to come into England, and to stay there, and to pass as well by lands as by water, for buying and selling by the ancient and allowed customs." The law merchant eventually became part of the common law and was incorporated into American law.

Codification of Commercial Law

In the interests of uniformity and reform, the legal profession, under the leadership of the American Law Institute, has suggested comprehensive codes of laws to be adopted by the states. The most important of these to business students is the Uniform Commercial Code, which is the basis of many chapters in this book. Its origins will be briefly examined here.

The National Conference of Commissioners on Uniform State Laws started to meet in the late 1800s to draft uniform statutes. Once these uniform codes were drawn up, the commissioners urged each state legislature to adopt them. The first such code, or act, was the Negotiable Instruments Act, which was finally approved in 1896 and by the early 1920s was adopted in every state (though not all states used exactly the same wording). Afterwards, other acts were drawn up in a similar manner; they included the Uniform Sales Act, the Uniform Warehouse Receipts Act, the Uniform Bills of Lading Act, the Uniform Partnership Act (drafted by the American Bar Association), the Model Business Corporation Act, and the Uniform Stock Transfer Act. Recently, a Uniform Probate Code was prepared. The most ambitious uniform act of all, however, is the Uniform Commercial Code.

The Uniform Commercial Code (UCC)

The National Conference of Commissioners on Uniform State Laws and the American Law Institute sponsored and directed the preparation of the Uniform Commercial Code. These two organizations were assisted by literally hundreds of law professors, businesspersons, judges, and lawyers. The work on the UCC began in 1942, and the finished draft was completed in 1952. The complete text of the Code can be found in Appendix C in this book. All fifty states, the District of Columbia, and the Virgin Islands have adopted the Uniform Commercial Code in whole or in part.[6]

The UCC consists of ten articles:
1. General Provisions.
2. Sales.
3. Commercial Paper.
4. Bank Deposits and Collections.
5. Letters of Credit.
6. Bulk Transfers.
7. Documents of Title.
8. Investment Securities.
9. Secured Transactions.
10. Effective Date and Repealer.

When each of the states adopted the Code, it repealed numerous statutes, such as the Uniform Sales Act, the Uniform Bills of Lading Act, the Uniform Warehouse Receipts Act, the Uniform

6. Louisiana has adopted only Articles 1, 3, 4, and 5, however.

Negotiable Instruments Act, the Uniform Conditional Sales Act, the Uniform Trust Receipts Act, the Uniform Stock Transfer Act, the Bulk Sales Act, and the Factors Lien Act.

The Code does not greatly change the basic principles of commercial law derived from the law merchant and common law but expands and codifies them in order to modernize, clarify, standardize, and liberalize the rules. The Code also helps state the legal relationship of the parties in modern commercial transactions. The Code is designed to help determine the intentions of the parties to a commercial contract and to give force and effect to their agreement. The Code further is meant to encourage business transactions by assuring businesspersons that their contracts, if validly entered into, will be enforced.

CLASSIFICATION OF LAW

The body of law is huge. In order to study it, one must break it down by some means of classification. No single system of classification can cover such a large mass of information; consequently, those systems that have been devised tend to overlap. Moreover, they are, of necessity, arbitrary in some respects. A discussion of the best known systems follows.

Substantive versus Procedural Law

Substantive law includes all of those laws that define, describe, regulate, and create legal rights and obligations. A rule stating that promises are enforced only where each party receives something of value from the other party is part of substantive law. So, too, is a rule stating that a person who injures another through negligence must pay damages.

Procedural law (or adjective law) establishes the methods of enforcing the rights that are established by substantive law. Questions about how a lawsuit should begin, what papers need to be filed, to which court the suit should go, which witnesses can be called, and so on are all questions of procedural law. In brief, substantive law tells us our rights; procedural law tells us how to get the benefit of them.

Exhibit 1–1 classifies law in terms of its subject matter, dividing it into law covering substantive issues and law covering procedural issues. Most of this text concerns substantive law.

EXHIBIT 1–1 SUBJECT MATTER DIVIDED INTO SUBSTANTIVE AND PROCEDURAL[a]

SUBSTANTIVE	PROCEDURAL
Agency	Evidence
Commercial paper	Civil procedure
Contracts	Criminal procedure
Corporation law	Administrative procedure
Property	Appellate procedure
Torts	
Taxation	
Sales	
Real property	
Personal property	
Partnerships	
Trusts and Wills	
Criminal law	
Constitutional law	
Administrative law	

a. The importance of this distinction is more than academic: the *result* of a case may well depend upon the determination that a rule is substantive rather than procedural.

Public versus Private Law

Public law addresses the relationship between persons and their government; **private law** addresses direct dealings between persons. Criminal, constitutional, and administrative laws are generally called public law because they deal with persons and their relationships to government. Criminal acts, though they may involve only one victim, are seen as offenses against society as a whole, and are prohibited by governments in order to protect the public. (The violation of a criminal law may also violate a private right.)

Constitutional law involves questions of whether the government—federal, state or local—has the power to act in a particular fashion; often the issue is whether a law, duly passed, exceeds the limits set on the government. In other words, governments receive their power from the Constitution. Additionally, constitutional law limits the exercise of governmental power in certain ways usually designed to protect the people's life, liberty, or property from improper governmental action. Most students are aware, for example, that the Fourth and Fifth Amendments to the U.S. Constitution (see Appendix B) protect citizens against unreasonable searches, coerced confessions, and similar types of improper conduct by police.

Administrative law details the procedures that govern the activities of various government commissions and administrative agencies. Whether a regulated business may stop a proposed action by OSHA that will raise costs excessively is an administrative law problem. Other areas of the law, such as contract rights and duties, fall within the private law category. (See Chapters 6 through 15.) Thus, a businessperson who sues a supplier for breaking a contract, or a pedestrian who sues a motorist for striking him or her is using private law. See Exhibit 1–2 for some examples of public and private law.

EXHIBIT 1–2 EXAMPLES OF PUBLIC AND PRIVATE LAW

PUBLIC LAW	PRIVATE LAW
Administrative law	Torts
Constitutional law	Contracts
Criminal law	Partnerships
Civil, criminal, and	Corporation law
appellate procedure	Real property
Evidence	Personal property
Taxation	Agency
	Commercial paper
	Sales
	Trusts and Wills

Civil versus Criminal Law

Civil law spells out the duties that exist between persons or between citizens and their governments, excluding the duty not to commit crimes. Contract law, for example, is part of civil law. The whole body of tort law, which has to do with the infringement by one person of the legally recognized rights of another, is an area of civil law. (Tort law is treated in Chapters 3 and 4.)

Criminal law is concerned with a wrong committed against the public as a whole. Crim-

inal acts are proscribed by local, state, or federal government by statute. (Criminal law is treated in Chapter 5.) Criminal law is always public law, whereas civil law is sometimes public and sometimes private. In a criminal case, the government seeks to impose a penalty upon an allegedly guilty person. In a civil case, one party (sometimes the government) tries to make the other party comply with a duty or pay for the damage caused by failure to so comply.

REMEDIES AT LAW VERSUS REMEDIES IN EQUITY

The distinction between law and equity is primarily of historical interest, but it has special relevance to students of business law. In the early king's courts, the kinds of *remedies* (legal means to recover a right or redress a wrong) that the courts could grant were severely restricted. If one person wronged another in some way, the king's court could award one or more of the following: (1) land, (2) items of value, or (3) money as compensation. The courts that awarded these compensations became known as *courts of law*. The three remedies were called *remedies at law*. Such a system introduced uniformity in the settling of disputes, but when *plaintiffs* (parties suing) wanted a remedy other than economic compensation, the courts of law could do nothing, so "no remedy, no right."

Equity Courts: Going to the King for Relief

When individuals could not obtain their preferred remedy in a court of law because of strict technicalities, they petitioned the king for relief. Most of these petitions were decided by an adviser of the king, called a *chancellor*. The chancellor was said to be the "keeper of the king's conscience." When the chancellor thought that the claim was a fair one, new and unique remedies were granted. In this way, a new body of chancery rules and reliefs, or remedies, came into being. Eventually formal chancery courts were established. These were known as *courts of equity*.

Equity is that branch of unwritten law, founded in justice and fair dealing, that seeks to supply a more equitable and adequate remedy than any available at law. Thus, two distinct systems were created, each having a different set of judges. There were two bodies of rules and remedies that existed at the same time, *remedies at law* and *remedies in equity*. Plaintiffs had to specify whether they were bringing an "action at law" or an "action in equity," and they chose their courts accordingly. Only one remedy could be granted for a particular wrong, and even in equity the wrong had to be of a type the court would recognize as remediable.

Courts of equity had the responsibility of using discretion in supplementing the common law. Even today, when the same court can award both legal and equitable remedies, such discretion is often guided by so-called *equitable principles and maxims*. Some of them are:

1. Whoever seeks equity must do equity.
2. Equality is equity.
3. Where there is equal equity, the law must prevail.
4. One seeking the aid of an equity court must come to the court with clean hands.
5. Equity will not suffer a right to exist without a remedy.
6. Equity aids the vigilant, not those who rest on their rights.

The last maxim is worthy of discussion. It means that individuals who fail to look out for their rights until after a reasonable time has passed will not be helped. This has become known as the equitable doctrine of **laches.**

The equitable doctrine of laches can be used as a defense. The doctrine arose to encourage people to bring lawsuits while the evidence is fresh. What constitutes a reasonable time, of course, varies according to the circumstances of the case. Time periods for different types of cases are now usually fixed by **statutes of limitations.** After the time allowed under a statute of limitations has expired, no action can be brought no matter how strong the case was originally.

Equitable Relief

Decrees of Specific Performance A plaintiff might come into a court of equity asking it to order a defendant to perform within the terms of a contract. A *court of law* could not issue such an order because its remedies were limited to payment of money or property as compensation for damages. A *court of equity*, however, could issue a decree of *specific performance*—an order to perform what was promised.

Injunctions If a person wanted a certain activity prevented, he would have to go to the chancellor in equity to ask that the person doing the wrongful act be ordered to stop. The order was called an *injunction*—a court order requiring that a person stop doing something. An **injunction** is an order to any person to refrain from doing something. An order forcing a contracting party to live up to his duties is specific performance.

Rescission Often the legal remedy of the payment of money for damages is unavailable or inadequate for disputes over agreements among persons. In such cases, the equitable remedy of rescission is frequently given. **Rescission** is an action to undo an agreement—to return to the *status quo*. It returns a person to the position he or she occupied before the other person acted wrongfully. It abolishes all duties created by the agreement that was rescinded. For example, if a sales agreement is made because a seller misrepresents the quality of goods, but the fraud is discovered before any money changes hands, the buyer might want merely to rescind the agreement. If, however, money has been exchanged and the buyer has already resold some of the goods, the buyer might want damages for harm suffered.

Today the distinction between courts of law and courts of equity has largely disappeared. Trial courts normally can grant remedies at law or in equity. The distinction is still important to the student of business law, however, because one must know the remedies available in order to request the proper one.

QUESTIONS AND CASE PROBLEMS

1. What is the difference between common law and statutory law? Should judges have the same authority to overrule statutory law as they have to overrule common law?

2. What is the difference between common law and *stare decisis*? Should judges have the same power to adopt a rule contrary to common law as they do to depart from *stare decisis*?

3. What is substantive law? What is procedural, or adjective, law? Are there reasons for the two existing side by side?

4. The concept of *equity* was mentioned in this chapter. Courts of equity tend to follow general rules or maxims rather than following common law or *stare decisis* as courts of law do. Some of those maxims are: whoever seeks equity must do equity; one seeking the aid of an equity court must come to the court with clean hands; and equity aids the vigilant, not those who rest on their rights. (The last maxim is the equitable doctrine of laches, and it refers to those who do not pursue a remedy within a reasonable time.) Why would equity courts give more credence to such maxims than to a hard and fast body of law?

5. The U.S. Constitution is a document in which the people of the United States give the government the "power to govern." Yet the Constitution was written by a handful of men who represented the aristocracy of the time. Surprisingly, this group of aristocrats wrote a document giving more freedoms to common people than any other constitution in existence. Name some of the basic guarantees found in the Constitution.

6. The Uniform Commercial Code took years to develop and has only recently been adopted by all the states (although Louisiana did not adopt all the articles). The UCC attempts to establish uniformity throughout the states in every conceivable area of commercial law. What are some of the advantages of such a document?

CHAPTER 2

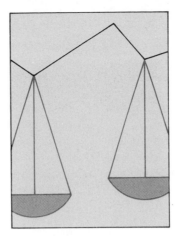

Courts
and Procedures

INTRODUCTION

In the United States, each of the states has its own court system. There is also a separate federal court system. This chapter will look at both the state and federal systems and will then follow a typical case from beginning to end. Remember that an important step in the use of the courts or the process of adjudication is *determining which rules apply to the facts in the case*. These rules can be *substantive* or *procedural*. They can come from several sources and can cover several areas of the law.

In studying the courts and their procedures, the first question should be which courts have the power to decide a particular case—that is, which courts have jurisdiction.

JURISDICTION

Juris means "law"; *diction* means "to speak." Thus, the power to speak the law is the literal meaning of the term *jurisdiction*. Before any court can hear a case, it must have jurisdiction—the power to decide that case. Otherwise it cannot exercise any authority in the case. In order for a court to exercise valid authority, it must have jurisdiction over the person against whom the suit is brought and over the subject matter of the case.

Jurisdiction over the Person

In order to consider a case, a court must also have power over the person or, in some cases, the property of the person against whom a suit is brought. Generally, a court's power is limited to the territorial boundaries of the state in which it is located. Therefore, a court has jurisdiction over the person of anyone who can be served with a summons within those boundaries. Additionally, if a person is a resident of the state or does business within the state, there will be jurisdiction over that person. Finally, in some cases where an individual has committed a wrong, such as an automobile injury or the sale of defective goods within the state, a court can exercise jurisdiction using the authority of a *long arm statute* even if the individual is outside the state. A court can exercise jurisdiction over a corporation in the state where it is incorporated, in the state where it has its main plant or office, and in any state where it does business.

If an individual owns property within a state, and the property is the subject of the suit, a court can exercise jurisdiction by virtue of its authority over property within the state even if the owner is outside the state. A court can also use property within a state to help satisfy a general debt.

In all cases where a court exercises jurisdiction, the parties must be served either with actual notice that they are involved in a suit (usually by service of a summons) or, where the parties cannot be located, by publication of notice in a newspaper or other manner if permitted by statute.

Subject Matter Jurisdiction

Subject matter jurisdiction is a limitation on types of cases a court can hear. For example, probate courts—courts that handle only matters relating to wills and estates—are a common example of limited subject matter jurisdiction. The subject matter jurisdiction of a court is usually defined in the statute or constitution creating the court. A court's subject matter jurisdiction can be limited not only by the subject of the lawsuit, but also by the amount of money in controversy, by whether a case is a felony or misdemeanor, or by whether the proceeding is a trial or an appeal.

Venue

Jurisdiction is concerned with whether a court has authority over a specific subject matter or individual. **Venue** is concerned with the particular geographic area within a judicial district where a suit should be brought.

Basically, the concept of venue reflects the policy that a court trying a suit should be in the geographic neighborhood where the incident leading to the suit occurred or where the parties involved in the suit reside. That neighborhood is usually the county where the incident oc-

curred or where the parties live. However, pretrial publicity or other factors may require a change of venue to another community, especially in criminal cases, if the defendant's right to a fair and impartial jury is impaired.

The proper venue for a suit is defined by statute. Improper venue does not deprive the court of power to hear a case, but a party can request a change of venue if venue is not proper.

General Jurisdiction and Special, or Limited, Jurisdiction

The distinction between courts of general jurisdiction and courts of special, or limited, jurisdiction lies in the subject matter of cases heard. A court of general jurisdiction can decide virtually any type of case. Every state has one level of such courts, which may be called county courts, circuit courts, district courts, or some other name. On the other hand, at both federal and state levels there are courts that hear only cases of specialized, or limited, subject matter. For example, one court may handle only cases dealing with divorce or child custody. Another may handle disputes over relatively small amounts of money (a small claims court). Courts of general jurisdiction will not handle cases that are appropriate for these courts of special, or limited, jurisdiction.

Original and Appellate Jurisdiction

The distinction between courts of original jurisdiction and courts of appellate jurisdiction normally lies in whether the case is being heard for the first time. Courts having original jurisdiction are those of the first instance. In other words, they are where the trial of a case begins. In contrast, courts having appellate jurisdiction act as reviewing courts. In general, cases can be brought to them only on appeal from an order or a judgment of a lower court.

THE COURT SYSTEMS IN THE UNITED STATES

Today in the United States there are fifty-two separate court systems. Each of the fifty states, in addition to the District of Columbia, has its own fully developed, independent system of courts. Additionally, there is a separate federal court system. It is important to understand that the federal courts—the system taken as a whole—are not superior to the state courts. They are simply an independent system authorized by Article 3, Section 2, of the United States Constitution. The federal courts were set up to handle matters of particular federal interest. As we shall see, the United States Supreme Court is the final controlling voice over all these fifty-two systems, at least when questions of U.S. constitutional law are involved.

A Typical Court System

Most court systems, including the federal system, are based on a three-tiered model. Any person who is a party to a lawsuit typically has the opportunity to plead the case before a trial court and then, if he or she loses, before two levels of appellate courts. Therefore, in most states a case may proceed first through a trial court, with an automatic right to review by a state appellate court, and then, if accepted, to the state supreme court. (Finally, if a federal constitutional issue is involved in the decision of the state supreme court, that decision may be appealed to the United States Supreme Court.)

Consider the typical state court system represented in Exhibit 2–1. It has three main tiers: (1) the state trial court of general or limited jurisdiction, (2) the state appellate court, and (3) the state supreme court.

One can view the typical state system presented in Exhibit 2–1 as being made up of trial courts and of appellate courts, or courts of appeal and review. Trial courts are exactly what their name implies—courts in which trials are held and testimony is taken. Trial courts may be courts of record, where a written record is taken, or courts not of record. Most are of record today. Most states have trial courts of both limited and general jurisdiction.

Limited-Jurisdiction Trial Courts Every state has trial courts that have original jurisdiction. Those with limited jurisdiction as to subject matter are often called special inferior trial courts or minor judiciary courts. Some typical courts

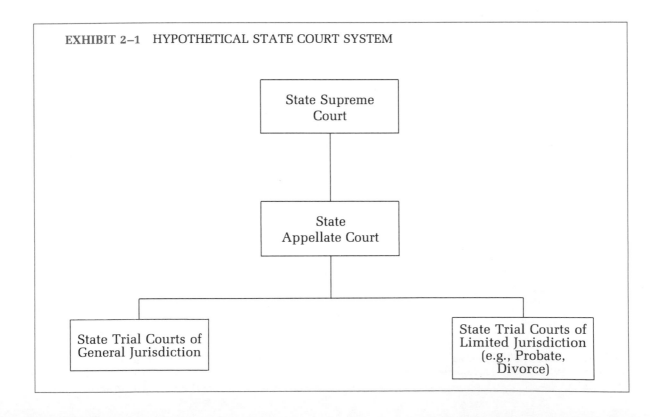

EXHIBIT 2–1   HYPOTHETICAL STATE COURT SYSTEM

State Supreme Court

State Appellate Court

State Trial Courts of General Jurisdiction

State Trial Courts of Limited Jurisdiction (e.g., Probate, Divorce)

of limited jurisdiction are domestic relations courts, which handle only divorce actions and child custody cases; local municipal courts, which handle mainly traffic cases; probate courts, which handle the administration of wills and estate settlement problems; and small claims and justice of the peace courts. Typically, the minor judiciary courts do not keep complete written records of trial proceedings.

General-Jurisdiction Trial Courts   Trial courts that have general jurisdiction as to subject matter may be called county, district, superior, or circuit courts.[1] The jurisdiction of these courts of general and original jurisdiction is often determined by the size of the county in which the court sits. These courts of general jurisdiction may be supplemented by the courts of limited jurisdiction or the minor judiciary courts just discussed above.

One should understand that many important cases involving businesses originate in these general trial courts. Thus, a study of corporate law, contract law, and commercial law must start here.

Appellate Courts, or Courts of Appeal and Review

Although in some states trial courts of general jurisdiction also have limited jurisdiction to hear appeals from the minor judiciary—for example, small claims and traffic cases—when one discusses courts of review, or appellate courts, one usually means courts that are not trial courts.

Every state has at least one court of review, or appellate court. The subject matter jurisdiction of these courts is substantially limited to hearing appeals. Many states have intermediate reviewing courts and one supreme court. The intermediate appellate, or review, court is often called the court of appeals. The highest court of the state is normally called the supreme court.[2] Appellate courts try few cases. They examine the record of the case on appeal and determine

whether the trial court committed an error. They look at questions of law and procedure, not questions of fact.[3] The decisions of each state's highest court in all questions of state law are final. It is only when questions of federal law are involved that a state's highest court can be overruled by the Supreme Court of the United States.

THE FEDERAL COURT SYSTEM— CASES AND CONTROVERSIES

The federal court system is similar in many ways to most state court systems. It is also a three-tiered model consisting of: (1) trial courts, (2) intermediate courts of appeals, and (3) the Supreme Court. Exhibit 2–2 shows the organization of the federal court system in some detail.

District Courts

At the federal level, the equivalent of a state trial court of general jurisdiction is the district court. There is at least one federal district court in every state. Congress has divided the country and territories into ninety-five federal judicial districts. This will be reduced to ninety-four as the District Court in the Canal Zone is being phased out. The number of judicial districts can vary over time primarily due to population changes and corresponding case loads. Large states, such as California, have more than one. Thus, an entire state can comprise a single district, or a state can be divided into several districts. With one exception, the districts do not cross state lines.[4] United States district courts are often called federal trial courts. Most federal cases originate in these courts. Whenever there are two or more district courts within a single state, there is limited geographical jurisdiction in each court. The state of Florida, for example, has district courts for northern, middle, and southern Florida.

---

1. The name in Ohio is Court of Common Pleas, and the name in New York is Supreme Court.
2. In New York it is called the Court of Appeals.

3. The only times an appellate court tampers with a trial court's findings of fact are when the finding is clearly erroneous (that is, when it is contrary to the evidence presented at trial) or when there is no evidence to support the finding.
4. The one exception is the District of Wyoming, which includes sections of Yellowstone National Park located in Montana and Idaho.

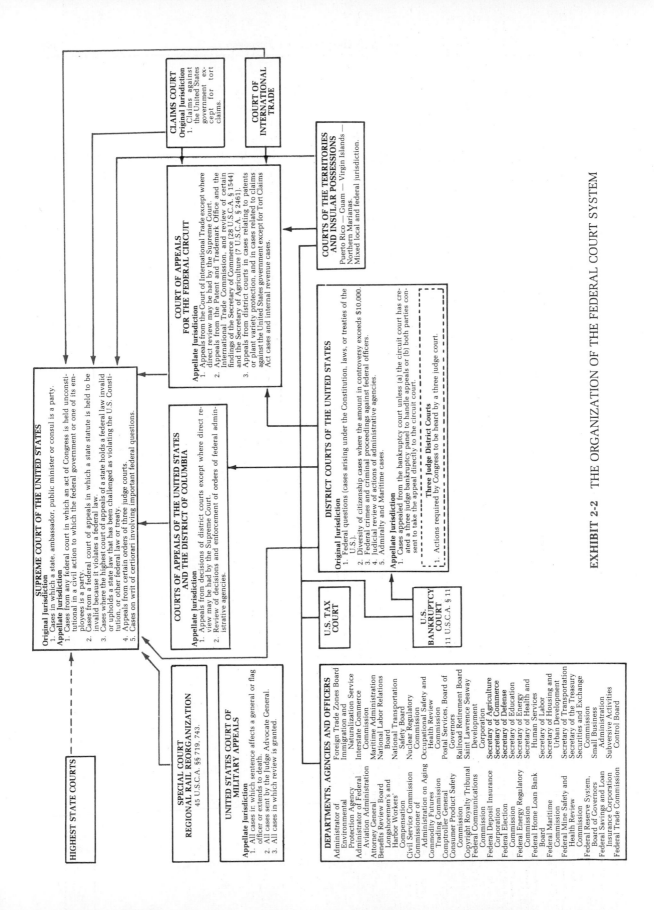

EXHIBIT 2-2 THE ORGANIZATION OF THE FEDERAL COURT SYSTEM

U.S. district courts have original jurisdiction in federal matters. In other words, this is where federal cases start. There are other trial courts with original, albeit special (or limited), jurisdiction, such as the U.S. Tax Court, the U.S. Bankruptcy Court, and the U.S. Claims Court. Certain administrative agencies and departments having judicial power also have original jurisdiction. These agencies and departments are listed in Exhibit 2–2.

U.S. Courts of Appeals

Congress has established twelve judicial circuits that hear appeals from the district courts located within their respective circuits. The decisions of the courts of appeals are final in most cases, but appeal to the Supreme Court is possible. Appeals from federal administrative agencies, such as the Federal Trade Commission, are also made to the U.S. circuit courts of appeals.

The Supreme Court of the United States

The highest level of the three-tiered model of the federal court system is the Supreme Court of the United States. According to the language of Article III of the U.S. Constitution, there is only one Supreme Court. All other courts in the federal system are considered "inferior." Congress is empowered to create such other inferior courts as it deems necessary. Thus, according to this language, the inferior courts that Congress has created include the second tier in our model— the U.S. courts of appeal, as well as the district courts and any other courts of limited, or specialized, jurisdiction.

The Supreme Court of the United States consists of nine justices; like federal judges, they are appointed by the president of the United States.[5] They receive lifetime appointments (under Article III, they "hold their offices during Good Behavior") and must be confirmed by the Senate. The Supreme Court was created by the U.S. Con-

stitution. Although it has original, or trial, jurisdiction in rare instances, set forth in Article III, Section 2, most of its work is as an appeals court. The Supreme Court can review any case decided by any of the federal courts of appeals, and it also has appellate authority over some cases decided in the state courts.

JURISDICTION OF FEDERAL COURTS

Since the federal government is a government of limited powers, the jurisdiction of the federal courts is limited. Article III of the U.S. Constitution established the boundaries of federal judicial power:

Section 1. The judicial power of the United States shall be vested in one supreme Court and in such inferior Courts as the Congress may from time to time ordain and establish. * * *

Section 2. The judicial power shall extend to all Cases, in Law and Equity, arising under this Constitution, the Laws of the United States, and Treaties made, or which shall be made, under their Authority;—to all Cases affecting Ambassadors, other public Ministers and Consuls;—to all Cases of admiralty and maritime Jurisdiction;—to Controversies to which the United States shall be a Party;—to Controversies between two or more States; between a State and Citizens of another State;[6]—between Citizens of different States;—between Citizens of the same State claiming Lands under the Grants of different States, and between a State, or the Citizens thereof, and foreign States, Citizens or Subjects.

In all Cases affecting Ambassadors, other public Ministers and Consuls, and those in which a State shall be a Party, the supreme Court shall have original Jurisdiction. In all the other Cases before mentioned, the supreme Court shall have appellate Jurisdiction, both as to Law and Fact, with such Exceptions, and under such Regulations as the Congress shall make.

In line with the checks and balances system of the federal government, Congress has the power to control the number and kind of inferior courts

---

5. Members of the Supreme Court and of some appellate courts are called justices, whereas members of trial courts are called judges. The same distinction often applies in state court systems.

6. Amendment XI, passed in 1798, prohibits any exercise of federal judicial power in cases brought against a state by citizens of another state.

in the federal system. Except in those cases where the Constitution gives the Supreme Court original jurisdiction, Congress can also regulate the jurisdiction of the Supreme Court. Therefore, although the Constitution sets the outer limits of federal judicial power, Congress can set other limits on federal jurisdiction. Furthermore, the courts themselves can promulgate rules that limit the types of cases they will hear.

Federal Questions

"The Judicial Power shall extend to all cases * * * arising under this Constitution, the laws of the United States and Treaties made * * * under their authority." Whenever a plaintiff's cause of action is based, at least in part, on the United States Constitution, a treaty, or a federal law, then a *federal question* arises, and the case comes under the judicial power of federal courts. People whose claims are based on rights granted by an act of Congress can sue in a federal court. People who claim that their constitutional rights have been violated can originate their suits in federal court.

Any lawsuit involving a federal question can originate in a federal court. Lawsuits involving diversity of citizenship (discussed later) must, however, be in excess of $10,000 to originate in federal court. There is no dollar amount requirement where federal courts have exclusive jurisdiction—that is, where the suit can only be brought in federal court.

Diversity of Citizenship

Another basis for federal district court jurisdiction is *diversity of citizenship.* Diversity of citizenship cases involve (1) citizens of different states, (2) a foreign country as plaintiff and citizens of a state, or different states, and (3) citizens of a state and citizens or subjects of a foreign country. Regarding money limits, under Title 28, Section 1332, the amount in controversy must be more than $10,000 before a federal court can take jurisdiction. For purposes of diversity of citizenship jurisdiction, a corporation is a citizen of the state where it is incorporated and of the state where it has its principal place of business. Cases involving diversity of citizen-

ship can commence in the appropriate federal court or, if they have started in a state court, can sometimes be transferred.

Diversity jurisdiction originated in 1789 with the authors of the Constitution, who felt that a state might be biased toward its own citizens. The option of using the federal courts provided by the principle of diversity of citizenship is a means of protecting the out-of-state party. A large percentage of the 70,000 cases filed in federal courts each year are based on diversity of citizenship.

Consider some examples. Smith is driving from his home state, New York, to Florida. In Georgia he runs into a car owned by Able, a citizen of Georgia. Able's new Mercedes is demolished, and as a result of the personal injuries she sustained in the accident, Able is unable to work for six months. Thus, the case in question involves more than $10,000 worth of damages. Georgia has *in personam* jurisdiction through a long arm statute (a state law permitting courts to obtain jurisdiction over nonresident defendants), but Smith can have the suit removed to a federal district court on the basis of diversity of citizenship.

Jones, who resides in Texas, is owed $25,000 by Corporation XYZ, which is incorporated and has its principal place of business in Louisiana. XYZ does enough business in Texas to allow Texas courts to exercise *in personam* jurisdiction over it. Since, for purposes of diversity of citizenship jurisdiction, XYZ is a citizen of Louisiana, Jones can begin her suit in a federal district court in Texas or Louisiana or in a Texas or Louisiana state court.

Concurrent versus Exclusive Jurisdiction

When both federal and state courts have the power to hear a case, such as in cases of diversity of citizenship of the parties, jurisdiction is *concurrent.* When cases can be tried only in federal courts, jurisdiction is *exclusive.* Federal courts have exclusive jurisdiction in cases involving federal crimes, bankruptcy, patents, and copyrights; in suits against the United States; and in some areas of admiralty law. (States have exclusive jurisdiction in certain subject matters also—for example, in divorce, and in adoptions.)

WHICH CASES REACH THE SUPREME COURT?

Many people are surprised to learn that in a typical case there is no absolute right of appeal to the United States Supreme Court. The Supreme Court is given original, or trial court, jurisdiction in a small number of situations. In all other cases, its jurisdiction is appellate "with such Exceptions, and under such Regulations as the Congress shall make." Today the exceptions and rules set by Congress and some rules that the court has set for itself are quite complex. Over 4,500 cases are filed with the Supreme Court each year; yet it hears an average of only 300.[7] There are basically two procedures for bringing a case before the Supreme Court: by *appeal* or by *writ of certiorari.*

Appeal

Under rules set out by Congress, the Supreme Court must review a decision (that is, an individual has an absolute right to appeal) in the following situations:

1.   When a federal court of appeals holds a state statute to be invalid because it violates federal law.
2.   When the highest state court of appeals holds a federal law invalid or upholds a state law that has been challenged as violating federal law.
3.   When a federal court holds an act of Congress unconstitutional and the federal government or one of its employees is a party.
4.   When the hearing under appeal is for an injunction in a civil (as opposed to criminal) ac-

tion that Congress requires a district court of three judges to determine.

Theoretically, the Supreme Court is required to hear any appeal that falls within one of these four categories, but it can decide which of these cases require full consideration, including written briefs from the lawyers and oral arguments before the Court. The Court will give full consideration only if four of the nine justices vote to do so. Otherwise the case will be dismissed. A case can be dismissed because the Court agrees with the lower court's decision, because the federal question presented is not a substantial one, or on some other procedural ground. When a case is dismissed for reasons of substantive law—that is, when the higher court agrees with the lower court or when a substantial federal question is lacking—the Court's decision has value as precedent, and the dismissal can be cited in later cases.[8]

Writ of Certiorari

With a **writ of certiorari,** the Supreme Court orders a lower court to send it the record of a case for review. Parties whose cases do not fall into one of the appeal categories can petition the Supreme Court to issue a *writ of certiorari,* but whether the Court will issue one is entirely at its discretion. In no instance is the Court required to issue a *writ of certiorari.*

The following situations indicate when the Court will issue a writ, although they are not a limit on the Court's discretion:

1.   When a state court has decided a substantial federal question that has not been determined by the Supreme Court before, or the state court has decided it in a way that is probably in disagreement with the trend of the Supreme Court's decisions.
2.   When two federal courts of appeals are in disagreement with each other.
3.   When a federal court of appeals has decided an important state question in conflict with state law, has decided an important federal question

---

7.   There has been some discussion about establishing a new national appellate court to relieve the Supreme Court's workload. The new court would take cases that the Supreme Court felt it should not spend its time deciding so that it could take on more cases that had important public policy implications. Commission on Revision of the Federal Court Appellate System, Structure and Internal Procedures: Recommendations for Change (1975).

---

8.   Hicks v. Miranda, 422 U.S. 332, 95 S.Ct. 2281 (1975).

not yet addressed by the Court but which should be decided by the Court, has decided a federal question in conflict with applicable decisions of the Court, or has departed from the accepted and usual course of judicial proceedings.

Most petitions for *writs of certiorari* are denied. A denial is not a decision on the merits of a case, nor does it indicate agreement with the lower court's opinion. Therefore, denial of the writ has no value as precedent.[9] The Court will not issue a writ unless at least four justices approve of it. This is called the "rule of four." Typically, only the petitions that raise the possibility of important constitutional questions are granted *writs of certiorari*.

JUDICIAL PROCEDURES: FOLLOWING A CASE THROUGH THE COURTS

American and English courts follow the *adversary system of justice*. The judge's role is viewed as nonbiased and mostly passive. The lawyer functions as the client's advocate, presenting the client's version of the facts in order to convince the judge or the jury (or both) that they are true. Judges do not have to be entirely passive. They are responsible for the appropriate application of the law. They do not have to accept the legal reasoning of the attorneys. They can base a ruling and a decision on a personal study of the law. Judges sometimes ask questions of witnesses and even suggest types of evidence to be presented. For example, if an indigent defendant chooses to act as his or her own counsel, the judge will often play less of a passive role and more of an advocate role, intervening during the trial proceedings to help the defendant.[10]

Procedure

Procedure involves the way disputes are handled in the courts. A large body of law, procedural law, establishes the rules and standards for

determining disputes in courts. The rules are very complex, and they vary from court to court. There is a set of federal *rules of procedure*, and there are various sets of procedural rules in the state courts. Rules of procedure differ in criminal and civil cases.

We will now follow a civil case through the state court system. The case involves an automobile accident in which Jones, driving a Cadillac, has struck Adams, driving a Ford. The accident has occurred at an intersection in New York City. Adams has suffered personal injuries, incurring medical and hospital expenses as well as four months of lost wages. Jones and Adams are unable to agree on a settlement, and Adams sues Jones. Adams is the *plaintiff*, and Jones is the *defendant*. Both have lawyers.

The Pleadings

Complaint and Summons Adams's suit, or action, against Jones will commence when her lawyer files a *complaint* (sometimes called a petition or declaration) with the clerk of the trial court in the appropriate geographic area (the proper venue). In most states it will be a court having general jurisdiction; in others it may be a court having special jurisdiction with regard to subject matter. The complaint will contain: (1) a statement alleging the facts necessary for the court to take jurisdiction, (2) a short statement of the facts necessary to show that the plaintiff is entitled to a remedy, and (3) a statement of the remedy the plaintiff is seeking.

A typical complaint is shown in Exhibit 2–3.

The complaint will state that Adams was driving her Ford through a green light at the specified intersection, exercising good driving habits and reasonable care, when Jones carelessly drove his Cadillac through a red light and into the intersection from a cross street, striking Adams and causing serious personal injury and property damage. The complaint will go on to state that she is entitled to $85,000 to cover medical bills, $10,000 to cover lost wages, and $5,000 to cover property damage to the car.

After the complaint has been filed, the sheriff or a deputy of the county will serve a summons and a copy of the complaint on the defendant

9. Singleton v. Commissioner of Internal Revenue, 439 U.S. 940, 99 S.Ct. 335 (1978).
10. See Faretta v. California, 422 U.S. 806, 95 S.Ct. 2525 (1975).

EXHIBIT 2–3   EXAMPLE OF A TYPICAL COMPLAINT

IN THE UNITED STATES DISTRICT COURT
FOR THE ____Southern____ DISTRICT OF ___New York___

CIVIL NO. _9–1047_

_____Jane Adams_____ ,
Plaintiff

vs.   COMPLAINT

_____John Jones_____ ,
Defendant.

Comes now the plaintiff and for his cause of action against the defendant alleges and states as follows:

1. This action is between plaintiff, who is a resident of the State of New York, and defendant, who is a resident of the State of New Jersey. There is diversity of citizenship between parties.

2. The amount in controversy, exclusive of interest and costs, exceeds the sum of $10,000.00.

3. On September 10th, 1982 plaintiff, Jane Adams, was exercising good driving habits and reasonable care in driving her car through the intersection of Broadwalk and Pennsylvania Ave. when defendant, John Jones, negligently drove his vehicle through a red light at the intersection and collided with plaintiff's vehicle.

4. As a result of the collision plaintiff suffered severe physical injury, that prevented her from working, and property damage to her car. The cost she incurred included: $85,000 in medical bills, $10,000 in lost wages, $5,000 automobile repair.

WHEREFORE, plaintiff demands judgment against the defendant for the sum of $100,000 plus interest at the maximum legal rate and the costs of this action.

By   _____

Joseph Roe
Attorney for Plaintiff
100 Main Street
New York, New York

1/2/83

Jones. The *summons* notifies Jones that he is required to prepare an answer to the complaint and to file a copy of his answer with both the court and the plaintiff's attorney within a specified time period (usually twenty to thirty days after the summons has been served). The summons also informs Jones that failure to answer will result in a judgment by default for the plaintiff—the plaintiff would be awarded the damages alleged in her complaint. A typical summons is shown in Exhibit 2–4.

Rules governing the service of a summons vary, but usually *service* is made by handing the summons to the defendant personally or by leaving it at the defendant's residence or place of business. In a few states a summons can be served by mail. When the defendant cannot be reached, special rules sometimes permit serving the summons by leaving it with a designated person, such as the secretary of state.

Choices Available after Receipt of the Summons and Complaint   Once the defendant is served with a copy of the summons and complaint, the defendant must file a responsive pleading. This filing must be done within the stipulated time period. The choices are to file (1) a motion to dismiss, (2) any answer containing an affirmative defense, (3) a counterclaim, or (4) an answer denying the allegations and containing both an affirmative defense and a counterclaim.

Motion to Dismiss   If the defendant challenges the sufficiency of the plaintiff's complaint, the defendant can present to the court a **motion to dismiss,** or **demurrer.** (The rules of civil procedure in many states do not use the term *demurrer;* they use only *motion to dismiss.*) The motion to dismiss is an allegation that even if the facts presented in the complaint are true, their legal consequences are such that there is no reason to go further with the suit and no need for the defendant to present an answer. It is a contention that the defendant is not legally liable even if the facts are as the plaintiff alleges. If, for example, Adams's complaint alleges facts that exclude the possibility of negligence on Jones's part, Jones can move to dismiss, and he will not be required to answer because his motion will

be granted. The motion to dismiss is often used for purposes of delay.

If Adams wishes to discontinue the suit because, for example, an out-of-court settlement has been reached, she can likewise move for dismissal. The court can also dismiss on its own motion. If the court grants the motion to dismiss, the judge is saying that the plaintiff has failed to state a recognized cause of action. The plaintiff generally is given time to file an amended complaint. If the plaintiff does not file this amended complaint, a judgment will be entered against the plaintiff solely on the basis of the pleadings, and the plaintiff will not be allowed to bring suit on the matter again. On the other hand, if the court denies the motion to dismiss, the judge is indicating that the plaintiff has stated a recognized cause of action, and the defendant is given an extension of time to file a further pleading. If the defendant does not do so, a judgment will normally be entered for the plaintiff.

Answer and Counterclaim   If the defendant has not chosen to file a motion to dismiss or has filed a motion to dismiss that has been denied, then an **answer** must be filed with the court. This document either admits the statements or allegations set out in the complaint or denies them and sets out any defenses that the defendant may have. If Jones admits all of Adams's allegations in his answer, a judgment will be entered for Adams. If Jones denies Adams's allegations, the matter will proceed to trial.

Jones can deny Adams's allegations and set forth his own claim that Adams was in fact negligent and therefore owes Jones money for damages to the Cadillac. This is appropriately called a **counterclaim,** or a **cross-complaint.** If Jones files a counterclaim, Adams will have to answer it with a pleading, normally called a *reply,* that has the same characteristics as an answer.

Answer and Affirmative Defenses   Jones can also admit the truth of Adams's complaint but raise new facts that will result in dismissal of the action. This is called raising an *affirmative defense.* For example, Jones could admit that he was negligent but plead that the time period for raising the claim has passed and that Adams's

EXHIBIT 2–4   A TYPICAL SUMMONS

SUMMONS IN A CIVIL ACTION

United States District Court

FOR THE ____Southern____ DISTRICT OF: New York

CIVIL ACTION FILE No. _94047_

Jane Adams

Plaintiff

v.

John Jones

Defendant

SUMMONS

To the above named Defendant:

    You are hereby summoned and required to serve upon   Joseph Roe

plaintiff's attorney, whose address is   100 Main Street
                                                          New York, New York

an answer to the complaint which is herewith served upon you, within 20* days after service of this summons upon you, exclusive of the day of service. If you fail to do so, judgment by default will be taken against you for the relief demanded in the complaint.

                                        _____Tom Smith_____
                                                Clerk of Court

                                        _____Mary Doakes_____
                                                Deputy Clerk.

Date: 1/10/83   [Seal of Court]

NOTE:—This summons is issued pursuant to Rule 4 of the Federal rules of Civil Procedure.

complaint must therefore be dismissed because it is barred by the statute of limitations (a statutory limit to the time during which one can raise a claim).

The complaint and answer (and the counterclaim and reply) taken together are called the **pleadings.** The pleadings inform each party of the claims of the other and specify the issues (disputed questions) involved in the case. Pleadings remove the element of surprise from a case. They allow lawyers to gather the most persuasive evidence and to prepare better arguments, thus increasing the probability that a just and true result will be forthcoming from the trial.

Dismissals and Judgments before Trial

Many actions for which pleadings have been filed never come to trial. There are numerous procedural avenues for disposing of a case without a trial. Many of them involve one or the other party's attempts to get the case dismissed through the use of pretrial motions. We have already mentioned the motion to dismiss, or the demurrer. Another equally important motion is the motion for a judgment on the pleadings.

Motion for Judgment on the Pleadings   After the pleadings are closed—after the complaint, answer, and any counterclaim and reply have been filed—either of the parties can file a *motion for a judgment on the pleadings*. This motion is basically the same as a motion to dismiss and may be granted or denied on the same grounds.

Motion for Summary Judgment   A lawsuit can be shortened or a trial can be avoided if there are no disagreements about the facts in a case and the only question is which laws apply to those facts. Both sides can agree to the facts and ask the judge to apply the law to them. In this situation, it is appropriate for either party to move for *summary judgment*. Summary judgment will be granted when there are no genuine issues of fact in a case and the only question is one of law. When the court considers a motion for summary judgment, it can take into account evidence outside the pleadings. This distinguishes the motion for summary judgment from the motion to dismiss. In a pretrial setting, one party can bring in a sworn statement, or affidavit, that refutes the other party's claim. Unless the second party brings in affidavits of conflicting facts, the first party will receive summary judgment.

Jones, for example, can bring in the sworn statement of a witness that Jones was in California at the time of the accident. Unless Adams can bring in other statements raising the possibility that Jones was at the scene of the accident, Jones will be entitled to dismissal on a motion for summary judgment. Motions for summary judgment can be made before or during a trial, but they will be granted only if it is plain that there are no factual disputes.

Discovery

Before a trial begins, the parties can use a number of procedural devices to obtain information and gather evidence about the case. Adams, for example, will want to know how fast Jones was driving, whether he had been drinking, whether he saw a red light, and so on. The process of obtaining information from the opposing party or from other witnesses is known as **discovery**. Discovery serves several purposes. It preserves evidence from witnesses who might not be available at the time of the trial or whose memories will fade as time passes. It can pave the way for summary judgment if it is found that both parties agree on all facts. It can lead to an out-of-court settlement if one party decides that the opponent's case is too strong to challenge. Even if the case does go to trial, discovery prevents surprises by giving parties access to evidence that might otherwise be hidden, and it serves to narrow the issues so that trial time is spent on the main questions in the case. In addition, discovery serves to establish a witness's testimony so that the witness's credibility can be attacked at trial if that testimony is changed. The federal rules of civil procedure and similar rules in the states set down the guidelines for discovery activity. Discovery includes gaining access to witnesses, documents, records, and other types of evidence.

Depositions and Interrogatories   Discovery can involve the use of depositions or interrogatories, or both. *Depositions* are sworn testimony by the opposing party or any witness, recorded by a court official. The person deposed appears before a court officer and is sworn. That person then answers questions asked by the attorneys from both sides. The questions and answers are taken down, sworn to, and signed. These answers will, of course, help the attorneys prepare their cases. They can also be used in court to impeach a party or witness who changes testimony at the trial. Finally, they can be used as testimony if the witness is not available at trial. Depositions can also be taken with written questions from both sides prepared ahead of time.

Interrogatories are a series of written questions for which written answers are prepared and then signed under oath. The main difference between interrogatories and depositions with written questions is that interrogatories are directed to a party, not to a witness, and the party can prepare answers with the aid of an attorney. The scope of interrogatories is broader because parties are obligated to answer questions even if the answer requires disclosing information from their records and files. Interrogatories are also usually less expensive than depositions.

Request for Admissions A party can serve a written request to the other party for an admission of the truth of matters relating to the trial. Any matter admitted under such a request is conclusively established for the trial. For example, Adams can ask Jones to admit that he was driving at a speed of forty-five miles an hour. A request for admission saves time at trial because parties will not have to spend time proving facts on which they already agree.

Documents, Objects, and Entry upon Land A party can gain access to documents and other items not in possession in order to inspect and examine them. Likewise, the party can gain entry upon land to inspect the premises. Jones, for example, can gain permission to inspect and duplicate Adams's medical records and repair bills.

Physical and Mental Examination Where the physical or mental condition of a party is in question, a party can ask the court to order a physical or mental examination. If the court is willing to make the order, the party can obtain the results of the examination. It is important to note that the court will make such an order only when the need for the information outweighs the right to privacy of the person to be examined.

The rules governing discovery are designed to make sure that a witness or party is not unduly harassed, that privileged material is safeguarded, and that only matters relevant to the case at hand are discoverable.

Pretrial Hearing

Either party or the court can request a pretrial conference or hearing. Usually the hearing consists of an informal discussion between the judge and the opposing attorneys after discovery has taken place. The purpose of the hearing is to identify the matters that are in dispute and to plan the course of the trial. The pretrial hearing is not intended to compel the parties to settle their case before trial, although judges may encourage them to settle out of court if circumstances suggest that a trial would be a waste of time.

Jury Trials

A trial can be held with or without a jury. If there is no jury, the judge determines the truth of the facts alleged in the case. The Seventh Amendment to the U.S. Constitution guarantees the right to a jury trial for cases at law in federal courts when the amount in controversy exceeds $20. Most states have similar guarantees in their own constitutions, although many states put a higher minimum dollar amount restriction on the guarantee. For example, Iowa requires the dollar amount of damages to be at least $1,000 before there is a right to a jury trial.

The right to a trial by jury does not have to be exercised, and many cases are tried without one. In most states and in federal courts, one of the parties must request a jury or the right is presumed to be waived.

In the case between Adams and Jones, both parties want a jury trial. The jurors are questioned by the judge and by both attorneys to ensure that their judgment will be impartial. After the jurors are selected, they are impaneled, sworn in, and the trial is ready to begin.

The Trial

Both attorneys are allowed to make *opening statements* concerning the facts that they expect to prove during the trial. Since Adams is the plaintiff and has the burden of proving that her case is correct, Adams's attorney begins the case by calling the first witness for the plaintiff and examining (questioning) the witness. (For both attorneys, the type of question and the manner of asking are governed by the rules of evidence.) This examination is called *direct examination.* After Adams's attorney is finished, the witness will be questioned by Jones's attorney on *cross-examination.* After that, Adams's attorney has another opportunity to question the witness in *redirect examination,* and Jones's attorney can then follow with *recross examination.* When both attorneys have finished with the first witness, Adams's attorney will call the succeeding witnesses in the plaintiff's case, each of whom is subject to cross-examination (and redirect and recross, if necessary).

At the conclusion of the plaintiff's case, the defendant's attorney has the opportunity to ask the judge to direct a verdict for the defendant on the ground that the plaintiff has presented no evidence that would justify the granting of the plaintiff's remedy. This is called a *motion for a directed verdict.* In considering the motion, the judge will look at the evidence in the light most favorable to the plaintiff and will grant the motion only if there is insufficient evidence to raise an issue of fact. (Motions for directed verdicts at this stage of trial are seldom granted.)

The defendant's attorney will then present the evidence and witnesses for the defendant's case. Witnesses are called and examined. The plaintiff's attorney has a right to cross-examine them, and there is a redirect and recross examination if necessary. At the end of the defendant's case, either attorney can again move for a directed verdict, and the test will again be

whether the jury can, under any reasonable interpretation of the evidence, find for the party against whom the motion is made.

After the defendant's attorney has finished the presentation of evidence, the plaintiff's attorney can present additional evidence to refute the defendant's case in a *rebuttal.* The defendant's attorney can meet that evidence in a *rejoinder.* After both sides have rested their cases, the attorneys each present a *closing argument,* urging a verdict in favor of their respective clients. The judge instructs the jury (assuming it is a jury trial) in the law that applies to the case. The instructions to the jury are often called *charges.* Then the jury retires to the jury room to deliberate a verdict. In the Adams v. Jones case the jury will not only decide for the plaintiff or for the defendant but, if it finds for the plaintiff, it will also decide on the amount of money to be paid her.

Motion for New Trial   At the end of the trial, a motion can be made to set aside an adverse verdict and any judgment, and to hold a new trial. The motion will be granted if the judge is convinced, after looking at all the evidence, that the jury was in error. A new trial can also be granted on the grounds of newly discovered evidence, misconduct by the participants during the trial, or error by the judge.

Judgment N.O.V. (Notwithstanding the Verdict)   If Adams wins, and if Jones's attorney had previously moved for a directed verdict, Jones's attorney can now make a motion for a *judgment n.o.v. (notwithstanding the verdict).* In other words, Jones can state that even if the evidence is viewed in the light most favorable to Adams, a reasonable jury should not have found a verdict in Adams's favor. If the judge finds this contention to be correct or decides that the law requires the opposite result, the motion will be granted. The standards for granting a judgment n.o.v. are the same as those for granting a motion to dismiss. Assume here that this motion is denied and that Jones appeals the case. (If Adams wins but receives a smaller money award than she sought, she can appeal also). These events are illustrated in Exhibit 2–5.

EXHIBIT 2–5 A TYPICAL LAWSUIT

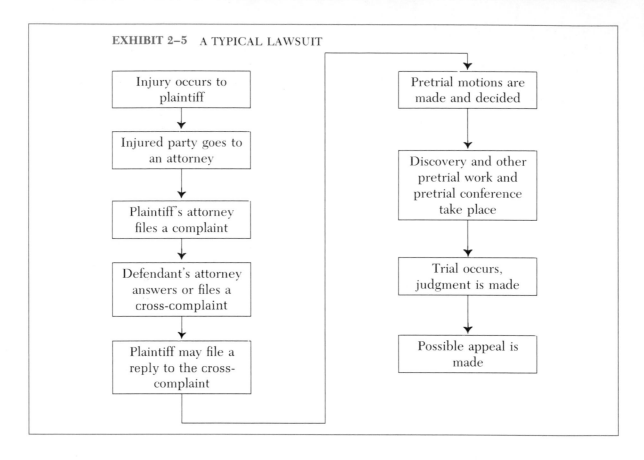

The Appeal

A notice of appeal must be filed with the clerk of the trial court within the prescribed time. Jones then becomes the *appellant* or *petitioner*. His attorney files in the reviewing court (usually an intermediate court of appeals) the record on appeal, which contains the following: (1) the pleadings, (2) a transcript of the trial testimony and copies of the exhibits, (3) the judge's rulings on motions made by the parties, (4) the arguments of counsel, (5) the instructions to the jury, (6) the verdict, (7) the posttrial motions, and (8) the judgment order from which the appeal is taken. Jones may also be required to post a bond for the appeal.

Jones's attorney is required to prepare a condensation of the record, known as an *abstract.* The abstract, the brief, and the arguments are filed with the reviewing court. The brief contains (1) a short statement of the facts, (2) a statement of the issues, (3) the rulings by the trial court that Jones contends are erroneous and prejudicial, (4) the grounds for reversal of the judgment, (5) a statement of the applicable law, and (6) arguments on Jones's behalf, citing applicable statutes and relevant cases as precedent. The attorney for the *appellee,* or *respondent,* Adams, must now file an answering brief and argument. Jones's attorney can now file a reply (although this is not required). The reviewing court then considers the case.

No Evidence Heard Appeals courts do not hear any evidence. Their decision concerning a case is based upon the abstracts, the record, and the briefs. The attorneys can present oral arguments, after which the case is taken under advisement. When the court has reached a decision, the decision is written. It contains the opinion (the court's reasons for its decision), the rules of law that apply, and the judgment. In general, the appellate courts do not reverse findings of fact unless the findings are unsupported or contradicted by the evidence. Rather, they review the record for errors of law. If the reviewing court believes that a reversible error was committed during the trial or that the jury was improperly instructed, the judgment will be reversed. Sometimes the case will be *remanded* (sent back to the court that originally heard the case) for a new trial. In many cases the decision of the lower court is *affirmed*, resulting in enforcement of that court's judgment or decree.

Higher Appeals Courts If the reviewing court is an intermediate appellate court, the losing party (in that court) may seek a reversal of its decision by filing within the prescribed time period a petition for leave to appeal to the state supreme court.[11] Such a petition corresponds to a petition for a *writ of certiorari* in the United States Supreme Court. The winning party in the intermediate appellate court can file an answer to the petition for leave to appeal. If the petition is granted, the complete record is certified and forwarded to the higher court. New briefs must be filed before the state supreme court and the attorneys may be allowed or requested to present oral arguments. Whenever the state supreme court concludes that the judgment of the intermediate appellate court is correct, it affirms. If it decides otherwise, it reverses the appellate court's decision and enters an appropriate order of remand. At this point, unless a federal question is at issue, the case has reached its end. If a new trial is ordered, it will start again at the court of origin.

It is important to know that the vast majority of disputes are settled out of court mainly because of the time and expense of trying a case. Furthermore, of those cases that go to trial, about 97 percent are finally resolved at the trial level, as relatively few trial court decisions are changed on appeal.

HOW TO FIND CASE LAW

Most trial court decisions are not published. Except for the federal courts and New York and a

few other states that publish selected opinions of their trial courts, decisions in trial courts are merely filed in the office of the clerk of the court, where they are available for public inspection.

On the other hand, the written decisions of appellate courts are published and distributed (these reported cases paradoxically are called *unwritten law*, as contrasted with the *written*, or statutory, law). Virtually all of the cases in this book have been taken from these decisions. It is therefore important to understand the case reporting system. The study of law is enhanced by using the so-called *case method* for presentation of subject matter. When students of law study cases, they are engaging in the inductive method of learning.

The reported appellate decisions are published in volumes called *Reports*, which are numbered consecutively. State court decisions are found in the state reports of that particular state. Additionally, state reports appear in regional units of the *National Reporter System*, published by West Publishing Company. Most lawyers and libraries have the West reporters because they report cases more quickly and they are distributed more widely than the state-published reports. In fact, many states have eliminated their own reports in favor of West's *National Reporter System*.

Geographical Areas

West Publishing Company has divided the states into geographical areas: Atlantic (A. or A.2d), Southeastern (S.E. or S.E.2d), Southwestern (S.W. or S.W.2d), Northwestern (N.W. or N.W.2d), Northeastern (N.E. or N.E.2d), Southern (So. or So.2d), and Pacific (P. or P.2d). After appellate decisions are published, they are normally referred to (cited) by giving the name of the case; the volume, name, and page of the state report (if any), the volume and page of the National Reporter; and the volume, name, and page of any other selected case series. For example, consider the following case: Quality Motors, Inc. v. Hays, 216 Ark. 264, 225 S.W.2d 326 (1950). After the names of the parties, we see that the opinion in this case may be found in Volume 216 of the official *Arkansas Reports* on page 264; and in

---

11. In most states, the appeal from the court of original jurisdiction to the state supreme court is a matter of right.

Volume 225 of the *Southwestern Reporter*, Second Series on page 326. (Additionally, when we cite cases in this text, we give the name of the court and the year of filing of the appellate court decision.)

Federal court decisions are found in the *Federal Reporter* (F. or F.2d), *Federal Supplement* (F.Supp.), *Federal Rules Decisions* (F.R.D.), *West's Bankruptcy Reporter* (B.R.), *United States Supreme Court Reports* (U.S.), *Supreme Court Reporter* (S.Ct.), and the *Lawyer's Edition* (L.Ed.).

In the title of a case such as *Adams v. Jones*, the v. or vs. stands for versus, which means against. In the trial court, Adams was the plaintiff—the person who filed the suit. Jones was the defendant. When the case is appealed, however, the appellate court will sometimes place the name of the party appealing the decision first, so that the case will be called *Jones v. Adams*. Since some appellate courts retain the trial court order of names, it is often impossible to distinguish the plaintiff from the defendant in the title of a reported appellate court decision. The student must carefully read the facts of each case in order to identify each party. Otherwise, the discussion by the appellate court will be difficult to understand.

The study of reported cases requires an understanding and application of legal analysis. For students who want to learn how to brief a case, Appendix A on this subject is presented at the end of the regular text chapters.

A SUPREME COURT CASE

The following case involves a federal question. The Supreme Court granted a *writ of certiorari* to determine whether a federal law permitted a student to sue a university. The Court decided what Congress intended. Note the use of prior cases (precedent) to resolve the question before the Court. The issue to be decided was whether Congress intended the withdrawal of federal funds to be the sole punishment for educational institutions with discriminatory admissions policies or whether a student who was denied admission could recover damages (a private remedy).

CANNON v.
UNIVERSITY OF
CHICAGO

United States Supreme Court,
1979. 441 U.S. 677,
99 S.Ct.1946.

Mr. Justice STEVENS delivered the opinion of the Court.

Petitioner's complaints allege that her applications for admission to medical school were denied by the respondents because she is a woman.[1] Accepting the truth of those allegations for the purpose of its decision, the Court of Appeals held that petitioner [Cannon] has no right of action against respondents [University of Chicago, et al.] that may be asserted in a federal court. We granted certiorari to review that holding.

Only two facts alleged in the complaints are relevant to our decision. First, petitioner was excluded from participation in the respondents' medical education programs because of her sex. Second, these education programs were receiving federal financial assistance at the time of her exclusion. These facts establish a violation of § 901(a) of Title IX of the Education Amendments of 1972 (hereinafter Title IX). That section, in relevant part, provides:

---

1. Each of petitioner's two complaints names as defendant a private university—the University of Chicago and Northwestern University—and various officials of the medical school operated by that university. In addition, both complaints name the Secretary, and the Region V Director of the Office for Civil Rights, of the Department of Health, Education, and Welfare. Although all of these defendants prevailed below, and are respondents here, the federal defendants have taken a position that basically accords with the position advanced by petitioner.

"No person in the United States shall, on the basis of sex, be excluded from participation in, be denied the benefits of, or be subjected to discrimination under any education program or activity receiving Federal financial assistance. . . ."

The statute does not, however, expressly authorize a private right of action by a person injured by a violation of § 901. For that reason, and because it concluded that no private remedy should be inferred, the District Court granted the respondents' motions to dismiss.

The Court of Appeals agreed that the statute did not contain an implied private remedy. Noting that § 902 of Title IX establishes a procedure for the termination of federal financial support for institutions violating § 901, the Court of Appeals concluded that Congress intended that remedy to be the exclusive means of enforcement. It recognized that the statute was patterned after Title VI of the Civil Rights Act of 1964 (hereinafter Title VI), but rejected petitioner's argument that Title VI included an implied private cause of action.

*   *   *   *

The Court of Appeals quite properly devoted careful attention to this question of statutory construction. As our recent cases—particularly *Cort v. Ash*, 422 U.S. 66—demonstrate, the fact that a federal statute has been violated and some person harmed does not automatically give rise to a private cause of action in favor of that person. Instead, before concluding that Congress intended to make a remedy available to a special class of litigants, a court must carefully analyze the four factors that *Cort* identifies as indicative of such an intent. Our review of those factors persuades us, however, that the Court of Appeals reached the wrong conclusion and that petitioner does have a statutory right to pursue her claim that respondents rejected her application on the basis of her sex. After commenting on each of the four factors, we shall explain why they are not overcome by respondents' countervailing arguments.

First, the threshold question under *Cort* is whether the statute was enacted for the benefit of a special class of which the plaintiff is a member. That question is answered by looking to the language of the statute itself. *   *   *

*   *   *   *

Unquestionably, therefore, the first of the four factors identified in *Cort* favors the implication of a private cause of action. Title IX explicitly confers a benefit on persons discriminated against on the basis of sex, and petitioner is clearly a member of that class for whose special benefit the statute was enacted.

Second, the *Cort* analysis requires consideration of legislative history. We must recognize, however, that the legislative history of a statute that does not expressly create or deny a private remedy will typically be equally silent or ambiguous on the question. Therefore, in situations such as the present one "in which it is clear that federal law has granted a class of persons certain rights, it is not necessary to show an intention to *create* a private cause of action, although an explicit purpose to *deny* such cause of action would be controlling." *Cort*, 422 U.S., at 82 (emphasis in original). But this is not the typical case. Far from evidencing any purpose to *deny* a private cause of action, the history of Title IX rather plainly indicates that Congress intended to create such a remedy.

Title IX was patterned after Title VI of the Civil Rights Act of 1964. Except for the substitution of the word "sex" in Title IX to replace the words "race, color, or national origin" in Title VI, the two statutes use identical language to describe the benefited class. Both statutes provide the same administrative mechanism for terminating federal financial support for institutions engaged in prohibited discrimination. Neither statute expressly mentions a private remedy for the person excluded from participation in a federally funded program. The drafters of Title IX explicitly assumed that it would be interpreted and applied as Title VI had been during the preceding eight years.

In 1972 when Title IX was enacted, the critical language in Title VI had already been construed as creating a private remedy. Most particularly, in 1967, a distinguished panel of the Court of Appeals for the Fifth Circuit squarely decided this issue in an opinion that was repeatedly cited with approval and never questioned during the ensuing five years. In addition, at least a dozen other federal courts reached similar conclusions in the same or related contexts during those years. It is always appropriate to assume that our elected representatives, like other citizens, know the law; in this case, because of their repeated references to Title VI and its modes of enforcement, we are especially justified in presuming both that those representatives were aware of the prior interpretation of Title VI and that that interpretation reflects their intent with respect to Title IX.

* * * *

* * * We have no doubt that Congress intended to create Title IX remedies comparable to those available under Title VI and that it understood Title VI as authorizing an implied private cause of action for victims of the prohibited discrimination.

Third, under *Cort*, a private remedy should not be implied if it would frustrate the underlying purpose of the legislative scheme. On the other hand, when that remedy is necessary or at least helpful to the accomplishment of the statutory purpose, the Court is decidedly receptive to its implication under the statute.

Title IX, like its model Title VI, sought to accomplish two related, but nevertheless somewhat different, objectives. First, Congress wanted to avoid the use of federal resources to support discriminatory practices; second, it wanted to provide individual citizens effective protection against those practices. Both of these purposes were repeatedly identified in the debates on the two statutes.

* * * *

Fourth, the final inquiry suggested by *Cort* is whether implying a federal remedy is inappropriate because the subject matter involves an area basically of concern to the States. No such problem is raised by a prohibition against invidious discrimination of any sort, including that on the basis of sex. Since the Civil War, the Federal Government and the federal courts have been the " 'primary and powerful reliances' " in protecting citizens against such discrimination. * * *

In sum, there is no need in this case to weigh the four *Cort* factors; all of them support the same result. Not only the words and history of Title IX, but also its subject matter and underlying purposes, counsel implication of a cause of action in favor of private victims of discrimination.

* * * *

When Congress intends private litigants to have a cause of action to support their statutory rights, the far better course is for it to specify as much when it creates those rights. But the Court has long recognized that under certain limited circumstances the failure of Congress to do so is not inconsistent with an intent on its part to have such a remedy available to the persons benefited by its legislation. Title IX presents the atypical situation in which *all* of the circumstances that the Court has previously identified as supportive of an implied remedy are present. We therefore conclude that petitioner may maintain her lawsuit, despite the absence of any express authorization for it in the statute.

The judgment of the Court of Appeals is reversed, and the case is remanded for further proceedings consistent with this opinion.

Review of Case

1. The name of the case, also known as the *style*, is *Cannon v. University of Chicago*. Cannon was the plaintiff at the trial level, where her complaint was dismissed for failure to state a cause of action.
2. The court that heard this case was the Supreme Court of the United States, the highest appellate court in the United States. That this was a Supreme Court opinion can be determined from the citation that will be discussed here.
3. The justice who delivered the opinion of the court was Justice Stevens. The Supreme Court has a chief justice and eight associate justices.
4. The numbers and letters found below the case name or party names, such as 441 U.S. 677 (1979), constitute the citation. This is what lawyers use to locate the case. This case can be found in volume 441 of *United States Reports*, on page 677. The case was decided in 1979.
5. The *opinion* usually begins with a recital of the facts followed by a discussion of the law.
6. The triple asterisks (*   *   *) indicate that the authors of this book have deleted part of the opinion to make the case more concise and readable. Quadruple asterisks (*   *   *   *) indicate that a paragraph (or more) has been omitted. Where an opinion cites another case, the citations to the referenced case have been omitted without leaving asterisks so as to save space and improve readability.
7. This case came to the Supreme Court after the district court dismissed Cannon's complaint. The Court of Appeals for the Seventh Circuit affirmed the dismissal. Cannon petitioned the Supreme Court for a *writ of certiorari*, and the Court agreed to hear the case.
8. The judgment of the Court of Appeals was reversed by the Supreme Court. This ruling does not mean that Cannon wins her suit against the

University of Chicago. The case was remanded to the trial court. That means that the case was sent back to the court from which it came for the purpose of having further action taken there. At trial at that time, Cannon must establish that she was discriminated against and prove her damages.

QUESTIONS AND CASE PROBLEMS

1. The American system of government is unique in that it has essentially two sets of governments—state and federal. This is called the dual, or federal, system. One problem that arises in a federal system is that each government tends to duplicate the other's efforts. Can you see any way to avoid such problems of duplication?
2. When a person commits an act that violates both state and federal law, quite often both the federal and the state government have jurisdiction. What problems do you see here?
3. The Constitution says that a person cannot be tried twice for the same crime. Does this problem arise when both the federal and the state government try the same person for the same crime? Explain.
4. a. Before two parties go to trial, there is an involved process called pleadings and discovery. Until recently, pleadings were very formal, and trials often turned on elements of surprise. For example, a plaintiff would not necessarily know until the trial what the defendant's defense was going to be. Does this seem like a fair way to conduct a trial?

b. Within the last twenty years, new rules of pleadings and discovery have substantially changed all this. Now each attorney can discover practically all the evidence that the other will be presenting at trial. However, certain information is still not available to the parties—namely, each attorney's work product. *Work product* is not a clear concept. Basically, it includes all the attorney's thoughts on the case. Can you see any reason why such information should not be made available to the opposing attorney?

5.   Quite often, trials are concluded before they are begun. If the parties do not disagree on the facts, they simply relate those facts to the judge, and then, through a motion for judgment on the pleadings, they ask the judge to decide what the law is and how it applies to this set of facts. How is it possible that two parties can agree on the facts yet disagree as to which party is liable?

6.   If a judge enters judgment on the pleadings, the losing party can usually appeal but cannot present evidence to the appellate court. Does this seem fair? Explain.

7.   Once a case is appealed, most appellate courts do not have the power to enter judgment or to award damages to a party who should have received them at trial. Consequently, if the appellate court disagrees with the trial court's decision, it will reverse and remand—in effect, ordering the trial court judge to change the judgment. Why should an appellate court not take a judge's word as final?

8.   Sometimes on appeal there are questions of whether the facts presented in a trial support the conclusion reached by the judge or the jury. The appellate court will reverse on the basis of the facts only when so little evidence was presented at trial that no reasonable person could have reached the conclusion that the judge or jury reached. Appellate courts normally defer to a judge's decision with regard to the facts. Can you see any reason for this?

CHAPTER 3

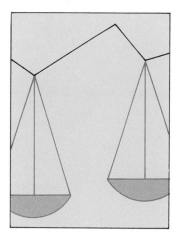

Torts

Part of doing business today and, indeed, part of everyday life is the risk of being involved in a lawsuit. A normal and ever-increasing business operating cost is that of liability insurance to protect against lawsuits. The list of circumstances in which businesspeople can be sued is long and varied. An employee injured on the job may attempt to sue the employer because of an unsafe working environment. The consumer who is injured while using a product may attempt to sue the manufacturer because of a defect in the product. The patient who has received negligent treatment may attempt to sue the doctor. The issue in all of these examples is alleged wrongful conduct by one person that causes injury to another. Such wrongful conduct is covered by the law of **torts.**

Tort law covers a broad variety of injuries. Society recognizes an interest in personal physical safety, and tort law provides a remedy for acts causing physical injury or interfering with physical security and freedom of movement. So-

ciety recognizes an interest in protecting personal property, and tort law provides a remedy for acts causing destruction or damage to property. Society recognizes other, more intangible interests in such things as personal privacy, family relations, reputation, and dignity. Tort law provides a remedy for invasion of protected interests in these areas. Tort law is constantly changing and growing with society. Although many torts have their origin in the old common law, new torts are recognized in order to protect new interests that develop with social change.

KINDS OF TORTS

Determining whether or not some action is a tort involves, in essence, a decision on how losses should be allocated in an increasingly complex society. Thus, the many factors that make up social policy are weighed against one another. Torts are traditionally divided into three categories:

1. *Intentional torts.*
2. *Negligence.*
3. *Strict liability.*

Intentional torts, as the name implies, are injuries caused by intentional acts. Negligence is harm from careless acts. Strict liability rules require someone to compensate the injured party without regard to fault; generally, strict liability is imposed by law.

TORT LAW
VERSUS CRIMINAL LAW

Two notions serve as the basis of all torts: wrongs and compensation. The word *tort* is French for "wrong." Tort law recognizes that some acts are wrong because they cause injury to someone. The actor is to blame, or bears the fault for these injuries. Of course, this is not the only type of wrong that exists in the law; crimes involve wrongs also. A crime, however, is an act so reprehensible that it is considered to be a wrong against the state or against society as a whole, as well as against the individual victim. Therefore, the *state* prosecutes the criminal. On the other hand, a tort action is a *civil* action, in which one person brings a suit of a personal nature against another. The state is not a party to the suit. Thus, for example, an assault could be the basis for a criminal prosecution as well as the basis of an action in tort. In such a case the same act can be a criminal wrong and a civil wrong.

The function of tort law is to provide the injured party with some remedy. The law of torts is used to decide when victims must bear the loss themselves and when the responsibility belongs to someone else. A typical tort action involves a negligent act of one party that causes personal or property damage to another.

The law of torts is ever-changing. For example, until recently it was not a legally recognizable tort for a husband to negligently injure his wife or child because of old notions of family structure. But today minors get much more protection, as do spouses. Traditionally, one could not recover for psychological injury unless one had personally risked physical harm. That rule is changing, with more and more courts allowing recovery for emotional damage to those who witness traumatic injury to another.

INTENTIONAL TORTS:
WRONGS AGAINST THE PERSON

An **intentional tort** arises from an act which the defendant consciously desired to perform, either in order to harm another or knowing with substantial certainty that injury to another could result. Note that it is *intent* to perform the original act that is important. The nature of the damage ultimately caused is irrelevant in determining whether there was intent. If Johnson intentionally pushes Adams and Adams falls to the ground and breaks her arm, it does not matter that Johnson never wished to break Adams's arm. Johnson did intend to push Adams, and that in itself is a tortious act; Johnson is liable for the consequences, including injury to Adams's arm. If the push were accidental, there would not be an intentional tort, but there might be a negligent injury.

Because intent is a subjective concept, the law generally assumes that one intends the normal consequences of his or her actions. Thus, an angry push is an intentional tort because the object of the push will go flying; however, a playful pat on the shoulder is not an intentional tort even though, in drawing away suddenly, the person touched may be injured. When injury is not a normal consequence of the act, the injured person must prove real harm has occurred in order to recover damages.

Assault

Any intentional, unexcused act that creates in another person a reasonable apprehension or fear of immediate harmful or offensive contact is an assault. Apprehension is not the same as fear. If a contact is such that a reasonable person would want to avoid it, and if there is a reasonable basis for believing the contact is coming, then the plaintiff suffers apprehension whether or not he or she is afraid.

The interest protected in assault is the freedom from having to expect harmful or offensive contact. The arousal of apprehension is enough to justify compensation. Of course, the *completion* of the act that caused apprehension, if it results in harm to the plaintiff, is a battery, discussed next. For example, Jones threatens Smith with a gun, then shoots him. The pointing of the gun at Smith is an assault; the firing of the gun is a battery.

Battery

A battery is an unexcused, harmful or offensive physical contact intentionally performed. If Jones intentionally punches Smith in the nose, it is a battery. The interest this tort protects is the right to personal security and safety. The contact can be harmful, or it can be merely offensive (such as an unwelcome kiss). Physical injury does not have to occur. The contact can be to any part of the body or anything attached to it—for example, a hat or other clothing, a purse, a chair, or an automobile in which one is sitting. Whether the contact is offensive or not is determined by the *reasonable person* standard. The contact can be made by the defendant or by some force that the defendant sets in motion—for example, a rock thrown, food poisoned, or a stick swung.

If the plaintiff shows that there was a contact, and the jury agrees that the contact was offensive, that is enough to have a right to some compensation. Furthermore, there is no need to show that the defendant acted out of malice. The person could have been joking or playing or could even have had some benevolent motive. The underlying motive does not matter, only the intent to do the act. In fact proving a motive is never necessary (but is always relevant). Damages from a battery can be for emotional harm or loss of reputation as well as for physical harm.

Assault and Battery Defenses A number of legally recognized defenses can be raised by a defendant who is sued for assault or battery, or both. The defenses to be discussed here are (1) **consent,** (2) **self-defense,** (3) **defense of others,** and (4) **defense of property.**

Consent When a person consents to the act that damages him or her, there is generally no liability for the damage done. A person who voluntarily signs up for a touch football team implicitly consents to the *normal* physical punishment

that takes place during such activities. This defense is good only so long as the defendant remains within the boundaries of the consent given—that is, plays football by the normal rules.

Self-defense An individual who is defending his or her life or physical well-being may use the defense of self-defense. A person is privileged to use whatever force is *reasonably* necessary to prevent harmful contact. This defense extends not only to *real* danger, but also to *apparent* danger. However, reasonable ground must exist for believing the danger is real. Also, force cannot be used once the danger has passed, and revenge is always prohibited.

Defense of Others An individual can act reasonably to protect others who are in real or apparent danger.

Defense of Property Individuals who use reasonable force in attempting to remove intruders from their homes can use the defense of property to counter tort lawsuits for assault or battery, or both. The law does value life, though, more than it values property. In principle, force that is likely to cause death or great bodily injury may never be used just to protect property. Setting a trap that fires a gun if an intruder enters an empty house is not considered reasonable by most courts.

False Imprisonment

False imprisonment, sometimes called false arrest, is defined as the intentional confinement or restraint of another person. It involves interference with the freedom to move without restraint. The confinement can be accomplished through the use of physical barriers, physical restraint, or threats of physical force. Moral pressure or future threats are not restraints sufficient to constitute false imprisonment. It is essential that the person being restrained not comply with the restraint willingly. On the other hand, a person is under no duty to risk personal harm in trying to escape.

Businesspeople are often confronted with suits for false imprisonment after they have attempted to confine a suspected shoplifter for questioning. Consider, for example, the case in which a store detective locks an alleged shoplifter in one of the store's offices. If the customer can prove his or her innocence or that the detention was totally unreasonable, the store can be sued for false imprisonment.

The loss to business from shoplifting is estimated to exceed 10 billion dollars a year. Almost all states have adopted so-called merchant protection legislation, which allows a merchant to detain any suspected shoplifter, provided that there is reasonable cause for suspicion and provided that the confinement is carried out in a

reasonable way. However, the risk of real injury to an innocent person is great. Educational programs are often offered to all employees; these programs explain the exact procedures to be followed when a customer is suspected of shoplifting. Harm to reputation and the mental distress from a wrongful imprisonment are believed by the law to be so real that damages are presumed and need not be proven to make a case.

A merchant can use the defense of probable cause to justify delaying a suspected shoplifter, but the delay must be *reasonable*. The following case provides a good example.

FAULKENBERRY v. SPRINGS MILLS, INC.

Supreme Court of South Carolina, 1978. 271 S.C.377, 247 S.E.2d 445.

BACKGROUND AND FACTS   *Barbara Faulkenberry brought this action against her employer, Springs Mills, Inc., for false imprisonment. On two separate occasions, fellow employees had reported to supervisory personnel that Faulkenberry had been seen secreting cloth in her pocketbook. After the second report, her supervisors and some plant security guards delayed her for about fifteen minutes at the mill gatehouse as she attempted to leave work. The delay was to investigate whether she had any cloth in her possession.*

Faulkenberry refused to open her pocketbook at the request of her supervisors. After some discussion and her continued refusal to open her pocketbook to reveal its contents, she left the mill gatehouse without further hindrance. Subsequently, she filed this action for false imprisonment based upon the delay at the gatehouse.

The trial court found the employer guilty of false imprisonment.

LEWIS, Chief Justice.

*   *   *   *

[T]he essence of the tort of false imprisonment consists in depriving the plaintiff of his or her liberty without lawful justification.

Since we conclude that the actions of appellant's [Springs Mills's] agents were done with legal justification we need not determine whether the delay or restraint of respondent at the gatehouse as she left work constituted the restraint required to make out false imprisonment. If appellant [Springs Mills] was legally justified in restraining respondent [Ms. Faulkenberry], she is not entitled to recover. The following from 32 Am.Jur.2d, False Imprisonment, Section 74, soundly states the applicable principles:

> Ordinarily the owner of property, in the exercise of his inherent right to protect it, is justified in restraining another who seeks to interfere with or injure it where the restraint or detention is reasonable in time and manner. Thus, where a person has reasonable grounds to believe that another is taking his property, he is justified in detaining the suspect for a reasonable length of time for the

purpose of making an investigation in a reasonable manner. In such cases, probable cause is a defense, even though the injury which is about to be inflicted constitutes only a misdemeanor, for it is the existence of a reasonable ground to suppose that one's property is in danger which gives right to the protection. It follows that the owner of a store or other premises has a right to detain a customer or patron, for a reasonable time for a reasonable investigation, whom he has reasonable grounds to believe has not paid for what he has received, or is attempting to take goods without payment *   *   * Moreover, the right to detain the person suspected of wrongdoing exists only during commission of the offense, and does not arise where the offense was completed at some prior time.

Probable cause is *   *   * a defense *   *   * to actions arising from a merchant's delay of suspected shoplifters. [The relevant law] provides:

> In any action brought by reason of having been delayed by a merchant or merchant's employee or agent on or near the premises of a mercantile establishment for the purpose of investigation concerning the ownership of any merchandise, it shall be a defense to such action if: (1) The person was delayed in a reasonable manner and for a reasonable time to permit such investigation, and (2) reasonable cause existed to believe that the person delayed had committed the crime of shoplifting.

We find no sound reason to deny the [same] defense, *   *   * to employers who reasonably delay employees in an attempt to determine the ownership of property. Such actions, of course, must be supported by probable cause; and the delay must be reasonable in time and manner and can only be justified during the commission of the suspected wrongdoing.

Appellant's [Springs Mills's] actions met the requirements of the foregoing rule. The evidence conclusively shows probable cause or legal justification for the restraint of [respondent, Barbara Faulkenberry]. Appellant's supervisory personnel acted only after the second report from an eyewitness that respondent was seen placing cloth in her purse. She was detained immediately thereafter at the gatehouse for the purpose of investigating the report that she was removing appellant's property from the Mill, an act which the information indicated was then in progress.

Respondent was not physically restrained, but was asked to come into the gatehouse so that the security officer could talk to her. The gatehouse was respondent's intended destination to complete her work check-out sheet. When she had completed "checking out" from work, she was asked to open her pocketbook and was told the reason for the request. She refused the request and after about twenty minutes discussion left without hindrance.

The record conclusively shows that respondent was delayed by appellant's security officers for only about twenty minutes for the purpose of making the legitimate inquiry into the charge that respondent was then in the act of unlawfully taking appellant's property. The information from fellow employees (eyewitnesses), upon which appellant acted in making the inquiry of respondent, was properly deemed reliable. The inquiry or investigation made was reasonable in nature, consisting solely of requests that respondent open her pocketbook.

The legal justification for the investigation by appellant into the alleged taking of its property by respondent is conclusively shown. The evidence therefore fails to sustain the finding of false imprisonment.

JUDGMENT AND REMEDY   *The state supreme court reversed the trial court's finding of false imprisonment. Springs Mills had legal justification for stopping Faulkenberry to investigate the reports that she was stealing from her employer. Hence, Faulkenberry was not entitled to recover on her action for false imprisonment. The decision of the lower court was reversed and the case was remanded to the trial court for entry of a judgment in favor of the appellant, Springs Mills.*

Infliction of Mental Distress

Recently the courts have begun to recognize an interest in freedom from mental distress as well as an interest in physical security. The tort of infliction of *mental distress* can be defined as an intentional act that amounts to extreme and outrageous conduct resulting in severe emotional distress to another. For example, a prankster telephones an individual and says that the individual's spouse has just been in a horrible accident. As a result, the individual suffers intense mental pain or anxiety. This is deemed to be extreme and outrageous conduct that exceeds the bounds of decency accepted by society and is therefore actionable.

Intentional infliction of mental distress is defined as intentionally causing severe emotional distress in those situations in which the actor's conduct has gone beyond all reasonable bounds of decency.[1]

As this is a relatively new tort, it poses some problems. One major problem is that it could flood the courts with lawsuits asserting this basis of recovery. A society in which individuals are rewarded if they are unable to endure the normal mental stresses of day-to-day living is obviously undesirable. Therefore, the law usually focuses on the nature of the acts that come under this tort. Indignity or annoyance alone are usually not enough for a lawsuit based on intentional infliction of emotional distress. Many times, however, repeated annoyances, coupled with threats, are enough. Also, an unusually severe emotional reaction, such as the extreme distress of a woman incorrectly informed that her husband and two sons have been killed, may be ac-

tionable. Because it is difficult to prove the existence of mental suffering, a few states (such as Texas) require that the mental disturbance be evidenced by some physical illness.

Defamation

The protection of a person's body is involved in the torts of assault, battery, and false imprisonment. **Defamation** of character involves wrongfully hurting a person's good reputation. The law has imposed a general duty on all persons to refrain from making false, defamatory statements about others. Breaching this duty orally involves the tort of **slander;** breaching it in writing involves the tort of **libel.**[2]

The basis of the tort is the publication of a statement or statements that hold an individual up to contempt, ridicule, or hatred. *Publication* here means that the defamatory statements are made to or within the hearing of persons other than the defamed party. If Thompson writes Andrews a private letter accusing him of embezzling funds, that does not constitute libel. If Peters calls Gordon dishonest, unattractive, and incompetent when no one else is around, that does not constitute slander. In neither case was the message communicated to a third party. Interestingly, the courts have generally held that dictating a letter to a secretary constitutes publication. Moreover, if a third party overhears defamatory statements by chance, the courts have generally held that this also constitutes publication. Note further that any individual who republishes or repeats defamatory statements is liable even if that person reveals the source of

---

1. Restatement, Second, Torts, § 46, Comment d.

2. This distinction between oral and written defamation is becoming less meaningful.

such statements. Most radio stations have instituted seven-second delays for live broadcasts such as talk shows, to avoid this kind of liability.

The common law has defined four types of false utterances that are considered torts *per se*, or on their face. That means that no proof of damages is required before these false utterances become actionable. They are:

1. A statement that another has a loathsome communicable disease.
2. A statement that another has committed improprieties while engaging in a profession or trade.
3. A statement that another has committed or has been imprisoned for a serious crime.
4. A statement that an unmarried woman is unchaste.

Defenses against Defamation Truth is normally an absolute defense against a defamation charge. Furthermore, there may be a privilege involved. For example, statements made by attorneys and judges during a trial are privileged and therefore cannot be the basis for a defama-

tion charge. Members of Congress making statements on the floor of Congress have an absolute privilege. Legislators have complete immunity from liability for false statements made in debate, even if they make such statements maliciously—that is, knowing them to be untrue. In general, false and defamatory statements that concern public figures and are published in the press are privileged if they are made without malice.[3] Under this rule of privilege, public figures are defined as those who "thrust" themselves into the forefront of public controversy.

In order to prove malice, a plaintiff must show that the defendant had either actual knowledge of falsity or a reckless disregard of the truth. The balance between free speech and the torts of slander and libel is delicate. The following two cases illustrate the issue of when a person is a public figure and, in the Burnett case, the extent of liability when malice is proved.

The following case illustrates the issue of when a person is a public figure.

---

3. New York Times Co. v. Sullivan, 376 U.S. 254, 84 S.Ct. 710 (1964).

BACKGROUND AND FACTS *Carol Burnett, the famous comedienne, believed she was libeled by an article in The National Enquirer. She decided to sue the Enquirer for substantial punitive damages. At trial, she was awarded $300,000 in general damages and $1,300,000 in punitive damages. The National Enquirer moved for judgment notwithstanding the verdict and a new trial. The court replied:*

BURNETT v. NATIONAL ENQUIRER
California Superior Court, Los Angeles County, 1981.
7 Med.L.Rptr. 1321.

SMITH, J.

It is not the intention of the court to deal at great length with every issue raised by defendant in its motion for judgment notwithstanding the verdict and motion for new trial, but simply to articulate the reasons for denying defendant's motions, save and except the motion for new trial as it relates to the issue of damages.

Initially, defendant contends that its publication of March 2, 1976 about plaintiff was not libelous per se. It is clear to the court that the average reader, viewing the article in its entirety, would conclude that plaintiff was intoxicated and causing a disturbance. The evidence is undisputed that the article was false. There can be little question that the described conduct of plaintiff holds her up to ridicule within the meaning of California Civil Code section 45.

The National Enquirer's protestation that it was not guilty of actual malice borders on absurdity. Not only did plaintiff establish actual malice by clear and convincing evidence, but she proved it beyond a reasonable doubt. At the very minimum Brian Walker, the de facto gossip columnist, had serious doubts as to the truth of the publication. There is a high degree of probability that Walker fabricated part of the publication—certainly that portion relating to plaintiff's row with Henry Kissinger.

Walker received information from Couri Hay, a free lance tipster for the National Enquirer, that Carol Burnett had been in the Rive Gauche restaurant, that she ordered a Grand Mariner souffle and that she passed her dessert to other parties in a boisterous or flamboyant manner; that she had been drinking, *but was not drunk.* Hay contends that this was verified through the maitre 'd. On the other hand, Hay related to Walker that he had received *unverified* information that Burnett had spilled wine on a customer and the customer had returned the favor by spilling water on her.

Shortly after receiving the information from Hay, Walker called Steve Tinney, the nominal gossip columnist, to see if he had any contacts in Washington who could verify Hay's tip. Walker expressed doubts to Tinney about Hay's trustworthiness. Tinney agreed with Walker's assessment of Hay, but told him he had no contacts in Washington.

Next Walker asked Greg Lyon, defendant's employee, to verify the "incident at the Rive Gauche". Walker told Lyon he had a one hour deadline to meet even though the publication was not due to "hit the streets" for thirteen days.

Lyon was asked to verify the following information: That Carol Burnett had been in a Washington, D.C. restaurant, that she had some sort of interchange with other customers and that an altercation took place with another customer—to wit, "the wine spilling and water throwing incident".

Lyon reported to Walker that he had not been able to verify anything other than the fact that plaintiff had passed dessert to other patrons. Additionally, he told Walker a fact *not* previously disclosed to him by Hay—that Henry Kissinger and plaintiff had carried on a good-natured conversation at the Rive Gauche that same night.

Confronted with this disappointing revelation, Walker expressed concern to Lyon as to whether he should publish the article. He kept pushing Lyon for his opinion. Lyon became angry and told him that he (Walker) was being paid to make those decisions.

At this point, it is fair to infer that Walker decided that there was little news value in the fact that Burnett and Kissinger had a good-natured conversation and that Burnett distributed her dessert to other patrons. A little embellishment was needed to "spice up" the item.

An entire afternoon was devoted to the issue of whether the National Enquirer was a newspaper or magazine. The court reaffirms its finding that the defendant does not qualify for the protection of California Civil Code section 48a because, when Exhibits 21, 22, 174 and 175 are viewed as a whole, the predominant function of the publication is the conveying of news which is neither timely nor current. Additionally, the defendant has been registered as a magazine with the Audit Bureau of Circulation since 1963, and carries a designation as a magazine or periodical in eight mass media directories.

In *Werner v. So. Calif. etc. Newspapers,* 35 Cal.2d 121, 128 (1950) our Supreme Court upheld the constitutionality of California Civil Code section 48a against an attack that it unfairly discriminated in favor of newspaper and radio stations. The court articulated its rationale as follows:

"In view of the complex and far flung activities of the news services upon which newspapers and radio stations must largely rely and the necessity of publishing *news while it's new* (emphasis mine), newspapers and radio stations may in good faith publicize items that are untrue but whose falsity they have neither the time nor the opportunity to ascertain."

Since the defendant rarely deals with news while it's new", it is not entitled to the protection of Civil Code section 48a.

Defendant has gone to great lengths to blame the adverse jury verdict on prejudicial trial publicity and, in particular, the blast by entertainer Johnny Carson. Some will question the sagacity of Carson's timing, but no one can question his constitutional right to air his grievance with defendant. While the defendant had the right to publish an article about Carson, it exercised incredibly poor judgment in publishing the article on the eve of the trial.

The National Enquirer successfully challenged two jurors who viewed or heard the Carson tirade. It did not see fit to challenge any others even though the trial could have proceeded with as few as eight jurors. Accordingly, defendant cannot now complain about three other jurors being tainted. The court questioned all jurors individually in chambers in the presence of counsel. Counsel were afforded an opportunity to question the jurors. The court denied the defendant's motion for a mistrial because it was satisfied, without any reservation whatsoever, that the remaining eleven jurors could render a fair trial to defendant.

*   *   *   *

While the record is clear that she suffered no actual pecuniary loss as a result of the libelous article, she had every right to suffer anxiety reactions in the immediate aftermath of the March 2, 1976 article and the ineffectual correction. Emotional distress is more difficult to quantify than pain and suffering, but it is no less real. A review of other verdicts for emotional distress is not particularly helpful since the facts of each case vary significantly. The fact that defendant's false publication was communicated to sixteen million readers coupled with an inadequate correction, is of substantial significance in measuring the extent of plaintiff's emotional distress. Finally, the only residual aspect of emotional distress which has lingered with plaintiff since the immediate aftermath of the publication is the fact she occasionally gets a little paranoid about talking too loudly in restaurants.

Defendant points to the fact that Burnett never sought the services of a psychiatrist, psychologist or counselor. Plaintiff acknowledged that she was able to set aside her anxiety to the point where she was able to function in her profession. Miss Burnett should be commended for not seeking the unnecessary services of some "phony build up artist" in order to inflate her damages. She should not be penalized for self-treating.

The court finds that plaintiff was a highly credible witness who did not exaggerate her complaints. Nevertheless, the jury award is clearly excessive and is not supported by substantial evidence. The court finds that the sum of $50,000.00 is a more realistic recompense for plaintiff's emotional distress and special damage.

An award of $1,300,000 will probably not amount to "capital punishment" (bankruptcy), as publicly espoused by defendant's counsel after the jury verdict, because of the defendant's strong cash position. The court finds that it is excessive because it does not bear a reasonable relationship to the compensatory damages that amount to only $50,000. A review of California case law indicates that appellate courts have not sanctioned any particular ratio of general and punitive damages. Each case turns on its own set of facts.

JUDGMENT AND REMEDY

The court found that there was substantial evidence to support an award of punitive damages, but reduced the award to $760,000, a sum the judge felt was sufficient to deter further misconduct. The judge also reduced the amount of general damages to $50,000. Motions for judgment n.o.v. and for a new trial were denied.

HUTCHINSON v. PROXMIRE

Supreme Court of the
United States, 1979.
443 U.S. Ill., 99 S.Ct. 2675.

BACKGROUND AND FACTS   *Professor Ronald R. Hutchinson received federal funding for animal studies on aggression. United States Senator William Proxmire bestowed his Golden Fleece of the Month Award on the federal agency that funded Hutchinson's research. The purpose of the award was to publicize wasteful government spending. Senator Proxmire announced the award in a speech prepared for the Senate. The speech was reprinted in a press release mailed to 275 members of the news media and in a newsletter sent to 100,000 people. Proxmire described the federal grants for Hutchinson's research, concluding with the following comments:*

The funding of this nonsense makes me almost angry enough to scream and kick or even clench my jaws. It seems to me it is outrageous.

Dr. Hutchinson's studies should make the taxpayers as well as his monkeys grind their teeth. In fact, the good doctor has made a fortune from his monkeys and in the process made a monkey out of the American taxpayer.

It is time for the Federal Government to get out of this 'monkey business.' In view of the transparent worthlessness of Hutchinson's study of jaw-grinding and biting by angry or hard-drinking monkeys, it is time we put a stop to the bite Hutchinson and the bureaucrats who fund him have been taking of the taxpayer.

Hutchinson sued Proxmire for defamation. The District Court held that Proxmire's speech was protected under the speech and debate clause of the Constitution, that Hutchinson was a public figure, and that he had not proven there was malice. The Court of Appeals affirmed the judgment in favor of Proxmire. The case finally reached the Supreme Court.

Mr. Chief Justice BURGER delivered the opinion of the Court.

*   *   *   *

The Speech or Debate Clause has been directly passed on by this Court relatively few times in 190 years. Literal reading of the Clause would, of course, confine its protection narrowly to a "Speech or Debate in either House." But the Court has given the Clause a practical rather than a strictly literal reading which would limit the protection to utterances made within the four walls of either Chamber. Thus, we have held that committee hearings are protected, even if held outside the Chambers; committee reports are also protected.

*   *   *   *

*   *   * Claims under the Clause going beyond what is needed to protect legislative independence are to be closely scrutinized. In *Brewster* we took note of this:

> The authors of our Constitution were well aware of both the need for the privilege *and the abuses that could flow from too sweeping safeguards. In order* to preserve other values, they wrote the privilege so that it tolerates and protects behavior on the part of Members not tolerated and protected when done by other citizens, *but the shield does not extend beyond what is necessary to preserve the integrity of the legislative process.*

Indeed, the precedents abundantly support the conclusion that a Member may be held liable for republishing defamatory statements originally made in either House. We perceive no basis for departing from that long-established rule.

* * * A speech by Proxmire in the Senate would be wholly immune and would be available to other Members of Congress and the public in the Congressional Record. But neither the newsletters nor the press release was "essential to the deliberations of the Senate" and neither was part of the deliberative process. * * * *

* * * Voting and preparing committee reports are the individual and collective expressions of opinion within the legislative process. As such, they are protected by the Speech or Debate Clause. Newsletters and press releases, by contrast, are primarily means of informing those outside the legislative forum; they represent the views and will of a single Member. It does not disparage either their value or their importance to hold that they are not entitled to the protection of the Speech or Debate Clause.

Since *New York Times v. Sullivan*, this Court has sought to define the accommodation required to assure the vigorous debate on public issues that the First Amendment was designed to protect while at the same time affording protection to the reputations of individuals. In *Gertz v. Robert Welch, Inc.*, the Court offered a general definition of "public figures":

> For the most part those who attain this status [of public figure] have assumed roles of especial prominence in the affairs of society. Some occupy positions of such persuasive power and influence that they are deemed public figures for all purposes. More commonly, those classed as public figures have thrust themselves to the forefront of particular public controversies in order to influence the resolution of the issues involved. In either event, they invite attention and comment.

It is not contended that Hutchinson attained such prominence that he is a public figure for all purposes. Instead, respondents have argued that the District Court and the Court of Appeals were correct in holding that Hutchinson is a public figure for the limited purpose of comment on his receipt of federal funds for research projects. That conclusion was based upon two factors: first, Hutchinson's successful application for federal funds and the reports in local newspapers of the federal grants; second, Hutchinson's access to the media, as demonstrated by the fact that some newspapers and wire services reported his response to the announcement of the Golden Fleece Award. Neither of those factors demonstrates that Hutchinson was a public figure prior to the controversy engendered by the Golden Fleece Award; his access, such as it was, came after the alleged libel.

On this record Hutchinson's activities and public profile are much like those of countless members of his profession. His published writings reach a relatively small category of professionals concerned with research in human behavior. To the extent the subject of his published writings became a matter of controversy it was a consequence of the Golden Fleece Award. Clearly those charged with defamation cannot, by their own conduct, create their own defense by making the claimant a public figure.

* * * *

Finally, we cannot agree that Hutchinson had such access to the media that he should be classified as a public figure. Hutchinson's access was limited to responding to the announcement of the Golden Fleece Award. He did not have the regular and continuing access to the media that is one of the accouterments of having become a public figure.

JUDGMENT AND REMEDY *The judgment in favor of Senator Proxmire was reversed. The case was remanded to the Court of Appeals for further review consistent with the Supreme Court's decision that Proxmire's speech was not protected and that Hutchinson was not a public figure.*

Slander of Title, Disparagement of Goods, and Defamation by Computer

There are three torts, typically called business torts, that involve defamation. Defamation arising from a false statement made about a person's product, business, or title to property is called *slander of title* or *disparagement of goods*, depending on the case. Erroneous information from a computer about a person's credit standing or business reputation can impair that person's ability to obtain further credit and is called *defamation by computer*. These torts are treated in more detail in the following chapter.

Invasion of the Right to Privacy

A person's right to solitude and freedom from prying public eyes is the interest protected by the tort of invasion of privacy. Four different acts qualify as an invasion of privacy:

1. The use of a person's name or picture for commercial purposes without permission.
2. Intrusion upon an individual's affairs or seclusion.
3. Publication of information that places a person in a false light. This could be a story attributing to the person ideas that are not held or actions that were not taken. (Publishing such a story could involve the tort of defamation as well.)
4. Public disclosure of private facts about an individual that an ordinary person would find objectionable.

Misrepresentation (Fraud, Deceit)

The tort of misrepresentation involves the use of fraud and deceit for personal gain. It includes several elements:

1. Misrepresentation of facts or conditions with knowledge that they are false or with reckless disregard for the truth.
2. Intent to induce another to rely on the misrepresentation.
3. Justifiable reliance by the deceived party.
4. Damages suffered as a result of reliance.
5. Causal connection between the misrepresentation and the injury suffered.

In general, the reliance must be upon a statement of fact. Reliance on a statement of opinion is not justified unless the person making the statement has a superior knowledge of the subject matter. A lawyer's opinion of the law, for instance, is an example of superior knowledge, and reliance on that opinion will be regarded as reliance upon a statement of fact.

Seller's Talk versus Facts In order for fraud to occur, more than mere *seller's talk* must be involved. Fraud exists only when a person represents as a material fact something he or she knows is untrue. For example, it is fraud to claim that a building does not leak when one knows it does. Facts are objectively ascertainable, whereas seller's talk is not. "I'm the best lawyer in town," is seller's talk, or "puffing." The speaker is not trying to represent something as fact, because "best" is a subjective, not an objective, term.

The topic of fraud in contracts is important enough to merit an entire chapter. (See Chapter 11.)

INTENTIONAL TORTS: WRONGS AGAINST PROPERTY

Wrongs against property include (1) trespass to land and to personal property, (2) conversion, and (3) nuisance. The wrong is against the individual who has legally recognized rights with regard to land or personal property.[5]

Trespass to Land

Any time a person enters onto land that is owned by another, or causes anything to enter onto the land, or remains on the land, or permits anything to remain on it, such action constitutes a **trespass to land.** Note that actual harm to the land is not an essential element of this tort, because the tort is designed to protect the right of an owner to exclusive possession. If no harm is done, usually only nominal—in name only, not significant—damages (such as $1) can be recovered by the landowner. Examples of common types of trespass to land include walking or driving on the land, shooting across it with a gun, throwing rocks or spraying water on a building in the possession of another, building a dam across a river that causes water to back up on someone else's land, and placing part of one's building on the adjoining landowner's property.

In the past, the right to land gave exclusive possession of a space that extended from "the center of the earth to the heavens," but this rule has been relaxed. Today, reasonable intrusions are permitted. Thus, aircraft can normally fly over privately owned land. The temporary invasion

of the air space over such land is, in effect, considered privileged as to the aircraft owner. Society's interest in air transportation preempts the individual's interest in the air space.

Trespass Criteria, Rights and Duties   Before a person can be a trespasser, the real property owner (person who legally controls the realty) must expressly or impliedly establish that person as a trespasser. For example, "Posted" trespass signs expressly establish a person as a trespasser when that person ignores these signs and enters upon the property. However, a guest in your home is not a trespasser. Should the guest become unruly, you could *ask* your guest to leave and at that moment establish your guest as a trespasser. Any person who enters upon your property to commit an illegal act (thief enters a lumberyard at night to steal lumber) is impliedly established as a trespasser without verbal establishment or posted signs.

Once a person is established as a trespasser, certain rights and duties are applied to both the owner of the realty and to the trespasser. Some of these are:

1.   A trespasser is liable for any damage caused to the property. The owner does not have to prove negligence.

2.   A trespasser assumes the risks of the premises and cannot hold the owner for injuries sustained. This rule does not permit the owner to lay traps with the intent to injure a trespasser. Also, generally, young persons do not assume the risks of the premises if they are attracted to the premises, called the "attractive nuisance" doctrine. Under some circumstances an owner may even have a duty to warn of dangers on the property, such as guard dogs.

3.   As previously discussed, a trespasser can be removed from the premises through the use of reasonable force without the owner being liable for assault and battery. This same basic concept allows an owner to remove, without liability, another's property which constitutes a trespass, if the removal is accomplished by the exercise of reasonable care.

In the following case, a trespasser, even though innocent, is liable for damages.

---

5.   The law distinguishes real property from personal property. *Real property* is land and things "permanently" attached thereto. *Personal property* is all other things that are basically movable. Thus, a house and lot are real property, whereas the furniture inside a house is personal property. Money and securities are also personal property.

ROSSI v. VENTRESCA BROS. CONST. CO., INC.

City Court of the City of White Plains, Westchester County, New York. Small Claims Part, 1978. 94 Misc.2d 756, 405 N.Y.S.2d 375.

BACKGROUND AND FACTS *During a severe snowstorm Ronald Rossi parked his car in the privately owned parking lot of a shopping center. The car was towed from the lot. Rossi sued the shopping center owners and the towing company to recover the $113.40 he paid to retrieve his car.*

BLAUSTEIN, Judge

* * * *

This Court reluctantly finds that the plaintiff was trespassing in parking on private property and the snowstorm does not justify the trespass. Further, the owner of the shopping center has the corollary right to remove any car so parked. The rule is stated in 87 C.J.S. Trespass § 45a:

"He [the owner] may remove chattels which are wrongfully on his land, if he uses due care in the removal. The removal should be effected with as little injury to the chattels removed as is possible, and without the exercise of excessive force."

* * * *

While plaintiff here is not a willful trespasser considering the severity of the storm, still, he was violating the owner's property and is liable for damages. The measure of damages is actual or special damages incurred. Even the most innocent of trespassers is liable for nominal damages as a minimum. (87 C.J.S. Trespass § 117).

JUDGMENT AND REMEDY *Plaintiff was allowed to recover $27 of the towing charge. The court found the $113.40 charge to be excessive damages for the plaintiff's trespass.*

Defenses against Trespass to Land Trespass to land involves wrongful interference with another person's real property rights. But if one can show that the trespass was warranted, as when a trespasser enters to assist someone in danger, a complete defense exists. Another defense is to show that the purported owner did not actually have the right to possess the land in question.

In some situations, courts can easily assess damages for trespass to land, especially when the trespasser damages or wrongfully destroys items of value on the land. For example, land purchasers can recover the value of destroyed trees when avoidable errors caused construction crews to knock them down.

Trespass to Personal Property

Whenever any individual unlawfully injures the personal property of another or otherwise inter-feres with the personal property owner's right to exclusive possession and enjoyment of that property, **trespass to personalty, or personal property,** occurs. Trespass to personal property involves intentional meddling. If a student takes another student's business law book as a practical joke and hides it so that the owner is unable to find it for several days prior to the final examination, the student has engaged in a trespass to personal property.

Defenses against Trespass to Personal Property If it can be shown that trespass to personal property was warranted, then a complete defense has been made. Many states, for example, allow automobile repair shops to hold a customer's car when he has refused to pay for repairs rendered (under what is called an artisan's, or possessory, lien).

Conversion Whenever personal property is taken from its rightful owner or possessor and placed in the service of another, the act of **conversion** occurs. Conversion is the civil side of those crimes relating to stealing.[6] A store clerk who steals merchandise from the store commits a crime and the tort of conversion at the same time. Of course, when conversion occurs, the lesser offense of trespass to personal property usually occurs as well. If the initial taking of the property was unlawful, there is trespass. Then, retention of that property is conversion. Even if the initial taking of the property was permitted by the owner or, for some other reason, is not a trespass, failure to return it may be conversion.

A person who unlawfully takes goods is liable for the tort of conversion even if the person mistakenly believed that he or she was entitled to them. In other words, good intentions are not a defense against conversion, and conversion can be an entirely innocent act. ABC Hardware allowed Samuels to take a lawn mower home to try it out. Samuels used the lawn mower once. He then lent it to his neighbor, Nichols. A thief stole the lawn mower from Nichols. When ABC Hardware learned what had happened to the mower, it demanded that Samuels pay for it. Samuels is guilty of conversion because he had no right to lend the mower to Nichols. His misuse of the mower renders him liable. He obviously did not intend for the mower to be stolen, but he intentionally took the mower from ABC and intentionally and knowingly lent it to his neighbor.

Whoever suffers a conversion is generally entitled to recover the reasonable value of the goods that have been lost. If Henries deliberately smashes a vase that Arts, Inc., exhibits for sale in its store, then Henries is liable for the value of the vase. Deliberate destruction of the personal property of another is conversion. Henries treated the vase as if he owned it when he asserted a right to destroy it. (When the goods are not destroyed, the owner can either try to get them back through a lawsuit or ask for damages for conversion. The court will not give the owner full value for the goods and return the property as well.)

Simple interference with another's personal property is less serious than conversion. It is called a trespass to the chattel, and the trespasser must pay for any damage done or for the owner's loss of use of the property.

The following case illustrates the concept of the tort of conversion.

---

6. Theft requires intent, but conversion does not.

BACKGROUND AND FACTS *Plaintiff Rouse was negotiating a new car purchase with defendant's salesmen. Rouse gave the salesmen the keys to the car he then owned, which was to be traded for the new automobile. When Rouse decided not to purchase a new car, the salesmen said they had lost the keys. Rouse summoned police, and when they arrived, the salesmen produced the missing keys and stated that they "just wanted to see him cry a while."*

RUSSELL-VAUGHN FORD, INC. v. ROUSE
Supreme Court of Alabama, 1968.
281 Ala. 567, 206 So. 2d 371.

SIMPSON, Justice.

*   *   *   *

*   *   * Initially it is argued that the facts of this case do not make out a case of conversion. It is argued that the conversion if at all, is a conversion of the keys to the automobile, not of the automobile itself. It is further contended that there was not under the case here presented a conversion at all. We are not persuaded that the law of Alabama supports this proposition.

"It has been held by this court that the fact of conversion does not necessarily import an acquisition of property in the defendant. The conversion may consist, not only in an appropriation of the property to one's own use, but in its destruction, *or in exercising dominion over it in exclusion or defiance of plaintiff's right.* *   *   * ''

It is not contended that the plaintiff here had no right to demand the return of the keys to his automobile. Rather, the appellants seem to be arguing that there was no conversion which the law will recognize under the facts of this case because the defendants did not commit sufficient acts to amount to a conversion. We cannot agree.

We see nothing in our cases which requires in a conversion case that the plaintiff prove that the defendant appropriated the property to his own use; rather, as noted in the cases referred to above, it is enough that he show that the defendant exercised dominion over it in exclusion or defiance of the right of the plaintiff. *   *   *

Further, appellants argue that there was no conversion since the plaintiff could have called his wife at home, who had another set of keys and thereby gained the ability to move his automobile. We find nothing in our cases which would require the plaintiff to exhaust all possible means of gaining possession of a chattel which is withheld from him by the defendant, after demanding its return. On the contrary, it is the refusal, without legal excuse, to deliver a chattel, which constitutes a conversion.

We find unconvincing the appellants contention that if there were a conversion at all, it was the conversion of the automobile keys, and not of the automobile. In Compton v. Sims, supra, this court sustained a finding that there had been a conversion of cotton where the defendant refused to deliver to the plaintiff ''warehouse tickets'' which would have enabled him to gain possession of the cotton. The court spoke of the warehouse tickets as a symbol of the cotton and found that the retention of them amounted to a conversion of the cotton. So here, we think that the withholding from the plaintiff after demand of the keys to his automobile, without which he could not move it, amounted to a conversion of the automobile.

It is next argued by appellants that the amount of the verdict is excessive. It is not denied that punitive damages are recoverable here in the discretion of the jury.

"If the conversion was committed in known violation of the law and of plaintiff's rights with circumstances of insult, or contumely, or malice, punitive damages were recoverable in the discretion of the jury."

We think that the evidence justifies the jury's conclusion that these circumstances existed in this case.

JUDGMENT AND REMEDY   *The jury verdict for Rouse was upheld. The jury had awarded Rouse $5,000 in damages for the conversion of his property, and the Alabama supreme court ruled that this amount was not excessive.*

Stolen Goods Here again, intent to engage in a wrongdoing is not necessary for conversion to exist. Rather, it is the intent to exercise control over property when such control is inconsistent with the plaintiff's rights that constitutes conversion. Therefore, someone who buys stolen goods is guilty of conversion even if he or she did not know the goods were stolen. If the true owner brings a tort action against the buyer, the buyer must pay the owner the full value of the property, despite having already paid some money to the thief.

Defenses against Conversion　A successful defense against the charge of conversion is that the purported owner has no title, or right to possess, superior to the holder's rights.

Necessity is another possible defense against conversion. If Abrams takes Stephens's cat, Abrams is guilty of conversion. If Stephens sues Abrams, Abrams must return the cat and pay damages. If, however, the cat has rabies and Abrams took the cat to protect the public, Abrams has a valid defense—necessity (and perhaps even self-defense if he can prove he was in danger from the cat).

Nuisance

It is possible to commit a tort and be liable because of unreasonable uses of your own property. A **nuisance** is an improper activity that interferes with another's enjoyment or use of his or her property. Nuisances can be either public or private. A public nuisance disturbs or interferes with the public in general, whereas a private nuisance interferes with the property interest of a limited number of individuals. Reasonable limitations are placed on the use of property in all situations. Such limitations prevent the owner from unreasonably interfering with the health and comfort of neighbors or with their right to enjoy their own private property. One who suffers as a result of a nuisance can have it stopped by seeking an injunction in the courts. An injunction is an equitable remedy. The court, if it grants the injunction, will prohibit the continuation of the undesirable activity.

Nuisances can also involve indecent, improper, or unlawful personal conduct. Obviously, there is an extremely subjective element in any definition of nuisance, particularly when it involves personal conduct. Moreover, a nuisance may be a tort or a crime, and the dividing line is difficult to ascertain. Finally, nuisances may result from intentional types of conduct as well as from negligent (careless) conduct. The

defendant may even be held liable on the ground of strict liability. The difficulties in applying the nuisance doctrine are apparent.

NEGLIGENCE

Intentional torts normally involve a particular mental state. In negligence, for example, the actor neither wishes to bring about the consequences of the act nor believes that they will occur. The actor's conduct merely creates a *risk* of such consequences. Without the creation of a risk, there can be no negligence. Moreover, the risk must be foreseeable; that is, it must be such that a reasonable person would anticipate it and guard against it. In determining what is reasonable conduct, courts consider the nature of the possible harm. A very slight risk of a dangerous explosion might be unreasonable, whereas a distinct possibility of burning one's fingers on a stove might be reasonable.

In examining a question of negligence, one should ask six questions:

1.　Does (or did) the defendant owe a duty of care to the plaintiff?
2.　What did the person do (act)?
3.　Did the act create a foreseeable risk of harm (breach of duty of care)?
4.　Was harm done (damages)?
5.　Did the act *cause* the harm (causation in fact, or actual cause)?
6.　At what point should liability cease (proximate cause)?

Many of the actions discussed in the section on intentional torts would constitute negligence if they were done carelessly, but without intent. For instance, carelessly bumping into someone who falls and breaks an arm constitutes negligence. Likewise, carelessly, as opposed to intentionally, flooding someone's land constitutes negligence. In a sense, negligence is a way of committing a tort rather than a distinct category of torts.

Negligence involves the allocation of loss between an innocent plaintiff and an innocent, albeit careless, defendant. The extent of duty and liability of both the plaintiff and the defendant is determined by social policy. For example, suppose that XYZ Corporation—selling $600 million of products a year—is sued by Simperman for negligent manufacturing. Simperman cannot afford to pay his medical expenses, but XYZ Corporation can spread the cost of the damages among all its customers. If there is a policy of spreading such costs, a court may find for the plaintiff. In a similar situation, however, the court might not find for the plaintiff if the defendant is an individual rather than a large corporation.

Negligence has been committed when someone has suffered injury caused by the failure of another to live up to a required duty of care. Three elements must be examined here: (1) breach (failure) of duty of care, (2) injury, and (3) causation. Certain defenses must also be examined.

Breach of Duty of Care

The first element in a tort of negligence can also be broken into a two-part question:

1. Is there a duty of care?
2. Did the defendant's action breach (fail to live up to) that duty?

Duty of Care Basically, the concept of duty arises from the notion that if we are to live in society with other people, some actions can be tolerated and some cannot, some actions are right and some are wrong, and some actions are reasonable and some are not. The basic rule of duty is that people are free to act as they please as long as their actions do not infringe on the interests of others.

Tort law measures duty by a standard of reasonableness—the *reasonable person standard.* In determining whether a tort has been committed, the courts ask how a reasonable person would have acted in the same circumstances. The reasonable person standard is said to be (though in an absolute sense it cannot be) objective. It is not necessarily how a particular person would act. It is society's judgment on how people should act. If the so-called reasonable person existed, he or she would be the most careful, most conscientious, most even-tempered, and most honest of people. This hypothetical "reasonable person" is frequently used in discussions of law.

Breach of Duty When someone intentionally harms another, or fails to comply with the duty of exercising reasonable care, a tortious act may have been committed (but not necessarily a completed tort, since that will depend on whether there is damage and proximate cause). Failure to live up to the standard of care may be an act (setting fire to a building) or an omission (neglecting to put out a fire). It may be an intentional act, a careless act, or a carefully performed but nevertheless dangerous act that results in injury.

Whether or not a person's act or failure to act is unreasonable depends on the interaction of a number of factors. One factor is the nature of the act. Some actions—spitting on someone, for instance—are so outrageous that the actor should pay for what has been done regardless of physical damage. Other acts, like blasting with dynamite, are so dangerous that any damage caused should be paid for. Another factor in determining whether damages should be awarded is the manner in which an act is performed. Intentionally hitting someone on the back probably should be paid for; accidentally doing so probably should not be. A third factor is the nature of the injury—whether it is serious or slight, extraordinary, or simply part of everyday life. Other factors to be considered are whether or not the activity causing the injury was socially useful and how easily the injury could have been guarded against.

Injury

In order for a tort to have been committed, there must be a *legally* recognizable injury to the plaintiff. The plaintiff must have suffered some loss, harm, wrong, or invasion of a protected interest to recover damages (that is, to receive compensation). The reason for the requirement of injury is obvious. Without an injury of some kind, there can be no compensation. Essentially, the purpose of torts is to compensate for legally recognized injuries resulting from wrongful acts, not to punish these acts. However, for some torts the injured person may be given extra compensation as punitive damages, because society tries to discourage these acts. But few negligent acts are so reprehensible that punitive damages are available.

Causation

The second element necessary to a tort is causation. If a person fails in a duty of care and someone suffers injury, the wrongful activity must have caused the harm for a tort to have been committed. In deciding whether there is causation, the court must actually address two questions:

1.   Is there *causation in fact?*
2.   Was the act the *proximate cause* of the injury?

Causation in Fact   Did the injury occur because of the defendant's act, or would it have occurred anyway? If an injury would not have occurred without the defendant's act, then there is **causation in fact.** If Johnson carelessly leaves a campfire burning, and the fire burns down the forest, there is causation in fact. If Johnson carelessly leaves a campfire burning, but it burns out, and then lightning causes a fire that burns down the forest, there is no causation in fact. In both cases there is a wrongful act and damage. In the second case, however, there is no causal connection and thus no liability. Causation in fact can usually be determined by use of the *but for* test: But for the wrongful act, the injury would not have occurred.

In some cases, causation in fact is difficult to determine. What if Johnson's campfire did spread, but at the same time lightning also started a fire? In this type of situation, the courts apply the *substantial factor* test. If Johnson's conduct was a substantial factor in bringing about the damage, Johnson will be held liable.

Determining causation in fact entails examining the facts portrayed in evidence at a trial. The plaintiff has the burden of proving causation in fact as well as other elements, such as damages. The plaintiff need not prove causation in fact beyond a reasonable doubt but must prove only that the causal connection is more likely than not. The plaintiff must prove the case by a *preponderance of the evidence* in a civil suit.

Proximate Cause   How far should a defendant's liability extend for a wrongful act that was a substantial factor in causing injury? For example, Johnson's fire not only burns down the forest but also sets off an explosion in a nearby chemical plant that spills chemicals into a river, killing all the fish for a hundred miles downstream and ruining the economy of a tourist resort. Should Johnson be liable to the resort owners? To the tourists whose vacations were ruined? These are questions about the limitation of liability, which is the second element in the general issue of causation. The courts use the term **proximate cause** (or sometimes legal cause) to describe this element. Proximate cause is a question not of fact but of law and policy. The question is whether the connection between an act and an injury is strong enough to justify imposing liability. Probably the most cited case on proximate cause is the *Palsgraf* case.

BACKGROUND AND FACTS   *The plaintiff, Palsgraf, was waiting for a train on a station platform. A man carrying a package was rushing to catch a train that was already moving. As the man attempted to jump aboard the moving train, he seemed unsteady and about to fall. A railroad guard on the car reached forward to grab him, and another guard on the platform pushed him from behind to help him on the train. The man's package, which contained fireworks, fell on the railroad tracks and exploded. There was nothing about the package to indicate its contents.*

PALSGRAF v. LONG ISLAND R.R. CO.
Court of Appeals of New York
1928.
248 N.Y. 339, 162 N.E. 99.

The explosion caused scales located on the platform to fall upon Palsgraf, causing injuries for which she sued the railroad company. At the trial, the jury found that the railroad guards were negligent in their conduct to the plaintiff.

CARDOZO, Chief Justice.

*   *   *   *

The conduct of the defendant's guard, if a wrong in its relation to the holder of the package, was not a wrong in its relation to the plaintiff, standing far away. Relatively to her it was not negligence at all. Nothing in the situation gave notice that the falling package had in it the potency of peril to persons thus removed. *Negligence is not actionable unless it involves the invasion of a legally protected interest, the violation of a right.* "Proof of negligence in the air, so to speak, will not do." [Emphasis added.] *   *   * If no hazard was apparent to the eye of ordinary vigilance, an act innocent and harmless, at least to outward seeming, with reference to her, did not take to itself the quality of a tort because it happened to be a wrong, though apparently not one involving the risk of bodily insecurity, with reference to some one else. "In every instance, before *negligence* can be predicated of a given act, *back of the act must be* sought and found a *duty to the individual complaining*, the observance of which would have averted or avoided the injury." [Emphasis added.]

A different conclusion will involve us, and swiftly too, in a maze of contradictions. A guard stumbles over a package which has been left upon a platform. It seems to be a bundle of newspapers. It turns out to be a can of dynamite. To the eye of ordinary vigilance, the bundle is abandoned waste, which may be kicked or trod on with impunity. Is a passenger at the other end of the platform protected by the law against the unsuspected hazard concealed beneath the waste? If not, is the result to be any different, so far as the distant passenger is concerned, when the guard stumbles over a valise which a truckman or a porter has left upon the walk? The passenger far away, if the victim of a wrong at all, has a cause of action, not derivative, but original and primary. His claim to be protected against invasion of his bodily security is neither greater nor less because the act resulting in the invasion is a wrong to another far removed. In this case, the rights that are said to have been violated, the interests said to have been invaded, are not even of the same order. The man was not injured in his person nor even put in danger. The purpose of the act, as well as its effect, was to make his person safe. If there was a wrong to him at all, which may very well be doubted it was a wrong to a property interest only the safety of his package. Out of this wrong to property, which threatened injury to nothing else, there has passed, we are told, to the plaintiff by derivation or succession a right of action for the invasion of an interest of another order, the right to bodily security. The diversity of interests emphasizes the futility of the effort to build the plaintiff's right upon the basis of a wrong to someone else. The gain is one of emphasis, for a like result would follow if the interests were the same. Even then, the orbit of the danger as disclosed to the eye of reasonable vigilance would be the orbit of the duty. One who jostles one's neighbor in a crowd does not invade the rights of others standing at the outer fringe when the unintended contact casts a bomb upon the ground. The wrongdoer as to them is the man who carries the bomb, not the one who explodes it without

suspicion of the danger. Life will have to be made over, and human nature transformed, before prevision so extravagant can be accepted as the norm of conduct,
the customary standard to which behavior must conform.

   *   *   * What the plaintiff must show is "a wrong" to herself; i.e., a violation
of her own right, and not merely a wrong to some one else, nor conduct "wrongful" because unsocial, but not "a wrong" to any one. *   *   * The risk reasonably
to be perceived defines the duty to be obeyed[.] *   *   * This does not mean, of
course, that one who launches a destructive force is always relieved of liability,
if the force, though known to be destructive, pursues an unexpected path. "It was
not necessary that the defendant should have had notice of the particular method
in which an accident would occur, if the possibility of an accident was clear to
the ordinarily prudent eye." Some acts, such as shooting are so imminently dangerous to any one who may come within reach of the missile however unexpect-
edly, as to impose a duty of prevision not far from that of an insurer. Even today, and much oftener in earlier stages of the law, one acts sometimes at one's
peril. *   *   * Here, by concession, there was nothing in the situation to suggest
to the most cautious mind that the parcel wrapped in newspaper would spread
wreckage through the station. If the guard had thrown it down knowingly and
willfully, he would not have threatened the plaintiff's safety, so far as appearances
could warn him. His conduct would not have involved, even then, an unreasonable probability of invasion of her bodily security. Liability can be no greater
where the act is inadvertent.

   *   *   * One who seeks redress at law does not make out a cause of action by
showing without more that there has been damage to his person. *If the harm was
not willful, he must show that the act as to him had possibilities of danger so
many and apparent as to entitle him to be protected against the doing of it though
the harm was unintended.* [Emphasis added.] *   *   * The victim does not sue
derivatively, or by right of subrogation, to vindicate an interest invaded in the
person of another. *   *   * He sues for breach of a duty owing to himself.

   *   *   * [To rule otherwise] would entail liability for any and all consequences, however novel or extraordinary.

*Palsgraf's complaint was dismissed. The railroad was not negligent to-
ward her because injury to her was not foreseeable. Had the owner of the
fireworks been harmed, there could well be a different result if he filed
suit.*

**JUDGMENT
AND REMEDY**

Foreseeability Since the decision in the *Palsgraf* case, the courts have used *foreseeability* as
the test for proximate cause. The railroad guards
were negligent, but the railroad's duty of care
did not extend to Palsgraf because she was an
unforeseeable plaintiff. If the consequences of
the harm done or the victim of the harm are unforeseeable, there is no proximate cause. Of
course, it is foreseeable that people will stand
on railroad platforms and that objects attached
to the platforms will fall as the result of explosions nearby. However, this is not a chain of
events against which a reasonable person will
normally guard. It is difficult to predict when a
court will say that something is foreseeable and
when it will say that something is not. This
difficulty stems from the fact that proximate cause
is tied up with the notion of duty and public
policy. (This point is obvious from Chief Justice
Cardozo's opinion.) How far a court stretches

foreseeability will be determined in part by the extent to which the court is willing to stretch the defendant's duty of care.

Defenses to Negligence

Three basic defenses in negligence cases are: (1) superseding or intervening forces, (2) assumption of risk, and (3) contributory and comparative negligence.

Superseding or Intervening Forces A superseding or intervening force may break the connection between a wrongful act and injury to another. If so, it cancels out the wrongful act. For example, keeping a can of gasoline in the trunk of one's car creates a foreseeable risk and is thus a negligent act. If lightning strikes the car, exploding the gas tank *and* can, injuring passing pedestrians, the lightning supersedes the original negligence as a cause of the damage, since it was not foreseeable. This example illustrates that the doctrine of superseding or intervening forces is also a question of proximate cause and legal duty.

In other situations, the intervention of a force may not relieve one of liability. If medical maltreatment of an injury aggravates the injury, the person whose negligence originally caused the injury is not relieved of liability. If subsequent disease or a subsequent accident is proximately caused by the original injury, the person who caused the original injury will be liable for the injury caused by the subsequent disease or accident. Where negligence endangers property, and the owner is injured in an attempt to protect the property, the negligent party will be liable for the injury.

In negligence cases, the negligent party will often attempt to show that some act has intervened after his or her action and that this second act was the proximate cause of injury. Typically, in cases where an individual takes a defensive action, such as attempting to escape by swerving or leaping from a vehicle, the original wrongdoer will not be relieved of liability even if the injury actually resulted from the escape attempt. The same is true under the "danger invites rescue" doctrine. Under this doctrine, if Smith commits an act that endangers Jones, and Brown sustains an injury trying to protect Jones, then Smith will be liable for Brown's injury. Rescuers can injure themselves, or the person rescued, or even a stranger, but the original wrongdoer will still be liable. The following case illustrates this doctrine.

GUARINO v. MINE SAFETY APPLIANCE CO.

Court of Appeals of New York, 1969. 25 N.Y.2d 460, 306 N.Y.S.2d 942, 255 N.E.2d 173.

BACKGROUND AND FACTS *This case arose out of an accident that killed three men and seriously injured five others. All were sewage treatment workers. After they had corrected a water leakage problem in a New York City sewer, one of the workers, Rooney, was fatally stricken by lethal gas present in the sewer when the oxygen-type protective mask he was wearing failed to operate properly. A companion worker shouted for help. Two other workers responded to the cries for help and were stricken by the gas when they entered the sewer tunnel without masks. The plaintiffs sued the manufacturer of the oxygen masks.*

JASEN J., Judge.

* * * *

This appeal presents for our review the "danger invites rescue" doctrine.

* * * *

Here the defendant committed a culpable act against the decedent Rooney, by manufacturing and distributing a defective oxygen-producing mask * * * By virtue of this defendant's culpable act, Rooney was placed in peril, thus inviting his rescue by the plaintiffs who were all members of Rooney's sewage treatment crew. There was no time for reflection when it became known that Rooney was in need of immediate assistance in the dark tunnel some 30 to 40 feet below the street level. These plaintiffs responded to the cries for help in a manner which was reasonable and consistent with their concern for each other as members of a crew. To require that a rescuer answering the cry for help make inquiry as to the nature of the culpable act that imperils someone's life would defy all logic.

As Judge Cardozo so eloquently stated in Wagner v. International Ry. Co.: "Danger invites rescue. The cry of distress is the summons to relief. * * * The *wrong* that imperils life is a wrong to the imperilled victim; it is a wrong also to his rescuer." [Emphasis added.]

* * * *

We conclude that a person who by his culpable act, whether it stems from negligence or breach of warranty, places another person in a position of imminent peril, may be held liable for any damages sustained by a rescuer in his attempt to aid the imperilled victim.

The manufacturer of the malfunctioning oxygen mask was held liable for damages sustained by the plaintiffs who sought to rescue the individual overcome by sewer gas when the mask failed. **JUDGMENT AND REMEDY**

Assumption of Risk A plaintiff who voluntarily enters into a risky situation, knowing the risk involved, will not be allowed to recover. This is the defense of **assumption of risk.** For example, a driver who enters a race knows that there is a risk of being killed or injured in a crash. The driver has assumed the risk of injury. The two requirements of this defense are: (1) knowledge of the risk and (2) voluntary assumption of the risk.

The risk can be assumed by express agreement, or the assumption of risk can be implied by the plaintiff's knowledge of the risk and subsequent conduct. Of course, the plaintiff does not assume a risk different from or greater than the risk normally carried by the activity. In our example, the race driver assumes the risk of being injured in the race but not the risk that the banking in the curves of the racetrack will give way during the race because of a construction defect.

Risks are not deemed to be assumed in situations involving emergencies. Neither are they assumed where a statute protects a class of people from harm and a member of the class is injured by the harm.

Contributory and Comparative Negligence All individuals are expected to exercise a reasonable degree of care in looking out for themselves. In some jurisdictions, recovery for injury resulting from negligence is prevented by failure of the injured person to exercise such care over himself or herself. This is the defense of **contributory negligence** where both parties have been negligent, and their combined negligence has contributed to cause the injury. When one party sues the other in tort for damages for negligence, the defendant can claim contributory negligence, which is a complete defense under common law rules. (Contributory negligence is not, however, a defense to intentional torts or to suits based on strict liability, a topic that will be covered later.)

The modern trend is toward narrowing the scope of the defense of contributory negligence. Instead of allowing contributory negligence to negate a cause of action completely, an increasing number of states allow recovery based on the doctrine of **comparative negligence.**[7] This doctrine enables computation of both the plaintiff's and the defendant's negligence. The plaintiff's damages are reduced by a percentage that represents the degree of his or her contributing fault. In an extreme case, if the plaintiff's negligence is found to be greater than the defendant's, the plaintiff will receive nothing. Indeed, the plaintiff may be subject to counterclaim by the defendant. In jurisdictions that follow the contributory negligence doctrine, negligence on the part of the plaintiff will bar any recovery of damages. In comparative negligence jurisdictions, however, the plaintiff will be able to recover the percentage of damages that was due to the defendant's negligence.

"Last clear chance" is a doctrine that can excuse the effect of a plaintiff's contributory negligence. If applicable, the last clear chance rule allows the plaintiff to recover full damages despite failure to exercise care. This doctrine, or rule, operates when, through his or her own negligence, the plaintiff is endangered (or his or her property is endangered) by a defendant who has an opportunity to avoid causing damage. For example, if Murphy walks across the street against the light, and Lewis, a motorist, sees her in time to avoid hitting her but hits her anyway, Lewis (the defendant) is not permitted to use Murphy's (the plaintiff's) prior negligence as a defense. The defendant negligently missed the opportunity to avoid injuring the plaintiff.

This rule is not easy to apply. Court decisions in which it appears are often in conflict. Its correct application requires knowledge of the nature and time span of the negligence of two or more persons, as well as knowledge of split-second sequences of events and perceptions. The principal variables for last clear chance cases are (1) the nature of the plaintiff's predicament and (2) the degree of the defendant's attentiveness to the plaintiff's peril. The classic last clear chance situation is one with a helpless plaintiff and an observant defendant. In any event, the defen-

dant's ability to have prevented the injury must be proved. It is the existence of this last clear chance that allows a plaintiff to recover damages for injury despite his or her negligence.

STRICT LIABILITY

The final category of torts is called **strict liability** or *liability without fault.* Intentional or negligent torts involve an act that departs from a reasonable standard of care and causes an injury. Under the doctrine of *strict liability,* liability for injury is imposed for reasons other than fault.

Abnormally Dangerous Activities

Strict liability for damages proximately caused by abnormally dangerous activities is one application of this doctrine. Abnormally dangerous activities have three characteristics:

1. The activity involves potential harm of a serious nature.
2. The activity involves a high degree of risk that cannot be completely guarded against by exercising reasonable care.
3. The activity is not commonly performed in the community or area.

Strict liability is applied because of the extreme risk of the activity. Although an activity such as blasting with dynamite is performed with all reasonable care, there is still a risk of injury. Balancing that risk against the potential for harm, it is fair to ask the person engaged in the activity to pay for injury caused by engaging in the activity. Although there is no fault, there is still responsibility because of the nature of the activity. In other words, it is reasonable to require the person engaged in the activity to carry the necessary insurance or otherwise stand prepared to compensate anyone who suffers. The following case illustrates a type of abnormally dangerous activity.

---

7. Comparative negligence has been adopted in about half the states.

BACKGROUND AND FACTS   *The Yommers operated a gasoline station. In December 1967 their neighbors, the McKenzies, noticed a smell in their well water, which proved to be caused by gasoline in the well water. McKenzie complained to the Yommers, who arranged to have one of their underground storage tanks replaced. Nevertheless, the McKenzies were unable to use their water for cooking or bathing until they had a filter and water softener installed. At the time of the trial, in December 1968, they were still bringing drinking water in from an outside source.*

The McKenzies sued the Yommers for nuisance and recovered damages of $3,500. The Yommers appealed the verdict on the grounds that the McKenzies did not prove that there was any negligence and that a gas station is not a nuisance.

YOMMER v. McKENZIE

Court of Appeals of Maryland, 1969.

255 Md. 220, 257 A.2d 138.

SINGLEY, Judge.

*   *   *   *

We have previously held that the establishment of a gasoline filling station does not constitute a nuisance *per se*, but that it may become a nuisance because of its location or manner in which it is operated.

The argument that the McKenzies must prove negligence in order to recover fails to take into account the doctrine of strict liability imposed by the rule of Rylands v. Fletcher which has been adopted by our prior decisions.

*   *   *   *

The black letter of new § 520 sets out the definition:

"520.   *Abnormally Dangerous Activities*

In determining whether an activity is abnormally dangerous, the following factors are to be considered:

(a)   Whether the activity involves a high degree of risk of some harm to the person, land or chattels of others;

(b)   Whether the gravity of the harm which may result from it is likely to be great;

(c)   Whether the risk cannot be eliminated by the exercise of reasonable care;

(d)   Whether the activity is not a matter of common usage;

(e)   Whether the activity is inappropriate to the place where it is carried on; and

(f)   The value of the activity to the community."

We believe that the present case is clearly within the ambit of this definition. Although the operation of a gasoline station does not of itself involve "a high degree of risk of some harm to the person, land or chattels of others," the placing of a large underground gasoline tank in close proximity to the appellees' residence and well does involve such a risk, since it is not a matter of common usage.* The

---

*   "An activity is a matter of common usage if it is customarily carried on by the great mass of mankind, or by many people in the community. *   *   * Gas and electricity in household pipes and wires [are examples of common usage], as contrasted with large gas storage tanks or high tension power lines." Restatement, Torts 2d, *supra*, comment on clause (d) at 65–66.

harm caused to the appellees was a serious one, and it may well have been worse if the contamination had not been detected promptly.

Although there is no evidence of negligence on the part of the Yommers (indeed such a showing is not required as will be discussed below), it is proper to surmise that this risk cannot, or at least was not, eliminated by the exercise of reasonable care.

The fifth and perhaps most crucial factor under the Institute's guidelines as applied to this case is the appropriateness of the activity in the particular place where it is being carried on. No one would deny that gasoline stations as a rule do not present any particular danger to the community. However, when the operation of such activity involves the placing of a large tank adjacent to a well from which a family must draw its water for drinking, bathing and laundry, at least that aspect of the activity is inappropriate to the locale, even when equated to the value of the activity.

*   *   *   *

We accept the test of appropriateness as the proper one: that the unusual, the excessive, the extravagant, the bizarre are likely to be non-natural uses which lead to strict liability.

*   *   *   *

It is apparent to us that the storage of large quantities of gasoline immediately adjacent to a private residence comes within this rule and relieved the McKenzies of the necessity of proving negligence. *   *   *

JUDGMENT
AND REMEDY   *The Yommers lost on appeal; the judgment for the McKenzies was upheld. There was no need to prove negligence in the case because the nature of the activity and the location of the tank caused the Yommers to be held strictly liable for the gasoline seepage.*

Other Applications of Strict Liability

There are other applications of the strict liability principle, notably in the workers' compensation acts and in the area of products liability. Liability here is a matter of social policy, and it is based on two factors: (1) the ability of the employer and manufacturer to better bear the cost of injury by spreading it out to society through an increase in the cost of goods and services and (2) the fact that the employer and manufacturer are making a profit from their activities and therefore should bear the cost of injury as an operating expense. Products liability will be considered in depth in Chapter 21.

QUESTIONS AND
CASE PROBLEMS

1.   Richards is an employee of the Dun Construction Corporation. While delivering materials to a construction site, he carelessly runs Dun's truck into a passenger vehicle driven by Green. This is Richards's second accident in six months. When Dun learns of this latest accident, a heated discussion ensues, and Dun fires Richards. Dun is so angry that he immediately writes

a letter to the union of which Richards is a member and to all other construction outfits in the community, stating that Richards is the "worst driver in the city" and that "anyone who hires him is asking for legal liability." Richards files suit against Dun, alleging libel on the basis of the statements made in the letters. Discuss the results.

2. It is a cold, wintry day. Ken needs to do some shopping on his way home from work. He is running late and is in a hurry. He stops at a drugstore to buy a tube of toothpaste on sale. He sticks the toothpaste in his overcoat pocket, laying the correct amount of change for the purchase on the counter. He is proceeding home when he suddenly remembers his wife's request that he pick up some much-needed groceries. He stops at a grocery store and rushes through the store picking up the groceries. He checks out and in a slow trot starts to leave the store when the checkout clerk sees the toothpaste in his overcoat pocket. Believing Ken was attemping to leave the store without declaring the item, the clerk yells, "Stop, thief!" Two bagboys grab Ken and haul him, struggling and protesting, to a small, dark back room, where he is locked in. One hour later, the store manager gets back from dinner, learns of the events and, after questioning a distraught Ken, lets him go. Ken starts having nightmares, acquires backaches, and becomes extremely nervous when friends and neighbors look at him. Discuss fully whether any torts have been committed against Ken.

3. Frank is a former employee of ABC Auto Repair Company. He enters the property of ABC, claiming the company owes him $150 in back wages. An argument ensues, and the ABC general manager, Steward, orders Frank off the property. Frank refuses to leave, and Steward orders two mechanics to throw him off the property. Frank runs to his truck, but on the way he grabs some tools valued at $150. Frank gets into his truck and, in his haste to drive away, destroys a gatepost. Frank refuses to return the tools.

(a) Discuss whether Frank has committed any torts.

(b) If the mechanics had thrown Frank off the property, would ABC be guilty of assault and battery? Explain.

4. John is a delivery employee for Crystal Glass, Inc. He is making a delivery when, at an intersection, his van and the passenger car of Jane collide. Jane wants to hold both John and Crystal Glass liable for the damages she has sustained. John claims that Jane was also at fault, at least as much at fault as he, and therefore neither he nor Crystal should be liable. Discuss fully these claims.

5. Ruth carelessly parks her car on a tall hill, leaving the car in neutral and failing to engage the parking brake. The car rolls down the hill, knocking down an electric line. The sparks from the broken line ignite a grass fire. The fire spreads until it reaches a barn one mile away. The barn has dynamite inside, and the burning barn explodes, causing part of the roof to fall upon and injure a passing motorist, Jim. Can Jim recover from Ruth? Why or why not?

6. A grocery cart in Waldbaum's Store was missing the protective flap in the "jump seat," or "baby seat," that can be raised to cover the opening when the seat is not in use. A shopper using the cart placed a large bottle of soda in the jump seat; the bottle fell through the opening and hit Mrs. Gross's foot, causing her injuries. Is Waldbaum's Store liable for this injury on the ground of negligence? Was the other shopper's act of placing heavy or breakable items in the jump seat foreseeable? [Gross v. Waldbaum, Inc., 102 Misc. 2d 175, 423 N.Y.S.2d 123 (Civ.Ct.N.Y.1979)]

7. Hodgeden purchased a stove from the Tyson Warehouse in Montpelier, Vermont. He gave Hubbard, the clerk, a promissory note for the stove, payable in six months. When Hubbard subsequently learned of Hodgeden's irresponsibility about paying his debts, he and Ayres, another clerk, started in pursuit of Hodgeden and overtook him about two miles outside of Montpelier. Hodgeden refused at first to give back the stove, claiming that he had paid good money for it. Hodgeden drew a knife and was then forcibly held by one of the clerks while the other took the stove. Hodgeden sued Hubbard and Ayres for assault and battery. Hubbard and Ayres claimed as a defense that since the goods were fraudulently purchased, they could use such force as was necessary to recover them. Are they right? [Hodgeden v. Hubbard, 18 Vt. 504 (1846)]

8. Gulf Refining Company sold a drum of gasoline to a farmer for use in his farm tractor. When Williams, an employee of the farmer, attempted to open the drum, he found that the bunghole cap was stuck because the threads were in disrepair. Movement of the worn threads produced a spark that caused an explosion and a fire. When Williams sued Gulf, Gulf admitted that it knew that the threads in the bung cap were in a state of disrepair from repeated hammering on the bung cap over the course of several years. Gulf claimed, however, that it should not be held liable for the injury sustained by Williams because it was so unusual, extraordinary, and improbable that it was not reasonably foreseeable. Is Gulf correct? [Gulf Refining Co. v. Williams, 183 Miss. 723, 185 So. 234 (1938)]

9. Butterfield was riding his horse rapidly down the road at about dusk. Shortly before this, Forrester, who

was making some repairs to his home, had laid a long pole partially across the road. Because of his speed, Butterfield did not see the pole. The horse collided with it, and Butterfield was thrown from the horse and injured. At trial, evidence showed that the pole could be seen from approximately a hundred yards away at that time of night. The facts also showed that Butterfield would have seen the pole and could have avoided hitting it if he had been riding at a normal rate of speed. If the court finds that both Butterfield and Forrester were negligent, can Butterfield collect any damages at all? [Butterfield v. Forrester, 11 East 60, Eng.Rep. 926, Huntsey (1809)]

10. Fletcher owned and operated a mill that needed a large reservoir of water to operate. Fletcher dug a large surface reservoir and filled it with water. A number of mines operated within the general area of the reservoir. Eventually, water started to leak through the ground into an underground mine shaft owned and operated by Rylands. Rylands sued Fletcher for the damage that Fletcher's reservoir had caused to Ryland's mining operation. Rylands, however, did not allege that Fletcher had been negligent in constructing or in operating his reservoir or mill. Can Rylands sue Fletcher without claiming that Fletcher has been negligent in any way? [Rylands v. Fletcher, L.R. 3 H.L. 330 (1868)]

CHAPTER 4

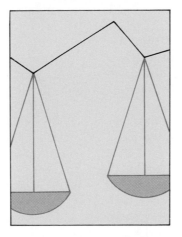

Torts Related to Business

Our economic system of free enterprise is predicated on the ability of individuals, acting either as individuals or as business firms, to compete for customers and for sales. Unfettered competitive behavior has been shown to lead to economic efficiency and economic progress. On the other hand, overly enthusiastic competitive efforts sometimes fall into the realm of intentional torts. Businesses may, generally speaking, engage in whatever is *reasonably* necessary to obtain a fair share of a market or to recapture a share that has been lost. But they are not allowed to use the motive of completely eliminating competition in order to justify certain business activities. Thus, an entire area of what is called business torts has arisen. **Business torts** are defined as wrongful interference with another's business rights. Included in business torts are such vaguely worded concepts as *unfair competition* and *interfering with the business relations of others*. Because the field is so broad, it is necessary to restrict this discussion to the following causes of action,

which are presented in terms of general categories:

1.   Wrongful interference with a contractual relationship.
2.   Wrongful interference with a business relationship.
3.   Wrongfully entering into business.
4.   Infringement of trademarks, patents, and copyrights.
5.   Disparagement of property or reputation.

WRONGFUL INTERFERENCE WITH A CONTRACTUAL RELATIONSHIP

Tort law relating to *intentional interference with a contractual relationship* has increased greatly in recent years. A landmark case in this area involved an opera singer, Joanna Wagner, who was under contract to sing for a man named Lumley for a specified period of years.[1] A man named Gye, who knew of this contract, nonetheless "enticed" Wagner to refuse to carry out the agreement, and Wagner began to sing for Gye. Gye's action constituted a tort because it interfered with the contractual relationship between Wagner and Lumley.

In principle, any lawful contract can be the basis for an action of this type. The plaintiff must prove that the defendant actually induced a breach of contractual relationship, not merely that the defendant reaped the benefits of a broken contract. If Jones has a contract with Smith that calls for Smith to mow Jones's lawn every week for a year at a specified price, Jones cannot sue Miller when Smith breaches the contract merely because Miller now receives gardening services from Smith.

Elements of Wrongful Interference with a Contractual Relationship

Three basic elements are necessary to the existence of wrongful interference with a contractual relationship:

1. A valid, enforceable contract must exist between two parties.

2. A third party must *know* that this contract exists.

3. This third party must *intentionally* cause either of the two parties who have the contract to break the contract. Whether this third party acts in bad faith or with malice is immaterial to establishing this tort, even though in most cases malice or bad faith is in evidence. However, the interference must be for the purpose of advancing the economic or pecuniary interest of the inducer.

The contract rights interfered with may be those between a firm and its employees or a firm and its customers. Sometimes the competitor of a firm may attempt to draw away a key employee, even to the extent of paying the damages for breach of contract. If the original employer can show that the competitor induced the breach—that is, that the employee would not normally have broken the contract—damages can be recovered.

The following case illustrates the necessity of proving that it was the action of the third party that induced the breach of contract.

---

1. Lumley v. Gye, 118 Eng.Rep. 749 (1853).

KNELL v. STATE FARM MUTUAL AUTO. INS. CO.

Appellate Court of Illinois, First District, Third Division, 1975. 32 Ill.App.3d 491, 336 N.E.2d 568.

BACKGROUND AND FACTS *Masterson retained two attorneys, Knell and Lezak, to represent him on a claim arising from an auto collison. The defendant, an insurance company, settled directly with Masterson even though it knew that he was represented by counsel. Knell and Lezak sued the insurance company for malicious interference with the attorney-client contractual relationship.*

McGLOON, J., Presiding Justice.

*   *   *   *

In the case at bar, there are no competent allegations tending to show that the client was induced by or conspired with the defendant to breach or terminate his contract with plaintiffs.

Although in the case at bar plaintiffs have alleged facts tending to show that the defendant insurance company knew of the attorney-client relationship and obtained a release by negotiating directly with the client, and that plaintiffs' client never paid plaintiffs their proportionate share of the fee, these facts alone are not enough to support a cause of action for malicious interference with the attorney-client relationship. A client has a right to negotiate a settlement on his own behalf, and without alleging facts supporting the allegation that defendant insurance company induced plaintiffs' client to breach or terminate his contract with plaintiffs, no cause of action is stated.

Cases in which actions for malicious interference with the attorney-client contract have been successfully maintained clearly contain facts not alleged in the instant case. For example, in *State Farm Insurance Co. v. Gregory*, there was evidence that the defendant insurance company induced the client to settle for less than the face value of the policy by representing that this would be more advantageous to him than proceeding with a lawsuit and dividing the recovery with his attorney. In *Employers Liability Assurance Corp. v. Freeman*, there was evidence that the insurer's claim adjuster told the attorney's client that he did not need an attorney, that the insurance company would take care of everything and that certain payments the insurer was to make to the client would be stopped if the client got involved in a lawsuit. In *Luric v. New Amsterdam Casualty Co.*, agents of the insurance company threatened plaintiff's client saying that unless he repudiated his retainer with the plaintiff he would receive no compensation for his injuries. In *Herron v. State Farm Mutual Insurance Co.*, the insurance company told plaintiff's client that he did not need an attorney and that a satisfactory settlement would be made. The insurance company in *Herron* even assisted the client in informing counsel of his dismissal.

In all of the above cases, there is some conduct on the part of the insurance company which induced the client to breach or terminate his contract with his attorney. In the case at bar no such conduct on the part of the insurance company is alleged. On the basis of the facts alleged we can only conclude that the client exercised his right to negotiate a settlement on his own behalf.

The trial court's judgment in favor of the insurance company was affirmed.   **JUDGMENT AND REMEDY**

WRONGFUL INTERFERENCE WITH A BUSINESS RELATIONSHIP

Individuals devise countless schemes to attract business, but they are forbidden by the courts to interfere unreasonably with another's business in their attempts to gain a share of the market. There is a difference between *competition* and *predatory behavior*. The distinction usually depends on whether a business is attempting to attract customers in general or to solicit only those customers who have already shown an interest in the similar product or service of a specific competitor. If a shopping center contains two shoe stores, an employee of Store A cannot be positioned at the entrance of Store B for the purpose of diverting customers to Store A. This type of activity constitutes the tort of wrongful interference with a business relationship, or what is commonly considered to be an unfair trade practice. If this type of activity were permitted, Store A would reap the benefits of Store B's advertising.

A salesperson cannot follow another company's salesperson through the city, soliciting the same prospective customers. Even though the people contacted may have purchased nothing from the first salesperson, that salesperson still has a business relationship with them. Courts will issue injunctions against this kind of behavior and will award damages when the business alleging interference can prove it suffered a monetary loss. In the following case a salesman's activities exceeded the bounds of fair competition.

AZAR v. LEHIGH CORP.

District Court of Appeal of
Florida, Second District, 1978.
364 So. 2d 860.

BACKGROUND AND FACTS   *Lehigh Corporation, a developer of real estate, obtained a restraining order against one of its former salesmen, Leroy Azar. Lehigh brought prospective customers to its development, Lehigh Acres, and provided accommodations at its company-owned motel. Azar pursued a practice of following Lehigh purchasers and persuading them to rescind their contracts with Lehigh and purchase less expensive property from him.*

The Circuit Court issued the following order:

IT IS HEREBY ORDERED AND ADJUDGED that the Defendant, Leroy Azar, is hereby restrained and enjoined from directly or indirectly contacting or soliciting the Plaintiff's perspective [sic] or actual customers on the premises of the Lehigh Resort Motel or at the sales offices of the Plaintiffs if such purchasers are in Lee County as guests of the Plaintiffs. "Guests" of the Plaintiffs shall mean persons who have been invited by the Plaintiffs, either directly or indirectly, to view the Lehigh Acres community and real estate situate therein. "Invited" shall mean those persons who have come to the Lehigh Acres community as a result of any promotional activities of the Plaintiffs wherein some incentive of value has been given or offered to said persons. The "Defendant", Leroy Azar, shall include any person or entity acting in the Defendant's behalf or at the urging of the Defendant, Leroy Azar.

Azar contended that Lehigh's customers had a right under federal law to rescind their contracts within three days and that he was merely providing them with an opportunity to be relieved of their contract and to obtain comparable property for lower prices. Lehigh asserted that Azar was tortiously interfering with the advantageous business relationship between them and their customers.

GRIMES, Chief Judge.

*   *   *   *

[T]he elements of [the tort of interference with business are] as follows:
(1) the existence of a business relationship under which the plaintiff has legal rights, (2) an intentional and unjustified interference with that relationship by the defendant, and (3) damage to the plaintiff as a result of the breach of the business relationship.   .   .   .
It is not essential, however, that the business relationship be founded upon an enforceable contract. *   *   *

There is a narrow line between what constitutes vigorous competition in a free enterprise society and malicious interference with a favorable business relationship. Under the heading of "Interference with prospective advantage," Prosser states:

Though trade warfare may be waged to the bitter end, there are certain rules of combat which must be observed.   .   . W. Prosser, Law of Torts (4th ed. 1971) at 956.

He goes on to say that the courts have generally prohibited such activities as defamation of the competitor, disparagement of his goods and his business methods, and intimidation, harassment and annoyance of his customers. In the final analysis, the issue seems to turn upon whether the subject conduct is considered to be "unfair" according to contemporary business standards.

Keeping in mind the trial judge's broad discretion to enter temporary restraining orders, we believe there is sufficient evidence in this record to support the court's decision. Moreover, we believe the terms of the order are precise enough for the appellant to understand what he cannot do. Considering appellant's knowledge of Lehigh's operation, we are confident that he will have no difficulty in ascertaining which of the motel patrons constitute appellees' guests as defined in the temporary restraining order.

The restraining order against Azar was allowed to stand. Azar remained under court order not to solicit business from those customers brought to Lehigh Acres by Lehigh Corporation.   **JUDGMENT AND REMEDY**

Defenses to Wrongful Interference with a Contractual or Business Relationship

Justification is the defense used most often against the accusation of the tort of wrongful interference with a contractual or business relationship. For example, bona fide competitive behavior is a privileged interference even if it results in the breaking of a contract. If Jones Meats advertises so effectively that it induces Sam's Restaurant Chain to break its contract with Paul's Meat Company, Paul's Meat Company would be unable to recover against Jones Meats on a wrongful interference theory. After all, the public policy that favors free competition in advertising definitely outweighs any possible instability that such competitive activity might cause in contractual relations.

Permissive Interferences

Permissive interferences are interfering actions that the courts have not held to be tortious interferences. The most common example is a labor union's freedom to encourage a strike. Encouraging a strike interferes with the contractual relationship between employer and employee and may interfere with business relationships; yet it is permitted by the courts.

WRONGFULLY ENTERING INTO BUSINESS

In a freely competitive society it is usually true that any person can enter into any business in order to compete for the customers of extant businesses. Two situations in which this general notion of free competition does not hold, however, are (1) when entering into a business is in violation of law and (2) when competitive behavior is predatory in nature.

Entering a Business in Violation of the Law

Although we live in a free enterprise system, government at all levels—local, state, and federal—restricts who may enter certain businesses. Indeed, there exists a whole area of regulated economic activities in which people cannot engage unless they first obtain permission from a regulatory agency or commission. True, today is an era of increasing deregulation; yet the number of businesses under such regulation is still large. For example, a group of people cannot simply agree among themselves to start a business competitive with their local electric company or natural gas company. First they would have to gain approval from the public utility, or service, commission in their particular state, approval which would be highly unlikely. As another example, one cannot simply put up a radio or television transmitter and start transmitting on some frequency believed to be open. A license is necessary. The Federal Communications Commission grants all licenses for both television and radio, and these are only for designated frequencies.

Many occupations require licenses in the United States. Not only are lawyers, physicians, and dentists licensed, but so are palm readers and astrologists. In many states the licensed member of a profession is allowed to bring action on behalf of the entire profession in order to prevent an unlicensed individual from practicing that occupation.

Predatory Competitive Activities

Any business or profession not subject to regulatory agencies or occupational licensing standards is open to an individual; however, no one can open a business for the sole purpose of driving another firm out of business. Such a predatory motive for opening a business is considered to constitute *simulated competition.* What the courts consider normal competitive activity is not always easy to ascertain. One might ask when the normal desire to compete and obtain profits ends and when a tortious action begins. The landmark case that follows illustrates how a Minnesota court grappled with the question of malicious injury to business.

TUTTLE v. BUCK

Supreme Court of Minnesota,
1909.
107 Minn. 145, 119 N.W. 946.

BACKGROUND AND FACTS *The plaintiff, a barber, filed suit against the defendant for malicious interference with his business. The plaintiff had owned and operated a barbershop for the previous ten years and had been able to maintain himself and his family comfortably from the income of the business.*

The defendant was a banker in the same community. During the past twelve months, the defendant had "maliciously" established a competitive barbershop, employed a barber to carry on the business, and used his personal influence to attract customers from the plaintiff's barbershop. Apparently, the defendant had circulated false and malicious reports and accusations about the plaintiff and had personally solicited, urged, threatened, and otherwise persuaded many of the plaintiff's patrons to stop using the plaintiff's services and to use the defendant's shop instead. The plaintiff charged that the defendant undertook this entire plan with the sole design of injuring the plaintiff and destroying his business, not for serving any legitimate business interest or as fair competition.

ELLIOTT, Justice.

*   *   *   *

*   *   * It is not at all correct to say that the motive with which an act is done is always immaterial, providing the act itself is not unlawful. *   *   *

*   *   * It must be remembered that the common law is the result of growth, and that its development has been determined by the social needs of the community which it governs. It is the resultant of conflicting social forces, and those forces which are for the time dominant leave their impress upon the law. It is of judicial origin, and seeks to establish doctrines and rules for the determination, protection, and enforcement of legal rights. Manifestly it must change as society changes and new rights are recognized. To be an efficient instrument, and not a mere abstraction, it must gradually adapt itself to changed conditions. Necessarily its form and substance has been greatly affected by prevalent economic theories. For generations there has been a practical agreement upon the proposition that competition in trade and business is desirable, and this idea has found expression in the decisions of the courts as well as in statutes. But it has led to grievous and manifold wrongs to individuals, and many courts have manifested an earnest desire to protect the individuals from the evils which result from unrestrained business competition. The problem has been to so adjust matters as to preserve the principle of competition and yet guard against its abuse to the unnecessary injury to the individual. So the principle that a man may use his own property according to his own needs and desires, while true in the abstract, is subject to many limitations in the concrete. Men cannot always, in civilized society, be allowed to use their own property as their interests or desires may dictate without reference to the fact that they have neighbors whose rights are as sacred as their own. The existence and well-being of society requires that each and every person shall conduct himself consistently with the fact that he is a social and reasonable person. The purpose for which a man is using his own property may thus sometimes determine his rights. "If there exists, then, a positive duty to avoid harm, much more, then, exists the negative duty of not doing willful harm, subject, as all general duties must be subject, to the necessary exceptions. The three main heads of duty with which the law of torts is concerned, namely, to abstain from willful injury, to respect the property of others, and to use due diligence to avoid causing harm to others, are all alike of a comprehensive nature." Pollock, Torts, (8th Ed.) p. 21.

To divert to one's self the customers of a business rival by the offer of goods at lower prices is in general a legitimate mode of serving one's own interest, and justifiable as fair competition. But when a man starts an opposition place of business, not for the sake of profit to himself, but regardless of loss to himself, and for the sole purpose of driving his competitor out of business, and with the intention of himself retiring upon the accomplishment of his malevolent purpose, he is guilty of a wanton wrong and an actionable tort. In such a case he would not be exercising his legal right, or doing an act which can be judged separately from the motive which actuated him. To call such conduct competition is a perversion of terms. It is simply the application of force without legal justification, which in its moral quality may be no better than highway robbery.

The plaintiff's cause of action was recognized under Minnesota law. The Supreme Court of Minnesota concluded that modern business requires certain protection against abusive business practices. The plaintiff then returned to the trial court to prove his case. From that point forward, Minnesota recognized a cause of action for tortious interference with business relations.

JUDGMENT AND REMEDY

INFRINGEMENT OF TRADEMARKS, PATENTS, AND COPYRIGHTS

Infringement of Trademarks

A **trademark** is a distinctive mark, motto, device, or implement that a manufacturer stamps, prints, or otherwise affixes to the goods it pro-

duces, so that they may be identified on the market and their origin vouched for. At common law, the person who used a symbol or mark to identify a business or product was protected in the use of that trademark. Clearly, if one used the trademark of another, one would mislead consumers into believing that one's goods were made by the other. The law seeks to avoid this kind of confusion. Normally, personal names, words, or places that are descriptive of an article or its use cannot be trademarked; they are available to anyone. Words that are used as part of a design or device, however, or words that are uncommon or fanciful may be trademarked.

Consider an example. *English Leather* may not be trademarked to describe leather processed in England. On the other hand, *English Leather* may be, and is, trademarked as a name for aftershave lotion, since this constitutes a *fanciful* use of the words. Consider also that even the common name of an individual may be trademarked if that name is accompanied by a picture or some fanciful design that allows for easy identification of the product—for example, Smith Brothers' Cough Drops.

When Infringement Occurs   Once a trademark has been registered, a firm is entitled to the exclusive use of it for marketing purposes. Whenever that trademark is copied to a substantial degree or used in its entirety by another, intentionally or unintentionally, the trademark has been infringed. The trademark need not be registered with the state or with the federal government in order to obtain protection from the tort of trademark infringement, but registration does furnish proof of the date of inception of its use. Moreover, registration may prolong the life of the trademark.

The defendant in the following case was liable for trademark infringement even though he did not manufacture the article.

VUITTON ET FILS, S.A. v. CROWN HANDBAGS

District Court, Southern District of New York, 1979. 492 F.Supp. 1071.

BACKGROUND AND FACTS   *Plaintiff, Vuitton, a French corporation that manufactures expensive handbags, sued the defendant for infringement of its registered trademark. The defendant had offered to sell six of the handbags to a private investigator hired by plaintiff.*

BRIEANT, District Judge

*   *   *   *

The goal of the framers of the Lanham Trade-Mark Act was to secure to the owner of a trademark the goodwill of his business, and at the same time protect the buying public against spurious and falsely marked goods. The Vuitton trademark has been used in connection with the advertising and sale of goods in commerce for over 46 years since its entry upon the Principal Trademark Register of the United States Patent Office in 1932. The trademark, #297,594, specifically refers to "handbags and pocketbooks" as items to which the mark would be affixed. Defendant makes no effort to challenge the validity or ownership of the Vuitton mark.

It remains to be determined whether defendant's actions in offering for sale copies of genuine Vuitton handbags was an infringement of plaintiff's registered mark within the meaning of 15 U.S.C. § 1114 which provides in pertinent part:

"1) Any person who shall, without the consent of the registrant—

(a) use in commerce any reproduction, counterfeit, copy, or colorable imitation of a registered mark in connection with the sale, offering for sale, distribution, or advertising of any goods or services on or in connection with which such use is likely to cause confusion, or to cause mistake, or to deceive . . . shall be liable in a civil action by the registrant for the remedies hereinafter provided."

Where an alleged infringing mark is used in connection with the sale of similar goods, the long standing rule in this Circuit has been that the second comer to the marketplace "has a duty to so name and dress his product as to avoid all likelihood of consumers confusing it with the product of the first comer." Harold

F. Ritchie, Inc. v. Chesebrough Ponds, Inc., 281 F.2d 755, 758, 120 USPQ 310, 312–313 (2d Cir. 1960). The second comer has no right to trade upon the good will of the first comer developed over a period of time and at considerable expense. As our Court of Appeals in this Circuit ruled many years ago:

"It is so easy for the honest business man, who wishes to sell his goods upon their merits, to select from the entire material universe, which is before him, symbols, marks and coverings which by no possibility can cause confusion between his goods and those of his competitors, that the courts look with suspicion upon one who, in dressing his goods for the market, approaches so near to his successful rival that the public may fail to distinguish between them."

The great weight of the evidence in the case leads to the conclusion that the Vuitton trademark is a strong mark, and as such is entitled to broad protection. The strength of the mark stems from its conspicuously distinctive nature. It is unique in its design and color, and during the more than 46 years of its continuous use in this country it has come to represent a source of product of perceived quality and prestige. *   *   *

It would be impossible for one engaged in the same trade as plaintiff is, and defendant is so engaged, to be unaware of the presence of the counterfeits in the trade. Nor could such a person be unaware of the plaintiff's rights to its valued mark. I find that defendant was a willful violator.

*   *   *   *

Both Vuitton and consumers in general would suffer by the purchase of counterfeit bags of inferior quality. Vuitton would soon lose its reputation for quality and exclusivity, and consumers would be deceived into believing they were getting something they were not.

Defendant clearly infringed upon plaintiff's registered trademark in violation of 15 U.S.C. § 1114, by offering for sale a combination of product and trademark which exactly mimics that of plaintiff, resulting in the type of confusion and deception which the Lanham Act was designed to prevent. In doing so, defendant acted willfully and with knowledge of the fact that these handbags which it offered for sale infringed upon the trademark rights of plaintiff. Defendant was in the business of manufacturing leather handbags in New York. As noted earlier, logic dictates that it must be charged with actual as well as constructive knowledge of plaintiff's mark and merchandise. The counterfeit bags were manufactured with the intention to trade upon the plaintiff's established reputation for quality merchandise. Although defendant apparently did not itself manufacture the infringing articles, it took an active part in their distribution and sale, making use of plaintiff's trademark in the process.

JUDGMENT AND REMEDY

Vuitton was granted permanent injunctive relief from Crown Handbag's commercial practices that violated Vuitton's trademark rights. Crown had to pay damages amounting to the sales price of the six handbags offered to Vuitton's investigator. Crown also had to pay Vuitton's attorney's fees.

Infringement upon Trade Names   The term *trade name* is used to indicate part or all of a business's name, whether that business be a sole proprietorship, a partnership, or a corporation. Generally, a trade name is directly related to a business and to its goodwill. As with trademarks, words must be unusual or fancifully used in order to be protected as trade names. The word

Safeway was held by the courts to be sufficiently fanciful to obtain protection as a trade name.[2] The decisions of the courts do not give entirely clear guidelines as to when the name of a corporation can be regarded as a trade name. A particularly thorny problem arises when a trade name

---

2. Safeway Stores v. Suburban Foods, 130 F.Supp. 249 (E.D.Va. 1955).

acquires generic use. Originally, the following were used only as trade names: Frigidaire, Scotch Tape, Xerox, and Kleenex. Today, a secondary meaning has been acquired by these names. Even so, the courts will not allow another firm to use those names in such a way as to deceive a potential consumer. Consider, for example, the following famous case concerning Coca-Cola, decided by the Supreme Court.

THE COCA-COLA CO. v. THE KOKE CO. OF AMERICA ET AL.

United States Supreme Court, 1920.
254 U.S. 143, 41 S.Ct. 113.

BACKGROUND AND FACTS *Coco-Cola Company sought to enjoin other beverage companies from using the words "Koke" or "Dope" for their products. The defendants contended that the Coca-Cola trademark was a fraudulent representation and that Coca-Cola was therefore not entitled to any help from the courts.*

MR. JUSTICE HOLMES delivered the opinion of the court.

This is a bill in equity brought by the Coca-Cola Company to prevent the infringement of its trade-mark Coca-Cola and unfair competition with it in its business of making and selling the beverage for which the trade-mark is used. The District Court gave the plaintiff a decree [an injunction]. This was reversed by the Circuit Court of Appeals. Subsequently a writ of certiorari was granted by this Court.

*   *   *   *

Of course a man is not to be protected in the use of a device the very purpose and effect of which is to swindle the public. But the defects of a plaintiff do not offer a very broad ground for allowing another to swindle him. The defense relied on here should be scrutinized with a critical eye. The main point is this: Before 1900 the beginning of the good will was more or less helped by the presence of cocaine, a drug that, like alcohol or caffein or opium, may be described as a deadly poison or as a valuable item of the pharmacopœa according to the rhetorical purposes in view. The amount seems to have been very small, but it may have been enough to begin a bad habit and after the Food and Drug Act of June 30, 1906, if not earlier, long before this suit was brought, it was eliminated from the plaintiff's compound. Coca leaves still are used, to be sure, but after they have been subjected to a drastic process that removes from them every characteristic substance except a little tannin and still less chlorophyl. The cola nut, at best, on its side furnishes but a very small portion of the caffein, which now is the only element that has appreciable effect. That comes mainly from other sources. It is argued that the continued use of the name imports a representation that has ceased to be true and that the representation is reinforced by a picture of coca leaves and cola nuts upon the label and by advertisements, which however were many years before this suit was brought, that the drink is an "ideal nerve tonic and stimulant," &c., and that thus the very thing sought to be protected is used as a fraud.

The argument does not satisfy us. We are dealing here with a popular drink not with a medicine, and although what has been said might suggest that its attraction lay in producing the expectation of a toxic effect the facts point to a different conclusion. Since 1900 the sales have increased at a very great rate corresponding to a like increase in advertising. The name now characterizes a beverage to be had at almost any soda fountain. It means a single thing coming from a single source, and well known to the community. It hardly would be too much to say that the drink characterizes the name as much as the name the drink. In other words Coca-Cola probably means to most persons the plaintiff's familiar product to be had everywhere rather than a compound of particular substances. The coca leaves and whatever of cola nut is employed may be used to justify the continuance of the name or they may affect the flavor as the plaintiff contends, but before this suit was brought the plaintiff had advertised to the public that it must not expect and would not find cocaine, and had eliminated everything tending to suggest cocaine effects except the name and the picture of the leaves and nuts, which probably conveyed little or nothing to most who saw it. It appears to us that it would be going too far to deny the plaintiff relief against a palpable fraud because possibly here and there an ignorant person might call for the drink with the hope for incipient cocaine intoxication. The plaintiff's position must be judged by the facts as they were when the suit was begun, not by the facts of a different condition and an earlier time.

The decree of the District Court restrains the defendant from using the word Dope. The plaintiff illustrated in a very striking way the fact that the word is one of the most featureless known even to the language of those who are incapable of discriminating speech. In some places it would be used to call for Coca-Cola. It equally would have been used to call for anything else having about it a faint aureole of poison. It does not suggest Coca-Cola by similarity and whatever objections there may be to its use, objections which the plaintiff equally makes to its application to Coca-Cola, we see no ground on which the plaintiff can claim a personal right to exclude the defendant from using it.

The product including the coloring matter is free to all who can make it if no extrinsic deceiving element is present.

The competing beverage companies were enjoined from calling their products "Koke," but the Court would not prevent them from calling their products "Dope."   **JUDGMENT AND REMEDY**

Infringement of Patents

A patent is a grant from the government that conveys and secures to an inventor the exclusive right to make, use, and sell an invention for a period of seventeen years. Patents for a lesser period are given for designs, as opposed to inventions. For either a regular patent or a design patent, the applicant must demonstrate to the satisfaction of the patent office that the invention, discovery, or design is genuine, novel, useful, and not obvious in the light of technology of the time. A patent holder gives notice to all that an article or design is patented by placing on it the word "Patent" or "Pat." plus the patent number.

When Infringement Occurs   If a firm uses a substantial identity of operation and result between its device and a patented device, the tort of patent infringement exists. Patent infringement may exist even though not all features or parts of an invention are copied. (With respect to a patented process, however, all steps or their equivalent must be copied in order for infringement to exist.) Often, litigation for patent infringement is so costly that the patent holder will instead offer to sell to the infringer a license to use the patented design, product, or process. Indeed, in many cases the costs of detection, prosecution, and monitoring are so high that patents are valueless to their owners, since they cannot afford to protect them.

Infringement of Copyright

A copyright is an intangible right granted by statute to the author or originator of certain literary or artistic productions. Works created after January 1, 1978, are automatically given statutory copyright protection for the life of the author plus fifty years. Note that it is not possible to copyright an idea. What is copyrightable is the particular way in which an idea is expressed.

When an Infringement Occurs Whenever the form of expression of an idea is copied, an infringement of copyright has occurred. The production does not have to be exactly the same as the original; nor does it have to reproduce the original in its entirety. If a substantial part of the original is reproduced, a copyright infringement exists.

Theft of Trade Secrets

Some processes or items of information that are not patented, or not patentable, are nevertheless protected by law against appropriation by a competitor. Businesses that have *trade secrets* generally protect themselves by having all employees who use the process or information agree in their contracts never to divulge it. Thus, if a salesperson tries to solicit the company's customers for non-company business, or if an employee copies the employer's unique method of manufacture, he or she has appropriated a trade secret and has also broken a contract, two separate wrongs. Theft of confidential data by industrial espionage, as when a business taps into a competitor's computer, is a theft of trade secrets without any contractual violations and is actionable in itself.

DISPARAGEMENT OF PROPERTY OR REPUTATION

Business firms are encouraged to compete in our society, but they have the right to be reasonably free from disparagement of their products and their reputations.

Disparagement of Product

Disparagement of product or, more generally, disparagement of property, refers to common law torts of *slander of quality* and *slander of title*. Unprivileged publication of false information about another's product, alleging it is not what its seller claims, constitutes a tort of slander of quality. This tort has also been given the name *trade libel*. Actual damages must be proved by the plaintiff to have proximately resulted from the slander of quality. It must be shown that a third person refrained from dealing with the plaintiff because of the improper publication. It is possible for an improper publication to be both a slander of quality and a defamation. For example, a statement that disparages the quality of an article may also, by implication, disparage the character of the person who would sell such a product.

When a publication denies or casts doubt upon another's legal ownership of any property, and when this results in financial loss to that property owner, the tort of slander of title may exist. Usually this is an intentional tort in which someone knowingly publishes an untrue statement about property, with the intent of discouraging a third person from dealing with the person slandered. For example, it would be difficult for a car dealer to attract customers after competitors put out a rumor that the dealer's stock consisted of stolen autos.

Disparagement of Reputation

In Chapter 3 we discussed defamation, breaking it down into its component parts of libel in written or printed form and slander in oral form. Defamation becomes a business tort when the defamatory matter injures someone else in a profession, business, or trade or when it adversely affects a business entity in its credit rating and other dealings.

THE FUTURE

Torts relating to business, long recognized at common law, are becoming increasingly important in today's competitive world. Courts are ordering redress for more and more of these torts. Suits claiming violation of one or more of the rights of the owners of businesses are proliferating. Computerization, rapid communications, and mass media advertising multiply the means of committing such torts and magnify the effects they can have on the injured party's business. Since the law in this area is primarily case law rather than statutory law, it is free to change to accommodate the new developments that are transforming the business world.

QUESTIONS AND CASE PROBLEMS

1.   Stevens owns a bakery. He has been trying to obtain a long-term contract with the owner of Martha's Tea Salons for some time. Stevens starts a local advertising campaign on radio and television and in the newspaper. This advertising campaign is so persuasive that Martha decides to break the contract she has had with Hank's Bakery so that she can patronize Stevens's bakery. Is Stevens liable to Hank's Bakery for the tort of wrongful interference with contractual relations? Is Martha liable for this tort? For anything?

2.   An Atlanta theater group produced a musical entitled "Scarlett Fever." The production opened with Shady Charlotte O'Mara at her plantation, Tiara, and moved through the major episodes of the film *Gone With The Wind.* This was not a parody or a farce, but another "play." The play also utilized backdrops reminiscent of the settings in the film. Original songs and dances were performed. Did this production infringe copyright interests in the film and the novel *Gone with the Wind?* [Metro-Goldwyn-Mayer, Inc. v. Showcase

Atlanta Coop. Productions, Inc., 479 F.Supp. 351 (N.D.Ga.1979)]

3.   While Dennis Prince was attempting to sell his restaurant, he learned that his former sister-in-law was telling prospective buyers that Prince was crooked and dishonest in his business dealings and that he was cheating his own children out of their shares of ownership in the business. What action, if any, can Prince take against his former sister-in-law? [Prince v. Peterson, 538 P.2d 1325 (Utah 1975)]

4.   Franchisees of a "T.G.I. Friday's" restaurant in Jackson, Mississippi, opened a restaurant in Baton Rouge, Louisiana. They named the new restaurant "E.L. Saturday's" or "Ever Lovin' Saturday's." The Baton Rouge restaurant was physically similar to T.G.I. Friday's, in Jackson. Both used a turn-of-the-century motif. "T.G.I. Friday's" is registered as a trademark with the United States patent office. Was the opening of the Baton Rouge restaurant a trademark infringement? [T.G.I. Friday's, Inc. v. International Restaurant Group, Inc., 569 F.2d 895 (5th Cir. 1978)]

5.   Southard was stranded in Hawaii as the result of an airline strike. He had purchased a round-trip ticket before leaving his home in Denver. He sued the union for tortious interference with his contract with the airline and sought to recover the additional expense he incurred on another airline. Was the union liable to Mr. Southard? [International Ass'n of Machinists v. Southard, 170 Colo. 119, 459 P.2d 570 (1969)]

6.   California Consumers Company purchased from S. L. Coker an ice distributing business in the city of Santa Monica. In the purchase agreement Coker agreed that he would not engage in the business of selling or distributing ice either directly or indirectly in the city of Santa Monica, so long as the purchasers or anyone later purchasing the business remained in the business. Imperial Ice Company acquired the ice distributing business from California Consumers. Coker subsequently began selling ice in the same territory. The ice was supplied to him by a company owned by Rossier and Matheson on very attractive terms, because they wished to break into that area. Imperial Ice sued to obtain an injunction to restrain Coker from violating his original contract. Did Rossier and Matheson induce Coker to violate his contract, and were they therefore guilty of the tort of wrongful interference with contractual relations? [Imperial Ice Co. v. Rossier et al., 18 Cal.2d 33, 112 P.2d 631 (1941)]

7.   Stiffel manufactured a floor lamp that he had patented. Sears, Roebuck and Co. made an identical lamp that it sold at a lower price. Stiffel sought an injunction against Sears, claiming that his patent had been

infringed. The patent, however, had expired. Was Sears guilty of infringement of patent and unfair competition? [Sears, Roebuck & Co. v. Stiffel Co., 376 U.S. 225, 84 S.Ct. 784 (1964)]

8.   Roto-Rooter was granted a federal registration in 1954 for its service mark "Roto-Rooter" for sewer, pipe, and drain cleaning services. In 1973 O'Neal opened a business with the name "Rotary D-Routing." Roto-Rooter sued for damages for trademark infringement. Could O'Neal continue using the name "Rotary D-Routing?" [Roto-Rooter Corp. v. O'Neal 513 F.2d 44 (5th Cir. 1975)]

CHAPTER 5

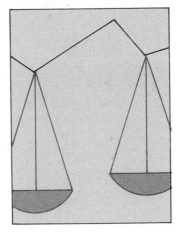

Criminal Law

Previously in this text we referred to a *crime* as being a wrong perpetrated against society as defined by society. A discussion of criminal law is appropriate to a study of business law because the prevention of crime and the effort of capturing and prosecuting criminals are time-consuming and costly activities. Since so much of a government's resources must be diverted to combat criminal activity, it is important that we understand the nature and extent of such activity.

The sanctions used to bring about a peaceful society, in which individuals engage in business and can compete and flourish, include those imposed by the civil law, such as tort damages for various types of conduct, as discussed in the previous chapters, and contract damages, to be discussed in detail later. Chapter 1 also pointed out that courts of equity may restrain certain unlawful conduct by issuing injunctions.

These remedies have not been sufficient. Consequently, additional sanctions have been developed for some activities. As a result, a criminal law element exists within the legal environment of business. The prerequisites of fault or guilt in this area are different from those in the civil law, as are the sanctions and penalties.

THE NATURE OF CRIME

Crimes can be distinguished from other wrongful conduct in that they are offenses against society as a whole. Crimes are prosecuted by a public official, not by their victims. In addition, criminals are punished. Tort remedies—remedies for civil wrongs—are generally intended to compensate the injured (except when damages of a punitive nature are assessed), but criminal law is directly concerned with punishing (and ideally rehabilitating) the wrongdoer. The act of punishment is intended to accomplish four aims:

1. Punishment is supposed to deter not only the wrongdoer in a particular instance, but also

all other members of society who might commit a similar wrong. In other words, this theory holds that publicly known acts of punishment indicate to other members of society that costs will be involved if they commit a similar wrong. Thus, punishment of a particular criminal will, according to this theory, prevent other crimes.

2. Punishment protects society by incapacitating the criminal through imprisonment. If a criminal is likely to commit other crimes, imprisonment will remove him or her from potential victims.

3. Punishment serves as a substitute for private vengeance. A society will become chaotic if private means of "settling the score" are allowed when criminal acts have taken place.

4. Punishment, in theory, will rehabilitate criminals. The American penal system has programs for treatment and education of inmates.

A final factor distinguishing criminal sanctions from tortious remedies is that the source of criminal law is primarily statutory. Both the acts that constitute crimes and the resulting punishments are formally and very specifically set out in statutes. A **crime** can thus be defined as a wrong against society proclaimed in a statute and punishable by society if committed.

Classifications of Crimes

Felonies and Misdemeanors Crimes are classified as felonies or misdemeanors according to their seriousness. **Felonies** are more serious than misdemeanors and are punishable by death or by imprisonment in a federal or state penitentiary for more than a year. The definition of a felony derives from the common law crimes of arson, rape, grand larceny, and murder. Felonies can be divided by degrees of seriousness. The Model Penal Code, for example, provides for four degrees of felony: capital offenses where the maximum penalty is death, first degree felonies punishable by a maximum penalty of life imprisonment, second degree felonies punishable by a maximum of ten years' imprisonment, and third degree felonies punishable by up to five years' imprisonment. (It is important to note that these are maximum penalties. The actual sentence served can be less than the maximum.)

When death occurs during or as the result of certain felonious crimes, many states have laws whereby the criminal is charged with *felony murder* in addition to the crime that was intended. State legislatures determine which crimes can lead to felony murder charges. Most states do not impose the death penalty in felony murder cases. The following case illustrates a felony murder statute.

STATE OF NEW JERSEY v. CANOLA

Superior Court of New Jersey, Appellate Division, 1975. 135 N.J.Super. 224, 343 A.2d 110.

BACKGROUND AND FACTS *The defendant, Canola, and three other men robbed a jewelry store. During the robbery, the owner of the store, Bahtiarian, and one of the robbers, Lloredo, were killed. Canola did not shoot either man, but he was found guilty of their deaths in accordance with the New Jersey felony murder statute.*

COLLESTER, Presiding Justice of the Appellate Division.

*   *   *   *

Defendant contends the trial court erred in denying his motion to dismiss the second count of the indictment charging him with the felony murder of Harold Lloredo. He argues here, as he did below, that he cannot be held for felony murder as a matter of law because Lloredo was shot and killed by Bahtiarian, one of the victims of the armed robbery. In denying the motion the trial court held the language of N.J.S.A. 2A:113-1, particularly the clause, "if the death of anyone ensues from the committing or attempting to commit any such crime or act," (hereinafter referred to as the "ensues clause") indicated a legislative policy which holds one (and others in concert with him) who deliberately commits an inherently violent act fully responsible for the probable consequences of the act.

The question of whether a participant in an armed robbery can be held liable for murder when his co-participant is killed by an intended victim in an attempt to abort an armed robbery has not heretofore been considered by our appellate courts. The resolution of the question depends upon the Legislature's intent when N.J.S.A. 2A:113–1 was enacted.

The statute, in pertinent part, reads as follows:

If any person, in committing or attempting to commit arson, burglary, kidnapping, rape, robbery, sodomy or any unlawful act against the peace of this state, of which the probable consequences may be bloodshed, kills another, or if the death of anyone ensues from the committing or attempting to commit any such crime or act; * * * then such person so killing is guilty of murder.

At both common law and today by statute all participants in any of the felonies referred to in the statute are equally guilty as principals.

* * * *

N.J.S.A. 2A:113–1 has no counterpart among the felony murder statutes in other jurisdictions which have considered murder prosecutions predicated upon a killing of an accomplice by one resisting a felony. The distinguishing feature in our statute is the "ensues clause," referred to above. Thus cases of other states are of no aid in deciding the question presented in the instant case.

* * * *

In *State v. Burton*, 130 N.J.Super. 174, 325 A.2d 856 (Law Div.1974), defendant was indicted for the murder of two of his accomplices who were killed by the police while they and the defendant were committing an armed robbery. In denying a motion to dismiss the indictment the trial judge stated that a reading of the statute indicated the Legislature intended to extend criminal accountability beyond that imposed upon a felon under the common law. The judge held that the "ensues clause" evidenced a legislative intent to adhere to the proximate cause theory of felony murder and to extend the culpability of a defendant to all deaths which occurred during the commission of any of the offenses designated in the statute.

* * * *

The proximate cause theory simply stated is that when a felon sets in motion a chain of events which were or should have been within his contemplation when the motion was initiated, the felon, and those acting in concert with him, should be held responsible for any death which by direct and almost inevitable consequences results from the initial criminal act.

We agree with the court's interpretation of the statute in *State v. Burton, supra.* In our view the statute indicates an intention on the part of the Legislature to extend criminal responsibility beyond that imposed upon a felon at common law and to hold liable all participants in an armed robbery for deaths which occur during the commission of the crime. We conclude that the trial judge properly denied the motion to dismiss the indictment.

Canola's conviction, as well as his sentence of two concurrent terms of life imprisonment, was upheld.   **JUDGMENT AND REMEDY**

Misdemeanors are crimes punishable by a fine or by confinement for up to a year. Misdemeanors are also sometimes defined as offenses where incarceration takes place in a local jail instead of in a penitentiary. In practice, the jail confinement is usually for no more than a year. Disorderly conduct and trespass are common misdemeanors. Some states have different classes of misdemeanors. For example, in Illinois there are Class A misdemeanors (confinement for up to a year), Class B (not more than six months), and Class C (not more than thirty days). Whether a crime is a felony or a misdemeanor can also determine whether the case is tried in a magistrate court or a general trial court.

Violations   Another kind of wrong is termed a petty offense and often is not classified as a crime. Petty offenses include many traffic violations or violations of building codes. Even for petty offenses, a guilty party can be put in jail for a few days, or fined, or both.

Federal and State Crimes   Criminal law is primarily the province of the states, but the federal government also has a criminal code. Federal crimes relate to federal government functions or involve federal personnel or institutions. Counterfeiting, unlawful immigration, spying, robbing a federally insured bank, or assaulting a federal officer are examples of federal crimes. In other instances, the federal government can use its general regulatory powers to aid state law enforcement agencies in combating crimes that have a national impact. Transportation of stolen vehicles across state lines, kidnapping, and civil rights violations are areas that fall under federal criminal law.

Classification by Nature   Crimes can be classified according to their nature. For example, there are crimes against property (theft, burglary, arson), crimes against the person (murder, assault, rape), and crimes against the government (perjury, bribery). These classifications are used to group crimes within a statutory code.

THE ESSENTIALS OF CRIMINAL LIABILITY

Three elements are necessary for a person to be convicted of a crime: (1) the performance of a prohibited act, (2) a specified state of mind or intent on the part of the actor, and (3) the absence of circumstances that the law deems sufficient to excuse actions that would otherwise be criminal.

Prohibited Acts

Every criminal statute prohibits certain behavior.[1] Most crimes require an act of commission; that is, the criminal must do something. In some cases an act of omission can be a crime, but only if what is omitted is a legal duty. Failure to file a tax return is an example of an omission that is a crime.

The *guilty act* requirement is based on one of the premises of criminal law—that a person is punished for *harm done* to society. Thinking about killing someone or about stealing a car may be wrong, but these thoughts in themselves do no harm until they are translated into action. Of course, a person can be punished for attempting murder or robbery, but only if substantial steps toward the criminal objective have been taken.

Even a completed act that harms society is not legally a crime unless the court finds that the required state of mind was present.

State of Mind

A wrongful mental state[2] is as necessary as a wrongful act to establish criminal liability. What constitutes such a mental state varies according to the wrongful action. Thus, for murder, the *actus reus* (act) is the taking of a life, and the *mens rea* (mental state) is the intent to take life. For theft, the *actus reus* is the taking of another person's property, and the *mens rea* involves both the knowledge that the property belongs to another and the intent to deprive the owner of it.

1. Called the *actus reus*, or guilty act.
2. Called the *mens rea*, or evil intent.

Without the mental state required by law for a particular crime, there can be no crime.

The *mens rea* in which a particular act is committed can vary in the degree of its wrongfulness. The same act—shooting someone—can be committed with varying mental states. It can be done coldly, after premeditation, as in murder in the first degree. It can be done in the heat of passion, as in voluntary manslaughter. Or it can be done as the result of negligence, as in involuntary manslaughter. In each of these situations the law recognizes a different degree of wrongfulness, and the punishment differs accordingly.

The Model Penal Code[3] recognizes four categories of *mens rea*:

1. Purpose or intent.
2. Knowledge (both formerly covered under the term *specific intent*).
3. Recklessness.
4. Negligence (both formerly covered by the term *general intent*).

The following case illustrates the requirement of *mens rea* and the resulting different wrongs in the taking of another's life.

---

3. American Law Institute Model Penal Code, official draft 1962. This Code contains four parts relating to general provisions, definitions of specific crimes, treatment and correction, and organization of correction.

BACKGROUND AND FACTS *The defendants, who were convicted of second degree murder, contended that their jury had been improperly instructed on the state of mind necessary for murder. The trial court had instructed the jury that malice could be presumed in any unlawful killing. The appellate court reviews the concepts of malice and* mens rea.

STATE OF NEW JERSEY v. ROBINSON
Superior Court of New Jersey, Appellate Division, 1976.
139 N.J.Super. 475,
354 A.2d 374.

BOTTER, Justice of the Appellate Division.

*   *   *   *

Malice has been variously defined. In some contexts it is described as merely the intentional doing of an unlawful act without justification or excuse, regardless of consciousness of wrongdoing. *   *   * The real difficulty is that the meaning of malice in common understanding and usage, as well as in law, is not suitably exact for defining crimes as serious as murder and manslaughter. In fact, the term "malice aforethought" which had various particular meanings in the law of homicide has given way to mere "malice" with all its loose connotations.

A knowing intention to do an unlawful act constitutes *mens rea*, criminal intent—an "evil intention." One can intend less than serious bodily injury and still act with an evil-meaning mind. This was illustrated in *State v. Madden*, where a police officer was attacked and killed by a mob composed of persons who may have had diverse criminal, evil intents, ranging from an intent to kill, to injure, to interfere with the officer's performance of his duty or merely to harass or humiliate. However, the court said that if death resulted from an act not performed with the intention to do some injury to the officer, the crime would be involuntary manslaughter, not murder. Thus, unlawful acts causing death which are performed with evil intention or hatred may constitute murder or manslaughter—or possibly only a *quasi*-criminal offense.

*   *   *   *

Thus, when distinguishing murder from manslaughter it is desirable to define murder as a killing committed (a) with the intent to kill or to do grievous bodily harm to any person or (b) with knowledge of the likelihood of death or grievous bodily injury accompanied by an indifference to the result. Involuntary manslaughter is distinguished by an intent to inflict less than serious injury, and it includes an unintentional killing such as results from the reckless handling of a firearm. Voluntary manslaughter is a killing committed in a sudden transport of passion induced by provocation sufficient to inflame an ordinary, reasonable person. These definitions are not complete, but they illustrate a proper focus upon essential elements of the crimes without the distortion engendered by concepts of evil. To say that malice can be inferred from circumstances which prove an intention corresponding to the conditions of murder is tautological at the very least. Nothing is lost by omitting the term "malice" in instructing a jury and [prior cases] strongly suggest the need to emphasize specific acts and intents in differentiating murder from manslaughter.

JUDGMENT AND REMEDY   *The defendants were granted a new trial. A defendant's state of mind must be proved in criminal cases; it is not presumed from actions.*

DEFENSES TO CRIMINAL LIABILITY

The law recognizes certain conditions that will relieve a defendant of criminal liability. These conditions are called defenses, and among the important ones are infancy, intoxication, insanity, mistake, consent, duress, justifiable use of force, entrapment, and statute of limitations. A criminal defendant can also be given immunity from prosecution.

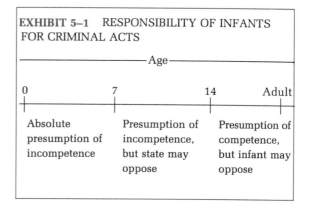

EXHIBIT 5–1   RESPONSIBILITY OF INFANTS FOR CRIMINAL ACTS

	————————Age————————	
0	7	14 Adult
Absolute presumption of incompetence	Presumption of incompetence, but state may oppose	Presumption of competence, but infant may oppose

Infancy

In the common law, children up to seven years of age were considered incapable of committing a crime because they did not have the moral sense to understand that they were doing wrong. Children between the ages of seven and fourteen were presumed to be incapable of committing a crime, but this presumption could be rebutted by showing that the child understood the wrongful nature of the act. (See Exhibit 5–1.) Today, states vary in their approaches, but all retain the defense of infancy as a bar to criminal liability. Most states retain the common law approach, although age limits vary from state to state. Other states have rejected the rebuttable presumption and simply set a minimum age required for crim-inal responsibility. All states have juvenile court systems that handle children below the age of criminal responsibility who commit delinquent acts. Their aim is allegedly to reform rather than to punish. In states that retain the rebuttable presumption approach, children who are beyond the minimum age but are still juveniles can be turned over to the criminal courts if the juvenile court determines that they should be treated as adults.

Intoxication

The law recognizes two types of intoxication, whether from drugs or from alcohol: *voluntary* and *involuntary*. Involuntary intoxication occurs when a person is either physically forced to ingest or inject an intoxicating substance or is unaware that a substance contains drugs or alcohol. Involuntary intoxication is a defense to crime if its effect was to make a person either incapable of understanding that the act committed was wrong or incapable of obeying the law.

Voluntary intoxication can also be used as a defense where intoxication precludes having the required *mens rea*. Thus, if Johnson shoots Peters while too drunk to know what she is doing, she cannot be convicted of *murder* because she did not have the required *intent* to kill when she shot Peters.

Voluntary intoxication, however, does not serve as a defense for crimes requiring recklessness or negligence. The law requires that people be aware that intoxication can make it impossible to behave as a reasonable person. Therefore, becoming intoxicated and committing a reckless or negligent act is a crime. In the example above, Johnson could be convicted of the lesser crime of *manslaughter*.

Insanity

Just as a child is judged incapable of the state of mind required to commit a crime, so also is someone suffering from mental illness. Thus, insanity is a defense to a criminal charge. The courts have had difficulty deciding what the test for legal insanity should be, and psychiatrists, as well as lawyers, are critical of the tests used. Almost all federal courts and some states use the standard in the Model Penal Code:

> A person is not responsible for criminal conduct if at the time of such conduct as a result of mental disease or defect he lacks substantial capacity either to appreciate the wrongfulness of his conduct or to conform his conduct to the requirements of the law.

Other states use the *M'Naghten* test, which excuses a criminal act if a mental defect makes a person incapable of appreciating the nature of the act or incapable of knowing that it was wrong. Some states that follow the *M'Naghten* rule have also adopted the irresistible impulse test. A person operating under an irresistible impulse may

know that an act is wrong but may still be unable to keep from doing it. Even if a mental illness is not grave enough to serve as a complete defense, it may render a person legally incapable of certain crimes if the illness precludes the possibility of the required *mens rea*. Some defense attorneys have shown great ingenuity in pleading that factors in the defendant's environment inevitably led to his crime.

Mistake

Everyone has heard the saying "ignorance of the law is no excuse." It may seem harsh to presume that everyone knows or should know the law, but the result of a different rule would be unmanageable. Ordinarily, ignorance of the law or a mistaken idea about what the law requires is not a valid defense. In some states, however, that rule has been modified. A person who claims that he or she honestly did not know that a law was being broken may have a valid defense if: (1) the law was not published or reasonably made known to the public or (2) the person relied on an official statement of the law that was erroneous. An official statement is a statute, judicial opinion, administrative order, or statement by someone responsible for administering, interpreting, or enforcing the law (which does not normally include private attorneys). Statements in newspapers or textbooks are not official statements.

A mistake of fact, as opposed to a mistake of law, will operate as a defense if it negates the required *mens rea*. If, for example, John Jones mistakenly drives off in Mary Thompson's car because he thinks that it is his, there is no theft. Theft requires knowledge that the property belongs to another. (Of course, this has no bearing on a civil action for the tort of conversion.)

Consent

What if a victim consents to a crime or even encourages a criminal to commit it? The law will allow consent as a defense if the consent cancels the harm that the law is designed to prevent. In each case, the question is whether the law forbids an act against the victim's will or forbids the act without regard to the victim's wish. The law forbids murder, prostitution, and drug use whether the victim consents to it or not. Consent operates as a defense most successfully in crimes against property, since one can always give away one's property. Of course, if the act operates to harm a third person who has not consented, there will be no escape from criminal liability. Consent or forgiveness given after a crime has been committed is not really a defense, though it can affect the likelihood of prosecution.

Duress

A person who is asked or instructed to commit a crime is not excused from criminal liability, but committing a crime under duress is a valid defense. The courts use a number of requirements to measure duress. First, the threat must be of serious bodily harm or death. A person who was threatened with failing a course or losing a job cannot plead duress as a defense. Second, the harm that is threatened must be greater than the harm that will be caused by the crime. A threat to shoot a woman's husband unless she robs a bank would be sufficient; a threat to hit her over the head might not be. The third requirement is that the threat must be immediate and inescapable. Finally, people who plead duress as a defense must have been involved in the situation through no fault of their own. If, for example, a person committing a burglary forces an accomplice to kill someone, the accomplice cannot use duress as an excuse. Participating in the burglary in the first place carries with it the possibility of being forced to commit a greater crime. The situation is the accomplice's fault.

The threat in a duress defense can be to the person under duress or to someone close to him or her, such as a spouse. One crime that cannot be excused by duress is murder. It is difficult to justify taking a life even if one's own life is threatened.

Justifiable Use of Force

Probably the most well known defense to criminal liability is self-defense. But there are other situations that justify the use of force: the defense of one's dwelling, the defense of other property, and the prevention of a crime. In all of these situations it is important to distinguish between the use of deadly and nondeadly force. Deadly force is likely to result in death or serious bodily harm. Nondeadly force is force that reasonably appears necessary to prevent the imminent use of criminal force.

Generally speaking, people can use the amount of nondeadly force that seems necessary to protect themselves, their dwellings or other property, or to prevent the commission of a crime. Deadly force can be used in self-defense if there is a reasonable belief that imminent death or grievous bodily harm will otherwise result, if the attacker is using unlawful force (an example of lawful force would be that exerted by a police officer), and if the person has not initiated or provoked the attack. Deadly force can be used to defend a dwelling only if the unlawful entry is violent and the person believes that deadly force is necessary to prevent imminent death, great bodily harm, or—in some jurisdictions—if the person believes deadly force is necessary to prevent commission of a felony in the dwelling.

In defense of other property, the use of nondeadly force is justified to prevent or to end the criminal's attempt to take away or otherwise interfere with the property. Deadly force usually is justifiable only when used in self-defense.

Force reasonably necessary to prevent a serious crime is permissible but, in the majority view, deadly force can be used to prevent only crimes that involve a substantial risk of death or great bodily harm.

Entrapment

Entrapment is a defense designed to prevent the police or other government agents from encouraging criminal acts in order to apprehend criminals. In the typical entrapment case, an undercover agent suggests that a crime be committed and somehow pressures or induces an individual to commit it. The agent then arrests the individual for the crime. Both the suggestion and the inducement must take place. The defense is not intended to prevent the police from setting a trap for an unwary criminal. It is intended to prevent them from pushing the criminal into it. The crucial issue is whether a criminal was pre-disposed to commit the crime or committed the crime because the agent induced it. This is often a question of fact, as illustrated by the following case.

BACKGROUND AND FACTS *This case involves a cocaine transaction that resulted in the defendant's conviction for selling the narcotic to a government Drug Enforcement Administration (DEA) agent, Sylvestri. An informer, Clegg, initiated a relationship with the defendant. The informer encouraged the defendant to supply a quantity of cocaine to an out-of-town buyer. The defendant agreed to meet the buyer and make the exchange. After the defendant delivered the cocaine to the agent, the agent arrested him. The defendant was subsequently found guilty on various charges, including possession and distribution of cocaine. The defendant claimed entrapment on the part of the government agents.*

UNITED STATES v. BOWER

United States Court of Appeals, Fifth Circuit, 1978.
575 F.2d 499.

RONEY, Circuit Judge.

* * * *

Defendant contends the evidence established an entrapment as a matter of law. In support of this claim, defendant relies primarily on his own trial testimony that he had agreed to participate in the criminal enterprise in a moment of extreme depression. Defendant had recently turned 30 and, reflecting upon an uneventful past and contemplating a similar future, had decided to return to college and finish his education. Unfortunately, a year of voluntary unemployment had so depleted his personal finances that he could not return to school without working at least part time. Having hoped to be able to focus his undivided attention on his studies, defendant began to recognize Clegg's proposals as an opportunity to finance his schooling. His depression at this time was heightened by the fact that he and his girlfriend had recently severed their long-standing relationship. Consequently, although he had repeatedly rejected Clegg's earlier entreaties, he could no longer resist the temptation of the promised "exorbitant gains" to be reaped from a single cocaine sale.

Since Clegg did not testify at trial, defendant's account of Clegg's repeated attempts to persuade defendant to procure narcotics is uncontradicted. The record nevertheless contains evidence weighing against the contention that defendant was "an innocent seduced by a government agent." Defendant admitted that he saw the sale as a source of "easy money" and that he expected to make a $1,000 profit on the transaction. He purchased the cocaine from a nongovernment source who trusted defendant enough to defer payment until defendant had resold the drug. Indeed, while negotiating the actual exchange, defendant assured DEA agent Sylvestri that he could handle Sylvestri's future cocaine needs if the amounts were not too large. Both agent Sylvestri and defendant testified that during the transaction, defendant received a telephone call from his source. Defendant interrupted his telephone conversation to ask Sylvestri if he was interested in buying another four ounces of cocaine. When the DEA agent expressed interest, defendant requested his source "not to lock up the other four" and offered to produce the additional cocaine for Sylvestri in 30 minutes.

On this evidence, the trial court did not err in submitting the entrapment issue to the jury. The crucial issue in entrapment cases is whether the defendant was predisposed to commit the crime. The Government's provisions of aid, incentive, and opportunity for commission of the crime amounts to an entrapment only if it appears that the defendant has done that which he would never have done were it not for the inducement of Government operatives. Although the record contains evidence upon which a jury might conclude that defendant was induced by a Government informer to commit a crime that he was not otherwise predisposed to commit, the evidence was not "so overwhelming that it was 'patently clear' or 'obvious' that [defendant] was entrapped as a matter of law."

JUDGMENT AND REMEDY *The appellate court affirmed the defendant's convictions. The evidence supported the jury's verdict that defendant was predisposed to commit the crime.*

Statute of Limitations

An individual can be excused from criminal liability by a statute of limitations. Such statutes provide that the state has only a certain amount of time to prosecute a crime. If the state does not do so within the allotted time, it has lost its opportunity, and the suspect is free from prosecution. The idea behind these statutes is that people should not have to live under the threat of criminal prosecution indefinitely. Also, if prosecution is delayed for too long, it becomes difficult to find out what the truth is because witnesses die or disappear and evidence is destroyed.

Time limits vary from state to state. Felonies usually have a longer statute of limitations than misdemeanors, and there is no time limitation placed on murder. For all other crimes, the time limit runs from the time the crime is committed, unless it is a crime that is difficult to discover. In those cases, the time begins to run when the crime is discovered. A time limitation will be suspended, however, if the suspect leaves the state or hides. Normally, statutes will provide for subtraction of time if the suspect cannot be found or is not available to stand trial.

Immunity

At times, the state may wish to obtain information from a criminal. Criminals, of course, have an absolute privilege against self-incrimination and are understandably reluctant to give information if it will be used to prosecute them. In these cases, the state can grant immunity from prosecution or agree to prosecute for a less serious offense in exchange for the information. Once immunity is given, the person can no longer refuse to testify on Fifth Amendment grounds, since self-incrimination is then impossible. Often a grant of immunity from prosecution for a serious crime is part of the plea-bargaining negotiations between defense and prosecution. The criminal may still be convicted of a lesser offense, but the state uses his or her testimony to prosecute accomplices for serious crimes carrying heavy penalties.

CRIMINAL PROCEDURE

Our criminal justice system operates on the premise that it is far worse for an innocent person to be punished than for a guilty person to go free. A person is innocent until proven guilty, and guilt must be proven beyond a reasonable doubt. The procedure of the criminal legal system is designed to protect the rights of the individual and preserve the presumption of innocence.

Constitutional Safeguards

Criminal law brings the weighty force of the state, with all its resources, to bear against the individual. Recognizing this fact, the Founding Fathers provided specific safeguards in the Constitution for the accused criminal. The Supreme Court has ruled that most of these safeguards apply not only in federal but also in state courts by virtue of the due process clause of the Fourteenth Amendment. The safeguards include:

1. Fourth Amendment protection from unreasonable searches and seizures.
2. Fourth Amendment requirement that no warrants for a search or an arrest can be issued without probable cause.
3. Fifth Amendment requirement that no one can be deprived of "life, liberty, or property without due process of law."
4. Fifth Amendment prohibition against double jeopardy (trying someone twice for the same criminal offense).
5. Sixth Amendment guarantees of a speedy trial, trial by jury, a public trial, the right to confront witnesses, and the right to a lawyer for serious charges.
6. Eighth Amendment prohibitions against excessive bails and fines, and cruel and unusual punishment.[4]

In recent years the Supreme Court has been active in interpreting these rights. Some of the cases are widely known. The *Miranda* decision, for example, established the rule that individuals who are arrested must be informed of their right to remain silent, of the fact that anything they say can be used against them in court, of their right to have a lawyer present, and of the duty of the state to provide lawyers if individuals cannot pay for them.[5]

Criminal Process

A criminal prosecution differs significantly from a civil case in several respects. These differences reflect the desire to safeguard the rights of the individual against the state.

---

4. See Appendix B on the U.S. Constitution.
5. Miranda v. Arizona, 384 U.S. 436, 86 S.Ct. 1602 (1966).

Arrest Before a warrant for arrest can be issued, there must be a finding of probable cause for believing that the individual has committed a crime. **Probable cause** can be defined as a substantial likelihood that the individual has committed or is about to commit a crime. Note that probable cause involves a likelihood, not just a possibility. Arrests may sometimes be made without a warrant when there is no time to get one, but the action of the arresting officer is still judged by the standard of probable cause.

Indictment Individuals must be formally charged with having committed specific crimes before they can be brought to trial. This charge is called an **indictment** if issued by a grand jury and an **information** if issued by a magistrate. Before a charge can be issued, the grand jury or the magistrate must determine that there is sufficient evidence to justify bringing the individual to trial. The standard used to make this determination varies from jurisdiction to jurisdiction. Some courts use the probable cause standard. Others use the preponderance of evidence standard, which is a belief based on evidence provided by both sides that it is more likely than not that the individual committed the crime. Still another standard is the *prima facie* case standard, which is a belief based only on the prosecution's evidence that the individual is guilty.

Trial At the trial the accused criminal does not have to prove anything. The entire burden of proof is on the prosecution (the state). Guilt is judged on the basis of the **reasonable doubt** test. The prosecution must show that, based on all the evidence, the defendant's guilt is established beyond all reasonable doubt. Note that a verdict of "not guilty" is not the same as a statement that the defendant is innocent. It merely means that not enough evidence was properly presented to the court to prove guilt beyond all reasonable doubt. Courts have complex rules about what types of evidence may be presented and how the evidence may be brought out, especially in jury trials. These rules are designed to ensure that evidence in trials is relevant, reliable, and not unfairly prejudicial to the defendant. The defense attorney will cross-examine the witnesses who present evidence against his or her client in an attempt to show that their evidence is not reliable. Of course, the state may also cross-examine any witnesses presented by the defendant.

CRIMES AFFECTING BUSINESS

Forgery

The fraudulent making or alteration of any writing that changes the legal liability of another is **forgery.** If Smith signs Brown's name without authorization to the back of a check made out to Brown, Smith has committed forgery. Forgery also includes changing trademarks, falsifying public records, counterfeiting, and, the alteration of any legal document.

Most states have a special statute, often called a *credit card statute,* to cover the illegal use of credit cards. Thus, the state attorney can prosecute a person who misuses a credit card for violating either the forgery statute or the special credit card statute.

Robbery

At common law, **robbery** was defined as forcefully and unlawfully taking personal property of any value from another. The use of force or fear is usually necessary for an act of theft to be considered a robbery. Thus, pickpocketing is not robbery because the action is unknown to the victim. Typically, states have more severe penalties for *aggravated* robbery—robbery by use of deadly weapon.

Burglary

At common law, **burglary** was defined as breaking and entering the dwelling of another at night with the intent to commit a felony. Originally, the offense was aimed at protecting an individual's home and its occupants. Most state statutes have eliminated some of the requirements found in the common law definition. Thus, the time at which the breaking and entering occurs is usually immaterial. State statutes frequently omit the element of breaking, and some states do not require that the building be a dwelling. Aggravated burglary, which is defined as burglary with the use of a deadly weapon, or burglary of a dwelling, or both, incurs a greater penalty.

Larceny

The wrongful or fraudulent taking and carrying away by any person of the personal property of another is **larceny.** It includes the fraudulent intent to permanently deprive an owner of property. Many business-related larcenies entail fraudulent conduct.

The place from which physical property is taken is generally immaterial. However, statutes usually prescribe a stiffer sentence for property taken from buildings such as banks or warehouses. Larceny is differentiated from robbery by the fact that robbery involves force or fear, and larceny does not. Therefore, pickpocketing is larceny, not robbery.

Distinguishing between Grand and Petit Larceny The common law distinction between grand and petit larceny depends on the value of the property taken. Many states have abolished this distinction, but in those that have not, grand larceny is a felony and petit larceny a misdemeanor.

What Constitutes Property? As society has grown more complex, the definition of the property that is subject to larceny statutes has been expanded. Stealing computer programs now constitutes larceny, even though the programs consist of magnetic impulses. Trade secrets can be subject to larceny statutes. Stealing the use of telephone wires by the device known as a "blue box" is subject to larceny statutes. So, too, is the theft of natural gas.

Embezzlement

The fraudulent conversion of property or money owned by one person but entrusted to another is **embezzlement.** Typically, it involves an employee who fraudulently appropriates money. Banks face this problem, and so do a number of businesses in which corporate officers or accountants "jimmy" the books to cover up the fraudulent conversion of money for their own benefit. Embezzlement is not larceny because the wrongdoer does not physically take the property from the possession of another, and it is not robbery because there is no taking by use of force or fear.

It does not matter whether the accused takes the money from the victim or from a third person. If, as the comptroller of a large corporation, Saunders pockets a certain number of checks from third parties that were given to her to deposit into the account of another company, she has committed embezzlement.

Misapplication of Trust Funds   Often the owner of property will remit money to a contractor specifically for the contractor to pay various persons who worked on the owner's building. The contractor who does not use the money for this purpose commits a special form of embezzlement called misapplication of trust funds. The funds were entrusted to the contractor for a specific purpose and that trust has been violated. The fact that the accused intended eventually to return the embezzled property does not constitute a sufficient defense. In practice, though, an embezzler who returns what has been taken will not ordinarily be prosecuted, because the owner usually will not take the time to make a complaint, give depositions, and appear in court.

Arson

The willful and malicious burning of a building (and in some states personal property) owned by another is the crime of **arson.** At common law, arson applied only to burning down the dwelling house of another. Such law was designed to protect human life. Today, arson statutes apply to other kinds of buildings. Also, if someone is killed as a result of arson, the act is murder because of the application of the murder-felony rule.

Burning to Defraud Insurers   Every state has a special statute that covers burning a building in order to collect insurance. If Allison owns an insured apartment building that is falling apart and burns it himself or pays someone else to set fire to it, Allison is guilty of burning to defraud insurers. Of course, the insurer need not pay the claim when insurance fraud is proven.

Obtaining Goods by False Pretenses

It is a criminal act to obtain goods by means of false pretenses—for example, buying groceries with a check, knowing that one has insufficient funds to cover it. Statutes covering such illegal activities vary widely from state to state.

Receiving Stolen Goods

It is a crime to receive stolen goods. The recipient of such goods need not know the true identity of the owner or of the thief. All that is necessary is that the recipient knows or should have known that the goods are stolen, which implies intent to deprive the owner of those goods.

Use of the Mails to Defraud

It is a federal crime to use the mails to defraud the public. Illegal use of the mails must involve (1) mailing or causing someone else to mail a writing for the purpose of executing a scheme to defraud and (2) a contemplated or organized scheme to defraud by false pretenses. If, for example, Johnson advertises the sale of a cure for cancer that he knows to be fraudulent because it has no medical validity, he can be prosecuted for fraudulent use of the mails. Federal law also makes it a crime to use a telegram to defraud.

False Measures, Labels, and Weights

Numerous federal and state regulations have been adopted to prevent and prosecute those who cheat, defraud, or mislead the public by using false labels, false measures, or false weights.

Lotteries

A number of state governments, including New York, New Jersey, and Arizona, are currently running lotteries. Nonetheless, lotteries are generally illegal even if they appear to be a legitimate form of business or advertising or are called by some other name. There are three necessary elements for a lottery to exist: a prize, a lot by chance, and payment of something of value in order to have the opportunity to win. Often, contest advertisements will say that participants can send in either a box top (or label) or a facsimile. This keeps the contest from being a lottery because contestants can enter without paying anything.

WHITE-COLLAR CRIMES

Although no official definition exists for *white-collar crime*, the term is popularly used to mean an illegal act or series of acts committed by an individual or corporation using some nonviolent means to obtain a personal or business advantage. Usually this kind of crime is committed in the course of a legitimate occupation. The cost to the public of so-called white-collar crimes ranges between $40 billion and $110 billion a year.

Since it is impossible to cover the vast range of what are considered to be white-collar crimes, the efforts in this chapter will center on four areas: (1) computer crimes, (2) bribery, (3) bankruptcy fraud, and (4) corporate crimes.

Computer Crimes

The age of the computer is now upon us. An increasing percentage of business is carried on via computers. Virtually all of the financial transactions of the government and most large businesses are computer handled. Many of the transfers of money from business to business, from individual to business, from business to individual, and from individual and business to and from government involve not the physical circulation of money but rather the changing of digital information within computer memories.

Clearly, the manipulation of computers for personal or business gain is possible. Detection is often difficult. Certain companies, and even the government, have discovered multimillion dollar thefts made this way only after a significant amount of time has elapsed. Employees of accounting and computer departments have been known to make extra copies of paychecks, trans-

fer monies among accounts, and have fictitious insurance policies pay out dividends.

The Problem of Secrecy The full extent of computer crime in our business society is unrevealed. Firms adversely affected by such crime rarely publicize the fact, because they are afraid that their customers will then doubt the accuracy of computer-generated material. Trials of apprehended perpetrators of computer crimes are rare. The affected business usually allows the case to be *plea bargained* instead of going to trial. Sometimes, for fear of publicity, the business will not even report the crime and may be blackmailed into giving the criminal a reference for another job.

The law involving computer crime is still in its formative stage. In the years to come, the courts and legislative bodies will be applying this area of criminal law more and more often.

Bribery

Basically, three types of actions called bribery are considered crimes. They involve: (1) bribery of foreign officials, (2) bribery of public officials, and (3) commercial bribery.

Bribery of Foreign Officials Until the 1970s, bribery of foreign officials to obtain business contracts was rarely, if ever, discussed. Indeed, payments in cash or in-kind benefits to government officials for such purposes are often considered normal practice. This is not to say that the practice is legal. In order to reduce the number of such bribes given to foreign government officials by representatives of American corporations, Congress passed the Foreign Corrupt Practices Act in 1977 (15 U.S.C. 78). The Act clearly states that any offer to give anything of value to a foreign govenment official to influence that government's official acts for business purposes is illegal. The Act provides fines of up to $1 million. It also provides for incarceration of officers or directors of convicted companies for up to a maximum of five years. Those officers and directors can also be fined up to $10,000, and the fine cannot be paid by the company.

Bribery of Public Officials The attempt to influence a public official to act in a way that serves a private interest is a crime. As an element of this crime, *intent* must be present and proved. The bribe that is offered can be anything that the recipient of the offer considers to be valuable. *The commission of a crime of bribery occurs when the bribe is tendered.* The recipient does not have to agree to perform whatever action is desired by the person tendering the bribe; nor does the recipient have to accept the bribe.

Commercial Bribery   In some states, so-called kickbacks and payoffs from an individual working for one company to another individual or individuals working for another company are crimes. No public official need be involved. Such commercial bribes are typically given with the intent of obtaining proprietary information, covering up an inferior product, or securing new business. Industrial espionage sometimes involves this kind of activity—for example, a payoff of some type to an employee in a competitor firm in exchange for trade secrets and pricing schedules.

BACKGROUND AND FACTS   *Defendant Tilton was responsible for locating repair shops to perform work for his employer, Sea-Land Incorporated. Tilton requested and received from the repair shop owners a $20 "commission" on each item sent to the shops. The trial court found Tilton guilty of mail fraud, interstate travel to facilitate an unlawful activity, and conspiracy.*

UNITED STATES v. TILTON

United States Court of Appeals, Fifth Circuit, 1980.
610 F.2d 302.

THORNBERRY, Circuit Judge.

* * * *

Appellant *   *   * contends that the evidence was not sufficient to support his convictions for conspiracy, mail fraud, and violating the Travel Act. This claim is without merit.

We will first examine appellant's claim with respect to the alleged Travel Act violation. The Travel Act provides in part:

(a) Whoever travels in interstate or foreign commerce or uses any facility in interstate or foreign commerce, including the mail, with intent to—

(1) distribute the proceeds of any unlawful activity; *   *   * shall be fined not more than $10,000 or imprisoned for not more than five years, or both.

(b) As used in this subsection "unlawful activity" means *   *   * (2) extortion, *bribery*, or arson in violation of the laws of the State in which committed or of the United States.

The Supreme Court recently held, in an opinion affirming a decision of this court, that "bribery," as mentioned in the Act, includes not only bribery of a public official but also bribery of a private employee in violation of a state criminal statute. The payment of $1,400 by Brenner to Tilton in the lounge of a Charleston, South Carolina motel constituted the offense of bribery, punishable under South Carolina law. Therefore, the only remaining question is whether Tilton's interstate travel from Florida to South Carolina was accomplished with the *intent* to facilitate this unlawful activity. It is enough that the intent is motivated in part by the unlawful activity even if one motivating factor involves a legitimate purpose. Tilton's acceptance of the bribe soon after arriving in South Carolina supports the inference that the trip was motivated, at least in part, by the bribe. The fact that Tilton travelled in part for an improper reason may be inferred from his actions immediately after the travel. Therefore, the evidence appears sufficient to support Tilton's conviction for violation of the Travel Act.

* * * *

The evidence is also sufficient to support a finding that Tilton conspired to commit mail fraud. This court has stated that to sustain a conviction for conspiracy to commit mail fraud, the evidence must merely show a scheme or artifice to defraud, use of the mails caused by someone associated with the scheme, and use of the mails in executing the fraud. The scheme of inflating the invoices that were mailed to Sea-Land in order to generate the "commissions" to be paid to Tilton defrauded Sea-Land by increasing the cost of each chassis by at least $20. The UTS conspirators (Gillespie, Cotrone) executed this fraudulent scheme by mailing the padded invoices to Sea-Land. It is not necessary to demonstrate which invoices were fraudulent. Since the defrauded funds were used to pay Tilton his "commissions," the evidence is clearly sufficient to demonstrate that Tilton participated in the *conspiracy* to commit mail fraud through a scheme to defraud and use of the mails to execute that fraud.

JUDGMENT AND REMEDY   *Tilton's conviction and sentence were upheld. The punishment was one year's imprisonment for violation of the Travel Act, four years' probation on the mail fraud and conspiracy counts, and a $2,000 fine for his part in the conspiracy.*

Bankruptcy Frauds

When a business finds itself with an oppressive amount of debt, its creditors may seek to have the court adjudge it a bankrupt. Alternatively, the individual or business entity may seek voluntary bankruptcy. Today, individuals or businesses can be relieved of oppressive debt by federal law under the Bankruptcy Reform Act of 1978. We discuss this Act in more detail in Chapter 33. In short, the Act requires that the debtor disclose all assets. The assets are then taken into possession by a trustee, unless they are exempt. The trustee must follow certain rules in distributing those assets to creditors. Following are examples of some of the numerous white-collar crimes that can be perpetrated throughout the many phases of a bankruptcy proceeding.

False Claims of Creditors   Creditors are required to file their individual claims against the debtor who is in bankruptcy proceedings. A creditor who files a false claim commits a crime.

Transfer of Property   Obviously, a debtor, knowing that he or she will be in bankruptcy proceedings, has an incentive to transfer assets to favored parties before or after the petition for bankruptcy is filed. For example, a company-owned automobile can be "sold" at a bargain price to a trusted friend or relative. Closely related to the crime of fraudulent transfer of property is fraudulent concealment of property. The number of ways in which debtors have fraudulently concealed assets would require several books to outline.

Scam Bankruptcies   The term *scam bankruptcy* has been used to indicate a swindle in which a bankruptcy is planned in advance. The perpetrators purchase a legitimate business that sells highly liquid goods, such as jewelry or electronic home entertainment equipment. Numerous items are purchased on credit by the new owners. The creditors are paid off within a relatively short period of time. This activity continues until the creditors are willing to offer larger and larger amounts of credit to the new owners. Finally, the new owners order a very large amount of merchandise on credit, sell it at whatever price is necessary to unload it quickly for cash, and then close down the business. Of course, creditors file an involuntary petition in bankruptcy against the business. The amount that those creditors will recover, however, is typically very small. And the scam operators are nowhere to be found.

Corporate Crimes

Corporations are "artificial" persons created by law. Clearly, they cannot harbor the criminal intent that is required for conviction of a crime, but their officers can. The modern tendency is to hold corporations criminally responsible for their acts or omissions if the assigned penalty is a fine, and if intent either is not an element of the crime or can be implied.

Obviously, a crime such as perjury cannot be committed by a corporation but can be committed by a natural person, such as an officer of the corporation. Furthermore, crimes punishable by imprisonment or corporal punishment cannot be committed by corporations. However, when a statute allows a fine in addition to, or in the place of, these penalties, a corporation can be convicted of that crime. If, for example, a statute requires that adequate safety equipment be installed on machines, and a corporation fails to do so—and if the result is the death of a worker—the corporation can be fined for committing criminal manslaughter. In addition, the corporate officers who were in a position to prevent the wrong can be prosecuted under specific federal and state statutes.

QUESTIONS AND CASE PROBLEMS

1. Civil trials and criminal trials are conducted under essentially the same format. There are, however, several important differences. In criminal trials, the defendant must be proven guilty beyond all reasonable doubt, whereas in civil trials, the defendant need only be proven guilty by a preponderance of the evidence. Can you see any reason for this difference?

2. Crimes are classified as either felonies or misdemeanors. Determine from the facts below what type of crime has been committed and whether the crime is a felony or a misdemeanor.

   (a) John is walking through an amusement park when his wallet, with $2,000 in it, is "picked" from his pocket.

   (b) Allen and George become involved in a shouting argument. Allen knocks George down, causing a serious head injury to George.

   (c) Darrell continually crosses Mary's backyard without permission, despite Mary's notice to Darrell to get off her land.

   (d) Harold walks into a camera shop. Without force and without the owner noticing, Harold walks out of the store with a camera.

3. The following fact situations are similar (the theft of Jean's television set); yet three different crimes are described. Identify the three crimes, noting the differences among them.

   (a) While passing Jean's house one night, Sam sees a portable television set left unattended on Jean's lawn. Sam takes the television set, carries it home, and tells everyone he owns it.

   (b) While passing Jean's house one night, Sam sees Jean outside with a portable television set. Holding Jean at gunpoint, Sam forces her to give up the set. Then Sam runs away with it.

   (c) While passing Jean's house one night, Sam sees a portable television set in a window. Sam breaks the front door lock, enters, and leaves with the set.

4. Jack, an undercover police officer, stops Patricia on a busy street. Jack offers to sell Patricia an expensive wristwatch for a fraction of its value. After some questioning, Jack admits that the watch is stolen property, although he says that he was not the thief. Patricia pays for and receives the wristwatch and is immediately arrested by Jack for receiving stolen property. At trial, Patricia contends entrapment. What is the result of the trial?

5. Two basic elements are needed for a person to be convicted of a crime. The first element is called *actus reus*, and the second is called *mens rea*. Explain what these terms mean, and discuss how each is applied to the following:

   (a) Murder or manslaughter.
   (b) Forgery.
   (c) Arson.

6. Faulkner was a seaman on the ship Zemindar. One night while on duty, Faulkner went in search of the rum that he knew the ship was carrying. He found it and opened one of the kegs, but because he was holding a match at the time, he inadvertently ignited the rum and set fire to the ship. Faulkner was criminally prosecuted for setting fire to the ship. At the trial, it was determined that even though he had not intended to set fire to the rum, he had been engaged in the unlawful act of stealing it. Does Faulkner's theft of the

rum make him criminally liable for setting fire to the ship? [Regina v. Faulkner, 13 Cox C.C. 550 (Ireland)]

7. In 1965 Rybicki failed to pay the complete amount of income tax he owed the federal government. Attempts by the IRS to collect the tax proved fruitless. Therefore, the IRS, through lawful means, obtained a tax lien on Rybicki's personal property, which included his truck. In February 1967 Rybicki's wife, upon hearing the motor of the truck, awoke her sleeping husband. Wielding a shotgun, Rybicki went to his front door and told the two men who were attempting to take his truck to stop. Rybicki claimed that he did not know that the two men were IRS agents. Subsequently, the federal government indicted Rybicki for obstructing justice. Can Rybicki be held criminally liable if he did not know that the men were IRS agents performing their duty? [United States v. Rybicki, 403 F.2d 599 (6th Cir. 1968)]

8. Pivowar agreed to lend Mills approximately $9,000, and Mills agreed to repay the loan and further agreed that the loan would be secured by two houses that he owned. Mills showed Pivowar the two houses but falsely represented that Pivowar was to get a first mortgage on the houses. Pivowar later learned that the mortgages he held were not on the two houses but on two vacant lots and, further, that the mortgages were second mortgages and not first mortgages as Mills had promised. Can Mills be prosecuted criminally for false pretenses if he contends that he intended to pay back the loan and that Pivowar never demanded payment on the note? [State v. Mills, 96 Ariz. 377, 396 P.2d 5 (1964)]

9. McCracken was employed by Hastings Co-op Elevator to manage its fertilizer operation. While employed by Hastings, McCracken and two other individuals associated with Hastings formed a chemical and fertilizer corporation, Upper Midwest, naming themselves as officers. Thereafter a series of transactions took place in which McCracken diverted direct sales of fertilizer to Hastings through Upper Midwest at increased prices to Hastings. McCracken, as agent for Upper Midwest, also purchased from Hastings eighteen carloads of fertilizer at considerably less than market prices, reselling on behalf of Upper Midwest (at substantial profits) to customers who thought they were dealing with Hastings. Charged with use of United States mails to defraud, McCracken testified at trial that the various sales and purchases were made to keep Hastings's profit margins at a minimum in order to preserve its tax-exempt status. Because he had assumed his acts were proper, McCracken had failed to inform the Hastings board of directors of his dual role as an employee of Hastings and an agent for Upper Midwest. The government contended that intent to defraud need not be specifically proved since it could be inferred from McCracken's participation in the various transactions. Was the government's contention upheld? [United States v. McCracken, 581 F.2d 719 (8th Cir. 1978)]

10. Lund was working on his doctoral dissertation in statistics at Virginia Polytechnic Institute in Blacksburg, Virginia. He was required to use the computer facilities at the university. His faculty adviser neglected to arrange for the use of the computer. Nonetheless, Lund went ahead and used it without obtaining proper authorization. At trial, Lund was convicted of grand larceny for obtaining approximately $30,000 worth of computer services without authorization. At trial, four faculty members testified that computer time "probably would have been" or "would have been" assigned to Lund if properly requested. Lund appealed his conviction. What was the result? [Lund v. Commonwealth of Virginia, 217 Va. 688, 232 S.E.2d 745 (1977)]

FOCUS ON ETHICS

The Central Problem: Defining Business Ethics

Business people face complicated decisions. A course of action that may mean relatively high short-run profits may also involve conduct that, though legal, is not ethical. How indeed does a manager know that he or she is facing an ethical issue in reaching a particular business decision? To answer this question, we must first define *ethics*, bearing in mind that what constitutes an ethical concern of a society may change as the values of that society change. What was ethical conduct in the United States ten years ago may be considered unethical today, although ten years from now it may again be considered ethical.

Essentially, an ethical issue is one that transcends its subject matter to pose a fundamental, structural question such as, What is fair? What is just? or What makes this outcome more socially desirable than another? One of the best definitions of *ethics* from a business point of view appeared in *Ethics in the Corporate Policy Process: An Introduction:* "Ethics is a process by which individuals, social groups, and societies evaluate their actions from the perspective of moral principles and values. This evaluation may be on the basis of traditional convictions, of ideals sought, of goals desired, of moral laws to be obeyed, of an improved quality of relations among humans and with the environment. When we speak of "ethics" and ethical reflection, we mean the activity of applying these various yardsticks to the actions of persons and groups." (C. McCoy et al., *Ethics in the Corporate Policy Process: An Introduction*, Berkeley, Calif.: Center for Ethics and Social Policy, Graduate Theological Union, 1975, p. 2.)

For business people, ethical issues arise because of competing interests in the business world among buyers, sellers, managers, and nonmanagers, and so on. Hence, business ethics attempts to reconcile the divergent goals arising from the different perspectives of these different groups.

A society's ethics, whether related to business or otherwise, rests on a collection of shared beliefs. Indeed, it is shared beliefs that cause people to organize as groups. This collection of basic values accepted by all members of the society is the morality of that society. In the United States, the collection of shared beliefs may be called the capitalist morality.

PROBLEMS WITH ACCEPTED SOLUTIONS

The capitalist morality and the business ethics contained within that morality have not been perpetuated and taught through the use of explicit rules or theories. Rather, the use of accepted solutions to certain recurring problems has perpetuated the capitalist morality. Think, for example, of how the typical accounting course or calculus course is taught: Problems with accepted solutions are presented. The system of shared beliefs in the United States will probably continue to thrive within a business context as long as the accepted solutions of the capitalist morality continue to be applied to problems.

These solutions, however, change as the morality of society changes.

For example, it was only recently that the commercial bribery of foreign government officials was raised as an ethical issue. It took several scandals involving large payoffs to bring this issue to the fore. Values in the United States finally changed sufficiently that Congress felt impelled to pass a law making it illegal, under most circumstances, for any corporate official to offer bribes to foreign government officials for the purpose of obtaining business. Corporate leaders have since complained that such legislation has kept U.S. businesses from competing on an equal footing with the corporations of other countries. They argue that other countries have no such law and that corporate officials (or government officials) of other countries feel no compunction about paying bribes in order to consummate business deals.

This issue illustrates that the shared beliefs that constitute a society's ethics are not only time-sensitive (changing with the passage of time) but also country-sensitive (varying from country to country).

THE PHILOSOPHY OF ETHICAL INQUIRIES

Any discussion of business ethics rests on philosophic principles contained in literature reaching back two thousand years or more. Those principles focus on a central question: All things considered, what ought I do? If we apply the "all things considered" phrase to issues that arise in the legal-economic structure of today (that is, the capitalist morality), we will have a basis for defining *business ethics*. Business ethics involves an analysis of the fundamental values of capitalism. Such an analysis is based upon the shared values of the capitalist morality. These shared values are, at a minimum:

1. The freedoms we believe everyone should enjoy.
2. The sanctity of private property.
3. The proper role of government.
4. The acceptance of technology.
5. The importance of the individual.

By examining these values in the light of current business reality, we are able to evaluate the "fairness" of current practices.

THREE TRAPS TO AVOID

In an ethical analysis of capitalist morality and actions in the business world, three traps await the analyst. The first is the tendency to assume that whenever certain components of capitalism are judged faulty, the only current alternative—socialism—must therefore be advocated. It is entirely possible to ask illuminating questions about capitalism and the fundamental values of its economic and legal system without suggesting that socialism is a superior system.

The second trap is the tendency to trivialize ethical questions by focusing on behavioral as opposed to structural economic or legal anomalies. For example, the question "Should I take a few office supplies for personal use?" may be an ethical question, but unless office supplies are to be the center of discussion, it somehow misses the point. If we decide to consider the question, then it should be discussed in light of another question: What is there about our economic or social system that makes this a significant question? In an analysis of business ethics, we are concerned with the moral standards of a society, not of particular individuals.

Remember that law reflects societal values, and thus it changes when these values change. However, since law is a response, there is a time lag between any changes in society's values and corresponding changes in the law. Before any change in the law occurs, someone must question the fairness of existing laws. Someone must ask whether those laws represent the society's values. Too often, students of law and business focus on understanding what current laws state without questioning why these laws exist or whether they should exist in their current form. Thus, the third trap in an ethical analysis is to assume that the law is always right as it stands and that it should be only learned, not evaluated. Throughout this book we will see how the law has been changed when it was revealed to be in conflict with society's prevailing standards of fairness and justice.

DISCUSSION QUESTIONS

1. Should businesses have ethics? In other words, should companies have social or ethical goals in addition to profit-making goals?
2. If companies should have goals other than making profits, who in the company should set those goals?
3. Should the decision on who sets the goals depend on the type of business conducted by the company or on the current political and environmental climate?
4. Should ethics be a concern of top management alone, or should it be a shared concern of all employees, distributors, suppliers, and so on?

UNIT II

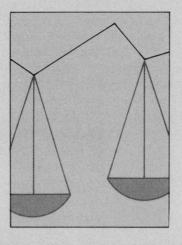

CONTRACTS

CHAPTER 6

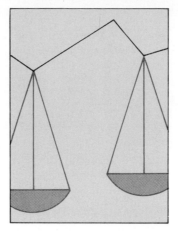

CONTRACTS
Nature, Form, and Terminology

SOME PERSPECTIVES

In the legal environment of business, contracts are one of the most significant bodies of law. Contract law shows to what extent our society allows people to make promises or commitments that are legally binding. It shows what excuses our society will accept for breaking such promises. And it shows what kinds of promises will be considered as being against public policy and therefore legally void.

As a general rule, a promise will be enforced by a court (or damages will be imposed for not keeping the promise) as long as it was made knowingly and voluntarily. Sometimes, however, enforcing a promise will transgress an important public policy. If the promise is against the interests of society as a whole, it will be invalidated. Also, if it was made by a child, or by an insane person, or on the basis of false information, a question will be raised about whether

the promise should be enforced. Resolving such questions is the essence of contract law.

Contract law, in effect, governs the relationships between those who make promises to one another. The use of contract principles dates back thousands of years. Very early in history the importance of contracts was recognized and given legal effect. The following chapters will explain how contracts are formed, how they are discharged, and what happens when they are not performed. The rules relating to the formation, discharge, and breach of enforceable promises are called *the law of contracts.*

Society's need of contracts is obvious. The foundation for almost all commercial activity is the contract. The purchase of goods, such as automobiles, is governed by a sales contract; the lease of an apartment or office by a lease agreement; the hiring of people to work for us or to make repairs by service contracts; the sharing of risks on our property by insurance contracts—

the list is endless. In short, we could not order our daily activities without them.[1] Contract law helps us predict the future because it looks to the future.

THE FUNCTION OF CONTRACTS

Contract law assures the parties to private agreements that the promises they make will be enforced. Not all promises or obligations are enforceable. Sometimes the promises exchanged create *moral* rather than *legal* obligations. Failure to perform a moral obligation, such as an agreement to take a friend to lunch, does not create a legal liability. Nonperformance of a contract generally does. The promise of a father to pay for the college education of his daughter may be a legal, as well as a moral, question.

Clearly, many promises are kept because of a sense of duty, or because keeping them is to the mutual self-interest of the parties involved, not because the **promisor** (the person making the promise) is conscious of the rules of contract law. Nevertheless, the rules of contract law are often followed in business agreements in order to avoid potential problems.

By providing procedures for enforcing private agreements, contract law provides an essential condition for the existence of a market economy. Without a legal framework for reasonably assured expectations within which to plan and venture, businesspersons would be able to rely only on the good faith of others. Duty and good faith are usually sufficient, but when price changes or adverse economic factors make it

costly to comply with a promise, these elements may not be enough. Contract law is necessary in order to ensure compliance with a promise or to entitle the innocent party to some form of relief.

Contract law also provides a foundation upon which more specialized areas of law are built. The sale of goods (Chapters 18 to 23); the transfer and negotiation of checks, notes, and drafts (Chapters 24 to 29); the giving of security in goods or land (Chapters 30 to 31); the rights of debtors and creditors (Chapter 32); the rights of agents, employees, and their employers (Chapters 34 to 35); the creation, operation, and termination of partnerships and corporations (Chapters 37 to 46); the regulation of trade and monopolies (Chapters 47 to 52); and the transfer of property (Chapters 53 and 56) all require a basic understanding of contract law.

Since contract law underlies virtually all business relationships, knowledge of it is essential to avoid costly mistakes. Some familiarity with legal thinking can be a valuable asset for anyone dealing with lawyers.

FREEDOM OF CONTRACT AND FREEDOM FROM CONTRACT

As a general rule, the law recognizes everyone's ability to enter freely into contractual arrangements. This recognition is called *freedom of contract*, and this freedom is protected by the U.S. Constitution in Article I, Section 10. But as the character of institutions and society changes, the functions of contract law and its enforcement must also change. Such change can be perceived today in the fact that certain types of agreements are no longer considered valid. For example, illegal bargains, agreements unreasonably in restraint of trade, and contracts made between one party with an inordinate amount of bargaining power and another with little power are generally not enforced. In addition, certain contracts with consumers, as well as certain clauses within those contracts, are not enforceable under the rationale of public policy, fairness, and justice (see Chapter 10 for details). The law of contracts is broadening to include new controls on the manner of contracting and on the allowable terms

---

1. The Soviet Union attempted to eliminate the need for contracts by dispensing with the private ordering of activities. The state required everyone to engage in certain specified activities—work, education, recreation—in the hope of redistributing wealth according to administrative standards and norms. The experiment failed, and Lenin explicitly recognized this when he wrote in 1921, "The private market proved to be stronger than we [thought]. * * * We ended up with ordinary * * * trade." Ultimately, contracts were reintroduced, and contract law was codified along traditional lines. See Loeber, *"Plan and Contract Performance in Soviet Law"*, reprinted in LaFave, *Law in the Soviet Society*, Wayne R. LaFave, ed. Urbana, University of Illinois Press [1965].

of agreements. These controls are meant to provide freedom from contract for certain members of society who heretofore may have been forced into making contracts unfavorable to them.

THE BASIC REQUIREMENTS OF A CONTRACT

The many topics that will be discussed in this unit on contracts require an understanding of the basic requirements of a contract and the processes by which one is created. The following list gives a brief description of these requirements. Each will be explained more fully in later chapters.

1.   **Agreement.** An agreement includes an offer and an acceptance. One party must offer to enter into a legal agreement, and another party must accept the terms of the offer.
2.   **Consideration.** Any promises made by parties must be supported by legally sufficient and bargained-for consideration.
3.   **Contractual capacity.** Both parties entering into the contract must have the contractual capacity to do so; they must be recognized by the law to possess characteristics qualifying them as competent parties.
4.   **Legality.** The contract must be made to accomplish some goal that is legal and not against public policy.
5.   **Reality of assent.** Apparent consent of both parties must be genuine.
6.   **Form.** The contract must be in whatever form the law requires, such as in writing.

The first four items given in this list constitute what are formally known as the elements of a contract. The last two are formally known as defenses to the formation or enforcement of a contract.

NATURE AND TYPES OF CONTRACTS

In order for the detailed elements of a contract to be understood, certain terms and certain types

of contracts must be defined. When reading subsequent chapters, refer to the definitions given in this chapter. This effort should enhance and reinforce your understanding of the language of contract law.

Definition of a Contract

A **contract** is simply any agreement that can be enforced in a court of law or equity. It is formed by two or more parties who agree to perform or refrain from performing some act now or in the future.[2] Generally, contract disputes arise when there is a promise of future performance. A **promise** is an undertaking that something either will or will not happen in the future. If the contractual promise is not fulfilled, the party who made it is subject to the sanctions of a court of law or equity. That party may be required to pay money damages for failing to perform or, in limited instances, may be required to perform the promised act.

TYPES OF CONTRACTS EXPLAINED

This section will explain the various types of contracts by comparing them to each other. They are:

(1)   express versus implied;
(2)   quasi-contracts, or contracts implied-in-law;
(3)   bilateral versus unilateral;
(4)   formal versus informal;
(5)   executed versus executory;
(6)   valid versus void, voidable, and unenforceable.

Express versus Implied Contracts

An **express contract** is one in which the terms of the agreement are fully and explicitly stated

---

2.   As defined by the American Law Institute, a *contract* is "a promise or a set of promises for the breach of which the law gives a remedy, or the performance of which the law in some way recognizes as a duty." Restatement, Second, Contracts, Section 1.

in words, oral or written. A signed lease for an apartment or house is an express written contract. If a classmate calls you on the phone and agrees to buy your textbooks from last semester for $50, an express oral contract has been made.

A contract that is implied from the conduct of the parties is called an **implied-in-fact contract,** or an implied contract. Implied-in-fact contracts differ from express contracts in that the *conduct* of the parties, rather than their words, creates and defines the terms of the contract. For example, suppose you need a tax consultant or an accountant to fill out your tax return this year. You look through the phone book and find both an accountant and a tax consultant at an office in your neighborhood, so you drop by to see them. You go into the office and explain your problem; and they tell you what their fees are. The next day you return, giving the secretary all of the necessary information such as cancelled checks, W-2 copies, and so on. You say nothing expressly to the secretary; rather, you walk out the door. Nonetheless, you have entered into an implied-in-fact contract to pay the tax consultant and accountant their usual and reasonable fees for their services. The contract is implied by your conduct and by the consultants' conduct. They expect to be paid for preparing your tax return. By bringing in all of the necessary records that will allow them to do so, you have implied an intent to pay them for their work.

Objective Theory of Contracts The intent or apparent intent to enter into a contract is of prime importance in the formation of the contract. This intent is determined by what is called the **objective theory of contracts,** not by the personal or subjective intent, or belief, of a party. This is illustrated by the tax preparation example. The theory is that a party's intention to enter into a contract is judged by outward, objective facts as interpreted by a **reasonable offeree** (one to whom the offer is being made), rather than by the party's own secret, subjective intentions. Objective facts include: (1) what the party said when entering into the contract, (2) how the party acted or appeared, and (3) the circumstances surrounding the transaction.

Courts need verifiable evidence in order to determine whether a contract has been made, so they usually rely only on subjective facts when passing judgment on a contract dispute. Using this approach, they often determine that the parties have entered into contracts that are *implied-in-fact*. In other words, courts examine all the objective facts, conduct, and circumstances surrounding a particular transaction in order to determine if the parties have made a contract.

Summary of Steps Necessary for an Implied-in-Fact Contract The following four steps establish an implied-in-fact contract:

1. The plaintiff furnished some service or property.
2. The plaintiff expected to be paid for that service or property.
3. The defendant knew or should have known that payment was expected (by using the objective theory of contracts test).
4. The defendant had a chance to reject the services or property and did not.

In the following case, do you agree with the court that an implied-in-fact contract existed?

BACKGROUND AND FACTS *Plaintiff Day had a vacant lot that was next to defendant Caton's vacant lot. Day decided to build a brick wall between the adjoining lots. Caton claimed that there was no express agreement between him and Day and that even though Caton knew that the wall was being constructed, his silence and subsequent use of the wall did not raise an implied promise to pay anything for it. In the trial court, the jury found for the plaintiff, Day. Caton took his case to the Supreme Judicial Court of Massachusetts to have the judgment overruled.*

DAY v. CATON
Supreme Judicial Court of Massachusetts, 1876.
119 Mass. 513.

DEVENS, Judge

The ruling that a promise to pay for the wall would not be implied from the fact that the plaintiff, with the defendant's knowledge, built the wall, and that the defendant used it, was substantially in accordance with the request of the defendant, and is conceded to have been correct.

The defendant, however, contends that the presiding judge incorrectly ruled that such promise might be inferred from the fact that the plaintiff undertook and completed the building of the wall with the expectation that the defendant would pay him for it, the defendant having reason to know that the plaintiff was acting with that expectation, and allowed him thus to act without objection.

The fact that the plaintiff expected to be paid for the work would certainly not be sufficient of itself to establish the existence of a contract, when the question between the parties was whether one was made. It must be shown that in some manner the party sought to be charged assented to it. If a party, however, voluntarily accepts and avails himself of valuable services rendered for his benefit, when he has the option whether to accept or reject them, even if there is no distinct proof that they were rendered by his authority or request, a promise to pay for them may be inferred. His knowledge that they were valuable, and his exercise of the option to avail himself of them, justify this inference. And when one stands by in silence, and sees valuable services rendered upon his real estate by the erection of a structure (of which he must necessarily avail himself afterwards in his proper use thereof), such silence, accompanied with the knowledge on his part that the party rendering services expects payment therefor, may fairly be treated as evidence of an acceptance of it, and as tending to show an agreement to pay for it.

* * * [I]f silence may be interpreted as assent where a proposition is made to one which he is bound to deny or admit, so also it may be if he is silent in the face of facts which fairly call upon him to speak.

If a person saw day after day a laborer at work in his field doing services, which must of necessity inure to his benefit, knowing that the laborer expected pay for his work, when it was perfectly easy to notify him if his services were not wanted, even if a request were not expressly proved, such a request, either previous to or contemporaneous with the performance of the services, might fairly be inferred. But if the fact was merely brought to his attention upon a single occasion and casually, if he had little opportunity to notify the other that he did not desire the work and should not pay for it, or could only do so at the expense of much time and trouble, the same inference might not be made. The circumstances of each case would necessarily determine whether silence with a knowledge that another was doing valuable work for his benefit and with the expectation of payment indicated that consent which would give rise to the inference of a contract. The question would be one for the jury, and to them it was properly submitted in the case before us by the presiding judge.

JUDGMENT AND REMEDY   *Caton did not convince the reviewing court that his exceptions were valid. The trial court's decision was upheld; there was indeed an implied-in-fact contract.*

Quasi-Contracts, or Contracts Implied-in-Law

Quasi-contracts, or **contracts implied-in-law,** should be distinguished from contracts *implied-in-fact.* Quasi-contracts, as their name suggests, are not true contracts. They arise in order to achieve justice rather than from a mutual agreement between the parties. A quasi-contract is imposed on the parties in order to avoid *unjust enrichment.* The doctrine of unjust enrichment holds that people should not be allowed to profit or enrich themselves inequitably at the expense of others. The doctrine is equitable rather than contractual in nature.

The quasi-contract is, in essence, a legal fiction. It is based neither on an expressed promise by the defendant to pay for the benefit received nor on conduct of the defendant implying such a promise. Indeed, the recipient of such a benefit (the defendant) not only has not solicited it but often may be unaware that it has been conferred.

Distinction between Contract Implied-in-Law and Contract Implied-in-Fact The contract implied-in-fact is a true contract. The parties have expressed their agreement to its terms by their conduct. The only way a contract implied-in-fact differs from an express contract is in its lack of express words or writings. In contrast, a contract implied-in-law (a quasi-contract) exists in the absence of both words and conduct from which a court could imply that a contract had been formed. Rather, a fictional contract is created by the court for reasons of social policy.

Example of a Quasi-Contract Suppose Steve enters into an oral agreement with Diane, agreeing to work with Diane for two years to develop a noise reduction turbine for fixed-wing commercial jets. Diane agrees to pay Steve a "fair share of the profit" derived from the sale of the device. After working six months on the project and making considerable headway, Diane tells Steve she will not pay him anything because the terms of the contract are too indefinite. Diane claims that there is no way to "objectively" determine "fair share of the profit." Assuming Diane is correct, Steve cannot sue on the contract itself, since there is no contract. Instead Steve sues on the theory of quasi-contract for the reasonable value of his services. Obviously, it would be unfair to allow Diane to pay nothing for Steve's work, so the court will imply a quasi-contract. Thus, Diane will be required to pay Steve a fair wage for the six months of work.

In the following case, we see the court's reasoning concerning the doctrine of a quasi-contract.

BACKGROUND AND FACTS *Matarese, the plaintiff, was a dock worker employed as a part-time stevedore on the pier of defendant Moore-McCormack Lines. He invented a device for loading and unloading cargo that would save the defendant company large sums of money. The company sent a representative, Furey, to Matarese's home, where Matarese demonstrated the system. Furey promised Matarese one-third of what the company would save by using the device. He offered Matarese the job of supervising the construction of the device on the company premises with the company's materials. The plaintiff accepted the job and began full-scale testing. When the testing proved successful, the company installed a large number of the devices at the pier and subsequently allowed other companies to acquire them for use at other piers. The plaintiff was never compensated. At trial court a jury awarded the plaintiff $90,000. The district judge required that Matarese accept a reduction to the sum of $40,000. Matarese agreed, and the judgment was entered on his behalf. Moore-McCormack Lines appealed.*

MATARESE v. MOORE-McCORMACK LINES
Circuit Court of Appeals, Second Circuit, 1946.
158 F.2d 631, 170 A.L.R. 440.

CLARK, Circuit Judge.

*   *   *   *

The main legal issue of the appeal turns *   *   * upon the validity of plaintiff's claim of unjust enrichment under the circumstances of this case. *   *   *

The doctrine of unjust enrichment or recovery in quasi-contract *   *   * is applicable to a situation where, as here, the product of an inventor's brain is knowingly received and used by another to his own great benefit without compensating the inventor. This is recognized in the leading New York case of Bristol v. Equitable Life Assur. Soc. of New York, 132 N.Y. 264, 267, 30 N.E. 506, 507, 28 Am.St.Rep. 568 (1892). In that case the New York Court of Appeals dismissed a complaint based on the use by defendant of an advertising scheme of which plaintiff had apprised it, because the scheme was not original and because it was not alleged to be marketable. The court, however, was careful to distinguish the situation in which an invention is involved, saying: "In such cases [of inventions] there is a production which can by multiplying copies be put to marketable use, *   *   *. Whoever infringes takes benefits or profits which otherwise would naturally come to the producer." *   *   *

Courts have justly been assiduous in defeating attempts to delve into the pockets of business firms through spurious claims for compensation for the use of ideas. Thus to be rejected are attempts made by telephoning or writing vague general ideas to business corporations and then seizing upon some later general similarity between their products and the notions propounded as a basis for damages. Such schemes are quite different from the situations envisaged in [this case]. Here the relationship between the parties before and after the disclosure, the seeking of disclosure by Furey [the company's representative], Furey's promise of compensation, the specific character, novelty, and patentability of plaintiff's invention, the subsequent use made of it by defendants, and the lack of compensation given the plaintiff—all indicate that the application of the principle of unjust enrichment is required. *   *   *

Defendants, relying upon the concession of lack of proof of Furey's authority to make the contract as originally alleged, claim a like lack of authority to accept the benefit of plaintiff's ideas to such an extent as to make them liable to pay reasonable compensation therefor. Such liability, they assert, could be based only on an extensive and fearsome corporate responsibility to pay for all chance ideas of an employee unwittingly utilized by the corporation. We may pass the interesting question how far an unwitting appropriation of property in ideas may create liability, since the case was presented and admitted to the jury on the theory of valuable services rendered by the plaintiff either to the knowledge of the defendants or "at the instance of someone authorized to obtain such services for the defendant." The court in its first reference to this issue stated it thus alternatively. Then at the close of its charge, it granted the defendants' request for a charge, indeed repeating it twice in colloquy with counsel, that the defendants "must have knowingly used it, knowing that it was plaintiff's device."

This charge, it seems to us, was justified upon the record. [A review of the record on this point is omitted.] *   *   *

JUDGMENT AND REMEDY   *The Circuit Court of Appeals affirmed the lower court's judgment. The doctrine of unjust enrichment, or recovery in quasi-contract, applied to this situation.*

A Limitation on the Quasi-Contract The principle underlying quasi-contractual obligations is based on the notion of "unjust enrichment." Nonetheless, there are situations in which the party obtaining the "unjust enrichment" is not liable. Basically, the quasi-contractual principle cannot be invoked by the party who has conferred a benefit on someone else unnecessarily or as a result of misconduct or negligence. Consider the following example. You take your car to the local car wash and ask to have it run through the washer and to have the gas tank filled. While it is being washed, you go to a nearby shopping center for two hours. In the meantime, one of the workers at the car wash has mistakenly believed that your car is the one that he is supposed to hand wax. When you come back, you are presented with a bill for a full tank of gas, a wash job, and a hand wax. Clearly, a benefit has been conferred on you. But this benefit has been conferred because of a mistake by the car wash employee. You have no liability. You have not received an *unjust* benefit under these circumstances. People cannot normally be forced to pay for benefits "thrust" upon them.

Also, the doctrine of quasi-contract cannot normally be used when there is a contract that covers the area in controversy. For example, Gonzales delivers a stove to a building project and does not get paid. Contractor Mott goes bankrupt. Gonzales cannot collect from Mitchell—the owner of the building—in quasi-contract because Gonzales has an existing contract with Mott.

Bilateral versus Unilateral Contracts

Every contract involves at least two parties. The **offeror** is the party making the offer, and the **offeree** is the party to whom the offer is made. The offeror always promises to do or not to do something and thus is also a promisor. Whether the contract is classified as *unilateral* or *bilateral* depends on what the offeree must do to accept the offer and bind the offeror to a contract. If the offer requires as acceptance only that the offeree promise to perform, the contract formed is called a **bilateral contract.** Hence, a bilateral contract is a "promise for a promise." If the offer is phrased so that the offeree can accept only by complete performance, the contract formed by completion of the act (performance) is called a **unilateral contract.** Hence, a unilateral contract is a "promise for an act."

A problem arises in unilateral contracts when the promisor attempts to revoke the offer after the promisee has begun performance. Acceptance can occur only upon full performance, and offers are normally revocable until accepted. The modern view, however, is that an offer becomes irrevocable once performance begins.

The classic illustration of a unilateral contract is that in which Alan says to Barbara, "If you walk across the Brooklyn Bridge, I'll give you $10." Alan promises to pay only if Barbara walks the entire span of the bridge. Only upon Barbara's complete crossing does she accept Alan's offer to pay $10. If she chooses not to walk at all, there are no legal consequences.

BACKGROUND AND FACTS *The plaintiffs entered into a contract to purchase land from the defendant, Conte. She refused to proceed with the transaction, and the buyers brought suit for specific performance. Conte defended her actions by asserting that the contract was void because it imposed no legal obligation on the buyers.*

BLEECHER v. CONTE

Supreme Court of California, 1981.
173 Cal.Rptr. 278, 626 P.2d 1051.

BIRD, Chief Justice.

*   *   *   *

The first issue to be decided is whether the agreement lacked mutuality of obligation and, therefore, was unenforceable. A bilateral contract is one in which there are mutual promises given in consideration of each other. The promises of each party must be legally binding in order for them to be deemed consideration for each other.

If a party is not assuming a legal duty in making a promise, the agreement is not binding as a bilateral contract. This court expressed the rule in Mattei v. Hopper: "[w]hen the parties attempt * * * to make a contract where promises are exchanged as the consideration, the promises must be mutual in obligation. In other words, for the contract to bind either party, both must have assumed some legal obligations. Without this mutuality of obligation, the agreement lacks consideration and no enforceable contract has been created.

*   *   *   *

In the present case, the seller contends that the buyers' promise was illusory since they assumed no real obligations under the agreement. Therefore, she argues, the contract lacked mutuality of obligation and was unenforceable. She claims that the buyers could decline to have a tract map prepared or to obtain city approval for development, renege on the agreement, and still get back their $1,000 escrow deposit. *   *   *

There is one fatal flaw in the seller's argument that this contract lacked mutuality of obligation. She overlooks the buyers' promise to "do everything in their power to expedite the recordation of the final map" and to "proceed with diligence."

The present contract would have no value to the buyers if they did not proceed in good faith and obtain the necessary reports and approvals. The buyers do not have an unfettered right to cancel their contract or ignore their contractual obligations. More importantly, the buyers expressly promised to diligently pursue their obligations and to refrain from withholding their approval unreasonably.

*   *   *   *

In light of the express and implied obligations to proceed in good faith, the buyers here had an enforceable obligation to proceed diligently with the recordation of the tract map and to obtain the city's approval to develop the property.

*   *   *

*   *   *   *

This land sale contract does not lack mutuality of obligation. The buyers are under an express duty to proceed diligently and to refrain from unreasonably denying approval. They have an implied duty to proceed in good faith and to act fairly.

JUDGMENT AND REMEDY   *The trial court's award of specific performance to the buyers was upheld.*

Formal versus Informal Contracts

Formal contracts are contracts that require a special form or method of creation (formation) to be enforceable. They include: (1) contracts under seal, (2) recognizances, and (3) negotiable instruments and letters of credit. **Contracts un-** der seal are formalized writings with a special seal attached.[3] The significance of the seal has

---

3. A seal is usually an impression made on a thin wafer of wax firmly affixed to the writing. In some instances, the word *seal* or the letters *L.S.* appear at the end of the document. *L.S.* stands for *locus sigilli* and means "the place for the seal."

eroded, although about ten states require no consideration when a contract is under seal. (See Chapter 8 for details.) A **recognizance** is an acknowledgment in court by a person that he or she will pay a certain sum if a certain event occurs. The most common form of recognizance is the surety bond or criminal recognizance bond. Negotiable instruments and letters of credit are special methods of payment that are designed for use in many commercial settings. **Negotiable instruments** include checks, notes, drafts, and certificates of deposit. **Letters of credit** are agreements to pay contingent on the purchaser's receipt of invoices and bills of lading. Negotiable instruments and letters of credit are discussed at length in subsequent chapters.

Informal contracts include all other contracts. (Such contracts are also called *simple contracts*.) No special form is required (except for certain types of contracts that must be in writing), as the contracts are usually based on their substance rather than their form. Informal contracts can be written or oral, bilateral or unilateral, executory or executed.

Executed versus Executory Contracts

Contracts are also classified according to their stage of performance. A contract that has been fully performed on both sides is called an **executed contract.** A contract that has not been fully performed on either side is called an **executory contract.** If one party has fully performed but the other has not, the contract is said to be executed on one side and executory on the other. For example, assume you agree to buy ten tons of coal from the Wheeling Coal Company. Further assume that Wheeling has delivered the coal to your steel mill, where it is now being burned. At this point, the contract is executed on the part of Wheeling and executory on your part. After you pay Wheeling for the coal, the contract will be executed on both sides.

Valid versus Void, Voidable, and Unenforceable Contracts

A **valid contract** is one with the necessary elements to entitle at least one of the parties to enforce it in court. Those elements consist of an offer and an acceptance, supported by legally sufficient consideration, for a legal purpose, and made by parties who have the legal capacity to enter into the contract. Each element is discussed in detail in the following chapters.

A **void contract** is no contract at all. The terms *void* and *contract* are contradictory. A void contract produces no legal obligations by any of the parties. For example, a contract can be void because one of the parties was adjudged by a court to be legally insane or because the purpose of the contract was illegal.

A **voidable contract** is a valid contract in which one of the parties has the option of avoiding his or her legal obligations. The party having this option can elect to avoid any duty to perform or can elect to *ratify* the contract. If the contract is avoided, both parties are released from it. If it is ratified, both parties must fully perform their respective legal obligations.

As a general rule, but subject to exceptions, contracts made by minors are voidable at the option of the minor. (See Chapter 9 for details.) Contracts entered into under fraudulent conditions are voidable at the option of the defrauded party. (See Chapter 11 for details.) In addition, some contracts entered into because of mistakes, and all contracts entered into under legally defined duress (undue influence) are voidable.

An **unenforceable contract** is one that cannot be enforced because of certain legal defenses against it. It is not unenforceable because of failing to satisfy any of the legal requirements of a contract; rather, it is a valid contract rendered unenforceable by some statute or law. For example, a valid contract barred by a statute of limitations is an unenforceable contract.[4] Likewise, oral contracts under the Statute of Frauds are unenforceable. (See Chapter 12 for details.)

---

4. A statute of limitations prevents a party from suing on a contract after a certain period of time has elapsed.

QUESTIONS AND CASE PROBLEMS

1.   Suppose Felix, a local businessman, is a good friend of Miller, the owner of a local candy store. Every day at his lunch hour Felix goes into Miller's candy store and usually spends about five minutes looking at the candy. After examining Miller's candy and talking with Miller, Felix usually buys one or two candy bars. One afternoon, Felix goes into Miller's candy shop, looks at the candy, picks up a $1 candy bar and, seeing that Miller is very busy at the time, waves the candy bar at Miller without saying a word and walks out. Is there a contract? If so, classify it within the categories presented in this chapter.

2.   Mary is a minor, age sixteen. By letter, Mary offers to buy John's bicycle for $100. John, an adult, accepts by telegram. Mary pays John $100, and John delivers the bicycle to Mary. How would this contract be classified, and what is the legal effect on Mary?

3.   James is confined to his bed. He calls a friend who lives across the street and offers to sell her his watch next week for $100. If his friend wishes to accept, she is to put a red piece of paper in her front window. The next morning, she places a red piece of paper in her front window. Is the contract formed bilateral or unilateral? Explain.

4.   Air Advertising employed Red, a World War II flying ace, to fly its advertisements above Long Island Sound beaches. Burger Baby restaurants engaged Air Advertising to fly an advertisement above the Connecticut beaches. The advertisement offered $1,000 to any person who could swim from the Connecticut beaches to Long Island across Long Island Sound in less than a day. On Saturday, October 10, at 10:00 a.m., Red flew a sign above the Connecticut beaches that read: "Swim across the Sound and Burger Baby pays $1,000." Upon seeing the sign, Davison dove in. About four hours later, when he was about halfway across the Sound, Red flew another sign over the Sound that read: "Burger Baby revokes." Is there a contract between Davison and Burger Baby? Can Davison recover anything?

5.   Susan contacts Joe and makes the following offer: "When you finish mowing my yard, I'll pay you $25." Joe responds by saying, "I accept your offer." Is there a contract? Is it a bilateral or unilateral contract? What is the legal significance of the distinction?

6.   Sosa Crisan, an eighty-seven-year-old widow of Romanian origin, collapsed while shopping at a local grocery store. The Detroit police took her to the Detroit city hospital. She was admitted, and she remained there fourteen days. Then she was transferred to another hospital, where she died some eleven months later. Crisan had never regained consciousness after her collapse at the local grocery store. After she died, the city of Detroit sued her estate to recover the expenses of both the ambulance that took her to the hospital and the expenses of her hospital stay. Is there a contract between Sosa Crisan and the hospital? If so, how much can the Detroit hospital recover? [In Re Crisan Estate, 362 Mich. 569, 107 N.W.2d 907 (1961)]

7.   On April 1, 1969, McLouth Steel Corporation entered into a contract with Jewell Coal and Coke Company under which Jewell agreed to supply all Mc-Louth's coal requirements for the next thirty years. The contract mentioned no specific quantities. The price was set at $14.25 a ton for the first six months and was subject to an escalation clause whereby in each subsequent six months the original price would be increased by the cost increases encountered by Jewell. Ten years later Jewell found that even with those cost increases, the price it could charge McLouth was far less than the price it could receive in the open market. Jewell therefore stopped shipping coal. Is the contract executory or nonexecutory on the ground of indefiniteness? [McLouth Steel Corp. v. Jewell Coal and Coke Co., 570 F.2d 594 (6th Cir. 1978)]

CHAPTER 7

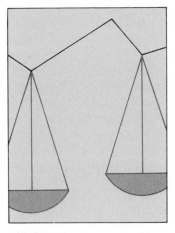

CONTRACTS
Agreement

Essential to any contract is an **agreement;** that is, an offer must be made by one party and accepted or assented to by the other party. The agreement does not necessarily have to be in writing. However, both parties must exhibit what is called a manifestation of assent to the same bargain.[1] If the agreement is supported by legally sufficient consideration,[2] is not illegal,[3] and is entered into freely by parties with contractual capacity,[4] a valid contract is formed, generally creating enforceable rights and duties between the parties.

---

1. Under early English and American law, many contracts were not enforced unless they complied with rigid legal standards requiring a writing and in many cases a seal or impression made on wax, which was firmly affixed to the writing. Today, some contracts must still be in writing (see Chapter 12). The seal has been almost entirely done away with. [UCC, 2–203]

2. See Chapter 8.

3. See Chapter 9.

4. See Chapter 10.

A contract must include the following terms, either expressed or capable of reasonable implication from the agreement:

1. Identification of the parties.

2. Identification of the object or subject matter of the contract, with specific identification of such items as goods, services, and land.

3. The consideration to be paid.

4. The time of performance.

If these terms are expressly stated in the agreement, the contract is definite. Although terms and intent are equally important in both offer and acceptance, for simplicity's sake we will discuss the relevant laws only in terms of the offer.

MUTUAL ASSENT— IDENTIFICATION OF THE PARTIES

Ordinarily, mutual assent is established by an **offer** and an **acceptance.** One party offers a certain bargain to another party, who then accepts that bargain. The parties are required to manifest to each other their **mutual assent** to the same bargain.[5] Because words often fail to convey the precise meaning intended, the law of contracts generally adheres to the objective theory of contracts, as discussed in Chapter 6. Under this theory, a party's words and conduct are held to mean whatever a reasonable person in the offeree's position would think they mean. The court will give words their usual meaning even if "it were proved by twenty bishops that [the] party * * * intended something else." [6]

REQUIREMENTS OF THE OFFER

The parties to a contract are the **offeror,** the one who makes an offer or proposal to another party, and the **offeree,** the one to whom the offer or proposal is made. An **offer** is a promise or commitment to do or refrain from doing some specified thing in the future. Three elements are necessary for an offer to be effective:

1. There must be a serious *intention* by the offeror to become bound by the offer.
2. The terms of the offer must be reasonably *certain*, or definite, so that the parties and the court can ascertain the terms of the contract.
3. The offer must be communicated to the offeree.

Once an effective offer has been made, the offeree has the power to accept the offer. If the offeree accepts, the offer is translated into an agreement (and thus into a contract if other essential elements are present).

Intention

The first element for an effective offer to exist is serious intent on the part of the offeror. But se-

rious intent is not determined by the *subjective* intentions of the offeror. It is determined instead by whether the offer created a *reasonable* impression in the mind of the offeree. Serious intent is therefore determined from the words and actions of the parties as interpreted by a reasonable person. Offers made in obvious anger, jest, or undue excitement do not meet the serious intent test. Since these offers are not effective, an offeree's acceptance would not create an agreement.

For example, you and three classmates ride to school each day in Jane's new automobile, which has a market value of $8,000. One cold morning the four of you get into the car, but Jane cannot get the car started. She yells in anger, "I'll sell this car to anyone for $500!" You drop $500 in her lap. Given these facts, a reasonable person, taking into consideration Jane's frustration and the obvious difference in value between the car and purchase price, would declare that her offer was not made with serious intent and that you do not have an agreement.

The concept of intention can be further explained by distinguishing between offers and various kinds of non-offers. Consider the following:

1. Expressions of opinion.
2. Statements of intention.
3. Preliminary negotiations.
4. Certain kinds of advertisements, catalogues, and circulars.

In each of these cases, an offer (as legally defined) probably does not exist, because the legal requirement of intention is probably not met.

Expressions of Opinion   An expression of opinion is not an offer. It does not evidence an intention to enter into a binding agreement. Hawkins took his son to McGee, a doctor, and asked McGee to operate on the son's hand. McGee said the boy would be in the hospital three or four days and that the hand would *probably* heal within a few days afterward. The son's hand did not heal for a month, but the father did not win

---

5. Restatement, Second, Contracts, Section 22.
6. Learned Hand in Hotchkiss v. National City Bank of N.Y., 200 F. 287 (2d Cir. 1911), aff'd 231 U.S. 50, 34 S.Ct. 20, (1913).

a suit for breach of contract. The court held that McGee did not make an offer to heal the son's hand in three or four days. He merely expressed an opinion as to when the hand would heal.[7]

Statements of Intention If Henry says "I *plan* to sell my stock in Ryder Systems for $150 per share," a contract will not be created if Fred "accepts" and tenders the $150 per share for the stock. Henry has merely expressed his intention to enter into a future contract for the sale of the stock. No contract is formed, because a reasonable person would conclude that Henry was only *thinking* about selling his stock, not promising to sell, even if Fred accepts and pays the $150 per share. Henry is stating a future contractual intent, not a present one.

----

7. Hawkins v. McGee, 84 N.H. 114, 146 A. 641 (1929).

Preliminary Negotiations A request or invitation to negotiate is not an offer. It only expresses a willingness to discuss entering into a contract. Included are statements such as "Will you sell Blythe Estate?" or "I wouldn't sell my car for less than $1,000." A reasonable person in the offeree's position would not conclude that these statements evidence an intention to enter into a binding obligation. Likewise, when construction work is done for the government and private firms, contractors are invited to submit bids. The *invitation* to submit bids is not an offer, and a contractor does not bind the government or private firm by submitting a bid. (The bids that the contractors submit *are* offers, however, and the government or private firm can bind the contractor by accepting the bid.)

Consider whether the court was dealing with preliminary negotiations or an actual offer in the following case.

BACKGROUND AND FACTS *Defendant Johnson is the owner of real estate. Johnson's real estate agent wrote a letter to plaintiff Mellen, indicating that certain seashore property that Mellen had expressed an interest in purchasing would be placed on the market. The letter further indicated that several other people who had expressed an interest in purchasing the property were also being informed at the same time before the property went on the open market. Mellen interpreted the letter as an "offer" and promptly "accepted." Mellen, thinking he was entitled to buy the property, sued Johnson to force her to go through with the sale (specific performance). The trial court upheld Mellen's position that the letter was an offer.*

MELLEN v. JOHNSON
Supreme Judicial Court of
Massachusetts, Essex, 1948.
322 Mass. 236, 76 N.E. 2d 658.

WILKINS, Justice.
*   *   *   *

The defendant is the owner of two parcels of land with the buildings thereon at 74 and 75 Willow Road, Nahant. On March 27, 1947, the defendant's son-in-law, Edward Hicks, who was her agent to sell the property, wrote the following letter to the plaintiff's brother-in-law, who was his agent as to this subject matter: "You will perhaps remember that we spent a pleasant visit *   *   * on the break water at Nahant last summer. On that occasion either you or your brother-in-law expressed an interest in my Mother's property which is the Johnson cottage. I told you that I would contact you if and when my Mother expressed a desire to dispose of her property. Well, that time has arrived and her health is such that she will not be able to open the cottage this year. She has, therefore, decided that it will be best to place the property on the market, however, before turning it over to the real estate agents, I am writing the several people, including yourself, who have previously expressed an interest in the property. Our price is $7,500. This property consists of the lot and cottage on the south side of Willow Road, and also a very large plot on which a two car garage is situated running from Willow Road clear through the block to the next street. Just how much property there is in this tract, I cannot tell you at the moment. I can say, however, that it is a large tract which would offer possibilities for further building. The price of $7,500 would include the entire property on both sides of Willow Road. The cottage is in very good condition. There are three rooms downstairs with a large entry hall, and a sun porch, also three good sized bedrooms upstairs, with bath. Hardwood floors throughout, hot water, heat and is suitable for all year round occupancy if desired. The oil burner is in good condition and the house is far better built than most of the new constructions of today. *I will be interested in hearing from you further if you have any interest in this property, for as I said before, I am advising those who have asked for an opportunity to consider it.* [Emphasis added.] I might just add that the property would be available for immediate occupancy. By that I mean within such time as the present furnishings could be removed and title transferred."

On March 28 Hicks received a telegram from the plaintiff's brother-in-law which read: "We are interested in your offer. Will look at house tomorrow. Communicate with you first of week." On the same day shortly after the telegram was received Hicks telegraphed the plaintiff's brother-in-law: "Have heard from three interested buyers tonight which means we must accept highest bid for Nahant property. Suggest you wire or phone us Elmsford N.Y. 7292 Saturday your best offer on cash basis." Before this was received the plaintiff's brother-in-law telegraphed Hicks: "I accept your offer on Nahant cottage. Letter in mail."

It is unnecessary to recount the subsequent communications of the parties other than to state that the defendant entered into a written contract to sell the property to someone other than the plaintiff. This sale has not been completed pending this suit.

* * * *

The letter of March 27 was not an offer. It expressed "a desire to dispose of" the property. It announced that the agent was "writing the several people, including yourself, who have previously expressed an interest in the property." Its conclusion, in part, was "I will be interested in hearing further from you if you have any interest in this property, for as I said before, I am advising those who have asked for an opportunity to consider it." The recipient could not reasonably understand this to be more than an attempt at negotiation. It was a mere request or suggestion that an offer be made to the defendant.

JUDGMENT AND REMEDY   *The trial court was found in error; its decision was reversed. The court of appeals decided that the letter was merely a negotiation, and Johnson was not required to sell the property to Mellen.*

COMMENTS   *It is often difficult to distinguish an actual "offer" from preliminary negotiations, or what lawyers call "invitations to offer." The key distinction between preliminary negotiations and offers is that an offer is a definite commitment, whereas a preliminary negotiation is noncommital.*

Advertisements, Catalogues, and Circulars In general, advertisements, mail order catalogues, price lists, and circular letters are treated not as offers to contract but as invitations to negotiate. Suppose Loeser & Co. advertises a used paving machine. The ad is mailed to hundreds of firms and reads, "Used Case Construction Co. paving machine. Builds curbs and finishes cement work all in one process. Price $11,250 firm." If Star Paving calls Loeser and says, "We accept your offer," no contract is formed. Any reasonable person would conclude that Loeser was not promising to sell the paving machine but rather that it was soliciting offers to buy it.

The same result occurs when a new car dealership advertises, "New Lincoln Continentals; loaded with options; now only $13,899." The ad is intended to draw customers who will make offers. If Bill Weinberg goes to the dealership with a check for $13,899, the dealership is not legally bound to sell the Lincoln. (However, federal and state statutes prohibit "false and misleading advertising" that is intended solely to draw customers to the retail outlet.)

Most advertisements are not offers, because the seller never has an unlimited supply of goods. If advertisements were offers, then everyone who "accepted" after the retailer's supply was exhausted could sue for breach of contract. Suppose you put an ad in the classified section of your local newspaper offering to sell a guitar for $75. Suppose further that seven people called and "accepted" your "offer" before you could remove the ad from the newspaper. If the ad were truly an offer, you would be bound on seven contracts to sell your guitar. But since initial advertisements are treated as *invitations* to make offers, rather than as offers, you would have seven offers to choose from, and you could accept the best one without incurring any liability for the six you reject.

Price lists are another form of invitation to negotiate or trade. The price list of the seller is not an offer to sell at that price. It merely invites the buyer to offer to buy at that price. As further evidence of the lack of intent to offer to sell at the listed prices, the words "prices subject to change" are usually printed somewhere on the price list.

Although most advertisements and the like are treated as invitations to negotiate, this does not mean that an advertisement can never be an offer. If the advertisement makes a promise so definite in character that it is apparent that the offeror is binding himself or herself to the conditions stated, the advertisement is treated as an offer. This is particularly true when the advertisement solicits performance—for example, by offering a reward for the capture of a criminal or for the return of a lost article.

Suppose an advertisement states, "To the first five persons in our store at 8:00 A.M. on May 1, we offer to sell Singer Sewing Machines, Model X, at $50." This statement invites an acceptance of terms stated rather than an offer to buy. If you were one of the first five in the store at the time specified, your acceptance creates a contract. Another example is a reward offered in a newspaper for the return of a lost dog. The finder's return of the dog in response to the advertisement creates a unilateral contract, as the reward obviously invited an acceptance, not an offer, from the offeree.

In the following case, the court had to decide whether a newspaper advertisement announcing a "special sale" in a department store should be construed as an offer, the acceptance of which would complete a contract. (Today the Federal Trade Commission has a set of rules governing such ads.)

BACKGROUND AND FACTS *Plaintiff Lefkowitz read a newspaper advertisement offering certain items of merchandise for sale on a first come-first served basis. Plaintiff went to the store twice and was the first person to demand the merchandise and indicate a readiness to pay the sale price. On both occasions, the defendant department store refused to sell the merchandise to the plaintiff, saying that the offer was intended for*

LEFKOWITZ v. GREAT MINNEAPOLIS SURPLUS STORE, INC.
Supreme Court of Minnesota, 1957.
251 Minn. 188, 86 N.W.2d 689.

women only, even though the advertisement was directed to the general public. The plaintiff sued the store for breach of contract, and the trial court awarded him damages.

MURPHY, Justice.

*   *   *   *

This case grows out of the alleged refusal of the defendant to sell to the plaintiff a certain fur piece which it had offered for sale in a newspaper advertisement. It appears from the record that on April 6, 1956, the defendant published the following advertisement in a Minneapolis newspaper:

> "Saturday 9 A.M. Sharp
> 3 Brand New
> Fur
> Coats
> Worth to $100.00
> First Come
> First Served
> $1
> Each"

On April 13, the defendant again published an advertisement in the same newspaper as follows:

> "Saturday 9 A.M.
> 2 Brand New Pastel
> Mink 3-Skin Scarfs
> Selling for $89.50
> Out they go
> Saturday. Each . . . $1.00
> 1 Black Lapin Stole
> Beautiful,
> worth $139.50 . . . $1.00
> First Come
> First Served"

The record supports the findings of the court that on each of the Saturdays following the publication of the above-described ads the plaintiff was the first to present himself at the appropriate counter in the defendant's store and on each occasion demanded the coat and the stole so advertised and indicated his readiness to pay the sale price of $1. On both occasions, the defendant refused to sell the merchandise to the plaintiff, stating on the first occasion that by a "house rule" the offer was intended for women only and sales would not be made to men, and on the second visit that plaintiff knew defendant's house rules.

*   *   *   *

The defendant contends that a newspaper advertisement offering items of merchandise for sale at a named price is a "unilateral offer" which may be withdrawn without notice. He relies upon authorities which hold that, where an advertiser publishes in a newspaper that he has a certain quantity or quality of goods which he wants to dispose of at certain prices and on certain terms, such advertisements are not offers which become contracts as soon as any person to whose notice they may come signifies his acceptance by notifying the other that he will take a certain quantity of them. Such advertisements have been construed as an invitation for an offer of sale on the terms stated, which offer, when received, may be accepted or rejected and which therefore does not become a contract of sale until accepted by the seller; and until a contract has been so made, the seller may modify or revoke such prices or terms.

*   *   *   *

[However] *   *   * [t]here are numerous authorities which hold that a particular advertisement in a newspaper or circular letter relating to a sale of articles may be construed by the court as constituting an offer, acceptance of which would complete a contract.

The test of whether a binding obligation may originate in advertisements addressed to the general public is "whether the facts show that some performance was promised in positive terms in return for something requested."

The authorities above cited emphasize that, where the offer is clear, definite, and explicit, and leaves nothing open for negotiation, it constitutes an offer, acceptance of which will complete the contract. *   *   *

Whether in any individual instance a newspaper advertisement is an offer rather than an invitation to make an offer depends on the legal intention of the parties and the surrounding circumstances. We are of the view on the facts before us that the offer by the defendant of the sale of the Lapin fur was clear, definite, and explicit, and left nothing open for negotiation. The plaintiff having successfully managed to be the first one to appear at the seller's place of business to be served, as requested by the advertisement, and having offered the stated purchase price of the article, he was entitled to performance on the part of the defendant. We think the trial court was correct in holding that there was in the conduct of the parties a sufficient mutuality of obligation to constitute a contract of sale.

The defendant contends that the offer was modified by a "house rule" to the effect that only women were qualified to receive the bargains advertised. The advertisement contained no such restriction. This objection may be disposed of briefly by stating that, while an advertiser has the right at any time before acceptance to modify his offer, he does not have the right, after acceptance, to impose new or arbitrary conditions not contained in the published offer.

The Supreme Court affirmed the trial court's judgment, awarding the plaintiff the sum of $138.50 ($139.50 for the Lapin stole less the $1 purchase price) in damages for breach of contract against the defendant department store.

JUDGMENT AND REMEDY

Other Non-Offer Situations Sometimes what appears to be an offer is not sufficient to serve as the basis for formation of a contract.

Auctions In an auction, a seller "offers" goods for sale through an auctioneer. This is not, how-ever, an offer for purposes of contract. The seller is really only expressing a willingness to sell. He or she may withdraw the goods at any time before the auctioneer closes the sale and may even refuse the highest bid. There is no obligation to sell. The bidder is actually the offeror. The auctioneer accepts a bid and completes a contract by knocking the hammer. A bidder can retract an offer while the auctioneer sings "going once, going twice, third and last call." If the bid is not withdrawn and the hammer falls, the contract is formed.[8]

Agreements to Agree   Agreements to agree are not contracts and cannot be enforced. Suppose Zahn Consulting gets together with Leon Construction Company to discuss plans for designing a shopping mall. Zahn and Leon agree further to meet in a month and work out the terms of the contract. The agreement to agree "or make a contract at a future time" is not enforceable. There is nothing to enforce in an agreement to agree because the terms have not yet been agreed upon.

Sham Transactions   A sham transaction is entered into by two parties in order to deceive a third person and is unenforceable. For example, a sham transaction might involve the alleged sale or transfer of a house to make one party's net worth appear larger than otherwise. Suppose that Sneed is trying to get a loan to buy a new BMW. In order to increase his unimpressive net worth on paper, he agrees in a personal letter to a close friend to sell his power boat for $50,000 (it's actually worth only about $25,000), and his friend agrees in a letter to pay that much. In filling out his net worth statement, Sneed claims that his boat is worth $50,000, and, if questioned, he can

produce a personal letter from his friend to show that that is the price at which it will be sold. Sneed and his friend entered into the sham transaction knowing that they were not actually going to perform their respective obligations. Sneed cannot attempt now to enforce that transaction by requesting payment of $50,000 for his boat.

Definiteness

The second element for an effective offer is the definiteness of its terms. An offer must have reasonably definite terms so that a court can determine if a breach has occurred and can give an appropriate remedy.[9] An offer may invite an acceptance to be worded in such specific terms that the contract is made definite. For example, assume D'Onfro contacts your corporation and offers to sell "from one to ten sheet metal presses for $1,750 each, state number desired in acceptance." Your corporation agrees to buy two presses. If the quantity had not been specified in the acceptance, the contract would be unenforceable because the terms of the contract would have been indefinite. But since the acceptance stated that your corporation wanted two presses, the contract is definite and can be enforced.

Is an employment contract that provides for a salary plus "a share of the profits" too vague and indefinite for a court to enforce? The following case tells the plight of a plaintiff, Victor Petersen, who worked first as construction supervisor and then as manager for the Pilgrim Village Company, the defendant.

---

8.   See UCC 2–328. At auctions announced as "without reserve," goods must be sold to the highest bidder.

9.   Restatement, Second, Contracts, Section 33.

PETERSEN v. PILGRIM VILLAGE

Supreme Court of Wisconsin, 1950.
256 Wis. 621, 42 N.W.2d 273.

BACKGROUND AND FACTS   *Petersen was employed by Pilgrim Village for nearly ten years. His contract of employment provided that he was to be paid a stated salary. Petersen claimed that Pilgrim told him when he began work that he would share in the profits of the corporation and promised him repeatedly throughout the term of his employment that he would share in the profits.*

When Petersen left Pilgrim Village, Pilgrim paid him all but $666.67 of his salary for the time he had worked the previous year.

Petersen sued Pilgrim for the back salary of $666.67 and for $20,000, which he declared was his "reasonable" share of corporate profits. Pilgrim *agreed to pay Petersen the salary but objected to paying any amount based on Petersen's claim that he was entitled to "a share of the profits." The trial court allowed the jury to award Petersen whatever part of the $20,000 they thought corresponded to "the reasonable value of services" Petersen had rendered to Pilgrim. The jury decided on $8,000. Pilgrim appealed, arguing that the parties had never come to any definite agreement as to what, if any, the percentage of profits was to be. The Supreme Court of Wisconsin reviewed Pilgrim's arguments.*

FRITZ, Chief Justice.

*   *   *   *

As stated in Restatement of the Law on Contracts, sec. 32, pp. 40, 41.

"An offer must be so definite in its terms, or require such definite terms in the acceptance, that the promises and performances to be rendered by each party are reasonably certain.

*   *   *   *

As stated in 12 Am.Jur. sec. 70, p. 561, "The general rule is that price is an essential ingredient of every contract for the transfer of property or rights therein or for the rendering of services. Accordingly, an agreement must be definite as to compensation. In order that an executory agreement may be valid, it is generally necessary that the price must be certain or capable of being ascertained from the agreement itself. By this is not meant that the exact amount in figures must be stated in the agreement; however, where that is not the case, the price must, by the terms of the agreement, be capable of being definitely ascertained. An agreement leaving the price for future determination is not binding. *   *   * (p. 562) Although there is some authority to the contrary, a promise to pay a reasonable sum for goods or services is generally held valid. *   *   * On the other hand, a promise to pay a fair share of profits has been held too indefinite to be valid." Varney v. Ditmars, 217 N.Y. 223, 111 N.E. 822, 823, Ann.Cas. 1916B 758 (1916).

In Varney v. Ditmars, supra, the employer promised to pay plaintiff $40 a week and "the first of January next year I will close my books and give you a fair share of my profits." The court said:

"The statement alleged to have been made by the defendant about giving the plaintiff and said designer a fair share of his profits is vague, indefinite, and uncertain, and the amount cannot be computed from anything that was said by the parties or by reference to any document, paper, or other transaction. The minds of the parties never met upon any particular share of the defendant's profits to be given the employes or upon any plan by which such share could be computed or determined. The contract so far as it related to the special promise or inducement was never consummated. It was left subject to the will of the defendant or for further negotiation. It is urged that the defendant by the use of the word 'fair,' in referring to a share of his profits, was as certain and definite as people are in the purchase and sale of a chattel when the price is not expressly agreed upon, and that if the agreement in question is declared to be too indefinite and uncertain to be enforced, a similar conclusion must be reached in every case where a chattel is sold without expressly fixing the price therefor. The question whether the words 'fair' and 'reasonable' have a definite and enforceable meaning when used in business transactions is dependent upon the intention of the parties in the use of such words and upon the subject-matter to which they refer. In cases of merchandising and in the purchase and sale of chattels the parties may use the words 'fair and reasonable value' as synonymous with 'market value.' *   *   *

"The contract in question, so far as it relates to a share of the defendant's profits, is not only uncertain, but it is necessarily affected by so many facts that are in themselves indefinite and uncertain that the intention of the parties is pure conjecture. *   *   * The courts cannot aid parties in such a case when they are unable or unwilling to agree upon the terms of their own proposed contract." *   *   *   *

Consequently, *   *   * plaintiff's [claim] *   *   * was merely that he was to be paid "some share of the profits," and as the parties never came to any definite agreement as to what that percentage of the profits was to be, the [trial] court erred.

JUDGMENT AND REMEDY   *Petersen left the appellate court without any of the $8,000 in "reasonable profits" the trial court jury had awarded him originally. Even assuming Petersen had been offered some share of the profits, the parties never showed that they had come to any definite agreement as to what that percentage of the profits ought to be. Note, however, that the appellate court allowed Petersen a new trial to establish sufficient evidence that he was entitled to payment of "the reasonable value" of any additional services he had rendered to Pilgrim over and above what he had been paid in his actual salary.*

COMMENTS   *Because an offer must be definite, a court can determine and award a monetary remedy if the offer is accepted and thus becomes a contract that is subsequently breached. The terms of the agreement forming the contract between the parties must be specific and firm enough for the court to measure which damages are directly related to the breach of the contract in question.*

Relaxation of Definiteness under the Uniform Commercial Code   Even before the adoption of the Uniform Commercial Code (UCC), courts were reluctant to declare a contract invalid because of the indefiniteness of its terms when both parties manifested a clear intention to enter into the contract. Therefore, the courts inserted reasonable terms wherever possible to resolve ambiguous or missing terms. In some cases this was impossible.

Clearly, in commercial situations contract law is supposed to aid business, not hinder it. For this reason, the UCC has liberalized the requirement of definiteness as to essential terms, although the common law continues to be much stricter in its interpretation.

Even though one or more of its terms are left open, a contract for sale does not fail for indef-

initeness, under the UCC, if the parties have clearly intended to make a contract and if a reasonably certain basis exists for giving an appropriate remedy. [UCC 2-204] Some of the ways in which the UCC fills in missing terms follow:

If no price is stated, or if the price is left open to be agreed on, "the price is a reasonable price at the time for delivery." [UCC 2-305] If no place of delivery is specified, then delivery is to occur at the seller's place of business. [UCC 2-308(a)][10] If the time for shipment or delivery is not provided for, then the time shall be a reasonable time after the contract is formed. [UCC 2-309] If

---

10.   But if both parties know the goods are elsewhere when the contract is formed, then the place of delivery is the place where the goods are located.

the time for payment is not specified, then payment is due at the time and place of delivery. [UCC 2-310(a)]

In addition, under the UCC, omitted terms may be supplied by custom and usage in trade and by prior dealings. If the parties have dealt with each other previously, their past conduct may be used to supply the omitted terms. For example, assume Steven's Poultry has purchased spring chickens from Robinson Farms for the last ten years, and the chickens have always been paid for on credit. Steven's Poultry then enters into a contract to buy 150 chickens, but no mention is made of the terms of payment. Because of prior dealings, Steven's may pay on credit, since the understandings of the past may be implied in the current contract.

Indefiniteness may be cured by *partial performance*, that is, by performance that has already begun. Assume Brown-Crummer, Inc., agrees to buy beans at $4 per bushel from Arkansas Grains. Arkansas Grains, however, has four different grades of beans. This is an indefinite contract since its subject matter is insufficiently described. But if Arkansas Grains ships No. 3 beans and Brown-Crummer accepts them, the indefiniteness is cured. This contract becomes enforceable when Brown-Crummer accepts the beans because Brown-Crummer's acceptance (partial performance) identifies the subject matter of the contract. [UCC 2-606]

In the following case, when the plaintiff bought chicken, he meant broiling and frying chickens—not stewing chickens. The defendant contended that any kind of chicken is chicken. This case illustrates how a federal district court applied New York law to decide the weighty question, "What is a chicken?"

BACKGROUND AND FACTS   *The plaintiff, a purchaser of fresh frozen chicken, sued for breach of contract, claiming that the goods sold did not correspond to the contract description.*

Plaintiff, a Swiss corporation, bought chicken from defendant, a New York sales corporation. The two contracts involved were negotiated predominantly through an exchange of cablegrams written for the most part in German but using the English word "chicken." Both contracts were identical except that there were different prices quoted for the 2½ to 3 pound chickens and the 1½ to 2 pound chickens. When the initial shipment arrived in Switzerland, plaintiff found that the birds were not young chickens suitable for broiling and frying but were stewing chickens or "fowl." Plaintiff protested, but more and more "birds" were shipped.

FRIGALIMENT IMPORTING CO. LTD. v. B.N.S. INT'L SALES CORP.
United States District Court of New York, 1960.
190 F.Supp. 116.

FRIENDLY, Circuit Judge.
*   *   *   *

The issue is, what is chicken? Plaintiff says "chicken" means a young chicken, suitable for broiling and frying. Defendant says "chicken" means any bird of that genus that meets contract specifications on weight and quality, including what it calls "stewing chicken" and plaintiff pejoratively terms "fowl." Dictionaries give both meanings, as well as some others not relevant here. To support its [claim], plaintiff sends a number of volleys over the net; defendant essays to return them and adds a few serves of its own. Assuming that both parties were acting in good faith, the case nicely illustrates Holmes' remark "that the making of a contract depends not on the agreement of two minds in one intention, but on the agreement of two sets of external signs—not on the parties' having *meant* the same thing but on their having *said* the same thing." The Path of the Law, in Collected Legal Papers, p. 178. *   *   *

Two contracts are in suit. In the first, dated May 2, 1957, defendant, a New York sales corporation, confirmed the sale to plaintiff, a Swiss corporation, of

"U.S. Fresh Frozen Chicken, Grade A, Government Inspected, Eviscerated 2½–3 lbs. and 1½–2 lbs. each

all chicken individually wrapped in cryovac, packed in secured fiber cartons or wooden boxes, suitable for export

75,000 lbs. 2½–3 lbs. .... @$33.00
25,000 lbs. 1½–2 lbs. .... @$36.50
per 100 lbs. FAS New York"

scheduled May 10, 1957

The second contract, also dated May 2, 1957, was identical save that only 50,000 lbs. of the heavier "chicken" were called for, the price of the smaller birds was $37 per 100 lbs., and shipment was scheduled for May 30. The initial shipment under the first contract was short but the balance was shipped on May 17. When the initial shipment arrived in Switzerland, plaintiff found, on May 28, that the 2½–3 lbs. birds were not young chicken suitable for broiling and frying but stewing chicken or "fowl"; indeed, many of the cartons and bags plainly so indicated. Protests ensued. Nevertheless, shipment under the second contract was made on May 29, the 2½–3 lbs. birds again being stewing chicken. Defendant stopped the transportation of these at Rotterdam.

This action followed. *   *   *

Since the word "chicken" standing alone is ambiguous, I turn first to see whether the contract itself offers any aid to its interpretation. Plaintiff says the 1½–2 lbs. birds necessarily had to be young chicken since the older birds do not come in that size, hence the 2½–3 lbs. birds must likewise be young. This is unpersuasive—a contract for "apples" of two different sizes could be filled with different kinds of apples even though only one species came in both sizes. Defendant notes that the contract called not simply for chicken but for "US Fresh Frozen Chicken, Grade A, Government Inspected." It says the contract thereby incorporated by reference the Department of Agriculture's regulations, which favor its interpretation; I shall return to this after reviewing plaintiff's other contentions.

[A]n exchange of cablegrams *   *   * preceded execution of the formal contracts. Plaintiff stresses that, although these and subsequent cables between plaintiff and defendant, which laid the basis for the additional quantities under the first and for all of the second contract, were predominantly in German, they used the English word "chicken"; it claims this was done because it understood "chicken" meant young chicken whereas the German word, "Huhn," included both "Brathuhn" (broilers) and "Suppenhuhn" (stewing chicken), and that defendant, whose officers were thoroughly conversant with German, should have realized this. *   *   *

Plaintiff's next contention is that there was a definite trade usage that "chicken" meant "young chicken." Defendant showed that it was only beginning in the poultry trade in 1957, thereby bringing itself within the principle that "when one of the parties is not a member of the trade or other circle, his acceptance of the standard must be made to appear" by proving either that he had actual knowledge of the usage or that the usage is "so generally known in the community that his actual individual knowledge of it may be inferred." Here there was no proof of actual knowledge of the alleged usage; indeed, it is quite plain that defendant's belief was to the contrary. In order to meet the alternative requirement, the law of New York demands a showing that "the usage is of so long continuance, so well established, so notorious, so universal and so reasonable in itself, as that the presumption is violent that the parties contracted with reference to it, and made it a part of their agreement."

Plaintiff endeavored to establish such a usage by the testimony of three witnesses and certain other evidence. Strasser, resident buyer in New York for a large chain of Swiss cooperatives, testified that "on chicken I would definitely understand a broiler." * * * Niesielowski, an officer of one of the companies that had furnished the stewing chicken to defendant testified that "chicken" meant "the male species of the poultry industry. That could be a broiler, a fryer or a roaster," but not a stewing chicken; * * * Dates, an employee of Urner-Barry Company, which publishes a daily market report on the poultry trade, gave it as his view that the trade meaning of "chicken" was "broilers and fryers." * * *

Defendant's witness Weininger, who operates a chicken eviscerating plant in New Jersey, testified "Chicken is everything except a goose, a duck, and a turkey." * * * Its witness Fox said that in the trade "chicken" would encompass all the various classifications. Sadina, who conducts a food inspection service, testified that he would consider any bird coming within the classes of "chicken" in the Department of Agriculture's regulations to be a chicken:

"*Chickens.* The following are the various classes of chickens:

(a) Broiler or fryer . . .   (d) Stag . . .
(b) Roaster . . .   (e) Hen or stewing chicken or fowl . . .
(c) Capon . . .   (f) Cock or old rooster . . ,"

Defendant argues, as previously noted, that the contract incorporated these regulations by reference.

* * * *

When all the evidence is reviewed, it is clear that defendant believed it could comply with the contracts by delivering stewing chicken in the 2½–3 lbs. size.

* * *

[P]laintiff has the burden of showing that "chicken" was used in the narrower rather than in the broader sense, and this it has not sustained.

The plaintiff's complaint was dismissed. The court held that plaintiff failed to sustain the burden of proving that the word "chicken" in the contract referred only to chickens suitable for broiling and frying and did not include stewing chickens.

JUDGMENT AND REMEDY

Output and Requirements Contracts The UCC also validates output and requirements contracts.[11] **Output contracts** are agreements to sell all production during a specified period to a buyer. **Requirements contracts** are agreements to buy all production needs, or "requirements," during a specified period from a seller. These contracts do not specifically state the quantity of output or requirements at the time of contract formation, but the quantity may be definitely ascertainable after the time of contract formation, within reasonable limits. The courts have a reasonably certain basis for giving an appropriate remedy if either type of contract is breached.

11. UCC 2-306(1): A term which measures the quantity by the output of the seller or the requirements of the buyer means such actual output or requirements as may occur in good faith, except that no quantity unreasonably disproportionate to any stated estimate or to any normal or otherwise comparable prior output or requirements may be tendered or demanded.

Communication

A third element for an effective offer is communication, resulting in the offeree's knowledge of the offer. One cannot agree to a bargain without knowing that the bargain exists. Suppose Emerman advertises a reward for the return of her lost dog. Baldwin, not knowing of the reward, finds the dog and returns it to Emerman. Baldwin cannot recover the reward because he did not know it was offered.[12]

Rewards   A reward is a unilateral contract. It can be accepted only by performance. An essential element to the reward contract is that the one who claims the reward must have known that it was offered. Otherwise there can be no contract. This rule follows because it is impossible to have an acceptance under contract law unless the offeree knows that the offer exists. The following case is one of the classic reward cases in the common law.

---

12.   A few states will allow recovery of the reward but not on contract principles. Since Emerman wanted her dog returned, and Baldwin returned it, these few states would allow Baldwin to recover on the basis that it would be unfair to deny him the reward just because he did not know about it.

GLOVER v. JEWISH
WAR VETERANS OF
THE UNITED STATES,
POST NO. 58
Municipal Court of Appeals for
the District of Columbia, 1949.
68 A.2d 233.

BACKGROUND AND FACTS   *The Jewish War Veterans of the United States offered a reward of $500 in a newspaper "to the person or persons furnishing information resulting in the apprehension and conviction of the persons guilty of the murder of Maurice L. Bernstein." A day or so after the notice appeared, one of the men suspected in the crime was arrested and the police received information that the other murderer was the "boyfriend" of a daughter of Mary Glover, the plaintiff and claimant in the present case. That evening, the police visited Mary Glover. She provided names and addresses and possible locations where her daughter and the suspect might be found. The suspect was arrested at one of the places suggested by Glover, and all suspects were subsequently convicted of the crime.*

Glover claimed the $500 reward from the Jewish War Veterans, arguing that the information she gave to the police officers led to the arrest and conviction of the murderers. But there was some question as to whether she was entitled to the reward. At the time she gave the information to the police officers, she did not know that any reward had been offered for information leading to the arrest and conviction of the guilty persons. In fact, she did not learn about the reward until several days afterward. The trial court denied Glover the $500 reward. The appellate court reviewed the law of contracts concerning rewards.

CLAGETT, Associate Judge.

*   *   *   *

The issue determinative of this appeal is whether a person giving information leading to the arrest of a murderer without any knowledge that a reward has been offered for such information by a nongovernmental organization is entitled to collect the reward. The trial court decided the question in the negative and instructed the jury to return a verdict for defendant.

*   *   *   *

We have concluded that the trial court correctly instructed the jury to return a verdict for defendant. While there is some conflict in the decided cases on the subject of rewards, most of such conflict has to do with rewards offered by governmental officers and agencies. So far as rewards offered by private individuals and organizations are concerned, there is little conflict on the rule that questions regarding such rewards are to be based upon the law of contracts.

Since it is clear that the question is one of contract law, it follows that, at least so far as private rewards are concerned, *there can be no contract unless the claimant when giving the desired information knew of the offer of the reward and acted with the intention of accepting such offer* (emphasis added); otherwise the claimant gives the information not in the expectation of receiving a reward but rather out of a sense of public duty or other motive unconnected with the reward. "In the nature of the case," according to Professor Williston, "it is impossible for an offeree actually to assent to an offer unless he knows of its existence." After stating that courts in some jurisdictions have decided to the contrary, Williston adds, "It is impossible, however, to find in such a case [that is, in a case holding to the contrary] the elements generally held in England and America necessary for the formation of a contract. If it is clear the offeror intended to pay for the services, it is equally certain that the person rendering the service performed it voluntarily and not in return for a promise to pay. If one person expects to buy, and the other to give, there can hardly be found mutual assent. These views are supported by the great weight of authority, and in most jurisdictions a plaintiff in the sort of case under discussion is denied recovery."

The American Law Institute in its Restatement of the Law of Contracts follows the same rule, thus: "It is impossible that there should be an acceptance unless the offeree knows of the existence of the offer." The Restatement gives the following illustration of the rule just stated: "A offers a reward for information leading to the arrest and conviction of a criminal. B, in ignorance of the offer, gives information leading to his arrest and later, with knowledge of the offer and intent to accept it, gives other information necessary for conviction. There is no contract."

We have considered the reasoning in state decisions following the contrary rule. Mostly, as we have said, they involve rewards offered by governmental bodies and in general are based upon the theory that the government is benefited equally whether or not the claimant gives the information with knowledge of the reward and that therefore the government should pay in any event. We believe that the rule adopted by Professor Williston and the Restatement and in the majority of the cases is the better reasoned rule and therefore we adopt it. We believe furthermore that this rule is particularly applicable in the present case since the claimant did not herself contact the authorities and volunteer information but gave information only upon questioning by the police officers and did not claim any knowledge of the guilt or innocence of the criminal but only knew where he probably could be located.

JUDGMENT AND REMEDY

The trial court judgment was affirmed. The Jewish War Veterans did not have to pay the reward to Glover. No contract existed because Glover's performance was not induced by the offer as she had no knowledge of the offer.

COMMENTS

In this case, the court indicated that there is some conflict concerning rewards offered by government officers and agencies. Some courts provide a remedy when a government body offers a reward on the theory that the government is benefited equally whether or not the claimant gave it the information while knowing about the reward. The public good is served regardless. Another rationale is that knowledge of government actions is imputed. Whichever theory the courts use, the result is the same—the government pays the reward.

TERMINATION OF THE OFFER

The communication of an effective offer to an offeree creates a power in the offeree to transform the offer into a binding legal obligation (a contract). This power of acceptance, however, does not continue forever. It can be terminated by either *operation of law* or *action of the parties.*

Termination by Operation of Law

The power in the offeree to transform the offer into a binding, legal obligation can be terminated by operation of the law through the following:

1. Lapse of time.
2. Destruction of the subject matter of the contract.
3. Death or incompetency of the offeror or the offeree.
4. Supervening illegality of the proposed contract.

Lapse of Time   An offer terminates when the period of time specified in the offer has passed. For example, suppose Anna offers to sell her boat to Bob if he accepts within twenty days. Bob must accept within the twenty-day period or the offer will lapse (terminate). The period of time specified in an offer begins to run when the offer is actually received by the offeree, not when it is sent or drawn up. When the offer has been delayed, the period begins to run from the date the offeree would have received the offer, but only if the offeree knew or should have known the offer was delayed.[13] For example, if Anna had used improper postage when mailing the offer to Bob, but Bob knew Anna had used improper postage, the offer would lapse twenty days after the day Bob would ordinarily have received the offer had Anna used proper postage.

If no time for acceptance is specified in the offer, the offer terminates at the end of a *reasonable* period of time. A reasonable period of time is determined by the subject matter of the contract, business and market conditions, and other relevant circumstances. An offer to sell farm produce, for example, will terminate sooner than an offer to sell farm equipment because farm produce is perishable and subject to greater fluctuations in market value. The question of reasonable period of time arises in the next case.

_____

13.   Restatement, Second, Contracts, Section 49.

CORCORAN v. LYLE SCHOOL DISTRICT NO. 406, KLICKITAT COUNTY, WASHINGTON

Court of Appeals of Washington, Division 3, Panel Four, 1978.
20 Wash.App. 621, 581 P.2d 185

BACKGROUND AND FACTS   *Bradley T. Corcoran, plaintiff, appealed his dismissal from the Lyle School District for his failure to accept his employment contract for the 1976–1977 school year in a timely manner. Corcoran is a certified teacher. He received an unsigned copy of his proposed employment contract on June 4, 1976. It provided: "If this contract is not signed by said employee and returned to the Secretary of the school district on or before June 14, 1976, the Board reserves the right to withdraw this offer."*

In addition, the superintendent of schools personally called Corcoran's attention to the time provision contained within the contract. At that time, Corcoran informed the superintendent that he was considering other employment. In any event, Corcoran did not return the contract with his signature on it until June 16. Two days later, he received a letter from the superintendent stating that the school board had decided not to accept any contracts returned after the June 14 deadline. Therefore, Corcoran would not be rehired for the forthcoming school year.

McINTURFF, Judge.

* * * *

Beyond the statutory rights contained in the continuing contract law, the relationship between the school district and its employees is a contractual one governed by general principles of law. *It is well settled that an offeror may require acceptance within a specified reasonable time and that failure of the offeree to so accept constitutes a rejection of the offer.* [Emphasis added.] By his failure to timely return the contract in the face of express written and personal notice that such conduct could result in the school board's rejection of its offer, Mr. Corcoran effectively waived his continuing contract rights.

While certified teachers who have not been given notice of non-retention are entitled to contracts containing terms and conditions substantially identical to those of the previous year, they may not desire such employment. If they fail to accept or reject those contracts within a reasonable time, school districts should be released from their obligations to rehire them under their former contracts. Unless a reasonable contract-return deadline is established and enforced, school districts, as a practical matter, may not know until classes begin how many of their retained teachers will return to the classroom each fall.

Mr. Corcoran does not contend the 10-day contractual limit was unreasonable, nor has he alleged any circumstances which would have prevented him from returning his signed contract within the time established. Therefore, we need not determine the reasonableness of the 10-day return provision.

* * * [B]y his own conduct Mr. Corcoran foreclosed the potential contractual relationship between himself and the school district. * * *

Judgment of the lower court was affirmed. The school district was not required to rehire Corcoran.

JUDGMENT AND REMEDY

Destruction of the Subject Matter An offer is automatically terminated if the specific subject matter of the offer is destroyed before the offer is accepted. For example, if Watts offers to sell her race horse to Teagle, but the horse dies before Teagle can accept, the offer is automatically terminated. Likewise, an offer to sell a particular lathe is terminated if the lathe is destroyed in a fire before the offer is accepted.

Death or Incompetency of the Offeror or Offeree An offeree's power of acceptance is

terminated when the offeror or offeree dies or is deprived of legal capacity to enter into the proposed contract.[14] An offer is personal to both parties and cannot pass to the decedent's heirs, guardian, or estate. Furthermore, this rule applies whether or not the other party had notice of the death or incompetency of the party. For example, on June 4, Manne offers to sell Clark a rowboat for $300, telling Clark that he, Manne, needs the answer by June 20. On June 10, Manne

---

14. Restatement, Second, Contracts, Section 48.

dies. On June 18, Clark informs the executor of Manne's estate that he has accepted the offer. The executor can refuse to sell the rowboat because the death of the offeror has terminated the offer.

There is an exception to the rule that the death of either the offeror or the offeree before acceptance terminates an offer. The exception applies to **irrevocable offers**—offers that legally cannot be withdrawn by the offeror once made. An *option* is an example of an irrevocable offer. Although some disagree, many legal scholars believe that the exception also applies to *firm offers* (irrevocable under the UCC). The issue is discussed in detail later in this chapter.

Supervening Illegality of the Proposed Contract   A statute or court decision that makes an offer illegal will automatically terminate the offer. If Barker offers to loan Jackson $20,000 at 15 percent annually, and a usury statute is enacted prohibiting loans at interest rates greater than 14 percent before Jackson can accept, the offer is automatically terminated. (If in the above hypothetical case, the usury statute had been passed after Jackson accepted the offer, a valid contract would have been formed, but the contract may be unenforceable.)

Termination by Action of the Parties

The power of the offeree to transform the offer into a binding, legal obligation can usually be terminated by any of the following actions:

1. Revocation of the offer by the offeror.
2. Rejection of the offer by the offeree.
3. Counteroffer by the offeree.

Revocation of the offer by the offeror   Revocation is the withdrawal of the offer by the offeror. An offer may be terminated by the offeror if a revocation is communicated to the offeree before the offeree accepts. Revocation may be accomplished by expressly repudiating the offer (such as "I withdraw my previous offer of October 17") or by acts inconsistent with the existence of the offer, which are made known to the offeree.

The revocation must be communicated to the offeree before acceptance, or the revocation will be ineffective and a valid contract will be formed. The general rule followed by most states is that a revocation is effective only upon actual receipt of the revocation by the offeree or offeree's agent. Therefore, a letter of revocation that is deposited in a mailbox on April 1 and that arrives at the offeree's residence or place of business on April 3 becomes effective on April 3. If the offeree accepts the offer on April 2, a valid contract will be formed, and the contract will be enforceable in a court of law.

Alternatively, communication to the offeree exists if the offeree indirectly discovers that the offer is revoked. This indirect discovery may occur when a third person tells the offeree that the offer has been revoked prior to the offeree's acceptance, or when the offeree learns that the subject matter of the contract has been sold to a third party.

Offers made to the general public may be revoked by communicating a revocation in the same manner that the offer was originally communicated. For example, suppose Macy's offers a $10,000 reward for anyone giving information leading to the apprehension of the persons who burglarized Macy's downtown store. The offer is published in three local papers and in four papers in neighboring communities. In order to revoke the offer, Macy's must publish the revocation in all seven papers for the same number of days as it published the offer. The revocation will then be accessible to the general public, even if some particular offeree does not know about it.

Irrevocable Offers   Although most offers are revocable, certain offers can be made irrevocable. Three such types of irrevocable offers deserve discussion. They are:

1. Option contracts.
2. Firm offers under the UCC.
3. Offeree's detrimental reliance on the offer (promissory estoppel).

Option Contracts   As a general rule, offerors may revoke their offers even if they expressly agreed to hold them open for a specified period of time.

When an offeror promises to hold an offer open for a *specified* period of time, however, and the offeree pays for the promise (gives consideration), an **option contract** is created. An option contract takes away the offeror's power to revoke the offer for the period of time specified in the option. If no time is specified, then a reasonable period of time is implied.

For example, suppose Brennan offers to sell one hundred shares of stock in Texas Instruments to Columbus for $189 per share. Brennan promises to keep the offer open for thirty days. After fourteen days Brennan calls Columbus on the telephone and says that the offer is revoked. If Columbus has not given any consideration (say $25 in cash) for the offer up to this time, Brennan may revoke the offer despite his promise to keep it open for thirty days. But if Columbus has given some consideration for the offer, Brennan must hold it open for the stated thirty days. This particular option contract (for the purchase of common stock) is becoming increasingly popular, and similar options are traded publicly on numerous exchanges.

When the offer is in the form of an option and the decedent was not required to perform an essential part of the contract, the offer survives the death or incompetency of the offeror.[15] For example, assume Vendrick executes an option to Carney entitling Carney to purchase Vendrick's hundred-acre ranch in Costa Rica. Carney pays $750 for the option, but before she can exercise it, Vendrick dies. Carney can still exercise the option against Vendrick's estate, since Vendrick is not required to perform the act of conveying the ranch to Carney personally. In sum, option contract rights and duties are not discharged by the death of either party unless performance is of a personal nature—that is, consists of personal services.

Firm Offers   Under the UCC, certain offers may be irrevocable even if no consideration is given. These are called **firm offers.**[16] If a merchant makes a written, signed offer to buy or sell goods and states that the offer is not revocable, the offer

cannot be revoked regardless of the lack of consideration. The offer will remain open for the period of time specified in the offer or, if no time is specified, for a reasonable period; but the period of irrevocability cannot exceed three months (unless it is paid for). Note the various elements necessary for a firm offer:

1. The offer must be for the purchase or sale of goods.
2. The offer must be made by a merchant dealing in those goods.
3. The offer must be written and signed by the merchant.
4. The offer must give assurance that it will be held open for some period of time.

Detrimental Reliance on the Offer   Increasingly, courts are refusing to allow an offeror to revoke an offer when the offeree has changed position in justifiable reliance on the offer. In such cases, revocation is considered unjust to the offeree. Consider an example. Feinberg has worked for Pfeiffer for thirty-five years. Pfeiffer tells her that whenever she quits, she will be paid $150 a month for the rest of her life. There is no indication by Pfeiffer that she should quit now. In fact, she works for a couple more years. She quits and Pfeiffer starts sending her checks for $150 every month. Five years later, Pfeiffer dies and his son takes over the business. The son says the $150 checks are ridiculous and attempts to avoid the promise. He will not be able to do so because Feinberg has been relying on the promise to pay her $150 a month. Had the promise not been made, she would have rearranged her affairs to obtain other retirement funds. This is a case of a detrimental reliance on a promise, which therefore cannot be revoked. This situation is normally called **promissory estoppel. To estop** means to bar or impede, or to preclude. Thus, promissory estoppel means that the promisor (the offeror) is barred or prevented from revoking the offer, in this case because the offeree has already changed her actions in reliance on the offer. We will cover the doctrine of promissory estoppel again in Chapter 8.

Another situation in which an offer becomes irrevocable is when there is *partial performance*

15. Restatement, Second, Contracts, Section 37.
16. UCC 2-205.

by the offeree in response to a *unilateral* offer prior to revocation, thereby causing detrimental reliance on the part of the offeree. The offer of a unilateral contract invites acceptance only by full performance or forbearance; merely promising to perform does not constitute acceptance. Obviously, injustice can result if an offeree expends time and money in partial performance, and then the offeror revokes the offer before performance is complete. Consequently, many courts will not allow the offeror to revoke after the offeree has performed some substantial part of his or her duties.[17] In effect, partial performance renders the offer irrevocable, giving the original offeree reasonable time to complete performance. Of course, when performance is complete, a unilateral contract exists.

Rejection of the Offer by the Offeree   The offer may be rejected by the offeree, in which case the offer is terminated. Any subsequent attempt by the offeree to accept will be construed as a new offer, giving the original offeror (now the offeree) the power of acceptance. A rejection is ordinarily accomplished by words or conduct evidencing an intent to reject the offer.

As in the case of revocation of the offer, rejection is effective only when actually received by the offeror or the offeror's agent.

Suppose you offer to sell Procter & Gamble twenty-five tons of linseed oil at 35 cents per gallon. Procter & Gamble could reject your offer by writing or telephoning you, expressly rejecting the offer (perhaps by saying, "We are sufficiently stocked in linseed oil and do not need any more"). Alternatively, the company could mail your offer back to you, evidencing an intent to reject the offer. Or it could offer to buy the oil at 20.3 cents per gallon, which would operate as a counteroffer, necessarily rejecting the original offer.

Merely inquiring about the offer does not constitute rejection. For example, a friend offers to buy your bicycle for $75. If you respond, "Is this your best offer?" or "Will you pay me $100 for it?" a reasonable person would conclude that you did not reject the offer but merely made an inquiry for further consideration of the offer. You can still accept and bind your friend to the $75 purchase price. When the offeree merely inquires as to the firmness of the offer, there is no reason to presume that he or she intends to reject it.

Some responses are borderline in nature. For example, if you respond to your friend's offer with, "The price seems low; I'll bet you can do better than that," it could be argued that you are inquiring about the offer or rejecting it.

Counteroffer by the Offeree   A counteroffer is usually, but not always, a rejection of the original offer and simultaneously the making of a new offer. Suppose Stewart offers to sell his home to Twardy for $70,000. Twardy responds, "Your offer is too high. I'll offer to purchase your house for $65,000." Twardy's response is termed a counteroffer, since it terminates Stewart's offer to sell at $70,000 and creates a new offer by Twardy to purchase at $65,000. At common law, the *mirror image* rule requires the offeree's acceptance to match the offeror's offer exactly— to mirror the offer. Any change in, or addition to, the terms of the original offer automatically terminates that offer and substitutes the counteroffer, which, of course, need not be accepted. The original offeror can, however, accept the terms of the counteroffer and create a valid contract.

Variance in terms between the offer and the offeree's acceptance, violating the mirror image rule, has caused considerable problems in commercial transactions. This is particularly true in contracts for the sale of goods where different standardized purchase forms of the seller and buyer are exchanged in the process of offer and acceptance. Seldom do the terms of both purchase forms match each other exactly. This phenomenon has been called the "battle of the forms" because of the problem of whose form will prevail.

Dealing with contracts for the sale of goods, the UCC in Sec. 2-207 has addressed this problem by providing that a contract is formed if the offeree makes a definite expression of acceptance, even though the terms of the acceptance

---

17.   Restatement, Second, Contracts, Section 25.

modify or add to the terms of the original offer.[18] *Between merchants*, the new terms become part of the contract automatically unless:

1. The original offer expressly required acceptance of its terms.
2. The new or changed terms materially alter the contract.
3. The offeror rejects the new or changed terms.

The Code further provides that if one or both parties are nonmerchants, the contract is formed according to the terms of the offer, not according to the additional terms of the acceptance.

It is possible for an offeree to make a new offer without intending to reject the original offer. In such a case two offers exist, each capable of acceptance. To illustrate, suppose Frank offers to sell his bicycle for $100. Irene's response is, "I do not have $100 but will try to raise that sum. I do have $75 and will offer to purchase your bicycle for that price." Since the offeree did not reject the $100 offer, that offer remains effective. But the offeree did offer to purchase the bicycle for $75. Thus, two offers exist, and the first to be accepted binds the parties to a contract for that amount.

ACCEPTANCE

Acceptance is a voluntary act (either words or conduct) by the offeree that shows assent (agreement) to the terms of an offer. The acceptance must ordinarily be made in the manner requested by the offeror. This is called *express authorized means of acceptance*. In addition, the acceptance must be unequivocal and communicated to the offeror.

Who Can Accept?

Generally, a third person cannot interpose himself or herself as a substitute for the offeree and effectively accept the offer. After all, the identity of the offeree is as much a condition of a bargaining offer as any other term contained therein. Thus, except in certain special circumstances to be discussed, only the person to whom the offer is made can accept the offer and create a binding contract. For example, Jones makes an offer to Hanley. Hanley is not interested, but Smith accepts the offer. No contract is formed.

Exceptions The special circumstances in which a third party can accept an offer in place of the offeree are as follows:

1. If the offer is an option contract, the right to exercise the option is generally considered a contract right. As such, it is assignable or transferable to third persons (with exceptions—see Chapter 13).
2. If the offeree is an agent for an undisclosed principal, the acceptance may be made by the principal and will bind both the principal and the offeror (see Chapter 35).

When the Offer Is Made to Two or More Persons If an offer is made to two or more persons, it must be accepted by all of them. If individual offers are made to two or more persons individually, then contracts are created only with those persons who accept the offer.

Unequivocal Acceptance

In order to exercise the power of acceptance effectively, the offeree must accept unequivocally. If the acceptance is subject to new conditions, or if the terms of the acceptance change the original offer, the acceptance may be considered a counteroffer that implicitly rejects the original offer. An acceptance may be unequivocal even though the offeree expresses dissatisfaction with the contract. For example, "I accept the goods, but I wish I could have gotten a better price" will operate as an effective acceptance. So, too, will "I accept, but can you shave the price?" On the other hand, the statement "I accept the goods, but only if I can pay on ninety days' credit" is not an unequivocal acceptance and operates as a counteroffer, rejecting the original offer.

---

18. For example, Sylvestre v. Minnesota, 289 Minn. 142, 214 N.W.2d 658 (1973). See UCC 2-207.

Certain conditions, when added to an acceptance, will not qualify the acceptance sufficiently to reject the offer. Suppose Childs offers to sell her sixty-five-acre cotton farm to Sharif. Sharif replies, "I accept your offer to sell the farm, provided you can supply good title." This condition (providing a good title) does not make the acceptance equivocal. A warranty of good title is normally implied in every offer for the sale of land, so the condition does not add any new or different terms to the offer.

Or suppose that in response to an offer to sell a motorcycle, the offeree replies, "I accept; please send written contract." The offeree has requested a written contract but has not made it a condition for acceptance. Therefore, the acceptance is effective without the written contract. However, if the offeree replies, "I accept if you send a written contract," the acceptance is expressly conditioned on the request for a writing, and the statement is not an acceptance but a counteroffer. (Notice how important *each* word is!) As noted above, under the UCC, an acceptance is still valid even if terms are added. The additional terms are then simply treated as proposals or additions to the contract.[19]

Silence as Acceptance

Ordinarily, silence cannot be acceptance, even if the offeror states, "By your silence and inaction you will be deemed to have accepted this offer." This general rule applies because an offeree should not be put under a burden or liability to act affirmatively in order to reject an offer. No consideration has passed to the offeree to impose such a liability.

On the other hand, silence can operate as an acceptance when an offeree takes the benefit of offered services even though he or she had an opportunity to reject them and knew that they were offered with the expectation of compensation. Suppose Holmes watches while her daughter is given piano lessons. The piano instructor has not been requested to give the daughter lessons but plans to give a series of fifteen. Holmes knows the instructor expects to be paid but lets the lessons continue nonetheless. Here, her silence constitutes an acceptance, and she is bound to pay a reasonable value for the lessons. This rule applies only to services and goods for which the offeree has received a benefit.

Silence can also operate as acceptance when the offeree has had prior dealings with the offeror. To illustrate: Brodsky, a salesman, has previously ordered goods from Morales and paid without notifying Morales of his acceptance. Whenever Brodsky receives a shipment from Morales, he sells it and simply sends a check to Morales. Only if the goods are defective does he notify Morales. The last shipment, however, has been neither paid for nor rejected. Nonetheless, Brodsky is bound on a contract and must pay Morales for this last shipment of goods.[20]

In the past, at common law, silence could constitute acceptance in the following situation: Books or magazines are sent to an individual through the mails. The individual did not order the books or magazines and is under no duty to reship them to the seller. However, if he or she uses the books or magazines, acceptance is established, and he or she must pay reasonable value for them. Note that silence does not constitute an acceptance unless the receiver exercises control over the goods. This common law rule of contract law has been changed by statute. The Postal Reorganization Act of 1970 provides that unsolicited merchandise sent by U.S. mail may be retained, used, discarded, or disposed of in any manner deemed appropriate, without the individual incurring any obligation to the sender.[21] In addition, the mailing of unordered merchandise (except for free samples) constitutes an unfair trade practice and is not permitted. (Exceptions are mailings by charitable agencies and those made by mistake.)

Another situation involving this issue of acceptance is that in which the offeree solicits the offer. In such a case the offeree is placed under a *duty to speak*, meaning to reject. Failure to reject operates as acceptance by silence. For ex-

---

19. Restatement, Second, Contracts, Section 61 and UCC 2-207.

20. Restatement, Second, Contracts, Section 72.

21. 39 U.S.C.A. § 3009.

ample, Able tells Sallor she is interested in purchasing a complete textbook on business law for approximately $25. Sallor responds that he has just the book Able is looking for, published by West and costing $22. Sallor further informs Able that he has sent the book to Able and unless he hears from Able to the contrary in thirty days, he will bill Able. Since Able solicited Sallor's offer, Able has a duty to reject, and her failure to do so during the thirty-day period will constitute an acceptance.

A similar situation occurs with such organizations as the Book-of-the-Month Club. Once an individual has agreed to this kind of offer, merchandise is shipped periodically (usually every month) unless the customer sends a card indicating that he or she does not want the merchandise. Failure to reject the offered merchandise in this manner operates as acceptance by silence.

To summarize, silence *alone* is never equivalent to acceptance. But combined with prior dealings that place the offeree under a duty to speak, silence often does operate as acceptance.

Communication of Acceptance

Whether the offeror must be notified of the acceptance depends on the nature of the contract. In a unilateral contract, notification or communication is generally not necessary. Since a unilateral contract calls for the full performance of some act, acceptance is not complete until the act has been fully performed. Therefore, notice of acceptance is unnecessary. To illustrate: Beta offers to pay Gamma $150 to paint Beta's garage. Gamma can accept only by painting the garage. Once the garage is completely painted (and hence the acceptance is complete), notification of the acceptance is superfluous. Exceptions do exist. When the offeror requests notice of acceptance or has no adequate means of determining whether the requested act has been performed, or when the law requires such notice of acceptance, then notice is necessary.[22]

In a bilateral contract, *communication* of acceptance is necessary because acceptance is in the form of a promise (not performance), and the contract is formed when the promise is made (rather than when the act is performed). The offeree must use reasonable efforts to communicate the acceptance to the offeror. In a bilateral contract, however, *notification* of acceptance is not necessary if the offer dispenses with the requirement. In addition, if the offer can be accepted by silence, no communication or notification is necessary. (Communication refers to the legal test of proper dispatch, whereas notification is the actual notice, in fact, to the other party.)

Under the UCC, an order or other offer to buy goods for prompt shipment may be accepted by either a promise to ship or by actual shipment.[23]

Consider an example. Peters receives a telegram that he is to ship certain goods to Johnson. The UCC provides that Peters can accept by either promptly shipping the goods or sending a telegram to Johnson, saying that he is going to ship the goods. (Obviously, if the shipment will take a considerable amount of time, Peters would be wise to telegraph Johnson that the goods are in transit.)

Mode and Timeliness of Acceptance in Bilateral Contracts

The general rule is that an acceptance is timely if it is effective within the duration of the offer. Problems arise, however, when the parties involved are not dealing face to face. In such cases, the offeree must use an authorized mode of communication. Acceptance takes effect, thus completing formation of the contract, at the time that communication is sent by the mode expressly or impliedly authorized by the offeror. This is the so-called acceptance-upon-dispatch rule, which the majority of courts uphold. (Note that this is an exception to the normal rule of bilateral contracts that acceptance requires a completed communication.) What becomes an issue is the *authorized* means of communicating the acceptance. Authorized means can be either expressly stated in the offer or impliedly authorized by facts or by law. In any case, the acceptance becomes effective at the time that it is sent by an author-

---

22. UCC 2–206(2).

23. UCC 2–206(1)(b).

ized means of communication, whether or not the offeror receives that communication.[24]

When an offeror specifies how acceptance should be sent (for example, by first-class mail or by telegram), *express authorization* is said to exist, and the contract is not valid unless the offeree uses that specified means of acceptance. Moreover, both offeror and offeree are bound in contract the moment such means of acceptance are employed. Thus, if telegraph is expressly authorized as the means for acceptance, a contract is established as soon as the offeree gives his or her message to Western Union. Even if Western Union for some reason fails to deliver the message, the contract still exists.

Most offerors do not specify expressly the means by which the offeree is to accept. Thus, the common law and statutes recognize what are called implied authorized means of acceptance. In the absence of expressly authorized means, three implied authorized means have been designated, as follows:

1.   The means chosen by the offeror to make the offer implies that the offeree is authorized to use the *same* or a *faster* means for acceptance.
2.   When two parties are at a distance, unless otherwise inferred, *mailing* (the so-called depository rule) is impliedly authorized.[25]
3.   Under the UCC, acceptance of an offer for sale of goods can be made by any *medium* that is *reasonable* under the circumstances.[26]

Any acceptance sent by means not expressly or impliedly authorized is often not effective until it is received by the offeror.[27] To illustrate authorized means of acceptance, note the following cases:

1.   On January 1, Jones makes an offer to sell Smith his motorcycle for $450, stipulating that Smith should send acceptance by telegram. On January 2, Jones mails Smith a letter of revocation that is received by Smith at noon on January 4. On January 3, Smith delivers to Western Union his telegram of acceptance. The telegram is missent and is not received by Jones until January 5. Are Jones and Smith bound in contract? The answer is yes. Telegram was the expressly stated means of acceptance in the offer; therefore, acceptance is effective the moment Smith delivers his acceptance to Western Union on January 3. A revocation is not effective until it is received by the offeree, in this case on January 4. This is subsequent to the acceptance, and the revocation is ineffective.

2.   On January 1, Jones by telegram offers to sell Smith his motorcycle for $450. The offer contains no expressly stated means for Smith to make his acceptance. The telegram is received by Smith the same day it is sent. On January 2, Smith delivers his acceptance to Western Union. The telegram is lost and is never received by Jones. Jones sells the motorcycle to Green on January 20, believing Smith was not interested in his offer. Can Smith hold Jones liable for breach of contract? The answer is yes. Although the offer did not expressly state a means for Smith's acceptance, telegraph was impliedly authorized. The court here could use either the common law "same or faster means" rule of implied authorization or the UCC "reasonable medium" rule dealing with the sale of goods. Either way, Smith formed a contract with Jones on January 2.

---

24.   Restatement, Second, Contracts, Section 30 provides that an offer invites acceptance "by any medium reasonable in the circumstances", unless the offer is specific about the means of acceptance. Under Section 65, a medium is reasonable if it is one used by the offeror or one customary in similar transactions, unless the offeree knows of circumstances that would argue against the reasonableness of a particular medium (e.g., the need for speed because of rapid price changes). Acceptance by mail is ordinarily reasonable where the parties are negotiating at a distance even though the offer was transmitted by telephone or telegraph. However, care must be taken to insure a safe transmission. Under Section 66, "[a]n acceptance by mail or otherwise from a distance is not operative when dispatched, unless it is properly addressed and such other precautions taken as are ordinarily observed to insure safe transmission of similar messages." See also UCC 2-206(1)(a).

25.   Adams v. Lindsell, 106 Eng.Rep. 250 (K.B. 1818).

26.   UCC 2–206(1)(a) changes the common law rule from "authorized means" to "a reasonable medium."

27.   An exception to this rule is given in Restatement, Second, Contracts, Section 67. Under the Restatement, an acceptance is effective upon dispatch even though the means of transmission is improper or the offeree fails to use care in insuring safe transmission (e.g., wrong address or postage) if (1) the acceptance sent is timely and (2) the offeror receives the communication within the same period of time that a properly transmitted acceptance would have arrived.

There are three basic exceptions to the rule that a contract is formed when acceptance is sent by authorized means:

1. If the acceptance is not properly dispatched, it usually will not be effective until received by the offeror.[28] For example, if mail is the authorized means for acceptance, the offeree's letter must be properly addressed and have the correct postage.

2. The offeror can specifically condition his or her offer on receipt of acceptance by a certain time. For example, an offer may be worded thusly: "Acceptance is not binding unless received by the offeror in her office by 5:00 P.M. on May 1." In this case it is immaterial how the offeree sends acceptance, as the acceptance is effective only when received.

3. Sometimes an offeree sends a rejection first, then later changes his or her mind and sends an acceptance. Obviously, this chain of events could cause confusion and even detriment to the offeror, depending on whether the rejection or the acceptance arrived first. Because of this, the law cancels the rule of acceptance upon dispatch, and the first communication to be received by the offeror determines whether a contract is formed.

QUESTIONS AND CASE PROBLEMS

1. As a bank officer, you have been given the responsibility of purchasing word processing equipment. On May 6, the ABC Manufacturing Corporation sends you a letter offering to sell your bank some word processing equipment at a price of $10,000, to be shipped via LM Truck Lines. The letter states that the offer is to remain open until May 20. On May 12, you write ABC a letter stating, "Offer appears a little high; I am sure you can do better. I'll need presidential approval for the $10,000 offer. I have authority to purchase word processing equipment for $8,500 and will

buy your products at that price." ABC receives this letter on May 16. On May 15, the president of your bank approves the $10,000 purchase. On that same date, ABC sends you a letter revoking its offer. The letter of revocation is received at your bank at 11:00 A.M. on May 19. On May 19 at 11:15 A.M. you send ABC the following telegram: "Accept your offer for $10,000." Because of a delay by the telegraph company, this letter is not delivered until May 21.

    (a) Discuss the legal effect of ABC's revocation sent on May 15.

    (b) Discuss fully the legal effect of your response sent on May 12.

    (c) Discuss whether your bank has a contract in light of the fact that the telegram was not delivered until May 21.

2. Beyer writes Sallor and inquires how much Sallor is asking for a specific forty-acre tract of land Sallor owns. In a letter received by Beyer, Sallor states, "I will not take less than $60,000 for the forty-acre tract as specified." Beyer immediately sends Sallor a telegram stating, "I accept your offer for $60,000." Discuss whether Beyer can hold Sallor to a contract for the land.

3. Smith, operating a sole proprietorship, has a large piece of used equipment for sale. He offers to sell the equipment to Barry for $10,000. Discuss the legal effect of the following events on the offer.

    (a) Smith dies prior to Barry's acceptance, and at the time Barry accepts, she is unaware of Smith's death.

    (b) The night before Barry accepts, fire destroys the equipment.

    (c) Barry pays $100 for a thirty-day option to purchase the equipment. During this period Smith dies and Barry accepts the offer, knowing of Smith's death.

    (d) Barry pays $100 for a thirty-day option to purchase the equipment. During this period Barry dies, and Barry's estate accepts Smith's offer within the stipulated time period.

4. Perez sees an advertisement in the newspaper that the ABC Corporation has for sale a two-volume set of *How to Make Repairs around the House* for $12.95. All Perez has to do is send in a card requesting delivery of the books for a thirty-day trial period of examination. If he does not ship the books back within thirty days of delivery, ABC will bill him for $12.95. Discuss whether or not Perez and ABC have a contract under either of the following circumstances.

    (a) Perez sends in the card and receives the books in the U.S. mail. He uses the books to make repairs and fails to return them within thirty days.

---

28. But see exception in footnote 27.

(b) Perez does not send in the card, but ABC sends him the books anyway through the U.S. mail. Perez uses the books and fails to return them within thirty days.

5. A plaintiff is attempting to recover death benefits under a life insurance policy. The policy contained a provision that allowed the policy's owner to terminate the policy and receive its cash value. All that the company required was a written request received at the home office. The owner of the policy died after having sent a letter requesting the cash value of the policy (which was much less than the face value). The letter was received *after* the policyowner died. The representative of the deceased owner contended that the estate was entitled to the death benefits of the life insurance policy. What result? [Franklin Life Ins. Co. v. Winney, 469 S.W.2d 21 (Tex.Civ.App. 1971)]

6. University announced plans to construct a hospital. The deadline for submission of contractors' bids was December 18, 1973, at 2:00 P.M. Thomas, a general contractor, planned to submit a bid and therefore solicited bids from numerous suppliers and subcontractors, including Trans Vac, a manufacturer and installer of sophisticated trash disposal systems. Trans Vac's lowest bid to Thomas was $287,000, and Thomas used this figure in computing its own bid, which was submitted to University just prior to the deadline. On January 10, 1974, University officially awarded Thomas the contract. On January 15, Trans Vac informed Thomas that a mistake had been made in its bid to Thomas, and it refused to perform its subcontract unless an increase in price was granted. Unable to find an acceptable alternative, Thomas agreed to a $32,500 increase. After completion of Trans Vac's work, however, Thomas refused to pay more than the amount of Trans Vac's original bid. Was Trans Vac's insistence on an increase in price permissible? Is Thomas's refusal to pay the price increase legally acceptable? [Montgomery Indus. Int'l, Inc. v. Thomas Constr. Co., 620 F.2d 91 (5th Cir. 1980)]

7. McKittrick Co. employed Embry under a written contract at a fixed annual salary. Several times before the contract expired, Embry approached McKittrick's president, seeking to have his employment contract extended another year. The president did not make any firm commitments to Embry, and Embry continued working. Eight days after his employment contract had run out, Embry again approached the president, this time threatening to quit if his contract was not extended. The president responded, "Go ahead, you're all right. Get your men out, and don't let that worry you." Two months later Embry was laid off. Can Embry recover his salary under the contract for the entire year? [Embry v. Hargadine, McKittrick Dry Goods Co., 127 Mo.App. 383, 105 S.W. 777 (1907)]

8. On October 28, 1891, Sanders submitted the following proposition to Pottlitzer Bros.: "We offer you ten carloads of apples, 175 to 200 barrels per car, . . . to be shipped as follows: 1st car by December 15th, 2nd car by December 30th and one car each day ten days after January 1." To this Pottlitzer Bros. replied: "We accept your proposition on apples, provided you will change it to read—car every eight days from January first, none in December." On the same day, Sanders responded that he could not accept Pottlitzer's changes and had to insist on the original offer. Several days later, Pottlitzer Bros. wrote a detailed letter to Sanders explaining why the requested changes were important and reiterating that it could not do business on Sanders's terms. Sanders then responded: "Letter received. Will accept conditions. If satisfactory, answer, and will forward contract." Pottlitzer Bros. replied by telegraph: "All right. Send contract as stated in our message." Sanders sent the contract as modified by Pottlitzer Bros. But Pottlitzer refused to accept the contract unless it also included provisions that Sanders furnish stoves on the carrier and take other precautions to protect the apples from freezing. Can Sanders enforce the agreement as originally modified? [Sanders v. Pottlitzer Bros. Fruit Co., 144 N.Y. 209, 39 N.E. 75 (1894)]

9. John H. Surratt was one of John Wilkes Booth's alleged accomplices in the murder of President Lincoln. On April 20, 1865, the Secretary of War issued and caused to be published in newspapers the following proclamation: "$25,000 reward for the apprehension of John H. Surratt and liberal rewards for any information that leads to the arrest of John H. Surratt." On November 24, 1865, President Johnson revoked the reward and published the revocation in the newspapers. Henry B. St. Marie learned of the reward but left for Rome prior to its revocation. In Rome, St. Marie discovered Surratt's whereabouts; and, in April of 1866, unaware that the reward had been revoked, he reported this information to United States officials. Pursuant to receiving this information, the officials were able to arrest Surratt. Should St. Marie have received the reward? If so, was he entitled to the full $25,000? [St. Marie v. United States, 92 U.S. 73, 23 L.Ed. 697 (1875)]

10. Dodds signed and delivered to Dickinson the following memorandum on Wednesday, June 10:

"I hereby agree to sell to Mr. George Dickinson the whole of the dwelling houses, garden ground, stabling, and outbuildings these to belonging, situated at Croft, belonging to me, for the sum of £800.

As witness my hand this tenth day of June, 1874.''
"£88 [signed] John Dodds."
"P.S. this offer to be left over until Friday, 9 o'clock
A.M. 12th June, 1874."
[Signed] J. Dodds."

The next afternoon (Thursday) Dickinson learned
that Dodds was negotiating with a man named Allan.
That evening Dickinson went to the house of Dodds'
mother-in-law and left her a written acceptance. This
document never reached Dodds. The next morning, at
7 A.M., Dickinson's agent gave Dodds a copy of the
acceptance. Dodds replied that it was too late as he
had already sold the property. Was the memorandum
signed by Dodds a binding contract? If it was merely
an offer, was Dickinson's acceptance sufficient to form
a binding contract? [Dickinson v. Dodds, 2 Div. 463
(1876)]

CHAPTER 8

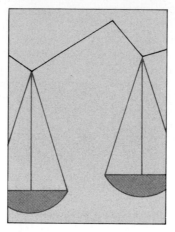

CONTRACTS
Consideration

As a general rule, a contract cannot be formed without legally sufficient consideration. **Consideration** is defined as the price for a promise. In other words, consideration is something that is exchanged for something else.

Often consideration is broken into two elements: (1) that something of legal value must be given, and (2) that there must be a bargained-for exchange. The "something of legal value" may consist of a *return* promise that is bargained for. If it consists of performance, that performance may consist of:

1. An act other than a promise.
2. A forbearance.
3. The creation, modification, or destruction of a legal relation.[1]

Suppose Earl says to his son, "In consideration of the fact that you are not as wealthy as your brothers, I will pay you $500." This promise is not enforceable because Earl's son has not given any consideration for the $500 promised.[2] Earl has simply stated his *motive* for giving his son a gift. The fact that the word "consideration" is used does not, alone, make it consideration.

REQUIREMENTS OF CONSIDERATION

Legal Sufficiency

To create a binding contract, the elements of consideration must not only exist but must be legally sufficient. To be *legally sufficient*, consideration of a promise must be either legally *detrimental to the promisee*—the one receiving the promise—or legally *beneficial to the promisor*—the one making the promise, or both. Legal

---

1. Restatement, Contracts, Second, Section 71.

2. Fink v. Cox, 18 Johns. 145, 9 Am.Dec. 191 (N.Y.1820).

detriment occurs when one does or promises to do something which there was no prior legal duty to do. It also includes refraining or promising to refrain from doing something that there was no prior legal duty to refrain from doing. Conversely, legal benefit is obtaining something that there was no prior legal right to obtain. *Legal* detriment or benefit is not synonymous with *actual* (economic) detriment or benefit. In most cases, the promisor's legal benefit is the same as the promisee's legal detriment. However, the existence of *either* a legal detriment or a legal benefit constitutes legally sufficient consideration.

Suppose Myers owns a brickhouse that causes considerable air pollution in and around his property. Myers has been thinking about getting out of the brick-making business since he has not made much profit and his property is constantly enveloped in a thick layer of smoke. Bernard, his neighbor, is sick of the smoke and pollution and offers Myers $1,500 to stop making bricks (and thus stop the smoke). Myers agrees. The consideration flowing from Myers to Bernard is the promise to refrain from doing an act that Myers is legally entitled to do, that is, to earn a living by making bricks. The consideration flowing from Bernard to Myers is the promise to pay a sum of money that is not otherwise legally required to be paid. (Consideration is sufficient even though Myers may have gone out of business without Bernard's offer.)

In one of the classic cases in contract law, the court found that refraining from certain behavior at the request of another was sufficient consideration to support a promise to pay a sum of money.

BACKGROUND AND FACTS   *William E. Story, Sr., was the uncle of William E. Story II. In the presence of family members and guests invited to a family gathering, Story, Sr., promised to pay his nephew $5,000 if he would refrain from drinking, using tobacco, swearing, and playing cards or billiards for money until he became 21. The nephew agreed and fully performed his part of the bargain. When he reached 21, he wrote and told his uncle that he had kept his part of the agreement and was thereby entitled to $5,000. The uncle replied that he was pleased with his nephew's performance, writing, "I have no doubt but you have, for which you shall have five thousand dollars, as I promised you. I had the money in the bank the day you was twenty-one years old that I intend for you, and you shall have the money certain.* * * P.S. You can consider this money on interest."*

The nephew received his uncle's letter and thereafter consented that the money should remain with his uncle according to the terms and conditions of the letter. The uncle died about two years later without having paid his nephew any part of the $5,000 and interest. The executor of the uncle's estate (the defendant in this action) did not want to pay the $5,000 (with interest) to the nephew, claiming that there had been no valid consideration for the promise.

The court disagreed with the executor and reviewed the doctrine of detriment-benefit as valid consideration under the law.

HAMER v. SIDWAY
Court of Appeals of New York, Second Division, 1891.
124 N.Y. 538, 27 N.E. 256.

PARKER, Justice.
*   *   *   *

The defendant contends that the contract was without consideration to support it, and therefore invalid. He asserts that the promisee, by refraining from the use of liquor and tobacco, was not harmed, but benefited; that that which he did was best for him to do, independently of his uncle's promise,—and insists that it follows that, unless the promisor was benefited, the contract was without consideration,—a contention which, if well founded, would seem to leave open for controversy in many cases whether that which the promisee did or omitted to do was in fact of such benefit to him as to leave no consideration to support the enforcement of the promisor's agreement. Such a rule could not be tolerated, and is without foundation in the law. The exchequer chamber in 1875 defined "consideration" as follows: "A valuable consideration, in the sense of the law, may consist either in some right, interest, profit, or benefit accruing to the one party, or some forbearance, detriment, loss, or responsibility given, suffered, or undertaken by the other." Courts "will not ask whether the thing which forms the consideration does in fact benefit the promisee or a third party, or is of any substantial value to any one. It is enough that something is promised, done, forborne, or suffered by the party to whom the promise is made as consideration for the promise made to him. In general a waiver of any legal right at the request of another party is a sufficient consideration for a promise. Any damage, or suspension, or forbearance of a right will be sufficient to sustain a promise." *   *   * Now, applying this rule to the facts before us, the promisee used tobacco, occasionally drank liquor, and he had a legal right to do so. That right he abandoned for a period of years upon the strength of the promise of the testator that for such forbearance he would give him $5,000. We need not speculate on the effort which may have been required to give up the use of those stimulants. It is sufficient that he restricted his lawful freedom of action within certain prescribed limits upon the faith of his uncle's agreement, and now, having fully performed the conditions imposed, it is of no moment whether such performance actually proved a benefit to the promisor, and the court will not inquire into it; but, were it a proper subject of inquiry, we see nothing in this record that would permit a determination that the uncle was not benefited in a legal sense.

JUDGMENT AND REMEDY   *The court ruled that the nephew had provided legally sufficient consideration by giving up smoking, drinking, swearing, and playing cards or billiards for money, until he became twenty-one and was therefore entitled to the money.*

COMMENTS   *The Hamer v. Sidway case is a good illustration of the distinction between benefits to the promisor and detriment to the promisee. Here the court did not inquire as to whether a benefit flowed to the promisor, but required only that there was a legally sufficient detriment to the promisee.*

MORAL OBLIGATIONS

Promises based on moral duty or obligation are not enforceable because a moral obligation is not legally sufficient consideration. Suppose your friend is injured in a distant city and a grocer takes care of him during his injury. Thereafter, feeling a moral obligation to help your friend and aid the grocer, you promise the grocer to pay for your friend's expenses. The promise is unenforceable since it is supported only by your moral obligation, and a moral obligation cannot be legally sufficient consideration.

Sometimes people feel a moral obligation to make a promise to loved ones. A father may promise to pay $10,000 to his daughter "in consideration of the love and affection that I have for you." An employer may promise to give a sum of money to a trusted employee "in consideration of the many acts of kindness and thoughtfulness over the years" that the employee has performed. This is generally called "good consideration." It is founded on natural duty and affection or on a strong moral obligation. Such consideration is not legally sufficient consideration, however. Therefore, promises made in exchange for it are unenforceable.

Another example of a promise made out of a moral obligation is a promise to pay the debts of one's parents or a promise to pay for the care rendered to relatives one was under no duty to support. A minority of states enforce such promises supported only by a moral obligation—but only to the extent of the actual obligation or of the services or care rendered. For an example, see California Civil Code, Sec. 1606.

ADEQUACY OF CONSIDERATION

Adequacy of consideration refers to the fairness of the bargain. This is a potential issue when the values of the items that are exchanged are unequal. If Bryant and Kowalewski make an agreement whereby Bryant is to pay $1 for Kowalewski's car (with a market value of $1,000), is the agreement supported by consideration? There is no question that $1 is legal value and that Kowalewski is giving up her legal title to the car. Thus, it appears that the requirements of legal value, bargained-for exchange, and legally sufficient consideration have been met. However, the consideration is far from adequate, since Kowalewski does not appear to be getting a fair bargain.

In general, a court of law will not question the adequacy of consideration if the consideration is legally sufficient. Under the doctrine of freedom of contract, parties are normally free to bargain as they wish. If people could sue merely because they entered into an unwise contract, the courts would be overloaded with frivolous suits. In extreme cases, a court of law may look to the amount or value (the adequacy) of the consideration because inadequate consideration can indicate fraud, duress, or undue influence. Suppose Lansky has a house worth $25,000, and he sells it for $5,000. The consideration would probably be legally sufficient but possibly not adequate. A $5,000 sale could indicate that the buyer unduly pressured Lansky into selling or that Lansky was defrauded into selling the house at far below market value.

In an equity suit, courts will more likely question the adequacy of consideration. (Remember from Chapter 1 that actions at law allow for remedies that consist of some form of compensation. Actions in equity allow for remedies that involve specific performance, injunction, or rescission.) The parties in an equity suit must show that the transaction was fair and that consideration was exchanged. For example, a suit to compel specific performance is equitable and requires the losing party to perform the contract duties rather than pay damages for breach of contract. Assume McMichael agrees to sell land worth $45,000 to Price for only $7,500. After signing the contract, McMichael refuses to deliver possession, and Price sues for specific performance. The court may now look at the relative values of the consideration exchanged in light of the circumstances and may refuse to allow specific performance since the consideration is inadequate.

As a general principle of contract law, the courts will not ordinarily attempt to evaluate the adequacy of the consideration in an agreed upon exchange. In the following case, however, the court would not allow "peace of mind" and $1.05 to constitute adequate consideration for a $12,000 land sale.

BACKGROUND AND FACTS *When the Rose family ran into marital difficulties, Robert Rose sought the advice and help of his sister, Norma Lurvey. Robert's estranged wife, Barbara, had failed to make several mortgage payments, and was in danger of defaulting on the family home as well as being in arrears on taxes. Norma Lurvey suggested to Robert that her son (his nephew), Wyman Lurvey, might assist financially.*

ROSE v. LURVEY
Court of Appeals of Michigan, 1972.
40 Mich.App. 230, 198 N.W.2d 839.

Robert and Wyman discussed transferring the house, but no price was ever mentioned. Wyman agreed that following such a transfer, he would make the back mortgage payments and pay the taxes that were owing. An attorney drew up the necessary papers. The instruments were executed despite the fact that they failed to specify a sale price. The only money mentioned was $1.05 recited as consideration in the documents. Subsequently, Robert and Barbara Rose reconciled and continued to live in the house, anticipating that Wyman would be paying them some additional money. Wyman instead served them with notice to vacate the premises. The Roses ignored the notice. A month or so later, Robert Rose entered the hospital. During the short time the house was unoccupied, Wyman moved in and began remodeling the interior.

The Rose family (plaintiffs) contended that the quit claim deed and the contract assigning the land to Wyman Lurvey (defendant) should be thrown out because the consideration was so grossly inadequate as to shock the conscience.

LESINSKI, Chief Judge.
*   *   *   *

It is a general principle of contract law that courts will not ordinarily look into the adequacy of the consideration in an agreed exchange. Equity will, however, grant relief where the inadequacy of consideration is particularly glaring. Thus the Michigan Supreme Court stated the rule that:

"Mere inadequacy of consideration, unless it be so gross as to shock the conscience of the court, is not ground for rescission."

In the case at bar [the one under consideration], the trial judge found that plaintiffs received more than just the $1.05 recited consideration from defendants. This additional consideration was said to have been the peace of mind plaintiffs obtained from knowing that they did not have to worry about the ramifications of defaulting on the land contract. This Court believes that this finding of additional consideration was erroneous. What the trial court mistakenly referred to as consideration was in actuality nothing more than the inducements and motives which influenced plaintiffs into making the contract. Inducements and motives are merely the subjective manifestation of plaintiffs' own desires. They are not that bargained for exchange or legal detriment to defendants which is necessary to establish a legally valid contract.

"The motive which prompts one to enter into a contract and the consideration for the contract are distinct and different things. [Emphasis added.] Parties are led into agreements by many inducements, such as the hope of profit, the expectation of acquiring what they could not otherwise obtain, the desire of avoiding a loss, etc. These inducements are not, however, either legal or equitable consideration, and actually compose no part of the contract."

In light of the fact that $1.05 represented the entire consideration for the transfer of an equity in the property worth approximately $12,000, we find ourselves called upon to decide whether such consideration was so grossly inadequate as to "shock the conscience of the court." We believe it was.

[T]he South Carolina Supreme Court *   *   * stated:

" 'Grossly inadequate consideration does not mean simply less than the actual value of the property. It means a consideration so far short of the real value of property as to shock a correct mind.' "

[T]he Virginia Supreme Court of Appeals cited * * * grossly inadequate consideration as:

" 'An inequality so strong, gross and manifest that it must be impossible to state it to a man of common sense without producing an exclamation at the inequality of it,' * * *."

This Court reaches the conclusion that the transfer of an equity in property worth $12,000 for $1.05 exhibited an inequality so strong as to amount to a gross inadequacy of consideration.

"Inadequacy of price paid for real property is not sufficient alone to authorize a court of equity to set aside a deed of conveyance, unless it is so gross as to shock a conscientious person; but, if the inadequacy is so great as to shock a conscientious person, it alone may furnish sufficient ground for annulling the conveyance."

The court held that the gross inadequacy of the consideration mandated the cancellation of the quit claim deed and of the contract of assignment. Wyman Lurvey was required to vacate the house. A new trial was ordered to determine whether Wyman owed the Roses rent for the time he occupied the house and whether the Roses owed Wyman the amount of back taxes and mortgage payments he had made on their behalf.

JUDGMENT AND REMEDY

Preexisting Duty Rule

Under most circumstances, a promise to do what one already has a legal duty to do is not legally sufficient consideration because no legal detriment or benefit has been incurred.[3] The preexisting legal duty may arise out of a previous contract or may be imposed by law. A sheriff cannot collect a reward for information leading to the capture of a criminal if the sheriff is under a duty to capture the criminal. Similarly, assume Healey agrees to hire Brewster for one year at $175 per week. Brewster begins working. After two months, Healey agrees orally to increase the wages to $195 per week. Healey's promise is unenforceable because it is not supported by legally sufficient consideration. Brewster was under a preexisting duty to work for one year, and the performance of that duty cannot serve as consideration for the wage increase.

The harshness of the preexisting duty rule is evident. In the examples above, the sheriff is denied a reward that anyone else could have received, and Brewster, the employee, can be denied his pay raise. Therefore, the courts are alert to finding any legal detriment or benefit that may

exist, no matter how small or insignificant it may be, so that the promise will be enforceable. Hence, if Brewster was required to perform any extra duties, the promise modifying his employment contract would be enforceable.[4]

Because of the harshness of the preexisting duty rule, the law recognizes three basic exceptions. They are:

1. Rescission and new contract.
2. Sale of goods—modification of contract without consideration.
3. Unforeseen difficulties.

Rescission and New Contract The law recognizes that two parties can mutually agree to rescind their contract, at least to the extent that it is executory. For example, suppose Jones contracts with Abel to purchase Abel's watch for $100. Later Jones tells Abel that he would prefer not to purchase the watch. As it happens, Abel no longer desires to sell it, so they call off the

---

3. Foakes v. Beer, 9 App. Cas. 605 (1884).

---

4. Note, however, that in the example of the sheriff, the person taking the job as sheriff knows ahead of time that he or she is not allowed to take rewards. Similarly, any sports figure knows his or her contract. But since the modern view of courts seems to skirt the preexisting duty rule, the courts' attitude has broken down much of contract validity.

deal. This is called **rescission**, defined as the un-making of a contract in which the parties to it remain in status quo.

Suppose one day later Jones decides he really wants the watch and offers to purchase it once again. Abel is willing to sell, but this time for a price of $125. Jones agrees, and a new contract is formed.

Based on these circumstances, the courts are frequently given a choice of using the preexisting duty rule (not enforcing the new promise) or rescission and new contract. To illustrate, suppose Bauman-Bache, Inc., begins construction on a seven-floor office building and after three months demands an extra $75,000 on its contract or it will stop working. The owner of the land, having no one else to complete construction, agrees to pay the extra $75,000. The agreement is not enforceable because it is not supported by legally sufficient consideration; Bauman-Bache was under a preexisting duty to complete the building. Some courts, however, have held such a modifying agreement enforceable. The conflicting policies are: (1) people should be able to modify their legal relations; and (2) modification in some cases will resemble duress, as in the Bauman-Bache example.

Most of the time, a promise to modify a construction contract without new consideration will not be enforced, but in some cases courts have said that the original contract was rescinded and replaced with the new agreement.[5] Some courts even hold that the original consideration carries over into the new agreement.[6]

Sale of Goods—Modification   The UCC deals with the problem of preexisting duty or modification of an existing contract very simply: "[A]n agreement modifying a contract within this Article needs no consideration to be binding." [UCC 2-209(1)]

To illustrate, Smith and Jones have entered into a one-year requirements contract whereby Smith is to supply Jones with all her flour needs for her bakery at $50 per barrel. Subsequently,

the price of wheat to Smith increases so sharply that the cost of producing a barrel of flour is now $56. Smith tells Jones he will not ship Jones any more flour unless Jones agrees to pay $58 per barrel. Jones agrees. This modification of an existing sales contract is enforceable under the UCC even though Smith was under a preexisting duty to supply flour at $50 per barrel. Jones must pay the additional $8 per barrel. The UCC simply eliminates the consideration requirement if both parties agree to a modification.

Unforeseen Difficulties   Sometimes a party to a contract runs into *unforeseen* and substantial difficulties that could not have been anticipated at the time the contract was entered into. If the parties later agree to pay extra compensation for overcoming these unforeseen difficulties, the court may enforce the agreement. It should be noted that these unforeseen difficulties do not include the types of risks ordinarily assumed in business. For example, the increase in the price of wheat in the preceding example would not normally be deemed an unforeseen hardship or difficulty.

Suppose you contract with Carvelli to dig a basement on your vacant lot for $1,000. Carvelli starts to dig the basement and encounters an unforeseen concrete slab reinforced with steel. He will now require special equipment and additional time to finish digging the basement. He asks for an additional $200 to dig the basement, and you agree. Many courts will enforce the modification, even though you receive no additional benefit; indeed, you have an additional burden, relative to the initial contract, under the unforeseen difficulty exception.

PROBLEM AREAS IN BUSINESS CONCERNING CONSIDERATION

Because of the difficulty in clearly defining the requirements for consideration, numerous exceptions have been created in order to enforce contracts without consideration or to emphasize the intent of the parties to contract with one another, rather than to emphasize the existence or nonexistence of consideration.

---

5.   Armour & Co. v. Celic, 294 F.2d 432 (2d Cir. 1961).
6.   Holly v. First Nat'l Bank, 218 Wis. 259, 260 N.W. 429 (1935).

Businesses face a great deal of uncertainty (risk) in the form of changing market conditions. This uncertainty makes it difficult to define the future rights and duties of parties who contract today. As a result, some output and requirements contracts may not call for any performance in the future under certain market considerations. Yet this does not mean that the contract fails for lack of consideration. Problems concerning the issue of consideration usually fall into one of the following categories:

1. Promises exchanged where total performance by the parties is uncertain.
2. Settlement of claims.
3. Certain promises enforceable without consideration.

The court's solutions to these types of problems can give you insights into how the law views the complex concept of consideration.

Uncertain Performance— Illusory versus Non-illusory

An exchange of promises where performance may never take place suggests that there is no consideration because there is no detriment or benefit. If the terms of the contract express such uncertainty of performance that the promisor has not actually promised to do anything, the promise is said to be *illusory*—without consideration and unenforceable. For example, suppose the president and sole owner of ABC Corporation says to his employees: "All of you have worked hard, and if profits continue to remain high, a 10 percent bonus at the end of the year will be given—if management thinks it is warranted." The employees continue to work hard, and profits remain high, but no bonus is given. This is an illusory promise, or no promise at all, because performance is solely within the discretion of the president. There is no bargained-for consideration. The statement declares merely that the president may or may not do something in the future. The president is not obligated (incurs no detriment) now or in the future.

The following four types of business contracts have a certain degree of uncertainty as to the amount of performance legally required:

1. Requirements contracts.
2. Output contracts.
3. Exclusive dealing contracts.
4. Option to cancel clauses.

Frequently the determination of whether the promise is illusory or non-illusory is dependent on all the surrounding facts, not just on the terms of the agreement.

Requirements Contracts A **requirements contract** is a contract in which the buyer agrees to purchase and the seller agrees to sell all or up to a stated amount of what the buyer *needs* or *requires*. If the contract terms permit the buyer to purchase only if the buyer *wishes* or *desires* to do so, or if the buyer reserves the right to buy the goods from someone other than the seller, the promise is illusory (without consideration), and the agreement is unenforceable.

For example, a manufacturer uses coal to operate and to heat his plant. The manufacturer agrees to purchase from a coal producer all the coal that the manufacturer will require or need to heat and to run his plant for one year at a set price per ton. Since the agreement is based on the *established* needs of the buyer, and since the contract requires the buyer to purchase those needs from this seller, the contract is non-illusory (with consideration) and enforceable, even though the exact amount of coal tonnage to be purchased is unknown. If the agreement stated that the buyer had to buy only the coal he "wanted" or "wished" or "desired," or if the buyer reserved the right to purchase his needs "from any seller whose delivery price is lowest," there is no contract, because the buyer is not obligated to buy any coal from this seller and thus has incurred no legal detriment.

But, one might ask, is there not a possibility that the manufacturer will go out of business and thus have no requirements? Where, then, is the detriment, or consideration? The detriment is that the buyer gives up the opportunity (legal right) to purchase from other sellers, and the seller gives up the opportunity (legal right) to sell to other buyers (who do not have requirements contracts) until he or she has satisfied the obligation under the requirements contract.

Output Contracts An **output contract** is a contract in which the seller agrees to sell and the buyer agrees to buy all or up to a stated amount of what the seller produces.

For example, if U.S. Steel agrees to sell to Boeing Aircraft all I-beams it produces during the month of March at an agreed price per beam, a binding, non-illusory promise will be made. If the contract terms permit a seller to sell output to others besides the buyer, or if the seller's obligation to produce is based on the seller's want, desire, or wish, the contract is illusory. Therefore, the criteria for a non-illusory output contract are basically the same as for a requirements contract, except that the criteria are applied to the seller's obligation to produce rather than to the buyer's obligation to purchase.

The UCC imposes a *good faith limitation* on output and requirements contracts. The quantity under such contracts is the amount of output or the amount of requirements that occur during a *normal* production year. The actual quantity sold or purchased cannot be unreasonably disproportionate to normal or comparable prior output or requirements.[7]

Exclusive Dealing Contracts—"Best Efforts" Rule An **exclusive dealing contract** gives a party the sole right to deal in or with the product of the other party. For example, an exclusive dealing contract requires a buyer to carry only products made by the seller. Wood agrees to market only the fabrics, millinery, and dresses upon which Lady Duff-Gordon places her endorsement. Lady Duff-Gordon receives no promise that Wood will market any dresses, but she gives Wood an exclusive right to market whatever number of items Wood deems appropriate. At first blush, Wood's promise appears illusory. He has not agreed to sell anything. However, as in the output and requirements contracts, Wood is under a duty to use his "best efforts" to market the dresses.[8] This duty, or obligation, is consideration for the promise to either supply or sell.

Consider another example, that of a real estate broker who obtains a thirty-day exclusive contract from the seller of a house. The broker has the duty to perform his or her best efforts in selling the house within thirty days and in dealing with potential buyers. The seller's detriment is the loss of the opportunity (legal right) to hire another broker. In return for this detriment the law imposes a legal obligation of "best efforts" on the broker.

Option to Cancel Clauses A term or time contract may include a clause in which one or both parties may reserve the right to cancel the contract prior to the stated period. For example, consider a three-year lease (a term contract) in which the tenant reserves the right to cancel, with notice, at any time after one year's occupancy. The uncertainty of performance is that the contract may or may not last for the entire three-year period.

The basic rule of law is that, although it is immaterial if one or both parties have the option, the contract with an option to cancel will be enforced if the party having the option has given up an opportunity (legal right). The loss of the opportunity is a detriment and thus constitutes consideration. This point will become clearer as we look at several more examples.

Suppose I contract to hire you for one year at $4,000 per month, reserving the right to cancel the contract at any time. Upon close examination of these words, you can see that I have not actually agreed to hire you, as I could cancel without liability before you start performance. I have not given up the opportunity of hiring someone else. This contract, therefore, is illusory.

Now compare this situation to the previous one. I contract to hire you for one year at $4,000 per month, reserving the right to cancel the contract at any time after you begin performance by giving you thirty days' notice. By saying that I will give you thirty days' notice, I am relinquishing the opportunity (legal right) to hire someone else instead of you for a thirty-day period. Therefore, if you work for one month, at the end of which I give you thirty days' notice, you will be entitled to enforce the contract for $4,000 in salary.

---

7. UCC 2-306.
8. Wood v. Lucy, Lady Duff-Gordon, 222 N.Y. 88, 118 N.E. 214 (1917). See UCC 2-306(2).

Settlement of Claims

An understanding of the enforceability of agreements to settle claims or discharge debts is important in the business world. The following agreements are the most frequent transactions:

1. Accord and Satisfaction.
2. Release, or Covenant Not to Sue.

Accord and Satisfaction The concepts of accord and satisfaction deal with a debtor's offer of payment and a creditor's acceptance of a lesser amount than the debt the creditor purports to be owed. The accord is defined as the agreement whereby one of the parties undertakes to give or perform, and the other to accept, in satisfaction of a claim, something other than that which was originally agreed upon. Satisfaction takes place when the accord is executed, after which there has been an accord and satisfaction. Accord and satisfaction deal with an attempt by the obligor to extinguish an obligation. A basic rule is that there can be no satisfaction unless there is first an accord.

This rule does not apply if the debtor presumably has a preexisting legal obligation to perform according to the contract. In other words, the creditor is owed full performance—that is, payment of the debt as per contract terms. When the amount of money in question is not in dispute, we have a situation of a preexisting legal obligation with respect to payment of a liquidated debt, where the legal term *liquidated* means ascertained, agreed-upon, fixed, settled, and determined. For example, if Baker signed an installment loan contract with her banker in which she agreed to pay a specified rate of interest on a specified sum of money borrowed, at timely monthly intervals in the form of a $100-per-month payment for two years, that is a liquidated debt. Reasonable persons will not differ over the amount owed.

The opposite of a liquidated debt is an unliquidated debt. Here reasonable persons may differ over the amount owed. It is not settled, fixed, agreed-upon, ascertained, or determined.

The process of accord and satisfaction normally is a compromise used exclusively in cases of unliquidated debts. In the majority of states, accord (acceptance of a lesser sum) of a liquidated debt is not satisfaction, and the balance of the debt is still legally owed. The rationale for this rule is that no consideration is given by the debtor to satisfy the obligation of paying the balance to the creditor, since the debtor has a preexisting legal obligation to pay the entire debt.

To illustrate, suppose a debtor, by agreement, borrows $100, payable at the end of one year at 10 percent interest. At the end of the year, the debtor sends the creditor a check for $100 (not $110), marked clearly "payment in full." The creditor, under the majority rule, could cash the check and still legally sue for the balance of $10. The following case illustrates precisely this point.

BACKGROUND AND FACTS *The creditor, Gibble Oil Company, brought the following action against Carl Widmer, the defendant and debtor. Gibble attempted to collect the $67.80 due on Widmer's credit card account. Widmer sent a check to Gibble Oil Company for $9.01 and marked on the check "full payment of all accounts to date." Because Gibble cashed the check, Widmer contended that Gibble had accepted the $9.01 check in full payment of his bill.*

WIDMER v. GIBBLE OIL CO.

Supreme Court of Arkansas, 1967.
243 Ark. 735, 421 S.W.2d 886.

HARRIS, Chief Justice.

*   *   *   *

Gibble Oil Company instituted a suit on November 23, 1966, asking judgment for $67.80, plus costs and interest, from the appellant. On November 30, 1966, Widmer sent his check to appellee in the amount of $9.01, the check being marked, "Full payment of all accounts to date." Gibble then cashed the check. This is the only factual difference between this case and Widmer v. Price Oil Company, for in that case, the check sent in a less amount (than that owed) was not cashed. This fact, however, is immaterial. As pointed out in *Price*, there must be a disputed amount involved, and a consent to accept less than that amount in settlement of the whole before there can be an accord and satisfaction.

* * * *

This holding is in accord with 6 Corbin on Contracts, Section 1277, Page 123, where it is said:

"It is not enough for the debtor merely to write on a voucher or on his check such words as 'in full payment' or 'to balance account,' where there has been no such dispute or antecedent discussion as to give reasonable notice to the creditor that the check is being tendered as full satisfaction."

In addition, we have held that a dispute or controversy about the amount of an account must be made in good faith, i.e., there must be a *bona fide* dispute. In [a similar case this court said]:

" 'While it is not necessary that the dispute or controversy should be well founded, it is necessary that it should be made in good faith.' "

As stated in *Price*, there is no evidence that Widmer denies that he actually owed the full amount demanded. In fact, it is stipulated that "as of November 23, 1966, the defendant Carl Widmer owed the amount of $67.80 to the Gibble Oil Company as a result of credit card purchases made by said defendant from the plaintiff." Further, that "prior to November 30, 1966 [the date of the sending of the check], no communication was exchanged between plaintiff, Gibble Oil Company, and defendant, Carl Widmer, in regard to the correctness or validity of said account."

JUDGMENT AND REMEDY *The trial court judgment was affirmed. The $9.01 check was not deemed "accord and satisfaction" of Widmer's debt to Gibble Oil Company.*

COMMENT *Some states might allow this transaction to act as a release. The majority rule is that there is no accord and satisfaction if a lesser amount is given in satisfaction for a liquidated debt. This majority rule is based on the absence of consideration so as to work a discharge of an undisputed balance.*

Accord and Satisfaction and Unliquidated Debt As stated before, an unliquidated debt is one in which there is a bona fide dispute as to the amount. That is, it is a debt in which reasonable persons could differ as to the exact amount owed. In these circumstances the accord of the lesser sum is also satisfaction, discharging the purported debt. Suppose that Devereaux goes to the dentist's office. The dentist tells him that he needs three gold inlays. The price is not discussed. The dentist performs the work. Dever-

eaux leaves the office. At the end of the month, the dentist sends him a bill for $1,500. Devereaux, believing that this amount is grossly out of proportion with what a reasonable person would believe to be the debt owed, sends a check for $1,000. On the back of the check he writes "payment in full for three gold inlays." The dentist cashes the check. Since we are dealing with an unliquidated debt—the amount has not been agreed upon—partial payment accepted by the dentist will wipe out the debt. One argument to support this rule is that the parties give up a legal right to contest the amount in dispute, and thus consideration passes.

Release, or Covenant Not to Sue   A **release** serves to bar any further recovery beyond the terms stated in the release. For example, suppose you are involved in an automobile accident due to the negligence of Jean. Jean offers you $500 if you will release her from any further liability resulting from the accident. You believe that the damages to your car will not exceed $400. You agree to the release. Later you discover that the damage to your car is $600. Can you collect the balance? The answer is no, you are limited to the $500 in the release. Therefore it is important to know the extent of your injuries or damages before signing a release.

Generally, releases are binding if three criteria are proved:

1. The release is secured and given in good faith—that is, in absence of fraud and the like.
2. In many states, the release must be in a signed writing.
3. Consideration for the release is given.

Consideration in the above case is Jean's promised payment of $500 in return for your promise not to bring an action for a larger amount. Under the UCC, a written, signed waiver or renunciation by an aggrieved party discharges any further liability for a breach even without consideration.[9]

A **covenant not to sue**, in contrast to a release, does not always bar further recovery. The parties simply substitute a contractual obligation for some other type of action. For example, assume that in the accident just described, you say that you are going to sue the negligent party,

Jean, in tort (negligence) for your damages. Jean and you agree that if you will refrain from bringing a tort action, she will pay for all damages to your car. Therefore, a contract is substituted for the tort action. If Jean fails to pay for your damages as agreed, your action is for breach of contract (you do not have to prove negligence). This does not prevent you from bringing a tort-negligence suit; but if you do so, you have breached your contract. Except for UCC 1-107, the same elements for a binding release apply for a valid covenant not to sue.

Past Consideration

Promises made for events that have already taken place are unenforceable. These promises lack consideration in that the element of bargained-for exchange is missing. In short, you can bargain for something to take place now or in the future, but not for something that has already taken place. Therefore, **past consideration** is no consideration.

Suppose a father tells his son, "In consideration of the fact that you named your son after me when he was born, I promise to pay you $1,000." The promise is for an event that already has taken place, so it is unenforceable. A similar example is a promise to pay for "past love and affection given." Although there are strong moral obligations to fulfill those promises, there is no legal obligation to do so.

Consider instead that the father tells his son, "In consideration of your promise to name your next child after me, I promise to pay you $1,000." The son names his next child after his father. Here is a bargained-for exchange with legally sufficient consideration binding the father to pay.

In the following case, we see an illustration of how "past" and "moral" issues can be involved in consideration.

---

9. UCC 1-107.

BACKGROUND AND FACTS *This suit concerned title to certain real property. The plaintiff-appellee was a minor bringing suit through his father. The defendants were the heirs of August Schultz and the administratrix of his estate. The case came to court on the basis of an oral contract allegedly made between Schultz and the plaintiff (through the plaintiff's mother).*

LANFIER v. LANFIER

Supreme Court of Iowa, 1939.
227 Iowa 258, 288 N.W. 104.

Schultz agreed to give the plaintiff certain real estate if plaintiff's mother would name plaintiff after him. He also agreed to reserve to the plaintiff's parents a life estate in that real estate. The plaintiff's parents accepted the proposal and named plaintiff after Schultz. Schultz neglected to perform his oral contract and never arranged for title to the property to pass to plaintiff. However, he did deliver possession of the real estate to plaintiff's parents, who held possession for about twelve years. Among other things, the plaintiff wanted the court to adjudge him the absolute owner of the real estate.

The administratrix of Schultz's estate and the other beneficiaries challenged plaintiff's right to the property. The trial court awarded the property to the plaintiff based on the alleged oral contract between decedent and plaintiff's mother.

MILLER, Justice.

*   *   *   *

"The general principle of the law of contracts, that to be valid and legally enforceable, as between the parties thereto an agreement or undertaking of any kind must be supported by a consideration, is too elementary to call for citation of authorities."

Under the record herein, there is a total absence of any evidence of a legal consideration to support the alleged contract plaintiff seeks to enforce. The evidence is undisputed that plaintiff was born on December 17, 1925, and, two days later, December 19, 1925, he was named August Dwayne Lanfier. He was named August after his grandfather, the decedent herein. *   *   * There is no evidence of any request on the part of the decedent that plaintiff be named after him until the latter part of March, 1926, over three months after plaintiff had been named. There are several witnesses who testified to conversations between plaintiff's mother and the decedent at that time, the substance of which was that, if plaintiff's mother would name plaintiff after the decedent, decedent would make a will and would thereby devise to plaintiff the real estate in question, subject to a life estate in plaintiff's parents. At the time these conversations were had, plaintiff and his parents were already in possession of the property, as tenants of the decedent.

*   *   *

Counsel for plaintiff assert that the contract was supported by sufficient consideration, in that the prior naming of the plaintiff for the decedent constituted a past or moral consideration, and further that the contract should be supported on the basis of love and affection being good consideration. The contentions of counsel are without merit.

This court has repeatedly held that past or moral consideration is not sufficient to support an executory contract. *   *   * If the services are gratuitous, no obligation, either moral or legal, is incurred by the recipient. No one is bound to pay for that which is a gratuity. No moral obligation is assumed by a person who receives a gift. Suppose the plaintiff had given the defendant a horse, was he morally bound to pay what the horse was reasonably worth? We think not. In such case there never was any liability to pay, and therefore a subsequent promise would be without any consideration to support it.

*   *   *   *

The contentions of counsel to the effect that love and affection constitute sufficient consideration to support the contract here asserted are likewise without

merit. No such consideration is expressed in the contract, and we seriously doubt that the record supports any claim that such might have been consideration for the alleged contract. However, in any event, the proposition of law contended for by counsel has no support in the decisions of this court or in the courts generally.
*   *   *   *

"Although love and affection is a 'good' consideration, it is not a sufficient consideration for a promise. Promises or contracts made on the basis of mere love and affection, unsupported by a pecuniary or material benefit, create at most bare moral obligations, and a breach thereof presents no cause for redress by the court."

JUDGMENT AND REMEDY

Plaintiff was not awarded title to the property. Love and affection are not legally sufficient consideration to support a promise, and thus breach of such a promise presents no legally recognizable cause of action.

COMMENTS

In rare cases, courts are willing to recognize a moral obligation of the promisor as a substitute for consideration where the promisor receives a material benefit and subsequently expresses a promise to pay for it. For example, in Webb v. McGowin, 27 Ala.App. 82, 168 So. 196 (1935), Webb was maimed for life when he diverted the course of a falling block of wood that otherwise would have killed McGowin. McGowin was so grateful to Webb that he agreed to send him $15 every two weeks for the remainder of Webb's life. But McGowin died before Webb. Ultimately, the court ruled that McGowin's estate was responsible for continuing to pay Webb the $15 every other week. McGowin's promise became a valid and enforceable contract.

Promises Enforceable Without Consideration

There are exceptions to the rule that only promises supported by consideration are enforceable. Other circumstances in which promises will be enforced despite the lack of what one normally considers legal consideration are as follows:

1. Composition of creditors' agreements.
2. Promises to pay debts barred by the statute of limitations or discharged by bankruptcy.
3. Detrimental reliance, or promissory estoppel.
4. Charitable subscriptions.

Composition of Creditors' Agreements A composition with creditors is an agreement between an insolvent or embarrassed debtor and his or her creditors that the creditors will accept either a specified amount or a percentage of the full amount owed. A creditors' composition agreement is fully enforceable without consideration, although courts sometimes find consideration in the mutual promises of the creditors to accept less than the full amount owed.

Promises to Pay Debts Barred by the Statute of Limitations Statutes of limitations in all states require a creditor to sue within a specified period to recover debts. If the creditor fails to sue in time, recovery of the debt is barred by the statute of limitations. A debtor who promises to pay a previous debt barred by the statute of limitations makes an enforceable promise. *The promise needs no consideration.* (Some states, however, require that it be in writing.) In effect, the promise extends the limitations period, and the creditor can sue to recover the entire debt. The promise can be implied if the debtor acknowledges the barred debt by making a partial payment.

Suppose you borrow $5,000 from First National Bank of San Jose. The loan is due in November 1980. You fail to pay, and the bank does not sue you until December 1985. If California's statute of limitations for this debt is five years, recovery of the debt is barred. If you then agree to pay the loan off, First National Bank can sue for the entire amount. This is an example of an express promise, which extends the limitations period. Likewise, you can make a monthly payment and implicitly acknowledge the existence of the debt. Again First National Bank can sue you for the entire debt. This is an example of acknowledgment. Suppose instead that you expressly promise First National Bank to pay it $2,500. This promise is generally enforceable only to the extent of $2,500 (and usually must be in writing).

Promises to Pay Debts Barred by Discharge in Bankruptcy The Bankruptcy Reform Act of 1978 has made substantial changes in the law concerning reaffirmations of debts barred by a discharge in bankruptcy. Prior to enactment of the law, a former debtor could make a promise in writing to repay a debt totally discharged by a bankruptcy decree, and that promise would be enforced without consideration.

The law severely restricts such reaffirmations, which are permitted only under the following conditions:

1. The agreement must be made before the debtor's discharge in bankruptcy. Even here the debtor can rescind within thirty days from the date of the agreement.
2. There must be a hearing by the Bankruptcy Court whereby the debtor is informed of the consequences of such agreement.

Detrimental Reliance, or the Doctrine of Promissory Estoppel The doctrine of detrimental reliance, or promissory estoppel, involves a promise given by one party that induces another party to rely on that promise to his or her detriment. When the promisor (the person making the promise) can reasonably expect the promisee (the person receiving the promise) to act on the promise, and injustice cannot be avoided any other way, the promise will be enforced.[10] Additionally, the promisee must act with justifiable reliance on the promise—that is, must be justified in relying on it—and the act must be of a substantial nature.

The promise is enforced by refusing to allow the promisor to set up the defense of no consideration. The promisor is estopped (prevented) from asserting the lack of consideration. The estoppel arises from the promise, hence **promissory estoppel** is the term used. (This doctrine is not used in some jurisdictions.)

Imagine that your grandfather tells you "I'll pay you $75 per week so you won't have to work anymore." Then you quit your job, and your grandfather refuses to pay. You may be able to enforce the promise since you have justifiably relied on it to your detriment.[11]

Traditionally, promissory estoppel has been applied only to gratuitous promises, that is, when the parties are not bargaining in a commercial setting. The trend, however, is to apply it in any situation if justice so requires. A classic case illustrates this point.

---

10. Restatement, Second, Contracts, Section 90 provides: A promise which the promisor should reasonably expect to induce action or forbearance on the part of the promisee or a third person and which does induce such action or forbearance is binding if injustice can be avoided only by enforcement of the promise.
11. Ricketts v. Scothorn, 57 Neb. 51, 77 N.W. 365 (1898).

HOFFMAN v. RED OWL STORES, INC.
Supreme Court of Wisconsin, 1965.
26 Wis.2d 683, 133 N.W.2d 267.

BACKGROUND AND FACTS *Red Owl Stores, Inc. (defendant), induced the Hoffmans (plaintiffs) to give up their current business and run a Red Owl franchise. The Hoffmans relied on the representations of Red Owl, and when the deal ultimately fell through because of Red Owl's failure to keep its promise concerning the operation of the franchise agency store, the Hoffmans brought this suit to recover their losses.*

CURRIE, Chief Justice.

*   *   *   *

Recognition of a Cause of Action Grounded on Promissory Estoppel.

Sec. 90 of Restatement, 1 Contracts, provides (at p. 110):

"A promise which the promisor should reasonably expect to induce action or forbearance of a definite and substantial character on the part of the promisee and which does induce such action or forbearance is binding if injustice can be avoided only by enforcement of the promise."

*   *   *   *

Because we deem the doctrine of promissory estoppel, as stated in sec. 90 of Restatement, 1 Contracts, is one which supplies a needed tool which courts may employ in a proper case to prevent injustice, we endorse and adopt it.

Applicability of Doctrine to Facts of this Case.

The record here discloses a number of promises and assurances given to Hoffman by Lukowitz in behalf of Red Owl upon which plaintiffs relied and acted upon to their detriment.

Foremost were the promises that for the sum of $18,000 Red Owl would establish Hoffman in a store. After Hoffman had sold his grocery store and paid the $1,000 on the Chilton lot, the $18,000 figure was changed to $24,100. Then in November, 1961, Hoffman was assured that if the $24,100 figure were increased by $2,000 the deal would go through. Hoffman was induced to sell his grocery store fixtures and inventory in June, 1961, on the promise that he would be in his new store by fall. In November, plaintiffs sold their bakery building on the urging of defendants and on the assurance that this was the last step necessary to have the deal with Red Owl go through.

We determine that there was ample evidence to sustain the answers of the jury to the questions of the verdict with respect to the promissory representations made by Red Owl, Hoffman's reliance thereon in the exercise of ordinary care, and his fulfillment of the conditions required of him by the terms of the negotiations had with Red Owl.

There remains for consideration the question of law raised by defendants that agreement was never reached on essential factors necessary to establish a contract between Hoffman and Red Owl. Among these were the size, cost, design, and layout of the store building; and the terms of the lease with respect to rent, maintenance, renewal, and purchase options. This poses *the question of whether the promise necessary to sustain a cause of action for promissory estoppel must embrace all essential details of a proposed transaction between promisor and promisee so as to be the equivalent of an offer that would result in a binding contract between the parties if the promisee were to accept the same.* [Emphasis added.]

Originally the doctrine of promissory estoppel was invoked as a substitute for consideration rendering a gratuitous promise enforceable as a contract. In other words, the acts of reliance by the promisee to his detriment provided a substitute for consideration. If promissory estoppel were to be limited to only those situations where the promise giving rise to the cause of action must be so definite with respect to all details that a contract would result were the promise supported by consideration, then the defendants' instant promises to Hoffman would not meet this test. However, sec. 90 of Restatement, 1 Contracts, does not impose the requirement that the promise giving rise to the cause of action must be so comprehensive in scope as to meet the requirements of an offer that would ripen into a contract if accepted by the promisee. Rather the conditions imposed are:

(1) Was the promise one which the promisor should reasonably expect to induce action or forbearance of a definite and substantial character on the part of the promisee?

(2) Did the promise induce such action or forbearance?

(3) Can injustice be avoided only by enforcement of the promise?

We deem it would be a mistake to regard an action grounded on promissory estoppel as the equivalent of a breach of contract action. As Dean Boyer points out, it is desirable that fluidity in the application of the concept be maintained. While the first two of the above listed three requirements of promissory estoppel present issues of fact which ordinarily will be resolved by a jury, the third requirement, that the remedy can only be invoked where necessary to avoid injustice, is one that involves a policy decision by the court. Such a policy decision necessarily embraces an element of discretion.

We conclude that injustice would result here if plaintiffs were not granted some relief because of the failure of defendants to keep their promises which induced plaintiffs to act to their detriment.

JUDGMENT AND REMEDY   *Trial court's judgment was affirmed. Hoffman was entitled to damages, the exact amount to be determined when the case was returned to the trial court.*

COMMENTS   *Promissory estoppel does not mean that each and every gratuitous promise will be binding merely because the promisee has changed position. Liability is created only when there is "justifiable reliance on the promise." The promisor must have known or had reason to believe that the promisee would likely be induced to change position as a result of the promise.*

Charitable Subscriptions   Subscriptions to religious, educational, and charitable institutions are promises to make a gift and are unenforceable on traditional contract grounds because they are not supported by legally sufficient consideration. A gift is the opposite of bargained-for consideration. However, the modern view is to enforce these promises under the doctrine of promissory estoppel, a substitute for consideration.

The premise for enforcement is that a promise is made, and an institution changes its position because of reliance on that promise. For example, suppose a church solicits and receives donative subscriptions to build a new church. On the basis of these pledges, the church purchases land, employs architects, and makes other contracts that change its position. Courts may enforce the pledges under promissory estoppel, or find consideration in the fact that each promise is made in reliance on the other promises of support, or that the trustees, by accepting the subscription, impliedly promise to complete the proposed undertaking. Such cases represent exceptions to the general rule that consideration must exist for the formation of a contract. And these exceptions come about as a result of public policy.

QUESTIONS AND
CASE PROBLEMS

1.   D'Albergo is the owner of a large bakery. She contracts to purchase from XYZ Flour, Inc., all the flour she might desire for a one-year period at $30 per barrel. Payment terms call for a billing at the end of each month for shipments made, with a 3 percent discount if paid within twenty days of the billing date. During the first month D'Albergo orders and XYZ delivers 1,000 barrels of flour. On the third day of the next month, XYZ sends D'Albergo a bill for $30,000 dated that same day. A dispute develops between the two parties. XYZ refuses to ship any more flour to D'Albergo, and on the thirtieth day of the month, D'Albergo sends XYZ a check for $29,100, marked clearly, "payment in full." Discuss whether XYZ's refusal to ship any more flour places it in breach of contract. Also, if XYZ cashes D'Albergo's check, can XYZ recover in a lawsuit the balance of $900?

2.   Tabor is the buyer of widgits manufactured by Martin. Martin's contract with Tabor calls for delivery of 10,000 widgits at $1 per widgit in ten equal installments. After delivery of two installments, Martin informs Tabor that because of inflation, Martin is losing money and will promise to deliver the remaining 8,000 widgits only if Tabor will pay $1.20 per widgit. Tabor agrees in writing. Discuss whether Martin can legally collect the additional $200 upon delivery to Tabor of the next installment of 1,000 widgits.

3.   Star Furniture Company manufactures summer lawn furniture. Its sole product consists of webbed aluminum frame furniture used mainly on outdoor patios and on beaches. As of October 1, Star Furniture was heavily indebted to its three main suppliers—Aluminum Pole, Inc., Plastic Webbing, Ltd., and The Little Steel Rivet Company. Star owed each of these suppliers approximately $10,000. Star's president met with the presidents of the three suppliers to work out some arrangement whereby the company could avoid declaring bankruptcy. Since all the parties desired that Star Furniture not go bankrupt, an agreement was made among the four parties that Star would pay each supplier $7,000, which would be accepted as full payment of all outstanding debts as of October 1. Discuss whether this agreement is enforceable.

4.   Beyer owns a lot and wants to build a house according to a specific set of plans and specifications. She solicits bids from building contractors and receives three bids: one from Carlton for $60,000, one from Friend for $58,000, and one from Shade for $53,000. She accepts Shade's bid. One month after construction of the house has begun, Shade contacts Beyer and informs her that because of inflation and a recent price hike in materials, he will not finish the house unless Beyer agrees to pay an extra $3,000. Beyer reluctantly agrees to pay the additional sum. After the house is finished, however, Beyer refuses to pay the additional $3,000. Discuss whether Beyer is legally required to pay this additional amount.

5.   Daniel, a recent college graduate, is on his way home for the Christmas holidays from his new job. Daniel gets caught in a snowstorm and is taken in by an elderly couple, who provide him with food and shelter. After the snowplows have cleared the road, Daniel proceeds home. Daniel's father, Fred, is most appreciative of the elderly couple's action and in a letter promises to pay them $500. The elderly couple, in need of money, accept Fred's offer. Because of a dispute between Daniel and Fred, Fred refuses to pay the elderly couple the $500. Discuss whether they can hold Fred in contract for the services rendered to Daniel.

6.   Greenwood, an established professional football player, signed a contract on May 31, 1974, to play football for three years, beginning in 1975, for the Birmingham Americans. The Birmingham Americans were a team operated by Alabama Football, Inc. (AFI), under a franchise agreement with the World Football League. The contract provided for an initial payment to Greenwood of $25,000 upon signing the contract, a $25,000 payment in September 1974, and a $25,000 payment in April, 1975. In addition, the parties contracted for additional sums as salary for each of the three years Greenwood was to play. Greenwood received the first two payments of $25,000 each. During the 1974 season, however, AFI experienced extreme financial difficulties, and in January of 1975 it lost its franchise to operate a team in the World Football League. Greenwood subsequently cancelled his agreement with AFI. AFI sued Greenwood to recover the $50,000 already paid, on the theory that Greenwood had not yet earned any compensation under the contract. Greenwood countered that the $50,000 constituted payment for his signing the contract and for the promotional value that AFI derived from the use of his name during 1974. Does the signing of the contract and the use of Greenwood's name during 1974 constitute sufficient consideration to support the early

payments made to Greenwood? Was AFI contractually obligated to make those payments, or were they merely unearned advances that must be returned upon cancellation of the contract? [Alabama Football, Inc. v. Greenwood, 452 F.Supp. 1191 (W.D.Pa.1978)]

7. Martino is a police officer in Atlantic City. Gray, who lost a significant amount of her jewelry during a burglary of her home, offered a reward for the recovery of the property. Incident to his job, Martino possessed certain knowledge concerning the theft of Gray's jewelry. When Martino informed Gray of his knowledge of the theft, Gray offered Martino $500 to help her recover her jewelry. As a result of Martino's police work, the jewelry was recovered and returned to Gray. Martino sued Gray for the reward he claimed she promised him. Was there a valid contract between Gray and Martino? [Gray v. Martino, 91 N.J.L. 462, 103 A. 24 (1918)]

8. Feinberg was employed as bookkeeper, office manager, and assistant treasurer of Pfeiffer Company. After she had worked there for forty-seven years, the board of directors, in recognition of her "long and faithful service," passed a resolution whereunder she would be paid $200 a month for the rest of her life at any time she decided to retire. Shortly thereafter, Feinberg retired and for several years received the $200 per month as promised. The president of Pfeiffer eventually died and was succeeded by his son-in-law, who reduced the payments to $100 a month. Feinberg sued Pfeiffer Company. Was she able to recover under contract theory? [Feinberg v. Pfeiffer Co., 322 S.W.2d 163 (Mo.App. 1959)]

9. Nees owned two parcels of land. One parcel, located on Atlantic Avenue, he held exclusively in trust for two of his children, Sophia and George. The other parcel, known as the Sackett Street property, passed to all five of Nees's children upon his death. None of the children learned that only Sophia and George were to receive the Atlantic Avenue property until they were

informed by Nees's attorney at the time the attorney opened Nees's strongbox. Sophia and George, seeing that their brothers and sisters were disappointed that none of them had received any interest in the Atlantic property, promised to give them their share in the Sackett Street property, "if you don't bother us about the Atlantic Avenue property." Was this promise enforceable against Sophia and George? [Springstead v. Nees, 125 App.Div. 230, 109 N.Y.S. 148 (1908)]

10. A group of developers in Alabama were planning the development of approximately seventy-five acres as an office park. Part of the proposed development was in the Mountain Brook police jurisdiction, and part was in the Homewood police jurisdiction. In order to facilitate administrative dealings, the developers sought to have Mountain Brook annex the part of the proposed development that was in Homewood. In order to convince the county legislature to introduce a bill authorizing the annexation, the developers requested the Mountain Brook Planning Commission to pass a resolution containing certain assurances to the homeowners in both Homewood and Mountain Brook who would be affected by the development. In part, the resolution that was passed stated that a buffer zone of about one hundred feet would surround the houses in Homewood. The zone would be maintained at all times, there would be no building or parking permitted in it, and it would be left as natural woodland. Twenty years later, only the hundred-foot buffer zone of natural woodlands separated the homeowners' backyards from the office park that had been developed. The developers announced plans to eliminate the buffer zone and to construct an additional office park. They claimed that the homeowners had no ground for preventing such additional development because there was no detrimental reliance on the alleged promises about maintaining the buffer zone. What was the result? [Mazer v. Jackson Ins. Agency, 340 So.2d 770 Ala. (1976)]

CHAPTER 9

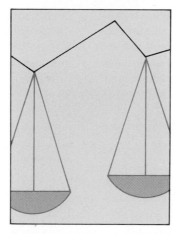

CONTRACTS
Contractual Capacity

Historically, the law has concerned itself with the relative strength of the bargaining power of each contracting party. Thus, special protection is afforded those who bargain with the inexperience of youth or those who lack legally defined mental competence.

Contractual capacity—the competence (legal ability) of the parties—is one element of a valid contract. Full competence exists when both parties have full legal capacity to enter into a contract and to have the contract enforced against them. No competence exists when one or both of the parties have been adjudged by a proper court to be insane and therefore have no legal capacity to contract. In this event, an essential element for a valid contract is missing, and the contract is void. Limited competence exists when one or both parties are minors in age, intoxicated, or insane (but not yet adjudicated officially as such by a proper court). These parties have full and legal capacity to enter into a contract, but if they so wish, they can avoid liability

under the contract. This kind of contract is said to be voidable.

MINORS

At common law, a minor was defined as a male who had not attained the age of twenty-one or a female who had not attained the age of eighteen. Today, in most states, the age of majority (when a person is no longer a minor) for contractual purposes has been changed by statute to eighteen years for both sexes.[1] In addition, some states provide for the termination of minority upon marriage. Subject to certain exceptions, the contracts entered into by a minor are voidable at the

---

1. Although the age of majority applicable in contracts has been changed to eighteen in many states, it may still be twenty-one for some purposes, including the purchase and consumption of alcohol. The word "infant" is usually used synonymously with the word "minor."

option of that minor. A **voidable contract** is one in which the minor may avoid legal obligations by exercising the option to *disaffirm* the contract. On the other hand, an adult who enters into a contract with a minor cannot avoid his or her contractual duties on the ground that the minor can do so. Unless the minor exercises the option to avoid the contract, the adult party is bound by it.

Minors' Rights to Disaffirm

The general rule of law is that a minor can enter into any contract that an adult can enter into, provided that the contract is not one prohibited by law for minors (for example, the sale of alcoholic beverages). Although minors can enter into contracts, they also have the right to disaffirm their contracts. (However, if so-called necessaries are contracted, the minor is liable for their reasonable value. This liability is *quasi-contractual*. Also, if a minor affirms a previously entered contract after reaching the age of majority, the minor loses the right to disaffirm.

Disaffirmance in General In order for a minor to exercise the option to avoid a contract, he or she need only manifest an intention not to be bound by it. The minor "avoids" the contract by "disaffirming" it. The technical definition of **disaffirmance** is the legal avoidance, or setting aside, of a contractual obligation. Words or conduct may express this intent. Suppose James Caldwell, a seventeen-year-old, enters into a contract to sell his car to Joseph Reed, an adult. Caldwell can avoid the contract and avoid his legal duty to deliver possession of the car to Reed by either telling Reed that he refuses to abide by the contract or by selling the car to a third person. In other words, Caldwell can disaffirm the contract by expressing his intention in words or by acting inconsistently with his duties under the contract.

The contract can ordinarily be disaffirmed at any time during minority or for a reasonable time after the minor comes of age. However, in some states an exception exists in the case of a contract for the sale of land by a minor. There, a minor cannot disaffirm the contract until he or she reaches majority.

If a minor fails to disaffirm a contract within a reasonable time after reaching the age of majority, the court must determine whether the conduct constitutes *ratification*, binding the minor in contract, or *disaffirmance*, allowing the minor's avoidance. Generally, if the contract is fully performed by both parties (executed), the contract is considered ratified. If the contract is still executory (not yet fully performed by both parties), it is considered disaffirmed.

For example, assume that the age of majority in your state is eighteen. Your sister, age seventeen, contracts to purchase a bicycle from an adult for $125. Your sister then turns eighteen. If she has not taken possession of the bicycle or paid the $125 purchase price, an executory contract exists, and most courts would hold her conduct to be an act of disaffirmance. On the other hand, if she has taken possession of the bicycle and paid the purchase price, an executed contract exists, and most courts would hold her failure to actively disaffirm within a reasonable time after her eighteenth birthday as an act of *ratification*, removing her right of avoidance.

Duty of Restoration When a contract has been executed, minors cannot disaffirm without returning whatever goods they may have received, or paying for their reasonable value, or at least making an offer to pay. This is called the minor's *duty of restoration*. Although many states recognize this duty, most place certain limitations on it. Under the majority view, the minor need only return the goods (or other consideration), provided such goods are in the minor's possession or control. Suppose Pat Boland, a seventeen-year-old, purchases a used Ford Fairmont from Jane Crow, an adult. Boland is a bad driver and negligently runs the car into a telephone pole. The next day he returns the car to Crow and disaffirms the contract. Under the majority view, this return fulfills Boland's duty even though the auto is now wrecked.

On the other hand, a few states, either by statute or by court decision, have placed an additional duty on the minor—the *duty of restitution*. The theory is that the adult should be returned to his or her position before the contract was made. The duty of restitution requires

Boland to pay Crow for the damage done to the car in addition to returning it. Some states do not require full restitution. A minor must pay only a "reasonable" amount to compensate the adult.

A minor must disaffirm the entire contract in order to disaffirm it at all. The minor cannot decide to keep part of the goods and return the remainder. When a minor disaffirms, all property that he or she has transferred to the adult as consideration can be recovered, even if it is then in the hands of a third party. If the property itself cannot be returned, the other party must pay the minor its equivalent value. Under UCC 2-403, the rule about recovering property does not apply if the transfer was a sale subject to the provisions of the UCC and the transfer was to a bona fide purchaser.[2]

In the following case, a minor's father brought an action to disaffirm the minor's purchase of an automobile and to recover the purchase price. The court reviewed the contract with the minor and took into account the fact that the seller knew the buyer was a minor when the contract was made.

---

2. Defined as "a purchaser for a valuable consideration paid or parted with in the belief that the vender had a right to sell, and without any suspicious circumstances to put him on inquiry." [Merritt v. Railroad Co., 12 Barb., N.Y. 605 (1852)].

BACKGROUND AND FACTS *Johnny Hays, the plaintiff, was a sixteen-year-old minor. He went to Quality Motors, Inc. (the defendant), to inspect and test a car. When the Quality Motors salesman raised the question of Hays's age, he was told that Hays's father in New York had sent him the money to buy the car. The salesman refused to sell the car unless the purchase was made by an adult. Hays left the salesman and returned shortly with a young man of twenty-three, whom he had met that day for the first time.*

The salesman then accepted Hays's cashier's check in payment for the car. The bill of sale was made out to the twenty-three-year-old. The salesman then recommended a notary public to prepare the necessary papers for transfer of the title to Hays, and he drove the two into town for this purpose. The young man did transfer title, and the car was delivered by the salesman to Hays at his college.

When Hays's father, Dr. D. J. Hays, learned of the transaction, he called Quality Motors and asked it to take the car back. The company refused to do so. Dr. Hays was unable at that time to deliver the car back to Quality Motors, since his son had taken it out of town. However, the next day, Dr. Hays retrieved the car from his son and once again called Quality Motors to ask it to take the car back. It again refused. Dr. Hays then went to his attorney's office and, through his attorney, once more attempted to have the company accept the car back. The company refused but said it would try to sell the car for the Hayses if it could. The car was put into storage.

The following week this lawsuit was filed. Plaintiff's attorney indicated in writing to the defendant that the return of the automobile had been refused but that the automobile was now in storage and would be turned over to the defendant any time it would be accepted. Meanwhile, the son found the keys to the car and the bill of sale, took the car out of state, and damaged it in two accidents. At the time of trial, the car was subject to various repair bills and was not in running condition. The defendant continually refused to take the car back.

QUALITY MOTORS, INC. v. HAYS
Supreme Court of Arkansas, 1949.
216 Ark. 264, 225 S.W.2d 326.

The special chancellor in the trial court found that, for all intents and purposes, the defendant sold the car to the plaintiff, knowing the plaintiff was a minor. The use of a third person adult was merely a sham.

DUNAWAY, Justice.

*   *   *   *

Johnny M. Hays [plaintiff], by his [father], Dr. D. J. Hays, brought this suit to disaffirm his purchase of a Pontiac automobile and recover the purchase price of $1,750 from defendant Quality Motors, Inc.

*   *   *   *

In the case at bar Johnny Hays testified positively that he desired to disaffirm his purchase and return the car to the seller. *   *   *

The law is well settled in Arkansas that an infant may disaffirm his contracts, except those made for necessaries, without being required to return the consideration received, except such part as may remain in specie in his hands. *   *   *

We do not find any merit in [Quality Motors's] contention that no proper tender of the car was made when [Johnny Hays through his father] sought to disaffirm his purchase. The undisputed testimony shows that Dr. Hays and his attorney offered to return the car on several occasions, but were informed that [defendant] would not accept it. That it was not actually delivered to Quality Motors when the suit was filed, is [defendant's] own fault. The law does not require that a tender be made under circumstances where it would be vain and useless.

[Quality Motors's] most serious contention is that the plaintiff is liable for damages to the car which occurred while he was driving over the country, after he had slipped the car from its storage place and while the suit to disaffirm was pending. In order to obtain any relief on this score, it must be shown that plaintiff was guilty of conversion in taking the automobile. [See Chapter 3 on torts.] Conversion is the exercise of dominion over property in violation of the rights of the owner or person entitled to possession. In advancing this argument [defendant] is in an inconsistent position. In its answer, [defendant] denied selling the car to [plaintiff] and was stoutly insisting that it did not have to take the car back. If that was true [defendant] was not the owner of nor entitled to possession of the car. Until the court decreed return of the car and recovery of the consideration paid, plaintiff still had title to the car. One cannot be liable for conversion in taking his own property.

*   *   *   *

[I]n the instant case Quality Motors, Inc. was insisting at the time of the alleged conversion by Johnny Hays, that it did not have to accept return of the car. Ebbert, one of the owners of Quality Motors, Inc., testified that during his conversation with his employees in regard to keeping the car in the shop after the first wreck, he told them they could not make Johnny leave it. "Well, it's not our car," was his statement at that time. In these circumstances it certainly cannot be said [plaintiff's] possession was that of a bailee or trustee.

[Defendant] knowingly and through a planned subterfuge sold an automobile to a minor. It then refused to take the car back. Even after the car was wrecked once, it was in [defendant's] place of business, and [defendant] was still resisting disaffirmance of the contract. The loss which [defendant] has suffered is the direct result of its own acts.

The court affirmed the minor's right to avoid the contract. The plaintiff, Johnny Hays, was ordered to return the car to the defendant within seven days. When the wrecked car was returned, plaintiff was allowed to recover the purchase price from the defendant.

JUDGMENT AND REMEDY

Minors comprise a particular category of persons the law protects from economic exploitation. A minor is not compelled to avoid contracts made before attaining majority. Rather, the minor has the option of keeping the bargain or avoiding it.

COMMENTS

The Effect of a Minor's Misrepresentation of Age Suppose a minor tells a seller that she is twenty-one years old when she is actually only seventeen. Ordinarily, the minor can disaffirm the contract even though she has misrepresented her age. Moreover, the minor is not liable in certain jurisdictions for the tort of deceit for such misrepresentation, the rationale being that such a tort judgment might indirectly force the minor to perform the contract.

In certain circumstances, though, a minor can be bound by a contract when age has been misrepresented. First, several states have enacted statutes for precisely this purpose. In these states misrepresentation of age is enough to prohibit disaffirmance. Other statutes prohibit disaffirmance by a minor who has engaged in business as an adult.[3]

Second, some courts refuse to allow minors to disaffirm executed contracts unless they can

return the consideration received. The combination of their misrepresentation and their unjust enrichment has persuaded several courts to estop (prevent) minors from asserting contractual incapacity.

Third, some courts allow a misrepresenting minor to disaffirm the contract but hold the minor liable for damages in tort. Here, the defrauded party may sue the minor for misrepresentation or fraud. A split in authority exists on this point, since some courts, as previously pointed out, have recognized that allowing a suit in tort is equivalent to the indirect enforcement of the minor's contract.

Basically, a minor's ability to avoid a contractual obligation is allowed by the law as a shield for the minor's defense, not as a sword for his or her unjust enrichment.

In the following case, an Ohio appellate court reviewed the trial court's decision regarding a purported disaffirmation of a purchase contract by a minor. The court was impressed mainly by the fact that the contract had been induced by a false representation of the age of the minor.

---

3. See, for example, statutes in Iowa, Kansas, Utah, and Washington.

BACKGROUND AND FACTS *The plaintiff is Haydocy Pontiac, a seller of automobiles. The defendant, Lee, was twenty years of age when she contracted to purchase the automobile, but she represented to the plaintiff, seller, that she was twenty-one years old. The defendant purchased the car by making a trade-in and financing the rest of the purchase price. She executed a note for the unpaid purchase price, including financing charges and insurance charges. The total amount of the note was approximately $2,000.*

Immediately following delivery of the automobile, Lee turned the car over to a third person. She never at any time thereafter had possession

HAYDOCY PONTIAC, INC. v. LEE

Court of Appeals of Ohio, Franklin County, 1969.
19 Ohio App.2d 217, 250 N.E.2d 898.

of the automobile. She made no further attempt to make payment on the contract, and she attempted to rescind it. She did not return the automobile to the plaintiff-seller; nor did she offer to return it. She merely announced that she was a minor at the time of purchase, that she had not ratified the agreement to purchase the car, and that she was repudiating her contract and would not be bound by it. The trial court applied the general rule of law permitting a minor to avoid a transaction without being required to restore the consideration received.

STRAUSBAUGH, Judge.

*   *   *   *

The cases we have examined in this regard all relate to the question whether the infant can recover from the vendor the purchase price paid and the right of the vendor to counterclaim rather than the facts of this case where the vendor, in the original petition, seeks to recover the property or, in lieu thereof, the balance due on the purchase price. Many of the cases use language to the effect that when the property received by the infant is in his possession, or under his control, to permit him to rescind the contract without requiring him to return or offer to return it would be to permit him to use his privilege as a "sword rather than a shield."

*   *   *   *

To allow infants to avoid a transaction without being required to restore the consideration received where the infant has used or otherwise disposed of it causes hardship on the other party. We hold that where the consideration received by the infant cannot be returned upon disaffirmance of the contract because it has been disposed of the infant must account for the value of it, not in excess of the purchase price, where the other party is free from any fraud or bad faith and where the contract has been induced by a false representation of the age of the infant. *Under this factual situation the infant is estopped [prevented] from pleading infancy as a defense where the contract has been induced by a false representation that the infant was of age. [Emphasis added.]*

The necessity of returning the consideration as a prerequisite to obtaining equitable relief is still clearer where the infant misrepresents age and perpetrated an actual fraud on the other party. The disaffirmance of an infant's contract is to be determined by equitable principles, whether sought in a proceeding in equity or a case at law.

The common law has bestowed upon the infant the privilege of disaffirming his contracts in conservation of his rights and interests. Where the infant, 20 years of age, through falsehood and deceit enters into a contract with another who enters therein in honesty and good faith and, thereafter, the infant seeks to disaffirm the contract without tendering back the consideration, no right or interest of the infant exists which needs protection. The privilege given the infant thereupon becomes a weapon of injustice.

JUDGMENT AND REMEDY

Judgment of the trial court was reversed. The Ohio Appellate Court allowed the seller, Haydocy Pontiac, Inc., to recover the fair market value of the automobile from the defendant, Lee. The only restriction imposed by the court was that the fair market value could not be in excess of the original purchase price of the automobile.

The theory behind protecting minors is that a young person lacks the   **COMMENTS**
maturity of judgment and experience to be able to avoid the pitfalls of
the marketplace. Yet, the magical age of eighteen years is no longer an
indication of contractual maturity that has its basis in fact or in public
policy.

Liability for Necessaries A minor who enters into a contract for *necessaries* may disaffirm the contract but will still remain liable for the reasonable value of the goods. The legal duty to pay a reasonable value does not arise from the contract itself but is imposed by law under a theory of quasi-contract. One theory is that the minor should not be unjustly enriched and should therefore be liable for those things that fulfill basic needs, such as food, clothing, and shelter.

Another theory is that the minor's right to disaffirm a contract has economic ramifications in that sellers are likely to refuse to deal with minors because of it. If minors can at least be held liable for the reasonable value of the goods, sellers' reluctance to enter into contracts with minors will be offset. This theory explains why the courts narrow the subject matter to necessaries. Without such a rule, minors might be denied the opportunity to purchase necessary goods.

Note, though, that the minor is liable only for the reasonable value of the goods (because there is no contract and therefore no contract price to which the court can refer). Suppose Hank Olsen, a minor, purchases a suit that is list priced at $150. After wearing the suit for several weeks, Olsen wants to disaffirm his contract with the clothier. He can do so, but he is liable for the reasonable value of the suit. If the market value is actually $115, then the clothier can recover only that amount, even if this deprives the clothier of all profit on the sale.

For an agreement to be classified as a contract for necessaries, three basic criteria are reviewed by a court. First, the item must be for the minor's very existence. Second, the value of the item must be in accordance with the minor's station in life (that which the minor is accustomed to). Third, the minor must not be under the care of a parent or guardian who has adequately supplied the minor the items of necessity.

There is no firm, universally accepted definition of necessaries. At a minimum, necessaries include food, clothing, shelter, medicine, and hospital care. However, the term is not construed to be limited to items required for physical support of life, but extends to whatever is needed to maintain a person in his or her established lifestyle. Thus, what are necessaries for one person may not be for another in a different station in life. Moreover, necessaries include education as well as services that are reasonably necessary to enable a minor to earn a living (such as an employment agency fee for obtaining a job).

Insurance and Loans Traditionally, insurance has not been viewed as a *necessary*, so minors can ordinarily disaffirm their contract and recover all premiums paid. However, some jurisdictions prohibit the right to disaffirm—for example, when minors contract for life or health insurance on their own lives. Other jurisdictions allow a minor to disaffirm but limit recovery to the value of premiums paid, less the insurance company's actual cost of protecting the minor under the policy. Suppose Bob Berzak takes out an automobile insurance policy and pays $125 in premiums. Bob has an accident for which his insurance company, State Farm, pays a claim of $85. In states following the traditional rule, Bob's recovery upon disaffirmance will be $125, the full value of the premiums. In states limiting his recovery, Bob can recover only $40, the excess of the value of the premiums over State Farm's actual cost under the policy.

In and of itself, a loan is seldom viewed as a necessary, even if the minor spends the money on necessaries. However, if the lender makes a loan for the express purpose of enabling the minor to purchase necessaries, and the lender personally makes sure the money is so spent, the minor is normally obligated to repay the loan.

GASTONIA PERSONNEL
CORP. v. ROGERS
Supreme Court of North
Carolina, 1970.
276 N.C. 279, 172 S.E.2d 19.

BACKGROUND AND FACTS   *Bobby L. Rogers, defendant, was nineteen years old, married, and nearing completion of his associate of arts degree when he went to the office of plaintiff, an employment agency, and signed a contract for assistance in obtaining suitable employment. The contract contained the following provision:*

> "If I ACCEPT employment offered me by an employer as a result of a lead (verbal or otherwise) from you within twelve (12) months of such lead even though it may not be the position originally discussed with you, I will be obligated to pay you as per the terms of the contract."

Under the contract, the defendant was otherwise free to continue his own quest for employment. He became obligated to the plaintiff only if he accepted a job to which the plaintiff agency had referred him.

After several telephone calls to prospective employers, the employment agency arranged an interview with an employer who ultimately hired the defendant. The service charge to defendant of $295 was never paid. Plaintiff attempted to collect its fee. Defendant attempted to disaffirm the contract on the theory that services of a professional employment agency are not "necessaries" and hence can be disaffirmed. The trial court agreed with the defendant.

BOBBITT, Chief Justice.

*   *   *   *

Under the common law, persons, whether male or female, are classified and referred to as *infants* until they attain the age of twenty-one years. [Under modern law, the age is lowered to eighteen years.]

*   *   *   *

An early commentary on the common law, after the general statement that contracts made by persons (infants) before attaining the age of twenty-one "may be avoided," sets forth "some exceptions out of this generality," to wit: "*An infant may bind himselfe to pay for his necessary meat, drinke, apparell, necessary physicke, and such other necessaries,* and likewise for his good teaching or instruction, whereby he may profit himselfe afterwards." (Our italics.) Coke on Littleton, 13th ed. (1788), p. 172. If the infant married, "necessaries" included necessary food and clothing for his wife and child.

In accordance with this ancient rule of the common law, this Court has held an infant's contract, unless for "necessaries" or unless authorized by statute, is voidable by the infant, at his election, and may be disaffirmed during infancy or upon attaining the age of twenty-one.

*   *   *   *

The nature of the common law requires that each time a rule of law is applied it be carefully scrutinized to make sure that the conditions and needs of the times have not so changed as to make further application of it the instrument of injustice.

In general, our prior decisions are to the effect that the "necessaries" of an infant, his wife and child, include only such necessities of life as food, clothing, shelter, medical attention, etc. In our view, the concept of "necessaries" should be enlarged to include such articles of property and such services as are reasonably necessary to enable the infant to earn the money required to provide the necessities of life for himself and those who are legally dependent upon him.

*   *   *   *

The evidence before us tends to show that defendant, when he contracted with plaintiff, was nineteen years of age, emancipated, married, a high school graduate, within "a quarter or 22 hours" of obtaining his degree in applied science, and capable of holding a job at a starting annual salary of $4,784.00. To hold, as a matter of law, that such a person cannot obligate himself to pay for services rendered him in obtaining employment suitable to his ability, education and specialized training, enabling him to provide the necessities of life for himself, his wife and his expected child, would place him and others similarly situated under a serious economic handicap.

In the effort to protect "older minors" from improvident or unfair contracts, the law should not deny to them the opportunity and right to obligate themselves for articles of property or services which are reasonably necessary to enable them to provide for the proper support of themselves and their dependents. The minor should be held liable for the reasonable value of articles of property or services received pursuant to such contract.

The services of a professional employment agency were construed to be a "necessary." The case was remanded to the lower court for a new trial. The defendant could be expected to pay the reasonable value of the services rendered to him pursuant to the employment contract.

JUDGMENT AND REMEDY

Although the doctrine of voidability of a minor's contract often seems necessary for the protection of the young person, there are situations in which such a result is unjust. This is consistent with the policy of law that promotes business by allowing contracts to develop between parties whenever possible. Some states allow the parties to submit a proposed contract to a court that removes a minor's right to disaffirm if the court finds the particular contract to be fair or just.

COMMENTS

Ratification

Ratification is an act or expression of words by which a minor, upon or after reaching majority, indicates an *intention* to become bound by the contract. Ratification must necessarily occur, if at all, after the individual comes of age, since any attempt to become legally bound prior to majority is no more effective than the original contractual promise. This protects the minor and is consistent with the theory that the contracts of a minor are voidable at his or her option.

Express Ratification   Suppose John Lawrence enters into a contract to sell a house to Carol Ogden. At the time of the contract Carol is a minor. Naturally, Carol can avoid her legal duty to pay for the house by disaffirming the contract. Imagine, instead, that Carol reaches majority and writes a letter to John stating that she still agrees to buy the house. Carol thus ratifies the contract and is legally bound. John can sue for breach of contract if Carol refuses to perform her part of the bargain. This is an example of *express ratification.*

Implied Ratification   The contract can also be ratified by *conduct.* Suppose, after reaching majority. Carol lives in the house. This conduct evidences an intent to abide by the contract and is a form of *implied* ratification. Again, Carol is legally bound, and John can sue her for breach of contract if she fails to perform her duty to pay the purchase price. Another example of implied ratification occurs when an individual, after reaching majority, continues to use and make payments on property purchased as a minor. The continued use and payment is inconsistent with disaffirmance and implicitly indicates an intention to be bound by the contract.

In general, any act or conduct showing an intention to affirm the contract will be deemed to be ratification. However, as previously discussed, silence after reaching the age of majority does not in and of itself constitute ratification of an executory contract in most situations. If Carol had said nothing to John and had not entered into possession or made payment, she would not have ratified the contract, since she had expressed no intention to abide by it. On the other hand, the minor may have a duty to speak in some circumstances. Suppose that after coming of age, a former minor seller fails to disaffirm, knowing that the purchaser is making improvements on the property sold. In this case the minor cannot disaffirm the contract.

Non-voidable Contracts and Torts

Minors Many states have passed statutes restricting the ability of minors to avoid certain contracts. For example, as previously discussed, some states prohibit minors from disaffirming certain insurance contracts. Other states hold that loans for education or medical care received by minors create binding legal duties that they cannot avoid.[4]

In addition, certain statutes specifically require minors to perform legal duties. Suppose James Dornan, a minor, wants to legally seize the property of Davis Snowden for default of a loan. In some states, Dornan is required to file a bond before the legal seizure, or attachment, can occur. After filing the bond, Dornan cannot avoid

the obligations of the bonding agreement, since the bond is a legal duty imposed by state statute. In such situations, a minor cannot rely on the common law rule that the bonding contract is voidable. Similar legal duties are imposed on minors with respect to bank accounts and transfers of stocks. A contract to enlist in the armed forces is also non-voidable by a minor.

Torts In Chapters 3 and 4, we discussed the area of law called torts, defined as private wrongs committed upon a person or property independent of contract. Generally, minors are liable for their torts. Courts do, however, weigh the factors of age, mental capacity, and maturity before determining a minor's liability. As has been pointed out, a breach of contract is normally not treated as a tort for which the minor is liable. However, when the tort is more than a simple misfeasance in the performance of a contract, and when it is separate from and independent of the contract, the court may rule against the minor. The test of action against the minor is whether liability exists without taking notice of the contract. For example, suppose a minor rents a boat. The rental agreement provides that the minor will use due care to prevent damage to the boat. Nonetheless, the minor's careless use of the boat damages it. Will a court uphold an action in tort for negligence? The answer to this question depends on whether imposing tort liability on the minor will directly or indirectly enforce the minor's promise, which, because of a lack of contractual capacity, is voidable.

Parents' Liability

As a general rule, parents are not liable for the contracts made by their minor children. This is why businesses ordinarily require parents to sign any contract made with a minor. The parents then become personally obligated under the contract to perform the conditions of the contract, even if their child avoids liability.

Parents who have neglected the care of their minor child can be held liable for the reasonable value of necessaries supplied to the child, even when they have not signed a contract. In other

---

4. New York Education Law, Sec. 281 (McKinney 1969); Cal. Civil Code Sec. 36 [West 1982].

words, if a child purchases shoes because his or her parents refuse to provide any shoes, the parents can be held liable for the reasonable value of the shoes.

INTOXICATED PERSONS

A contract entered into by an intoxicated person can be either voidable or valid. If the person was drunk enough to lack mental capacity, then the transaction is voidable at the option of the intoxicated person even if the intoxication was purely voluntary. In order for the contract to be voidable, it must be proved that the intoxicated person's reason and judgment were impaired to the extent that he or she did not comprehend the legal consequences of entering into the contract. If, despite intoxication, the person understands these legal consequences, the contract will be enforceable. Simply because the terms of the contract are foolish or obviously favor the other party does not mean that the contract is voidable (unless the other party *fraudulently* induced the person to become intoxicated). Problems often arise in determining whether a party was drunk enough to avoid legal duties. Many courts prefer to look at objective indications to determine whether the contract is voidable because of intoxication rather than inquiring into the intoxicated party's mental state.

The following case shows an unusual business transaction in which boasts, brags, and dares "after a few drinks" resulted in a binding sale and purchase transaction. It should be noted that avoidance for intoxication is very rare.

BACKGROUND AND FACTS   *W. O. Lucy and J. C. Lucy filed suit against A. H. Zehmer and Ida Zehmer, the defendants, to compel the Zehmers to perform a contract by which it was alleged that the Zehmers had sold to the Lucys their property, known as the Ferguson Farm, for $50,000. The transaction had come about in a most unusual manner. Lucy had known Zehmer for fifteen or twenty years and for the last eight years or so had been anxious to buy the Ferguson Farm from Zehmer. One night, Lucy stopped in to visit the Zehmers in the restaurant, filling station, and motor court they operated. While there, Lucy tried to buy the Ferguson Farm once again. This time he tried a new approach. According to the trial court transcript, Lucy said to Zehmer, "I bet you wouldn't take $50,000 for that place." Zehmer replied, "Yes, I would too; you wouldn't give fifty."*

Throughout the evening the conversation returned to the sale of the Ferguson Farm for $50,000. At the same time, the parties continued to drink whiskey and engage in light conversation. The conversation repeatedly returned to the subject of the Ferguson Farm. Eventually, Lucy enticed Zehmer to write up an agreement to the effect that Zehmer would agree to sell to Lucy the Ferguson Farm for $50,000 complete. Zehmer first wrote that out on the back of a restaurant check. He tore up the first copy because he had written "I do hereby agree" and thought it had better read "we" because Mrs. Zehmer would have to sign it too. Zehmer rewrote the agreement and asked Mrs. Zehmer to sign it. She agreed.

Lucy sued Zehmer to go through with the sale. Zehmer argued that he was drunk and that the offer was made in jest and hence was unenforceable. The trial court agreed with the Zehmers.

W. O. LUCY AND J. C. LUCY v. A. H. ZEHMER AND IDA S. ZEHMER
Supreme Court of Appeals of Virginia, 1954.
196 Va. 493, 84 S.E.2d 516.

BUCHANAN, Justice.

*   *   *   *

The instrument sought to be enforced was written by A. H. Zehmer on December 20, 1952, in these words: "We hereby agree to sell to W. O. Lucy the Ferguson Farm complete for $50,000.00, title satisfactory to buyer," and signed by the defendants, A. H. Zehmer and Ida S. Zehmer.

A. H. Zehmer admitted that *   *   * W. O. Lucy offered him $50,000 cash for the farm, but that he, Zehmer, considered that the offer was made in jest; that so thinking, and both he and Lucy having had several drinks, he wrote out "the memorandum" quoted above and induced his wife to sign it; that he did not deliver the memorandum to Lucy, but that Lucy picked it up, read it, put it in his pocket, attempted to offer Zehmer $5 to bind the bargain, which Zehmer refused to accept, and realizing for the first time that Lucy was serious, Zehmer assured him that he had no intention of selling the farm and that the whole matter was a joke. Lucy left the premises insisting that he had purchased the farm.

*   *   *   *

The discussion leading to the signing of the agreement, said Lucy, lasted thirty or forty minutes, during which Zehmer seemed to doubt that Lucy could raise $50,000. Lucy suggested the provision for having the title examined and Zehmer made the suggestion that he would sell it "complete, everything there," and stated that all he had on the farm was three heifers.

Lucy took a partly filled bottle of whiskey into the restaurant with him for the purpose of giving Zehmer a drink if he wanted it. Zehmer did, and he and Lucy had one or two drinks together. Lucy said that while he felt the drinks he took he was not intoxicated, and from the way Zehmer handled the transaction he did not think he was either.

*   *   *   *

The defendants insist that *   *   * the writing sought to be enforced was prepared as a bluff or dare to force Lucy to admit that he did not have $50,000; that the whole matter was a joke; that the writing was not delivered to Lucy and no binding contract was ever made between the parties.

It is an unusual, if not bizarre, defense. *   *   *

In his testimony, Zehmer claimed that he "was high as a Georgia pine," and that the transaction "was just a bunch of two doggoned drunks bluffing to see who could talk the biggest and say the most." That claim is inconsistent with his attempt to testify in great detail as to what was said and what was done. *   *   * The record is convincing that Zehmer was not intoxicated to the extent of being unable to comprehend the nature and consequences of the instrument he executed, and hence that instrument is not to be invalidated on that ground. *   *   *

*   *   *   *

The appearance of the contract, the fact that it was under discussion for forty minutes or more before it was signed; Lucy's objection to the first draft because it was written in the singular, and he wanted Mrs. Zehmer to sign it also; the rewriting to meet that objection and the signing by Mrs. Zehmer; the discussion of what was to be included in the sale, the provision for the examination of the title, the completeness of the instrument that was executed, the taking possession of it by Lucy with no request or suggestion by either of the defendants that he give it back, are facts which furnish persuasive evidence that the execution of the contract was a serious business transaction rather than a casual, jesting matter as defendants now contend.

* * * *

Not only did Lucy actually believe, but the evidence shows he was warranted in believing, that the contract represented a serious business transaction and a good faith sale and purchase of the farm.

In the field of contracts, as generally elsewhere, *"We must look to the outward expression of a person as manifesting his intention rather than to his secret and unexpressed intention. [Emphasis added.] 'The law imputes to a person an intention corresponding to the reasonable meaning of his words and acts.'"*

* * * *

Whether the writing signed by the defendants and now sought to be enforced by the complainants was the result of a serious offer by Lucy and a serious acceptance by the defendants, or was a serious offer by Lucy and an acceptance in secret jest by the defendants, in either event it constituted a binding contract of sale between the parties.

The Supreme Court of Virginia determined that the writing was an enforceable contract and reversed the lower court. The Zehmers were required by court order to carry through with the sale of the Ferguson Farm to the Lucys.

JUDGMENT AND REMEDY

Avoidance or Ratification

If a contract is held to be voidable because of a person's intoxication, that person has the option of disaffirming (avoiding) it—the same option available to a minor. However, the vast majority of courts require the intoxicated person to make full restitution (fully return consideration received) as a condition of disaffirmance. For example, a person contracts to purchase a set of encyclopedias while intoxicated. If the books are delivered, the purchaser can disaffirm the executed contract (getting back payment made) only by returning the encyclopedias.

Like a minor, an intoxicated person, after becoming sober, may ratify expressly or implicitly. Implied ratification occurs when a person enters into a contract while drunk and fails to disaffirm the contract within a *reasonable* time after becoming sober. Acts or conduct inconsistent with an intent to disaffirm will also ratify the contract—for example, if a person continues to use property purchased under a voidable contract.

In addition, contracts for necessaries are voidable (as in the case of minors), but the in-

toxicated person is liable in quasi-contract (implied-in-law contract) for the reasonable value of the consideration received.

The lack of contractual capacity due to intoxication while the contract is being made must be distinguished from capacity (or the lack thereof) of an alcoholic. If a contract is made while an alcoholic is sober, there is no lack of capacity.[5]

INSANE PERSONS

Contracts made by insane persons can be either void, voidable, or valid. If a person has been adjudged insane by a court of law and a guardian has been appointed, any contract made by the insane person is void—no contract exists. Only the guardian can enter into binding legal duties on behalf of the insane person.

Insane persons not so adjudged by a court may enter into voidable contracts if they do not

---

5. Olsen v. Hawkins, 90 Idaho 28, 408 P.2d 462 (1965).

know they are entering into the contract, or if they lack the mental capacity to comprehend its subject matter, nature, and consequences. In such situations the contracts are voidable at the option of the insane person, although the other party does not have this option.[6]

The contract may be disaffirmed or ratified. Ratification must occur after the person is mentally competent or after a guardian is appointed and ratifies the contract. As in the case of minors and intoxicated persons, insane persons are liable in quasi-contract for the reasonable value of necessaries they receive.

A contract entered into by an insane person may also be valid. A person can understand the nature and effect of entering into a certain contract, yet simultaneously lack capacity to engage in other activities. In such cases the contract will be valid, since the person is not legally insane for contractual purposes.

In some circumstances, some states refuse to allow disaffirmance of a contract entered into by an insane person. If the contract is fair and reasonable and the other party had no knowledge or reason to believe the person was insane, the contract will be enforced. However, the majority of states allow disaffirmance even here, provided the insane person restores any consideration received and makes restitution to the other party.[7]

CONVICTS

Persons convicted of a major criminal offense (a felony or treason) often lack full contractual capacity. Laws pertaining to their ability to contract vary from state to state. In some states the convicted felon can make a valid transfer of his or her property or contract for services of others, or both, while in prison. In other states, the convicted felon is either partially or totally unable to contract during the period of incarceration.

---

6. This applies to all voidable contracts.
7. Modern courts no longer require a person to be *legally* insane to disaffirm contracts. See Ortelere v. Teachers' Retirement Bd., 25 N.Y.2d 196, 303 N.Y.S.2d 362, 250 N.E.2d 460 (1969). The court sets out what the tests for mental incompetency are.

ALIENS

An alien is a citizen of another country who resides in this country. Generally, aliens who are legally in this country have the same contractual rights as U.S. citizens. They may be sued and they may sue in the courts in order to enforce their contractual rights. Some states restrict the right of an alien to own real property. In virtually all cases, an enemy alien during time of war will not be able to enforce a contract, although the contract can be held in abeyance until the war is over.

MARRIED WOMEN

At common law, a married woman could not make binding contracts even if she lived apart from her husband. In other words, married women's contracts were void rather than voidable. Even after the death of the husband, the married woman was incapable of ratifying a previously drawn contract because that contract was invalid from the beginning. Virtually all states have abolished common law restrictions on the contractual capacity of married women.[8] A few restrictions do remain in certain states.

QUESTIONS AND CASE PROBLEMS

1. For most contractual purposes in State X, age eighteen is the age of majority. Martin, age seventeen, contracts to purchase adult Smith's car for $1,200, paying $200 down, with the balance plus interest to be paid at $75 per month. The car is to be used primarily to go back and forth to college and for pleasure. Martin takes possession and starts making payments. He turns eighteen and then makes one additional pay-

---

8. These statutes are normally called Married Women's Property Acts.

ment before discovering some defects in the automobile. Martin tenders the car back to Smith, demanding back all payments made, claiming his right to disaffirm the contract. Smith refuses the tender, claiming Martin is legally liable for the remaining payments. Discuss who is correct and why.

2. Seling, a minor, sold her bicycle to Adam, an adult, for $100. Adam took possession and paid Seling. Two months later, Adam sold the bicycle to Bonnet, a bona fide purchaser, for value. Seling's parents became upset when they learned of her sale. Seling, before reaching the age of majority, seeks to disaffirm the contract with Adam and recover the bicycle from Bonnet. Discuss whether Seling can recover the bicycle from Bonnet, *and* discuss Adam's liability to Seling.

3. Treat is a seventeen-year-old minor who has just graduated from high school. She is attending a university 200 miles from home and has contracted to rent an apartment near the university for one year at $250 per month. She is working at a convenience store to earn enough money to be self-supporting. She moves into the apartment and has paid four months' rent when a dispute arises between her and the landlord. Treat, still a minor, moves out and returns the key to the landlord. The landlord wants to hold Treat for the balance on the lease, $2,000. Discuss fully Treat's liability on the lease.

4. If a college student who is a minor seeks to rent an apartment, he or she may be asked to sign a lease in which there is a clause certifying that the person signing the lease is an adult. What are the possible legal ramifications of such a signed lease?

5. Smith has been the owner of a car dealership for a number of years. One year ago, Smith sold one of his most expensive cars to Beyer. At the time of the sale, Smith thought Beyer acted in a peculiar manner; however, Smith had not thought further about the transaction until today, when Beyer's court-appointed guardian appeared at his office, tendered back the car, and demanded Beyer's money back. The guardian informed Smith that Beyer had been adjudged insane two months ago by a proper court.
   (a) Discuss the rights of the parties.
   (b) If Beyer had been adjudicated insane at the time of the contract, what would be the legal effect of the contract?

6. Robertson, a minor, entered into a conditional sales agreement whereby he purchased a pickup truck from Julian Pontiac Company for the agreed price of $1,743.85. Robertson traded in a passenger car for which he was given a credit of $723.85 on the purchase price, leaving a balance of $1,020, which he agreed to pay in twenty-three monthly installments. Robertson had already paid one of the installments when the pickup truck began to experience electrical wiring difficulties. Less than a month after the purchase of the truck, Robertson turned eighteen. About two weeks later, as a result of the electrical wiring defects, the truck caught fire and was practically destroyed. Robertson refused to make any further payments under the installment agreement. Julian Pontiac Company sued Robertson to recover the truck. Robertson filed a cross-complaint to rescind the contract and recover the amounts he had paid. Who prevails? [Robertson v. King, 225 Ark. 276, 280 S.W.2d 402 (1955)]

7. Pankas was the owner and operator of a hair styling boutique in downtown Pittsburgh, Pennsylvania. He had maintained his shop in the same location for a number of years and had built up a substantial clientele. In March 1962, Pankas hired Bell, who was about seventeen years old at the time. Part of Bell's employment included an agreement (called a restrictive covenant) that if he should leave Pankas's employ, he would not work at another beauty parlor within a ten-mile radius of downtown Pittsburgh. Shortly after reaching majority, Bell left Pankas's employ and, along with another Pankas employee, opened a beauty shop only a few blocks away from Pankas's business. In addition, Bell advertised the fact that he and his partner were former employees of Pankas. Pankas sued Bell to enjoin him from further breach of their restrictive covenant. Bell claimed that as a minor he could rescind the agreement. Was he correct? [Pankas v. Bell, 413 Pa. 494, 198 A.2d 312 (1964)]

8. Peddy and Montgomery entered into a contract under which Montgomery agreed to sell a certain parcel of her land to Peddy. At the time of the transaction, Montgomery was a resident of the state of Alabama. Alabama, by statute, prohibited married women from selling real estate without the consent of their husbands. Montgomery's husband refused to consent to the deal, and Montgomery in turn refused to transfer the land to Peddy. Montgomery claimed that because of the statute she was not obligated under the contract since the contract was invalid from the beginning. Peddy responded that the statute violated the equal protection clause of the Constitution since it treated men and women differently with no reasonable basis for the difference in treatment. Was the contract between Montgomery and Peddy void or voidable? What do you think of the constitutional claim? [Peddy v. Montgomery, 345 So.2d 631 (Ala.1977)]

9. Spaulding, a minor, was married and living with his wife and child when he entered into a contract with New England Furniture Co. for the purchase of bedroom furniture and a stove. The purchase included

a three-piece bedroom set that was priced significantly higher than most other three-piece bedroom sets and an expensive combination oil-and-gas stove. After making several payments, Spaulding defaulted, disaffirmed his contract, and allowed the company to remove all the furniture and the stove. New England Furniture, however, refused to return the money that Spaulding had already paid. Was Spaulding able to recover these payments? [Spaulding v. New England Furniture Co., 154 Me. 330, 147 A.2d 916 (1959)]

CHAPTER 10

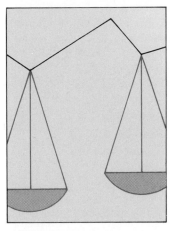

CONTRACTS
Legality

In order for a contract to be enforced in court, the contract must call for the performance of a legal act. A contract is illegal if either its formation or its performance is criminal, tortious, or otherwise opposed to public policy. The first part of this chapter will consider what makes a bargain illegal—when the contract is contrary to state or federal statutes and when the contract is contrary to public policy. The second part will consider the *effects* of an illegal bargain. Such contracts are normally void—that is, they really are not contracts.

CONTRACTS CONTRARY TO STATUTE

Usury

Every state has statutes that set the maximum rates of interest that can be charged for different types of transactions, including ordinary loans. A lender who makes a loan at an interest rate above the lawful maximum is guilty of **usury**. The maximum rate of interest varies from state to state.

In order to determine the amount of interest being charged on a loan, many states require service charges, credit insurance, and "points" to be included in the calculation. For example, suppose you are charged $100 per year to borrow $1,000. In addition, the lender charges you $25 in service charges and requires you to take out credit insurance that costs another $25. The true annual rate of interest is then 15 percent (the total of $150 in charges divided by the principal amount of $1,000). A discount from the principal amount (points) should also be included in the calculation if appropriate. If you receive only $950 for the $1,000 loan, you are paying $50 in points. Points are prorated over the life of the loan and then added to the other charges to determine the true rate of interest.

If the above loan were to be paid in five annual installments, then the effective interest rate would be increased by 1 percent, thereby increasing the total interest charged to 16 percent. If the statutory maximum interest rate were 15 percent, then the loan would be usurious.

Not all charges are included in the calculation for interest. Many statutes provide that charges for additional services primarily of benefit to the borrower should not be included if they are reasonable. Examples of such charges are certain filing fees, attorneys' fees, and inspection or investigation charges.

Exceptions   Because usury statutes place a ceiling on the allowable rates of interest, exceptions have been made in order to facilitate business transactions. For example, many states exempt corporate loans from the usury laws. In addition, almost all states have adopted special statutes allowing much higher interest rates on small loans. In some cases the interest (including other charges) can exceed 100 percent of the loan. Such high rates are allowed because many borrowers simply cannot get loans at interest rates below the lawful maximum and might otherwise be forced to turn to loan sharks.

Installment Loans   Many states have special statutes dealing with allowable charges and interest on installment loans. This is particularly true of retail and motor vehicle installment sales. Each state statute must be checked, as the rates and amounts vary substantially. For example, in some states the maximum amount permitted by law may depend on the age of the motor vehicle and subject to the loan agreement.

In addition, many states permit what are called add-on interest rates (charges) on installment loans. For example, you purchase a car for $1,000, payable in twelve monthly installments at a rate of 9 percent interest. The seller takes the $90 in interest, adds this amount to the $1,000 (for a total of $1,090), and divides this amount by 12, which yields a monthly payment figure of $90.83. Since you do not receive the full value of the loan of $1,000 during the twelve-month period (you are paying back part of the principal each month), your actual annual simple interest

rate is approximately 18 percent, double the stated 9 percent.[1]

Retail Charge Agreements—Revolving Charge Accounts   Sales agreements often give the purchaser an opportunity to pay all charges from a particular seller or lender by means of a revolving charge account. This means that the purchaser can make numerous credit purchases at a department store (on a credit card, for example) and, upon receiving the bill, can either pay it in full or pay a minimum monthly amount, extending the balance to be paid in the future. For the privilege of paying the balance later, the purchaser is charged a monthly interest on the balance. For example, purchases on a revolving credit account or purchases made with Visa or MasterCard credit cards usually call for interest payments of 1.5 percent per month on the outstanding balance. Some courts have interpreted these transactions as not being "loans of money" and therefore not subject to the usury laws. Some states have passed installment sales statutes that expressly permit such practices.

Effects of Usury   The effects of a usurious loan differ from state to state. A number of states allow the lender to recover the principal of a loan along with interest up to the legal maximum. In effect, the lender is denied recovery of the excess interest. In other states the lender can recover the principal amount of the loan but not the interest. In a few states, a usurious loan is a void transaction, and the lender cannot recover either the principal or the interest (which is very harsh).

Gambling

In general, wagers, lotteries, and games of chance are illegal. All states have statutes that regulate

---

1.   The complexities of determining the true interest rate for comparative loan shopping led to passage of the federal Truth-in-Lending Law, which primarily requires a seller or lender to disclose not only the charges associated with the loan, or installment sale, but the *annual percentage rate* (APR) by standard procedures. This law does not set maximum rates (state law controls what is usury), but it does provide information on the interest actually being charged.

gambling—defined as any scheme for the distribution of property by chance, among persons who have paid a valuable consideration for the opportunity to receive the property.[2] Gambling is the creation of risk for the purpose of assuming it. A few states do permit gambling as long as the prizes or winnings do not exceed $100 to $500.[3] In addition, a number of states have recognized the substantial revenues that can be obtained from gambling and have legalized state-operated lotteries, horseracing, and lotteries arranged for charitable purposes (such as bingo).

Sometimes it is difficult to distinguish a gambling contract from the risk-sharing inherent in almost all contracts. Suppose Adams takes out a life insurance policy on Ziegler, naming himself as beneficiary under the policy. At first blush, this may seem entirely legal; but further examination shows that Adams is simply gambling on how long Ziegler will live. In order to prevent this type of practice, insurance contracts can be entered into only by someone with an **insurable interest.** An insurable interest, discussed in Chapter 55, is a property or ownership right in the thing being insured. Adams cannot take out an insurance policy on Ziegler's home or auto because Adams does not have an insurable interest in Ziegler's property. But if Adams has a mortgage on Ziegler's house, he can take out an insurance policy because he has a property interest in the house.

Futures contracts, or contracts for the future purchase or sale of commodities such as corn and wheat, are not illegal gambling contracts. It might appear that a person selling or buying a futures contract is essentially gambling on the future price of the commodity. However, since the seller of the futures contract can purchase the commodity elsewhere and deliver the commodity as required in the futures contract, courts have upheld the legality of such contracts.

---

2. See Wishing Well Club v. Akron, 112 N.E.2d 41 (1951).
3. Iowa and Florida are two such states.

BACKGROUND AND FACTS   *The Seattle Times* ran a football forecasting contest that it named "Guest-Guesser." The Seattle chief of police claimed that the contest was illegal because it was a lottery. When the *Times* asked for a declaratory judgment action to determine the legality of the contest, the trial court found that the contest was an illegal lottery. The *Times* appealed.

SEATTLE TIMES CO. v. TIELSCH
Supreme Court of Washington, En Banc, 1972.
80 Wash.2d 502, 495 P.2d 1366.

ROSELLINI, J.
* * * *

The result of a football game may depend upon weather, the physical condition of the players and the psychological attitude of the players. It may also be affected by sociological problems between and among the members of a football team. The element of chance is an integral part of the game of football as well as the skill of the players.

The lure of the "Guest-Guesser" contest is partially the participant's love of football, partially the challenge of competition and partially the hope enticingly held out, which is often false or disappointing, that the participant will get something for nothing or a great deal for a very little outlay. . . .

The elements of a lottery are prize, consideration and chance. . . .

The appellant maintains that chance is not a dominant element in football forecasting contests. * * * The trial court found to the contrary upon that evidence, and we think the finding is justified. The appellant's expert statistician who testified at the trial did not state that chance plays no part in the outcome of such a contest or even that it does not play a dominant role. He merely testified that such a contest is not one of "pure chance." Pure chance he defined as a 50-50 chance. He acknowledged that a contestant who consistently predicted the outcome of 14 out of 20 games correctly would be a "highly skilled" contestant.

* * * *

Where a contest is multiple or serial, and requires the solution of a number of problems to win the prize, the fact that skill alone will bring contestants to a correct solution of a greater part of the problems does not make the contest any the less a lottery if chance enters into the solution of another lesser part of the problems and thereby proximately influences the final result. . . .

Our research has revealed only one case involving a football forecasting game and the game there was a "pool," that is, a gambling game wherein wagers were placed. The Superior Court of Pennsylvania held that it was a lottery. What is most relevant in the case for our consideration here is the court's discussion of the element of chance in forecasting the result of football games. That court said: It is true that for an avid student of the sport of football the chance taken is not so great as for those who have little interest in the game. However, it is common knowledge that the predictions even among these so-called "experts" are far from infallible. Any attempt to forecast the result of a single athletic contest, be it football, baseball, or whatever, is fraught with chance. This hazard is multiplied directly by the number of predictions made. The operators of the scheme involved in this case were all cognizant of this fact for the odds against a correct number of selections were increased from 5 to 1 for three teams picked up to 900 to 1 for fifteen teams.

The trial court in the instant case recognized the same basic realities attendant upon the enterprise of football game-result forecasting. We are convinced that it correctly held that chance, rather than skill, is the dominant factor in the Times' "Guest-Guesser" contest. The very name of the contest conveys quite accurately the promoter's as well as the participants' true concept of the nature of the contest.

We conclude that the contest, however harmless it may be in the opinion of the participants and the promoters, is a lottery. * * *

JUDGMENT AND REMEDY *The trial court was upheld. The "Guest-Guesser" game was indeed illegal as a lottery. The contest, even though harmless in the opinion of the participants and the promoters, was illegal.*

Sabbath Laws

Statutes called Sabbath, or Sunday, laws prohibit the formation or performance of certain contracts on a Sunday. At common law, in the absence of this statutory prohibition, such contracts are legal. Most states, however, have enacted some type of Sunday statute.

Some states have statutes making all contracts entered into on a Sunday illegal. Statutes in other states prohibit only the sale of merchandise, particularly alcoholic beverages, on a Sunday. (These are often called blue laws.) A number of states have laws that forbid the carrying on of "all secular labor and business on The Lord's Day". In such states, it would appear that all contracts made on a Sunday are illegal and unenforceable *as long as they remain executory.*

Exceptions to Sunday laws permit works of necessity and works of charity. In addition, a contract entered into on a Sunday that has been fully performed (that is, an *executed* contract) cannot be rescinded, or cancelled. Active enforcement of Sunday laws varies from state to state and even among communities within a particular state. Many do not enforce the Sunday laws, and many such laws have been held to be unconstitutional.

Licensing Statutes

All states require members of certain professions or callings to obtain licenses allowing them to practice. Doctors, lawyers, real estate brokers, construction contractors, electricians, and stockbrokers are but a few of the people who must be licensed. Some licenses are obtained only after extensive schooling and examinations, which indicates to the public that a special skill is involved. Others require only that the particular person be of good moral character.

When a person enters into a contract with an unlicensed individual, the contract may be enforceable despite the lack of a license. The nature of the statute itself often tells if such a contract is enforceable. Some statutes expressly provide that the lack of a license for people engaged in certain occupations will bar enforcement of any work-related contracts they enter into.

If the statute does not expressly state this, one must look to the underlying purpose of the licensing requirements for that occupation. If the underlying purpose is to protect the public from unauthorized practitioners, then the contract will be illegal and unenforceable. For example, if you enter into a contract involving the professional services of an unlicensed chiropractor, the chiropractor cannot enforce the contract. The licensing of chiropractors is designed to protect the public from persons who are not capable (or who have not shown their capability) of practicing their trade. On the other hand, if the underlying purpose of the licensing statute is to raise revenues, contracts entered into with an unlicensed practitioner will be enforceable. The sanction instead will usually be a fine on the unlicensed practitioner.

Assume you live in a state where anybody can be a television repairman. The only require-

ment for a license is the payment of $50 a year. Since there are no restrictions on who can get a license, it obviously is used only to raise revenue. If Hyde has his television fixed in a reasonable manner by Jenkins and is charged a reasonable price, Hyde cannot escape his contractual liability to pay Jenkins simply because Jenkins does not have a valid license.

Contracts to Commit a Crime

Any contract to commit a crime is a contract in violation of a statute.[4] Thus, a contract to sell an illegal drug (sale is prohibited by statute) is not enforceable. Should the object or performance of the contract be rendered illegal by statute after the contract has been entered into, the contract is said to be discharged by law. (See discussion under "Impossibility of Performance" in Chapter 14).

CONTRACTS CONTRARY TO PUBLIC POLICY

Although contracts are entered into by private parties, some are not enforceable because of the negative impact they would have on society. These contracts are said to be *contrary to public policy*. Numerous examples exist. Any contract to commit an immoral act is in this category. Contracts that prohibit marriage have been held illegal on this basis. Suppose Dangerfield promises a young man $500 if he will refrain from marrying Dangerfield's daughter. If the young man accepts, the resulting contract is not formed (is void). Thus, if he married Dangerfield's daughter, Dangerfield could not sue him for breach of contract.

In the following case, a famous movie star was party to an unusual suit brought to enforce an oral contract for property and support growing out of a nonmarital relationship.

---

4. See, for example, McConnell v. Commonwealth Pictures Corp., 7 N.Y.2d 465, 199 N.Y.S.2d 483, 166 N.E.2d 494 (1960). In this famous case, the majority view and the dissent clearly showed two different ideas about illegality.

MARVIN v. MARVIN
Supreme Court of California,
1976.
18 Cal.3d 660, 134 Cal.Rptr.
815, 557 P.2d 106.

BACKGROUND AND FACTS *Michelle Marvin lived with Lee Marvin for seven years without marriage and then brought suit to enforce an alleged oral contract existing between them. Michelle Marvin, the plaintiff, claimed that, according to their agreement, she was entitled to half the property that had been acquired in Lee Marvin's name during the seven years, and she sought support payments.*

The aspect to be dealt with here is the Supreme Court of California ruling that a court can enforce a contract between nonmarital parties unless the contract was explicitly founded on the consideration of meretricious sexual services, which are illegal.

TOBRINER, Justice.

*   *   *   *

During the past 15 years, there has been a substantial increase in the number of couples living together without marrying.[1] Such nonmarital relationships lead to legal controversy when one partner dies or the couple separates. Courts of Appeal, faced with the task of determining property rights in such cases, have arrived at conflicting positions. We [the Supreme Court] take this opportunity to resolve that controversy and to declare the principles which should govern distribution of property acquired in a nonmarital relationship.

*   *   *   *

Although the past decisions hover over the issue in the somewhat wispy form of the figures of a Chagall painting, we can abstract from those decisions a clear and simple rule. *The fact that a man and woman live together without marriage, and engage in a sexual relationship, does not in itself invalidate agreements between them relating to their earnings, property, or expenses.* [Emphasis added.] Neither is such an agreement invalid merely because the parties may have contemplated the creation or continuation of a nonmarital relationship when they entered into it. Agreements between nonmarital partners fail only to the extent that they rest upon a consideration of meretricious sexual services. *   *   *

*   *   *   *

In summary, we base our opinion on the principle that adults who voluntarily live together and engage in sexual relations are nonetheless as competent as any other persons to contract respecting their earnings and property rights. Of course, they cannot lawfully contract to pay for the performance of sexual services, for such a contract is, in essence, an agreement for prostitution and unlawful for that reason [because the action is illegal; hence the contract would be illegal and void]. But they may agree to pool their earnings and to hold all property acquired during the relationship in accord with the law governing community property; conversely they may agree that each partner's earnings and the property acquired from these earnings remains the separate property of the earning partner. So long as the agreement does not rest upon illicit meretricious consideration, the parties may

---

1. 'The 1970 census figures indicate that today perhaps eight times as many couples are living together without being married as cohabited ten years ago." [Comment, *In re Cary: A Judicial Recognition of Illicit Cohabitation* (1974) 25 Hastings L.J. 1226.]

order their economic affairs as they choose, and no policy precludes the courts from enforcing such agreements.

In the present instance, plaintiff alleges that the parties agreed to pool their earnings, that they contracted to share equally in all property acquired, and that defendant agreed to support plaintiff. The terms of the contract as alleged do not rest upon any unlawful consideration. We therefore conclude that the complaint furnishes a suitable basis upon which the trial court can render declaratory relief.

*   *   *   *

We conclude that the judicial barriers that may stand in the way of a *policy based upon the fulfillment of the reasonable expectations of the parties to a nonmarital relationship should be removed.* [Emphasis added.] As we have explained, the courts now hold that express agreements will be enforced unless they rest on an unlawful meretricious consideration. We add that in the absence of an express agreement, the courts may look to a variety of other remedies in order to protect the parties' lawful expectations.

The courts may inquire into the conduct of the parties to determine whether that conduct demonstrates an implied contract or implied agreement of partnership or joint venture or some other tacit understanding between the parties. *   *   * Finally, a nonmarital partner may recover in quantum meruit for the reasonable value of household services rendered less the reasonable value of support received if he can show that he rendered services with the expectation of monetary reward.

The court recognized that a contract can exist between nonmarital parties with regard to their earnings and property rights and that such an agreement can be enforced by the court as long as it is not explicitly founded on the consideration of sexual services. The case was sent back to the trial court to determine if an implied or an express contract existed between the parties and the nature of the terms. In trial court, the original verdict was reversed.

JUDGMENT AND REMEDY

Contracts in Restraint of Trade

An example of contracts that adversely affect the public are contracts in restraint of trade. Public policy favors competition in the economy. In addition, contracts in restraint of trade usually violate one or more statutes.[5] However, prior to the adoption of these federal statutes, case law prohibiting certain contracts had the effect of restraining trade.

Although most contracts in restraint of trade are illegal, an exception is recognized when the restraint is *reasonable* and is an integral part of certain contracts. Many such exceptions are a type of restraint that is called a covenant not to compete, or a restrictive covenant.

Covenants Not to Compete *Covenants not to compete* are often contained in contracts for the sale of an ongoing business. The seller agrees not to open up a new store within a certain geographical area surrounding the old store. When covenants, or agreements, not to compete are accompanied by the sale of an ongoing business, the agreements are usually upheld as legal if they are "reasonable," usually in terms of time and area. The purpose of these covenants is to enable

---

5.   Some of these statutes are the Sherman Antitrust Act, the Clayton Act, and the Federal Trade Commission Act. States also have separate antitrust statutes. Antitrust and contracts in restraint of trade are discussed in Chapters 50 and 51.

the seller to sell, and the purchaser to buy, the "good will" and "reputation" of an ongoing business. If these covenants were not valid, then the valuable business interest of "good will" and "reputation" could not be transferred. For example, suppose the seller has built up an established clientele because the business is known for its high-quality product and service. If the buyer desires to keep the opportunity to serve the established clientele, he or she will include a covenant that imposes reasonable restrictions on the seller—for example, that the seller shall not establish a similar business within a two-mile radius for a period of five years. The seller, in turn, receives consideration in return for giving up his legal right to compete under the conditions proscribed. In this way, the seller is prevented from opening a similar business right down the block and drawing away the buyer's customers.

If the agreement not to compete is made without an accompanying sales agreement, it is void. When no business is being sold, there is no reason for a person to agree not to compete in a certain geographical area. Such an agreement tends to restrain trade and is contrary to public policy.

Even when ancillary to a primary agreement, agreements not to compete can be contrary to public policy if they are unreasonably broad or restrictive. Suppose Orian Capital, doing business in San Francisco, sells its loan and finance business to Bankers Life Company. If Orian Capital agrees not to open another business in the whole state of California, the agreement not to compete is unreasonably broad. After all, the threat of losing customers to Orian is not very severe in San Diego. On the other hand, if the agreement covers only the San Francisco Bay area, it will probably be upheld.

Ancillary agreements not to compete can also be held contrary to public policy if they last for an unreasonably long period of time. In the preceding example, if Orian agrees not to compete for a hundred years, the contract will be contrary to public policy. On the other hand, a five-year agreement is reasonable and enforceable (and in some cases depending on the situation, up to twenty years would be reasonable).

Agreements not to compete can be ancillary to employment contracts. It is common for many middle and upper level management personnel to agree not to work for competitors or not to start a new business for a specified period of time after terminating employment. If such an agreement is not ancillary to an employment contract, it is illegal. If ancillary, it is legal as long as it is not excessive in scope or duration. (The courts are reluctant to enforce these contracts, however.)

On occasion, where the covenant not to compete is unreasonable in its essential terms, the court may *reform* the covenant, converting its terms into reasonable ones. Instead of declaring the covenant illegal and unenforceable, the court applies the rule of reasonableness, to change the contract so that its basic, original intent can be enforced. For example, in the Orian Capital case, if Orian is forbidden to open another business anywhere in California for a period of one hundred years, the court could either declare the entire covenant null and void or could reform the covenant terms to cover only the San Francisco Bay area for a period of five years. (This presents a problem, however, in that the judge becomes a party to the contract. Consequently, contract reformation is usually carried out by a court only when necessary to prevent undue burdens or hardships.)

Resale Price Maintenance Agreements Another contract in restraint of trade is the resale price maintenance contract between a manufacturer and a dealer or a set of dealers. The dealer or dealers agree not to sell a product at a price below some specified minimum, thereby assuring a certain price level for the product. Between 1937 and 1977, manufacturers could require resale price maintenance on the part of dealers throughout the country (subject to state control). Today, however, such laws (called fair trade laws) are against public policy as expressed by federal statute. They are illegal.[6]

---

6. There are exceptions, however. The states can regulate the sale of alcoholic beverages in virtually any way they wish, and many have resale price maintenance for alcoholic beverages. Insurance is also regulated by state law.

BACKGROUND AND FACTS *Budget Rent-A-Car, the plaintiff, fran-chises and services operators in the discount automobile rental business. Budget brought this lawsuit to enforce a restrictive covenant not to com-pete against Fein, the defendant.*

Defendant Fein was a prospective purchaser of a Budget franchise. It is standard practice for Budget to require prospective purchasers to sign a standard agreement with many provisions, among them "not to enter into any daily discount automotive rental business in the western hem-isphere for a period of two years" without the written permission of Budget. The agreement also prevents the franchisee from disclosing any information about the operational aspects of the business to any other business or organization.

After Fein signed the standard agreement, Budget divulged to him much of its confidential literature describing its operating technique. Budget believed its knowledge of how to start and operate a local rental agency successfully was akin to a trade secret. Consequently, when the franchise deal between Fein and Budget fell through and Fein acquired another franchise from a competitor, Budget charged that Fein was op-erating his agency similarly to a Budget agency, apparently using some of the confidential information he had seen after signing the agreement.

BUDGET RENT-A-CAR CORP. OF AMERICA v. FEIN
United States Court of Appeals, Fifth Circuit, 1965.
342 F.2d 509.

BROWN, Circuit Judge.

* * * *

[A]s a matter of public policy, * * * this restrictive covenant would be unenforceable—primarily because of the "unreasonable" breadth of the territorial restriction. * * *

Of course the equitable doctrine of restrictive covenants is the law's reflex to the needs of the businessman and the commercial world. Consequently it is the business judgment on the value of the relationship, the nature of acquired trade confidences, the uniqueness of skills and the like which counts for much. In that process it is not for Judges, certainly not initially, to determine independent of the practical appraisal of business what is reasonably necessary to protect these several interests. These practical judgments carry great weight. But in the final analysis a court has to evaluate the competing factors to determine whether the legal sanction sought unduly interferes with personal economic freedom of in-dividuals or the flow of goods and services free of monopolistic restraints. * * *

For the covenantee to obtain judicial relief, he must show more than the mere promise of the covenantor. He must bare the soul of the business, or parts of it, even though this breaches for a time or a limited extent the confidences, trade secrets, etc. sought to be protected. * * * Before the law will foreclose economic opportunity to an individual for a long period of time because of a covenant exacted as a prelude to the consideration of whether a new relationship is to come into being, it is obvious that what is to be revealed has to be something which is of demonstrable value and deserving of protection.

* * * *

There is another important aspect. *Budget, by extracting this covenant from everyone it talks turkey with, deleteriously affects a far wider range of people* than a covenant ancillary to a sale of business where only two parties—the seller and the buyer—are involved. [Emphasis added. Here the court is saying that true ancillary restrictive agreements are acceptable.] Of course Budget can say that there are only two parties to this particular agreement. The difference is that when a business changes hands, a transaction economically beneficial to the community occurs, but when an individual signs the Budget agreement, looks the deal over, and then does not buy, the only result of economic significance to the community—here the wide, wide world, or at least the half wide world—is that one less individual is free to choose how he will make his living.

*   *   *   *

If Fein had actually bought the franchise and this covenant pertained to the eventuality of his selling out and thereafter competing, *   *   * a much stronger argument could be made for the enforceability of the covenant. But such is not this case.

*   *   * Obviously this [covenant] has an anti-competitive effect since anyone talking to Budget is nailed down for two years—anywhere in the western hemisphere. Business necessities justifying such a consequence are not revealed in this record.

Another basis—independent of those already mentioned—why this covenant cannot be enforced is that the territory encompassed is unreasonably large. [Emphasis added.] *   *   * Since Budget does not do business throughout the western hemisphere and the papers utterly fail to demonstrate that there is any reasonably foreseeable likelihood that it will in the near future, it follows that the territorial limitation is unreasonably broad. The covenant is therefore unenforceable.

JUDGMENT AND REMEDY   *Both the trial court and the appellate court agreed that the restrictive covenant was unenforceable. Budget could not prohibit Fein from engaging in the rental car franchise business.*

COMMENTS   *The current view of restraints of trade is that reasonable restraints contained in an employment agreement are enforceable if the purpose of the restraint is to protect a property interest of the promisee (usually the employer) and the conditions of the restraint are reasonable in terms of geographical limitations, duration, and so on. In addition, where confidential or secret information is involved, the courts will occasionally imply a noncompetition agreement where one is not expressly provided.*

Unconscionable Contracts (Clauses) and Exculpatory Clauses

Ordinarily, a court will not look at the fairness or equity of a contract. That is, the courts will generally not inquire into the adequacy of consideration, as discussed in Chapter 8. Persons are assumed to be reasonably intelligent, and the courts will not come to their aid just because they have made an unwise or foolish bargain. In certain circumstances, however, bargains are so oppressive that the courts will relieve innocent parties of part or all of their duties. Such bargains are called **unconscionable contracts or clauses.**

Contracts attempting to absolve parties of negligence are often held to be unconscionable. For example, suppose Jones and Laughlin Steel Company hires a laborer and has him sign a contract stating:

Said employee hereby agrees with employer, in consideration of such employment, that he will take upon himself all risks incident to his position and will in no case hold the company liable for any injury or damage he may sustain, in his person or otherwise, by accidents or injuries in the factory, or which may result from defective machinery or carelessness or misconduct of himself or any other employee in service of the employer.

Such clauses, which may also be found in rental or ordinary sales agreements, are called **exculpatory clauses.** They are defined as clauses that release a party from all liability in the event of monetary or physical injury *no matter who is at fault.* This contract provision attempts to remove Jones and Laughlin's potential liability for injuries occurring to the employee, and it is usually contrary to public policy.[7]

---

7. For a case with similar facts, see Little Rock & Ft. Smith Ry. Company v. Eubanks, 48 Ark. 460, 3 S.W. 808 (1887). In such a case the clause may also be illegal on the basis of a violation of the state workers' compensation law.

BACKGROUND AND FACTS *Norma McCutcheon was a tenant in a multi-family dwelling complex owned by United Homes Corp. She was injured one evening when she fell down an unlighted flight of stairs leading from her apartment. She claimed that defendant, United Homes Corp., was negligent because the lights at the top and bottom of the stairwell were not operating. At trial, the defendant claimed that it was not liable since the plaintiff had signed a form called a "month-to-month rental agreement." In the agreement the following exculpatory clause existed:*

    Neither the Lessor nor his Agent shall be liable for any injury to Lessee, his family, guests, or employees, or any other person entering the premises or the building of which the demised premises are a part.

The trial court granted a summary judgment of dismissal.

McCUTCHEON v. UNITED HOMES CORP.
Supreme Court of Washington, En Banc, 1971.
79 Wash.2d 443, 486 P.2d 1093.

STAFFORD, Justice.

*   *   *   *

The question is one of first impression. The issue is whether the lessor of a residential unit within a multi-family dwelling complex may exculpate itself from liability for personal injuries sustained by a tenant, which injuries result from the lessor's own negligence in maintenance of the approaches, common passageways, stairways and other areas under the lessor's dominion and control, but available for the tenants' use. (Hereinafter called the "common areas".)

Basic to the entire discussion is the common law rule that one who leases a portion of his premises but retains control over the approaches, common passageways, stairways and other areas to be used in common by the owner and tenants, has a duty to use reasonable care to keep them in safe condition for use of the tenant in his enjoyment of the demised premises. The landlord is required to do more than passively refrain from negligent acts. He has a duty of affirmative conduct, an affirmative obligation to exercise reasonable care to inspect and repair the previously mentioned portions of the premises for protection of the lessee.

It is readily apparent that the exculpatory clause was inserted in defendant's form "Month to Month Rental Agreement" to bar its tenants from asserting actions for personal injuries sustained through the landlord's own negligence. It was adopted to negative the result of the lessor's failure to comply with its affirmative duty to the tenants.

The defendant asserts that a lessor may contract, in a rental agreement, to exculpate itself from liability to its lessee, for personal injuries caused by lessor's own negligence. It contends such exculpatory clauses are not contrary to public policy because the landlord-tenant relationship *is not a matter of public interest, but relates exclusively to the private affairs of the parties concerned and that the two parties stand upon equal terms. Thus, there should be full freedom to contract.*

* * * *

The importance of "freedom of contract" is clear enough. However, the use of such an argument for avoiding the affirmative duty of a landlord to its residential tenant is no longer compelling in light of today's multi-family dwelling complex wherein a tenant merely rents some space with appurtenant rights to make it more usable or livable. Under modern circumstances the tenant is almost wholly dependent upon the landlord to provide reasonably for his safe use of the "common areas" beyond the four walls demised to him.

* * * *

In other words, such an exculpatory clause may be legal, when considered in the abstract. However, when applied to a specific situation, one may be exempt from liability for his own negligence *only when the consequences thereof do not fall greatly below the standard established by law.*

In the landlord-tenant relationship it is extremely meaningful to require that a landlord's attempt to exculpate itself, from liability for the result of its own negligence, *not fall greatly below the standard of negligence set by law.* As indicated earlier, a residential tenant who lives in a modern multi-family dwelling complex is almost wholly dependent upon the landlord for the reasonably safe condition of the "common areas". However, a clause which exculpates the lessor from liability to its lessee, for personal injuries caused by lessor's own acts of negligence, not only lowers the standard imposed by the common law, it effectively *destroys* the landlord's affirmative obligation or duty to keep or maintain the "common areas" in a reasonably safe condition for the tenant's use.

When a lessor is no longer liable for the failure to observe standards of affirmative conduct, or for *any* conduct amounting to negligence, by virtue of an exculpatory clause in a lease, *the standard ceases to exist.* In short, such a clause *destroys* the concept of negligence in the landlord-tenant relationship. Neither the standard nor negligence can exist in abstraction.

* * * *

* * * Furthermore, one must ignore present day realities to say that such an exculpatory clause, which relieves a lessor of liability for personal injuries caused by its own negligence, is purely a "personal and private affair" and "not a matter of public interest".

We no longer live in an era of the occasional rental of rooms in a private home or over the corner grocery. In the relatively short span of 30 years the public's use of rental units in this state has expanded dramatically. In the past 10 years alone, in the state of Washington, there has been an increase of over 77,000 rental units. It takes no imagination to see that a business which once had a minor impact upon the living habits of the citizenry has developed into a major commercial enterprise directly touching the lives of hundreds of thousands of people who depend upon it for shelter.

Thus, we are not faced merely with the theoretical duty of construing a provision in an isolated contract specifically bargained for by *one landlord and one tenant* as a purely private affair. Considered realistically, we are asked to construe an exculpatory clause, the generalized use of which may have an impact upon thousands of potential tenants.

Under these circumstances it cannot be said that such exculpatory clauses are "purely a private affair" or that they are "not a matter of public interest." The real question is whether we should sanction a technique of immunizing lessors of residential units within a multi-family dwelling complex, from liability for personal injuries sustained by a tenant, which injuries result from the lessor's own negligence in maintaining the "common areas"; particularly when the technique employed destroys the concept of negligence and the standard of affirmative duty imposed upon the landlord for protection of the tenant.

An exculpatory clause of the type here involved contravenes long established common law rules of tort liability that exist in the landlord-tenant relationship. As so employed, it offends the public policy of the state and will not be enforced by the courts. It makes little sense for us to insist, on the one hand, that a workman have a safe place in which to work, but, on the other hand, to deny him a reasonably safe place in which to live.

The trial court was reversed and the case was remanded for a new trial.   **JUDGMENT**
This particular exculpatory clause was deemed unenforceable.   **AND REMEDY**

Contracts entered into because of one party's vastly superior bargaining power may also be deemed unconscionable. For example, if every auto manufacturer inserts an exculpatory clause (a clause freeing the manufacturer from liability for personal or monetary damage) in contracts for the sale of autos, consumers presumably have no chance to bargain for the elimination of the clause in a given contract. (These contracts are also called adhesion contracts.) Essentially, the consumer's choice is to take it or leave it. In order to combat such clauses, courts have recently held them to be unconscionable.[8] The consumer has no choice, so the contract is contrary to public policy.

Another example of an unconscionable contract is where the terms of the agreement "shock the conscience" of the court. Suppose a welfare recipient with a fourth-grade education agrees to purchase a refrigerator for a price of $2,000, signing a two-year, non-usurious installment contract. The same type of refrigerator usually sells for $400 on the market. Some courts have held this type of contract unconscionable despite the general rule that the courts will not inquire into the adequacy of consideration.[9]

Both the Uniform Commercial Code (UCC) and the Uniform Consumer Credit Code (UCCC) embody the unconscionability concept—the former with regard to the sale of goods [10] and the latter with regard to consumer loans and the waiver of rights.[11]

To illustrate, UCC 2-302, dealing with the sale of goods, basically provides that as a matter of law a court can declare an entire contract or any clause in a contract illegal because it is unconscionable. Whether the court will so hold depends frequently upon the commercial setting and all the circumstances of the transaction, such as the education, income, and position of the buyer relative to the seller (as in the refrigerator example).

---

8. See Henningsen v. Bloomfield Motors, Inc., 32 N.J. 358, 161 A.2d 69 (1960).

9. Jones v. Star Credit Corp., 59 Misc.2d 189, 298 N.Y.S.2d 264 (1969).
10. See, for example, UCC Secs. 2-302 and 2-719.
11. See, for example, UCCC Secs. 5.108 and 1.107.

Discriminatory Contracts

Contracts in which a party promises to discriminate in terms of color, race, religion, national origin, or sex are contrary to statute and contrary to public policy.[12] For example, if a property owner promises in a contract not to sell the property to a member of a particular race, the contract is unenforceable. Public policy underlying these prohibitions is very strong and the courts are quick to invalidate discriminatory contracts. Thus, the law attempts to ensure that people will be treated equally.

Contracts for the Commission of a Tort

Contracts that require a party to commit a civil wrong, or a tort, are illegal. Remember that a *tort* is an act that is wrongful to another individual in a private sense, even though it may not necessarily be criminal in nature.

Contracts Injuring Public Service

Contracts that interfere with a public officer's duties are contrary to public policy. For example, contracts to pay legislators for favorable votes are obviously harmful to the public. Often, a fine line is drawn between lobbying efforts and agreements to influence voting. When a lobby group provides certain factual information in order to influence the outcome of legislation, the lobby is not engaging in an illegal activity. But if the lobby enters into a contingency fee agreement, whereby the legislator receives a certain amount of money if a certain bill is passed or a certain contract is awarded, the agreement is illegal because it is deemed contrary to public policy. In the United States, people are not entitled to buy and sell votes. Therefore, agreements like that are illegal.

Agreements that involve a *conflict of interest* are often illegal. Public officers cannot enter into contracts that cause conflict between their official duties as representatives of the people and their private interests. Statutes require many public officers to liquidate their interests in private businesses before serving as elected representatives. Other statutes merely require them to put their businesses in blind trusts, so that private and public responsibilities remain separate.

Suppose Ladd is a county official in charge of selecting land for the building of a new courthouse. He makes a contract for the state to buy land that he happens to own. This is a conflict of interest. If the state discovers later that Ladd owned the land, it can normally use this information to show a conflict of interest and to void the contract.

Agreements Obstructing Legal Process

Any agreement that intends to delay, prevent, or obstruct the legal process is illegal. For example, an agreement to pay some specified amount if a criminal prosecution is terminated is illegal. Likewise, agreements to suppress evidence in a legal proceeding or to commit fraud upon a court are illegal. Tampering with a jury by offering jurors money in exchange for their votes is illegal.

In a trial, most witnesses (except expert witnesses) are paid a flat fee to compensate them for their expenses. Offering to pay one witness more than another is contrary to public policy, since the extra payment can provide an incentive for the witness to lie.

A promise to refrain from prosecuting a criminal offense in return for a reward is void because it is against public policy. A reward given under the threat of arrest or prosecution is also void.

Forum Selection and Arbitration Clauses Agreements that do not obstruct the legal process include agreements for the preselection of a forum or agreements for the arbitration of a dispute. **Forum selection clauses** are often contained in contracts where the parties are large multinational firms. For example, a contract for the sale of construction machinery made between a French corporation and a Colombian corporation can provide for the resolution of dis-

---

12. Federal Civil Rights Act of 1964; 42 U.S.C.A., Sec. 2000e, et seq.

putes in London, England. Agreements to pre-select a forum are usually upheld unless they are designed to discourage litigation (for example, where a consumer in Florida buys an auto from General Motors Corp. and the contract contains a forum selection clause requiring any lawsuit to be brought in Detroit, Michigan).

Arbitration is the negotiation of a dispute before an arbitrator or a panel of arbitrators. Both sides present their stories, and the arbitrator makes the decision. Essentially, arbitration is similar to a trial, although formal rules of pleading, discovery, and evidence are not recognized. After arbitration, the losing party may appeal the arbitrator's decision to a court of law, but with rare success. **Arbitration clauses** (clauses in the contract calling for the settlement of disputes through arbitration) are generally upheld today, although courts previously invalidated such clauses on the basis that they interfered with the jurisdiction of the court.

EFFECT OF ILLEGALITY

In general, an illegal contract is void. That is, the contract is deemed never to have existed, and the courts will not aid either party. In most illegal contracts both parties are considered to be equally at fault—in **pari delicto.** In such cases the contract is void. If it is executory (not yet fulfilled), neither party can enforce it. If it is executed, there can be neither contractual nor quasi-contractual recovery.

Suppose Sonatrach, Algeria's national oil company, contracts to sell oil to Tenneco without government approval. Algeria has a law that prohibits the export of oil without government approval. Therefore, the contract is illegal and unenforceable. If Tenneco sues to enforce delivery of the oil, the suit will be dismissed since the contract is void. Even if Tenneco has paid for some of the oil, the contract cannot be enforced. Tenneco cannot even get back the money it paid under the illegal contract. In general, the courts take a hands-off attitude toward illegal contracts.

That one wrongdoer in an illegal contract is unjustly enriched at the expense of the other is of no concern to the law—except under certain special circumstances that will be discussed later. The major justification for this hands-off attitude is that it is improper to place the machinery of justice at the disposal of a plaintiff who has broken the law by entering into an illegal bargain. Another justification is the hoped-for deterrent effect of this general rule. A plaintiff who suffers loss because of it should presumably be deterred from entering into similar illegal bargains. But one might ask whether the defendant who has been unjustly enriched is not given an incentive to find someone else to dupe.

Exceptions to the General Rule

Some persons are excepted from the general rule that neither party to an illegal bargain can sue for breach and neither can recover for performance rendered:

1. Persons unaware or ignorant of facts that make the agreement illegal.
2. Persons protected by statutory law.
3. Persons who withdraw from an illegal agreement before the transaction is performed (partial performance).
4. Persons induced to enter into an illegal contract through fraud, duress, or undue influence.

Justifiable Ignorance of the Facts   When one of the parties is relatively innocent, that party can often obtain restitution or recovery of benefits conferred in a partially executed contract. In this case, the courts will not enforce the contract but will allow the parties to return to their original position.

It is also possible for an innocent party who has fully performed under the contract to enforce the contract against the guilty party. For example, a truck carrier contracts with Gillespie to carry goods to a specific destination for a normal fee of $500. The truck carrier delivers the goods and later finds out that the contents of the shipped crates were illegal. The law specifies that the shipment, use, and sale of the goods are all illegal. The carrier, being an innocent party, could still legally collect the $500.

Members of Protected Classes   An illegal contract can be enforced by a member of a group of persons specifically protected by statute. When a statute is clearly designed to protect certain classes of people, a member of that class can enforce an illegal contract even though the other party cannot. A statute that prohibits employees from working more than a specified number of hours per month is designed to protect those employees. An employee who works more than the maximum can recover for those extra hours of service. Flight attendants are subject to a federal statute that prohibits them from flying more than a certain number of hours every month. Even if an attendant exceeds the maximum, the airline must pay for those extra hours of service.

Another example of statutes designed to protect a particular class of people concerns **Blue Sky Laws,** legislation that regulates and supervises investment companies for the protection of the public. Such laws are intended to stop the sale of stock in fly-by-night concerns like visionary oil wells and distant gold mines. Investors are protected as a class and can sue to recover the purchase price of stock issued in violation of such laws.

Most states also have statutes regulating the sale of insurance. If the insurance company violates a statute when selling insurance, *the purchaser can nevertheless enforce the policy.* For example, assume Indemnity Insurance Company is not qualified to sell insurance in Montana but does so anyway. A purchaser who buys a policy to insure his auto has an accident and seeks to recover. The insurer cannot resist payment under the policy, even though the contract is illegal. The statutes regulating insurance companies are designed to protect policyholders, so the buyer can recover from the insurer.

Withdrawal from Illegal Agreement If the illegal agreement has been only partly performed and the illegal part of the bargain has not yet been performed, the party rendering performance can withdraw from the bargain. That party can recover the performance or its value. For example, Sam and Jim decide to wager (illegally) on the outcome of a boxing match. They each deposit money with a stakeholder, who agrees to pay the winner of the bet. At this point, each party has performed part of the agreement, but the illegal part of the agreement will not occur until the money is paid to the winner. Before such payment occurs, either party is entitled to withdraw from the agreement by giving notice of repudiation to the stakeholder.

Illegal Contract through Fraud, Duress, or Undue Influence Often illegal contracts involve two blameworthy parties, but one party is more at fault than the other. Whenever the plaintiff has been induced to enter into an illegal bargain by fraud, duress, or undue influence of the other party to the agreement, that party will be allowed to recover for performance or its value. Consider the following example: Mildred Pfeiffer runs several businesses that are about to be closed down through involuntary bankruptcy. Her accountant has been counseling her for some time. He suggests that she "sell" to him her Mercedes for a nominal fee. He promises to "sell" it back to her after she has gone through full bankruptcy proceedings. (This is a so-called sham transaction used explicitly to hide assets from creditors in a bankruptcy proceeding.) After the bankruptcy proceeding, the accountant refuses to "sell" back the Mercedes. Although Pfeiffer's transfer of property was for the purpose of defeating her creditors and was thus illegal, the court will allow her to recover her property.

Severable, or Divisible, Contracts

If a contract is severable into legal and illegal portions, and the illegal portion does not go to the essence of the bargain, the legal portion can be enforced. A *severable contract* consists of distinct parts that can be performed separately, with separate consideration provided for each part.

Suppose Norman Harrington contracts to buy ten pounds of bluegrass seed for $25 and five gallons of herbicide for $30. At the time, Harrington does not know that the Food and Drug Administration has banned sale of the herbicide and that the contract for its sale is therefore illegal. Here, the contract is severable because separate considerations were stated for the bluegrass seed ($25) and the herbicide ($30). Therefore, the portion of the contract for the sale of bluegrass seed is enforceable; the other portion is not.

Another example of a severable contract would be one involving the sale of a business in which a restrictive covenant not to compete is included. The courts may find that the restrictive covenant is too broad and therefore illegal. This part of the contract would then become void, but the remainder of the contract for the sale of the business would stand.

QUESTIONS AND
CASE PROBLEMS

1.   A famous New York City hotel, Hotel Lux, is noted for its food as well as its luxury accommodations. Hotel Lux contracts with a famous chef, Chef Perlee, to become its head chef at $6,000 per month. The contract states that should Perlee leave the employment of Hotel Lux for any reason, he agrees he will not work as a chef for any hotel or restaurant in the states of New York, New Jersey, or Pennsylvania for a period of one year. During the first six months of the contract, Hotel Lux substantially advertises Perlee as its head chef, and business at the hotel is excellent. Then a dispute arises between the hotel management and Perlee, and Perlee terminates his employment. One month later, he is hired by a famous New Jersey restaurant just across the New York state line. Hotel Lux learns of Perlee'e employment through a large advertisement in a New York City newspaper. It seeks to enjoin Perlee from working in that restaurant as a chef for one year. Discuss how successful Hotel Lux will be in its action.

2.   State X requires a person to be eighteen years old before being permitted to purchase alcoholic beverages. The state also has passed a law that persons who prepare and serve liquor in the form of drinks in commercial establishments must be licensed. The only requirement for obtaining a yearly license is that the person be at least eighteen years old. Michael, age 35, is hired as a bartender for the Lone Star Restaurant. George, a staunch alumnus of a nearby university, brings twenty of his friends to the restaurant to celebrate a football victory that afternoon. George has ordered four rounds of drinks, and the bar bill exceeds $150. George learns that Michael failed to renew his bartender's license, and George refuses to pay, claiming the contract is unenforceable. Discuss if George is correct.

3.   The Constitution provides for the separation of church and state. The government can in no way support or affiliate itself with any particular religion or group of religions. [Note that across-the-board legislation, such as tax exemptions for religious organizations, is not prohibited by this constitutional provision.] Illinois enacted a law requiring all nonfood retailers to remain closed on Sunday. A local retailer challenged the law as a violation of the constitutional provision calling for separation of church and state. Do you think such a "Sunday closing law" is unconstitutional? Discuss fully.

4.   Walsh was shopping at W. T. Grant Co. when she was approached by a saleswoman, who asked her if she wanted to open a charge account. The saleswoman's "pitch" was that she needed points for a contest. Walsh agreed to open a charge account and was given a booklet of coupons totaling $200. She was told by the saleswoman that she would be charged only for the coupons she used. In reality, the agreement Walsh signed was an installment sales contract, obligating her to pay a total of $246.01 over a twenty-month period at $10 per month. Walsh failed to make the first payment. W. T. Grant Co. filed suit. Is the agreement illegal? If so, for what reasons? [W. T. Grant Co. v. Walsh, 100 N.J.Super. 60, 241 A.2d 46 (1968)]

5.   Womack was a well-known gambler in Saline County. Judge Maner, a friend of Womack, not only knew of Womack's gambling enterprises, but approved of them. From time to time over a period of several years, Womack paid money to the judge to ensure that he would not be prosecuted. As a result of this long-standing agreement, Womack paid the judge a total of $1,675. Womack then claimed that the consideration for his paying the judge was void and unlawful at the time the contract was entered into as well as at the present time. Therefore, Womack sued Judge Maner to rescind the contract and to get back the $1,675 he had paid. Should Womack recover? [Womack v. Maner, 277 Ark. 786, 301 S.W.2d 438 (1957)]

6.   McCall and Frampton entered an oral agreement whereby McCall was to leave her husband and her employment and was to live and be intimate with Frampton and to work toward the promotion of his musical career. In return, McCall was to receive, as equal partner, 50 percent of all proceeds from Frampton's work as a musician. McCall did in fact leave her husband, live with Frampton, and devote all her resources, time, and effort to the promotion of Frampton's career. As agreed, they shared all benefits as equal partners from 1973 through July 1978, at which time

Frampton unilaterally terminated the agreement. McCall sued to recover 50 percent of Frampton's earnings since 1978 and to obtain an interest in certain real property held by Frampton. McCall relied on *Marvin v. Marvin* to support her argument that the agreement is an enforceable one. Did McCall win? [McCall v. Frampton, 99 Misc.2d 159, 415 N.Y.S.2d 752 (Sup. Ct. 1979)]

7. Williams, a woman of limited education who was separated from her husband and living on welfare, entered into a series of installment contracts with Walker-Thomas Furniture Company. During the period 1957 to 1962 she purchased various items from Walker-Thomas, including curtains, rugs, chairs, mattresses, a washing machine, and a stereo set. With each purchase, she paid part in cash and signed an installment agreement for the balance. Included in the installment agreement was a paragraph, in extremely fine print, that provided that payments, after the first purchase, were to be prorated on all purchases then outstanding. In other words, each time Williams made an additional purchase from Walker-Thomas under an installment agreement, her payments were credited against the total of all outstanding installment purchases from the company. This had the effect of keeping a balance due on every item until the total bill was paid. Prior to her final purchase, Williams had reduced her outstanding balance to $164. The last purchase, a stereo, increased her balance due to $678. After making several more payments, Williams defaulted. Walker-Thomas attempted to enforce the installment provision allowing it to repossess all the goods previously purchased by Williams. Was this contract enforceable? [Williams v. Walker-Thomas Furniture Company, 198 A.2d 914 (D.C.App.1964)]

8. In 1970 Overbeck received a Sears credit card. In 1974 he charged several purchases on the credit card. If Overbeck had paid for each purchase within thirty days, no service charge would have been added to the outstanding balance. But he chose to let the account "revolve." Therefore, under the credit card agreement between Overbeck and Sears, a service charge of 1.5 percent (18 percent annually) was added each month. Overbeck claimed that the 18 percent annual interest was usurious and contrary to the laws of Indiana that set the maximum legal rate at 6 percent. Was Overbeck correct? [Overbeck v. Sears, Roebuck and Company, 169 Ind.App. 501, 349 N.E.2d 286 (1976)]

9. Ferguson and Coleman entered into an agreement for the sale of land to be used for growing cotton. The agreement stated two alternative prices. The land was to be sold for $902.58 "if cotton should rise to 8 cents by the first of November . . ." If not, the selling price was to be $500. Before the first of November, cotton rose to 8½ cents, but Coleman refused to pay the higher price for the land. Was this an illegal gambling contract? Do you see any possible usury here? What if the contract had read: "Price of the land $500 if Russia lands a man on the moon by the first of November, otherwise price $900"? [Ferguson v. Coleman, 3 Rich. 99, 45 Am.Dec. 761.]

10. Roeber and the Swift & Courtney & Beecher Company were both engaged in the business of manufacturing matches. Swift desired to purchase Roeber's business, which was quite lucrative. Pursuant to the sale agreement between Swift and Roeber, Roeber agreed not to engage in the match business in any state in the United States other than Nevada and Montana for ninety-nine years. Was the contract enforceable? [Diamond Match Company v. Roeber, 106 N.Y. 473, 13 N.E. 419 (1801)]

CHAPTER 11

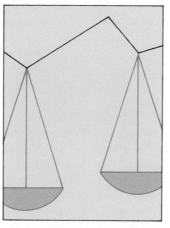

CONTRACTS
Genuineness of Assent

It is possible for a contract to be unenforceable even though two parties, with full legal capacity, have entered into an agreement for a legal purpose and even though it is supported by consideration. This can occur when (1) there is no *genuine assent* to the terms of the contract because of misrepresentation, mistake, duress, or undue influence; and (2) when written evidence is lacking for certain contracts that require it. This chapter will examine the problems of genuine assent, and the next chapter will deal with contracts that require a writing under the Statute of Frauds.

Historically, the law has stressed the necessity of people conducting their affairs in a way that is not injurious to others. This philosophy has already been discussed in the chapters on tort and criminal law. Although parties to a contract must assume certain risks, the law has determined that neither party should be allowed to benefit in contract from deceit, from undue influence, from duress, or from making certain

types of mistakes. (The law views different types of mistakes in different ways, as will be discussed in this chapter.) Therefore, certain contracts are voidable either by both parties when there is mutual mistake or by the innocent party in contracts formed by deceit, undue influence, or duress.

MISTAKES

It is important to distinguish between mistakes *as to facts* and mistakes *in judgment as to value or quality*. Only the former have legal significance. Suppose Jane Simpson plans to buy ten acres of land in Montana. If she believes the land is worth $10,000, and it is worth only $4,000, her mistake is one of value or quality. However, if she believes the land is the ten acres owned by the Boyds, and it is actually the ten acres owned by the Deweys, her mistake is one of fact. Only a mistake as to fact allows a contract to be avoided.

Mistakes occur in two forms—*unilateral* and *mutual,* or *bilateral.* A unilateral mistake is made by only one of the contracting parties; a mutual mistake is made by both.

Unilateral Mistakes

A unilateral mistake involves some *material fact* that is important to the subject matter of the contract. In general, a unilateral mistake does not afford the mistaken party any right to relief from the contract.[1]

There are two exceptions to the general rule. First, the rule is not applied when the *other* party to the contract knows or should have known that a mistake was made. Second, some states will not enforce the contract against the mistaken party if the error was due to a mathematical mistake in addition, subtraction, division, or multiplication and if it was done inadvertently and without gross negligence.

For an example of how these exceptions are applied, consider the following case. Odell Construction Co. made a bid to install the plumbing in a proposed apartment building. When Herbert Odell, the president, added up his costs, his secretary forgot to give him the figures for the pipe fittings. Because of the omission, Odell's bid was $6,500 below that of the other bidders. The prime

contractor, Sunspan Inc., accepted Odell's bid. If Sunspan was not aware of Odell's mistake and could not reasonably have been aware of it, the contract will be enforceable, and Odell will be required to install the plumbing at the bid price. However, if it can be shown that Odell's secretary mentioned her error to Sunspan, or if Odell's bid was so far below the others' that, as a contractor, Sunspan should reasonably have known the bid was a mistake, the contract can be rescinded. Sunspan would not be allowed to accept the offer knowing it was made by mistake.[2] The law of contracts protects only *reasonable* expectations.

Mutual Mistakes of Material Fact

When both parties are mistaken as to a material fact, the contract can be rescinded by either party.[3] The mistake must be about a material fact—that is, a fact that is important and central to the contract.

The classic case on mutual mistake of fact involved a ship named "Peerless" that was to sail from Bombay with certain cotton goods on board. However, more than one ship named "Peerless" sailed from Bombay that winter. The mistake was mutual, and it was about a material fact.

---

1. Restatement, Second, Contracts, Section 153, liberalizes this rule to take into account the modern trend of allowing avoidance although only one party has been mistaken.

2. Peerless Glass Co. v. Pacific Crockery Co., 121 Cal. 641, 54 P. 101 (1898).
3. Restatement, Second, Contracts, Section 152.

RAFFLES v.
WICHELHAUS AND
ANOTHER

2 Hurl. & C. 906,
159 Eng. Rep. 375 (1864).
Court of Exchequer (Per Curiam)

BACKGROUND AND FACTS   *The defendant purchased a shipment of Surat cotton from the plaintiff "to arrive ex 'Peerless' from Bombay." The defendant expected the goods to be shipped on the Peerless sailing from Bombay in October. The plaintiff expected to ship the goods on another Peerless, which sailed from Bombay in December. By the time the goods arrived and the plaintiff tried to deliver them, the defendant was no longer willing to accept them.*

*   *   *   *

Declaration. For that it was agreed between the plaintiff and the defendants, to wit, at Liverpool, that the plaintiff should sell to the defendants, and the defendants buy of the plaintiff, certain goods, to wit, 125 bales of Surat cotton, guaranteed middling fair merchant's Dhollorah, to arrive ex "Peerless" from Bombay; and that the cotton should be taken from the quay, and that the defendants would pay the plaintiff for the same at a certain rate, to wit, at the rate of 17¼d. per pound, within a certain time then agreed upon after the arrival of the said goods in England. Averments: that the said goods did arrive by the said ship from Bombay in England, to wit, at Liverpool, and the plaintiff was then and there ready, and willing and offered to deliver the said goods to the defendants, &c. Breach: that the defendants refused to accept the said goods or pay the plaintiff for them.

Plea. That the said ship mentioned in the said agreement was meant and intended by the defendants to be the ship called the "Peerless," which sailed from Bombay, to wit, in October; and that the plaintiff was not ready and willing and did not offer to deliver to the defendants any bales of cotton which arrived by the last mentioned ship, but instead thereof was only ready and willing and offered to deliver to the defendants 125 bales of Surat cotton which arrived by another and different ship, which was also called the "Peerless", and which sailed from Bombay, to wit, in December.

*   *   *   *

There is nothing on the face of the contract to show that any particular ship called the "Peerless" was meant; but the moment it appears that two ships called the "Peerless" were about to sail from Bombay there is a latent ambiguity, and parol evidence may be given for the purpose of shewing that the defendant meant one "Peerless," and the plaintiff another. That being so, there was no consensus ad idem, and therefore no binding contract.

The judgment was for the defendants.

JUDGMENT AND REMEDY

The effect of a mistake upon the formation of a contract is a difficult area of law to understand. In order to find mutual assent, the courts employ the following objective test: Persons are bound by the reasonable impressions they create in the mind of the other party, regardless of whether that impression is the same as their subjective intentions. (In Chapter 7, on Agreement, we also make reference to objective intent.)

COMMENTS

Mutual Mistake in Identity and Mistake in Value

If a mistake concerns the *value* or *quality* of the object of the contract rather than some material fact, the contract can be enforced by either party. This rationale evolves from the theory that certain risks are assumed by both parties who enter into a contract. Without this rule, almost any party who did not receive what he or she considered a fair bargain could argue bilateral mistake. In essence, this would make *adequacy* of consideration a factor in determining whether a contract existed. As discussed in chapter 8, the courts normally do not inquire into the adequacy of consideration.

Obviously, the distinction between a mistake *in identity* and a mistake *in value* is central to this issue. Suppose Daniel Murray, after seeing Beverly Beale's violin, buys it for $250 and neither party knows that it is a Stradivarius built in 1717. Here there is no mistake that will warrant rescission or reformation. Both parties knew what the subject matter of the contract was—the violin that Murray had seen. Both Murray and Beale mistook the value of that particular violin. Therefore, the contract cannot be rescinded.

Modern courts still apply the "Peerless" theory of mutual mistake in evaluating whether or not a contract exists.

In the following case the court applied the mutual mistake doctrine to a situation where a contract was canceled and the cancellation was accepted on the basis of a mutual mistake of fact.

BOYD v. AETNA LIFE INS. CO.

Appellate Court of Illinois, Fourth District, 1941.
310 Ill.App. 547, 35 N.E.2d 99.

BACKGROUND AND FACTS *The plaintiff, Christine Boyd, was named beneficiary in a policy insuring her husband's life. The policy, issued by Aetna Life (the defendant), contained a provision for payment of benefits in the event of the husband's permanent total disability. The couple separated, but the policy was still in force, and Mrs. Boyd continued to pay the premiums. However, she eventually agreed to surrender the policy. She did not know the whereabouts of her husband and was uninformed about his state of health. After she surrendered the policy, Mrs. Boyd learned that her husband had become disabled. His disability had occurred before she surrendered the policy, and had she known about it, she would not have surrendered the policy. She asked the court to rescind her surrender agreement with the Aetna Life Insurance Co. and to pay her the disability (and death) benefits due under the policy on the ground of "mutual mistake of fact."*

STONE, Presiding Justice.

* * * *

The decisive and practically sole question for the consideration of this court is whether the facts alleged in the amended complaint, set forth a sufficient mistake of fact, in the legal acceptation of the term, as to justify the intervention of a court of equity, and relieve against the consequences of that alleged mistake of fact, in the entering into the contract of recision.

"Mistake of fact" has been defined to be a mistake, not caused by the neglect of a legal duty on the part of the person making the mistake, and consisting in an unconscious ignorance or forgetfulness of a fact past or present material to the contract, or belief in the present existence of a thing material to the contract which does not exist, or in the past existence of a thing which has not existed. [Emphasis added.]

* * * [A]t the time of cancellation plaintiff had a perfectly valid claim, but she and the company were both at that time, * * * ignorant of the fact that there was a claim in existence, due to the total permanent disability of insured. The supposed element of doubt as to the health of Boyd never entered into the contemplation of either party, nor did it form any part of the consideration for the cancellation and surrender of the policy. It would be quite natural that they would assume as they evidently did, that the insured was in good health. As matter of fact such is the express allegation of the amended complaint.

* * * *

In the instant case, the insured's state of health was not merely incidental, nor was it a matter that would merely enhance the amount of damages. The subject matter of the mistake was intrinsic to the transaction. As set forth in plaintiff's amended complaint, "if she had known the true facts as to said Jimmie Boyd's total permanent disability * * * she would not have surrendered same (the policy) to the defendant." This policy was in full force and effect at the time of total permanent disability. Upon that contingency coming to pass the liability of defendant was fixed. The cancellation was not intended to reach back and absolve defendant from any liability which it had already incurred.

Aetna was held liable to Mrs. Boyd as a beneficiary for payment of benefits under the policy, since she had been paying the policy up to and including the point when her ex-husband became disabled. At the time of his disability, Aetna became indebted to Mrs. Boyd as beneficiary for those payments. Therefore, there was indeed a mutual mistake of fact, since neither she nor Aetna knew of her ex-husband's disability entitling her to payment. The court permitted Mrs. Boyd to rescind her surrender agreement with Aetna and ordered Aetna to pay her the disability benefits.

JUDGMENT AND REMEDY

FRAUDULENT MISREPRESENTATION

Although fraud is a tort, it also affects the genuineness of the innocent party's consent to the contract. Thus, the transaction is not voluntary in the sense of "mutual assent." When an innocent party consents to a contract with fraudulent terms, the contract normally can be voided because that party has not *voluntarily* consented to its terms.[4] Normally, the innocent party can either rescind the contract and be restored to the original position or can enforce the contract and seek damages for any injuries resulting from the fraud.

When a Misrepresentation Is Fraudulent

The word *fraudulent* is used in various senses in the law. Generally, fraudulent misrepresentation refers only to misrepresentation that is consciously false and is intended to mislead another. That is, the perpetrator of the fraudulent misrepresentation must know or believe that the assertion is not true, or must be lacking the confidence that he or she states or implies in the

truth of the assertion, or must know that he or she does not have the basis stated or implied for the assertion.

What is at issue is whether the defendant believes that the plaintiff is substantially certain to be misled as a result of the misrepresentation. For example, Jones makes a statement to ABC Credit Rating Company about his financial condition that he knows is untrue. Jones realizes that ABC will publish this information for its subscribers. Marchetti, a subscriber, receives the published information. Relying on that information, Marchetti is induced to make a contract to lend money to Jones. Jones's statement is a fraudulent misrepresentation. The contract is voidable by Marchetti.

The Four Elements of Fraud

Typically, there are four elements of fraud:

1. A misrepresentation of a material fact has occurred.
2. There is an attempt to deceive.
3. The innocent party has justifiably relied on the misrepresentation.
4. The innocent party has been injured.

In the following four sections we will examine each of these elements.

---

4. Restatement, Second, Contracts, Sections 162, 163, and 164.

Misrepresentation Has Occurred   The first element of proving fraud is to show that misrepresentation of a material fact has occurred. This misrepresentation can be in words or actions. For example, the statement "This sculpture was made by Michelangelo" is an express misrepresentation of fact if the statue was made by another artist.

Suppose Quid contracts to buy a racehorse from Ray. The horse is blind in one eye, but when Ray shows the horse, he skillfully keeps its head turned so that Quid does not see the defect. The concealment constitutes fraud because of Ray's *conduct*. Likewise, if a salesperson shows a sample from the top of a large box, but does not show the inferior samples at the bottom, a misrepresentation *by conduct* has occurred if there is a marked difference in quality between the top and the bottom merchandise.

Representations of future facts (predictions) or statements of opinion are generally not subject to a claim of fraud. Every person is expected to exercise care and judgment when entering into contracts, and the law will not come to the aid of one who simply makes an unwise bargain. For example, statements like, "This land will be worth twice as much next year" or "This car will last for years and years," are statements of opinion, not fact. Hence, contracting parties should recognize them as such and not rely on them. An opinion is usually subject to contrary or conflicting views; a fact is objective and verifiable. Therefore, a seller of goods is allowed to "huff and puff" his wares without liability for fraud.

In certain cases, however, opinions may entitle the innocent party to rescission or reformation. These cases almost always involve some sort of "expert" giving a naive purchaser some opinion, and they are decided on equitable grounds. The courts usually hold it to be unfair to allow an expert to take advantage of a novice, especially if the expert knows the novice is relying on the expert's opinion. Thus, an expert's statement of opinion to a layperson is treated as fact.

The following case illustrates how a dance instructor with superior knowledge made statements of opinion concerning plaintiff's dance potential, and such were treated as a misrepresentation of a material fact.

VOKES v. ARTHUR MURRAY, INC.

District Court of Appeal of
Florida, Second District, 1968.
212 So.2d 906.

BACKGROUND AND FACTS   *The defendant, Arthur Murray, Inc., operated dancing schools throughout the nation through local franchised operators, one of whom was the defendant. The plaintiff, Audrey E. Vokes, a widow without family, wished to become "an accomplished dancer" to find "a new interest in life." In 1961 she was invited to attend a "dance party" at J. P. Davenport's "School of Dancing." Vokes went to the school and received elaborate praise from her instructor for her grace, poise, and potential as "an excellent dancer." The instructor sold her eight half-hour dance lessons for $14.50 each, to be utilized within one calendar month.*

Subsequently, over a period of less than sixteen months, Vokes bought a total of fourteen dance courses, which amounted to 2,302 hours of dancing lessons for a total cash outlay of $31,090.45, all at Davenport's school.

PIERCE, Judge.

*   *   *   *

These dance lesson contracts and the monetary consideration therefor of over $31,000 were procured from her by means and methods of Davenport and his associates which went beyond the unsavory, yet legally permissible, perimeter of "sales puffing" and intruded well into the forbidden area of undue influence, the suggestion of falsehood, the suppression of truth, and the free exercise of rational judgment, if what plaintiff alleged in her complaint was true. From the time of her first contact with the dancing school in February, 1961, she was influenced unwittingly by a constant and continuous barrage of flattery, false praise, excessive compliments, and panegyric encomiums, to such extent that it would be not only inequitable, but unconscionable, for a Court exercising inherent chancery power to allow such contracts to stand.

She was incessantly subjected to overreaching blandishment and cajolery. She was assured she had "grace and poise"; that she was "rapidly improving and developing in her dancing skill"; that the additional lessons would "make her a beautiful dancer, capable of dancing with the most accomplished dancers"; that she was "rapidly progressing in the development of her dancing skill and gracefulness", etc., etc. She was given "dance aptitude tests" for the ostensible purpose of "determining" the number of remaining hours instructions needed by her from time to time.

At one point she was sold 545 additional hours of dancing lessons to be entitled to award of the "Bronze Medal" signifying that she had reached "the Bronze Standard", a supposed designation of dance achievement by students of Arthur Murray, Inc.

Later she was sold an additional 926 hours in order to gain the "Silver Medal", indicating she had reached "the Silver Standard", at a cost of $12,501.35.

At one point, while she still had to her credit about 900 unused hours of instructions, she was induced to purchase an additional 24 hours of lessons to participate in a trip to Miami at her own expense, where she would be "given the opportunity to dance with members of the Miami Studio".

She was induced at another point to purchase an additional 126 hours of lessons in order to be not only eligible for the Miami trip but also to become "a life member of the Arthur Murray Studio", carrying with it certain dubious emoluments, at a further cost of $1,752.30.

At another point, while she still had over 1,000 unused hours of instruction she was induced to buy 151 additional hours at a cost of $2,049.00 to be eligible for a "Student Trip to Trinidad", at her own expense as she later learned.

Also, when she still had 1100 unused hours to her credit, she was prevailed upon to purchase an additional 347 hours at a cost of $4,235.74, to qualify her to receive a "Gold Medal" for achievement, indicating she had advanced to "the Gold Standard".

On another occasion, while she still had over 1200 unused hours, she was induced to buy an additional 175 hours of instruction at a cost of $2,472.75 to be eligible "to take a trip to Mexico".

Finally, sandwiched in between other lesser sales promotions, she was influenced to buy an additional 481 hours of instruction at a cost of $6,523.81 in order to "be classified as a Gold Bar Member, the ultimate achievement of the dancing studio".

All the foregoing sales promotions, illustrative of the entire fourteen separate contracts, were procured by defendant Davenport and Arthur Murray, Inc., by false representations to her that she was improving in her dancing ability, that she had excellent potential, that she was responding to instructions in dancing grace, and that they were developing her into a beautiful dancer, whereas in truth and in fact she did not develop in her dancing ability, she had no "dance apti- tude", and in fact had difficulty in "hearing the musical beat". The complaint alleged that such representations to her "were in fact false and known by the defendant to be false and contrary to the plaintiff's true ability, the truth of plain- tiff's ability being fully known to the defendants, but withheld from the plaintiff for the sole and specific intent to deceive and defraud the plaintiff and to induce her in the purchasing of additional hours of dance lessons". It was averred that the lessons were sold to her "in total disregard to the true physical, rhythm, and mental ability of the plaintiff". In other words, while she first exulted that she was entering the "spring of her life", she finally was awakened to the fact there was "spring" neither in her life nor in her feet.

* * * *

It is true that "generally a misrepresentation, to be actionable, must be one of fact rather than of opinion". But this rule has significant qualifications, applicable here. It does not apply where there is a fiduciary relationship between the parties, or where there has been some artifice or trick employed by the representor, or where the parties do not in general deal at "arm's length" as we understand the phrase, or where the representee does not have equal opportunity to become apprised of the truth or falsity of the fact represented.

" * * * A statement of a party having * * * superior knowledge may be regarded as a statement of fact although it would be considered as opinion if the parties were dealing on equal terms."

It could be reasonably supposed here that defendants had "superior knowl- edge" as to whether plaintiff had "dance potential" and as to whether she was noticeably improving in the art of terpsichore. And it would be a reasonable inference from the undenied averments of the complaint that the flowery eulo- giums heaped upon her by defendants as a prelude to her contracting for 1944 additional hours of instruction in order to attain the rank of the Bronze Standard, thence to the bracket of the Silver Standard, thence to the class of the Gold Bar Standard, and finally to the crowning plateau of a Life Member of the Studio, proceeded as much or more from the urge to "ring the cash register" as from any honest or realistic appraisal of her dancing prowess or a factual representation of her progress.

* * * *

" * * * [W]hat is plainly injurious to good faith ought to be considered as a fraud sufficient to impeach a contract", and that an improvident agreement may be avoided" * * * because of surprise, or mistake, *want of freedom, undue influence, the suggestion of falsehood, or the suppression of truth*". (Emphasis supplied.)

JUDGMENT AND REMEDY *Vokes's complaint, which had originally been dismissed from the trial court, was reinstated, and the case was returned to the trial court to allow Vokes to prove her case.*

COMMENTS *Fraud is an ambiguous concept in law. It includes various degrees of misrepresentation that can be separated into three tort categories: (1) intentional behavior, (2) negligent behavior, and (3) strict liability for certain behavior. In all cases involving the tort of misrepresentation and* *the contract defense of fraud, the defendant must misrepresent a fact or facts, and the plaintiff must believe the misrepresentation to be true and must rely on it with resulting damages.*

Misrepresentation of Law Misrepresentation of law does not ordinarily entitle the party to relief from a contract. For example, Sarah has a parcel of property that she is trying to sell to Brad. Sarah knows that a local ordinance prohibits building anything on the property higher than three stories. Nonetheless, she tells Brad, "You can build a condominium fifty stories high if you want to." Brad buys the land and later discovers that Sarah's statement is false. Normally Brad cannot avoid the contract because at common law people are assumed to know state and local law where they reside. Additionally, a layperson should not rely upon a statement made by a nonlawyer about a point of law.

Exceptions to this rule occur when the misrepresenting party is in a profession that is known to require greater knowledge of the law than the average citizen possesses. The courts are recognizing an increasing number of such professions. For example, the courts recognize that real estate brokers are expected by their clients to know the law governing real estate sales, land use, and so on. If Sarah, in the preceding example, were a lawyer or a real estate broker, her misrepresentation of the area's zoning status would probably constitute fraud.

Silence Ordinarily, neither party to a contract has a duty to come forward and disclose facts. Therefore, a contract cannot be set aside because certain pertinent information is not volunteered.

For example, suppose you own a car and have an accident that requires extensive body work on one side of the car. After the repair, the car's appearance and operation are the same as they were prior to the accident. One year later you decide to sell your car. Do you have a duty to volunteer the information about the accident to the seller? The answer is no. In this case, silence does not constitute misrepresentation. On the other hand, if the purchaser asks you if the car

has had extensive body work and you lie, you have committed a fraudulent misrepresentation.

Some exceptions to this rule exist. If a *serious* defect or *serious* potential problem is known to the seller but cannot reasonably be suspected by the buyer, the seller may have a duty to speak. Expanding the example just given, suppose your car occasionally vibrates dangerously because of the earlier accident. In this case, you would have a duty to speak. In another example, if the foundation of a factory is cracked, creating a potential for serious water damage, the seller must reveal this fact. Likewise, when a city fails to disclose to bidders subsoil conditions that will cause great expense in constructing a sewer, the city is guilty of fraud.[5]

Failure to disclose important facts also constitutes fraud if the parties have a relationship of trust and confidence called a *fiduciary relationship*. In such a relationship, if one party knows any facts that materially affect the other's interests, they must be disclosed. An attorney, for example, has a duty to disclose material facts to a client. Other such relationships include partners in a partnership, directors of corporations and the shareholders, and guardians and wards.

Knowledge of the Fact's Falsity—Attempt to Deceive The *second* element of fraud is knowledge on the part of the misrepresenting party that facts have been falsely represented. This element, normally called **scienter**, or "guilty knowledge," signifies that there was an *intent to deceive*. Proof of intent is not necessary if the

---

5. City of Salinas v. Souza & McCue Constr. Co., 66 Cal.2d 217, 57 Cal.Rptr. 337, 424 P.2d 921 (1967). Normally the seller must disclose only "latent" defects—that is, ones that would not readily be discovered even by an expert. Thus, termites in a house would not be a latent defect, since an expert could readily discover their presence.

circumstances surrounding a transaction are such that one can *infer* the intent. The act of misrepresentation combined with the knowledge of its falsity normally constitutes an intent to deceive.

Suppose that Roper has owned a 1980 Oldsmobile for two years and suddenly, for no apparent reason, quits driving it. Roper then advertises the automobile for sale. Chipper asks Roper how the engine runs, and Roper says, "This Olds runs like a Swiss watch; there is nothing wrong with it." So Chipper buys the Olds, only to discover the next day that there is a crack in the engine block requiring replacement of the entire engine. Here a court can *infer* that Roper knew that the engine block was cracked (at least in the absence of another explanation from Roper), since he suddenly quit driving the two-year-old car and put it up for sale.

Innocent Misrepresentation   If a person makes a statement that he or she believes to be true, but that actually misrepresents material facts, the person is guilty only of an **innocent misrepresentation,** not of fraud. If an innocent misrepresentation occurs, the aggrieved party can rescind the contract but usually cannot seek damages in tort caused by the misrepresentation (because there was a lack of knowledge and therefore of intent). Basically, an innocent misrepresentation, in the contract sense, is viewed as a mistake rather than as a fraud.

Negligent Misrepresentation   Suppose a salesperson tells a customer, "This air conditioner will cool your whole house," without knowing the size of the house. This person is acting in a negligent manner with reckless disregard for the truth. Consider another example: A real estate broker assures Sneed that a particular house is insulated, even though the broker does not know whether the house is insulated. In virtually all states, such *negligent misrepresentation* is equal to *scienter*, or to knowingly making a misrepresentation. In other words, culpable ignorance of the truth supplies the intention to mislead, even if the defendant can claim, "I didn't know."

Reliance on the Misrepresentation   The *third* element of fraud is reasonably *justifiable reliance* on the misrepresentation of fact. The de-

ceived party must have justifiable reason for relying on the misrepresentation, and the misrepresentation must be an important factor in inducing the party to enter into the contract. It need not be the sole factor in order to satisfy the requirement of reliance.

Reliance is not justified if the innocent party knows the true facts or relies on obviously extravagant statements. Suppose a used-car dealer tells you, "This old Cadillac will get fifty miles to the gallon." You would not normally be justified in relying on the statement. Or suppose Phelps, a bank director, induces Scott, a co-director, into signing a guarantee that the bank's assets will satisfy its liabilities, stating, "We have plenty of assets to satisfy our creditors." If Scott knows the true facts, he will not be justified in relying on Phelps's statement. However, if Scott does not know the true facts *and has no way of finding them out*, he will be justified in relying on the statement. The same rule applies to defects in property sold. If the defects are obvious, the buyer cannot justifiably rely on the seller's representations. If the defects are hidden or latent, that is, (not appearing on the surface), the buyer is justified in relying on the seller's statements.

Injury to the Innocent Party   The final element of fraud is injury to the innocent party. The courts are divided on this issue, and some do not require a showing of injury when the action is to *rescind* or *cancel* the contract. Since rescission returns the parties to the position they were in prior to the contract, showing injury to the innocent party has been held to be unnecessary.[6]

In an action to recover *damages* caused by the fraud, proof of an injury is universally required. The measure of damages is ordinarily equal to what the value of the property would have been if it had been delivered as represented, less the actual price paid for the property. In effect, this gives the innocent [nonbreaching] party the benefit of the bargain, rather than reestablishing the party's position prior to the contract. In actions based on fraud, courts

---

6. For example, Kaufman v. Jaffee, 244 App.Div. 344, 279 N.Y.S. 392 (1935).

will often award **exemplary**, or **punitive**, **damages**, which are defined as those damages awarded to a plaintiff over and above what will be just compensation for the loss. Punitive damages are based on the public policy consideration of *punishing* the defendant or setting an example for similar wrongdoers.

In the following case, Hazel Gales applied for auto insurance, stating falsely that she had not been in an auto accident in the past five years and had not received a ticket for a moving vio-

lation in the past three years. The defendant, Plains Insurance Co., claimed that such false representations made her policy void from the beginning [void *ab initio*]. The company contended that it would not have sold the policy at the specified rate and perhaps would not have sold it at all if Gales had provided true information about her driving record. Thus, the insurance company contended that it had not engaged in a genuine assent (that is, there was no reality of consent).

BACKGROUND AND FACTS   *The plaintiff in this action, D. C. Miller, is suing the insurance company of the owner and driver of the automobile in which his wife was killed. The owner and operator of the automobile, Hazel Gales, also perished in the crash. She was insured by Plains Insurance Company, the defendant. The policy provided, among other things, $500 medical expense coverage and up to $10,000 uninsured motorists coverage. This coverage provides for payment to the insured in case the insured is involved in an accident where someone else is at fault and does not have any insurance.*

At the trial, Miller was awarded both $500 in medical expenses and $10,000 under the uninsured motorists provision. On appeal, the defendant argued that had it known certain representations were untrue, it would not have undertaken the risk in insuring Gales, who had a record for moving traffic violations and, in particular, for hazardous driving and did not disclose it when applying for the policy.

MILLER v. PLAINS INS. CO.
Springfield Court of Appeals, Missouri 1966.
409 S.W.2d 770.

TITUS, Judge.

*   *   *   *

What is a material misrepresentation? *A misrepresentation that would likely affect the conduct of a reasonable man in respect to his transaction with another is material.* [Emphasis added.] Materiality, however, is not determined by the actual influence the representation exerts, but rather by the possibility of its so doing. A representation made to an insurer that is material to its determination as to what premium to fix or to whether it will accept the risk, relates to a fact actually material to the risk which the insurer is asked to assume. The word "risk" does not relate to an actual increase in danger but to a danger determined by the insurer's classification of the various circumstances affecting rates and insurability. That the fact misrepresented has no actual subsequent relation to the manner in which the event insured against occurred, does not make it any the less material to the risk. Thus, whether a misrepresentation is material in an application for an automobile insurance policy, is determined by whether the fact, if stated truthfully, might reasonably have influenced the insurance company to accept or reject the risk or to have charged a different premium, and not whether the insurer was actually influenced.

*   *   *   *

It is a well-known fact insurance companies rely on expense, loss, and other statistical data to measure differences among risks and thus ascertain rates to be charged for individual risks in accordance with standards for measuring variations in hazards. This is recognized and, to some extent, controlled by our statutes. Questions as to traffic violations of prospective insureds and as to previous accidents in which they have been involved are legitimate fields of research for insurance companies, for these are not only rate-determining facts but may also determine if the risk will even be insured. In consideration of the authorities previously cited, * * * we are of the opinion the misrepresentations involved in this case might reasonably be expected to have influenced the insurance company to have accepted or rejected Mrs. Gales as an insured or to have charged her a different premium for issuing her a policy. As the only evidence in this case is that if defendant had known the truth it would have declined the risk, we are drawn to the conclusion the misrepresentations were material and should permit defendant to avoid its liability under the policy.

JUDGMENT
AND REMEDY

The trial court was reversed. The defendant, Plains Life Insurance Company, did not have to pay the $10,000 uninsured motorists claim or the $500 medical expense coverage because of the material misrepresentation of fact made by Hazel Gales when she filled out the application on which her insurance policy was issued. In essence, the court decided there was no true assent by the insurance company to insure Gales under that premium for that policy. No insurance contract ever came into existence.

UNDUE INFLUENCE

Undue influence arises from special kinds of relationships in which one party can greatly influence another party, thus overcoming that party's free will. Minors and elderly people are often under the influence of guardians. If the guardian induces a young or elderly ward to enter into a contract that benefits the guardian, undue influence is likely being exerted. Undue influence can arise from a number of fiduciary or confidential relationships: attorney-client, doctor-patient, guardian-ward, parent-child, husband-wife, or trustee-beneficiary. The essential feature of undue influence is that the party being taken advantage of does not, in reality, exercise free will in entering into a contract. A contract entered into under excessive or undue influence lacks genuine assent and is therefore voidable.[7]

In the final analysis, the court must ask the following question in order to determine undue influence: To what extent was the transaction induced by dominating the mind or emotions of the person in question? It follows, then, that the mental state of the person in question will often show to what extent the persuasion from the outside influence was "unfair."

Whenever a contract is challenged on the basis of the particular relationship between the parties, the court will often *presume* that the contract was made under undue influence. For example, if a ward challenges a contract made with his or her guardian, the presumption will normally be that the guardian has taken advantage of the ward. To rebut this presumption successfully, the guardian has to show that full disclosure was made to the ward, that consideration was adequate, and that the ward received independent and competent advice before completing the transaction.

In cases where the relationship is one of trust and competence, such as between an attorney and a client, the dominant party (the attorney) is held to extreme or utmost good faith in dealing with the subservient party. Suppose a long-time attorney for an elderly man induces him to

_____

7. Restatement, Second, Contracts, Section 177.

sign a contract for the sale of some of his assets to a friend of the attorney at below-market prices. The contract is probably voidable. The attorney has not upheld good faith in dealing with the man (unless this presumption can be rebutted).

DURESS

Assent to the terms of a contract is not genuine if one of the parties is *forced* into agreement. Recognizing this, the courts allow that party to rescind the contract. Forcing a party to enter a contract under the fear of threats is legally defined as **duress.**[8] For example, if Piranha Loan Co. threatens to harm you or your family unless you sign a promissory note for the money that you owe, Piranha is guilty of using duress. In addition, threatening blackmail or extortion to induce consent to an informal contract constitutes duress. Duress is both a defense to the enforcement of a contract and a ground for rescission or cancellation. Therefore, the party upon whom the duress is exerted can choose to carry out the contract or to avoid the entire transaction. (This is true in most cases in which assent is not real.)

Generally, the threatened act must be wrongful or illegal. Threatening civil litigation (if the claim is bona fide) does not constitute duress, but threatening a criminal suit does.

Suppose that Donovan injures Jaworski in an auto accident. The police are not called. Donovan has no automobile insurance, but she has substantial assets. Jaworski is willing to settle the potential claim out of court for $3,000. Donovan refuses. After much arguing, Jaworski loses her patience and says, "If you don't pay me $3,000 right now, I'm going to sue you for $35,000." Donovan is frightened and gives Jaworski a check

for $3,000. Later in the day she stops payment on the check. Jaworski comes back to sue her for the $3,000. Donovan argues that she was the victim of duress. However, the threat of a civil suit is normally not duress. Had Jaworski threatened to have Donovan arrested unless Donovan paid her $3,000, Donovan's check would have been secured under duress.

Suppose Nelson and Dice belong to a fashionable social club. Nelson watches Dice cheating in a game of bridge and threatens to expose him unless Dice agrees to sign a contract with Nelson. In fear of being expelled from the club, Dice signs. The contract is entered into under duress.

Economic need is generally not sufficient to constitute duress, even when one party exacts a very high price for an item the other party needs. However, if the party exacting the price also creates the need, duress may be found. For example, the Internal Revenue Service assessed a large tax and penalty against Sam Thompson. Thompson retained Earl Eyman to resist the assessment. The last day before the deadline for filing a reply with the Internal Revenue Service, Eyman declined to represent Thompson unless he signed a very high contingency fee agreement for his services. The agreement was unenforceable.[9] Although Eyman had threatened only to withdraw his services, something that he was legally entitled to do, he was responsible for delaying the withdrawal until the last day. Since it would have been impossible at that late date to obtain adequate representation elsewhere, Thompson was forced into either signing the contract or losing his right to challenge the IRS assessment. (Thompson may also bring a cause of action for a breach of good faith.)

---

8. Restatement, Second, Contracts, Sections 174 and 175.

9. Thompson Crane & Trucking Co. v. Eyman, 123 Cal.App.2d 904, 267 P.2d 1043 (1954).

BACKGROUND AND FACTS *Union Pacific paid a large fee to the State of Missouri in order to obtain a certificate authorizing the railroad to issue bonds. The railroad then sought a partial refund of the fee, claiming it was paid under duress. The Missouri courts held the fee was paid voluntarily.*

UNION PAC. R.R. CO. v. PUBLIC SERV. COMM'N
United States Supreme Court, 1918.
248 U.S. 67, 39 S.Ct. 24.

MR. JUSTICE HOLMES delivered the opinion of the court.

This case concerns the validity of a charge made by the Public Service Commission of Missouri for a certificate authorizing the issue of bonds secured by a mortgage of the whole line of the Union Pacific road. The statutes of Missouri have general prohibitions against the issue of such bonds without the authority of the Commission, impose severe penalties for such issue and purport to invalidate the bonds if it takes place. Moreover the bonds would be unmarketable if the certificate were refused. Upon these considerations the plaintiff in error applied, in all the States through which its line passed, for a certificate authorizing the issue of bonds to the amount of $31,848,900. The Missouri Commission granted the authority and charged a fee of $10,962.25. The Railroad Company accepted the grant as required by its terms, but protested in writing against the charge as an unconstitutional interference with interstate commerce, and gave notice that it paid under duress to escape the statutory penalties and to prevent the revocation of the certificate. *   *   *
*   *   *   *

The Supreme Court of the State *   *   * [held] that the application to the Commission was voluntary and hence that the Railroad Company was estopped to decline to pay the statutory compensation. *   *   * [A]s conduct under duress involves a choice, it always would be possible for a State to impose an unconstitutional burden by the threat of penalties worse than it in case of a failure to accept it, and then to declare the acceptance voluntary[.]

On the facts we can have no doubt that the application for a certificate and the acceptance of it were made under duress. The certificate was a commercial necessity for the issue of the bonds. The statutes, if applicable, purported to invalidate the bonds and threatened grave penalties if the certificate was not obtained. The Railroad Company and its officials were not bound to take the risk of these threats being verified. Of course, it was for the interest of the Company to get the certificate. It always is for the interest of a party under duress to choose the lesser of two evils. But the fact that a choice was made according to interest does not exclude duress.

JUDGMENT
AND REMEDY

The Supreme Court ruled that the railroad company's application for the certificate was not a voluntary act.

ADHESION CONTRACTS AND UNCONSCIONABILITY

Modern courts are beginning to strike down terms that are dictated by one of the parties with overwhelming bargaining power. **Adhesion contracts** arise when one party forces the other party to adhere to dictated terms or go without the commodity or service in question. An adhesion contract is written *exclusively* by one party (the dominant party) and presented to the other party (the adhering party) with no opportunity to ne-

gotiate. Adhesion contracts usually contain copious amounts of fine print disclaiming the maker's liability for everything imaginable. Standard lease forms are often called adhesion contracts. Many automobile retailers have used contracts containing several pages of fine print when selling a car. In the past, nearly every company excluded liability for personal injuries suffered as a result of using the product. The average consumer buying a car for $5,000 or $6,000 was in no position to bargain for personal injury coverage. The consumer could either go without an automobile or buy the auto, risking personal injury for which he could not hold the auto manufacturer liable.

Standard form contracts are used by a variety of businesses and include life insurance policies, residential leases, loan agreements, and employment agency contracts. In order to avoid enforcement of the contract or of a particular clause, the aggrieved party must show substantially unequal bargaining positions and show that enforcement would be "manifestly unfair" or "oppressive." If the required showing is made, the contract or particular term is deemed *unconscionable* and not enforced. Technically, unconscionability under the UCC applies only to contracts for the sale of goods.[10] Many courts, however, have broadened the concept and applied it in other situations.

Although unconscionability was discussed in the preceding chapter under the subject of legality, it is important to note here that the great degree of discretion permitted a court to invalidate or strike down a contract or clause as being unconscionable has met with resistance. As a result, some states have not adopted Section 2-302 of the UCC. In those states the legislature and the courts prefer to rely on traditional notions of fraud, undue influence, and duress. In one respect, this gives certainty to contractual relationships, since parties know they will be held to the exact terms of their contracts. But on the other hand, public policy does dictate that there be some limit on the power of individuals and businesses to dictate terms of a contract.

QUESTIONS AND CASE PROBLEMS

1. In front of witnesses, Juanita informs Sue that she is going to offer to sell her car to Nick for $950. That evening, Juanita types a letter offering to sell her car to Nick, but in her haste she types the figure $900 instead of $950. Nick receives the letter and by return letter accepts. At the time for transfer of title, Nick tenders $900, but Juanita refuses to transfer title to the car unless he pays $950. She claims she has witnesses to her intent. Discuss whether, despite the witnesses, Nick can hold Juanita to a contract for $900. Would your answer be any different if Juanita in her haste had typed $95 instead of $950? Explain.

2. Pam owns two 1981 Buicks, one valued at $8,000 and the other valued at $9,000. She needs money and decides to sell one of her cars. Mary knows of this and offers to purchase Pam's Buick for $8,500. Pam signs a contract for the purchase price. At the time for transfer and payment, Pam attempts to deliver the Buick valued at $8,000. Mary believes she is buying the Buick valued at $9,000. Pam wants to hold Mary in contract for the 1981 Buick valued at $8,000, and Mary wants to hold Pam in contract for the 1981 Buick valued at $9,000. Discuss who can hold the other in contract.

3. Martin owns a forty-room motel on Highway 100. Tanner is interested in purchasing the motel. During the course of negotiations, Martin tells Tanner that the motel netted $30,000 last year and that it will net at least $45,000 next year. The motel books, which Martin turns over to Tanner, clearly show that Martin's motel netted only $15,000 last year. Also, Martin fails to tell Tanner that a bypass to Highway 100 is being planned that will redirect most traffic away from the front of the motel. Tanner purchases the motel. During the first year under Tanner's operation, the motel nets only $18,000. It is at this time that Tanner learns of the previous low profitability of the motel and the planned bypass. Tanner wants his money back from Martin. Discuss fully Tanner's probable success in getting his money back.

4. Discuss which of the following contracts are fully enforceable:

    (a) Simmons finds a stone in his pasture that he believes to be quartz. Jenson, who also believes that the stone is quartz, contracts to purchase it for $10. Just before delivery, the stone is discovered to be a diamond worth $1,000.

    (b) Jacoby's barn is burned to the ground. He accuses Goldman's son of arson and threatens to bring criminal action unless Goldman agrees to pay him $5,000. Goldman agrees to pay.

    (c) Student Velikovski threatens to tell teacher O'Brien's wife that O'Brien is having a sexual relationship with a student—unless O'Brien agrees to pay Velikovski $200. O'Brien agrees to pay.

    (d) Sallor is a new salesperson and innocently tells Beyer that a lawn mower he is selling has a five-year manufacturer's warranty. Beyer con-

---

10. See UCC 2-302.

tracts to purchase the lawn mower in reliance thereon. Beyer and Sallor are transacting business for the first time. At the time of delivery, it is discovered that the manufacturer only warrants the lawn mower for one year.

5. Joshua and Adam are brothers and have been close for many years. Adam is the oldest and has been acting as a father figure for fifteen years, since the death of their father. Joshua married Mary, and Adam and Mary do not get along together. During the past year, Adam has told Joshua that Mary is unfaithful and is out to get all his worldly possessions. Furthermore, he advises Joshua to sell his lake property (held in Joshua's name) before Mary moves in. Adam suggests that Joshua sell the property to a friend of Adam's immediately, and that although the value of the property is $20,000, a sale of $14,000 is better than nothing. Joshua contracts with his brother's friend at that price, but before the closing to transfer title, Joshua dies. Mary is executrix of his estate and wants to set aside the contract to sell the lake property. Discuss how successful she will be.

6. Plaintiff publishes a directory entitled *New York Yellow Pages*, which is strikingly similar in format, print style, and paper color to the *New York Telephone Company Yellow Pages*, but which in fact is part of an independent business enterprise. In addition, the *New York Yellow Pages* has on its cover the legend "Let your fingers do the walking!" along with the familiar logo of walking fingers that appears on the *Telephone Company Yellow Pages*. Plaintiff's representative, stating that this publication would replace the bulkier *New York Telephone Company Yellow Pages*, sold advertising space to Grossman for $1,492.80. Grossman made a down payment of $118.40 and one installment payment of $65.20 and thereafter refused to make payments. Plaintiff sued. Grossman claims that plaintiff fraudulently induced him to enter into the contract by leading him to believe plaintiff's book was a new, improved version of the *New York Telephone Company Yellow Pages*. Can Grossman rescind the contract on grounds of fraudulent inducement? [New York Yellow Pages, Inc. v. Growth Personnel Agency Inc., 98 Misc.2d 541, 414 N.Y.S.2d 260 (Civ.Ct. 1979)]

7. Stronach was a salesman for National Cash Register Company. Over the years he had sold cash registers to a number of retail establishments. Stronach approached Townsend, a retail merchant, to sell him a cash register. Stronach told Townsend that he would save the cost of a bookkeeper and perhaps half the cost of a sales clerk if he bought a cash register. Relying on this, Townsend bought the cash register. After several months, he realized that the cash register was not bringing about the savings that Stronach had promised. Can Townsend rescind the agreement? [See National Cash Register Co. v. Townsend Grocery Store, 137 N.C. 652, 50 S.E. 306 (1905)]

8. Laemmar was an employee of J. Walter Thompson Co. During the years of his employment, he purchased shares of common stock from the company. Laemmar's stock was to be subject to repurchase by the company if Laemmar's employment were terminated for any reason. The officers and directors of the company decided to increase their control and demanded that Laemmar and several other employees sell their stock back or lose their jobs. Although Laemmar did not wish to sell his stock, he did so to keep his job. The officers and directors never made any physical threats or suggestions of physical harm to Laemmar. Several years later Laemmar instituted a lawsuit to rescind his sale of the stock. Can Laemmar rescind? [Laemmar v. J. Walter Thompson Co., 435 F.2d 680 (7th Cir. 1970)]

9. W & B Realty Company owned and operated an apartment building in Chicago and rented one of the apartments to O'Callaghan. O'Callaghan signed a lease with a clause relieving W & B from all liability for any injuries that O'Callaghan might sustain anywhere on the premises of the apartment area, regardless of any negligence by W & B Realty. One evening, while crossing the courtyard, O'Callaghan fell because the pavement in the courtyard had been improperly maintained. O'Callaghan sued W & B for her injuries. W & B claimed that it was not liable because of the exculpatory clause contained in the lease. Is W & B correct? [O'Callaghan v. Waller & Beckwith Realty Co., 15 Ill.2d 436, 155 N.E.2d 545 (1958)]

10. Rollins was a prisoner in Rhode Island State Prison. While he was incarcerated, a prisoners' uprising occurred in which prison personnel were held as hostages. Rollins and other prisoners were promised immunity from prosecution by the director of the Department of Corrections if they would stop their violent actions and release the hostages. They did so. Nonetheless, they were later indicted and prosecuted for the crimes they committed during the prison revolt. Can Rollins and the others raise the defense that the promise of immunity had been made to them? [State v. Rollins, 116 R.I. 528, 359 A.2d 315 (1976)]

CHAPTER 12

CONTRACTS
Writing and Form

I agree to mow your lawn. You agree to pay me $25. I mow your lawn. You give me $15. I threaten to sue. After all, we did have an *oral* contract. Is it enforceable? In most cases, it is, but the party seeking to enforce it must establish the existence of the contract as well as its actual terms. Naturally, when the parties have no writing or memorandum about the contract, only oral testimony can be used in court to establish the existence of the terms of the contract. The problem with oral testimony is that parties are sometimes willing to perjure themselves in order to win lawsuits. Therefore, at early common law, parties to a contract were not allowed to testify. This led to the practice of hiring third party witnesses. As early as the seventeenth century, the English recognized this practice as a problem and enacted a statute to help deal with it. The statute was known as "An Act for the Prevention of Frauds and Perjuries."[1] The act required certain types of contracts to be evidenced by a writing

and signed by the party against whom enforcement was sought. For example, the act covered agreements that could not be performed within a year and the sale of real property involving a mortgage.

CONTRACTS THAT MUST BE IN WRITING

Today almost every state has a Statute of Frauds, modeled after the English act. The actual name of the Statute of Frauds is misleading since it neither applies to fraud nor invalidates any type of contract. Rather, it denies enforceability to certain contracts that do not comply with its requirements. Although the statutes vary slightly from state to state, they all require the following types of contracts to be in writing or evidenced by written memorandum.[2]

---

1. The English Parliament passed the act in 1677.

2. Restatement, Second, Contracts, Section 110.

1.   Contracts involving an interest in land.
2.   Contracts that cannot *by their terms* be performed within one year from date of formation.
3.   Collateral contracts such as promises to answer for the debt or duty of another and promises by the administrator or executor of an estate
to pay a debt of the estate personally, that is, out
of his or her own pocket.
4.   Promises made in consideration of marriage.
5.   Contracts for the sale of goods for more than
$500.

CONTRACTS INVOLVING AN INTEREST IN LAND

Sale of Land

A contract calling for the sale of land is not enforceable unless it is in writing or evidenced by
a written memorandum. Land is real property
and includes all physical objects that are permanently attached to the soil, such as buildings,
plants, trees, and the soil itself. The Statute of
Frauds operates as a *defense* to the enforcement
of an oral contract for the sale of land. Therefore,
even if both parties acknowledge the existence
of an oral contract for the sale of land, under
most circumstances the contract will still not be
enforced.[3] If S contracts orally to sell Blackacre
to B but later decides not to sell, B cannot enforce the contract. Likewise, if B refuses to close
the deal, S cannot force B to pay for the land by
bringing a lawsuit. The Statute of Frauds is a
defense to the enforcement of this type of oral
contract.

Frequently it is necessary to distinguish between real property, which is property affixed
to the land, and personal property. A contract
for the sale of land ordinarily involves the entire
interest in the real property, including buildings, growing crops, vegetation, minerals, timber, and anything else affixed to the land. Therefore, a fixture (personal property so affixed or so
used as to become a part of the realty) is treated

as real property. But anything else, say a couch,
is treated as personal property.

The Statute of Frauds requires written contracts for the transfer of other interests in land.
Interests in land include life estates, real estate
mortgages, easements, and leases.

Life Estates   A **life estate** is an ownership interest in land that lasts for a person's lifetime.
For example, if Sally Manne sells Edenfarm to
Mary Johnson "for life, then after Johnson's death,
to Nancy Smole," Johnson has a life estate in the
farm. This means that Johnson can live on and
farm the land during her lifetime, but when
Johnson dies Smole will have a full estate in the
farm—that is, she will own it entirely.[4]

Mortgages   A real estate **mortgage** is a conveyance of an interest in land as a security for repayment of a loan. If Nancy Smole, now full
owner of Edenfarm, wants to borrow money from
First National Bank, First National will require
collateral for the loan. By giving conditional title
of Edenfarm to the bank, Smole can get the loan.[5]
When Smole pays off the debt, Edenfarm will be
hers once again in total ownership.

Easements   An **easement** is a legal right to use
land without owning it. Easements are created
expressly or impliedly. An express easement
arises when the owner of land expressly agrees
to allow another person to use the land. To be
enforceable the agreement must be in writing.
Implied easements can arise from the past conduct of the parties. For example, when a farmer
has used a certain path to reach the back forty
acres of his farm for twenty years, and the path
goes across a neighbor's property, the farmer has
an *implied* easement to cross the neighbor's
property. Implied easements need not be in writing and rarely are, because of the way they are

---

3.   However, the contract will be enforced if the parties admit to the existence of the oral contract in court or admit to
its existence pursuant to discovery before trial.

---

4.   Full ownership like Nancy Smole's is called a fee simple
absolute. See Chapter 53.
5.   Technically, only in "title" states will Nancy Smole be
required to convey title to First National Bank. In "lien" states,
she can enter into a mortgage giving the bank a lien against
the farm. Today, many of the distinctions between title states
and lien states have essentially been eliminated.

created. Another example of an implied ease-ment involves the ownership of adjacent prop-erties by one person. The owner establishes an apparent and permanent use of, say, a road through one property onto the other. He or she then sells that property without specifying the road as an easement to the other property. It is implied nonetheless if the other property is otherwise landlocked without ingress or egress.

Leases   A lease is a transfer without title of real property for a certain period of time.[6] Most states have statutes dealing specifically with leases apart from the Statute of Frauds and exempt leases of less than one year from the writing require-ments. Thus, any lease lasting more than one year must be in writing. Some states extend this period. For example, Indiana allows leases to be oral for up to three years.

Partial Performance—Exception

Since the Statute of Frauds is a defense against the enforcement of an oral contract for the sale of land or an interest in land, problems arise when an oral contract has been partially per-formed. For example, the buyer may have paid part of the purchase price and then taken pos-session of the premises or made permanent im-provements to the property.[7] If the parties can-not be returned to their status quo, the courts are likely to grant *specific performance* of the oral contract (if they enforce it at all).

   When the purchase price has been paid, but the buyer has not taken possession, the parties can be returned to their original positions, so the courts will usually not grant specific perfor-mance. When the buyer has paid part of the pur-chase price and entered into possession, some states allow enforcement of the contract since the parties cannot be restored to their status quo. When part of the purchase price has been paid,

possession has been taken by the buyer, and per-manent improvements have been made to the land, most states allow enforcement of the con-tract. Once these three things have been done, the courts can be fairly sure there was actually a contract in existence, even if it was an oral con-tract. Otherwise the parties would not have taken the steps they did. Furthermore, it would be un-fair to allow the seller to retake possession after a substantial part of the purchase price had been paid and the buyer had made valuable improve-ments.[8]

CONTRACTS WHOSE TERMS CANNOT POSSIBLY BE PERFORMED WITHIN ONE YEAR FROM DATE OF FORMATION OR THE MAKING THEREOF

Contracts that cannot, by their own terms, be performed within one year from the date the contract is formed must be in writing to be en-forceable. Since disputes over such contracts are unlikely to occur until some time after the con-tracts are made, resolution of these disputes is difficult unless the contract terms have been put in writing.

   In order for a particular contract to fall into this category, contract performance must be ob-jectively impossible to perform within a year from the date of contract formation. If the contract, by its terms, is *possible* (not probable) to perform within the year, the contract is not within the Statute of Frauds and need not be in writing.

   Suppose Bankers Life orally contracts to loan $40,000 to Janet Lawrence "as long as Lawrence and Associates operates its financial consulting firm in Omaha, Nebraska." The contract is not within the Statute of Frauds—no writing is re-quired—because Lawrence and Associates could possibly go out of business in less than one year. In this event, the contract would be fully per-formed in less than one year. Although this oc-currence is unlikely, it is nevertheless possible,

---

6.   Although a lease is technically a conveyance of an inter-est in land, it is usually accompanied by a contract, rather than a deed.

7.   Executed contracts—that is, contracts that have been fully performed—are not subject to the Statute of Frauds.

---

8.   In some states, mere *reliance* on an oral contract is enough to remove it from the Statute of Frauds.

and that possibility removes the contract from the province of the Statute of Frauds.[9]

Suppose, on the other hand, that Bankers Life agrees to loan the money to Lawrence "for a period of two years with the provision that there will be no acceleration or prepayment for the period." Lawrence and Associates could go out of business in less than one year. Since the debtor is not allowed to accelerate payments on the loan or prepay the remainder at any time, he or she cannot perform the contract in less than one year without breaching the contract's terms. Therefore, this contract is subject to the Statute of Frauds and must be evidenced by a writing. Compare the specified two years in this contract to the statement in the preceding example, where the words "as long as" were used.

Next assume that the contract states that the loan will last for two years "terminable at the end of six months, subject to review of Lawrence and Associates' financial condition." Here the contract is not subject to the Statute of Frauds because, by the terms of the contract, it can be fully performed within one year.

The one-year period begins to run *the day after the contract is made.*[10] Suppose you graduate from college on June 1. An employer orally contracts to hire you immediately (June 1) for one year at $2,000 per month. This contract is not subject to the Statute of Frauds (need not be in writing to be enforceable) because the one-year period to measure performance begins on June 2. Since your performance of one year can begin immediately, it would take you exactly one year from the date of entering the contract to perform.

Suppose that on March 1 the dean of your college, in your presence, orally contracts to hire your professor for the next academic year (a nine-month period) at a salary of $35,000. The academic year begins on September 1. Does this contract have to be in writing to be enforceable? The answer is yes. The one-year period used to measure whether performance by contract terms is possible begins on March 2. Since the nine-month contract could not begin until September 1 and would end on May 31 of the next year, the contract performance period exceeds the one-year measurement period by three months. Thus, this contract is within the Statute of Frauds. But if this oral contract had been entered into at any time between June 1 and September 1, the contract, by its terms, would be performed within one year of the date of contract formation (acceptance of the offer), and the oral contract would be enforceable.

In summary, the test to determine whether an oral contract is enforceable under the one-year rule of the Statute of Frauds is not whether an agreement is *likely* to be performed within a year from the date of making the contract. Rather, the question revolves around whether performance within a year is *possible.* Conversely, when performance of an oral contract is impossible during a one-year period, this provision of the Statute of Frauds will bar recovery on an oral contract.

---

9. See Warner v. Texas & Pac. Ry. Co., 164 U.S. 418, 17 S.Ct. 147 (1896).

10. 2 Corbin on Contracts, Sec. 444.

ADAMS v. WILSON
Court of Appeals of Maryland, 1971.
264 Md. 1.284 A.2d 434.

BACKGROUND AND FACTS *This suit involved the enforceability of an oral contract to purchase a one-third interest and become a partner in an accounting firm. Robert C. Wilson and Vernon Robbins, both Certified Public Accountants, formed an accounting firm as a partnership in 1956. Ten years later, the firm employed the defendant, Thomas H. Adams, Jr., also a Certified Public Accountant. Adams desired to become a partner. After much discussion, the two partners, Robbins and Wilson, agreed to permit Adams to purchase a one-third interest in the partnership.*

By the terms of the oral purchase agreement, Adams was to pay a total of $30,000 for his interest—$20,000 to be paid immediately ($10,000 *each to Wilson and Robbins) and the remaining $10,000 to be paid from Adams's earnings in any fiscal year (June 1 to May 31) that his earnings exceeded $20,000. Adams was then admitted as a member of the partnership.*

Subsequently, the partnership was dissolved. Wilson asked Adams what he was going to do about the $5,000 Adams still owed him. Adams also owed Robbins $5,000, but Robbins made no demand for it.

After the dissolution of the partnership, Robbins and Adams formed a new partnership and continued in the accounting business. Meanwhile, Wilson filed this action against Adams to recover $5,000, alleging that it was part of the purchase price of the one-third interest in the old partnership. Adams refused to pay the $5,000, claiming, among other arguments, that recovery by Wilson was barred by the Statute of Frauds because the oral contract was unenforceable.

The trial court ruled against Adams's contention that his obligation was unenforceable under the Statute of Frauds as a contract not to be performed within a year.

BARNES, Judge.

*   *   *   *

Section IV, Clause 5 of the Statute of Frauds, 29 Car. II C. 3 (enacted 1676, effective 1677), Alexander's British Statutes (Coe ed. 1912), in force in Maryland subsequent to July 4, 1776, by the provisions of Article 5 of the Declaration of Rights of the Maryland Constitution, requires a memorandum signed by the party to be charged for the enforcement of contracts "not to be performed within the Space of one Year from the making thereof."

Adams contends that in view of the finding that the oral contract in regard to the deferred payment of $10,000 was conditioned upon his share of the profits from the partnership exceeding $20,000 *in any one year*, the contract was within the meaning of Section IV, Clause 5 of the Statute of Frauds.

There are two answers to this contention. The first answer is that, as construed by the English Courts and by this Court, it is only when performance of the oral contract is *impossible* during the year period will this provision of the Statute of Frauds bar recovery.

*   *   * The second answer is that Adams testified at the hearing that this was a provision of the oral contract, and this is sufficient memorandum to satisfy the Statute of Frauds. As Chief Judge Brune stated, for the Court, in Pollin v. Perkins, 223 Md. 532, 539–540, 165 A.2d 908, 911 (1960):

*   *   * "[T]he admissions of a party in the form of testimony constitute sufficient "memoranda" or "writings" under the Statute of Frauds, for recorded testimony is regarded as equivalent to signed depositions."

JUDGMENT AND REMEDY

Adams had to pay Wilson the $5,000. Not only was the oral contract performable during the one-year period, but Adams's testimony at a prior legal proceeding constituted sufficient legal "memoranda" to satisfy the Statute of Frauds.

COMMENTS

The year is measured from the time the agreement is made, not from the time performance begins. Note the court's very narrow interpretation of *the one-year rule. Courts in England and in the United States have been notorious for choosing the narrowest possible meaning for this rule. Adams's income could have sufficiently exceeded $20,000 within one year from the date of the agreement so that it would have been possible for him to pay the $10,000 within one year.*

COLLATERAL PROMISES

A collateral, or secondary, promise is one ancillary to an integrated contractual relationship. This term is used to refer to any promise that is ancillary to a principal transaction. Two collateral promises are covered by the Statute of Frauds. They are:

1.   Promises by the administrator or executor of an estate to pay the debts of the estate personally.
2.   Promises to answer for the debt or duty of another.

Promises by the Administrator or Executor of an Estate to Pay the Debts of the Estate Personally

The administrator (or executor) of an estate has the duty of paying the debts of the deceased and distributing any remainder to the deceased's heirs. The administrator can contract orally on behalf of the estate. A writing is required only when the administrator promises to pay the debts of the estate personally. Suppose Edward Post (administrator) contracts with Martha Lynch for legal services. If Post contracts on behalf of the estate, an oral contract is valid, and the estate is bound to pay Lynch for her legal services. But if Post agrees to pay Lynch's legal fees personally out of his own pocket, the contract must be in writing. Otherwise it is not enforceable, and Lynch cannot recover.

Promises to Answer for the Debt or Duty of Another

Promises made by one person to pay the debts or discharge the duties of another if the latter fails to perform are subject to the Statute of Frauds

and must be in writing. Three elements must be present in this collateral promise situation in order to require that the agreement be in writing. They are:

1.   Three parties are involved.
2.   Two promises are involved.
3.   The secondary, or collateral, promise is to pay a debt or fulfill a duty only if the first promisor fails to do so.

This set of requirements is illustrated in Exhibit 12–1.

The Statute of Frauds applies only to contracts that are promises of guaranty or suretyship. An oral promise to answer for the promisor's own debt is not within the statute, even if by its performance the completion of the promise will discharge the debt of another. Obviously, the promise must be made to the cred-

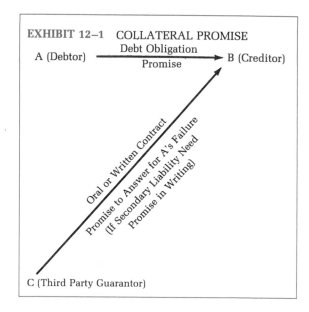

EXHIBIT 12–1   COLLATERAL PROMISE

itor. When the promise is made to the debtor, it is never within the Statute of Frauds.

The key point here is that the debt of the guarantor is secondary. The debtor's obligation is primary. The Statute of Frauds applies if, and only if, the guarantor's obligation is contingent upon the debtor's refusal or inability to pay the creditor. Consider some examples.

Suppose that Occidental Petroleum has signed an agreement with Husky Oil to ship 40,000 barrels of crude oil to Husky for a specified price. In other words, Husky has incurred an initial, or primary, obligation to Occidental Petroleum. Now a vice-president of European Caveham Ltd. makes a *collateral* promise with Occidental Petroleum that, if Husky does not pay for the oil, European will pay for it. If the collateral promise to pay the debt of Husky is not in writing, it is not enforceable. The nature of European's liability is secondary (European is liable only if Husky Oil does not pay). When the promise creates secondary liability, it falls under this section of the Statute of Frauds.

As another example, suppose John orally contracts with Green Florist to send his mother a dozen roses for Mother's Day. John's oral contract with Green Florist provides that he will pay for the roses if his mother does not do so. Is the contract enforceable against John? The answer is yes. John's mother is not a debtor; nor is she obligated to pay Green Florist. John's obligation is primary, not secondary, because John's mother has no obligation as a promisor under the contract. The third element that makes writing necessary is missing, and John's oral contract is supported by legally sufficient consideration to be enforceable.[11]

Now suppose John's mother owes $1,000 to the Third Bank of Austin on a promissory note payable on June 1. John knows that his mother cannot pay on the due date. John orally contracts with the Third Bank for the bank to extend the note payment for six months. Should the note not be paid at the end of that period by John's mother, John agrees to pay the note. Does this oral contract fall within the Statute of Frauds?

The answer is yes. The contract was express, made between the guarantor, John, and the creditor, Third Bank, and John's obligation is secondary—he is obligated to pay only if his mother does not pay. Therefore, this contract is not enforceable unless it is supported by a writing. Had John co-signed the note (and become a co-maker), allowing the bank to collect from either John or his mother, John's obligation would be *primary* and the contract would fall outside the Statute of Frauds and would not need to be in writing. Had John secured his mother's release from the debt from the bank for his promise to pay, the release being a discharge of her primary obligation to pay, John's promise to pay would become the *primary* liability and would fall outside the Statute of Frauds and would not need to be in writing in order to be enforceable.

The "Main Purpose" Rule—Consideration of Benefit to Promisor   The promise to answer for the debt of another is covered by the Statute of Frauds unless the oral promisor is effectively a debtor because his or her main purpose is to secure a pecuniary benefit. This type of contract need not be in writing.[12] The assumption is that a court can infer from the circumstances of any given case whether the "leading objective" of the promisor was to secure a pecuniary advantage and thus, in effect, to answer for his or her own debt. The question is: What did the promisor expect to get in exchange for the promise? If the beneficial consideration received is equivalent to, or is bargained for as the equivalent to, the obligation undertaken, then the oral promise is outside the Statute of Frauds, since it is a promise to answer for a debt of another.

Consider an example. The General Contracting Corporation agrees to build a home for Oswald. General Contracting subcontracts part of its work to Ace Construction Company. After several weeks, Ace refuses to supply further labor or materials because General is in shaky financial condition and Ace is worried about being paid. Oswald is anxious to inhabit the house so that his children may start school on time in their new neighborhood. Therefore, Oswald or-

---

11.   Restatement, Second, Contracts, Section 112.

12.   Restatement, Second, Contracts, Section 116.

ally agrees to pay General's debts if General fails to pay. Oswald's oral promise is enforceable (even though collateral) because the primary, or main, purpose in making the guarantee was to get the house built.[13] (This holds true even though it was General's *original* obligation and General was the *original* promisor.)

Another typical application of the so-called main purpose doctrine is when one creditor guarantees the debtor's debt to another creditor for the purpose of forestalling litigation so as to allow the debtor to remain in business long enough to generate enough profits to pay *both* creditors.

---

13. Kampman v. Pittsburgh Contracting and Engineering Co., 316 Pa. 502, 175 A.396 (1934).

WILSON FLOORS CO. v. SCIOTA PARK, LTD.

Supreme Court of Ohio, 1978.
54 Ohio St.2d 451, 377 N.E.2d 514.

BACKGROUND AND FACTS   *Wilson Floors contracted to provide flooring materials for a residential and commercial development known as "The Cliffs," which was owned by the defendant. When Unit, the general contractor for Sciota, fell behind in payments to Wilson, Wilson stopped work on the project. The bank financing the development assured Wilson that he would be paid if he returned to work. After Wilson's final bill was not paid by Unit, he proceeded with this action against the bank.*

SWEENEY, Justice.

The central issue in this cause is whether the bank's oral promise to Wilson that payments would be forthcoming upon a resumption of work at The Cliffs project constituted an enforceable oral contract.

R.C. 1335.05 provides:

"No action shall be brought whereby to charge the defendant, upon a special promise, to answer for the debt, default, or miscarriage of another person * * * unless the agreement upon which such action is brought, or some memorandum or note thereof, is in writing and signed by the party to be charged therewith or some other person thereunto by him or her lawfully authorized."

"When the leading object of the promisor is not to answer for another, but to subserve some pecuniary or business purpose of his own, involving a benefit to himself, or damage to the other contracting party, his promise is not within the statute of frauds, although it may be in form a promise to pay the debt of another, and its performance may incidentally have the effect of extinguishing that liability."

In applying the leading object rule to the facts in this cause, the Court of Common Pleas, finding that the bank assumed a "direct undertaking" when it guaranteed Wilson payment for future services rendered, held that the bank's promise was enforceable by Wilson. No significance was given to the fact that Unit remained primarily liable for the debt owed Wilson; *i.e.*, that Wilson continued to send its progress billings to Unit for reimbursement.

The Court of Appeals, on the other hand, finding that the bank became only secondarily liable to Wilson when it guaranteed payment to the subcontractor, held that the bank's promise came within the provisions of the statute of frauds and therefore was unenforceable. The fact that the promise by the bank to guarantee payments was made to further the bank's own business interest was found not to be determinative of the cause.

* * * *

"In many cases the test whether a promise is or is not within the statute of frauds is to be found in the fact that the original debtor does or does not remain liable on his undertaking; if he is discharged by a new arrangement made on sufficient consideration, with a third party, this third party may be held on his promise though not in writing; but if the original debtor remains liable and the promise of the third party is only collateral to his, it will in strictness be nothing more than a promise to answer for the other's debt. But where the third party is himself to receive the benefit for which his promise is exchanged, it is not usually material whether the original debtor remains liable or not."

The above explanation of the leading object rule indicates that, in a determination of whether an oral promise is enforceable to pay the debt of another, the court may employ one of two tests. The court may inquire as to whether the promisor becomes primarily liable on the debt owed by another to a third party. If it is found that the promisor does not become primarily liable for payment of the debt, the court may inquire as to whether the promisor's leading object was to subserve his own business or pecuniary interest.

Because it is unquestioned that the bank in the instant cause did not become primarily liable when it guaranteed the subcontractors that they would be paid the court must apply the second test * * * to determine the enforceability of the verbal agreement.

Under the second test, it is of no consequence that when such promise is made, the original obligor remains primarily liable or that the third party continues to look to the original obligor for payment. So long as the promisor undertakes to pay the subcontractor whatever his services are worth irrespective of what he may owe the general contractor, and so long as the main purpose of the promisor is to further his own business or pecuniary interest, the promise is enforceable. Thus, under this test it is not required to show as a condition precedent for enforceability of the oral contract that the original debt is extinguished.

The facts in the instant cause reflect that the bank made its guarantee to Wilson to subserve its own business interest of reducing costs to complete the project. Clearly, the bank induced Wilson to remain on the job and rely on its credit for future payments. To apply the statute of frauds and hold that the bank had no contractual duty to Wilson despite its oral guarantees would not prevent the wrong which the statute's enactment was to prevent, but would in reality effectuate a wrong.

Judgment was entered in favor of Wilson. The bank's main purpose (leading object) was to derive a benefit for itself. Therefore, the promise to pay Unit's debts was not within the Statute of Frauds.   **JUDGMENT AND REMEDY**

PROMISES MADE IN CONSIDERATION OF MARRIAGE

A unilateral promise to pay a sum of money or to give property in consideration of a promise to marry must be in writing. If Bill MacAdams promises $10,000 to Bruce Coby if Coby promises to marry his daughter, Sally MacAdams, MacAdams's promise must be in writing. The same rule applies to prenuptial agreements (agreements made before marriage), which define the ownership rights of each partner in the other partner's property. For example, a prospective husband may wish to limit the amount his prospective wife could obtain if the marriage should end in divorce. Another common situation involving prenuptial agreements occurs when a man and woman who wish to get married both have separate assets and children from prior marriages. A prenuptial arrangement may be highly desirable in this case, particularly in a community property state. Prenuptial arrangements must be in writing to be enforceable, and there must be consideration. (Some states do not require consideration—Florida, for example.)

CONTRACTS FOR THE SALE OF GOODS

The UCC contains several Statute of Frauds provisions that require written evidence of a contract. Section 2-201 contains the major provision, which generally requires a writing or memorandum for the sale of goods priced at $500 or more.[14] A writing that will satisfy the Code requirement need only state the quantity term, and that need not be stated "accurately," as long as it adequately reflects both parties' intentions. The contract will not be enforceable, however, for any quantity greater than that set forth in the writing. In addition, the writing must be signed by the person to be charged—that is, the person who refuses to perform or the one being sued. Beyond these two requirements, the writing need not designate the buyer or seller, the terms of payment, or the price.

Exceptions to the writing requirements, contained in UCC 2–201, are discussed in detail in Chapter 18. A few of the more important exceptions are also discussed in this chapter.

Partial Performance

The Statute of Frauds provides that an oral contract will be enforceable to the extent a seller accepts payment or to the extent a buyer accepts delivery of the goods contracted for.[15] For example, Windblown Sailboats makes an oral contract with Sunset Sails to have Sunset make 750 sails for Windblown's new nineteen-foot Day Sailer. Windblown repudiates the agreement after the sails have been made and after two dozen have been delivered. The contract will be enforceable to the extent of the two dozen sails accepted by Windblown.

Goods Made Specially to Order

Contracts for goods made specially for the buyer—that is, goods that could not be resold by the seller in the ordinary course of the seller's business —are enforceable even when not in writing, provided that the seller has made a substantial beginning of manufacture or commitment for their procurement.[16] Suppose that Wilt Chamberlain orally contracts with a furniture factory for $1 million of furniture specially designed on a larger than normal scale to accommodate his larger than normal physique. Once the factory has committed itself to the manufacture or has made a substantial beginning in manufacturing the furniture, the oral contract is enforceable.

Consider another example. Smith orally contracts with Green for 10,000 calendars at a price of $10,000 imprinted with Smith's business name and address. Once Green has made a substantial beginning in the printing of the calendars, the oral contract is enforceable.

Confirmation of an Oral Contract between Merchants

If one merchant sends another written confirmation of an oral contract, the merchant receiving the confirmation (with knowledge of its terms) must object in writing within ten days of its receipt, or the oral contract will be enforceable by either party.[17]

Suppose Rodriguez in Los Angeles calls Cohen in New York City on June 1, and an oral contract is formed for Cohen's purchase of a new $10,000 machine. The next day Rodriguez

---

14. UCC 2-201, reads in part:

[A] contract for the sale of goods for the price of $500 or more is not enforceable by way of action or defense unless there is some writing sufficient to indicate that a contract for sale has been made between the parties and been signed by the party against whom enforcement is sought. * * * A writing is not insufficient because it omits or incorrectly states a term agreed upon but the contract is not enforceable under this paragraph beyond the quantity of goods shown in the writing. * * *

15. UCC 2-201(3)(c).

16. UCC 2-201(3)(a).

17. UCC 2-201(2).

sends Cohen a telegram that states, "This is to confirm our telephone contract of June 1 for * * * machine at $10,000. Thank you for your order." Cohen receives the telegram the same day. On June 15 Cohen discovers that a similar machine can be purchased for $9,000. Cohen claims the Statute of Frauds as a defense for his refusal of Rodriguez's tender of the machine. Cohen will lose against Rodriguez's suit for breach because he failed to object within ten days of receiving Rodriguez's confirmation.

Admissions

If a party to an oral contract "admits" in "pleading, testimony or otherwise in court that a contract for sale was made," the contract will be enforceable, but only to the extent of the quantity admitted.[18] Thus, if the president of Windblown Sailboats admits under testimony that an oral agreement was made for fifty sails, the agreement will be enforceable to that extent.

SUFFICIENCY OF THE WRITING

To be safe, all contracts should be fully set forth in a writing signed by all the parties. This assures that if any problems arise concerning performance of the contract, a written agreement can be introduced into court. The Statute of Frauds and the UCC require either a written contract or a *written memorandum* signed by the party against whom enforcement is sought. In other words, any confirmation, invoice, sales slip,

---

18. UCC 2-201(3)(b).

check, or telegram can constitute a writing sufficient to satisfy the Statute of Frauds.[19] The signature need not be placed at the end of the document but can be anywhere in the writing. It can even be an initial rather than the full name.

A memorandum evidencing the oral contract need only contain the essential terms of the contract. Under the UCC, for the sale of goods, the writing need only name the quantity term and be signed by the party to be charged. Under most provisions of the Statute of Frauds, the writing must ordinarily name the parties, subject matter, consideration, and quantity. Contracts for the sale of land are exceptions. The memorandum must, in addition, state the *essential* terms of the contract, such as location and price, with sufficient clarity to allow the terms to be determined from the memo itself, without reference to any outside sources.[20]

Only the party to be charged need sign the writing. Therefore, a contract may be enforceable by one of its parties but not by the other. Suppose Ota and Warrington orally contract for the sale of Ota's lake house and lot for $25,000. Ota writes Warrington a letter confirming the sale by identifying the parties and the essential terms—price and method of payment—and object of the sale and signs the letter. Ota has made a written memorandum of the oral land contract. Since she signed the letter, she can be held to the oral contract by Warrington. However, since Warrington has not signed or entered into a written contract or memorandum, he can plead the Statute of Frauds as a defense, and Ota cannot enforce the contract against him.

---

19. Even if the Statute of Frauds is satisfied, the existence and terms of the contract must be proven in court.

20. Rhodes v. Wilkins, 83 N.M. 782, 498 P.2d 311 (1972).

BACKGROUND AND FACTS *The Lamberts (plaintiffs) brought suit against Home Federal Savings and Loan Association and Marx & Bensdorf (defendants) for breach of an alleged promise to make a long-term loan of $2,910,000. The Lamberts were constructing ninety-six apartment units. Marx & Bensdorf, Home Federal's agent, made a construction loan of $672,000. This loan was evidenced by a one-year note in trust deed, which, by its terms, became null and void in October 1968 upon payment and release. Clearly, by the terms of the construction loan, it in no way*

LAMBERT v. HOME FED. SAV. AND LOAN ASS'N

Supreme Court of Tennessee, 1972.

481 S.W.2d 770.

involved the $2,910,000 permanent loan that was to follow, even though the permanent loan was to be made by the same organization.

When the Lamberts tried to obtain the $2,910,000, the defendants refused to make the loan. The Lamberts claimed that the permanent loan was tied into the construction loan, and they alleged that there were memoranda indicating the terms of the permanent financing transaction sufficient to satisfy the Statute of Frauds. Thirteen documents were produced at the trial, none of which had any bearing on the permanent loan. The lower court dismissed the case, finding that neither Home Federal nor Marx & Bensdorf had made any commitment to lend that money to the Lamberts.

The Lamberts tried to convince the appellate court that the permanent loan was evidenced by a writing sufficient to satisfy the Statute of Frauds. Furthermore, they argued that since the permanent loan was related to the construction loan, testimony about discussions and negotiations should be permitted to show the court the relationship between the loans and permit the original construction loan agreement to be modified to include the permanent loan.

HUMPRHEYS, Justice.

*   *   *   *

To meet the requirements of the Statute of Frauds, the Lamberts produced memoranda which they contended would, when considered in connection with this [original construction] mortgage to Marx & Bensdorf, furnish written memoranda of the transaction which would satisfy the Statute of Frauds.

The memoranda relied on by the Lamberts consists of thirteen documents which, considered separately, and collectively, made no commitments whatsoever by Home Federal or Marx & Bensdorf to lend [an additional $2,910,000 of] money to the Lamberts and take a trust deed as security. Nor is any commitment made by the Lamberts to Home Federal and Marx & Bensdorf to accept such a loan and to give a trust deed to secure the same on any described real property. [In other words, there was no written document specifically showing a bilateral agreement, or a "promise for a promise."]

Marx & Bensdorf is not involved in the memoranda other than by the note and deed of trust for the construction loan of $672,000.00. [Moreover], this deed of trust by its terms became null and void upon payment and release, which was done October 1, 1968; and contains no terms which considered alone or with the thirteen instruments satisfies the statute.

The deed of trust does not, and could not, under its terms, secure any greater amount than the $672,000.00 for which it was intended to furnish security. No other amounts are mentioned in the instrument and there is no language therein indicating any intention that it shall apply to any other loan than the single one mentioned.

A mortgage, or a deed of trust, in its legal aspect is a conveyance of an estate or an interest in land and as such within the meaning of the Statute of Frauds. A mortgage or deed of trust of land cannot be made by parol [orally]. A promise to make another the owner of a lien or charge upon land is equivalent to selling him such an interest therein, and is within the statute.

* * * It is also the rule that a mortgage cannot be modified or extended by an oral agreement to secure further indebtedness.

On the basis of this authority the Lamberts' contention that the trust deed to Marx & Bensdorf to secure the single $672,000.00 loan can be looked to as memorandum satisfying the Statute of Frauds must be rejected.

The rule by which the thirteen instruments exhibited to the bill as memoranda satisfying the Statute of Frauds must be tested is well stated thusly: "The general rule is that the memorandum, in order to satisfy the statute, must contain the essential terms of the contract, expressed with such certainty that they may be understood from the memorandum itself or some other writing to which it refers or with which it is connected, without resorting to parol evidence. A memorandum disclosing merely that a contract had been made without showing what the contract is, is not sufficient to satisfy the requirement of the Statute of Frauds that there be a memorandum in writing of the contract."

Considered in the light of this statement of what is required of memoranda to satisfy the statute, the conclusion is unavoidable that the memoranda does not satisfy the statute.

The appeal was dismissed. The Lamberts could not enforce the loan contract for $2,910,000. The court required that in order to satisfy the Statute of Frauds, the writing had to include the essential terms of the contract.

JUDGMENT AND REMEDY

The writing should specify the parties, subject matter, and any special conditions or terms with certainty. Documenting consideration is a matter of state law. Some states require it; some do not. If the writing consists of several pages, each page should be signed separately and clearly identified as part of the same transaction.

COMMENTS

THE PAROL EVIDENCE RULE

The **parol evidence rule** prohibits the introduction of words (parol) that contradict or vary the terms of written contracts. The written contract is ordinarily assumed to be the complete embodiment of the parties' agreement. Courts are reluctant to recognize oral or other written evidence of prior or contemporaneous agreements that conflict with the terms of the written agreement. Therefore, courts assume that all prior negotiations and oral agreements are embodied in the written contract.

Because of the rigidity of the parol evidence rule, courts make several exceptions.

First, when the parties *modify* the existing written agreement orally, evidence of the modification can be introduced into court. Since courts assume all prior negotiations and oral agreements are merged in the written contract, there is no reason to forbid changes in the written contract as long as they occur after the writing. Keep in mind that the oral modifications may not be enforceable if they come under the Statute of Frauds—for example, if they increase the price of the goods for sale to over $500 or increase the term for performance to more than one year. Also, oral modifications will not be enforceable if the original contract provides that any modification must be in writing.[21]

Second, oral evidence can be introduced in all cases to show that the contract was voidable

---

21. UCC 2-209(2)(3).

or void (for example, induced by mistake, fraud, or misrepresentation). In this case, if one of the parties was deceived into agreeing to the terms of a written contract, oral evidence attesting to fraud should not be excluded. Courts frown upon bad faith and are quick to allow such evidence when it establishes fraud.

Third, when the terms of a written contract are ambiguous, oral evidence is admissible to show the meaning of the terms.

Fourth, oral evidence is admissible when the written contract is incomplete in that it lacks one or more of the essential terms. The courts allow oral evidence to fill in the gaps in this case.

Fifth, under the UCC, oral evidence can be introduced to explain or supplement a written contract by showing a prior course of dealing or usage of trade.[22] When buyers and sellers deal with each other over extended periods of time, certain customary practices develop. They are often overlooked when writing the contract, so courts allow the introduction of oral evidence to show how the parties have acted in the past.

Lastly, the parol evidence rule does not apply if the existence of the entire written contract is subject to an orally agreed upon condition. Proof of the condition does not *alter* or *modify* the written terms but involves the very *enforceability* of the written contract. Suppose Carvelli agrees in writing to buy Jackson's real property for $100,000. The terms are written on a note pad, and the pad is signed by both parties. Prior to the signing, the parties orally agree that the contract is binding *only on condition* that the terms as written are approved by Carvelli's attorney. Evidence of the oral condition can be proved and is not a violation of the parol evidence rule. What is at issue here is the intention of the parties to have an enforceable agreement.

---

22. UCC 1-205, 2-202.

MASTERSON v. SINE

Supreme Court of California, 1968.

68 Cal.2d 222, 65 Cal.Rptr. 545, 436 P.2d 561.

BACKGROUND AND FACTS *Masterson sold his ranch to Sine, his brother-in-law. Their contract of purchase included a clause giving Masterson a ten-year option to repurchase the ranch for the same price plus a percentage of the cost of any improvements Sine might have made over the course of the years. Masterson went bankrupt sometime after the sale. His trustee in bankruptcy attempted to exercise this option clause to repurchase the ranch to obtain funds to satisfy Masterson's debts. The trial court refused to allow Sine to introduce extrinsic evidence showing the meaning the parties attached to the option clause, specifically that it was personal to Masterson. Thus, the trial court permitted the trustee to enforce the option to repurchase on Masterson's behalf. Defendant Sine appealed.*

TRAYNOR, Chief Justice.

*   *   *   *

When the parties to a written contract have agreed to it as an "integration"—a complete and final embodiment of the terms of an agreement—parol evidence cannot be used to add to or vary its terms. *   *   * When only part of the agreement is integrated, the same rule applies to that part, but *parol evidence may be used to prove elements of the agreement not reduced to writing.*[Emphasis added.]

*   *   *   *

The crucial issue in determining whether there has been an integration is whether the parties intended their writing to serve as the exclusive embodiment of their agreement. The instrument itself may help to resolve that issue. It may state, for example, that "there are no previous understandings or agreements not contained in the writing," and thus express the parties' "intention to nullify antecedent understandings or agreements." Any such collateral agreement itself must be examined, however, to determine whether the parties intended the subjects of negotiation it deals with to be included in, excluded from, or otherwise affected by the writing. Circumstances at the time of the writing may also aid in the determination of such integration.

* * * *

In formulating the rule governing parol evidence, several policies must be accommodated. One policy is based on the assumption that written evidence is more accurate than human memory. This policy, however, can be adequately served by excluding parol evidence of agreements that directly contradict the writing. Another policy is based on the fear that fraud or unintentional invention by witnesses interested in the outcome of the litigation will mislead the finder of facts.

Legal authorities have suggested that the party urging the spoken as against the written word is most often the economic underdog, threatened by severe hardship if the writing is enforced. [This] view [of] the parol evidence rule arose to allow the court to control the tendency of the jury to find through sympathy and without a dispassionate assessment of the probability of fraud or faulty memory that the parties made an oral agreement collateral to the written contract, or that preliminary tentative agreements were not abandoned when omitted from the writing. [It] recognizes, however, that if this theory were adopted in disregard of all other considerations, it would lead to the exclusion of testimony concerning oral agreements whenever there is a writing and thereby often defeat the true intent of the parties.

Evidence of oral collateral agreements should be excluded only when the fact finder [the judge or the jury] is likely to be misled. The rule must therefore be based on the credibility of the evidence. One such standard, adopted by section 240(1)(b) of the Restatement of Contracts, permits proof of a collateral agreement if it "is such an agreement as might *naturally* be made as a separate agreement by parties situated as were the parties to the written contract." The draftsmen of the Uniform Commercial Code would exclude the evidence in still fewer instances: "If the additional terms are such that, if agreed upon, they would *certainly* have been included in the document in the view of the court, then evidence of their alleged making must be kept from the trier of fact." [UCC Sec. 2-202] (italics added.)

The option clause in the deed in the present case does not explicitly provide that it contains the complete agreement, and the deed is silent on the question of assignability. Moreover, the difficulty of accommodating the formalized structure of a deed to the insertion of collateral agreements makes it less likely that all the terms of such an agreement were included. The statement of the reservation of the option might well have been placed in the recorded deed solely to preserve the grantors' rights against any possible future purchasers and this function could well be served without any mention of the parties' agreement that the option was personal. There is nothing in the record to indicate that the parties to this family transaction, through experience in land transactions or otherwise, had any warning of the disadvantages of failing to put the whole agreement in the deed. This case is one, therefore, in which it can be said that a collateral agreement such as that alleged "might naturally be made as a separate agreement." *A fortiori,* the case is not one in which the parties "would certainly" have included the collateral agreement in the deed.

JUDGMENT AND REMEDY

Since the writing did not have an integration clause, extrinsic (parol) evidence could be used to show that the option was personal to the grantors and, therefore, not assignable. As a result, the trial court judgment was reversed because that court had excluded parol evidence improperly.

COMMENTS

In numerous situations, the parol evidence rule does not apply: (1) when obvious and gross clerical or typographical errors exist; (2) when a written offer is verbally accepted and nothing further is reduced to writing; (3) when the underlying contract is voidable, unenforceable, or never arose because of lack of capacity of a party, fraud, duress, or illegality; and (4) when supplemental materials do not change the terms of the contract by evidence of custom and usage.

QUESTIONS AND CASE PROBLEMS

1. On May 1, by telephone, Yu offers to hire Benson to perform personal services. On May 5, Benson returns Yu's call and accepts the offer. Discuss fully whether this contract falls under the Statute of Frauds under the following circumstances:

   (a) The contract calls for Benson to be employed for one year, with the right to begin performance immediately.

   (b) The contract calls for Benson to be employed for nine months, with performance of services to begin on September 1.

   (c) The contract calls for Benson to submit a written research report, with a deadline of two years for submission.

2. In December 1980, Kaplin ordered 11,000 yards of madras at 75 cents a yard from Reich. The order was made over the telephone. On January 9, 1981, Reich sent Kaplin a bill that included a statement of the quantity that Reich had sent Kaplin. On February 18, 1981, Kaplin wrote to Reich, stating:

Replying to your letter of the 18th, please be advised that we examined a few pieces of merchandise that were billed to us against your invoice No. 10203, and found that it was not up to our standard. We are, therefore, unable to accept this shipment. * * * Very truly yours, (signed) Isador Kaplin.

Reich sued Kaplin for payment owed under the contract. Kaplin defended on the ground that the contract was entered into over the telephone and therefore failed to meet Statute of Frauds requirements. Is Kaplin's argument convincing?

3. William Rowe was admitted to General Hospital, suffering from the effects of a severe gastric hemorrhage. On the day Rowe was admitted, Rowe's son informed an agent for the hospital that his father had no financial means but that he would pay for his father's medical services. Subsequently, the son stated, "Well, we want you to do everything you can to save his life, and we don't want you to spare any expense. Whatever he needs, Doctor, you go ahead and get it, and I will pay you." After Rowe was discharged from the hospital, his son refused to pay the medical bills. Can the hospital enforce the son's oral promise?

4. Roger is interested in starting a restaurant on Lake Faithful. He locates an old, vacant mansion on the lake, which, with alterations, would be ideal for the restaurant. The mansion is owned by Striker. Roger calls Striker on the telephone and contracts to lease the mansion, to be used as a restaurant with agreed alterations, for ten years at a lease price of $12,000 per year, with Roger to pay six months' rent in advance. Roger is to have immediate right to possession. He sends Striker a check for $6,000, noting on the check,

"six months advance payment on ten-year lease—Striker mansion." Striker cashes the check upon receipt. Roger does not take immediate possession, but he does contract with Smith & Associates to make alterations to the mansion. Work on the alterations had not yet begun when, one month later, Striker has an opportunity to sell the mansion to a buyer at a substantial price. Striker tenders back to Roger $6,000, claiming the ten-year lease is unenforceable under the Statute of Frauds. Is Striker correct? Discuss fully.

5. The following oral contracts deal with the sale of goods. Discuss fully which of them are enforceable and which are unenforceable under the Statute of Frauds:

> (a) Carrigan contracts to purchase for $2,000 napkins and tablecloths with the name of his restaurant, "Harvest House," embroidered on each.
>
> (b) Harper, a merchant, sends Proctor, another merchant, a confirmation of their oral contract. Proctor receives this confirmation on May 1 and does not respond until May 20, at which time he refutes the contract.

6. "Man's Country," a health club and bathhouse in Manhattan, leased a billboard from Christopher at a monthly rental of $400. The lease allowed termination by either party on ninety days' notice. In August 1978, Christopher threatened to terminate the lease if the club did not agree to a higher rental. The club alleges that it agreed to the higher rental in exchange for a new lease agreement that was to last seven and one-half years and that did not include a termination provision. It sent a written version of this oral lease agreement to Christopher for execution, and it immediately began paying the higher rental of $600 per month. In addition, the club undertook to make changes in the artwork on the billboards. In June 1979, Christopher again demanded a rent increase and threatened to terminate the lease if the club refused. The club sued for enforcement of the new lease agreement, which precluded such increases and gave Christopher no right of termination. Christopher countered that the Statute of Frauds barred the club's suit. Christopher, not wanting to relinquish its right of termination, had never executed the written lease that the club had drawn up. Can the new lease agreement be enforced? [Club Chain of Manhattan, Ltd. v. Christopher & Seventh Gourmet, Ltd., 74 A.D.2d 277, 427 N.Y.S.2d 627 (Sup.Ct. 1980)]

7. Wasatch Orchard Company entered into an oral agreement with Fabian to have him sell its canned asparagus for a three-year period. Wasatch agreed to pay Fabian a 2.5 percent commission on all sales he made. Within six months, Fabian had secured orders totaling $30,000. Thereafter, Wasatch refused to honor its oral commitment. Can Fabian sue under the oral agreement? What, if anything, can Fabian recover? [Fabian v. Wasatch Orchard Co., 41 Utah 404, 125 P. 860 (1912)]

8. Butler Brothers was the main contractor for a highway construction project near Minneapolis. Butler hired another contractor, Ganley Brothers, to perform some of the highway construction work. At the time the contract was formed, Butler made several false representations to Ganley. If Ganley had known Butler's statements were fraudulent, Ganley would never have entered into the contract. The written contract between Butler and Ganley included the following clause: "The contractor [Ganley] has examined the said contracts * * * and is not relying upon any statement made by the company in respect thereto." In light of this clause, can Ganley introduce evidence of Butler's fraudulent misstatements at trial? [Ganley Bros. Inc. v. Butler Bros. Bldg. Co., 170 Minn. 373, 212 N.W. 602 (1927)]

9. Rimshot, director of a local basketball camp, wished to increase his business by advertising his camp. He discussed with Lyal, a local printer, the possibility of Lyal printing up flyers about the camp. Rimshot told Lyal that not only did he want Lyal to print the flyers, he wanted him to distribute them to local merchants. Lyal said that he usually distributed about 20 flyers to each one and charged a small publication fee. Subsequently, Lyal and Rimshot entered into a written agreement under which Lyal agreed to print 1,000 flyers for Rimshot and to "publish the same locally." Lyal printed the flyers but distributed them to only four merchants, giving 250 to each. After the poorest turnout in his basketball camp's history, Rimshot sued Lyal for breach of contract. Can he introduce parol evidence concerning Lyal's statements about how he normally distributed flyers? [See similar fact pattern in Stoops v. Smith, 100 Mass. 63, 97 Am.Dec. 76 (1868)]

10. Ramsey Products Corporation, a manufacturer, entered into negotiations with Williams & Associates, architects, to design a new factory for Ramsey. After several days of negotiations, Ramsey and Williams signed a contract under which Williams promised to design the factory. The contract was brief, containing a short description of the type of plant as well as the number of offices that Ramsey wanted. Over the next several months, Williams drew up plans for a new factory that would cost between $400,000 and $500,000. Since this was much more than what Ramsey expected to pay, Ramsey officials changed their minds and refused to compensate Williams for his plans.

Williams sued Ramsey to recover for his services. Ramsey wished to defend against Williams's claim on the ground that Williams had not performed the contract as discussed by the parties. Specifically, Ramsey wanted to introduce evidence about oral negotiations made before the written contract, which said that Williams would design a building costing about $250,000. Since the building Williams had actually designed would cost much more, Ramsey argued that Williams had breached his contract. Can Ramsey introduce this evidence? [Williams & Associates v. Ramsey Products Corp., 19 N.C.App. 1, 198 S.E.2d 67 (1973)]

CHAPTER 13

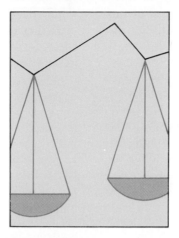

CONTRACTS
Third Party Rights

Once it has been determined that a valid and legally enforceable contract exists, attention can be turned to the rights and duties of the parties to the contract. Since a contract is a private agreement between the parties who have entered into it, it is fitting that these parties alone should have rights and liabilities under the contract. This idea is referred to as "privity" of contract, and it establishes the basic concept that third parties have no rights in a contract to which they are not a party.

Suppose I offer to sell you my watch for $100, and you accept. Later, I refuse to deliver the watch to you even though you tender the $100. You decide to overlook my breach, but your close friend, Ann, is unhappy with my action and files suit. Can she receive a judgment? The answer is obviously no, as she was not a party to the contract. You, as a party, have rights under the contract and could file a successful suit, but Ann has *no standing in court.*

There are two exceptions to this rule. The first involves an **assignment of rights** or **delegation of duties**. Here, one of the original parties transfers contractual rights or obligations to a third party, giving the third party the rights or obligations of the transferor. The second involves a **third party beneficiary contract.** Here, the rights of a third party against the promisor arise from the original contract, and the parties to the original contract normally make it with the intent to benefit the third party.

ASSIGNMENT OF RIGHTS AND DELEGATION OF DUTIES

When third parties acquire rights or assume duties arising from a contract to which they were not parties, the rights are transferred to them by *assignment* and the duties are transferred by *delegation*. Assignment, or delegation, occurs after the original contract is made, when one of the parties transfers an interest or duty in the contract to another party.

A distinction must also be made between assignment, or delegation, and *novation* (see Chapter 14). A novation is a written agreement entered into by *all* the parties whereby one party is substituted for another party, that is, one party is completely dismissed from the contract, and another is substituted. The dismissed party is no longer liable under the original contract. In an assignment, or delegation, the original party remains liable on the contract.

Assignments

In every bilateral contract the two parties have corresponding rights and duties. One party has a *right* to require the other to perform some task, and the other has a *duty* to perform it. The transfer of rights to a third person is known as an *assignment*. When rights under a contract are assigned unconditionally, the rights of the assignor (the party making the assignment) are extinguished.[1] The third party (the assignee, or party receiving the assignment) has a right to demand performance from the other original party to the contract (the obligor). This is illustrated in Exhibit 13–1.

Once Able has assigned her rights under the original contract with Baker to Carlson, Carlson can enforce the contract against Baker if Baker fails to perform. (The assignee takes only those rights that the assignor originally had. Furthermore, the assignee's rights are subject to the defenses that the obligor has against the assignor.)

Statute of Frauds   In general, an assignment can take any form, oral or written. Naturally, it is more difficult to prove the occurrence of an oral assignment, so it is practical to put all assignments in writing.

Assignments covered by the Statute of Frauds must be in writing to be enforceable. As noted

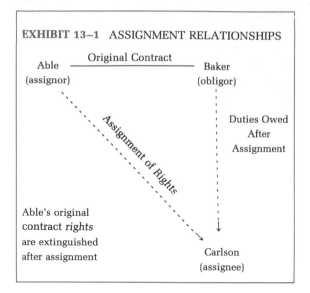

EXHIBIT 13–1   ASSIGNMENT RELATIONSHIPS

Original Contract

Able (assignor) ——————— Baker (obligor)

Assignment of Rights

Duties Owed After Assignment

Able's original contract *rights* are extinguished after assignment

Carlson (assignee)

in Chapter 12, assignments of an interest in land, contracts not to be performed within one year, promises to answer for the debts of another, promises in consideration of marriage, and promises of an administrator or an executor to personally pay the debts of an estate must also be in writing. In addition, most states require contracts for the assignment of wages to be in writing.[2]

Consideration   An assignment need not be supported by *legally sufficient consideration* to be effective. A gratuitous assignment is just as effective as an assignment made for money. However, the absence of consideration becomes significant when the assignor wants to revoke the assignment. If the assignment was made for consideration, the assignor cannot revoke it. If no consideration is involved, the assignor can revoke, thereby cancelling the right of the third party to demand performance or to sue for failure to render that performance.[3] Gratuitous assignments can be revoked by:

---

1.   Restatement, Second, Contracts, Section 331.

2.   See, for example, California Labor Code Sec. 300.
3.   Restatement, Second, Contracts, Section 332.

1. The subsequent assignment of the same right to another third party.
2. The death of the assignor.
3. The bankruptcy of the assignor.
4. A notice of revocation given to the assignee.

Rights That Can Be Assigned

As a general rule, all rights can be assigned, except in the following special circumstances:

1. If a statute expressly prohibits assignment, the particular right in question cannot be assigned.
2. If a contract stipulates that the rights cannot be assigned, then, ordinarily, they cannot be assigned.[4]
3. When a contract is *personal* in nature, the rights under the contract cannot be assigned unless all that remains is a money payment.
4. Finally, a right cannot be assigned if assignment will materially increase or alter the duties of the obligor.

Recall Exhibit 13–1, where Able is the assignor, Baker the obligor, and Carlson the assignee. Suppose Baker owes Able $50, and Able assigns to Carlson the right to receive the $50. Here, a valid assignment of a debt exists, and Baker must pay the $50 to Carlson, or Carlson will be entitled to enforce payment in a court of law.

The following examples illustrate the above exceptions to the general rule.

1. Suppose John is a new employee of Craft, Inc. Craft is an employer under Workers' Compensation statutes in this state, and thus John is a covered employee. John has a relatively high risk job. In need of a loan, John borrows the money from Shady, assigning to Shady all Workers' Compensation benefits due him should he be injured on the job. This type of assignment of *future* Workers' Compensation benefits is prohibited by state statute and thus cannot be assigned.

2. Suppose Baker agrees to build a house for Able. The contract between Able and Baker states: "The contract cannot be assigned by Able. Any assignment renders this contract void, and all rights hereunder will thereupon terminate." Able then attempts to assign her rights to Carlson. Carlson cannot enforce the contract against Baker by trying to get Baker to build the house because the contract expressly prohibits the assignment of rights. (But once the house is built, the rights to the monetary payment are assignable.)

3. Suppose Baker signs a contract to be a tutor for Able's children. Able then attempts to assign her right in Baker's services to Carlson. Carlson cannot enforce the contract against Baker because the contract called for the rendering of a personal service.[5]

4. Assume Able takes out an insurance policy on her hotel with Preventive Casualty, an insurance company. The policy insures against fire, theft, floods, and vandalism. Able then attempts to assign the insurance policy to Carlson, who also owns a hotel. The assignment is ineffective because it substantially alters Preventive Casualty's *duty of performance.* Insurance companies evaluate the particular risk of a certain party and tailor their policies to fit the exact risk of that party. If the policy is assigned to a third party, the insurance risk will be materially altered. Therefore, the assignment will not operate to give Carlson any rights against Preventive Casualty.

In the following two cases the court grappled with the question of which rights can be assigned. In both cases, the question of whether the contract was personal in nature arose.

4. Several exceptions to this rule exist. First, a contract cannot prevent assignment of the right to receive money. This exception exists to encourage the free flow of money and credit in modern business settings. Second, the assignment of rights in real estate normally cannot be prohibited because this would be contrary to public policy. Such prohibitions are called *restraints against alienation.* Third, the assignment of negotiable instruments cannot be prohibited. Fourth, see UCC 2-210(2).

5. Restatement, Second, Contracts, Sections 317 and 318.

NOLAN v. WILLIAMSON MUSIC, INC.

United States District Court, Southern District of New York, 1969.
300 F.Supp. 1311.

BACKGROUND AND FACTS *The plaintiff in this case was Robert Nolan, who composed the song "Tumbling Tumbleweeds." Nolan entered into an agreement with the Sam Fox Publishing Company whereby he conveyed his interest in the song to the publisher, Sam Fox, and the publisher's successors and assigns. The agreement stated that it was Nolan's intention to transfer to the publisher all rights of every kind, nature, and description (including the rights generally known in the field of literary and musical endeavor as the moral rights of the authors) throughout the world. No right of any kind, nature, or description was to be reserved by the composer.*

In consideration of this agreement, Sam Fox agreed to pay Nolan certain royalties on a pre-agreed schedule. Sam Fox Publishing Company published and exploited the song "Tumbling Tumbleweeds." Several years later, the company assigned all of its rights and interests in the song to the defendant, Williamson Music, Inc. Sam Fox never notified Nolan that the assignment had been made. When Nolan subsequently learned of the assignment, he attempted to rescind the contract.

EDELSTEIN, District Judge.

*   *   *   *

Nolan also seeks:

(a) an injunction permanently enjoining defendants from asserting any rights in or to the song;

*   *   *   *

The assignment to Sam Fox Publishing Company was dated July 11, 1934, and it provided, *inter alia*, that the "Composers" (defined as Nolan, Walker and Hall) conveyed to the "Publisher (defined as Sam Fox Publishing Company), its successors and assigns forever, all the right, title and interest of every kind, nature and description, including the copyright therein, throughout the world, of the Composers in 'Tumbling Tumbleweeds.' " This agreement also recites that it was the intention of the parties:

to transfer to the Publisher all rights of every kind, nature and description (including the rights generally known in the field of literary and musical endeavor as the moral rights of the authors) throughout the world which the Composers have, own and possess in and to the said musical composition and no right of any kind, nature or description is [to be] reserved by the Composers.

The "Composers" also agreed to renew the copyright on the song and then to assign the renewal term to the "Publisher."

In consideration of these undertakings, the "Publisher" agreed to pay to the "Composers" royalties[.]

*   *   *   *

Subsequently, by an agreement dated January 28, 1946, Sam Fox assigned all of its right and interest in and to the song to defendant, Williamson Music, Inc., (Williamson) and agreed to use its best efforts to obtain the renewal copyright of the song and then to assign the renewal term to Williamson.

*   *   *   *

The instant action followed a letter dated May 29, 1963, which Nolan sent to Fox and Williamson seeking to terminate any and all agreements relating to "Tumbling Tumbleweeds" between Nolan and Fox.

*   *   *   *

The basic claim which plaintiff has urged in this suit is that he had the legal right to, and, in fact, did rescind his agreements with Fox by the May 29, 1963, notice. Plaintiff argues that rescission is justified in this case because over the years Fox has allegedly committed the following breaches:

*   *   *   *

assignment of the copyright and its renewal term to Williamson; payment of royalties by Fox based only on Fox's receipts from Williamson;

*   *   *   *

In addition *   *   * plaintiff argues that Fox has generally acted fraudulently towards plaintiff and that in particular it was fraudulent not to have revealed to plaintiff Fox's relationship with Williamson.

The court finds that it was not a breach of contract for Sam Fox to assign the copyright to Williamson. The 1934 transfer from plaintiff to Sam Fox of "all rights of every kind, nature and description" which plaintiff had in the copyright was clearly absolute on its face. Furthermore, the agreement specifically provided that the conveyance was to the "Publisher, its successors and assigns." Whether a contract is assignable or not is, of course, a matter of contractual intent, and one must look to the language used by the parties to discern that intent. Clearly the language just quoted contemplated that the agreement was to be assignable.

The plaintiff, by citing Paige v. Faure, seems to be saying, however, that this contract involved such personal elements of trust and confidence that it was not assignable without the consent of the parties despite the clear language to the contrary. This argument, though, is not premised upon any reliable evidence adduced at the trial which would demonstrate that Nolan entered into his agreement with Fox because of any personal trust and confidence which he placed in Fox. Further, rescission of copyright exploitation agreements much like the one in issue in the case at bar was also sought in the case of In re Waterson, Berlin & Snyder Co., when the original assignee of the copyrights at issue there attempted to assign them to other publishers. The District Court granted rescission in that case on the ground that the agreements were not assignable because of the degree of personal trust involved in them. The Court of Appeals, however, reversed that decision and held that the copyrights could be assigned further.

Plaintiff's assertions of fraud are based in part upon the allegation that Fox concealed from plaintiff its relationship with Williamson by never giving plaintiff actual notice of the assignment. The evidence, however, does not support a finding of fraud in this regard. It is true that Fox never gave plaintiff actual notice of the assignment, but the court has already held that the contract was assignable without Fox's first having to obtain the plaintiff's consent.

An injunction was denied. The court declared that Sam Fox had every right under the terms of the contract to make the assignment to Williamson Music, Inc. Nolan had no right to rescind the contract or refuse to comply with its terms.

JUDGMENT AND REMEDY

MACKE CO. v. PIZZA OF GAITHERSBURG, INC.

Court of Appeals of Maryland, 1970.

259 Md. 479, 270 A.2d 645.

BACKGROUND AND FACTS *The Pizza of Gaithersburg (the Pizza Shop) arranged to have cold-drink machines installed in several of its pizza establishments. The Pizza Shop (appellee) originally contracted with Virginia Coffee Service, Inc., to install the vending machines. The Macke Company (appellant) bought out the Virginia company's assets and took over its vending operations. The Pizza Shop wanted to rescind the contracts. It argued that the assignment amounted to such a "material change" in the performance of the obligations under the agreements that it resulted in a breach of the contract. The lower court agreed with the Pizza Shop and granted it the right to rescind the contract, but the appellate court held that the assignment was permissible under the terms of the contract.*

SINGLEY, Judge.

*   *   *   *

In the absence of a contrary provision—and there was none here—rights and duties under an executory bilateral contract may be assigned and delegated, subject to the exception that duties under a contract to provide personal services may never be delegated, nor rights be assigned under a contract where *delectus personae* was an ingredient of the bargain.[1] [It has been] held that the right of an individual to purchase ice under a contract which by its terms reflected a knowledge of the individual's needs and reliance on his credit and responsibility could not be assigned to the corporation which purchased his business. [It has been] held that an advertising agency could not delegate its duties under a contract which had been entered into by an advertiser who had relied on the agency's skill, judgment and taste.

We cannot regard the agreements as contracts for personal services. They were either a license or concession granted Virginia by the appellees, or a lease of a portion of the appellees' premises, with Virginia agreeing to pay a percentage of gross sales as a license or concession fee or as rent and were assignable by Virginia unless they imposed on Virginia duties of a personal or unique character which could not be delegated.

The appellees earnestly argue that they had dealt with Macke before and had chosen Virginia because they preferred the way it conducted its business. Specifically, they say that service was more personalized, since the president of Virginia kept the machines in working order, that commissions were paid in cash, and that Virginia permitted them to keep keys to the machines so that minor adjustments could be made when needed. Even if we assume all this to be true, the agreements with Virginia were silent as to the details of the working arrangements and contained only a provision requiring Virginia to "install * * * the above listed equipment and * * * maintain the equipment in good operating order and stocked with merchandise." We think the Supreme Court of California put the problem of personal service in proper focus a century ago when it upheld the assignment of a contract to grade a San Francisco street:

---

1. Like all generalizations, this one is subject to an important exception. Uniform Commercial Code § 9-318 makes ineffective a term in any contract prohibiting the assignment of a contract right: i.e., a right to payment. Compare Restatement, Contracts § 151(c) (1932).

"All painters do not paint portraits like Sir Joshua Reynolds, nor landscapes like Claude Lorraine, nor do all writers write dramas like Shakespeare or fiction like Dickens. Rare genius and extraordinary skill are not transferable, and contracts for their employment are therefore personal, and cannot be assigned. But rare genius and extraordinary skill are not indispensable to the workmanlike digging down of a sand hill or the filling up of a depression to a given level, or the construction of brick sewers with manholes and covers, and contracts for such work are not personal, and may be assigned."

*   *   *   *

Restatement, Contracts § 160(3) (1932) reads, in part:

"Performance or offer of performance by a person delegated has the same legal effect as performance or offer of performance by the person named in the contract, unless,

(a) performance by the person delegated varies or would vary materially from performance by the person named in the contract as the one to perform, and there has been no *   *   * assent to the delegation *   *   *"

*   *   * As we see it, the delegation of duty by Virginia to Macke was entirely permissible under the terms of the agreement *   *   *

[T]he Pizza Shops had no right to rescind the agreements.

Pizza of Gaithersburg could not rescind the vending machine contracts without being liable to Macke for damages.   **JUDGMENT AND REMEDY**

This case could have gone either way. Had the court accepted parol evidence, it might have ruled differently.   **COMMENT**

Anti-Assignment Clauses

Rights under a contract can be rendered nonassignable by an express prohibition against assignment in the contract promise that creates the right. If the promisor, in clear language, evidences the intention to create a right in the promisee that is not to be assignable, no subsequent assignment can affect the promisor or third parties.

Anti-assignment clauses have appeared in leases for many years. Now they are being used more frequently in other types of contracts as well. Recently, they have appeared in mortgage contracts in an attempt to restrict the assumption of mortgages by new owners of real property. The typical lease or mortgage today cannot be assigned without the landlord's or mortgagee's consent.

Typical clauses in mortgages are due-on-sale (DOS) provisions. This means that an owner of realty with a lower than market interest rate cannot sell the property to a buyer with an assumption of this low interest rate mortgage. The due-on-sale provision accelerates the entire loan, making the mortgage fully payable. Therefore the loan would have to be fully paid (by the buyer) or the buyer would have to secure a new mortgage (at the current interest rate). The Supreme Court has upheld such clauses for federally insured financial institutions. Such is the case in Massachusetts, among other states. But in California, mortgages for residential property cannot be due upon an assignment. In other words, in California, virtually all residential mortgages can be assumed by a new purchaser of the real estate.

Certain contracts provide that if the promisee assigns his or her rights under the contract to a third party, the contract itself should be void. These contract provisions are frequently found in insurance policies. They stipulate the forfeiture of the policy rights if the policyholder assigns the policy. If the assignment is attempted before a loss is incurred, the company can declare that the policy is void. (On the other hand, if the assignment is made after the loss, the assignee can recover.)

Typically, when an anti-assignment clause restrains the alienation of property, the clause can become subject to judicial review. In the following case the court examined an anti-assignment clause in terms of its reasonableness and its effect on public policy.

The following illustrates an anti-assignment clause in a franchise agreement which was held enforceable.

HANIGAN v. WHEELER
Court of Appeals of Arizona,
Division 2, 1972.
19 Ariz.App. 49, 504 P.2d 972.

BACKGROUND AND FACTS *This case centered around an anti-assignment clause in an agreement for a franchise business that required the consent of the area franchise holder before the business could be transferred. The proceeding was brought for a declaratory judgment. (In a declaratory judgment, a court merely declares the rights and duties of parties without awarding damages. Such judgments are given to prevent disputes from arising.)*

The appellant, George Hanigan, entered into a "Dairy Queen Store Agreement" with the appellee, Eileen A. LeMoines. The contract contained a provision that read as follows: "Second Party shall not assign or transfer this Agreement without the written approval of First Party." Subsequently, LeMoines entered into a deposit and receipt agreement with Wheeler for the sale of the Dairy Queen franchise as well as the real property located at and built specifically for the franchise.

A few days later, Hanigan was told about the sale, and an attempt was made to gain his approval. Hanigan refused to approve the sale. He stated that the price of $90,000 was too high and that, in his experience, an inflated sale price was detrimental to the Dairy Queen business. Hanigan also stated that the Wheelers were inexperienced in business and that they were too young to run the franchise properly. (Mr. Wheeler was a dentist, and Mrs. Wheeler was a housewife.) The trial court declared that the clause disallowing assignment without Hanigan's consent was unenforceable as against public policy. The franchise holder, Hanigan, appealed.

HOWARD, Judge.
* * * *

The primary question dispositive of this appeal is whether the trial court erred in determining that the contract provision precluding the franchise transfer without the area franchise holder's approval is unenforceable as against public policy. A review of the record and the relevant law leads us to answer this question in the affirmative. Given the instant fact situation, the law in this area does not warrant the trial court's order requiring Hanigan to consent to the subject transaction:

> "As a general rule, a contract is not assignable where the nature or terms of the contract make it nonassignable, [footnote omitted] unless such provision is waived. * * * The parties may in terms, by a provision in the contract, prohibit an assignment thereof, * * *" 6 C.J.S. Assignments § 24.b (1937).

"Provisions in bilateral contracts which forbid or restrict assignment of the contract without the consent of the obligor have generally been upheld as valid and enforceable when called into question, [footnote omitted] although the meaning of such terms becomes a matter of interpretation. *   *   *" 6 Am.Jr.2d Assignments § 22 (1963).

These general statements are in accord with the Restatement of the Law of Contracts § 151, which reads as follows:

"A right may be the subject of effective assignment unless, *   *   * (c) the assignment is prohibited by the contract creating the right."
*   *   *   *

A leading case stated the law as follows:

*   *   *   * we think it is reasonably clear that, while the courts have striven to uphold freedom of assignability, they have not failed to recognize the concept of freedom to contract. In large measure they agree that, where appropriate language is used, assignments of money due under contracts may be prohibited. When 'clear language' is used, and the 'plainest words *   *   * have been chosen' parties may 'limit the freedom of alienation of rights and prohibit the assignment.'
*   *   *   *

In opposition to the above principles, appellees contend that more than a contract right is involved in the case at bench in that the subject clause restricting assignment without Hanigan's approval serves as an unreasonable and unlawful restraint on the right of alienation of property, since the Store Agreement provides no guidelines by which the area franchise holder is to base his approval or disapproval of potential buyers, and that hypothetically, through the whim or arbitrariness of the holder, the LeMoines could be prevented from ever selling their franchise and the property associated with the franchise.

We accept the fundamental principle that one of the primary incidents inherent in the ownership of property is the right of alienation or disposition. However, this right is not limitless. The right to make an assignment of property can be defeated where there is a clear stipulation to that effect. The current state of the law in this area appears to be that a restraint on the alienation of property may be sustained when the restraint is reasonably designed to attain or encourage accepted social or economic ends.
*   *   *   *

We also perceive that despite the restriction on assignment of the store agreement, the LeMoines are not entirely powerless. Where a contract contains a *promise* to refrain from assigning, an assignment which violates it would not be ineffective. "The promise creates a *duty* in the promisor not to assign. It does not deprive the assignor of the *power* to assign and its breach, therefore, would simply subject the promisor to an action for damages while the assignment would be effective. *   *   *"

In summary, we hold that the law as set forth above demonstrates that the contract limitation against assignment of the Store Agreement without the approval of the area franchise holder is proper and valid. The trial court erred in concluding that the provision limiting assignability was unenforceable as against public policy. The court also erred in ruling that defendants had a duty to consent to the franchise sale, for this is contrary to the manifested intention of the parties to the contract. The general proposition is that " 'a covenantor [promisor] is not to be held beyond his undertaking and he may make that as narrow as he likes.' "

JUDGMENT AND REMEDY   *The trial court was incorrect. The appellate court declared that it was the right of the area franchise holder to consent or refuse to consent to the sale (assignment) of a franchise.*

COMMENTS   *The trial court had ordered Hanigan to consent to the transaction. Hanigan wanted the appeals court to declare affirmatively that, as a matter of law, he was not required to approve the transfer. The court had to use a declaratory judgment because no sale had occurred yet. In this particular case, judicial scrutiny was fact oriented rather than public policy oriented.*

Notice of the Assignment   Once a valid assignment of rights has been made to a third party, the third party should notify the obligor (Baker in Exhibit 13–1) of the assignment. This is not legally necessary because an assignment is effective immediately, whether or not notice is given, but it protects all of the parties. The following examples illustrate some of the problems that can arise when a third party fails to give notice of an assignment.

First, suppose A delivers eight ounces of high grade uranium to B, a nuclear energy cooperative. B is to pay a specified sum for the uranium. Before B pays, A assigns the right to receive payment for the uranium to C, one of A's suppliers in South Africa. C fails to notify B of the assignment, and B makes the payment to A. Since C failed to give notice of the assignment, C lost the right to collect the money from B. Before notice of the assignment, B is free to fulfill its obligation by paying A directly. If C had given notice of the assignment to B, B would have been required to pay C instead of A.

Second, suppose further that, after A assigned the right to receive payment to C, A also assigned the right to receive payment to D. Further assume that D then notified B of the second assignment. Many states will allow D to recover the money from B because of timely notification. Suppose several days after D notified B of the second assignment, C notified B of the first assignment. Here B is in a touchy situation, since it has received notice from two different people

that payment is to be made to each. In this case, a majority of states will require payment to be made to D. D gave notice first and should be entitled to prevail over C, who was delinquent. However, some states would allow C to recover the money even though C failed to give notice before D.[6]

Delegation of Duties

Just as a party can transfer rights under a contract through an assignment, a party can also transfer duties. Duties are not assigned, however. They are delegated. Normally, a delegation of duties does not relieve the party making the delegation—the delagator—of the obligation to perform in the event that the party who has been delegated the duty—the delagatee—fails to perform.

Form of the Delegation   No special form is required to create a valid delegation of duties. As

---

6.   At common law, there were three different rules. The first rule was called the English rule. Assignees, second in time to the first assignee, prevailed in every case in which they had paid value, had taken the assignment without notice of the prior assignment, and had given the *obligor* notice of the assignment before the first assignee gave such notice. Another rule, called the New York rule, essentially stated that the first assignment in time is first in right. Finally, the third rule was the Massachusetts rule. The first assignee prevailed provided the first assignment was not revokable at the time the second assignment was made.

long as the delegator (the party delegating the duty) expresses a present intention to make the delegation, it will be effective. The delegator need not even use the word "delegate."

Duties That Can Be Delegated   As a general rule, any duty can be delegated. Exhibit 13–2 illustrates the relationships involved in a delegation. There are, however, some exceptions to this rule. Delegation is prohibited:

1. When performance depends on the *personal* skill or talents of the obligor.
2. When special trust has been placed in the obligor.
3. When performance by a third party will vary materially from that expected by the obligee under the contract.

Suppose B contracts with A to tutor A in the various aspects of financial underwriting and investment banking. B is an experienced businessman who is well known for his expertise in finance. Further, assume that B wants to delegate his duties to teach A to a third party, C. This delegation would be ineffective since B has contracted to render a service to A that is founded upon B's *expertise*. It is a change from A's ex-

pectancy under the contract. Therefore, C cannot perform B's duties.

Suppose B, an attorney, contracts with A, a bank, to advise A on a proposed merger with a savings and loan association. B wishes to delegate her duty to advise the bank to C, a law firm across town. Services of an attorney are *personal in nature.* B's delegation will be ineffective.

Finally, assume that B contracts with A to pick up and deliver heavy construction machinery to A's property. B then delegates this duty to C, who is in the business of delivering heavy machinery. The delegation is effective. The performance required is of a *routine* and *nonpersonal nature* and does not change A's expectancy under the contract.

Effect of a Delegation of Duties   If a delegation of duties is enforceable, the obligee (A in the exhibit) must accept performance from the delegatee. The obligee can legally refuse performance from the delegatee only if the duty is one that may not be delegated. A valid delegation of duties does *not relieve* the delegator (B in the exhibit) of obligations under the contract.[7] If the delegatee (C in the exhibit) fails to perform, the delegator is still liable to the obligee.

The liability of the delegatee to the obligee depends on whether the agreement between delegatee and delegator is interpreted as a "mere delegation" or a delegation plus an "assumption of duty" by the delegatee. Where the delegatee has made no promise to perform the duty *for the benefit of the obligee*, there is a "mere delegation." In these cases, the obligee cannot compel the delegatee to perform or hold the delegatee liable for non-performance. Common examples are cases where the delegatee is an employee or a subcontractor of the obligor.

Suppose B contracts to build a house for A. B is the obligor. A is the obligee. B then contracts with C for C to supply the necessary construction materials. C fails to deliver. A can sue B, but cannot sue C. This is a clear case where C's promise to deliver the materials was for the ben-

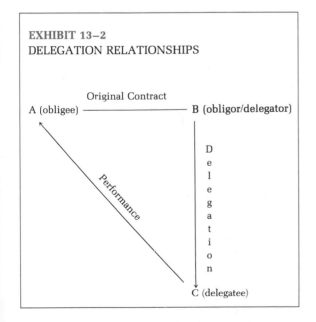

EXHIBIT 13–2
DELEGATION RELATIONSHIPS

A (obligee) ——— Original Contract ——— B (obligor/delegator)

Performance

Delegation

C (delegatee)

---

7.   Crane Ice Cream Co. v. Terminal Freezing Co., 147 Md. 588, 128 A. 280 (1925).

efit of the obligor, B, but not for the benefit of the obligee, A.

Where the delegatee does make a promise to perform the duty for the benefit of the obligee, there is an "assumption of duty." The obligee is then in the position of third party creditor beneficiary and can hold the delegatee liable for nonperformance.

Suppose B contracts to build a house for A. B is unable to build the house, so B contracts with C to build the house for A. C does not build the house. Here, the delegatee, C, entered into a contract for the benefit of the obligee, A. A can sue both B and C.

Whenever one party assigns rights to another, there is a question of whether such assignment also involves a delegation or an assumption of duties, or both. For example, B assigns a contract with the words, "I assign this contract to C." C has not *expressly* assumed any duties. Is C liable to perform these duties anyway?

The traditional view was that under this type of assignment, C did not assume any duties. This view was based on the theory that the acceptance of the benefits of the contract was not sufficient to imply a promise to assume the duties of the contract. Modern authorities, however, take the view that the probable intention in using such general words is to create both an assignment of rights and an assumption of duties.[8] Therefore, when general words are used (for example, "I assign the contract" or "all my rights under the contract"), the contract is construed as implying both an assignment of rights and an assumption of duties. Naturally, this result occurs only when the parties have not expressly provided otherwise. When the agreement making the assignment and delegations specifically states that the delegatee is not assuming the duties, the delegatee cannot be sued for failure to perform those duties.

Suppose a contract for the sale of B's boutique to C stated, "B does hereby sell, transfer, and assign to C all of B's rights with regard to

the Honneywell Boutique." Under the traditional view, C would not be obligated to pay B's business debt to A. In the modern view, a promise to pay B's debt to A would be implied, and A could require C to pay.

THIRD PARTY BENEFICIARY CONTRACTS

Able contracts with Baker to pave Baker's driveway upon Baker's promise to pay Carlson $375. Carlson is the third party beneficiary (since he is benefiting from Baker's promise). See Exhibit 13–3.

In general, the law recognizes three types of beneficiaries—creditor, donee, and incidental.[9] The courts will usually uphold Baker's promise if Carlson is a creditor or donee beneficiary but not if Carlson is an incidental beneficiary. In order to determine whether the third party beneficiary has enforceable rights, the **intent** of Able in Exhibit 13–3 must be examined.

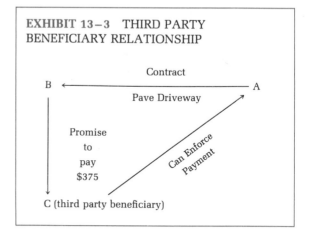

EXHIBIT 13–3 THIRD PARTY BENEFICIARY RELATIONSHIP

Creditor Beneficiaries

If a promisee's main purpose in making a contract is to discharge a duty or debt he or she

---

8. UCC 2-210 (where there is a general assignment of a contract for the sale of goods). Restatement, Second, Contracts, Section 328.

9. Restatement, Second, Contracts, Section 302. This is the traditional terminology used to describe the various types of third party beneficiaries. Under the Restatement of Contracts, the term, "intended beneficiary" replaces "creditor beneficiary" and "donee beneficiary." However, a majority of state courts still distinguish between donee and creditor beneficiaries, so the traditional terms will be used here.

already owes to a third party, then the third party is a **creditor beneficiary.**[10] There must be a debtor-creditor relationship established or existing. The debtor then makes a contract with another person, which is intended to discharge the debt of the debtor and at the same time confer a benefit on the debtor's creditor. The creditor, although not a party to the contract between the debtor and the other person, was intended to benefit. The creditor becomes a creditor beneficiary and therefore can enforce the promise against the other person (the promisor).

Suppose that several months ago, Duval Copper Company delivered 75,000 pounds of copper cathode to Pensoil Corporation. Pensoil still owes Duval $24,000, so Pensoil arranges to sell the copper cathode to Kennecott Copper Corp. Kennecott, in turn, agrees to pay the $24,000 purchase price to Duval. Duval is a creditor beneficiary and can enforce payment of the $24,000 against Kennecott. (See Exhibit 13–4.)

The following case is a classic illustration of the third party beneficiary theory.

---

10.   Restatement, Second, Contracts, Section 302(1)(a).

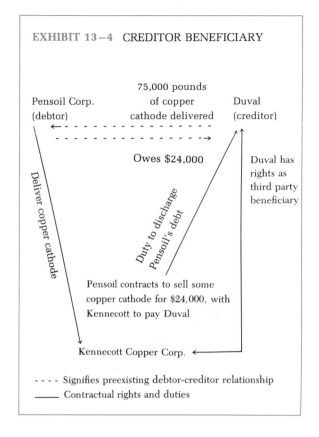

EXHIBIT 13–4   CREDITOR BENEFICIARY

- - - - Signifies preexisting debtor-creditor relationship
——— Contractual rights and duties

BACKGROUND AND FACTS   *Holly owed the plaintiff $300. The defendant suggested that Holly give him the money and promised to pay it to the plaintiff to discharge Holly's debt. (Sufficient consideration was present in this transaction to create a contract between Holly and the defendant.) The defendant never paid the plaintiff, so the plaintiff sued the defendant, considering himself a third party beneficiary of the contract between Holly and the defendant. The court decided that the plaintiff had a legal right to sue the defendant for failing to pay the $300 as promised, even though the plaintiff was never "in privity"; that is, he was never a direct participant or party to the contract.*

LAWRENCE v. FOX
Court of Appeals of New York,
1859, 20 N.Y. 268.

H. GRAY, Justice.

*   *   *   *

In this case the promise was made to Holly and not expressly to the plaintiff; *   *   * As early as 1806 it was announced by the Supreme Court of this State, upon what was then regarded as the settled law of England, "That where one person makes a promise to another for the benefit of a third person, that third person may maintain an action upon it." *Schermerhorn v. Vanderheyden* (1 John. R., 140), has often been re-asserted by our courts and never departed from.

*   *   *   *

In *Hall v. Marston* the court [said]: "It seems to have been well settled that if A promises B for a valuable consideration to pay C, the latter may maintain assumpsit [the agreement] for the money;" and in *Brewer v. Dyer*, the recovery was upheld, as the court said, "upon the principle of law *long recognized and clearly established*, that when one person, for a valuable consideration, engages with another, by a simple contract, to do some act for the benefit of a third, the latter, who would enjoy the benefit of the act, may maintain an action for the breach of such engagement; that it does not rest upon the ground of any actual or supposed relationship between the parties as some of the earlier cases would seem to indicate, but upon the broader and more satisfactory basis, that the law operating on the act of the parties creates the duty, establishes a privity, and implies the promise and obligation on which the action is founded."

*   *   *   *

In this case the defendant, upon ample consideration received from Holly, promised Holly to pay his debt to the plaintiff; the consideration received and the promise to Holly made it as plainly his duty to pay the plaintiff as if the money had been remitted to him for that purpose, and as well implied a promise to do so as if he had been made a trustee of property to be converted into cash with which to pay.

*   *   *   *

No one can doubt that he [Holly] owes the sum of money demanded of him, or that in accordance with his promise it was his duty to have paid it to the plaintiff; nor can it be doubted that whatever may be the diversity of opinion elsewhere, the adjudications in this State, from a very early period, approved by experience, have established the defendant's liability *   *   * "

The judgment should be affirmed.

JUDGMENT AND REMEDY   *Judgment was for the plaintiff. The defendant was required to pay the plaintiff $300 to fulfill his original contract with Holly.*

Assumption of a Mortgage   The assumption of a real estate mortgage is a type of third party creditor beneficiary contract. Suppose some years ago your parents purchased their home. Unable to pay cash, they contracted to borrow the money from Thrift Home and Loan at a rate of 8.5 percent interest, with Thrift taking a mortgage on the home purchased. Today your parents decide to sell their home to Braico. Braico is interested in the 8.5 percent loan rate of interest and agrees to pay your parents for their equity (value of the home less the mortgage amount) and to assume the mortgage held by Thrift. Even though Thrift is not a party to the present contract for the sale of the home to Braico, does Thrift have any rights in this contract?

The answer is yes, if the assumption is not prohibited in the mortgage contract. When your parents purchased the home through a mortgage, they became debtors and Thrift a creditor. When your parents sold the home to Braico, her assumption of their mortgage created a benefit for Thrift in that Thrift could then hold Braico personally liable on the loan—in addition to holding your parents liable or gaining the property should there be a default. Thus, Thrift is a creditor beneficiary of certain terms of the contract between your parents and Braico and can enforce the monthly mortgage payments against Braico.

Donee Beneficiaries

If a promisee's main purpose in making a contract is to confer a gift upon a third party, then the third party is a *donee beneficiary*.[11] A donee beneficiary can enforce the promise of a promisor just as a creditor beneficiary can. To illustrate: Suppose Able goes to her attorney, Baker, and enters into a contract in which Baker promises to draft a will naming Able's son, Carl, as an heir. Carl is a donee beneficiary, and if Baker does not prepare the will properly, Carl can sue Baker.[12] Or suppose Able offers to paint Baker's house if Baker pays $750 to Carl, Able's son. Able wants to give the money to Carl as a gift. Carl is a donee beneficiary and can enforce Baker's promise to pay $750.

The most common third party beneficiary contract involving a donee beneficiary is a life insurance contract. In a typical contract, Able, the promisee, pays premiums to Old Life, a life insurance company, and Old Life promises to pay a certain amount of money upon Able's death to anyone Able designates as beneficiary. The designated beneficiary, Carl, is a donee beneficiary under the life insurance policy and can enforce payment against the insurance company upon Able's death. (A donee beneficiary cannot sue the promisee, whereas a creditor beneficiary probably can.)

Incidental Beneficiaries

The benefit that an *incidental beneficiary* receives from a contract between two parties is unintentional. Therefore, an incidental beneficiary cannot enforce a contract to which he or she is not a party. Several factors must be examined to determine whether a party is an incidental beneficiary. The presence of one or more of the factors listed below strongly indicates an *intended* (rather than an incidental) benefit to the third party.

1. Performance rendered directly to the third party.
2. The rights of the third party to control the details of performance.
3. Express designation in the contract.

The following are examples of incidental beneficiaries. The third party has no rights in the contract and cannot enforce it against the promisor.

1. B contracts with A to build a factory on A's land. B's plans specify that Ad Pipe Company pipe fittings must be used in all plumbing. Ad Pipe Company is an incidental beneficiary and cannot enforce the contract against B by attempting to require B to purchase its pipe.
2. B contracts with A to build a recreational facility on A's land. Once the facility is constructed, it will greatly enhance the property values in the neighborhood. If B subsequently refuses to build the facility, C, a neighboring property owner, cannot enforce the contract against B by attempting to require B to build the facility.
3. B is an employee of A. B has been promised a promotion if his employer obtains a contract with C. A is unable to obtain the contract with C. B is an incidental beneficiary to that contract. B has no right to sue C for being the cause of his nonpromotion to a better-paying position. Indeed, B cannot sue C even if B loses his job as the result of the failure of A and C to reach an agreement.

WHEN THE RIGHTS OF A THIRD PARTY VEST

Until the rights of a third party *vest*, the third party cannot enforce a contract against the original parties. When a right is vested, it is fixed or it takes effect. The rights of a third party vest

---

11. Restatement, Second, Contracts, Section 302(1)(b).
12. Lucas v. Hamm, 56 Cal.2d 583, 15 Cal.Rptr. 821, 364 P.2d 685(1961).

when the original parties *cannot rescind or change the contract without the consent of the third party.* Older cases distinguish between vesting in the case of a donee beneficiary and a creditor beneficiary, but modern courts no longer make this distinction.[13]

The rights of a third party beneficiary (donee or creditor) vest (and the power of the original contracting parties to change, alter, or rescind the contract terminates) whenever one of the following three things happen:

1. The third party beneficiary learns of and consents to the contract.[14]
2. The third party beneficiary brings suit upon the contract.
3. The third party materially alters his or her position in detrimental reliance on the contract.

Suppose, for example, that Carlson learns of Baker's intention to give $375 to Carlson after the driveway is paved. Before Carlson agrees to accept the payment, however, Baker decides to make payment elsewhere. Carlson's rights to the payment will not have been vested since Carlson did not assent prior to the contract revision.

If the contract expressly reserves the right to cancel, rescind, or modify the contract, the rights of the third party beneficiary are subject to any change that results. In such a case, the vesting of the third party's rights will not terminate the power of the original contracting parties to alter their legal relationships.[15] This is particularly true in most life insurance contracts, where the right to change the beneficiary is reserved.

---

13. According to the original Restatement of Contracts as well as a number of courts (some of which make these distinctions), a donee beneficiary's rights vest immediately upon the creation of a contract, and knowledge or assent to the contract is unnecessary. Creditor beneficiaries, on the other hand, must have relied on a contract detrimentally or must bring suit upon the contract in order for their rights to vest.

14. Restatement, Second, Contracts, Section 311(3), says that the promisor and the promisee have to request assent.

15. Defenses raised against third party beneficiaries are given in Restatement, Second, Contracts, Section 309.

QUESTIONS AND CASE PROBLEMS

1. John has been accepted as a freshman to attend a college 200 miles from his home for the fall semester. John's roommate is his close friend, Daniel. John's father, Michael, makes a contract with auto dealer Jackson to purchase a new car for $10,000 to be delivered to John, with the title in John's name. Daniel is delighted to hear of Michael's purchase for John, since Daniel will not have a car of his own at college and will benefit from John's having a car. Michael pays the full purchase price and takes off for a six-month vacation in Europe. Jackson never delivers the car, and John files an action against Jackson. Discuss fully whether John can recover for Jackson's breach of contract. Would your answer be any different if Daniel sued Jackson for breach of contract?

2. Five years ago Jane purchased a house. At that time, being unable to pay the full purchase price, she borrowed money from Thrift Savings and Loan, which in turn took an 8 percent mortgage on the house. The mortgage contract did not prohibit the assignment of the mortgage. Now Jane has secured a new job in another city and sells the house to Sylvia. The purchase price includes payment to Jane of the value of her equity and the assumption of the mortgage held by Thrift. At the time of this contract, Thrift did not know of or consent to the sale. On the basis of these facts, if Sylvia defaults in making the house payments to Thrift, what are Thrift's rights?

3. Thomas is a student attending college. He signs a one-year lease agreement that runs from September 1 to August 31. The lease agreement specifies that the lease cannot be assigned without the landlord's consent. Thomas decides not to go to summer school and assigns the balance of the lease (three months) to a close friend, Fred. The landlord objects to the assignment and denies Fred access to the apartment. Thomas claims Fred is financially sound and should be allowed the full rights and privileges of an assignee. Discuss fully whether the landlord or Thomas is correct.

4. Ben Cartwright sells the mineral rights to 1,000 acres on the Ponderosa to Ajax Mining Company for royalty payments of $1,000 per month for the term of the agreement. One month later, Ben assigns the roy-

alties to his son, Little Joe, as a gift. Later, Little Joe's actions around the Ponderosa cause him to fall out of favor with his father. Ben, in need of working capital, contracts with banker John for a loan of $50,000, with Ben assigning the royalty payments to John for the repayment of this loan. The next royalty payment arrives. Discuss who is entitled to the royalty payment, Little Joe or banker John?

5.   Diane has a specific set of plans to build a sailboat. The plans are detailed in nature, and any boat builder can build the boat. Diane secures bids, and the low bid is by the Whale of a Boat Corporation. Diane contracts with Whale to build the boat for $4,000. Whale then receives unexpected business from elsewhere. In order to meet the delivery date in the contract with Diane, Whale assigns (delegates) the contract, without Diane's consent, to Quick Brothers, a reputable boat builder. When the boat is ready for delivery, Diane learns of the assignment and refuses to accept delivery, even though the boat is built to specifications. Discuss fully whether Diane is obligated to accept and pay for the boat. Would your answer be any different if Diane did not have a specific set of plans but instead contracted with Whale to design and build a sailboat for $4,000? Explain.

6.   Christopher wrote a letter to Donald claiming that Donald owed him $3,000 for the shipment of string bikinis sent Donald three months ago. Donald wrote back, saying that the bikinis were defective and that therefore he refused to pay. Christopher wrote back that his lawyer had advised him that it was questionable whether Donald had informed him of the defect in time and that Christopher might have a valid claim for the purchase price of $3,000 despite any defects. About a month later, Donald wrote back to Christopher informing him that Jerry, who owed Donald $3,000 from a previous contract, had agreed with Donald to make the payment to Christopher. Thereafter, Jerry failed to make the payment to Christopher. Can Christopher sue Jerry?

7.   Owens, a federal prisoner, was transferred from federal prison to the Nassau County Jail pursuant to a contract between the U.S. Bureau of Prisons and the county. The contract included a policy statement that required the receiving prison to provide for the safekeeping and protection of transferred federal prisoners. While in the Nassau County Jail, Owens was beaten severely by prison officials, suffering lacerations, bruises and a lasting impairment that caused blackouts. Can Owens, as a third party beneficiary, sue

the county for breach of its agreement with the U.S. Bureau of Prisons? [Owens v. Haas, 601 F.2d 1242 (2d Cir. 1979)]

8.   Beman wrote his wife's will as she was about to die. When he read the will to her, she said that it was not the way she wanted it and that she wanted to leave her house to her niece, Seaver. Beman offered to write her another will, but she said she was afraid she would not hold out long enough to sign it. Beman told her that if she would sign the will, he would leave Seaver enough in his will to make up the difference. When Beman died, no provision was made for Seaver to receive the monetary value of the house. Seaver brought an action against Beman's estate, claiming a contract right for the value of the house. What was the result? [Seaver v. Ransom, 224 N.Y. 233, 120 N.E. 639 (1918)]

9.   For several years, Eastern Company and Hudson Company had made a number of transactions with each other. By January 1963 Eastern owed Hudson $2,200, and Hudson owed Eastern $1,034. Eastern assigned the accounts Hudson owed it to Home Factors Corporation. Home Factors Corporation conducts a business known as factoring. Factoring involves the purchase, at a discount, of accounts receivable from various companies. Most businesses offer their goods or services on credit. Therefore, at any given time, most businesses will have accounts receivable. When cash flow becomes tight—when a business requires cash, for example, to cover payroll checks—it may resort to selling its accounts receivable to factorers. They in turn take an assignment of the right to payment from the seller. Home Factors attempted to collect the $1,034 debt from Hudson, but Hudson refused to pay because of the $2,200 debt Eastern owed it. Is this a valid defense? [Hudson Supply and Equipment Co. v. Home Factors Corp., 210 A.2d 837 (D.C.App. 1965)]

10.   Lea and Parkgate entered into a lease agreement whereby Lea rented certain wagons from Parkgate for a number of years. Part of the rental agreement provided that Parkgate would keep the wagons in good repair. During the term of the lease, Parkgate decided to liquidate its business. With several years left in the lease agreement, Parkgate assigned the rights and delegated the duties under its contract with Lea to British Waggon Company. When Lea learned of the transfer, it claimed that Parkgate had no right to sell the contract to British Waggon and that it did not have to accept services from British Waggon. Can British Waggon enforce the contract? [British Waggon Co. v. Lea & Co., 5 Q.B. 149 (1880)]

CHAPTER 14

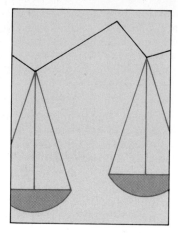

CONTRACTS
Performance and Discharge

Just as rules are necessary to determine when a legally enforceable contract exists, so rules are also necessary to determine when one of the parties can justifiably say, "I have fully performed, so I am now discharged from my obligations on this contract." The legal environment of business requires some point at which one or both parties can reasonably know their duties are at an end. This chapter deals with this issue.

The **discharge** (termination) of a contract is ordinarily accomplished when both of the parties perform those acts promised in the contract. For example, a buyer and seller have a contract for the sale of a bicycle for $50. This contract will be discharged upon buyer's payment of $50 to the seller, and the seller's transfer of possession of the bicycle to the buyer.

However, discharge can occur in other ways. Some of the more important of these, which will be discussed later in this chapter, are: [1]

1. The occurrence or failure of a *condition*.
2. *Agreement*.
3. *Breach of contract*.
4. *Impossibility of performance*.

CONDITIONS

In certain contracts, promises of performance are not *expressly* conditioned or qualified. They are called *absolute promises*. They must be performed, or the party promising the act will be in breach of contract. For example, I contract to sell you my watch for $100. Our promises are unconditional: my transfer of the watch to you and your payment of $100 to me. The $100 does not have to be given if the watch is not.

However, in some cases performance may be beneficial only if a certain event either does or does not occur. Therefore, *a condition* is inserted into the contract, either expressly by the parties or impliedly by courts, which, if not held

---

1. Looking at *all* of them would take an entire book.

to be satisfied, will discharge the obligations (promises) of the parties.

Suppose I offer to purchase a tract of your land on the condition that your neighbor to the south agrees to sell me her land. You accept my offer. Our obligations (promises) are conditioned upon your neighbor's willingness to sell her land. Should this condition not be satisfied (for example, if your neighbor refuses to sell), our obligations to each other are discharged and cannot be enforced.

Thus, a **condition** is a possible future event, the occurrence or nonoccurrence of which will trigger the performance of a legal obligation. The occurrence or nonoccurrence of a condition can also terminate an existing obligation under a contract.

Although there is a fundamental distinction between the breach or performance of an absolute promise and the failure or nonoccurrence of an express condition, both can occur in a single contract.

For example, suppose you promise to buy a corn futures contract from Merrill Lynch *if the price of number 2 yellow corn reaches $2.25 per bushel.* The condition to your promise to buy is that the price of number 2 yellow corn will reach $2.25 per bushel. If there is a failure of that condition—if number 2 yellow corn never reaches $2.25 per bushel and, therefore, you do not buy—

the contract is not breached. However, once the price of corn does reach $2.25, your promise to buy becomes absolute, and if you do not buy, the contract is breached.

Types of Conditions

Three types of conditions can be present in any given contract—conditions *precedent*, conditions *subsequent*, and conditions *concurrent*.

Conditions Precedent A condition that must be fulfilled before a party's promise becomes absolute is called a **condition precedent.**[2] The condition precedes the absolute duty to perform. For example, if Craig promises to pay Davis $500 if Davis installs a tile roof on Craig's house, Craig's promise is subject to the (implied) condition precedent of Davis's installing the tile roof. Or if Fisher promises to contribute $1,000 to the Salvation Army if Calvin completes college, Fisher's promise is subject to the (express) condition precedent of Calvin's completing college. Until the conditions are fulfilled or satisfied, Craig's promise to pay Davis and Fisher's promise to donate to charity do not become absolute.

---

2. Restatement, Second, Contracts, Section 224, eliminates the terms *condition precedent* and *condition subsequent*.

BACKGROUND AND FACTS *In the following case, a contract for the sale of a tract of land by the appellee (seller) to the appellant (buyer) was subject to a condition precedent that certain zoning variances be obtained. Generally, applications for zoning can be filed only during each of two specified months of the year, six months apart. The parties had included in their contract a provision that "this sale [is] subject to the obtaining of necessary zoning for the erection of general offices for use of doctors within the next zoning application term." The parties had further agreed that the provision meant the six-month period following the first day of the month in which zoning applications could be filed after the signing of the contract.*

The zoning application was timely filed (that is, within the legal, necessary, or reasonable period) but not obtained "within the next zoning application term." The sellers then notified the buyer in writing that the contract was terminated and the buyer's 10 percent deposit was being returned. The land was sold to another purchaser. The buyer (appellant)

BARNES v. EUSTER
Court of Appeals of Maryland, 1965.
240 Md. 603, 214 A.2d 807.

attempted to obtain damages from the seller (appellee) for having sold the land to another purchaser. The buyer took the position that the contract was still in force.

HAMMOND, Judge.

* * * *

Although the contract did not expressly make time of the essence, it may well be, as appellees contend, that by reason of the condition as to rezoning, the contract was like a unilateral contract, such as an option, in which the law makes time of the essence and *that time ran out with the expiration of the then current "zoning application term," and the contract then ended,* * * * *without further obligation on either party.* [Emphasis added.]

* * * * .

The contract provision was that it was "subject" to the specified rezoning being obtained within the current zoning application term, and "where a contractual duty is subject to a condition precedent, whether express or implied, there is no duty of performance and there can be no breach by nonperformance until the condition precedent is either performed or excused." Here it was not performed, and, if the further assumption be made that the condition * * * was for the protection only of the buyer, it could have been excused or waived by him as being a provision for his benefit, but the excusing or waiving would have had to be done before the expiration of the current zoning application term or within a reasonable time thereafter.

* * * *

In mid-1960 the buyer knew the condition had not been met, but it was not until three years later, * * * that he first indicated by word or act that he was willing to excuse or waive the condition and take the land as it was. Some sixteen months after the last day of the critical zoning application term, when the sellers wrote that the contract had terminated, he took the position it was still in force, subject to the condition.

* * * *

His delay in excusing or waiving the condition was unreasonable as a matter of law in light of the notification of termination by the sellers and the rapidly rising prices of real estate. * * *

JUDGMENT AND REMEDY   *The appellate court affirmed the trial court's order. The prospective buyer had no right to damages from the seller for sale of the land to another purchaser since the condition precedent had never been fulfilled or excused within a reasonable time.*

Conditions Subsequent   When a condition operates to terminate a party's absolute promise to perform, it is called a **condition subsequent.**[3] The condition follows, or is subsequent to, the absolute duty to perform. If the condition occurs, the party need not perform any further. For example, if Hartman promises to work for the San Pedro Company for one year unless he is called into military service, the absolute duty to work is conditioned upon not being drafted. Hart-

---

3. Restatement, Second, Contracts, Section 224. It is possible that a condition may be subsequent in form but precedent in fact. Further, if there is any difference at all between the two, it is as to burdens of proof and pleading. For this reason, the draft of the Restatement, Second, Contracts drops the distinction between the two.

man's promise to work for San Pedro continues to be absolute until he is drafted or otherwise inducted. Once Hartman is drafted, the absolute duty to work for San Pedro ends, and Hartman is released from the contract.[4]

Concurrent Conditions　Where each party's absolute duty to perform is conditioned on the other party's absolute duty to perform, there are **concurrent conditions.** Concurrent conditions occur only when the parties expressly or impliedly are to perform their respective duties simultaneously. For example, if a buyer promises to pay for goods if they are delivered by the seller, each party's absolute duty to perform is conditioned upon the other party's absolute duty to perform. The buyer's duty to pay for the goods does not become absolute until the seller either delivers or tenders the goods—that is, makes an unconditional offer to perform, coupled with the manifested ability to carry out the offer. Accordingly, the seller's duty to deliver the goods does not become absolute until the buyer tenders or actually makes payment. Therefore, neither can recover from the other for breach unless he or she first tenders his or her own performance.

Express and Implied Conditions　Conditions can also be classified as:

1. Express.
2. Implied-in-fact.
3. Implied-in-law.

Express conditions are provided for by the parties' agreement. An express condition is usually prefaced by "if," "provided," "after," or "when." Conditions *implied-in-fact* are similar to express conditions because they are understood to be part of the agreement, but they are not expressly found in the language of the agreement. The court infers them from the promises.

Suppose Silverman and Lyon enter into two agreements. The first states, "Silverman promises to pay Lyon $1,500 *if* Lyon delivers 100 cases of oranges to Silverman's business office. Lyon promises to deliver 100 cases of oranges to Sil-

verman's business office *if* Silverman pays $1,500 for the oranges." The second agreement states, "Silverman promises to pay $1,500 for 100 cases of Lyon's oranges to be delivered at Silverman's business office."

In the first agreement, Silverman's promise to pay is expressly conditioned on Lyon's promise to deliver. Also, Lyon's promise to deliver is expressly conditioned on Silverman's promise to pay. As noted above, these are *concurrent conditions.*

In the second agreement, Silverman's promise to pay is conditioned on Lyon's promise to deliver, and Lyon's promise to deliver is conditioned on Silverman's promise to pay. The conditions are implied-in-fact because they are necessarily implied by the promise contained in the contract. In other words, it is obvious from custom and context that the duties here are conditional.

Finally, *implied-in-law*, or *constructive*, conditions are imposed by the law in order to achieve justice and fairness. They are not contained in the language of the contract or even necessarily implied.[5] For example, a contract in which a builder is supposed to build a house for a buyer can omit the date on which the buyer is supposed to pay the builder. Nonetheless, the court will imply a condition that the buyer is not obliged to pay the builder until the house is fully or substantially completed. This is done because the buyer should not be compelled to perform unless the builder has performed.

The distinction between conditions is important because if these conditions are expressed, the plaintiff has a duty to allege that all conditions antecedent to his or her responsibility have occurred. Thus, when they are expressed, the burden of proof is on the plaintiff.

DISCHARGE BY PERFORMANCE

The great majority of contracts are discharged by performance. The contract comes to an end when both parties fulfill their respective duties by performing the acts they have promised. Perfor-

---

4. Hartman v. San Pedro Commercial Co., 66 Cal.App.2d 935, 153 P.2d 212 (1945).

5. Restatement, Second, Contracts, Section 226.

mance can also be accomplished by tender. **Tender** is an unconditional offer to perform by one who is ready, willing, and able to do so. Therefore, a seller who places goods at the disposal of a buyer has tendered delivery and can demand payment. A buyer who offers to pay for goods has tendered payment and can demand delivery of the goods. Once performance has been tendered, the party making the tender has done everything possible to carry out the terms of the contract. If the other party then refuses to perform, the party making the tender can consider the duty discharged and sue for breach of contract.

The Degree of Performance Required

It is important to distinguish among three types of performance:

1. Complete.
2. Substantial.
3. Definitely inferior and constituting a material breach of the contract.

One typically uses a *reasonable expectations test* for determining which of these categories a performance fits. *Complete performance* occurs when performance is within the bounds of reasonable expectations. *Substantial performance* occurs when performance is slightly below reasonable expectations. A *material breach* occurs when performance is far below reasonable expectations.

Although in most contracts the parties fully discharge their obligations by complete performance, sometimes a party fulfills most, but not all, the duties or completes the duties in a manner contrary to the terms of the contract. The issue then arises as to whether this failure of complete performance acts as a discharge of performance for the other party.

For example, a home building contract specifies installation of Fuller brand plasterboard for the walls. The builder cannot secure the Fuller brand and installs Honeyrock. All other aspects of construction conform to the contract. Does this

deviation discharge the buyer from paying for the house upon completion?

The answer usually depends on one or two basic factors:

1. Does the term in dispute constitute an express condition?
2. Can only "complete performance" discharge the promise?

If both factors are present, only *complete* performance acts as a discharge of performance. If the terms of the contract do not fit both these categories, *substantial*, not complete, performance is required. In this event, it must be determined whether the performance is substantial. If it is not, the party is then in *material breach* (a topic to be discussed later).

Conditions and Complete Performance Normally, conditions expressly stated in the contract must fully occur in all aspects. Any deviation operates as a discharge. In the most recent illustration, if the terms in the specifications had stated that *only Fuller brand* plasterboard was to be used, a court could construe this term as a condition. The builder's use of the Honeyrock brand, even though it is of equal quality to Fuller, would not fulfill this express condition precedent to payment, and therefore the builder would not be entitled to payment.

A typical illustration of a condition precedent to payment is a life insurance policy in which one of the conditions for enforcing the policy is the payment of the life insurance premium. The premium must be paid prior to the death of the insured, or the insurance company will not be obligated to pay benefits.

Substantial Performance Most terms or promises are not made or construed as conditions. Human nature dictates that performance will not always fully satisfy the parties. Therefore, for the sake of justice and fairness, the courts hold that a party's obligation is not discharged as long as the other party has fulfilled the terms of the contract with *substantial performance*. In order to qualify as substantial, the performance must not vary greatly from the performance promised in the contract. If performance is substantial, the other party's duty to perform remains absolute, less damages, if any, for the minor deviations.

In the "Fuller" illustration, if the specification for Fuller plasterboard is not construed as a condition, then the only issue is whether the substitution of Honeyrock plasterboard is substantial performance. Obviously, if Honeyrock is of similar quality, substantial performance by the builder has taken place, and either the buyer is obligated to pay,[6] or the contractor is required to tear out all the Honeyrock brand plasterboard and replace it with the Fuller brand. However, this kind of deviation from the terms of a contract must not be willful or grossly negligent but must result only from an oversight.

Substantial performance does not operate to eliminate any breach of contract arising from less than full performance. Although substantial performance does not prevent discharge (as the breach is not material), a breach of contract—however slight—has occurred. If the plasterboard substituted for Fuller brand had been of a somewhat lesser quality than Fuller, reducing the value of the house by $300, the builder would still be allowed to recover the contracted building price but less the $300. Remedies will be discussed in detail in the next chapter.

---

6. For an excellent analysis of substantial performance, see Judge Cardozo's opinion in Jacob & Youngs v. Kent, 230 N.Y. 239, 129 N.E. 889 (1921).

BACKGROUND AND FACTS *The Jacobs entered into a written contract with the plaintiff, Plante, to furnish the materials and construct a house on their lot, in accordance with plans and specifications, for a sum of $26,765. During the course of construction, the plaintiff was paid $20,000. Disputes arose between the parties concerning the work being done. The Jacobses refused to continue paying. The plaintiff did not complete the house. The trial court found that the contract was substantially performed. The Jacobses were told to pay $4,152.90 plus interest and court costs.*

PLANTE v. JACOBS

Supreme Court of Wisconsin, 1960.

10 Wis.2d 567, 103 N.W.2d 296.

HALLOWS, JUSTICE.

*   *   *   *

The defendants argue the plaintiff cannot recover any amount because he has failed to substantially perform the contract. The plaintiff conceded he failed to furnish the kitchen cabinets, gutters and downspouts, sidewalk, closet clothes poles, and entrance seat amounting to $1,601.95. This amount was allowed to the defendants. The defendants claim some 20 other items of incomplete or faulty performance by the plaintiff and no substantial performance because the cost of completing the house in strict compliance with the plans and specifications would amount to 25 or 30 per cent of the contract price. The defendants especially stress the misplacing of the wall between the living room and the kitchen, which narrowed the living room in excess of one foot. The cost of tearing down this wall and rebuilding it would be approximately $4,000. The record is not clear why and when this wall was misplaced, but the wall is completely built and the house decorated and the defendants are living therein. Real estate experts testified that the smaller width of the living room would not affect the market price of the house.

*   *   *   *

Substantial performance as applied to construction of a house does not mean that every detail must be in strict compliance with the specifications and the plans. Something less than perfection is the test of specific performance unless all details are made the essence of the contract. This was not done here. There may be situations in which features or details of construction of special or of great personal importance, if not performed, would prevent a finding of substantial performance of the contract. In this case the plan was a stock floor plan. No detailed construction of the house was shown on the plan. There were no blueprints. The specifications were standard printed forms with some modifications and additions written in by the parties. Many of the problems that arose during the construction had to be solved on the basis of practical experience. No mathematical rule relating to the percentage of the price, of cost of completion or of completeness can be laid down to determine substantial performance of a building contract. Although the defendants received a house with which they are dissatisfied in many respects, the trial court was not in error in finding the contract was substantially performed.

The next question is what is the amount of recovery when the plaintiff has substantially, but incompletely, performed. For substantial performance the plaintiff should recover the contract price less the damages caused the defendant by the incomplete performance. Both parties agree. Venzke v. Magdanz, 1943, 243 Wis. 155, 9 N.W.2d 604, states the correct rule for damages due to faulty construction amounting to such incomplete performance, which is the difference between the value of the house as it stands with faulty and incomplete construction and the value of the house if it had been constructed in strict accordance with the plans and specifications. This is the diminished-value rule. The cost of replacement or repair is not the measure of such damage, but is an element to take into consideration in arriving at value under some circumstances. The cost of replacement or the cost to make whole the omissions may equal or be less than the difference in value in some cases and, likewise, the cost to rectify a defect may greatly exceed the added value to the structure as corrected. The defendants argue that under the Venzke rule their damages are $10,000. The plaintiff on review argues the defendants' damages are only $650. Both parties agree the trial court applied the wrong rule to the facts.

JUDGMENT AND REMEDY   *The reviewing court upheld the trial court's judgment. Substantial performance was evident.*

Performance to the Satisfaction of Another
Contracts will often state that completed work must personally satisfy one of the parties or a third person. The question then arises as to whether this satisfaction becomes a condition precedent, requiring actual personal satisfaction or approval for discharge, or whether the test of satisfaction is an absolute promise requiring such performance as would satisfy a "reasonable person" (substantial performance).

When the subject matter of the contract is personal, a contract to be performed to the satisfaction of one of the parties is conditioned, and performance must actually satisfy that party. For example, contracts for portraits, works of art, medical or dental work, and tailoring are considered personal. Therefore, only the personal satisfaction of the party will be sufficient to fulfill the condition. Suppose Williams agrees to paint a portrait of Hirshon's daughter for $500.

The contract provides that Hirshon must be satisfied with the portrait. If Hirshon is not, she will not be required to pay for it. The only requirement imposed on Hirshon is that she act honestly and in good faith. If she expresses dissatisfaction only to avoid paying for the portrait, the condition of satisfaction is excused, and her duty to pay becomes absolute. (Of course, the jury, or judge acting as a jury, will decide whether she is acting honestly.)

Contracts that involve mechanical fitness, utility, or marketability need only be performed to the satisfaction of a reasonable person unless they *expressly state otherwise.* For example, construction contracts or manufacturing contracts are usually *not* considered to be personal, so the party's personal satisfaction is normally irrelevant. As long as the performance will satisfy a reasonable person, the contract is fulfilled. For example, assume Duplex Safety Boiler Company agrees to rebuild Garden's boiler "to Garden's satisfaction." After rebuilding the boiler, it operates properly, but Garden is dissatisfied and refuses to pay for the repair work. Most courts would not construe these terms as a condition and if a reasonable person would be satisfied with the boiler's operation, Duplex is entitled to be paid for the repair work.[7]

At times, contracts also require performance to the satisfaction of a third party (not a party to the contract). For example, assume you contract to pave several city streets. The contract provides that the work will be done "to the satisfaction of Phil Hopper, the supervising engineer." In this situation, the courts are divided. A minority of courts require the personal satisfaction of the third party, here Phil Hopper. If Hopper is not satisfied, you will not be paid, even if a reasonable person would be satisfied. Again, the personal judgment must be made honestly or the condition will be excused. A majority of courts require the work to be satisfactory to a reasonable person. So even if Hopper were dissatisfied with the cement work, you

would be paid, as long as a qualified supervising engineer would have been satisfied.

All of the above examples demonstrate the necessity for *clear, specific wording in contracts.* That is, in all states the parties could provide that the performance must meet the *personal and subjective* satisfaction of the party who is paying for the work being done. One must never underestimate the importance of reading the small print in contracts.

Material Breach of Contract

A **breach of contract** is the nonperformance of a contractual duty. When the breach is *material,* or performance is not substantial, the nonbreaching party is excused from the performance of contractual duties and has a cause of action to sue for damages caused by the breach. If the breach is *minor* (not material), the nonbreaching party's duty to perform can sometimes be suspended until the breach is remedied but is not entirely excused. Once the minor breach is cured, the nonbreaching party must then resume performance of the contractual obligations undertaken. Any breach entitles the nonbreaching party to sue for damages, but only a material breach discharges the nonbreaching party from the contract. The policy underlying these rules allows contracts to go forward when only minor problems occur but terminates them if major problems occur.[8]

Suppose Raytheon Corp. contracts with the United States government to build an all-weather tactical strike force system and to test equipment for the Hawk missile system. Raytheon is to complete the project in two years and has certain schedules to meet for each stage of the production. Every six months Raytheon is to receive $3.8 million of the total $15.2 million contract price. If Raytheon is four months late in completing the first stage of production, the government will be entitled to treat the contract as discharged. Taking ten months to complete a stage that was scheduled for six months is a material breach of contract. In addition, the government

---

7.   If, however, the contract specifically states that it is to be fulfilled to the "personal" satisfaction of one or more of the parties, and the parties so intended, the outcome will probably be different.

8.   See UCC 2-612 dealing with installment contracts for the sale of goods.

can sue Raytheon for breach of contract and recover damages caused by the four-month delay. If, on the other hand, Raytheon is two days late in completing the first stage, the government will not be entitled to treat the contract as discharged. Two days is only a minor breach. However, the government can sue Raytheon for damages caused by the minor delay.

A nonbreaching party need not treat a material breach as a discharge of the contract, but can treat the contract as being in effect and simply sue for damages. In the above example, if Raytheon delays four months on the first stage, the government can treat the contract as still being in effect and sue for damages caused by the delay.

Time for Performance

If no time for performance is stated in the contract, a reasonable time is implied.[9] If a specific time is stated, the parties must usually perform by that time. However, unless time is expressly stated to be vital, a delay in performance will not destroy the performing party's right to payment. When time is expressly stated to be vital, or when "time is of the essence," the time for performance must usually be strictly complied with. The time element becomes a condition.

For example, a contract for the sale of soybeans must be performed within a reasonable time, even if it does not mention time. A contract for the sale of soybeans "on or before April 1" may be performed by April 2 or 3. (But the party rendering late performance will have to pay for any damages caused by the delay.) A contract for the sale of soybeans "on or before April 1—necessary for immediate shipment abroad on April 2" must be performed by April 1. Time is of the essence because the buyer plans on immediate resale. Delivery after April 1 will prevent the buyer from exporting the soybeans.

DISCHARGE BY AGREEMENT

Any contract can be discharged by agreement of the parties. The agreement can be contained in

the original contract, or the parties can form a new contract for the express purpose of discharging the original contract.

Discharge by Rescission

Rescission is the process whereby the parties cancel the contract and are returned to the positions they occupied prior to forming it. In order to mutually rescind a bargain, the parties must make another agreement, which must also satisfy the legal requirements for a contract. There must be an *offer*, an *acceptance*, and *consideration*. Ordinarily, if the parties agree to rescind the original contract, their promises not to perform those acts promised in the original contract will be legal consideration for the second contract. This occurs when the performance of each is executory, in whole or in part.

The rescission agreement is generally enforceable even if made orally. This applies even if the original agreement was in writing. There are two basic exceptions. One applies to transfers of realty. The other applies to the sale of goods under the UCC, where the sales contract requires written rescission.[10]

When one party has fully performed, however, an agreement to call off the original contract will not normally be enforceable. Because the performing party has received no consideration for the promise to call off the original bargain, additional consideration will be necessary.

To illustrate: Suppose Beatrice Foods Company contracts to buy forty truckloads of oranges from Tropicana Products Inc. Later, representatives of Beatrice and Tropicana get together and decide to call off the deal or rescind the original contract. This agreement is enforceable since neither party has yet performed. The consideration that Tropicana receives for calling off the deal is freedom from performing what it was legally bound to perform under the contract—that is, not having to deliver the forty truckloads of oranges. The consideration Beatrice receives for calling off the deal is not having to pay for the oranges, an obligation it otherwise had to honor.

9. See UCC 1-204.

10. UCC 2-209(2)(4).

On the other hand, if Tropicana had already delivered the oranges, an agreement to call off the deal would not normally be enforceable. In this case, Tropicana would receive no consideration for its promise to call off the deal.

In sum, contracts that are *executory* on *both* sides (contracts where neither party has performed) can be rescinded solely by agreement.[11] But contracts that are *executed on one side* (contracts where one party has performed) can be rescinded only if the party who has performed receives consideration for the promise to call off the deal.

Discharge by Novation or Substituted Agreement

The process of **novation** substitutes a new party for one of the original parties. Essentially, the parties to the original contract and one or more new parties all get together and agree to substitute the new party for one of the original parties. The requirements of a novation are:

1. A previous valid obligation.
2. An agreement of all the parties to a new contract.
3. The extinguishment of the old obligation (discharge of the prior party).
4. A new contract that is valid.

Suppose Union Carbide Corp. decides to sell its petrochemical business in Europe. Union Carbide contracts with British Petroleum Company to sell Bakelite Xylonite Ltd. stock to British Petroleum for $200 million in cash. The contract is signed by both parties. After British Petroleum consults its tax and securities experts, it decides to substitute BP Chemicals as the purchaser instead. In order to accomplish this, the parties agree to a novation. Union Carbide, British Petroleum, and BP Chemicals all get together and agree that BP Chemicals will buy the Bakelite Xylonite stock from Union Carbide. As long

as the new contract is supported by consideration, the novation will discharge the original contract (between Union Carbide and British Petroleum) and replace it with the new contract (between Union Carbide and BP Chemicals). See Exhibit 14–1.

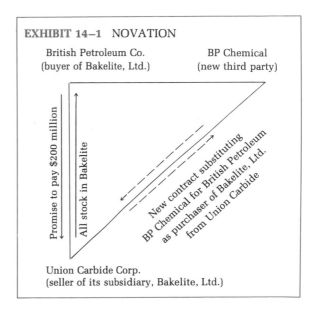

EXHIBIT 14–1   NOVATION

British Petroleum Co.
(buyer of Bakelite, Ltd.)

BP Chemical
(new third party)

Promise to pay $200 million

All stock in Bakelite

New contract substituting BP Chemical for British Petroleum as purchaser of Bakelite, Ltd. from Union Carbide

Union Carbide Corp.
(seller of its subsidiary, Bakelite, Ltd.)

A *substituted* agreement is a new contract that expressly or impliedly revokes and discharges a prior contract.[12] The parties involved may simply want a new agreement with somewhat different terms. So they expressly state in a new contract that the old contract is now discharged. They can also make the new contract without expressly stating that the old contract is discharged. If the parties do not expressly discharge the old contract, it will be *impliedly* discharged due to the change or different terms of the new contract.

For example, suppose Triangle Pacific Corp. contracts to sell its lumber manufacturing facilities in Slocan, British Columbia, to a Canadian investor group for $7.9 million in cash and $800,000 in five-year subordinated debentures. Before the sale is closed, however, Triangle Pacific Corp. decides that it wants $6.9 million in

---

11. Certain sales made to consumers at their homes can be rescinded by the consumer within three days for no reason at all. This three-day "cooling-off" is designed to aid consumers who are susceptible to high-pressure door-to-door sales tactics. See Chapter 48 and 15 USC § 1635(a).

12. It is this immediate discharge of the prior contract that distinguishes a substituted contract from accord and satisfaction, discussed in the next section.

cash and $1.8 million in five-year subordinated debentures. The Canadian investor group agrees, and the parties draw up a new contract with these terms of sale. If the second agreement states, "Our previous contract to accept payment of $7.9 million in cash, balance in five-year subordinated debentures is hereby revoked," the original contract will be expressly discharged by substitution. If the second agreement does not state this, the original contract will nevertheless be discharged by implication. Triangle Pacific Corp. cannot sell the same lumber manufacturing facilities under two different terms of payment. Since the terms are inconsistent, a court will enforce the terms that were decided upon most recently. In this case, the sale would be for $6.9 million in cash and $1.8 million in five-year subordinated debentures.

A *compromise*, or settlement agreement, that arises out of a bona fide dispute over the obligations under an existing contract will be recognized at law. Such an agreement will be substituted as a new contract, and it will either expressly or impliedly revoke and discharge the obligations under any prior contract.

Discharge by Accord and Satisfaction

For a contract to be discharged by *accord* and *satisfaction*, the parties must agree to accept performance different from the performance originally promised. An *accord* is defined as an executory contract (that is, one that has not yet been performed) to perform some act to satisfy an existing contractual duty.[13] The duty is not yet discharged. A *satisfaction* is the performance of the accord agreement. An **accord** *and* its **satisfaction** (performance) discharge the original contractual obligation. However, an accord is not binding until the satisfaction is made. Thus, either party can revoke an accord before payment or performance has been made and the original promise(s) remain in effect.

To illustrate, suppose Matthews obtains a judgment against Elizabeth Brown for $3,000. Thus, Brown owes Matthews $3,000 in cash. Later both parties agree that the judgment can be sat-

isfied if Brown pays $2,000 in cash and transfers her automobile to Matthews in lieu of the $1,000 balance. Brown pays $2,000 in cash and then offers the car to Matthews, but he refuses it. The subsequent agreement for $2,000 in cash and the transfer of the automobile is the accord. However, the satisfaction does not occur, and the $3,000 debt is not discharged until it is fully completed by both parties. As long as any part of the accord and satisfaction remains to be performed, it does not constitute satisfactory payment of the debt. A disputed amount, or unliquidated debt, must be involved before there can be an accord and satisfaction, or else one runs into preexisting legal obligation problems, as seen in Chapter 8 on consideration.

DISCHARGE BY OPERATION OF LAW

Alteration of the Contract

In order to discourage parties from altering written contracts, the law operates to discharge an innocent party when the other party has materially altered a written contract without consent. For example, contract terms such as quantity or price might be changed without the knowledge or consent of all parties. If so, the party who was unaware of the change can treat the contract as discharged or terminated.[14]

Statutes of Limitations

Statutes of limitations limit the period of time during which a party can sue on a particular cause of action. A cause of action is a cause or reason for suing or bringing an action. After the applicable limitations period has passed, suit can no longer be brought in a court of law or equity.

For example, the limitations period for oral contracts is usually two to three years; for written contracts, four to five years; for recovery of judgments, ten to twenty years.

---

13. Restatement, Second, Contracts, Section 281.

14. The innocent party can also treat the contract as in effect, either on the original terms or on the terms as altered. A buyer who discovers that a seller altered the quantity of goods in a sales contract from 100 to 1,000 by secretly inserting a zero can purchase either 100 or 1,000 of the items.

Section 2-725 of the UCC deals with the statute of limitations applicable to contracts for the sale of goods. The UCC does not distinguish between oral and written contracts. Section 2-725 provides that an action for the breach of any contract for sale must be commenced within four years after the cause of that action has occurred. The cause of action starts to accrue when the breach occurs, regardless of the aggrieved party's lack of knowledge of the breach. By original agreement, the parties can reduce this four-year period to a one-year period. They cannot, however, extend the statute beyond the four-year limitation period.

Technically, the running of a statute of limitations bars access only to *judicial* remedies; it does not extinguish the debt or the underlying obligation. The statute precludes access to the courts for collection. But if the party who owes the debt or obligation agrees to perform (that is, makes a new promise to perform), the cause of action barred by the statute of limitations will be revived. For the old agreement to be revived by a new promise in this manner, many states require that the promise be in writing or that there be evidence of part performance.

For example, suppose Burlington Northern Railroad contracts for sixty-three new miles of track to be laid between Dalhart and Amarillo, Texas. Martin Marietta Corp. supplies four tons of cast iron railway for the project and is paid $22,000 of the $30,000 purchase price. Texas's statute of limitations for collection of this debt is five years, but Martin Marietta Corp. fails to collect the debt or sue for collection during that five-year period after delivery of the iron. Therefore, Martin Marietta Corp. can no longer sue. It is barred by the statute of limitations. But if Burlington Northern Railroad agrees, in writing, to pay the remaining $8,000, or if it actually pays part of the $8,000, Marietta Corp. can again sue to collect the full debt. The statute of limitations is no longer a bar, and the cause of action for recovery of the full debt is revived.

Bankruptcy

A discharge in bankruptcy will ordinarily bar enforcement of a debtor's contract by the creditor. (Bankruptcy is fully discussed in Chapter 33.) Bankruptcy can be entered into voluntarily or involuntarily. A proceeding in bankruptcy attempts to allocate the assets the debtor owns at bankruptcy to the creditors in a fair and equitable fashion. Once the assets are allocated, the debtor receives a **discharge in bankruptcy.** Partial payment of a debt barred after discharge in bankruptcy will not revive the debt.

ANTICIPATORY BREACH

Duties of the nonbreaching party can be discharged by a *material* breach of contract or by *anticipatory repudiation* of the contract by the other party.

Before either party to a contract has a duty to perform, one of the parties may refuse to perform his or her contractual obligations. This is called **anticipatory breach, or repudiation.**[15] For example, De La Tour made a contract with Hochester in March to employ Hochester as a courier for three months—June, July, and August. On April 1, De La Tour told Hochester, "I am going abroad this summer and will not need a courier." This is an anticipatory breach of the employment contract. Since De La Tour repudiated the contract, Hochester could treat the act as a present, material breach. Furthermore, he could sue to recover damages *immediately*, without having to wait until June 1 to sue.[16]

There are two reasons for treating an anticipatory breach as a present, material breach:

1. The nonbreaching party should not be required to remain ready and willing to perform when the other party has already repudiated the contract.
2. The nonbreaching party should have the opportunity to seek a similar contract elsewhere.

---

15. Restatement, Second, Contracts, Section 253, and UCC 2-610.
16. The doctrine of anticipatory breach first arose in the landmark case of Hochester v. De La Tour, 2 Ellis and Blackburn Reports 678 (1853) when the English court recognized the delay and expense inherent in a rule requiring a nonbreaching party to wait until the time for performance to sue on an anticipatory breach.

Thus, Hochester should not be required to remain ready to serve as De La Tour's courier until June 1 since that would be a waste of time. In the meantime, Hochester could be working elsewhere.

It is important to note that until the non-breaching party treats this early repudiation as a breach, the breaching party can retract his or her anticipatory repudiation by proper notice and restore the parties to their original obligations.[17]

The following case illustrates an anticipatory breach and the resulting measurement of damages.

---

17. See UCC 2-611.

RELIANCE COOPERAGE CORP. v. TREAT

United States Court of Appeals, Eighth Circuit, 1952. 195 F.2d 977.

BACKGROUND AND FACTS *Often, cases of anticipatory breach, or repudiation, arise when a sharp fluctuation in market prices makes a contract price either very favorable to the buyer or very favorable to the seller. In the case that follows, the market price of "white oak bourbon staves" rose sharply, and the sales contract called for a fixed price for the staves. As the market price rose, the seller tried to improve his position by informing the buyer that he would not deliver the staves under the agreement unless the buyer agreed to pay whatever the market price was when the deliveries were made. The trial court found the seller liable for breach by anticipatory repudiation, but the buyer appealed the trial court's judgment with regard to damages.*

SANBORN, Circuit Judge.

The parties to this action entered into a contract which, so far as pertinent, reads as follows:

"This Agreement entered into in St. Louis, Missouri this 12th day of July, 1950 by and between Reliance Cooperage Corporation, an Illinois corporation, Party of the First Part, and A. R. Treat, of Marshall, Arkansas, Party of the Second Part; Witnesseth:

"Party of the First Part hereby agrees to purchase and Party of the Second Part hereby agrees to sell a quantity of staves sufficient to aggregate three hundred thousand (300,000) white oak bourbon staves of four and one-half average width, to be produced by, or purchased by, Second Party in Arkansas, Missouri, or Oklahoma, upon the following terms and conditions:

"1.   Said staves when shipped shall be not less than 90% bourbon grade. Production shall commence as soon as possible and shall be completed not later than December 31, 1950. First Party agrees that on each final inspection, not more than 3% of the bourbon staves shall be less than two inches in width and none shall be less than one and one-half inches in width. The price to be paid Second Party by First Party shall be $450.00 per thousand for said bourbon grade staves of four and one-half inch average width, and $40.00 per thousand for oil grade staves of four and one-half inch average width, all f.o.b. freight cars nearest mill-site where staves were produced, *   *   *.
*   *   *   *

"4.   This agreement shall be governed by the laws of the State of Missouri."

Treat [the defendant] produced and delivered no staves to the Reliance Cooperage Corporation. After the time for performance specified in the contract had expired, the Corporation brought this action against Treat to recover the difference between the contract price of the staves and their market price at the time delivery was due under the contract. This difference was alleged to be $90,000. Treat, the defendant, admitted having entered into the contract, but denied that his non-performance had caused the plaintiff any damage.

* * * *

The evidence indicated that there had been, between the date of the contract and the date when performance was due, a rise in the market price of staves.

* * * *

It was admitted that the defendant had on August 12, 1950, sent to Ralph Ettlinger, an officer of the plaintiff, the following letter:

"Marshall, Arkansas
August 12, 1950

"Dear Mr. Ralph Ettlinger:

"I have been trying to get a letter to you for some time but they return to me. I went to Harrison yesterday and got Tom Burns Co. adress [sic] trying to get in touch with you. We got a mill at Hallaster, Mo. trying to get started. Have a few Bolts will have a time getting any more. I can't make these staves up there or any where else at the price I haft to pay for Bolts. Every one else are paying $475.00 to $500.00 per M. You see I can't compete with them so if you want those staves I will haft to get around what ever the market is from time to time. You can see your seff that I can get bolts say 70¢ a price when others paying $100.00 per foot. I think the boys can make a lot of staves fast up there if they can pay as much as others are paying if not they will haft to quit. Now you can see where I am at. The other to co. that I am making for with my other 3 mills have raised from $75.00 to $100.00 on the 1000 4½" staves and said they would cancel out as the market raises. So you do just what you want to. I can't make them unless I can buy the timber so let me hear at once. I will have a car before long.

"Yours as ever,
A. R. Treat."

* * * *

The following letter written by the plaintiff to the defendant, which he admitted having received, was introduced in evidence:

"October 6, 1950

"Mr. A. R. Treat
Marshall, Arkansas.
Dear Mr. Treat:

"Last week you advised our Mr. Ralph Ettlinger that you would not deliver staves under our agreement with you dated July 12, 1950, until he came down to Marshall and talked to you about revising the price at which the staves are to be sold to us.

"Under date of August 14, 1950, we wrote you requesting that you reconsider your decision, stated in your letter of August 12, 1950, not to deliver staves under our agreement unless we would pay 'whatever the market is from time to time.' We have not had a formal reply to our letter of August 14, 1950, and the substance of your phone conversation with Mr. Ralph Ettlinger certainly does not permit us to feel confident that you will perform in accordance with your agreement.

"We want to make it very clear to you at this point that we are looking forward to your strict compliance with all of the obligations which you have undertaken in your agreement with us. Over two months have elapsed since we met in St. Louis and worked out the terms of our present contract and to this date you have not advised us that you have produced a single stave for delivery to us under this agreement.

"Information reaching us discloses that you are cutting staves in several different locations. There is, therefore, no reason at all why you cannot deliver to us the staves contracted for in accordance with the terms of our agreement. Please let us hear from you at once on the matter of our agreement or we shall be obliged to take some action to protect our rights in the matter.

> "Very truly yours,
> "Reliance Cooperage Corp.,
> By Adolf Loeb.

"AL:vg"

*   *   *   *

In [a prior case], this Court said: "The general doctrine of anticipatory breach by repudiation has, however, been clearly recognized in that state [Missouri]." The leading case on the general subject adopted the views which are expressed in part as follows: "The man who wrongfully renounces a contract into which he has deliberately entered cannot justly complain if he is *immediately* sued for a compensation in damages by the man whom he has injured [emphasis added]; and it seems reasonable to allow an option to the injured party, either to sue immediately or to wait till the time when the act was to be done, still holding it as prospectively binding for the exercise of this option, which may be advantageous to the innocent party, and cannot be prejudicial to the wrongdoer."
*   *   *   *

"*   *   * The law is that, where the promisor before the time of performance expressly renounces his contract, the promisee is thereby entitled either to treat the contract as broken and sue at once for its breach without averring an offer or readiness to perform, or he may wait until the time of performance has expired, and then sue for the consequences of nonperformance."

[W]hile as a general rule an action upon an executory contract [one that has still not been performed] cannot be maintained until the time for performance has expired, the repudiation of the contract by one of the parties before that time gives to the other party the option to treat the contract as ended and to sue for the damages resulting from the anticipatory breach. In other words, unless the injured party chooses to treat the contract as breached by the anticipatory repudiation, his claim for damages does not accrue until the expiration of the time for performance.

There is no doubt that a party to an executory contract such as that in suit may refuse to accede to an anticipatory repudiation of it and insist upon performance, and, if he does so, the contract remains in existence and is binding on both parties, and no actionable claim [cause of action] for damages arises until the time for performance expires.

It is our opinion that, under the undisputed facts in this case, the unaccepted anticipatory renunciation by the defendant of his obligation to produce and deliver staves under the contract did not impair that obligation or affect his liability for damages for the nonperformance of the contract, and that the measure of those damages was no different than it would have been had no notice of renunciation been given by the defendant to the plaintiff. If there had been no anticipatory repudiation of the contract, the measure of damages for nonperformance by the seller would have been the difference between the contract price and the market price of the staves on the date when delivery was due, and that is the measure which should have been applied in assessing damages in this case.

Moreover, the measure of damages would have been the same had the plaintiff accepted the anticipatory repudiation as an actionable breach of the contract. The plaintiff would still have been entitled to recover what it had lost by reason of the defendant's failure to produce and deliver by December 31, 1950, the staves contracted for, namely, the difference between the market price and the contract price of the staves on that date. The Comment in Restatement of the Law of Contracts, § 338, Measure of Damages for Anticipatory Breach, contains the following statement (page 549): "The fact that an anticipatory repudiation is a breach of contract (see § 318) does not cause the repudiated promise to be treated as if it was a promise to render performance at the date of the repudiation. Repudiation does ʟot accelerate the time fixed for performance; nor does it change the damages to be awarded as the equivalent of the promised performance."

*　*　*　*

The doctrine of anticipatory breach by repudiation is intended to aid a party injured as a result of the other party's refusal to perform his contractual obligations, by giving to the injured party an election to accept or to reject the refusal of performance without impairing his rights or increasing his burdens. Any effort to convert the doctrine into one for the benefit of the party who, without legal excuse, has renounced his agreement should be resisted.

*　*　*　*

The plaintiff is entitled to recover as damages the amount by which on December 31, 1950, the market price of the staves contracted for exceeded their contract price. What the market price of such staves was on that date is a question of fact [to be determined at the new trial].

A new trial, in which the market price of wooden staves on the date in question was to be established, was ordered. The difference between that market price and the contracted-for market price times the number of staves in question would determine the actual damages to be awarded the plaintiff, Reliance Cooperage Corp.	**JUDGMENT AND REMEDY**

DISCHARGE BY IMPOSSIBILITY OF PERFORMANCE

After a contract has been made, performance may become impossible in an objective sense. This is known as **impossibility of performance** and may discharge a contract.[18] This *objective impossibility* ("It can't be done") must be distinguished from *subjective impossibility* ("I can't do it"). Examples of subjective impossibility include contracts in which goods cannot be delivered on time because of freight car shortages[19] and contracts in which money cannot be paid on time because the bank is closed.[20] In effect, the party

---

18. Restatement. Second, Contracts, Section 261.

19. Minneapolis v. Republic Creosoting Co., 161 Minn. 178, 201 N.W. 414(1924).
20. Ingham Lumber Co. v. Ingersoll & Co., 93 Ark. 447, 125 S.W. 139 (1910).

in these cases is saying "It is impossible for *me* to perform," not "It is impossible for anyone to perform." Accordingly, such excuses will not discharge a contract, and the nonperforming party will normally be held in breach of contract.

Objective Impossibility

Four basic types of situations generally qualify under the objective impossibility of performance rules that discharge contractual obligations:

1. Where one of the parties to a personal contract *dies prior* to performance.[21]
2. Where the *specific* subject matter of the contract is destroyed.[22]
3. Where a change in *law* renders performance illegal.[23]
4. Where performance becomes *commercially impracticable*.[24]

To illustrate the first type of impossibility, suppose Jane, a famous actress, contracts to play the leading role in a movie. Before the picture starts, she becomes ill and dies. Her personal performance was essential to the completion of the contract. Thus her death discharges the contract and her estate's liability for her nonperformance.

The second type of impossibility can occur when, for example, Pappagoras contracts to sell 10,000 bushels of apples to be harvested "from his Green Valley apple orchard in the state of Washington." Volcanic ash from Mount St. Helens destroys his apples. Because the contracted apples were to come specifically from his Green Valley orchard, his performance has been rendered impossible by Mount St. Helens. Thus this contract is discharged.

Another example of the second type of impossibility is a contract to lease a building where the building is destroyed by fire, or a contract to sell oil from a particular well where the well goes dry.

Examples of the third type include a contract to loan money at 20 percent where the usury rate is changed to make loans in excess of 12 percent illegal, or a contract to build an apartment building where the zoning laws are changed to prohibit the construction of residential rental property. Both changes render the contracts impossible to perform.

The fourth type of impossibility is the result of a growing trend to allow parties to discharge contracts in which the performance that was originally contemplated turns out to be more difficult or more expensive than anticipated. This is known as the doctrine of commercial impracticability. In order for someone to successfully invoke this doctrine, the anticipated performance must become extremely difficult or costly.

To illustrate, the California Supreme Court held that a contract was discharged because it would cost ten times more than the original estimate to excavate a certain amount of gravel.[25] In another case, commercial impracticability was not found where a carrier of goods was to deliver wheat from the West Coast of the United States to a safe port in Iran.[26] The Suez Canal, the usual route, was nationalized by Egypt and closed, forcing the carrier to travel around Africa and the Cape of Good Hope, through the Mediterranean and on to Iran. The added expense was approximately $42,000 above and beyond the contract price of $306,000, and the original journey of 10,000 miles was extended by an additional 3,000 miles. Nevertheless, the court held that the contract was not commercially impracticable to perform because the closing of the Suez Canal was foreseeable. Therefore, caution should be used in invoking commercial impracticability. The added burden of performing must be extreme and, more importantly, must not be within the cognizance of the parties when the contract was made.

---

21. Restatement, Second, Contracts, Section 262.
22. Restatement, Second, Contracts, Section 263.
23. Restatement, Second, Contracts, Section 264.
24. Restatement, Second, Contracts, Sections 265 and 266, and UCC 2–615.

25. Mineral Park Land Co. v. Howard, 172 Cal. 289, 156 P. 458 (1916).
26. Transatlantic Financing Corp. v. United States, 363 F.2d 312 (D.C. Cir. 1966).

BACKGROUND AND FACTS *In November 1959, the plaintiff, Parker, went to the Arthur Murray Dance Studio to redeem a certificate entitling him to three free dance lessons. At the time, Parker was a thirty-seven-year-old college-educated bachelor who lived alone in a one-room attic apartment. During the free lessons, the instructor told Parker that he had exceptional potential to become an accomplished dancer and generally encouraged him to take more lessons. Parker signed a contract for seventy-five hours of lessons at a cost of $1,000. At the bottom of the contract, "NON-CANCELLABLE NEGOTIABLE CONTRACT" was printed in boldface type.*

Parker attended lessons regularly. He was praised and encouraged by the instructors despite his lack of progress. Contract extensions and new contracts for additional instructional hours were executed. Each contract and each extension contained the same boldface words: "NON-CANCELLABLE CONTRACT." Some of the agreements contained the statement, "I UNDERSTAND THAT NO REFUNDS WILL BE MADE UNDER THE TERMS OF THIS CONTRACT," also in boldface.

On September 24, 1961, Parker was seriously injured in an automobile collision. The accident rendered him incapable of continuing his dance lessons. By that time, he had contracted for a total of 2,734 hours of lessons for which he had paid $24,812.80. Despite repeated written demand, the defendants, the Arthur Murray Dance Studio, refused to return any of Parker's money. This lawsuit ensued.

STAMOS, Presiding Justice.

The sole issue raised by defendants is whether the terms of the contracts barred plaintiff from asserting the doctrine of impossibility of performance as the basis for seeking recision.

*   *   *   *

Plaintiff was granted recision [by the trial court] on the ground of impossibility of performance. The applicable legal doctrine is expressed in the Restatement of Contracts, § 459, as follows:

> A duty that requires for its performance action that can be rendered only by the promisor or some other particular person is discharged by his death or by such illness as makes the necessary action by him impossible or seriously injurious to his health, unless the contract indicates a contrary intention or there is contributing fault on the part of the person subject to the duty.

Similarly, § 460 of the Restatement states:

> (1) Where the existence of a specific thing or person is, either by the terms of a bargain or in the contemplation of both parties, necessary for the performance of a promise in the bargain, a duty to perform the promise . . . (b) is discharged if the thing or person subsequently is not in existence in time for seasonable performance, unless a contrary intention is manifested, or the contributing fault of the promisor causes the nonexistence.

In Illinois impossibility of performance was recognized as a ground for recision [sic] in Davies v. Arthur Murray, Inc., 124 Ill.App.2d 141, 260 N.E.2d 240, wherein the court nonetheless found for the defendant because of the plaintiff's failure adequately to prove the existence of an incapacitating disability.

PARKER v. ARTHUR MURRAY, INC.
Appellate Court of Illinois, Second Division, First District, 1973.
10 Ill.App.3d 1000, 295 N.E.2d 487.

Defendants do not deny that the doctrine of impossibility of performance is generally applicable to the case at bar. Rather they assert that certain contract provisions bring this case within the Restatement's limitation that the doctrine is inapplicable if "the contract indicates a contrary intention." It is contended that such bold type phrases as "NON-CANCELLABLE CONTRACT," "NON-CANCELLABLE NEGOTIABLE CONTRACT" and "I UNDERSTAND THAT NO REFUNDS WILL BE MADE UNDER THE TERMS OF THIS CONTRACT" manifested the parties mutual intent to waive their respective rights to invoke the doctrine of impossibility. This is a construction which we find unacceptable. Courts engage in the construction and interpretation of contracts with the sole aim of determining the intention of the parties. We need rely on no construction aids to conclude that plaintiff never contemplated that by signing a contract with such terms as "NON-CANCELLABLE" and "NO REFUNDS" he was waiving a remedy expressly recognized by Illinois courts. Were we also to refer to established tenets of contractual construction, this conclusion would be equally compelled. An ambiguous contract will be construed most strongly against the party who drafted it. Exceptions or reservations in a contract will, in case of doubt or ambiguity, be construed least favorably to the party claiming the benefit of the exceptions or reservations. Although neither party to a contract should be relieved from performance on the ground that good business judgment was lacking, a court will not place upon language a ridiculous construction. We conclude that plaintiff did not waive his right to assert the doctrine of impossibility.

Defendants have also contended, albeit indirectly, that plaintiff failed to establish the existence of an incapacitating disability. In contrast to Davies v. Arthur Murray, Inc., supra, wherein the plaintiff relied solely upon his own uncorroborated testimony, plaintiff in the case at bar produced both lay witnesses and expert medical testimony corroborating the severity and permanency of his injuries. That testimony need not be recited; suffice it to say that overwhelming evidence supported plaintiff's contention that he was incapable of continuing his lessons.

JUDGMENT AND REMEDY

The trial court's ruling that impossibility of performance was grounds for rescission was upheld. Parker was entitled to recover the prepaid sums of money representing unused lessons.

COMMENTS

A closely allied theory is the doctrine of frustration of purpose. In principle, a contract will be discharged if supervening circumstances make it impossible to attain the purpose both parties had in mind when making the contract. The origins of the doctrine lie in the old English "coronation cases." A coronation procession was planned for Edward VII when he became king of England following the death of his mother, Queen Victoria. Hotel rooms along the coronation route were rented at exorbitant prices for that day. When the king became ill and the procession was cancelled, the purpose of the room contracts was "frustrated." A flurry of lawsuits resulted. Hotel and building owners sought to enforce the room rent bills against would-be parade observers, and would-be parade observers sought to be reimbursed for rental monies paid in advance on the rooms. It was from this situation that the court developed its theory of recovery known as frustration of purpose.

Temporary Impossibility

An occurrence or event that makes it temporarily impossible to perform the act for which a party has contracted will operate to suspend performance until the impossibility ceases. Then, ordinarily, the parties must perform the contract as originally planned. However, if the lapse of time and the change in circumstances surrounding the contract make it substantially more burdensome to perform the promised acts, the parties will be discharged.

The leading case on this subject, Autry v. Republic Productions,[27] involved an actor who was drafted into the army in 1942. Being drafted rendered his contract temporarily impossible to perform, and it was suspended until the end of the war. When the actor got out of the army, the value of the dollar had so changed that performance of the contract would have been substantially burdensome for him. Therefore, the contract was discharged.

QUESTIONS AND CASE PROBLEMS

1. The Rosenbergs own a real estate lot, and they contract with Faithful Construction, Inc., to build a house thereon for $60,000. The specifications list "all plumbing bowls and fixtures . . . to be Crane brand." The Rosenbergs leave on vacation, and during their absence Faithful is unable to buy and install Crane plumbing fixtures. Instead, Faithful installs Kohler brand fixtures, an equivalent in the industry. Upon completion of the building contract, the Rosenbergs, on inspection, discover the substitute and refuse to accept the house, claiming Faithful had breached the conditions set forth in the specifications. Discuss fully the Rosenbergs' claim.

2. Junior owes creditor Carlton $1,000, which is due and payable on June 1. Junior has been in a car accident, missed a great deal of work, and consequently will not have the money on June 1. Junior's father, Fred, offers to pay Carlton $1,100 in four equal installments if Carlton will discharge Junior from any further liability on the debt. Carlton accepts. Discuss the following:

    (a) Is the transaction a novation, or is it accord and satisfaction? Explain.

    (b) Does the contract between Fred and Carlton have to be in writing to be enforceable? (Review the Statute of Frauds.) Explain.

3. ABC Clothiers, Inc., has a contract with retailer Taylor & Sons to deliver 1,000 summer suits to Taylor's place of business on or before *May 1*. On *April 1*, Taylor senior receives a letter from ABC informing him that ABC will not be able to make the delivery as scheduled. Taylor is very upset, as he had planned a big ad sale campaign. He wants to file suit against ABC immediately (April 2). Taylor's son, Tom, tells his father that a suit is not proper until ABC actually fails to deliver the suits on May 1. Discuss fully who is correct, Taylor or his son Tom?

4. The following events take place after the formation of the contracts. Discuss which of these contracts are now discharged by virtue of the events rendering the contracts impossible of performance.

    (a) Jimenez, a famous singer, contracts to perform in your nightclub. He dies prior to performance.

    (b) Raglione contracts to sell you her land. Just before title is to be transferred, she dies.

    (c) Oppenheim contracts to sell you 1,000 bushels of apples from her orchard in the state of Washington. Because of a severe frost, she is unable to deliver the apples.

    (d) Maxwell contracts to lease a service station for ten years. His principal income is from the sale of gasoline. Due to an oil embargo by foreign oil nations, gasoline is rationed, cutting sharply into Maxwell's gasoline sales. He cannot make his lease payments.

5. Murphy contracts to purchase from Lone Star Liquors six cases of French champagne for $1,200. The contract states that delivery is to be made at the Murphy residence "on or before June 1, to be used for daughter's wedding reception on June 2." The champagne is carried regularly in Lone Star's stock. On June 1, Lone Star's delivery van is involved in an accident, and the champagne is not delivered that day. On the morning of June 2, Murphy discovers the nondelivery. Unable to reach Lone Star because its line is busy, Murphy purchases the champagne from another dealer. That afternoon, just before the wedding reception, Lone Star tenders delivery of the champagne at Murphy's

27. 30 Cal.2d 144, 180 P.2d 888 (1947).

residence. Murphy refuses tender, and Lone Star sues for breach of contract. Discuss fully the result.

6. In 1972 Allyn & Bacon, publishers, contracted with two authors, Goldman and Traschen, to produce a second edition of their drama anthology. After the authors had selected the plays, obtained copyright consents, and completed the editorial comment, they received two letters from Allyn & Bacon discouraging them from going forward with the revision. The first letter stated that the company was phasing out its English department and urged the authors to consider submitting their work to another publisher. The second letter advised them that there would be little funding for promotion or advertising of the book. It stated that "from a business and financial standpoint, we are simply not in a position to launch your revision."

Goldman and Traschen, alleging anticipatory repudiation, sued for breach of contract. Will their claim succeed? Alternatively, could they recover for their own substantial performance of the contract? [Goldman v. Allyn & Bacon, Inc., 482 F. Supp. 963 (D.C. Mass. 1979)]

7. Miller, a general contractor, contracted with Village Apartments, Inc., to build a number of apartments. Miller hired a subcontractor, Mascioni, to construct certain walls and agreed to pay him 55 cents per cubic foot for the walls. The contract between Miller and Mascioni contained the following clause: "Payments to be made as received from the owner." In compliance with his contract with Miller, Mascioni completed construction of the walls. However, the owner never paid Miller, and Miller therefore refused to pay Mascioni. Mascioni sued Miller. What was the judgment? [Mascioni v. I. B. Miller, Inc., 261 N.Y. 1, 184 N.E. 473 (1933)]

8. Beck & Pauli Lithographing Company agreed in a contract with Colorado Milling & Elevator Company to furnish 10,000 business cards and 5,000 checks, letterheads, noteheads, billheads, and envelopes bearing Colorado Milling's logo. Beck was to design and deliver these items to Colorado Milling by the end of the year. Beck failed to tender or deliver the items contracted for until six or eight days after the expiration of the year. Colorado Milling refused to accept them and refused to pay any part of the contract price. Was Colorado Milling justified in doing this? [Beck and Pauli Lithographing Co. v. Colorado Milling and Elevator Co., 52 F. 700 (10th Cir. 1892)]

9. Nicholson hired Howard Construction Company to build a building for use as a bridal salon. At the time, Nicholson had arranged that Honey's International would be the tenant. Once built, the building would be suitable only for a bridal salon. After Nicholson and Howard had entered into their contract but before construction had begun, Honey's International went bankrupt. Nicholson thereafter refused to pay Howard to go through with the contract since Nicholson's intended tenant was no longer in existence. Howard sues Nicholson for breach of contract. Can Howard recover? [Howard v. Nicholson, 556 S.W.2d 477 (Mo.App.1977)]

10. The city of Fort Lauderdale hired La Gasse Pool Company to renovate a swimming pool owned and operated by the city. When La Gasse was about three-quarters finished, the pool was vandalized. The damage to the pool required La Gasse to redo part of its work. Thereafter, La Gasse completed the renovation project. Who should pay for the extra work caused by the vandalism? [La Gasse Pool Constr. Co. v. Fort Lauderdale, 288 So.2d 273 (Fla.App.1974)]

CHAPTER 15

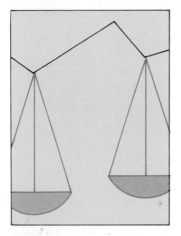

CONTRACTS
Breach of Contract and Remedies

Whenever a party fails to perform part or all of the duties under a contract, that party is in *breach of contract*. Breach of contract is the failure to perform what a party is under an absolute duty to perform.[1] Once a party fails to perform or performs inadequately, the other party— the nonbreaching party—can choose one or more of several remedies. A *remedy* is the relief provided for an innocent party when the other party has breached the contract. It is the means employed to enforce a right or redress an injury. Strictly speaking, the "remedy" is not a part of a lawsuit, but the result thereof, the object for which the lawsuit is presented and the end to which all litigation is directed. The most common remedies available to a nonbreaching party include:

1. damages.
2. rescission and restitution.
3. specific performance.
4. reformation.

DAMAGES

A breach of any contract entitles the nonbreaching party to sue for money damages. *Damages* are designed to compensate the nonbreaching party for the loss of the bargain. When a party loses the benefit of the bargain or contract, the breaching party must make up this loss to the nonbreaching party. Often, courts say that innocent parties are to be placed in the position they would have occupied had the contract been fully performed.[2]

---

1. Restatement, Second, Contracts, Section 235(2).

2. Restatement, Second, Contracts, Section 347, and UCC 1-106(1).

Types of Damages

There are four broad categories of damages that will be discussed in this chapter. They are:

1. Compensatory.
2. Consequential.
3. Nominal.
4. Punitive.

Compensatory Damages Damages compensating the nonbreaching party for the *loss* of the bargain are known as **compensatory damages.** These damages compensate the injured party only for injuries actually sustained and proved to have arisen directly from the contract. They simply replace the loss caused by the wrong or injury. In a breach of contract, compensatory damages are usually the only damages recoverable. To illustrate: Wilcox contracts to perform certain services exclusively for Hernandez during the month of March for $2,000. Hernandez cancels the contract and is in breach. Wilcox is able to find another job during the month of March, but can only earn $500. He can sue Hernandez for breach and recover $1,500 as compensatory damages.

The measurement of compensatory damages varies by type of contract. Certain types of contracts deserve special mention. They are contracts for the sale of goods, land contracts, and construction contracts.

Sale of Goods In a contract for the sale of goods, the usual measure of compensatory damages is an amount equal to the difference between the contract price and the market price.[3] Suppose Chrysler Corporation contracts to buy ten model UTS 400 computer terminals from Sperry Rand Corporation for $8,000 apiece. If Sperry Rand fails to deliver the ten terminals, and the current market price of the terminals is $8,150, Chrysler's measure of damages in this case is $1,500 (ten times $150).

Sale of Land The measure of damages in a contract for the sale of land is ordinarily the same as the measure in contracts for the sale of goods—that is, the difference between the contract price and the market price of the land. The majority of states follow this rule regardless of whether it is the buyer or the seller who breaches the contract. A minority of states, however, follow a different rule when the seller breaches the contract and the breach is not deliberate.[4] In such a case, these states allow the prospective purchaser to recover any down payment plus any expenses incurred (such as fees for title searches, attorneys, and escrows). This minority rule effectively places purchasers in the position they occupied prior to the sale.

Construction Contracts The measure of damages in a building or construction contract varies depending upon which party breaches and at what stage the breach occurs. The owner can breach at three different stages of the construction:

1. Before performance begins.
2. During performance.
3. After performance is complete.

If the owner breaches *before performance begins,* the contractor can recover only the profits that would have been made on the contract (that is, the total contract price less the cost of materials and labor). To illustrate: Goodyear Tire & Rubber Co. wants to build an international research center at its industrial and film products plant in Craigavon, Northern Ireland. Goodyear makes a contract for the 54,000-square-foot center with your corporation. The contract price is $5 million, and your company plans to spend $4.3 million in materials and labor. However, before construction begins, Goodyear's president calls you and unequivocally repudiates the contract. Your measure of damages is $700,000.

---

3. At the time and place where the goods were to be delivered or tendered. See UCC 2-708 and UCC 2-713.

4. A deliberate breach includes the vendor's failure to convey the land because the market price has gone up. A nondeliberate breach includes the vendor's failure to convey the land because an unknown easement rendered title unmarketable. See Chapter 53.

If the owner breaches *after performance begins*, the contractor can recover the profits plus the costs incurred in partially constructing the building. Assume you begin work on the research center, but after you spend $1.2 million, Goodyear throws your crews off the land and refuses to allow any more construction to go on. Your measure of damages is $1.9 million ($700,000 of lost profit plus $1.2 million in costs).

If the owner breaches *after the construction is complete*, the contractor can recover the entire contract price.[5] Assume you are able to complete the research center, but Goodyear breaches the contract by refusing to pay. Your measure of damages is $5 million (the full contract price).

When the *construction contractor breaches the contract* by stopping halfway through the project, the measure of damages is the cost of completion. If the contractor substantially performs, the courts may use the cost of completion formula, but only if there is no substantial economic waste in requiring completion.[6] If the contractor finishes late, the measure of damages will be the *loss of use*. As examples, assume three situations:

1. The builder of a house quits working after the foundation is built.
2. The builder of a house completes the construction, but the paneling is one-quarter-inch thick instead of five-sixteenths-inch thick.
3. The builder completes the house one week late.

In situation 1, the measure of damages equals the cost of getting another builder to complete the house. In situation 2, the cost to complete the house includes the cost of tearing out the walls and installing the thicker paneling. This additional cost is economic waste and a needless expense (which the owner probably would not incur anyway), so the courts will usually give the owner the difference between the value of the house as it is and the value of the house if it had been completed as promised. If the house is worth $2,000 less because of the thinner paneling, that will be the amount of damages recoverable. In situation 3, the measure of damages is the cost incurred by the owner to live elsewhere for a week and any other costs incident to the delay.

Often, the party suing for compensatory damages has failed to perform completely his or her part of the bargain. Faced with this situation in the following case, two courts arrived at the same figure for damages but used different theories. The trial court used the theory of *substantial performance*; the appellate court insisted that the proper action was *quantum meruit* (recovery of fair value). In either event, a contractor who did not live up to the requirements of his contract was not entitled to full payment of the contract price.

---

5. Actually, this is true for most contracts; the nonbreaching party is normally owed the contract profit plus the cost of performance.
6. Economic waste occurs when the cost of additional resources to finish the project exceeds any conceivable value placed on the additional work done. For example, if a contractor discovers that it will cost $10,000 to move a large coral rock eleven inches as specified in the contract, and the change in the rock's position will alter the appearance of the project only a trifle, full completion will involve an economic waste.

BACKGROUND AND FACTS   *Armstead Masonry Company brought this action against Roper (and Reynolds), the defendants, to collect $535.25 damages for nonpayment of an oral contract whereby Roper agreed to pay Armstead to do some brick veneer work on Roper's house. The record showed that the parties entered into this oral contract, and Armstead expressly promised to use new brick matching as closely as possible the color and appearance of the existing brick on Roper's house. Armstead failed to use brick that conformed reasonably to Roper's existing brick work, although Armstead's veneer work was sound in all other respects.*

REYNOLDS v.
ARMSTEAD
Supreme Court of Colorado,
1968.
166 Colo. 372, 443 P.2d 990.

Since work was completed, Armstead was entitled to a certain amount of payment on the contract. However, the trial court assessed Roper's damages at $267.63 and awarded Armstead $267.62—the contract price of $535.25 less damages of $267.63.

MOORE, Chief Justice.

* * * *

This court has repeatedly held that a contractor may recover the agreed price for substantial performance of his contract, subject to a deduction for damages for the contractor's failure to adhere to the contract in minor details.

The question presented here, however, is whether as a matter of law Armstead substantially performed his contract with Roper, and therefore became entitled to a recovery on the contract. Our authorities judiciously decline to state a formula determining with mathematical certainty what constitutes substantial performance, but instead rely upon the application of general principles. Thus, in Morris v. Hokosona, supra, we stated:

"* * * substantial performance permitting a recovery on the contract means an attempt in good faith to strictly and fully perform and is not satisfied unless there has been only slight or inadvertent omissions or departures which have not affected the value of the structure and which are capable of remedy and for which the employer may be compensated by a reduction of the contract price."

* * * "Substantial compliance with reference to contracts, means that although the conditions of the contract have been deviated from in trifling particulars not materially detracting from the benefit the other party would derive from a literal performance, he has received substantially the benefit he expected, and is, therefore, bound to pay."

* * * *

In the instant case the trial court, in legal effect, found that there had not been a substantial compliance with the terms of the contract, and that to the extent of fifty per cent of the contract price there was a failure to perform. Armstead's failure to install brick which reasonably matched the existing veneer damaged the appearance of Roper's house to the extent of half the value of the contract. The parties entered into their agreement with the acknowledged intent that Armstead's brickwork should be aesthetically, as well as functionally, acceptable. Consequently, we hold that as a matter of law Armstead's breach was material and cannot be deemed a "slight and trivial defect" "not materially detracting from the benefit the other party would derive from a literal performance."

Armstead's failure to substantially perform his contract deprived him of the right to recover under the "theory" of express contract.

* * * *

Upon a "theory" of quantum meruit the plaintiff, under the evidence, was entitled to the judgment entered by the trial court.

JUDGMENT AND REMEDY   *The trial court's judgment was affirmed. Armstead was entitled to collect for the work he did, but his failure to perform in compliance with the terms of his agreement with Roper resulted in a substantial reduction in the amount of money he could collect from Roper.*

Consequential (Special) Damages Damages resulting from a party's breach of contract are called *consequential damages*. They differ from compensatory damages in that they are caused by special circumstances beyond the contract itself. They flow only from the consequences or results of a breach.

For example, if a seller fails to deliver goods with knowledge that a buyer is planning to resell these goods *immediately*, consequential damages will be awarded for the loss of profit from the planned resale. The buyer will also recover compensatory damages for the difference between the contract price and the market price of the goods.

In order to recover consequential damages, the breaching party must know (or have reason to know) that special circumstances will cause the nonbreaching party to suffer an additional loss. The rationale here is to give the nonbreaching party the whole benefit of the bargain, provided the breaching party knew of the special circumstances when the contract was made.

For example, Leed contracts to have a specific part shipped to her—one that she desperately needs to repair her printing press. In contracting with the shipper who is to return the part, Leed tells the shipper that she must receive it by Monday or she will not be able to print her paper and will lose $750. If the shipper is late, Leed can recover the consequential damages caused by the delay (that is, the $750 in lost profits).

Likewise, when a bank wrongfully dishonors a check, the drawer of the check (customer of the bank) may recover consequential damages (such as those resulting from slander of credit or reputation) if he or she is arrested or prosecuted.[7] Another example of consequential damages is when an ice company fails to deliver ice to keep a butcher's meat cold. The ice company can be held liable for meat spoilage if it does not deliver the ice on time.

A leading case on the necessity of giving notice of "consequential" circumstances is *Hadley v. Baxendale*, decided in 1854. The case involved a broken crankshaft used in a mill operation. In the mid-1800s, it was very common for large mills, such as the one the plaintiffs operated, to have more than one crankshaft in case the main one broke and had to be repaired, as it did in this case. Also, in those days it was common knowledge that flour mills had spares. It is against this background that the parties argued whether or not the damages resulting from lost profits while the crankshaft was out for repair were "too remote" to be recoverable.

---

7. Weaver v. Bank of America, 59 Cal.2d 428, 30 Cal.Rptr. 4, 380 P.2d 644 (1963). A checking account is a contractual arrangement. See UCC 4-402.

BACKGROUND AND FACTS *The plaintiffs ran a flour mill in Gloucester. The crankshaft attached to the steam engine broke, causing the mill to shut down. The shaft had to be sent to a foundry located in Greenwich so that the new shaft could be made to fit the other parts of the engine. The defendants were common carriers, who transported the shaft from Gloucester to Greenwich. The plaintiffs claimed that they had informed the defendants that the mill was stopped and that the shaft must be sent immediately. The freight charges were collected in advance, and the defendants promised to deliver the shaft the following day. They did not do so, however. As a consequence, the mill was closed for several days. The plaintiffs sued to recover their lost profits during that time. The defendants contended that the loss of profits was "too remote." The court held for the plaintiffs, and the jury was allowed to take into consideration the lost profits.*

HADLEY v. BAXENDALE
9 Exch. 341, 156 Eng.Rep. 145, 1854.

ALDERSON, B.

*   *   *   *

We think that there ought to be a new trial in this case; but, in so doing, we deem it to be expedient and necessary to state explicitly the rule which the Judge, at the next trial, ought, in our opinion, to direct the jury to be governed by when they estimate the damages.

*   *   *   *

Now we think the proper rule in such a case as the present is this:—Where two parties have made a contract which one of them has broken, the damages which the other party ought to receive in respect of such breach of contract should be such as may fairly and reasonably be considered either arising naturally, i.e., according to the usual course of things, from such breach of contract itself, or such as may reasonably be supposed to have been in the contemplation of both parties, at the time they made the contract, as the probable result of the breach of it. Now, if the special circumstances under which the contract was actually made were communicated by the plaintiffs to the defendants, and thus known to both parties, the damages resulting from the breach of such a contract, which they would reasonably contemplate, would be the amount of injury which would ordinarily follow from a breach of contract under these special circumstances so known and communicated. But, on the other hand, if these special circumstances were wholly unknown to the party breaking the contract, he, at the most, could only be supposed to have had in his contemplation the amount of injury which would arise generally, and in the great multitude of cases not affected by any special circumstances, from such a breach of contract. For, had the special circumstances been known, the parties might have specially provided for the breach of contract by special terms as to the damages in that case; and of this advantage it would be very unjust to deprive them. Now the above principles are those by which we think the jury ought to be guided in estimating the damages arising out of any breach of contract.

*   *   *.   *

Now, in the present case, if we are to apply the principles above laid down, we find that the only circumstances here communicated by the plaintiffs to the defendants at the time the contract was made, were, that the article to be carried was the broken shaft of a mill, and that the plaintiffs were the millers of that mill. But how do these circumstances show reasonably that the profits of the mill must be stopped by an unreasonable delay in the delivery of the broken shaft by the carrier to the third person? Suppose the plaintiffs had another shaft in their possession put up or putting up at the time, and that they only wished to send back the broken shaft to the engineer who made it; it is clear that this would be quite consistent with the above circumstances, and yet the unreasonable delay in the delivery would have no effect upon the intermediate profits of the mill. Or, again, suppose that, at the time of the delivery to the carrier, the machinery of the mill had been in other respects defective, then, also, the same results would follow. Here it is true that the shaft was actually sent back to serve as a model for a new one, and that the want of a new one was the only cause of the stoppage of the mill, and that the loss of profits really arose from not sending down the new shaft in proper time, and that this arose from the delay in delivering the broken one to serve as a model. But it is obvious that, in the great multitude of cases of millers sending off broken shafts to third persons by a carrier under ordinary circumstances, such consequences would not, in all probability, have occurred; and these special circumstances were here never communicated by the plaintiffs to the defendants. It follows, therefore, that the loss of profits here cannot reasonably be considered such a consequence of the breach of contract as could have been fairly and reasonably contemplated by both the parties when they made this contract.

The Court of Exchequer ordered a new trial. According to the court, the special circumstances that caused the loss of profits had never been sufficiently communicated by the plaintiffs to the defendants. The plaintiffs would have to have given express notice of these circumstances in order to collect consequential damages.

JUDGMENT AND REMEDY

In awarding damages, compensation is given only for those injuries that the defendant could reasonably have foreseen as a probable result of the usual course of events following a breach. If the injury complained of is outside the usual and foreseeable cause of events, it must be shown specifically that the defendant had reason to know the facts and foresee the injury.

In this case, the plaintiff claimed that he gave express notice to the carrier's clerk that the shaft was needed immediately because "the mill was stopped." Today this would be considered adequate notice. At the time that the case was decided, however, notice to the clerk of the common carrier was not considered to be notice to the common carrier.

COMMENTS

Punitive Damages Punitive, or exemplary, damages are generally not recoverable in a breach of contract action. Punitive damages are designed to punish a guilty party and to make an example of the party in order to deter similar conduct in the future. Such damages have no legitimate place in contract law since they are, in essence, penalties, and a breach of contract is not unlawful in a criminal or societal sense. A contract is simply a civil relationship between the parties. The law may compensate one party for the loss of bargain, no more and no less.

In a few situations a person's actions can cause both a breach of contract and a tort. For example, the parties can establish by contract a certain reasonable standard or duty of care. Failure to live up to that standard is a breach of contract, and the act itself may constitute negligence.

A careful review of Chapter 3, dealing with torts, will indicate that some intentional torts could also be tied to a breach of the terms of the contract. In these cases it is possible for the non-

breaching party to recover punitive damages for the commission of the tort in addition to compensatory and consequential damages for breach of contract.

Nominal Damages Nominal damages have been defined as those that recognize only a technical injury where no true damages have been suffered. In other words, when no financial loss is involved because of a breach of contract, the court may award nominal damages to the innocent party. Nominal damage awards are often trifling, such as a dollar, but they do establish that the defendant acted wrongfully. For example, suppose that Jackson contracts to buy potatoes from Stanley at 50 cents a pound. Stanley breaches the contract and does not deliver the potatoes. In the meantime, the price of potatoes has fallen. Jackson is able to buy them in the open market at half the price he contracted for with Stanley. He is clearly better off because of Stanley's breach. Thus, in a breach of contract suit, Jackson may be awarded only nominal damages for the technical injury he sustained, because no monetary loss was involved.

Mitigation of Damages

In most situations, when a breach of contract occurs, the innocent injured party is held to a duty to mitigate, or reduce, the damages that he or she suffers. Whatever duty is owed depends on the nature of the contract. For example, some states require the lessor to use reasonable means to find a new tenant if the lessee abandons the premises and fails to pay rent. If an acceptable tenant becomes available, the landlord is required to lease the premises to this tenant to mitigate the damages recoverable from the former lessee. The former lessee is still liable for the difference between the amount of the rent under the original lease and the rent received from the new lessee. If the lessor had not taken reasonable means necessary to find a new tenant, presumably a court could reduce the award made by the amount of rent he or she could have received had such reasonable means been taken.

In the majority of states, wrongfully terminated employees owe the duty to mitigate damages suffered by their employers' breach. The damages they receive are their salaries less the incomes they would have received in similar jobs that they could have obtained by reasonable means. It is the employer's burden to prove the existence of such a job and to prove that the employee could have been hired. (The employee is, of course, under no duty to take a job that is not of the same type and rank.)

Liquidated Damages versus Penalties

A **liquidated damages** provision in a contract specifies a certain amount to be paid in the event of a future default or breach of contract. For example, a provision requiring a construction contractor to pay $100 for every day he is late in completing the construction is a liquidated damages provision. Liquidated damages differ from penalties. **Penalties** specify a certain amount to be paid in the event of a default or breach of contract *and are designed to penalize* the breach-

ing party. Liquidated damage provisions are enforceable; penalty provisions are not.

In order to determine if a particular provision is for liquidated damages or for a penalty, two questions must be answered. First, were the damages difficult to estimate when the contract was entered into? Second, was the amount set as damages a reasonable estimate and not excessive? [8] If both answers are yes, the provision will be enforced. If either answer is no, the provision will not be enforced.

In a construction contract, it is difficult to estimate the amount of damages caused by a delay in completing construction, so liquidated damage clauses are often used. On the other hand, the damage caused by failure to pay rent is easily estimated, so in leases, liquidated damage clauses are normally not enforced.[9]

The amount that a nonbreaching party can recover from a breach of contract depends upon whether the provision is held to be a liquidated damage provision or a penalty. If the liquidated damage provision is determined to be enforceable, the nonbreaching party can recover the amount specified in the provision. If the provision is determined to be a penalty, it is not enforceable (no matter what it is called in the contract). Therefore, the nonbreaching party can recover only compensatory and consequential damages actually proved.

RESCISSION AND RESTITUTION

Rescission is essentially an action to undo, or cancel, a contract—to return the contracting parties to the positions they occupied prior to the transaction.[10] Where fraud, a mistake, duress, or failure of consideration are present, rescission is

---

8. Restatement, Second, Contracts, Section 356(1).

9. But compare with K. W. Clarkson, R. L. Miller, and T. J. Muris, "Liquidated Damages vs. Penalty: Sense or Nonsense?" *Wisconsin Law Review*, Spring 1978.

10. The rescission discussed here refers to *unilateral* rescission, where only one party wants to undo the contract. In mutual rescission, both parties agree to undo the contract. Mutual rescission discharges the contract; unilateral rescission is generally available as a remedy for breach of contract.

available.[11] The failure of one party to perform entitles the other party to rescind the contract. The rescinding party must give prompt notice to the breaching party. In order to rescind a contract, both parties must make **restitution** to each other. If the goods or property received can be restored *in specie*—that is, if the actual goods or property can be returned—they must be. If the goods or property have been consumed, restitution must be made in an equivalent amount of money.

Essentially, restitution refers to the recapture of a benefit conferred on the defendant through which the defendant has been unjustly enriched. It is what the court had to grapple with in the following case, which concerns the promotion of a singer and composer of country and western music.

---

11.   States often have statutes allowing consumers to rescind unilaterally contracts made at home with door-to-door salespersons. Rescission is allowed within three days for any reason or for no reason at all. See, for example, California Civil Code, § 1689.5.

BACKGROUND AND FACTS   *Linda Osteen was a singer and composer of country and western music. Her father made an oral agreement with Johnson, the defendant, to promote Linda. Johnson was to advertise her through various mailings for a period of one year and to arrange and furnish the facilities necessary for her to record several songs. At a minimum, Johnson was to prepare two records from the songs recorded and to press and mail copies of one of the records to disc jockeys throughout the country.*

At trial, Johnson proved that he did arrange for several recording sessions, at which Linda recorded four songs. One thousand copies of a record of two of the songs were then pressed; 340 of them were mailed to disc jockeys, and 200 were mailed to Linda's parents. Various mailings were made to advertise Linda, including flyers sent to disc jockeys throughout the country. Her name was advertised in trade magazines. At issue was the fact that Johnson wrongfully caused the name of another party to appear on the label of the record as co-author of a song that had been written solely by Linda. The trial court, finding that Johnson had substantially performed the agreement, awarded only $1 in nominal damages in the judgment in favor of Linda's father. The reviewing court now takes up the question of the right of restitution.

OSTEEN v. JOHNSON

Colorado Court of Appeals, 1970.

473 P.2d 184.

DUFFORD, Judge.

*   *   *   *

1.   Right of Restitution

Although plaintiffs' reasons are not clearly defined, they argue here that the award of damages is inadequate, and that the trial court erred in concluding that the defendant had substantially performed the agreement. However, no evidence was presented during the trial of the matter upon which an award of other than nominal damages could be based. In our opinion, the remedy which plaintiffs proved and upon which they can rely is that of restitution. See 5 A. Corbin, Contracts § 996. This remedy is available where there has been a contract breach of vital importance, variously defined as a substantial breach or a breach which goes to the essence of the contract. See 5 A. Corbin, Contracts § 1104, where the author writes:

"In the case of a breach by non-performance, * * * the injured party's alternative remedy by way of restitution depends upon the extent of the non-performance by the defendant. The defendant's breach may be nothing but a failure to perform some minor part of his contractual duty. Such a minor non-performance is a breach of contract and an action for damages can be maintained. The injured party, however, can not maintain an action for restitution of what he has given the defendant unless the defendant's non-performance is so material that it is held to go to the 'essence' * * *. A minor breach by one party does not discharge the contractual duty of the other party; and the latter being still bound to perform as agreed can not be entitled to the restitution of payments already made by him or to the value of other part performances rendered." * * *

2. Breach of Contract

The essential question here then becomes whether any breach on the part of the defendant is substantial enough to justify the remedy of restitution. Plaintiffs argue that the defendant breached the contract in the following ways: First, the defendant did not promote Linda for a period of one year as agreed; secondly, the defendant wrongfully caused the name of another party to appear on the label as co-author of the song which had been composed solely by Linda; and thirdly, the defendant failed to press and mail out copies of the second record as agreed.

The first argument is not supported by the record. Plaintiffs brought the action within the one-year period for which the contract was to run. There was no evidence that during this period the defendant had not continued to promote Linda through the use of mailings and advertisements. Quite obviously the mere fact that the one-year period had not ended prior to the commencement of the action does not justify the conclusion that the defendant had breached the agreement. Plaintiffs' second argument overlooks the testimony offered on behalf of the defendant that listing the other party as co-author of the song would make it more likely that the record would be played by disc jockeys.

The plaintiffs' third argument does, however, have merit. It is clear from the record and the findings of the trial court that the first record had met with some success. It is also clear that copies of the second record were neither pressed nor mailed out. In our opinion the failure of the defendant to press and mail out copies of the second record after the first had achieved some success constituted a substantial breach of the contract and, therefore, justifies the remedy of restitution. Both parties agree that the essence of their contract was to publicize Linda as a singer of western songs and to make her name and talent known to the public. Defendant admitted and asserted that the primary method of achieving this end was to have records pressed and mailed to disc jockeys * * *.

3. Determining Damages

It is clear that the defendant did partially perform the contract and, under applicable law, should be allowed compensation for the reasonable value of his services. See 5 A. Corbin, Contracts § 1114, where the author writes:

"[A]ll courts are in agreement that restitution by the defendant will not be enforced unless the plaintiff returns in some way what he has received as a part performance by the defendant."

The trial court's judgment was reversed, and the case was remanded with directions that a new trial be held to determine the issue of the amount to which the plaintiffs were entitled by way of restitution. That amount was to be the original $2,500 paid by Linda's father less the reasonable value of the services that Johnson performed on behalf of the plaintiffs.

JUDGMENT AND REMEDY

SPECIFIC PERFORMANCE

The remedy of *specific performance* calls for the performance of the act promised in the contract. This remedy is quite attractive to the nonbreaching party since it provides the exact bargain promised in the contract. It also avoids some of the problems inherent in a suit for money damages. (Specific performance is a rare remedy, only available in unique situations.)

There are three basic reasons for the attractiveness of the remedy of specific performance. First, the nonbreaching party need not worry about collecting the judgment.[12] Second, the nonbreaching party need not look around for another contract. Third, the actual performance is more valuable than the money damages.

Although the equitable remedy of specific performance is often preferable to other remedies, specific performance will not be granted unless the party's legal remedy (money damages) is inadequate. For example, contracts for the sale of goods rarely qualify for specific performance. The legal remedy, money damages, will ordinarily be adequate in such situations because substantially identical goods can be bought or sold in the market. If the goods are unique, however, a court of equity will decree specific performance. For example, paintings, sculptures, or rare books or coins are so unique that money damages will not enable a buyer to obtain substantially identical substitutes in the market.

Sale of Land

Specific performance is granted to a buyer in a contract for the sale of land. The legal remedy for breach of a land sales contract is inadequate because every piece of land is considered to be unique. Money damages will not compensate a buyer adequately because the same land in the same location obviously cannot be obtained elsewhere.

Contracts for Personal Services

Personal service contracts require one party to work personally for another party. Courts of equity uniformly refuse to grant specific performance of personal service contracts. If the contract is not deemed personal, the remedy at law may be adequate if substantially identical service is available from other persons (for example, if you hire someone to mow your lawn). In most personal services contracts, courts are very hesitant to order specific performance by a party because public policy strongly discourages involuntary servitude.[13] Moreover, the courts do not want to have to monitor a continuing service contract.

Therefore, specific performance will be denied if it is impossible or impractical to enforce

---

12. Courts enter judgments as final dispositions of cases. The judgment, of course, must be collected. Collection, however, poses problems. For example, the judgment debtor may be broke or have only a very small net worth.

13. The Thirteenth Amendment to the United States Constitution prohibits involuntary servitude, but *negative injunctions* (that is, prohibiting rather than ordering certain conduct) are possible. Thus, whereas you may not be able to compel a person to perform under a personal service contract, you may be able to restrain that person from engaging in similar contracts for a period of time.

performance. Courts do not want to become entangled in personal service transactions and will not decree specific performance if supervision will be prolonged or difficult. For this reason, courts refuse to order specific performance that requires the exercise of personal judgment or talent.

If you contract with a brain surgeon to perform brain surgery on you, and the surgeon refuses to perform, the court would not compel (and you certainly would not want) the surgeon to perform under these circumstances. There is no way the court can assure meaningful performance in such a situation.[14] In the following case, the question of specific performance in the sale of goods is at issue. The court had to determine whether a legal remedy was sufficient or whether the equitable relief of performance was required.

---

14. Similarly, courts often refuse to order specific performance of construction contracts because they are not set up to operate as construction supervisors or engineers.

CAMPBELL SOUP CO. v. WENTZ

United States Court of Appeals, Third Circuit, 1948.
172 F.2d 80.

BACKGROUND AND FACTS *Campbell Soup Company, the plaintiff, entered into a contract for the sale of carrots with farmers who grew and produced the particular variety of carrots used in the company's canned goods. Under the terms of the contract, a farmer was required to cut, clean, and bag the produce. When the carrots were delivered, the company determined if they conformed to company specifications. Another provision in the contract excused the company from accepting carrots under certain circumstances but retained the right to prohibit the sale of those carrots elsewhere unless the company agreed. The carrots involved in this case were Chantenay red carrots.*

Campbell Soup made a written contract with the defendant, Wentz, a Pennsylvania farmer. Wentz was to deliver all the Chantenay red carrots he grew on his fifteen-acre farm that year for $30 per ton. During the year, the market price of the carrots rose sharply to about $90 per ton, and Chantenay red carrots became virtually unobtainable. The defendant told a Campbell representative that he would not deliver his carrots at the contract price. Then, he sold the rest of his carrots to a neighboring farmer. Campbell bought about half the shipment from the neighboring farmer and then realized that it was purchasing its own "contract carrots." Campbell refused to purchase any more and sought an injunction against both the defendant and the neighboring farmer to prohibit them from selling any more of the contract carrots to others. In addition, Campbell sought to compel specific performance of the contract against Wentz. The trial court denied the equitable relief requested by Campbell.

GOODRICH, Circuit Judge.

*   *   *   *

The trial court denied equitable relief. We agree with the result reached, but on a different ground from that relied upon by the District Court.

*   *   *   *

We think that on the question of adequacy of the legal remedy the case is one appropriate for specific performance. It was expressly found that at the time of the trial it was "virtually impossible to obtain Chantenay carrots in the open market." This Chantenay carrot is one which the plaintiff uses in large quantities, furnishing the seed to the growers with whom it makes contracts. It was not claimed that in nutritive value it is any better than other types of carrots. Its blunt shape makes it easier to handle in processing. And its color and texture differ from other varieties. The color is brighter than other carrots. The trial court found that the plaintiff failed to establish what proportion of its carrots is used for the production of soup stock and what proportion is used as identifiable physical ingredients in its soups. We do not think lack of proof on that point is material. It did appear that the plaintiff uses carrots in fifteen of its twenty-one soups. It also appeared that it uses these Chantenay carrots diced in some of them and that the appearance is uniform. The preservation of uniformity in appearance in a food article marketed throughout the country and sold under the manufacturer's name is a matter of considerable commercial significance and one which is properly considered in determining whether a substitute ingredient is just as good as the original.

*   *   *   *

Judged by the general standards applicable to determining the adequacy of the legal remedy we think that on this point the case is a proper one for equitable relief. There is considerable authority, old and new, showing liberality in the granting of an equitable remedy. We see no reason why a court should be reluctant to grant specific relief when it can be given without supervision of the court or other time-consuming processes against one who has deliberately broken his agreement. Here the goods of the special type contracted for were unavailable on the open market, the plaintiff had contracted for them long ahead in anticipation of its needs, and had built up a general reputation for its products as part of which reputation uniform appearance was important. We think if this were all that was involved in the case specific performance should have been granted.

*   *   *   *

We are not suggesting that the contract is illegal. Nor are we suggesting any excuse for the grower in this case who has deliberately broken an agreement entered into with Campbell. We do think, however, that a party who has offered and succeeded in getting an agreement as tough as this one is, should not come to a chancellor and ask court help in the enforcement of its terms. That equity does not enforce unconscionable bargains is too well established to require elaborate citation.

Campbell Soup Company's petition for an injunction and for specific performance, denied by the district court was upheld by the appellate court but on different grounds. The court recognized that if the contract had not been unconscionable (see Chapter 10), specific performance would have been available to the company. The unique nature of the product involved meant that there was no adequate legal remedy. **JUDGMENT AND REMEDY**

REFORMATION

Reformation is an equitable remedy used when the parties have *imperfectly* expressed their agreement in writing. Reformation allows the contract to be rewritten to reflect the parties' true intentions. It applies most often where fraud or mutual mistake (for example, a clerical error) are present. If Gilge contracts to buy a certain piece of land from Cavendish, but both parties are mistaken about what piece of land is to be sold, a mutual mistake has occurred. Accordingly, a court of equity could reform the contract so that Gilge and Cavendish can agree on which piece of land is being sold.

Two other examples deserve mention. The first involves two parties who have made a binding oral contract. They further agree to reduce the oral contract to writing, but in doing so, they make an error in stating the terms. Universally, the courts will allow into evidence the correct terms of the oral contract, thereby reforming the written contract.

The second example deals with written agreements (covenants) not to compete (see Chapter 10, Legality). If the covenant is for a valid and legitimate purpose (such as the sale of a business) but the area or time restraints of the covenant are unreasonable, some courts will reform the restraints by making them reasonable and will enforce the entire contract as reformed. Other courts, however, will throw the entire restrictive covenant out as illegal.

Before a court will grant reformation, one or both of the parties must present clear and convincing evidence of either fraud or mistake.

RECOVERY BASED ON QUASI-CONTRACT

As stated in Chapter 6, a quasi-contract is not a true contract but an equitable theory *imposed* on the parties to obtain justice and to prevent unjust enrichment. Hence, a quasi-contract becomes an equitable basis for equitable relief. The legal obligation, or duty, arises because the law *implies* a promise to pay for benefits received by a party. Generally, when one party has conferred a benefit on another party, justice requires the party receiving the benefit to pay the reasonable value of it. The party receiving the benefit should not be unjustly enriched at the other party's expense.

In order to recover on a quasi-contract, the party seeking recovery must show that:

1. A benefit has been conferred on the other party.

2. The benefit was conferred with the expectation of being paid.
3. The party seeking recovery did not act as a volunteer in conferring the benefit.
4. Retention of the benefit without being paid would result in unjust enrichment of the party receiving the benefit.

Quasi-contractual recovery is useful where one party has *partially* performed under a contract that is unenforceable. It can be used as an alternative to a suit for damages and will allow the party to recover the reasonable value of the partial performance.

For example, suppose Abrams contracts to build two oil derricks for the Texas Gulf Sulfur Co. The derricks are to be built over a period of three years, but the parties do not make a written contract. Enforcement of the contract will therefore be barred by the Statute of Frauds.[15] If Abrams completes one derrick before Texas Gulf Sulfur tells him that the contract is unenforceable, Abrams can sue in quasi-contract because: First, a benefit has been conferred on Texas Gulf Sulfur, since one oil derrick has been built. Second, Abrams built the derrick (conferred the benefit) expecting to be paid. Third, Abrams did not volunteer to build the derrick; he built it under an unenforceable oral contract. Fourth, allowing Texas Gulf Sulfur to retain the derrick would enrich the company unjustly. Therefore, Abrams should be able to recover the reasonable value of the oil derrick (under the theory of *quantum meruit*—"as much as he deserved"). This is ordinarily equal to the fair market value of the derrick.

ELECTION OF REMEDIES

In many cases, a nonbreaching party will have several remedies available, but they may be inconsistent with each other. Therefore, the party must choose which remedy to pursue. For example, a person who buys a fraudulently rep-

15. Contracts which by their terms cannot be performed within one year must be in writing to be enforceable. See Chapter 12.

resented car can sue either to cancel (rescind) the sales contract or to recover damages. Obviously, these remedies are inconsistent. An action to rescind undoes the contract; an action for damages affirms it.

The purpose of the *election of remedies* doctrine is to prevent double recovery. Suppose McCarthy agrees to sell his land to Tally. Then McCarthy changes his mind and repudiates the contract. Tally can sue for compensatory damages or for specific performance. If she receives damages caused by the breach, she should not be able to get specific performance of the sales contract, since failure to deliver possession of the land was the cause of the injury for which she received damages. If Tally could seek compensatory damages in addition to specific performance, she would recover twice for the same breach of contract. The doctrine of election of remedies requires Tally to choose the remedy she wants, and it eliminates any possibility of double recovery.

Unfortunately, the doctrine has been applied in a rigid and technical manner, leading to some harsh results.[16] Therefore, the doctrine of election of remedies has been eliminated in contracts for the sale of goods. The UCC expressly rejects the doctrine. (See UCC 2-703 and UCC 2-711.) Remedies under the UCC are essentially cumulative in nature and include all the available remedies for breach of contract.

WAIVER OF BREACH

Under certain circumstances, a nonbreaching party may be willing to accept a defective performance of the contract. This knowing relinquishment of a legal right (that is, the right to require satisfactory and full performance) is called a **waiver**.[17] When a waiver of a breach of contract occurs, the party waiving the breach cannot take any later action on the theory that the contract was broken. In effect, the waiver erases the past breach; the contract continues as if the breach had never existed. Of course, the waiver of breach of contract extends only to the matter waived and not to the whole contract. Businesspersons often waive breaches of contract by the other party in order to get whatever benefit possible out of the contract.

For example, a seller contracts with a buyer to deliver to the buyer 10,000 tons of coal on or before November 1. The contract calls for the buyer's payment to be made by November 10 for coal delivered. Because of a coal miners' strike, coal is scarce. The seller breaches the contract by not tendering delivery until November 5. The buyer may well be advised to waive the seller's breach, accept delivery of the coal, and pay as contracted.

Ordinarily, the waiver by a contracting party will not operate to waive subsequent, additional, or future breaches of contract. This is always true when the subsequent breaches are unrelated to the first breach. For example, an owner who waives the right to sue for late completion of a stage of construction does not waive the right to sue for failure to comply with engineering specifications.

A waiver will be extended to subsequent defective performance if a reasonable person would conclude that similar defective performance in the future would be acceptable. Therefore, a *pattern of conduct* that waives a number of successive breaches will operate as a continued waiver. In order to change this result, the nonbreaching party should give notice to the breaching party that full performance will be required in the future.

To illustrate: Suppose the construction contract above was to be completed in six stages, each two months apart, spanning a period of one

---

16. For example, in a Wisconsin case, Carpenter was fraudulently induced to buy a piece of land for $100. He spent $140 moving onto the land and then discovered the fraud. Instead of suing for damages, Carpenter sued to rescind the contract. The court denied recovery of the $140 because the seller, Mason, did not receive the $140 and was therefore not required to reimburse Carpenter for his moving expenses. So Carpenter suffered a net loss of $140 on the transaction. If Carpenter had sued for damages, he could have recovered the $100 and the $140. See Carpenter v. Mason, 181 Wis. 114, 193 N.W. 973 (1923).

---

17. Restatement, Second, Contracts, Sections 84, 246, and 247. The Restatement uses the term *promise* rather than *waiver*.

year. The question is whether the waiver of the right to object to lateness of performance of stage 1 will operate as a waiver of the time requirements of performance for stages 2 through 6. If only stage 1's time requirements have been waived, the waiver will not extend to the other five stages. However, if the first five stages were all late (and the right to object to the lateness was always waived), the waivers will extend to stage 6 unless the owner has given proper notice that future performance is to be on time.

The party who has rendered defective or less than full performance remains liable for the damages caused by the breach of contract. In effect, the waiver operates to keep the contract going. The waiver prevents the nonbreaching party from calling the contract to an end or rescinding the contract. The contract continues, but the nonbreaching party can recover damages caused by defective or less than full performance.

CONTRACT PROVISIONS LIMITING REMEDIES

A contract can include provisions stating that no damages can be recovered for certain *types* of breaches or that damages must be limited to a *maximum amount*. In addition, the contract can provide that the only remedy for breach is replacement, repair, or refund of the purchase price. Provisions stating that no damages can be recovered are called *exculpatory clauses*. (See Chapter 10). Provisions that affect the availability of certain remedies are called *limitation of liability clauses*.

Because of the importance of these clauses and their uses, some discussion and illustrative situations will follow. It is important to keep in mind that the following is an overview, not an exhaustive explanation or a complete coverage of this topic.

Mutual Assent of Limitation Required

Initially, a court must determine if the provision has been made a part of the contract by offer and acceptance. In order for a term or provision to become part of a contract, both parties must consent to it. Therefore, courts will analyze whether the provision was noticed by the parties—whether, for example, the provision was in fine print or on the back of a lengthy contract. If either party did not know about the provision, it will not be a part of the contract and will not be enforced.[18]

For example, motorists often park their cars in lots and receive a small ticket stub that excludes liability for damages to cars parked in the lot. If a reasonable person would have noticed such an exculpatory clause, it will be enforced. If the clause is not conspicuous and a reasonable person would not have noticed it, the clause will not be enforced, and the motorist can sue for damage caused to his or her car.[19]

Type of Breach Covered

Once it has been determined that the provision or clause is part of the contract, the analysis must focus on the type of breach that is exculpated. For example, a provision excluding liability for fraudulent or intentional injury will not be enforced. Likewise, a clause excluding liability for illegal acts or violations of law will not be enforced. On the other hand, a clause excluding liability for negligence may be enforced in appropriate cases. When an exculpatory clause for negligence is contained in a contract made between parties with roughly equal bargaining positions, the clause usually will be enforced.

For example, assume Delta Airways buys six DC-9s from Douglas Aircraft. In the contract for sale, a clause excludes liability for errors in design and construction of the aircraft. The clause will be upheld because both parties are large corporations with roughly equal bargaining positions. The equality of bargaining power assures that the exculpatory clause was not dictated by one of the parties and forced upon the other.

---

18. See, for example, the Magnuson-Moss Warranty Act discussion in Chapter 20.
19. See California State Auto v. Barrett Garages, Inc., 257 Cal.App.2d 84, 64 Cal.Rptr. 699(1967).

Limited Remedies—UCC

Under the UCC, in a contract for the sale of goods, remedies can be limited, but rules different from those just discussed apply. If only a certain remedy is desired, the contract must state that the remedy is exclusive. Suppose you buy an automobile, and the sales contract limits your remedy to repair or replacement of defective parts. Under the UCC, the sales contract must state that the *sole* and *exclusive* remedy available to the buyer is repair and/or replacement of the defective parts.[20] If the contract states that the remedy is exclusive, then the specified remedy will be the only one ordinarily available to the buyer (provided the contract is not unconscionable).

When circumstances cause an exclusive remedy to fail in its essential purpose, then it will not be exclusive. [See UCC 2-719(2).] In the preceding example, if your car breaks down several times, and the dealer is unable to fix or replace the defective parts, the exclusive remedy fails in its essential purpose. Then all the other remedies under the UCC become available.

Under the UCC, a sales contract may also limit or exclude consequential damages, provided the limitation is not *unconscionable*.[21] Where the buyer is purchasing consumer goods, the limitation of liability for personal injury is *prima facie* unconscionable and will not normally be enforced. Where the buyer is purchasing goods for commercial use, the limitation of liability for personal injury is not necessarily unconscionable.

Suppose that you have purchased a small printing press for your teenage son. It is a present to him for his birthday. He will be using it to print leaflets and pamphlets for his social club. The contract for purchase states that consequential damages, arising from personal injury as a result of a defect in the small printing press, are excluded. This exclusion or limitation of liability is *prima facie* unconscionable (illegal). It will not be enforced. On the other hand, if you buy a printing press for your business, the limitation will not necessarily be unconscionable and may be enforceable.

QUESTIONS AND CASE PROBLEMS

1. Discuss fully under which of the following breach of contract situations specific performance would be an appropriate remedy:

(a) Thompson contracts to sell her house and lot to Cousteau. Then upon finding another buyer willing to pay a higher purchase price, she refuses to deed the property to Cousteau.

(b) Amy contracts to sing and dance in Fred's nightclub for one month, beginning May 1. She then refuses to perform.

(c) Hoffman contracts to purchase a rare coin owned by Erikson, as Erikson is breaking up his coin collection. At the last minute, Erikson decides to keep his coin collection intact and refuses to deliver the coin to Hoffman.

(d) There are three shareholders of the ABC Corporation: Panozzo, who owns 48 percent of the stock; Chang, who owns another 48 percent; and Ryan, who owns 4 percent. Ryan contracts to sell her 4 percent to Chang. Later, Ryan refuses to transfer the shares to Chang.

2. Cohen contracts to sell his house and lot to Windsor for $100,000. The terms of the contract call for Windsor to put up 10 percent of the purchase price as "earnest money," a down payment. The terms further stipulate that should the buyer breach the contract, the earnest money would be treated as liquidated damages. Windsor puts up the earnest money, but because her expected financing of the $90,000 balance falls through, she breaches the contract. Two weeks later Cohen sells the house and lot to Ballard for $105,000. Windsor demands her $10,000 back, but Cohen refuses, claiming that Windsor's breach and contract terms entitle him to keep the "earnest money" payment. Discuss who is correct.

3. Ken owns and operates a famous candy store. He makes most of the candy sold in the store, and business is particularly heavy during the Christmas season. Ken contracts with Sweet Inc. to purchase 10,000 pounds of sugar to be delivered on or before November

---

20. UCC 2-719(1).

21. See Chapter 10 for discussion of unconscionability and UCC 2-719(3).

15. Ken has informed Sweet that this particular order is to be used for the Christmas season business. Because of production problems and change of transportation managers at Sweet, the sugar is not tendered to Ken until December 10, at which time Ken refuses it as being too late. Ken has been unable to purchase the quantity of sugar needed to meet the Christmas orders and has had to turn down numerous regular customers, some of whom have indicated that they will purchase candy elsewhere in the future. What sugar Ken has been able to purchase has cost him 10 cents per pound above the contracted price with Sweet. Ken sues Sweet for breach of contract, claiming as damages the higher price paid for sugar from others, lost profits from this year's lost Christmas sales, future lost profits from customers who have indicated that they will discontinue doing business with him, and punitive damages for failure to meet the contracted delivery date. Sweet claims Ken is limited to compensatory damages only. Discuss who is correct.

4. Wallechinsky purchases an automobile from Anderson Motors, paying $1,000 down and agreeing to pay off the balance in thirty-six monthly payments of $200 each. The terms of the agreement call for Wallechinsky to make each payment on or before the first of each month. During the first six months, Anderson receives the $200 payments before the first of each month. During the next six months, Wallechinsky's payments are never made until the fifth of each month. Anderson has accepted and cashed the payment check each time. When Wallechinsky tenders the thirteenth payment on the fifth of the next month, Anderson refuses to accept the check, claiming that Wallechinsky is in breach of contract and demands the entire balance owed. Wallechinsky claims that Anderson cannot hold her in breach. Discuss the result fully.

5. Putnam contracts to buy a new Oldsmobile from Old Century Motors, paying $2,000 down and agreeing to make twenty-four monthly payments of $350 each. He takes the car home and, after making one payment, learns that his Oldsmobile has a Chevrolet engine in it rather than the famous Olds Super V-8 engine. Old Century never informed Putnam of this fact. Putnam immediately notifies Old Century of his dissatisfaction and tenders back the car to Old Century. Old Century accepts the car and returns to Putnam the $2,000 down payment plus the one $350 payment. Two weeks later Putnam, without a car and angry, files a suit against Old Century, seeking damages for breach of warranty and fraud. Discuss the effect of Putnam's actions.

6. The Grady-Gould Watershed Improvement District contracted with Kellett Company to have twenty miles of ditches sprayed to remove vegetation. Kellett guaranteed a 95 percent kill rate. The contract required that the level of kill be determined by inspection of the ditches after notice to Kellett. Kellett completed spraying and was paid the full contract price. Grady-Gould subsequently had representatives of the Soil Conservation Service appraise the kill level. No notice of this inspection was given to Kellett. However, Kellett conducted its own inspection, determined that a 95 percent kill had not been achieved, and promised Grady-Gould that the area would be resprayed. Kellett never resprayed, and Grady-Gould subsequently sued. Kellett asserts by way of defense Grady-Gould's failure to give notice of inspection, as required by the contract, in order that Kellett's representative could be present at such inspection. Is this defense valid? [Grady-Gould Watershed Improvement Dist. v. Transamerica Ins. Co., 570 F.2d 720 (8th Cir. 1978)]

7. Ballard was working for Eldorado Tire Company. He was discharged and sued for breach of the employment contract. The trial court awarded damages to Ballard, and Eldorado Tire appealed. In the appeal, Eldorado claimed that the trial court failed to reduce Ballard's damages by the amount that he might have earned in other employment during the remainder of the breached contract. Eldorado Tire introduced as evidence the fact that there was an extremely low rate of unemployment for professional technicians and managers in the area. The implication was that Ballard had not taken advantage of the opportunity for mitigating damages. Was Eldorado correct? [Ballard v. Eldorado Tire Co., 512 F.2d 901 (5th Cir. 1975)]

8. Westinghouse entered into a contract with New Jersey Electric to manufacture and install a turbine generator for producing electricity. The contract price was over $10 million. The parties engaged in three years of negotiations and bargaining before they agreed on a suitable contract. The ultimate contract provided, among other things, that Westinghouse would not be liable for any injuries to the property belonging to the utility or to its customers or employees. Westinghouse warranted only that it would repair any defects in workmanship and materials appearing within one year of installation. After installation, part of New Jersey Electric's plant and several of its employees were injured because of a defect in the turbine. New Jersey Electric sued Westinghouse, claiming that Westinghouse was liable for the damages because the exculpatory provisions in the contract were unconscionable. What was the result? [Royal Indem. Company v. Westinghouse Elec. Corp., 385 F.Supp. 520 (D.C.N.Y.1974)]

9. Evergreen Amusement Corporation purchased a parcel of land for use as a drive-in movie theater. Evergreen contracted with Milstead to have the lot cleared and graded according to specifications that would make it adequate for a drive-in theater. Milstead was supposed to complete the work by June 1, and Evergreen planned to open the theater at about that time. However, Milstead did not finish clearing and grading the lot until the third week in August. Evergreen sued Milstead, claiming as damages the profits that it could have made on the drive-in theater had it been in operation. Are lost profits the proper measure of damages here? [Evergreen Amusement Corp. v. Milstead, 206 Md. 610, 112 A.2d 901 (1955)]

10. Kerr Steamship Company delivered to RCA a twenty-nine-word coded message to be sent to Kerr's agent in Manila. The message included instructions on loading cargo onto one of Kerr's vessels. Kerr's profits on the carriage of the cargo were to be about $6,600. RCA mislaid the coded message, and it was never sent. Kerr sued RCA for the $6,600 in profits that it lost because RCA never sent the message. Can Kerr recover? [Kerr Steamship Co. v. Radio Corp. of America, 245 N.Y. 284, 157 N.E. 140 (1927)]

FOCUS ON ETHICS

Contract Law and the Application of Ethics

Numerous areas of contract law lend themselves to ethical analysis. Certainly business people face ethical questions as they deal with the application of black-letter law. For example, courts usually do not examine the consideration for a contract in terms of whether or not it is equal to the value received in an economic exchange. A businessperson could knowingly arrange an exchange in which consideration is greatly less than value received and successfully argue in court that the consideration was legally good and sufficient. Nonetheless, that person still might be violating the ethics of the society.

CONTRACT LAW AND CHANGE

Much of contract law has changed to coincide with changing ideas of fairness. Consider several examples that are, of course, not exhaustive of ethical concerns in contract law.

Impossibility
The doctrine of impossibility is based to some extent on the ethical question of whether one party should suffer economic loss when it is impossible to perform a contract. The rule that one is "bound by his or her contracts" is clearly negated when the doctrine of impossibility of performance is applied to relieve a contracting party of liability for failure to perform.

Mistake
The notion that mistake in contracts should release the contracting parties from their obligations has gained strength as the ethics of society have changed. If one were to peruse the cases of several hundred years ago, one would find much less acceptance of mistake as an excuse to avoid a contractual obligation than exists today.

Sales
Contract law has also changed to meet the demands of merchants. Society places special rules in the sale of goods when the seller or buyer, or both, are merchants. Thus, certain sections of Article 2 of the Uniform Commercial Code apply only when one or both parties are merchants. See, for example, UCC 2-314(1) and UCC 2-205.

Contractual Capacity
Chapter 9 pointed out that in order for a contract to be valid, the individuals entering into it must have contractual capacity.

Consequently, except under certain circumstances, minors can avoid contractual obligations. The question of whether or not a minor should be held responsible for his or her acts is clearly an ethical one. Our set of shared beliefs currently dictates that minors should not be held responsible for contracts except under special circumstances.

For example, in most states minors are allowed to avoid contracts for the sale of nonnecessaries. Merely by making a good faith attempt to return the purchased goods, a minor can receive a full refund of any monies paid. An ethical issue arises, however, when the minor has diminished the value of the goods prior to returning them or is unable to return them. Because it does not seem "fair" to most people that the merchant should suffer because of the minor's actions, some states require that the merchant be compensated for any reduction in value of the goods.

The Equitable Remedy of Quasi-Contract
Quasi-contracts, or contracts implied-in-law, arise to establish justice and fairness rather than from mutual agreement between

parties. They are imposed on the parties in order to prevent unjust enrichment. The doctrine against unjust enrichment holds that individuals should not be allowed to profit or enrich themselves inequitably at the expense of others. This is a fundamental belief in our society. Clearly, imposing contract liability on an unconsenting party in order to prevent a result perceived by society as unfair (unjust enrichment) is an action inspired by ethical considerations rather than by the existing body of contract law.

ETHICS VERSUS EFFICIENCY

Contracts can be analyzed in terms of economic efficiency, Economic efficiency exists when, *ex ante*, no change in the current use of resources will result in the material welfare of the society increasing. It can be argued that the law of contracts leads to economic efficiency because it establishes a set of rules that businesspersons can rely on when they engage in commercial transactions. When such persons know what the outcome of court cases will be, they try to minimize the amount of their resources going into litigation.

Much litigation about contracts has as its end result a reduction in the wealth of one party and an increase in the wealth of the other. Consider the following example: An individual enters into a contract with a merchant. For a specified sum of money, the merchant is to provide a certain tool. The tool is to be used for a specified activity. The purchaser of the tool uses it for another activity and in so doing permanently injures himself. He sues the merchant, which is an extremely large company. If the trier of fact rules in favor of the

merchant, the wealth of the injured plaintiff will be decreased; if the trier of fact rules in favor of the plaintiff, the plaintiff's wealth will be increased. From an ethical point of view, one might argue that since the merchant can more easily "afford" to lose wealth (in payment to the injured plaintiff for the injuries), the trier of fact should rule in favor of the plaintiff.

However, from an economic efficiency point of view, such a decision would lead to less efficiency. After all, the contract between the two parties was for a tool to be used in a specified activity. The plaintiff did not use the tool in that activity. If, because of injury from improper use of the tool, the plaintiff is awarded damages, a signal will be generated to other individuals in society that they will be compensated for any injuries sustained by careless or negligent use of such tools. This will lead to greater carelessness by consumers in using the product. Economic efficiency will suffer.

The results of recent court cases involving personal injuries indicate a greater concern in our society today about proper compensation for injuries (an ethical concern), than about economic efficiency no matter how careless the plaintiff.

CONTRACT LAW, THE INDIVIDUAL, AND BIG BUSINESS

According to one school of legal and economic thought, contract law as interpreted in this unit does not mesh with reality. This school holds that the individual as a consumer no longer contracts in the traditional sense with multi-billion-dollar companies such as Exxon and General Motors. Consequently, it is suggested that

the traditional contract notions of offer, acceptance, consideration, and so on, may not be the most appropriate way to analyze consumer purchases. Indeed, some argue that consumers today buy on the merchant's terms or not at all. If this is correct, then ethical considerations no longer play as important a part in understanding common law contract doctrine as they did a hundred years ago.

Another approach argues that no matter how big the firm, it must please the consumer in order to maximize profits. That is, the ultimate "director" of the firm is the consumer, who still has the choice of buying a smaller quantity or, none at all, of whatever products are offered in the marketplace. And in those markets where more than one firm exists, competition forces the firms to offer the consumer products at a price and quality that will maximize profits. To some extent, the ethical issues here are hidden by the results of the producers' notion of profit maximization. Because most producers make the highest profits by inducing repeat sales, they have a profit incentive to treat their clients ethically—in a way that pleases them.

Since both schools of thought are convinced that they are right, the debate may continue indefinitely.

DISCUSSION QUESTIONS

1. Is the nature of a company's business an ethical concern? That is, is it ethical for a company to produce and market goods of varying quality and to place the burden of purchasing goods of the desired quality on the consumer?
2. U.S. automobile manufacturers have recently been attempting

to produce higher-quality cars. Did this result from an ethical concern of the companies? If so, why did this concern not exist before? Or is the attempt to produce higher-quality cars merely a result of Japanese competition, and will such an attempt cease when and if the Japanese competition disappears?

3. To what extent should a company offer advantageous prices and pursue a high standard of honesty by refraining from advertising only its loss leader articles?

UNIT III

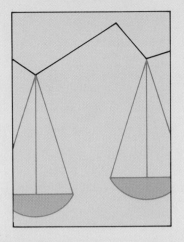

PERSONAL PROPERTY AND BAILMENTS

CHAPTER 16

Personal Property

Property is the legally protected rights and interests a person has in anything with an ascertainable value that is subject to ownership. Property would have little value (and the word would have little meaning) if the law did not define the right to use it, to sell or dispose of it, and to prevent trespassing upon it. In the United States, the ownership of property receives unique protection under the law. The Bill of Rights states that "no person shall . . . (by any Act of Congress) be deprived of life, liberty, or property, without due process of law; nor shall private property be taken for public use, without just compensation." The Fourteenth Amendment provides that "no State shall . . . deprive any person of life, liberty, or property, without due process of law."

THE NATURE
OF PERSONAL PROPERTY

Property can be divided into real property and personal property. *Real property* (sometimes

called "realty" or "real estate") means the land and everything permanently attached to the land. Where structures are permanently attached to the land, then everything meant to be attached permanently to the structures is also realty. Everything else is *personal property* ("personalty").

Personal property and real property differ significantly, so the law has developed different sets of rules to deal with their acquisition and disposition. For example, a lease of real property conveys a *property interest* from the landlord (lessor) to the tenant (lessee). A lease of personal property merely transfers a *possessory interest*, creating a bailment (to be discussed in the next chapter).

There are occasions when it is difficult to determine whether the items transferred are realty or personalty. This can be particularly important when dealing with the sale of the item. For example, two such issues deal with *fixtures* and contracts for the sale of *minerals* (including oil, gas, and the like), *structures, crops,* and *timber* to be removed from the realty. Because of these ambiguous areas, special rules have evolved recently to clarify and even change past rules (for example, the UCC with respect to timber—UCC 2–107[2]).

A **fixture** is personal property attached to the realty or used in such a manner that it becomes a part of the realty. Fixtures pass as part of the realty, unless the seller expressly excludes them from the sale. Until the personal property becomes a fixture, it remains personal property and does not pass as part of the realty.

For example, whether a dishwasher is part of the realty as a fixture or is a piece of personal property owned by a seller can be important in the sale of a house. If the dishwasher is built into a kitchen counter, it probably will be considered a fixture and pass with the title of the house from the seller to the buyer. If it is not so attached (that is, if it is portable), it remains personalty and will not pass with the title of the house.

Personal property can be tangible or intangible. *Tangible personal property*, like a TV set, heavy construction equipment, or a car, has physical substance. *Intangible personal property* represents some set of rights and duties, but it has no real physical existence. Stocks and bonds are intangible personal property.

Attorneys sometimes refer to all personal property as **chattel,** a more comprehensive term than *goods* because it includes living as well as inanimate property. Often, instead of saying personal property, the law will refer to goods as chattel.

THE EXPANDING NATURE OF PERSONAL PROPERTY

In a dynamic society, the concept of personal property must expand to take account of new types of ownership rights. For example, gas, water, and telephone services are now considered personal property for the purpose of criminal prosecution when they are stolen or used without payment. Federal and state statutes protect against the copying of musical compositions. It is a crime now to engage in "bootlegging"—illegal copying for resale—of records and

tapes. The theft of computer programs is usually considered a theft of personal property.

PROPERTY RIGHTS AND OWNERSHIP TITLE

Property can be viewed as a bundle of rights. These rights include:

1. Possession.
2. Disposition—sale, gift, rental, lease, and so on.

There are two principal ways for more than one person to hold this bundle at one time:

1. Tenancy in common.
2. Joint tenancy with right of survivorship, commonly called joint tenancy.

Fee Simple

When a person or persons holds the entire bundle of rights, they are said to be the owner or owners in **fee simple.** They have the right to possession of the property and to dispose of the property as they choose.

Tenancy in Common

Tenancy in common is co-ownership in which two or more persons own an undivided fractional interest in the property, but upon one tenant's death, that interest passes to his or her heirs. For example, Reband and Charnock own a rare stamp collection as tenants in common. Should Reband die before Charnock, one-half of the stamp collection would become the property of Reband's heirs. If Reband sold her interest to French before she died, French and Charnock would be co-owners as tenants in common. If French died, his interest in the personal property would pass to his heirs, and they in turn would own the property with Charnock as tenants in common.

Joint Tenancy with Right of Survivorship

In a **joint tenancy with right of survivorship,** each party owns an undivided fractional interest in the personal property. Joint tenancy with right of survivorship can be terminated any time before the joint tenant's death by gift or by sale. But if no termination occurs, then upon the death of a joint tenant, his or her interest passes to the remaining joint tenants, not to the heirs of the deceased joint tenant. In the preceding example, if Reband dies before Charnock, the entire collection becomes the property of Charnock. Reband's heirs receive absolutely no interest in the collection. If, prior to Reband's death, she sells her interest to French, French and Charnock become co-owners. Reband's sale, however, terminates the joint tenancy with the right of survivorship, and French and Charnock become owners as tenants in common.

Less Common Ways of Holding Property

There are two less common ways of holding property. One is tenancy by the entireties, and the other is community property.

Tenancy by the Entireties   The form of co-ownership called tenancy by the entireties is less common today than it used to be. Typically, it is created by a conveyance (transfer) to a husband and wife. It is distinguished from joint tenancy with right of survivorship by the inability of either spouse to transfer separately his or her interest during his or her life. In states where statutes give the wife the right to convey her property, this form of concurrent ownership has been effectively abolished. A divorce will terminate tenancy by the entireties. A partitioning of the property will create separate interests in it.

Community Property   The form of ownership called community property applies only to Arizona, California, Idaho, Louisiana, Nevada, New Mexico, Texas, and Washington. Each spouse technically owns an *undivided* one-half interest in the property. This type of ownership applies to most personal property acquired by the husband and/or wife during the course of marriage.

It generally does not apply to property acquired prior to the marriage.

ACQUIRING OWNERSHIP OF PERSONAL PROPERTY

Possession

A particularly interesting example of acquiring ownership by possession is the capture of wild animals. Wild animals belong to no one in their natural state, and the first person to take possession of a wild animal normally owns it. The killing of a wild animal amounts to assuming ownership of it. Merely being in hot pursuit does not give title, however. There are two exceptions to this basic rule. First, any wild animals captured by a trespasser are the property of the landowner, not the trespasser. Second, if wild animals are captured or killed in violation of wild game statutes, the captor does not obtain title to the animals. Other illustrations of acquiring ownership by possession are presented later in this chapter.

Purchase

Purchase is one of the most common means of acquiring and transferring ownership of personal property. The purchase or sale of personal property (called goods) is covered in depth in Chapters 18 to 23, on the Uniform Commercial Code.

Production

Production—the fruits of labor—is another means of acquiring ownership of personal property. Nearly everyone in the United States today is involved in some sort of production. For example, writers, inventors, and manufacturers all produce personal property and thereby acquire title to it. (In some situations—for example, where researchers are hired for that purpose—the producer does not own what is produced.)

Gifts

A **gift** is another fairly common means of both acquiring and transferring ownership of real and personal property. A gift is essentially a *voluntary* transfer of property ownership. It is not supported by legally sufficient consideration since the very essence of a gift is giving without consideration. A gift must be transferred or delivered in the present rather than in the future. For example, suppose that your aunt tells you she is going to give you a new Mercedes-Benz for your next birthday. This is simply a *promise* to make a gift. It is not enforceable unless the Mercedes-Benz is delivered to the donee.

The Requirements of an Effective Gift: There are three requirements of an effective gift:

1. Delivery.
2. Donative intent.
3. Acceptance by the donee.

Delivery   Delivery is obvious in most cases, but some objects cannot be relinquished physically. Then the question of delivery depends upon the surrounding circumstances. When the physical object cannot be delivered, a symbolic or **constructive delivery** will be sufficient. Constructive delivery does not confer actual possession of the object in question. It is a general term for all those acts that the law holds to be equivalent to acts of real delivery. Suppose that you want to make a gift of various old rare coins that you have stored in a safety deposit box. You certainly cannot deliver the box itself to the donee, and you do not want to take the coins out of the bank. Instead, you can simply deliver the key to the box to your donee. This is symbolic, or constructive, delivery of the contents of the box.

Delivery of intangible personal property must be accomplished by symbolic or constructive delivery. For example, ownership interests in firms are often represented by stock certificates, and delivery of the certificate entitles the holder to dividends. Other examples of intangible personal property that must be constructively delivered include insurance policies, contracts, promissory notes, and chattel mortgages.

An effective delivery also requires giving up *complete dominion and control* (ownership rights) over the subject matter of the gift. The outcome of disputes often turns on the retaining or relinquishing of control over the subject matter of the gift. The Internal Revenue Service scrutinizes transactions between relatives when one relative has given away income-producing property. A relative who does not relinquish complete control over a piece of property will have to pay taxes on the income from that property. Under the tax laws, it may be illegal to assign or give away income while retaining control over the property that produces the income (unless a special trust is set up).

Delivery can be accomplished by means of a third person. The third person may be the agent of the donor or the donee. If the person is the agent of the donor, the gift is effective when the agent delivers to the donee. If, on the other hand, the third person is the agent of the donee, the gift is effective when the donor delivers to the donee's agent.[1] Where there is doubt as to whose agent the third party is, he or she is generally presumed to be the agent of the donor. Naturally, no delivery is necessary if the gift is already in the hands of the donee. All that is necessary to complete the gift in such a case is the required intent and acceptance by the donee.

Donative Intent   Donative intent is determined from the language of the donor and the surrounding circumstances. For example, when a gift is challenged in court, the court may look at the relationship between the parties and the size of the gift in relation to the donor's other assets. A gift to an archenemy will be viewed with suspicion. Likewise, when people give away a large portion of their assets, the courts will scrutinize the transaction to determine the mental capacity of the donor and whether there is any fraud or duress.

In the following case, the Supreme Court of New York looks at the validity of a gift of certificates of stock and the question of constructive, or symbolic, delivery.

---

1.   Bickford v. Mattocks, 95 Me. 547, 50 A. 894 (1901).

MATTER OF COHN

Supreme Court of New York, 1919.

187 App.Div. 392, 176 N.Y.S. 225.

BACKGROUND AND FACTS *On September 20, 1911, his wife's birthday, Leopold Cohn wrote out and delivered to his wife, in the presence of his entire family, the following paper:*

"West End, N.J., Sept. 20, 1911.

"I give this day to my wife, Sara K. Cohn, as a present for her (46) forty-sixth birthday (500) five hundred shares of American Sumatra Tobacco Company common stock.

"Leopold Cohn."

That instrument was delivered to Sara. Six days later, Leopold died. At that time, Leopold owned 7,213 shares of the common stock of the company in question, but the stock was in the name and possession of his firm, A. Cohn & Co. The certificates were deposited in a New York City safe deposit box in the name of and belonging to the firm. Prior to his death, Leopold was negotiating with the partners in the firm—his brother and his nephew—to enter into a new partnership, to which he would contribute some of the shares as an asset. Indeed, two days before his death, Leopold asked his attorney to speed up completion of the new partnership agreement because he wanted to get the Sumatra stock belonging to him so that he could in fact deliver it to his wife.

SHEARN, Judge.

*   *   *   *

There being no rights of creditors involved, no suggestion of fraud, the intention to make the birthday gift being conclusively established, the gift being evidenced by an instrument of gift executed and delivered to the donee on her birthday, and ever since retained by her, and the circumstances surrounding the making of the gift affording a reasonable and satisfactory excuse for not making actual delivery of the certificates at the time the gift was made, there was in my opinion a valid and effectual gift of the certificates mentioned in the instrument of gift.

There is no doubt that it has been held in a long line of cases in this State that delivery of the thing given is, as a general rule, one of the essential elements to constitute a valid gift. *   *   *

As the rule requiring delivery is clearly subject to exceptions, in order to apply it correctly in varying circumstances resort should be had to the reason for the rule. Under the civil law delivery was not requisite to a valid gift, but it was made a requisite by the common law as a matter of public policy, to prevent mistake and imposition. The necessity of delivery where gifts resting in parol are asserted against the estates of decedents is obvious; but it is equally plain that there is no such impelling necessity when the gift is established by the execution and delivery of an instrument of gift. An examination of a large number of cases in this State discloses the significant facts that (1) in every case where the gift was not sustained, the gift rested upon parol evidence; and (2) in every case of a gift evidenced by the delivery of an instrument of gift, the gift has been sustained. *   *   * It is interesting to note that in Matson v. Abbey, 70 Hun 475, 24 N.Y.S. 284, 53 N.Y.St.Rep. 794; affd., as to the gift, 141 N.Y. 179, 36 N.E. 11, sustaining a gift evidenced by an instrument of assignment without delivery of the property assigned, the court quotes with approval the statement of the English law in Irons v. Smallpiece, 2 Barn. & Ald. 551, 552, made by Abbott, C. J.: "I am of opinion that by the law of England, in order to transfer property by gift, there must either be a deed or instrument of gift, or there must be an actual delivery of the thing to the donee." Based upon decisions in numerous other jurisdictions, it is stated in 20 Cyc. 1197 that: "The general rule is that a gift of property evidenced by a written instrument executed by the donor is valid without a manual delivery of the property." I am inclined to think that this is a broader statement than the New York cases would justify * * * for it does not assume a delivery of the instrument of gift. * * * It seems to me beyond serious question that the delivery of the instrument of gift in the instant case constituted a good symbolical delivery. * * *

Therefore, applying the rule of delivery in the light of the reason which gave birth to it, and finding here no possibility of fraud or imposition, and no doubt whatever concerning the intention of the donor, and finding full support in * * * precedent * * * it is my opinion that there was a good constructive or symbolical delivery, consisting of the delivery of the instrument of gift, and that the gift should be sustained. * * *

Sara Cohn received her 500 shares of American Sumatra Tobacco Company common stock.

JUDGMENT AND REMEDY

Symbolic delivery is a substitute for delivery of the chattel only where delivery of the chattel is impossible or extremely inconvenient. A dissenting opinion in the above case stressed that there was no physical impossibility of actual delivery of the stock in question.

COMMENTS

Acceptance The final requirement of a valid gift is acceptance by the donee. This rarely presents any problems since most donees readily accept their gifts. The courts generally assume acceptance unless shown otherwise.

***Inter Vivos* Gifts and *Causa Mortis* Gifts** **Inter vivos gifts** are made during one's lifetime. **Causa mortis gifts** are made in contemplation of imminent death. *Causa mortis* gifts do not become absolute until the donor dies from the illness or disease that was contemplated. The donee must survive to take the gift, and the donor must not have revoked the gift prior to death. A *causa mortis gift* is revocable at any time up to the death of the donor and is automatically revoked if the donor recovers.

Suppose Stevens is to be operated on for a cancerous tumor. Before the operation, he delivers an envelope to a close business associate. The envelope contains a letter saying "I realize my days are numbered and I want to give you this check for $1,000,000 in the event of my death from this operation." It also contains a check for $1,000,000 which the business associate cashes. The surgeon begins the operation and decides not to remove the tumor. Stevens recovers from the operation but dies from a heart attack several months later. If Stevens's personal representative tries to recover the $1,000,000, she will succeed. The *causa mortis gift* is automatically revoked if the donor recovers. The *specific event* that was contemplated in making the gift was death from a particular operation. Since Stevens's death was not the result of a cancerous tumor, the gift is revoked and the $1,000,000 passes to Stevens's personal representative when Stevens dies.[2]

WILL OR INHERITANCE

Ownership of property may be transferred by will or by inheritance under state statutes. These transfers, called bequests, devices, or inheritances, are dealt with in Chapter 56.

ACCESSION

Accession means "adding on" to something. It occurs when someone adds value to a piece of personal property by either labor or materials. Generally, there is no dispute about who owns the property after accession has occurred, especially when the accession is accomplished with the owner's consent.

For example, a Corvette customizing specialist comes to Smith's house. Smith has all the materials necessary. The customizing specialist uses them to add a unique bumper to Smith's Corvette. Smith simply pays the customizer for the value of the labor in improving the property, obviously retaining title to the property.

Two situations in which ownership can be in issue after occurrence of an accession are:

1. Where a party has wrongfully caused the accession.
2. Where the materials added or labor expended greatly increase the value of the property or change the identity of the property.

Some general rules can be applied when either or both situations occur.

If the accession was caused wrongfully (without the owner's consent) and in bad faith, the courts would generally favor the owner over the improver even if the value of the property was increased substantially. In addition, many

courts would deny the improver (wrongdoer) any compensation for the value added; for example, a car thief who put new tires on the stolen car would obviously not be compensated for the value of the new tires.

If the accession is performed in good faith, however, even without the owner's consent, ownership of the improved item most often depends on the actual increase in value of the property by the accession or change of identity of the property. The greater the increase, the more likely ownership will pass to the improver. Obviously, when this occurs, the improver must compensate the original owner for the value of the property prior to the accession. If the increase in value is not sufficient to pass ownership to the improver, most courts require the owner to compensate the improver for the value added.

To illustrate: Suppose Angelo is walking in a large country field and discovers a huge stone lying near a fence that is shaped approximately like the Lone Ranger's horse, Silver. Angelo comes back for twenty-seven weeks and transforms the stone into an exact replica of Silver. Angelo's artist friends are very impressed and convince him to move the stone horse to a gallery, where it is valued at $50,000. The owner of the field where Angelo found the stone now wants to claim title to it. Normally, the courts will give Angelo title to the stone because the changes he made caused it to greatly increase in value and the accession was performed in good faith. But Angelo will have to pay the owner of the field for the reasonable value of the stone before it was altered.

CONFUSION

When the personal property of two persons becomes intermingled, this is called **confusion.** Confusion is defined as the commingling of goods such that one person's personal property cannot be distinguished from another's. It frequently occurs when the goods are fungible.[3] *Fungible goods are goods of which each particle is identical with*

---

2. Brind v. International Trust Co., 66 Colo. 60, 179 P. 148 (1919).

3. See UCC 1-201(17).

every other particle, such as grain and oil. For example, if two farmers put their number 2 grade winter wheat in the same silo, confusion will occur. If the confusion of goods is caused by a person who wrongfully and willfully mixes goods with those of another in order to render them indistinguishable, the innocent party acquires title to the total.

This rule does not apply when confusion occurs by:

1. Agreement.
2. Honest mistake.
3. The act of some third party.

When any of these three events occurs, the owners all share ownership equally as tenants in common. Suppose that you enter into a cooperative arrangement with six other farmers in your local community of Midway, Iowa. Each fall everyone harvests the same amount of number 2 yellow corn. The corn is stored in silos that are held by the cooperative. Each farmer owns one-sixth of the total corn in the silos. If anything happens to the corn, each will bear the loss in equal proportions of one-sixth.

Often, though, each owner will not have an interest equal to the other owners. In such a case, the owners must keep careful records of their respective proportions. If a dispute over ownership or loss arises, the courts will presume that everyone has an equal interest or proportion of the goods. So you must be prepared to prove that you own more or less than an equal part.

Suppose you own two-thirds of the corn in the Midway Co-op silos above. Further assume that the silos are partially damaged by a tornado and thunderstorm. How much have you lost of your total if one-half of the corn is blown away by the storm? You have lost one-half of your two-thirds, or one-third. When corn is stored by several owners, each owning a different proportion of the total, any loss is suffered proportionally.

Confusion that results from intentional wrongdoing or negligent conduct creates a different problem when there is a loss by fire, theft, or destruction. The person responsible for the commingling must bear the entire loss if any of the goods are lost, stolen, or destroyed. However, if the wrongdoer can show that no injury occurred and can show the specific portion contributed to the whole, then the wrongdoer can recover that portion.

Suppose you are the vice-president in charge of purchasing for a salad oil company. You buy 10,000 gallons of high-grade salad oil and have it delivered to a field warehouse and company. The warehouse and company stores many grades of oil, and your oil is negligently mixed with a much lower grade of oil. The oil was worth $.64 per gallon before it was confused, but now it is worth only $.32 per gallon. Here you should be entitled to claim your 10,000 gallons of oil and sue the warehouse for $3,200 in damages caused by the negligent confusion. On the other hand, suppose the grades of oil were exactly the same but you contracted to have your oil stored in a separate bin? There may have been a technical breach of contract, but you will not recover any damages because there has been no injury.[4]

MISLAID, LOST, AND ABANDONED PROPERTY

Mislaid Property

Property that has been placed somewhere by the owner voluntarily and then inadvertently forgotten is **mislaid property.** Suppose you go to the theater and leave your gloves on the concession stand. The gloves are mislaid property, and the theater owner is entrusted with the duty of reasonable care for the goods. Whenever mislaid property is found, the finder does not obtain title or possession of the goods.[5] Instead, the owner of the place where the property was mislaid becomes the caretaker of the property because it is highly likely that the true owner will return.[6]

---

4. As a matter of commercial reality, very few, if any, warehouses contract for storage in separate facilities. If they did, many people would want separate facilities for fear of confusion. But, this would negate the savings in warehouse storage. Here we are really dealing with *fungible* goods.
5. The finder is an involuntary bailee. See Chapter 17.
6. He or she is a bailee with right of possession against all except the true owner. See Chapter 17.

Lost Property

Property that is *not* voluntarily left and forgotten is **lost property.** A finder of lost property can claim title to the property against the whole world, *except the true owner*. If the true owner demands that the lost property be returned, the finder must do so. In addition, when a third party attempts to take possession of lost property from a finder, the third party cannot assert that the title lies with yet another person.

Whenever a finder knows who the true owners of property are and fails to return it to them, that finder is guilty of a tort known as *conversion* (see Chapter 3). Finally, many states require the finder to make a reasonably diligent search to locate the true owner of lost property.

Suppose Arnolds works in a large library at night. In the courtyard on her way home, she finds a piece of gold jewelry that looks like it has several precious stones in it. Arnolds decides to take it to a jeweler to have it appraised. While pretending to weigh the jewelry, an employee of the jeweler removes several of the stones. If Arnolds brings an action to recover the stones from the jeweler, she will win because she found lost property and holds valid title against everyone *except the true owner*. Since the property was *lost* and not *mislaid*, the owner of the library is not the caretaker of the jewelry. Instead, Arnolds acquires title good against the whole world (except the true owner.)[7]

Many states have **estray statutes** to encourage and facilitate the return of property to its true owner and then to reward a finder for honesty if the property remains unclaimed. Such statutes provide an incentive for finders to report their discoveries by making it possible for them, after passage of a specified period of time, to acquire legal title to the property they have found. The statute usually requires the county clerk to advertise the property in an attempt to enhance the opportunity of the owner to recover what has been lost.

There are always some preliminary questions to be resolved before the estray statute can be employed. The item must be *lost property*, not merely mislaid or abandoned property. When the situation indicates that the property was probably lost and not mislaid or abandoned, as a matter of public policy, loss is presumed and the estray statute applies. Such a situation occurred in the following case.

---

7. See Armory v. Delamire, 1 Strange 505 (K.B. 1722). However, if Arnolds had found the jewelry during the course of her employment, her employer would be the involuntary bailee. Further, many courts now say that lost property recovered in a private place allows the owner of the place, *not* the finder, to become the bailee (even if the finder is not a trespasser).

PASET v. OLD ORCHARD BANK & TRUST CO.

Appellate Court of Illinois, First District, Third Division, 1978. 62 Ill.App.3d 534, 19 Ill.Dec. 389, 378 N.E.2d 1264.

BACKGROUND AND FACTS *A safety deposit box subscriber brought this action against a bank, seeking a declaratory judgment that the state estray statute applied to her finding $6,325 on a chair in the examination booth in the bank's safety deposit vault area. The money was not claimed within the statutory time period of one year. Hence, the plaintiff petitioned the court to grant her ownership of the money. The trial court entered an order refusing to determine ultimate ownership of the money.*

SIMON, Justice.

On May 8, 1974, the plaintiff, Bernice Paset, a safety deposit box subscriber at the defendant Old Orchard Bank (the bank), found $6,325 in currency on the seat of a chair in an examination booth in the safety deposit vault. The chair was partially under a table. The plaintiff notified officers of the bank and turned the money over to them. She then was told by bank officials that the bank would try to locate the owner, and that she could have the money, if the owner was not located within 1 year.

The bank wrote to everyone who had been in the safety deposit vault area either on the day of, or on the day preceding, the discovery, stating that some property had been found and inviting the customers to describe any property they might have lost. No one reported the loss of currency, and the money remained unclaimed a year after it had been found. However, when the plaintiff requested the money, the bank refused to deliver it to her, explaining that it was obligated to hold the currency for the owner.

*   *   *   *

The bank's position is that the estray statute is not applicable because the money was not lost in the sense the word "lost" is used in that statute. The bank contends that, under the common law, the money was mislaid by its owner rather than lost, and that the estray statute does not apply to mislaid property. In the alternative, the bank argues that the money was discovered not in a public place, but in a private area with access restricted to safety deposit box subscribers. The bank claims, therefore, that the money always was in its constructive possession or custody, either as owner of the premises or as bailee for an unknown and unidentified safety deposit box subscriber, and that property in someone's constructive possession or custody cannot be lost. As against the plaintiff, the bank claims to have the superior right to hold the money indefinitely, and in fact is required to do so until the true owner puts in his appearance.

*   *   *   *

The estray statute provides in [relevant part]:

"If any person or persons find any lost goods, money, bank notes, or other choses in action, of any description whatever, such person or persons shall inform the owner thereof, if known. *   *   * If the owner is unknown and if such property found is of value of $15 or upwards, the finder or finders shall, within 5 days after such finding as aforesaid, appear before some circuit judge residing in the county, and make affidavit of the description thereof, the time and place when and where the same was found, that no alteration has been made in the appearance thereof since the finding of the same, that the owner thereof is unknown to him and that he has not secreted, withheld or disposed of any part thereof. The judge shall enter an order stating the value of the property found as near as he can ascertain. A certified copy of such order and the affidavit of the finder shall, within 10 days after the order has been entered, be transmitted to the county clerk to be recorded in his estray book, and filed in his office.

"*   *   * If the value thereof exceeds the sum of $15, the county clerk, within 20 days after receiving the certified copy of the judge's order shall cause an advertisement to be set up on the court house door, and in 3 other of the most public places in the county, and also a notice thereof to be published for 3 weeks successively in some public newspaper printed in this state and if the owner of such goods, money, bank notes, or other choses in action does not appear and claim the same *   *   * within one year after the advertisement thereof as aforesaid, the ownership of such property shall vest in the finder."

*   *   *   *

Traditionally, the common law has treated lost and mislaid property differently for the purposes of determining ownership of property someone has found. Mislaid property is that which is intentionally put in a certain place and later forgotten; at common law a finder acquires no rights to mislaid property. The element of intentional deposit present in the case of mislaid property is absent in the case of lost property, for property is deemed lost when it is unintentionally separated from the dominion of its owner. The general rule is that the finder is entitled to possession of lost property against everyone except the true owner. We are not concerned in this case with abandoned property where the owner, intending to relinquish all rights to his property, leaves it free to be appropriated by any other person. Although at common law the finder is entitled to keep abandoned property, the plaintiff has not taken the position that the money here was abandoned.

* * * *

[W]e do not accept the bank's initial argument that the money was mislaid rather than lost. It is complete speculation to infer, as the bank urges, that the money was deliberately placed by its owner on the chair located partially under a table in the examining booth, and then forgotten. If the money was intentionally placed on the chair by someone who forgot where he left it, the bank's notice to safety deposit box subscribers should have alerted the owner. The failure of an owner to appear to claim the money in the interval since its discovery is affirmative evidence that the property was not mislaid.

Because the evidence, though ambiguous, tends to indicate that the money probably was not mislaid, and because neither party contends that the money was abandoned, we conclude that the ambiguity should, as a matter of public policy, be resolved in favor of the presumption that the money was lost. * * * Accordingly, we reject the bank's first contention that the money was mislaid and the estray statute irrelevant, and conclude that the money was "lost," and so encompassed by the Illinois estray statute.

We also reject the bank's alternative argument that the money, having been found in a place from which the general public was excluded, was always in the bank's constructive custody or possession, and therefore could not have been "lost," as that word is used in the estray statute.

* * * *

* * * The bank's record of its safety deposit box subscribers who visited the vault on the day of or the day preceding the plaintiff's discovery gave the bank the opportunity to search for the owner among this limited group. The bank also had sufficient time to contact any subscriber who had not been in his box since the date the plaintiff discovered the money. Consequently, in view of the opportunities the bank had to search out the owner of the money among this limited group, of the notice the bank gave to that group and of the plaintiff's undisputed compliance with the estray statute, vesting the ownership of the money in the finder is a more pragmatic and sensible solution than having the bank continue to hold the money indefinitely.

JUDGMENT AND REMEDY	*The appellate court decided that the estray statute should be applied and that the ownership of the money should be vested in the finder.*

Abandoned Property

Property that has been *discarded* by the true owner with *no intention* of claiming title to it is **abandoned property.** Someone who finds abandoned property acquires title to it, and such title is good against the whole world, *including the original owner.* The owner of lost property who eventually gives up any further attempt to find the lost property is frequently held to have abandoned the property.

To illustrate the concept of lost property becoming abandoned property, we will assume that Starr is driving with the windows down in her car. Somewhere along her traveled route, a valuable scarf blows out the window. Despite retracing her route, she cannot find the scarf. She finally decides that any further search is useless and proceeds to her destination 500 miles away. Starr makes no further attempt to find the scarf. Six months later, Frye, a hitchhiker, finds the scarf. Frye has acquired title, which is good even against Starr. (Of course, the same result would occur if Starr had deliberately discarded the scarf along the highway.)

If, however, a finder is trespassing and finds abandoned property, title does not become vested in the finder but vests with the owner of the land. This is also true of lost property. Suppose Callahan employs Allen and Billheimer to clean out a henhouse. Callahan has recently purchased a home that previously had changed hands a number of times. Allen and Billheimer find a tin can full of gold buried in a corner of the henhouse. The can is extremely old and rusty, suggesting that it has been buried there for quite some time. Callahan, the owner of the land, takes the coins from Allen and Billheimer and claims that they belong to her. Allen and Billheimer bring suit to recover the coins. Allen and Billheimer may be able to recover the coins because they were lost articles found concealed in the earth. Such articles, commonly known as *treasure trove*, are usually coin, gold, or silver found hidden in the earth or other private place. In England, treasure trove belongs to the crown, but in the United States, it is treated like lost property and becomes the property of the finder, subject to the rights of the true owner. Note in this example that Allen and Billheimer are not trespassers. If they were trespassers, they would not be entitled to retain the title to the treasure trove.[8]

PATENTS

A patent is a grant from the government that conveys and secures to an inventor the exclusive right to make, use, and sell an invention for seventeen years. Patents are typically given for new articles, but *design patents* are given for manu-

factured articles that have been changed in a way that will enhance their sale. *Plant patents* are given to individuals who invent, discover, or reproduce a new variety of plant. Patent law has been evolving with respect to computer programs. Initially, computer programs could not be patented, but the commercial necessity of protecting them has led to a revised view.

TRADEMARKS

A trademark is a distinctive mark, model, device, or emblem that manufacturers stamp, print, or otherwise affix to the goods they produce so that the goods can be identified in the market and their origin verified. Federal statute allows a trademark to be registered by its owner or user. Exclusive use of the trademark can be perpetual. Protection depends on adoption and use; if the owner continues use, no one can infringe upon the trademark. International protection can also be afforded by various registrations. Registration is made before using the trademark in most other countries.

A trademark must be distinctive in order to be registered. It is not enough to merely describe an article or to name a city. For example, it would be hard to register the trademark "New York Clothes." Exceptions to this rule, of course, exist. When particular words have been used for such a long time that the public identifies them with a particular product and its origin, then those words can be registered as a trademark. The same holds for geographic terms that have acquired a meaning other than their location.

Trademarks can become so common that they become generic names. For example, "Thermos" was originally a brand name for a thermal food-storage container. Now the term has become synonymous with such containers and therefore can no longer be used solely as one company's trademark.

COPYRIGHTS

A copyright is an intangible right granted by statute to the author or originator of certain literary or artistic productions. With a copyright, the

---

8. Danielson v. Roberts, 44 Or. 108, 74 P.913 (1904).

owner is vested for a limited time period with the sole and exclusive privilege of reproducing copies of the work for publication and sale.

At common law, any author or compiler of data who prevented others from using the work without permission by keeping it secret had a common law copyright. Such a copyright ended when the work was published. (Publication meant any communication to others, not necessarily in written or printed form.) Federal statutes now govern virtually all copyright law in this country.

On January 1, 1978, a new copyright law became effective, completely replacing Title 17 of the United States Code, which had been used since 1909. The new law is divided into eight chapters, beginning with a discussion of the subject matter and scope of copyright. It includes chapters relating to copyright duration, notice, deposit and registration requirements, infringement, manufacturing requirements, administration, and the like. The new copyright law has four essential purposes:

1. To maximize the availability of creative works to the public.
2. To give creators of copyrighted works a fair return and to provide users of copyrighted works with a fair income.
3. To balance the interest of copyright users and owners.
4. To minimize any negative impact on industries regulated by change in the copyright law.

Works created after January 1, 1978, are given statutory copyright protection for the life of the author plus fifty years. Pseudonymous and anonymous publications, as well as those done "for hire" (ghosted), have a copyright term of seventy-five years from publication or one hundred years from creation, whichever is shorter. For those works already under copyright protection, their present term of twenty-eight years from date of first publication will remain. If a renewal is asked for, the second term will be increased to forty-seven years.

Exclusive Use of Copyright

The copyright holder is entitled to the exclusive use of all those materials that are copyrighted,

subject to a number of exceptions, such as fair use and library reproduction.

Fair Use   Under the doctrine of fair use, some copying is allowed without payment of fees or permission of the copyright holder. "Fair use" allows reproduction of copyrighted material without permission if the use of the material is "reasonable" and not harmful to the rights of the copyright owner. Section 107 of the new copyright law mentions permissible purposes such as criticism, comment, news reporting, teaching (including multiple copies for classroom use), scholarship, or research. Four criteria are used in considering whether a particular use is reasonable:

1. The purpose and character of the use, including whether it is of a nonprofit, educational nature or of a commercial nature.
2. The amount and importance of the material used in relation to the work as a whole.
3. The nature of the copyrighted work.
4. The effect of the use on the potential market or value of the copyrighted work.

Library Reproduction   Libraries and archives can reproduce single copies of certain copyrighted items for noncommercial purposes without violating the copyright law. Notice of copyright on the library or archive reproduction is necessary, however. Wholesale copying of periodicals is not permitted.

QUESTIONS AND CASE PROBLEMS

1. John has a severe heart attack and is taken to the hospital. He is not expected to live, and he knows it. As a bachelor without close relatives nearby, John gives his car keys to his close friend and chess partner, Fred, telling Fred that he is expected to die and that the car is Fred's. John survives the heart attack, but two months later he dies from pneumonia. Uncle Sam is executor of John's estate and wants Fred to return the car. Fred

refuses, claiming the car was given to him by John as a gift. Discuss whether Fred will be required to return the car to John's estate.

2.   Sally goes into Meyer's Department Store to do some Christmas shopping. She becomes engrossed in looking over a number of silk blouses when she suddenly realizes she has a dinner engagement. She hastily departs from the store, inadvertently leaving her purse on a sales counter. Julie, a sales clerk at the store, notices the purse on the counter but leaves it there, expecting Sally to return for it. Later, when Sally returns, the purse is gone. Sally files an action against Meyer's Department Store for the loss of her purse. Discuss the probable success of her suit.

3.   Bill Heise is a janitor for the First Mercantile Department Store. While walking to work, Bill discovers an expensive watch lying on the curb. Later that day, while Bill is cleaning the aisles of the store, he discovers a wallet containing $500 but no identification. Bill turns over the wallet to his superior, Joe Frances. Bill gives the watch to his son, Gordon. Two weeks later, Martin Avery, the owner of the watch, discovers that Bill found the watch and demands it back from Gordon. Bill decides now to claim the wallet with its $500, but Joe refuses to turn it over, saying that Bill is not the true owner and that the money is really the property of the store. Discuss who is entitled to the watch and who is entitled to the wallet containing $500.

4.   Fred McDuff has a son named Don. Fred wants to give his son a new car that he has recently purchased. Fred and his son have not gotten along during the past few years, and Fred feels part of this is his fault. He goes to his son's house, wanting to make amends by giving the car to Don. When Fred arrives at Don's house, his daughter-in-law (Don's wife) tells Fred that Don is out of town and will return the next day. Fred gives the keys to the new car to his daughter-in-law, tells her to hold the keys for his son, and says that he will return the next day. Two hours later, Fred has second thoughts about giving Don a car. He retrieves the keys from his daughter-in-law before she can turn them over to Don. Don returns from his trip, learns of the events, and demands possession of the car, claiming a gift was made. Is Don entitled to the car?

5.   James DeCante owns a 1967 Chevy. The car has been having continual mechanical problems, and James's repair expenses have been considerable. One day, in disgust, James parks the car on a city-owned vacant lot two blocks from his house. The car sits there for four months. During this period Sam Green observes the car, which has been unattended by James. Sam takes the car and makes improvements and re-

pairs valued at $500. Later, James learns that Sam has the car, has it running smoothly, and is treating the car as if it were his. James demands the car, claiming title. Sam refuses to surrender the car, claiming that he has title. Discuss who is correct and what rights, if any, each person has against the other.

6.   Ethel Yahuda had an extensive library of rare books and manuscripts. Several years before her death, Yahuda announced at a public luncheon attended by a head of state that she was donating her library to Hebrew University. Her public announcement was accompanied by the delivery of an itemized memorandum of the books and manuscripts contained in her library. Hebrew University Association accepted the list. No books were ever tendered by Yahuda to the university. Is there a completed gift? [Hebrew Univ. Assn. v. Nye (executors of estate of Ethel S. Yahuda), 26 Conn.Sup. 342, 223 A.2d 397 (1966)]

7.   McAvoy owned a barbershop. Medina, a regular customer, spotted a pocketbook lying on one of the tables where McAvoy kept magazines for his customers. Medina pointed out the pocketbook to McAvoy. McAvoy put the purse aside and told Medina that he would hold it until its owner returned. Several weeks passed, and no one claimed the pocketbook. Medina returned to the barbershop and claimed that, since the pocketbook was lost property and he was the finder, and since the owner had not reclaimed it, it was his. Who should get possession of the pocketbook—McAvoy or Medina? [McAvoy v. Medina, 93 Mass. (11 Allen) 548 (1866)]

8.   Troop and Rust were partners in an oil and gas operation. Troop owned a three-fourths interest in the operation, and Rust owned a one-fourth interest. After eight years of operation, a dispute arose as to whether Rust had contributed his share of the expenses. As a result of the dispute, the partnership was dissolved. In attempting to divide up the oil, Rust learned that Troop had commingled the partnership's oil with oil from another lease that Troop owned. At trial, Troop was unable to show how much of the commingled oil had come from his other operation. How much of the oil should each of the parties receive? [Troop v. St. Louis Union Trust Co., 25 Ill.App.2d 143, 116 N.E.2d 116 (1960)]

9.   Richard Coddington, a single man, opened a joint savings account with his mother. They signed a signature card that stated that the account was owned by them as joint tenants with the right of survivorship. New York banking law provides that joint tenancy has been created when a bank account is opened in the names of two persons and is "payable to either or the survivor." However, there was no statement made on the passbook as to survivorship. Later, Richard mar-

ried Margaret. Richard died. Margaret claimed a share of the savings account on the ground that it was not a joint tenancy because the passbook did not contain words of survivorship. She also claimed that the statutory presumption of a joint tenancy was negated by Richard's past behavior—his withdrawal of substantial sums from the account throughout his life. At trial, the court awarded the entire account to Richard's mother. Margaret appealed. What was the result? [Matter of Estate of Coddington, 56 App.Div.2d 697, 391 N.Y.S.2d 760 (1977)]

10. In 1945 Lieber, then in the U.S. Army, was one of the first soldiers to occupy Munich, Germany. He and some of his friends entered Adolf Hitler's apartment and removed various items of his personal belongings. Lieber brought home his share, including Hitler's uniform jacket and cap and some of his decorations and personal jewelry. Lieber's possession of these articles was publicly known because Louisiana newspapers published pictures and stories about the collection. Lieber was the subject of a feature story in the Louisiana State University Alumni News of October 1945. In 1968 Lieber's collection was stolen by his chauffeur. The chauffeur sold it to a New York dealer. The dealer then sold it to Mohawk Arms, who purchased it in good faith. When Lieber discovered the whereabouts of his stolen property, he made a demand for it that was refused. The trial court granted summary judgment to Lieber. Mohawk Arms then appealed. What was the result? [Lieber v. Mohawk Arms, Inc., 64 Misc.2d 206, 314 N.Y.S.2d 510 (1970)]

CHAPTER 17

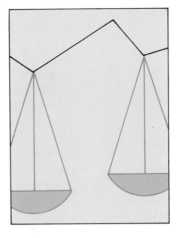

Bailments

Virtually every individual and business is affected by the law of bailments at one time or another (and sometimes even on a daily basis). When individuals deal with bailments, whether they realize it or not, they are subject to the obligations and duties that arise from the bailment relationship. A **bailment** is formed by the delivery of personal property, without transfer of title, by one person, called a **bailor,** to another, called a **bailee,** usually under an agreement for a particular purpose (for example, loan, storage, repair, or transportation). Upon completion of the purpose, the bailee is obligated to return the bailed property to the bailor or to a third person or to dispose of it as directed. Most bailments are created by agreement, but not necessarily by contract, because in many bailments not all of the elements of a contract (such as mutual assent or consideration) are present. For example, if you loan your business law text to a friend so that your friend can read tomorrow's assignment, a bailment is created, but not by contract, because there is no consideration. On the other hand, many commercial bailments, such as delivery of your suit or dress to the cleaners for dry cleaning, are based on contract.

A bailment is distinguished from a sale or a gift in that the transfer is without passage of title or intent to transfer title. In a sale or a gift, title is transferred from the seller or donor to the buyer or donee.

The number, scope, and importance of bailments created daily in the business community and in everyday life make it desirable for any person to understand the elements necessary for the creation of a bailment and to know what rights, duties, and liabilities flow from bailments.

ELEMENTS OF A BAILMENT

Not all transactions involving the delivery of property from one person to another create a bailment. The basic elements of bailment creation are:

1. Personal property.
2. Delivery of possession (without title).
3. Agreement.

Personal Property Requirement

Bailment involves only personal property. A bailment of persons is not possible. Although a bailment of your luggage is created when it is transported by an airline, you as a passenger are not the subject of a bailment. Also, you cannot bail realty; thus, leasing your house to a tenant is not bailment.

Bailments involving *tangible* items, such as jewelry, cattle, or automobiles, are more frequent than bailments of *intangible* personal property, such as promissory notes and shares of corporate stock.

Delivery of Possession

Delivery of possession means transfer of possession of property to the bailee in such a way that:

1. The bailee is given exclusive possession and control over the property.
2. The bailee must *knowingly* accept the personal property.[1]

Suppose that Stevenson is in a hurry to catch his plane. He has a package he wants to check at the airport. He arrives at the airport check-in office, but the man in charge has gone on a coffee break. Stevenson decides to leave the package on the counter.

Even though there has clearly been physical transfer of the package, the person in charge of the check-in station did not knowingly accept the personal property and therefore there was no effective delivery. The same result would occur in the following example: Delacroix checks her coat at a restaurant. In the coat pocket is a $20,000 diamond necklace. By accepting the coat, the bailee does not *knowingly* accept the necklace.

If either delivery of possession or knowing acceptance is lacking, there is no bailment relationship. To illustrate: As a general rule valet parking constitutes a bailment, but self-park parking does not. The difference is found in the control of the car keys. When a car owner is required to leave the car keys with the parking attendant, the owner transfers a sufficient amount of control over the car to the parking company to constitute a bailment. When the car is parked and locked and the keys retained by the owner, the parking garage is merely a *lessor* of space and the car owner a lessee.

The following case distinguishes a lease of space and a bailment.

---

1. We are dealing here with *voluntary* bailments.

NELSON v. SHROEDER
AEROSPORTS, INC.
Supreme Court of South Dakota,
1979.
280 N.W.2d 107.

BACKGROUND AND FACTS   *Plaintiff Nelson parked his airplane at a facility owned and operated by the defendant. The parking spaces contained tie-down facilities to secure the aircraft. Nelson tied his plane down when he left it at the facility. The defendant later moved Nelson's plane to another space and tied it down. A later attempt was made by the defendant to move the aircraft, but the tie-down knots were so secure that the aircraft was not disturbed. At all times Nelson retained the keys to the plane. After the weather bureau issued a storm warning, the defendant checked all aircraft in tie-down spaces and found that the tie-downs for Nelson's plane were securely tied. During the storm, Nelson's plane was turned over by high winds, and Nelson sought recovery for the damage from the defendant.*

DUNN, Justice.

Plaintiff argues that a bailor-bailee relationship arose between the parties in that a prima facie case was presented for the existence of a bailment. Plaintiff correctly states the elements for a showing of such a prima facie case, to wit: (1) the delivery of the property to defendant, (2) its value, (3) defendant's failure to return the property in good condition upon demand, and (4) the damages resulting from the failure to deliver.

Plaintiff fails, however, to recognize that the delivery contemplated above for the existence of a bailment turns on whether possession and control of the property is retained by the owner or is delivered to defendant. To constitute sufficient delivery, the generally recognized test is whether there is a full transfer of the property so as to amount to relinquishment of exclusive possession, control and dominion over the property for the duration of the relationship so that the person to whom delivery is made can exclude the possession of the owner and all other persons within the limits of the agreement between the parties.

*   *   *   *

The evidence shows that plaintiff kept the keys to the aircraft and gave a third party permission to fly the aircraft. This exhibits plaintiff's retained control over the aircraft. *   *   *

We must conclude that plaintiff did not relinquish exclusive possession, control and dominion over the aircraft. We hold that under the circumstances present in this case, where plaintiff's aircraft was placed in the airport parking or tie-down space and defendant was not given and did not assert exclusive control over the aircraft, there was no delivery giving rise to a bailor-bailee relationship and only a lease relating to the space occupied by the aircraft was created as opposed to a bailment of the aircraft into the hands of defendant.

*The trial court's judgment for the defendant was upheld. There are, however, cases dealing with **paid-for** parking privileges in which the court has held that a bailment is created even though the car owner locks up the car and retains the keys.*	**JUDGMENT AND REMEDY**

There are two types of delivery that will result in the bailee's exclusive possession of and control over the property. One is a *physical delivery*, and the other is a *constructive delivery*.

Physical Delivery A distinction is made between a restaurant patron who checks a coat with an attendant and a patron who hangs the coat on a coatrack. The coat given to the attendant constitutes a physical delivery and therefore a bailment. The attendant (hence the restaurant) has exclusive possession and control over the retention and removal of the coat. By contrast, the self-hung coat can be removed at any time by the patron or anyone else so inclined. The restaurant does not have substantial control over the property and is not considered a bailee.

Constructive Delivery—Bailment without Physical Delivery Constructive delivery is a substitute delivery or symbolic delivery. What is physically delivered to the bailee is not the actual property bailed, but something so related to the property that the requirement of delivery is satisfied. For example, Lyssenko owns a boat that she loans to Brady for the weekend. It is moored at a municipal marina. Lyssenko gives Brady the boat registration papers so that the harbor master will allow Brady to board the boat. Lyssenko has made constructive delivery of the boat to Brady.

There are certain unique situations in which a bailment is found despite the apparent lack of the requisite elements of control or knowledge. In particular, safe deposit box rental is usually held to constitute a bailor-bailee relationship between the bank and its customer, despite the bank's lack of knowledge of the contents and its inability to have exclusive control of the property.[2]

Another example is where the bailee acquires the property accidentally, by mistake, and fortuitously—such as in finding someone else's lost or mislaid property. A bailment is created even though the bailor did not voluntarily deliver the property to the bailee. These are called *constructive* or *involuntary* bailments.

The Bailment Agreement

A bailment agreement can be *express* or *implied*. Although a written agreement is not required for bailments of less than one year (that is, the Statute of Frauds does not apply), it is a good idea to have one, especially when valuable property is involved. However, if there is a writing that appears to be *complete*, missing terms cannot be proven by parol evidence because of the parol evidence rule. (See Chapter 12.)

The bailment agreement expressly or impliedly provides for the return of the bailed property to the bailor or to a third person, or provides for disposal by the bailee. The agreement presupposes that the bailee will return the identical goods originally given by the bailor. However, in bailment of *fungible goods*—uniform identical goods—or bailments with the *option to purchase*, only equivalent property must be returned.

Fungible goods are defined in UCC 1-201(17) as units of goods that are by nature equivalent to one another—for example, grain or gasoline. UCC 7-207(1) states clearly, "Fungible goods may be commingled."

For example, Sanchez, Basen, and Kerlly each store 1,000 pounds of grain in Hansen's Warehouse every year, and each receives receipts. When Sanchez returns to reclaim "his grain," Hansen's Warehouse is obligated to give him 1,000 pounds of wheat grain—but not necessarily the particular kernels he originally deposited. Sanchez cannot claim that Hansen's Warehouse is guilty of conversion (see Chapter 3) in not returning to him the exact wheat that he put into storage. As long as it returns goods of the same *type, grade,* and *quantity,* Hansen's Warehouse—the bailee—has performed its obligation.

A bailment with an option or offer to purchase allows the prospective buyer the right to hold or use the property while deciding whether to purchase. At the end of an agreed period, the bailee must either return the property to the bailor-seller or agree to purchase (such as by paying cash to the seller). In the latter case, the bailee-buyer returns to the seller-bailor "equivalent" property (promise or payment of money), terminating the bailment and creating a sale.

A typical example is a *sale on approval*. Suppose Rand is interested in buying a lawn mower. The seller gives him possession of a new model, telling him to take it home and try it out. The sales price is $280. If Rand does not like the lawn mower, he can bring it back within two weeks. If he does not bring it back within this period, or if he approves the offer, the seller will bill him. Thus, a bailment is created, and Rand has the duty to either return the lawn mower or approve the offer and return the equivalent in the form of the purchase price.

TYPES OF BAILMENTS

Bailments are either "ordinary" or "special" ("extraordinary"). There are three types of ordinary bailments. The distinguishing feature among them is *which party receives a benefit from the bailment.* Ultimately, the courts will use this factor to determine the standard of care owed by the bailee handling the goods or chattel (personal property), and this factor will dictate

---

2. By statute or by express contract, however, a safe deposit box may be a lease of space or license depending on the jurisdiction or the facts or both.

the rights and liabilities of the parties. (Modern courts tend to use *reasonable standards of care* regardless of the type of bailment arrangement in effect.)

Bailments for the Sole Benefit of the Bailor (Gratuitous Bailments)

When one person takes delivery of personal property for safekeeping as a favor to another, a bailment for the sole benefit of the bailor is in effect. It is a *gratuitous bailment* for the convenience and benefit of the bailor. In such a situation, the bailee is expected to use *slight care* to preserve the bailed property.

Consider an example. Michael is leaving for a two-week trip to Jamaica. He asks Susan if he can store his Celebrity automobile in her garage. He gives her the keys. She promises not to use the car for personal use. She is not paid any rent. One day, her children happen to be playing in her garage. When the children leave the garage, they fail to close and lock the door. Michael's car is stolen.

When Michael returns, he complains that Susan should pay for the loss of the car. She probably will not have to unless he can prove that she was guilty of negligence. The fact that the children failed to lock the garage door would not normally be considered negligence.

Bailments for the Sole Benefit of the Bailee

The loan of an article to a person (the bailee) solely for that person's convenience and benefit is the essence of a *bailment for the sole benefit of the bailee*. Under such circumstances, the bailee must use *great care* to preserve the bailed item from damage. If your best friend loans you a car so you can go out on a date, you must exercise great care in driving that car. If the car gets scratched because you parked it in a crowded parking lot, you will have trouble proving that you used great care, and, normally, you will be liable.

Bailments for the Mutual Benefit of the Bailee and the Bailor (Contractual Bailments)

Mutual benefit bailments are by far the most common kind, and they involve some form of compensation (although not necessarily money) between the bailee and the bailor for the service provided—for example, repair work, transporting goods, storing items, renting goods, or holding property.

A mutual benefit bailment need not involve the payment of a fee. All that is required is that both bailor and bailee receive a benefit. For example, many corporations provide locker and cloakroom facilities for their employees' personal belongings because employees are not permitted to bring these items into the work area. The employee (bailor) benefits by receiving storage facilities. The employer (bailee) benefits by keeping the work area uncluttered, thus decreasing the chances of minor accidents.

The duty of care required in a mutual benefit bailment is that of *reasonable care*. Obviously, the exact measurement of that standard depends on the facts of each situation. A general rule, however, is that the standard of care required will be more than what would be expected in a bailment for the sole benefit of the bailor but less than what would be expected in a bailment for the sole benefit of the bailee.

RIGHTS AND DUTIES OF A BAILEE (BAILEE'S RESPONSIBILITIES)

Rights of the Bailee

The bailee takes possession of personal property for a specified purpose after which that property is returned (in the same or prespecified altered form). Thus, implicit in the bailment agreement is the right of the bailee to take possession, to utilize the property in accomplishing the purpose of the bailment, and to receive some form of compensation (unless the bailment is intended to be gratuitous). Depending upon the nature of the bailment and the terms of the bailment agreement, these bailee rights are present (with some limitations) in varying degrees in all bailment transactions.

Right of Possession Temporary control and possession of property that ultimately is to be returned to the owner is the hallmark of a bailment. The meaning of "temporary" depends upon the terms of the bailment. If a specified period is expressed in the bailment agreement, then the bailment is continuous for that time period. Earlier termination by the bailor is a breach of contract (if it is for consideration), and the bailee can recover damages from the bailor. If no duration is specified, the bailment ends when either the bailor or the bailee so demands.

A bailee's right of possession, even though temporary, permits the bailee to recover damages from any third persons for damage or loss to the property. For example, No Spot Dry Cleaners sends all suede leather garments to Cleanall Company for special processing. If Cleanall loses or damages any leather goods, No Spot has the right to recover against Cleanall. (The customer can also recover from No Spot.)

If goods or chattel are stolen from the bailee during the bailment, the bailee has a legal right to regain possession (recapture) of the goods or obtain damages from any third person who has wrongfully interfered with the bailee's possessory rights.

Right to Use Bailed Property Naturally, the extent to which bailees can use the goods or chattel entrusted to them depends upon the terms of the bailment contract. Where no provision is made, the extent of use depends upon how necessary it is to have the goods at the bailee's disposal in order to carry out the ordinary purpose of the bailment. For example, when leasing drilling machinery, the bailee is expected to use the equipment to drill. On the other hand, in long-term storage of a car, the bailee is not expected to use the car because the ordinary purpose of a storage bailment does not include use of the property.

Right of Compensation A bailee has a right to be compensated as provided for in the bailment

agreement or reimbursed for costs and services rendered in the keeping of the bailed property, or both. In commercial mutual benefit bailments, the amount of compensation is often expressed in the bailment contract. For example, in a rental (bailment) of a car, the contract provides charges on a basis of time, mileage, or a combination of the two, plus other possible charges. In nonrental bailments, such as leaving your car for an oil change, the bailee makes a service charge.

Even in gratuitous bailments, a bailee has a right to be reimbursed or compensated for costs incurred in the keeping of the bailed property. For example, Ann loses her pet dog, which is found by Jesse. Jesse takes Ann's dog to his home and feeds it. Even though he takes good care of the dog, it becomes ill, and a veterinarian is called. The bill for the veterinarian's services and the medicine is paid for by Jesse. Jesse is normally entitled to be reimbursed by Ann for all reasonable costs incurred in the keeping of her dog.

To enforce a bailee's right of compensation, the bailee has a right to place a *possessory* lien (claim) on the specific bailed property until he or she has been fully compensated. This lien on specific bailed property is sometimes referred to as an **artisan's lien**. The lien is effective only as long as the bailee retains possession over the bailed property.

If the bailor refuses to pay or cannot pay the charges (compensation), the bailee is entitled in most states to foreclose on the lien. This means that the bailee can sell the property and be paid out of the proceeds for the amount owed from the bailment, returning any excess to the bailor.

For example, Peter takes his car (that he has just paid cash for) to the garage and enters into an agreement for repairs. The repairs are to be paid in cash. Upon completion of the repairs, the garage tenders Peter his car, but because of unexpected bills he cannot pay the garage. The garage has a right to retain possession of Peter's car, exercising a *bailee's lien*. Unless Peter can make arrangements for payment, the garage will be entitled to sell the car in order to be compensated for the repairs.

Right to Limit Liability "Ordinary" bailees have the right to limit their bailment liability by type of risk or by monetary amount, or both, as long as:

1. The limitations are called to the attention of the bailor.
2. The limitations are not against public policy.

Any enforceable limitation imposed by the ordinary bailee must be brought to the bailor's attention. Although the bailee is not required to read or interpret the limitation to the bailor, it is essential that the bailor in some way know of the limitation. Thus, a sign in Joe's garage stating that Joe will not be responsible "for loss due to theft, fire, or vandalism" may or may not be held to be notice to the bailor. Whether the notice will be effective will depend on the size of the sign, its location, and other circumstances. The same holds true with limitations placed on the back of identification receipts (stubs) for parked cars, checked coats, or stored bailed goods. Most courts would require additional notice, since the bailor rarely reads the receipt and usually treats it merely as an identification number to get back the bailed goods.

Even if the bailor has notice, certain types of disclaimers of liability are declared as being against public policy and therefore illegal. These clauses are called *exculpatory clauses*. The classic illustration of an exculpatory clause is found on parking receipts: "We assume no risk for damage to or loss of automobile or its contents regardless of cause. It is agreed that the vehicle owner assumes all such risks." Even though the language may vary, if the bailee attempts to exclude liability for the bailee's own negligence, the result is the same—the clause is unenforceable as being against public policy. This is especially true in the case of bailees providing quasi-public services.

Duties of the Bailee

The bailee has two basic responsibilities: (1) to take proper care of the property and (2) to surrender or dispose of the property at the end of the bailment. The bailee's duties are based on a mixture of tort law and contract law. The duty of care involves the standards and principles of tort law discussed in Chapter 3. A bailee's failure to exercise appropriate care in handling the bailor's property results in tort liability. The duty to relinquish the property at the end of the bailment is grounded in contract law principles. Failure to return the property is a breach of contract, and, with one exception, the bailee is liable for damages. The exception exists when the obligation is excused because the goods or chattel have been destroyed, lost, or stolen through no fault of the bailee (or claimed by a third party with a superior claim).

Duty of Care   As previously discussed, bailees must exercise proper care over the property in their possession to prevent its loss or damage. The three types of bailments demand different degrees of care (although the trend is toward a uniform standard of care). When a bailment exists for the sole benefit of the bailee, great care, or the highest level of care, is required. When the bailment exists for the mutual benefit of the bailor and the bailee, reasonable care is the standard. When the bailment exists for the sole benefit of the bailor, slight care, or something less than ordinary or reasonable care, is expected.

Duty to Return Bailed Property   At the end of the bailment, the bailee normally must relinquish the identical undamaged property (unless it is fungible) to either the bailor or someone the bailor designates or otherwise dispose of it as directed. This is a *contractual* duty arising from the bailment agreement (contract). Failure to give up possession at the time the bailment ends is breach of a contract term.

As noted previously, there are recognized exceptions from tort law that will excuse contract liability. If the bailee does not or cannot return the property at the end of the bailment because it has been lost, stolen, or damaged *through no negligence* (fault) on the part of the bailee, then the contractual obligation to return the property is excused. (There are a number of exceptions to this rule that concern common carriers, public warehouse companies, and innkeepers. They usually cannot limit liability except as provided by statute because they have a higher duty of care. Exceptions also exist when the bailee de-viates from the bailment agreement.) Also, if a third party with a superior claim takes the property, the bailee normally is not liable.

Delivery of Goods to the Wrong Person A bailee may be liable if the goods being held or delivered are given to the wrong person. Hence, a bailee must be satisfied that the person to whom

the goods are being delivered is the actual owner or has authority from the owner to take possession of the goods. Should the bailee be in error, particularly when the bailee knows the goods are stolen or that there is another claim of ownership against the goods, then the bailee may be liable for conversion or mis-delivery. The following case presents an example of this principle.

CAPEZZARO v.
WINFREY
Superior Court of New Jersey,
1977.
153 N.J.Super. 267, 379 A.2d
493.

BACKGROUND AND FACTS *The plaintiff was a robbery victim who sued the city and its police officers after the police arrested a suspect who the plaintiff claimed had stolen money. During their apprehension of the suspect, the police had removed the money from the suspect's clothing, and the police department kept it.*

When the suspect was released from custody, she went to the police station and demanded return of the money. The police officers gave it to her. The robbery victim claimed to be the rightful owner of the money and sued the city for negligence because police officers in the city's employ had released the money.

The jury found for the robbery victim, and the police officers and the city appealed this judgment.

LORA, SEIDMAN and MILMED, Judges.
PER CURIAM
*   *   *   *

It has been said that a constructive bailment or a bailment by operation of law may be created when a person comes into possession of personal property of another, receives nothing from the owner of the property, and has no right to recover from the owner for what he does in caring for the property. Such person is ordinarily considered to be a gratuitous bailee, liable only to the bailor for bad faith or gross negligence.

Where possession has been acquired accidentally, fortuitously, through mistake or by an agreement for some other purpose since terminated, the possessor, "upon principles of justice," should keep it safely and restore or deliver it to its owner. Under such circumstances, the courts have considered the possessions quasi-contracts [implied contracts created by law] of bailment or constructive and involuntary bailments.

Here the police seized and obtained custody of the money which was found in Winfrey's [the robbery suspect's] girdle during a search in her cell after her arrest on the robbery charge and after plaintiff claimed Winfrey had stolen it from him. It is undisputed that the money was being kept by the police as evidence for use in Winfrey's prosecution. It follows, then, that the City of Newark, through its police department, was holding the money for its own benefit as well as for the benefit of its rightful owner.

Ordinarily, a person who has possession of property may be presumed by another to be the rightful owner thereof in the absence of any knowledge to the contrary. However, here the police were fully aware of plaintiff's adverse claim, but notwithstanding such knowledge and without notice to plaintiff turned the money over to Winfrey.

In view of the mutual benefit attendant upon custody of the money in the case before us, we find no error in the trial judge's refusal to charge that the police department was a gratuitous bailee. *   *   *

Defendants further contend that when the indictment was dismissed any claim by plaintiff lost its validity and they were obligated to return the monies in question to Winfrey as bailor. We disagree. A bailee with knowledge of an adverse claim makes delivery to the bailor at his peril, and only if he is ignorant of such a claim will he be protected against a subsequent claim by the rightful owner. The position of a bailee in such situation and his possible courses of action are set forth in 9 *Williston on Contracts* (3 ed. 1967), § 1036 at 897–898:

> *   *   * If a bailee knows goods are stolen, or that the bailor is acting adversely to a clearly valid right, even though the true owner has as yet made no demand for them, the bailee will be liable to him for conversion if delivery is made to the bailor. In case, therefore, that the bailee knows or has been notified of an adverse claim, he will deliver to the bailor at his peril. The bailee must, for his own protection, choose one of two courses:
>
> First, he may satisfy himself of the validity of one of the two claims and obtain authority from the owner of the claim to refuse delivery to all other claimants. In such a case he may plead at law to an action by any but the rightful owner the title of the latter, or the right of one having a superior right to immediate possession. If this title or right can be proved, a perfect defense is established. Second, if no actual adverse claim has been made, but the bailee knows of the existence of an adverse right, or if the bailee cannot determine which of two claimants has the better title, and neither claimant will give a bond indemnifying the bailee from all damage caused by delivery to him, the only course open to the bailee is to file a bill of interpleader against the several possible owners, praying a temporary injunction against actions against himself until the true ownership of the goods is determined. And it should be added that a bailee who redelivers the goods to the bailor, or upon his order, in ignorance of his lack of title, is fully protected against subsequent claims of the rightful owner.

The police returned the money to Winfrey after being informed by the warden of the county jail that the indictments had been dismissed. They did not contact plaintiff before doing so, even though they were on notice of his adverse claim. The dismissal of the indictment for the reasons here present did not vitiate plaintiff's adverse claim to the money. Inherent in the jury's verdict is a finding that defendants were negligent in releasing the money without a determination of the validity of the adverse claim. Such finding and the verdict are amply supported by the evidence.

The judgment of the trial court was affirmed. The police officers and the city were liable to the robbery victim.

JUDGMENT AND REMEDY

Presumption of Negligence Sometimes the duty to return and duty of care are combined to determine bailee liability. At the end of the bailment, a bailee has the duty to return the bailor's property in the condition it was received (allowing for ordinary wear and aging). In some cases, the bailor can sue the bailee in tort (as well as contract) for damages or lost goods on the theory of *negligence*. But often it is not possible for the bailor to discover and prove the specific acts of negligence committed by the bailee that caused damage or loss to the property.[3] Thus, the law of bailments recognizes a rule whereby a bailor's proof that damage or loss to the property has occurred will, in and of itself, raise a *presumption* that the bailee is guilty of negligence. Once this is shown, the bailee must prove that he or she was not at fault. A bailee who is able to *rebut* (contradict) the presumption of negligence is not liable to the bailor. When damage to goods is normally of the type that results only from someone's negligence, and when the bailee had full control of the goods, it is more likely than not that the damage was caused by the bailee's negligence. Therefore, the bailee's negligence is presumed.

Determining whether a bailee exercised an appropriate degree of care is usually a question of fact. This means that the trier-of-fact (a judge or a jury) weighs the facts of a particular situation and concludes that the bailee did or did not exercise the requisite degree of care at the time the loss or damage occurred. The failure to exercise appropriate care is negligence, and the bailee is liable for the loss or damage in tort. The following case illustrates a duty of care supplied by the terms of the bailment contract, and the failure of the warehouseman to exercise that care resulted in negligence.

---

3. The basic formula for finding negligence requires proof that (1) a duty exists, (2) a breach of that duty occurred, and (3) the breach is the proximate cause of damage or loss.

F-M POTATOES, INC. v. SUDA

Supreme Court of North Dakota, 1977.
259 N.W.2d 487.

BACKGROUND AND FACTS *The plaintiff, F-M Potatoes, Inc., sued the defendant, Paul Suda, asserting that Suda owed F-M $6,500 pursuant to an oral contract for air conditioned storage of a large number of potatoes from October 1974 through March 1975. The storage agreement provided for a reasonable rental rate in the F-M warehouse facilities. Each storage bin contained a fan, heater, and humidifying equipment. The temperature and ventilation of each bin was controlled by a thermostat. Such conditioning capabilities permit the warehouse to store potatoes for about twelve months. The potatoes that Suda stored with F-M were to be used for potato chips. Therefore, during the conditioning process at the warehouse, they were to be kept at a temperature higher than normal to change the proportion of sugars to starches within each potato.*

Starting in December 1974, Suda's potatoes were taken to a laboratory for testing; they never attained an acceptable potato chip color shade. Thus, no buyer would purchase them. In March 1975, F-M hauled Suda's potatoes from its warehouse and disposed of them. Suda claimed at the trial that the potatoes were not marketable because F-M failed to provide proper air conditioned storage. F-M asserted that the potatoes were not marketable because of other factors.

PAULSON, Judge.

*   *   *   *

Prior to discussing the issues raised by F-M on this appeal, it is necessary to determine whether the legal relationship which existed between Suda and F-M, pursuant to the oral storage agreement, was that of landlord-tenant or that of bailor-bailee. " ' *   *   * [T]he test is whether the person leaving the property has made such a delivery to the owner of the premises as to amount to a relinquishment, for a time, of his exclusive possession, control, and dominion over the property, so that the latter can exclude, within the limits of the agreement, the possession of all others. If he has, the general rule is that the transaction is a bailment. If there is no such delivery and relinquishment of exclusive possession, and control and dominion over the goods is dependent in no degree upon the cooperation of the owner of the premises, and access to the goods is in nowise subject to the latter's control, it is generally held that the owner of the goods is a tenant or lessee of the space upon the premises where they are left.' "

In the instant case, F-M agreed to provide conditioned storage for Suda's potatoes and to control all of the mechanical equipment for maintaining the temperature and other conditioning factors. F-M received an additional 30¢ per cwt. for conditioned storage which it would not have received if it had simply rented to Suda unconditioned storage space. *   *   * Under these facts, we conclude that the agreement between Suda and F-M created a bailment for hire and that they were in the relationship of bailor-bailee.

*   *   *   *

[UCC 7-204] *Duty of care—Contractual limitation of warehouseman's liability.*—1. A warehouseman is liable for damages for loss of or injury to the goods caused by his failure to exercise such care in regard to them as a reasonably careful man would exercise under like circumstances but unless otherwise agreed he is not liable for damages which could not have been avoided by the exercise of such care.

Although a warehouseman is not an insurer of the stored goods, he must exercise a degree of skill and care that a reasonable man would exercise requisite to the operation of the business in which he is engaged. F-M contracted to provide Suda "conditioned storage" for his potatoes. Modern day conditioned storage of potatoes is a complicated process requiring the proper combinations of temperature, humidity, and ventilation to condition the potatoes for market while at the same time preventing deterioration of the potatoes. F-M was required, therefore, to exercise the degree of skill and care that a reasonable warehouseman would have exercised in providing conditioned storage for potatoes. [Several instances of negligent care were cited by the court.]

*   *   *   *

F-M *   *   * failed to exercise the degree of care in providing conditioned storage for Suda's potatoes that a reasonable warehouseman would have exercised under like circumstances.

The Supreme Court of North Dakota affirmed the trial court's findings that F-M acted negligently in providing storage for Suda's potatoes. F-M had to compensate Suda for 75 percent of the damaged potatoes, the loss the court attributed to F-M's negligence.   **JUDGMENT AND REMEDY**

RIGHTS AND
DUTIES OF A BAILOR

Rights of a Bailor

The bailor's rights are essentially a complement to each of the bailee's duties. A bailor has the right to expect the following:

1. The property will be protected with reasonable care while in the possession of the bailee.
2. The bailee will utilize the property as agreed in the bailment agreement (or not at all).
3. The property will be relinquished at the conclusion of the bailment according to directions given by the bailor.
4. The bailee will not convert (alter) the goods except as agreed.
5. The bailor shall not be bound by any bailee limitations of liability unless such are known and are enforceable by law.
6. Repairs or service on the property will be completed without defective workmanship.

Duties of a Bailor

A bailor has a single, all-encompassing duty to provide the bailee with goods or chattel that are free from hidden defects that could cause injury to the bailee. This duty translates into two rules:

1. In a *mutual benefit bailment*, the bailor must notify the bailee of all known defects and any hidden defects that the bailor could have discovered with reasonable diligence and proper inspection.
2. In *bailments for the sole benefit of the bailee*, the bailor must notify the bailee of any known defects.

The bailor's duty to reveal defects is based on a negligence theory of tort law. A bailor who fails to give the appropriate notice is liable to the bailee and to any other person who might reasonably be expected to come into contact with the defective article.

To illustrate: Rentco (bailor) leases four tractors to Hopkinson. Unknown to Rentco (but discoverable by reasonable inspection), the brake mechanism on one of the tractors is defective at the time the bailment is made. Hopkinson uses the defective tractor not knowing of the brake problem and injures herself and two other field workers when the tractor rolls out of control. Rentco is liable on a negligence theory for injuries sustained by Hopkinson and the two employees.

This is the analysis: Rentco has a mutual benefit bailment and a *duty* to notify Hopkinson of the discoverable brake defect. Rentco's failure to notify is the *proximate cause* of injuries to farm workers who might be expected to use or have contact with the tractor. Therefore, Rentco is *liable* for the resulting injuries.

A bailor can also incur *warranty liability* based on contract law for injuries resulting from bailment of defective articles. Property leased by a bailor must be *fit for the intended purpose of the bailment*. The bailor's knowledge or ability to discover any defects is immaterial. Warranties of fitness arise by law in sales contracts and by judicial interpretation in the case of bailments "for hire."

Termination of Bailment

Bailments for a specific term end when the stated period lapses. When no duration is specified, the bailment can be terminated any time by the following events:

1. The mutual agreement of both parties.
2. A demand by either party.
3. The completion of the purpose of the bailment.
4. An act by the bailee that is inconsistent with the terms of the bailment.
5. The operation of law.

SPECIAL BAILMENTS

Most of this chapter has concerned itself with ordinary bailments. Special, or extraordinary, bailments include (1) common carriers, (2) warehouse companies, and (3) innkeepers or hotel keepers.

Common Carriers

Common carriers are publicly licensed to provide transportation services to the general public. They are distinguished from private carriers that operate transportation facilities for a select clientele. A private carrier is not bound to provide service to every person or company making a request. The common carrier, however, must arrange carriage for all who apply, within certain limitations.[4] The delivery of goods to a common carrier creates a bailment relationship between the shipper (bailor) and the common carrier (bailee).

The common carrier contract of transportation creates a *mutual benefit bailment*. But, unlike ordinary mutual benefit bailments, the common carrier is held to a standard of care based on *strict liability*, rather than reasonable care, in protecting the bailed personal property. This means that the common carrier is absolutely liable for all loss or damage to goods except damage caused by one of the five common law exceptions:

1. An act of God.
2. An act of a public enemy.
3. An order of a public authority.
4. An act of the shipper.
5. The inherent nature of the goods.

Common carriers are treated as if they were absolute insurers for the safe delivery of goods to the destination, but actually they are not. They cannot contract away this liability for damaged goods; but, subject to government regulations, they are permitted to limit their dollar liability to an amount stated on the shipment contract.[5]

Except for the five exceptions given, any damage to goods in shipment, even that caused by the willful acts of third persons or sheer accident, does not relieve the common carrier from liability. Thus, a common carrier trucking company moving cargo is liable for acts of vandalism, mechanical defects in refrigeration units, or a dam bursting, if any of these acts results in damage to the cargo. But damage caused by acts of God—earthquake or lightning striking, for example—are the shipper's loss.

There are many interesting cases concerning what constitutes an "act of God." The following extract is from a case in which a common carrier learned that a flood was *not* necessarily enough of an "act of God" to excuse liability:

> The only acts of God that excuse common carriers from liability for loss or injury to goods in transit are those operations of the forces of nature that could not have been anticipated and provided against and that by their super human force unexpectedly injure or destroy goods in the custody or control of the carrier. Extreme weather conditions which operate to foil human obligations of duty are regarded as acts of God. However, every strong wind, snowstorm, or rainstorm cannot be termed an act of God merely because it is of unusual or more than average intensity. Ordinary, expectable, and gradual weather conditions are not regarded as acts of God even though they may have produced a disaster, because man had the opportunity to control their effects.[6]

Shipper's Loss   The shipper bears any loss occurring through its own faulty or improper crating or packaging procedures. For example, if a bird dies because its crate was poorly ventilated, the shipper bears the loss, not the carrier.

In the following case, the U.S. Supreme Court deals with the question of whether a common carrier that has exercised reasonable care and has complied with the instructions of the shipper is nonetheless liable to the shipper for spoilage in transit of an interstate shipment of perishable commodities.

---

4. A common carrier is not required to take any and all property anywhere in all instances. Public regulatory agencies, such as the Interstate Commerce Commission, govern commercial carriers, and carriers can be restricted to geographical areas. They can also be limited to carrying certain kinds of goods or to providing only special types of transportation equipment.

5. For example, federal laws and Interstate Commerce Commission regulations require common carriers to offer shippers the opportunity to obtain higher dollar limits for loss by paying a higher fee for the transport.

---

6. Southern Pac. Co. v. Loden, 508 P.2d 347 (Ariz. App.1972).

MISSOURI PAC. RY. CO. v. ELMORE & STAHL

United States Supreme Court, 1964.
377 U.S. 134, 84 S.Ct. 1142.

BACKGROUND AND FACTS   *Elmore & Stahl, a fruit shipper, contracted with Missouri P. R. Co. to ship melons from Rio Grande City, Texas, to Chicago. At trial, the jury was convinced that Missouri P. R. Co. and its connecting carriers performed all the required transportation services without negligence. The jury also found that a preponderance of evidence showed that the condition of the melons on arrival in Chicago was defective and that the defective condition was not due solely to an inherent defect in the melons. The trial judge ruled against the carrier, and the Texas Court of Appeals affirmed, as did the Texas Supreme Court. The ground for affirmation was that as a matter of federal law, the carrier cannot exonerate itself by showing that no negligence on its part occurred. Rather, the carrier needs to establish that the loss or damage was caused by one of the accepted perils recognized at common law. Basically, Missouri P. R. Co. did not show that the spoilage or decay was due entirely to the inherent nature of the goods or, in other words, that the damage was caused solely by natural deterioration. The U.S. Supreme Court reviewed the case.*

Mr. Justice STEWART delivered the opinion of the Court.

*   *   *   *

The parties agree that the liability of a carrier for damage to an interstate shipment is a matter of federal law controlled by federal statutes and decisions. The Carmack Amendment of 1906, § 20(11) of the Interstate Commerce Act, makes carriers liable "for the full actual loss, damage, or injury *   *   * caused by" them to property they transport, and declares unlawful and void any contract, regulation, tariff, or other attempted means of limiting this liability. It is settled that this statute has two undisputed effects crucial to the issue in this case: First, the statute codifies the common-law rule that a carrier, though not an absolute insurer, is liable for damage to goods transported by it unless it can show that the damage was caused by "(a) the act of God; (b) the public enemy; (c) the act of the shipper himself; (d) public authority; (e) or the inherent vice or nature of the goods." *   *   * Second, the statute declares unlawful and void any "rule, regulation, or other limitation of any character whatsoever" purporting to limit this liability. *   *   * Accordingly, under federal law, in an action to recover from a carrier for damage to a shipment, the shipper establishes his prima facie case when he shows delivery in good condition, arrival in damaged condition, and the amount of damages. Thereupon, the burden of proof is upon the carrier to show both that it was free from negligence and that the damage to the cargo was due to one of the excepted causes relieving the carrier of liability *   *   *.

The disposition of this case in the Texas courts was in accordance with these established principles. It is apparent that the jury were unable to determine the cause of the damage to the melons. "[T]he decay of the perishable cargo is not a cause; it is an effect. It may be the result of a number of causes, for some of which, such as the inherent defects of the cargo *   *   * the carrier is not liable." But the jury refused to find that the carrier had borne its burden of establishing that the damaged condition of the melons was due solely to "inherent vice," as defined in the instruction of the trial judge—including "the inherent nature of the commodity which will cause it to deteriorate with a lapse of time." The petitioner [Missouri P. R. Co.] does not challenge the accuracy of the trial judge's instruction or the jury's finding. Its position is simply that if goods are perishable, and the nature of the damage is spoilage, and the jury affirmatively find that the carrier was free from negligence and performed the transportation services as required by the shipper, then the law presumes that the cause of the spoilage was the natural tendency of perishables to deteriorate even though the damage might, in fact, have resulted from other causes, such as the acts of third parties, for which no exception from carrier liability is provided. Consequently, it is argued, the question of "inherent vice" should not have been submitted to the jury, since the carrier in such a case does not bear the affirmative burden of establishing that the damage was caused by the inherent vice exception of the common law.

The petitioner appears to recognize that, except in the case of loss arising from injury to livestock in transit—a well-established exception to the general common-law rule based on the peculiar propensity of animals to injure themselves and each other—no distinction was made in the earlier federal cases between perishables and non-perishables. It is said, however, that the "large-scale development, in relatively recent years, of long distance transportation of fresh fruit and vegetables in interstate commerce has led to the evolution" of a new federal rule governing the carrier's liability for spoilage and decay of perishables, similar to the "livestock rule," which absolves the carrier from liability upon proof that the carrier has exercised reasonable care, and has complied with the shipper's instructions.

We are aware of no such new rule of federal law. As recently as 1956, in Secretary of Agriculture v. United States, 350 U.S. 162, 76 S.Ct. 244, 100 L.Ed. 173, this Court gave no intimation that the general rule placing on the carrier the affirmative burden of bringing the cause of the damage within one of the specified exceptions no longer applied to cases involving perishable commodities.
*   *   *   *

Finally, all else failing, it is argued that as a matter of public policy, the burden ought not to be placed upon the carrier to explain the cause of spoilage, because where perishables are involved, the shipper is peculiarly knowledgeable about the commodity's condition at and prior to the time of shipment, and is therefore in the best position to explain the cause of the damage. Since this argument amounts to a suggestion that we now carve out an exception to an unquestioned rule of long standing upon which both shippers and carriers rely, and which is reflected in the freight rates set by the carrier, the petitioner must sustain a heavy burden of persuasion. The general rule of carrier liability is based upon the sound premise that the carrier has peculiarly within its knowledge "[a]ll the facts and circumstances upon which [it] may rely to relieve [it] of [its] duty. *   *   * In consequence, the law casts upon [it] the burden of the loss which [it] cannot explain or, explaining, bring within the exceptional case in which [it] is relieved from liability." Schnell v. The Vallescura, 293 U.S. 296, 304, 55 S.Ct. 194, 196, 79 L.Ed. 373. We are not persuaded that the carrier lacks adequate means to inform itself of the condition of goods at the time it receives them from the shipper, and it cannot be doubted that while the carrier has possession, it is the only one in a position to acquire the knowledge of what actually damaged a shipment entrusted to its care.

JUDGMENT
AND REMEDY

The U.S. Supreme Court upheld the judgment of the Texas Supreme Court, which had affirmed the Texas Court of Civil Appeals judgment, which had affirmed the trial judge's judgment for damages against the carrier. Even if a common carrier exercises reasonable care, it is liable for spoilage in transit unless it can prove that the cause of the spoilage was the natural tendency of the commodities to deteriorate. That is to say, the carrier is not relieved from liability simply by showing its freedom from negligence.

Connecting Carriers Where connecting carriers are involved in transporting goods, the shipper can recover from the original carrier or any connecting carrier. In all cases of carrier liability, the shipper must prove that the cargo was in good condition at the time it was shipped. Normally, the *last* carrier is presumed to have received the goods in good condition.

Warehouse Companies

Warehousing is the business of providing storage of property for compensation. A warehouse company is a professional bailee whose responsibility differs from an ordinary bailee in two important aspects. First, a warehouse company is empowered to issue documents of title, in particular, warehouse receipts.[7] Second, warehouse companies are subject to an extraordinary network of state and federal statutes and Article 7 of the UCC (as are carriers).

Like ordinary bailees, a warehouse company is liable for loss or damage to property and possession resulting from *negligence* (and therefore does not have the same liability as a common carrier). The duty is one of reasonable care to protect and preserve the goods. A warehouse

company can limit the dollar amount of liability, but the bailor must be given the option of paying an increased storage rate for an increase in the liability limit.

A warehouse company accepts goods for storage and issues a warehouse receipt describing the property and the terms of the bailment contract. The warehouse receipt can be negotiable or nonnegotiable depending on how it is written. The warehouse receipt is negotiable if its terms provide that the warehouse company will deliver the goods "to the bearer" of the receipt, or "to the order of" a person named on the receipt.

The warehouse receipt serves multiple functions. It is a receipt for the goods stored; it is a contract of bailment; it also represents the goods (that is, it indicates title) and hence has value and utility in financing commercial transactions. For example, Oakner, a processor and canner of corn, delivers 6,000 cases of corn to Shaw, the owner of a warehouse. Shaw issues a negotiable warehouse receipt payable "to bearer" and gives it to Oakner. Oakner sells the warehouse receipt to a large supermarket chain, "I. M. Plenty." Oakner delivers the warehouse receipt to I. M. Plenty. I. M. Plenty is now the owner of the corn and has the right to obtain the cases from Shaw. It will present the warehouse receipt to Shaw, who in return will release the cases of corn to the chain.

Innkeepers

At common law, innkeepers, hotel owners, or similar operators were held to the same strict liability as common carriers with respect to

---

7. Document of title is defined in UCC 1-201(15) as any "document which in the regular course of business or financing is treated as adequately evidencing that the person in possession of it is entitled to receive, hold, and dispose of the document and the goods it covers. To be a document of title, a document must purport to be issued by or addressed to a bailee and purport to cover goods in the bailee's possession * * *"

property brought into the rooms by guests. Now, only those who provide lodging to the public for compensation as a *regular* business are covered under this rule of strict liability. Moreover, the rule applies only to those who are *guests*, as opposed to *lodgers*. A lodger is a permanent resident of the hotel or inn, whereas a guest is a traveler.

Statutory Changes   In many states, innkeepers can avoid strict liability for loss of guests' valuables and money by providing a safe in which to keep them. Each guest must be clearly notified of the availability of such a safe. When articles are not kept in the safe, or when they are of such a nature that they are not normally kept in a safe, statutes will often limit innkeepers' liability.

Consider an example covering personal property that cannot be put in a safe. Jackson stays for a night at Hideaway Hotel. When he returns from eating breakfast in the hotel restaurant, he discovers that the people in the room next door have forced the lock on the door between the two rooms and stolen his suitcase. Jackson claims that the hotel is liable for his loss. The hotel denies liability due to the lack of negligence on its part. At common law, innkeepers are actually insurers of the property of their guests and the hotel will be liable.

Today, however, state statutes limit the strict liability of the common law. These statutes vary from state to state. In many states, the monetary damages for which the innkeeper is liable are limited in amount. Indeed, these statutes may even provide that the innkeeper has no liability in the absence of negligence. Many statutes require these limitations to be posted or the guest to be notified, and the posting (notice) is frequently found on the door of each room in the motel or hotel.

Normally, the innkeeper assumes no responsibility for the safety of a guest's automobile because the guest usually retains possession and control. If, on the other hand, the innkeeper provides parking facilities, and the guest's car is entrusted to the innkeeper or to an employee, the innkeeper will be liable under the rules that pertain to parking lot bailees (ordinary bailments).

QUESTIONS AND CASE PROBLEMS

1. Curtis is an executive on a business trip to the West Coast. He has driven his car on this trip and checks into the Hotel Ritz. The hotel has a guarded underground parking lot. Curtis gives his car keys to the parking lot attendant but fails to notify the attendant that his wife's $10,000 fur coat is in a box in the trunk. The next day, upon checking out, he discovers that his car has been stolen. Curtis wants to hold the hotel liable for both the car and the coat. Discuss the probable success of his claim.

2. Discuss the standard of care required from the bailee for the bailed property in the following situations, and determine whether the bailee breached that duty:

    (a) Adam borrows Tom's lawn mower because his own lawn mower needs repair. Adam mows his front yard. In order to mow the back yard, he needs to move some hoses and lawn furniture. He leaves the mower in front of his house while doing so. When he returns to the front, he discovers the mower has been stolen.

    (b) Mary owns a valuable speedboat. She is going on vacation and asks her neighbor, Regina, to store the boat in one stall of Regina's double garage. Regina consents, and the boat is moved to the garage. Regina, in need of some grocery items for dinner, drives to the store. In doing so, she leaves the garage door open, as is her custom. While she is at the store, the speedboat is stolen.

3. Lee owns and operates a service station. Walter notes from his records and car mileage that his car needs an oil change. Walter's car also needs some minor repairs. Walter takes his car to Lee's station for the oil change and minor repairs. Lee tells Walter that he will be unable to do the work until the next day and that Walter can either bring the car back at that time or leave it overnight. Walter leaves the car with Lee. The next afternoon Walter comes to pick up his car. Lee presents Walter with a bill for $220 and refuses to return the car until he is paid. Upon inspecting the car, Walter discovers that the mileage indicator shows 150 more miles on the car than when he brought it in. Lee claims he was legally allowed to let one of

his employees road-test the car by taking it to his home and driving it last evening. Discuss Walter's and Lee's legal rights under these circumstances.

4. Paul borrows from his neighbor, Max, a gasoline-driven lawn edger. Max has not used the lawn edger for two years. Paul is not familiar with using a lawn edger since he has never owned one. Max previously used this edger numerous times, and if he had made a reasonable inspection, he would have discovered that the blade was loose. Paul is injured when the blade becomes detached while he is edging his yard.

(a) Can Paul hold Max liable for his injuries?
(b) Would your answer be any different if Paul had rented the edger from Max and paid a fee? Explain.

5. Franklin Washer Inc. delivered to the Western Central Railroad one hundred crated washing machines to be shipped to Rocky High Appliance Store in Denver, Colorado. Western Central received the goods on Thursday and stored them in its warehouse pending loading into boxcars the next day. On the shipping invoice, Western Central had a clause printed in big bold type that excluded the carrier from liability resulting from loss of goods under control of the carrier because of acts of vandalism, fire, or theft. The clause also limited liability to $500 per shipment unless a higher evaluation was declared and a fee paid. That evening a riot broke out, and in the process some of the one hundred crated washing machines were stolen, some were damaged by the rioters, and some were destroyed by fire. Franklin wants to hold the carrier liable for the entire value of the one hundred machines. Western claims, first, that it has no liability by virtue of the contractual limitation against liability for loss by fire, theft, or vandalism; and second, that if there was liability, its damage cost responsibility would be only $500. Discuss the validity of Western's claims.

6. In the early 1970s, New York City was engaged in extensive urban renewal, and many individuals were forced to relocate. Phillips was a resident of an apartment building that the city planned to tear down. He was forced to move his belongings to an apartment that was not yet ready for occupancy. Most of his belongings were stolen from this apartment while he was out of town. Phillips attempted to sue New York City for his lost property. Did the city owe a duty to Phillips? [Phillips v. City of New York, 71 Misc.2d 861, 337 N.Y.S.2d 303 (1972)]

7. Procter & Gamble was a distributor of soybean oils. Its buyer, Allied Crude Vegetable Oil Refining Corp., persuaded Procter & Gamble to engage in a practice known as field warehousing. Under this arrangement, Procter & Gamble shipped oil to Field Warehousing Corp., which stored the oil in its tanks. In exchange for the oil, Field Warehousing gave Procter & Gamble "warehousing receipts." This allowed Procter & Gamble to sell the oil to Allied by merely selling the receipts (which were evidence of title to the oil). Thus, Procter & Gamble did not have to ship any of the oil in order to make a sale. About six months after it began storing oil at Field Warehousing, Procter & Gamble sold a large number of its warehouse receipts to Allied. Sometime after the delivery of the designated oil to Field Warehousing, but prior to the delivery to Allied, the oil was stolen. After a year-long investigation, neither Field Warehousing nor Procter & Gamble could determine how the oil disappeared. Who was liable for the missing oil? [Procter & Gamble Distributing Co. v. Lawrence American Field Warehousing Corp., 16 N.Y.2d 344, 266 N.Y.S.2d 785, 213 N.E.2d 873 (1965)]

8. Buchanan entered into an agreement with Byrd and Barksdale in which Buchanan would pay $40 a month for Byrd and Barksdale to feed and keep Buchanan's horse on their five-acre tract in Irving, Texas. One night, the horses were in one of the pastures rather than in their stalls. All of them escaped around midnight, apparently through an open gate. Two were killed by a train a mile away. One of them was Buchanan's. He sued for damages. The trial court ruled that a mutual benefit bailment had been entered into and that judgment was for the plaintiff, because there was a presumption that Byrd and Barksdale, as bailees, were guilty of negligence. The Court of Civil Appeals reversed the judgment. Buchanan appealed to the Supreme Court of Texas. What was the result? [Buchanan v. Byrd, Supreme Court of Texas, 519 S.W.2d, 841 (1975)]

9. The Birmingham Television Corporation had stored some equipment with Harris Warehouse Company. The city's water main burst, flooding the warehouse and destroying much of the equipment. When Birmingham sued the warehouse (and the city waterworks), the warehouse raised the defense that the suit was not commenced within nine months after notice was given of the damage. This was expressly required by the terms of the warehouse receipt. Birmingham claimed that the provision was not binding because it was not communicated except by being marked on the back of the warehouse receipt. At trial, a summary judgment was entered in favor of the warehouse. What was the result on appeal? [Birmingham Television Corp. v. Waterworks, 292 Ala. 147, 290 So.2d 636 (1974)]

FOCUS ON ETHICS

Personal Property and Bailments

Some of the ethical considerations associated with mislaid and lost property, patents, trademarks and copyrights, and bailments are addressed below. Ethical questions that have developed in light of the expanding nature of personal property are also briefly discussed.

MISLAID AND LOST PROPERTY

Owners of businesses can often become finders of mislaid property. As a matter of law and perhaps of ethics, the finder of such mislaid property is entrusted with the duty of reasonable care for the goods. The extent to which the finder of mislaid property actually engages in exercising reasonable care depends in part on individual ethical standards. A problem arises when an employee finds the mislaid property. Who should get the property when no one claims it— the owner of the business or the employee? There also exists a conflict when a customer finds the mislaid property. Should the customer be the recipient of such property if it is never claimed?

The same issues arise with regard to lost property. The finder of lost property may attempt to hide the fact that the property was found. When the true owner demands return of the lost property, the finder can, in many circumstances, avoid relinquishing the lost property. Estray statutes have been enacted as a substitute for a higher code of ethics. Finders are thus encouraged to report discoveries because, by statute, they can acquire legal title to the property after a specified time period.

Note that businesses are aware that if they place enough hurdles before a person who is entitled to possession, the individual will often not pursue the matter and will thus lose the item by default. Is such conduct to be condoned or encouraged? Alternatively, should businesses be expected to strive for a higher standard or merely to rely on the law to determine a *minimum* code of conduct?

PATENTS, TRADEMARKS, AND COPYRIGHTS

Personal property includes the rights associated with the ownership of patents, trademarks, and copyrights. In the world of business, it is always possible that one person may intentionally infringe on someone else's patent, trademark, or copyright. The "infringer" reaps the rewards of another's creativity without incurring those expenses associated with the protection of the original item or idea. In turn, the original owner suffers a decrease in profits. Consider a competitor that takes aerial photographs of a plant's layout. The court ultimately deemed such conduct improper and ordered the defendant not to use any of the information so obtained.

The fact is, though, that many businesses will infringe on copyrights and patents when they know that the cost of enforcement is prohibitive. In other words, it is economically infeasible for the owner of a patent, trademark, or copyright to enforce such ownership rights. When an infringement occurs, owners of patents, trademarks, and copyrights will pursue litigation only if expected benefits exceed expected costs. The expected costs involve legal fees, as well as time spent engaging in such a lawsuit. The expected benefits include any damages awarded in a successful lawsuit, plus any future increase in revenues if the patent, trademark, or copyright were no longer violated. Because of this cost-benefit computation and because litigation costs are normally high, the majority of patent, trademark, and copyright infringements in the United States are probably not prosecuted. The ones that are usually involve extremely successful products.

Finally, note that in the area of trademarks, the law has evolved in the following way: when the use of a trademark or trade name becomes so common, it eventually belongs to society rather than to the trademark or trade name owner. Certainly an ethical question is at issue here.

THE EXPANDING NATURE OF PERSONAL PROPERTY

Recently a new set of ethical questions has arisen with regard to personal property. Today computer software programs are considered personal property. The incidence of "theft" of computer programs is indeed astounding. Unfortunately, to some individuals, personal property means only *tangible* personal property. These individuals do not consider ethical questions when the theft involves nontangible personal property. How many people think nothing of illegally duplicating copyrighted diskettes? How many people feel compunction about reproducing copyrighted movies? This issue is currently being debated in the courts and will eventually make its way to the Congress. Makers of videocassette recorders contend that owners of their products have the right to copy all television presentations. On the other hand, actors, producers, directors, and others who receive residual payments for movies, sitcoms, and the like, believe that their rights are being violated. In particular, those who hold proprietary rights in movies maintain that they should be awarded continuing royalties for all copies of the movie in question.

BAILMENTS

Ethical issues must be considered each time a bailment occurs. The bailee's duties often arise because of the *implied* responsibility in the bailment agreement. That the bailee take proper care of the property and surrender it at the end of the bailment seems eminently acceptable and indeed ethically appropriate given the nature of a bailment contract.

To a large extent, the courts have rejected numerous standard exculpatory clauses in bailment contracts simply on a public policy basis. Our collection of shared beliefs requires that bailees be responsible for the bailed items. The notion that a bailee can avoid *all* liability for damage to bailed items violates our common ethical standard of respect for the property of others. Courts often reject exculpatory clauses excusing parties from responsibility for any harm that they intentionally cause.

DISCUSSION QUESTIONS

1. Given the expanding nature of personal property today, an appropriate question is "What is the true nature of property?" And indeed, "What is ownership?"

2. Should the bailee be liable for damages to a rented car simply because the agreement says that such a person is responsible, even when the person renting the item was not aware of the terminology within the contract? Should the bailor of rental cars be allowed to require, as a practical matter, the purchase of insurance from the bailee before the car can be rented?

3. What property interests should be protected by law? Does one have a personal property interest in a job? In a spouse? In children?

UNIT IV

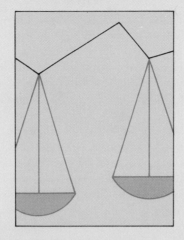

COMMERCIAL
TRANSACTIONS
AND THE
UNIFORM
COMMERCIAL
CODE

CHAPTER 18

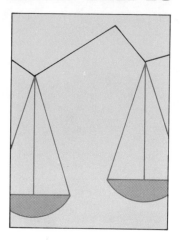

SALES
Introduction to Sales Contracts and Their Formation

Almost every day of our lives we make purchases—the daily newspaper, groceries, clothes, textbooks, a stereo, a car, and so on. Most of our purchases are of "goods" rather than real property. Thus, studying the law of sales of goods is relevant to our daily lives.

The people from whom we buy our goods are, to us, "sellers." But our "sellers" are in turn "buyers" from their suppliers, who are in turn, "buyers" from manufacturers. The law of sales is the study of the rights and responsibilities of those in the purchase-and-sale of goods chain, from the original maker of the item to the ultimate user. A **sale** is a contract that, by its terms, transfers title to goods from a seller to a buyer for a price.

HISTORICAL PERSPECTIVE

Today's law of sales originated centuries ago in the customs and traditions of merchants and traders. The *Lex Mercantoria* (Law Merchant) was a system of rules, customs, and usages self-imposed by early commercial traders and merchants to settle disputes and to enforce obligations among themselves. These rules were established at "fairs," where merchants met to exchange goods and settle differences through "fair courts" established and operated by the merchants themselves.

By the end of the seventeenth century, the principles of the Law Merchant were widely accepted and quite naturally became part of the common law. From that time on, judges, not merchants, refined the principles of mercantile law into the modern commercial law of sales.

Numerous attempts were made in the United States to produce a uniform body of laws relating to commercial transactions. Two major enactments, the Uniform Negotiable Instruments Law (1896) and the Uniform Sales Act (1906), were followed by several other "uniform acts," none of which were widely adopted by the states.

In the 1940s the need to integrate the half-dozen or so uniform acts covering commercial transactions into a single, comprehensive body of statutory law was recognized. Accordingly, the Uniform Commercial Code (UCC, or simply "the Code") was developed to serve that purpose.

Shift from Common Law to Statutory Law

It is important to note that when we focus on sales contracts, the subject of this chapter, we move away from common law principles and into a statutory body of law. The UCC is the statutory framework we will use, since it has been adopted as law by all states (with the exception of Louisiana, which has adopted only part of it). Relevant sections of the UCC are noted in the following discussion of sales contracts. The reader should refer to the appendix in the back of the book while examining these notations. Many similarities to the contract law previously studied in Chapters 6 through 15 will be apparent. Indeed, such similarities should be expected, since the UCC represents the codification of much of the existing common law of contracts.

The Uniform Commercial Code

The UCC is the single most comprehensive codification of the broad spectrum of laws involved in a total commercial transaction. The Code views the entire "commercial transaction for the sale of and payment for goods" as a single legal occurrence having numerous facets.

To illustrate: Review the ten articles of the UCC as listed in Chapter 1. Now consider a consumer who buys a refrigerator from an appliance store and agrees to pay for it on an installment plan. The following articles of the UCC could be applied to this single commercial transaction. Since there is a contract for sale of goods, Article 2 would apply. If a check is given as the down payment on the purchase price, it will be negotiated and ultimately passed through one or more banks for collection. This process is the subject matter of Article 3, Commercial Paper, and Article 4, Bank Deposits and Collections. If the ap-

pliance store extends credit to the consumer through the installment plan, and if it retains a right in the refrigerator (collateral), then Article 9, Secured Transactions, will be applicable.

Suppose, in addition, the appliance company must first obtain the refrigerator from its manufacturer's warehouse, after which it is to be delivered by common carrier to the consumer. The storage and shipment of goods is the subject matter of Article 7, Documents of Title. If the appliance company arranges to pay the manufacturer, located in another state, for the refrigerator supplied, a letter of credit, which is the subject matter of Article 5, may be used.

Thus, the Code attempts to provide a consistent and integrated framework of rules to deal with all the phases *ordinarily arising* in a commercial sales transaction from start to finish.[1]

THE SCOPE OF ARTICLE 2: THE SALE OF GOODS

No body of law operates in a vacuum removed from other principles of jurisprudence. A sales contract is governed by the same common law principles applicable to all contracts—offer, acceptance, consideration, and capacity—and these principles should be reexamined when studying sales. The law of sales, found in Article 2 of the UCC, is a part of the law of contracts.

Two things should be kept in mind. First, Article 2 deals with the sale of *goods*, not real property (real estate), services, or intangible property such as stocks and bonds. Second, in some cases, the rules may vary quite a bit, de-

---

1. Two articles of the UCC seemingly do not fit into the "ordinary" commercial sales transaction. Article 6, Bulk Transfers, involves merchants who sell off the major part of their inventory (often pocketing the money and disappearing, leaving creditors unpaid). Since such "bulk sales" do not "ordinarily arise" in a commercial transaction for the sale of goods, they are treated separately. Article 8, Investment Securities, deals with negotiable securities (stocks and bonds), transactions that do not fall within the concept of sale of or payment for *goods*. However, the subject matter of Articles 6 and 8 was considered by the Code's drafters to be related *sufficiently* to commercial transactions to warrant inclusion in the UCC.

pending upon whether the buyer or seller is a *merchant*.

It is always a good idea to note the subject matter of a dispute and the kind of people involved. If the subject is goods, then the UCC will govern. If it is real estate or services, then the common law alone will apply. Although the vast majority of the rules under Article 2 apply to all sellers and buyers of goods, some specific rules apply only if the seller or buyer, or both, are merchants.

What Is a Sale?

Section 2-102 of the Code states that Article 2 "applies to transactions in goods." This implies a broad scope for this article, ranging over leases, gifts, bailments, and purchases of goods. However, for the purposes of this chapter (and most authorities and courts would agree), we will treat Article 2 as applicable only to an actual sale.

The word "sale" is a shorthand way of saying "a sales contract which by its terms transfers goods from seller to buyer for a price." A sale is officially defined ". . . as the passing of title from the seller to the buyer for a price." [UCC 2-106(1)] The price may be payable in money or in other goods, services, or realty (real estate).

What Are Goods?

To be characterized as a *good*, an item must be *tangible*, and it must be *movable*.

A tangible item has physical existence—it can be touched or seen, as a horse, a car, or a chair. Thus, intangible property such as corporate stocks and bonds, promissory notes, bank accounts, patents and copyrights, or ordinary contract rights have only conceptual existence and do not come under Article 2.

A *movable* item can be carried from place to place. Hence, real estate is excluded from Article 2. Two basic areas of dispute arise in determining whether the object of the contract is goods, and thus whether Article 2 is applicable. One dispute concerns goods *associated with realty*, such as crops or timber, and the other concerns contracts involving a combination of *goods and services*.

Goods Versus Realty   *Goods associated with real*

estate fall under Article 2. Section 2-107 provides the following rules:

1.   A contract for the sale of minerals or the like (including oil and gas) or a structure (such as a building) is a contract for the sale of goods *if severance is to be made by the seller*. If the buyer is to sever them from the land, the contract is considered a sale of real estate governed by the principles of real property law, not the UCC.

To illustrate: S agrees to sell B a quantity of oil that is located under S's property. If B is to drill the wells to remove the oil, the contract is a sale of real estate. If the agreement provides that S is to drill the wells to obtain the oil, the transaction is a sale of goods. Similarly, if S agrees to sell B an old barn located on S's farm with B to remove the barn, it is a contract for the sale of real estate. If S is to remove the barn, the contract is characterized as a sale of goods under UCC Article 2.

2.   A sale of growing crops or timber to be cut is a contract for the sale of goods regardless of who severs them.

3.   Other "things attached" to realty but capable of severance without material harm to the land are considered goods regardless of who severs them.[2]

Examples of such things are a furnace or window air-conditioner in a house, or counters and stools in a luncheonette. The test is whether removal will cause *material harm* to the realty to which the item is attached. Removal of a window air-conditioner would be a sale of goods, but removal of a central air-conditioning system would probably do a great deal of damage to the realty and would be treated as a sale of real estate. When the parties do not envision any items being removed (severed) from the realty, such as in the sale of "ten acres with corn standing," then the transaction is characterized as the sale of real estate.

Goods Versus Services   Where goods and services are combined, courts have disagreed over whether a particular transaction involves the sale of goods or the rendering of a service. For ex-

---

2.   The Code avoids using the word "fixtures" here because of the numerous definitions of this term. (See Chapter 53.)

ample, is the blood furnished to a patient during an operation a "sale of goods" or the "performance of a medical service"? Some courts say "a good"; some say "a service." In discussing their decisions, the courts try to determine which factor is predominant—the good or the service.

The same kind of "mixed transaction" problem is encountered when a beautician applies hair dye to a customer in a beauty shop. The Code does not provide the answer, and court decisions are in conflict.

The Code does stipulate, however, that serving food or drink to be consumed either on or off restaurant premises is the "sale of goods," at least for the purpose of an implied warranty of merchantability. [UCC 2-314(1)] Whether the transaction in question involves the sale of goods or services is important because the majority of courts treat services as being excluded by the UCC.

Also, a contract for specially manufactured goods is one for goods, not services. [UCC 2-105(1)] Several other special cases are explicitly characterized as goods by the Code, including the unborn young of animals and rare coins and other forms of money as a commodity.

Who Is a Merchant?

Article 2 governs the sale of goods in general. It applies to sales transactions between all buyers and sellers. In a limited number of instances, however, the Code presumes that in certain phases of sales transactions involving *professional merchants*, special business standards ought to be imposed because of the merchants' degree of commercial expertise.[3] Such standards do not apply to the casual or inexperienced seller or buyer. Section 2-104 defines three ways that *merchant* status occurs:

1.   A merchant is a person who *deals in goods*

of the kind involved in the sales contract. Thus, a retailer, a wholesaler, or a manufacturer is a merchant of those goods sold in the business. A merchant for one type of goods is not necessarily a merchant for any other type. For example, a sporting equipment retailer is a merchant when buying tennis equipment but not when buying stereo equipment.

2.   A merchant is a person who, by occupation, *holds himself or herself out as having knowledge and skill peculiar to the practices or goods involved in the transaction.* This is a broad definition that can include banks or universities as merchants.

3.   A person who employs a merchant as a broker, agent, or other intermediary has the status of merchant in that transaction. Hence, if a "gentleman farmer" who ordinarily does not run the farm hires a broker to purchase livestock, the farmer is considered a merchant in the livestock transaction.

In summary, a person is a merchant when that person, acting in a mercantile capacity, possesses or uses an expertise specifically related to the goods being sold. This basic distinction, however, is not always clear-cut. For example, disagreement has arisen over whether a farmer is a merchant. The answer depends upon the particular goods involved, the transaction, and whether, in the particular situation, the farmer has special knowledge concerning the goods involved in the transaction. The following case illustrates how the courts decide whether or not a person is a merchant and therefore subject to the UCC version of the Statute of Frauds.

---

3.   The provisions that apply only to merchants deal principally with the Statute of Frauds, firm offers, confirmatory memoranda, warranties, and contract modification. These special rules reflect expedient business practice commonly known to merchants in the commercial setting. They will be discussed later in this chapter.

BACKGROUND AND FACTS   *The plaintiff, a grain company, brought this action against a farmer for the farmer's failure to deliver grain pursuant to an alleged oral contract. The grain company had issued, and the farmer had received, a written confirmation for the sale. This was the only writing, and it was for more than $500. The trial court entered a judgment for the farmer, and the grain company appealed.*

TERMINAL GRAIN CORP. v. FREEMAN
Supreme Court of South Dakota, 1978.
270 N.W.2d 806

HANSON, Retired Justice.

*   *   *   *

Terminal Grain *   *   * alleges error on the refusal of the trial court to instruct the jury on the Uniform Commercial Code provisions contained in [UCC 2-201(1) and (2)]. [UCC 2-201(1)] is a general statute of frauds providing as follows:

Except as otherwise provided in [this section] a contract for the sale of goods for the price of five hundred dollars or more is not enforceable by way of action or defense unless there is some writing sufficient to indicate that a contract for sale has been made between the parties and signed by the party against whom enforcement is sought or by his authorized agent or broker. A writing is not insufficient because it omits or incorrectly states a term agreed upon but the contract is not enforceable under this section beyond the quantity of goods shown in such writing.

The above statute of frauds has been held applicable in similar actions for damages involving oral contracts in excess of $500.00 between an elevator/buyer and a farmer/seller for nondelivery of grain at a future date. However, the court had no occasion to consider the application of [UCC 2-201(2)] in either case. This exception to the Uniform Commercial Code general statute of frauds provides:

Between merchants if within a reasonable time a writing in confirmation of the contract and sufficient against the sender is received and the party receiving it has reason to know its contents, it satisfies the requirements of [subsection (1)] against such party unless written notice of objection to its contents is given within ten days after it is received.

As a farmer, Freeman contends he is not a "merchant" within the contemplation of the above statute and it, therefore has no application to him. The term "merchant" is defined in [UCC 2-104(1)] as meaning

a person who deals in goods of the kind or otherwise by his occupation holds himself out as having knowledge or skill peculiar to the practices or goods involved in the transaction or to whom such knowledge or skill may be attributed by his employment of an agent or broker or other intermediary who by his occupation holds himself out as having such knowledge or skill.

Also, the term "between merchants" is defined to mean "in any transaction with respect to which both parties are chargeable with the knowledge or skill of merchants."

The official comment to § 2-104 of the Uniform Commercial Code definition of "Merchant" and "Between Merchants" states in part:

1. This Article assumes that transactions between professionals in a given field require special and clear rules which may not apply to a casual or inexperienced seller or buyer. *   *   *

2. The term 'merchant' as defined here roots in the 'law merchant' concept of a professional in business. The professional status under the definition may be based upon specialized knowledge as to the goods, specialized knowledge as to business practices, or specialized knowledge as to both and which kind of specialized knowledge may be sufficient to establish the merchant status is indicated by the nature of the provisions.

In similar factual cases the courts which have considered whether or not a "farmer" is or may be considered a "merchant" under the above Uniform Commercial Code provisions are almost equally divided in their opinions. The courts in Illinois, Texas, Missouri, Ohio, and North Carolina have held farmers to be merchants under various facts and circumstances [.]

On the other hand the courts in Iowa, New Mexico, Utah, Kansas, Arkansas, and Alabama have held that a farmer is not a merchant[.]

In arriving at its conclusion that the defendant farmer/seller was not a "merchant" within the meaning of the Uniform Commercial Code, the Kansas Court said:

> [T]he appellee neither 'deals' in wheat, as that term is used in 2-104 nor does he by his occupation hold himself out as having knowledge or skill peculiar to the practices or goods involved in the transaction. The concept of professionalism is heavy in determining who is a merchant under the statute. The writers of the official UCC comment virtually equate professionals with merchants—the casual or inexperienced buyer or seller is not to be held to the standard set for the professional in business. The defined term 'between merchants', used in the exception proviso to the statute of frauds, contemplates the knowledge and skill of professionals on each side of the transaction. The transaction in question here was the sale of wheat. Appellee as a farmer undoubtedly had special knowledge or skill in raising wheat but we do not think this factor, coupled with annual sales of a wheat crop and purchases of seed wheat, qualified him as a merchant in that field. The parties' stipulation states appellee has sold only the products he raised. There is no indication any of these sales were other than cash sales to local grain elevators, where conceivably an expertise reaching professional status could be said to be involved.

We agree with the reasoning of the Kansas Court and with the other courts which hold the average farmer, like Freeman, with no particular knowledge or experience in selling, buying, or dealing in future commodity transactions, and who sells only the crops he raises to local elevators for cash or who places his grain in storage under one of the federal loan programs, is not a "merchant" within the purview of the exception provision to the Uniform Commercial Code statute of frauds. Through training and years of experience a farmer may well possess or acquire special knowledge, skills, and expertise in the production of grain crops but this does not make him a "professional," equal in the marketplace with a grain buying and selling company, whose officers, agents, and employees are constantly conversant with the daily fluctuations in the commodity market, the many factors affecting the market, and with its intricate practices and procedures. Accordingly, the trial court did not err in refusing to instruct the jury on this issue.

JUDGMENT AND REMEDY

The decision was affirmed for the farmer, and the grain company could not recover damages for the farmer's failure to deliver the wheat. The Statute of Frauds was applicable to the transaction. Since the farmer was not a "merchant," the confirmation sent by the grain company was insufficient to bind the farmer to the alleged oral contract.

COMMENT

Whether a farmer is a merchant will be decided on the facts of each case. If the farmer deals extensively in contracts for future delivery, the courts are more likely to determine that he or she is a merchant than if the farmer deals only in cash sales to grain elevators.

FORMATION OF
A SALES CONTRACT

The policy of the UCC is to recognize that the law of sales is part of the general law of contracts. The Code often restates general principles or is silent on certain subjects. In those situations, the common law of contracts and applicable state statutes govern. The following sections summarize the ways that UCC provisions *change* the effect of the general law of contracts.

Offer

In general contract law, the moment a definite offer is met by an unqualified acceptance, a binding contract is formed. In commercial sales transactions, the verbal exchanges, the correspondence, and the actions of the parties may not reveal exactly when a binding contractual obligation arises. The Code states that an agreement sufficient to constitute a contract can exist even if the moment of its making is undetermined. [UCC 2-204(2)]

Open Terms According to contract law, an offer must be definite enough for the parties (and the courts) to ascertain its essential terms when it is accepted. The UCC states that a sales contract will not fail for indefiniteness even if one or more terms are left open as long as: (1) the parties intended to make a contract and (2) there is a reasonably certain basis for the court to grant an appropriate remedy. [UCC 2-204(3)]

The Code provides numerous *open term* provisions that can be used to fill in the gaps in a contract. Two factors should be kept in mind. The more terms left open, the less likely the courts will find that the parties intended to form a contract. As a general rule, if the *quantity* term is left open, the courts will have no basis for determining a remedy, and the sales contract will

fail unless the contract is either an output or a requirement contract. [UCC 2-306]

Open Price Term If the parties have not agreed on a price, the court will determine "a reasonable price *at the time for delivery*." [UCC 2-305(1)] If either the buyer or the seller is to determine the price, it means a price fixed in good faith. [UCC 2-305(2)]

Sometimes the price fails to be fixed through the fault of one of the parties. In that case, the other party can treat the contract as cancelled or fix a reasonable price. For example, Axel and Beatty enter into a contract for the sale of goods and agree that Axel will fix the price. The agreement becomes economically burdensome to Axel, and Axel refuses to fix the price. Beatty can either treat the contract as cancelled or can set a reasonable price. [UCC 2-305(3)]

Open Payment Term When parties do not specify payment terms, payment is due at the time and place at which the buyer is to receive the goods. [UCC 2-310(a)] Generally, cash, not credit, is used. The buyer can tender payment using any commercially normal or acceptable means, such as a check, credit card and the like. If the seller demands payment in cash, however, the buyer must be given a reasonable time to obtain it. [UCC 2-511(2)] This would be especially important when a definite and final time for performance is stated in the contract.

Although the UCC has radically lessened the requirements for definiteness of essentials in contracts of sale, it has not removed the common law requirement that the contract be at least definite enough for the court to identify the agreement, so that it can either enforce it or award appropriate damages if it is breached. In the following case, the absence of the price term and of the specific goods to be purchased caused the court to find that there was no contract.

ROYAL STORE
FIXTURE CO. v. BUCCI
Pennsylvania County Court,
1969.
7 UCC Rep. Serv. 1193.

BACKGROUND AND FACTS *Bucci, the defendant, purchased some land, intending to build a combination restaurant and delicatessen on it, and contacted several contractors and suppliers for estimates. Bucci ultimately made a written agreement with the Royal Store Fixture Co., the plaintiff, "to purchase the store fixtures and refrigeration equipment re-*

quired" for the new store. Subsequently, the plaintiff submitted various proposals for an equipment layout to the defendant. The defendant also received bids from other companies and ultimately purchased the required equipment from one of the plaintiff's competitors. The plaintiff insisted that the defendant was bound by the writing—that is, by a valid agreement to buy all store fixtures and equipment requirements through the plaintiff at competitive prices. The defendant argued, on the other hand, that the document signed by the parties was too vague and indefinite to be a binding contract.

MEADE, Judge.

*   *   *   *

The Uniform Commercial Code *   *   * (UCC) § 2-204. *   *   * provides that "(3) Even though one or more terms are left open a contract for sale does not fail for indefiniteness if the parties have intended to make a contract and there is a *reasonably certain basis for giving an appropriate remedy.*" (Italics supplied.) The commentary to the code *   *   * points out that, as to contract rules "The prime test is simply that the parties intended to make a contract and that 'there is a reasonably certain basis for giving an appropriate remedy'. It is specifically provided that the price, particulars of performance, the time for performance and the duration of the contract must not necessarily be fixed by the agreement of the parties." The authors of the code itself point out in the comment to § 2-204 that "The more terms the parties leave open, the less likely it is that they have intended to conclude a binding agreement, but their actions may be frequently conclusive on the matter despite the omissions."

The subject matter in the case sub judice [the case at bar or the case under study] is described only as "store fixtures and refrigeration equipment." This description is wholly inadequate to give the requisite clarity to the agreement so as to make it an enforceable contract.

*   *   *   *

Nor do we believe that the price of the unspecified store fixtures and refrigeration equipment could ever be reduced to reasonable certainty. While § 2-305 of the UCC dealing with "open price term", has been construed to call for a reasonable price (Kuss Machine Tool & Die Co. v. El-Tronics, Inc., 393 Pa 353 (1958)), this may not necessarily be the same as the "competitive prices" called for in the writing. The testimony is clear that the parties left open the term of price, because it was to be agreed upon at a later date. Whether the court could arrive at a "reasonable" price is doubted in view of plaintiff's testimony on that question.

*   *   *   *

For the foregoing reasons, we hold that the instrument signed by the parties was not an enforceable agreement. *   *   *

Judgment must be entered in favor of defendant and against plaintiff.

JUDGMENT AND REMEDY

Judgment was for the defendant. Bucci was allowed to purchase store fixtures and refrigeration equipment from another supplier. The sales contract, or agreement, was too vague because it did not state the price of the unspecified goods that were to be sold, and, more importantly, it was not possible for the court to determine exactly what goods Bucci was to purchase under the agreement.

Open Delivery Term When no delivery terms are specified, the buyer normally takes delivery at the seller's place of business. [UCC 2-308(a)] If the seller has no place of business, then the seller's residence is used. When goods are located in some other place and both parties know it, then delivery is made there. When the time for shipment or delivery has not been clearly specified in the sales contract, the court will infer a "reasonable" time under the circumstances for performance. [UCC 2-309(1)] The following case concerns reasonable time.

MENDELSON-ZELLER
CO., INC. v. JOSEPH
WEDNER & SON CO.
U.S. Department of Agriculture,
1970.
7 UCC Rep. Serv. 1045.

BACKGROUND AND FACTS *The dispute here concerned 400 cartons of lettuce.*

The contract provided that the lettuce would be shipped from El Centro, California, on January 18 and that lemons would be loaded at Yuma, Arizona. The parties estimated that delivery to Pittsburgh, Pennsylvania, would be in time for the market of Monday morning, January 22, 1968.

Mendelson-Zeller, the plaintiff, shipped the lettuce on January 18, 1968, at 9:40 P.M. from El Centro, California, and the lemons on January 19, 1968, at 4:30 A.M. from Yuma, Arizona, in a truck. The truckload of produce arrived at Wedner & Son's (the defendant's) place of business at 12:30 P.M., January 22, 1968. Wedner's docking superintendent refused to unload the truck and instructed the driver to return the next morning at 2:00 A.M. to have the truck unloaded for Tuesday's market. The driver locked the truck and did not return until 6:30 A.M. on Tuesday. Thus, the produce was delivered on the scheduled delivery date, but, according to Wedner, it arrived nine and one-half hours late. Wedner claimed that the agreement indicated that the goods would arrive between 2:00 and 3:00 A.M. so they would be available when the produce market opened. Mendelson-Zeller claimed that neither the time of loading nor the time of arrival was guaranteed.

Wedner eventually sold the lettuce and remitted the net proceeds of $1,028.93 to Mendelson-Zeller, along with the net proceeds from the consignment sale of the lettuce. Mendelson-Zeller sued for the difference between the contract price and the amount remitted.

FLAVIN, Judicial Officer.

* * * *

There is evidence that the trucker was under some pressure to get the lettuce to respondent [Wedner & Son] for Monday morning's market.

* * * *

It is evident * * * that [seller] * * * distinguishes between an estimated delivery time and a delivery time which is specified as a part of the contract terms. Neither party submitted a broker's memorandum covering the sale which would presumably show whether there was a specified contract delivery time. In addition the bill of lading does not disclose a specified arrival time though a blank space is provided in which such information can be entered. All of the statements relevant to arrival time other than [buyer] Wedner's statement can be interpreted to mean estimated or anticipated arrival time rather than a time specified as a contract condition.

Respondent [Wedner] as the party alleging that a specified arrival time was a part of the contract of sale had the burden of proving by a preponderance of the evidence that its allegation was true. In view of the foregoing discussion we conclude that respondent has not met its burden of proof.

Section 2-309(1) of the Uniform Commercial Code provides that the time for delivery in the absence of an agreed time shall be a reasonable time. Section 2-503(1) provides that tender of delivery must be at a reasonable hour. The evidence shows that the truck left Yuma at 4:30 a.m. January 19 and arrived at respondent's warehouse at 12:30 p.m. January 22. Although the trucker offered to pay overtime for unloading, respondent's docking superintendent refused to unload. Wedner testified that he thought the truck arrived well after business hours. However, he also testified that respondent's office hours are 9 a.m. to 5 p.m. and the hours at its warehouse and terminal on Mondays are 4 a.m. to anywhere from 11:30 to 12:30 p.m. There is no evidence as to the exact time the warehouse closed on January 22. It is unnecessary to resolve whether the tender on January 22 was within a reasonable hour or whether, as complainant contends, respondent accepted delivery by ordering the truckers to return the next morning. The load was tendered and accepted at 6:30 a.m. January 23, about 97 hours after the truck left Yuma. Although there was some testimony indicating that the normal transit time is 72 hours, the trucking company states that this is an impossibility in the winter time. The truck was actually in transit about 80 hours between Yuma and Pittsburgh. Under the circumstances, we are unable to say that delivery on January 23, was not within a reasonable time.

JUDGMENT AND REMEDY The seller, Mendelson-Zeller Co., prevailed. The delivery was made in reasonable time; hence Wedner's failure to pay the full contract price of the lettuce was a breach of contract. The court awarded Mendelson-Zeller damages plus interest on the amount owing.

Duration of an Ongoing Contract A single contract might specify successive performances, but may not indicate how long the parties are required to deal with one another. Although either party may terminate the ongoing contractual relationship, principles of good faith and sound commercial practice call for reasonable notification before termination so as to give the other party reasonable time to seek a substitute arrangement. [UCC 2-309(2)(3)]

Options and Cooperation Regarding Performance When specific shipping arrangements have not been made but the contract contemplates shipment of the goods, the seller has the right to make these arrangements in good faith, using commercial reasonableness in the situation. [UCC 2-311]

When terms relating to the assortment of goods are omitted from a sales contract, the buyer can specify the assortment. For example, Able and Baker contract for the sale of 1,000 pens. The pens come in a variety of colors, but the contract is silent on which color is ordered. Baker, the buyer, has the right to take 600 blue pens and 400 green pens if he wishes. However, Baker must make the selection in good faith and must use commercial reasonableness. [UCC 2-311]

Merchant's Firm Offer The firm offer is in the special category of rules applicable only to *merchants*. Under regular contract principles, an offer can be revoked any time before acceptance. The major common law exception is an option contract in which the offeree pays consideration for the offeror's irrevocable promise to keep the offer open for a stated period.

The UCC creates a second exception that applies only to *firm offers* for the sale of goods made *by a merchant* (regardless of whether or not the offeree is a merchant). If the merchant gives *assurances* in a *signed writing* that the offer will remain open for the stated period or, if no definite period is specified, a reasonable period, (neither to exceed three months), the *merchant's firm offer* is irrevocable without the necessity of consideration.[4] [UCC 2-205]

To illustrate: Daniels, a used-car dealer, writes a letter to Peters on January 1 stating, "I have a 1974 Dodge Dart on the lot that I'll sell you for $2,200 any time between now and the end of the month." By January 18, Daniels has heard nothing from Peters so he sells the Dodge Dart to another person. On January 23, Peters tenders $2,200 to Daniels and asks for the car. When Daniels tells him the car has already been sold, Peters claims that Daniels has breached a good contract. Peters is right. Since Daniels is a merchant of used cars, he is obligated to keep his offer open until the end of January. Since he has not done so, he is liable for breach.

It is necessary, however, that the offer be both *written and signed* by the offeror.[5] Where a firm offer is contained in a form contract prepared by the offeree, a *separate* firm offer assurance must be signed in addition. The purpose of the merchant's firm offer rule is to give effect to a merchant's deliberate intent to be bound to a firm offer. If the firm offer is buried in one of the pages of the offeree's form contract amid copious language, the offeror might inadvertently sign the contract without realizing it, thus defeating the purpose of the rule.

ACCEPTANCE

Methods of Acceptance The general common law rule is that an offeror can specify, or authorize, a particular means of acceptance, making that means the only one effective for the contract. The common law rule has been altered recently, however, so that even unauthorized

means of communication are effective as long as the acceptance is received by the specified deadline. For example, suppose the offer states, "Answer by telegraph within five days." If the offeree sends a letter, and it is received by the offeror within five days, a valid contract is formed.

When the offeror does not specify a means of acceptance, the Code provides that acceptance can be made by any means of communication reasonable under the circumstances, even if the acceptance is not received within the designated time. [UCC 2-206(1)] For example, Alpha Corporation writes Beta Corporation a letter offering to sell Beta $1,000 worth of goods. The offer states that Alpha will keep the offer open for only ten days from the date of the letter. Before the ten days have lapsed, Beta sends Alpha a telegram of acceptance. The telegram is misdirected by the telegraph company and does not reach Alpha until after the ten-day deadline. Is a valid contract formed? The answer is probably yes, since telegraph appears to be a commercially reasonable medium of acceptance under the circumstances. Acceptance would be effective upon Alpha's delivery of the message to the telegraph office, which occurred before the offer lapsed.

The UCC permits acceptance of an offer to buy goods for current or prompt shipment by either a *promise* to ship or *prompt shipment* of the goods to the buyer. [UCC 2-206(1)(b)] This provision of the Code retains the common law acceptance of an offer (performance by delivery of conforming goods to the carrier) and adds as acceptance the commercial practice of sellers who send promises to ship conforming goods. These promises are effective when sent, if they meet the test of being sent by a medium that is commercially reasonable under the circumstances.

The Code goes one step further and provides that if the seller does not promise to ship conforming goods but instead ships (in response to the order) *nonconforming goods*, this shipment constitutes both an acceptance (contract) and a breach. This specific rule (dealing with nonconforming goods shipped) does not apply if the seller seasonably notifies the buyer that the nonconforming shipment is offered only as an accommodation. The notice of accommodation

---

4. If the offeree pays consideration, then an *option contract* and not a *merchant's firm offer* is formed.

5. "Signed" includes any symbol executed or adopted by a party with present intention to authenticate a writing. [UCC 1-201(39)]

must clearly indicate to the buyer that the shipment does not constitute an acceptance and that, therefore, no contract has been formed at this time.

For example, Beyer orders 1,000 *blue* widgets from Sallor. Sallor ships 1,000 *black* widgets to Beyer, notifying Beyer that since Sallor has only black widgets in stock, these are sent as an accommodation. The shipment of black widgets is not an acceptance, but an offer (usually a counter-offer), and a contract will be formed only if Beyer accepts the black widgets.

If, however, Sallor ships 1,000 black widgets instead of blue without notifying Beyer that the goods are being shipped *as an accommodation*, Sallor's shipment acts as both an acceptance of Beyer's offer and a *breach* of the resulting contract. Beyer may sue Sallor for any appropriate damages.

At common law, since a unilateral offer invites acceptance by a performance, the offeree need not notify the offeror of performance unless the offeror would not otherwise know about it. The UCC is more stringent than common law, stating that "Where the beginning of requested performance is a reasonable mode of acceptance an offeror who is not notified of acceptance within a reasonable time may treat the offer as having lapsed before acceptance." [UCC 2-206(2)]

To illustrate: Johnson writes the Scroll Bookstore on Monday, "Please send me a copy of *West's Book of Business Law* for $30, C.O.D.," signed "Johnson." Scroll receives the request on Tuesday. Scroll immediately prepares the book for shipment but does not ship it for four weeks. Upon its arrival, Johnson rejects the shipment, claiming that the book has arrived too late to be of value.

In this case, since Johnson heard nothing from Scroll for a month, he was justified in assuming that the store did not intend to deliver *West's Book of Business Law*. Johnson could consider that the offer lapsed because of the length of time.

Additional Terms   Under traditional common law, if Able makes an offer to Baker, and Baker in turn accepts but adds some slight qualification, there is no contract. The so-called "mirror-image rule" of offer-to-acceptance makes Baker's

action a rejection of and a counter-offer to Able's offer.

The UCC generally takes the position that if the offeree's response indicates a *definite* acceptance of the offer, a contract is formed, even if the acceptance includes terms in addition to or different from the original offer. [UCC 2-207(1)] However, the Code provides that the offeree's expression cannot be construed as an acceptance if the modifications are subject to (conditional on) the offeror's "assent."

For example, Sallor offers to sell Beyer 500 pounds of chicken breasts at a specified price and on specified delivery terms. Beyer responds, "I accept your offer for 500 pounds of chicken breasts, *as evidenced by a city scale weight certificate*, at the price and delivery terms stated in your offer."

Beyer's response constitutes a contract even though the acceptance adds the words "as evidenced by a city scale weight certificate." However, if Beyer says, "I accept your offer for 500 pounds of chicken breasts on condition that the weight be evidenced by a city scale weight certificate," there will be no contract unless Sallor so agrees.

If it is determined that a contract exists, the issue then becomes one of under whose terms we measure performance: the offeror's or the offeree's (with modifications)? The Code also addresses this issue in an attempt to solve the so-called battle of the forms between commercial buyers and sellers. (See Exhibit 18-1 for a sample purchase order.)

Rules Where Seller or Buyer Is a Non-merchant   When either the seller or the buyer is a non-merchant, or when both are non-merchants, the additional terms are construed as mere proposals (suggestions), and the modified terms do not become a part of the contract. Thus, the contract is formed on the offeror's terms. [UCC 2-207(2)]

For example, Smith offers to sell his *personal* car to Green for $1,000. Green replies, "I accept your offer to purchase your car for $1,000. I would like a new spare tire to be included as part of the purchase price." Green has given Smith a definite expression of acceptance, creating a

EXHIBIT 18–1 SAMPLE PURCHASE ORDER

ABC MANUFACTURING COMPANY
WORK PURCHASE ORDER

TO: ___XYZ Widget Co.___   DATE: ___1/18/83___

___123 Marlett Ave.___

___Richmond, Wisconsin___   REG.#: _____403_____

Please supply the following services within the schedule and cost frame as listed below. A copy of your final quotation is attached for reference and verification of projected costs for this project. This purchase order covers those items listed on your quotation as well as those items listed below:

We accept your final quotation of $19.20 per widget for delivery of one thousand widgets to be delivered within thirty days of the date listed above. Freight cost to be paid by you.

THIS ORDER constitutes a contract and our authorization for you to commence work on the above project, subject to conditions listed below which hereby become a part of this contract. (It also recognizes acceptance of quotations submitted by you on the items attached and listed above within the limits of our conditions of contract and your specified terms of delivery.)

Payment shall be made for the work completed, delivered to and accepted by ABC Manufacturing Company at each stage, and no other form of partial payment or advance payment shall be made without prior written authorization by ABC Manufacturing Company.

If a delay occurs for reasons under the control of the supplier and if the specified completion dates are not met, or are not likely to be met, by any supplier of services, then this contract shall be void, unless written notice of new, specified dates is given to and accepted by ABC Manufacturing Company, and unless there is issued a new Work Purchase Order which replaces the original Work Purchase Order.

Final acceptance of all work and materials rests with ABC Manufacturing Company, which retains the right at all times to secure mutually acceptable modifications or changes to or to reject work and materials which, in its opinion, does not meet the standards of good and reasonably workmanlike quality.

_____   SIGNED: _____
Authorized Supplier Signature   Department Manager

contract, even though Green's acceptance also suggests an added term for the offer. Since Green is not a merchant, the additional term is merely a proposal (suggestion), and Green is not legally obligated to comply. On the other hand, if Smith made the spare tire a *condition* of acceptance, then Smith would be making a counteroffer and rejecting the original offer.

Rules between Merchants   The Code rule for additional terms in the acceptance is a little different when the transaction occurs between merchants (that is, when both buyer and seller are merchants). Between merchants the additional proposed terms *automatically* become part of the contract unless:

1. They *materially alter* the original contract.
2. The *offer expressly states* that no terms other than those in the offer will be accepted.
3. The offeror timely objects to the modified terms. [UCC 2-207(2)]

Suppose Sallor and Beyer are merchants. Sallor offers to sell Beyer 1,000 ballpoint pen and pencil sets at a price of $10 per set *plus* freight. Beyer responds, "I accept your offer. Price is $10.01 per set, *including* freight." There is a contract between Sallor and Beyer because Beyer made a definite expression of acceptance. Unless Sallor objects to the freight modification within a reasonable time after receiving notice of the change, Sallor is bound to the $10.01 per set price including freight.

Such is not the case, however, if the modification is one that materially alters the contract. What constitutes a material alteration is frequently a question of fact that only a court can decide. Generally, if the modification involves no unreasonable element of surprise or hardship for the offeror, the court will hold that it did not materially alter the contract. If, in the example just presented, the actual freight charge and the 1¢ per set are within a reasonable range of each other, the modification would *probably* not be considered material.

Now suppose that Sallor's offer states, "1,000 ballpoint pen and pencil sets at a price of $10 per set plus freight. Your acceptance on these terms and these terms only." Beyer's definite expression of acceptance with the modified freight terms still constitutes a contract, but because Sallor's offer specifically restricts his obligations to the terms of his offer, the contract is formed on Sallor's terms of "$10 per set plus freight."

In this next case, the court grapples with the question of whether a carpet manufacturer's written confirmation of a carpet dealer's oral orders for carpet was an "acceptance expressly conditioned on the buyer's consent to additional terms" (specifically, an arbitration provision), which would bring their situation within UCC 2-207(1), and whether the written confirmation between merchants automatically became part of the contract unless they "materially altered it," which would bring the action within the provisions of UCC 2-207(2).

BACKGROUND AND FACTS   *The Carpet Mart was a carpet dealer, and Collins & Aikman Corp. was a carpet manufacturer. Typically, the parties did business orally, followed with acknowledgment forms that were generally recognized as confirmations of prior oral agreements. In this particular instance, Collins & Aikman attempted to introduce in their confirmation form an additional term concerning an arbitration provision. The court was not able to resolve who should prevail because a final decision required additional findings of fact from the trial court. So, the court merely provided a framework within which the trial court could proceed after the additional information had been gathered. The case should be read for an understanding of the law.*

DORTON v. COLLINS & AIKMAN CORP.

United States Court of Appeals, Sixth Circuit, 1972.
453 F.2d 1161.

CELEBREZZE, Circuit Judge.

*   *   *   *

    *   *   * *Under the common law, an acceptance or a confirmation which contained terms additional to or different from those of the offer or oral agreement constituted a rejection of the offer or agreement and thus became a counter-offer.* [Emphasis added.] The terms of the counter-offer were said to have been accepted by the original offeror when he proceeded to perform under the contract without objecting to the counter-offer. Thus, a buyer was deemed to have accepted the seller's counter-offer if he took receipt of the goods and paid for them without objection.

    Under Section 2-207 the result is different. This section of the Code recognizes that in current commercial transactions, the terms of the offer and those of the acceptance will seldom be identical. Rather, under the current "battle of the forms", each party typically has a printed form drafted by his attorney and containing as many terms as could be envisioned to favor that party in his sales transactions. Whereas under common law the disparity between the fine-print terms in the parties' forms would have prevented the consummation of a contract when these forms are exchanged, Section 2-207 recognizes that in many, but not all, cases the parties do not impart such significance to the terms on the printed forms. *   *   *
*   *   *   *

    Assuming, for purposes of analysis, that the arbitration provision was an addition to the terms of The Carpet Mart's oral offers, we must next determine whether or not Collins & Aikman's acceptances were "expressly made conditional on assent to the additional *   *   * terms" therein, within the proviso of Subsection 2-207(1).

    Because Collins & Aikman's acceptances were not expressly conditional on the buyer's assent to the additional terms within the proviso of Subsection 2-207(1) a contract is recognized under Subsection (1), and the additional terms are treated as "proposals" for addition to the contract under Subsection 2-207(2). Since both Collins & Aikman and The Carpet Mart are clearly "merchants" as that term is defined in Subsection 2-104(1), the arbitration provision will be deemed to have been accepted by The Carpet Mart under Subsection 2-207(2) unless it materially altered the terms of The Carpet Mart's oral offers.

JUDGMENT
AND REMEDY

If Collins & Aikman's acknowledgments are in fact acceptances and the arbitration provision is additional to the terms of Carpet Mart's oral orders, the contracts will be recognized under the provisions of UCC 2-207(1). The arbitration clause will then be viewed as a "proposal" under UCC 2-207(2), and it will be deemed to have been accepted by Carpet Mart, as both parties are merchants, unless it materially altered the oral agreement.

Consideration

The UCC radically changes the common law rule that contract modification must be supported by new consideration. Section 2-209(1) states that "an agreement modifying a contract needs no consideration to be binding." Of course, contract modification must be sought in good faith. [UCC 1-203] Modifications *extorted* from the other party are in bad faith and, therefore, unenforceable.

For example, Hal agrees to manufacture and sell certain goods to Betty for a stated price. Subsequently, a sudden shift in the market makes it difficult for Hal to sell the items to Betty at the given price without suffering a loss. Hal tells Betty of the situation, and Betty agrees to pay an additional sum for the goods. Later Betty reconsiders and refuses to pay more than the original price. Under Section 2-209(1) of the UCC, Betty's promise to modify the contract needs no consideration to be binding. Hence, Betty is bound by the modified contract.

In the example above, a shift in the market provides an example of a *good faith* reason for contract modification. In fact, Section 1-203 states that "Every contract or duty within this act imposes an obligation of good faith in its performance or enforcement." Good faith in the case of a merchant is defined to mean honesty in fact and the observance of reasonable commercial standards of fair dealing in the trade. [UCC 2-103(1)(b)] But what if there really were no shift in the market, and Hal knew that Betty needed the goods immediately but refused to deliver unless Betty agreed to pay an additional sum of money? This sort of extortion of a modification without a legitimate commercial reason would be ineffective because it would violate the duty of good faith. Hal would not be permitted to enforce the higher price.

When Modification Without Consideration Requires a Writing There are situations in which modification without consideration must be written in order to be enforceable. For example, the contract itself may prohibit any modification or rescission of the contract unless such is in a signed writing. Therefore, only those changes agreed to in the signed writing are enforceable. [UCC 2-209(2)] If a consumer (nonmerchant buyer) is dealing with a merchant, *and* the merchant supplies the form that contains a prohibition against oral modification, the consumer must sign a separate acknowledgment of such a clause.

Also, any modification that brings the contract under the Statute of Frauds will usually require the modification to be in writing to be enforceable. Thus, if an oral contract for the sale

of goods priced at $400 is modified so that the contracted goods are now priced at $600, the modification will have to be in writing to be enforceable. [UCC 2-209(3)] If, however, the buyer accepts delivery of the goods after the modification, he or she is bound to the $600 price. [UCC 2-201(3)(c)]

Statute of Frauds

Section 2-201(1) of the UCC contains a Statute of Frauds provision that applies to contracts for the sale of goods. The provision requires a writing for the contract to be enforceable if the price is $500 or more. The parties can have an initial oral agreement, however, and satisfy the Statute of Frauds by having a subsequent written memorandum of their oral agreement. In each case the writing must be signed by the party against whom enforcement is sought.

Between Merchants — Written Confirmation Once again the UCC provides a special rule for a contract for the sale of goods between merchants. Merchants can satisfy the requirements of a writing for the Statute of Frauds if, after the parties have agreed orally, one of the merchants sends a signed written confirmation to the other merchant. The communication must indicate the terms of the agreement, and the merchant receiving the confirmation must have reason to know of its contents. Unless the merchant who receives the confirmation gives written notice of objection to its contents within ten days after receipt, the writing will be sufficient against the receiving merchant even though he or she has not signed anything.

For example, Beyer is a Miami merchant buyer. He contracts over the telephone to purchase $5,000 worth of goods from Sallor, a New York City merchant seller. Two days later Sallor sends written confirmation detailing the terms of the oral contract, and later Beyer receives it. If Beyer wishes to use the Statute of Frauds as a defense against enforcement of the contract against him, Beyer must give Sallor written notice of objection to the contents of the written confirmation within ten days of receipt.

Relaxed Requirements   The UCC has greatly relaxed the requirements for the sufficiency of a writing to satisfy the Statute of Frauds. A written contract or a memorandum will be sufficient as long as a sales contract (agreement) is indicated and as long as it is signed by the party (or agent) against whom enforcement is sought. The single term that must be included in the writing is the quantity (except in the case of output and requirements contracts). All other terms can be proved in court by oral testimony. Often, terms that are not agreed upon can be supplied by the open term provisions of Article 2 itself.

Exceptions   Section 2-201 defines three exceptions to the Statute of Frauds requirement. [UCC 2-201(3)] A contract, if proved to exist, will be enforceable despite the absence of a writing even if it involves a sale of goods for over $500 if:

1.   *The oral contract is for (a) specially manufactured goods for a particular buyer, (b) these goods are not suitable for resale to others in the ordinary course of the seller's business, and (c) the seller has substantially started to manufacture the goods or made commitments for the manufacture of the goods.* In this situation, once the seller has taken action, the buyer cannot repudiate the agreement claiming the Statute of Frauds as a defense.

To illustrate: Archer ordered a uniquely styled cabinet from Collins, a cabinetmaker. The price of the cabinet is $1,000, and the contract is oral. Collins finishes the cabinet and tenders delivery to Archer. Archer refuses to pay for it even though the job is completed on time. Archer claims that he is not liable because the contract is oral. Clearly, if the unique style of the cabinet makes it improbable that Collins can find another buyer, then Archer is liable to Collins. Also, Collins must have made a substantial beginning in manufacturing the specialized item prior to Archer's repudiation. Of course, the court must still be convinced that there was an oral contract.

2.   *A party to a contract can admit in pleadings (written complaints), testimony, or other court proceedings that a contract for sale was made.* In this case the contract will be enforceable even though it was oral.

To illustrate: Archer and Collins negotiate an agreement over the telephone. During the negotiations, Archer requests a delivery price for 500 gallons of gasoline and a separate price for 700 gallons of gasoline. Collins replies that the price would be the same, $1.10 per gallon. Archer verbally orders 500 gallons. Collins honestly believes that Archer has ordered 700 gallons and tenders that amount. Archer refuses shipment of 700 gallons, and Collins sues for breach. Archer's answer and testimony admit an oral contract was made, but only for 500 gallons. Since Archer admits the existence of the oral contract, Archer cannot plead the Statute of Frauds as a defense. However, the contract is enforceable only to the extent of the quantity admitted, 500 gallons.

3.   *An oral agreement will be enforceable to the extent that payment has been made and accepted or to the extent that goods have been received and accepted.* This is the "partial performance" exception. The oral contract will be enforced at least to the amount of performance that *actually* took place.

For example, Archer orally contracts to sell Collins ten chairs at $100 each. Before delivery, Collins sends Archer a check for $500, which Archer cashes. Later, when Archer attempts to deliver the chairs, Collins refuses delivery, claiming the Statute of Frauds as a defense, and demands the return of his $500. Under the UCC's partial performance rule, Archer can enforce the oral contract by tender of delivery of five chairs for the $500 accepted. Similarly, if Collins had made no payment but had accepted delivery of five chairs from Archer, the oral contract would have been enforceable against Collins for $500, the price of the five chairs delivered.

Parol Evidence

If the parties to a contract set forth its terms in a confirmatory memorandum (a writing expressing offer and acceptance of the deal) or in a writing intended as their final expression, the terms of the contract cannot be contradicted by evidence of any prior or contemporaneous oral or written agreements. However, the terms of the contract can be explained or supplemented by consistent additional terms, or by *course of deal-*

ing, usage of trade, or course of performance. [UCC 2-202]

Consistent Additional Terms   If the court finds an ambiguity in a writing that is supposed to be a complete and exclusive statement of the agreement between the parties, it may accept evidence of consistent additional terms to clarify and remove the ambiguity. The court will not, however, accept evidence of contradictory terms. This is the rule under both the Code and the common law of contracts.

Course of Dealing and Usage of Trade   In construing a commercial agreement, the court will assume that the course of prior dealing between the parties and the usage of trade were taken into account when the agreement was phrased. [UCC 2-202 and 1-201(3)] The Code states, "A course of dealing between the parties and any usage of trade in the vocation or trade in which they are engaged or of which they are or should be aware give particular meaning to [the terms of an agreement] and supplement or qualify the terms of [the] agreement." [UCC 1-205(3)]

The Code has determined that the meaning of any agreement, evidenced by the language of the parties and by their action, must be interpreted in light of commercial practices and other surrounding circumstances.

A *course of dealing* is a sequence of previous conduct between the parties to a particular transaction that establishes a common basis for their understanding. [UCC 1-205(1)] Course of dealing is restricted, literally, to the sequence of conduct between the parties that has occurred prior to the agreement in question.

Usage of trade is defined as any practice or method of dealing having such regularity of observance in a place, vocation, or trade as to justify an expectation that it will be observed with respect to the transaction in question. [UCC 1-205(2)] Further, the expressed terms of an agreement and an applicable course of dealing or usage of trade will be construed to be consistent with each other whenever reasonable. However, when such construction is *unreasonable*, the expressed terms in the agreement will prevail. [UCC 1-205(4)]

In the following case, the court permitted the introduction of evidence of usage and custom in the trade to explain the meaning of quantity figures that the parties took for granted when the contract was formed.

BACKGROUND AND FACTS   *Heggblade-Marguleas-Tenneco (HMT) entered into two contracts with Sunshine Biscuit (referred to in this opinion as Bell Brand). Under the terms of the contract, HMT was to supply Bell Brand with potatoes to be used in the production of potato-snack foods, such as chips and french fries. It was understood that the amount of potatoes to be supplied would vary because of HMT's commitments to its other customers. HMT was a newly merged company. One of its constituent companies had been engaged in the business of marketing agricultural products, and the other had grown potatoes but never marketed them. HMT had no prior marketing experience with this type of potato processing. HMT did, however, conduct a market study concerning the feasibility of growing, marketing, and processing potatoes. Based on the results of this study, it decided to plant between one and two thousand acres of potatoes.*

HMT informed Bell Brand that, after analyzing its needs and obligations to other customers, it would probably be able to supply Bell Brand with 100,000 sacks of potatoes to start. A Bell Brand potato buyer read HMT's estimates and became concerned that the quantity was too high. HMT hired an expert with over twenty years experience in the potato

**HEGGBLADE-
MARGULEAS-
TENNECO, INC. v.
SUNSHINE BISCUIT,
INC.**

Court of Appeals of California, 5th District, 1976.
59 Cal.App.3d 948,
131 Cal.Rptr. 183.

processing industry to obtain more marketing contacts and to assist in selling the potatoes HMT was planning to grow.

Because of the decline in demand for Bell Brand products from May to July 1971, Bell Brand's sales for the late spring and summer of 1971 went down substantially, and its need for potatoes was severely reduced. Bell Brand prorated this reduced demand among its suppliers, including HMT, as fairly as possible. By the end of the harvest season, Bell Brand was able to take only 60,105 hundredweight sacks out of the 100,000 estimated by HMT on the contracts in dispute.

HMT sued Bell Brand for damages on the difference between the 100,000 estimated and 60,105 actual sacks of potatoes purchased. The trial court held for Bell Brand on the basis that it was understood and agreed "* * * as is customary in the potato processing industry, that the numbers of potatoes specified in each of said contracts were reasonable estimates of the respective requirements of [Bell Brand] only during said period, and did not constitute the exact number of potatoes to be ordered by [Bell Brand] * * * and delivered by plaintiff under said contracts."

FRANSON, Acting Presiding Justice.

*   *   *   *

California Uniform Commercial Code section 2202 states the parol evidence rule applicable to the sale of personal property:

"Terms with respect to which the confirmatory memoranda of the parties agree or which are otherwise set forth in a writing intended by the parties as a final expression of their agreement with respect to such terms as are included therein may not be contradicted by evidence of any prior agreement or of a contemporaneous oral agreement but may be explained or supplemented "(a) By course of dealing or usage of trade (Section 1205) *   *   *;"

California Uniform Commercial Code section 2202, subdivision (a), permits a trade usage to be put in evidence "as an instrument of interpretation." The Uniform Commercial Code comment to subdivision (a) of section 2202 states that evidence of trade usage is admissible "*   *   * in order that the true understanding of the parties as to the agreement may be reached. Such writings are to be read on the assumption that *   *   * the usages of trade were taken for granted when the document was phrased. Unless *carefully negated* they have become an element of the meaning of the words used. Similarly, the course of actual performance by the parties is considered the best indication of what they intended the writing to mean."

A case factually similar to the instant case is *Columbia Nitrogen Corporation v. Royster Company* (4th Cir. 1971), 451 F.2d 3. There the seller sued the buyer for breach of contract for the purchase of a specified quantity of phosphate. The buyer's defense was a trade usage which imposed no duty to accept at the quoted prices the minimum quantity stated in the contract. The trial court had excluded this evidence because "*   *   * 'custom and usage *   *   * are not admissible to contradict the express, plain, unambiguous language of a valid written contract, which by virtue of its detail negates the proposition that the contract is open to variances in its terms. *   *   *' " The Court of Appeal interpreted Virginia Uniform Commercial Code section 2-202, which is identical to California Uniform

Commercial Code section 2202(a), as meaning that where the contract does not expressly state that trade usage cannot be used to explain or supplement the written terms, the evidence of trade usage should be admitted to interpret the contract. "The contract is silent about adjusting prices and quantities to reflect a declining market. It neither permits nor prohibits adjustment, and this neutrality provides a fitting occasion for recourse to usage of trade and prior dealing to supplement the contract and explain its terms."

We find *Columbia Nitrogen Corporation* persuasive. Under subdivision (a) of section 2202, established trade usage and custom are a part of the contract unless the parties agree otherwise. Since the contracts in question are silent about the applicability of the usage and custom, evidence of such usage and custom was admissible to explain the meaning of the quantity figures.

*   *   *   *

Appellant's [HMT] argument that the evidence of custom should not have been considered by the jury in interpreting the contracts because the officers of HMT were inexperienced in the marketing of processing potatoes and lacked knowledge of the custom is similarly without merit. Mr. Hoffman was knowledgeable in the processing potato business and was aware of the trade custom. Since appellant pleaded that the contracts had been entered into on October 15, 1970, and Hoffman had been employed by HMT on October 1, 1970, his knowledge was imputed to HMT.

Moreover, persons carrying on a particular trade are deemed to be aware of prominent trade customs applicable to their industry. The knowledge may be actual or constructive, and it is constructive if the custom is of such general and universal application that the party must be presumed to know of it.

*   *   * Because potatoes are a perishable commodity and their demand is dependent upon a fluctuating market, and because the marketing contracts are signed eight or nine months in advance of the harvest season, common sense dictates that the quantity would be estimated by both the grower and processor. Thus, it cannot be said as a matter of law that HMT was ignorant of the trade custom.

We conclude that the trial court properly admitted the evidence of usage and custom to explain the meaning of the quantity figures in the contracts.

JUDGMENT AND REMEDY

The trial court's judgment was affirmed. Bell Brand did not have to pay HMT for the difference between the 100,000 estimated hundredweight sacks of potatoes and the 60,105 actual sacks of potatoes that were purchased.

COMMENTS

Parol evidence of usage and custom that is not inconsistent with the terms of the written agreement can be introduced in situations where both parties knew or should have known of the existence of the particular custom or usage in that industry in that locality. Such evidence is supplemental and shows the meaning that the parties attach to the particular language. It does not alter or change the contract terms. Just as a previous course of dealing between parties can be regarded as establishing a common basis for interpreting their expressions and conduct [UCC 1-205(1)], so, too, a usage of trade is a regularly observed practice or method of dealing that is normally accepted and followed in a place, vocation, or trade and that establishes a common basis for interpreting expressions or conduct. [UCC 1-205(2)]

Course of Performance   Course of performance is the conduct that occurs under the terms of a particular agreement. The course of performance actually undertaken is the best indication of what the parties to an agreement intended it to mean. Presumably, the parties themselves know best what they meant by their words, and their action under that agreement is the best indication of what they meant. [UCC 2-208]

To illustrate: Able Lumber Company contracts with Baker to sell Baker a specified number of "2-by-4s". The lumber in fact does not measure 2 inches by 4 inches but rather 1⅞ inches by 3¾ inches. If Baker objects to the lumber delivered, Able can prove that "2-by-4s" are never exactly 2 inches by 4 inches by applying usage of trade or course of prior dealings, or both. Able can show in previous transactions that Baker took 1⅞ inch by 3¾ inch lumber without objection. In addition, Able can show that in the trade, 2-by-4s are commonly 1⅞ inches by 3¾ inches. Both usage of trade and course of prior dealings are relevant in determining and explaining what the parties meant by 2-by-4s.

Using the same example, suppose that Able agrees to deliver the lumber in five separate deliveries. The fact that Baker has accepted lumber without objection in three previous deliveries under the agreement (course of performance) is relevant in determining that the words 2-by-4 actually mean 1⅞ by 3¾.

The Code provides *rules of construction.* Express terms, course of performance, course of dealing, and usage of trade are to be construed together when they do not contradict one another. When such construction is unreasonable, however, the following order of priority controls: (1) express terms, (2) course of performance, (3) course of dealing, and (4) usage of trade. [UCC 1-205(4) and 2-208(2)]

Unconscionability

An unconscionable contract is one that is so unfair and one-sided that it would be unreasonable to enforce it. Section 2-302 allows the court to evaluate a contract or any clause in a contract, and if the court deems it to be unconscionable *at the time it was made,* the court can (1) refuse to enforce the contract, or (2) enforce the remainder of the contract without the unconscionable clause, or (3) limit the application of any unconscionable clauses to avoid an unconscionable result.

The court, in determining whether a contract or clause is unconscionable, must decide whether, in light of general commercial practice and the commercial needs of the particular trade involved, the clauses are so one-sided as to be unconscionable under the circumstances at the time the contract was made. In this day of consumer law, more and more consumer sales contracts are being attacked as unconscionable. Typical cases involve high pressure salespersons and uneducated consumers who contract away their basic rights. In general, the courts have concluded that unequal bargaining power, coupled with unscrupulous dealings by one party, will result in an unenforceable, unconscionable contract.

It is noteworthy that the doctrine of unconscionability expressed explicitly in Section 2-302 is a codification of a pre-UCC notion that was of uncertain application. The right of the courts to refuse to enforce all of the terms agreed to by the parties to a contract has been recognized for centuries. Equity courts have refused to grant performance of a contract deemed unfair (unconscionable). One of the leading cases involved Campbell Soup Company.[6] The form contract prepared by Campbell Soup contained a clause that excused Campbell Soup from accepting goods under certain circumstances. Additionally, though, the clause prohibited the seller of the goods from selling them elsewhere without Campbell's written consent. The court refused

---

6.   Campbell Soup Co. v. Wentz, 172 F.2d 80 (3d Cir. 1948). See Chapter 15 for case excerpts.

to grant specific performance in this classic case on the basis that this clause was unconscionable.

The inclusion of Section 2-302 in the UCC reflects an increased sensitivity to certain realities of modern commercial activities. Classical contract theory holds that a contract is a bargain in which the terms have been worked out *freely* between parties that are equals. In many modern commercial transactions, this premise is invalid.

Standard form contracts are often signed by consumer-buyers who understand few of the terms used and who often do not even read them. Virtually all of the terms are advantageous to the parties supplying the standard form contract. With Section 2-302, the courts have a powerful weapon for policing such transactions, as the next case illustrates.

BACKGROUND AND FACTS   *The purchasers of a freezer brought this action to reform the contract of sale. The purchasers alleged the contract was unconscionable.*

JONES v. STAR CREDIT CORP.

Supreme Court of New York, Nassau County, 1969.

59 Misc. 2d 189, 298 N.Y.S.2d 264.

WACHTLER, Justice.

On August 31, 1965 the plaintiffs, who are welfare recipients, agreed to purchase a home freezer unit for $900 as the result of a visit from a salesman representing Your Shop At Home Service, Inc. With the addition of the time credit charges, credit life insurance, credit property insurance, and sales tax, the purchase price totalled $1,234.80. Thus far the plaintiffs have paid $619.88 toward their purchase. The defendant claims that with various added credit charges paid for an extension of time there is a balance of $819.81 still due from the plaintiffs. The uncontroverted proof at the trial established that the freezer unit, when purchased, had a maximum retail value of approximately $300. The question is whether this transaction and the resulting contract could be considered unconscionable within the meaning of Section 2-302 of the Uniform Commercial Code which provides in part:

(1) If the court as a matter of law finds the contract or any clause of the contract to have been unconscionable at the time it was made the court may refuse to enforce the contract, or it may enforce the remainder of the contract without the unconscionable clause, or it may so limit the application of any unconscionable clause as to avoid any unconscionable result.

(2) When it is claimed or appears to the court that the contract or any clause thereof may be unconscionable the parties shall be afforded a reasonable opportunity to present evidence as to its commercial setting, purpose and effect to aid the court in making the determination.

There was a time when the shield of "caveat emptor" would protect the most unscrupulous in the marketplace—a time when the law, in granting parties unbridled latitude to make their own contracts, allowed exploitive and callous practices which shocked the conscience of both legislative bodies and the courts.

The effort to eliminate these practices has continued to pose a difficult problem. On the one hand it is necessary to recognize the importance of preserving the integrity of agreements and the fundamental right of parties to deal, trade, bargain, and contract. On the other hand there is the concern for the uneducated and often illiterate individual who is the victim of gross inequality of bargaining power, usually the poorest members of the community.

* * * *

The law is beginning to fight back against those who once took advantage of the poor and illiterate without risk of either exposure or interference. From the common law doctrine of intrinsic fraud we have over the years, developed common and statutory law which tells not only the buyer but also the seller to beware. This body of laws recognizes the importance of a free enterprise system but at the same time will provide the legal armor to protect and safeguard the prospective victim from the harshness of an unconscionable contract.

Section 2-302 of the Uniform Commercial Code enacts the moral sense of the community into the law of commercial transactions. It authorizes the court to find, as a matter of law, that a contract or a clause of a contract was "unconscionable at the time it was made," and upon so finding the court may refuse to enforce the contract, excise the objectionable clause or limit the application of the clause to avoid an unconscionable result. "The principle", states the Official Comment to this section, "is one of the prevention of oppression and unfair surprise". It permits a court to accomplish directly what heretofore was often accomplished by construction of language, manipulations of fluid rules of contract law and determinations based upon a presumed public policy.

There is no reason to doubt, moreover, that this section is intended to encompass the price term of an agreement. In addition to the fact that it has already been so applied, the statutory language itself makes it clear that not only a clause of the contract, but the contract in toto, may be found unconscionable as a matter of law. Indeed, no other provision of an agreement more intimately touches upon the question of unconscionability than does the term regarding price.

Fraud, in the instant case, is not present; nor is it necessary under the statute. The question which presents itself is whether or not, under the circumstances of this case, the sale of a freezer unit having a retail value of $300 for $900 ($1,439.69 including credit charges and $18 sales tax) is unconscionable as a matter of law. The court believes it is.

Concededly, deciding the issue is substantially easier than explaining it. No doubt, the mathematical disparity between $300, which presumably includes a reasonable profit margin, and $900, which is exhorbitant on its face, carries the greatest weight. Credit charges alone exceed by more than $100 the retail value of the freezer. These alone, may be sufficient to sustain the decision. Yet, a caveat is warranted lest we reduce the import of Section 2-302 solely to a mathematical ratio formula. It may, at times, be that; yet it may also be much more. The very limited financial resources of the purchaser, known to the sellers at the time of the sale, is entitled to weight in the balance. Indeed, the value disparity itself leads inevitably to the felt conclusion that knowing advantage was taken of the plaintiffs. In addition, the meaningfulness of choice essential to the making of a contract, can be negated by a gross inequality of bargaining power.

There is no question about the necessity and even the desirability of instalment sales and the extension of credit. Indeed, there are many, including welfare recipients, who would be deprived of even the most basic conveniences without the use of these devices. Similarly, the retail merchant selling on instalment or extending credit is expected to establish a pricing factor which will afford a degree of protection commensurate with the risk of selling to those who might be default prone. However, neither of these accepted premises can clothe the sale of this freezer with respectability.

Support for the court's conclusion will be found in a number of other cases already decided. In American Home Improvement, Inc. v. MacIver, the Supreme Court of New Hampshire held that a contract to install windows, a door and paint, for the price of $2,568.60, of which $809.60 constituted interest and carrying charges and $800 was a salesman's commission was unconscionable as a matter of law. In State by Lefkowitz v. ITM, Inc., a deceptive and fraudulent scheme was involved, but standing alone, the court held that the sale of a vacuum cleaner, among other things, costing the defendant $140 and sold by it for $749 cash or $920.52 on time purchase was unconscionable as a matter of law. Finally, in Frostifresh Corp. v. Reynoso, the sale of a refrigerator costing the seller $348 for $900 plus credit charges of $245.88 was unconscionable as a matter of law. . . .

Having already paid more than $600 toward the purchase of this $300 freezer unit, it is apparent that the defendant has already been amply compensated. In accordance with the statute, the application of the payment provision should be limited to amounts already paid by the plaintiffs and the contract be reformed and amended by changing the payments called for therein to equal the amount of payment actually so paid by the plaintiffs.

Judgment was entered for the plaintiffs. The contract was reformed so that no further payments were required to be made.   **JUDGMENT AND REMEDY**

SUMMARY OF SPECIAL RULES

The special rules outline for contracts of sale of goods and the Code sections of Article 2 that apply are presented in summary form on the next page in Exhibit 18–2. All of these rules have either been treated in this chapter or will be treated in Chapters 19 through 23.

EXHIBIT 18-2 UCC RULES FOR CONTRACTS FOR THE SALE OF GOODS

	RULE	UCC SECTION
OFFER AND ACCEPTANCE	1. The acceptance of unilateral offers can be made by a promise to ship or by shipment itself.	2-206(1)(b)
	2. Not all terms have to be included for a contract to result.	2-204
	3. Particulars of performance can be left open.	2-311(1)
	4. Firm written offers by *merchants* for three months or less cannot be revoked.	2-205
	5. Acceptance by performance requires notice within a reasonable time; otherwise the offer can be treated as lapsed.	2-206(2)
	6. The price does not have to be included to have a contract.	2-305
	7. Variations in terms between the offer and the acceptance may not be a rejection but may be an acceptance.	2-207
	8. Acceptance can be made by any reasonable means of communication; it is effective when deposited.	2-206(1)(a)
CONSIDERATION	1. A modification of a contract for the sale of goods does not require consideration.	2-209(1)
	2. Adding a seal has no effect on the validity of the contract.	2-203
ILLEGALITY	1. Unconscionable bargains will not be enforced.	2-302
VOIDABLE CONTRACTS	1. Rescission for fraud does not prevent a lawsuit for monetary damages.	2-721
	2. A person with voidable title has power to transfer a good title to a good faith purchaser for value.	2-403
FORM OF THE AGREEMENT	1. The Statute of Frauds covers: (a) All sales of goods for a price of $500 or more. (b) Written confirmations between merchants. (c) Specially manufactured goods. (d) Memoranda that do not include all the agreement terms. (e) Goods for which payment has been made and accepted; goods which have been received and accepted. (f) Admission in pleadings or court proceedings that a contract for sale was made.	2-201
RIGHTS OF THIRD PARTIES	1. Delegation of duties is included when a contract, or the rights under a contract, are assigned.	2-210
PERFORMANCE OF CONTRACTS	1. Tender of payment is a condition precedent to a tender of delivery, unless a credit sale was agreed upon.	2-511
	2. Anticipatory breach cannot be withdrawn if the other party gives notice that it is final.	2-611
	3. Claims and rights can be waived without consideration.	1-107
DISCHARGE	1. The statute of limitations is four years. Mutual agreement can reduce it to not less than one year.	2-725

QUESTIONS AND
CASE PROBLEMS

1.   A. B. Smith Inc. is the manufacturer of washing machines. Over the *telephone*, Smith offers to sell Radar Appliances 100 Model-Z washers at a price of $150 per unit. Smith agrees to keep this offer open for ninety days. Radar tells Smith that the offer appears to be a good one and that Radar will let Smith know of its acceptance within the next two to three weeks. One week later, Smith sends and Radar receives notice that Smith has withdrawn its offer. Radar immediately thereafter telephones Smith and accepts the $150 per unit offer. Smith claims, first, that there never was a sales contract formed between it and Radar and, second, that if there was a contract, the contract is unenforceable. Discuss Smith's contentions.

2.   Beyer, a retailer of television sets, orders 100 Model Color-X sets from manufacturer Martin. The order specifies the price and that the television sets are to be *shipped* by Humming Bird Express on or before October 30. The order is received by Martin on October 5. On October 8 Martin writes Beyer a letter indicating the order was received and that the sets will be shipped as directed, at the specified price. This letter is received by Beyer on October 10. On October 28 Martin, in preparing the shipment, discovers it has only 90 Color-X sets in stock. Martin ships the 90 Color-X sets and 10 television sets of a different model, stating clearly on the invoice that the 10 are being shipped only as an accommodation. Beyer claims Martin is in breach of contract. Martin claims the shipment was not an acceptance, and therefore no contract was formed. Explain who is correct and why.

3.   Beyer has a requirements contract with Sallor that obligates Sallor to supply Beyer with all the gasoline Beyer needs for his delivery trucks for one year at $1 per gallon. A clause inserted in small print in the contract by Beyer, and not noticed by Sallor, states, "The buyer reserves the right to reject any shipment for any reason without liability." For six months Beyer has ordered and Sallor has delivered under the contract without any controversy. Because of price actions by OPEC, the price of gasoline to Sallor has increased substantially. Sallor contacts Beyer and tells Beyer he cannot possibly fulfill the requirements contract unless Beyer agrees to pay $1.10 per gallon. Beyer, in need of the gasoline, agrees in writing to modify the contract. Later that month, Beyer learns he can buy gasoline at $1.05 per gallon from Collins. Beyer refuses delivery of his most recent order to Sallor, claiming, first, that the contract allows Beyer to do so without liability and second, that he is required to pay only $1 per gallon if he accepts the delivery. Discuss fully Beyer's contentions.

4.   Sallor owns 360 acres of land in Bear County. Sallor makes three separate contracts, in writing, with Beyer concerning the land. First, Sallor contracts to sell to Beyer 500 tons of gravel from a quarry located on the land for a stated price. The contract calls for Beyer to remove the gravel. The second contract sells to Beyer all the wheat presently growing on a forty-acre tract. Sallor is obligated under the contract to harvest and deliver the wheat to Beyer. The third contract is the sale of the northeast ninety acres with all corn standing. Discuss fully which of these contracts, if any, fall under the UCC.

5.   Sallor offers to sell Beyer 1,000 shirts for a stated price. The offer states that shipment will be by the ABC Truck Line. Beyer replies, "I accept your offer for 1,000 shirts at the price quoted. Delivery to be by Yellow Express Truck Line." Both Sallor and Beyer are merchants. Three weeks later, Sallor ships the shirts by the ABC Truck Line, and Beyer refuses shipment. Sallor sues for breach of contract. Beyer claims, first, that there never was a contract because the modification of carriers did not constitute an acceptance and, second, even if there was a contract, Sallor is in breach by shipping the shirts by ABC contrary to the contract terms. Discuss fully Beyer's claims.

6.   Pemberton went to Tradesmens Bank to secure a loan to buy a car. The bank would loan Pemberton the money only under the conditions that the car would serve as collateral for the loan, that the car would be insured, and that the car dealer who was to sell the car to Pemberton would guarantee payment of the loan if Pemberton defaulted. Both Pemberton and the car dealer agreed to these conditions, and Pemberton secured the loan and purchased the car. The insurance on the car was subsequently cancelled. The bank was given notice of this cancellation, but contrary to local custom and its own past course of dealing with the car dealer, it failed in turn to notify the car dealer. Pemberton was involved in an auto accident. Pemberton's financial situation was such that he could not pay the balance of the loan. Therefore, the bank sued the car dealer based on the guarantee that the car dealer had given under the loan agreement. At trial, the car dealer defended on the grounds that it was not liable under the guarantee because the bank had failed to

give the car dealer notice of the cancellation of the insurance. The bank claimed that it was under no obligation to give notice to the car dealer because such a term was not included in the written loan guarantee agreement. In light of the parol evidence rule, can the car dealer prove that there was an implied promise on the part of the bank to give notice of cancellation of insurance? [Provident Tradesmens Bank & Trust Co. v. Pemberton, 196 Pa.Super. 180, 173 A.2d 780 (1961)]

7.   In 1961 Clark and American Sand & Gravel discussed the possibility of a purchase by Clark of 25,000 tons of sand at 45 cents per ton. Although both parties found the terms of the possible sale agreeable, no sale was ever made. About eighteen months later, Clark requested his truck driver to obtain about 1,500 tons of sand from American Sand & Gravel. American Sand & Gravel supplied the sand, but no purchase price was ever mentioned. Subsequently, American charged Clark 55 cents per ton for the sand. Is there a contract between American and Clark? If so, what price can American charge for the sand? [American Sand & Gravel, Inc. v. Clark and Fray Constr. Co., 2 Conn.Cir. 284, 198 A.2d 68 (1964)]

8.   Loeb & Company entered into an oral agreement with Schreiner, a farmer, whereby Schreiner was to sell Loeb 150 bales of cotton, each weighing 480 pounds. Shortly thereafter, Loeb sent Schreiner a letter confirming the terms of the oral contract. Schreiner neither acknowledged receipt of the letter nor objected to its terms. When delivery came due, Schreiner ignored the oral agreement and sold on the open market because the price of cotton had more than doubled (from 37 cents to 80 cents per pound) since the oral agreement was made. In a lawsuit by Loeb & Company

against Schreiner, can Loeb & Company recover? [Loeb & Co. v. Schreiner, 294 Ala. 722, 321 So.2d, 199 (1975)]

9.   McNabb agreed to sell soybeans to Ralston Purina Company. Severe weather damaged a significant portion of all soybean crops that year. When McNabb was unable to meet the November 30th delivery deadline, Ralston Purina modified the contracts monthly without additional consideration to allow delivery as late as February 28th of the following year. Between November and February, the price of soybeans rose substantially. If Ralston Purina's extensions of the delivery date were intended to *maximize* damages in the event of McNabb's breach, would the modifications to the contract be enforceable? [Ralston Purina Co. v. McNabb, 381 F.Supp. 181 (D.Tenn.1974)]

10.   The LTV Aerospace Corporation publicly solicited bids from local suppliers to manufacture shipping containers to specifications and in quantities to 8,000. The containers were to be delivered on a periodic basis to be specified by LTV to fit its production schedule. Bateman, having obtained a copy of the invitation to bid from a third party, submitted a detailed written bid to LTV. After some oral changes on both specifications and price, an agreement was reached, and the bid was accepted by LTV. Bateman made substantial beginnings in the production of the packing cases. LTV refused to take delivery of the cases after it stopped production of the specific product for which the cases were needed. When Bateman sued for breach of contract, LTV claimed that there was no writing to satisfy the Statute of Frauds. The trial court ruled against LTV, and LTV appealed. What was the result? [LTV Aerospace Corp. v. Bateman, 492 S.W.2d 703 (Tex.Civ.App. 1973)]

CHAPTER 19

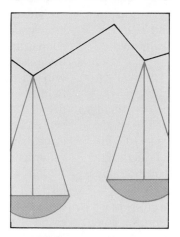

SALES
Title, Risk, and
Insurable Interest

The sale of goods transfers ownership (title) from seller to buyer. Often a sales contract will be signed before the actual goods are available. For example, a sales contract for oranges is signed in May, but the oranges are not ready for picking and shipment until October. Any number of things can happen between the time that a sales contract is signed and the time that the goods are actually transferred to the buyer's possession. Fire, flood, or frost can destroy the orange groves. The oranges may be lost or damaged in transit. The parties may want to obtain casualty insurance on the goods. The government may levy a tax on the oranges.

Before the UCC, *title*—right of ownership— was the central concept in sales law, controlling all issues of rights and remedies of the parties to a sales contract. However, it was difficult to determine when title actually passed. Therefore, the UCC divorced the question of title as completely as possible from the question of the rights and obligations of buyers, sellers, or third per-

sons (such as subsequent purchasers, creditors, or the tax collector).

In some situations title is still relevant under the Code, and the UCC has special rules for locating title. These rules will be discussed in the materials that follow. In most situations, however, the Code replaces the concept of title with three other concepts: (1) identification, (2) risk of loss, and (3) insurable interest.

PASSAGE OF TITLE

Sales and Contracts to Sell

Before any interest in specific goods can pass from the seller to the buyer, two conditions must prevail: (1) The goods must be in existence, and (2) they must be identified to the contract. If either condition is lacking, only a contract *to sell* (not a sale) exists. [UCC 2-105(2)] Goods that are not both existing and identified to the contract are called "future goods." For example, a contract to purchase next year's crop of hay would be a contract for future goods, a crop yet to be grown.

Identification

For passage of title, the goods must be identified in a way that will distinguish the particular goods to be delivered under the sales contract from all other similar goods.[1] **Identification** is a designation of goods as the subject matter of the sales contract.

In many cases identification is simply a matter of specific designation. For example, you contract to purchase a fleet of five cars by the serial numbers listed for the cars, or you agree to purchase all the wheat in a specific bin at a stated price per bushel. Problems usually occur only when a quantity of goods is purchased from a larger mass, such as 1,000 cases of peas from a 10,000-case lot.

There is a general rule that when a purchaser buys a quantity of goods to be taken from a larger mass, identification can be made only by separating the contracted goods from the mass. Therefore, until the seller separates the 1,000 cases of peas from the 10,000-case lot, title and risk of loss remain with the seller.

There are a few exceptions to this general rule. For example, a seller owns approximately 5,000 chickens (hens and roosters). A buyer agrees to purchase all the hen chickens at a stated price. Most courts would hold that "all the hen chickens" is a sufficient identification, and title and risk can pass to the buyer without the goods identified in the contract being physically separated from the other goods (the hens from the roosters). The reasoning is that the contract identification serves as sufficient separation.

---

1.   According to UCC 2-401, each provision of Article 2 "with respect to the rights, obligations, and remedies of the seller, the buyer, purchasers or other third parties applies irrespective of title to the goods except where the provisions refer to such title." These provisions referring to title include: UCC 2-312, warranty of title by seller; UCC 2-326(3), consignment sales; UCC 2-327(1)(a), sale on approval and "risk of loss"; UCC 2-403(1), entrustment; UCC 2-501(2), insurable interest in goods; and UCC 2-722, who can sue third parties for injury to goods.

The most common exception deals with fungible goods. [UCC 1-201(17)] Fungible goods are goods that are alike naturally, by agreement or trade usage. Typical examples are wheat, oil, and wine. If these goods are held or intended to be held as tenants in common (owners have an undivided share of the entire mass), a seller-tenant can pass title and risk of loss to the buyer without an actual separation. The buyer replaces the seller as a tenant in common. [UCC 2-105(4)]

For example, Able, Baker, and Clark are farmers. They deposit, respectively, 5,000 bushels, 3,000 bushels, and 2,000 bushels of the same grade of grain in a bin. The three become tenants in common, with Able owning 50 percent of the 10,000 bushels, Baker 30 percent, and Clark 20 percent. Able could contract to sell 5,000 bushels of grain to Thomas and, since the goods are fungible, pass title and risk of loss to Thomas without physically separating 5,000 bushels. Thomas now becomes a tenant in common with Baker and Clark.

Identification is significant because it gives the buyer the right to obtain insurance (insurable interest) on the goods and the right to recover from third parties who damage the goods. In certain circumstances, identification allows the buyer to take the goods from the seller. In other words, the concept of identification is easier to understand if one looks at its consequences.

Parties can agree on when identification will take place in their contract; but if they do not so specify, in addition to the preceding rules, the following rules apply:

1.   Identification takes place at the time the contract is made *if the contract calls for the sale of specific and ascertained goods already existing.*
2.   If the sale involves unborn young animals that will be born within twelve months from the time of the contract, or if it involves crops to be harvested within twelve months (or the next harvest season occurring after contracting, whichever is longer), identification will take place, in the first case, when the young are conceived and, in the second case, when the crops are planted or begin to grow.
3.   In other cases, identification takes place when the goods are marked, shipped, or somehow des-

ignated by the seller as the particular goods to pass under the contract. The seller can delegate the right to identify goods to the buyer.

When Title Passes

Once goods exist and are identified, the provisions of UCC 2-401 apply to the passage of title.

By Agreement   Parties can expressly agree to the conditions under which title will pass to the buyer and to the time. In virtually all subsections of UCC 2-401, the words "unless otherwise explicitly agreed" appear, meaning that any explicit understanding between the buyer and the seller will determine when title passes.

In Absence of Agreement   Unless another agreement is explicitly made, title passes to the buyer at the time and the place the seller performs the *physical* delivery of the goods. [UCC 2-401(2)] The delivery arrangements determine when this occurs.

Shipment Contracts   Under shipment contracts, the seller is required only to deliver the goods into the hands of a carrier (like a trucking company), and title passes to the buyer at the time and place of shipment. [UCC 2-401(2)(a)]

Destination Contracts   With destination contracts, the seller is required to deliver the goods to a particular destination, usually directly to the buyer but sometimes to the buyer's designate. Title passes to the buyer when the goods are tendered at that destination. [UCC 2-401(2)(b)]

Contracts for Delivery without Seller Moving the Goods   Where the contract of sale does not call for the seller's shipment or delivery (buyer to pick up), the passage of title depends on whether the seller must deliver a document of title, such as a bill of lading or a warehouse receipt, to the buyer. When a document of title is required, title passes to the buyer *when and where the document is delivered.* Thus, if the goods are stored in a warehouse, title passes to the buyer when the appropriate documents are delivered. The goods never move. In fact, the buyer can

choose to leave the goods at the same warehouse for a period of time, and the buyer's title to those goods will be unaffected.

When no documents of title are required, and delivery is made without moving the goods, title passes at the time and place the sales contract was made, if the goods have already been identified. If the goods have not been identified, then title does not pass until identification occurs. Consider an example: Fein sells lumber to Ozo. It is agreed that Ozo will pick up the lumber at the yard. If the lumber has been identified (segregated, marked, or in any other way distinguished from all other lumber), title will pass to Ozo when the contract is signed. If the lumber is still in storage bins at the mill, however, title will not pass to Ozo until the particular pieces of lumber to be sold under this contract are identified. [UCC 2-401(3)]

RISK OF LOSS

Under the UCC, several concepts replace the concept of title in determining the rights and remedies of parties to a sales contract. For example, risk of loss does not necessarily pass with title. The question of who suffers a financial risk if goods are damaged, destroyed, or lost is resolved primarily under Sections 2-509 and 2-319. Risk of loss depends on whether or not a sales contract has been breached at the time of loss. [UCC 2-510]

Passage of Risk of Loss Absent a Breach of Contract

By Agreement   Risk of loss can be assigned through an agreement by the parties, preferably in writing. Therefore, the parties can generally control the exact moment risk of loss passes from the seller to the buyer. Of course, at the time so agreed, the goods must be in existence and identified to the contract for this contract provision to be enforceable.

Carrier Cases—Sales Requiring Delivery by Movement of Goods   Assuming that there is no specification in the agreement, the following rules will apply to so-called carrier cases.

Shipment Contracts

In a shipment contract, if the seller is required or authorized to ship goods by carrier (not required to deliver them to a particular destination), risk of loss passes to the buyer when the goods are duly delivered to the carrier. [UCC 2-509(1)(b)]

For example, a seller in New York sells 10,000 tons of sheet metal to a buyer in California, F.O.B. New York (free on board in New York—that is, buyer pays the transportation charges from New York). The contract authorizes a shipment by carrier; it does not require the seller to tender the metal in California. Risk passes to the buyer when the conforming goods are properly placed in the possession of the carrier. If the goods are damaged in transit, the loss falls on the buyer. (Actually, buyers have recourse against carriers, subject to tariff rule limitations, and they usually insure the goods from the time they leave the seller.) Generally, all contracts are assumed to be shipping contracts if nothing is stated in the contract.

Destination Contracts

In a destination contract, the seller is required to deliver the goods at a particular destination. The risk of loss passes to the buyer when the goods are tendered to the buyer at that destination. In the preceding example, if the contract had been F.O.B. California, risk of loss during transit to California would have fallen on the seller.

Specific terms in the contract, even though used in connection with a stated price, assist one in determining when risk of loss passes to the buyer. Four such terms should be noted:

1. **F.O.B.** (free on board) can be either at place of shipment (for example, seller's city or place of business) or at place of destination (for example, buyer's city or place of business). In absence of agreement, the risk of loss rules pertaining to shipment and destination as stated above basically apply. [UCC 2-319(1)]
2. **F.A.S.** (free alongside) vessel requires the seller at his own expense and "risk" to deliver the goods alongside the vessel before risk passes to the buyer. [UCC 2-319(2)]
3. **CIF or C&F** (cost, insurance, and freight, or just cost and freight) requires, among other things, the seller to "put the goods in possession of a carrier" before risk passes to the buyer. [UCC 2-320(2)] (These are basically pricing terms and remain shipment contracts, not destination contracts.)
4. **Delivery ex-ship** (from the carrying vessel) means that risk of loss does not pass to the buyer until the goods leave the ship or are otherwise properly unloaded. [UCC 2-322]

In the following case the court reviewed UCC 2-509(1) as it relates to passage of the risk of loss. Under the Code, an F.O.B. term indicates whether the contract is a "shipment" contract or a "destination" contract, with the risk of loss passing at different times in each of these contracts. The F.O.B. terminology controls. In this case a "shipment" contract shifted the risk of loss to the buyer when the goods were delivered to a carrier. The fact that there was a "ship to" address had no significance in changing the UCC presumption that the contract was a "shipment" contract.

PESTANA v. KARINOL CORP.

District Court of Appeal of Florida, Third District (1979). 367 So. 2d 1096.

BACKGROUND AND FACTS *The plaintiff-buyer sought a refund of the deposit he had made on goods that were lost in transit. The trial court determined that the plaintiff owed the defendant-seller the balance of the purchase price of the goods.*

HUBBART, Judge.

*   *   *   *

The central issue presented for review is whether a contract for the sale of goods, which stipulates the place where the goods sold are to be sent by carrier but contains (a) no explicit provisions allocating the risk of loss while the goods are in the possession of the carrier and (b) no delivery terms such as F.O.B. place of destination, is a shipment contract or a destination contract under the Uniform Commercial Code. We hold that such a contract, without more, constitutes a shipment contract wherein the risk of loss passes to the buyer when the seller duly delivers the goods to the carrier under a reasonable contract of carriage for shipment to the buyer. Accordingly, we affirm.

*   *   *   *

There are two types of sales contracts under Florida's Uniform Commercial Code wherein a carrier is used to transport the goods sold: a shipment contract and a destination contract. A shipment contract is considered the normal contract in which the seller is required to send the subject goods by carrier to the buyer but is not required to guarantee delivery thereof at a particular destination. Under a shipment contract, the seller, unless otherwise agreed, must: (1) put the goods sold in the possession of a carrier and make a contract for their transportation as may be reasonable having regard for the nature of the goods and other attendant circumstances, (2) obtain and promptly deliver or tender in due form any document necessary to enable the buyer to obtain possession of the goods or otherwise required by the agreement or by usage of the trade, and (3) promptly notify the buyer of the shipment. On a shipment contract, the risk of loss passes to the buyer when the goods sold are duly delivered to the carrier for shipment to the buyer.

A destination contract, on the other hand, is considered the variant contract in which the seller specifically agrees to deliver the goods sold to the buyer at a particular destination and to bear the risk of loss of the goods until tender of delivery. This can be accomplished by express provision in the sales contract to that effect or by the use of delivery terms such as F.O.B. (place of destination). Under a destination contract, the seller is required to tender delivery of the goods sold to the buyer at the place of destination. The risk of loss under such a contract passes to the buyer when the goods sold are duly tendered to the buyer at the place of destination while in the possession of the carrier so as to enable the buyer to take delivery. The parties must explicitly agree to a destination contract; otherwise the contract will be considered a shipment contract.

Where the risk of loss falls on the seller at the time the goods sold are lost or destroyed, the seller is liable in damages to the buyer for non-delivery unless the seller tenders a performance in replacement for the lost or destroyed goods. On the other hand, where the risk of loss falls on the buyer at the time the goods sold are lost or destroyed, the buyer is liable to the seller for the purchase price of the goods sold.

In the instant case, we deal with the normal shipment contract involving the sale of goods. The defendant Karinol pursuant to this contract agreed to send the goods sold, a shipment of watches, to the plaintiff's decedent in Chetumal, Mexico. There was no specific provision in the contract between the parties which allocated the risk of loss on the goods sold while in transit. In addition, there were no delivery terms such as F.O.B. Chetumal contained in the contract.

All agree that there is sufficient evidence that the defendant Karinol performed its obligations as a seller under the Uniform Commercial Code if this contract is considered a shipment contract. Karinol put the goods sold in the possession of a carrier and made a contract for the goods safe transportation to the plaintiff's decedent; Karinol also promptly notified the plaintiff's decedent of the shipment and tendered to said party the necessary documents to obtain possession of the goods sold.

The plaintiff Pestana contends, however, that the contract herein is a destination contract in which the risk of loss on the goods sold did not pass until delivery on such goods had been tendered to him at Chetumal, Mexico—an event which never occurred. He relies for this position on the notation at the bottom of the contract between the parties which provides that the goods were to be sent to Chetumal, Mexico. We cannot agree. A "send to" or "ship to" term is a part of every contract involving the sale of goods where carriage is contemplated and has no significance in determining whether the contract is a shipment or destination contract for risk of loss purposes. As such, the "send to" term contained in this contract cannot, without more, convert this into a destination contract.

JUDGMENT AND REMEDY   *The buyer was liable to the seller for the full contract price of the watches.*

Delivery without Movement of Goods   The Code also addresses situations in which the seller is required neither to ship nor to deliver the goods. Frequently the buyer is to pick up the goods from the seller, or the goods remain in a warehouse, or they are held by a bailee (the person to whom they are entrusted). [UCC 2-509(2)(3)]

When the goods are held by a bailee, they are usually represented by a negotiable or nonnegotiable document of title (a bill of lading or warehouse receipt). If the goods are held by the seller, a document of title is usually not used. This distinction is important in applying the rules governing passage of risk of loss to the buyer. [UCC 2-509(2)(3)]

Merchant Seller   If the seller is a merchant, risk of loss to goods held by the seller passes to the buyer when the buyer actually takes physical possession of the goods. [UCC 2-509(3)] For example, a merchant sells goods to a buyer who is supposed to pick them up. Risk of loss does not pass to the buyer until the goods are actually picked up. (Tender is not enough.)

Nonmerchant Seller   If the seller is not a merchant, the risk of loss to goods held by the seller passes to the buyer upon *tender of delivery.* [UCC 2-509(3)] A tender of delivery is the seller's placing or holding of conforming goods at the buyer's disposition (with any necessary notice), enabling the buyer to take delivery. [UCC 2-503(1)]

To illustrate: Jones has cut down a tree in her backyard. The tree has been cut into a pile of firewood. On May 1, Jones contracts to sell the wood to Farber. At the time of their contract, Jones tells Farber that he can take the wood with him on that day if he wishes. Farber tells Jones to keep the wood until May 15, so that he, Farber, can arrange for a place to keep it after taking possession. The firewood burns up three days later through no fault of Jones. Jones claims that Farber is obligated to pay for the wood, even though it has been destroyed. Jones is right. Jones, a nonmerchant, tendered delivery when she offered to let Farber take the wood with him on May 1. The question of tender of delivery arises in the following case.

LUMBER SALES, INC. v. BROWN

Court of Appeals of Tennessee, 1971.
63 Tenn.App. 189, 469 S.W.2d 888.

BACKGROUND AND FACTS   *The court provided a concise statement of the facts as follows.*

PURYEAR, Judge.

* * * *

The uncontroverted evidence shows that during the early morning hours of November 27, 1968, the Louisville and Nashville Railroad Company, to which we will hereinafter refer as the carrier, placed a boxcar loaded with lumber consigned to the defendant on this siding at track location 609-A.

This boxcar was designated as NW54938 and it was inspected by an employee of the carrier between 8:00 A.M. and 8:30 A.M. on November 27, 1968, at which time it was found loaded with cargo and so designated upon the carrier's records.

At 11:07 A.M. on November 27, 1968, the carrier notified one of defendant's employees that the carload of lumber had been delivered at track location 609-A.

At approximately 4:00 P.M. on that same day an employee of the carrier again inspected this boxcar at track location 609-A, found one of the seals on it to be broken and resealed it at that time. The evidence does not show whether the car was still loaded with cargo at that time or not.

The following day, November 28th, was Thanksgiving Day and the record does not disclose that the carrier inspected the boxcar on that date. But on November 29, 1968, between 8:00 A.M. and 8:30 A.M. an employee of the carrier inspected the car and found it empty.

* * * *

The particular Code Section applicable here is Sub-section (1) of [the Tennessee Code] as follows:

"47-2-509. *Risk of loss in the absence of breach.*—(1) Where the contract requires or authorizes the seller to ship the goods by carrier (a) (this portion not applicable) (b) if it does require him to deliver them at a particular destination and the goods are there duly tendered while in the possession of the carrier, the risk of loss passes to the buyer when the goods are there duly so tendered as to enable the buyer to take delivery."

* * * *

Counsel for defendant argues that the lumber in question was not duly so tendered *as to enable the buyer to take delivery"* as required by [UCC Sec. 2-509(1)(b)]

However, this argument seems to be based upon the premise that it was not convenient for the defendant to unload the lumber on November 27th, the day on which it was delivered at track location 609-A and defendant was duly notified of such delivery.

This was an ordinary business day and the time of 11:07 A.M. was a reasonable business hour. If it was not convenient with the defendant to unload the lumber within a few hours after being duly notified of delivery, then he should have protected himself against risk of loss by directing someone to guard the cargo against loss by theft and other hazards.

To hold that the seller or the carrier should, under the circumstances existing in a case of this kind, continue to protect the goods until such time as the buyer may find it convenient to unload them would impose an undue burden upon the seller or the carrier and unnecessarily obstruct the channels of commerce.

The language of subsection (1)(b) of [the Tennessee Code] does not impose such a burden upon the seller, in the absence of some material breach of the contract for delivery, and we think a reasonable construction of such language only requires the seller to place the goods at the buyer's disposal so that he has access to them and may remove them from the carrier's conveyance without lawful obstruction, with the proviso, however, that due notice of such delivery be given to the buyer.

JUDGMENT AND REMEDY   *The trial court judgment was affirmed. Risk of loss had passed to the buyer, and the buyer was liable to the seller for the contract price of the carload of lumber. Basically, the UCC and the court indicated that the buyer should have provided insurance in kind by having someone physically protect the lumber, or he should have purchased a regular insurance policy against theft.*

Cases Involving Bailees   When a bailee is holding goods for a person who has contracted to sell them, and the goods are to be delivered without being moved, the risk of loss passes to the buyer when: (1) the buyer receives a negotiable document of title for the goods, or (2) the bailee acknowledges the buyer's right to possess the goods, or (3) the buyer receives a nonnegotiable document of title *and* has had a *reasonable time* to present the document to the bailee and demand the goods. Obviously, if the bailee refuses to honor the document, the risk of loss remains with the seller. [UCC 2-509(2) and 2-503(4)(b)]

To illustrate: McKee stores goods in Hardy's warehouse and takes a negotiable warehouse receipt for them. On the following day, McKee endorses and sells the receipt to Byne for cash. The day after that, Hardy's warehouse burns down, and the goods are completely destroyed. At the time of the fire, Hardy had not been informed of the sale of the warehouse receipt. The risk of loss is on Byne because it accompanies the negotiable warehouse receipt that gave him title to the goods.

Sale on Approval and Sale or Return Contracts

A **sale on approval** is not a sale until the buyer accepts (approves) the offer. A **sale or return** is a sale that can be rescinded by the buyer without liability. In each case, passage of title and risk of loss depend upon the happening or nonhappening of the conditional event, since these transactions are conditional by their very nature.

Sale on Approval   When a seller offers to sell goods to a buyer and permits the buyer to take the goods on a trial basis, a sale on approval is made. The term *sale* here is a misnomer, since only an *offer* to sell has been made, along with a bailment created by the buyer's possession.

Therefore, title and risk of loss (from causes beyond the buyer's control) remain with the seller until the buyer accepts (approves) the offer. Acceptance can be made expressly, by any act inconsistent with the *trial* purpose or seller's ownership, or by the buyer's election not to return the goods within the trial period. If the buyer does not wish to accept, the buyer may notify the seller of such fact within the trial period, and the return is at the seller's expense and risk. [UCC 2-327(1)] Goods held on approval are not subject to the claims of the buyer's creditors until acceptance.

Sale or Return   The sale or return (sometimes called *sale and return*) is a species of contract by which the seller delivers a quantity of goods to the buyer, on the understanding that if the buyer wishes to retain any portion of those goods (for use or resale), the buyer will consider the portion retained as having been sold to him or her and will pay accordingly. The balance will be returned to the seller or will be held by the buyer as a bailee subject to the seller's order. When the buyer receives possession at the time of sale, the title and risk of loss pass to the buyer. Both remain with the buyer until the buyer returns the goods to the seller within the time period specified. If the buyer fails to return the goods within this time period, the sale is finalized. The return of the goods is at the buyer's risk and expense. The goods held on a sale or return contract are subject to the claims of the buyer's creditors while they are in the buyer's possession.

Under a contract of sale or return, the title vests immediately in the buyer, who has the privilege of rescinding the sale. [UCC 2-326] It is often difficult to determine from a particular transaction which exists—a sale on approval or a contract for sale or return. The Code states that (unless otherwise agreed) if the goods are for the buyer to use, the transaction is a sale on approval; if the goods are for the buyer to resell, the transaction is a sale or return. [UCC 2-326(1)]

Risk of Loss in a Breached Sales Contract

There are many ways to breach a sales contract, and the transfer of risk operates differently depending on whether the seller or the buyer breaches.

Seller's Breach If the goods are so nonconforming that the buyer has the right to reject them, the risk of loss will not pass to the buyer until the defects are cured or until the buyer accepts the goods in spite of their defects (thus waiving the right to reject). For example, a buyer orders blue widgets from a seller, F.O.B. seller's plant. The seller ships black widgets, giving the buyer the right to reject. The widgets are damaged in transit. The risk of loss falls on the seller (although the risk would have been on the buyer if blue widgets had been shipped under a shipment contract). [UCC 2-510]

If a buyer accepts a shipment of goods and later discovers a latent defect, acceptance can be revoked. Revocation allows the buyer to pass the risk of loss back to the seller, at least to the extent that the buyer's insurance does not cover the loss. [UCC 2-510(2)]

Buyer's Breach The general rule is that when a buyer breaches a contract, the loss *immediately* shifts to the buyer. There are three important limitations to this rule:

1. The seller must have already identified the goods under the contract. (Regardless of the delivery arrangements, the risk will shift.)
2. The buyer will bear the risk for only a *commercially reasonable time* after the seller learns of the breach.
3. The buyer will be liable only to the extent of any *deficiency* in the seller's insurance coverage. [UCC 2–510(3)]

The following case is a good example of the disastrous effect a buyer's breach can have when it results in a shift of the risk of loss for a shipment that becomes a total loss when fire destroys the seller's plant.

BACKGROUND AND FACTS *A manufacturer of plastic pellets (the plaintiff) brought this action against a buyer (the defendant) for breach of contract to purchase plastic pellets. The buyer breached its contract by failing to accept the goods when acceptance became due after the seller had made a proper tender of delivery. The seller was entitled to acceptance of the goods and to payment in accordance with the contract terms. However, the buyer failed to provide delivery instructions. The buyer sent the seller a confirming order containing the following notation: "Make and hold for release. Confirmation."*

The seller had manufactured 40,000 pounds of brown polystyrene plastic pellets within two weeks of the order and had requested release orders from the buyer. The buyer repeatedly refused to issue these release orders, citing labor difficulties and vacation schedules.

MULTIPLASTICS INC. v. ARCH INDUSTRIES, INC.

Supreme Court of Connecticut, 1974.
166 Conn. 280, 348 A.2d 618.

The buyer finally agreed to issue the release orders on August 20, 1971, but never actually released them. On September 22, 1971, the seller's plant, which contained the pellets manufactured for the buyer, was destroyed by fire, and the seller's fire insurance did not cover the loss of the pellets. The seller then brought this action against the buyer to recover the contract price. The buyer argued that, because the risk of loss had not passed, the seller could not recover the contract price.

The trial court concluded that the seller had made a valid tender of delivery and that the buyer had repudiated and breached the contract by refusing to accept delivery on August 20, 1971. Moreover, the trial court found that the month between August 20 and September 22, 1971, was not a "commercially unreasonable time" for the seller to treat the risk of loss as having shifted to the buyer. Hence, the trial court concluded that the seller was entitled to recover the contract price plus interest from the buyer.

BOGDANSKI, Associate Justice.

* * * *

General Statutes § 42a-2-510, entitled "Effect of breach on risk of loss," reads, in pertinent part, as follows: "(3) Where the buyer as to conforming goods already identified to the contract for sale repudiates or is otherwise in breach before risk of their loss has passed to him, the seller may to the extent of any deficiency in his effective insurance coverage treat the risk of loss as resting on the buyer for a commercially reasonable time." The defendant contends that § 42a-2-510 is not applicable because its failure to issue delivery instructions did not constitute either a repudiation or a breach of the agreement.

* * * *

The plaintiff's requests for delivery instructions cannot be said to have misled the defendant into thinking that the plaintiff did not consider their contract breached. In fact, General Statutes § 42a-2-610, entitled "Anticipatory repudiation," specifically provides that the aggrieved seller may "resort to any remedy for breach as provided by section 42a-2-703 * * *, even though he has notified the repudiating party that he would await the latter's performance and has urged retraction." * * * The plaintiff's conduct after the defendant refused to accept delivery was not inconsistent with his claim that the contract was breached.

The remaining question is whether, under General Statutes § 42a-2-510(3), the period of time from August 20, 1971, the date of the breach, to September 22, 1971, the date of the fire, was a "commercially reasonable" period within which to treat the risk of loss as resting on the buyer. The trial court concluded that it was "not, on the facts in this case, a commercially unreasonable time," which we take to mean that it was a commercially reasonable period. The time limitation is designed to enable the seller to obtain the additional requisite insurance coverage. The trial court's conclusion is tested by the finding. Although the finding is not detailed, it supports the conclusion that August 20 to September 22 was a commercially reasonable period within which to place the risk of loss on the defendant. As already stated, the trial court found that the defendant repeatedly agreed to transmit delivery instructions and that the pellets were specially made to fill the defendant's order. Under those circumstances, it was reasonable for the plaintiff to believe that the goods would soon be taken off its hands and so to forego procuring the needed insurance.

We consider it advisable to discuss one additional matter. The trial court concluded that "title" passed to the defendant, and the defendant attacks the conclusion on this appeal. The issue is immaterial to this case. General Statutes § 42a-2-401 states: "Each provision of this article with regard to the rights, obligations and remedies of the seller, the buyer, purchasers or other third parties applies irrespective of title to the goods except where the provision refers to such title." As one student of the Uniform Commercial Code has written: "The single most important innovation of Article 2 [of the Uniform Commercial Code] is its restatement of *   *   * [the parties'] responsibilities in terms of operative facts rather than legal conclusions; where pre-Code law looked to 'title' for the definition of rights and remedies, the Code looks to demonstrable realities such as custody, control and professional expertise. This shift in approach is central to the whole philosophy of Article 2. It means that disputes, as they arise, can focus, as does all of the modern law of contracts, upon actual provable circumstances, rather than upon a metaphysical concept of elastic and endlessly fluid dimensions."

The trial court was correct. The risk of loss had passed to the defendant buyer. The plaintiff seller was entitled to recover the full contract price plus interest from the defendant because the seller had no insurance to offset the loss.

    The court of appeals ignored entirely any dispute that the parties tried to raise over who had clear title to the merchandise. Under the Code, the passage of title does not determine who is responsible for the risk of loss.

JUDGMENT AND REMEDY

BULK TRANSFERS

Special problems arise when a major portion of a business's assets are transferred. This is the subject matter of UCC Article 6, Bulk Transfers, which are defined as any transfer of a major part of the material, supplies, merchandise, or other inventory *not made in the ordinary course of the transferor's business.* [UCC 6-102(1)] Problems arise, for example, when a business owing numerous creditors sells a substantial part of its equipment and inventories to a buyer. If the merchant uses the proceeds to pay off debts, no problems arise. But what if the merchant spends the money on a trip around the world, leaving the creditors without payment? Can the creditors lay any claim to the goods that were transferred in bulk to the buyer? To prevent this problem from arising, Article 6 lays out certain requirements for bulk transfer.

Requirements of Article 6

A bulk transfer of assets is ineffective against any creditor of the transferor unless the following requirements are met:

1. The seller (transferor) must furnish to the transferee a sworn list of the person's existing creditors. This list must include those whose claims are disputed, stating names, business addresses, and amounts due. [UCC 6-104(1)(a)]
2. The buyer and the seller must prepare a schedule of the property transferred. [UCC 6-104(1)(b)]
3. The buyer must preserve the list of creditors and the schedule of property for six months. He or she must permit inspection thereof by any creditor of the seller or file the list and the schedule of property in a designated public office. [UCC 6-104(1)(c)]

4. Notice of the proposed bulk transfer must be given by the buyer to each creditor of the seller at least ten days before the buyer takes possession of the goods or makes payments for them, whichever happens first. [UCC 6-105]

If all four steps are undertaken, then the bulk transfer complies with statute. The buyer acquires the goods free of all claims of creditors of the seller.

Notice to Creditors

The specific requirements for the contents of the notice to creditors are:

1. A statement that a bulk transfer is about to be made.
2. Names and business addresses of the seller in bulk and buyer in bulk.
3. Information about whether all debts of the seller in bulk are to be paid in full as a result of the bulk transfer and if so, the addresses to which creditors should send their bills. [UCC 6-107(1)]

Whenever the debts of the transferor in bulk are not to be paid in full as they fall due, the notice to creditors must also state such things as the location and general description of the property to be transferred, the address where the schedule of property and list of creditors may be inspected, and whether the transfer is for new consideration. [UCC 6-107(2)]

When Failure to Comply Occurs

When the requirements of Article 6 are not complied with, goods in possession of the transferee continue to be subject to the claims of the unpaid creditors of the seller for a period of six months. [UCC 6-111] Nonetheless, a bona fide purchaser of these goods from the transferee who pays value in good faith, not knowing that the goods are still subject to the claims of the transferor's creditors, acquires the goods free of any claim of those creditors.

If the creditor did not receive notice and such is due to the fault of the seller (such as not being on the seller's list), the seller is liable to the buyer

for any loss incurred by the buyer. If the failure to receive notice is the buyer's fault and the seller's creditor satisfies his or her claim from the property transferred, the buyer can only recover from the seller the amount of the debt the seller owed to that creditor (quasi-contractual theory).

SALES BY NONOWNERS

Special problems arise when persons who acquire goods with imperfect titles attempt to resell them. UCC 2-402 and 2-403 deal with the rights of two parties who lay claim to the same goods, sold with imperfect titles.

Imperfect Title

Void Title   A buyer acquires at least whatever title the seller has to the goods sold. A buyer may unknowingly purchase goods from a seller who is not the owner of the goods. If the seller is a thief, the seller's title is *void*—legally, no title exists. Thus, the buyer acquires no title, and the real owner can reclaim the goods from the buyer.

For example, if Thomas steals goods owned by Able, Thomas has *void title* (no legally recognized title) to those goods. If Thomas sells the goods to Beyer, Able can reclaim them from Beyer even though Beyer acted in good faith and honestly had no knowledge that the goods were stolen.

Voidable Title   A seller will have a *voidable title* if the goods that he or she is selling were obtained by fraud; paid for with a check that is later dishonored; purchased on credit, when the seller was insolvent; or if the goods were purchased from a minor. Purchasers of goods acquire all title that their transferors either had or had the power to transfer. However, a purchaser of a limited interest acquires rights only to the extent of the interest purchased. A seller with *voidable title* has power, nonetheless, to transfer a good title to a **good faith purchaser** for value.

A good faith purchaser is one who buys without knowledge of the circumstances that would make a person of ordinary prudence inquire about the title of the seller of the goods. In other words, such circumstances exist, but the purchaser is unaware of them. The real owner cannot recover goods from a good faith purchaser for value. [UCC 2-403(1)] If the buyer of the goods is not a good faith purchaser for value, then the actual owner of the goods can reclaim them from the buyer (or from the seller if the goods are still in the seller's possession).

To illustrate: Martin, a minor, sells his bicycle to Able, an adult. Since Martin is a minor, with the right to avoid this contract, Able has a voidable title. If Able sells the bicycle to Beyer, a good faith purchaser, Martin cannot use his minority, when he later disaffirms his contract with Able, to recover the bicycle from Beyer.

The defendant in the following case had some warning that there was something suspicious about the transaction in which he was participating.

BACKGROUND AND FACTS   *The plaintiff was engaged in the business of selling boats, motors, and trailers. He sold a new boat, motor, and trailer to a person who called himself John W. Willis. Willis took possession of the goods and paid for them with a check for $6,285. The check was later dishonored.*

About six months later, the defendant bought the boat, motor, and trailer from a man identified as "Garrett," who was renting a summer beach house to the defendant that year. The defendant had known Garrett for several years.

The plaintiff sought to recover the boat, motor, and trailer from the defendant. The defendant's sole defense was that he was a good faith purchaser, and therefore the plaintiff should not be able to recover from him.

LANE v. HONEYCUTT

Court of Appeals of North Carolina, 1972.

14 N.C.App. 436, 188 S.E.2d 604.

VAUGHN, Judge.

*   *   *   *

Plaintiff has been engaged in the business of selling boats, motors and trailers in Carteret County for a number of years. On 21 February 1970, he sold a new 20-foot Critchfield boat, a new 120 hp motor and a new 1970 Cox boat trailer to a person who represented himself as John W. Willis. The purchaser took possession of the goods in exchange for a check in the amount of $6,285.00. The check was later dishonored. Contrary to the contentions of plaintiff, we hold that the goods were delivered under a transaction of purchase and that the consequences of this purchase are governed by G.S. [General Statutes] § 25-2-403, which, in part, is as follows:

"*Power to transfer; good faith purchase of goods; 'entrusting.'*—(1) A purchaser of goods acquires all title which his transferor had or had power to transfer except that a purchaser of a limited interest acquires rights only to the extent of the interest purchased. A person with voidable title has power to transfer a good title to a good faith purchaser for value. When goods have been delivered under a transaction of purchase the purchaser has such power even though

(a) the transferor was deceived as to the identity of the purchaser, or

(b) the delivery was in exchange for a check which is later dishonored, or

(c) it was agreed that the transaction was to be a 'cash sale,' or

(d) the delivery was procured through fraud punishable as larcenous under the criminal law."

* * * *

The question * * * which we consider to be determinative of this appeal is whether there is any evidence to support the following findings of fact by the court. "(2) The Defendant, Jimmy Honeycutt, did not purchase the boat, motor and trailer in good faith."

* * * *

[Next, the court carefully reviewed the defendant's testimony concerning "Mr. Garrett," who had sold the defendant a boat, motor, and trailer worth over $6,000 for a mere $2,500.]

"Mr. Garrett first approached me about buying his house on the beach that I was staying in, and told me he wanted $50,000.00 for it, and I told him I couldn't afford anything like that. He said, 'Well, let me sell you a boat out there.' And I said, 'Well, I couldn't afford that either.' * * *"

* * * *

"* * * As to whether or not, in other words, this boat looked like it was fairly expensive, well, I thought it would be a little more than it was. He told me the price and I was very pleasantly surprised. ... * * * ... (H)e sells fishing tackle and stuff of that nature, and beer. He also sells gasoline for boats. Yes, sir, that is about all he sells down there. He rents small fishing boats and motors too. No, he doesn't sell them, he doesn't sell boats as far as I know. ... * * *"

Garrett told defendant he would let defendant have the boat for $2500. Defendant then paid Garrett a deposit of $100. Garrett had nothing to indicate that he was the owner of the boat, motor or trailer. Garrett told defendant he was selling the boat for someone else. "This guy comes down, you know, and does some fishing."

Two weeks later defendant returned to Garden City, South Carolina, with $2400, the balance due (on a boat, motor and trailer which had been sold new less than six months earlier for $6,285.00). On this occasion,

"Mr. Garrett had told me—well, he always called him, 'this guy' see, so I really didn't know of any name or anything, but he told me, 'this guy does a lot of fishing around here but I can't seem to get ahold of him.' He said, 'I've called him, but I can't get ahold of him, so since you have the money and you're here after the boat' * * * '(s)ince you have the money and I can't seem to find him,' he said, 'I don't believe he would object, so I'll just go ahead and sign this title for you so you can go on and get everything made out to you.' He then signed the purported owner's name on the documents and he signed the title over to me then."

The so-called "document" and "title," introduced as defendant's exhibit No. 8, was nothing more than the "certificate of number" required by G.S. § 75A-5 and issued by the North Carolina Wildlife Resources Commission. This "certificate of number" is not a "certificate of title" to be compared with that required by G.S. § 20-50 for vehicles intended to be operated on the highways of this State. Upon the change of ownership of a motor boat, G.S. § 75A-5(c) authorizes the issuance of a new "certificate of number" to the transferee upon proper application. The application for transfer of the number, among other things, requires the seller's *signature*. A signature is "the name of a person written with his own hand." Webster's Third New International Dictionary (1968). Defendant observed Garrett counterfeit the signature of the purported owner, John P. Patterson, on the exhibit. Following the falsified signature on defendant's exhibit No. 8, the "date sold" is set out as "June 12, 1970" and the buyer's "signature" is set out as "George (illegible) Williams." There was no testimony as to who affixed the "signature" of the purported buyer, George Williams, and there is no further reference to him in the record.

*   *   *   *

We hold that the evidence was sufficient to support the court's finding that defendant was not a good faith purchaser. *   *   *

The trial court's ruling was affirmed. The defendant was not a good faith purchaser. The plaintiff was determined to be the owner and was entitled to immediate possession of the boat, motor, and trailer. The plaintiff was also awarded damages against the defendant for wrongful detention of the property.

JUDGMENT AND REMEDY

Entrustment   According to Section 2-403(2), entrusting goods to a merchant *who deals in goods of that kind* gives the merchant the power to transfer all rights to a *buyer in the ordinary course of business. Entrusting* includes both delivering the goods to the merchant and leaving the purchased goods with the merchant for later delivery or pickup. [UCC 2-403(3)] A "buyer in the ordinary course" is a person who buys in good faith from a person who deals in goods of that kind. The buyer cannot have knowledge that the sale violates the ownership rights of a third person.

For example, Sue leaves her watch with a jeweler to be repaired. The jeweler sells both new and used watches. The jeweler sells the watch to Ann, a customer, who does not know that the jeweler has no right to sell it. Ann gets *good title* against Sue's claim of ownership.[2]

The good faith buyer, however, obtains only those rights that the person entrusting the goods has. For example, Sue's watch is stolen by Thomas. Thomas leaves the watch with a jeweler for repairs. The jeweler sells the watch to Betty, who does not know that the jeweler has no right to sell it. Betty gets good title against Thomas, the entrustor, but not against Sue, who

neither entrusted the watch to Thomas nor authorized Thomas to entrust it.

Seller's Retention of Sold Goods   Ordinarily, sellers do not retain goods in their possession or their use after the goods are sold. A seller who retained goods after they were sold could mislead creditors into believing that the seller's assets were more substantial than they really were.

Retention of the goods, and particularly their use by the seller, is basic evidence of an intent to defraud creditors. If a creditor can prove that the retention is in *fact* fraud, or if the state has a *statute* providing that such retention creates a *presumption* of fraud (and if such is unrebutted), the creditor can set aside the sale to the buyer.

However, UCC 2-402(2) recognizes that it is not necessarily a fraud upon creditors if a *merchant* seller retains possession in good faith for a "commercially reasonable time" in order to accomplish some legitimate purpose (for example, repairs or adjustments). In such situations, the seller's unsecured creditors cannot void the sale.

A seller can defraud creditors by selling items at something substantially less than "fair consideration," thereby depleting the seller's assets. This is fraud on the seller's creditors if the seller is insolvent at the time of the sale, is made insolvent by the sale, or actually intended to defraud or delay actions by the creditors. Assets sold at less than "fair consideration" often are sold to a friend or relative of the seller. Such

---

2.   In the case of entrustment, no transaction of purchase is required between the entrustor (true owner) and the entrustee in order for the good faith purchaser to prevail.

sales are considered sham transactions used to conceal assets.

For example, suppose that FL Boat Company is on the verge of bankruptcy. Many of the loans that FL's owner had taken out were personally secured by him, so his creditors can go after his personal assets to recover what he owes them. Knowing this, FL's owner sells several expensive cars to his father for only $3,000 apiece, and he sells his personal yacht to his brother-in-law for $10,000 (when it is worth $110,000). He has an implicit understanding with his father and his brother-in-law that he will retain control over these assets but that they will have title. If the creditors find out about the sham transactions, they can void the sales.

INSURABLE INTEREST

Buyers and sellers often obtain insurance policy coverage to protect against damage, loss, or destruction of goods. But any party purchasing insurance must have a "sufficient interest" in the insured item to obtain a valid policy. Insurance laws—not the Code—determine "sufficiency." (See Chapter 55.) However, the Code is helpful because it contains certain rules regarding a buyer's and a seller's insurable interest in goods on a sales contract.

Buyer's Insurable Interest

Buyers have an insurable interest in *identified* goods. The moment the goods are identified to the contract by the seller, the buyer has this "special" property interest that allows the buyer to obtain necessary insurance coverage for those goods even before the risk of loss has passed. [UCC 2-501(1)]

Consider an example: In March a farmer sells a cotton crop he hopes to harvest in October to a buyer. After the crop is planted, the buyer insures it against hail damage. In September a hailstorm ruins the crop. When the buyer files a claim under her insurance policy, the insurer refuses to pay the claim, asserting that the buyer has no insurable interest in the crop. The insurer is not correct. The buyer acquired an insurable interest

in the crop when it was planted, since she had a contract to buy it. The rule in UCC 2-501(1)(c) states that a buyer obtains an insurable interest in the goods by identification, which occurs "when the crops are planted or otherwise become growing crops * * * if the contract is * * * for the sale of crops to be harvested within twelve months or the next normal harvest season after contracting, whichever is longer."

Seller's Insurable Interest

Sellers have an insurable interest in goods as long as they retain title to the goods. However, even after title passes to a buyer, a seller who has a "security interest" in the goods (a right to secure payment) still has an insurable interest and can insure the goods. [UCC 2-501(2)]

Hence, both a buyer and a seller can have an insurable interest in identical goods at the same time. In all cases, one must sustain an actual loss in order to have the right to recover from an insurance company.

QUESTIONS AND CASE PROBLEMS

1. On May 1 Beyer goes into Smith's retail clothing store to purchase a suit. Beyer finds the suit he is interested in for $190 and buys it. The suit needs alteration. Beyer is to pick up the altered suit at Smith's store on May 10. Assume separately:
    (a) One of Smith's major creditors has a judgment against Smith and levies execution on that judgment against all clothing in Smith's possession.
    (b) On May 9, through no fault of Smith, his store burns down, and all contents are a total loss.
    Discuss *Beyer's* rights to the suit on which the major creditor has levied. Between Smith and Beyer, who suffers the loss of the suit destroyed by fire? Explain.
2. Beyer orders from Sallor 1,000 cases of Greenie brand peas from Lot A at list price to be shipped F.O.B. Sallor's city via Fast Freight Lines. Sallor receives the order and immediately sends Beyer an acceptance of

the order with a promise to ship promptly. Sallor later separates the 1,000 cases of Greenie peas and prints Beyer's name and address on each case. The peas are placed on Sallor's dock, and Fast Freight is notified to pick up the shipment. The night before the pickup by Fast Freight, through no fault of Sallor, a fire destroys the 1,000 cases of peas. Sallor claims title passed at the time the contract was made, and risk of loss passed to Beyer upon the marking of the goods with Beyer's name and address. Discuss Sallor's contentions.

3. Sallor sells lawn mowers. Beyer is a regular customer who comes in to see Sallor. Sallor has a special promotional campaign. He tells Beyer about it. It involves a down payment of $50. Upon receipt of the down payment, Sallor will sell Beyer a new Universal lawn mower for $200, even though it normally sells for $350. Sallor further states to Beyer that if Beyer does not like the performance of the lawn mower, Beyer can return the mower within thirty days and Sallor will refund the $50 down payment. Beyer pays the $50 and takes the mower. On the tenth day the lawn mower is stolen through no fault of Beyer. Beyer calls Sallor and demands the return of his $50. Sallor claims Beyer should suffer the risk of loss and that he still owes Sallor the remainder of the purchase price, or $150. Discuss whether Beyer or Sallor is correct.

4. In the following situations, two parties lay claim to the same goods sold. Discuss which of the parties would prevail in this claim to the television set in each situation.

(a) Thomas steals Able's television set and sells the set to Beyer, an innocent purchaser, for value. Able learns Beyer has the set and demands its return.

(b) Able takes her television set for repair to Martin, a merchant who sells new and used television sets. By accident, one of Martin's employees sells the set to Beyer, an innocent purchaser-customer, who takes possession. Able wants her set back from Beyer.

5. Crump, a television fanatic, purchased a television antenna and antenna tower from Lair Company. Crump purchased the antenna and tower under a ten-year conditional sales contract that obligated him to make monthly payments. The sales contract provided that Lair Company would retain title until Crump had completed all payments under the contract. The purchase contract stated, among other things, that Crump was not to move or tamper with the antenna during the ten-year payment period. About a year later, lightning struck and destroyed Crump's new antenna. At Crump's request, Lair Company performed extensive repairs on the antenna. Crump refused to pay, claiming that risk of loss or damage resulting from the lightning should be borne by Lair Company. Will Lair be successful in a suit for the cost of its repairs? [Lair Distributing Co. v. Crump, 48 Ala.App. 72, 261 So. 2d 904 (1972)]

6. As one of the benefits of working with A&Z Motor Company, Knotts received a model car at dealer cost to use both for family and business purposes. Knotts was to be the sole user of the car, and A&Z retained the certificate of title. Knotts retained the use of the dealer's plates. The car was insured by Safeco Insurance Company, and Knotts was named in the policy as the owner of the car. Knotts made payments at a rate of $70 per month to the First National Bank, which had financed the dealer's original purchase. Several weeks after A&Z gave Knotts the use of the car, he had an accident. Knotts sued the insurance company to recover for damages which were covered by the insurance policy. Safeco refused to pay, claiming that Knotts was not the owner of the car and that, since A&Z was the owner, the insurance policy necessarily ran in favor of it. Can Knotts recover from Safeco? [Knotts v. Safeco Ins. Co. of America, 78 N.M. 395, 432 P.2d 106 (1967)]

7. A new car owned by a New Jersey car rental agency was stolen in 1967. The agency collected the full price of the car from its insurance company, Home Indemnity Company, and assigned all its interest in the automobile to the insurer. Subsequently, a thief sold the car to an automobile wholesaler, who in turn sold it to a retail car dealer. Schrier purchased the automobile from the car dealer without knowledge of the theft. Home Indemnity Insurance Company sued Schrier to recover the car. Can Home Indemnity recover? [Schrier v. Home Indemnity Co., 273 A.2d 248 (D.C.App. 1971)]

8. Shook ordered three reels of burial cable from Graybar Electric Company. Graybar delivered one reel of burial cable and by mistake delivered two reels of aerial cable. The aerial cable was unsuited to Shook's use. Shook notified Graybar of the mistake, and Graybar requested that the nonconforming reels be returned. Graybar did not collect the cable. Shook could not return it because there was a truckers' strike. The cable was left at the Six Run Grocery Store directly beside the building. The two reels of cable were eventually stolen. Graybar was notified. Graybar sued Shook for the purchase price. At trial, Shook prevailed. Graybar appealed. What was the result? [Graybar Electric Co. v. Shook, 283 N.C. 213, 195 S.E.2d 514 (1973)]

9. The Ryans borrowed money from Evanston Building & Loan Company to buy a modular home

manufactured by Fuqua Homes. They purchased the home from a partnership acting as an intermediary-dealer for Fuqua. After receiving the proceeds of the sale, the partners in the intermediary-dealership disappeared without making any payment to Fuqua Homes. Fuqua claimed that since it had not been paid, it was still the holder of the certificate of origin of the modular home, and it still had title to the home. Is Fuqua correct? [Fuqua Homes, Inc. v. Evanston Building & Loan Co., 52 Ohio App.2d 399, 370 N.E.2d 780 (1977)]

10.   A men's clothing manufacturer in Los Angeles sold $2,216 of men's clothing to a store in Westport, Connecticut. The contract stated that the shipment was to be "F.O.B. Los Angeles." The Los Angeles manufacturer arranged for shipping via common carrier to Connecticut. Upon arrival of the clothes, the purchaser's agent refused to unload them, as did the carrier's agent, indicating that it was the purchaser's obligation to unload. The carrier left with the shipment, which subsequently disappeared. The Los Angeles manufacturer sued the purchaser for the contract price. Had the risk of loss passed to the Connecticut purchaser at the time of delivery of the clothes to the common carrier? [Ninth Street East Ltd. v. Harrison, 5 Conn. Cir. 597, 259 A.2d 772 (1968)]

CHAPTER 20

SALES
Introduction to
Sales Warranties

Until recently, *caveat emptor*—let the buyer beware—was the prevailing philosophy in sales contract law. In twentieth century America, however, this outlook has given way to a more enlightened consumer approach (although many sellers argue that today's standards of liability are unrealistic and excessive). This chapter will review the concept of product warranty as it occurs in a sales contract under the UCC.

The concept of *warranty* is based upon the seller's assurance to the buyer that the goods will meet certain standards. The UCC designates five types of warranties that can arise in a sales contract:

1. Warranty of title. [UCC 2-312]
2. Express warranty. [UCC 2-313]
3. Implied warranty of merchantability. [UCC 2-314]
4. Implied warranty of fitness for a particular purpose. [UCC 2-315]

5. Implied warranty arising from the course of dealing or trade usage. [UCC 2-314(3)]

In the law of sales, since a warranty imposes a duty upon the seller, a breach of warranty is a breach of the seller's promise, and a buyer can sue to recover damages against the seller. Also, a breach can allow the buyer to rescind the agreement.[1]

WARRANTY OF TITLE

Title warranty arises automatically in most sales contracts. UCC 2-312 imposes three types of warranties of title.

---

1. Rescission can occur in two ways: It can refer either to rejection of goods before acceptance or to revocation by the buyer after acceptance, returning the parties to their original positions.

Good Title

In most cases, sellers warrant that they have good and valid title to the goods sold and that transfer of the title is rightful. [UCC 2-312(1)(a)] For example, Alice steals goods from Ophelia and sells them to Betty, who does not know that they are stolen. If Ophelia discovers that Betty has the goods, then Ophelia has the right to reclaim them from Betty. Under this Code provision, however, Betty can then sue Alice for breach of warranty, because a thief has no title to stolen goods and thus cannot give good title in a subsequent sale. When Alice sold Betty the goods, Alice *automatically* warranted to Betty that the title conveyed was valid and that its transfer was rightful. Since this was not in fact the case, Alice has breached the warranty of title imposed by UCC 2-312(1)(a), and Alice becomes liable to the buyer for appropriate damages.

No Liens

A second warranty of title provided by the Code protects buyers who are *unaware* of any encumbrances (claims or liens) against goods at the time of the contract. [UCC 2-312(1)(b)] This warranty protects buyers who, for example, unknowingly purchase goods that are subject to a creditor's security interest. (See Chapters 30 and 31.) If a creditor legally reposseses the goods from a buyer who *had no actual knowledge of the security interest,* then the buyer can recover from the seller for a breach of warranty. (The buyer who has *actual knowledge* of a security interest has no recourse against a seller.)

To illustrate: Henderson buys a used color television set from Sneed for cash. A month later, Reynolds repossesses the set from Henderson, proving that she, Reynolds, has a valid security interest in the set. She proves that Sneed is in default, having missed five payments. Henderson demands his money back from Sneed. Under Section 2-312(2)(b), Henderson will be able to recover because the seller of goods warrants that the goods shall be delivered free from any security interest or other lien of which the buyer has no knowledge.

No Infringements

A third "category" of title warranty is the warranty against infringement. A merchant is deemed to warrant that the goods delivered are free from any patent, trademark, or copyright claims of a third person.[2] [UCC 2-312(3)] If this warranty is breached and the buyer is sued by the claim holder, the buyer *must notify the seller* of litigation within a reasonable time to enable the seller to decide whether to defend the lawsuit. If the seller in writing decides to defend and agrees to bear all expenses, including that of an adverse judgment, then the buyer must let the seller undertake litigation; otherwise the buyer loses all rights against the seller if any infringement liability is established. [UCC 2-607(3)(b)]

To illustrate: Green buys a machine from Brown, a manufacturer of such machines, for use in his factory. Three years later, Patton sues Green for damages for patent infringement. Patton claims that he has a patent on the machine and that it cannot be used without his permission. At once, Green informs Brown of this suit and demands that Brown take over the defense. Brown refuses to do so, claiming that Patton has no case. Green goes to court and loses. Patton obtains a judgment against Green, which Green pays off. Green now demands that Brown reimburse him for the amount. Brown must reimburse Green because merchant sellers of goods warrant to buyers that the goods they regularly sell are free of infringement claims by third parties.

This infringement warranty does not apply to buyers who furnish specifications for the goods to be made in a particular way. In fact, it is the buyer who must hold the seller harmless (i.e., not liable) against any third person's claims of infringement arising out of the goods manufactured to the buyer's specifications. [UCC 2-312(3)] The same requirements of notice apply to a seller who is sued for breach of an infringement war-

---

2. Recall from Chapter 18 that a *merchant* is defined in UCC 2-104(1) as a person who deals in goods of the kind involved in the sales contract or who, by occupation, presents himself or herself as having knowledge or skill peculiar to the goods involved in the transaction.

ranty for which the buyer is answerable by virtue of the "hold harmless" agreement. [UCC 2-607(6)]

To illustrate: Green orders a custom-made machine from Brown, who is a manufacturer of such machines. It is built strictly to Green's specifications. While the machine is being built, Patton files a suit against Brown for patent infringement. Brown immediately informs Green in writing of this suit and demands that Green take over the expense of the litigation. Green refuses to do so. Brown settles with Patton out of court by paying Patton modest damages. Brown now wishes to be reimbursed by Green. Brown will be able to collect because a buyer who orders custom-built goods from a seller, and who furnishes the seller with the specifications, warrants to the seller that the specifications do not infringe any patent.

Disclaimer of Title Warranty In an ordinary sales transaction, the title warranty can be disclaimed or modified only by *specific language* in a contract. For example, sellers assert that they are transferring only such rights, title, and interest as they have in the goods.

In certain cases, the circumstances of the sale are sufficient to indicate clearly to a buyer that no assurances as to title are being made. The classic example is a sheriff's sale, where buyers know that the goods have been seized to satisfy debts and it is apparent that the goods are not the property of the person who is selling them. [UCC 2-312(2)]

WARRANTIES OF QUALITY

Express Warranties

A seller can create an **express warranty** by making representations concerning the quality, condition, description, or performance potential of the goods. Under UCC 2-313, express warranties arise when a seller indicates that:

1. The goods will conform to any *affirmation or promise* of fact that the seller makes to the buyer about the goods. Such affirmations or promises are usually made during the bargaining process. Statements such as "These drill bits will *easily* penetrate stainless steel—and without dulling" constitute an express warranty.

2. The goods will conform to any *description* of them. For example, "Crate contains one 150-horsepower diesel engine."

3. The goods will conform to any *sample* or *model.*

Basis of the Bargain The Code requires that for any express warranty to be created, the affirmation, promise, description, or sample must become part of the "basis of the bargain." Just what constitutes the basis of the bargain is hard to say. The Code does not define the concept, and each case presents a question of fact to determine whether a representation came at such a time and in such a way that it induced the buyer to enter the contract.

Are certain vague telephone statements part of the basis of the bargain? That is the question addressed in the following case.

BACKGROUND AND FACTS *Riegle sold a standardbred race horse to Sessa for $25,000. Prior to the sale, Sessa sent a friend, Maloney, to examine the horse. Maloney reported that he "liked him." Additionally, during a telephone conversation, Riegle stated to Sessa that Sessa would like the horse and that he was a "good one" and "sound." After the sale was consummated and after delivery, the horse almost immediately went lame in the hind legs. Experts were unable to identify the cause. They could not establish if the condition was present before Riegle shipped the horse. Even though the horse—Tarport Conaway—was later able to race, Sessa sued for damages.*

SESSA v. RIEGLE

United States District Court,
Eastern District of Pennsylvania,
1977.
427 F.Supp. 760, affirmed
without opinion 568 F.2d 770
(3d Cir. 1978).

HANNUM, District Judge.

*   *   *   *

Sessa contends that certain statements made by Riegle during that conversation constitute express warranties on which Riegle is liable in this action. The most important of these is Riegle's alleged statement that, "the horse is sound," or words to that effect.

In deciding whether statements by a seller constitute express warranties, the court must look to UCC § 2-313 which presents three fundamental issues. First, the court must determine whether the seller's statement constitutes an "affirmation of fact or promise" or "description of the goods" under § 2-313(1)(a) or (b) or whether it is rather "merely the seller's opinion or commendation of the goods" under § 2-313(2). Second, assuming the court finds the language used susceptible to creation of a warranty, it must then be determined whether the statement was "part of the basis of the bargain." If it was, an express warranty exists and, as the third issue, the court must determine whether the warranty was breached.

With respect to the first issue, the court finds that in the circumstances of this case, words to the effect that "The horse is sound" spoken during the telephone conversation between Sessa and Riegle constitute an opinion or commendation rather than express warranty. This determination is a question for the trier of fact. There is nothing talismanic or thaumaturgic about the use of the word "sound." Whether use of that language constitutes warranty, or mere opinion or commendation depends on the circumstances of the sale and the type of goods sold. While § 2-313 makes it clear that no specific words need be used and no specific intent need be present, not every statement by a seller is an express warranty.

Several older Pennsylvania cases dealing with horse sales show that similar statements as to soundness are not always similarly treated under warranty law. In Wilkinson v. Stettler, 46 Pa.Super. 407 (1911), the statement that a horse "was solid and sound and would work any place" was held not to constitute an express warranty. This result was followed in Walker v. Kirk, 72 Pa.Super. 534 (1919) which considered the statement, "This mare is sound and all right and a good worker double." Walker was decided after the passage of § 12 of the Uniform Sales Act, the precursor of U.C.C. § 2-313 and thus presumably rests on the standard there established. The Official Comments to U.C.C. § 2-313 indicate that no changes in the law of warranties under Uniform Sales Act § 12 were intended.

However, in Flood v. Yeager, 52 Pa.Super. 637 (1912) an express warranty was found where the plaintiff informed the defendant that, " he did not know anything at all about a horse and that he did not want *   *   * the defendant to make a mean deal with him; whereupon the defendant said that the horse was solid and sound; that he would guarantee him to be solid and sound" 52 Pa.Super. at 638. While all three of these cases are premised partly on the now displaced rule that specific intent to warrant is a necessary concomitant of an express warranty, they do show that statements of the same tenor receive varying treatment depending on the surrounding circumstances.

The results in these cases are also consistent with custom among horse traders as alluded to by Gene Riegle. He testified that it is "not a common thing" to guarantee a horse, that he has never guaranteed a horse unless he had an "understanding" with the buyer and that he did not guarantee Tarport Conaway. In other words, because horses are fragile creatures, susceptible to myriad maladies, detectable and undetectable, only where there is an "understanding" that an ignorant buyer is relying totally on a knowledgeable seller not "to make a mean deal," are statements as to soundness taken to be anything more than the seller's opinion or commendation.

The facts suggest no special "understanding" between Sessa and Riegle. Sessa was a knowledgeable buyer, having been involved with standardbreds for some years. Also, Sessa sent Maloney, an even more knowledgeable horseman, as his agent to inspect the horse.

Also mitigating against a finding of express warranty is the nature of the conversation between Sessa and Riegle. It seemed largely collateral to the sale rather than an essential part of it. Although Sessa testified that Riegle's "personal guarantee" given during the conversation was the quintessence of the sale, the credible evidence suggests otherwise. While on the telephone, Riegle made statements to the effect that "the horse is a good one" and "you will like him." These bland statements are obviously opinion or commendation, and the statement, "The horse is sound," falling within their penumbra takes on their character as such.

Under all the facts and circumstances of this case, it is clear to the court that Riegle's statements were not of such a character as to give rise to express warranties under § 2-313(1) but were opinion or commendation under § 2-313(2).

Even assuming that Riegle's statements could be express warranties, it is not at all clear that they were "part of the basis of the bargain," the second requisite of § 2-313. This is essentially a reliance requirement and is inextricably intertwined with the initial determination as to whether given language may constitute an express warranty since affirmations, promises and descriptions tend to become part of the basis of the bargain. It was the intention of the drafters of the U.C.C. not to require a strong showing of reliance. In fact, they envisioned that all statements of the seller became part of the basis of the bargain unless clear affirmative proof is shown to the contrary. See Official Comments 3 and 8 to U.C.C. § 2-313, 12A P.S. § 2-313.

It is Sessa's contention that his conversation with Riegle was the principal factor inducing him to enter the bargain. He would have the court believe that Maloney was merely a messenger to deliver the check. The evidence shows, however, that Sessa was relying primarily on Maloney to advise him in connection with the sale. Maloney testified that he had talked to Sessa about the horse on several occasions and expressed the opinion that he was convinced "beyond the shadow of a doubt" that he was a good buy. With respect to his authority to buy the horse he testified

"Well, Mr. Sessa said he had enough confidence and faith in me and my integrity and honesty that I, what I did say about the horse, I was representing the horse as he is or as he was, and that if the horse, in my estimation, was that type of a horse and at that given price, the fixed price of $25,000 he would buy the horse."

When, at the airport, Maloney protested that he did not want to accept full responsibility to go to Ohio alone, Sessa told him "* * * I take your word. I—I trust your judgment and I trust your—your honesty, that if this horse is right, everything will be all right." In Ohio, Maloney examined the horse, jogged him and reported to Sessa over the telephone that he "liked him."

The court believes that Maloney's opinion was the principal, if not the only, factor which motivated Sessa to purchase the horse. The conversation with Riegle played a negligible role in his decision.

**JUDGMENT
AND REMEDY**   *The final conclusion of the court was that even if an express warranty had been made, Sessa accepted it and was unable to prove by a preponderance of the evidence that the horse was not sound at the time of tender.*

Statements of Opinion and Value—Use of Formal Words Not Required   According to Section 2-313(2), "It is not necessary to the creation of an express warranty that the seller use formal words such as 'warrant' or 'guarantee' or that he has a specific intention to make a warranty * * *." It is necessary only that a reasonable buyer would regard the representation as part of the basis of the bargain.

On the other hand, if the seller merely makes a statement that relates to the value or worth of the goods, or makes a statement of opinion or recommendation about the goods, the seller is not creating an express warranty. [UCC 2-313(2)] For example, a seller claims, "This is the best used car to come along in years; it has four new tires and a 350-horsepower engine just rebuilt this year." The seller has made several *affirmations of fact* that can create a warranty: The automobile has an engine; it is a 350-horsepower engine; it was rebuilt this year; there are four tires on the automobile; the tires are new. But the seller's *opinion* that it is "the best used car to come along in years" is known as "puffing" and creates no warranty. (Puffing is an expression of opinion by a seller that is not made as a representation of fact.) A statement relating to the value of the goods, such as "it's worth a fortune" or "anywhere else you'd pay $10,000 for it," will not normally create a warranty.

The ordinary seller can give an *opinion* that is not a warranty. However, if the seller is an expert and gives an opinion as an expert, then a warranty can be created. For example, Saul is an art dealer and an expert in seventeenth century painting. If Saul states to Beyer, a purchaser, that in his opinion a particular painting is a Rembrandt, and Beyer buys the painting, Saul has warranted the accuracy of his opinion.

What constitutes an express warranty and what constitutes puffing is not easy to resolve. Merely recognizing that some statements are not warranties does not tell us where one should draw the line between puffs and warranties. The reasonableness of the buyer's reliance appears to be the controlling criterion in many cases. For example, a salesperson's statements that a ladder "will never break" and will "last a lifetime" are so clearly improbable that no reasonable buyer should rely on them. Also, the context within which a statement is made might be relevant in determining the reasonableness of the buyer's reliance. For example, any statement made in a written advertisement is more likely to be relied upon by a reasonable person than a statement made orally by a salesperson.

The following case involves the question of puffing. It is a classic pre-UCC case that is not inconsistent with the Code.

**WAT HENRY PONTIAC
CO. v. BRADLEY**
Supreme Court of Oklahoma,
1949.
202 Okl. 82, 210 P.2d 348.

BACKGROUND AND FACTS   *This action was brought to recover $324.56 in damages for breach of an express oral warranty made by a used car dealer. The dealer (defendant) assured his customer (the plaintiff) that the automobile was in fine mechanical condition and that it would take the plaintiff anywhere she wanted to go. The trial court held that such an assertion was more than an expression of mere opinion. It constituted a warranty.*

The plaintiff alleged that on October 22, 1944, she purchased a used Buick automobile from the defendant, paying $890 in cash. At that time, the defendant assured her orally that the vehicle was in first-class con-

dition, usable and serviceable in every respect. The plaintiff relied on that representation and purchased the vehicle. But as it turned out, the car was not in first-class usable condition. In fact, it was necessary to have the vehicle repaired and have parts replaced. Ultimately, the plaintiff spent $249.56 in repair and replacement and suffered damages, expenses, and inconvenience in the sum of $75.

The defendant argued, in the first place, that the expression was mere opinion and did not constitute a warranty and, in the second place, that no implied warranty of quality or fitness is ever present in the sale of a secondhand automobile.

JOHNSON, Justice.

* * * *

We now consider defendant's proposition one: "Generally, no implied warranty of quality or fitness is present in sale of a secondhand automobile, but doctrine of caveat emptor applies."

This is the general rule as to implied warranties however, the plaintiff in this case does not rely on an implied warranty, but upon an express verbal warranty, and the rule of caveat emptor does not apply where there is an express warranty of condition, and does not apply to hidden defects which are not open to discovery by the buyer.

[The court thus found that the rule of *caveat emptor* did not apply in this case. The court looked next at the defendant's other contention—that he had not asserted a warranty but merely stated an opinion.]

The salesman who sold the car testified in substance that he had been an auto mechanic for about twelve years before becoming a salesman; that he was engaged in demonstrating and selling cars; that he did not warrant the car, but explained to the buyer that the sale was without a warranty, but did state that after the deal was closed that he told plaintiff, "I would not be afraid to start, and I wouldn't have been afraid to start any place in the car, because it run as nice as you would expect a car that age to run. There wasn't anything to indicate to me that there was anything wrong with the car, if there was anything wrong with it."

The evidence adduced as to the issues involved was in conflict, each side having witnesses to substantiate their theory. Now, did these facts as stated by plaintiff, if true, constitute an oral warranty?

The rule is that to constitute an express warranty no particular form of words is necessary, and any affirmation of the quality or condition of the vehicle, not uttered as a matter of opinion or belief, made by a seller at the time of sale for the purpose of assuring the buyer of the truth of the fact and inducing the buyer to make the purchase, if so received and relied on by the buyer, is an express warranty.

This court * * * [has stated the rule of law as follows:]

" 'Warranty' is a matter of intention. A decisive test is whether the vendor assumes to assert a fact of which the buyer is ignorant, or merely states an opinion, or his judgment, upon a matter of which the vendor has no special knowledge, and on which the buyer may also be expected to have an opinion and to exercise his judgment. In the former case there is a warranty; in the latter case there is not.

* * *

"The buyer knew nothing about the capacity of the automobile purchased. The seller was an expert in the handling of automobiles, and was engaged in the business of demonstrating and selling the same. Held, a statement made by the seller that the automobile could be driven over the roads in a certain vicinity satisfactorily constituted a warranty and was not the expression of a mere opinion."

The facts in this case bring it squarely within the above well-settled principles of law, and the jury was justified in finding that there was an oral warranty.

JUDGMENT AND REMEDY

The court held that the defendant's statements about the mechanical condition of the car constituted a warranty. The defendant was liable to the plaintiff, who was awarded $324.56 in damages for breach of the express oral warranty of the used car.

COMMENT

A similar case, Frederickson v. Hackney, 159 Minn. 234, 198 N.W. 806 (1924), was decided differently. In that case, the seller of a bull calf stated to the buyer that the purchase would put "the buyer on the map" and that the father of the bull calf was "the greatest living dairy bull." The bull proved sterile, so the buyer sued. The Minnesota court considered the statements made by the seller only trade talk, not a warranty of productive capacity. Apparently, the most persuasive difference between the two cases was that in the Wat Henry case it was a woman who bought the car to make a trip with her seven-month-old child in 1944 to visit her husband in the Army, and the car broke down en route. Presumably, it was the natural compassion that the trier of fact felt for a World War II service wife who was stranded with a seven-month-old child that distinguishes this case from the Frederickson case. This analysis is supported by the fact that oral statements by used car salespeople are notoriously unreliable and, indeed, archetypal puffs.

Implied Warranties

An *implied warranty* is one that *the law derives* by implication or inference from the nature of the transaction or the relative situation or circumstances of the parties.

For example: Kaplan buys an axe at Enrique's Hardware Store. There are no express warranties made. The first time she chops wood with it, the axe handle breaks, and Kaplan is injured. She immediately notifies Enrique. Examination shows that the wood in the handle was rotten but that the rottenness could not have been noticed by either Enrique or Kaplan. Nonetheless, Kaplan notifies Enrique that she will hold him responsible for the medical bills. Enrique is responsible because a merchant seller of goods warrants that the goods he sells are fit for normal use. This axe was obviously not fit for normal use.

Implied Warranty of Merchantability

An **implied warranty of merchantability** arises in every sale of goods made *by a merchant* who deals in goods of the kind sold. [UCC 2-314] Thus, a retailer of ski equipment makes an implied warranty of merchantability every time the retailer sells a pair of skis, but a neighbor selling skis at a garage sale does not.

Goods that are *merchantable* are "reasonably fit for the ordinary purposes for which such goods are used." They must be of at least average, fair, or medium-grade quality. The quality must be comparable to quality that will pass without objection in the trade or market for goods of the same description. In addition, the goods to be merchantable must be adequately packaged and labeled as provided by the agreement, and they must conform to the promises or affirmations of fact made on the container or label, if any.

Some examples of nonmerchantable goods include: light bulbs that explode when switched on, pajamas that burst into flames upon slight contact with a stove burner, high heels that break off shoes under normal use, or shotgun shells that explode prematurely.

A sale is always accompanied by an implied warranty of merchantability that imposes on the merchant liability for the safe performance of the product. It makes no difference whether the merchant knew of or could have discovered a defect that makes the product unsafe. (Of course, merchants are not absolute insurers against *all* accidents arising in connection with the goods.

For example, a bar of soap will not be unmerchantable merely because a user can slip and fall by stepping on it.) In an action based on breach of warranty, it is necessary to show: (1) the existence of the implied warranty, (2) that the warranty was broken, and (3) that the breach of warranty was the proximate cause of the injury sustained.

The serving of food or drink to be consumed on or off the premises is recognized as a sale of goods subject to the warranty of merchantability. [UCC 2-314(1)] "Merchantable" food means food that is fit to eat. Therefore, any object within the food that a buyer would ordinarily expect to accompany the food would not render the food nonmerchantable. Thus, a pearl swallowed by a buyer eating oysters would not subject the merchant seller to liability, but a nail would.

The following is a classic case of a court's interpretation of whether a fish bone in fish chowder is a foreign substance rendering the chowder unwholesome or not fit to be eaten.

BACKGROUND AND FACTS *Webster brought the following action against the Blue Ship Tea Room for personal injuries she sustained when consuming a bowl of their fish chowder. Her theory was breach of implied warranty of merchantability. A jury rendered a verdict for the plaintiff.*

WEBSTER v. BLUE SHIP TEA ROOM
Supreme Judicial Court of Massachusetts, 1964.
347 Mass. 421, 198 N.E.2d 309.

REARDON, Justice.

This is a case which by its nature evokes earnest study not only of the law but also of the culinary traditions of the Commonwealth [Massachusetts] which bear so heavily upon its outcome. It is an action to recover damages for personal injuries sustained by reason of a breach of implied warranty of food served by the defendant in its restaurant. * * *

* * * On Saturday, April 25, 1959, about 1 P.M., the plaintiff, accompanied by her sister and her aunt, entered the Blue Ship Tea Room operated by the defendant. The group was seated at a table and supplied with menus.

This restaurant, which the plaintiff characterized as "quaint," was located in Boston "on the third floor of an old building on T Wharf which overlooks the ocean."

The plaintiff, who had been born and brought up in New England (a fact of some consequence), ordered clam chowder and crabmeat salad. Within a few minutes she received tidings to the effect that "there was no more clam chowder," whereupon she ordered a cup of fish chowder. Presently, there was set before her "a small bowl of fish chowder." She had previously enjoyed a breakfast about 9

A.M. which had given her no difficulty. "The fish chowder contained haddock, potatoes, milk, water and seasoning. The chowder was milky in color and not clear. The haddock and potatoes were in chunks" (also a fact of consequence). "She agitated it a little with the spoon and observed that it was a fairly full bowl * * *. It was hot when she got it, but she did not tip it with her spoon because it was hot * * * but stirred it in an up and under motion. She denied that she did this because she was looking for something, but it was rather because she wanted an even distribution of fish and potatoes." "She started to eat it, alternating between the chowder and crackers which were on the table with * * * [some] rolls. She ate about 3 or 4 spoonfuls then stopped. She looked at the spoonfuls as she was eating. She saw equal parts of liquid, potato and fish as she spooned it into her mouth. She did not see anything unusual about it. After 3 or 4 spoonfuls she was aware that something had lodged in her throat because she couldn't swallow and couldn't clear her throat by gulping and she could feel it." This misadventure led to two esophagoscopies at the Massachusetts General Hospital, in the second of which, on April 27, 1959, a fish bone was found and removed. The sequence of events produced injury to the plaintiff which was not insubstantial.

We must decide whether a fish bone lurking in a fish chowder, about the ingredients of which there is no other complaint, constitutes a breach of implied warranty under applicable provisions of the Uniform Commercial Code,[1] the annotations to which are not helpful on this point. As the judge put it in his charge, "Was the fish chowder fit to be eaten and wholesome? * * * [N]obody is claiming that the fish itself wasn't wholesome. * * * But the bone of contention here—I don't mean that for a pun—but was this fish bone a foreign substance that made the fish chowder unwholesome or not fit to be eaten?"

The defendant asserts that here was a native New Englander eating fish chowder in a "quaint" Boston dining place where she had been before; that "[f]ish chowder, as it is served and enjoyed by New Englanders, is a hearty dish, originally designed to satisfy the appetites of our seamen and fishermen"; that "[t]his court knows well that we are not talking of some insipid broth as is customarily served to convalescents." We are asked to rule in such fashion that no chef is forced "to reduce the pieces of fish in the chowder to miniscule size in an effort to ascertain if they contained any pieces of bone." "In so ruling," we are told (in the defendant's brief), "the court will not only uphold its reputation for legal knowledge and acumen, but will, as loyal sons of Massachusetts, save our world-renowned fish chowder from degenerating into an insipid broth containing the mere essence of its former stature as a culinary masterpiece." Notwithstanding these passionate entreaties we are bound to examine with detachment the nature of fish chowder and what might happen to it under varying interpretations of the Uniform Commercial Code.

* * * It is not too much to say that a person sitting down in New England to consume a good New England fish chowder embarks on a gustatory adventure

---

1. "(1) Unless excluded or modified by section 2-316, a warranty that the goods shall be merchantable is implied in a contract for their sale if the seller is a merchant with respect to goods of that kind. Under this section the serving for value of food or drink to be consumed either on the premises or elsewhere is a sale. (2) Goods to be merchantable must at least be such as * * * (c) are fit for the ordinary purposes for which such goods are used * * *." G.L. c. 106, § 2-314.

which may entail the removal of some fish bones from his bowl as he proceeds. We are not inclined to tamper with age old recipes by any amendment reflecting the plaintiff's view of the effect of the Uniform Commercial Code upon them. We are aware of the heavy body of case law involving foreign substances in food, but we sense a strong distinction between them and those relative to unwholesomeness of the food itself, e.g., tainted mackerel (Smith v. Gerrish, 256 Mass. 183, 152 N.E. 318), and a fish bone in a fish chowder. Certain Massachusetts cooks might cavil at the ingredients contained in the chowder in this case in that it lacked the heartening lift of salt pork. In any event, we consider that the joys of life in New England include the ready availability of fresh fish chowder. We should be prepared to cope with the hazards of fish bones, the occasional presence of which in chowders is, it seems to us, to be anticipated, and which, in the light of a hallowed tradition, do not impair their fitness or merchantability. While we are bouyed up in this conclusion by Shapiro v. Hotel Statler Corp., 132 F.Supp. 891 (S.D.Cal.), in which the bone which afflicted the plaintiff appeared in "Hot Barquette of Seafood Mornay," we know that the United States District Court of Southern California, situated as are we upon a coast, might be expected to share our views. We are most impressed, however, by Allen v. Grafton, 170 Ohio St. 249, 164 N.E.2d 167, where in Ohio, the Midwest, in a case where the plaintiff was injured by a piece of oyster shell in an order of fried oysters. Mr. Justice Taft (now Chief Justice) in a majority opinion held that "the possible presence of a piece of oyster shell in or attached to an oyster is so well known to anyone who eats oysters that we can say as a matter of law that one who eats oysters can reasonably anticipate and guard against eating such a piece of shell *   *   *."

The court "sympathized with a plaintiff who has suffered a peculiarly New England injury," but entered a judgment for the defendant.   **JUDGMENT AND REMEDY**

Implied Warranty of Fitness for a Particular Purpose   The implied warranty of fitness for a particular purpose arises when *any seller* (merchant or nonmerchant) knows the particular purpose for which a buyer will use the goods *and* knows that the buyer is relying upon the seller's skill and judgment to select suitable goods. [UCC 2-315]

A "particular purpose of the buyer" differs from the "ordinary purpose for which goods are used" (merchantability). Goods can be merchantable but still not fit for the buyer's particular purpose. For example, house paints suitable for ordinary walls are not suitable for painting over stucco walls.

A contract can include both a warranty of merchantability *and* a warranty of fitness for a particular purpose, which relates to the specific use or special situation in which a buyer intends to use the goods. For example, a seller recommends a particular pair of shoes, *knowing* that a customer is looking for mountain climbing shoes. The buyer purchases the shoes *relying* on the seller's judgment. If the shoes are found to be not only improperly made but suitable only for walking, not for mountain climbing, the seller has breached both the warranty of fitness for a particular purpose, and the warranty of merchantability.

A seller does not need "actual knowledge" of the buyer's particular purpose. It is sufficient if a seller "has reason to know" the purpose. However, the buyer must have *relied* upon the seller's skill or judgment in selecting or furnishing suitable goods in order for an implied warranty to be created.

For example, Josephs buys a shortwave radio from Radio Shack, telling the salesperson that she wants a set strong enough to pick up Radio Luxemburg, which is 8,000 miles away. Radio Shack sells Josephs a Model XYZ set. The set works, but it will not pick up Radio Luxemburg. Josephs wants her money back. Here, since Radio Shack is guilty of a breach of implied warranty of fitness for the buyer's particular purpose, Josephs will be able to recover. The salesperson knew specifically that she wanted a set that would pick up Radio Luxemburg. Furthermore, Josephs relied upon the salesperson to furnish a radio that would fulfill this purpose. Radio Shack did not do so. Therefore, the warranty was breached.

In the next case, a seller helped a buyer solve a painting problem and became the defendant in a lawsuit for breach of an implied warranty of fitness.

CATANIA v. BROWN

Circuit Court of Connecticut, Appellate Division, 1967. 4 Conn.Cir. 344, 231 A.2d 668.

BACKGROUND AND FACTS *The defendant, Brown, was engaged in the retail paint business. Catania, the plaintiff, asked Brown to recommend a paint to cover the exterior stucco walls of his house. Brown recommended and sold to Catania a certain brand of paint called "Pierce's Shingle and Shake" paint. Brown also advised Catania how to prepare the walls before applying the paint and how to mix the paint in proper proportion to the thinner. Catania followed Brown's instructions, but the paint blistered and peeled soon after it was applied.*

JACOBS, Judge.

*   *   *   *

Under the statute governing implied warranty of fitness for a particular purpose (§ 42a-2-315), two requirements must be met: (a) the buyer relies on the seller's skill or judgment to select or furnish suitable goods; and (b) the seller at the time of contracting has reason to know the buyer's purpose and that the buyer is relying on the seller's skill or judgment. "It is a question of fact in the ordinary case whether these conditions have been met and the warranty arises."

*   *   * "The raising of an implied warranty of fitness depends upon whether the buyer informed the seller of the circumstances and conditions which necessitated his purchase of a certain character of article or material and left it to the seller to select the particular kind and quality of article suitable for the buyer's use. *   *   * So when the buyer orders goods to be supplied and trusts to the judgment or skill of the seller to select goods or material for which they are ordered, there is an implied warranty that they shall be reasonably fit for that purpose." "Reliance can, of course, be more readily found where the *retailer* selects the product or recommends it."

*   *   * [T]he buyer, being ignorant of the fitness of the article offered by the seller, justifiably relied on the superior information, skill and judgment of the seller and not on his own knowledge or judgment, and under such circumstances an implied warranty of fitness could properly be claimed by the purchaser.

JUDGMENT AND REMEDY *The plaintiff prevailed on the theory of implied warranty of fitness for a particular purpose. The defendant had created and breached a warranty* *of fitness by recommending the particular paint as suitable for stucco walls.*

Overlapping Warranties

Sometimes two or more warranties are made in a single transaction. An implied warranty of merchantability or of fitness for a particular purpose, or both, can exist in addition to an express warranty. For example, where a sales contract for a new car states that "this car engine is warranted to be free from defects for 12,000 miles or 12 months, whichever occurs first," there is an express warranty against all defects and an implied warranty that the car will be fit for normal use.

The rule of Section 2-317 is that express and implied warranties are construed as *cumulative* if they are consistent with one another. If the warranties are *inconsistent*, the courts will usually hold that:

1. *Express* warranties will displace inconsistent *implied* warranties other than implied warranties of fitness for a particular purpose.
2. Samples will take precedence over inconsistent general descriptions.
3. Technical specifications will displace inconsistent samples or general descriptions.

Suppose that when Josephs buys a shortwave radio at Radio Shack, the contract expressly warrants radio receivership to a maximum range of 4,000 miles. She tries to pick up Radio Luxemburg—the stated purpose of her purchase—which is 8,000 miles away. The set cannot perform that well. Josephs claims that Radio Shack is guilty of breach of warranty of fitness. The express warranty, however, takes precedence over any implied warranty of merchantability that a shortwave set should pick up any station anywhere in the world. Josephs does have a good claim for the breach of implied warranty of fitness for a specific purpose because she had made it clear that she was buying the set to pick up Radio Luxemburg. In cases of inconsistency between an express warranty and a warranty of fitness for a buyer's particular purpose, the warranty of fitness for the buyer's particular purpose normally prevails. [UCC 2-317(c)]

Warranty Disclaimers

Since each warranty is created in a special way, the manner in which each one can be disclaimed or qualified by the seller varies.

Express Warranties Any affirmation of fact or promise, description of the goods, or use of samples or models by a seller will create an express warranty. Obviously, then, express warranties can be excluded if the seller has carefully refrained from making any promise or affirmation of fact relating to the goods, or describing the goods, or selling by means of a sample model. [UCC 2-313]

The Code does permit express warranties to be negated or limited by specific and unambiguous language, provided this is done in a manner that protects the buyer from surprise. Therefore, a written disclaimer in language that is clear and conspicuous, called to a buyer's attention, could negate all oral express warranties not included in the written sales contract. This permits the seller to avoid false allegations that oral warranties were made, and it ensures that only representations by properly authorized individuals are included as part of the bargain. [UCC 2-316(1)]

Implied Warranties Generally speaking, and unless circumstances indicate otherwise, implied warranties (merchantability and fitness) are disclaimed by the expressions "as is," "with all faults," or other similar expressions that in common understanding for *both* parties call the buyer's attention to the fact that there are no implied warranties. [UCC 2-316(3)(a)]

The Code also permits a seller to specifically disclaim the implied warranty either of fitness or of merchantability. [UCC 2-316(2)] To disclaim the implied warranty of fitness, the dis-claimer *must* be in writing and conspicuous. The word "fitness" does not have to be mentioned in the writing; it is sufficient if, for example, the disclaimer states, "There are no warranties that extend beyond the description on the face hereof."

A *merchantability disclaimer* must be more specific; it must mention *merchantability*. It need not be written; but if it is, the writing must be conspicuous. According to UCC 1-201(10):

> A term or clause is conspicuous when it is so written that a reasonable person against whom it is to operate ought to have noticed it. A printed heading in capitals is conspicuous. Language in the body of a form is conspicuous if it is in large or other contrasting type or color.

To illustrate: Merchant Smith sells Beyer a particular lawn mower selected by Smith with the characteristics clearly requested by Beyer. At the time of the sale, Smith orally tells Beyer that he does not warrant the merchantability of the mower, as it is last year's model. The mower proves to be defective and will not work. Beyer wishes to hold Smith for breach of implied war-ranty of merchantability and of fitness for a par-ticular purpose.

Beyer can hold Smith for breach of the war-ranty of fitness but not of the warranty of mer-chantability. Smith's oral disclaimer mentioning the word *merchantability* is a proper disclaimer. For Smith to have disclaimed the implied war-ranty of fitness, a conspicuous writing would have been required. Since no written disclaimer was made, Smith can still be held liable.

Buyer's Refusal to Inspect   If a buyer actually examines the goods (or a sample or model) as fully as desired before entering a contract, or if the buyer refuses to examine the goods, *there is no implied warranty with respect to defects that a reasonable examination will reveal.*

Suppose, in the illustration concerning Kap-lan's purchase of the axe from Enrique's Hard-ware Store, the defect in Kaplan's axe could eas-ily have been spotted by normal inspection. Kaplan, even after Enrique asκs, refuses to in-spect the axe before buying it. After being hurt

by the defective axe, she will not be able to hold Enrique for breach of warranty of merchantabil-ity because she could have spotted the defect during an inspection. [UCC 2-316(3)(b)]

Failing to examine the goods is not a refusal to examine them; it is not enough that the goods were available for inspection and the buyer failed to examine them. A "refusal" occurs only when the seller *demands* that the buyer examine the goods. Of course, the seller always remains lia-ble for all latent (hidden) defects that ordinary inspection would not reveal. What the exami-nation ought to reveal depends on a particular buyer's skill and method of examination. There-fore, an auto mechanic purchasing a car should be responsible for the discovery of some defects that a nonexpert would not be expected to find. The circumstances of each case determine what defects a so-called reasonable inspection should reveal.

Usage of Trade   The Code recognizes in Section 2-314(3) that implied warranties can arise (or be excluded or modified) from course of dealing, course of performance, or usage of trade. [UCC 2-316(3)(c)] In the absence of evidence to the contrary, when both parties to a sales contract have knowledge of a well-recognized trade cus-tom, the courts will infer that they both intended that custom to apply to their contract. For ex-ample, in the sale of a new car, where the in-dustry-wide custom includes lubricating the car before delivery, a seller who fails to do so can be held liable to a buyer for resulting damages for breach of implied warranty. This, of course, would also be negligence on the part of the dealer.

Unconscionability and Warranty Disclaimers

The Code sections dealing with warranty dis-claimers do not refer specifically to unconscion-ability as a factor. Eventually, however, the courts will test warranty disclaimers with reference to the unconscionability standards of Section 2-302. Such things as lack of bargaining position, "take it or leave it" choices, and failure of a buyer to understand or know of a warranty disclaimer provision will become relevant to the issue of unconscionability. Note in the following pre-UCC landmark decision the court's recognition of the consumer's "bargaining" position with respect to large auto manufacturers.

BACKGROUND AND FACTS   *This case involves the recovery of damages from an automobile manufacturer for injuries sustained by the owner and driver of a new car manufactured by Chrysler. The standard form purchase order used in the transaction contained an express warranty by which the manufacturer warranted the vehicle free from defects in material or workmanship. If any defects were found, the manufacturer promised to correct them without cost to the purchaser for a ninety-day period or four thousand miles, whichever occurred first. In addition, the purchase order contained a disclaimer in fine print, of any and all other express or implied warranties. The disclaimer purported to absolve Chrysler and the dealer from all liability for the implied warranty of merchantability against injuries suffered because of negligent manufacture. The standard form purchase order became part of the Chrysler contract when a consumer purchased an automobile. Hence, the express warranty that was offered instead of all other warranties, express or implied, was intended to provide the limits of Chrysler's liability.*

HENNINGSEN v. BLOOMFIELD MOTORS, INC.
Supreme Court of New Jersey, 1960.
32 N.J. 358, 161 A.2d 69.

FRANCIS, Justice.

*   *   *   *

Plaintiff Claus H. Henningsen purchased a Plymouth automobile, manufactured by defendant Chrysler Corporation, from defendant Bloomfield Motors, Inc. His wife, plaintiff Helen Henningsen, was injured while driving it and instituted suit against both defendants to recover damages on account of her injuries. *   *   * The complaint was predicated upon breach of express and implied warranties and upon negligence. *   *   *

The facts are not complicated, but a general outline of them is necessary to an understanding of the case.

On May 7, 1955 Mr. and Mrs. Henningsen visited the place of business of Bloomfield Motors, Inc., an authorized De Soto and Plymouth dealer, to look at a Plymouth. They wanted to buy a car and were considering a Ford or a Chevrolet as well as a Plymouth. They were shown a Plymouth which appealed to them and the purchase followed. The record indicates that Mr. Henningsen intended the car as a Mother's Day gift to his wife. He said the intention was communicated to the dealer. When the purchase order or contract was prepared and presented, the husband executed it alone. His wife did not join as a party.

The purchase order was a printed form of one page. On the front it contained blanks to be filled in with a description of the automobile to be sold, the various accessories to be included, and the details of the financing. The particular car selected was described as a 1955 Plymouth, Plaza "6", Club Sedan. The type used in the printed parts of the form became smaller in size, different in style, and less readable toward the bottom where the line for the purchaser's signature was placed. The smallest type on the page appears in the two paragraphs, one of two and one-quarter lines and the second of one and one-half lines, on which great stress is laid by the defense in the case. These two paragraphs are the least legible and the most difficult to read in the instrument, but they are most important in the evaluation of the rights of the contesting parties. They do not attract attention and there is nothing about the format which would draw the reader's eye to them. In fact, a studied and concentrated effort would have to be made to read them. De-emphasis seems the motive rather than emphasis. More particularly, most of the printing in the body of the order appears to be 12 point block type, and easy to read. In the short paragraphs under discussion, however, the type appears to be six point script and the print is solid, that is, the lines are very close together.

The two paragraphs are:

"The front and back of this Order comprise the entire agreement affecting this purchase and no other agreement or understanding of any nature concerning same has been made or entered into, or will be recognized. I hereby certify that no credit has been extended to me for the purchase of this motor vehicle except as appears in writing on the face of this agreement.

"I have read the matter printed on the back hereof and agree to it as a part of this order the same as if it were printed above my signature. I certify that I am 21 years of age, or older, and hereby acknowledge receipt of a copy of this order."

*   *   *   *

The testimony of Claus Henningsen justifies the conclusion that he did not read the two fine print paragraphs referring to the back of the purchase contract. And it is uncontradicted that no one made any reference to them, or called them to his attention. With respect to the matter appearing on the back, it is likewise uncontradicted that he did not read it and that no one called it to his attention.

The reverse side of the contract contains 8½ inches of fine print. It is not as small, however, as the two critical paragraphs described above. The page is headed "Conditions" and contains ten separate paragraphs consisting of 65 lines in all. *   *   * In the seventh paragraph, about two-thirds of the way down the page, the warranty, which is the focal point of the case, is set forth. It is as follows:

"7. It is expressly agreed that there are no warranties, express or implied, *made* by either the dealer or the manufacturer on the motor vehicle, chassis, or parts furnished hereunder except as follows.

" 'The manufacturer warrants each new motor vehicle (including original equipment placed thereon by the manufacturer except tires), chassis or parts manufactured by it to be free from defects in material or workmanship under normal use and service. Its obligation under this warranty being limited to making good at its factory any part or parts thereof which shall, within ninety (90) days after delivery of such vehicle *to the original purchaser* or before such vehicle has been driven 4,000 miles, whichever event shall first occur, be returned to it with transportation charges prepaid and which its examination shall disclose to its satisfaction to have been thus defective; *this warranty being expressly in lieu of all other warranties expressed or implied, and all other obligations or liabilities on its part,* and it neither assumes nor authorizes any other person to assume for it any other liability in connection with the sale of its vehicles. *   *   *.' " [Emphasis ours.]

After the contract had been executed, plaintiffs were told the car had to be serviced and that it would be ready in two days. *   *   *

*   *   *   *

The new Plymouth was turned over to the Henningsens on May 9, 1955. No proof was adduced by the dealer to show precisely what was done in the way of mechanical or road testing beyond testimony that the manufacturer's instructions were probably followed. Mr. Henningsen drove it from the dealer's place of business in Bloomfield to their home in Keansburg. On the trip nothing unusual appeared in the way in which it operated. Thereafter, it was used for short trips on paved streets about the town. It had no servicing and no mishaps of any kind before the event of May 19. That day, Mrs. Henningsen drove to Asbury Park. On the way down and in returning the car performed in normal fashion until the accident occurred. She was preceeding north on Route 36 in Highlands, New Jersey, at 20–22 miles per hour. The highway was paved and smooth, and contained two lanes for north-bound travel. She was riding in the right-hand lane. Suddenly she heard a loud noise "from the bottom, by the hood." It "felt as if something cracked." The steering wheel spun in her hands; the car veered sharply to the right and crashed into a highway sign and a brick wall. No other vehicle was in any way involved. A bus operator driving in the left-hand lane testified that he observed plaintiffs' car approaching in normal fashion in the opposite direction; "all of a sudden [it] veered at 90 degrees *   *   * and right into this wall." As a result of the impact, the front of the car was so badly damaged that it was impossible to determine if any of the parts of the steering wheel mechanism or workmanship or assembly were defective or improper prior to the accident. The condition was such that the collision insurance carrier, after inspection, declared the vehicle a total loss. It had 468 miles on the speedometer at the time.

I.

The Claim of Implied Warranty against the Manufacturer.

In the ordinary case of sale of goods by description an implied warranty of merchantability is an integral part of the transaction. If the buyer, expressly or by implication, makes known to the seller the particular purpose for which the article is required and it appears that he has relied on the seller's skill or judgment, an implied warranty arises of reasonable fitness for that purpose. The former type of warranty simply means that the thing sold is reasonably fit for the general purpose for which it is manufactured and sold. *   *   *

*   *   *   *

Of course such sales, whether oral or written, may be accompanied by an express warranty. *   *   * [A]ny affirmation of fact relating to the goods is an express warranty if the natural tendency of the statement is to induce the buyer to make the purchase.

*   *   *   *

*   *   * [A] question of first importance to be decided is whether an implied warranty of merchantability by Chrysler Corporation accompanied the sale of the automobile to Claus Henningsen.

*   *   *   *

Chrysler points out that an implied warranty of merchantability is an incident of a contract of sale. It concedes, of course, the making of the original sale to Bloomfield Motors, Inc., but maintains that this transaction marked the terminal point of its contractual connection with the car. Then Chrysler urges that since it was not a party to the sale by the dealer to Henningsen, there is no privity of contract between it and the plaintiffs, and the absence of this privity eliminates any such implied warranty.

*   *   *   *

Under modern conditions the ordinary layman, on responding to the importuning of colorful advertising, has neither the opportunity nor the capacity to inspect or to determine the fitness of an automobile for use; he must rely on the manufacturer who has control of its construction, and to some degree on the dealer who, to the limited extent called for by the manufacturer's instructions, inspects and services it before delivery. In such a marketing milieu his remedies and those of persons who properly claim through him should not depend "upon the intricacies of the law of sales. The obligation of the manufacturer should not be based alone on privity of contract." *   *   *

Accordingly, we hold that under modern marketing conditions, when a manufacturer puts a new automobile in the stream of trade and promotes its purchase by the public, an implied warranty that it is reasonably suitable for use as such accompanies it into the hands of the ultimate purchaser. [Emphasis added.] Absence of agency between the manufacturer and the dealer who makes the ultimate sale is immaterial.

II.

The Effect of the Disclaimer and Limitation of Liability Clauses on the Implied Warranty of Merchantability.

*   *   * In a society such as ours, where the automobile is a common and necessary adjunct of daily life, and where its use is so fraught with danger to the driver, passengers and the public, the manufacturer is under a special obligation in connection with the construction, promotion and sale of his cars. Consequently, the courts must examine purchase agreements closely to see if consumer and public interests are treated fairly.

What influence should these circumstances have on the restrictive effect of Chrysler's express warranty in the framework of the purchase contract? As we have said, *warranties originated in the law to safeguard the buyer and not to limit the liability of the seller or manufacturer.*[Emphasis added.] *   *   * But does the doctrine that a person is bound by his signed agreement, in the absence of fraud, stand in the way of any relief?
*   *   *   *

The traditional contract is the result of free bargaining of parties who are brought together by the play of the market, and who meet each other on a footing of approximate economic equality. *   *   * But in present-day commercial life the standardized mass contract has appeared. It is used primarily by enterprises with strong bargaining power and position. *   *   *
*   *   *   *

The warranty before us is a standardized form designed for mass use. It is imposed upon the automobile consumer. He takes it or leaves it, and he must take it to buy an automobile. No bargaining is engaged in with respect to it. In fact, the dealer through whom it comes to the buyer is without authority to alter it; his function is ministerial—simply to deliver it. The form warranty is not only standard with Chrysler but, as mentioned above, it is the uniform warranty of the Automobile Manufacturers Association. *   *   *

The gross inequality of bargaining position occupied by the consumer in the automobile industry is thus apparent. *   *   *
*   *   *   *

*   *   * Having in mind the situation in the automobile industry as detailed above, and particularly the fact that the limited warranty extended by the man-

ufacturers is a uniform one, there would appear to be no just reason why the principles of all of the cases set forth should not chart the course to be taken here.

*   *   *   *

*   *   * Courts keep in mind the principle that the best interests of society demand that persons should not be unnecessarily restricted in their freedom to contract. But they do not hesitate to declare void as against public policy contractual provisions which clearly tend to the injury of the public in some way.

*   *   * *[W]e are of the opinion that Chrysler's attempted disclaimer of an implied warranty of merchantability and of the obligations arising therefrom is so inimical to the public good as to compel an adjudication of its invalidity.* [Emphasis added.]

*   *   *   *

III.
The Dealer's Implied Warranty.

The principles that have been expounded as to the obligation of the manufacturer apply with equal force to the separate express warranty of the dealer. This is so, irrespective of the absence of the relationship of principal and agent between these defendants, because the manufacturer and the Association establish the warranty policy for the industry. The bargaining position of the dealer is inextricably bound by practice to that of the maker and the purchaser must take or leave the automobile, accompanied and encumbered as it is by the uniform warranty.

*   *   *   *

For the reasons set forth in Part I hereof, *we conclude that the disclaimer of an implied warranty of merchantability by the dealer, as well as the attempted elimination of all obligations other than replacement of defective parts, are violative of public policy and void.* [Emphasis added.]

The court upheld the right of the plaintiffs, the Henningsens, to recover damages for injuries notwithstanding the attempted warranty disclaimer on the part of the defendants, Chrysler Corporation and Bloomfield Motors, Inc.

**JUDGMENT
AND REMEDY**

MAGNUSON-MOSS
WARRANTY ACT

The Magnuson-Moss Warranty Act was designed to prevent deception in warranties by making them easier to understand.[3] The Magnuson-Moss Warranty Act is mainly enforced by the Federal Trade Commission (FTC). Additionally, the attorney general or a consumer who has been injured can enforce the Act if informal procedures for settling disputes prove to be

ineffective. The Magnuson-Moss Warranty Act modifies UCC warranty rules to some extent where *consumer* sales transactions are involved. However, the UCC remains the primary codification of warranty rules for industrial and commercial transactions.

No seller is *required* to give a written warranty for consumer goods sold under the Warranty Act. But if a seller chooses to make an express written warranty, and the cost of the consumer goods is more than $10, the warranty must be labeled as "full" or "limited." In addition, if the cost of the goods is more than $15 (FTC regulation), the warrantor is required to

---

3.   15 U.S.C.A. Sections 2301-12.

make certain disclosures fully and conspicuously in a single document in "readily understood language." This disclosure states the names and addresses of the warrantor(s), what specifically is warranted, procedures for enforcement of the warranty, any limitations on warranty relief, and that the buyer has legal rights.

Although a *full warranty* may not cover every aspect of the consumer product sold, what it covers ensures some type of buyer satisfaction in case the product is defective. Full warranty requires free repair or replacement of any defective part; if it cannot be repaired within a reasonable time, the consumer has the choice of either a refund or a replacement without charge. The full warranty does not have a time limit on it. Any limitation on consequential damages must be *conspicuously* stated. Also, the warrantor need not perform warranty services if the problem with the product was caused by damage to the product or unreasonable use by the consumer.

A *limited warranty* arises when the written warranty fails to meet one of the minimum requirements for a full warranty. The fact that a seller is giving only a limited warranty must be conspicuously designated. If it is only a time limitation that distinguishes a limited warranty from a full warranty, then the Warranty Act allows the seller to indicate it by such language as "full 12-month warranty."

Creating an express warranty under the Warranty Act differs from creating one under the UCC.[4]

1. An express warranty is *any written promise* or *affirmation of fact* made by the seller to a consumer indicating the quality or performance of the product and affirming or promising that the product is either free of defects or will meet a specific level of performance over a period of time. For example, "this watch will not lose more than one second a year."

2. An express warranty is a written agreement to refund, repair, or replace the product if it fails to meet written specifications. This is typically a service contract.

Implied warranties do not arise under the Magnuson-Moss Warranty Act. They continue to be created according to the UCC provisions. Where an express warranty is made in a sales contract or a combined sales and service contract (where the service contract is undertaken within ninety days of the sale), the Magnuson-Moss Warranty Act prevents sellers from disclaiming or modifying the implied warranties of merchantability and fitness for a particular purpose. However, sellers can impose a time limit on the duration of an implied warranty, but such time limit has to correspond to the duration of the express warranty.[5]

QUESTIONS AND CASE PROBLEMS

1.   Beyer contracts to purchase a used car from Johnson's Quality Used Cars. During the oral negotiations for the sale, Johnson told Beyer that this used car was in "A-1 condition" and would get sixteen miles to the gallon. Beyer asked if the car used oil. Johnson replied that he had personally checked the car, and in his opinion the car did not use oil. After delivery, Beyer has used the car for one month (400 miles of driving) and is unhappy with it. The car needs numerous repairs, does not get sixteen miles to the gallon, and has used two quarts of oil. Beyer claims Johnson is in breach of express warranties as to the condition of the car, gas mileage, and oil use. Johnson claims no express warranties were made. Discuss who is correct.

2.   Beyer is a farmer who needs to place a 2,000 pound piece of equipment in his barn. This will require lifting the equipment 30 feet up into a hayloft. Beyer goes to Davidson Hardware and tells Davidson that he needs some heavy-duty rope to be used on his farm. Davidson recommends a one-inch thick nylon rope, and Beyer purchases 200 feet of the rope. Beyer ties the rope around the piece of equipment, puts it through a pulley, and, with a tractor, he lifts the equip-

---

4.   For example, express warranties created by description or sample or model will continue to be governed under UCC provisions because only written promises or affirmations of fact are covered by the Magnuson-Moss Warranty Act.

5.   The time limit on an implied warranty occurring by virtue of the seller's express warranty must, of course, be reasonable, conscionable, and set forth in clear and conspicuous language on the face of the warranty.

ment off the ground. Suddenly the rope breaks. In the crash to the ground the equipment is severely damaged. Beyer files suit against Davidson for breach of implied warranty of fitness. Discuss how successful Beyer will be with his suit.

3. Beyer purchases a new car from Smith Motors. The retail installment contract states immediately above the buyer's signature in large, bold type, "There are no warranties that extend beyond the description on the face hereof" and "There are no express warranties that accompany this sale unless expressly written in this contract." In purchasing the car, Beyer specifically informed Smith's salesperson that he wanted a car that could be driven in a dusty area without needing mechanical repairs. Smith's salesperson said to Beyer, "Nothing will go wrong with this car, but if it does, return it to us, and we will repair it without cost to you." Neither this statement nor any similar to it appears in the retail sales contract. Beyer drives the car into a dust storm. The air filter gets plugged up and the car engine overheats, causing motor damage. Smith refuses to repair the engine under any warranty. Beyer claims Smith is liable for breach of the implied warranty of fitness, that such cannot be disclaimed because of the Magnuson-Moss Warranty Act, and that there is a breach of the salesperson's express warranty. Discuss Beyer's claims.

4. Sallor has a used television set that she wishes to sell. Beyer contracts to purchase the set. At the time of the making of the contract, Sallor demands that Beyer inspect the set to be sure it is exactly what he wants. Beyer tells Sallor that he does not have the time to do so. The set is delivered and paid for. Beyer, upon using the set, discovers that the picture has a tendency to "jump" and that the vertical control does not always correct that tendency. The cost to repair the set is $50. Beyer claims that the set is neither merchantable nor fit for its purpose. Sallor claims no liability. Discuss who is correct.

5. John buys a one-carat diamond ring from Shady Sallor for $500. John is assured by Shady that the ring belonged to his deceased mother and that the only reason the price is so low is that he is behind in making payments on his car. John has no reason to believe differently. Beyer, a neighbor, admires the ring and offers to purchase it for $1,000. John agrees to sell the ring to Beyer, stating that he is transferring only such right and title as he has. Two months later, the police confiscate the ring as property stolen in a burglary of Owen's home. Beyer seeks to hold John liable. Discuss Beyer's action under warranty laws.

6. Myrtle Carpenter purchased hair dye from a drugstore. The use of the dye caused an adverse skin reaction. She sued the local drugstore and the manu-

facturer of the dye, Alberto Culver Company. She claimed that a sales clerk indicated that several of Myrtle's friends had used the product and that their hair came out "very nice." The clerk purportedly also told Myrtle that she would get very fine results. On the package, there were cautionary instructions telling the user to make a preliminary skin test to determine if the user was susceptible in any unusual way to the product. Myrtle stated that she did not make the preliminary skin test. Did the seller make an express warranty about the hair dye? [Carpenter v. Alberto Culver Co., 28 Mich.App. 399, 184 N.W.2d 547 (1970)]

7. McCarty purchased four tires from a Korvette store. The sales invoice clearly stated that the tires were guaranteed for 36,000 miles against all road hazards, including blowouts, when the tires were used in normal, noncommercial passenger car service. One of the rear tires on McCarty's car blew out. The car swerved and turned over. McCarty and his wife were injured, and the car was severely damaged. McCarty claimed that the clause in the sales invoice was an express warranty against blowouts. Was it? [McCarty v. E. J. Korvette, Inc., 28 Md.App. 421, 347 A.2d 253 (1975)]

8. In July 1959, McMeekin purchased a lawn mower from Gimbel Brothers. In June of the next year, while McMeekin was mowing his lawn, his son was struck in the eye by an unknown object and subsequently lost sight in the eye. In a suit filed by McMeekin on behalf of his son against Gimbels, McMeekin sought recovery on the theory that Gimbels had breached its warranty of merchantability. McMeekin claimed that "somehow, part of the lawn mower broke off and flew into my son's eye." Can McMeekin recover? [McMeekin v. Gimbel Brothers, Inc., 223 F.Supp. 896 (W.D.Pa.1963)]

9. Lewis purchased a used hydraulic system for his sawmill in Ark Cove, Arkansas. He requested from his local Mobil Oil dealer the proper hydraulic fluid to operate the machinery. The Mobil dealer said he did not know what the proper lubricant for Lewis's machinery was but would find out. The only information given to the dealer by Lewis was that the machinery was operated by a gear-type pump; the Mobil dealer did not request any further information. He apparently contacted a Mobil representative for a recommendation and then sold Lewis a particular product that was straight mineral oil with no chemical additives. Within a few days after operating the equipment, Lewis began experiencing difficulty with its operation. The oil changed color, foamed over, and got hot. The oil was changed a number of times with no improvement. Six months later the system broke down, and a complete new system was installed. Lewis asked the Mobil dealer if he was sure he was supplying the right kind of oil.

The Mobil dealer said he was. During a two-year period, Lewis continued to have trouble with the system and required six new pumps. A new type of pump was installed, and the Mobil dealer recommended the same oil. The new pump broke down three weeks later. Finally, the brand of pump was changed. A Mobil representative came to see the new pump and recommended a new oil. When the new oil was used, Lewis had no problems with his pumping system. Lewis sued for breach of implied warranty of fitness for a particular purpose. Did he prevail? [Lewis v. Mobil Oil Corp., 438 F.2d 500 (8th Cir. 1971)]

10. A disclaimer of the implied warranty of fitness must be in writing and must be conspicuous. If the implied warranty of merchantability is to be excluded by means of a writing, it must also be conspicuous. The following paragraph appeared in a sales contract. The page contained other type of larger and smaller sizes and boldface print, but no other words on the page were printed in italics.

The equipment covered hereby is sold subject only to the applicable manufacturer's standard printed warranty, if any, in effect at the date hereof, receipt of a copy of which is hereby acknowledged, and no other warranties, express or implied, including without limitation, the implied warranties of *merchantability and fitness for a particular purpose shall apply.*

Is this an effective disclaimer of the implied warranties according to UCC 2-316? [Dorman v. International Harvester Co., 46 Cal.App.3d 11, 120 Cal.Rptr. 516 (1975)]

11. Robinson purchased a truck from Branch Moving and Storage Company "as it was" without inspecting the truck. Branch diligently and repeatedly advised Robinson of the risk he was taking by purchasing the unit without inspection. When the truck required a number of repairs because of defects in it, Robinson sued Branch for breach of warranty. At trial, Robinson won. Branch appealed. What was the result? [Robinson v. Branch Moving and Storage Co., 28 N.C.App. 244, 221 S.E.2d 81 (1976)]

CHAPTER 21

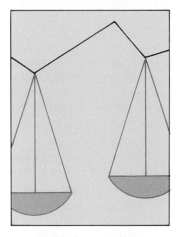

SALES
Products Liability

Often retailers serve simply as go-betweens, selling the manufacturer's goods to consumers in prepackaged, sealed containers. Even so, retailers may be liable to purchasers on express or implied warranties despite the fact that they cannot always examine the goods prior to resale. In the past, courts frequently addressed the question of whether the injured party should recover from the manufacturer, the processor, or the retailer, for damages caused by a defective product. Today, liability has been extended to manufacturers and processors through the application of new and old principles of the law.

Manufacturers and sellers of goods can be held liable to consumers, users, and bystanders for physical harm or property damage that is caused by the goods. This is called *products liability* and it encompasses tort theories such as *strict liability* and *negligence* as well as the contract theory of *warranty*.

WARRANTY THEORY

As we learned in Chapter 20, consumers and other purchasers of goods can recover *from any seller* for losses resulting from breach of implied and express warranties. Thus, since a manufacturer is a *seller*, a person who purchases goods from a retailer can recover either from the retailer or the manufacturer if the goods are not merchantable. This was not always the case. Until enactment of the UCC, *privity of contract* was normally required for a purchaser to bring an action for breach of warranty against a manufacturer.

Privity of Contract

One of the general principles of contract law is that unless you are one of the parties to a contract, you have no rights under the contract. (Notable exceptions are assignments and third party beneficiary contracts. See Chapter 13.) In short, common law established that **privity** must exist between a plaintiff and a defendant with respect to the matter under dispute in order to maintain any action based upon a contract.

For example, I purchase a ham from retailer Ralph. I invite you to my house that evening. I prepare the ham properly. You are served first, since you are my guest, and you become severely ill because the ham is tainted. Can you sue retailer Ralph for breach of the implied warranty of merchantability? Since warranty is based on a contract for sale of goods, under the common law you would normally have warranty rights only if you were a party to the purchase of the ham. Therefore, the warranty would extend only to me, the purchaser.

In the past this hardship was sometimes resolved by court decisions removing privity as a requirement to hold manufacturers and sellers liable for certain defective products (notably food, drugs, and cosmetics) sold. The UCC, reflecting some of these decisions, has addressed the problem of privity, at least to the extent of giving the state the option to determine with whom privity is no longer required.

Third Party Beneficiaries of Warranties: Express or Implied

There is sharp disagreement over how far warranty liability should extend. In order to satisfy opposing views of the various states, the drafters of the UCC proposed three alternatives for liability under UCC 2-318. Accordingly, some states have adopted alternative A; others, alternative B; and still others, alternative C. All three alternatives are intended to eliminate the privity requirement with respect to certain enumerated types of injuries (personal versus property) for certain beneficiaries (for example, household members, bystanders).

Alternative A   All sellers' warranties (express or implied) extend to any *natural person* in the buyer's family or household or to anyone who is a guest in the home, when it is reasonable to expect that such persons will use, consume, or be affected by the goods or be personally injured

because of a breach of the warranty. Consider this example: Anderson buys an electric washing machine from E-Z Appliances. One month after the purchase, Anderson's mother-in-law, who has been living with his family for a year, receives a severe electric shock from a defective wire while using the machine. Anderson's mother-in-law claims damages from E-Z Appliances for breach of warranty of merchantability. She can recover because the defective wire made the washing machine unfit for normal use. Since she was living with Anderson's family, she naturally would use the washing machine if she helped with housekeeping chores. Anderson's mother-in-law therefore qualifies as a third party beneficiary of the warranty.

Alternative B   Alternative B extends the seller's warranty (express or implied) to any *natural person* who can reasonably be expected to use, consume, or be affected by the goods and who suffers personal injury because of the breach of warranty. This is a broader basis for liability than alternative A since protection is not limited to family or household members.

Note the restrictions here. As with alternative A, the seller's warranty extends only to persons, not corporations. It also limits the right of recovery to personal injury damages and therefore eliminates the possibility of suing for property damages. A seller may not exclude or limit the warranties given under alternatives A or B.

Alternative C   Alternative C offers the broadest coverage of all. It extends to any person who is injured. (It also extends the rule to damages beyond injuries to the person.) It does not allow the seller to exclude or limit the operation of liability for personal injury of an individual to whom the warranty extends.

LIABILITY BASED ON NEGLIGENCE

Chapter 3 defined *negligence* as failure to use that degree of care that a reasonable, prudent person would have used under the circumstances. The failure to exercise reasonable care under the circumstances that cause an injury is the basis of liability for negligence. Thus, the manufacturer of a product must exercise "due care" to make that product safe to be used as it was intended. Due care must be exercised in designing the product, in selecting the materials, in using the appropriate production process, in assembling and testing the product, and in placing adequate warnings on the label of dangers of which an ordinary person might not be aware. The duty of care extends to the inspection and testing of purchased products used in the final product sold by the manufacturer.

The opposite of due care is negligence. In the following case, the New York court dealt with the liability of a manufacturer who failed to use due care in manufacturing a finished product.

BACKGROUND AND FACTS　*The MacPherson case is the classic negligence case in which privity of contract was not required between plaintiff and defendant to establish liability. This is a forerunner to products liability, although it does not use products liability theory. Its subject matter, defectively manufactured wooden wheels for automobiles, is dated, but the principles involved are not.*

The defendant, Buick Motor Company, was sued by Donald C. MacPherson, the plaintiff, who suffered injuries while riding in a Buick automobile that suddenly collapsed because one of the wheels was made of defective wood. The spokes crumbled into fragments, throwing MacPherson out of the vehicle and injuring him.

The wheel itself had not been made by Buick Motor Company; it had been bought from another manufacturer. There was evidence, however, that the defects could have been discovered by reasonable inspection and that inspection had not taken place. Although there was no charge that Buick knew of the defect and willfully concealed it, MacPherson charged Buick with negligence for putting a human life in imminent danger.

Keep in mind that MacPherson sued the manufacturer directly, despite the fact that the automobile was purchased from a retail Buick dealer.

MacPHERSON v. BUICK MOTOR CO.

Court of Appeals of New York, 1916.

111 N.E. 1050, 217 N.Y. 382.

CARDOZO, Justice.

*　*　*　*

The question to be determined is whether the defendant owed a duty of care and vigilance to any one but the immediate purchaser.

The foundations of this branch of the law, at least in this state, were laid in Thomas v. Winchester, 6 N.Y. 397, 57 Am.Dec. 455. A poison was falsely labeled. The sale was made to a druggist, who in turn sold to a customer. The customer recovered damages from the seller who affixed the label. "The defendant's negligence," it was said, "put human life in imminent danger." A poison, falsely labeled, is likely to injure any one who gets it. *Because the danger is to be foreseen, there is a duty to avoid the injury.* [Emphasis added.] *　*　* Thomas v. Winchester became quickly a landmark of the law. In the application of its principle there may, at times, have been uncertainty or even error. There has never in this state been doubt or disavowal of the principle itself. *　*　*

These early cases suggest a narrow construction of the rule. Later cases, however, evince a more liberal spirit. First in importance is Devlin v. Smith, 89 N.Y. 470, 42 Am.Rep. 311. The defendant, a contractor, built a scaffold for a painter.

The painter's servants were injured. The contractor was held liable. He knew that the scaffold, if improperly constructed, was a most dangerous trap. He knew that it was to be used by the workmen. He was building it for that very purpose. Building it for their use, he owed them a duty, irrespective of his contract with their master, to build it with care.

From Devlin v. Smith we *   * turn to the latest case in this court in which Thomas v. Winchester was followed. That case is Statler v. Ray Mfg. Co., 195 N.Y. 478, 480, 88 N.E. 1063. The defendant manufactured a large coffee urn. It was installed in a restaurant. When heated, the urn exploded and injured the plaintiff. We held that the manufacturer was liable. We said that the urn "was of such a character inherently that, when applied to the purposes for which it was designed, it was liable to become a source of great danger to many people if not carefully and properly constructed."

It may be that Devlin v. Smith and Statler v. Ray Mfg. Co. have extended the rule of Thomas v. Winchester. If so, this court is committed to the extension. The defendant argues that things imminently dangerous to life are poisons, explosives, deadly weapons—things whose normal function it is to injure or destroy. But whatever the rule in Thomas v. Winchester may once have been, it has no longer that restricted meaning. A scaffold (Devlin v. Smith, supra) is not inherently a destructive instrument. It becomes destructive only if imperfectly constructed. A large coffee urn (Statler v. Ray Mfg. Co., supra) may have within itself, if negligently made, the potency of danger, yet no one thinks of it as an implement whose normal function is destruction. *   *   *

*   *   *   *

We hold, then, that the principle of Thomas v. Winchester is not limited to poisons, explosives, and things of like nature, to things which in their normal operation are implements of destruction. If the nature of a thing is such that it is reasonably certain to place life and limb in peril when negligently made, it is then a thing of danger. Its nature gives warning of the consequences to be expected. If to the element of danger there is added knowledge that the thing will be used by persons other than the purchaser, and used without new tests, then, irrespective of contract, the manufacturer of this thing of danger is under a duty to make it carefully. *   *   * It is possible to use almost anything in a way that will make it dangerous if defective. That is not enough to charge the manufacturer with a duty independent of his contract. *   *   * There must also be knowledge that in the usual course of events the danger will be shared by others than the buyer. Such knowledge may often be inferred from the nature of the transaction. But it is possible that even knowledge of the danger and of the use will not always be enough. The proximity or remoteness of the relation is a factor to be considered. We are dealing now with the liability of the manufacturer of the finished product, who puts it on the market to be used without inspection by his customers. If he is negligent, where danger is to be foreseen, a liability will follow.

We are not required, at this time, to say that it is legitimate to go back of the manufacturer of the finished product and hold the manufacturers of the component parts. To make their negligence a cause of imminent danger, an independent cause must often intervene; the manufacturer of the finished product must also fail in his duty of inspection. It may be that in those circumstances the negligence of the earlier members of the series is too remote to constitute, as to the ultimate user, an actionable wrong. *   *   * There is here no break in the chain of cause and effect. In such circumstances, the presence of a known danger, attendant upon a known use, makes vigilance a duty. *   *   *

From this survey of the decisions, there thus emerges a definition of the duty of a manufacturer which enables us to measure this defendant's liability. Beyond all question, the nature of an automobile gives warning of probable danger if its construction is defective. This automobile was designed to go 50 miles an hour. Unless its wheels were sound and strong, injury was almost certain. It was as much a thing of danger as a defective engine for a railroad. The defendant knew the danger. It knew also that the car would be used by persons other than the buyer. This was apparent from its size; there were seats for three persons. It was apparent also from the fact that the buyer was a dealer in cars, who bought to resell. The maker of this car supplied it for the use of purchasers from the dealer just as plainly as the contractor in Devlin v. Smith supplied the scaffold for use by the servants of the owner. *   *   *

*   *   *   *

It is true that *   *   * "an automobile is not an inherently dangerous vehicle." *   *   * The meaning is that danger is not to be expected when the vehicle is well constructed. The court left it to the jury to say whether the defendant ought to have foreseen that the car, if negligently constructed, would become "imminently dangerous." Subtle distinctions are drawn by the defendants between things inherently dangerous and things imminently dangerous, but the case does not turn upon these verbal niceties. If danger was to be expected as reasonably certain, there was a duty of vigilance, and this whether you call the danger inherent or imminent. *   *   *

We think the defendant was not absolved from a duty of inspection because it bought the wheels from a reputable manufacturer. It was not merely a dealer in automobiles. It was a manufacturer of automobiles. It was responsible for the finished product. It was not at liberty to put the finished product on the market without subjecting the component parts to ordinary and simple tests. *   *   * The obligation to inspect must vary with the nature of the thing to be inspected. The more probable the danger the greater the need of caution.

JUDGMENT AND REMEDY

The New York Court of Appeals, the highest court in the New York state system, affirmed the judgment of the original trial court and the intermediate review court that the defendant, Buick Motor Company, was liable in damages to Donald C. MacPherson for the injuries he sustained when he was thrown from the vehicle.

COMMENT

This case has been interpreted to cover all articles that imperil life whenever negligently made. Prior to MacPherson, manufacturers escaped liability to consumers whenever their contractual dealings were with middlemen or retailers. Since MacPherson, that is no longer the case.

Privity of Contract Not Required   An action based upon negligence does not require privity of contract between the injured plaintiff and the negligent defendant-manufacturer. Section 395 of the Restatement, Second, Torts states:

A manufacturer who fails to exercise reasonable care in the manufacture of a chattel [movable good] which, unless carefully made, he should recognize as involving an unreasonable risk of causing substantial bodily harm to those who lawfully used it for a purpose for which it was manufactured and to those whom the supplier should expect to be in the vicinity of its probable use, is subject to liability for bodily harm caused to them by its lawful use in a manner and for a purpose for which it is manufactured.

Simply stated, a manufacturer is liable for its failure to exercise due care to any person who sustained an injury proximately caused by a negligently made (defective) product regardless of whether there was a sale or contract to sell.

Defenses to Negligence Any manufacturer, seller, or processor who can prove due care was used in the manufacture of its product has an appropriate defense against a negligence suit, since failure to exercise due care is one of the major elements of negligence.

But there are other defenses, and their use and application vary from state to state. One area of variation is the tying of the breach (failure to exercise reasonable care) to the injury, referred to as causation (see Chapter 3). Numerous events, involving different people, take place between the time a product is manufactured and the time of use. Thus, if any of these events can be shown to have caused or contributed to the injury, the manufacturer will claim no liability on the basis of this intervening cause.

Two other defenses are contributory negligence and, where recognized, assumption of risk (both also discussed in Chapter 3). For example, assume a person used a lotion on her or his body, knowing that the ingredients of that lotion would cause the skin to blister. The plaintiff files suit claiming that the manufacturer was negligent in failing to warn of the possibility of blisters on the label. The manufacturer-defendant would claim that the plaintiff's own knowledge of the risk and voluntary use of the product with such knowledge was an unreasonable assumption of risk and was the proximate cause of the injury.

Likewise, anytime a plaintiff misuses a product or fails to make a reasonable effort at preserving his or her own welfare, the manufacturer or seller will claim that the plaintiff contributed to causing the injuries. The claim is that the plaintiff's negligence offsets the negligence of the manufacturer or seller. In some states, the contributory negligence of the plaintiff is an absolute defense for the defendant manufacturer or seller. In many others, the negligence of each is compared (comparative negligence), and damages are based on the proportion of negligence attributed to the defendant.

Basis of Liability— Violation of Statutory Duty

Numerous federal and state laws impose duties upon manufacturers of cosmetics, drugs, foods, toxic substances, and flammable materials. These duties involve appropriate description of contents, labeling, branding, advertising, and selling. For example, federal statutes include the Federal Flammable Fabrics Act; the Federal Food, Drug, and Cosmetics Act; and the Federal Hazardous Substances Labeling Act. In a civil action for damages (tort), a violation of statutory duty is often held to constitute *negligence per se*.

Consider an example: Jason Manufacturing Company produces pipe fittings *specifically* for use in the construction of homes in Monroe County only. The fittings do not comply with county building codes. One of the pipe fittings bursts in a home, allowing hot water to spray on the homeowner. The homeowner can bring a negligence action for personal damages on the ground that failure to comply with the building codes is in and of itself an automatic breach of the manufacturer's duty of reasonable care. Of course, the homeowner has to show proximate cause, that is, relate the injury to the careless act.

Fraudulent and Nonfraudulent Misrepresentation

When a fraudulent misrepresentation has been made to a user or consumer, and that misrepresentation ultimately results in an injury, the basis of liability may be the tort of **fraud.** Examples are the intentional mislabeling of packaged cosmetics or the intentional concealment of a product's defects. A more interesting basis of liability is nonfraudulent misrepresentation, when a merchant *innocently* misrepresents the character or quality of goods.

A famous example involved a drug manufacturer and a victim of addiction to a prescription medicine called Talwin. The manufacturer, Winthrop Laboratories, a division of Stirling Drug, Inc., innocently indicated to the medical profession that the drug was not physically addictive. Using this information, a physician prescribed the drug for his patient, who developed an addiction that turned out to be fatal. Even though the addiction was a highly unusual reaction resulting from the victim's highly unusual susceptibility to this product, the drug company was still held liable.[1]

THE DOCTRINE OF STRICT LIABILITY

A recent development of tort law is the revival of the old doctrine of strict liability. Under this doctrine, people are liable for the results of their acts regardless of their intentions or their exercise of reasonable care. For example, a company that uses dynamite to blast for a road is strictly liable for any damages that it causes, even if it takes reasonable and prudent precautions to prevent such damages. In essence, the blasting company becomes liable for any personal injuries it causes and thus is an absolute insurer.

The English courts accepted the doctrine of strict liability for many years. Often persons whose conduct resulted in the injury of another were held liable for damages, even if they had not intended to injure anyone and had exercised reasonable care. This approach was abandoned around 1800 in favor of the *fault* approach in which an action was considered tortious only if it was wrongful or blameworthy in some respect.

Strict liability was reapplied to manufactured goods in several landmark cases in the 1960s and has since become a common method of holding manufacturers liable. Basically, if the purchaser of a product is injured through use of the product, that person can show a cause of action against the manufacturer by proving (1) that the product was defective, (2) that the defect made the product unreasonably dangerous, and (3) that the defect was the proximate cause of the injury.

The Restatement of Torts

The Restatement, Second, Torts designates how the doctrine of strict products liability should be applied. It is a precise and widely accepted statement of the liabilities of sellers of goods (including manufacturers) and deserves close attention. Section 402A of Restatement, Second, Torts states:

> (1) One who sells any product in a defective condition unreasonably dangerous to the user or consumer or to his property is subject to liability for physical harm thereby caused to the ultimate user or consumer or to his property, if
>> (a) the seller is engaged in the business of selling such a product, and
>> (b) it is expected to and does reach the user or consumer without substantial change in the condition in which it is sold.
> (2) The rule stated in Subsection (1) applies although
>> (a) the seller has exercised all possible care in the preparation and sale of his product, and
>> (b) the user or consumer has not bought the product from or entered into any contractual relation with the seller.

Thus, liability is imposed by law as a matter of public policy. It does not depend on privity of contract or on proof of negligence. The manufacturer's liability to an injured party is virtually unlimited.[2] The injured party does not have to be the buyer or a third party beneficiary, as required under contract warranty theory. [UCC 2-318] Indeed, this type of liability in law is not governed by the provisions of the UCC.

An important case that started the trend toward strict liability involved the use of a power tool.

---

1. Crocker v. Winthrop Laboratories, Div. of Stirling Drugs, Inc., 514 S.W.2d 429 (Tex. 1974).

2. Many state laws, Nebraska's, for example, are limiting the manufacturer's liability.

GREENMAN v. YUBA
POWER PRODUCTS,
INC.

Supreme Court of California,
1962.

27 Cal.Rptr. 697, 377 P.2d 897.

BACKGROUND AND FACTS *California was the first state to impose strict liability in tort on manufacturers. In this landmark decision, the California Supreme Court sets out the reasons for applying tort law rather than contract law to cases in which a consumer is injured by a defective product.*

TRAYNOR, Justice.

*   *   *   *

Plaintiff brought this action for damages against the retailer and the manufacturer of a Shopsmith, a combination power tool that could be used as a saw, drill, and wood lathe. He saw a Shopsmith demonstrated by the retailer and studied a brochure prepared by the manufacturer. He decided he wanted a Shopsmith for his home workshop, and his wife bought and gave him one for Christmas in 1955. In 1957 he bought the necessary attachments to use the Shopsmith as a lathe for turning a large piece of wood he wished to make into a chalice. After he had worked on the piece of wood several times without difficulty, it suddenly flew out of the machine and struck him on the forehead, inflicting serious injuries. About ten and a half months later, he gave the retailer and the manufacturer written notice of claimed breaches of warranties and filed a complaint against them alleging such breaches and negligence.

*   *   *   *

Plaintiff introduced substantial evidence that his injuries were caused by defective design and construction of the Shopsmith. His expert witnesses testified that inadequate set screws were used to hold parts of the machine together so that normal vibration caused the tailstock of the lathe to move away from the piece of wood being turned permitting it to fly out of the lathe. They also testified that there were other more positive ways of fastening the parts of the machine together, the use of which would have prevented the accident. The jury could therefore reasonably have concluded that the manufacturer negligently constructed the Shopsmith. The jury could also reasonably have concluded that statements in the manufacturer's brochure were untrue, that they constituted express warranties, and that plaintiff's injuries were caused by their breach.

The manufacturer contends, however, that plaintiff did not give it notice of breach of warranty within a reasonable time and that therefore his cause of action for breach of warranty is barred[.] *   *   *

*   *   *   *

[The Calif. Sales Act] does not provide that notice must be given of the breach of a warranty that arises independently of a contract of sale between the parties. Such warranties are not imposed by the sales act, but are the product of common-law decisions that have recognized them in a variety of situations. It is true that in many of these situations the court has invoked the sales act definitions of warranties in defining the defendant's liability, but it has done so, not because the statutes so required, but because they provided appropriate standards for the court to adopt under the circumstances presented.

The notice requirement is not an appropriate one for the court to adopt in actions by injured consumers against manufacturers with whom they have not dealt. *   *   * We conclude, therefore, that even if plaintiff did not give timely notice of breach of warranty to the manufacturer, his cause of action based on the representations contained in the brochure was not barred.

Moreover, to impose strict liability on the manufacturer under the circumstances of this case, it was not necessary for plaintiff to establish an express warranty[.] A manufacturer is strictly liable in tort when an article he places on the market, knowing that it is to be used without inspection for defects, proves to have a defect that causes injury to a human being. Recognized first in the case of unwholesome food products, such liability has now been extended to a variety of other products that create as great or greater hazards if defective.

*   *   * [S]trict liability has usually been based on the theory of an express or implied warranty running from the manufacturer to the plaintiff, the abandonment of the requirement of a contract between them, the recognition that the liability is not assumed by agreement but imposed by law, and the refusal to permit the manufacturer to define the scope of its own responsibility for defective products make clear that the liability is not one governed by the law of contract warranties but by the law of strict liability in tort. Accordingly, rules defining and governing warranties that were developed to meet the needs of commercial transactions cannot properly be invoked to govern the manufacturer's liability to those injured by their defective products unless those rules also serve the purposes for which such liability is imposed.

*   *   * The purpose of such liability is to insure that the costs of injuries resulting from defective products are borne by the manufacturers that put such products on the market rather than by the injured persons who are powerless to protect themselves. Sales warranties serve this purpose fitfully at best. In the present case, for example, plaintiff was able to plead and prove an express warranty only because he read and relied on the representations of the Shopsmith's ruggedness contained in the manufacturer's brochure. Implicit in the machine's presence on the market, however, was a representation that it would safely do the jobs for which it was built. Under these circumstances, it should not be controlling whether plaintiff selected the machine because of the statements in the brochure, or because of the machine's own appearance of excellence that belied the defect lurking beneath the surface, or because he merely assumed that it would safely do the jobs it was built to do. It should not be controlling whether the details of the sales from manufacturer to retailer and from retailer to plaintiff's wife were such that one or more of the implied warranties of the sales act arose. "The remedies of injured consumers ought not to be made to depend upon the intricacies of the law of sales." To establish the manufacturer's liability it was sufficient that plaintiff proved that he was injured while using the Shopsmith in a way it was intended to be used as a result of a defect in design and manufacture of which plaintiff was not aware that made the Shopsmith unsafe for its intended use.

The jury verdict for the plaintiff was upheld.   JUDGMENT
                                                                                    AND REMEDY

Requirements of Strict Products Liability

The six basic requirements of strict products liability are:

1.   The defendant must sell the product in a defective condition.
2.   The defendant must normally be engaged in the business of selling that product.
3.   The product must be unreasonably danger-

ous to the user or consumer because of its defective condition.[3]

4. The plaintiff must incur physical harm to self or property by use or consumption of the product.

5. The defective condition must be the proximate cause of the injury or damage.

6. The goods must not have been substantially changed from the time the product was sold to the time the injury was sustained.

---

3. This element is no longer required in some states, for example, California.

Thus, in any action against a manufacturer or seller, the plaintiff does not have to show why or in what manner the product became defective. The plaintiff does, however, have to show that at the time the injury was sustained, the condition of the product was essentially the same as it was when it left the hands of the defendant manufacturer or seller.

In the following case, the question of strict liability comes into play. The court attempts to answer the question of whether the product was manufactured in such a way that it would become unreasonably dangerous.

ROGERS v. UNIMAC COMPANY, INC.

Supreme Court of Arizona, 1977.
115 Ariz. 304, 565 P.2d 181.

BACKGROUND AND FACTS *Plaintiff Rogers, a car wash employee, brought this action against the manufacturer of a commercial washer-extractor (an appliance used for drying towels). When the lid of the machine was raised, a mechanical brake stopped the spinning basket. The extractor also had a timer that stopped the basket at a pre-set time. During peak hours, the employees used the lid-activated brake. The brake frequently failed to operate, and the employees pressed down on the rim of the spinning basket to stop its motion. In November 1972, while Rogers was attempting to stop the extractor in this manner, his arm became entangled in the machine. An examination of the brake unit after the accident revealed that it had not been properly maintained. Rogers contended that the machine was defectively designed and that the manufacturer should have placed a warning on the extractor to indicate this type of hazard.*

CAMERON, Chief Justice.

* * * *

The Unimac 202, when shipped to the Country Club Car Wash in 1967, was equipped with two safety features. First, a micro switch cut off the electrical current to the motor when the lid was raised. This prevented the motor from running while the lid was open. Second, raising the lid applied a mechanical brake which stopped the cylinder within ten seconds. That the Unimac Company could have adopted a different type of safety device, i.e., a lid lock, is not in itself sufficient evidence to establish defective design. Under strict liability principles, a manufacturer is required to adopt those safety devices which would prevent the product from becoming unreasonably dangerous.

We do not believe the evidence showed a defect in design which made the Unimac 202 unreasonably dangerous. The most the evidence presented by the plaintiff showed was improper maintenance and repair of the machine and not defective design. The safety features of the Unimac 202 were a reasonable preventative of injury so long as the machine was properly maintained. The manufacturer is not liable for lack of normal maintenance.

* * * *

The plaintiff * * * contends that the Unimac Company should have placed a warning on the extractor of the hazard involved in reaching into the spinning cylinder. He argues that a warning was necessary because the machine was so designed that the operator had to lift the lid to apply the brake, and was thus exposed to the spinning cylinder for at least ten seconds or longer, depending upon the condition of the brake.

The brake design of the Unimac 202 was, at the time of manufacture and is today, a common and accepted safety design. But we need not decide whether this ten-second interval was an unreasonably dangerous defect because the lack of a warning was not the proximate cause of the injury. * * *

* * * *

Furthermore, we are unwilling to impose liability upon the manufacturer of an appliance for failure to warn of those dangers which may arise because of lack of normal repair.

* * * *

A warning on the Unimac 202 extractor would not have prevented this injury. The owners and managers of the County Club Car Wash required their young employees to work with an extractor made hazardous because of lack of repair. The Unimac 202 presented no unreasonable danger of injury so long as it was properly maintained.

The judgment for the defendant-manufacturer was affirmed. Rogers was unable to prove that a defect in the product was the proximate cause of his injury.

JUDGMENT AND REMEDY

A different court could have reached the opposite result.

COMMENT

Limitations on Recovery

Some courts have limited the application of the strict liability doctrine to cases in which personal injuries have occurred. Thus, when a defective product causes only *property damage,* the seller may not be liable under a theory of strict liability, depending on the law of the particular jurisdiction. In addition, until recently, recovery for *economic* loss was not available in an action based on strict liability (and even today this is rarely available). Note, however, that recovery for *breach of warranty* may be available, depending upon the type of injury and which alternative section of UCC 2-318 is in effect.

Lastly, statutes enacted by a number of states limit the seller's (manufacturer's) liability to injuries occurring within a specified period (for example, five to twelve years) from the date of *sale* or *manufacture* of the defective product.

Therefore, it is immaterial that the product is defective or causes injury if the injury occurs after the statutory period has lapsed. In addition, some of these legislative enactments have limited the application of the doctrine of strict liability to new goods. Some states, such as Massachusetts, have refused to recognize products liability. In these states, recovery is gained mainly via breach of warranty or negligence.

Defenses

Assumption of Risk Assumption of risk can be used as a defense in an action based on strict liability in tort. Whenever consumers or users use goods improperly under unreasonable circumstances, they assume the risk of injury. In order for such a defense to be established, the defendant must show the following basic elements (previously discussed):

1. That the plaintiff voluntarily engaged in the risk while realizing the potential danger.
2. That the plaintiff knew and appreciated the risk created by the defect.
3. That the plaintiff's decision to undertake the known risk was unreasonable.

Misuse of the Product   Similar to the defense of voluntary assumption of risk is that of misuse of the product. Here the injured party does not know that the product is dangerous for a partic-

ular use, but that use is not the one for which the product was designed. (Contrast this with assumption of risk.) This defense has been severely limited by the courts, however. Even if the injured party does not know about the inherent danger of using the product in a wrong way, if the misuse is foreseeable nonetheless, the seller must take measures to guard against it. In the following case, the court examines the question of whether the injured party's misuse of the product was foreseeable by the manufacturer.

MATA v. CLARK EQUIPMENT CO.
Appellate Court of Illinois, First District, Second Division, 1978.
58 Ill.App.3d 418, 15 Ill.Dec. 980, 374 N.E.2d 763.

BACKGROUND AND FACTS   *Lazaro Mata was injured when he lost his balance while standing on the seat of a forklift manufactured by the defendant.*

DOWNING, Justice.

*   *   *   *

[I]t has been consistently held that the doctrine of strict liability in tort does not make a manufacturer an insurer of the consumer's safety. The doctrine is one of liability without negligence, but it is not liability without fault.

Every product need not be accident proof, incapable of causing harm or accompanied by a warning against injury which may ensue from a mishap in its use.

The liability of a manufacturer properly encompasses only those situations where the product is being used for the purpose for which it was intended or for which it is reasonably foreseeable that it may be used. In retrospect, almost nothing is entirely unforeseeable. A test of foreseeability, however, does not bring within the scope of a defendant's liability every injury that might possibly occur. Foreseeability has been defined by our supreme court as that which is *objectively reasonable* to expect, not merely what might conceivably occur.

"[T]he question of what constitutes an ordinary use is clearly a question of fact and *   *   * the foreseeability of careless use is a matter for a jury unless the use of the product was, in fact, so unintended and unforeseeable that the case should be taken from the jury."

We believe that Mata's use of the forklift truck at the time of his injury was so unintended and unforeseeable that the trial judge should have taken the case from the jury. Foreseeability may be decided as a matter of law where the facts demonstrate that plaintiff could never be entitled to recovery.

The evidence showed that at the time he was injured, plaintiff, a forklift operator with 17 years experience, was operating the forklift truck in question without the benefit of the protective overhead guard which had been installed by Clark. When the bag of nuts fell and became wedged between the truck and the wall, Mata stood up on the seat (an act he would not have been able to accomplish had the overhead guard been in place) while the truck was still in operation, and attempted to remove it. He then lost his balance, grasped the stationary tie-bar, and was injured. It must be obvious that Mata knew the operational features of the forklift and the dangers that were present in its operation.

The trial court's judgment for Mata was reversed. Mata had assumed the risk of his injury and was not entitled to recover from the manufacturer.   **JUDGMENT AND REMEDY**

Contributory Negligence As pointed out in Chapter 3, at common law, in any action based on negligence, contributory negligence of the injured party either completely barred recovery or reduced the amount of recovery under the rule of comparative negligence. In principle, negligence and contributory negligence are immaterial in any action based on the theory of strict liability in tort. After all, strict liability assumes that the danger presented was foreseeable by the manufacturer of the product.

Some states are changing, however. For example, in California, contributory negligence is now a defense to an action based on strict liability in tort—even when the action itself has nothing to do with negligence.

Strict Liability to Bystanders

All courts extend the strict liability of manufac-turers and other sellers to injured bystanders, although the drafters of Restatement, Second, Torts, Section 402A did not take a position on bystanders. For example, the manufacturer of an automobile was held liable for injuries caused by the explosion of the car's motor while in traffic. A cloud of steam that resulted from the explosion caused multiple collisions because other drivers could not see well.[4]

In the following case, the court looks at the fact that bystanders as a class are purchasers of most of the same products to which they are exposed as bystanders. Thus, someone injured by an exploding bottle in a supermarket seems to be covered by Section 402A, Restatement, Second, Torts.

---

4. Giberson v. Ford Motor Co., 504 S.W.2d 8 (Mo.1974).

BACKGROUND AND FACTS *Embs was buying some groceries at Stamper's Cash Market. Unnoticed by her, a carton of 7-Up was sitting on the floor at the edge of the produce counter about one foot from where she was standing. Several of the 7-Up bottles exploded. Embs's leg was injured severely enough that Embs had to be taken to the hospital by a managing agent of the store. The trial court dismissed the claim pursuant to a directed verdict at the completion of her proof. The appellate court now takes up her case.*

EMBS v. PEPSI-COLA BOTTLING CO. OF LEXINGTON, KENTUCKY, INC.
Court of Appeals of Kentucky, 1975.
528 S.W.2d 703.

LUKOWSKY, Judge.

*   *   *   *

Our expressed public policy will be furthered if we minimize the risk of personal injury and property damage by charging the costs of injuries against the manufacturer who can procure liability insurance and distribute its expense among the public as a cost of doing business; and since the risk of harm from defective products exists for mere bystanders and passersby as well as for the purchaser or user, there is no substantial reason for protecting one class of persons and not the other. The same policy requires us to maximize protection for the injured third party and promote the public interest in discouraging the marketing of products having defects that are a menace to the public by imposing strict liability upon retailers and wholesalers in the distributive chain responsible for marketing the defective product which injures the bystander. The imposition of strict liability places no unreasonable burden upon sellers because they can adjust the cost of insurance protection among themselves in the course of their continuing business relationship.

We must not shirk from extending the rule to the manufacturer for fear that the retailer or middleman will be impaled on the sword of liability without regard to fault. Their liability was already established under Section 402A of the Restatement of Torts 2d. As a matter of public policy the retailer or middleman as well as the manufacturer should be liable since the loss for injuries resulting from defective products should be placed on those members of the marketing chain best able to pay the loss, who can then distribute such risk among themselves by means of insurance and indemnity agreements.

* * * *

The result which we reach does not give the bystander a "free ride." When products and consumers are considered in the aggregate, bystanders, as a class, purchase most of the same products to which they are exposed as bystanders. Thus, as a class, they indirectly subsidize the liability of the manufacturer, middleman and retailer and in this sense do pay for the insurance policy tied to the product.

Public policy is adequately served if parameters are placed upon the extension of the rule so that it is limited to bystanders whose injury from the defect is reasonably foreseeable.

For the sake of clarity we restate the extension of the rule. The protections of Section 402A of the Restatement, Second, Torts extend to bystanders whose injury from the defective product is reasonably foreseeable.

* * * *

It matters not that the evidence be circumstantial for as Thoreau put it "Some circumstantial evidence is very strong, as when you find a trout in the milk." There are some accidents, as where a beverage bottle explodes in the course of normal handling, as to which there is common experience that they do not ordinarily occur without a defect; and this permits the inference of a defect. This is particularly true when there is evidence in the case of the antecedent explosion of other bottles of the same product.

In cases involving multiple defendants the better reasoned view places the onus of tracing the defect on the shoulders of the dealers and the manufacturer as a policy matter, seeking to compensate the plaintiff and to require the defendants to fight out the question of responsibility among themselves.

JUDGMENT AND REMEDY *The appellate court reversed the trial court's directed verdict that dismissed Embs's claim. The case was remanded to the lower court for a new trial.*

Crash-worthiness Doctrine

Certain courts have adopted the doctrine of crash-worthiness, which imposes liability for defects in the design or construction of motor vehicles that increase the extent of injuries to passengers if an accident occurs. The doctrine holds even when the defects do not actually cause the accident.[5] By accepting the crash-worthiness doctrine, the courts reject the argument of automobile manufacturers that involving a car in a collision does not constitute "ordinary use" of a car. There are, in fact, strong differences of opinion among the courts on this issue.

Strict Liability of Suppliers of Component Parts and Lessors

Under the rule of strict liability in tort, the basis of liability has been expanded to include suppliers of component parts and lessors of movable goods. Thus, if General Motors buys brake pads from a subcontractor and puts them in Chevrolets without changing their composition, and those pads are defective, both the supplier of the brake pads and General Motors will be held strictly liable for the damages caused by the defects.

Liability for personal injuries caused by defective goods extends to those who lease such goods. Section 408 of the Restatement, Second, Torts states that:

> One who leases a chattel as safe for immediate use is subject to liability to those whom he should expect to use the chattel, or to be endangered by its probable use, for physical harm caused by its use in a manner for which and by a person for whose use it is leased, if the lessor fails to exercise reasonable care to make it safe for such use or to disclose its actual condition to those who may be expected to use it.

Some courts have held that a leasing agreement gives rise to a contractual *implied warranty* that the leased goods will be fit for the duration of the lease. Under this view, if Hertz Rent-a-Car leases a Chevrolet that has been improperly maintained, and a passenger is injured in an accident, the passenger can sue Hertz. (Liability is based on the contract theory of warranty, not tort.)

QUESTIONS AND CASE PROBLEMS

1. Susan buys a television set from Quality TV Appliance Associates. She is going on vacation, so she takes the set to her mother's house for her mother to use. Because the set is defective, it explodes, causing considerable damage to her mother's house. Susan's mother sues Quality for breach of implied warranty of merchantability. Quality claims Susan's mother has no standing in court because she did not buy the set from Quality. Discuss the defense claimed by Quality.

2. Acme Drug Company manufactures a drug for airsickness. Acme has placed the drug on the market. Beyer purchases the drug from Green's Drug Store. Beyer is going on a trip and takes two of the tablets as directed. Beyer loses consciousness because of the side effects of the drug, and he falls down a flight of stairs at the airport, breaking an arm and a leg. Acme knew of the possible side effects but did not place any warning on the label. Also, it is learned that Acme failed to meet minimum federal drug standards in the manufacture of the drug—standards that would have reduced the side effects. Beyer wants to file an action based on Acme's negligence.
    (a) Discuss Beyer's burden of proof.
    (b) Discuss how the situation would change if a warning had been placed on the package and minimum standards had been met.

3. Colt manufactures a new pistol. Firing of the pistol is dependent on an enclosed high-pressure device. The pistol has been thoroughly tested in two laboratories in the Midwest, and it has been designed and manufactured according to all known technology. Beyer purchases one of the new pistols from Smith's Gun and Rifle Emporium. When he uses the pistol in the high altitude of the Rockies, the difference in pressure

5. Turner v. General Motors Corp., 514 S.W.2d 497 (Texas Civ.App. 1974).

causes the pistol to misfire, resulting in serious injury to Beyer. Colt can prove that all due care was used in the manufacturing process, and it refuses to pay for Beyer's injuries. Discuss Colt's liability in tort.

4. Baxter manufactures electric hair dryers. Beyer purchases a Baxter dryer from her local Ace Drug Store. Green, a friend and guest in Beyer's home, has taken a shower and wants to dry her hair. Beyer tells Green to use the new Baxter hair dryer, which Beyer has just purchased. As Green plugs in the dryer, sparks fly out from the motor and continue to do so as she operates it. Despite this, Green begins drying her hair. Suddenly, the entire dryer ignites into flames, severely burning the scalp of Green. Green sues Baxter on the basis of the torts of negligence and strict liability. Baxter admits the dryer was defective but denies liability, particularly since Green did not purchase the dryer. Discuss the validity of any defense claimed by Baxter.

5. Green is standing on a street corner waiting for a ride to work. Beyer has just purchased a new car manufactured by Able Motors. Beyer is driving down the street when suddenly the steering mechanism breaks, causing Beyer to run over Green. Green suffers permanent injuries. Beyer's total income per year has never exceeded $15,000. Green files suit against Able under the theory of strict liability in tort. Able pleads no liability because (1) due care was used in the manufacture of the car, (2) Able is not the manufacturer of the steering mechanism (Smith is), and (3) the Restatement governing strict liability applies only to users or consumers, and Green is neither. Discuss the validity of the defenses claimed by Able.

6. Howmedica, Inc., manufactured and distributed artificial replacements for human bones and joints. Hoffman, who suffered from degenerative osteoarthritis, underwent surgery for repair to her hip. As part of the surgery, her doctor implanted a hip prosthesis. Several months later, Hoffman's hip fractured, causing severe pain and necessitating further surgery. Howmedica, Inc., argued that, even if it had been negligent in manufacturing and testing the hip and had breached its warranty of merchantability, it was not liable to Hoffman under UCC 2-318 (Alternative B) since Hoffman and Howmedica were not in privity of contract. Is this a sound argument? [Hoffman v. How-

medica, Inc., 364 N.E.2d 1215 (Mass.1977)]

7. Harry Scott purchased from Delta Oxygen Company a cylinder filled with oxygen to be used in welding operations. Tommy Scott, Harry's brother and employee, was attempting to connect the cylinder to an acetylene torch when an explosion occurred. Scott was seriously burned and was hospitalized as a result of the explosion. In an action by Scott for breach of implied warranty against Delta Oxygen Company, Scott relied on UCC 2-318. What was the result? [Delta Oxygen Co. v. Scott, 238 Ark. 534, 383 S.W.2d 885 (1964)]

8. Union Oil Company was engaged in drilling operations off the Alaskan coast. As a part of its operations, Union installed gas protection systems in its offshore drilling rigs. Over a period of less than a year, the salt water and spray caused the internal parts of the detection system to corrode, resulting in a failure in the system. Subsequently, because of an undetected gas leak, an explosion killed one of Union's employees, Haragan. Haragan's representative sued Baroid, the manufacturer and seller of the gas detection system. Can Haragan's representatives recover on a theory of strict liability? How would they argue that there was a defect? [Haragan v. Union Oil Co., 312 F.Supp. 1392 (D.C. Alaska, 1970)]

9. In 1961, Gillette Dairy, Inc. purchased a compressor from St. Regis Corp. for use in its dairy processing plant. In 1965 the compressor exploded, resulting in a fire that caused extensive damage to Gillette's plant. The explosion was caused by a defect in the manufacture of the pistons. Gillette sought to recover from St. Regis for damage done to the plant and for the profits it lost while the plant was closed for repairs. What was the result? [Norfolk Dev. Corp. v. St. Regis Pulp and Paper Corp., 338 F.Supp. 1213 (D.C.Neb. 1972)]

10. A two-year-old child lost his leg when he became entangled in a grain auger on his grandfather's farm. The auger had a safety guard that prevented any item larger than 4⅝ inches from coming into contact with the machine's moving parts. The child's foot was smaller than the openings in the safety guard. Was such an injury reasonably foreseeable? [Richelman v. Kewanee Machinery & Conveyor Co., 375 N.E.2d 885 (1978)]

CHAPTER 22

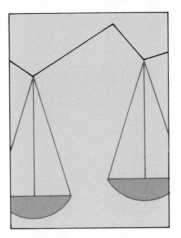

SALES
Performance and
Obligation

DUTY OF GOOD FAITH AND COMMERCIAL REASONABLENESS

To understand the performance that is required of a seller and of a buyer under a sales contract, it is necessary to know the duties and obligations each party has assumed under the terms of the contract. Keep in mind that "duties and obligations" under the terms of the contract here include those specified in the agreement, the custom, and the Code.

Sometimes the sales contract leaves open some particulars of performance and permits one of the parties to specify them. The obligations of "good faith" and "commercial reasonableness" underlie every sales contract within the UCC. They are objective obligations, and they can form the basis for a breach of contract suit later on. These standards are read into every contract, and they provide a framework in which the parties can specify particulars of performance. "Any such

specification must be made in good faith and within limits set by commercial reasonableness." [UCC 2-311(1)]

The duty of cooperation between the parties required by Section 2-311 must be read along with the Code's "good faith" provision, which can never be disclaimed. "Every contract or duty within this Act imposes an obligation of good faith in its performance or enforcement." [UCC 1-203] "Good faith" in the case of a merchant means honesty in fact and the observance of reasonable commercial standards of fair dealing in the trade. [UCC 2-103(1)(b)]

Thus, when one party delays specifying particulars of performance for an unreasonable period of time or fails to cooperate with the other party, the innocent party is excused from any resulting delay in performance. In addition, the innocent party can proceed to perform in any reasonable manner. If the innocent party has performed as far as is reasonably possible under the circumstances, then the other party's failure to specify particulars or failure to cooperate can be treated as a breach of contract.

Good faith can mean that one party must not take advantage of another party by manipulating contract terms. Good faith applies to both parties, even the nonbreaching party. The principle of good faith applies through both the performance and the enforcement of all agreements or duties within a contract. Good faith is a question of fact for the jury. As previously mentioned, it means honesty in fact.

ZAPATHA v. DAIRY MART, INC.

Massachusetts Supreme Judicial Court, 1980.
408 N.E.2d 1370, 29 UCC Rep. Serv. 1121.

BACKGROUND AND FACTS   *In 1973 the Zapathas entered into a franchise agreement with the defendant. The agreement permitted either party to terminate the relationship without cause on ninety days' written notice. A second franchise agreement was executed in 1974, when the Zapathas moved their store to a new location. In 1977 the Zapathas refused to sign a new agreement submitted by the defendant. Dairy Mart then gave written notice to the Zapathas that their contract would be terminated in ninety days. The Zapathas brought this action seeking to enjoin the termination of the agreement, alleging that the contract provision allowing termination without cause was unconscionable and that Dairy Mart had not acted in good faith.*

WILKINS, Judge.

*   *   *   *

We start with the recognition that the Uniform Commercial Code itself implies that a contract provision allowing termination without cause is not per se unconscionable. Section 2-309(3) provides that "[t]ermination of a contract by one party except on the happening of an agreed event requires that reasonable notification be received by the other party and an agreement dispensing with notification is invalid if its operation would be unconscionable." This language implies that termination of a sales contract without agreed "cause" is authorized by the Code, provided reasonable notice is given. There is no suggestion that the ninety days' notice provided in the Dairy Mart franchise agreement was unreasonable.

We find no potential for unfair surprise to the Zapathas in the provision allowing termination without cause. We view the question of unfair surprise as focused on the circumstances under which the agreement was entered into. The termination provision was neither obscurely worded, nor buried in fine print in the contract. The provision was specifically pointed out to Mr. Zapatha before it was signed; Mr. Zapatha testified that he thought the provision was "straightforward," and he declined the opportunity to take the agreement to a lawyer for advice. The Zapathas had ample opportunity to consider the agreement before they signed it. Significantly, the subject of loss of employment was paramount in Mr. Zapatha's mind. He testified that he had held responsible jobs in one company from 1952 to 1973, that he had lost his employment, and that he "was looking for something that had a certain amount of security; something that was stable and something I could call my own." We conclude that a person of Mr. Zapatha's business experience and education should not have been surprised by the termination provision and, if in fact he was, there was no element of unfairness in the inclusion of that provision in the agreement.

We further conclude that there was no oppression in the inclusion of a termination clause in the franchise agreement. We view the question of oppression as directed to the substantive fairness to the parties of permitting the termination provisions to operate as written. The Zapathas took over a going business on premises provided by Dairy Mart, using equipment furnished by Dairy Mart. As an investment, the Zapathas had only to purchase the inventory of goods to be sold but, as Dairy Mart concedes, on termination by it without cause Dairy Mart was obliged to repurchase all the Zapathas' saleable merchandise inventory, including items not purchased from Dairy Mart, at 80% of its retail value. There was no potential for forfeiture or loss of investment. There is no question here of a need for a reasonable time to recoup the franchisees' initial investment. The Zapathas were entitled to their net profits through the entire term of the agreement. They failed to sustain their burden of showing that the agreement allocated the risks and benefits connected with termination in an unreasonably disproportionate way and that the termination provision was not reasonably related to legitimate commercial needs of Dairy Mart. To find the termination clause oppressive merely because it did not require cause for termination would be to establish an unwarranted barrier to the use of termination at will clauses in contracts in this Commonwealth, where each party received the anticipated and bargained for consideration during the full term of the agreement.

We see no basis on the record for concluding that Dairy Mart did not act in good faith, as that term is defined in the sales article ("honesty in fact and the observance of reasonable commercial standards of fair dealing in the trade"). There was no evidence that Dairy Mart failed to observe reasonable commercial standards of fair dealing in the trade in terminating the agreement. If there were such standards, there was no evidence of what they were.

The question then is whether there was evidence warranting a finding that Dairy Mart was not honest "in fact." The judge concluded that the absence of any commercial purpose for the termination other than the Zapathas' refusal to sign a new franchise agreement violated Dairy Mart's obligation of good faith. Dairy Mart's right to terminate was clear, and it exercised that right for a reason it openly disclosed. The sole test of "honesty in fact" is whether the person was honest. We think that, whether or not termination according to the terms of the franchise agreement may have been arbitrary, it was not dishonest.

The judge concluded that bad faith was also manifested by Dairy Mart's introductory brochure, which made representations of "security, comfort, and independence." Although this brochure and Mr. Zapatha's mistaken understanding that Dairy Mart could terminate the agreement only for cause could not be relied on to vary the clear terms of the agreement, the introductory brochure is relevant to the question of good faith. However, although the brochure misstated a franchisee's status as the owner of his own business, it shows no lack of honesty in fact relating to the right of Dairy Mart to terminate the agreement. Furthermore, by the time the Zapathas executed the second agreement, and even the first agreement, they knew that they would operate the franchise, but that they would not own the assets used in the business (except the goods to be sold); that the franchise agreement could be terminated by them and, at least in some circumstances, by Dairy Mart; and that in fact the major investment of funds would be made by Dairy Mart. We conclude that the use of the brochure did not warrant a finding of an absence of "honesty in fact."

JUDGMENT AND REMEDY   *The lower court's judgment for the plaintiffs was reversed. Dairy Mart was allowed to terminate the agreement.*

PERFORMANCE OF A SALES CONTRACT

A seller has the basic obligation to *transfer and deliver conforming goods*. The buyer has the basic obligation to *accept and pay for conforming goods* in accordance with the contract. [UCC 2-301] Overall performance of a sales contract is controlled by the agreement between the buyer and the seller. When the contract is unclear, or when terms are indefinite in certain respects and disputes arise, the Code provides built-in standards and rules for interpreting their agreement.

CONCURRENT CONDITIONS OF PERFORMANCE

The delivery of goods by the seller and the payment of the purchase price by the buyer are said to be *concurrent conditions*—those that are mutually dependent and are to be performed at the same time. The theoretical assumption is that delivery and payment can occur simultaneously. In reality this rarely happens.

Section 2-301 of the Code provides that "the obligation of the seller is to transfer and deliver and that of the buyer is to accept and pay *in accordance with the contract*" (emphasis added). If the contract expressly provides that the seller must first deliver the goods before receiving payment or that the buyer must pay before receiving the goods, then the terms of the contract control. However, where the agreement does not specifically provide, the Code charges both parties with the duty to proceed. In other words, in order for either party to maintain an action against the other for breach, the party bringing suit must put the other party in default by performing. This is accomplished in one of three ways—through: (1) performance according to the contract, (2) tender

of performance according to the contract, or (3) excuse from tender of performance.[1]

For example, Laval agrees to deliver goods to Boyd on September 1, and Boyd agrees to pay on September 15. If Laval fails to deliver the goods, Boyd can sue Laval on or after September 2. Since Laval is in default, Boyd can proceed without first tendering the purchase price.

SELLER'S OBLIGATION OF TENDER OF DELIVERY

Tender of Delivery

Tender of delivery requires that the seller have and hold *conforming* goods at the buyer's disposal and give the buyer whatever notification is reasonably necessary to enable the buyer to take delivery. [UCC 2-503(1)]

Tender must occur at a *reasonable hour* and in a *reasonable manner*. In other words, a seller cannot call the buyer at 2:00 A.M. and say, "The goods are ready. I'll give you twenty minutes to get them." Unless the parties have agreed otherwise, the goods must be tendered for delivery at a reasonable time and must be kept available for a reasonable period of time in order to enable the buyer to take possession of them. [UCC 2-503(1)(a)]

All goods called for by a contract must be tendered in a single delivery unless the parties agree otherwise [UCC 2-612] or the circumstances are such that either party can rightfully request delivery in lots. [UCC 2-307] Hence, an order for 1,000 shirts cannot be delivered two at a time. If seller and buyer contemplated, though,

---

1.   To tender is to offer or make available money or property in pursuance of a contract in such a way that nothing further remains to be done to fulfill the obligation of the party tendering.

that the shirts would be delivered in four orders of 250 each as they are produced, for summer, winter, fall, and spring stock, and the price can be apportioned accordingly, it may be commercially reasonable to do so.

Place of Delivery

Non-Carrier Cases   If the contract does not designate where the goods will be delivered, and the buyer is expected to pick them up, the place of delivery is the *seller's place of business* or, if the seller has none, the *seller's residence*. [UCC 2-308] If the contract involves the sale of *identified goods* (see Chapter 19 for a discussion of such goods), and the parties know when they enter into the contract that these goods are located somewhere other than at the seller's place of business (such as at a warehouse or in the possession of a bailee), then the *location of the goods* is the place for their delivery. [UCC 2-308]

For example, Laval and Boyd live in San Francisco. In San Francisco, Laval contracts to sell to Boyd five used railroad dining cars, which both parties know are located in Atlanta. If nothing more is specified in the contract, the place of delivery for the railroad cars is Atlanta.

Assume further that the railroad cars are stored in a warehouse and that Boyd will need some type of document to show the warehouse (bailee) in Atlanta that Boyd is entitled to take possession of the five dining cars. The seller "tenders delivery" without moving the goods. The seller may "deliver" either by giving the buyer a *negotiable document of title* or by obtaining the *bailee's* (warehouse's) *acknowledgment* that the buyer is entitled to possession.[2]

Carrier Cases   There are many instances, resulting either from attendant circumstances or from delivery terms contained in the contract, when it is apparent that the parties intend that a carrier be used to move the goods. There are two ways a seller can complete performance of the obligation to deliver the goods—through a shipment contract or a destination contract.

Shipment Contracts   A shipment contract requires or authorizes the seller to ship goods by a carrier. The contract does not require the seller to deliver the goods at a particular destination. [UCC 2-509 and 2-319] Unless otherwise agreed, the seller must [UCC 2-504]:

1. Put the goods into the hands of the carrier.
2. Make a contract for their transportation that is reasonable according to the nature of the goods and their value.
3. Obtain and promptly deliver for tender to the buyer any documents necessary to enable the buyer to obtain possession of the goods from the carrier.
4. Promptly notify the buyer that shipment has been made.

If the seller fails to notify the buyer that shipment has been made or fails to make a proper contract for transportation, and a *material loss* of the goods or a *delay* results, the buyer can reject the shipment. Of course, the parties can agree that a lesser amount of loss or a delay will be grounds for rejection.

Destination Contracts   Under destination contracts, the seller agrees to see that the goods will be duly tendered to the buyer at a particular destination. Once the goods arrive, the seller must tender the goods at a reasonable hour and hold conforming goods at the buyer's disposal for a reasonable length of time, giving appropriate notice. The seller must also provide the buyer with any documents of title necessary to enable the buyer to obtain delivery from the carrier. This is often done by tendering the documents through ordinary banking channels. Although not a part of the seller's tender, unless otherwise agreed, the buyer must furnish facilities reasonably suited for the receipt of the goods. [UCC 2-503]

---

2. If the seller delivers a nonnegotiable document of title or merely writes instructions to the bailee to release the goods to the buyer without the bailee's *acknowledgment* of the buyer's rights, this will also be a sufficient tender, unless the buyer objects. [UCC 2-503(4)] But risk of loss would not pass until the buyer had a reasonable time to present the document or the instructions.

F.O.B. Contracts   In contracts specifying that the goods, price, or delivery are F.O.B. to a particular point, the F.O.B. point is the delivery point. [UCC 2-319(1)]

If the F.O.B. point is the seller's place of shipment, then it is a *shipment contract*, and the seller incurs only the risk and expense of putting the goods into the hands of the carrier under the four conditions described above. If the F.O.B. point is at a particular destination, then it is a *destination contract*, and the responsibilities to the seller are the same as those under any destination contract as just described. [UCC 2-319]

If the vehicle of transportation at the F.O.B. point is referred to, then the seller must pay the expense of loading the goods on board the vehicle. For example, "F.O.B. car X23JM, Balt. RR yard, Baltimore" means that the seller transports the goods to the carrier (Baltimore Railroad) at the railroad yard in Baltimore and loads the goods onto car X23JM.

F.A.S. Contracts   F.A.S. contracts involve transportation by ship or other seagoing vessel. In contracts specifying that the goods, price, or delivery are F.A.S. (free alongside ship), the seller must deliver the goods alongside the vessel, usually on a dock designated by the buyer. In effect, this is a *shipment contract*. The seller has no responsibility for loading the goods onto the vessel, only delivery alongside it. The seller must obtain and tender a receipt, which is delivered to the buyer, ordinarily through banking channels. Once delivered, the F.A.S. contract is complete; the consignor (seller) is then relieved of any liability for the goods. [UCC 2-319(2)]

Ex-ship Contracts   If the contract specifies for delivery of goods "ex-ship" (from the carrying vessel), a *destination contract* is in effect. This is the reverse of the F.A.S. contract. It requires the shipper not only to ship conforming goods, but also to unload the goods at the port of destination.

C.I.F. Contracts   Contracts specifying C.I.F. ("cost, insurance, and freight") indicate that the buyer's purchase price includes the *cost* of the goods, *insurance* during transit, and *freight*

charges. If a contract is merely C&F, then only the cost and freight charges, not insurance, are included in the purchase price. Both C.I.F. and C&F contracts are shipment contracts, not destination contracts.

Unless otherwise agreed, the seller is required to deliver and load the goods on board the carrier, obtain a bill of lading showing freight has been paid, obtain proper insurance coverage, prepare an invoice and other necessary documents, and forward all documents to the buyer. For the purposes of risk and title, delivery to the carrier is delivery to the buyer. [UCC 2-320 and 2-321]

THE PERFECT TENDER RULE

As previously noted, the seller has an obligation to ship or tender *conforming goods*, and this entitles the seller to acceptance by and payment from the buyer according to the terms of the contract. At common law the seller was obligated to deliver goods in conformity with the terms of the contract in every detail. This was called the *perfect tender* doctrine. The UCC, in Section 2-601, preserves the perfect tender doctrine by providing "if goods or tender of delivery fail *in any respect* to conform to the contract" (emphasis added), the buyer has the right to accept the goods, reject the entire shipment, or accept part and reject part.

For example, the buyer contracts to purchase 100 cases of brand X peas to be delivered at the buyer's place of business on or before October 1. On September 28 the seller discovers that there are only 99 cases of brand X in inventory, but there will be another 500 cases within the next two weeks. So the seller tenders delivery of the 99 cases of brand X on October 1, with the promise that the other case will be delivered within three weeks. Since the seller failed to make a perfect tender of 100 cases of brand X, the buyer has the right to reject the entire shipment and hold the seller in breach. Such a rigid rule seems uncharacteristic of the Code's philosophy of finding and preserving a contract whenever possible and inconsistent with the idea that good faith permeates the Code.

Exceptions to the Perfect Tender Rule

Agreement of the Parties If the parties have agreed, for example, that defective goods or parts will not be rejected if the seller is able to repair or replace them within a reasonable time, then the perfect tender rule does not apply.

Cure The term **cure** is not specifically defined in the Code, but it refers to the seller's right to repair, adjust, or replace defective or nonconforming goods. [UCC 2-508]

When any tender or delivery is rejected because of *nonconforming goods* and the time for performance has not yet expired, the seller can notify the buyer promptly of the intention to cure and can then do so *within the contract time for performance.* [UCC 2-508(1)]

For example, Horn sells Gill a white refrigerator, to be delivered on or before September 15. Horn delivers a yellow refrigerator on September 10, and Gill rejects it. Horn can cure by notifying Gill that he intends to cure and by delivering a white refrigerator on or before September 15.

Once the time for performance under the contract has *expired*, the seller can still exercise the right to cure if the seller had *reasonable grounds to believe that the nonconforming tender would be acceptable to the buyer.*

Although frequently the seller tenders nonconforming goods with some type of price allowance, he or she may still have a reasonable belief that the goods will be accepted by the buyer for other reasons. For example, Demsetz has been supplying auto body paint to Hall Body, an auto body paint shop, for several years. Demsetz and Hall have a contract for R-Z type paint. In the past, when Demsetz could not obtain R-Z type paint, he substituted R-Y type paint, and Hall accepted without any objection. Hall signs a new contract for R-Z type paint to be delivered on April 30. Demsetz realizes that, with the paint supply on hand, only half the order can be filled with R-Z type paint, so he completes the other half of the order with R-Y type paint. The order is delivered on April 30. Hall rejects. Demsetz, knowing from their prior course of dealing that

R-Y had always been an acceptable substitute, has "reasonable grounds to believe" that R-Y will be acceptable. Therefore, Demsetz can cure within a reasonable time, even though conforming delivery will occur after the actual time for performance under the contract.

As just pointed out, the seller may offer a price allowance with the tender of nonconforming goods. This frequently creates a presumption that a buyer will accept the fortuitous offer. Suppose a buyer contracts to purchase 100 model Z hand calculators at a price of $20 each from a seller, to be delivered on or before October 1. The seller cannot deliver 100 model Z calculators but tenders 100 new, more sophisticated, more expensive model A–1 calculators at the same price as the 100 model Z calculators contracted for on October 1. The buyer rejects the delivery. If the seller notifies the buyer of intent to cure, the seller has a *reasonable time* (after October 1) to substitute a conforming tender of model Z calculators.

The seller's right to cure substantially restricts the buyer's right to reject. If the buyer refuses a tender of goods as nonconforming but does not disclose the nature of the defect to the seller, the buyer cannot later assert the defect as a defense if the defect is one that the seller could have cured. The buyer must act in good faith and state specific reasons for refusing to accept the goods. [UCC 2-605]

Substitution of Carriers Where an agreed manner of delivery (berthing, loading, or unloading facilities) becomes impracticable or unavailable through no fault of either party, but a commercially reasonable substitute is available, this substitute performance is sufficient tender to the buyer. [UCC 2-614(1)]

For example, a sales contract calls for the delivery of a number of barrels of oil "F.O.B. Stanley Steamer at New York." War breaks out, and the shipping line is prohibited from sailing to New York due to an embargo. The seller will be entitled to make a reasonable substitute tender, perhaps by rail. Note that the seller here is responsible for any additional shipping costs, unless contrary arrangements have been made in the sales contract.

Installment Contracts An **installment contract** is a single contract that requires or authorizes delivery in two or more separate lots to be accepted and paid for separately. In an installment contract, a buyer can reject an installment *only if the nonconformity substantially impairs the value* of the installment and cannot be cured. [UCC 2-612(2) and 2-307] Notice, then, how this is a substantial limitation on the perfect tender rule.

The entire installment contract is breached only when one or more nonconforming installments *substantially* impair the value of the *whole contract*. If the buyer subsequently accepts a nonconforming installment and fails to notify the seller of cancellation, then the contract is reinstated, however. Also, if the buyer brings an action with respect only to past installments or demands performance as to future installments, the aggrieved party has reinstated the contract. [UCC 2-612(3)]

A major issue to be determined is what constitutes *substantial* impairment of the "value of the whole." For example, consider an installment contract for the sale of twenty carloads of plywood. The first carload does not conform to the contract because 9 percent of the plywood in the car deviates from the thickness specifications. The buyer cancels the contract, and immediately thereafter the second and third carloads of plywood arrive at the buyer's place of business. The court would have to grapple with the question of whether the 9 percent of nonconforming plywood substantially impaired the value of the whole.[3]

A more clear-cut example is an installment contract that involves parts of a machine. Suppose that the first part is delivered and is irreparably defective but necessary for the operation of the machine. The failure of this first installment will be a breach of the whole contract. Even when the defect in the first shipment is such that it gives the buyer only a "reasonable apprehension" about the ability or willingness of the seller to properly complete the other installments, the breach on the first installment may be regarded as a breach of the whole.

The point to remember in this discussion is that the UCC substantially alters the right of a buyer to reject the entire contract in installment sales contracts. Such contracts are broadly defined in the UCC, which strictly limits rejection to cases of substantial nonconformity. The following is one such case.

---

3. Forest Products v. White Lumber Sales, Inc., 256 Or. 466, 474 P.2d 1, 8 UCC 178 (1970). The court held that the deviation did not substantially impair the value of the whole contract. Additionally, the court stated that the nonconformity could be cured by an adjustment in the price.

REPUBLIC-ODIN APPLIANCE CORP. v. CONSUMERS PLUMBING & HEATING SUPPLY CO.

Court of Common Pleas of Ohio, 1963.
24 Ohio Opinions 2d 226, 192 N.E.2d 132.

BACKGROUND AND FACTS *Republic-Odin Appliance Corporation, a manufacturer of home water heaters, did a large-scale business with the defendant, Consumers Plumbing and Heating Supply Company, for about seven years. Over the years, however, Consumers Plumbing and Heating Supply engaged in frequent disputes about items on bills rendered by Republic. Consumers Plumbing's president, Friedman, held back $7,000 on a balance due. That was on December 10.*

HODDINOTT, Judge.
*   *   *   *

Then, on December 19th, plaintiff's vice president and general manager, William Lennon, wrote in a letter to Friedman, the following: *   *   *

"In light of your past record of arbitrary deductions, 'misunderstanding of terms,' arbitrary withholding of $7,000.00 and your violation of our selling agreement, and in keeping with our desire to improve our channels of distribution, we are hereby notifying you that we are unwilling to ship to your account for any and all of your four locations.

"Unless payment for your account in full is received in this office by December 23, 1958, we will be forced to take necessary legal action to insure collection."

* * *

Plaintiff brought this action on its account with defendant for heaters sold, freight and parcel post, and prayed for a judgment of $7,465.58 and interest.

* * *

The failure to pay the substantial amount due on this order, following on the heels of the troubled relations of the parties and the unprecedented demands of the defendant put forth as conditions for doing business in the future, is a material breach of contract within the purview of the statute. Plaintiff was justified in repudiating this order. * * *

Plaintiff was also justified in repudiating the other unfilled orders of defendant.

* * * To state it in its simplest terms: If there is one installment contract between seller and buyer and one party breaches it under circumstances indicating he will not perform his duties in the future, then the other party is excused from further performance.

The Uniform Commercial Code, which went into effect in 1962, recognizes that a party to an installment contract has a right to "a continuing sense of reliance and security that the promised performance will be forthcoming when due," the Code makes provision for an adequate assurance of performance. * * *

Consumers Plumbing lost. Republic was awarded $7,465.58 with interest. **JUDGMENT AND REMEDY**

Commercial Impracticability Whenever occurrences unforeseen by either party when the contract was made make performance commercially impracticable, the rule of perfect tender no longer holds. According to UCC 2-615(a), delay in delivery or nondelivery in whole or in part is not a breach when performance has been made impracticable "by the occurrence of a contingency the nonoccurrence of which was a basic assumption on which the contract was made * * *." However, the seller must notify the buyer as soon as it is practicable to do so that there will be a delay or nondelivery.

The notion of commercial impracticability is derived from contract law theories of impossibility and frustration of purpose. Increased costs resulting from inflation do not in and of themselves excuse performance. This is the kind of risk ordinarily assumed by a seller conducting business. The unforeseen contingency must be one that would have been impossible to contemplate in a given business situation.

For example, a major oil company that receives its supplies from the Middle East has a contract to supply a buyer with 100,000 gallons of oil. Because of an oil embargo by OPEC, the seller is prevented from securing oil supplies to meet the terms of this contract. Because of the same embargo, the seller cannot secure oil from any other source. This situation comes fully under the commercial impracticability exception to the perfect tender doctrine.

Sometimes the unforeseen event only *partially* affects the seller's capacity to perform. As a result, the seller is able to fulfill the contract *partially* but cannot tender total performance. In this event, the seller is required to allocate in a fair and reasonable manner any remaining production and deliveries among the contracted customers. The buyer must receive notice of the allocation, with the obvious right to accept or reject the allocation.

For example, a grower of cranberries in the state of Washington, Cran Plan, has contracted to sell this season's production to a number of customers, including the G & G grocery chain. G & G has contracted to purchase 2,000 crates of cranberries. Cran Plan has sprayed some of its bogs of cranberries with a chemical called Green. The Department of Agriculture discovers that there is a potential danger that persons who eat

products sprayed with Green may develop cancer. An order prohibiting the sale of these products is effected. Cran Plan has harvested all the bogs not sprayed with Green, but the production will not allow it to fully meet all contract deliveries. In this case, Cran Plan is required to allocate its production, notifying G & G of the amount it is able to deliver.

Does a picket line at a job site cause a party's performance to become so "impracticable" that the excuse of "impossibility" becomes a valid defense to performance? That is the question to be answered in the following case.

MISHARA CONSTR. CO., INC. v. TRANSIT-MIXED CONCRETE CORP.

Supreme Judicial Court of Massachusetts, 1974.
310 N.E.2d 363.

BACKGROUND AND FACTS *The plaintiff, Mishara Construction Company, Inc., was a general contractor. Mishara was under contract with the Pittsfield Housing Authority for the construction of Rose Manor, a housing project for the elderly. In September 1966, Mishara negotiated with the defendant, Transit-Mixed Concrete Corp., for the supply of ready-mixed concrete to be used on the project. An agreement was reached that Transit would supply all the concrete needed on the project at a price of $13.25 per cubic yard, with deliveries to be made at the times and in the amounts ordered by Mishara. The two parties signed a purchase order on September 21, 1966. The purchase order identified the Rose Manor project and indicated that delivery was to be made as required by the Mishara Construction Company. Performance under this contract was satisfactory to both parties until April 1967.*

In that month a labor dispute disrupted work on the job site. Although work resumed on June 15, 1967, a picket line was maintained on the site until the project was completed in 1969. Throughout this period, with very few exceptions, Transit delivered no concrete because of the picket line, despite frequent requests by Mishara. After notifying Transit of its intention, Mishara purchased the balance of its concrete requirements elsewhere. Mishara then sought damages for the additional cost of the replacement concrete and for the expenses it incurred in locating an alternate source of ready-mixed concrete.

REARDON, Justice.

*   *   *   *

The principal issue in the case was the defendant's claimed excuse of impossibility of performance. The determination of that issue depended on facts and circumstances which were for the jury to decide. *   *   *

*   *   *   *

The excuse of impossibility in contracts for the sale of goods is controlled by the appropriate section of the Uniform Commercial Code, *   *   * § 2-615. That section sets up two requirements before performance may be excused. First, the performance must have become "impracticable." Second, the impracticability must have been caused "by the occurrence of a contingency the non-occurrence of which was a basic assumption on which the contract was made." This section of the Uniform Commercial Code has not yet been interpreted by this court. Therefore it is appropriate to discuss briefly the significance of these two criteria.

With respect to the requirement that performance must have been impracticable, the official Code comment to the section stresses that the reference is to "*commercial* impracticability" as opposed to strict impossibility. [Emphasis added.] This is not a radical departure from the common law of contracts as interpreted by this court. Although a strict rule was originally followed denying any excuse for accident or "inevitable necessity," e.g., Adams v. Nichols, 19 Pick. 275 (1837), it has long been assumed that circumstances drastically increasing the difficulty and expense of the contemplated performance may be within the compass of "impossibility." By adopting the term "impracticability" rather than "impossibility" the drafters of the Code appear to be in accord with Professor Williston who [prior to enactment of the UCC] stated that "the essence of the modern defense of impossibility is that the promised performance was at the making of the contract, or thereafter became, impracticable owing to some extreme or unreasonable difficulty, expense, injury, or loss involved, rather than that it is scientifically or actually impossible."

The second criterion of the excuse, that the intervening circumstance be one which the parties assumed would not occur, is also familiar to the law of Massachusetts. The rule is essentially aimed at the distribution of certain kinds of risks in the contractual relationship. By directing the inquiry to the time when the contract was first made, we really seek to determine whether the risk of the intervening circumstance was one which the parties may be taken to have assigned between themselves. It is, of course, *the very essence of contract that it is directed at the elimination of some risks for each party in exchange for others. Each receives the certainty of price, quantity, and time, and assumes the risk of changing market prices, superior opportunity, or added costs.* [Emphasis added.] It is implicit in the doctrine of impossibility (and the companion rule of "frustration of purpose") that certain risks are so unusual and have such severe consequences that they must have been beyond the scope of the assignment of risks inherent in the contract, that is, beyond the agreement made by the parties. To require performance in that case would be to grant the promisee an advantage for which he could not be said to have bargained in making the contract. "The important question is whether an unanticipated circumstance has made performance of the promise vitally different from what should reasonably have been within the contemplation of both parties when they entered into the contract. If so, the risk should not fairly be thrown upon the promisor." Williston, Contracts (Rev. ed.) § 1931 (1938). The emphasis in contracts governed by the Uniform Commercial Code is on the commercial context in which the agreement was made. The question is, given the commercial circumstances in which the parties dealt: *Was the contingency which developed one which the parties could reasonably be thought to have foreseen as a real possibility which could affect performance?* [Emphasis added.] Was it one of that variety of risks which the parties were tacitly assigning to the promisor by their failure to provide for it explicitly? If it were, performance will be required. If it could not be so considered, performance is excused. The contract cannot be reasonably thought to govern in these circumstances, and the parties are both thrown upon the resources of the open market without the benefit of their contract.

With this backdrop, we consider Mishara's contention that a labor dispute which makes performance more difficult never constitutes an excuse for nonperformance. We think it is evident that in some situations a labor dispute would not meet the requirements for impossibility discussed above. A picket line might constitute a mere inconvenience and hardly make performance "impracticable." Likewise, in certain industries with a long record of labor difficulties, the nonoccurrence of strikes and picket lines could not fairly be said to be a basic assumption of the agreement. Certainly, in general, labor disputes cannot be considered extraordinary in the course of modern commerce. See Restatement: Contracts, § 461, illustration 7 (1932). Admitting this however, we are still far from the proposition implicit in the plaintiff's requests. Much must depend on the facts known to the parties at the time of contracting with respect to the history of and prospects for labor difficulties during the period of performance of the contract, as well as the likely severity of the effect of such disputes on the ability to perform. From these facts it is possible to draw an inference as to whether or not the parties intended performance to be carried out even in the face of the labor difficulty. *Where the probability of a labor dispute appears to be practically nil, and where the occurrence of such a dispute provides unusual difficulty, the excuse of impracticability might well be applicable.* [Emphasis added.] * * * "Rather than mechanically apply any fixed rule of law, where the parties themselves have not allocated responsibility, justice is better served by appraising all of the circumstances, the part the various parties played, and thereon determining liability."

JUDGMENT AND REMEDY
The plaintiff was unsuccessful in obtaining damages from the defendant. The jury determined that this labor dispute would be considered a commercial impracticability under the UCC. Therefore, the defendant was excused from performing under the terms of the contract.

COMMENT
Many commentators on this case do not agree with the judgment. Strikes in and of themselves do not normally excuse performance, so the outcome of this case cannot be considered the general rule.

Destruction of Identified Goods The Code provides that when a casualty occurs that totally destroys *identified goods* under a sales contract through no fault of either party and *before risk passes to the buyer*, the seller and buyer are excused from performance. [UCC 2-613(a)] However, if the goods are only partially destroyed, the buyer can inspect them and either treat the contract as void or accept the damaged goods with an allowance off the contract price.

Consider an example. Acme Appliances has on display six ABC dishwashers of a discontin-ued model. Five are white, and one is harvest gold. No others of that model are available. Jones, who is not a merchant, clearly specifies that she needs the harvest gold dishwasher because it fits into her kitchen's color scheme. Jones buys the harvest gold dishwasher. Unfortunately, before Acme can deliver it, it is destroyed by a fire. In such a case, under Section 2-613, Acme Appliance will not be liable to Jones for failure to deliver the harvest gold dishwasher. The goods here suffered a casualty without fault of either party before the risk of loss passed to the buyer, and the loss was total, so the contract is avoided. Clearly, Acme has no obligation to tender that dishwasher. Of course, Jones has no obligation to pay for it either.

Change the example somewhat. Jones purchases a discontinued dishwasher model but does not specify the color. If the harvest gold dishwasher is destroyed by fire, Acme is still obliged to tender one of the other discontinued models, and Jones is obligated to accept and to make payment. Only if Acme's entire stock of the discontinued model were destroyed by the fire would Acme be excused from performance in this instance.

Assurance and Cooperation   Two other exceptions to the perfect tender doctrine apply equally to the seller and buyer.

The right of assurance stems from the concept that the essential purpose of a contract is performance by both parties, and thus when one party has reason to believe the other party will not perform, it is an undue hardship to force the first party to perform.

The Code provides that should a seller (or buyer) have "reasonable grounds" to believe the buyer (or seller) will not perform as contracted, he or she may "in writing demand adequate assurance of due performance" from the other party; and until such assurance is received, he or she may "suspend" further performance without liability. The grounds for such belief and action must be reasonable. Between merchants, the grounds are determined by commercial standards. [UCC 2-609] The assurances requested also must be reasonable. If such assurances are not forthcoming within a reasonable time (not to exceed thirty days), the failure to respond may be treated as a *repudiation* of the contract.

For example, Sallor has contracted to ship Beyer 100 dozen shirts on or before October 1, with Beyer's payment due within thirty days of delivery. Sallor has made two previous shipments, neither of which has been paid for by Beyer. On September 20, Sallor demands in writing certain assurances of payment (such as payment of the last two orders to bring the account up to date) before Sallor will ship the 100 dozen shirts. If this assurance is reasonable, Sal-

lor can suspend shipment of the shirts without liability pending Beyer's compliance. If Beyer does not provide the payments within a reasonable time (no longer than thirty days), Sallor can hold Beyer in breach of contract without having made the contracted shipment.

Sometimes performance of one party depends on the cooperation of the other. The Code provides that when such cooperation is not forthcoming, the other party can suspend his or her own performance without liability and hold the uncooperative party in breach. [UCC 2-311(3)]

For example, Sallor is required by contract to deliver 1,200 model Z washing machines to locations within the state of California to be specified later by Beyer. Deliveries are to be made on or before October 1. Sallor has repeatedly requested the delivery locations, and Beyer has not responded. The 1,200 model Z machines are ready for shipment on October 1, but Beyer still refuses to give Sallor the delivery locations. Sallor does not ship on October 1. Can Sallor be held liable? The answer is no. Sallor is excused for any resulting delay of performance because of Beyer's failure to cooperate.

BUYER'S OBLIGATIONS

Once the seller has adequately tendered delivery, the buyer is obligated to accept the goods and pay for them according to the terms of the contract. In the absence of any specific agreements, the buyer must:

1. Furnish facilities reasonably suited for receipt of the goods. [UCC 2-503(1)(b)]
2. Make payment at the time and place the buyer *receives* the goods even if the place of shipment is the place of delivery. [UCC 2-310(a)]

Payment

When a sale is made on credit, the buyer is obliged to pay according to credit terms (for example, 60, 90, or 120 days), *not* when the goods are received. The credit period usually begins on the *date of shipment.* [UCC 2-310(d)]

Payment can be made by any means agreed upon between the parties. Cash can be used, but the buyer can also use any other method generally acceptable in the commercial world. If the seller demands cash when the buyer offers a check, credit card, or the like, then the seller must permit the buyer reasonable time to obtain legal tender. [UCC 2-511]

Right of Inspection

Unless otherwise agreed, or for C.O.D. (collect on delivery) goods, the buyer's right to inspect the goods is absolute. This right allows the buyer to verify, before making payment, that the goods tendered or delivered are what were contracted for or ordered. If the goods are not what the buyer ordered, there is no duty to pay. *An opportunity for inspection is therefore a condition precedent to the seller's right to enforce payment.* [UCC 2-513(1)]

Unless otherwise agreed, inspection can take place at any reasonable place and time and in any reasonable manner. Generally, what is reasonable is determined by custom of the trade, past practices of the parties, and the like. The Code also provides for inspection after arrival when goods are to be shipped.

Costs of inspecting conforming goods are borne by the buyer unless agreed otherwise. [UCC 2-513(2)]

C.O.D. Shipments If a seller ships goods to a buyer C.O.D. (or like terms), the buyer can rightfully *reject* them (unless the contract expressly provides for a C.O.D. shipment). The reason is C.O.D. does not permit inspection before payment, and the effect is a denial of the buyer's right of inspection. But when the buyer has agreed to a C.O.D. shipment in the contract or has agreed to pay for the goods upon the presentation of a bill of lading, no right of inspection exists because it was negated by the agreement. [UCC 2-513(3)]

Payment Due—Documents of Title Under certain contracts, payment is due on the receipt of the required documents of title even though the goods themselves may not have arrived at their destination. With C.I.F. and C&F contracts, payment is required upon receipt of the documents

unless the parties have agreed to the contrary. Thus, payment is required prior to inspection, and it must be made unless the buyer knows that the goods are nonconforming. [UCC 2-310(b) and 2-513(3)]

Acceptance

The buyer can manifest assent to the delivered goods in different ways:

1. The buyer can expressly accept the shipment by words or conduct. For example, there is an acceptance if the buyer, after having reasonable opportunity to inspect, signifies agreement to the seller that either the goods are conforming or that they are acceptable despite their nonconformity. [UCC 2-606(1)(a)]
2. Acceptance will be presumed if the buyer has had a reasonable opportunity to inspect the goods and has failed to reject them within a reasonable period of time. [UCC 2-606(1)(b) and 2-602(1)]
3. The buyer accepts the goods by performing any act inconsistent with the seller's ownership. For example, any use or resale of the goods will generally constitute an acceptance. Limited use for the sole purpose of testing or inspecting the goods is not an acceptance, however. [UCC 2-606(1)(c)]

Revocation of Acceptance

Acceptance of the goods by the buyer precludes the buyer from exercising the right of rejection. Acceptance does not in and of itself impair the right of the buyer to pursue other remedies, however. (Remedies are discussed in Chapter 23.) But if the buyer accepts the nonconforming goods and fails to notify the seller of the breach when it is discovered (or when it should have been discovered), then the buyer is barred from pursuing any remedy against the seller. What is at issue here is the necessity of the buyer informing the seller of the breach within a reasonable time. The burden is on the buyer to establish the existence of a breach of contract once the goods are accepted. [UCC 2-607(3)]

After a buyer accepts a lot or a commercial unit, acceptance can still be revoked if the nonconformity *substantially* impairs the value of the unit or lot and if one of the following factors also is present:

1. If acceptance was predicated on the reasonable assumption that the conformity would be cured, and it has not been cured within a reasonable time. [UCC 2-608(1)(a)]
2. If the buyer does not discover the nonconformity, either because it is difficult to discover

before acceptance or because the seller's assurance that the goods are conforming kept the buyer from inspecting the goods. [UCC 2-608(1)(a)]

In the following case, the court made clear that "substantial impairment of the value to the buyer" is the test of whether revocation of purchased goods can occur once the buyer has accepted the goods.

BACKGROUND AND FACTS   *Peckham purchased a new car from Larsen Chevrolet. During the first month and a half after the purchase of the car, he discovered that there was a dent in the hood, the gas tank contained no baffles, the emergency brake was inoperable, the clock and speedometer did not work, and there was no jack or spare tire. Peckham made repeated attempts to have those defects repaired. The repairs were finally completed three months after purchase. Then, a couple of days after that, a fire occurred in the dashboard of the car, damaging the dashboard and the carpeting and rendering the vehicle inoperable. Peckham took the car back to Larsen Chevrolet, demanding that the vehicle be repaired at Larsen's expense, or that the contract be rescinded, or that a new car be provided. A discussion between Peckham and Larsen Chevrolet did not satisfy Peckham, so he orally informed Larsen that he was electing to rescind the contract and demand the return of the purchase price. At a hearing for a summary judgment, Larsen Chevrolet argued that the alleged defects were known by Peckham at the time of purchase. Larsen further denied having received the alleged oral notice of rescission.*

A summary judgment was entered in favor of Larsen Chevrolet. The Idaho Supreme Court stated that "although the action was brought for 'rescission,' we treat it as one for revocation of acceptance under the Uniform Commercial Code."

PECKHAM v. LARSEN CHEVROLET
Supreme Court of Idaho, 1978.
99 Idaho 675, 587 P.2d 816.

SHEPARD, Chief Justice.

* * * *

Sale of the automobile here is a sale of goods governed by Article 2 of the Uniform Commercial Code. I.C. § 28-2-711 sets forth in general a buyer's remedies. It is provided therein that a buyer may cancel the contract if the seller's delivery is such that it gives the buyer a right to reject or a right to revoke acceptance of the goods.

As noted, this action was originally brought as one for "rescission" and Larsen Chevrolet and General Motors argue that because there is no provision in the Uniform Commercial Code for this remedy, it is unavailable to the buyer. The Code has, in most instances, abandoned the use of the term "rescission" in favor of terms such as "cancellation or termination." However, it has been held, and the commentators agree, that rescission and revocation of acceptance amount to the same thing under the Uniform Commercial Code, particularly since cancellation is a remedy available to a buyer who has established justifiable grounds for revocation of acceptance. I.C. § 28-2-711(1); We, therefore, view and treat Peckham's action for "rescission" as one for "revocation of acceptance" under I.C. § 28-2-608. The principal issue in this case is whether Peckham has sufficiently established the elements necessary for a revocation of acceptance under. I.C. § 28-2-608, so as to avoid a summary judgment in favor of the defendants.

Before a buyer may revoke acceptance under § 28-2-608, he must first show that the goods are nonconforming and that the nonconformity substantially impairs the value of the goods to the buyer. *   *   *

Thereafter, if the buyer knew of the nonconformity when he accepted the goods, it is necessary that he show he acted with a reasonable assumption that the nonconformity would be cured, but that it was not seasonally cured. I.C. § 28-2-608(1)(a). If the buyer did not know of the nonconformity when he accepted, he must show that his acceptance was reasonably induced, either by the difficulty of discovering the nonconformity before acceptance or by the seller's assurances. I.C. § 28-2-608(1)(b); [citation.] Finally, the revocation of acceptance by the buyer must occur within a reasonable time after the buyer discovers the defect or should have discovered it, and before any substantial change in condition of the goods which is not caused by their own defects. Such revocation of acceptance is not effective until the buyer notifies the seller. I.C. § 28-2-608(2).
*   *   *   *

Considering the requisite elements for a revocation of acceptance and the facts construed most favorably toward Peckham, a factual dispute exists as to whether Peckham orally notified Larsen Chevrolet of his desire to cancel or rescind the contract (revocation of acceptance) immediately following the fire. Such is denied by Larsen Chevrolet. Depending upon the resolution of that disputed fact, also unresolved is whether Peckham's alleged oral or written notice of cancellation of the contract took place within a reasonable time.

As explained by comment 4 to § 28-2-608(2) of the Uniform Commercial Code, revocation of acceptance is required within .   .   . a reasonable time after discovery of the grounds for such revocation. Since this remedy will be generally resorted to only after attempts at adjustment have failed, the reasonable time period should extend in most cases beyond the time in which notification of breach must be given, beyond the time for discovery of non-conformity after acceptance and beyond the time for rejection after tender. The parties may by their agreement limit the time for notification under this section, but the same sanctions and considerations apply to such agreements as are discussed in the comment on manner and effect of rightful rejection.

It would appear that no particular form or content of notice of revocation of acceptance is required if the notice is sufficient to inform the seller that the buyer has revoked and identify the particular goods as to which he has revoked.

A further factual issue appears to remain regarding the conformity of the goods. Here there appears to be a dispute as to whether the goods were accepted by Peckham in a defective nonconforming condition or whether he accepted the goods upon assurance by the seller that the defects would be remedied. As stated by I.C. § 28-2-608, comment 2:

[r]evocation of acceptance is possible only where the nonconformity substantially impairs the value of the goods to the buyer. For this purpose, the test is not what the seller had reason to know at the time of contracting; the question

is whether the nonconformity is such as will in fact cause a substantial impairment of value to the buyer though the seller had no advance knowledge as to the buyer's particular circumstances.

An exhaustive discussion of what constitutes substantial impairment to a buyer is unnecessary since it is held each case must be examined on its own merits to determine what is a substantial impairment of value to the particular buyer.

The court reversed the summary judgment in favor of the defendants.   **JUDGMENT**
The case was remanded for further proceedings consistent with the opin-   **AND REMEDY**
ion.

Notice of Revocation Required   Revocation of acceptance will not be effective until notice is given to the seller, and that must occur within a reasonable time after the buyer either discovers *or should have discovered* the grounds for revocation. Also, revocation must occur before the goods have undergone any substantial change that was not caused by their own defects (such as spoilage). [UCC 2-608(2)]

Partial Acceptance   If some of the goods delivered do not conform to the contract, and the seller has failed to cure, the buyer can make a *partial* acceptance. [UCC 2-601(c)] The same is true if the nonconformity was not reasonably discoverable before acceptance. A buyer cannot accept less than a single *commercial unit*, however. According to Section 2-105, "commercial unit" means a unit of goods that, by commercial usage, is viewed as a "single whole" for purposes of sale, division of which would materially impair the character of the unit, its market value, or its use. A commercial unit can be a single article (such as a machine), or a set of articles (such as a suite of furniture or an assortment of sizes), or a quantity (such as a bale, gross, or carload), or any other unit treated in the trade as a single whole.

Anticipatory Repudiation

The buyer and the seller have *concurrent* conditions of performance. But what if before the time for either performance, one party clearly communicates to the other the intention not to perform? Such an action is a breach of the contract by *anticipatory repudiation*. When this occurs, the aggrieved party can, according to UCC 2-610:

1.   For a commercially reasonable time await performance by the repudiating parties.
2.   Resort to any remedy for breach even if the aggrieved party has notified the repudiating party that he or she awaits the latter's performance and has urged retraction.
3.   In either case, *suspend performance* or proceed in accordance with the provisions of this article on the seller's right to identify goods notwithstanding breach or to salvage unfinished goods. [Emphasis added.]

The key to anticipatory breach is that the repudiation takes place *prior* to the time that the party is required under contract to tender performance. The nonbreaching party has a choice of two responses. He or she can treat the repudiation as a final breach by pursuing a remedy; or he or she can wait, hoping that the repudiating party will decide to honor the obligations required by the contract despite the avowed intention to renege.

Should the latter course be pursued, the Code permits the breaching party (subject to some limitations) to "retract" his or her repudiation. The retraction can be by any method that clearly indicates an intent to perform. Once retraction is made, the rights of the repudiating party under the contract are reinstated. [UCC 2-611]

To illustrate: Sallor has contracted to deliver to Beyer 100,000 tons of coal on or before October 1. On September 15, Sallor tells Beyer that he will not make delivery until December 1. This statement of intent not to deliver until two months after the required delivery date is an anticipatory breach, and Beyer could pursue any of the remedies discussed in the next chapter.

But suppose Beyer responds that he expects Sallor to perform as obligated. Then, on September 28, Sallor informs Beyer that the 100,000 tons will be delivered as contracted, and a tender is made on October 1. Beyer has learned in the meantime that the same amount of coal can be purchased elsewhere (later in October) at a lower price. Therefore, Beyer refuses the tender, claiming Sallor breached the contract on September 15.

In this case Beyer, not Sallor, is in breach of contract. Sallor's notice was a retraction of the earlier repudiation. Since Beyer had not resorted to a remedy, or materially changed his position, or indicated the repudiation was final, the retraction reinstated Sallor's rights under the contract. Therefore, Sallor's proper tender obligated Beyer to accept and pay for the coal tendered, and Beyer's refusal constitutes a breach.

QUESTIONS AND CASE PROBLEMS

1. Sallor contracts to ship to Beyer 100 model Z television sets. The terms of delivery are F.O.B. Sallor's city, by Green Truck Lines, with delivery on or before April 30. On April 15, Sallor discovers that because of an error in inventory control, all model Z sets have been sold and the stock has not been replenished. Sallor has model X, a similar but slightly more expensive unit, in stock. On April 16, Sallor ships 100 model X sets, with notice that Beyer will be charged the model Z price. Beyer (in a proper manner) rejects the model X sets tendered on April 18. Sallor does not wish to be held in breach of contract, even though he has tendered nonconforming goods. Discuss Sallor's options.

2. Sallor contracts to deliver to Beyer 1,000 bushels of corn at market price. Delivery and payment are to be made on October 1. On September 10, Beyer informs Sallor that because of financial reverses she cannot pay on October 1. Sallor immediately notifies Beyer that he is holding Beyer in breach of contract. On September 15, Sallor files suit for breach of contract. On October 3, Beyer files an answer to Sallor's lawsuit. Beyer claims that had Sallor tendered delivery on October 1, she would have paid for the corn. Since no delivery was tendered, Beyer claims she cannot be held liable. Discuss whether Sallor can hold Beyer liable in breach.

3. Sallor has contracted to deliver to Beyer 1,000 cases of brand Greenie peas on or before October 1. Beyer is to specify the means of transportation twenty days prior to date of shipment. Payment for the peas is to be made by Beyer upon tender of delivery. On September 10, Sallor prepares the 1,000 cases for shipment. Sallor asks Beyer how he would like the goods to be shipped, but Beyer does not respond. On September 21, Sallor demands in writing assurance that Beyer will be able to pay upon tender of the peas. Sallor's demand is that the money be placed in escrow prior to October 1 in a bank in Beyer's city named by Sallor. Beyer does not respond to any of the requests made by Sallor, but on October 5 he wants to file suit against Sallor for breach of contract for failure to deliver the peas as contracted. Discuss Sallor's liability for failure to tender delivery on October 1.

4. Sallor contracts to deliver 100 model X color television sets to a new retail customer, Beyer, on May 1, with payment to be made upon delivery. Sallor tenders delivery in her own truck. Beyer notices that one or two cartons have scrape marks on them. Beyer inquires of Sallor whether the sets might have been damaged upon loading. Sallor assures Beyer that the sets are in perfect condition. Beyer tenders Sallor a check, but Sallor refuses the check, claiming that the first delivery to new customers is always for cash. Beyer promises to have the cash within two days. Sallor leaves the sets with Beyer, who stores them in a warehouse pending an "opening sale" date. Two days later, Beyer opens some of the cartons and discovers that a number of the televisions are damaged beyond ordinary repair. Sallor claims Beyer has accepted the sets and is in breach by not paying on delivery. Discuss fully Sallor's claims.

5. Desilets Granite Company manufactures monuments. Stone Equalizer makes machinery. Desilets contracted for a stone splitting machine. When the machine was delivered, problems developed with its operation. By agreement between the two parties, the machine was returned for modifications and corrections. It was agreed that when the renovated stone splitter was redelivered, Desilets would make the final

payment on the contract. Stone Equalizer shipped the renovated machine but refused to unload it until payment was tendered. That day Desilets attached the machine and filed suit against Stone Equalizer for breach of warranty. Under order of the court, Desilets was subsequently allowed to operate the renovated machine, but the machine proved unsatisfactory and unfit for its purpose. Desilets therefore rejected the machine and sued Stone Equalizer for breach. Did Desilets justifiably revoke acceptance of the purchased product? [Desilets Granite Co. v. Stone Equalizer Corp., 340 A.2d 65 (Vt. 1975)]

6. On October 1, Ingle purchased a combine to be used on his farm from Marked Tree Equipment Company, which promised that the machine would be made to function on soft ground. The combine was delivered, and Ingle used it for about three days and then stopped. Wet soil from heavy rains caused the combine to bog down so that Ingle was unable to use it on his farm. Later, during the month of November, Ingle attempted to use the combine approximately fifteen times. When Ingle's first payment came due, on December 1, he made the payment, relying on the salesperson's promises that the machine would be made to work. Thereafter, Ingle did nothing with the combine until the following year, when he attempted once again to harvest with it. His attempts were unsuccessful, so he refused to make the second annual payment, which came due in December. Marked Tree sued Ingle for the balance of the purchase price. Will Marked Tree recover? [Ingle v. Marked Tree Equipment Co., 244 Ark. 1166, 428 S.W.2d 286 (1968)]

7. On October 2, 1956, the United States entered into a contract with Transatlantic under which Transatlantic promised to carry 10,000 tons of wheat from a port in the Gulf of Mexico to Iran. No route was specified in the contract. A month later, while en route to Iran, Transatlantic received notice that Egypt had just closed the Suez Canal. Transatlantic's anticipated route had been through the Suez, so it immediately changed its course and went to Iran by passing around the Cape of Good Hope. Transatlantic then sued the United States for the additional costs (15 percent) that it had incurred. The United States refused, claiming

that no route was ever specified in the agreement between the parties. Can Transatlantic recover? [Transatlantic Financing Corp. v. United States, 363 F.2d 312 (D.C.Cir. 1966)]

8. Goddard and Ishikawajima-Harima Heavy Industries entered into a contract under which Ishikawajima agreed to furnish Goddard with as many boats as Goddard would require. On January 28, 1965, Goddard sent a written order to Ishikawajima for a number of boats. On February 17, 1965, just after Ishikawajima had begun manufacturing the boats, its plant was completely destroyed by fire. Is Ishikawajima liable to Goddard for its failure to deliver the boats? [Goddard v. Ishikawajima-Harima Heavy Industries Co., 29 A.D.2d 754, 287 N.Y.S.2d 901 (1968)]

9. Fram Corp. furnished eighteen fuel filter/separator units called for by a contract with Crawford, who was constructing a building for the United States Navy. Crawford received and installed all eighteen units. The contract price for the units was $55,564.20. Crawford did not pay $6,298.50 of the total, claiming that he had not accepted the equipment because it was defective. Was Crawford right? [United States for the Use of Fram Corp. v. Crawford (C.A.5 Ga.) 443 F.2d 611 (1971)]

10. Holterbosch contracted with Groulich to provide quality food for a pavilion at the 1964 New York World's Fair. The food was to be equal in quality to that presented to agents of Holterbosch at a meeting (prior to the contract signing) where different platters of food were displayed and sampled. The contract was for 1 million units of food to be delivered over a one-year period. On April 23, 1964, the first delivery of food—955 units—was found to be inferior to the contract samples presented at the prior meeting and was therefore rejected as unacceptable. Holterbosch agreed to allow Groulich to tender another batch of food. Groulich delivered 2,520 units. Many of them were found to be unacceptable by both employees of Holterbosch and patrons at the New York World's Fair exhibit. Holterbosch cancelled the contract. Groulich sued for out-of-pocket expenses and lost profits. Who wins? [Groulich Caterer, Inc. v. Hans Holterbosch, Inc., 243 A.2d 253 (N.Y. 1968)]

CHAPTER 23

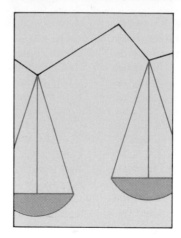

SALES
Remedies of Buyer and Seller for Breach of Sales Contracts

When a sales contract is breached, the aggrieved party may have a number of remedies from which to choose. [UCC 2-703 and 2-711] These remedies range from retaining the goods to requiring the breaching party's performance under the contract. The general purpose of these remedies is to put the aggrieved party "in as good a position as if the other party had fully performed." It is important not only that the nonbreaching party know what remedies are available but that he or she know which remedy is most appropriate for a given situation. [UCC 1-106(1)]

REMEDIES OF THE SELLER

The remedies available to a seller when the buyer is in breach under the UCC include:

1. The right to withhold delivery of the goods.
2. The right to stop a carrier or bailee from delivering goods to an insolvent or defaulting buyer.

3. A limited right to reclaim goods in the possession of an insolvent buyer.
4. The right to identify and/or resell goods to the contract.
5. The right to recover the purchase price plus incidental damages in certain cases.
6. The right to recover damages for the buyer's nonacceptance or repudiation of the contract.
7. The right to cancel the sales contract.

The Right to Withhold Delivery of the Goods

In general, sellers can withhold or discontinue performance of their obligations under a sales contract when buyers breach. If a seller discovers that the buyer is insolvent, the seller can refuse to deliver the goods unless the buyer pays in cash. [UCC 2-702(1)]

Consider an example. On September 1, Simpson receives an order from Bentley for ten cases of ballpoint pens to be shipped on September 13. Bentley wants the goods put on his thirty-day open account. On September 6, Bentley files involuntary bankruptcy. On September 9, Simpson learns of Bentley's bankruptcy and therefore refuses to ship the goods on September 13. The court-appointed trustee of Bentley's assets now claims that Simpson has breached his contract with Bentley by not shipping the goods on September 13 as agreed. The trustee will not prevail because Simpson was under no obligation to ship goods on credit to an insolvent buyer. The trustee could, of course, still obtain the goods for the benefit of Bentley's bankrupt estate by paying cash for them.

If a buyer has wrongfully rejected, revoked acceptance, failed to make proper and timely payment, or repudiated a part of the contract, the seller can withhold delivery of the particular goods in question. Furthermore, the seller can withhold the entire undelivered balance of the goods if the buyer's breach is material. [UCC Sec. 2-703]

The Right to Stop a Carrier or Bailee from Delivering Goods to an Insolvent Buyer

If the seller has delivered the goods to a carrier or bailee, but the buyer has not as yet received them, the goods are said to be *in transit*. If the seller learns of the buyer's insolvency while the goods are in transit, the seller can stop the carrier or bailee from delivering the goods to the buyer on the basis of the buyer's insolvency, regardless of the quantity shipped. A person is insolvent under the UCC when that person ceases to pay "his debts in the ordinary course of business or cannot pay his debts as they become due or is insolvent within the meaning of the federal bankruptcy law." [UCC 1-201(23)]

If the buyer is not insolvent but repudiates the contract or gives the seller some other right to withhold or reclaim the goods, the seller can stop the goods in transit only if the quantity shipped is at least a carload, a truckload, a planeload, or a larger shipment. [UCC 2-705(1)]

Consider an example. On January 1, Beel orders a carload of onions from Sneed. Sneed is to ship them on January 8, and Beel is to pay for them on January 10. Sneed ships on time, but Beel does not pay on January 10. As soon as Sneed learns of this, she orders the carrier to stop the carload in transit. Since the carload is still on its way to Beel's city, the carrier is able to stop shipment. Beel cannot claim that Sneed and the carrier have performed a wrongful act by stopping the shipment, for a seller can always stop a carload of goods in transit when a buyer commits some breach of contract that gives the seller the right to withhold or reclaim the goods. Had the contract called for a shipment of ten bags of onions, rather than a carload, Sneed could not have stopped the goods in transit unless Beel was unable to pay for the goods (insolvent).

In order to stop delivery, the seller must *timely notify* the carrier or other bailee that the goods are to be returned or held for the seller. If the carrier has sufficient time to stop delivery, then the goods must be held and delivered according to the instructions of the seller, who is liable to the carrier for any additional costs incurred. If the carrier fails to act properly, it will be liable to the seller for any loss. [UCC 2-705(3)]

The right of the seller to stop delivery is lost when:

1. The buyer obtains possession of the goods.
2. The carrier acknowledges the buyer's rights by reshipping or storing the goods for the buyer.
3. A bailee of the goods other than a carrier acknowledges that he or she is holding the goods for the buyer.
4. A negotiable document of title covering the goods has been negotiated to the buyer. [UCC 2-705(2)]

The Right to Reclaim Goods in the Possession of an Insolvent Buyer

Whenever a seller discovers that the buyer has *received* goods on credit while insolvent (as previously defined), the seller can demand return of the goods, if such demand is made within ten days of the buyer's receipt of the goods. The seller can demand and reclaim the goods at any time if the buyer misrepresented his or her solvency in writing within three months prior to the delivery of the goods. [UCC 2-702(2)]

The seller's right to reclaim, however, is subject to the rights of a good faith purchaser or other buyer in the ordinary course of business who purchases the goods from the buyer before the seller reclaims.[1]

---

1. *A buyer in the ordinary course of business* is a person who, in good faith and without knowledge that the sale violates the ownership rights or security interest of a third party, buys in ordinary course from a person (other than a pawnbroker) in the business of selling goods of that kind. [UCC 1-201(9)]

It is obvious that successful reclamation of goods under the UCC constitutes preferential treatment as against the buyer's other creditors. Because of this, the Code provides that reclamation *bars* the seller from pursuing any other remedy as to these goods. [UCC 2-702(3)] (This probably is irrelevant when the buyer is insolvent.)

In the following case, the court looks at the question of whether the trustee of a bankrupt company can prevail over the seller's right to reclaim goods under UCC 2-702(2).

IN RE FEDERAL'S INC.
United States Court of Appeals,
Sixth Circuit, 1977.
553 F.2d 509.

BACKGROUND AND FACTS On August 10, 1972, Panasonic delivered to Federal's Inc. on credit electronic goods valued at approximately $64,000. On August 16, Federal's filed for bankruptcy. Two days later, on August 18, Panasonic demanded, pursuant to UCC 2-702(2), a return of the merchandise delivered to Federal's. It was clearly stipulated at trial that Federal's had intended to pay for the goods at the time they were ordered and received. Federal's insolvency was clear at the time Federal's received Panasonic's goods. At trial, a district judge ruled in favor of the bankruptcy trustee on all issues. Panasonic appealed, claiming its right of reclamation under UCC 2-702(2). The appellate court examines the question of whether the UCC prevails over the Federal Bankruptcy Act.

ENGEL, Circuit Judge.

*   *   *   *

We have previously held that the rights of an unpaid seller of goods under § 2-702 are tantamount to those available to a defrauded seller under common law. However, we must agree with the district court's observation that § 2-702 is more than a mere codification of common law. Nevertheless, we are persuaded that the right asserted by the seller under § 2-702(2) is a valid state-created right of ownership. Because that right conceptually has its antecedents in the historical and equitable right of a defrauded seller to reclaim the goods he has sold to an insolvent buyer, we hold it cannot be said to arise "*solely* by force of statute" under § 1(29). (emphasis added).

*   *   *   *

The development of the Uniform Commercial Code, and its universal acceptance marks this provision as anything but spurious. The Code represents the combined empirical judgment of 49 states of the Union that the irrebuttable presumption of fraud in § 2-702(2) conforms to the experience in the majority of cases. While we should not flinch from upholding the primacy of the Bankruptcy Act if it is otherwise demanded, a construction of the Act which would invalidate the application of the U.C.C. must at least give pause. The Code is far more than a spurious state law created by special interests for their own special protection. As pointed out by Judge Friendly in United States v. Wegematic Corp., 360 F.2d

674, 676 (2d Cir. 1966), the Code was, even in 1966, "well on its way to becoming a truly national law of commerce *   *   *"

Likewise, we are undisturbed by the argument that under equitable principles in most jurisdictions, rescission was not available unless it was shown that the defrauding buyer did not intend to pay for the goods, an element absent here by stipulation of fact. Observation of traditional equity principles does not require, however, a blind adherence to an immutable rule. Quite the contrary, we see in the Code provision an adaptation of the historical equitable remedy to modern commercial life. Faced wth an expanding commercial community, state legislatures have recognized that contractual relations now require more certainty. By fixed rules, of uniform applicability, citizens are able to deal with one another more reliably and with greater dispatch. Thus proof of intent not to pay, always difficult to establish, is eliminated. Also the "reasonable time" for rescission under common law, which might vary greatly according to the equities of a particular case, is made certain by the flat imposition of a ten-day period.

The result, therefore, of the Code is not so much a multiplication of grounds on which a seller may rescind a sale, *   *   * as it is the achievement of certainty and reliability in the determination of rights. While the insolvent buyer (and thus his receiver or trustee) may face a greater risk of loss of the purchased goods where timely demand is made within the period, the right to retain them is more certain than under the common law where no demand is made within ten days and where there has been no express written misrepresentation of solvency. The Code thereby confers certain benefits upon the bankrupt estate by allowing the receiver more promptly to ascertain the rights of the bankrupt and in eliminating sources of litigation. Further, section 702(3) by providing that successful reclamation specifically excludes all other remedies, insures that the result is both predictable and final.

The Court of Appeals reversed the district court's ruling in favor of the bankruptcy trustee. Panasonic could reclaim the merchandise.

JUDGMENT AND REMEDY

*The 1978 Bankruptcy Code has a provision (Section 546(c)) which is directly on point. That section specifically provides that the rights and powers of the trustee are "subject to any statutory right or common law right of a seller *   *   * if the debtor has received such goods while insolvent *   *   *." The seller need only make a written demand for return within ten days after receipt by the buyer.*

COMMENTS

The Right to Identify and/or Resell Goods to the Contract after the Buyer Has Breached

Sometimes a buyer breaches or repudiates a sales contract while the seller is still in possession of finished or partially manufactured goods. In this event, the seller can identify to the contract the conforming goods that are still in his or her possession or control even if they were not identified at the time of the breach. Then the seller can resell the goods, holding the buyer liable for any loss. [UCC 2-704]

When the contracted goods are unfinished at the time of breach, the seller can treat the unfinished goods in two ways. First, the seller can cease manufacturing the goods and resell them for scrap or salvage value. Second, the seller can complete the manufacture, identify the goods to the contract, and resell them, holding the buyer liable for any deficiency. In choosing between these two alternatives, the seller must exercise reasonable commercial judgment in order to mitigate the loss and obtain maximum realization of value from the unfinished goods. [UCC 2-704(2)]

The Right to Resell the Goods

When a seller possesses or controls the goods at the time of the buyer's breach (because of the buyer's wrongful rejection or revocation of acceptance, failure to pay, or repudiation of the contract), or when the seller rightfully reacquires the goods by stopping them in transit, then the seller has the right to resell the goods. The resale must be made in good faith and in a commercially reasonable manner. The seller can recover any deficiency between the sales price and the contract price, along with **incidental damages,** defined as those costs to the seller resulting from the breach. [UCC 2-706(1) and 2-710] Obviously, it would be unfair for a buyer to profit from his or her own breach. Therefore, the Code encourages the seller's use of the remedy of resale by providing that the seller is *not liable* to the buyer for any profits made on the resale. [UCC 2-706(6)]

Consider some examples. Sallor contracts on Monday to sell his car to Beyer for $5,000, with delivery of the car and payment for it due on the following Monday. When Sallor tenders delivery on Monday, Beyer refuses to accept or pay for the car. Sallor informs Beyer that he will resell the car at a private sale. Sallor sells the car to Devins for $2,000 on Tuesday. The following day, Sallor sues Bayer for $3,200—$3,000 being the difference between the resale price and the contract price and $200 being the value of incidental damages—the expense of arranging the sale. In this example, the seller would be unlikely to recover the $3,000 difference between the resale price and the contract price, because the resale was obviously not made in good faith or in a commercially reasonable manner. But if Sallor can prove incidental damages of $200, he will be likely to recover them.

Now Sallor contracts with Beyer to sell a prize bull for $10,000, with delivery and payment due on Monday. On Monday, Sallor tenders delivery of the prize bull, but Beyer refuses to accept or pay for it. Sallor tells Beyer that he is going to sell the bull at an area livestock auction the next day. At the auction, there are few bidders for the prize bull. Beyer decides to bid on the bull himself and obtains it for $9,000. Sallor then demands $1,100 in damages from Beyer—$1,000 for the contract price less the resale price plus $100 for incidental expenses in getting the prize bull to the auction. In this example, the total sum could probably be recovered by Sallor, assuming he can substantiate his incidental expenses. The livestock auction was a reasonable place for resale, and the resale was done in a commercially reasonable manner.

Finally, Sallor contracts on Monday to sell 4,000 heads of romaine lettuce to Beyer for 30 cents per head, with delivery and payment due on Friday. On Wednesday, Sallor has 14,000 heads of romaine lettuce in his inventory, but he has not yet identified the 4,000 he intends to sell to Beyer. On that day, Beyer telephones Sallor to inform him that he will not accept or pay for the lettuce. Beyer claims that, since the 4,000 heads of romaine lettuce for his contract have not yet been identified, Sallor cannot resell and recover damages from Beyer. Beyer is incorrect here. Sallor has the right to identify the 4,000 heads of lettuce for Beyer's contract and the right to resell the lettuce. Sallor can recover the difference between the resale price received and the contract price of 30 cents per head, plus any incidental damages. [UCC 2-704(1), 2-706(1), and 2-710]

The resale can be private or public, and the goods can be sold as a unit or in parcels. The seller must give the original buyer reasonable notice of the resale, unless the goods are perishable or will rapidly decline in value. [UCC 2-706(2) and 2-706(3)] In the latter case, the seller has a duty to resell the goods as rapidly as possible in order to mitigate damages. A bona fide purchaser in a resale takes the goods free of any of the rights of the original buyer, even if the seller fails to comply with these requirements of the Code. [UCC 2-706(5)]

The Right to Recover the Purchase Price Plus Incidental Damages

Before the UCC was adopted, a seller could not sue for the purchase price of the goods unless title had passed to the buyer. Under the Code, an unpaid seller can bring an action to recover the purchase price and incidental damages, but this is only under the following unusual circumstances:

1. When the buyer has accepted the goods and has not revoked acceptance, in which case title would have passed.
2. When conforming goods have been lost or damaged after the risk of loss has passed to the buyer.
3. When the buyer has breached after the goods have been identified to the contract and the seller is unable to resell the goods. [UCC 2-709(1)]

An action to recover the purchase price and incidental damages, available to the seller only under the circumstances just described, is distinct from an action to recover damages for breach of the sales contract.

If a seller sues for the contract price of goods that he or she has been unable to resell, the goods must be held for the buyer. The seller can resell at any time prior to the collection of the judgment from the buyer, but the net proceeds from the sale must be credited to the buyer. This is just an example of the duty to mitigate damages.

To illustrate: Suppose Sallor has contracted to sell Beyer 200 tablecloths with the name of Beyer's restaurant inscribed on them. Sallor delivers the 200 tablecloths to Beyer, but Beyer refuses to pay. Or suppose Sallor tenders the 200 tablecloths to Beyer, but Beyer refuses to accept them. In either case, Sallor has, as a proper remedy, an action for the purchase price.

In the first situation, Beyer accepted conforming goods, but he is in breach by failure to pay. In the second situation, the goods have been identified to the contract, but it is obvious that Sallor could not sell the tablecloths inscribed with Beyer's restaurant's name to anyone else. Thus, both situations fall under UCC 2-709.

The Right to Damages for Buyer's Wrongful Repudiation or Non-acceptance

If a buyer repudiates a contract or wrongfully refuses to accept the goods, a seller can maintain an action to recover the damages that were sustained. Ordinarily, the amount of damages will equal the difference between the contract price and the market price (at the time and place of tender of the goods) plus incidental damages. [UCC 2-708(1)] The time and place of tender are frequently given by such terms as F.O.B., F.A.S., C.I.F., and the like, which determine whether there is a shipment or destination contract.

If the difference between the contract price and the market price is too small to place the seller in the position that he or she would have been in if the buyer had fully performed, the proper measure of damages is the seller's lost profits, including a reasonable allowance for overhead and other incidental expenses. [UCC 2-708(2)]

The question of wrongful repudiation of a sales contract concerning specially manufactured roller wheels for skateboards is the subject of the next case.

BACKGROUND AND FACTS   *Chicago Roller Skate Manufacturing Company entered into a sales contract with Sokol Manufacturing Company to provide the latter with truck and wheel assemblies with plates and hangers for use in the manufacture of skateboards. Chicago sent the requested goods to Sokol. At that time there was a balance due of $12,860. But since the skateboard fad had ended, Sokol decided to return, without Chicago's consent, a quantity of the goods purchased. These goods were not suitable for any other use; nor could they be resold. Chicago held them for seven months. Chicago offered Sokol a credit of 70 cents per*

CHICAGO ROLLER SKATE MANUFACTURING COMPANY v. SOKOL MANUFACTURING COMPANY
Supreme Court of Nebraska, 1970.
185 Neb. 515, 177 N.W.2d 25.

unit, which Sokol neither accepted nor rejected. Finally, Chicago disassembled, cleaned, and rebuilt the units to make them suitable on normal roller skates. The rebuilt units had a reasonable value of between 67 cents and 69 cents. Thus, the salvage operation cost Chicago Roller Skate $3,540.76. Profits lost amounted to an additional $2,572. Chicago, disregarding its expense, credited Sokol with 70 cents per unit and brought suit for the balance due of $4,285. It recovered this sum in a judgment in the trial court. Sokol appealed.

NEWTON, Justice.

*   *   *   *

Section 1-103, U.C.C., provides: "Unless displaced by the particular provisions of this act, the principles of law and equity, including the law merchant and the law relative to capacity to contract, *   *   * or other validating or invalidating cause shall supplement its provisions."

Section 1-106, U.C.C., provides in part: "(1) The remedies provided by this act shall be liberally administered to the end that the aggrieved party may be put in as good a position as if the other party had fully performed but neither consequential or special nor penal damages may be had except as specifically provided in this act or by other rule of law."

Section 1-203, U.C.C. states: "Every contract or duty within this act imposes an obligation of good faith in its performance or enforcement."

Section 2-718(4), U.C.C., provides: "Where a seller has received payment in goods their reasonable value or the proceeds of their resale shall be treated as payments *   *   *."

In accordance with section 2-709, U.C.C., plaintiff was entitled to hold the merchandise for defendant and recover the full contract price of $12,860. Plaintiff did not elect to enforce this right, but recognizing that there was no market for the goods or resale value and that they were consequently worthless for the purpose for which they were designed, it attempted to mitigate defendant's damages by converting the goods to other uses and credited defendant with the reasonable value of the goods as converted or rebuilt for use in roller skates. In so doing, plaintiff was evidencing good faith and conforming to the general rule requiring one damaged by another's breach of contract to reduce or mitigate damages. *   *   *

The Uniform Commercial Code contemplates that it shall be supplemented by existing principles of law and equity. It further contemplates that the remedies provided shall be liberally administered to the end that an aggrieved party shall be put in as good a position as it would have been in if the contract had been performed. Here the buyer was demanding of the seller credit for the full contract price for goods that had become worthless. The seller was the aggrieved party and a return of worthless goods did not place it in as good a position as it would have been in had the contract been performed by the buyer paying the contract price. On the other hand, the crediting to defendant of the reasonable value of the rebuilt materials and recovery of the balance of the contract price did reasonably reimburse plaintiff. This procedure appears to be contemplated by section 2-718(4), U.C.C., which requires that a seller paid in goods credit the buyer with the reasonable value of the goods.

It is the defendant's theory that since the goods were not resold or held for the buyer, the seller cannot maintain an action for the price. We agree with this proposition. We also agree with defendant in its contention that the controlling measure of damages is that set out in section 2-708(2), U.C.C. This section provides that the measure of damages is the profit which the seller would have made from full performance by the buyer, together with any incidental damages resulting from the breach and costs reasonably incurred. Defendant overlooks the provision for allowance of incidental damages and costs incurred. The loss of profits, together with the additional costs or damage sustained by plaintiff amount to $6,112.76, a sum considerably in excess of that sought and recovered by plaintiff. Although the case was tried by plaintiff and determined on an erroneous theory of damages, the error is without prejudice to defendant. There being no cross-appeal, the judgment of the district court is affirmed.

Sokol had to pay the $4,285 to Chicago Roller Skate Manufacturing Company.

JUDGMENT AND REMEDY

The Right to Cancel the Sales Contract

A seller can cancel a contract if the buyer wrongfully rejects or revokes acceptance of conforming goods, fails to make proper payment, or repudiates the contract in part or in whole. The contract can be canceled with respect to the goods directly involved, or the entire contract can be canceled if the breach is material. A material breach is one that substantially impairs the value of the entire contract. [UCC 2-703]

The seller must notify the buyer of the cancellation, and at that point all remaining obligations of the seller are discharged. The buyer is not discharged from all remaining obligations but is in breach and can be sued under any of the subsections mentioned in UCC 2-703 and in UCC 2-106(4).

If the seller's cancellation is not justified, then the seller is in breach of the contract, and the buyer can sue for appropriate damages.

Seller's Lien

In certain circumstances, a seller has a lien, or legal interest, in goods being sold. Technically, a lien is a right that is incident to the sale rather than a remedy for breach of contract.

A seller's lien enables the seller to retain possession of the goods until the buyer pays for them.

The seller's lien can be waived or lost by: (1) express agreement, (2) acts inconsistent with the lien's existence, (3) payment or tender of payment by the buyer, or (4) voluntary and unconditional delivery of the goods to a carrier or other bailee or to the buyer or an authorized agent of the buyer.

If the sales agreement provides for an extension of credit to the buyer, the seller normally has no lien on the goods, since the act of extending credit is inconsistent with the existence of the lien. The seller will have a lien on the goods, however, if the buyer becomes insolvent or if the credit period expires while the goods are still in the seller's possession.

The tender of payment or the actual payment of the debt that the lien secures will ordinarily discharge the lien. This occurs when the buyer pays the full price for the goods and the seller gives up possession. When the buyer gives a promissory note, the lien will ordinarily *not* be discharged until the note is paid even if the seller relinquishes possession of the goods.

Finally, sellers lose their liens when they voluntarily deliver possession of the goods to the buyer or to an authorized agent of the buyer. The lien is not lost, though, where delivery is qualified or where the buyer obtains possession fraudulently.

Consider the following illustration. Williams, the plaintiff, sold his Chevrolet sedan to the Greers, the defendants. The defendants paid $235 by check and $90 in cash. After the Greers received possession of the Chevy, they stopped payment on the check. Williams went to court to regain possession of the auto by enforcing his seller's lien. The court upheld his complaint, allowing him to regain possession of the auto and to keep it until the Greers paid the $235. Essentially, the Greers had obtained possession fraudulently; therefore, they had a voidable title. Williams could validly enforce his lien because he had the right to void the title.

REMEDIES OF THE BUYER

Under the UCC, the remedies available to the buyer include:

1. The right to reject nonconforming or improperly delivered goods.
2. The right to recover identified goods upon the seller's insolvency.
3. The right to obtain specific performance.
4. The right to replevy the goods.
5. The right to retain the goods and enforce a security interest in them.
6. The right to cancel the contract.
7. The right of cover.
8. The right to recover damages for nondelivery or repudiation by the seller.
9. The right to recover damages for breach in regard to accepted goods.

The Right to Reject Nonconforming or Improperly Delivered Goods

If either the goods or the seller's tender of the goods fails to conform to the contract in *any respect*, the buyer can reject the goods. If some of the goods conform to the contract, the buyer can keep the conforming goods and reject the rest. [UCC 2-601]

Timeliness and Reason for Rejection Required Goods must be rejected within a reasonable time and the seller must be seasonably notified. [UCC 2-602] Furthermore, the buyer must designate particular defects that are ascertainable by reasonable inspection. Failure to do so precludes the buyer from using such defects

to justify rejection or to establish breach when the seller could have cured the defects if they had been stated reasonably. [UCC 2-605] After rejecting the goods, the buyer cannot exercise any right of ownership over them. If the buyer acts inconsistently with the seller's ownership rights, the buyer will be deemed to have accepted the goods. [UCC 2-606]

Merchant Buyer's Duties When Goods Are Rejected If a *merchant* buyer rightfully rejects goods, and the seller has no agent or business at the place of rejection, the buyer is required to follow any reasonable instructions received from the seller with respect to the goods controlled by the buyer. The buyer is entitled to reimbursement for the care and cost entailed in following the instructions. [UCC 2-603] The same requirement holds if the buyer rightfully revokes acceptance. [UCC 2-608(3)]

If no instructions are forthcoming and the goods are perishable or threaten to speedily decline in value, the buyer can resell the goods in good faith, taking the appropriate reimbursement from the proceeds. [UCC 2-603(1)] If the goods are not perishable, the buyer may store them for the seller's account or reship them to the seller. [UCC 2-604]

The Right to Recover Identified Goods from an Insolvent Seller

If a buyer has made a partial or a full payment for goods that remain in the possession of the seller, the buyer can recover the goods if the seller becomes insolvent within ten days after receiving the first payment and if the goods are identified to the contract. To exercise this right, the buyer must tender to the seller any unpaid balance of the purchase price. [UCC 2-502]

The Right to Obtain Specific Performance

A buyer can obtain specific performance when the goods are unique or when the buyer's remedy at law is inadequate. [UCC 2-716(1)] Ordinarily, a suit for money damages will be sufficient to place a buyer in the position he or she would have occupied if the seller had fully performed. However, when the contract is for the purchase of a particular work of art, patent, copyright, or similarly unique item, money damages may not be sufficient. Under these circumstances, equity will require the seller to perform exactly (a remedy of specific performance) by delivering the particular goods identified to the contract.

To illustrate: Casey contracts to sell an antique car to Smith for $30,000, with delivery and payment due on June 14. Smith tenders payment on June 14, but Casey refuses to deliver. Can Smith force delivery of the car? Probably, because the antique car is unique. Therefore, Smith can obtain specific performance of the contract from Casey.

The Right to Replevy the Goods

Replevin is an action to recover specific goods in the hands of a breaching party who is unlawfully withholding them from the other party. The buyer can replevy goods identified to the contract if the seller has repudiated or breached the contract. *Additionally,* buyers must usually show that they were unable to cover for the goods after a reasonable effort.

Consider the following example. On July 1, Sallor contracts to sell her tomato crop to Beyer, with delivery and payment due on August 10. By August 1, it is clear that the local tomato crop will be bad and that the price of tomatoes is going to rise. Sallor therefore contracts to sell her tomato crop to Green for a higher price and then informs Beyer that she will not deliver on August 10 as agreed. Beyer indicates that cover is unavailable and that he is therefore going to bring a replevin action against Sallor to force her to deliver her tomatoes to Beyer on August 10.

This replevin action will succeed. Although a tomato crop is not unique, a buyer of scarce goods for which no cover is available has a right to a replevin. In a normal tomato year, cover would probably have been available and Beyer would be limited to an action for damages.

The Right to Retain and Enforce a Security Interest in the Goods

Buyers who rightfully reject goods or who jus-

tifiably revoke acceptance of goods that remain in their possession or control have a security interest in the goods. The security interest encompasses any payments the buyer has made for the goods as well as any expenses incurred with regard to inspection, receipt, transportation, care, and custody of the goods. [UCC 2-711(3)] A buyer with a security interest in the goods is a "person in the position of a seller." This gives the buyer the same rights as an unpaid seller. Thus, the buyer can resell, withhold delivery, or stop delivery of the goods. A buyer who chooses to resell must account to the seller for any amounts received in excess of the security interest. [UCC 2-711(3) and 2-706(6)]

The Right to Cancel the Contract

When a seller fails to make proper delivery or repudiates the contract, the buyer can cancel or rescind the contract. In addition, a buyer who has rightfully rejected or revoked acceptance of the goods can cancel or rescind. Under these circumstances, the buyer can cancel or rescind that portion of the contract directly involved in the breach. If the seller's breach is material and substantially impairs the value of the whole contract, the buyer can cancel or rescind the whole contract. Upon notice of cancellation, the buyer is relieved of any further obligations under the contract but still retains all remedy rights that can be assessed against the seller.

The Right of Cover

In certain situations, buyers can protect themselves by obtaining *cover,* that is, by substituting goods for those that were due under the sales contract. This option is available to a buyer who has rightfully rejected goods or revoked acceptance. It is also available where the seller repudiates the contract or fails to deliver the goods. In obtaining cover, the buyer must act in good faith without unreasonable delay. [UCC 2-712]

After purchasing substitute goods, the buyer can recover from the seller the difference between the cost of cover and the contract price, plus incidental and consequential damages less the expenses that were saved as a result of the seller's breach. [UCC 2-712 and 2-715]

Consequential damages are any loss suffered by the buyer that the seller could have foreseen (had reason to know) at the time of contract and any injury to the buyer's person or property proximately resulting from a breach of warranty. [UCC 2-715(2)]

Suppose Sallor contracts to sell Beyer 10,000 pounds of sugar at 20 cents per pound. Delivery is to be on or before November 15. Sallor knows that Beyer is going to use the sugar to make candy for Christmas sales. Beyer usually makes a $15,000 profit from these sales. Sallor fails to deliver on November 15. Beyer attempts to purchase the sugar on the open market, but she must pay 30 cents a pound and take delivery on December 8. Because of this late delivery date, Beyer can prepare and sell only half as much Christmas candy as usual.

Beyer can recover from Sallor the difference between the cover price and the contract price of sugar ($3,000 − $2,000 = $1,000) plus any incidental damages (costs incurred in effecting the cover). In addition, since Sallor knew the reason for Beyer's purchase (sale of Christmas candy), Beyer is entitled to consequential damages. In this case, Beyer could probably include as part of her damages against Sallor the lost profits from the Christmas candy sales ($7,500— half of the $15,000 profit usually made).

Buyers are not required to cover, and failure to do so will not bar them from using any other remedies that are available under the UCC. [UCC 2-712(3)] But a buyer who fails to cover may *not* be able to collect the consequential damages that could have been avoided by purchasing substitute goods. [UCC 2-715(2)(a)] Thus the UCC encourages buyers to cover in order to mitigate damages.[2] For example, if a wholesaler is supposed to supply a grocer wth eggs for resale, and the wholesaler is unable to deliver them, the grocer has the option of covering. If the grocer covers, he or she can recover any lost profits resulting from the wholesaler's breach of the contract. If the grocer does not cover, and has no eggs to sell, he or she cannot recover lost profits.

---

2. UCC 2-712(3) and UCC 2-715(2)(a) are inconsistent.

The Right to Recover Damages for Nondelivery or Repudiation

If a seller repudiates the sales contract or fails to deliver the goods, the buyer can sue for damages. The measure of recovery is the difference between the contract price and the market price of the goods at the time that the buyer *learned* of the breach. The market price is determined at the place where the seller was supposed to deliver the goods. In appropriate cases, the buyer can also recover incidental and consequential damages less the expenses that were saved as a result of the seller's breach. [UCC 2-713] Note that the damages here are based upon the time and place a buyer would normally obtain cover.

Consider an example. Billings orders 10,000 bushels of wheat from Sneed for $5 a bushel, with delivery due on June 14 and payment due on June 20. Sneed does not deliver on June 14. On June 14, the market price of wheat is $5.50 per bushel. Billings chooses to do without the wheat. He sues Sneed for damages for nondelivery. Billings can recover $5,000 plus any expenses the breach may have caused him to incur. Here the measure of damages is the market price less the contract price at the date that Billings was to have received delivery. (Any expenses Billings saved by the breach would have to be deducted from the damages.)

The Right to Recover Damages for Breach in Regard to Accepted Goods

A buyer who has accepted nonconforming goods must notify the seller of the breach within a reasonable time after the defect was or should have been discovered. Otherwise, the buyer cannot complain about defects in the goods. [UCC 2-607(3)] In addition, the parties to a sales contract can insert a provision requiring the buyer to give notice of any defects in the goods within a certain prescribed period. Such a requirement is ordinarily binding on the parties.

Measure of Damages If a Warranty is Breached
When the seller breaches a warranty, the measure of damages equals the difference between the value of the goods as accepted and their value

if they had been delivered as warranted. The buyer can recover all damages resulting from the breach of warranty as well as incidental and consequential damages. [UCC 2-714]

BACKGROUND AND FACTS   *Alafoss agreed to sell Premium Corp. of America (PCA) a large quantity of women's coats made of Icelandic sheep wool. PCA approved samples and ordered 8,200 coats. One of the special features of the samples was a detachable solid white fur collar. Several months after delivery of the coats, PCA discovered that, among other defects, the majority of the coats had discolored fur collars. After an unsuccessful attempt at treating the collars (paid for by Alafoss), PCA was able to obtain an offer of only $25 per coat, apparently because of the defects and discoloration. Alafoss was unable to produce a higher offer, so PCA sold 3,376 nonconforming coats to a third party for approximately $20 per coat. Alafoss then sued for the unpaid contract price. PCA counterclaimed for damages for breach of warranty. At trial, the court held that Alafoss had indeed breached warranties of quality, and it entered a net judgment for PCA in the amount of $133,275 (plus costs). The U.S. Court of Appeals now examines the question of whether PCA adequately proved its damages.*

ALAFOSS, H. F. v. PREMIUM CORP. OF AMERICA, INC.
United States Court of Appeals, Eighth Circuit, 1979.
599 F.2d 232.

BRIGHT, Circuit Judge.

*   *   *   *

The legal standard for determining PCA's damages in this case is set forth in Minn.Stat.Ann. § 336.2-714(2), which provides:

"(2) The measure of damages for breach of warranty is the difference at the time and place of acceptance between the value of the goods accepted and the value they would have had if they had been as warranted, unless special circumstances show proximate damages of a different amount."

In applying that standard, the district court took the unit cost of the wrap coats to PCA, $88.11, as the value of each coat as warranted, at the time and place of acceptance. The court determined the actual value of each nonconforming coat at the time and place of acceptance to be $25. The court then calculated PCA's damages from the breach by multiplying both unit values by 3,736, the number of nonconforming coats left over after the sales program ended, and subtracting the total value of the coats as accepted from the value they would have possessed if they had been as warranted. The resulting difference amounted to $238,758.96.

In calculating the damage PCA sustained because of the nonconforming coats in the above manner, the district court appears to have overlooked certain "special circumstances show[ing] proximate damages of a different amount." [UCC 2-714(2)] First, evidence introduced at trial indicates that PCA anticipated that, even if all of the wrap coats conformed to sample, it would be unable to sell somewhere between twenty-five and fifty percent of the coats during the mail-marketing program. Such "normal leftover" coats would have been sold in bulk at a price less than cost, precisely as PCA did here with the leftover nonconforming coats. To the extent that such normal leftover coats would have existed in the absence of any breach by Alafoss, the proper measure of damages proximately caused by Alafoss' breach is the difference between the value of leftover conforming coats if sold in bulk and the value of the nonconforming coats sold in bulk.

Second, because the nonconformities for which Alafoss is responsible may have caused more coats to be left over than would have been the case absent the breach, the district court should have distinguished between the number of coats that would normally have been left over and the number of additional coats left over due to the nonconformities. As to those additional leftover coats (but not as to the coats that would have been left over even if no breach existed), the proper measure of damages is that applied by the district court to all coats—that is, at the time and place of acceptance, the difference between the value of the coats if they had been as warranted and the coats' value as actually delivered.

Thus, the proper computation of PCA's damages proximately resulting from Alafoss' breach requires, in addition to the findings already made by the district court, a determination of (1) the number of coats that would have been left over absent any breach, and (2) the value of those normal leftover coats. The record as it stands does not reveal those quantities. We note, however, that the PCA customers' letters referred to above, indicating that coats were returned by customers for reasons other than the nonconformities attributable to Alafoss, constitute strong evidence that such returned coats would have been left over even if Alafoss had complied fully with the terms of the sales agreement. Therefore, the damage award should be substantially reduced to reflect the actual loss PCA sustained for coats that would have been left over regardless of the breach.

JUDGMENT
AND REMEDY

The Court of Appeals affirmed the district court's determination of the liability of Alafoss for breach of warranties. However, it reversed the damage award and remanded the case for further consideration of damages consistent with this opinion. In particular, the trial court was directed to receive additional evidence concerning the number of coats that normally would have been left over (unsold) absent any breach.

Suit by a Buyer's Customer Resulting from the Seller's Breach of Warranty   When a buyer resells defective goods that were originally sold by a breaching seller, the buyer's customer can sue the buyer. Under these circumstances the buyer has two alternatives:

1.   The buyer can notify the seller of the pending litigation. The notice should state that the seller can come in and defend, and it should also state that the seller will be bound by the buyer's action if the seller does not defend within a reasonable time after receipt of the notice. [UCC 2-607(5)(a)]
2.   The buyer can also defend against the customer's suit and later bring an action against the original seller. This situation arises most frequently where there is a manufacturer-dealer arrangement—for example, where a car dealer sells a defective automobile and the customer sues the dealer but not the manufacturer.

Other Measures of Damages   The Code also allows for two additional methods or remedies for damages for accepted goods. Both can also be applied where there has been a breach of warranty.

The first applies where the buyer has accepted *nonconforming* goods. The buyer is entitled to recover for any loss "resulting in the ordinary course of events *   *   * as determined in any manner which is reasonable." Thus, this remedy is available for both a breach of warranty situation and any other failure of the seller to perform according to the contracted obligations. [UCC 2-714(1)]

The second remedy is extremely important to a buyer, as the buyer not only has possession of the goods but also determines the amount of damages. The UCC permits the buyer, with proper notice to the seller, to deduct all or any part of the damages from the price still due and payable to the seller. [UCC 2-717]

Suppose Sallor is under contract to deliver 100 pairs of dress shoes at $50 each to Beyer. The shoes are tendered, and upon inspection Beyer discovers that 10 pairs are high-quality work shoes, not dress shoes. Beyer accepts all 100 pairs and notifies Sallor of the breach. At the time for contracted payment by Beyer, Beyer notifies Sallor that she will not be able to sell the work shoes as quickly or for the same price or profit as the dress shoes, and she is therefore tendering a check for $4,750 instead of the full $5,000 to reflect this loss. If Sallor accepts and cashes Beyer's check, Beyer's measurement of damages is final.

When the buyer still has the goods, the courts often must grapple with the interpretation of the basic damages formula in UCC 2-714(2) versus circumstances where damages of different amounts are proven.

STATUTE OF LIMITATIONS FOR ACTIONS BROUGHT UNDER THE UNIFORM COMMERCIAL CODE

An action brought by a buyer or seller for breach of contract must be commenced under the Code *within four years after the cause of action accrues.* By agreement in the contract, the parties can reduce this period to not less than one year, but they cannot extend the period beyond the stated four years. [UCC 2-725(1)]

A cause of action accrues for breach of warranty when the seller makes tender of delivery. This is the rule even if the aggrieved party is unaware that the cause of action has accrued. [UCC 2-725(2)] In addition to filing suit within the four-year period, an aggrieved party must ordinarily notify the breaching party of a defect within a reasonable time. [UCC 2-607(3)(a)]

Future performance warranties (those that expressly or impliedly take effect in the future)

are not breached until the time for performance begins. The statute of limitations also begins to run at that time.

For example, Beyer purchases a central air-conditioning unit for Beyer's restaurant. The unit is warranted to keep the temperature below a certain level. The unit is installed in the winter, but when summer comes, the restaurant does not stay cool. Therefore, this warranty was breached in the summer and not when the unit was delivered in the winter. The statute of limitations did not begin to run until the summer.

Actions Not Falling within the Uniform Commercial Code

When a buyer or seller brings suit on a legal theory unrelated to the Code, the limitations periods specified above do not apply, even though the claim relates to goods.

For example, Beyer buys tires for his automobile. The tires prove to have an inherently dangerous defect. Four years and one month after purchasing the tires, Beyer loses control of the car and injures several passengers as well as himself. Beyer can bring a suit against the tire manufacturer based on strict liability in tort. The suit will not be governed by the Code's statute of limitations, but rather by the state's tort statute of limitations.

CONTRACTUAL PROVISIONS AFFECTING REMEDIES

The parties to a sales contract can vary their respective rights and obligations by contractual agreement. Certain restrictions are placed on the ability of parties to contract to limit their rights and remedies under the Code, but the common provisions that the parties frequently include are:

1. The liquidation or limitation of damages.
2. The limitation of remedies.
3. The waiver of defenses.

Liquidated Damages and Limitation of Damages

The parties can provide that a specified amount of damages will be paid in the event that either party breaches. These damages, called liquidated damages, must be reasonable in amount and approximately equal to the anticipated or actual loss caused by the breach. If the provision is valid, the aggrieved party is limited to recovering only the amount of damages as agreed. If the amount of liquidated damages is unreasonably large, the provision is void as a penalty, and the court will determine the appropriate damage. [UCC 2-718]

Consider as an example the sale of an uncommon antique. Sallor contracts with Beyer to sell it for $3,000. The contract contains a liquidated damages clause that holds the breaching party liable for $1,000 in case of a breach by either party. Payment and delivery of the antique are due on January 1. Beyer tenders payment on that date, but Sallor refuses to deliver for no valid reason. Can Beyer demand $1,000 in damages? Because we are dealing with an uncommon antique, Beyer will probably be able to recover. Sallor's breach might cause Beyer a loss of $1,000 in that the object in question is probably not easily acquired on the open market for the price of $3,000. If, instead, the object in question were easily obtainable for the agreed price, then Beyer probably would not be able to recover the $1,000. The normal measure of damages would then be the market price of the object less the contract price. The $1,000 damage clause in the contract would, in essence, be imposing a penalty upon Sallor and therefore would be void under UCC 2-718(1). The court could determine that a smaller damage was appropriate, however.

A buyer often makes a down payment when a contract is executed. If the buyer defaults and the contract contains a liquidated damages provision, the buyer can recover only the part of the down payment that exceeded the amount specified as liquidated damages. The buyer is entitled to this sum as restitution. If the contract contains no provision for liquidated damages, the seller's damages are deemed to be 20 percent of the purchase price or $500, whichever is less. [UCC 2-718(2)(b)] The amount by which the buyer's down payment exceeded this sum must be returned to the buyer. If the seller can prove that his or her actual damages are higher, the buyer

can recover only the excess over the seller's actual damages.

For example, Beyer pays $1,250 down on a $10,000 lathe. Beyer then breaches, and Sallor offers no proof of the actual damages. In the absence of a liquidated damages clause, Beyer is entitled to restitution of $750 ($1,250 less $500). If Beyer had put $350 down on a $500 lathe, Beyer would be entitled to $250 ($350 less $100, which is 20 percent of the purchase price).

Limitation of Remedies

A seller and a buyer can expressly provide for remedies in addition to those provided in the Code. They can also provide remedies in lieu of those provided in the Code, or they can change the measure of damages. The seller can provide that the buyer's only remedy upon breach of warranty will be repair or replacement of the item, or the seller can limit the buyer's remedy to return of the goods and refund of the purchase price. A remedy that is so provided is in addition to remedies provided in the Code unless the parties expressly agree that the remedy is exclusive of all others. [UCC 2-719(1)]

If the parties state that a remedy is exclusive of all other remedies, then it is the sole remedy. But when circumstances cause an exclusive remedy to fail of its essential purpose, the remedy will no longer be exclusive. [UCC 2-719(2)]

For example, a sales contract that limits the buyer's remedy to repair or replacement fails of its essential purpose if the item cannot be repaired and no replacements are available.

For example, Bing buys a motorcycle from merchant Simple. The sales contract is accompanied by an express warranty stating that there is an exclusive remedy of repair or replacement of defective parts. The contract explicitly provides that Simple will not be responsible for consequential loss. Bing discovers numerous defects in her motorcycle after only a few days' use. After discovering each defect, she returns the motorcycle for repairs. Some of the parts are out of stock and will take months to arrive at Simple's repair station. Bing sues Simple. A trier of fact in this situation may return a verdict for Bing in an amount far exceeding the cost of repairs. The reason is that the exclusive remedy of repair or replacement of defective parts would have failed in its essential purpose, since the motorcycle could not operate as it should, free of defects.

In the following case, the court examines a limitation clause in a sales contract concerning *when* a claim can be brought for inferior quality wool.

BACKGROUND AND FACTS   *Wilson Trading Corp. entered into a contract with David Ferguson, Ltd. for the sale of yarn. A clause in the contract stated that "no claims relating to excessive moisture content, short weight, count variations, twist, quality or shade shall be allowed if made after weaving, knitting, or processing, or more than 10 days after receipt of shipment." In an apparent contradiction to this clause, defendant David Ferguson, Ltd., failed to make payment because, according to the defendant, after the yarn was cut and knitted into sweaters and then washed, the color changed in a way that made the sweaters unmarketable. At trial, plaintiff Wilson Trading Corp. won summary judgment for the contract price of the yarn, on the ground that the notice of the alleged breach of warranty for defect in the coloration of the yarn was not given within the time expressly limited by the contract. The appellate division affirmed the trial court's decision without an opinion and the buyer appealed.*

WILSON TRADING CORP. v. DAVID FERGUSON, LTD.
Court of Appeals of New York, 1968.
23 N.Y.2d 398, 297 N.Y.S.2d 108, 244 N.E.2d 685.

JASEN, Judge.
*   *   *   *

The defendant on this appeal urges that the time limitation provision on claims in the contract was unreasonable since the defect in the color of the yarn was latent and could not be discovered until after the yarn was processed and the finished product washed.

Defendant's affidavits allege that its sweaters were rendered unsaleable because of latent defects in the yarn which caused "variation in color from piece to piece and within the pieces." *   *   * Indeed, the plaintiff does not seriously dispute the fact that its yarn was unmerchantable, but instead *   *   * relies upon the failure of defendant to give notice of the breach of warranty within the time limits prescribed by paragraph 2 of the contract.

Subdivision (3) (par. [a]) of section 2-607 of the Uniform Commercial Code expressly provides that a buyer who accepts goods has a reasonable time after he discovers or should have discovered a breach to notify the seller of such breach. Defendant's affidavits allege that a claim was made immediately upon discovery of the breach of warranty after the yarn was knitted and washed, and that this was the earliest possible moment at which the defects could reasonably be discovered in the normal manufacturing process. *   *   *

However, the Uniform Commercial Code allows the parties, within limits established by the code, to modify or exclude warranties and to limit remedies for breach of warranty. *   *   *

We are, therefore, confronted with the effect to be given the time limitation provision in paragraph 2 of the contract.
*   *   *   *

Parties to a contract are given broad latitude within which to fashion their own remedies for breach of contract (Uniform Commercial Code, § 2-316, subd. [4]; §§ 2-718–2-719). Nevertheless, it is clear from the official comments to section 2-719 of the Uniform Commercial Code that it is the very essence of a sales contract that at least minimum adequate remedies be available for its breach. "If the parties intend to conclude a contract for sale within this Article they must accept the legal consequence that there be at least a fair quantum of remedy for breach of the obligations or duties outlined in the contract. Thus any clause purporting to modify or limit the remedial provisions of this Article in an *unconscionable manner* is subject to deletion and in that event the remedies made available by this Article are applicable as if the stricken clause had never existed." (Uniform Commercial Code, § 2-719, official comment 1; emphasis supplied.)

It follows that contractual limitations upon remedies are generally to be enforced unless unconscionable. *   *   *

However, it is unnecessary to decide the issue of whether the time limitation is unconscionable on this appeal for section 2-719 (subd. [2]) of the Uniform Commercial Code provides that the general remedy provisions of the code apply when "circumstances cause an exclusive or limited remedy to fail of its essential purpose". As explained by the official comments to this section: "where an apparently fair and reasonable clause because of circumstances fails in its purpose or operates to deprive either party of the substantial value of the bargain, it must give way to the general remedy provisions of this article." (Uniform Commercial Code, § 2-719, official comment 1.) Here, paragraph 2 of the contract bars all claims for shade and other specified defects made after knitting and processing. Its effect is to eliminate any remedy for shade defects not reasonably discoverable within the time limitation period. It is true that parties may set by agreement any time not manifestly unreasonable whenever the code "requires any action to be taken within a reasonable time" (Uniform Commercial Code, § 1-204, subd. [1]), but here the time provision eliminates all remedy for defects not discoverable before knitting and processing and section 2-719 (subd. [2]) of the Uniform Commercial Code therefore applies.

Defendant's affidavits allege that sweaters manufactured from the yarn were rendered unmarketable because of latent shading defects not reasonably discoverable before knitting and processing of the yarn into sweaters. If these factual allegations are established at trial, the limited remedy established by paragraph 2 has failed its "essential purpose" and the buyer is, in effect, without remedy. The time limitation clause of the contract, therefore, insofar as it applies to defects not reasonably discoverable within the time limits established by the contract, must give way to the general code rule that a buyer has a reasonable time to notify the seller of breach of contract after he discovers or should have discovered the defect. (Uniform Commercial Code, § 2-607, subd. [3], par. [a].) *   *   *

In sum, there are factual issues for trial concerning whether the shading defects alleged were discoverable before knitting and processing, and, if not, whether notice of the defects was given within a reasonable time after the defects were or should have been discovered. If the shading defects were not reasonably discoverable before knitting and processing and notice was given within a reasonable time after the defects were or should have been discovered, a further factual issue of whether the sweaters were rendered unsaleable because of the defect is presented for trial.

The judgment in favor of the seller was reversed. The case was remanded for a new trial.   **JUDGMENT AND REMEDY**

Limiting Consequential Damages   A contract can limit or exclude consequential damages provided the limitation is not unconscionable. When the buyer is a consumer, the limitation of consequential damages for personal injuries resulting from a breach of warranty is *prima facie* unconscionable. The limitation of consequential damages is not necessarily unconscionable where the loss is commercial in nature—for example, lost profits and property damage. [UCC 2-719(3)]

Waiver of Defenses

A buyer can be precluded from objecting to a breach of warranty by a seller in certain situations. For example, when a buyer purchases on credit, the seller usually assigns the note or account to a financial institution in order to obtain ready cash. In order to facilitate the assignment of these notes or accounts, the seller will include a waiver of defense clause in the sales contract. By entering into the contract, the buyer agrees not to assert against the assignee defenses that may apply to the seller. In essence, the buyer must complain directly to the seller, and the buyer cannot withhold payment for breach of warranty. If the owner of the assignment clause is a holder in due course of the buyer's note, no defenses can be asserted against the owner-assignee, even if the contract contains no waiver of defense clause. [UCC 9-206]

In such a case buyers are in the same position they would be in if they had signed a waiver. Because of this, many states, including those that have adopted the Uniform Consumer Credit Code, have invalidated such clauses when the sale is for consumer goods. In addition, Federal Trade Commission rules provide that in consumer purchases on credit, any personal defense of the debtor-buyer against the seller is equally applicable against *any* holder, including a holder in due course. Therefore, these clauses are invalid in consumer transactions.

QUESTIONS AND CASE PROBLEMS

1.   Sallor contracts to ship to Beyer via ABC Truck Line 100 cases of brand Knee High corn, F.O.B. Sallor's city, at $6.50 per case. Beyer is to make a 10 percent down payment on the date of shipment. The payment is to be received at Sallor's place of business before shipment occurs. Sallor ships the corn as contracted, although he has not yet received the down payment, and the goods arrive in Beyer's city. There they remain in the delivery van. Since Beyer failed to make the down payment, Sallor orders ABC not to make the delivery to Beyer's warehouse. Beyer claims that the transit had ended and that Sallor had no right to stop the delivery of the corn. Discuss the validity of Beyer's claim and Sallor's action.

2.   Sallor has contracted to sell Beyer 500 washing machines of a certain model at list price. Sallor is to ship the goods on or before December 1. Sallor produces 1,000 of this model washing machine but has not as yet prepared Beyer's shipment. On November 1, Beyer repudiates the contract. Discuss the remedies available to Sallor.

3.   Beyer has contracted with Sallor for the purchase and delivery of 100 model Z dryers. At the time for that contracted tender, Sallor tenders 80 model Z dryers and 20 model X dryers. Sallor does not have 100 model Z dryers in stock and does not expect to acquire any for at least three months. Beyer wants 100 model Z dryers or none at all. Discuss the remedies available to Beyer under these circumstances.

4.   Beyer has contracted to purchase 500 pairs of shoes from Sallor. Sallor manufactures the shoes and tenders delivery to Beyer. Beyer accepts the shipment. Later, upon inspection, Beyer discovers that 10 pairs of the shoes are poorly made and will have to be sold to customers as seconds. If Beyer decides to keep all 500 pairs of shoes, what remedies are available to her?

5.   Beyer is an antique car collector. He contracts to purchase spare parts for a 1938 engine from Sallor.

These parts are not made any more and are scarce. To get the contract with Sallor, Beyer has had to pay 50 percent of the purchase price in advance. On May 1, Beyer sends the payment, which is received on May 2. On May 3, Sallor, having found another buyer willing to pay substantially more for the parts, informs Beyer that he will not deliver as contracted. That same day Beyer learns that Sallor is insolvent. Sallor has the parts, and Beyer wants them. Discuss fully any possible remedies available to Beyer to get these parts.

6. As a result of inquiries by Sumitomo, a steel manufacturer, Goodson supplied Sumitomo with a written statement of its solvency on February 7, 1968. On February 25, 1968, Goodson and Sumitomo entered into a contract for the sale of steel to be shipped from Japan. Goodson received the steel on June 24, 1968, about two months after Sumitomo had shipped it. On July 30, 1968, Sumitomo learned that Goodson was insolvent and had been insolvent for the entire month of February 1968. The same day, Sumitomo attempted to reclaim the steel from Goodson's trustee in bankruptcy. Will Sumitomo succeed? In Re Goodson Steel Corp., 488 F.2d 776 (5th Cir. 1974).

7. Westmoreland Metal Manufacturing Company made school furniture. In 1955 Willred Company entered into a contract with Westmoreland to be its exclusive distributor of school furniture in the metropolitan New York area. Under this contract, Westmoreland made a number of shipments of furniture to Willred, which Willred resold to the New York Board of Education. The distributorship contract between Willred and Westmoreland was to end in December 1957, but Westmoreland, without legal justification, terminated the contract in February 1956. Just before Westmoreland breached the contract, it made a large shipment of furniture to Willred that amounted to about half the furniture that Willred had just ordered from Westmoreland. Much of the furniture was shipped in damaged condition, requiring Willred to repair it extensively before it could be resold. In addition, Willred was forced to purchase a large quantity of school furniture on the open market to satisfy a current contract with the New York Board of Education. Finally, Willred had to rent a small amount of furniture in order to satisfy its contractual obligations

to the New York Board of Education. Which of these expenditures, if any, can Willred recoup from Westmoreland? [Willred Co. v. Westmoreland Metal Mfg. Co., 200 F.Supp. 59 (E.D.Pa.1961)]

8. In a contract between Associated Metals & Minerals Corp. and Kaiser Trading Company, Associated promised to deliver to Kaiser 4,000 tons of cryolite over the next sixteen months. After Associated had delivered about one-eighth of the cryolite to Kaiser, it repudiated the contract. Kaiser sought to enforce the contract and requested the court to grant it specific performance against Associated. Kaiser presented convincing proof at trial that only a few hundred tons of cryolite were available on the open market and that Kaiser needed the 4,000 tons that Associated had promised to deliver in order for Kaiser to fulfill its contractual obligations to a number of other industrial companies. Should the court grant specific performance in this case? [Kaiser Trading Co. v. Associated Metals and Minerals Corp., 321 F.Supp. 923 (N.D.Cal. 1970)]

9. Kaiden placed a $5,000 deposit on a Rolls-Royce in August. The order form did not specify a delivery date, but correspondence between the parties indicated delivery was expected in November. On November 21, Kaiden notified the automobile dealer that she had purchased another Rolls-Royce elsewhere and requested a refund of her deposit. Under the liquidated damages clause of the written contract, the dealer was to retain the entire cash deposit in the event of a breach by the purchaser. The car was sold before Kaiden brought suit to recover her deposit. The dealer's actual damages amounted to $2,075. Should the court allow the dealer to retain the $5,000? [Lee Oldsmobile, Inc. v. Kaiden, 32 Md.App. 556, 363 A.2d 270 (1976)]

10. Rancher Baden purchased bull semen from Curtiss Breeding to use for artificial insemination. The semen was defective, so no calves were born. When Baden sued Curtiss, he contended that his consequential damages should include not only the value of the calf crop not born that year, but also the calf crop that would have been born the following year from the first calf crop. Should Baden be awarded these additional consequential damages? [Baden v. Curtiss Breeding Service, U.S. Dist. Ct. Mont. 280 F. Supp. 243 (1974)]

CHAPTER 24

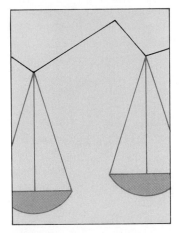

COMMERCIAL PAPER
Basic Concepts of Commercial Paper

To some extent, commercial law is a reflection of the customs and usages in the business world. The development of the law concerning commercial paper, for example, grew from commercial necessity. As early as the thirteenth century, merchants dealing in foreign trade were using commercial paper to finance and conduct their affairs. Problems in transportation and safekeeping of gold or coins had prompted this practice. Since the courts of these times did not recognize the validity of commercial paper, the merchants had to develop their own rules governing its use, and these rules were enforced by "fair" or "borough" courts. For this reason, the early law governing commercial paper is called the "Law Merchant." (See Chapter 1.)

Later, the Law Merchant was codified in England in the Bills of Exchange Act of 1882. In 1896, the National Conference of Commissioners on Uniform Laws drafted the Uniform Negotiable Instruments Law. This law was reviewed by the states, and by 1920 all the states had adopted

it. The Uniform Negotiable Instruments Law was the forerunner of Article 3 of the Uniform Commercial Code.

Commercial paper can be defined as any written promise or order to pay a sum of money. Drafts, checks, and promissory notes are typical examples. Commercial paper is transferred more readily than ordinary contract rights, and persons who acquire it are normally subject to less risk than the ordinary assignee of a contract right.

FUNCTIONS AND PURPOSES OF COMMERCIAL PAPER

Commercial paper has two functions. It serves as a substitute for money or as a credit device, or both.

A Substitute for Money

Debtors sometimes use currency, but for convenience and safety they often use commercial paper instead. For example, commercial paper is being used when a debt is paid by check. The substitute-for-money function of commercial paper developed in the Middle Ages. As mentioned previously, merchants deposited their precious metals with bankers to avoid the dangers of loss or theft. When they needed funds to pay for the goods that they were buying, they gave the seller a written order addressed to the bank. This authorized the bank to deliver part of the precious metals to the seller. These orders, called *bills of exchange,* were sometimes used as a substitute for money. Today people use checks the same way. They also use drafts, promissory notes, and certificates of deposit that are payable either on demand or on some specified date in the future. That some commercial paper is a substitute for money is further indicated by the Federal Reserve's official definition of what is called the "narrow" money supply (M1–B) currency (dollar bills and coins) in the hands of the public and checking-like account balances in all financial institutions, not just commercial banks.

A Credit Device

Commercial paper creates credit. When a buyer gives a seller a promissory note, the terms of which provide that it is payable within sixty days, the seller has essentially extended sixty days of credit to the buyer. The credit aspect of commercial paper was developed in the Middle Ages soon after bills of exchange began to be used as substitutes for money. Merchants were able to give to sellers bills of exchange that were not payable until a future date. Since the seller would wait until a maturity date to collect, this also was a form of extending credit to the buyer.

Discounting   The holder of a promissory note payable in sixty or ninety days who wishes to sell this instrument to a third party may do so for immediate cash. Typically, banks buy these instruments and wait until their maturity date to receive payment. In order to induce a bank to buy a promissory note, the holder of the instrument accepts a discount of, say, 5, 10, or 15 percent of the face amount. In effect, the bank pays

less than the amount it will eventually collect as a way of charging interest.

Collectibility   For commercial paper to operate *practically* either as a substitute for money or as a credit device or as both, it is essential that the paper be easily transferable without danger of being uncollectible. This is the function that characterizes commercial paper. Each rule studied in this chapter can be examined in light of this function. To the extent that the rule makes the paper more desirable—more easily transferable—it can be seen as a positive rule.

TYPES OF COMMERCIAL PAPER

UCC 3-104 specifies four types of instruments—drafts, checks, certificates of deposit, and notes.

Drafts

A **draft,** or bill of exchange, is an unconditional written order. The party creating it (the drawer) orders another party (the drawee) to pay money, usually to a third party (the payee). Exhibit 24–1 shows a typical draft (bill of exchange). The drawee must be obligated to the drawer either by agreement or through a debt relationship before the drawee is obligated to the drawer to honor the order.

Time and Sight Drafts   A time draft is a draft that is payable at a definite future time. A sight draft is payable on sight, that is, when the holder presents it for payment.[1] A draft can be both a time and sight draft; such a draft is one payable at a stated time after sight.

Trade Acceptances   The **trade acceptance** is a draft that is ordinarily used with the sale of goods. The seller is both drawer and payee on this draft.

---

1.   Or a sight draft is payable on acceptance. Acceptance is the drawee's written promise (engagement) to pay the draft when it comes due. The usual manner of accepting is by writing the word *accepted* across the face of the instrument, followed by the date of acceptance and the signature of the drawee.

Essentially, the draft orders the buyer to pay a specified sum of money to the seller usually at a stated time in the future.

To illustrate: Good Yard Company sells $50,000 of fabric to Lane Dresses, Incorporated, each fall on terms requiring payment to be made in ninety days. One year Good Yard needs cash, so it draws a *trade acceptance* that orders Lane to pay $50,000 to the order of Good Yard Company ninety days hence. Good Yard presents the paper to Lane. Lane *accepts* by signing the face

of the paper and returns it to Good Yard. Lane's acceptance creates an enforceable promise to pay the instrument when it comes due in ninety days. Good Yard can sell the trade acceptance in the commercial money market more easily than it can assign the $50,000 account receivable (for the reasons covered in Chapter 13, on assignments, and in subsequent chapters in this area). Thus, trade acceptances are the standard credit instruments in sales transactions. Exhibit 24–2 shows a trade acceptance.

EXHIBIT 24–1   TYPICAL TIME DRAFT: A BILL OF EXCHANGE

Whiteacre, Minn. _____ January 16 _____ 19 83 _____ $ $1,000.00———

Ninety days after above date ——— Pay to the order of **The First National Bank** 22-1
OF WHITEACRE, MINNESOTA

———————— One thousand and no/100 ——————————————————Dollars

VALUE RECEIVED AND CHARGE THE SAME TO ACCOUNT OF

To   Bank of Ourtown   *Stephen L. Eastman*
     Ourtown, Michigan   Stephen L. Eastman

EXHIBIT 24–2   TYPICAL TIME DRAFT: A TRADE ACCEPTANCE

TRADE ACCEPTANCE

Mytown, California   _____ March 15 _____ 19 83

To _____ The ABC Company

On _____ June 15, 1983 _____   Pay to the order of _____ XYZ Corporation

————— One thousand and no/100 —————————— Dollars ($——— 1,000.00 ———)

The obligations of the acceptor hereof arise out of the purchase of goods from the drawer. The drawee may accept this bill payable at any bank or trust company in the United States which such drawee may designate.

Accepted at Blackacre, N.Y.   on March 15   19 82
Payable at   Bank of Blackacre   XYZ Corporation
             Blackacre, New York

Buyer's Signature   ABC Company
By Agent or Officer *Tom Smith/V. Pres.*   By *Joe Jones/Pres.*

EXHIBIT 24–3   TYPICAL PROMISSORY NOTE

$ ---3,000.00---- Whiteacre, Minnesota ___April 30___ 19 _83_ Due _6/20/83_

-------- Sixty days -- after date,

for value received, the undersigned jointly and severally promise to pay to the order of payee at its office

in Whiteacre, Minnesota, $ _Three thousand and no/100_ Dollars with interest thereon from

date hereof at the rate of _-15-_ per cent per annum (computed on the basis of actual days and a year

of 360 days) indicated in No. _7_ below.

☒ 7 INTEREST IS PAYABLE AT MATURITY
☐ 8 INTEREST IS PAID TO MATURITY
☐ 9 INTEREST IS PAYABLE _____ BEGINNING ON _____ 19 ___
☐

SIGNATURE *Lawrence E. Roberts*   SIGNATURE *Margaret P. Roberts*

SIGNATURE _____   SIGNATURE _____

32-364 (8-71)

(side column) ☒ SECURITIES ☐ INSURANCE ☐ SAVINGS ☐ OTHER
☐ SEC. AGREEMENT 1. INV. & ACCTS. 2. CONSUMER GOODS 3. EQUIP.

(right box)
NO.
OFFICER   Clark
BY
ACCRUAL
☒ NEW   ☐ REN'L
☒ SECURED
☐ UNSECURED

Checks

A **check** is a distinct type of draft, *drawn* on a *bank* and payable on *demand*. Checks are discussed more fully in Chapter 29. Note here, however, that with certain types of checks, the bank is both the drawer and the drawee. For example, cashier's checks drawn by the bank on itself are payable on demand when issued. In addition, a check can be drawn by a bank on another bank. This instrument is known as a bank draft.

When traveler's checks are drawn on a bank, they are checks, but they require the payee's authorized signature before becoming payable. (Technically, most traveler's checks are not checks but drafts, because the drawee—for example, American Express—is ordinarily not a bank.)

Promissory Notes

The **promissory note** is a written promise between two parties. One party is the maker of the promise to pay, and the other is the payee, or the one to whom the promise is made. A promissory note, commonly referred to as a **note,** can have multiple makers or multiple payees. A note can be made payable at a definite time or on demand. It can name a specific payee or merely be payable to its bearer. A sample promissory note is shown in Exhibit 24–3.

Notes are used in a variety of credit transactions and often carry the name of the transaction involved. For example, in real estate transactions, promissory notes for the unpaid balance on a house, secured by a mortgage on the property, are called *mortgage notes*. A note that is secured by personal property is called a *collateral note*. And a note payable in installments, such as for payment of a color television set over a twelve-month period, is called an *installment note*.

Certificates of Deposit

A **certificate of deposit** (CD) is an acknowledgment by a bank of receipt of money with an engagement to repay it. [UCC 3-104(2)(c)] Certificates of deposit in small denominations are often sold by savings and loan associations, savings banks, and commercial banks. They are called small CDs and are for amounts up to $100,000.

Certificates of deposit for amounts over $100,000 are called large CDs.[2] Exhibit 24–4 shows a typical small CD.

Large certificates of deposit pay interest and are negotiable. Their negotiability allows them to be sold, to be used to pay debts or to serve as security (collateral) for a loan.

Letters of Credit

A **letter of credit** is neither a draft nor a note. It is an agreement that the issuer will pay drafts drawn by the creditor. Letters of credit are made by a bank or other person at the request of a customer.

OTHER WAYS OF CLASSIFYING COMMERCIAL PAPER

The preceding classifications of commercial paper follow the language of the UCC. There are

---

2. Large CDs are included in certain definitions of the money supply because they are fully negotiable and because the interest they pay is not regulated by the Federal Reserve. Large CDs may, however, be subject to regulation by the state banking authority of the state in which they are issued.

numerous other ways to classify commercial paper, two of which are treated here.

Demand Instruments and Time Instruments

Commercial paper can be classified as demand instruments or as time instruments. A demand instrument is payable on demand, that is, whenever the holder—a possessor *to whom the instrument runs*—chooses to present it to the maker in the case of a note or the drawee in the case of a draft. (Instruments payable on demand include those payable on sight or on presentation, and in which no time for payment is stated.) [UCC 3-108] All checks are demand instruments because, by definition, they must be payable on demand; therefore, checking accounts are called **demand deposits.** Time instruments are payable at a future date.

Orders to Pay and Promises to Pay

Commercial paper involving the payment of money must contain either a *promise* to pay or an *order* to pay. Thus, commercial paper can be classified as either promises to pay or orders to pay. Accordingly, a check is a draft and an order

---

EXHIBIT 24–4   TYPICAL SMALL CD

THE FIRST NATIONAL BANK OF WHITEACRE
NEGOTIABLE CERTIFICATE OF DEPOSIT

$\frac{22 \cdot 1}{960}$ Number 3999

WHITEACRE, MINNESOTA, ____February 15____ , 19 _83_

THIS CERTIFIES to the deposit in this Bank of the sum of $ _5,000.00 ——————_

———————— Five thousand and no/100 ———————————————————————————————— **DOLLARS**

which is payable to bearer on the __15th__ day of __July__ , 19 _83_ , against presentation and surrender of this certificate, and bears interest at the rate of _7 3/4_ % per annum, to be computed (on the basis of 360 days and actual days elapsed) to, and payable at, maturity. No payment may be made prior to, and no interest runs after, that date. Payable at maturity in federal funds, and if desired, at Manufacturers Hanover Trust Company, New York.

THE FIRST NATIONAL BANK OF WHITEACRE

BY ___John Doe___

SIGNATURE

to pay. On the other hand, a certificate of deposit and a promissory note are promises to pay.

Negotiable and Nonnegotiable Instruments

Since all commercial paper is either *negotiable* or *nonnegotiable*, this serves as another means of classification. Both its form and its content determine whether commercial paper is negotiable. All the elements listed in UCC 3-104 must be present for negotiability. This topic is of sufficient importance that all of Chapter 25 is devoted to it. Note that when an instrument is negotiable, its transfer from one person to another is governed by Article 3 of the UCC. Indeed, UCC 3-102(e) defines *instrument* as a "negotiable instrument." For that reason, wherever the term *instrument* is used in this book, it refers to a negotiable instrument. Transfers of nonnegotiable instruments are governed by rules of assignment. (See Chapter 13).

PARTIES TO COMMERCIAL PAPER

To review, a note (or a certificate of deposit) has two original parties—the maker and the payee. A draft, or check, has three original parties—the drawer, the drawee, and the payee. Sometimes two of the parties to a draft can be the same person (drawer-drawee or drawer-payee). Once an instrument is issued, additional parties can become involved. **Issue** is defined as the "first delivery of an instrument to a holder." [UCC 3-102(1)(a)][3]

Makers

A **maker** is the person who issues a promissory note or a CD promising to pay a certain sum of money to a payee. The maker's signature must appear on the face of the promissory note or CD for the maker to be liable on the note.

---

3. One can also refer to primary and secondary parties. Primary parties are makers of notes and acceptors of drafts. These parties promise to pay the instrument according to its terms. A signature of a person other than as the maker or the acceptor makes that person a secondary party.

Drawers, Drawees, and Payees

When a check or other draft is issued, the person who issues it, known as the **drawer**, orders the **drawee** (who is a bank in the case of a check) to pay a certain sum of money to a **payee** (or to the bearer of the instrument).

To illustrate: Smith has a checking account with West Wind Bank. At the end of the month, Smith receives his utility bill of $52 from the Tower Power and Light Corporation. Smith writes a check payable to the order of the utility, signing it in the lower right-hand corner. Smith is the *drawer* of the check. The West Wind Bank, which has been ordered to pay the check, is the *drawee*. Tower Power and Light, to which Smith has issued the check, is the *payee*.

Indorsers

The payee of a note or draft may transfer it by signing (indorsing) it and delivering it to another person. By doing this, the payee becomes an **indorser**. For example, Carol receives a graduation check for $25. She can transfer the check to her mother (or anyone) by signing it on the back. Carol is an indorser.

Indorsees

The person who receives the indorsed instrument is the **indorsee**. In the example above, Carol's mother is the indorsee. She is entitled to the $25 payment by virtue of Carol's indorsement. Carol's mother can indorse the check to someone else and thus become an indorser as well.

The Bearer

A **bearer** is any person who has physical possession of an instrument that either is payable to anyone without specific designation or is indorsed in blank. If a note is expressly made "payable to bearer," the person who possesses that note is the bearer. A person possessing a note or check payable to "cash" is also a bearer. A check payable to the order of a named person and indorsed by that named person in blank on the back makes its possessor a bearer also.

Holders

The term **holder** includes any person in possession of an instrument drawn, issued, or indorsed to him or her or to his or her order or to bearer or in blank.[4] To illustrate: A check made payable to the order of John Doe and in his possession makes John Doe a holder. A promissory note written by Sarah Smith promises to pay a sum of money to the order of Tom Jones. While the note is in Jones's possession, Jones is a holder. If Jones signs (indorses) the back of the note and transfers (negotiates) it to Adam White, the note becomes bearer paper, and White becomes the holder.

The holder and the owner of negotiable paper can often be the same person, but not necessarily. For example, a thief who steals a bearer instrument is a *holder* under commercial law principles (but obviously the thief is not the owner). Nonetheless, the thief can legally transfer (negotiate) the bearer instrument to another person, who then becomes a *holder*.

Holder in Due Course   Under UCC 3-302, a holder in due course (HDC) is a person who acquires an instrument for value in a good faith transaction without notice that it is defective or overdue. It is easier for an HDC to collect payment on an instrument than it is for an assignee of a contract to collect payment. The assignee is subject to all outstanding defenses of prior parties; the HDC is protected from all but a few defenses.[5]

Holder through a Holder in Due Course   An ordinary holder whose manner of acquisition fails to meet the requirements of a holder in due course can still be afforded HDC protection by proving that any prior holder qualified as a holder in due course. [UCC 3-201(1)]

Acceptors

An **acceptor** is a drawee of a draft or check who has by signature on the instrument manifestly agreed to pay the draft when due. For example, when the buyer "agrees" to pay the trade acceptance of the seller, drawn on the buyer (drawee), the buyer becomes an acceptor of the draft. (See Exhibit 24–2). The same result takes place when a drawee bank certifies a check drawn on that bank.

Accommodation Parties

An **accommodation party** is one who signs an instrument in any capacity to lend "his name to another party to it." [UCC 3-415(1)] The accommodation party actually lends his or her credit to the party to whom the accommodation is made and is classified accordingly.

For example, Barrow seeks a loan from the West Wind Bank. The bank will make the loan only if Barrow will get a third party with a good credit rating to co-sign the note. Able qualifies and agrees to accommodate Barrow by signing the note below Barrow's signature. Barrow is the *maker*, and Able is the *accommodation maker*. If, prior to the instrument's due date, Smith takes it for value, Able is still liable in the capacity in which she signed, even though Smith knows of the accommodation. [UCC 3-415(2)]

In any case, Able, as the accommodation party, is not liable to Barrow. Able is liable to Smith who took for value. She is normally liable only to the West Wind Bank. But if Able pays the instrument, she has the right of recourse on the instrument against Barrow. [UCC 3-415(5)]

QUESTIONS AND CASE PROBLEMS

1. Adam Smith, a college student, wished to purchase a new component stereo system from John Locke Stereo, Inc. Since Smith did not have the cash to pay

---

4. UCC 1-201(20) defines *holder* as "a person who is in possession of a document of title or an instrument or an investment security drawn, issued, or indorsed to him or to his order or to bearer or in blank."

5. The HDC is subject to real defenses. These generally involve the validity of the instrument, for example, legal capacity or certain sorts of forgery or alteration. [UCC 3-305] An HDC is free from all personal defenses between prior parties, for example, breach of contract.

for the entire stereo system, he offered to sign a note promising to pay $150 per month for the next six months. Locke Stereo, anxious to sell the system to Smith, agreed to accept the promissory note as long as Smith had one of his professors sign it. Smith did this and tendered a note to John Locke Stereo that stated, "I, Adam Smith, promise to pay John Locke Stereo or its order the sum of $150 per month for the next six months." The note was signed by Adam Smith and his business law professor. About a week later, John Locke Stereo, which was badly in need of cash, signed the back of the note and sold it to Fidelity Bank. How are each of the four parties designated in commercial paper parlance?

2. A partnership called Larson and Adkins is a law firm. Larson had just won a case for her client, Brown, against Bill Bucks. When Larson went to collect the judgment from Bucks, Bucks wrote out a check that read: "Pay to the order of Larson and Adkins $60,000 [Signed] Bill Bucks." On the top of the check were the words "Hanover Trust." When Larson went to deposit the check in the trust account that she had set up for her client, she signed the back of the check "L. Larson." How are each of these parties designated in commercial paper law?

3. Negotiable instruments play an important part in commercial transactions. Different needs can be fulfilled by using different types of instruments in certain ways. For instance, many insurance companies use a form of draft instead of a check to remit insurance benefits. The insurance company is both the drawer and the drawee; the beneficiary (the person receiving the money) is the payee; and the draft is made payable through a named bank in which the insurance company maintains a large account. What are the advantages of using such a draft?

4. Often when two parties to a sale are strangers to each other, and the sale is for a substantial amount of money, the selling party will insist that the purchaser make payment with a cashier's check. A cashier's check is a check for which the bank is both the drawer and the drawee. To purchase a cashier's check, a person goes to a bank teller, tenders the amount of money for

which the check is to be payable, and supplies the teller with the name of the person who is to be the payee of the check. Once the payee's name is inscribed on the check, only the payee (or a person to whom the payee negotiates the check) will be able to receive money for the check. What problem might arise if a seller asks a prospective buyer of goods to make payment with a cashier's check, and the buyer purchases the check, naming the seller as the payee? How can this problem be avoided?

5. Identify the following types of commercial paper or parties involved in commercial paper.
(a) A draft drawn on a bank payable to a payee on demand.
(b) A written acknowledgment by a bank of a receipt of money with an obligation to repay it.
(c) A written promise to pay another (or holder) a certain sum of money.
(d) An instrument drawn by a bank on itself payable on demand.
(e) Any person who acquires the instrument as a payee, by indorsement, or by delivery.
(f) A person who issues a promissory note payable to a named payee.
(g) A payee who transfers an order instrument by signing the instrument.
(h) A person who indorses a check on behalf of the payee upon the payee's transfer to an indorsee.

6. A California statute makes possession of a check with intent to defraud a crime. Norwood had in his possession an instrument that had the following title in the upper right-hand corner: "AUDITOR CONTROLLER'S GENERAL WARRANT COUNTY OF LOS ANGELES." Below this the instrument stated, "The treasurer of the County of Los Angeles will pay to the order of John Norwood $5,000." At trial the district attorney proved that Norwood had intended to defraud the County of Los Angeles of $5,000 while in possession of the above instrument. You are Norwood's attorney, and you are now appealing the case. What argument would appear to be the strongest to overturn Norwood's conviction? [People v. Norwood, 26 Cal.3d 148, 103 Cal.Rptr. 7 (1972)]

CHAPTER 25

COMMERCIAL PAPER
The Negotiable
Instrument

For businesses and commerce to operate smoothly, commercial paper must be generally accepted as money. For it to be so accepted, it must be freely transferable. The law creating and governing the negotiable instrument is primarily designed, therefore, to urge its use as a substitute for money.

In this chapter, we will examine the elements of a negotiable instrument. Whenever a dispute arises over the enforceability of an instrument, it is vital to know whether the instrument is negotiable. If it is, all disputes are resolved under Article 3 of the UCC. If it is not, disputes must be resolved under ordinary contract law. For example, the holder-in-due-course doctrine is recognized only under Article 3. Thus, anyone attempting to utilize this doctrine in enforcing an instrument must show that the instrument is negotiable. If it is not, transfer of such instrument is by assignment and is governed by the rules of contract law.

This chapter deals with the requirements of what must appear *on the face* of negotiable instruments. All matters relating to the requirements for a proper indorsement appear *on the back* of the instrument and are covered in Chapter 26.

THE REQUIREMENTS FOR
A NEGOTIABLE INSTRUMENT

UCC 3-104(1) specifies that for an instrument to be negotiable, it must:

1. Be in writing.
2. Be signed by the maker or drawer.
3. Be an unconditional promise or order.
4. Contain a specific sum of money.
5. Be payable on demand or at a definite time.
6. Be payable to order or to bearer.

A Writing

Negotiable instruments must be in *written form*. Clearly, an oral promise can create the danger of fraud or make it difficult to assign liability. Negotiable instruments must possess the quality of certainty that only formal written expression can give.

Practical Limitations on the Writing   There are certain practical limitations concerning the writing and the substance on which it is placed.

1.   The writing must be on material that lends itself to *permanence*. Instruments have been written on the sides of cows, carved in blocks of ice, and recorded on other impermanent surfaces. They are in writing, but only for a relatively short period of time. For example, if Mary writes in the sand, "I promise to pay $100 to the order of Tom," this is not a writing because it lacks permanence.

2.   The writing must have *portability*. This is not a legal requirement, but if an instrument is not movable, it cannot meet the requirement that it be freely transferable. A promise to pay written on the side of a cow is technically correct, but a cow cannot easily be transferred in the ordinary course of business.

Signed by the Maker or the Drawer

For an instrument to be negotiable, it must be signed by the maker if it is a note or certificate of deposit, or by the drawer if it is a draft or check. [UCC 3-104(1)(a)]

Extreme latitude is granted in determining what constitutes a **signature**. UCC 1-201(39) defines the word *signed* as "[including] any symbol executed or adopted by a party with present intention to authenticate a writing." UCC 3-401(2) expands upon this: "A signature is made by use of any name, including any trade or assumed name, upon an instrument, or by any word or mark used in lieu of a written signature." Thus, initials, an X, or a thumbprint will suffice. A trade name or an assumed name is sufficient even if it is false. A "rubber stamp" bearing a person's signature is permitted and frequently used in the business world. Parol evidence (Chapter 12) is admissible in identifying the signer. When the signer is identified, the signature becomes effective.

Placement of the Signature   The location of the signature on the document is unimportant. The usual place is the lower right-hand corner, but this is not required. A *handwritten* statement on the body of the instrument, such as "I, Mary Jones, promise to pay John Doe," is sufficient to act as Mary's signature.

There are virtually no limitations on the manner in which a signature can be made, but it is necessary to be careful when receiving an instrument that has been signed in an unusual way. The burden of proving the genuineness of a signature rests on the recipient. Furthermore, an unusual signature clearly decreases the marketability of an instrument because it creates uncertainty.

Signature by Authorized Representative   If a person signs an instrument as the agent for the maker or drawer, the maker or drawer has effectively signed the instrument if the agent had *authority* to do so. No particular form of appointment as an agent is necessary to show such authority; all that is needed is proof that the agent has such authority. [UCC 3-403]

If the agent has authority, the maker or drawer is liable on the instrument, just as if he or she had actually signed it. If the agent has authority and clearly has signed the instrument in a representative capacity, he or she will not be personally liable. If the agent has no such authority, or if the agent did not clearly sign in a representative capacity, the agent is personally liable. The importance of the liability of the parties in these situations will be discussed in detail in Chapter 35.

Unconditional Promise or Order

The terms of a promise or order must be included in the writing on the face of a negotiable instrument. These terms must not be conditioned upon the occurrence or nonoccurrence of some other event or agreement. Nor can the promise state that it is to be paid only out of a particular fund or source. [UCC 3-105(2)]

Promise or Order　In order for an instrument to be negotiable, it must contain an express order or promise to pay. A mere acknowledgment of the debt, which might logically *imply* a promise, is not sufficient under the UCC because the promise must be an *affirmative* undertaking. [UCC 3-102(1)(c)]

For example, the traditional I.O.U. is only an acknowledgment of indebtedness. Therefore, it is not a negotiable instrument. But if such words as *to be paid on demand* or *due on demand* are added, the need for an affirmative promise is satisfied. For example, if a buyer executes a promissory note using the words, "I promise to pay $1,000 to the order of the seller for the purchase of goods X, Y, Z," then the requirement for a negotiable instrument is satisfied.

A certificate of deposit is different. Here, the requisite promise is satisifed because the bank's acknowledgment of the deposit and the other terms of the instrument clearly indicate a promise.

An order is associated with three-party instruments, such as trade acceptances, checks, and drafts. An order directs a third party to pay the instrument as drawn. In the typical check, the word *pay* (to the order of a payee) is a command to the drawee bank to pay the check when presented, and thus it is an order. The order is mandatory even if it is written in a courteous form with words like *please pay* or *kindly pay*. However, precise language must be used. An order stating, "I wish you would pay," does not fulfill the requirement of precision.

In addition to being precise, an effective order must specifically identify the drawee (the person who must pay). [UCC 3-102(1)(b)] A bank's name printed on the face of a check, for example, sufficiently designates the bank as drawee.

Unconditional　A negotiable instrument's utility as a substitute for money or as a credit device would be dramatically reduced if it had *conditional* promises attached to it. It would be expensive and time-consuming to investigate such conditional promises, and, therefore, the free transferability of negotiable instruments would be greatly reduced. There would be substantial administrative costs associated with processing conditional promises. Furthermore, the payee would risk the possibility of the condition not occurring.

If Martin promises to pay Paula $10,000 only if a certain ship reaches port safely, anyone interested in purchasing the promissory note would have to investigate whether the ship arrived. Additionally, the facts that the investigation disclosed might be incorrect. To avoid such problems, the UCC provides that only unconditional promises or orders can be negotiable. [UCC 3-104(1)(b)]

However, the Code expands the definition of *unconditional* in order to make sure that certain conditions commonly used in business transactions do not render an otherwise negotiable instrument nonnegotiable. These are resolved by UCC 3-105:

A promise or order otherwise unconditional is not made conditional by the fact that the instrument

(a) is subject to implied or constructive conditions; or
(b) states its consideration * * * or the transaction which gave rise to the instrument * * *; or
(c) refers to or states that it arises out of a separate agreement * * *; or
(d) states that it is drawn under a letter of credit; or
(e) states that it is secured, whether by mortgage, reservation of title or otherwise; or
(f) indicates a particular account to be debited or any other fund or source from which reimbursement is expected; or
(g) is limited to payment out of a particular fund or the proceeds of a particular source, if the instrument is issued by a government or governmental agency unit; or
(h) is limited to payment out of the entire assets of a partnership, unincorporated association, trust or estate * * *.

Some of these conditions are very common and will be briefly discussed.

Implied or Constructive Conditions Without the rule allowing implied or constructive conditions, no instrument could be negotiable. Implied conditions, such as good faith and commercial reasonableness appear in virtually every example of a negotiable instrument.

Statements of Consideration Many instruments state the terms of the underlying agreement as a matter of standard business practice. Somewhere on its face, the instrument refers to the transaction or agreement for which it is being used in payment. The policy of the UCC is to integrate standard trade usages into its provisions.

For example, the words *as per contract* or *this debt arises from the sale of goods X and Y* do not render an instrument nonnegotiable.

If James Quinta writes, "On July 14, 1982, I promise to pay to the order of Louis Sneed $100 in full payment for the television set that Louis Sneed delivered to me on July 2, 1982, signed James Quinta," this promissory note is a negotiable instrument. The statement concerning the television set is not a condition. It describes the consideration for which the note is given. On the other hand, if the following words were added, the instrument would become nonnegotiable: "If this television set does not suit my tastes and preferences in any way whatsoever on July 13,

then the maker's obligation hereunder shall be null and void."

Reference to Other Agreements The UCC provides that mere reference to another agreement does not affect negotiability. If, on the other hand, the instrument is made subject to the other agreement, it will be nonnegotiable. [UCC 3-105(2)(a)] A reference to another agreement is normally inserted for the purpose of keeping a record or giving information to anyone who may be interested. Notes frequently refer to separate agreements that give special rights to a creditor for an acceleration of payment or to a debtor for prepayment. References to these rights do not destroy the negotiability of the instrument.

For example, an instrument states, "On January 23, 1985, I promise to pay to the order of Patricia Senior $1,000, this note being secured under a security agreement and lien upon my 1974 Dodge Dart, noted upon the title certificate thereof, signed Henry Winn." This instrument is negotiable. A statement that an instrument's payment is secured by collateral will not render an otherwise negotiable instrument nonnegotiable. [UCC 3-112(1)(b)] In fact, this statement adds to the salability and marketability of the instrument.

In the following case, a promissory note that incorporated another agreement was rendered nonnegotiable.

HOLLY HILL ACRES, LTD. v. CHARTER BANK OF GAINESVILLE

District Court of Florida, 1975.
314 So.2d 209.

BACKGROUND AND FACTS *A promissory note and purchase money mortgage were executed by the appellant, Holly Hill Acres, and given to a third party, Rogers and Blythe. Subsequently, Rogers and Blythe assigned the promissory note and mortgage in question to the appellee, Charter Bank of Gainesville, to secure its own note. Ultimately, the Holly Hill note went into default. The bank sued both Holly Hill and Rogers and Blythe to recover payment on the note. The trial court allowed the bank to recover. Holly Hill appealed that ruling, claiming that the note contained a stipulation that rendered it nonnegotiable. Hence, Holly Hill's defense against paying Rogers and Blythe was equally effective as a defense against paying the bank.*

The bank argued that it was a special type of assignee called a holder in due course because the promissory note was a negotiable instrument. On this basis, the bank claimed the unhampered right to recover on the note despite any underlying disputes between Holly Hill and Rogers and

Blythe. (A holder in due course takes a negotiable instrument free of most claims of other parties when negotiable commercial paper is involved. See Chapter 27.) Hence, the key to the bank's claim for recovery was that the promissory note was negotiable.

The trial court ruled that the note was negotiable and that the bank could recover. Holly Hill appealed this ruling, claiming that because the note was made subject to the mortgage agreement, it was nonnegotiable.

SCHEB, Judge.

*   *   *   *

The note, executed April 28, 1972, contains the following stipulation:

This note with interest is secured by a mortgage on real estate, of even date herewith, made by the maker hereof in favor of the said payee, and shall be construed and enforced according to the laws of the State of Florida. *The terms of said mortgage are by this reference made a part hereof.* [Emphasis supplied.]

*   *   *   *

The note having incorporated the terms of the purchase money mortgage was not negotiable. The appellee Bank was not a holder in due course. *   *   *

The note, incorporating by reference the terms of the mortgage, did not contain the unconditional promise to pay required by [U.C.C. Sec. 3-104(1)(b)]. Rather, the note falls within the scope of [U.C.C. Sec. 3-105(2)(a)]. Although negotiability is now governed by the Uniform Commercial Code, this was the Florida view even before the U.C.C. was adopted.

*   *   * Mere reference to a note being secured by mortgage is a common commercial practice and such reference in itself does not impede the negotiability of the note. There is, however, a significant difference in a note stating that it is "secured by a mortgage" from one which provides, "the terms of said mortgage are by this reference made a part hereof." In the former instance the note merely refers to a separate agreement which does not impede its negotiability, while in the latter instance the note is rendered non-negotiable.

The appellate court ruled that the note was nonnegotiable and that the bank was not a holder in due course. A new trial was ordered—one in which Holly Hill could assert its defenses against the bank. **JUDGMENT AND REMEDY**

Secured by a Mortgage   A simple statement in an otherwise negotiable note, indicating that the note is secured by a mortgage, does not destroy its negotiability. Actually, such a statement might make the note even more acceptable in commerce. Note that the statement that a note is secured by a mortgage must not stipulate that the maker's promise to pay is *subject* to the terms and conditions of the mortgage.

Indication of Particular Funds or Accounts   In many instruments, it is indicated expressly or impliedly that payment should come from a particular fund or that a particular account is to be debited. For example, a check is drawn impliedly on funds in a particular checking account.

Generally, mere reference to the account to be debited, or to the fund from which payment is preferred, will not affect the negotiability of the instrument. However, if payment is expressly limited to payment *only* from a particular fund, the instrument is rendered nonnegotiable. [UCC 3-105(2)(b)] The condition obviously restricts the acceptability of the instrument as a substitute for money, as a holder's payment now depends on whether such a fund exists and whether it is sufficient to pay the instrument.

For example, a note dated March 3, 1983, reads, "Gilbert Corporation promises to pay to the order of the Miami Herald $150 on demand, charged to advertising expense, signed Harold Henry, Treasurer, Gilbert Corporation." This note is negotiable. The phrase "charged to advertising expense" is merely a posting instruction to the corporation's accounting department. If a note states that "Jones plans to liquidate real estate to pay this obligation," the note is still considered negotiable.[1] On the other hand, if a note reads "payment to be made within the next thirty days from jobs now under construction," the note will be held nonnegotiable because it does not contain an unconditional promise.

Consider another example. A note states that "payment of said obligation is restricted to payment from accounts receivable." In this case, payment is conditioned from only one particular source—accounts receivable—and therefore renders the instrument nonnegotiable. This does not make the note uncollectible, however. The contract may still be assigned under contract rules of assignment.

The two exceptions to this rule are instruments issued by government agencies that are payable out of particular revenue funds and instruments limited to partnership, unincorporated association, estate, or trust assets. [UCC 3-105(1)(g) and (h)]

Sum Certain in Money

Negotiable instruments must state the amount to be paid in a *sum certain in money*. This requirement promotes clarity and certainty in determining the value of the instrument. [UCC 3-104(1)(b)] Any promise to pay in the future is risky because the value of money (purchasing power) fluctuates. Nonetheless, the present value of such an instrument can still be estimated with a reasonable degree of accuracy by financial ex-

perts. If the instrument's value were stated in terms of goods or services, it would be too difficult to ascertain the market value of those goods and services at the time the instrument was to be discounted.

The UCC mandates that negotiable commercial paper be paid wholly in money. For example, a promissory note that provides for payment in diamonds, or in 1,000 hours of services, would not be payable in money. Thus, the note would be nonnegotiable.

Sum Certain The term *sum certain* means an amount that is ascertainable from the instrument itself without reference to an outside source. A demand note payable with 12 percent interest meets the requirement of sum certain because its amount can be determined at the time it is payable. UCC 3-106(1) states that the sum is not rendered uncertain by the fact that it is to be paid:

> (a) with stated interest or by stated installments; or
> (b) with stated different rates of interest before and after default or a specified date; or
> (c) with a stated discount or addition if paid before or after the date fixed for payment; * * *

The basic test is whether any holder who receives the instrument can determine by calculation the amount required to be paid when the instrument is due. Thus, instruments that provide simply for payment of interest at prevailing bank rates are generally nonnegotiable, because bank rates fluctuate. A mortgage note tied to a variable rate of interest that fluctuates as a result of market conditions would not be negotiable. However, when an instrument is payable at the legal rate, or at judgment, or as fixed by state law, the instrument can be negotiable.

In international trade, notes that are to be paid in another currency satisfy the sum certain requirement. If X promises to pay 1,000 French francs, this note meets the certainty requirement even though the parties must refer to exchange rates that are not embodied in the instrument. The Code, therefore, makes an exception to its own general rule because of the realities of international trade. [UCC 3-107(2)]

---

1. Southern Baptist Hospital v. Williams, 89 So.2d 769 (La.App.1956).

Often, instruments have provisions authorizing collection costs and attorneys' fees upon default. UCC 3-106(1)(e) indicates that an instrument with such provisions still meets the sum certain requirement and is therefore still negotiable. Providing for collection costs and attorneys' fees lessens some of the costs and risks that a bank (or other institution) dealing in commercial paper would otherwise incur. Note, though,

that a few states have invalidated such provisions either by statute or by judicial decision. In states where such provisions are legal, the fees must be reasonable, or the clause will be voided as against public policy.

The elements that determine negotiability must be present on the face of the instrument. In the following case, the amount of a finance charge was not apparent from the face of the note.

BACKGROUND AND FACTS *This transaction involved a consumer credit sale in which a note and a security agreement, written on the same sheet of paper, were executed. The note provided that any unearned finance charges would be refunded if the consumer prepaid the full credit amount. The court had to determine whether the note and the security agreement, when read together, constituted a negotiable instrument. The defendant was a merchant and needed to know because a statute prohibits any seller of consumer goods from taking a negotiable instrument other than a check in conjunction with a consumer credit sale. If a merchant transgresses this statute, the purchaser can recover three times the amount of the credit charge from the merchant. Morris Chevrolet therefore used the defense that the paper signed by Walls did not include a negotiable instrument. The reasoning was that the note lacked a sum certain. Walls took the position that a sum certain could be ascertained by looking at the note and the security agreement, which were contained on the same piece of paper. The trial court agreed with the defendant, Morris Chevrolet, that the note was not negotiable. The trial court therefore dismissed plaintiff Walls' petition. Walls appealed.*

WALLS v. MORRIS CHEVROLET, INC.
Court of Appeals of Oklahoma, 1973.
515 P.2d 1405.

BAILEY, Presiding Judge.

*　*　*　*

First, both parties assume that the note, considered by itself, is not negotiable. So do we. The sum payable from the face of the note does not appear to be a sum certain because of the privilege stated in the note of refund of any unearned finance charge upon prepayment of the balance. The amount of the finance charge is not apparent from the face of the note and therefore the sum to be paid is uncertain in the event of prepayment. Under [UCC Sec. 3-106]: "(1) The sum payable is a sum certain even though it is to be paid * * * (c) with a stated discount * * * if paid before * * * the date fixed for payment * * *." In this instance the amount of the discount is not stated in the note and cannot be computed from its face. As is stated in the Uniform Commercial Code Comment to this section: "A stated discount or addition for early or late payment does not affect the certainty of the sum so long as the computation can be made * * * from the instrument itself * * *."

To overcome the absence of a sum certain on the face of the note, the plaintiff argues that the amount of the finance charge appears in the accompanying security agreement, that the security agreement and the note should be considered one instrument because on the same sheet of paper, that so construed the missing term is supplied and both note and security agreement are negotiable.

*   *   *   *

*   *   * We have been cited to no case, nor have we found one, in which a note on its face non-negotiable has been found to be negotiable by reference to an attached security agreement.

It is our opinion that a note cannot depend upon another agreement for elements of negotiability whether that agreement is attached to the note or separate from it except in those rare instances where such an incorporation is sanctioned by the Uniform Commercial Code expressly or by necessary implication. Negotiable notes are designed to be couriers without excess luggage under both the prior law and under the Code and so negotiability must be determined from the face of the note without regard to outside sources (with rare exceptions) so that the taker may know that he takes a negotiable instrument with the insurance of collectability provided by the Code and not an ordinary contract subject to the possibility of all defenses by the maker.

JUDGMENT AND REMEDY   *The note was not negotiable on its face. A separate agreement cannot supply the elements of negotiability to a note that, from its very nature, must be either negotiable or not from its face. Therefore, the merchant prevailed.*

Money and No Other Promise   UCC 3-104(1)(b) provides that a sum certain is to be payable in "money and no other promise." The Code defines money as "a medium of exchange authorized or adopted by a domestic or foreign government as a part of its currency." [UCC 1-201(24)]

Suppose that the maker of a note promises "to pay on demand $1,000 in U.S. gold." Since gold is not a medium of exchange adopted by the U.S. government, the note is not payable in money. The same result would occur if the maker promised "to pay $1,000 *and* fifty liters of 1964 Chateau Lafite-Rothschild wine," as the instrument is not payable *entirely* in money.

An instrument "payable in $1,000 U.S. currency or an equivalent value in gold" might render the instrument nonnegotiable, particularly if the maker reserved the option of paying in money or gold. If the option were left to the payee, the instrument would most likely be negotiable.

The UCC has a special provision for such instruments. [UCC 3-107(2)] Any instrument payable in the U.S. with a face amount stated in a foreign currency can be paid in the equivalent in U.S. dollars at the due date, unless the paper expressly requires payment in the foreign currency.

To summarize, only instruments payable in money are negotiable. An instrument payable in U.S. government bonds or in shares of IBM stock is not negotiable, because neither bonds nor stocks are a medium of exchange recognized by the U.S. government.

Payable on Demand or at a Definite Time

UCC 3-104(1)(c) requires that a negotiable instrument "be payable on demand or at a definite time." Clearly, in order to ascertain the value of a negotiable instrument, it is necessary to know when the maker, drawee, or acceptor is required to pay. It is also necessary to know when the obligations of secondary parties—drawers, indorsers and accommodation parties—will arise. Furthermore, it is necessary to know when an instrument is due in order to calculate when the statute of limitations may apply. And finally, with an interest-bearing instrument, it is necessary to know the exact interval during which the interest will accrue in order to determine the present value of the instrument.

Payable on Demand   Instruments that are payable on demand include those that contain the words *payable at sight* or *payable upon presentment* and those that say nothing about when payment is due. The very nature of the instrument may indicate that it is payable on demand. For example, a check, by definition, is payable on demand. [UCC 3-104(2)(b)] If no time for payment is specified and the person responsible for payment must pay upon the instrument's presentment, the instrument is payable on demand. [UCC 3-108]

Payable at a Definite Time   To be negotiable, time instruments must be payable at a definite time that is specified on the face of the instrument. The maker or drawee is under no obligation to pay until the specified time has elapsed.

Often instruments contain additional terms that seem to conflict with the definite time requirement. UCC 3-109 attempts to clear up some of these potential problems:

(1) An instrument is payable at a definite time if by its terms it is payable:
(a) on or before a stated date or at a fixed period after a stated date; or
(b) at a fixed period after sight; or
(c) at a definite time subject to any acceleration; or
(d) at a definite time subject to extension at the option of the holder, or to extension to a further definite time at the option of the maker or acceptor or automatically upon or after a specified act or event.
(2) An instrument which by its terms is otherwise payable only upon an act or event uncertain as to time of occurrence is not payable at a definite time even though the act or event has occurred.

To illustrate: An instrument dated June 1, 1981, states, "One year after the death of my grandfather, James Taylor, I promise to pay to the order of Henry Winkler $500. [Signed] Mary Taylor." This instrument is nonnegotiable. Because the date of the grandfather's death is uncertain, the maturity date is uncertain, even though the event is bound to occur.

When an instrument is payable on or before a stated date, it is clearly payable at a definite time, although the maker has the option of paying before the stated maturity date. This uncertainty does not violate the definite time requirement. If Lee gives Zenon an instrument dated May 1, 1981, which indicates on its face that it is payable on or before May 1, 1982, it satisfies the requirement. On the other hand, an instrument that is undated and made payable "one month after date" is clearly nonnegotiable. There is no way to determine the maturity date from the face of the instrument.

Drafts stating that they are payable at a fixed period after sight are considered payable at a definite time. [UCC 3-109(1)(b)] The term *sight* means the moment that the draft is presented for payment or for acceptance by the drawee. The Code further requires that such instruments be presented for acceptance to the drawee in order to determine the maturity date. [UCC 3-501(1)(a)] Presenting an instrument for acceptance to the drawee establishes the sight and the time period, which runs from the date the instrument is presented.

Acceleration Clauses   An **acceleration clause** is one that allows a payee or other holder of a time instrument to demand payment of the entire amount due, with interest, if a certain event occurs, such as a default in payment of an installment when due. There must, of course, be a good faith belief that payment will not be made before an acceleration clause is invoked.

For example, Carl lends $1,000 to Debra. Debra makes a negotiable note promising to pay $100 per month for eleven months. The note may contain a provision that permits Carl or any holder to accelerate all the payments plus interest if Debra fails to pay an installment in any given month. If, for example, Debra fails to make the third payment, the note will be due and payable in full. If Carl accelerates the unpaid balance, Debra will owe Carl the remaining principal plus interest.

Under UCC 3-109(1)(c), instruments that include acceleration clauses are negotiable because the exact value of the instrument can be ascertained, and the instrument will be absolutely payable on a fixed date if the event allowing acceleration does not occur. Thus, the fixed date is the outside limit used to determine the value of the instrument.

Furthermore, the payee or holder cannot accelerate the instrument even if it contains an acceleration clause unless it is done in good faith. Section 1-208 indicates that the acceleration clause "*   *   * shall be construed to mean that *   *   * [the holder of the instrument] shall have the power *   *   * [to accelerate] only if he in good faith believes that the prospect of payment or performance is impaired." But the burden of proving a lack of good faith is on the borrower—the maker of the note.

Extension Clauses The reverse of an acceleration clause is an extension clause, which allows the date of maturity to be extended into the future. To keep the instrument negotiable, the interval of the extension must be specified if the right to extend is given to the maker of the instrument. If, on the other hand, the holder of the instrument can extend it, the maturity date does not have to be specified.

Suppose a note reads, "The maker [obligor] has the right to postpone the time of payment of this note beyond its definite maturity date of January 1, 1983. However, this extension shall be for no more than a reasonable time." Any note with this language is not negotiable because it does not satisfy the definite time requirement. The right to extend is the maker's, and the maker has not indicated when the note will become due after the extension.

If a note reads, "The holder of this note at the date of maturity, January 1, 1985 can extend the time of payment until the following June 1 or later, if the holder so wishes," this is a negotiable instrument. The length of the extension does not have to be specified because the option to extend is solely that of the holder. After January 1, 1985, the note is, in effect, a demand instrument.

Payable to
Order or to Bearer

Since one of the functions of a negotiable instrument is to substitute for money, freedom to transfer is an essential requirement. To be sure that a proper transfer can be made, one of the requirements of a negotiable instrument is that it be "payable to order or to bearer." [UCC 3-104(1)(d)] These required words indicate that at the time of issuance it is expected that future unknown persons—not just the immediate party—will eventually be the owners. If these words are not present, the instrument is non-negotiable and therefore only assignable and governed by contract law.

Order Instruments UCC 3-110(1) defines an instrument as an order to pay "when by its terms it is payable to the order *   *   * of any person therein specified with reasonable certainty *   *   *." This section goes on to state that an order instrument can be payable to the order of:

(a) the maker or drawer; or

(b) the drawee; or

(c) a payee who is not maker, drawer, or drawee; or

(d) two or more payees together or in the alternative; or

(e) the representative of an estate, trust, or fund or his successor; or

(f) an office or officer by title [such as a tax assessor]; or

(g) a partnership or unincorporated association.

The purpose of order paper is to allow the maker or drawer to transfer the instrument to a specific person. This in turn allows that person to transfer the instrument to whomever he or she wishes. Thus the maker or drawer agrees to pay the person so specified or to pay whomever that person designates. In this way, the instrument retains its transferability.

Suppose an instrument states, "payable to the order of Sam Smith," or, "pay to Sam Smith or order." Clearly the maker or drawer has indicated that a payment will be made to Smith or to whomever Smith designates. The instrument is negotiable.

However, if the instrument states, "payable to Sam Smith," or, "pay to Sam Smith only," the instrument loses its negotiability. (The maker or drawer indicates only that Smith will be paid.)

In addition, except for bearer paper, the person specified must be named with *certainty* because the transfer of an order instrument requires an indorsement. (See Chapter 26.) If an instrument is "payable to the order of my kissing cousin," the instrument is nonnegotiable, as a holder could not be sure which cousin was intended to indorse and properly transfer the instrument.

Bearer Instrument   UCC 3-111 defines a bearer instrument as one that does not designate a specific payee. The term *bearer* means the person in possession of an instrument that is payable to bearer or indorsed in blank. [UCC 1-201(5)] This means that the maker or drawer agrees to pay anyone who presents the instrument for pay-

ment, and complete transferability is implied.

Any instrument containing the following terms is a bearer instrument: "Payable to the order of bearer," "Payable to Sam Sneed or bearer," "Payable to bearer," "Pay cash," or "Pay to the order of cash." The use of such designations can cause problems and should be avoided. Therefore, a check made payable to the order of "Uncle Sam" would probably be to a designated payee, the United States government, and be an order instrument. An instrument "payable to the order of a bucket of milk" would not be a designation of a specific payee, and the instrument would be a bearer instrument.

Where the instrument is made payable to order *and* to bearer, if the bearer words are handwritten or typewritten, the instrument is a bearer instrument. But if the bearer words are printed, it is an order instrument. [UCC 3-110(3)] The next case distinguishes bearer paper from order paper.

BACKGROUND AND FACTS   *Defendant Briggs signed a note that read in part "Ninety days after date, I, we, or either of us, promise to pay to the order of Three Thousand Four Hundred Ninety Eight and 45/100.......dollars." The italicized words and symbols were typed out. The remainder of the words in the quote were printed. No blanks had been left on the face of the instrument; any unused space had been filled in with hyphens. The note contained several clauses that permitted acceleration in the event the holder deemed itself insecure. When the note was not paid at maturity, Broadway Management Corp. brought suit on the note for full payment. Broadway prevailed at trial; Briggs appealed. The appeal centered on the question of whether the note was order or bearer paper.*

BROADWAY MANAGEMENT CORP. v. BRIGGS

Appellate Court of Illinois, Fourth District 1975.
30 Ill.App.3d 403, 332 N.E.2d 131.

CRAVEN, Justice.

*   *   *   *

The trial court determined this instrument to be non-negotiable paper, yet applied certain elements of the law of negotiable instruments in arriving at its conclusion. We believe the instrument to be negotiable. Uniform Commercial Code, section 3-109 establishes that an acceleration clause does not affect negotiability; *   *   *

Thus, the critical question of whether this is order or bearer paper is to be determined by section 3 of the Uniform Commercial Code, which governs negotiable instruments. If this is bearer paper, the plaintiff's possession was sufficient to make it a holder (Uniform Commercial Code, section 1-201(20))

*   *   *   *

On the other hand, if the instrument is order paper, it becomes apparent that the payee cannot be determined upon the face of the instrument.

*   *   *   *

Under the Code, an instrument is payable to bearer only when by its terms it is payable to:

(a) bearer or the order of bearer; or (b) a specified person or bearer; or (c) 'cash' or the order of 'cash', or any other indication which does not purport to designate a specific payee. (U.C.C., § 3-111.)

The official comments to the section note that an instrument made payable "to the order of _____" is not bearer paper, but an incomplete order instrument unenforceable until completed in accordance with authority. U.C.C., § 3-115.

The instrument here is not bearer paper. We cannot say that it "does not purport to designate a specific payee." Rather, we believe the wording of the instrument is clear in its implication that the payee's name is to be inserted between the promise and the amount, so that the literal absence of blanks is legally insignificant.

JUDGMENT AND REMEDY   *Because the payee's name was not inserted in the blank reserved for the payee's name, the instrument was an incomplete order instrument, so the holder could not be determined from the face of the instrument. The trial court's decision was reversed, and the case was remanded.*

OMISSIONS THAT DO NOT AFFECT NEGOTIABILITY

UCC 3-112 lists the following terms and omissions that do not affect negotiability:

1. The omission of a statement of any consideration.
2. The omission of the place where the instrument is drawn or payable.
3. The promise or power to maintain or protect collateral or to give additional collateral.
4. The term in a draft indicating that the payee, by indorsing or cashing the draft, acknowledges full satisfaction of the obligation of the drawer.

OTHER FACTORS NOT AFFECTING NEGOTIABILITY

There are other factors that do not affect the negotiability of an instrument, and the UCC provides rules for clearing up ambiguous terms. Some of these rules are:

1. Unless the date of an instrument is necessary to determine a definite time for payment, the fact that an instrument is undated does not affect its negotiability. A typical example is an undated check. [UCC 3-114(1)]
2. Postdating or antedating an instrument does not affect negotiability. [UCC 3-114(1)]
3. Handwritten terms outweigh typewritten and printed terms. [UCC 3-118(b)] For example, if your check is printed "Pay to the order of," and in handwriting you insert in the blank "John Smith or bearer," the check is a bearer instrument.
4. Words outweigh figures unless the words are ambiguous. [UCC 3-118(c)] This is important where the numerical amount and written amount on a check differ.
5. Where an interest rate is specified but not stated, "with interest," the interest rate is the judgment rate, not the legal rate. [UCC 3-118(d)]

QUESTIONS AND CASE PROBLEMS

1.　The following note is written by Mary Ellen on the back of an envelope: "I, Mary Ellen, promise to pay to Kathy Martin or bearer $100 on demand." Discuss fully if this constitutes a negotiable instrument.

2.　A promissory note is signed by Peter Paul. The note is dated May 1, 1983. Assuming that all other terms in the note meet the requirements for negotiability, discuss fully whether the following clause would render the note nonnegotiable: "This note is payable 100 years from date, but payment of principal plus interest is due and payable immediately upon the death of the maker."

3.　The following instrument was written on a sheet of paper by Moss Martin: "I, the undersigned, do hereby acknowledge that I owe Sam Smith one thousand dollars, with interest, payable out of the proceeds of the sale of my horse, Thundercloud, next month. Payment is to be made on or before six months from date." Discuss specifically why this instrument is nonnegotiable.

4.　You have signed a year's lease for an apartment near campus. The October rent is due and payable. You write a check for the rent due. On the check you write the following, "Payment for October rent as per lease agreement."

   (a)　Does this statement render the instrument nonnegotiable? Explain.

   (b)　Would your answer be any different if the written clause read, "Payment subject to signed lease dated September 1, 1983"?

5.　Martin Moss is in need of a loan. He borrows $500 from his friend, Paula Peters, signing a promissory note. Two clauses in the note are as follows:

   (a)　"On or before July 1, 1984, I promise to pay to Paula Peters or bearer $550 in cash or title to my 1970 car, at the holder's option."

   (b)　"The maker hereof reserves the right to extend the time of payment of said note for six months; however, the holder reserves the right to extend the time of payment indefinitely."

Explain whether either or both clauses render Martin's note nonnegotiable.

6.　Ingel entered into a contract with Allied Aluminum Associates, Inc., to have aluminum siding put on his home. Ingel executed a promissory note naming Allied as payee, and, at the same time, both Ingel and the Allied representative signed a completion certificate that bound Allied to complete the job satisfactorily. The completion certificate was not mentioned in nor attached to the promissory note. Allied Aluminum Associates later negotiated the promissory note to Universal C.I.T. Credit Corp. Allied never finished the aluminum siding work and was never heard from again. In a suit by Universal to collect on the note, Ingel's defense turned on whether the promissory note was negotiable. Ingel contended that it was not negotiable since it was accompanied by a completion certificate that contained promises other than the promise merely to pay a sum certain in money. Will Ingel's argument succeed? [Universal C.I.T. Credit Corp. v. Ingel, 347 Mass. 119, 196 N.E.2d 847 (1964)]

7.　Joe Jones Trucking Co. owed Mason, a lessor, $3,000 for the rental of certain trucking equipment. Mason informed the president of Joe Jones Trucking, Blayton, that unless he issued his personal check for $3,000 immediately, Mason would sue the company. Mason promised to hold onto the check for two days to allow Joe Jones Trucking time to pay the arrearages. When the company failed to do so, Mason attempted to deposit the check, but Blayton had stopped payment on it. Blayton claimed that the check was subject to a condition—that it would be void if the company failed to pay the arrearages within two days—and that therefore the check was not negotiable. If Mason's agreement not to cash the check was first made orally over the phone and later put in writing, will this affect the negotiability of the check issued by Blayton? [Mason v. Blayton, 119 Ga.App. 203, 166 S.E.2d 601 (1969)]

8.　Hotel Evans, Inc., issued two promissory notes, as maker, to A. Alport & Son, Inc., payee. One note contained a promise by Hotel Evans to pay Alport $1,600 "with interest at bank rates." The other note, for $900, had "bank rates" typed in after the printed word "interest." Are either of these promissory notes negotiable? [A. Alport & Son, Inc. v. Hotel Evans, Inc., 65 Misc.2d 374, 317 N.Y.S.2d 937 (1970)]

9.　In October 1970, Hall issued a draft that included the following: "Pay to L. Westmoreland and B. Bridges or order $1,000 on demand." Before he handed it to Bridges, Hall scratched out the words *or order* with his pen. Does the fact that the draft is payable to two payees destroy its negotiability? Does the scratching out of the words *or order* destroy the draft's negotiability? [First Federal Sav. and Loan Ass'n v. Branch Banking and Trust Co., 282 N.C. 44, 191 S.E.2d 683 (N.C.1972)]

10.　The Williamsons held a note secured by a second

mortgage on a farm they had sold to the Wanlesses. The Wanlesses sometimes made payments later than the first of the month, but they never missed a payment. The Williamsons brought suit to enforce the acceleration clause in the note. Could the Williamsons prove that they believed in good faith that payment or performance might be impaired? [Williamson v. Wanless, 545 P.2d 1145 (1976)]

CHAPTER 26

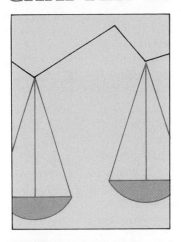

COMMERCIAL PAPER
Transferability and Negotiation

Commercial paper must be freely transferable. Once a negotiable instrument circulates beyond the original parties, the commercial law principles of negotiation come into play. The method of transfer that is used to pass a negotiable instrument from person to person determines the rights and duties that are passed with it.

Strictly speaking, negotiation occurs at the first delivery of a negotiable instrument to a holder, when the maker or drawer *issues* the instrument. [UCC 3-102(1)(a)] Typically, however, in commercial practice, the term *negotiation* is used to identify transfers occurring in a particular way after the instrument has been issued.

As already pointed out, the method of transfer determines the rights and duties that are passed with the negotiable instrument. Furthermore, whether the instrument is an order or bearer instrument (as discussed in Chapter 25) will determine how one *initially* negotiates it.

ASSIGNMENT AND NEGOTIATION

Once issued, a negotiable instrument can be transferred by *assignment* or by *negotiation*.

Assignment

Recall from Chapter 13 that under general contract principles, a transfer by assignment to an assignee gives the assignee only those rights that the assignor possessed. Assignment is a transfer of rights under a contract. Any defenses that can be raised against an assignor can be raised against the assignee (unless there is an enforceable antidefense clause). Article 3 applies only to negotiable instruments; there can be no *negotiation* of a nonnegotiable instrument. Furthermore, when a transfer fails to qualify as a negotiation, it becomes an assignment. The transferee is then an *assignee*, rather than a *holder*.

Negotiation

Negotiation is the transfer of an instrument in such form that the transferee becomes a holder. [UCC 3-202(1)] Under UCC principles, a transfer by negotiation creates a holder who, at the very least, receives the rights of the previous possessor. [UCC 3-201(1)] Unlike an assignment, a transfer by negotiation can make it possible for a holder to receive more rights in the instrument than the prior possessor. [UCC 3-305] (A holder who receives greater rights is known as a *holder in due course.* See Chapter 27). There are two methods of negotiating an instrument so that the receiver becomes a holder.

Negotiating Order Paper   Order paper contains the name of a payee capable of indorsing, as in "pay to the order of Jane Smith." Order paper is also paper that has as its last or only indorsement a *special* indorsement, as in "pay to Smith. [Signed] Jones." If the instrument is order paper, it is negotiated by delivery with any necessary indorsements. For example, the Transco Company issues a payroll check "to the order of Jane Smith." Smith takes the check to the supermarket, signs her name on the back (an indorsement), gives it to the cashier (a delivery), and receives cash. Smith has negotiated the check to the supermarket. [UCC 3-202(1)]

Negotiating Bearer Paper If an instrument is payable to bearer, it is negotiated by delivery— that is, by transfer into another person's possession. Indorsement is not necessary. [UCC 3-202(1)] The use of *bearer paper* involves more risk through loss or theft than the use of order paper.

Assume Bob Brown writes a check "payable to cash" and hands it to Debbie Myers (a delivery). Brown has negotiated the check (a bearer instrument) to Myers. Myers places the check in her wallet, which is subsequently stolen. The thief has possession of the check. At this point, negotiation has not occurred, because delivery must be voluntary on the part of the transferor. However, if the thief "delivers" the check to an innocent third person, negotiation will be complete. All rights to the check will be passed *absolutely* to that third person, and Myers will lose

all right to recover the proceeds of the check from that third person. [UCC 3-305] Of course, she can recover her money from the thief if the thief can be found.

Converting Order to Bearer Paper and Vice Versa The method used for negotiation depends upon the character of the instrument at the time the negotiation takes place. For example, a check originally payable to "Cash," but subsequently indorsed "Pay to X," must be negotiated as order paper (by indorsement and delivery) even though it was previously bearer paper. [UCC 3-204(1)]

An instrument payable to the order of a named payee and indorsed in blank (see Exhibit 26–1) becomes a bearer instrument. [UCC 3-204(2)] To illustrate: A check is made payable to the order of John Smith. The check is issued to Smith, and Smith indorses his name on the back of it. The instrument can now be negotiated by delivery only. Smith can negotiate the check to whomever he wishes by delivery, and that person in turn can negotiate by delivery without indorsement. If Smith, after such indorsement, loses the check, then the finder can negotiate it further.

EXHIBIT 26–1   BLANK INDORSEMENT

INDORSEMENTS

Indorsements are required whenever the instrument being negotiated is classified as an order instrument. (Many transferees of bearer paper require indorsement for identification purposes even though the UCC does not require it.) An **indorsement** is a signature with or without additional words or statements. It is most often written on the back of the instrument itself. If there is no room on the instrument, indorsements can be written on a separate piece of paper called an **allonge**. The allonge must be "so firmly affixed" to the instrument "as to become a part thereof." [UCC 3-202(2)] Pins or paper clips will not suffice. Staples are preferable.

One purpose of an indorsement is to effect the negotiation of order paper. Sometimes the transferee of bearer paper will request the holder-transferor to indorse. This is done to impose liability on the indorser. The liability of indorsers will be discussed later, in Chapter 28.

Once an instrument qualifies as a negotiable instrument, the form of indorsement will have no effect on the character of the underlying instrument. Indorsement relates to the right of the holder to negotiate the paper and the manner in which it must be done.

Types of Indorsements

We will examine four categories of indorsements:

1. Blank
2. Special
3. Qualified
4. Restrictive

Blank Indorsements A **blank indorsement** specifies no particular indorsee and can consist of a mere signature. [UCC 3-204(2)] Hence, a check payable "to the order of Rosemary White" can be indorsed in blank simply by having her signature written on the back of the check. Exhibit 26–1 shows a blank endorsement.

An instrument payable to order and indorsed in blank becomes payable to bearer and can be negotiated by delivery alone. [UCC 3-204(2)] In other words, a blank indorsement converts an order instrument to a bearer instrument, which anybody can cash. If De Wert indorses a check payable to her order in blank and then loses it on the street, Jones can find it and sell it to Smith for value without indorsing it. This constitutes a negotiation because Jones makes delivery of a bearer instrument (which was an order instrument until it was indorsed).

Special Indorsements A **special indorsement** indicates the specific person to whom the indorser intends to make the instrument payable; that is, it names the indorsee. [UCC 3-204(1)] No

special words of negotiation are needed. Words such as "pay to the order of Wilson" or "pay to Wilson" followed by the signature of the indorser are sufficient. When an instrument is indorsed in this way, it is order paper. Had the words "pay to Wilson" been used on the face of the instrument to indicate the payee, the instrument would not have been negotiable.

To avoid the risk of loss from theft, one may convert a blank indorsement to a special indorsement. This returns the bearer paper to order paper. UCC 3-204(3) allows a holder to "convert a blank indorsement into a special indorsement by writing over the signature of the indorser in blank any contract consistent with the character of the indorsement."

For example, a check is made payable to Arthur Engles. He indorses his name by blank indorsement on the back of the check and negotiates the check to Sam Wilson. Sam, not wishing to cash the check immediately, wants to avoid any risk should he lose the check. He therefore writes "pay to Sam Wilson" above Arthur's blank indorsement. In this manner Sam has converted Arthur's blank indorsement into a special indorsement. Further negotiation now requires Sam Wilson's indorsement plus delivery. (See Exhibit 26–2.)

EXHIBIT 26–2   SPECIAL INDORSEMENT

Qualified Indorsements Generally, an indorser, *merely by indorsing*, impliedly promises to pay the holder, or any subsequent indorser, the amount of the instrument in the event that the drawer or maker defaults on the payment [UCC 3-414(1)] A **qualified indorsement** is used by an indorser to disclaim or limit this liability on the instrument. In this form of indorsement, the notation *without recourse* is commonly used. A sample is shown in Exhibit 26–3.

EXHIBIT 26–3   QUALIFIED INDORSEMENT

A qualified indorsement is often used by persons acting in a representative capacity. For instance, insurance agents sometimes receive checks payable to them that are really intended as payment to the insurance company. The agent is merely indorsing the payment through to the principal and should not be required to make good on the check if it is later dishonored. The "without recourse" indorsement absolves the agent. If the instrument is dishonored, the holder cannot obtain recovery from the agent who indorsed "without recourse" unless the indorser has breached one of the warranties listed in UCC 3-417(2).

Generally speaking, blank and special indorsements are *unqualified* indorsements. That is, the blank or special indorser is guaranteeing payment of the instrument *in addition to* transferring title to it. The qualified indorser is not guaranteeing such payment. Nonetheless, the qualified indorsement ("without recourse") still transfers title to the indorsee; an instrument bearing a qualified indorsement can be further negotiated.

Qualified indorsements are accompanied by either a special or a blank indorsement that determines further negotiation. Therefore, a special qualified indorsement makes the instrument an order instrument, and it requires an indorsement plus delivery for negotiation. A blank qualified indorsement makes the instrument a bearer instrument, and only delivery is required for negotiation.

To illustrate: A check is made payable to the order of Mary Smith. Mary wants to negotiate the check specifically to Harold Hollis with a qualified indorsement. Mary would indorse the check, "Pay to Harold Hollis, without recourse. [Signed] Mary Smith." For Harold to further negotiate the check to George Green, Harold would have to indorse and deliver the check to George.

Restrictive Indorsements   Prior to the existence of the UCC, a restrictive indorsement was thought to prohibit the further negotiation of an instrument. Although some who indorse in this manner still believe the restrictive indorsement prevents any further transfer, the Code holds to the contrary. UCC 3-206(1) states that "no restrictive indorsement prevents further transfer or negotiation of the instrument." The **restrictive indorsement** requires indorsees to comply with certain instructions regarding the funds involved. Restrictive indorsements come in many forms. UCC 3-205 categorizes four separate types.

Conditional Indorsements   When payment is dependent on the occurrence of some specified event, the instrument has a conditional indorsement. [UCC 3-205(a)] For example, Ted Smith indorses a note to read as follows (Exhibit 26–4):

EXHIBIT 26–4   CONDITIONAL INDORSEMENT

Except against intermediary banks (defined later), the indorsement is enforceable, and neither Bob Block nor any subsequent holder has the right to enforce payment on the note before the condition is met. [UCC 3-206(3)]

It is important to note that a conditional indorsement does not prevent further negotiation of the instrument. However, if the conditional language had appeared on the face of the instrument, it would not have been negotiable because it would not have met the requirement that the note contain an unconditional promise to pay.

Indorsements Prohibiting Further Indorsement   An indorsement such as "pay to Bill Jones only. (Signed) X," does not destroy negotiability. Jones can negotiate the paper to a holder just as if it had read "pay to Bill Jones. (Signed) X." [UCC 3-206(1)] This type of restrictive indorsement has the same legal effect as a special indorsement. It is rarely used. [UCC 3-205(b)]

Indorsement for Deposit or Collection   A common type of restrictive indorsement is one that makes the indorsee (almost always a bank) a collecting *agent* of the indorser. (See Exhibit 26–5 for an illustration where the check is payable and issued to Mary Smith.)

In particular, a "Pay any bank or banker" indorsement has the effect of locking the instrument into the bank collection process. Only a bank can acquire rights of a holder following this indorsement until the item has been specially indorsed by a bank to a person who is not a bank.

EXHIBIT 26–5   FOR DEPOSIT–FOR COLLECTION INDORSEMENT

[UCC 4-201(2)] The court deals with a bank's special indorsement by an allonge after its restrictive indorsement in the next case.

BACKGROUND AND FACTS   *Defendant Commercial Credit Corporation issued two checks payable to the order of Rauch Motor Co. Rauch Motor indorsed the checks in blank and deposited them in its account with University National Bank. University National stamped the checks "pay any bank" and sent them through the collection process. The checks were subsequently returned to University National marked "payment stopped." Several months later, University National indorsed the checks to Lamson, who sued Commercial Credit Corporation for the face amount of the checks. The trial court entered judgment for Lamson. The Court of Appeals reversed, and the Supreme Court of Colorado agreed to hear the case.*

LAMSON v. COMMERCIAL CREDIT CORPORATION
Supreme Court of Colorado, 1975.
531 P.2d 966.

DAY, Justice.
*   *   *   *

In reversing the trial court the Court of Appeals held as a matter of law that the plaintiff Lamson was not a holder of the checks. It arrived at the decision by ruling that the Bank's indorsement to Lamson was not in conformance with the Uniform Commercial Code because it was stapled to the checks. It was this interpretation of [UCC] 3-202(2) which prompted us to grant certiorari. It is that holding of the Court of Appeals which we expressly reverse.

When Rauch deposited the checks, it indorsed them in blank, transforming them into bearer paper. [UCC] 1-201(5) and 3-204(2). The Bank in turn indorsed the checks "pay any bank." That is a restrictive indorsement. [UCC]3-205(c). After a check has been restrictively indorsed, "only a bank may acquire the rights of a holder *   *   * [u]ntil the item has been specially indorsed by a bank to a person who is not a bank." [UCC] 4-201(2)(b).

There is no question that the checks were indorsed to Lamson by name, thus qualifying as a special indorsement. [UCC] 3-204(1). The problem is whether the special indorsement was correctly and properly affixed to the checks under [UCC] 3-202(2). It provides *inter alia* that "[a]n indorsement must be written *   *   * on behalf of the holder and on the instrument or on a paper so firmly affixed thereto as to become a part thereof."

* * * *

We agree with the Court of Appeals' statement that a separate paper pinned or paper-clipped to an instrument is not sufficient for negotiation. [UCC] 3-202(2), comment 3. However, we hold, *contra* to its decision, that the section does permit stapling as an adequate method of firmly affixing the indorsement. * * * Therefore we hold that under the circumstances described, stapling an indorsement to a negotiable instrument is a permanent attachment to the checks so that it becomes "a part thereof."

[UCC] 1-201(20) defines a holder as "a person who is in possession of * * * an instrument * * * indorsed to him * * *." The Bank's special indorsement, stapled to the two checks, effectively made Lamson a holder, although not a holder in due course.

JUDGMENT AND REMEDY *The trial court's judgment for Lamson was reinstated.*

Trust or Agency Indorsements

Indorsements that are for the benefit of the indorser or a third person are trust, or agency, indorsements. Samples are shown in Exhibit 26–6.

The indorsement results in legal title vesting in the original indorsee. To the extent that the original indorsee pays or applies the proceeds consistently with the indorsement (for example, "in trust for Johnny North * * *"), the indorsee is a holder and can become a holder in due course. (See Chapter 27.) [UCC 3-205(d) and 3-206(4)]

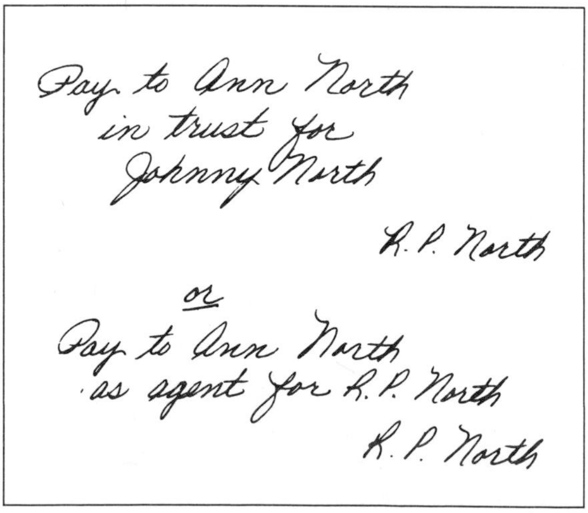

The fiduciary restrictions on the instrument do not reach beyond the original indorsee.[1] Any subsequent purchaser can qualify as a holder in due course unless he or she has actual notice that the instrument was negotiated in breach of the fiduciary duty.[2]

Bank's Liability for Restrictive Indorsements

Banks handling commercial paper in the normal course of *collection* are called *intermediary* banks [UCC 4-105(c)], and banks paying on commercial paper are called *payor* banks. [UCC 4-105(b)] Neither bank is bound by any restrictive indorsements of any person except the immediate holder who transfers or presents the instrument for payment. [UCC 3-206(2)] This means that only the first bank to which the item

EXHIBIT 26–6 TRUST INDORSEMENTS

Pay to Ann North
in trust for
Johnny North
                    R. P. North

or

Pay to Ann North
as agent for R. P. North
                    R. P. North

---

1. Compare this to the rule governing conditional indorsements. A conditional indorsement binds all subsequent indorsers (except certain banks) and primary parties to see that the money is applied consistently with the condition. Agency or trust indorsements limit this responsibility only to the original indorsee. Subsequent parties are not encumbered with this restriction.
2. See Quantum Dev. v. Joy, 397 F.Supp. 329 (D.C.Virgin Is. 1975).

is presented for collection must pay in a manner consistent with any restrictive indorsement. [UCC 3-206(3)] This bank is called the depository bank. [UCC 4-105(a)] This is true even if the depository bank is also the payor bank (that is, where only one bank is involved).

To illustrate: Elliot writes a check on his New York bank account and sends it to Barton. Barton indorses the check with a restrictive indorsement that reads, "For deposit into Account #4921 only." A Miami bank is the first bank to which this check is presented for payment (the depositary bank), and it must act consistently with the terms of the restrictive indorsement. Therefore, it must credit account #4921 with the money or be liable to Barton for conversion. Elliot's check leaves the Miami bank indorsed "for collection." As the check moves through the collection network of intermediary banks to Elliot's New York bank for payment, each intermediary bank is only bound by the preceding bank's indorsement to collect.

The division of responsibility between types of banks is necessary. Collecting banks process huge numbers of commercial instruments, and there is no practical way for them to examine and comply with the effect of each restrictive indorsement. Therefore, the only reasonable alternative is to charge the depositary bank with the responsibility of examining and complying with any restrictive indorsements.

Unauthorized Signatures

People are not normally liable to pay on negotiable instruments unless their signatures appear on the instruments. Hence, an unauthorized signature is wholly inoperative and will not bind the person whose name is forged.[3] There are exceptions to this rule, found in UCC 3-404(1). If the person whose unauthorized signature was used ratifies that signature or is in some way precluded from denying it, then the unauthorized signature is operative. Additionally, an un-

authorized signature will operate as "the signature of the unauthorized signer in favor of any person who in good faith pays the instrument or takes it for value." [UCC 3-404(1)]

Generally when there is a forged or unauthorized *indorsement*, the burden of loss falls on the first party to take the forged indorsement. However, there are two situations in which the resulting loss falls on the drawer or maker. These situations are:

1. When the imposter induces the maker or drawer of an instrument to issue it to the imposter.
2. When a person signs as or on behalf of a maker or drawer, intending that the payee will have no interest in the instrument, and an agent or employee of the maker or drawer has supplied him or her with the name of the payee, also *intending* the payee to have no such interest. [UCC 3-405(1)] These situations often involve an employee who wishes to swindle an employer by padding bills or payrolls. This is frequently referred to as the *fictitious payee* rule.

Imposters: Signature and Name of Payee

An **imposter** is one who, by use of the mails, telephone, or personal appearance, induces a maker or drawer to issue an instrument in the name of an impersonated payee. The maker or drawer honestly believes that the imposter is actually the named payee and issues the instrument to the imposter. Since the maker or drawer did issue and intend the imposter to receive the instrument, the indorsement by the imposter is not treated as unauthorized when transferred to an innocent party.

In these situations, the unauthorized indorsement of a payee's name can be as effective as if the real payee had signed. The *imposter rule* of UCC 3-405 provides that an imposter's indorsement will be effective—that is, not a "forgery"—insofar as the drawer goes.

For example, a man walks into John Green's clothing store and purports to be Jerry Lewis soliciting contributions for his annual fund raising for muscular dystrophy. John Green has heard

---

3. On the other hand, a drawee is charged with knowledge of the *drawer's* signature. The drawee cannot recover money it pays out on a negotiable instrument bearing a forged drawer's signature.

of the Lewis Telethon but has never met or seen Jerry Lewis. Wishing to support a worthy cause, Green writes out a check for $500 payable to Jerry Lewis and hands it to the imposter. The imposter forges the signature of Jerry Lewis and negotiates the check to a Stop and Shop convenience store. Green discovers the fraud and stops payment on the check, claiming the payee's signature is forged. Since the imposter rule is in effect, Green cannot claim a forgery against Stop and Shop, and he must seek redress from the imposter. If Green had sent the check to the real Jerry Lewis, but the check had been stolen and negotiated to the store by a forged indorsement, the imposter rule would not apply, and Stop and Shop would have to seek redress against the forger.

FICTITIOUS PAYEE

The so-called **fictitious payee** rule deals with the intent of the maker or drawer to issue an instrument to a payee who has *no interest* in the instrument. This most often takes place when (1) a dishonest employee deceives the employer-maker or drawer into signing an instrument payable to a party with no right to receive the instrument, or (2) the dishonest employee or agent has the authority to so issue the instrument on behalf of the maker or drawer. In these situations, the payee's indorsement is not treated as a forgery, and the maker or drawer is held liable on the instrument by an innocent holder.

Assume that the Revco Company gives its bookkeeper, Sam Snyde, general authority to issue checks in the company name drawn on Second Federal Bank so that Snyde can pay employees and pay other corporate bills. Snyde decides to cheat Revco out of $10,000 by issuing a check payable to Fanny Freid, an old acquaintance of his. Snyde does not intend Freid to receive any of the money, and Freid is not an employee or creditor of the company.

Snyde indorses the check in Freid's name, naming himself as indorsee. Snyde cashes the check with a local bank, which collects payment from the drawee bank, Second Federal. Second Federal then charges Revco's account $10,000.

Revco discovers the fraud and demands that its account be recredited. Who bears the loss? Neither the local bank that first accepted the check nor Second Federal are liable. The rule of UCC 3-405 provides the answer. Since Snyde's indorsement in the name of a payee with no interest in the instrument is "effective," there is no "forgery." Hence, the collecting bank is protected in paying on the check, and the drawee bank is protected in charging Revco's account. It is the employer-drawer, Revco, that bears the loss.[4]

Whether a dishonest employee actually signs the check or merely supplies his or her employer with names of fictitious creditors (or with true names of creditors having fictitious debts), the Code makes no distinction in result. For example, Ned Norris draws up the payroll list from which employee checks are written. Norris fraudulently adds the name Sue Swift (a fictitious person) to the payroll, thus causing checks to be issued to her. Again, it is the employer-drawer who bears the loss because the employer is in the best position to prevent such fraud.

In the following case, the court must determine whether an employer should bear the loss for checks wrongfully indorsed by an employee.

---

4. May Dept. Stores Co. v. Pittsburgh Nat. Bank, 374 F.2d 109 (3rd Cir. 1967).

DANJE FABRICS v. MORGAN GUARANTY TRUST CO.

New York Supreme Court, 1978.
24 UCC Rep. Serv. 188.

BACKGROUND AND FACTS *Danje Fabrics, a company that converted yarn into fabric, hired Caulder as its bookkeeper. Specialty Dyers dyed fabrics for Danje. Caulder prepared checks in payment of Specialty Dyers's invoices and submitted them to Danje's president for signature. After Caulder's employment was terminated, it was discovered that he had taken twenty-seven checks payable to Specialty Dyers and diverted them* *into an account he opened at Citibank in the name of Specialty Dyers. Danje sought recovery from Morgan, the drawee bank, for wrongfully deducting the amount of these checks from Danje's account.*

GROSSMAN, Judge.

*   *   *   *

Citibank contends that Morgan has a complete defense to the claim set forth by Danje in its complaint by reasons of the provisions of § 3-405 of the Uniform Commercial Code.

This section provides in pertinent part:

"Section 3-405. Imposters; Signatures in Name of Payee. (1) An indorsement by any person in the name of a named payee is effective if *   *   * (c) an agent or employee of the maker or drawer has supplied him with the name of the payee intending the latter to have no such interest."

Since it was Caulder who was responsible for the preparation of checks based upon invoices given to him by plaintiff Danje's production department and who presented such checks to the individual who was authorized to sign them, Citibank argues, and Morgan agrees, that, based upon the facts as herein set forth, Caulder "supplied" the plaintiff with the name of the payee intending the latter to have no such interest and therefore the endorsements in question are effective. Danje's position is that, since the twenty-seven checks in question were prepared as a result of bona fide business transactions between Dyers, the named payee, and Danje, Caulder did not "supply" plaintiff with the name of the payee but simply converted the checks to his own use, and that therefore § 3-405(1)(c) of the Uniform Commercial Code has no application to the instant case.

Therefore, the issue to be decided in this case is what scope the word "supplied", as used in § 3-405(1)(c) of the Uniform Commercial Code was intended to have. Was it the legislature's intent for it to cover all instances where an employee presents an instrument to the maker for signature or must a line be drawn to distinguish between those instances where the instrument is based upon a fraudulent transaction and those where the instrument is based upon a bona fide transaction occurring in the regular course of business?

*   *   *   *

Although the Official Comment [to UCC 3-405], makes mention only of "padded payroll" cases, it is clear that the provisions of the Code extend beyond these to other "padded" cases where the operative facts are present, i.e., where the drawer's agent or employee prepares the checks, presumably drawn for payroll or other valid purposes, for signature or otherwise furnishes the signing officer with the name of the payee.

*   *   *   *

In our present case, the checks stolen by Caulder were legitimate and bona fide payments due and owing to Dyers. The checks themselves involved in our case were not fraudulent in any respect and the facts herein indicate that proper and careful business procedures were followed in the drawing and making of said checks. The undisputed facts herein further show that it was only the criminal conduct of Caulder in appropriating, stealing and falsely endorsing said checks, which constituted legitimate payments to the named payee, that resulted in the loss herein incurred by Danje.

*   *   *   *

In our instant case, the checks involved were based upon bona fide transactions and obligations of the plaintiff which arose out of the normal business relationship with the payee named on said checks. In such instance, it cannot be claimed that the employee, Caulder, supplied his employer, Danje, with the name of the payee, Dyers, as said checks were legitimately based upon open invoices due and owing to the payee, Dyers.

JUDGMENT AND REMEDY   *The indorsements forged by Caulder were ineffective. Danje was entitled to have its account credited by Morgan. Morgan could then recover from Citibank under the warranties made by Citibank as the collecting bank.*

Miscellaneous Indorsement Problems

No Standard Category   Sometimes an indorsement does not seem to fit into any of the standard categories. For example, the indorsement can read: "I hereby assign all my right and title and interest in this note. (Signed) Bob Smith." The signature is an effective indorsement despite the additional language of transfer. Use of the word *assign* does not change the negotiation into a mere assignment. Clearly Bob Smith did not intend to limit the rights of the person to whom he was transferring the instrument. [UCC 3-202(4)]

Correction of Name   An indorsement should be identical to the name that appears on the instrument. The payee or indorsee whose name is misspelled can indorse with the misspelled name, or the correct name, or both. [UCC 3-203]

For example, Susan Lock receives a check payable to the order of "Susan Locke." She can indorse the check either "Susan Locke" or "Susan Lock." The usual practice is to indorse the name as it appears on the instrument and follow it by the correct name.[5]

Bank Indorsements   When a customer deposits a check with a bank and fails to indorse it, the bank has the right to supply any necessary indorsement for its customer unless the instrument *specifically prohibits it.* [UCC 4-205(1)]

For example, Bob Adams deposits his government check with First National Bank and forgets to indorse it. Since government checks typically state, "Payee's indorsement required," the bank will not supply the indorsement. The check will be returned to Adams for his signature.

Ordinarily, checks do not specifically require the payee's indorsement. The bank merely stamps or marks the check, indicating that it was deposited by the customer or credited to the customer's account. [UCC 4-205]

Commercial paper must move rapidly through banking channels. In the process of clearing through collection, a check can be transferred between banks using any agreed-upon method of indorsement that identifies the transferor bank. [UCC 4-206] For example, a bank can indorse using its Federal Reserve number instead of its name.

Multiple Payees   An instrument payable to two or more persons *in the alternative* (for example, "Pay to Able or Baker") requires the indorsement of one of the payees. [UCC 3-116(a)] However, if an instrument is payable to two or more persons *jointly* (for example, "Pay Carl and Doris" or "Pay Glenda, Harold"), then all the payees' indorsements are necessary for negotiation. [UCC 3-116(b)]

Unindorsed Order Paper   If order paper is transferred without indorsement, it is a transfer by assignment, not by negotiation. The receiver is merely a transferee, not a holder, and does not qualify as a holder in due course. If, however, the transfer is made for value given, the unqual-

5.   Watertown Federal Sav. and Loan v. Spanks, 346 Mass. 398, 193 N.E.2d 333 (1963).

ified indorsement of the transferor can be compelled by law unless the parties have agreed otherwise. The effect is the negotiation of the instrument. The transferee becomes a holder and can negotiate the instrument further. [UCC 3-201(3)] Compare this rule with that of the bank's right, upon deposit of an unindorsed check, as previously discussed.

Agents or Officers   A negotiable instrument can be drawn payable to a legal entity such as an estate, a partnership, or an organization. For example, if a check reads "Pay to the Red Cross," an authorized representative of the Red Cross can negotiate it.

Similarly, negotiable paper can be payable to a public officer. For example, checks reading "Pay to the order of the County Tax Collector," or "Pay to Larry White, Receiver of Taxes," can be negotiated by whoever holds the office. [UCC 3-110(1)(b)]

QUESTIONS AND CASE PROBLEMS

1.   A check drawn by Daniel for $200 is made payable to the order of Paula. The check is issued to Paula. Paula owes her landlord $200 in rent and transfers the check to her landlord with the following indorsement: "For rent paid. [Signed] Paula." Paula's landlord has contracted to have Peter Plumber repair a number of apartment leaks. The plumber insists on immediate payment. The landlord transfers the check to Peter without indorsement. Later, in order to pay for plumbing supplies at Facet's Store, Peter transfers the check with the following indorsement: "Pay to Facet's Store, without recourse. [Signed] Peter Plumber." Facet sends the check to its bank indorsed "For deposit only. [Signed] Facet's Store."

(a) Classify each of these indorsements.
(b) Was the transfer from Paula's landlord to Peter Plumber, without indorsement, an assignment or a negotiation? Explain.

2.   Dan David drafts a check for $500 payable to the order of Jane Petrie. Petrie wants to purchase Fred Flint's 1972 Chevy for $500 and contracts to do so, with payment to be immediate and delivery of the car to be seven days thereafter. Petrie indorses David's check to Flint as "Pay to Flint, upon condition of delivery of his 1972 Chevy. [Signed] Jane Petrie." Flint takes the check and indorses it, "For deposit. [Signed] Fred Flint."

On his way to the bank to deposit the check, Flint is sidetracked by a flea market sale. Flint purchases an old clock and gives the indorsed check to Gary Gambler, the seller of the clock. Gambler deposits the check with his bank.

Assume Dan David has a legal right to stop payment on the check, and assume that Flint has not delivered the car.

(a) How would each of the above indorsements be classified?
(b) What is the legal effect of Petrie's indorsement under the circumstances?
(c) Could Flint legally negotiate the check to Gambler with an indorsement "for deposit"? Explain.

3.   Able Ledger has been Ann Green's employee accountant for five years. During that time, Green has relied more and more on Ledger to prepare payment checks for suppliers, payroll checks, and the like. Unknown to Green, Ledger is a compulsive gambler and is deeply in debt. Ledger, believing that his life is at stake, prepares two checks payable to nonexistent suppliers. Green signs both checks without knowledge of these events. Ledger indorses both suppliers' names and adds "pay to Able Ledger" above both names. Ledger takes the checks and deposits them at his bank without indorsement. Later, he withdraws the funds from his bank. His bank sends the checks through the collection process. The checks are paid by Green's bank, the drawee. Green discovers Ledger's action after Ledger has left town. Green claims that Ledger's indorsement of the suppliers' names constituted a forgery, that Ledger's bank did not have Ledger's indorsement, and that therefore the bank must recredit her account. Discuss Green's contentions.

4.   John and Mary Smith ordered a clock from a catalog seller. John sent the seller a check for $50 with the order. The seller cashed the check. When the seller found she could not deliver the clock, she drew and sent a refund check to the Smiths. When the Smiths received the check, they noticed that it was made payable to Jonathan and Mary Smith. Mary Smith is now away visiting her mother, and John needs to negotiate the check to pay an overdue bill.

(a) Can John properly negotiate the check without Mary's indorsement? Explain.

(b) John is concerned that the check is made payable to Jonathan, not John. Would this prohibit John from negotiating the check under any circumstances? Explain.

5. Jay Jones is an Elevated Party candidate for City Council in a large city. It is common knowledge that Jones is personally soliciting funds throughout the neighborhood. Frank Francis has been a member of the Elevated Party for years. He receives a phone call from Sam Shady, who pretends to be Jay Jones and asks for financial help. Over the phone Francis agrees to write a check for $200 payable to Jay Jones. Shady gives Jones a post office box address. Francis writes the check and sends it to the box as directed. Shady has nothing to do with the campaign of Jones, and the box is his own. Shady immediately takes the check and indorses the name of Jones and then his own name. Shady now negotiates the check to a friend, Judy Green, who has no knowledge of Shady's activities. Shady leaves the country. Later, Francis learns of the fraud. Francis claims that since the signature of Jones was forged by Shady, Francis is not liable to Green on the check. Discuss the contention of Francis.

6. Dynamics Corp. and Marine Midland Bank had a long-standing agreement under which Marine Midland received checks payable to Dynamics and indorsed and deposited them in Dynamics' account. Dynamics never saw the checks. They were made out to the order of Dynamics and delivered directly to Marine Midland. Marine Midland stamped the backs of the checks with Dynamics' name and insignia and transferred them. Within the meaning of the UCC, is the act of sending checks to Marine Midland Bank a negotiation? If Marine Midland transfers the checks to other parties, is this a negotiation? [Marine Midland Bank–New York v. Graybar Electric Co., 41 N.Y.2d 703, 363 N.E.2d 1139 (1977)]

7. At one of the weekly auctions that Sweedler conducted, a purchaser bid for and received merchandise worth approximately $300. In return, the purchaser gave Sweedler a cashier's check that was payable to the purchaser. However, he failed to indorse the check, and Sweedler inadvertently failed to request the indorsement. Without the indorsement, the bank refused to pay Sweedler. The purchaser also refused to indorse the check because he was dissatisfied with the merchandise. If, at a trial between Sweedler and the bank, the purchaser admits that he gave Sweedler the cashier's check in exchange for certain merchandise, will Sweedler be allowed to recover against the bank? [Sweedler v. Oboler, 65 Misc.2d 789, 319 N.Y.S.2d 89 (1971)]

8. Davis, a Marine, often ran out of money and telegraphed his father to wire him extra cash. On August 1, 1945, the father received a telegram, purportedly from his son, requesting $250. The father wired a money order to the Western Union office nearest his son's base. Though the Western Union money order application contained an option whereby the father could require positive identification of the recipient at the other end, the father failed to sign for this special provision. Later, when the father learned that an imposter, not his son, had received the $250, he demanded his money back from Western Union. Western Union declined. Should the father recover? [Davis v. Western Union Telegraph Co., 4 D. & C.2d 264 (Pa.1956)]

9. F. Mitchell, assistant treasurer of Travco Corporation, caused two checks payable to a fictitious company, L. and B. Distributors, to be drawn on the corporation's account. Mitchell took both checks to his personal bank, indorsed them "F. Mitchell," and gave them to the teller. The teller cashed them. When Travco learned of the embezzlement, it demanded reimbursement from the bank. The bank contended that under the rule concerning fictitious payees and imposters, Mitchell's indorsement was valid and that therefore the bank should be allowed to collect. Is the bank's contention true? [Travco Corp. v. Citizens Federal Sav. & Loan Ass'n, 42 Mich.App. 291, 201 N.W.2d 675 (1972)]

10. Walker was a bookkeeper for O.K. Moving & Storage Company. She opened a checking account under her own name at Elgin National Bank. For one year, she took checks made payable to O.K. Moving & Storage and indorsed them "For deposit only, O.K. Moving & Storage Company." She then deposited them in her individual account at the bank. O.K. Moving & Storage discovered her actions. It sued Elgin National Bank for conversion of its checks. Will O.K. Moving prevail? [O.K. Moving & Storage Co. v. Elgin National Bank, 363 So.2d 160, Dist.Ct.App.Fla. (1978)]

CHAPTER 27

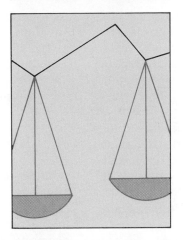

COMMERCIAL PAPER
Holder in Due Course

Commercial paper is not money; rather, it is an instrument that is payable in money. Litigation concerning commercial paper occurs when there is a dispute about who should be paid. Issues of litigation usually turn on which party can obtain payment on an instrument when it is due or on whether or not some defense can be asserted to discharge or to cancel liability on an instrument. For these reasons, it becomes important for a person seeking payment to have the rights of a holder in due course.

A holder in due course takes a negotiable instrument free of all claims and most defenses of other parties. That means that the holder in due course has the right to collect payment on that instrument, and this right will take priority over the claims of other parties.[1]

---

1. UCC 3-305(2) specifically sets forth the very limited number of real *defenses* that defeat payment to a holder in due course. A holder in due course takes commercial paper free from personal (as opposed to real) defenses. These are discussed more thoroughly in Chapter 28.

CONTRACT LAW VERSUS THE LAW OF COMMERCIAL PAPER

The basic principles of contract law govern when simple contract rights are assigned to a third party, when a nonnegotiable instrument is transferred to a third party, or when a negotiable instrument is improperly negotiated to a third party (transferee). The contract rights of assignees or transferees are burdened with every legal defense that existed between prior parties regardless of the extent of their knowledge of them. Persons who transfer or assign contractual or nonnegotiable rights pass on only the rights that they had.

For example, Martin contracts in writing to purchase a used word processor from Francis for $600. Martin needs the word processor in his business. Martin pays $200 down and agrees to pay the balance, plus 10 percent interest, in six equal installments. Francis, as part of the sale, made express warranties as to the amount of prior use and the condition of the word processor. Shortly after the sale and transfer, Francis sells and assigns the contract and balance to Arlene. Martin learns that Francis has lied about the prior use, and the processor is not in the condition warranted. Martin refuses to make any further payments on the contract, claiming breach of warranty. Arlene insists that she has no knowledge of the deceit, is an innocent party, and wants to enforce the contractually obligated payments against Martin. Because Arlene as assignee is subject to any defense Martin has against the assignor, Francis, Arlene is subject to the claims and defenses of Martin.

The body of rules contained in Article 3 of the UCC govern a party's right to payment of a check, draft, note, or certificate of deposit.[2] The third party is characterized as either an ordinary *holder* or a *holder in due course*.[3] (The party can also be a transferee according to UCC 3-201.) Our discussion of holders in due course will be concerned primarily with *negotiable* instruments that have been negotiated.

HOLDER

As pointed out in Chapter 24, a holder is a person who possesses a negotiable instrument "drawn, issued, or indorsed to him or his order or to bearer or in blank." [UCC 1-201(20)] In other words, the holder is the person who, by the terms of the instrument, is legally entitled to payment. The holder of an instrument need not be its owner in order to transfer it, negotiate it, discharge it, or enforce payment of it in his or her own name. [UCC 3-301]

A holder has the status of an assignee of a contract right. A transferee of a negotiable instrument who is characterized merely as a holder

(as opposed to a holder in due course) obtains only those rights that the predecessor-transferor had in the instrument. In the event that there is a conflicting, superior claim or defense to the instrument, an ordinary holder will not be able to collect payment.

HOLDER IN DUE COURSE

A **holder in due course** (HDC) is a special-status transferee of a negotiable instrument who, by meeting certain acquisition requirements, takes the instrument *free* of most defenses or adverse claims to it. Stated another way, an HDC can normally acquire a higher level of immunity to defenses against payment on the instrument or claims of ownership to the instrument by other parties.

Requirements for Holder-in-Due-Course Status

The basic requirements for attaining HDC status are set forth in UCC 3-302. An HDC must first be a holder of a negotiable instrument. The holder must take the instrument (1) for value, (2) in good faith, and (3) without notice that it is overdue, or that it has been dishonored, or that any person has a defense against it or a claim to it.

The underlying requirement of "due course" status is that a person must first be a holder on that instrument. Regardless of other circumstances surrounding acquisition, only a holder has a chance to become an HDC.

Taking for Value An HDC must have given *value* for the instrument. [UCC 3-303] A person who receives an instrument as a gift or who inherits it has not met the requirement of value. In these situations, the person becomes an ordinary holder and does not possess the rights of an HDC.[4]

---

2. The rights and liabilities on checks, drafts, notes, and certificates of deposit are determined under Article 3 of the UCC. Other kinds of commercial paper, such as stock certificates or bills of lading and other documents of title, meet the requirements of negotiable instruments, but the rights and liabilities of the parties on these documents are covered by Articles 7 and 8 of the Code.

3. A holder, as the term is used in Article 3 of the UCC, applies here only in the context of negotiable instruments.

---

4. There is one way an ordinary holder who fails to meet the value requirement can qualify as a holder in due course. The "shelter provision" of the Code allows an ordinary holder to succeed to HDC status if any prior holder was an HDC. This exception is discussed later in the chapter. [UCC 3-201(1)]

The concept of value in the law of negotiable instruments is not the same as the concept of consideration in the law of contracts. An executory promise (a promise to give value in the future) is clearly valid consideration to support a contract. [UCC 1-201(44)] It does not, however, normally constitute value sufficient to make one an HDC. UCC 3-303 provides that a holder takes the instrument for value only to the extent that the agreed-upon consideration has been performed. Therefore, if the holder plans to pay for the instrument later or plans to perform the required services at some future date, the holder has not yet given value. In that case, the holder is not yet a holder in due course.

Suppose Ted Green draws a $500 note payable to Roger Evans in payment for goods. Evans negotiates the note to Irene Franks, who promises to pay him for it in thirty days. During the next month, Franks learns that Evans breached the contract by delivering defective goods and that Green will not honor the $500 note. Evans has left town. Whether Franks can hold Green liable on the note will depend on Franks's status as a holder in due course. Since Franks has given no value at the time of having learned of Green's defense, Franks is a mere holder, not a holder in due course. Thus, Green's defense is valid not only against Evans but also against Franks. If Franks had paid Evans for the note on the transfer (which would mean the agreed-upon consideration had been performed), she would be a holder in due course and could hold Green liable on the note even though Green had a valid breach of contract or warranty defense against Evans.

The Code provides for a holder to take the instrument for value in one of three ways. Basically, a holder gives value:

1. To the extent that the agreed-upon consideration has been paid or a security interest or lien acquired.
2. By payment of or as security for an antecedent debt.
3. By giving a negotiable instrument or irrevocable commitment as payment.

The following case takes up the question of value. Donald Goldberg sold his interest in a corporation to Rothman and others for $7,500. Upon Goldberg's request, the buyers made four promissory notes payable to Ethel Goldberg, his wife.

BACKGROUND AND FACTS *The plaintiff, Ethel Goldberg, sought to recover the sum of $7,500 on four promissory notes in which she was designated the payee. The notes were executed by six individual defendants. At the time the notes were made, the plaintiff's husband, Donald Goldberg, and the defendants were all stockholders in a corporation known as 86th Street Bay 40th Corporation. The notes were given in consideration for the sale of Donald Goldberg's interest in the corporation to the defendants. At Donald Goldberg's request, the notes were made payable to his wife, the plaintiff, who otherwise had no interest in or connection with the corporation.*

The defendants alleged that they had a valid cause of action that they should be able to assert against Donald Goldberg and against Ethel Goldberg as payee on the promissory notes because, at the time the notes were executed, Donald Goldberg specifically said that certain monies would be paid for goods that had been sold pursuant to a business deal in which the corporation was involved.

The defendants claimed that a balance of $7,643.33 was due as a result of this other business deal and that they should be able to bring an action against Donald Goldberg as a counterclaim, or, at least, as a

GOLDBERG v. ROTHMAN

Civil Court of the City of New York, 1971.

66 Misc.2d 981, 322 N.Y.S.2d 931.

setoff against the plaintiff's cause of action. [Background and Facts substantially as stated by the court.]

BOYERS, Justice.

*   *   *   *

There is no explanation or reason as to why plaintiff was designated payee of the subject notes other than it was done in compliance with Donald Goldberg's request. Nor does it appear that plaintiff took the instruments for "value" as that term is defined by § 3-303 of the Uniform Commercial Code. For ought that appears Donald Goldberg gave these notes as a gift to the plaintiff, but such a determination is not relevant to the issues herein. It is clear that a payee may be a holder in due course (see § 3-302, Uniform Commercial Code), but since the plaintiff herein did not take the instruments for value she is an ordinary holder. Nonetheless she has the rights of a holder and may enforce payment in her own name (§ 3-301, Uniform Commercial Code). *   *   * [T]he court feels the merits or lack of merits of defendants' contention of an assignment and the promise of Donald Goldberg that the debt owing to [defendants] could be set off against the notes is not relevant to plaintiff's cause of action for reasons hereafter set forth.

Under § 3-306, Uniform Commercial Code, plaintiff not having the rights of a holder in due course takes the instrument here, the notes in question, "subject to (b) all defenses of any party which would be available in an action on simple contract."

*   *   *   *

Plaintiff sues herein in her own right. Defendants have not shown that any defenses exist against her in relation to the validity of the notes nor have they established that they have any right of setoff because of an alleged claim against plaintiff's husband.

JUDGMENT AND REMEDY   *The court held that Ethel Goldberg was entitled to recover $7,500 from the defendants. However, her award did not prejudice any cause of action the defendants had against Donald Goldberg. The court made it clear that the plaintiff's right to recover was independent of her husband's possible liability in another lawsuit.*

Agreed-upon Consideration Performed A holder takes an instrument for value to the extent that agreed-upon consideration has been performed. In the typical situation, the holder is a purchaser for money. For example, Morris executes a $300 note payable to the order of Paulson. Paulson sells the note to a bank which pays Paulson $285 (a discount is usual). The bank has given full value for Morris's note.

Performance of agreed-upon consideration can also include an act such as the delivery of goods. Harper holds a note from Barton and agrees to negotiate the note to Thompson in payment for a purchase of goods. Delivery of the goods is Thompson's agreed-upon performance, that is, the value given for the note.

UCC 3-303(a) provides that a holder takes an instrument for value only to the extent that the agreed-upon consideration has been performed. For example, Arnolds negotiates a $1,000 note to Raymonds for a total price of $950, with $700 payable now and $250 due in thirty days. Raymonds is immediately an HDC to the extent of $700, and when she completes payment of $250, she will become an HDC for the full $1,000 face amount of the note.

Do not be confused when the value of the agreed-upon consideration differs from the face amount of the instrument. When a time instrument is sold, it is usually discounted to allow for transfer costs, collection costs, and interest charges. Thus, a $1,000 note due in ninety days may be sold for $950 cash to a financial institution. The requirement of agreed-upon consideration is satisfied by the $950 payment. And when the instrument comes due, the holder will collect the full $1,000. If the discrepancy between the purchase amount and face value is great, however, this discrepancy can be considered along with other factors to indicate either that the purchaser lacks good faith or that only a partial payment is being made, reducing the HDC status to this amount. The good faith element will be discussed later in this chapter.

A holder takes an instrument for value to the extent that the holder acquires a security interest in or lien on the instrument.[5] It is not unusual for an instrument to be given as security for a loan or other obligation.

If, for example, Norris issues a $1,000 note payable to Lomond, Lomond can use the note to secure a $700 loan from Hilton. (Lomond gets $700 cash; Hilton holds the note as security.) Hilton's $700 loan qualifies her as a holder for value. If Lomond does not repay the $700, Hilton can collect the note. But what if Norris has a personal defense against Lomond? Hilton, as an HDC, is free and clear of the defense, but *only to the extent of $700*. Hence, the rule is, "a purchaser of a limited interest can be a holder in due course only to the extent of the interest purchased." [UCC 3-302(4)]

A holder can also take for value by acquiring a lien on the instrument through an agreement rather than through operation of law. For example, a payee of a note pledges it to a bank as security for a loan. The terms of the pledge agreement give the bank a lien on the instru-

ment. The bank is a holder for value to the extent of its lien.

Antecedent Claim   When an instrument is given in payment of an **antecedent claim** (or as security for an antecedent, or prior, debt), the value requirement is met. [UCC 3-303(b)] Here again, commercial law and contract law produce different results. An antecedent debt is not valid consideration under general contract law, but it does constitute value sufficient to satisfy the requirement for HDC status in commercial law.

Assume Cary owes Dwyer $2,000 on a past due account. If Cary negotiates a $2,000 note to Dwyer and Dwyer accepts it to discharge the overdue account balance, Dwyer has given value for the instrument.

Negotiable Instrument as Value   Merely promising to pay money or to perform an act in the future does not constitute giving value. However, if a purchaser's promise to pay money is made in the form of a negotiable instrument or irrevocable commitment (for example, a check or an irrevocable letter of credit), the requirement of value is met. UCC 3-303(c) provides that a holder takes the instrument for value "when he gives a negotiable instrument for it, or makes an irrevocable commitment to a third person."

To illustrate: Martin has issued a $500 negotiable promissory note to Paula. The note is due six months from the date issued. Paula's financial circumstances are such that she does not want to wait for the maturity date to collect. Therefore, Paula negotiates the note to her friend Susan, who pays Paula $200 in cash and writes Paula a negotiable check for the balance of $300. Susan has given full value for the note by paying $200 in cash and issuing Paula the check for $300.

A negotiable instrument has value when issued, not when the underlying obligation is finally paid. In the preceding example, assume that before Paula cashes Susan's check, Susan learns that the maker of the note has a personal defense against Paula. In this event, Susan has the protection of HDC status. Commercial practicality requires this rule because a negotiable instrument, by its nature, carries the possibility that it might be negotiated to a holder in due

---

5. A holder does not become an HDC of an instrument by purchasing it at a judicial sale or by taking it under legal process. [UCC 3-302(3)(a)]

course. If it is, the party that issued it generally cannot refuse to pay. [UCC 3-303]

In the following case, the plaintiff tried to claim that his action fit the definition of *taking for value* so that he could retain the proceeds of a check.

BENNETT v. UNITED STATES FIDELITY AND GUAR. CO.
Court of Appeals of North Carolina, 1973.
19 N.C.App. 66, 198 S.E.2d 33.

BACKGROUND AND FACTS   *Bennett, the plaintiff, sued to recover $4,400, the amount of a check issued by an insurance company in settlement of an automobile damage claim. The plaintiff's mother, Mabel, owned the car. The plaintiff had possession of it, and he allowed his friend, Wilbur Prince, to borrow it. While driving the car, Prince wrecked it. He reported the accident to his insurance company, the defendant, United States Fidelity and Guaranty Company.*

The insurance company negotiated a settlement for $4,400. It issued a check jointly payable to its insured, Prince, and to the owner of the car, Mabel Bennett. The two indorsed the check to the plaintiff, who then deposited it in his bank account, intending to use the money to purchase a new car.

During the time it took the check to clear, the insurance company issued a stop-payment order because it discovered that the insurance policy did not cover collision damage for nonowned vehicles. The plaintiff took the position that he was a holder in due course and had the right to recover from the insurance company, notwithstanding the company's dispute with Prince and Mable.

MORRIS, Judge.

*   *   *   *

Plaintiff [Bennett] contends that he is entitled, under [UCC 3-302], to the amount of the draft. [UCC 3-302] defines a holder in due course as one who takes an instrument for value, and in good faith, and without notice that it is overdue or has been dishonored or of any defense against or claim to it on the part of any person.

The undisputed evidence discloses that plaintiff was without notice of the defense of the issuer and that he took the instrument in good faith and for the purpose of purchasing an automobile to replace the one wrecked by defendant's insured. The only question about which the parties disagree is whether plaintiff took the check for value.

[UCC 3-303] defines taking for value as follows:

"A holder takes the instrument for value (a) to the extent that the agreed consideration has been performed or that he acquires a security interest in or a lien on the instrument otherwise than by legal process; or (b) when he takes the instrument in payment of or as security for an antecedent claim against any person whether or not the claim is due; or (c) when he gives a negotiable instrument for it or makes an irrevocable commitment to a third person."

Plaintiff earnestly contends that he comes within the purview of the definition for two reasons.

He first contends that the evidence discloses that he took the check in payment of an antecedent claim against Wilbur Lee Prince and, therefore, he took the check for value. There is no dispute about the fact that the car was registered in the name of plaintiff's mother. Plaintiff, therefore, had no claim against Prince for the damage to the car. On appeal he says, however, that he had a claim against Prince for damage to personal property in the car at the time of the wreck. A close examination of the record, and particularly the deposition and affidavit of plaintiff, reveals absolutely no evidence of whether plaintiff had any property in the car and if so, what it was. In his affidavit, plaintiff said: "The value given by him to Wilbur Lee Prince was full settlement of any claim that he might have against Wilbur Lee Prince for the loss of any personal property Wilbur Lee Prince was responsible for when the Datsun automobile was damaged," but nowhere does he contend that he did in fact have any personal property in the car. Plaintiff has failed to present any evidence which would tend to show any legal claim against either payee, which plaintiff had and relinquished.

He also contends that he gave value by virtue of the provisions of [UCC 3-303(c)] in that he made an irrevocable commitment to a third person. Plaintiff contends and the evidence reveals that he intended to use the amount of the check for the purchase of a new car. He stated in his deposition that the insurance draft was delivered to him; that he carried it to his mother and to Prince for endorsement and then deposited it in his checking account at Wachovia Bank and Trust Company; that he was told at the time he made the deposit that it would take "a couple of days to clear"; that he then called the insurance agent who suggested that he postdate the check he was to give in payment for the car he was buying; that he then went to the dealer and followed this suggestion.

The official comment to [UCC 3-303(c)] is as follows:

"Paragraph (c) is new, but states generally recognized exceptions to the rule that an executory promise is not value. A negotiable instrument is value because it carries the possibility of negotiation to a holder in due course, after which the party who gives it cannot refuse to pay. The same reasoning applies to any irrevocable commitment to a third person, such as a letter credit issued when an instrument is taken."

We are of the opinion that the wording of the statute contemplates a simultaneous transaction—a commitment to a third person made when the holder takes the instrument. We do not construe it to include a commitment made subsequent to the taking of the instrument. We hold, therefore, that plaintiff's subsequent reliance on the payment of the draft does not constitute a taking for value necessary to put plaintiff in the position of holder in due course.

The undisputed facts establish that plaintiff is not a holder in due course.

Bennett was unable to recover the $4,400, since the appellate court found that he was not a holder in due course of the insurance company's check.   **JUDGMENT AND REMEDY**

Check Deposits and Withdrawals Occasionally, a commercial bank can become an HDC when honoring other banks' checks for its own customers. In this situation the bank becomes an "involuntary" holder in due course, in that at the time of giving value the bank has no intention of becoming an HDC.

Assume that on Monday morning Pat Stevens has $200 in her checking account at the First National Bank. That morning Stevens deposits her payroll check for $300 drawn by her employer on the Second National Bank. During her lunch hour she issues a check to her landlord for $225. The landlord cashes the check at the First National Bank. Later, the Second National Bank returns the payroll check marked "insufficient funds." In most cases, First National would charge this check against Stevens's account. If such cannot be done, however, is the First National Bank an HDC of the employer's check? The answer is yes. According to what is referred to as the first-money-in, first-money-out rule, First National Bank has paid to the landlord $25 of its own funds. [UCC 4-208(2)] Therefore, First National is an HDC to the extent it has given value—$25.

Taking in Good Faith

The second requirement for HDC status is that the holder take the instrument in good faith. [UCC 3-302(1)(b)] This means that the purchaser-holder must have acted honestly in the process of acquiring the instrument. **Good faith** is defined in

UCC 1-201(19) as "honesty in fact in the conduct or transaction concerned."

The good faith requirement *applies only to the holder.* It is immaterial whether the transferor acted in good faith. Thus, a person who in good faith takes a negotiable instrument from a thief can be an HDC. The reason is simple. An inherent characteristic of negotiable paper is that any person in possession of an instrument that runs to him or her by its terms is a holder. Also, anyone can deal with the possessor as a holder.

Because of the good faith requirement, one must ask whether the purchaser, when acquiring the instrument, honestly believed the instrument was not defective. If a person purchases a $10,000 note for $100 from a stranger on a street corner, the issue of good faith can be raised on the grounds of the suspicious circumstances *and* the grossly inadequate consideration. The Code does not provide clear guidelines to determine good faith. Thus, each situation will be examined separately. The issue in the following case is whether a bank acquired a check in good faith.

MANUFACTURERS AND TRADERS TRUST COMPANY v. MURPHY

United States District Court, W.D. Pennsylvania, 1974. 369 F.Supp. 11.

BACKGROUND AND FACTS *Murphy gave Brownsworth a check for $15,000 for the purchase of carpeting that the two men intended to resell at a profit. The plaintiff, Manufacturers and Traders Trust Company (M&T), issued a cashier's check for $15,000 to Brownsworth to replace Murphy's personal check. Murphy had become suspicious of the proposed venture and had stopped payment on his check. The plaintiff, claiming to be a holder in due course, sued Murphy for recovery.*

KNOX, District Judge.

* * * *

M & T claims that it is a holder in due course in compliance with the requirements of 3-302 of the Uniform Commercial Code.

Under that section, plaintiff claims it gave value (its cashier's check for $15,000) in good faith (having contacted Murphy's Meadville Bank to verify account and the sufficiency of funds) and had no notice of defenses or claims against the instrument when taken (the stop payment order by Murphy was not made until later). M & T has presented the check and its evidence of being a holder in due course which it has the burden of establishing. At that point, the defendant, Murphy, must come forward with evidence which would establish, if believed, that plaintiff is not a holder in due course.

The defendant contends that M & T is not a holder in due course since it lacked the good faith required to be such a holder. In support of this proposition, Murphy advances two theories:

First, that because Brownsworth was not a regular customer at M & T bank that the cashing or giving of a cashier's check was not in good faith generally. This argument overlooks the fact that the Silvercreek manager of plaintiff's branch bank called Murphy's bank in Meadville to verify the account and the sufficiency of funds on this check which appeared authentic on its face. Therefore, we reject this argument. It must be kept in mind that the law favors negotiability of a negotiable instrument.

Second, that a lack of good faith is shown on plaintiff's part by the conflicting stories given by Brownsworth to two of the branch bank managers. This, defendant alleges, gave some type of notice to the bank generally which would make them suspicious and destroy any good faith in dealing with Brownsworth. This notice to the branch offices fails on its face to convince us but it furthermore lacks merit for the reason that the plaintiff bank was irrevocably committed on the $15,000 personal check of Murphy *prior to* a different story being given by Brownsworth at the Fredonia branch office. M & T became liable to pay on its $15,000 cashier's check immediately upon issuing it. It became a holder in due course at that moment and later events would make no difference in that status. Therefore, we reject this theory of defendant as well.

*   *   *   *

Furthermore, the defendant has failed within the totality of the circumstances in this case to show any bad faith on the part of M & T.

We therefore determine as a matter of law that plaintiff is a holder in due course of the Murphy check for $15,000.

Judgment was entered for the bank.

JUDGMENT
AND REMEDY

Taking without Notice

The third requirement for HDC status involves notice. [UCC 3-304] A person will not be afforded HDC protection if he or she acquires an instrument knowing, or having reason to know, that it is defective in any one of the following ways: [UCC 3-302(1)(c)]

1. It is overdue.
2. It has been dishonored.
3. There is a defense against it.
4. There is another claim to it.

The main provisions of UCC 3-304 spell out the common circumstances that, as a matter of law, constitute notice of a claim or defense and notice of an overdue instrument. However, UCC 3-304(4) specifies certain facts that a purchaser might know about an instrument but that do not constitute notice of a defense or claim. These facts do not disqualify the purchaser from HDC status.

Notice of a Fact   Notice of a fact involves [UCC 1-201(25)]: 1. Actual knowledge of it. 2. Receipt of a notice about it. 3. Reason to know that a fact exists, given all the facts and circumstances known at the time in question.

Overdue Instruments   All negotiable paper is either payable at a definite time (time instrument) or payable on demand (demand instrument). What will constitute notice that an instrument is overdue or has been dishonored will vary depending upon whether a person takes demand or time paper.

Time Instruments   A holder of a time instrument who takes the paper the day after its expressed due date is "on notice" that it is overdue. Nonpayment by the due date should indicate to any purchaser who is obligated to pay that the primary party has a defense to payment. Thus, a promissory note due on May 15 must be acquired before midnight on May 15. If it is purchased on May 16, the purchaser will be an ordinary holder, not an HDC.

Sometimes instruments read, "Payable in thirty days." A note dated December 1 that is payable in thirty days is due by midnight on December 31. But, what if a note is dated December 2 and is payable in thirty days? When is it due? If the payment date falls on a Sunday or holiday, the instrument is payable on the next business day, so the note is due on January 2.

A large debt is often broken down into successive payments. The debt can be evidenced by a single, large-denomination note payable in installments, or there can be a series of notes in smaller denominations issued, each identified as part of the same indebtedness. In the case of an installment note, notice that the maker has defaulted on any installment of principal (but not interest payments) will prevent a purchaser from becoming an HDC. [UCC 3-304(3)(a)] Some installment notes provide specifically that any payment made on the note shall be applied first to interest, with the balance to principal. Thus, any installment payment submitted that is less than the amount owed on that installment would put a holder on notice that the note is overdue.

The same result occurs when a series of notes, each with successive maturity dates, is issued at the same time for a single indebtedness. An uncured default in payment of any one note of the series will constitute overdue notice for the entire series. Prospective purchasers then know that they cannot qualify as HDCs.

Suppose a note reads, "Payable May 15, but may be accelerated if the holder feels insecure." A purchaser, unaware that a prior holder has elected to accelerate the due date on the instrument, buys the instrument prior to May 15. UCC 3-304(3)(b) provides that such a purchaser can be a holder in due course unless he or she has reason to know that the acceleration has occurred.

Demand Instruments A purchaser has notice that a demand instrument is overdue if he or she takes the instrument knowing that demand has been made or takes it an unreasonable length of time after its issue. "A reasonable time for a check

drawn and payable within the states and territories of the United States and the District of Columbia is *presumed* to be 30 days." [UCC 3-304(3)(c)] [Emphasis added]

Obviously, what constitutes a reasonable time period depends on the circumstances. Except for a domestic check, in which a reasonable time is presumed to be thirty days, there are no exact measurements for determining a reasonable time. Past cases indicate, however, that a reasonable time for payment of an interest-bearing demand instrument is longer than for one payable without interest.

Dishonored Instruments Only actual knowledge that an instrument was previously dishonored, or knowledge of facts that would lead a holder to suspect that such had happened, puts a holder on notice. Thus, a check clearly stamped "insufficient funds," taken by a person, would put that person on notice. No notice exists without this knowledge. For example, Burton holds a demand note dated March 1 on Kayto, Inc., a local business firm. On March 19, she demands payment, and Kayto refuses (that is, dishonors the instrument). On March 20, Burton negotiates the note to Reynolds, a purchaser who lives in another state. Reynolds does not know and has no reason to know that the note has been dishonored, so Reynolds is not put on notice and therefore can become an HDC.

Claims Against or Defenses to an Instrument Knowledge of claims or defenses can be imputed to the purchaser in certain situations because (1) they are apparent from an examination of the face of the instrument or (2) they are extraneous to the instrument but apparent from the facts surrounding the transaction.

The Code provides that a purchaser of a negotiable instrument has "notice of a claim or defense if *   * the instrument is so incomplete, bears such visible evidence of forgery or alteration, or is otherwise so irregular as to call into question its validity, terms of ownership *   * or *   * that the obligation of any party is voidable in whole or in part, or that all parties have been discharged." [UCC 3-304(1)(a)(b)]

Incomplete Instruments   A purchaser cannot expect to become an HDC when an instrument is so incomplete on its face that an element of negotiability is lacking (for example, the name of the payee on order paper is missing, or the amount is not filled in). Minor omissions are permissible because these do not call into question the validity of the instrument.

For example, omission of connective words, such as the "on" in "pay to Smith on order," does not affect negotiability and neither does omission of the date from a check that has the month and year. [UCC 3-304(1)(a) and 3-114(1)]

When a person accepts an instrument without knowing that it is incomplete, then that person can take as an HDC and enforce the instrument as completed. To illustrate: Stuart Morgan asks Joan Nelson to buy a textbook for him when she goes to the campus bookstore. Morgan writes a check payable to the campus store, leaves the amount blank, and tells her to fill in the price of the textbook. Assume the textbook costs $15.50 in each of the following situations.

1.   If Nelson gives the store the check with the amount entirely blank, the check is so incomplete that not only is it non-negotiable (it has no certain amount), but also the bookstore cannot qualify as an HDC.
2.   If the cashier sees that the check is blank, watches Nelson complete the amount as $65.50, and then gives her $50 in change, the store will probably still be an HDC if the cashier is without notice that the filling in of the amount is improper. [UCC 3-304(4)(d)]
3.   If Nelson fills in the check for $65.50 before she gets to the bookstore, the store sees only a properly completed instrument. Therefore it will take the check as an HDC and can enforce it for the full $65.50. The unauthorized completion is not a sufficient defense against the store in this situation. [UCC 3-407 and 3-115]

Irregular Instruments   Any noticeable irregularity on the face of an instrument that should indicate to a purchaser that something is wrong with the paper will bar HDC status. For example, a note bearing a payee's signature that has been lined through with bold strokes, with the second name penciled above it, is highly irregular and will disqualify a taker from HDC status. [UCC 3-304(1)(a)]

On the other hand, a note that is otherwise negotiable, containing the notation "payable at Newark," will not be the subject of inquiry because such notation does not raise questions essential to the terms, ownership, or validity of the note, nor does it create an ambiguity as to who is the party required to pay. [UCC 3-304(1)(a)]

Different handwriting used in the body of a check and in the signature will not in and of itself make an instrument irregular. Postdating or antedating a check, or stating the amount in digits but failing to write out the numbers, will not make a check irregular. [UCC 3-114(2)]

Visible evidence of forgery or alterations to material elements of negotiable paper will disqualify a purchaser from HDC status. Conversely, a careful forgery or alteration can go undetected by reasonable examination, and therefore, the purchaser can qualify as an HDC. [UCC 3-304(1)(a)] However, losses that result from careful forgeries usually fall on the party to whom the forger transferred the instrument (assuming, of course, that the forger cannot be found).

Voidable Obligations   It stands to reason that a purchaser who knows that a party to an instrument has a defense that entitles that party to avoid the obligation in any way cannot be a holder in due course. At the very least, good faith requires *honesty in fact* of the purchaser in a transaction. For example, a potential purchaser who knows that the maker of a note has breached the underlying contract with the payee cannot thereafter purchase the note as an HDC. [UCC 3-304(1)(b)]

Knowledge of one defense precludes a holder from becoming an HDC with respect to all other defenses. Jones, knowing that the note he has taken was previously forged, presents it to the maker for payment. The maker refuses to pay on the grounds of breach of the underlying contract by the payee, Smith. The maker can assert this defense against Jones even though Jones had no knowledge of the breach because his knowledge of the forgery alone prevents him from being an HDC in *all* circumstances.

Knowledge that a fiduciary has wrongfully negotiated an instrument is sufficient notice of a claim against the instrument to disqualify HDC status. Suppose Jordan, a trustee of a university, improperly writes a check on the university trust account to pay a personal debt. Farley knows that the check has been improperly drawn from university funds, but she accepts it anyway. Farley cannot claim to be an HDC. When a purchaser knows that a fiduciary is acting in breach of trust, HDC status is denied. [UCC 3-304(2)]

There is a strong policy against *imputing* notice to an otherwise good faith purchaser on a negotiable instrument. Not all knowledge charges the purchaser with notice of a claim or defense. UCC 3-304(4) contains a list of specific facts that do not in themselves constitute notice of a defense or claim. The list can be reviewed in the full text of the Code contained in Appendix C. In short, the Code's position is that certain kinds of information about the instrument or about parties to it can raise some suspicion regarding the ultimate enforceability of the paper, but the information falls short of indicating a defense or claim.

Finally, knowledge from a public notice, for example, through newspapers or official records, is not automatically imputed to a purchaser; it must be shown that the information was read. [UCC 3-304(5)]

Recall that the basic test of good faith is honesty in fact. The key concern is whether this particular purchaser honestly knew or had reason to know something was wrong with that particular instrument at the time it was acquired.

Payee as HDC   Under certain circumstances, a payee may qualify as an HDC. [UCC 3-302(2)] In order to be an HDC, a payee must exercise good faith, give value, and take the instrument without notice of a defense against it or claim to it.

To illustrate: Able is Martin's agent. Able fraudulently convinces Martin that Martin owes a friend, Paula, $500 and is legally required to give her a promissory note for that amount. Martin signs the negotiable promissory note payable to Paula and gives the note to Able. Able takes the note to Paula with the story that Martin is in

need of money and hopes his friend Paula can help. In good faith and without knowledge of Able's fraud, Paula gives Able the money, taking the note. Able absconds with the cash. Upon learning of these events, Martin refuses to pay Paula on the note when it comes due. Although Paula is the payee, she has met the criteria of an HDC, and she can enforce the note against Martin.

Logic dictates that in the majority of instances, if there are defenses to the instrument, the payee will know or have reason to know about them. To illustrate: Baker Painters contracts with Amex Company to paint the exterior of its new office building for $2,000. Amex issues a negotiable promissory note to Baker Painters for $2,000, due thirty days later. When the note comes due, Baker tries to collect the $2,000 from Amex. Amex refuses to pay the note, claiming that the paint was defective; it washed off during a rainstorm. Since Baker Painters obviously knows about the defective paint, Baker Painters is not an HDC. Amex can disavow liability on the note based on the breach of the underlying contract.

HOLDERS THROUGH A HOLDER IN DUE COURSE

A person who does not qualify as a holder in due course but who derives his or her title *through a holder in due course* can acquire the rights and privileges of a holder in due course. According to UCC 3-201(1):

Transfer of an instrument vests in the transferee such rights as the transferor has therein, except that a transferee who has himself been a party to any fraud or illegality affecting the instrument or who as a prior holder had notice of a defense or claim against it cannot improve his position by taking from a later holder in due course.

This is sometimes called the **shelter provision.** This rule seems to detract from the basic holder-in-due-course philosophy. It is, however, in line with the concept of marketability and free transferability of commercial paper, as well as contract law, which provides that assignees acquire the rights of assignors. The transfer rule extends the holder-in-due-course benefits, and it is designed to aid the HDC to dispose of the instrument readily. Since any instrument in the hands of an HDC is free from personal defenses (by definition), an HDC should reasonably have the privilege of transferring all rights in the instrument.

Consider an example: By fraud, Jensen induces Bonanza to write her a check payable to her order. Later Jensen negotiates the check to Gonzales, an HDC. Still later, Gonzales indorses it specially to Adams for value, but Adams knows of the original fraud. Adams is not an HDC because of such knowledge, but he is a holder because he has taken through an HDC and has the same rights as an HDC. Anyone, no matter how far removed from an HDC, who can trace his or her title ultimately back to an HDC, comes within the shelter provision. Normally, a person who acquires an instrument from an HDC or from someone with HDC rights gets HDC rights on the principle that the transferee of an instrument gets at least the rights that the transferor had.

Limitations on the Shelter Provision

However, UCC 3-201(1) explicitly indicates that certain persons who formerly held instruments cannot improve their positions by later reacquiring them from HDCs. Thus, if a holder was a party to fraud or illegality affecting the instrument, or if, as a prior holder, he or she had notice of a claim or defense against an instrument, that holder is not allowed to improve his or her status by repurchasing from a later HDC. In other words, a person is not allowed to "launder" the paper by passing it into the hands of an HDC and then buying it back.

To illustrate: Bailey and Zopa collaborate to defraud Manor. Manor is induced to give Zopa a negotiable note payable to Zopa's order. Zopa then specially indorses the note for value to Adams, an HDC. Bailey and Zopa split the proceeds. Adams negotiates the note to Stanley, another HDC. Stanley then negotiates the note for value to Bailey. Bailey, even though he got the note through an HDC, is not a holder through an

HDC, for he participated in the original fraud and can never acquire HDC rights in this note.

Special Cases

In a few exceptional circumstances, a holder can take an instrument even for value but still not be accorded HDC status. UCC 3-302(3) specifies the following situations:

1. Purchase at a judicial sale (for example, a bankruptcy sale) or taking under legal process.
2. Acquisition when taking over an estate (as administrator).
3. Purchase as part of a bulk transfer (for example, a corporation buying the assets of another corporation).

This provision limits the rights of the holder to that of an ordinary holder.

FEDERAL LIMITATIONS ON HOLDER-IN-DUE-COURSE RIGHTS

A relatively recent Federal Trade Commission (FTC) rule has severely limited the preferential position enjoyed by a holder in due course in certain circumstances. This so-called FTC Rule limits the rights of an HDC over an instrument that evidences a debt arising out of a consumer credit transaction. The rule, entitled "Preservation of Consumers' Claims and Defenses," is an attempt to prevent a situation in which a consumer is required to make payment for a defective product to a third party who is a holder in due course of a promissory note that formed part of the contract with the dealer who sold the defective good.

The FTC Rule[6] makes the following provision for any seller or lessor of goods or services who takes or receives a consumer credit contract or who accepts as full or partial payment for such sale or lease the proceeds of any purchase money loan made in connection with any consumer credit contract:

---

6. Section 433 of Title 15 U.S. Code, Sections 41 et seq., effective May 14, 1976.

NOTICE

ANY HOLDER OF THIS CONSUMER CREDIT CONTRACT IS SUBJECT TO ALL CLAIMS AND DEFENSES WHICH THE DEBTOR COULD ASSERT AGAINST THE SELLER OF GOODS OR SERVICES OBTAINED PURSUANT HERETO OR WITH THE PROCEEDS HEREOF. RECOVERY HEREUNDER BY THE DEBTOR SHALL NOT EXCEED AMOUNTS PAID BY THE DEBTOR HEREUNDER.

Obviously, the purpose of this notice is to inform any holder that upon acquisition of the negotiable commercial paper, he or she is subject to all claims and demands that the debtor could assert against the promisee or payee named in the paper. In essence, the FTC Rule places a holder in due course of the paper or of the negotiable instrument in the position of a contract assignee. The FTC Rule clearly reduces the degree of transferability of commercial paper resulting from consumer credit contracts.

QUESTIONS AND CASE PROBLEMS

1. Janice Smith issues a ninety-day negotiable promissory note payable to the order of Dennis Jones. The amount of the note is left blank, pending a determination of the amount of money Jones will need to purchase a bull for Smith. Smith authorizes any amount not to exceed $2,000. Jones, without authority, fills in the note in the amount of $5,000 and thirty days later sells the note to the First National Bank of Texas for $4,500. Jones not only does not buy the bull but has left the state. The First National Bank had no knowledge that the instrument was incomplete when issued or that Jones had no authority to complete the instrument in the amount of $5,000.

   (a) Does the bank qualify as a holder in due course, and, if so, for what amount? Explain.

   (b) If Jones had sold the note to a stranger in a bar for $500, would the stranger qualify as a holder in due course? Explain.

2. Dana draws and issues a $100 check to Peter. The check is dated and issued on May 1. On May 25, Peter indorses the check in blank to Sam as a gift. On June 5, Sam delivers the check for value without indorsement to Helen. Dana has stopped payment on the check, claiming that Peter is in breach of contract. Helen claims that she has the rights of a holder in due course. Discuss Helen's contention.

3. Daniel is a well-known industrialist in the community. He has agreed to purchase a rare coin from Helen's Coin Shop. The purchase price is to be determined by independent appraisal. Payment is to be by Daniel's check. Daniel is going out of town and informs Helen that his agent will bring her a check during his absence. Daniel draws up a check payable to Helen, leaves the amount blank, and gives the check to his agent, Able. Able, without authority, fills in the amount for $10,000, and presents it to Helen, who now has the appraisal. The appraisal price is $7,000. Able tells Helen that Daniel wanted to be sure the check would cover the appraisal and that he (Able) is authorized to receive the coin plus the balance in cash. Helen gives Able the coin plus $3,000. When Daniel discovers Able's fraud, Daniel stops payment on the check and offers Helen $7,000 for the coin. Helen claims she is a holder in due course and is entitled to the face value of the check, $10,000. Discuss whether Helen is an HDC and can therefore successfully pursue her claim.

4. Martha has just opened a small copy reproduction store. She has numerous clients, and she bills them at the end of the month. Her operation was begun with limited financial resources. Her bank balance with the First National Bank is $200. She receives in the morning mail two checks. One is from the Buckhorn Corporation for $500, and the other is from Shady Acres Magazine Sales for $300. Martha deposits both checks at the First National Bank. Later, a paper supply saleswoman presents Martha with an overdue bill of $800. Martha writes a check in that amount, and the check is paid by the First National Bank. Later, one of the checks deposited by Martha is returned to the First National Bank. It is from Shady Acres and is marked "insufficient funds." Can the First National Bank be a holder in due course to the check written by Shady Acres? Explain.

5. Daniel is going on a fishing trip with two friends. Upon packing, he discovers that his fishing rod and reel are broken. He immediately goes to George's Rod & Reel Store and purchases a rod and reel from Charles, a clerk, in the store. The cost of the rod and reel is $70. Daniel has always paid cash at this store in the past, but he has only $63 cash in his pocket. He pays the $63 in cash and gives the clerk a check intended to cover the balance. He signs the check but in his haste, leaves the payee's name and amount blank, tell-

ing the clerk to properly fill them in. Charles rings up a $63 sale on the cash register. He then inserts his name as payee on the check. George, the owner, owes Charles $7 in overtime pay. George fills in the amount on the check for $7. Charles negotiates the check to Altari in payment of a loan. Altari *cleverly* raises the amount of the check from $7 to $70 by adding a zero behind the 7 and a "ty" on the word seven. The changes are made in the same color ink. Altari transfers the check to Harold for value. Daniel's purchased rod and reel are defective, and he has stopped payment on the check. All the above events are now known. Harold claims that he has the status of an HDC. Discuss whether Harold is correct.

6.   The Sahara-Nevada Hotel billed Affinity Pictures for hotel charges in the amount of $3,046. Affinity's president, Saka, refused to pay the full amount, claiming that only $800 was owed. Saka signed a blank check and gave it to his agent. He instructed the agent to make the check out for $800, cash it, and give the cash to the Sahara-Nevada Hotel. Instead, the agent made the check payable for $3,046, the amount claimed by the hotel, and delivered it to the hotel's manager without mentioning the instructions. Is the Sahara-Nevada Hotel, the payee, a holder in due course? [Saka v. Sahara-Nevada Corp., 92 Nev. 703, 558 P.2d 535 (1976)]

7.   By making several fraudulent misrepresentations, a builder induced several homeowners in Washington, D.C., to sign contracts authorizing home improvements. The homeowners obtained financing to pay the builder's fees from Jefferson Federal Savings and Loan Association, a local lending institution. In exchange for the financing, the homeowners each issued promissory notes to Jefferson. The builder's fees were exorbitant, and the promissory notes were issued by the homeowners in the exact amounts of the fees charged. In addition, it was the builder's agent who introduced the homeowners to the loan manager of Jefferson Savings and Loan. The loan manager was aware of the fact that this person was the builder's agent. About a month later, after the homeowners realized that the prices for the home improvements were exorbitant, they refused payment on the notes held by Jefferson. If Jefferson qualifies as a holder in due course, it will have every right to payment. Does Jefferson qualify? [Slaughter v. Jefferson Federal Sav. and Loan Ass'n, 538 F.2d 397 (D.C.Cir. 1976)]

8.   Anderson entered into a contract with Atlantic Storm Window Company for the installation of storm windows in his home. He signed a promissory note and a contract. They were stapled together, and neither had any dollar amounts filled in. Atlantic Storm Window had orally agreed with Anderson that the price would be $744, but it later filled in both the contract and the promissory note for $895. Shortly thereafter, Atlantic sold the promissory note with the contract still attached to First National Bank. Atlantic installed the windows improperly, and Anderson refused to pay on the note. If First National Bank qualifies as a holder in due course, Anderson will be obligated on the promissory note. What was the result? [First Nat. Bank v. Anderson, 7 D. & C. 2d 661 (Pa.1956)]

9.   Mecham signed a note payable to Munson for a brokerage fee on a mortgage Munson's firm was obtaining for him. Munson gave the note to his bank as security for a debt. Mecham maintained that Munson did not obtain the type of mortgage on which they had agreed, and he refused to make payment on the note. Can the bank recover from Mecham? [Mecham v. United Bank of Arizona, 107 Ariz. 437, 489 P.2d 247 (1971)]

CHAPTER 28

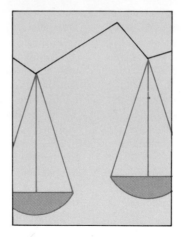

COMMERCIAL PAPER
Liability, Defenses, and Discharge

Two kinds of liability are associated with negotiable instruments: liability based on contract and warranty liability. *Liability based on contract* is likely to arise not from a specific contract but from UCC rules relating to the signature on the instrument. Those who sign commercial paper are potentially liable for payment of the amount stated on the instrument. *Warranty liability*, on the other hand, extends to both signers and nonsigners. A breach of warranty can occur when the instrument is transferred or presented for payment.

This chapter covers liability of the parties who sign the instrument—for example, drawers of drafts and checks, makers of notes and certificates of deposit, and indorsers. The liability of accommodation parties is also covered. Finally, warranty liability of those who *transfer* with or without a signature is discussed.

Since liability is not always absolute on a negotiable instrument, even for a holder in due course, in this chapter we will consider the de-

fenses available to prevent liability and then will review the various ways a person can be discharged from an obligation on a negotiable instrument. Note that the focus here is on liability *on the instrument itself* or on warranties connected with transfer or presentment of the instrument* as opposed to liability for the underlying contract.

LIABILITY BASED ON SIGNATURES

The key to liability on a negotiable instrument is a **signature,** which is defined in UCC 3-401(2) as "any name, including any trade or assumed name, upon an instrument, or * * * any word or mark used in lieu of a written signature." A signature can be handwritten, typed, or printed; or it can be made by mark, by thumbprint, or in virtually any manner. According to UCC 1-201(39), "signed" means any symbol executed or adopted by a party with the "present intention to authenticate a writing."

The requirement of a signature has its origin in the Law Merchant and is based simply on the need to know whose obligation the instrument represents. The critical element with any signature is a "present intention to authenticate a writing." Parol evidence can be used to identify the signer, and, once identified, the signature is effective against the signer no matter how it is made. UCC 3-401(1) states the general rule: "No person is liable on an instrument unless his [or her] signature appears thereon."

The few exceptions to the general rule are contained in UCC 3-404, covering unauthorized signatures:

1. Any unauthorized signature is wholly inoperative unless the person whose name is signed ratifies it or is precluded from denying it. [UCC 3-404(1)] For example, a signature made by an agent exceeding the scope of actual, implied or apparent authority can be ratified by the principal. A Pennsylvania court held that a wife's acceptance and retention of benefits from a promissory note constituted ratification of an otherwise unauthorized signature made by her husband.[1] Moreover, a person who writes and signs a check, leaving blank the amount and the name of the payee, and leaves the check in a place available to the public, can be estopped (prevented), on the basis of negligence, from denying liability for its payment. [UCC 3-115, 3-406, and 4-401(a)]

2. An unauthorized signature operates as the signature of the unauthorized signer in favor of an HDC. For example, a person who forges a check can be held personally liable by an HDC. [UCC 3-404 and 3-401(2)]

Agent's Signatures

The general law of agency applies to negotiable instruments. Agents can sign negotiable instruments and thereby bind their principals (see Chapter 35). [UCC 3-403(1)] Without such a rule, all corporate commercial business would stop. As Chapter 43 will show, every corporation can and must act through its agents. However, because of the critical function the signature plays in determining liability on a negotiable instrument, this chapter will go into some detail concerning the potential problems of agents' signatures.

Even an authorized agent will not normally bind a principal on the instrument unless the agent indicates that he or she is signing on behalf of a *clearly named* principal. The agent must write out the principal's name (by signature, mark, or some symbol) and his or her own name, or the agent can supply only the principal's signature.[2]

To illustrate: The following signatures by Able as agent for Peter would bind Peter on the instrument:

1. Peter, by Able, agent.
2. Peter.
3. Peter, Able.

If an authorized agent signs just his or her own name, the principal will not be bound on the instrument. The agent will be personally liable. In these situations, form prevails over intent.

Under UCC 3-403(2)(a), when an agent carelessly signs just his or her own name, the agent is *personally* liable on the instrument even though the parties know of the agency relationship. In addition, the parol evidence rule precludes the introduction of evidence to establish that the signature was made for a principal (see Chapter 12.)

Under UCC 3-403(2)(b), two other situations in which an agent is held personally liable on a negotiable instrument can arise. If the instrument is signed in both the agent's name and the principal's name—"John Jones, Bob Smith"—but nothing on the instrument indicates the agency relationship, the agent cannot be distinguished from the principal. In such a case, the form of the signature binds the agent (and it can also bind the principal). Since inclusion of both the agent's and the principal's names without indicating their relationship is ambiguous, parol

---

1. Rehrig v. Fortunak, 39 D. & C.2d 20, (Pa.1966).

2. If the agent signs the principal's name, the Code presumes that the signature is authorized and genuine. [UCC 3-307(1)(b)]

evidence is admissible *as between the original parties* to prove the agency relationship.

Another situation envisioned under UCC 3-403(2)(b) occurs when an agent signs a negotiable instrument and indicates agency status but fails to name the principal—for example, "Barry Scott, agent." Against any subsequent holder the agent is *personally* liable, but the unnamed principal cannot be held on the instrument. But, since the indication of agency status without naming the principal is ambiguous, parol evidence is admissible as between the *original parties* to prove the agency relationship and establish the liability of the unnamed principal. [UCC 3-403(2)(b)]

GRIFFIN v. ELLINGER

Supreme Court of Texas, 1976.
538 S.W.2d 97.

BACKGROUND AND FACTS *O. B. Ellinger, doing business as Ellinger Paint and Dry Wall, sued Percy Griffin on three checks drawn on the account of Greenway Building Company and signed by Griffin, the company president. The checks, totaling $3,950, were issued to Ellinger in payment for labor and materials furnished to Greenway for a construction project. Greenway was the prime contractor for the project, and Griffin was authorized to sign checks as president of the company. The bank refused to honor the checks because of insufficient funds in the Greenway account.*

The major question before the court was whether Griffin's signature on a corporate check, without any indication of his representative capacity, obligated him personally and individually for the amount of the check.

DOUGHTY, Justice.

The question presented by this case is whether a corporate officer who signs a check on a corporate account without designating the capacity in which he signs is personally liable as the drawer of the check. *   *   *
*   *   *   *

*   *   * [Defendant] contends that the drafts show conclusively on their face that he was signing in a representative capacity only. Second, petitioner contends that extrinsic evidence establishes as a matter of law that the parties understood his signature to be in a representative capacity.

*   *   * To determine whether an authorized representative is personally liable on an instrument which he signs on behalf of his principal, we must look to Section 3-403 of the Code[.] *   *   *

Each of the three drafts signed by Griffin were in essentially the same form. A copy of one of the drafts is reproduced below.

[C5606]

The first question is whether the draft shows on its face that Griffin signed in a representative capacity only. Although the draft clearly names the person represented, it does not show that Griffin signed only in his capacity as president of Greenway. Griffin contends, however, that considering the instrument as a whole, and taking into account the normal business usage of personalized checks, it should be apparent from the instrument itself that Griffin signed only as an authorized agent of Greenway. We disagree. We recognize that it is unusual to demand the individual obligation of a corporate officer on checks drawn on the corporate account, and that the more usual way of obtaining the personal obligation of an officer on such a check would be by endorsement. Business practice and usage are proper factors to be considered in construing the particular instrument under consideration. We also recognize that an instrument may disclose on its face that a signature was executed only in a representative capacity even though the particular office or position of the signer is not disclosed thereon.

* * * [W]e can find nothing on the face of the checks in the present case to show that Griffin intended to sign only in a representative capacity. [Defendant] points out that each check is stamped by a "check protector," which imprinted not only the amount of the draft but also the company's name. Although the stamp clearly reveals the name of the principal, it does not aid [Defendant] because it gives no information as to the capacity in which *he* signed the instrument.

The fact that the name of the corporation appears on the check indicates that the account drawn upon is that of the corporation and that the funds in the account are the corporation's. While the drawer of a check is ordinarily the owner of the funds in the account drawn upon, the Code does not require that this be so. Under Section 3.413, *any person* who signs a draft engages that, upon dishonor, he will pay the amount thereof to the holder. Indeed, under Section 3.404, the signer of a draft who has no authority to draw upon the account is nevertheless liable upon his contract as drawer to any person who takes the instrument in good faith for value. [Defendant] points out that, since a corporation can only act through its agents, a personal signature is always required to authorize withdrawal of funds from a corporate account. Under Section 3.403, however, one signing an instrument is personally liable thereon even though he is authorized to and does in fact bind his principal, if he does not disclose that he is signing only in a representative capacity. In short, the burden is on the signer to relieve himself of personal liability by disclosing his agency. The fact that the instrument is an authorized draft drawn on a corporate account is not enough to disclose the representative character of the signature thereon. Section 3.403(c) expressly provides that the signer of an instrument may avoid personal liability by disclosing both the name of the organization of which he is an agent and the office he holds with the organization. Absent such a disclosure or its equivalent, the signer is personally liable on the instrument according to its terms, unless, "otherwise established between the immediate parties" under subsection (b)(2). We hold that the checks in question do not show on their face that Griffin signed only in a representative capacity.

* * *

The plaintiff, Ellinger, was able to collect the $3,950 from Griffin personally because Griffin failed to disclose the representative character of his signature.

JUDGMENT AND REMEDY

COMMENTS *Although this case represents the majority rule, there are differences among states on the issue of personal liability. When the question of personal liability arises, the signer can offer evidence to prove that he or she acted in a representative capacity and may thus overcome the presumption that he or she is personally obligated.*

When a negotiable instrument is signed in the name of an organization, and the organization's name is preceded or followed by the name and office of an authorized individual, the organization will be bound; the individual who has signed the instrument in the representative capacity will not be bound. [UCC 3-403(3)]

If the agent had no authority, either apparent or implied, to sign the principal's name, the "unauthorized signature is wholly inoperative as that of the person whose name is signed * * *." [UCC 3-404(1)] Assume that Mary Night is the principal and Arthur King is her agent. King, without authority, signs a promissory note as follows: "Mary Night, by Arthur King, agent." Since Mary Night's "signature" is unauthorized, she cannot be held liable on the note, but King will be liable. This would be true even if King had merely signed the note "Mary Night," without indicating any agency. In either case, the unauthorized signer, King, is liable on the instrument.

Signature Liability

Primary and Secondary Liability　Every party who signs a negotiable instrument is either primarily or secondarily liable for payment of that instrument when it comes due. If a person is primarily liable on a negotiable instrument, then that person is absolutely required to pay the instrument, subject to certain real defenses. [UCC 3-305] Only *makers* and *acceptors* are primarily liable. [UCC 3-413(1)]

The liability of a party who is secondarily liable on a negotiable instrument is similar to that of a guarantor (surety) in a simple contract. Drawers and indorsers have secondary liability. Secondary liability is "contingent liability." In the case of notes, an indorser's secondary liability does not arise until the maker, who is pri-

marily liable, has defaulted on the instrument. [UCC 3-413(1) and 3-414]

With regard to drafts and checks, a drawer's secondary liability does not arise until the drawee fails to pay or to accept the instrument, whichever is required. Note, however, that a drawee is not primarily liable. Makers of notes promise to pay, but drawees are ordered to pay. Therefore, drawees are not primarily liable unless they promise to pay—for example, by certifying a check. Nor are drawees even secondarily liable on an instrument. As stated in UCC 3-409, "a check or draft does not of itself operate as an assignment of any funds in the hands of the drawee available for its payment * * *." Thus, unless a drawee *accepts*, the drawee's only obligation is to honor the drawer's orders.

The parties to a negotiable instrument are bound by all of the terms implied by their signatures by operation of law. Once it is established that a party signed the instrument (or that it was signed by that party's authorized agent), the Code defines the party's liability. The liability is contractual in the sense that each party voluntarily incurs it and thus can modify it.

Primary Liability of the Maker or Acceptor　The maker of a note promises to pay the note. The words "I promise to pay" embody the maker's obligation to pay the instrument according to the terms as written at the time of the signing. If the instrument is incomplete when the maker signs it, then the maker's obligation is to pay it as completed, assuming that the instrument is properly completed. [UCC 3-413(1) and 3-115]

A maker guarantees that certain facts are true by signing a promissory note. In particular, Section 3-413(3) specifies that a maker admits to all subsequent parties that the payee in fact exists and that the payee has current capacity to indorse the note (for example, that the payee is not a minor at the time the note is signed). Primary liability is unconditional. The primary party's liability is immediate when the note becomes due. No action by the holder of the instrument is required.

The drawee/acceptor is in virtually the same position as the maker of a note. [UCC 3-413(1)(3)] A drawee who does not accept owes a contractual duty to the drawer to pay in accordance with the drawer's orders, but a drawee owes no duty to either the payee or any holder.

For example, Beyer buys from Sallor goods costing $2,000. The goods will be shipped to arrive on September 1. Instead of giving Sallor cash, Beyer draws a draft on Finance Company for $2,000 payable to Sallor on September 1. At this point, Finance is not liable on the draft, and it will not become liable on the draft unless and until it accepts the draft.

Three situations under which a holder must present the instrument to a drawee for acceptance are:

1. Where the instrument requires such presentation (see trade acceptances, discussed in Chapter 24).
2. Where the draft is to be payable at an address different from that of the drawee.
3. Where the draft's payment date is dependent on such presentment [UCC 3-501(1)(a)]—for example, if the draft is payable thirty days after acceptance or sight.

Presentment in these situations is required to charge the drawer and indorsers with secondary liability.

If the drawee accepts the instrument as presented, the drawee becomes an acceptor and is primarily liable to all subsequent holders. A drawee who refuses to accept such a draft has dishonored the instrument. In refusing to accept, the drawee retains his original status and owes no duty to the payee or any holder.

A check is a special type of draft that is drawn on a bank and is payable on demand. Acceptance of a check is called certification. Certification is not necessary on checks, and a bank is under no obligation to certify. (See Chapter 29 for details.) However, upon certification, the drawee bank occupies the position of an acceptor and is primarily liable on the check to holders. [UCC 3-411]

Secondary Liability Dishonoring an instrument triggers the liability of secondarily liable parties on the instrument—that is, the drawer, "unqualified indorsers," and accommodation indorsers.[3] Parties who are secondarily liable on a negotiable instrument promise to pay on that instrument only if:

1. The instrument is properly and timely presented.
2. The instrument is dishonored.
3. Notice of dishonor is timely given to the secondarily liable party.[4]

These requirements are necessary for a secondarily liable party to have signature liability on a negotiable instrument, but they are not necessary to hold a secondarily liable party to warranty liability (to be discussed later). [UCC 3-414, 3-501, and 3-502]

UCC 3-413(2) provides that "upon dishonor of the draft and any necessary notice of dishonor * * * [the drawer] will pay the amount of the draft to the holder or to any indorser who takes it up." For example, Nancy Jones writes a check on her account at Third National Bank payable to the order of Joel Andrews. If Third National does not pay the check when Andrews presents it for payment, then Jones is liable to Andrews on the basis of her secondary liability. Drawers are secondarily liable on drafts unless they disclaim their liability by drawing the instruments "without recourse." [UCC 3-413(2)]

Since drawers are secondarily liable, their liability does not arise until presentment and notice of dishonor have been made *properly and*

---

3. A "qualified" indorser—one who indorses "without recourse," undertakes no obligation to pay. A qualified indorser merely assumes warranty liability which is discussed later in this chapter.

4. An instrument can be drafted to provide a waiver of the presentment, dishonor, and notice of dishonor requirements. Presume for simplicity's sake that such waivers have not been incorporated into the instruments described in this chapter.

in a *timely* way. If a draft (or check) is payable at a bank, improper presentment or notice relieves the drawer from secondary liability only when the drawee bank is insolvent. Since the days of the Great Depression, an insolvent bank has become a rare phenomenon.

An *unqualified indorser* promises that in the event of presentment, dishonor, and notice of dishonor, the indorser will pay the instrument. Thus, the liability of an indorser is much like that of a drawer, with one major exception: Indorsers are *relieved* of their contractual liability to the holder of the instrument by (1) improper (late) presentment or (2) late notice or failure to notify the indorser of dishonor. [UCC 3-414, 3-501, and 3-502]

When an indorser has actively caused an instrument to be dishonored, the requirements of presentment and notice of dishonor are excused. [UCC 3-511(2)(b)]

Proper Presentment   The Code spells out what constitutes a proper presentment. Basically, presentment by a holder must be to the proper person, must be in a proper manner, and must be timely. [UCC 3-503 and 3-504]

A note or CD must be presented to the maker for payment. A draft is presented by the holder to the drawee for acceptance or payment, or both, whatever is required. A check is presented to the drawee for payment. [UCC 3-504]

The proper manner for presentment can be in any one of the following three ways, depending on the type of instrument: [UCC 3-504(2)]

1.   By mail. But presentment is not effective until receipt of the mail.

2.   Through a clearinghouse procedure, such as deposited checks.

3.   At the place specified in the instrument for acceptance or payment—or, if the instrument is silent as to place, at the place of business or the residence of the person required to accept or pay.

One of the most crucial criteria for proper presentment is timeliness. [UCC 3-503] Failure to present on time is the most prevalent reason for improper presentment and consequent discharge of unqualified indorsers from secondary liability. See Exhibit 28–1, bearing in mind that its contents are somewhat oversimplified.

Proper Notice   Once the instrument has been dishonored, proper notice must be given to hold secondary parties liable. The rules of proper notice are basically [UCC 3-508]:

1.   Notice must be given to the party to be held secondarily liable, but such notice can come from any person who could be liable on the instrument. Once proper notice is received, that notice is effective for all subsequent holders. [UCC 3-508(8)]

2.   Except for dishonor of foreign drafts, notice may be given in any reasonable manner. This includes oral or written notice and notice written or stamped on the instrument itself. [UCC 3-508(3)] To give notice of dishonor of a foreign draft (a draft drawn in one country and payable in another country), a formal notice called a *protest* is required. [UCC 3-509]

3.   Any necessary notice must be given by a bank before its midnight deadline (midnight of the next banking day after receipt) [UCC 4-104(1)(h)] and by all others before midnight of the third busi-

---

EXHIBIT 28–1   TIME FOR PROPER PRESENTMENT

Type of Instrument	For Acceptance	For Payment
Time	On or before due date	On due date
Demand	Within a reasonable time (after date or issue, or after secondary party becomes liable thereon)	
Check (domestic)	Not applicable	Presumed to be: Within thirty days (of date of issue) to hold drawer secondarily liable Within seven days (of indorsement) to hold indorser secondarily liable

ness day after either dishonor or receipt of notice of dishonor [UCC 3-508(2)]. Written notice is effective when sent, not when received.

4. Notice to a partner is notice to a partnership. Similarly, when a party is deceased, incompetent, or bankrupt, notice may be given to his representative.

Accommodation Party An **accommodation party** is one who signs an instrument for the purpose of lending his or her name to another party in credit to the instrument. [UCC 3-415(1)] Accommodation parties are one form of security against nonpayment on a negotiable instrument.

For example, a bank about to lend money, a seller taking a large order for goods, or a creditor about to extend credit to a prospective debtor all want some reasonable assurance that the debts will be paid. A party's uncertain financial condition or the fact that the parties to a transaction are complete strangers can make a creditor reluctant to rely solely on the prospective debtor's ability to pay. To reduce the risk of nonpayment, the creditor can require the joining of a third person as an accommodation party on the instrument.

If the accommodation party signs on behalf of a maker, he or she will be an *accommodation maker* and will be primarily liable on the instrument. If the accommodation party signs on behalf of a payee or other holder (usually to make the instrument more marketable), he or she will be an *accommodation indorser* and will be secondarily liable. Any indorsement not in the ordinary chain of title is notice of its accommodation character. [UCC 3-415(2)(4)]

BACKGROUND AND FACTS *Donald Carty was refused a loan at the Bloomfield State Bank because of lack of collateral. When Carty obtained the signatures of the Stockwells, the bank approved the loan. The Stockwells and the Cartys executed the note. The loan proceeds, $10,000, were delivered to Donald Carty. The bank sued the Stockwells for the balance due on the second renewal of the note.*

STOCKWELL v. BLOOMFIELD STATE BANK

Court of Appeals of Indiana,
First District, 1977.
367 N.E.2d 42.

LYBROOK, Judge.

* * * *

The Stockwells' status in signing the notes must be determined in accord with [UCC] 3-415 which reads as follows:

"Contract of accommodation party.—(1) An accommodation party is one who signs the instrument in any capacity for the purpose of lending his name to another party to it. When the instrument has been taken for value before it is due the accommodation party is liable in the capacity in which he has signed even though the taker knows of the accommodation.

* * * *

An accommodation party is not liable to the party accommodated, and if he pays the instrument has a right of recourse on the instrument against such party."

The nature of a party's signature must therefore be based on the reason for which that signature was placed on the note. The nature of liability of an accommodation party is determined by the capacity in which he signed. Therefore, the question of Stockwells' status is relevant only for assertion of special suretyship defenses and failure of consideration.

In the case at bar Carty, the primary obligor, had attempted to obtain the loan in his own name. He had been refused for lack of security. Stockwells then lent their names to the note so Carty could obtain the loan, and thus one of the guidelines for determining accommodation status was settled. In addition, Stockwell added the words "Co-signed by" prior to his signature on the first renewal note. While it is true that the second renewal note is the subject of this action, the entire series of transactions may be examined in determining the status of Stockwell. The record also contains evidence that Carty intended, and in fact did, lease a building for the operation of his intended business from Stockwell. This would lend credence to the trial court's ruling that Stockwell was an accommodation maker. The use of the proceeds of the loan has also been held to be an indicator of a maker's status. Stockwell received only an indirect benefit (leasing his real estate to Carty) while Carty received the direct benefit (the funds to commence his business). While no one individual above mentioned factor would demand Stockwell be declared an accommodation party, when the entire transaction is viewed as a whole, the evidence preponderates with the decision of the trial court and we therefore affirm its ruling that the Stockwells are accommodation makers.

Stockwells next contend that they are not liable on the note by reason of failure of consideration. This contention is based on two foundations. First, to assert failure of consideration to them the Stockwells must be makers and not accommodation parties. An accommodation party's consideration is the primary obligor's receiving the proceeds of the loan and no separate consideration need run to the accommodation maker.

JUDGMENT AND REMEDY   *The trial court's judgment in favor of the bank was affirmed. The Stockwells had to repay the amount due on the note plus interest and attorney's fees.*

Warranty Liability of Parties

In addition to the signature liability discussed in the preceding sections, transferors make certain implied warranties regarding the instruments that they are negotiating. Liability under these warranties is not subject to the conditions of proper presentment, dishonor, and notice of dishonor. These warranties arise even when a transferor does not indorse the instrument (as in delivery of bearer paper). [UCC 3-417] Sometimes it is more expedient to compel a transferor to take back an instrument on the basis of breach of warranty than it is to prove a case of signature liability as a holder in due course against the maker or drawer. Warranties fall into two categories, those that arise upon the *transfer* of a negotiable instrument and those that arise upon *presentment*.

Transfer Warranties   The five *transfer warranties* are described in UCC 3-417(2). They provide that any person who *indorses* an instrument and

receives consideration warrants to all subsequent transferees and holders who take the instrument in good faith that:

1.   The transferor has good title to the instrument or is otherwise authorized to obtain payment or acceptance on behalf of one who does have good title.
2.   All signatures are genuine or authorized.
3.   The instrument has not been materially altered.
4.   No defense of any party is good against the transferor.
5.   The transferor has no knowledge of any insolvency proceedings against the maker, the acceptor, or the drawer of an unaccepted instrument.

A qualified indorser who indorses an instrument "without recourse" limits this fourth warranty to a warranty that he or she has "no knowledge" of such a defense rather than that there is no defense. [UCC 3-417(3)]

The Extent of Transfer Warranties The manner of transfer and the negotiation that is used determine how far and to whom a transfer warranty will run. Transfer by indorsement and delivery of order paper extends warranty liability to any subsequent holder who takes the instrument in good faith. However, the warranties of a person who transfers without indorsement (by delivery of bearer paper) will extend only to the immediate transferee. [UCC 3-417(2)]

For example, Able forges Martin's name as maker of a promissory note. The note is made payable to Able. Able indorses the note in blank and negotiates it to Paula. Able has left the country. Paula, without indorsement, delivers the note to Bill. Bill, in turn without indorsement, delivers the note to Helen. Upon presentment of the note to Martin, the forgery is discovered. Helen can hold Bill (the immediate transferor) liable for breach of warranty that all signatures are genuine. Helen cannot hold Paula liable, because Paula is not Helen's immediate transferor but is a prior non-indorsing transferor. This example shows the importance of the distinction between transfer by indorsement and delivery of order paper and transfer by delivery of bearer paper without indorsement.

Presentment Warranties When a person presents an instrument for payment or acceptance to a maker or a drawer, a **presentment warranty** will protect the person to whom the instrument is presented. As a general rule, when payment or acceptance of an instrument is made, it is final in favor of a holder in due course, or any person, who in good faith has changed his or her position in reliance on that payment. [UCC 3-418] Three exceptions to this general rule, under UCC 3-417(1), are often referred to as the presentment warranties. They provide the following:

1. The party presenting has good title to the instrument or is authorized to obtain payment or acceptance on behalf of a person who has good title.
2. The party presenting has no knowledge that the signature of a maker or the drawer is unauthorized.
3. The instrument has not been materially altered.

The second and third warranties do not apply in certain cases (to certain persons) where the presenter is a holder in due course. It is assumed, for example, that a drawer or maker will recognize his or her own signature or that a maker or acceptor will recognize whether an instrument has been materially altered.

Both transfer and presentment warranties attempt to shift liability back to a wrongdoer or to the person who dealt face to face with a wrongdoer and thus was in the best position to prevent the wrongdoing. The following case illustrates an accommodation indorser's possible signature and warranty liability.

BACKGROUND AND FACTS *Bugay came into the possession of a check drawn to the order of Henry Sherman, Inc. He fraudulently indorsed "Henry Sherman" on the back side of the check. Then Bugay asked the defendant, Maropoulos, to help him cash it. Maropoulos took Bugay to the Oak Park Currency Exchange, Inc., the plaintiff, because Maropoulos was known by the personnel of that company. While on the company premises, Maropoulos identified himself and induced the company to cash the check. Oak Park Currency Exchange agreed to cash the check only if Maropoulos would indorse it. He did so, received the money, and immediately gave it to Bugay. When Oak Park subsequently indorsed the check and deposited it in the Belmont National Bank, the "Henry Sherman" indorsement was found to be a forgery. The bank recovered full payment from plaintiff Oak Park. Plaintiff in turn attempted to receive reimbursement from defendant Maropoulos on his indorsement and for*

OAK PARK CURRENCY EXCHANGE, INC. v. MAROPOULOS

Appellate Court of Illinois, 1977.
48 Ill.App.3d 437, 6 Ill.Dec. 525, 363 N.E.2d 54.

breach of warranty. At trial, the court directed a verdict in favor of defendant Maropoulos. Oak Park appealed.

GOLDBERG, Presiding Justice.

* * * *

In this court, plaintiff urges that defendant breached his warranty of good title when he obtained payment of a check on which the payee's indorsement was forged and that there was sufficient evidence to support a directed verdict in favor of plaintiff. Plaintiff's contentions are based exclusively on Section 3-417(1) of the Code. Defendant contends that an accommodation indorser does not make warranties under Section 3-417(1) and that the trial court properly directed a verdict for the defendant.

A party who signs an instrument "for the purpose of lending his name to another party to * * *" that instrument is an accommodation party. Section 3-415(1). Such a party "is liable in the capacity in which he has signed * * *" Section 3-415(2). Therefore defendant is an accommodation indorser and would be liable to plaintiff under his indorser's contract, provided that he had received timely notice that the check had been presented to the drawee bank and dishonored. Section 3-414. Because these conditions precedent to the contractual liability of an indorser have not been met, defendant is not liable on his contract as an accommodation indorser.

Furthermore, the drawee bank, American National, did not dishonor the check but paid it. This operated to discharge the liability of defendant as an accommodation indorser.

The portion of the Code upon which plaintiff seeks to hold defendant liable is Section 3-417 entitled "Warranties on Presentment and Transfer." * * * Section 3-417(1) sets out warranties which run only to a party who "pays or accepts" an instrument upon presentment. We note that presentment is defined as "a demand for acceptance or payment made upon the maker, acceptor, drawee, or other payor * * *" Section 3-504(1). As applied to the instant case, the warranties contained in Section 3-417(1) * * * run only to the payor bank and not to any other transferee who acquired the check. In the case before us, plaintiff is not a payor or acceptor of the draft. * * * The case before us involves a transferee, not a party who paid or accepted the instrument.

* * * *

An additional theory requires affirmance of the judgment appealed from. Subsection 3-417(2) of the Code provides that one "who transfers an instrument and receives consideration warrants to his transferee * * *" that he has good title. * * * The evidence presented in the case at bar establishes that defendant received no consideration for his indorsement. Though [plaintiff's employee] testified that she saw Bugay hand defendant some money as the two left the currency exchange, she also testified that defendant stated that he was doing a favor for his friend; that she was not paying close attention to the two men and that she did not watch them as they walked away from her. Thus her testimony was considerably weakened by her own qualifying statements and it was strongly and directly contradicted by the positive and unshaken testimony of defendant that he received nothing in return for his assistance. The simple fact standing alone that this witness saw Bugay hand some money to defendant, even if proved, would have no legal significance without additional proof of some type showing that the payment was consideration for defendant's indorsement.

The appellate court affirmed the trial court's directed verdict in favor of Maropoulos. He was not required to repay Oak Park Currency Exchange, Inc.   **JUDGMENT AND REMEDY**

DEFENSES

Depending upon whether it is a holder or an HDC (or a holder through an HDC) who makes the demand for payment, certain defenses will be effective to bar collection from persons who would otherwise be primarily or secondarily liable on an instrument.

Defenses fall into two general categories—personal defenses and real (or universal) defenses. Personal defenses are used to avoid payment to an *ordinary holder* of a negotiable instrument. [UCC 3-306] Real defenses are used to avoid payment to all holders of a negotiable instrument (including an HDC or a holder through an HDC). [UCC 3-305(2)] (In all of these discussions, reference to an HDC includes a holder through an HDC.)

Personal Defenses

Breach of Contract   When there is a breach of the underlying contract for which the negotiable instrument was issued, the maker of a note can refuse to pay it or the drawer of a check can stop payment. Breach of the contract can be claimed as a defense to liability on the instrument. For example, Peter purchases several cases of imported wine from Walter. The wine is to be delivered in four weeks. Peter gives Walter a promissory note for $1,000, which is the price of the wine. The wine arrives, but many of the bottles are broken, and several bottles that are tested have turned to vinegar. Peter refuses to pay the note on the basis of breach of contract and breach of warranty. (Under sales law, a seller impliedly promises that the goods are at least merchantable; see Chapter 20.) If the note is no longer in the hands of the payee seller but is presented for payment by an HDC, the maker buyer will not be able to plead breach of contract as a defense against liability on the note.

Fraud in the Inducement   A person who issues a negotiable instrument based on false statements by the other party will be able to avoid payment on that instrument. To illustrate: Peter agrees to purchase Sam's used tractor for $2,800. Sam, knowing his statements to be false, tells Peter that the tractor is in good working order and that it has been used for only one harvest. In addition, he tells Peter that he owns the tractor free and clear of all claims. Peter pays Sam $500 in cash and issues a negotiable promissory note for the balance. As it turns out, Sam still owes the original seller $500 on the purchase of the tractor, and the tractor is subject to a filed security interest. In addition, the tractor is three years old and has been used in three harvests. Peter can refuse to pay the note if it is held by an ordinary holder; but if Sam has negotiated the note to an HDC, Peter must pay the HDC. Of course, Peter can then sue Sam directly.

The following case illustrates not only the importance of reading a contract before signing, but also that fraud in this case is only a personal defense and cannot be used against a holder in due course.

BACKGROUND AND FACTS   *Mr. and Mrs. Burchett and Mr. and Mrs. Beevers, the plaintiff appellees, signed contracts with Kelly to install aluminum siding on their homes. The original offer (made orally and accompanied by a written statement) indicated that each house would serve as a show house for advertising purposes and that the owners would receive $100 credit on each contract sold in a specific area of their town. Neither the Burchetts nor the Beeverses read their contract. In a few days,*   **BURCHETT v. ALLIED CONCORD FINANCIAL CORP.**
Supreme Court of New Mexico, 1964.
74 N.M. 575, 396 P.2d 186.

the first installment of the contract that they had actually signed—a mortgage contract that had been recorded against their property—came due. At that point, the appellees realized the nature of the contracts they had signed and brought this action against the finance company to have the notes and mortgages canceled and declared void. The trial court determined that since the notes and mortgages were obtained fraudulently, Allied Concord Financial Company could not recover.

CARMODY, Justice.

* * * *

Following the explanation by Kelly, both families agreed to the offer and were given a form of a printed contract to read. While they were reading the contract, Kelly was filling out blanks in other forms. After the appellees had read the form of the contract submitted to them, they signed, *without reading*, the form or forms filled out by Kelly, assuming them to be the same as that which they had read and further assuming that what they signed provided for the credits which Kelly assured them they would receive. Needless to say, what appellees signed were notes and mortgages on the properties to cover the cost of the aluminum siding, and contracts containing no mention of credits for advertising or other sales.

* * * *

Within a matter of days after the contracts were signed, the aluminum siding was installed, although in neither case was the job completed to the satisfaction of appellees. Sometime later, the appellees received letters from appellant, informing them that appellant had purchased the notes and mortgages which had been issued in favor of Consolidated Products and that appellees were delinquent in their first payment. Upon the receipt of these notices, appellees discovered that mortgages had been recorded against their property and they immediately instituted these proceedings.

* * * *

[The] trial court found that the notes and mortgages, although signed by the appellees, were fraudulently procured. The court also found that the appellant paid a valuable consideration for the notes and mortgages, although at a discount, and concluded as a matter of law that the appellant was a holder in due course.

* * *

* * * *

* * * The only real question in the case is whether, under these facts, appellees, by substantial evidence, satisfied the provisions of the statute relating to their claimed defense as against a holder in due course.

In 1961, by enactment of ch. 96 of the session laws, our legislature adopted, with some variations, the Uniform Commercial Code. The provision of the code applicable to this case is as follows:

"To the extent that a holder is a holder in due course he takes the instrument free from

"* * *

"(2) all defenses of any party to the instrument with whom the holder has not dealt except

"* * *

"(c) such misrepresentation as has induced the party to sign the instrument with neither knowledge nor reasonable opportunity to obtain knowledge of its character or its essential terms; *   *   *

We believe that the official comments following § 3-305(2)(c), Comment No. 7, provide an excellent guideline for the disposition of the case before us.
*   *   *   *

The test of the defense here stated is that of excusable ignorance of the contents of the writing signed. The party must not only have been in ignorance, but also have had no reasonable opportunity to obtain knowledge. In determining what is a reasonable opportunity all relevant factors are to be taken into account, including the age and sex of the party, his intelligence, education and business experience; his ability to read or to understand English, the representations made to him and his reason to rely on them or to have confidence in the person making them; the presence or absence of any third person who might read or explain the instrument to him, or any other possibility of obtaining independent information; and the apparent necessity, or lack of it, for acting without delay.

"Unless the misrepresentation meets this test, the defense is cut off by a holder in due course."
*   *   *   *

Applying the elements of the test to the case before us, Mrs. Burchett was 47 years old and had a ninth grade education, and Mr. Burchett was approximately the same age, but his education does not appear. Mr. Burchett was foreman of the sanitation department of the city of Clovis and testified that he was familiar with some legal documents. Both the Burchetts understood English and there was no showing that they lacked ability to read. Both were able to understand the original form of contract which was submitted to them. *   *   * (T)he Burchetts had never had any prior association with Kelly and the papers were signed upon the very day that they first met him. There was no showing of any reason why they should rely upon Kelly or have confidence in him. The occurrences took place in the homes of appellees, but other than what appears to be Kelly's "chicanery," no reason was given which would warrant a reasonable person in acting as hurriedly as was done in this case. None of the appellees attempted to obtain any independent information either with respect to Kelly or Consolidated Products, nor did they seek out any other person to read or explain the instruments to them. As a matter of fact, they apparently didn't believe this was necessary because, like most people, they wanted to take advantage of "getting something for nothing." There is no dispute but that the appellees did not have actual knowledge of the nature of the instruments which they signed, at the time they signed them. Appellant urges that appellees had a reasonable opportunity to obtain such knowledge but failed to do so, were therefore negligent, and that their defense was precluded.

We recognize that the reasonable opportunity to obtain knowledge may be excused if the maker places reasonable reliance on the representations. The difficulty in the instant case is that the reliance upon the representations of a complete stranger (Kelly) was not reasonable, and all of the parties were of sufficient age, intelligence, education, and business experience to know better. In this connection, it is noted that the contracts clearly stated, on the same page which bore the signatures of the various appellees, the following:

"No one is authorized on behalf of this company to represent this job to be 'A SAMPLE HOME OR A FREE JOB.' " *   *   *

Although we have sympathy with the appellees, we cannot allow it to influence our decision. They were certainly victimized, but because of their failure to exercise ordinary care for their own protection, an innocent party cannot be made to suffer.

JUDGMENT
AND REMEDY

The finance company, as holder in due course, took the instrument free from the defenses claimed. Thus, the Burchetts and the Beeverses were liable for the amount of the notes.

COMMENTS

Consumer protection legislation might alter the outcome of similar cases in some states. Also, had this action been brought after the FTC holder in due course rule was put into effect in 1976 (see Chapter 27), then the outcome might have been different. Remember that the FTC Rule requires that the subsequent holder of a promissory note resulting from a consumer credit contract be informed that he or she takes the note simply as a contract assignee and that the consumer credit contract is subject to all claims and demands that the debtor could assert against the promisee or payee named therein.

Illegality   Certain types of illegality constitute personal defenses. Other types constitute real defenses. Some transactions are prohibited under state statutes or ordinances, and some of these applicable statutes fail to provide that the prohibited transactions are void. If a statute provides that an illegal transaction is voidable, the defense is personal. If a statute makes an illegal transaction void, the defense is a real defense and can successfully be asserted against an HDC. For example, a state may make gambling contracts illegal and void, but be silent on payments of gambling debts. Thus, the payment of a gambling debt becomes voidable.

Ordinary Duress or Undue Influence   Duress involves threats of harm or force. Ordinary duress—for example, the threat of a boycott—is a personal defense. When the threat of force or harm becomes so violent and overwhelming that a person is deprived of his or her free will (aggravated duress), it becomes a real defense, good against all holders, including HDCs. [UCC 3-305]

Mental Incapacity   There are various types and degrees of incapacity. Incapacity is ordinarily only a personal defense. If a maker or drawer is so extremely incapacitated that the transaction

becomes a nullity, then the instrument is void. In that case, the defense becomes real, and it is good against an HDC as well. [UCC 3-305(2)(b)]

If the maker drafts a negotiable instrument while insane, but before a formal court hearing declares (adjudicates) him or her insane, many courts declare the obligation thereon as voidable. If, however, the maker has been declared by a court as being insane, a guardian has been appointed, and then the note is written, many courts would hold the obligation null and void.

Discharge by Payment or Cancellation   If commercial paper is paid before its maturity date, the maker will ordinarily demand the return of the instrument itself or will note on the face of the instrument that payment has been made. Otherwise, it is possible for the instrument to continue circulating. If it comes into the hands of an HDC who demands payment at maturity, the defense of discharge by payment, which is merely a personal defense, will not allow the maker to avoid paying a second time on the same note. [UCC 3-601(1)(a) and 3-602]

Unauthorized Completion of an Incomplete Instrument   It is unwise for a maker or drawer to sign any negotiable instrument that is not complete. For example, Daniel signs a check, leaves the amount blank, and gives it to Able, an employee, instructing Able to make certain purchases and to complete the check "for not more than $500." Able fills in the amount as $5,000 *contrary to instructions*. If Daniel can stop payment in time, Daniel *may* be able to assert the defense of unauthorized completion and avoid liability to an ordinary holder. However, if the check is negotiated to an HDC, the instrument is payable as completed. [UCC 3-115, 3-407, 3-304(4)(d), and 4-401(2)(b)]

Nondelivery   If a bearer instrument is lost or stolen, the maker or drawer of the instrument has the defense of nondelivery against an ordinary holder. Recall that delivery means "voluntary transfer of possession." [UCC 1-201(14)] This defense, however, is not good against an HDC. [UCC 3-805 and UCC 3-306(c)]

Real, or Universal, Defenses

Real, or universal, defenses are valid against *all* holders, including HDCs or holders who take through an HDC.

Forgery   Forgery of a maker's or a drawer's signature cannot bind the person whose name is used (unless that person ratifies the signature or is precluded from denying it). [UCC 3-401 and 3-404(1)] Thus, when a person forges an instrument, the person whose name is used has no liability to pay any holder or any HDC the value of the forged instrument. In addition, a principal can assert the defense of unauthorized signature against any holder or HDC when an agent exceeds his or her authority to sign negotiable paper on behalf of the principal. [UCC 3-403] (Forgery is discussed in Chapter 26, and unauthorized signatures have been discussed earlier in this chapter in the section on liability.)

Fraud in the Execution (in factum) or Inception   If a person is deceived into signing a negotiable instrument, believing that he or she is signing something other than a negotiable instrument (such as a receipt), fraud in execution is committed against the signer. For example, a

consumer unfamiliar with the English language signs a paper presented by a salesperson as a request for an estimate when in fact it is a promissory note. Even if the note is negotiated to an HDC, the consumer has a valid defense against payment. This defense cannot be raised, however, when a reasonable inquiry would have revealed the nature and terms of the instrument.[5] Thus the signer's age, experience, and intelligence are relevant, since they frequently determine whether the signer should have known the nature of the transaction before he signed.

Material Alteration   An alteration is material if it changes the contract terms between any two parties in any way. Examples of material alterations are [UCC 3-407(1)]:

1.   A change in the number or relations of the parties.
2.   The completion of an instrument in an unauthorized manner.
3.   Adding to the writing as signed or removing any part of it.

Thus, cutting off part of the paper of a negotiable instrument, adding clauses, or any change in the amount, the date, or the rate of interest—even if the change is only one penny, one day, or 1 percent—is material. But it is not a material alteration to correct the maker's address, to have a red line drawn across the instrument to indicate that an auditor has checked it, or to correct the total final payment due when a mathematical error is discovered in the original computation. If the alteration is not material, any holder is entitled to enforce the instrument according to its original terms.

Material alteration is a *complete* defense against an ordinary holder but only a *partial* defense against an HDC. An ordinary holder can recover nothing on an instrument if it has been materially altered. [UCC 3-407(2)] An HDC can enforce the instrument according to its original terms. [UCC 3-407(3)] If the alteration is readily apparent, then obviously the holder has

---

5.   Burchett v. Allied Concord Financial Corp., 74 N.M. 575, 396 P.2d 186 (1964), *supra.*

notice of some defect or defense, and such a holder cannot be an HDC. [UCC 3-302(1)(c) and 3-304(1)(a)]

Discharge in Bankruptcy Discharge in bankruptcy is an absolute defense on any instrument regardless of holder because the purpose of bankruptcy is to settle finally all of the insolvent party's debts. [UCC 3-305(2)(d)]

Minority Minority, or infancy, is a real defense only to the extent that state law recognizes it as such. [UCC 3-305(2)(a)] (See Chapter 9.) Thus, this defense renders the instrument voidable rather than void, as discussed in the next three sections ("Illegality," "Mental Incapacity," and "Extreme Duress"). Since state laws on minority vary, so do determinations on whether minority is a real defense as against an HDC.

For example, in some states, when a minor misrepresents his or her age, the minor is prohibited from exercising the right of disaffirmance. In those states, minority is not allowed as a real defense if a minor who signs a negotiable instrument misrepresents his or her age. (In those states a minor can disaffirm if no misrepresentation of age took place.) In other states, a minor is allowed to disaffirm (liable only for a tort of deceit) despite the misrepresentation of age, and therefore minority is a real defense.

Illegality When the law declares that an instrument is *void* because it has been executed in connection with illegal conduct, then the defense is absolute against both an ordinary holder and an HDC. If the law merely makes it *voidable*, as in the personal defense of illegality discussed previously, then it is still a defense against a holder, but not against an HDC. The courts are sometimes prone to treat the word *void* in a statute as meaning "voidable" in order to protect a holder in due course.[6] [UCC 3-305(2)(a)]

Mental Incapacity If a person is adjudicated mentally incompetent by state proceedings, then any instrument that person issues thereafter is

null and void. The instrument is *void ab initio* (from the beginning) and unenforceable by any holder or any HDC. [UCC 3-305(2)(a)]

Extreme Duress When a person signs and issues a negotiable instrument under such extreme duress as an immediate threat of force or violence (for example, at gunpoint), the instrument is *void* and unenforceable by any holder or HDC. (Ordinary duress, discussed previously, is only a personal defense.) [UCC 3-305(2)(a)]

DISCHARGE

Discharge from liability on an instrument can come from payment, cancellation, or material alteration as previously discussed. Discharge can also occur if a party reacquires an instrument, if a holder impairs another party's right of recourse, or if a holder surrenders collateral without consent. [UCC 3-601]

Discharge by Payment

According to UCC 3-601(1)(a) and 3-603, all parties to a negotiable instrument will be discharged when the party primarily liable on it pays to a holder the amount due in full.[7] The same is true if the drawee of an unaccepted draft or check makes payment in good faith to the holder. In these situations, all parties on the instruments are usually discharged. By contrast, such payment made by any other party (for example, an indorser) will discharge only the indorser and subsequent parties on the instrument. The party making such a payment still has the right to recover on the instrument from any prior parties.

---

6. Hawkland, *Commercial Paper and Bank Deposits and Collections* (Brooklyn: Foundation Press, 1979), p. 249.

7. This is true even if the payment is made "with knowledge of a claim of another person to the instrument unless prior to such payment or satisfaction the person making the claim either supplies indemnity deemed adequate by the party seeking the discharge or enjoins payment or satisfaction by order of a court of competent jurisdiction in an action in which the adverse claimant and the holder are parties." [UCC 3-603(1)]

Instruments Acquired by Theft or Restrictively Indorsed   A party will not be discharged when paying in bad faith to a holder who acquired the instrument by theft or who obtained the instrument from someone else who acquired it by theft (unless, of course, the person has the rights of a holder in due course). [UCC 3-603(1)(a)] Finally, a party who pays on a restrictively indorsed instrument cannot claim discharge if the payment is made in a manner inconsistent with the terms of the restrictive indorsement. [UCC 3-603(1)(b)]

Once payment or other satisfaction is made to the holder in return for the surrender of the instrument, the liability of the maker or drawer is discharged and the transaction comes to an end. There are numerous acts by which makers or drawers can fulfill payment or satisfaction.

In the following case, a dishonored check was satisfied when the purchaser returned to the seller the automobile for which the check had been given.

BACKGROUND AND FACTS   *The defendant, Senechal, wished to purchase a 1959 Ford automobile from the plaintiff, a dealer. Senechal borrowed $500 from his credit union and gave his promissory note for the repayment of the loan. The credit union issued a check in the amount of $500 payable to the order of Senechal and American Auto Sales, the plaintiff's trade name. Thereafter, Senechal indorsed and delivered the check to the plaintiff together with his 1950 truck as a trade-in.*

The plaintiff then transferred ownership of the 1959 Ford automobile to Senechal by bill of sale and possession. Neither the plaintiff nor the credit union had a security interest in the car.

*The credit union then learned that Senechal had been fired from his job and stopped payment on the check. Accordingly, when the plaintiff presented the check to the bank for payment, it was dishonored. Thereupon, as a result of the plaintiff's efforts to restore the parties to the **status quo**, Senechal agreed to return the car to the plaintiff, who accepted it. However, Senechal did not return the bill of sale to the plaintiff because he mistakenly believed that the credit union held a security interest in it.*

This lawsuit followed because the plaintiff took the position that the mere exchange of the automobile for the dishonored check was not satisfaction. The trial court found that the plaintiff was not entitled to any damages because the car had been returned to him, title could be perfected, and the car could be sold in satisfaction of the purchase price.

DUILIO v. SENECHAL
Massachusetts, 1969.
7 UCC Rep. Serv. 222.

COX, Justice.

*   *   *   *

In this action of contract the plaintiff seeks to recover, as a holder in due course, five hundred dollars, being the amount of a check he received from the above named defendant Credit Union in connection with the sale of a 1959 Ford automobile to the defendant Senechal.

The plaintiff claims as a holder in due course to be entitled to the amount of the check. He contends that he did not take title to the 1959 Ford and therefore was not made whole.

The plaintiff, contrary to his contentions, received not only possession but also a good title to the vehicle, notwithstanding redelivery was not accompanied by a bill of sale. The findings show that Senechal clearly intended a retransfer to the plaintiff of such title as he had, and because in fact there was no security interest outstanding, the title was unencumbered and was good. [UCC 2-401(2),(3)(b)]. *Whether the 1959 Ford was taken back by the plaintiff in satisfaction of the check presented a question of fact.* [Emphasis added.]

The conclusion is warranted that the check in the plaintiff's possession had been satisfied and therefore that the plaintiff may not recover the amount thereof. It is provided by [UCC 3-603], that "(1) The liability of any party is discharged to the extent of his payment or satisfaction to the holder *   *   *" and "(2) Payment or satisfaction may be made with the consent of the holder by any person including a stranger to the instrument."

The finding was warranted, if not required, that satisfaction of the check was made with the consent of the plaintiff as holder and that the liability of the defendant as drawer was thereby discharged.

Whether the plaintiff is a holder in due course is inconsequential, so far as recovery of the amount of the check is concerned, and there was no prejudicial error in denying the plaintiff's requested rulings to the effect that he is holder in due course or in allowing that of the defendant that he is not. It is enough that he is a holder, and that, as such, satisfaction was made with his consent, as the Uniform Commercial Code provides. [UCC 3-202(1); 3-301; 3-603(1),(2)]. The plaintiff has obtained restitution [loss value has been restored] by being restored to the position he formerly occupied by the return of the 1959 Ford sedan which he formerly had.

JUDGMENT AND REMEDY   *The trial court's ruling was affirmed. The plaintiff was not awarded any further recovery, and Senechal was not required to pay any damages, because he had restored the plaintiff to his former position.*

Discharge by Cancellation

The holder of a negotiable instrument can discharge any party to the instrument by cancellation. UCC 3-605(1)(a) explains how cancellation can occur: "The holder of an instrument may even without consideration discharge any party in a manner apparent on the face of the instrument or the indorsement, as by intentionally cancelling the instrument or the party's signature by destruction or mutilation, or by striking out the party's signature." For example, to write the word "Paid" across the face of an instrument constitutes cancellation. Tearing up a negotiable instrument cancels the instrument. Crossing out a party's indorsement cancels that party's liability and the liability of subsequent indorsers who have already indorsed the instrument, but not the liability of any prior parties.

Destruction or mutilation of a negotiable instrument is considered cancellation only if it is done with the intention of eliminating obligation on the instrument. [UCC 3-605(1)(a)] Thus, if destruction or mutilation occurs by accident, the instrument is not discharged, and the original terms can be established by parol evidence. [UCC 3-804]

Discharge by Reacquisition

A person reacquiring an instrument that he or she held previously discharges all intervening indorsers against subsequent holders who do not qualify as holders in due course. [UCC 3-208 and 3-601(3)(a)]

Discharge by Impairment of Recourse or of Collateral

Sometimes a party to an instrument will post or give collateral to secure that his or her performance will occur. When a holder surrenders that collateral without consent of the parties who would benefit from the collateral in the event of nonpayment, those parties to the instrument are discharged. [UCC 3-606(1)(b)]

QUESTIONS AND CASE PROBLEMS

1. On December 1, Daniel draws a check payable to Peter for $100 for services to be rendered on or before January 1. Peter indorses the check in blank to Smith on December 15 as payment of a debt he owed. Smith has been unable to cash the check during the Christmas holidays. Finally, on January 5 he negotiates the check to Harold, without indorsement, as payment for a cord of wood delivered. Peter never performs the services, and Daniel has stopped payment on the check by the time Harold attempts to cash it. Harold contends that he can hold Daniel liable on the check. Daniel claims that his defense is good against Harold. Discuss the contentions of Daniel and Harold.

2. Jim Hartman is vice-president of Harvey Waller's Construction Corporation. As vice-president, Hartman has authority to draft checks on behalf of the corporation. He draws two corporate checks, one for $20,000 to ABC Auto Inc. for a new Mercedes, signed "Harvey Waller's Construction Corporation," and the other to Suppliers, Inc., for $2,000 for purchase of materials, signed "Jim Hartman." Harvey Waller, president of Harvey Waller's Construction Corporation, learns of the purchases and stops payment on both checks, claiming no liability for the corporation, based on the fact that Hartman had no authority to purchase the car and that the corporation does not need the materials Hartman purchased. Discuss whether the corporation is liable on these checks.

3. Martin makes out a negotiable promissory note payable to the order of Peter. Peter indorses the note "without recourse, Peter" and transfers the note for value to Susan. Susan, in need of cash, negotiates the note to Helen by indorsing it "Pay to Helen, Susan." On the due date, Helen presents the note to Martin for payment, only to learn that Martin has filed for bankruptcy and will have all debts (including the note) discharged in bankruptcy. With these facts, discuss fully whether Helen can hold Martin, Peter, and Susan liable on the note.

4. Daniel draws a check on his bank, the First National West Bank, for $500, payable to Susan. She indorses the check in blank and negotiates it to Helen for value. Helen is about to purchase a piece of real estate in Daniel's city and goes to the First National West Bank to have the check certified. The bank refuses to certify the check and, after an argument, refuses even to cash the check, despite the fact that Daniel has sufficient funds in his checking account and has not issued a stop-payment order.

(a) Is the bank's refusal to certify the check a dishonor? Explain.

(b) Can the bank be held liable by Helen for its refusal to pay the check? Explain.

(c) If the bank does certify the check, what is the status of the bank as to the real estate agent to whom Helen would negotiate the check? Explain.

5. Martin makes out a $500 negotiable promissory note payable to the order of Peter. By special indorsement, Peter transfers the note for value to Susan. By blank indorsement, Susan transfers the note for value to Martha. By special indorsement, Martha transfers the note for value to Harold. In need of cash, Harold transfers the instrument for value by blank indorsement *back* to Susan. When told that Peter has left the country, Susan strikes out Peter's indorsement. Later she learns that Peter is a wealthy restaurant owner in Miami and that Martin is financially unable to pay the note. Susan contends she can hold either Peter, Martha, or Harold liable on the note as an HDC. Discuss fully Susan's contentions.

6. George Sackett is president of G & J Wood Products Company. On October 14, 1968, Sackett personally co-signed, along with a sawmill operator named Bennington, a promissory note to Deerfield State Bank. When Bennington went out of business because of financial difficulties, G & J Wood Products paid the balance due on the note. What status did G & J Wood Products have before and after it paid the note?

7. In January 1971 the law firm of Harkavy, Moxley, and Keane was dissolved. Keane left the firm, which continued under the names of the other two partners. Prior to its dissolution, the law firm maintained a business account at Pan American Bank in which the signature of any one of the partners was sufficient for the deposit or withdrawal of funds. After dissolution of the firm, the account was kept open to take care of the former firm's receivables. In May 1971 a check payable to Keane and Moxley in the amount of $16,500 was received by Harkavy for business carried on by the former firm. The check was deposited in the former firm's account after the bookkeeper for the firm had rubber-stamped the check "For Deposit Only, Har-

kavy, Moxley and Keane 035-602." The $16,500 was thereafter withdrawn by Harkavy and Moxley and deposited into the account of the new firm. If the stamping of the check is deemed to be an improper indorsement, then Keane cannot recover from Pan American Bank. Can Keane recover? [Keane v. Pan American Bank, 309 So.2d 579 (Fla.App.1975)]

8. Fidelity Mortgage Investors established a line of credit with Sterling National Bank and Trust Company in the amount of $2,000,000. In exchange for the credit, Fidelity issued a promissory note to Sterling for this same amount. Interest on the note was 9¼ percent. A notation "9¼" was penciled on the face of the note by Sterling. This accorded with standard bank practices in that locality. Fidelity later claimed that this notation constituted a fraudulent and material alteration of the instrument in that it represented an attempt by Sterling to set the post-maturity interest at the same rate as the pre-maturity interest. In the absence of agreement, the post-maturity rate would be 6 percent (by statute). What effect did the notation "9¼" have on each of the parties to the promissory note? [Sterling Nat'l Bank and Trust Co. v. Fidelity Mortgage Investors, 510 F.2d 870 (2d Cir. 1975)]

9. The LRZH Corporation borrowed from Langeveld and gave in exchange its promissory note, which was guaranteed by Joseph Higgins. The note was secured by a third mortgage on property owned by LRZH. Langeveld failed to record this mortgage until nearly one year after the loan was made. LRZH defaulted on the note. Foreclosure proceedings yielded only enough money to pay the holders of the first and second mortgages. Receiving nothing from the sale of the property, Langeveld sued Higgins on the basis of his guaranty. Higgins argued that Langeveld's failure to record the mortgage impaired the collateral held by Langeveld and hence discharged Higgins from liability. What was the result? [Langeveld v. LRZH Corp., 130 N.J.Super. 486, 327 A.2d 683 (1974)]

10. A bank sued an accommodation indorser for payment of a note. The indorser asserted as a defense that the bank could not collect because the purpose of the loan was to purchase the bank's own stock—a transaction prohibited under the Federal Banking Law. The federal statute does not make this type of loan void. Was the indorser's defense of illegality successful? [Pan American Bank of Tampa v. Sullivan, 375 So.2d 338 (Fla.App. 4th Dist. 1979)].

CHAPTER 29

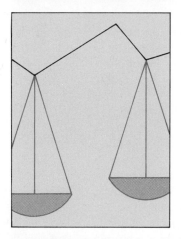

COMMERCIAL PAPER
Checks and the
Banking System

Checks are the most common kind of commercial paper regulated by the Uniform Commercial Code. Checks, credit cards, and charge accounts have replaced currency as a means of payment in almost all transactions for goods and services. It is estimated that Americans write over 38 billion checks a year, transferring about $40 trillion in checkbook dollars around the nation. Checks are more than a daily convenience; checkbook money is an integral part of the economic system.

This chapter will identify the legal characteristics of checks and the legal duties and liabilities that arise when a check is issued. Then it will consider the check deposit and collection process—that is, the actual procedure by which checkbook money moves through banking channels, causing the underlying cash dollars to be shifted from bank account to bank account.

CHECKS

A **check** is a special type of draft that is drawn on a *bank*, ordering it to pay a sum of money on *demand*. [UCC 3-104(2)(b)] The person who writes the check is called the drawer and is usually a depositor in the bank on which the check is drawn. The person to whom the check is payable is the payee. The bank or financial institution on which the check is drawn is the drawee. If Anne Gordon writes a check from her checking account to pay her school tuition, she is the *drawer*, her bank is the *drawee*, and her school is the *payee*.

The payee can indorse the check to another person, thereby making that receiver a holder. Recall from Chapter 27 that a holder is a person who is in rightful possession of an instrument that is drawn to that person's order (or drawn to bearer) or that is indorsed to that person (or in blank). [UCC 1-201(20)] The *payee as a holder* of a check has the right to transfer or negotiate it or to demand its payment in his or her own name, *as does any subsequent holder.*

A check does not, in and of itself, operate as an assignment [UCC 3-409(1)], because it does not show an intention to make present transfer of the right to the specified sum. Thus, the drawee bank is not liable to a payee or holder who presents the check for payment, even though the drawer has sufficient funds to pay the check. The payee's, or holder's, only recourse is against the drawer. (The drawer may subsequently hold the bank for its wrongful refusal to pay.)

Cashier's Checks

Checks are usually three-party instruments, but on certain types of checks, the bank can serve as both the drawer and the drawee. For example, when a bank draws a check upon itself, the check is called a **cashier's check** and is a negotiable instrument upon issue (see Exhibit 29–1). In effect, with a cashier's check, the bank lends its credit to the purchaser of the check, thus making it available for immediate use in banking circles. (The drawee is treated similar to an acceptor.) A

cashier's check is therefore an acknowledgment of a debt drawn by the bank upon itself.

Traveler's Checks

A traveler's check is generally not a check, but a straight draft. It is an instrument on which a financial institution is both the drawer and the drawee. (It is most often a regular draft since a bank is seldom the drawee.) On traveler's checks, however, there is an additional requirement that the payee must provide his or her authorized signature in order for it to become a negotiable instrument. A traveler's check has the characteristics of a cashier's check from the issuing bank. It is drawn by the issuer upon itself. (See Exhibit 29–2.)

Certified Checks

A personal check is only as good as the credit of the drawer. When a person writes a check, it is assumed that he or she has money on deposit to cover that check when it is presented for payment. To insure against dishonor for insufficient funds, a check may be certified by the drawee bank. A **certified check** is recognized and accepted by a bank officer as a valid appropriation of the specified amount that is drawn against the

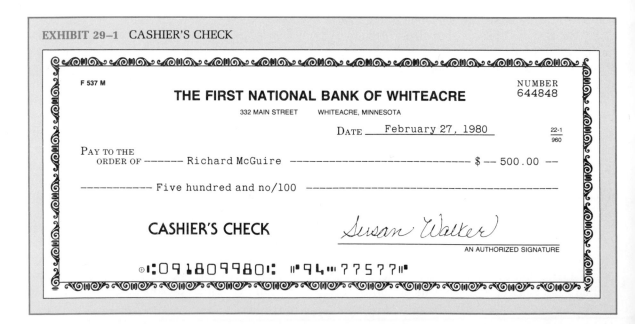

EXHIBIT 29–1   CASHIER'S CHECK

F 537 M

THE FIRST NATIONAL BANK OF WHITEACRE

332 MAIN STREET   WHITEACRE, MINNESOTA

NUMBER 644848

DATE ___February 27, 1980___   22-1 / 960

PAY TO THE ORDER OF ------- Richard McGuire ------------------------------------ $ -- 500.00 --

------------ Five hundred and no/100 ------------------------------------

CASHIER'S CHECK   *Susan Walker*

                                                            AN AUTHORIZED SIGNATURE

⑆⑈091809980⑈ ⑈94⑈77577⑈

funds held by the bank. (See Exhibit 29–3.) The usual method of certification is for the cashier or teller to write across the face of the check, over the signature, a statement that it is good when properly indorsed.

The certification should contain the date, the amount being certified, and the name and title of the person certifying. Certification prevents the bank from denying liability. It is a promise

that sufficient funds are on deposit and *have been set aside* to cover the check. Certified checks are used in many business dealings, especially when the buyer and seller are strangers. Sometimes, certified checks are the required form of payment under state law—for example, in purchases at a sheriff's sale.

A drawee bank is not obligated to certify a check, and failure to do so is not a dishonor of

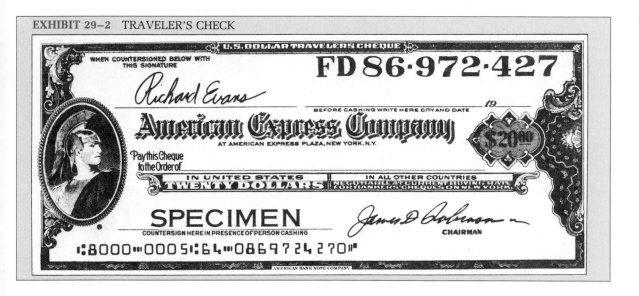

EXHIBIT 29–2   TRAVELER'S CHECK

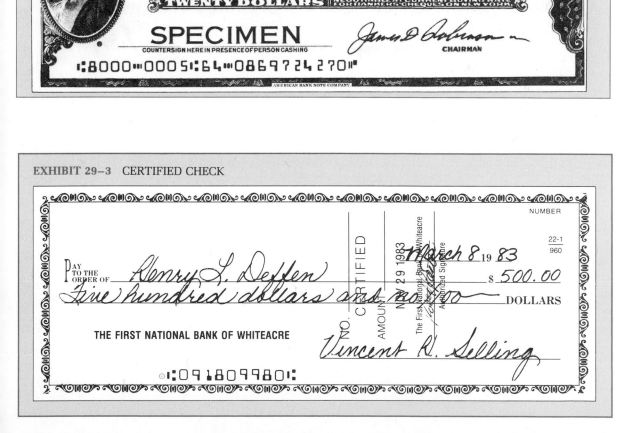

EXHIBIT 29–3   CERTIFIED CHECK

the check. [UCC 3-411(2)] When a bank agrees to certification, it immediately charges the drawer's account with the amount of the check and transfers those funds to its own certified check account. In effect, the bank is agreeing in advance to accept that check when it is presented for payment and to make payment from those funds reserved in the certified check account. [UCC 3-411(1)]

Drawer's Request for Certification   The legal liability of the drawer differs on the basis of whether the certification is requested by the drawer or the holder. The drawer who obtains certification remains *secondarily liable* on the instrument if for some reason the certifying bank cannot or does not honor the check when it is presented for payment.

For example, Epstein buys Stiple's car for $500. Epstein writes out a check for that amount and takes it to the bank to be certified. In the unlikely event that the bank fails to honor the check when it is presented for payment, Stiple can hold Epstein liable for payment of the $500.

Holder's Request for Certification   If the check is certified at the request of the holder, then the drawer and any indorsers prior to certification are completely discharged. A holder's request for certification is viewed as an affirmative choice for the bank's promise to pay over the drawer's and any indorser's promises. In this situation,

the holder can look only to the bank for payment. In the example above, Epstein writes a $500 check to Stiple, but Stiple takes the check to the drawee bank for certification. Upon certification, Epstein is released from all liability, and Stiple can look only to the bank for his $500. [UCC 3-411(1)]

Revocation of Certification   The bank's ability to revoke certification is extremely limited. If a good faith holder has changed position in reliance on that certification, the bank cannot revoke. Furthermore, since certification constitutes *acceptance* of an instrument under the Uniform Commercial Code, a bank can never revoke certification against an HDC regardless of whether the HDC has changed position in reliance on the certification. [UCC 3-418]

Alteration of a Certified Check   A bank will be liable for payment of an altered check only if the check was altered prior to certification. Upon certification, the drawee bank becomes an acceptor. An acceptor agrees that he or she will pay the instrument according to its tenor at the time of his or her engagement. Therefore, alterations after certification are not binding on the bank.

The following case involves a certified check that was altered. Because of the alteration, it was dishonored when presented to the bank.

SAM GOODY, INC. v.
FRANKLIN NAT'L
BANK OF LONG
ISLAND
Supreme Court of New York,
1968.
57 Misc.2d 193, 291 N.Y.S.2d
429.

BACKGROUND AND FACTS   *The Franklin National Bank (defendant) certified a check payable to Sam Goody, Inc., in the amount of $16. The certification stamp of the defendant bank did not show the amount for which the check was certified. The check had been presented to the defendant bank for certification by either the depositor or an accomplice. After the certification was procured, the amount of the check was altered from $16 to $1,600. The check was later presented to the plaintiff, Sam Goody, Inc., in payment for merchandise. The customer who presented the check represented that it was a bonus check. The customer had ordered the merchandise on the previous day and had stated that he would secure from his employer a certified check drawn directly to the plaintiff, Sam Goody, to pay the balance owing. Subsequently, the bank refused to honor the check because of the alteration. The plaintiff sued the bank* *for the full $1,600. The bank asserted that it was responsible only for the amount it had certified originally—that is, $16.*

FARLEY, Justice.

*   *   *   *

The unusual facts of this case give rise to the application of law that is rarely invoked.

*   *   *   *

The fraudulent scheme perpetrated in this case was obviously made possible by the knowledge that the certification stamp of the defendant Bank would not disclose the amount for which the check was certified. The plaintiff claims the negligence of the Bank in this respect caused the loss and that the Bank is estopped from asserting the defense of alteration under section 3-406 of the Uniform Commercial Code.

*   *   *   *

A bank, when certifying a check, does no more than to affirm the genuineness of the signature of the maker, that he has funds on deposit to meet the item, and that the funds will not be withdrawn to the prejudice of the holder. The certification constitutes an acceptance of the check to this extent (U.C.C., § 3-411), but the bank by its certification does not guaranty the body thereof *   *   * and engages only to pay the item according to its tenor at the time certification is procured (U.C.C., § 3-413). Furthermore, a holder of a check, by having it certified, is deemed to have warranted to the bank that the instrument has not been materially altered. The Code makes one exception to this rule by providing that the same warranty is not given by a holder in due course whether the alteration is made before or after certification (U.C.C., §§ 3-417 subd. (1) [c. iii, iv]; 3-413). Consequently, under the Code, where a check is certified *after the amount has been altered*, the bank runs the risk of sustaining the loss if the instrument passes into the hands of a holder in due course. [Emphasis added.] The Code in this respect changes the law which previously obtained in New York (National Reserve Bank of the City of New York v. The Corn Exchange Bank, supra).

The rule, however, is otherwise where the certification of the check is procured by the maker. In such case, the bank does not incur the risk of an alteration prior to its acceptance, and only agrees to pay the instrument according to its tenor at the time of certification even as to a holder in due course (U.C.C., § 3-413[1]).

The evidence in this case does not disclose whether the maker or his accomplice procured certification of the check, but the controlling fact that alteration occurred after certification of the instrument is not disputed. The bank, in checking its records, discovered the alteration and refused payment. Under these circumstances, the negligence of the bank, if any, is not a substantial or proximate cause of the loss, and in accordance with the rules mentioned above, it is not liable to the plaintiff except for the amount for which the check was originally drawn.

The defendant, Franklin National Bank, was liable for only $16, the   **JUDGMENT**
original amount of the certified check.   **AND REMEDY**

COMMENT   *Notice that the court did not discuss UCC 3-406 at length. Rather, the court made it clear that it did not believe that the bank was negligent.*

THE BANK–CUSTOMER RELATIONSHIP

The bank-customer relationship begins when the customer opens a checking account and deposits money that will be used to pay for checks written. The rights and duties of the bank and the customer are contractual and depend upon the nature of the transaction.

Article 4 of the UCC is a statement of the principles and rules of modern bank deposit and collection procedures. It governs the relationship of banks with one another as they process checks for payment, and it establishes a framework for the deposit and checking agreement between a bank and its customer.

Article 3 of the UCC, dealing with the use of commercial paper, sets forth the requirements for negotiable instruments. The extent to which any party is either charged or discharged from liability on a check is established according to the provisions of Article 3. Note that a check can fall within the scope of Article 3 as a negotiable instrument and yet be subject to the provisions of Article 4 while it is in the course of collection. In the case of a conflict between Articles 3 and 4, Article 4 controls. [UCC 4-102(1)]

A creditor-debtor relationship is created between a customer and a bank when, for example, the customer makes cash deposits into a checking account or when final payment is received for checks drawn on other banks.

A principal-agent relationship underlies the check collection process. A check does not operate as an immediate legal assignment of funds between the drawer and the payee. [UCC 3-409] The money in the bank represented by that check does not move from the drawer's account to the payee's account; nor is any underlying debt discharged until the drawee bank honors the check and makes final payment. To transfer checkbook dollars among different banks, each bank acts as the agent of collection for its customer. [UCC 4-201(1)]

DUTIES OF THE BANK

A commercial bank serves its customers primarily in two ways:

1.   Honoring checks for the withdrawal of funds on deposit in its customers' accounts.
2.   Accepting deposits in U.S. currency and collecting checks written to or indorsed to its customers that are drawn on other banks.

Honoring Checks

When a commercial bank provides checking services, it agrees to honor the checks written by its customers with the usual stipulation that there be sufficient funds available in the account to pay each check. When a drawee bank *wrongfully* fails to honor a check, it is liable to its customer for damages resulting from its refusal to pay. The Code does not attempt to specify the theory under which the customer may recover for wrongful dishonor; it merely states that the drawee is liable. Thus, the drawer customer no longer has to prove that the drawee bank breached its contractual commitment, or slandered the customer's credit, or was negligent. [UCC 4-402] When the bank properly dishonors a check for insufficient funds, it has no liability to the customer.

On the other hand, a bank may charge against a customer's account a check that is payable from that account even though the account contains insufficient funds to cover the check. [UCC 4-401(1)] Once a bank makes special arrangements with its customer to accept overdrafts on an account, the payor bank can become liable to its customer for damages proximately caused by its wrongful dishonor of overdrafts. The charging of overdrafts will be discussed later in this chapter.

The customer's agreement with the bank includes a general obligation to keep sufficient money on deposit to cover all checks written. The customer is liable to the payee or to the holder of a check in a civil suit if a check is not honored. If intent to defraud can be proved, the customer can also be subject to criminal prosecution for writing a bad check.

The following case illustrates that when a bank agrees with a customer to pay overdrafts, the bank's refusal to honor checks on an overdrawn account is a wrongful dishonor.

BACKGROUND AND FACTS   *Lawrence and Linda Kendall were officers and the principal shareholders of a corporation formed to build yachts upon special order from customers. The corporation had never issued stock and was undercapitalized.*

The corporation had a payroll checking account and a general business checking account with United California Bank. When the corporation ran into some financial problems, Mr. Kendall spoke with Ron Lamperts, a loan officer at the bank, in an effort to obtain financing for the corporation.

The bank agreed to honor overdrafts on the corporate account until such time as the corporation was out of the woods. The Kendalls continued to write checks for supplies, payroll, and other operating expenses of the corporation from about mid-October through December. The corporate bank account was badly overdrawn, and a number of the checks had been dishonored by the bank.

The Kendalls brought this lawsuit against United California Bank, charging that its wrongful dishonor of checks that it had initially agreed to accept as overdrafts caused damage to the Kendalls' personal and credit reputation.

KENDALL YACHT CORP. v. UNITED CALIFORNIA BANK
Court of Appeals of California, 1975.
50 Cal.3d 949, 123 Cal.Rptr. 848.

McDANIEL, Associate Justice.

* * * *

During October, November, and December, the Bank honored overdrafts of the Corporation totaling in excess of $15,000. There were also a number of overdrafts written during these months which were not honored by the Bank. Some of these were to suppliers and others were payroll checks to employees. In addition, the Bank failed to honor a check written to Insurance Company of North America to cover a premium for workmen's compensation insurance. The Kendalls were not aware that this check had been "bounced" until after one of their employees had been injured and they had been notified by Insurance Company of North America that their insurance had been terminated for nonpayment of premium.

After the collapse of the business, the Kendalls understandably had a number of enemies in the community. They were accused of having breached the trust of their former suppliers and employees and of having milked the Corporation of its funds and placed them in a Swiss bank account. They were repeatedly threatened with legal action and physical harm; they suffered acts of vandalism such as eggs and oil being thrown at their cars. Mr. Kendall's subsequent employer was contacted and threatened by creditors of the Corporation. Criminal charges were brought against Mrs. Kendall for writing checks against insufficient funds; the charges were dismissed shortly before she was brought to trial on them. The Kendalls were required to appear and answer charges in administrative proceedings involving dishonored payroll checks and the Corporation's failure to carry workmen's compensation insurance. Each testified to experiencing severe emotional distress and humiliation as a result of these matters. They also testified to marital problems which were allegedly caused by the stress brought on by the failure of the business.

*   *   *   *

The Bank contends first that under Commercial Code section 4402 the wrongful dishonor of a check of a *corporation* does not give a cause of action for damages to individual officers and shareholders of the corporation. Commercial Code section 4402, which represents section 4-402 of the Uniform Commercial Code, reads as follows: "A payor bank is liable to its customer for damages proximately caused by the wrongful dishonor of an item. When the dishonor occurs through mistake liability is limited to actual damages proved." [Footnote omitted.]

[It] was entirely foreseeable that the dishonoring of the Corporation's checks would reflect directly on the personal credit and reputation of the Kendalls and that they would suffer the adverse personal consequences which resulted when the Bank reneged on its commitments.

*   *   *   *

[It] has been held in this state that a cause of action for wrongful dishonor of a check sounds in tort as well as in contract (*Weaver v. Bank of America,* 59 Cal.2d 428, 431, 30 Cal.Rptr. 4, 380 P.2d 644), and "if the conduct is tortious, damages for emotional distress may be recovered despite the fact that the conduct also involves a breach of contract."

JUDGMENT AND REMEDY   *The court awarded the Kendalls $26,000 each as compensatory damages for the bank's wrongful dishonor of the checks.*

Stale Checks

The bank's responsibility to honor its customers' checks is not absolute. A bank is not obliged to pay an uncertified check presented more than six months from its date. [UCC 4-404] Commercial banking practice regards a check outstanding for longer than six months as *stale.* UCC 4-404 gives a bank the option of paying or not paying on a **stale check.** The usual banking practice is to consult the customer, but if a bank pays in good faith without consulting the customer, it has the right to charge the customer's account for the amount of the check.

The following case exemplifies this rule.

GRANITE EQUIPMENT LEASING CORP. v. HEMPSTEAD BANK
Supreme Court of New York, 1971.
68 Misc.2d 350, 326 N.Y.S.2d 881.

BACKGROUND AND FACTS   *Granite Equipment Leasing Corporation issued a check to Overseas Equipment Company. After five days, Overseas indicated that the check had not been received. Granite ordered payment on the check stopped and wired the funds to Overseas. Approximately one year later, the check cleared and Granite's account was charged. Granite sued the bank for return of the funds to its account, maintaining that the bank had a duty to inquire into the circumstances of the stale check. The bank based its defense on the premise that the stop-payment order had expired and that it had acted in good faith.*

HARNETT, Justice.

* * * *

Under the Uniform Commercial Code, does a bank have a duty of inquiry before paying a stale check? Does it matter that the stale check had been previously stopped under a stop payment order which expired for lack of renewal? So this case goes.

Granite Equipment Leasing Corp. kept a checking account with Hempstead Bank. On October 10, 1968 Granite drew a check payable to Overseas Equipment Co., Inc. Five days later, after Overseas advised that the check had not been received, Granite wrote the Bank on October 15, 1968 to stop payment on the check. On that same day Granite authorized the Bank to wire the payee funds in the same amount as the stopped check and the Bank did so. Granite never renewed its stop payment order between October 1968 and November 10, 1969. On November 10, 1969, without notice or inquiry to Granite, the Bank accepted the original check to Overseas which had been stopped the year before, paid the indicated funds to a collecting bank, and charged Granite's account.

Granite now seeks to recover from the Bank the amount charged because of the check paid to Overseas in November 1969. The Bank defends on the ground that under UCC § 4-403 the stop payment order had expired for want of renewal, and that acting in good faith it was entitled under UCC § 4-404 to pay the stale check.

There is no doubt the check is stale. There is no doubt the stop payment order was properly given at the outset, and that it was never renewed. Granite essentially maintains the Bank had a duty to inquire into the circumstances of that stale check, and should not have paid in face of a known lapsed stop order without consulting its depositor.

The Uniform Commercial Code, which became effective in New York on September 27, 1964, provides that:

"(1) A customer may by order to his bank stop payment of any item payable for his account * * * (2) * * * A written [stop] order is effective for only six months unless renewed in writing". UCC § 4-403.

* * * *

Granite cannot be permitted to predicate liability on the part of the Bank on its failure to inquire about and find a stop payment order which had become terminated in default of renewal.

* * * *

Neither may Granite predicate a claim of liability upon the Bank's payment of a stale check. The legal principles applicable to this circumstance are codified in UCC § 4-404, which provides that:

"[a] bank is under no obligation . . . to pay a check, other than a certified check, which is presented more than six months after its date, but *it may charge its customer's account for a payment made thereafter in good faith*". (Emphasis added.)

* * *

There is no obligation under the statute of the Bank to search its records to discover old lapsed stop payment orders. The Bank does not have to pay a stale check, but it may pay one in "good faith". Significantly, UCC § 1-201(19) defines "good faith" as "honesty in fact in the conduct or transaction concerned". In the absence of any facts which could justify a finding of dishonesty, bad faith, recklessness, or lack of ordinary care, in the face of circumstances actually known, or which should have been known, the Bank is not liable to Granite for its payment of the check drawn to Overseas.

Granite's complete remedy lies in its pending Florida action against Overseas to recover the extra payment.

JUDGMENT AND REMEDY — *The court dismissed the complaint and entered judgment in favor of the bank, which was not required to pay Granite Equipment the amount of the check. The court ruled that Hempstead Bank had acted in good faith.*

Missing Indorsements

Depositary institutions are allowed to supply any necessary indorsements of a customer. This rule does not apply if the item expressly requires the payee's indorsement. The depositary bank places a statement on the item to the effect that it was deposited by a customer or credited to that customer's account. [UCC 4-205(1)]

Death or Incompetence of a Customer

UCC 4-405 provides that if, at the time a check is issued or its collection has been undertaken, a bank does *not know* of an adjudication of incompetence, an item can be paid and the bank will not incur liability. Neither death nor incompetency revokes the bank's authority to pay an item until the bank knows of the situation and has had reasonable time to act. Even when a bank *knows* of the *death* of its customer, for ten days after the date of death, it can pay or certify checks drawn on or prior to the date of death—unless a person claiming an interest in that account, such as an heir or an executor of the estate, orders the bank to stop all payment. Without this provision, banks would constantly be required to verify the continued life and competency of their drawers.

Stop-Payment Orders

Only a customer can order his or her bank to pay a check, and only a customer can order payment to be stopped. This right does not extend to holders—that is, payees or indorsees—because the drawee bank's contract is only with its draw-

ers. A stop-payment order must be received in a reasonable time and in a reasonable manner to permit the bank to act on it. [UCC 4-403(1)]

A stop-payment order can be given orally, usually by phone, and it is binding on the bank for only fourteen calendar days unless confirmed in writing.[1] (See Exhibit 29–4.) A written stop-payment order or oral order confirmed in writing is effective for six months only, unless renewed in writing. [UCC 4-403(2)]

Should the drawee bank pay the check over the customer's properly instituted stop-payment order, the bank will be obligated to recredit the account of the drawer customer. However, the bank is liable for no more than the actual loss suffered by the drawer because of such wrongful payment.

For example, Pat Davis orders one hundred used typewriters at $50 each from Jane Smith. Davis pays in advance for the goods with her check for $5,000. Later that day, Smith tells Davis that she is not going to deliver any typewriters. Davis immediately calls her bank and stops payment on the check. Two days later, in spite of this stop-payment order, the bank inadvertently honors Davis's $5,000 check to Smith for the undelivered typewriters. The bank will be liable to Davis for the full $5,000.

The result would be different if Smith had delivered ninety-nine typewriters. Since Davis would have owed Smith $4,950 for the goods delivered, she would have been able to establish actual losses of only $50 resulting from the bank's payment over her stop-payment order. The bank would be liable to Davis for only $50.

---

1. Some states do not recognize oral stop-payment orders; they must be in writing.

EXHIBIT 29–4   STOP-PAYMENT ORDER

TO THE FIRST NATIONAL BANK
   OF SOUTH MIAMI
   SOUTH MIAMI, FLORIDA

DATE OF ORDER   ACCOUNT NUMBER

Please STOP PAYMENT on my (or our) check drawn on your bank, described as follows:

NO.:   DATED: PAYABLE TO: AMOUNT $

REASON: DUPLICATE ISSUED?

THIS REQUEST IS MADE WITH THE UNDERSTANDING THAT THE BANK WILL USE REASONABLE PRECAUTION IN FOLLOWING YOUR INSTRUCTION. BUT IN CONSIDERATION OF THE ACCEPTANCE OF THIS REQUEST IT IS EXPRESSLY AGREED THAT THE BANK WILL IN NO WAY BE LIABLE IN THE EVENT THE CHECK IS PAID IF PAID THE SAME DAY YOUR ORDER IS RECEIVED OR IF PAID BY OVERSIGHT OR INADVERTENCE OR IF BY REASON OF SUCH PAYMENT OTHER CHECKS DRAWN BY THE UNDERSIGNED ARE RETURNED FOR INSUFFICIENT FUNDS AND THE UNDERSIGNED FURTHER AGREES TO INDEMNIFY THE BANK AGAINST ALL EXPENSES AND COSTS THAT IT MIGHT INCUR BY REASON OF REFUSING PAYMENT ON SAID CHECK.

EXPIRATION DATE

IT IS HEREBY AGREED AND UNDERSTOOD THAT THIS ORDER WILL REMAIN IN EFFECT FOR A SIX-MONTH PE-RIOD UNLESS OTHERWISE DIRECTED AND THE BANK WILL CHARGE $5.00 FOR EACH SIX-MONTH PERIOD OR PORTION THEREOF THAT THIS ORDER IS IN EFFECT. THE BANK MAY CHARGE MY ACCOUNT WITH THIS AMOUNT.

ORDER RECEIVED BY   IN PERSON   BY LETTER   SIGNATURE OF MAKER

BANK NOT LIABLE IF CHECK HAS BEEN CASHED IN THE SAME DAY THIS ORDER WAS ACCEPTED.

A stop-payment order has its risks for a customer. The drawer must have a *valid legal ground* for issuing such an order; otherwise the holder can sue the drawer for payment. Moreover, defenses sufficient to refuse payment against a payee may not be valid grounds to prevent payment against a subsequent holder in due course. [UCC 3-305]

A person who wrongfully stops payment on a check will not only be liable to the payee for the amount of the check, but might also be liable for *special* damages resulting from the wrongful order. Special damages, however, must be separately pleaded and proven at trial. The following case illustrates the problem of proving special damages for wrongful stop payment of a check.

BACKGROUND AND FACTS   *Sanford was fired from a restaurant by his supervisor, Vickrey. Vickrey gave him a number of checks for wages due along with a check for $720 to reimburse him for shares of stock that he had purchased in one of Vickrey's other companies. After depositing the checks, Sanford returned to the restaurant and verbally insulted and threatened Vickrey. Following the incident, Vickrey stopped payment on the check for $720. Sanford sued Vickrey for $720 plus interest.*

VICKREY v. SANFORD
Court of Appeals of Texas,
1974.
506 S.W.2d 270.

BREWSTER, Justice.

*   *   *   *

On the occasion when Vickrey had given the $720.00 check to Sanford, Sanford had advised Vickrey that he needed the money to pay up bills and to get to Las Vegas, Nevada, at which place he could get a job.

After Sanford had done the cursing at the "Sirloin Stockade", he, on the same day, left for Las Vegas, Nevada, and was there hired at the Golden Nuggett as a dealer and to work at the roulette wheel.

A few days later Sanford called home and was told by his wife that payment had been stopped on the $720.00 check and that Mr. Allen, a vice-president of Denton County National Bank, where he had cashed it, wanted to get in touch with him. He called Allen and Allen wanted him to sign a note for the $720.00.

* * * *

Sanford sought in this case to recover the amount of the check ($720.00) plus interest thereon, plus the expenses that he incurred in making the two trips back to Denton, plus exemplary (punishment) damages.

* * * *

[The court had no trouble deciding that Vickrey was responsible for paying the $720 plus interest. It was Sanford's most unusual request for the cost of traveling between Nevada and Texas to straighten out the mess that gave the court cause for concern.]

If plaintiff, Sanford, is legally entitled to recover for expenses incurred in making the two trips from Nevada back to Texas plus the loss of salary due to losing his job, it would only be on the theory that they were special damages that were within the contemplation of the parties at the time the contract was executed. This is a necessary element if the expenses sought to be recovered are in the category of special damages.

* * * *

There was no evidence tending to show that the entire transaction with reference to Sanford signing the note to the Bank could not have been handled by mail, thus rendering both of Sanford's trips to Texas unnecessary. There was no evidence offered to the effect that it was necessary that this note be signed in Denton.

JUDGMENT AND REMEDY   *The court permitted Sanford to recover only the amount of the $720 check in damages. The court held that there was insufficient evidence to uphold Sanford's claim for special damages.*

Overdrafts

When the bank receives an item properly payable from its customer's checking account, but there are insufficient funds in the account to cover the amount of the check, the bank can either dishonor the item or it can pay the item and charge the customer's account, creating an overdraft. [UCC 4-401(1)] The bank can subtract the difference from the customer's next deposit because the check carries with it an enforceable implied promise to reimburse the bank.

When a check "bounces," a holder can resubmit the check, hoping that at a later date sufficient funds will be available to pay it. The holder must notify any indorsers on the check of the first dishonor; otherwise they will be discharged from their signature liability.

Payment on a Forged Signature of the Drawer

A forged signature on a check has no legal effect as the signature of a drawer. [UCC 3-404(1)] Banks require signature cards from each customer who opens a checking account. The bank is responsible for determining whether the signature on a customer's check is genuine. The general rule is that the bank must recredit the customer's account when it pays on a forged signature.

Customer Negligence When the customer's negligence substantially contributes to the forgery, the bank will not normally be obliged to recredit the customer's account for the amount of the check. Suppose Axelrod Corporation uses a mechanical check-writing machine to write its payroll and business checks. Axelrod discovers that one of its employees used the machine to write himself a check for $10,000 and that the bank subsequently honored it. Axelrod requests the bank to recredit $10,000 to its account for incorrectly paying on a forged check. If the bank can show that Axelrod failed to take reasonable care in controlling access to the check-writing equipment, Axelrod cannot require the bank to recredit its account for the amount of the forged check. [UCC 3-406]

Timely Examination Required   A customer has an *affirmative duty* to examine monthly statements and canceled checks promptly and with reasonable care and to report any forged signatures promptly. [UCC 4-406(1)]

When the bank sends to its customer, or makes available to the customer, a statement of account and returned checks, the customer has a duty to examine them and promptly report any forged or unauthorized signatures. This includes forged signatures of indorsers, to be discussed later. [UCC 4-406]

Failure to so examine and report, or any carelessness by the customer that results in a loss to the bank, makes the customer liable for the loss. [UCC 4-406(2)(a)] Even if the customer can prove that reasonable care was taken against forgeries, the Code provides that discovery of such forgeries and notice to the bank must take place within specific time frames, or the customer cannot require the bank to recredit his or her account.

When a series of forgeries by the same wrongdoer takes place, the Code provides that the customer in order to recover for all the forged items must discover and report the forgery to the bank within fourteen calendar days of the receipt of the bank statement and canceled checks that contain the forged item. [UCC 4-406(2)(b)] Failure to notify within this time discharges the bank's liability for all similar forged checks prior to notification.

For example, Middletown Bank sends out monthly statements and checks on the last day of each month. Bradley, owner of a small store, unknowingly has had a number of his blank checks stolen by employee Harry. On April 20 Harry forges Bradley's signature and cashes check number 1. On April 22, Harry forges and cashes check number 2. The checks canceled in April (including the forged ones) and the April statement from the Middletown Bank are received on May 1. Bradley sets aside the statement and does not reconcile his checking account. On May 20 Bradley forges check number 3. The checks canceled in May and the May statement are received by Bradley on June 1. Upon immediate examination of both statements, Bradley discovers the forgeries.

Can Bradley demand that the bank recredit his account for all forged checks? The answer is no, assuming the bank was not negligent in paying the forged checks. [UCC 4-406(3)] A series of forgeries by the same wrongdoer has been committed. The two forged checks in April were made available to Bradley for inspection on May 1. Liability for any forged check in the series written after May 15 (fourteen days after receipt of the April statement) falls on Bradley. In addition, if Bradley's negligence in failing to examine his April statement promptly results in a loss to the Middletown Bank, the bank's liability to recredit Bradley's account for any forged item would be reduced by the amount of any loss the bank suffered by reason of Bradley's failure to promptly notify the bank.

Had Bradley examined his April statement immediately upon receipt and reported the two April forgeries, the bank would have been obligated to fully recredit Bradley's account. However, if the bank can prove that Bradley's carelessness in permitting the blank checks to be stolen substantially contributed to the forgery, Bradley—not the bank—will be liable. [UCC 3-406 and 4-406]

Regardless of the degree of care exercised by the customer or the bank, the Code has placed an absolute time limit on the liability of a bank for forged customer signatures. UCC 4-406(4) provides that a customer who fails to report his or her forged signature one year from the date that the statement and canceled checks were made available for inspection loses the legal right to have the bank recredit his or her account.

Payment on a Forged Indorsement

A bank that pays a customer's check that bears a forged indorsement must recredit the customer's account or be liable to the customer-drawer for breach of contract.

For example, Baker issues a $50 check "to the order of Thelma." Larry steals the check, forges Thelma's indorsement and cashes the check. When the check reaches Baker's bank, the bank pays it and debits Baker's account. Under UCC 4-401, the bank must recredit Baker's account $50 because it failed to carry out Baker's order to pay "to the order of Thelma." (Baker's bank will in turn recover from the bank that cashed the check under breach of warranty principles.) [UCC 4-207(1)(a)]

By comparison, the bank has no right to recover from a holder who, without knowledge, cashes a check bearing a *forged drawer's signature*. The holder merely guarantees that he or she has no knowledge that the signature of the drawer is unauthorized. Unless the bank can prove such knowledge, its only recourse is against the forger. [UCC 3-418 and 4-207(1)(b)]

The customer, however, has a duty to examine the returned checks and statements received by the bank and report forged indorsements upon discovery or notice. Failure to report forged indorsements within a three year period after such forged items are made available to the customer relieves the bank of liability. [UCC 4-406(4)]

In the following case, the customer's duty to discover and report an unauthorized signature was at issue.

NU–WAY SERVICES, INC. v. MERCANTILE TRUST CO. NAT'L ASS'N

Missouri Court of Appeals 1975. 530 S.W.2d 743.

BACKGROUND AND FACTS   *Nu-Way is the customer-drawer in this case, and Mercantile Trust Company is the drawee bank. Nu-Way has sued Mercantile Trust for reimbursement for numerous altered and forged checks that the latter paid. The court gives a detailed rendition of the events leading up to this lawsuit.*

GUNN, Judge.

*   *   *   *

Nu-Way, a truck repair company, maintained a checking account with Mercantile. The signature card for Nu-Way's president, Mariano Costello, was kept on file by the bank. Each month, Nu-Way wrote approximately 175 checks on its account, and Mercantile sent Nu-Way a monthly statement indicating the fluctuating checking account balance as each check was charged against the account with the cancelled checks being returned with the statement.

In an altruistic gesture designed for the rehabilitation of a former convict, Mr. Costello hired James Ussery as night manager for Nu-Way. Part of Ussery's duties entailed obtaining automotive parts from parts companies. Mr. Costello would on occasion date and sign checks and fill in the name of the payee (always a parts company) for payment of parts used by Nu-Way, and the amount of the check would be left blank for Ussery to fill in when the cost of the parts was determined at the time they were picked up by him. On seven such checks which Mr. Costello had signed, Ussery made alterations to substitute his name as payee and cashed the checks for his own benefit. Ussery also had unauthorized access to Nu-Way's checkbook and removed a substantial number of blank checks therefrom. Ussery made use of 43 of the blank checks by forging Mr. Costello's signature on them after making himself the payee. The dates on the altered and forged checks were from July 29, 1971 to January 13, 1972.

Each of the forged checks was returned to Nu-Way by Mercantile along with an itemized statement of account at the end of each month the checks were cashed. And each month Mr. Costello would have a company clerk compare the amount of the checks with the statements. At Mr. Costello's direction the bookkeeping employee merely compared the amount of the checks with the statements looking only for mathematical computation errors by Mercantile. None of the Nu-Way employees, including Mr. Costello, examined any of the checks for forgeries or alterations nor compared the checks with the company checkbook. Ultimately, one of Nu-Way's vendors called Mr. Costello's attention to a check made payable to Ussery, and an investigation revealed the alterations and forgeries. Mercantile was notified of the irregularities and subsequently reimbursed Nu-Way for $231 to cover the amount of the first check altered by Ussery. Nu-Way brought suit to recover the amount paid out on its checking account on the forged and altered checks.

* * * *

In its argument that it has no liability to Nu-Way for the payments made on the altered and forged checks, Mercantile relies on [UCC 4-406] which in pertinent part provides:

"(1) When a bank sends to its customer a statement of account accompanied by items paid in good faith in support of the debit entries or holds the statement and items pursuant to a request or instructions of its customer or otherwise in a reasonable manner makes the statement and items available to the customer, the customer must exercise reasonable care and promptness to examine the statement and items to discover his unauthorized signature or any alteration on an item and must notify the bank promptly after discovery thereof.
"(2) If the bank establishes that the customer failed with respect to an item to comply with the duties imposed on the customer by subsection (1) the customer is precluded from asserting against the bank
(a) his unauthorized signature or any alteration on the item if the bank also establishes that it suffered a loss by reason of such failure; and
(b) an unauthorized signature or alteration by the same wrongdoer on any other item paid in good faith by the bank after the first item and statement was available to the customer for a reasonable period not exceeding fourteen calendar days and before the bank receives notification from the customer of any such unauthorized signature or alteration.
"(3) The preclusion under subsection (2) does not apply if the customer establishes lack of ordinary care on the part of the bank in paying the items."

Nu-Way concedes that under the facts of this case that § 400.4-406(3) places the burden upon it of proving that Mercantile lacked ordinary care in paying on the altered and forged checks. We find as a matter of law that Nu-Way failed in this case in its proof of lack of ordinary care by Mercantile as to the 43 forged checks.
* * *

* * *   The fundamental rule in the Uniform Commercial Code regarding unauthorized signatures is stated in [UCC 3-404(1)] as follows:

"Any unauthorized signature is wholly inoperative as that of the person whose name is signed unless he ratifies it or is precluded from denying it . . ." It is accepted that Ussery's forgeries of Mr. Costello's signature were unauthorized and would therefore be "wholly inoperative" as to Nu-Way unless Nu-Way is "precluded from denying it." [UCC 4-406] relates directly to the relationship between depositor and bank and affords an apt guide for determining whether a basis exists for precluding Nu-Way's denial of the signatures.

Initially, we find that Nu-Way failed to meet its obligation under subparagraph (1) of [UCC 4-406], in that it did not "exercise reasonable care and promptness to examine the statement and items to discover [the] unauthorized signature *　*　* on an item." In accordance with Mr. Costello's instructions, the Nu-Way clerk in charge of examining the bank statements examined Mercantile's statements to check the accuracy of the mathematics. The "items"—the cancelled checks—were not examined at all. Mr. Costello readily admitted that the checks were not scrutinized for forgeries as required by statute nor was reasonable notice given to Mercantile of any wrongdoing after the first check and statement was made available to Nu-Way within the meaning of [UCC 4-406(2)(b)]. Hence, Nu-Way failed in its duties to discover and report the forgeries under [UCC 4-406(2)] and is precluded from recovering against Mercantile *　*　*

After Mr. Costello notified Mercantile that there had been payments made on some forgeries and alterations, the clerk responsible for examining Nu-Way's account and her two supervisors made comparison between the authorized signature card and all Nu-Way's checks for the period covered by the forgeries and alterations and were unable to differentiate between the forgeries and the authorized signature. The forgeries were sufficiently adroit so as to escape detection even under the supervisors' scrutiny. However, the clerk was reprimanded for allowing the alterations to pass, as erasures appearing on the altered checks were perspicuous. [sic]

*　*　*　*

[We] have determined as a matter of law that the recovery against Mercantile on the 43 forged checks is precluded by [UCC 4-406].

JUDGMENT AND REMEDY   *Nu-Way was unable to recover against Mercantile on the forty-three forged checks.*

Payment on an Altered Check

The customer's instruction to the bank is to pay the exact amount on the face of the check to the holder. The bank must examine each check before making final payment. If it fails to detect an alteration, it is liable to its customer for the loss because it did not pay as the drawer customer ordered. The loss is the difference between the original amount of the check and the amount actually paid. Suppose a check written for $11 is raised to $111. The customer's account will be charged $11 (the amount the customer ordered it to pay). The bank will be responsible for the $100. [UCC 4-401(2)(a)]

The bank is entitled to recover the amount of loss from the transferor who, by presenting the check for payment, warrants that the check has not been materially altered. No customer or collecting bank or other holder in due course who acts in good faith gives this warranty to: (1) the maker of a note, (2) the drawer of a draft, (3) the acceptor of an item with respect to an alteration made prior to the acceptance if the holder in due course took the item after the acceptance, or (4) the acceptor of an item with respect to an alteration made after the acceptance. [UCC 4-207(1)(c) and 3-417(1)(c)]

A customer's negligence can shift the risk of loss. A common example occurs when a person carelessly writes a check, leaving large gaps around the numbers and words so that additional numbers and words can be inserted. (See, for example, Exhibit 29–5.)

Similarly, a person who signs a check and leaves the dollar amount for someone else to fill in is barred from protesting when the bank unknowingly and in good faith pays whatever amount is shown. [UCC 4-401(2)(b)] Finally, if the bank can trace its loss on successive altered checks to the customer's failure to discover the initial alteration, then the bank can alleviate its liability for reimbursing the customer's account.[2] [UCC 4-406] The law governing the customer's *duty* to examine monthly statements and canceled checks, to discover and report alterations to the drawee bank, is the same as that applied to forged customer signatures.

---

2. The bank's defense is the same whether successive payments were made on either a forged drawer's signature or an altered check. The bank must prove that prompt notice would have prevented its loss. For example, notification might have alerted the bank to stop paying further items or enabled it to catch the forger.

In every situation involving a forged drawer's signature or alteration, a bank must observe reasonable commercial standards of care in paying on a customer's checks. [UCC 4-406(3)] The customer's contributory negligence can be asserted only if the bank has exercised ordinary care.

ACCEPTING DEPOSITS

A second fundamental service a commercial bank provides for its checking account customers is to accept deposits of cash and checks. Cash deposits made in U.S. currency are received into the customer's account without being subject to further collection procedures. This section will focus on the check after it has been deposited. In the vast majority of cases, deposited checks are from parties who do business at different banks, but sometimes checks are written between customers of the same bank. Either situation brings into play the bank collection process as it operates within the statutory framework of Article 4 of the UCC.

Definitions

The first bank to receive a check for payment is the **depositary bank**.[3] When a person deposits

---

3. All definitions in this section are found in UCC 4-105.

EXHIBIT 29–5   A POORLY FILLED OUT CHECK

his or her IRS tax refund check into a personal checking account at the local bank, the bank acts as a *depositary* bank. The bank on which a check is drawn (the drawee bank) is called the **payor bank.** Any bank except the payor bank that handles a check during some phase of the collection process is a **collecting bank.** Any bank except the payor bank or depositary bank to which an item is transferred in the course of this collection process is called an **intermediary bank.** During the collection process, any bank can take on one or more of these roles.

For example, a buyer in New York writes a check on her New York bank and sends it to a seller in San Francisco. The seller deposits the check in her San Francisco bank account. The seller's bank is both a *depositary bank* and a *collecting bank.* The buyer's bank in New York is the *payor bank.* As the check travels from San Francisco to New York, any collecting bank (other than the depositary bank and the payor bank) handling the item in the collection process is also called an *intermediary bank.*

Check Collection between Customers of the Same Bank   An item that is payable by the depositary bank that receives it is called an "on-us item." If the bank does not dishonor the check by the opening of the second banking day following its receipt, it is considered paid. [UCC 4-213(4)(b)] For example, Harriman and Goldsmith each have a checking account at First National Bank. On Monday morning, Goldsmith deposits into his own checking account a $300 check from Harriman. That same day, First National issues Goldsmith a "provisional credit" for $300. When the bank opens on Wednesday, Harriman's check is considered honored and Goldsmith's provisional credit becomes a final payment.

Check Collection between Customers of Different Banks   Millions of checks circulate throughout the United States each day, and every check must be physically transported to its payor bank before final payment is made. Once a depositary bank receives a check, it must arrange to present it either directly or through intermediary banks to the appropriate payor bank. Each bank in the collection chain must pass the check on before

midnight of the next banking day following its receipt. [UCC 4-202(2)]

The bank has a duty to use ordinary care in performing its collection functions. [UCC 4-202(1)] This duty requires banks to conform to general banking usage as established in the Uniform Commercial Code, Federal Reserve regulations, clearinghouse rules, and so on.[4] [UCC 4-103(1)] Banks also have a duty to act seasonably. This means that a bank is generally required to take appropriate action before the midnight deadline following the receipt of a check, a notice, or a payment. [UCC 4-104(1)(h)] So, for example, a collecting bank that receives a check on Monday must forward it to the next collection bank prior to midnight on Tuesday.

Upon receipt of a check by a *payor* bank through the collection process, the midnight deadline for action becomes extremely important. Unless the payor bank dishonors the check or returns it by midnight on the next banking day following receipt, the payor bank is accountable for the face amount of the check. [UCC 4-302]

Because of this and of the need for an even work flow of the many items handled by banks daily, the Code permits what is called deferred posting, or delayed return. *Deferred posting* permits checks received after a certain time (say 2:00 P.M.) to be deferred until the next day. Thus, a check received by a payor bank at 3:00 P.M. on Monday would be deferred for posting until Tuesday. In this case, the payor bank's deadline would be midnight Wednesday. [UCC 4-301(1)].

The Federal Reserve System Clears Checks   The Federal Reserve System has greatly simplified the clearing of checks—that is, the method by which checks deposited in one bank are transferred to the banks on which they were written. Suppose Smith of Chicago writes a check to the Jones family in San Francisco. When the Joneses receive the check in the mail, they deposit it in their bank. Their bank then deposits the check in the Federal Reserve Bank of Chicago. That

---

4.   The Code is explicit that "the obligations of good faith, diligence, reasonableness and care * * * may not be disclaimed. * * *" [UCC 1-102(3)]

Federal Reserve Bank then sends the check to Smith's bank, where the amount of the check is deducted from Smith's account. Exhibit 29–6 illustrates this process.

Check Clearing Technology in Banking Operations

The present basis of the payment-collection process is the check, but banks are finding it increasingly difficult to cope with trillions of pieces of paper that evidence funds. New systems of automatic payments and direct deposits, known as electronic funds transfer systems (EFTS),

promise to rid banks of the burden of transferring money by moving mountains of paper. There are basically three parts to an EFTS system: (1) teller machines, (2) point-of-sale systems, and (3) automated clearinghouses.

Teller Machines A recent EFTS development has involved teller machines, which are also called customer bank communication terminals or remote service units. They are located either on the bank's premises or at convenient locations such as stores, supermarkets, drugstores, and shopping centers.

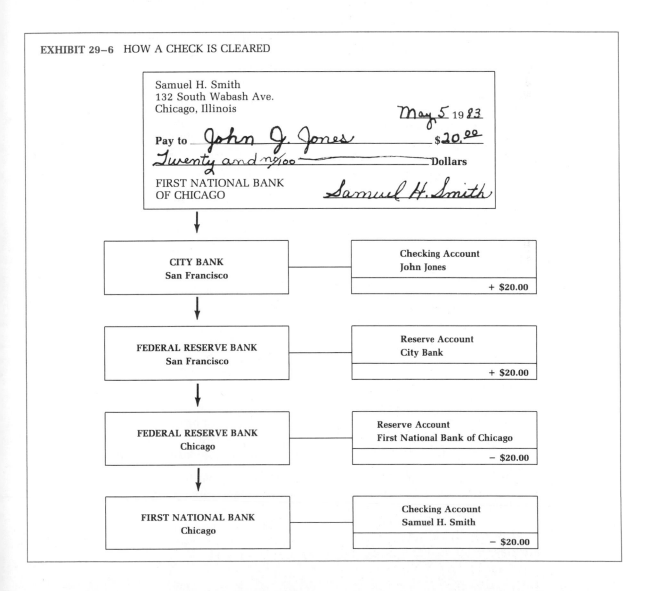

EXHIBIT 29–6   HOW A CHECK IS CLEARED

Automated teller machines receive deposits, dispense funds from checking or savings accounts, make credit card advances, and receive payment. The devices are connected on-line to the bank's computers.

Point-of-Sale Systems Point-of-sale systems allow the consumer to transfer funds to merchants in order to make purchases. On-line terminals are located at check-out counters in the merchant's store. When making a purchase, the customer's card is inserted into the terminal, which reads the data encoded on it. The computer at the customer's bank verifies that the card and identification code are valid and that there is enough money in the customer's account. After the purchase is made, the customer's account is debited for the amount of the purchase.

Automated Clearinghouses Automated clearinghouses are similar to ordinary clearinghouses in which checks are cleared between banks. The main difference is that entries are made in the form of electronic signals; no checks are used. These systems are not for further automating the handling of paper checks; they are replacements. Such systems are especially useful to businesspersons for recurrent payments, such as payroll, social security, or pension fund payments.

These systems have aroused some serious consumer concerns. For example:

1.   It is difficult to issue stop-payment orders.
2.   Fewer records are available.
3.   The possibilities for tampering and lack of privacy are increased.
4.   "Float"—the time between the writing of a check and its deduction from an account—is lost.
5.   There is a possibility of chicanery by the unscrupulous gaining access to the system.

The Bank's Liability in EFTS

In response to customer concern over EFTS, Congress has passed legislation affecting the liability of both customers and banks. These new rules relate to electronic funds transfer accounts that are operated by telephone, automatically, or by using a customer debit card that is presented to merchants when making purchases. Some of the major rules that apply are:

1.   If a customer's debit card is lost or stolen and used without his or her permission, the customer has to pay only $50. However, the customer must notify the bank of the loss or theft within *two* days of learning about it. Otherwise, the liability increases to $500. The customer is liable for more than $500 if the unauthorized use is not reported within sixty days after it appears on the customer's statement. (Even the $50 limit does not apply if the customer gives his or her card to someone who uses it improperly or if fraud is committed.)
2.   Any error on the monthly statement must be picked up by the customer within *sixty* days, and the bank must be notified. The bank then has *ten* days to investigate. If the bank takes longer than ten days, it must return the disputed amount of money to the customer's account until the error is found. If there is no error, the customer has to give the money back to the bank.
3.   The bank must furnish receipts for transactions made through computer terminals, but it is not obliged to do so for telephone transfers.
4.   A monthly statement must be made for every month in which there is an electronic transfer of funds. Otherwise, statements must be made every quarter. The statement must show the amount and date of the transfer, the names of the retailers involved, the location or identification of the terminal, and the fees. Additionally, the statement must give an address and phone number for inquiries and error notices.
5.   Any authorized prepayment for utility bills and insurance premiums can be stopped three days before the scheduled transfer.
6.   There are certain limitations to the federal government's access to these financial records, but a bank is not prohibited from giving the customer's records to a retailer who might want information on the customer's spending habits.

All of the above information must be given to the customer who opens an EFTS account.[5]

---

5.   The $50 limit on consumer liability went into effect February 10, 1978. The other provisions of this new law took effect in May 1980.

QUESTIONS AND
CASE PROBLEMS

1. Daniel drafts a check for $1,000 payable to Paula and drawn on the West Bank. After issue of the check, Paula, by blank indorsement, negotiates the check to Fred. Fred finds an ideal real estate lot for sale, but to close the deal he needs to make a $1,000 down payment by certified check. Fred takes the check to West Bank and requests West Bank to certify Daniel's check.

(a) If West Bank refuses to certify Daniel's check, can either Daniel or Fred hold it liable? Explain.

(b) If West Bank certifies the check, explain fully the liability to Fred of Daniel as drawer and Paula as indorser.

2. On January 5 Daniel drafts a check for $3,000 drawn on the East Bank and payable to his secretary, Sylvia, for services rendered. Daniel puts last year's date on the check by mistake. Before Sylvia can get to the East Bank to cash the check, on January 7, Daniel is killed in an automobile accident. The East Bank is aware of Daniel's death. On January 10 Sylvia presents the check to the East Bank, and the bank honors the check by payment to Sylvia. Daniel's widow, Martha, claims that the East Bank wrongfully paid Sylvia since it knew of Daniel's death and also paid a check that was by date over one year old. Martha, as executrix of Daniel's estate and sole heir by his will, demands that East Bank recredit Daniel's estate for the check paid Sylvia. Discuss fully East Bank's liability in light of Martha's demand.

3. Daniel goes grocery shopping and carelessly leaves his checkbook in his shopping cart. His checkbook, with two blank checks remaining, is stolen by Thomas. On May 5 Thomas forges Daniel's name on a check for $100 and cashes the check at Daniel's bank, the First of Jonestown Bank. Daniel has not reported the theft to his bank. On June 1 Daniel receives his monthly bank statement and cancelled checks from Jonestown Bank including the forged check by Thomas. Daniel does not reconcile his checking account. On June 20 Thomas forges Daniel's last check. This check is for $1,000 and is cashed at the West Bank, a bank with which Thomas has previously done business. The West Bank sends the check through the collection process, and the Jonestown Bank honors it. On July 1, upon receipt of Jonestown Bank's statement and cancelled checks, Daniel discovers both forgeries and immediately notifies Jonestown Bank. Thomas cannot be found. Daniel claims that Jonestown must recredit his account for both checks, as his signature was forged. Discuss fully Daniel's claim.

4. Diana takes her television set to Honest John's TV Service Store for repairs. The set is supposedly repaired, at a cost of $125. On Saturday Diana writes out a check payable to Honest John drawn on the First Greenville Bank. Diana takes the set home and discovers that virtually no repairs have been made. On Monday Diana calls Honest John to complain about his lack of performance. Honest John insists the repairs were made and refuses to even look at the television set. Diana immediately calls the First Greenville Bank and issues a stop-payment order over the phone. Three weeks later, Honest John cashes Diana's check at a drive-in window of the First Greenville Bank. Diana is furious upon discovery of the bank's payment to Honest John and wants the bank to recredit her account. Discuss fully the First Greenville Bank's liability in this matter.

5. Daniel has $5,000 in his checking account with the Second Bank of Fielder. Daniel writes a check for $500 payable to Peter. This check is in settlement of a long-standing dispute between the two. Peter deposits the check in his bank. Peter's bank sends the check through the collection process. The Second Bank, by mistake, returns the check to Peter's bank marked "insufficient funds." Peter's bank returns the check to Peter, charging his account for $500, plus the bank's service charge of $10 for returned checks. Peter is furious and files criminal charges against Daniel. Discuss fully the Second Bank of Fielder's liability for wrongful dishonor of Daniel's check.

6. Aetna Insurance Company received an insurance claim from Marie Porter and drew a draft on itself payable to Porter or her order. On the face of the draft appeared the words "payable through Hartford National Bank and Trust." When she received the draft, Porter negotiated it to Karen Bentley, her doctor. Bentley indorsed the draft "for deposit only, Karen Bentley," and gave it to her secretary, Mark Upton, to take to the bank. Upton took the check to the Traders Bank, which credited Bentley's savings account that evening and passed the check on to the district Federal Reserve bank the next morning. Almost immediately, the Federal Reserve bank transferred the draft to Hartford National Bank and Trust. Pursuant to Aetna's instructions, Hartford National paid the check from funds that Aetna kept in its account with Hartford. What is each of the parties in the above transaction called un-

der Article 4 of the UCC? [See Aetna Cas. & Sur. Co. v. Traders National Bank & Trust Co., 514 S.W.2d 860 (Mo. Ct. App. 1974)]

7. Rees Plumbing Company, Inc., and Weldon Douglas both maintained checking accounts at the Citizens Bank of Jonesboro. On August 19, 1966, Rees drew a check payable to Douglas in the amount of $1,000 and delivered it to Douglas. On that same day Douglas presented the check to Citizens Bank for deposit in his own checking account. Deposit slips were prepared, and a teller of the bank stamped the back of the check with the August 19 date, and a statement, "pay to any bank—prior indorsement guaranteed, Citizens Bank of Jonesboro, Jonesboro, Arkansas." On August 20, 1966, the bank dishonored the check because of insufficient funds and debited the amount of the check from Douglas's account. Did the bank, by stamping the indorsement upon the check deposited by Douglas and by delivering a deposit slip to Douglas, "accept" the check? Assume that instead of giving Douglas a provisional credit to his account, the Citizens Bank had cashed the check. Could it then have debited Douglas's account upon dishonor of the check? [Douglas v. Citizens Bank of Jonesboro, 244 Ark. 168, 424 S.W.2d 532 (1968)]

8. Reinhard purchased a cashier's check made payable to The Patchworks Co. from Marine Midland Bank. The check was delivered to The Patchworks in exchange for goods purchased by Reinhard. Because he was dissatisfied with the goods, Reinhard told the bank that he had lost the check and asked that payment be stopped. Can Reinhard stop payment? [Moon Over the Mountain, Ltd. v. Marine Midland Bank, 87 Misc.2d 918, 386 N.Y.S.2d 974 (1976)]

9. Northwest Shopping Center owned and operated a shopping center in Texas. Kaiser was one of its tenants. Pursuant to the rental agreement, Kaiser paid a monthly rent of $500 with a check that it mailed to Northwest. Northwest retained one of these rent checks for over nine months before presenting it to the bank for payment. If Northwest now presents to Kaiser's bank for payment, must the bank pay? If the bank refuses to pay, is Kaiser still liable? [Kaiser v. Northwest Shopping Center, 544 S.W.2d 785 (Tex. Civ. App. 1976)]

10. Ralston pledged stock certificates as collateral for a loan. The proceeds of the loan, $38,000, were used to open a new checking account at the lending bank. Ralston immediately had the bank certify a $21,000 check payable to a second bank. Later that day the lending bank learned that the stock certificates were stolen and notified the payee bank that certification of the check was rescinded. The payee bank had accepted the check for deposit to Ralston's account but had given no value for it (no checks had been honored against the deposit). As a holder of the certified check, could the payee bank prevent the lending bank's revocation of certification? [Rockland Trust Co. v. South Shore Nat'l Bank, 366 Mass. 74, 314 N.E.2d 438 (1974)].

CHAPTER 30

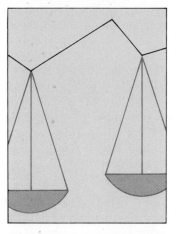

SECURED TRANSACTIONS
Introduction

The concept of a secured transaction is as basic to modern business practice as the concept of credit. Few purchasers (manufacturers, wholesalers, retailers, consumers) have the resources to always pay cash for goods being purchased. To a limited extent, consignment arrangements enable a retailer to maintain an adequate stock of goods without always advancing capital (cash), but credit is the most feasible and most common method used.

There are many credit devices available, such as securing credit with a chattel mortgage (tangible personal property) or a lien, giving a promissory note, or making an installment or time payment arrangement. Regardless of the credit method chosen, when the debtor-creditor relationship arises, the creditor often requires the debtor to provide some type of security beyond a mere promise that the debt will be paid. A credit transaction for goods coupled with security is known as a **secured transaction.** The cred-

itor has two major concerns if the debtor defaults on the obligation to repay:

1.   Can the debt be satisfied from some *specific property offered as security* (collateral) by the debtor?
2.   Will satisfaction of that particular debt from that collateral be given *priority* over the claims of other creditors?

These concerns form the basis for the law of secured transactions.

Virtually any transaction that is the subject of commercial financing when a security interest arises comes within the body of law known as *secured transactions.* For example, secured transactions are often involved in the sale of goods when a retailer purchases goods for inventory on credit, or when a business purchases equipment on credit, or when a consumer buys merchandise on a credit plan. The law of secured transactions tends to favor the rights of creditors, but to a lesser extent, it offers debtors some protection, too.

THE LAW BEFORE THE UCC

Prior to the adoption of the UCC, the law relating to secured transactions was concerned with the person who had *title* to the property and with the form of the transaction. The law of secured transactions was mystifying, and the terminology was unwieldy because of the great number of methods of obtaining a security interest in goods. The methods most commonly used were chattel mortgages, trust receipts, conditional sales, and pledges.

ARTICLE 9 OF THE UCC

The UCC eliminated the distinctions among the various forms of financing outlined above and simplified the terminology. Concern for title was eliminated or greatly lessened. Substance was elevated over form. Article 9 of the UCC provides a framework for the law of secured transactions, regardless of the terms used in a security agreement. In the following sections, the vocabulary used in secured transactions is explained. This terminology is unique to Article 9 of the Code and to secured transactions themselves.

DEFINITIONS

Under the UCC, not only has the terminology been simplified, but the particular credit devices used are irrelevant to determining the rules for establishing rights and priorities of creditors in the event of a default. The terminology used under the Code is now uniformly adopted in all documents drawn in a secured transaction situation:

1. **Security interest.** Every interest "in *personal property or fixtures* [emphasis added] which secures payment or performance of an obligation" is a security interest. [UCC 1-201(37)]

2. **Secured party.** A lender, seller, or any person in whose favor there is a security interest,

including a person to whom accounts[1] or chattel paper[2] have been sold, is a secured party. [UCC 9-105(1)(m)]

3. **Debtor.** The party who owes payment or performance of the secured obligation, whether or not that party actually owns or has rights in the collateral, is a debtor. The term *debtor* includes sellers of accounts or chattel paper. When the debtor and owner of the collateral are not the same person, the term *debtor* refers to the actual owner of the collateral or describes the obligor on an obligation, or both, depending upon the context in which the term is used. [UCC 9-105(1)(d)]

4. **Security agreement.** The agreement that creates or provides for a security interest between the debtor and a secured party is called a security agreement. [UCC 9-105(1)(l)]

5. **Collateral.** The property subject to a security interest, including accounts and chattel paper that have been sold, is collateral. [UCC 9-105(1)(c)]

These basic definitions form the concept under which a debtor-creditor relationship becomes a secured transaction relationship. See Exhibit 30–1.

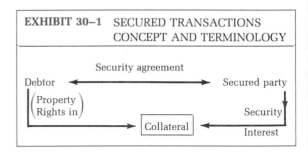

EXHIBIT 30–1   SECURED TRANSACTIONS CONCEPT AND TERMINOLOGY

6. **Goods.** "All things which are *movable* at the time the security interest attaches or which are *fixtures*" (emphasis added) come under the general category of goods. Goods include standing timber that is to be cut and removed, the unborn young of animals, and growing crops.

---

1. *Account* refers to any right to payment for goods sold or leased or for services rendered; in effect, it is the ordinary commercial accounts receivable. [UCC 9-106]

2. " 'Chattel paper' means a writing or writings which evidence both a monetary obligation and a security interest in or a lease of specific goods, * * *" [UCC 9-105(1)(b)]

[UCC 9-105(1)(h)] They do not include money, documents, instruments, accounts, chattel paper, general intangibles, minerals before extraction, or the like.

Article 9 classifies "goods" as (a) consumer goods, (b) equipment, (c) farm products, and (d) inventory.

A. *Consumer goods.* Goods are consumer goods if they are used or bought for use primarily for personal, family, or household purposes—for example, household furniture. [UCC 9-109(1)]

B. *Equipment.* Goods are equipment if they are used or bought for use primarily in business—for example, a delivery truck. [UCC 9-109(2)]

C. *Farm products.* Crops or livestock or supplies used or produced in farming operations are farm products. Also the products of crops or livestock in their unmanufactured state (such as ginned cotton, maple syrup, milk, eggs) are farm products. Farm products must be in the possession of a debtor engaged in farming operations. [UCC 9-109(3)]

D. *Inventory.* Goods held for disposition (that is, for sale or lease) and materials used or consumed in the course of business (raw materials, for example) are all considered inventory. [UCC 9-109(4)]

7. **Chattel paper.** A writing that evidences both a *monetary obligation and a security interest* in specific goods or leased goods is chattel paper. For example, when a security agreement relates to specific equipment, it is called chattel paper. When any transaction is evidenced both by a security agreement and by instruments evidencing the debt obligation, the group of writings put together constitutes chattel paper. For example, a retail installment contract plus a signed note is chattel paper. [UCC 9-105(1)(b)]

8. **Accounts and general intangibles.** An *account* is any right to payment for goods sold or leased or for services rendered that is not evidenced by an instrument or chattel paper, whether or not it has been earned by performance. [UCC 9-106] For example, a retailer sells goods to a consumer on an open account. The consumer has sixty days in which to pay. The retailer can assign the account receivable in an outright sale or use it to secure a loan. The transaction between the retailer and the lender based on this security is one type of *secured transaction.* The lender is the secured party, the retailer is the debtor, and the consumer is an account debtor.[3]

The definition of **general intangibles** is "* * * any personal property (including things in action) other than goods, accounts, chattel paper, documents, instruments, and money." [UCC 9-106] For example, a patent or copyright can be a valuable personal property right of the inventor or author. To secure a loan, an author can put up his or her copyright, with entitlement to royalties, as collateral for the loan. The copyright would be classified as a general intangible.

9. **Documents of title.** Documents of title include bills of lading, dock warrants, dock receipts, warehouse receipts, and any other documents that in the regular course of business or financing are treated as adequate evidence that the person in possession of them is entitled to receive, hold, and dispose of them and the goods they cover. [UCC 9-105(1)(f), 1-201(15), and 7-201]

10. **Instruments.** An instrument means a negotiable instrument or a certificated security or any other writing evidencing a right to the payment of money but which is not itself a security agreement or a lease. Also, it must be a writing of the type which, in the ordinary course of business, is transferred by delivery with any necessary indorsement or assignment. [UCC 9-105(1)(i)] Examples of instruments are therefore stocks, commercial paper, certificates of deposit, and banker's acceptances.

In order for the secured party to have priority over the debtor's collateral upon default as against claims of other creditors, the secured party must *perfect* his or her secured interest. **Perfection** is a method or procedure giving third parties notice of a secured party's claim (security interest). The sections that follow will discuss creating a

3. The account debtor is the person who is obligated on the account, chattel paper, or general intangible. [UCC 9-105(1)(a)] So, for example, when the account of a third person (the user) is assigned to the bank, the dealer becomes a debtor, the bank is the secured party, and the third party is the account debtor.

security interest and the steps that must be taken to perfect that interest.

CREATING A SECURITY INTEREST

The first concern in dealing with security interests is to determine whether the transaction falls within Article 9. That article applies to any transaction that is intended to create a security interest in personal property or fixtures. It also applies to any sale of accounts or chattel paper. Transactions that are excluded from Article 9 are real estate mortgages, landlords' liens, mechanics' liens, claims arising out of judicial proceedings, wage or salary claims, and so on. [UCC 9-104] In general, these transactions have been excluded because of their extensive treatment in other areas of the law. For example, landlords' liens against tenants who have defaulted are governed by rules of real property law.

Requirements for Attachment

Assuming that the transaction comes within the scope of Article 9, a businessperson must meet three requirements in order to have an enforceable security interest.

1. Generally, there must be an agreement in writing.
2. The secured party must give value to the debtor.
3. The debtor must have rights in the collateral.

Once these requirements are met, the creditor's rights are said to "attach" to the collateral. This means that the creditor's security interest is *enforceable* against the debtor. Attachment insures that the security interest between the debtor and the secured party is effective. [UCC 9-203]

Written Agreement   Unless the collateral is in the possession of the secured party, there must be a *written security agreement* describing the collateral and signed by the debtor. The security agreement creates or provides for a security interest. For example, it might read "Debtor hereby grants to secured party a security interest in the

following goods. *   *   *'' There are three requirements for the agreement to be valid:

1. The agreement must be signed by the debtor.
2. The agreement must contain a description of the collateral.
3. The description must reasonably identify the collateral. [UCC 9-203(1) and 9-110]

Value Given to Debtor   The secured party must give *value*. According to UCC 1-201(44), value is any consideration that supports a simple contract. In addition, value can be security given for a preexisting (antecedent) obligation or any binding commitment to extend credit. Normally, the value given by a secured party is in the form of a direct loan, or it involves a commitment to sell goods on credit.

Debtor Has Rights in Collateral   The debtor must have *rights* in the collateral; that is, the debtor must have some ownership interest or right to obtain possession of that collateral. The debtor's rights can represent either a current or a future legal interest in the collateral.

PURCHASE MONEY SECURITY INTEREST

Often, sellers of consumer durable goods, such as stereos and television sets, agree to extend credit for part of the purchase price of those goods. Also, lenders not necessarily in the business of selling such goods often agree to lend much of the purchase price for such goods. There is a special name for the security interest that the seller or the lender obtains when such a transaction occurs. It is called a **purchase money security interest.** Formally, such an interest obtains when:

1. A security interest is retained or taken by the seller of the collateral in order to secure part or all of its price; or
2. A security interest is taken by a person who, by making advances or incurring an obligation, gives something of value that enables the debtor to acquire rights in the collateral or to use it. [UCC 9-107]

In either case, a lender or seller has essentially provided a buyer with the "purchase money" to buy goods. To illustrate, suppose Barbara wants to purchase a combination color television-stereo set from Sallor. The purchase price is $900. Not being able to pay cash, Barbara signs a security agreement to pay $100 down and $50 per month until the balance plus interest is fully paid. Sallor is to retain a security interest in the purchased set until full payment has been made. Since the security interest was created as part of the purchase agreement, it is a purchase money security interest.

The same result would occur if Barbara went to the West Bank and borrowed the $900 to buy the combination set from Sallor. After Barbara signs a security agreement with West Bank, with the to-be-purchased set as collateral, West Bank has a purchase money security interest the moment the set is purchased from Sallor. Obviously if Barbara used the money for other purposes, West Bank would not have a security interest. For this reason, West Bank might arrange to pay the $900 directly to Sallor.

The importance of the distinction between a purchase money security interest and other types of security interests will be discussed in Chapter 31. In short, a purchase money security interest ordinarily has priority over a nonpurchase money security interest.

PERFECTING A SECURITY INTEREST

A creditor has two main concerns if the debtor defaults—satisfaction of the debt out of certain predesignated property and priority over other creditors. The concept of *attachment*, which establishes the criteria for creating an enforceable security interest, deals with the former concern; the concept of *perfection* deals with the latter.

Even though a security interest has attached, the secured party *must* take steps in order to protect its claim to the collateral over claims that third parties may have, such as other secured creditors, general creditors, trustees in bankruptcy, and purchasers of the collateral that is the subject matter of the security agreement. Per-

fection represents the legal process by which a secured party protects itself against the claims of third parties who may wish to have their debts satisfied out of the collateral.

Methods of Perfection

There are basically three methods of perfection:

1. *By transfer of collateral.* The debtor can transfer possession of the collateral itself to the secured party. This occurs, for example, when the debtor gives the secured party stocks or bonds, or even a piece of jewelry, provided that it is collateral securing the debt. With respect to instruments (negotiable as per UCC 3-104) or a certificated security (as defined in UCC 8-102), except for a few cases of temporary perfections, the only way for proper perfection is by possession by the secured party. This type of transfer is called a **pledge.** [UCC 9-302(1)(a), 9-304(1), 9-305]

Consider an example. Ulster borrows $2,000 from Levine, giving Levine possession of three antique guns as collateral for the loan. Several months later, before Ulster has repaid the loan, a creditor obtains a judgment against Ulster. The creditor seeks to have the sheriff take the valuable antique guns away from Levine. Even though no financing statement has been filed, the creditor cannot touch the antique guns because Levine perfected his security interest in them when he took possession of them.

2. *By purchase money security interest in consumer goods.* In certain circumstances, the security interest can be perfected automatically at the time of a credit sale—that is, at the time that the security interest is created under a written security agreement. Note that this *automatic perfection rule* with regard to purchase money security interests applies only when the goods are *consumer goods.* The seller in this situation need do nothing more to protect his or her interest. There are exceptions to this rule, however, that cover security interests in fixtures and in motor vehicles. [UCC 9-302(1)(d)] For those states that have not adopted the 1972 UCC amendments, a purchase money security interest in farm equipment under a certain statutory value is also automatically perfected by attachment.

Another instance of automatic perfection occurs when a person assigns a small portion of his or her accounts receivable—usually to a collecting agent known as a *factor.* Perfection is automatic as long as the assignment does not by itself or in conjunction with other assignments to the same assignee constitute a transfer of a significant part of the outstanding accounts of the debtor. Other situations where perfection is automatic (but which are somewhat less important) are listed in UCC 9-302(1).

3. *By filing.* The third and most common method of perfection is by filing a *financing statement.* The UCC requires a financing statement to have: (a) the signature of the debtor, (b) the addresses of both the debtor and the creditor, and (c) a description of the collateral by type or item.[4] [UCC 9-402(1)] Filing is the means of perfection to use in all cases—unless, of course, the collateral is the kind that a secured party can take possession of, or is required to take possession of, in order to perfect (such as a money pledge), or unless the creditor has a purchase money security interest in consumer goods. See Exhibit 30–2 for a sample financing statement.

Both the security agreement and the financing statement must contain a description of the collateral in which the secured party has a security interest. Generally, the description of the goods is more precise in the security agreement than in the financing statement. Sometimes, however, the description contained in the security agreement is usually the same as the one in the financing statement. This is true because the secured party often merely files a copy of the security agreement (in order to perfect). This practice of using a copy of the security agreement as the financing statement is generally valid, provided that the security agreement meets the criteria previously described and provided that the criteria for the financing statement (such as the inclusion of the addresses of both parties) are met.

The legal purposes for including a description in both the security agreement and financing statement differ.

The UCC requires that the security agreement include a description of the collateral because no security interest in goods could exist unless the parties agree on which goods are subject to the security interest and then describe these goods in writing. On the other hand, the purpose of including a description of collateral in a financing statement is to put persons who might later wish to lend to the debtor on notice that certain goods in the debtor's possession are already subject to a security interest. The following case demonstrates these different objectives for including a description of collateral in the security agreement and the financing statement.

---

4. Certain types of collateral—crops, timber to be cut, minerals, accounts, or goods that are to become fixtures—require more than mere description, i.e., a description of the real estate concerned. [UCC 9-402(1)(5), 9-103(5), and 9-313]

JONES & LAUGHLIN SUPPLY v. DUGAN PRODUCTION CORP.

Court of Appeals of New Mexico, 1973.
85 N.M. 51, 508 P.2d 1348.

BACKGROUND AND FACTS *The defendants, Dugan Production Corporation (Dugan) and George McDonald (McDonald), purchased oil drilling equipment at a sheriff's sale. The equipment was previously owned by Lucky Drilling Company, but Jones & Laughlin Supply, the plaintiff, held a security interest in these items. The plaintiff (Jones) claimed that the property purchased at the sheriff's sale was subject to the security interest. The defendants, Dugan and McDonald, argued that the disputed items were not listed in the security agreement. Jones argued that it had given a loan to the Lucky Drilling Company and in return had taken a perfected security interest on all of the company's equipment through a security agreement and a filed financing statement. The language used in the security agreement differed from the language used in the financing statement.*

EXHIBIT 30–2   SAMPLE FINANCING STATEMENT

This FINANCING STATEMENT is presented for filing pursuant to the California Uniform Commercial Code.

1. DEBTOR (LAST NAME FIRST—IF AN INDIVIDUAL)	1A. SOCIAL SECURITY OR FEDERAL TAX NO.	
1B. MAILING ADDRESS	1C. CITY, STATE	1D. ZIP CODE
2. ADDITIONAL DEBTOR (IF ANY) (LAST NAME FIRST—IF AN INDIVIDUAL)	2A. SOCIAL SECURITY OR FEDERAL TAX NO.	
2B. MAILING ADDRESS	2C. CITY, STATE	2D. ZIP CODE
3. DEBTOR'S TRADE NAMES OR STYLES (IF ANY)	3A. FEDERAL TAX NUMBER	

4. SECURED PARTY

     NAME

     MAILING ADDRESS

     CITY   STATE   ZIP CODE

4A. SOCIAL SECURITY NO., FEDERAL TAX NO. OR BANK TRANSIT AND A.B.A. NO.

5. ASSIGNEE OF SECURED PARTY   (IF ANY)

     NAME

     MAILING ADDRESS

     CITY   STATE   ZIP CODE

5A. SOCIAL SECURITY NO., FEDERAL TAX NO. OR BANK TRANSIT AND A.B.A. NO.

6. This FINANCING STATEMENT covers the following types or items of property **(include description of real property on which located and owner of record when required by instruction 4).**

As security for and in consideration of all present and any future advances or other obligations debtor hereby grants United California Bank a security interest in all of the following types or items of property ("Collateral" herein) in which the debtor now has or hereafter acquires any right, title, or interest, or rights present and future, wheresoever located and whether in the possession of the debtor, a warehouseman, bailee, trustee or any other person, and all increases, therein and replacements, products, and proceeds thereof. Proceeds include but are not limited to inventory, returned merchandise, accounts, chattel paper, general intangibles, insurance proceeds, documents, money, goods, equipment, instruments, and any other tangible or intangible property arising under the sale, lease or other disposition of collateral:

7. CHECK IF APPLICABLE [X]	7A. PRODUCTS OF COLLATERAL [ ] ARE ALSO COVERED	7B. DEBTOR(S) SIGNATURE NOT REQUIRED IN ACCORDANCE WITH INSTRUCTION 5(c) ITEM: [ ] (1) [ ] (2) [ ] (3) [ ] (4)

8. CHECK IF APPLICABLE   [X]   [ ] DEBTOR IS A "TRANSMITTING UTILITY" IN ACCORDANCE WITH UCC § 9105 (1) (n)

9. DATE: ▶ SIGNATURE(S) of DEBTOR(S)	C O D E	10. THIS SPACE FOR USE OF FILING OFFICER (DATE, TIME, FILE NUMBER AND FILING OFFICER)
TYPE OR PRINT NAME(S) OF DEBTOR(S)	1	
▶	2	
SIGNATURE(S) OF SECURED PARTY(IES)	3	
	4	
TYPE OR PRINT NAME(S) OF SECURED PARTY(IES)	5	
11. *Return copy to:*	6	
NAME	7	
ADDRESS		
CITY	8	
STATE	9	
ZIP CODE	0	
(1) FILING OFFICER COPY FORM UCC-1—FILING FEE $3.00 *Approved by the Secretary of State*		

MS-336   10-78

LOPEZ, Judge.

*   *   *   *

The case arose out of a sheriff's sale in which certain pieces of equipment belonging to Lucky Drilling Company were sold to the defendants [Dugan and McDonald]. At the sheriff's sale, Dugan *   *   * purchased the Whealand rotary table in question. The defendant, George McDonald, purchased the Waukesha gasoline engine. Prior to the sheriff's sale, Lucky Drilling Company mortgaged certain equipment to plaintiff and plaintiff took a security agreement and mortgage. *   *   * A review of the record reveals that this security agreement, together with an unsigned financing statement with exhibits was filed *   *   * in the office of the County Clerk of San Juan County, New Mexico and *   *   * in the office of the New Mexico Secretary of State.

*   *   * [T]he two items in question were not specifically described in the security agreement or in the financing statement. *   *   * The financing statement was not signed by the debtor or the secured party as required by [UCC] 9-402.

The financing statement contains the wording: "*   *   * all hand tools, drill collars, drill pipe, equipment, accessories, parts, exchanges, substitutions, additions, accretions, betterments, supplies and items that Debtor may now have or hereafter acquire and use with or as part of such collateral or in connection therewith. *   *   *" The financing statement further contains the wording: "Debtor's seven complete rotary drilling rigs identified as No. 1 *   *   *" through "No. 7 *   *   *, including all components as described on Exhibit 'A' and Exhibit 'B' attached hereto. *   *   *" This financing statement is not signed by the debtor or the mortgagee.

The security agreement which is signed by all the parties contains the wording: "Debtor's seven rotary drilling rigs Nos. 1 thru 7 including all components as described on Exhibit 'A' (6 pages) and Exhibit 'B' (7 pages), both of which are attached hereto and made a part hereof by this reference, *   *   *, together with all hand tools, drill collars, drill pipe and together with all equipment, accessories, parts, exchanges, additions, betterments, and appliances that Debtor may hereafter acquire and use with or as a part of the above described goods. *   *   *" *The security agreement does not contain the language "equipment, parts, supplies and items which the Debtor may now have" as does the financing statement.* [Emphasis added.]

The undisputed testimony is that the Whealand rotary table in question had been bought with Rig No. 2 originally and prior to the giving of the security agreement had been replaced by a Brewster rotary table. The Whealand rotary table was returned to the parts inventory in the Bloomfield yard and never used again. The inventory mentioned in the Exhibits "A" and "B" lists the Brewster rotary table as a component part of Rig No. 2. In respect to the V-12 gasoline Waukesha engine, the testimony reveals that this engine was purchased with Rig. No. 3 and later on was replaced by V-12 Waukesha diesel engine before the security agreement was executed. The inventory mentioned in the Exhibits "A" and "B" shows the V-12 diesel engine as a component of Rig. No. 3 and not the engine in question.

Plaintiff would have the two disputed items included within the security agreement on the basis of the "used with" language of the security agreement and on the basis of similar language included in certain of the exhibits referred to in the security agreement. This argument is without merit for two reasons. First, the "used with" phrase in the security agreement applies only to after-acquired property and the disputed items are not in that category. Second, the "used with" phrase in the exhibits applies only to rigs 4 through 7, and the evidence is undisputed that the disputed items were not used with those rigs. The disputed items cannot be included in the security agreement on the basis of "used with" language in the security agreement or the exhibits.

The financing statement was not signed pursuant to the provisions of [UCC Sec.] 9-402. There is a conflict in the language of the security agreement and the financing statement. We follow the reasoning in the Anderson Uniform Commercial Code, Vol. 4 at 124 (2d Ed. 1971) referring to Uniform Commercial Code which states:

"*   *   * § 9-110:17.—Conflicting descriptions in security agreement and financing statement:

"When there is a conflict between the financing statement on file and the security agreement as to the property involved, the latter prevails for the reason that no security interest can exist in the absence of a security agreement, and therefore a financing statement which goes beyond the scope of the agreement has no effect to that extent." Thus, the "may now have" language of the unsigned financing statement does not provide plaintiff with a security interest in the disputed items.

Plaintiff contends the disputed items were included within the security agreement because they were reasonably described therein. [UCC Sec.] 9-110. Plaintiff contends this reasonable description is provided by "external evidence." This "external evidence" consists of the unsigned financing statement and evidence at trial to the effect that Lucky Drilling Company mortgaged and plaintiff took, pursuant to the mortgage, security on *all* of the equipment of Lucky Drilling Company.

*   *   * Plaintiff's security agreement neither refers to "now owned equipment" or to "all" equipment of Lucky Drilling Company.

A security agreement is effective according to *its* terms. [UCC Sec.] 9-201. A security interest is not effective against third parties unless the debtor has signed a security agreement which contains a description of the collateral. [UCC Sec.] 9-203(1)(b). The disputed items cannot be included within the security agreement by the "outside evidence" relied on by plaintiff because the disputed items are not described in the security agreement. *   *   *

*   *   * We hold that the security agreement did not cover the two disputed items.

The plaintiff, Jones, did not have a security interest in the Whealand rotary table purchased by Dugan or in the Waukesha gasoline engine purchased by McDonald. The defendants had the right to these items bought at the sheriff's sale, and the plaintiff had no claim against them. **JUDGMENT AND REMEDY**

In the following case, a security agreement was executed to cover the sale of a guitar and an amplifier that were used by the buyer to perform in nightclubs. Hence they were not consumer goods. (Compare UCC 9-109(1) and (2).) The seller's perfection of the security interest required the filing of a security agreement or a financing statement. The seller filed the security agreement as the financing statement. Imperfections in the security agreement did not trouble the court, but the absence of the seller's address on the security agreement as the financing statement was fatal.

STREVELL-PATERSON FINANCE CO. v. MAY

Supreme Court of New Mexico, 1967.

77 N.M. 331, 422 P.2d 366.

BACKGROUND AND FACTS *The plaintiff in this case was a secured party who sold a guitar and amplifier to Elverio Chavez, to be used primarily in the performance of nightclub acts. Hence the goods were not consumer goods. The sale was made on credit, and a "conditional sales agreement" covering the transaction was executed. The sales agreement was entitled "chattel mortgage." Although the terminology was incorrect under the new terminology used in the UCC, the court found that the denomination "chattel mortgage" was immaterial and that a security agreement did exist between the seller and the buyer.*

The buyer took the goods with him on the day of purchase and ultimately defaulted on the credit payments. The seller attempted to recover the guitar and amplifier, but the buyer had pawned them to the defendant pawnshop owner. The plaintiff obtained possession of pawn tickets representing the guitar and amplifier and presented them to the defendant pawnshop, which refused to deliver the guitar and amplifier because they had been sold to a third party. The plaintiff claimed that he had a valid security interest in the property and that the interest was properly perfected before the goods had been pledged to the pawnshop. Thus, the plaintiff claimed that he had a right to possession of the guitar and amplifier.

HENSLEY, Chief Judge.

* * * *

At the outset we note that filing is not necessary to perfect a security interest taken or retained by a seller or other person who finances the actual purchase of consumer goods, [UCC] 9-302(1)(d). Here the guitar and amplifier, however, were not "consumer goods" as they were primarily used by Chavez to perform in night clubs and are "equipment", [UCC] 9-109(2). Consequently, perfection by filing of the security agreement was required.

* * * *

The fact that an agreement offered for filing is denominated a "chattel mortgage" is immaterial. The traditional forms of security agreements in use before the enactment of [UCC] 9-203, and [UCC] 9-102, supra, may continue to be used after their enactment. Uniform Commercial Code, § 9-101, comment 2. A "security agreement" is defined as "an agreement which creates or provides for a security interest. * * * " [UCC] 9-105(1)(h). A "security interest" is defined as " * * * an interest in personal property or fixtures which secures payment or performance of an obligation. * * * " [UCC] 1-201(37). It is clear that the old form "chattel mortgage" meets the definition of a "security agreement." [UCC] 9-402(1), specifically provides that a copy of the security agreement is sufficient as a financing statement if it is signed by the debtor and secured party, gives an address of the secured party from which information concerning the security interest may be obtained, gives a mailing address of the debtor and contains a statement indicating the types, or describing the items of collateral. Thus, an instrument denominated as a "chattel mortgage" may be filed as a financing statement so long as it contains the necessary information. We must now determine whether the instrument contained the information required by [UCC] 9-402(1).

[Defendant] contends that since the secured party did not sign the instrument that [UCC] 9-402(1) * * * was not satisfied. We note that the Uniform Commercial Code is to be construed liberally and applied to promote its underlying purposes and policies [UCC] 1-102(1). Professor Gilmore, Security Interests in Personal Property * * * says:

> "Confusingly, and unnecessarily, the formal requisites of the security agreement [§ 9-203] and the formal requisites of the financing statement [§ 9-402] are not the same. Under § 9-203, all that is required in the 'security agreement' is the debtor's signature and a description of the collateral * * * Under § 9-402, however, the 'financing statement' must contain the signatures of both the secured party and the debtor [Both were required prior to 1972 UCC Amendments.] and must also give addresses for both of them. The financing statement must also contain descriptions of collateral * * *."

Professor Gilmore's reasoning, page 347, in resolving the conflict is persuasive:

> "* * * There is no sensible reason for the discrepancies between the formal requisites of § 9-203 and § 9-402. With respect to signatures § 9-203 seems to be right: the debtor's signature on a document binding him to liability is obviously essential; there seems to be no reason for the secured party's signature to be required on either 'agreement' or 'statement' * * *."

We conclude that the lack of the secured party's signature does not make the instrument defective within the meaning of [UCC] 9-402(1). The defendant had due notice even though the secured party did not sign the instrument.

The lack of the secured party's address is more difficult. [UCC] 9-402(1) says:

> "A financing statement is sufficient if it * * * gives an address of the secured party from which information concerning the security interest may be obtained * * *."

As in the situation of no signature by the secured party, which we have already resolved, there is a conflict between [UCC] 9-203 and [UCC] 9-402. The latter requires the address of the secured party while the former does not.

Professor Gilmore, Security Interest in Personal Property, 347, supra, notes:

> "The addresses are required in the document which is filed for record and, for simplicity's sake, might as well be included in the underlying 'agreement' * * *"

In this case, the plaintiff's name appears only on the cover of the instrument of July 12, 1963. We cannot say that the plaintiff substantially complied with the requirements of [UCC] 9-403(1). Consequently, the instrument of July 12, 1963, is defective as a financing statement and did not give notice to the defendant of the plaintiff's security interest in the guitar and amplifier.

Our conclusion is not inconsistent with the intent of the Uniform Commercial Code to adopt a system of "notice filing." Section 9-402, Uniform Commercial Code, comment 2 says:

> "* * * The notice itself indicates merely that the secured party who has filed may have a security interest in the collateral described. Further inquiry from the parties concerned will be necessary to disclose the complete state of affairs. * * *"

If the secured party's address does not appear it would be an undue burden on the person seeking such information to find him. The filing system will perform its intended function only if secured party substantially complies with the requirements of [UCC] 9-402(1).

*   *   * The plaintiff did not perfect its security interest and cannot maintain an action against the pawnshop in conversion.

JUDGMENT AND REMEDY   *Judgment was for the defendant, the pawnshop. The plaintiff failed to perfect his security interest and was not able to maintain a claim against the pawnshop owner, who had sold the guitar and amplifier to a third party.*

Where to File   Depending upon the classification of collateral, filing is with either the secretary of state or the county clerk or other official, or both, according to state law. UCC 9-401 has three alternatives for states to choose from. In general, financing statements for consumer goods or for any collateral used or arising from a farmer's business should be filed with the county clerk. Other kinds of collateral require filing with the secretary of state. [UCC 9-401]

When the secured party obtains a security interest in *unissued* shares of stock, UCC 9-302(1) prevails, because unissued securities are categorized as general intangibles under UCC 9-106. "General intangibles means any personal property (including things in action) other than goods, accounts, chattel paper, documents, instruments, and money." Under UCC 9-301(1), a security interest in unissued stock is perfected by filing a financing statement with the secretary of state.

The following case illustrates the importance of the time and the place of filing in order to perfect a security interest priority over other creditors. This case involves a clause in a contract stating that "all property hereinafter acquired" is collateral. This means that even though property will be acquired by the debtor in the future, the creditor's security interest in it will automatically be perfected without a new filing.

CAIN v. COUNTRY CLUB DELICATESSEN OF SAYBROOK, INC.
Superior Court of Connecticut, 1964.
25 Conn. Sup. 327, 203 A.2d. 441.

BACKGROUND AND FACTS   *The defendant, Country Club Delicatessen of Saybrook, opened its restaurant business in Old Saybrook on July 26, 1962. At that time it was fully equipped. On August 16, 1962, the defendant borrowed $35,000 from First Hartford, giving a promissory note secured by a security agreement covering "All goods, personal property, equipment, machinery, fixtures, inventory, leasehold rights, including, but not limited to, the property described below, including all after acquired property of like kind." (Attached was a Schedule A listing all specific items included).*

The previous day, August 15, 1962, First Hartford had filed a financing statement with the secretary of state, Uniform Commercial Code division, showing the defendant as debtor and First Hartford as the secured party. This financing statement had the same description of property as did the security agreement. It also contained a provision covering after-acquired property and a description of the real estate and other data relating to the requirements as to fixtures, in the event any of the property was fixtures. Also, on August 15, 1962, First Hartford executed another financing statement, a duplicate of the one filed in the office of the secretary of state, and filed it with the town clerk of the town of Old Saybrook. The description of the property was exactly the same as in the financing statement filed with the secretary of state. Both these financing statements were executed by the defendant corporation.

On August 30, 1962, approximately fifteen days later, the defendant corporation and Hewitt executed a conditional sales contract covering certain property sold by Hewitt to the defendant. Some of this property was expressly mentioned in the financing statement and security agreement that First Hartford had filed. The defendant was in the process of purchasing property that it simultaneously gave as security for the First Hartford loan. Hewitt also filed a financing statement with the town clerk of the town of Old Saybrook showing Hewitt as the secured party, and General Electric Credit Corporation as an assignee of Hewitt and the defendant corporation as debtor. The description of the types of items of property covered by Hewitt's security agreement was of "complete restaurant and delicatessen including kitchen equipment and display equipment." No financing statement by Hewitt or General Electric was ever filed with the secretary of state, Uniform Commercial Code division. Hewitt filed only with the town clerk of Old Saybrook approximately fifteen days after First Hartford had filed its financing statement with the town clerk. (Background and Facts essentially as stated by the court.)

PASTORE, Judge.

*   *   *   *

No financing statement of either Hewitt Engineering, Inc., or General Electric was on file with either the secretary of state, Uniform Commercial Code division, or the town clerk of Old Saybrook against defendant corporation up to the time on August 15, 1962, when First Hartford first filed its financing statements respectively in both of said offices. Also, no financing statement of said Hewitt or General Electric was on file with the secretary of state up to September 23, 1962, when the instant proceeding was started.

Some of the property specifically mentioned in the conditional sale contract of Hewitt, assigned to General Electric, appears also in the description of the property covered by the financing statement and security agreement of First Hartford. *   *   *

The position of First Hartford is that it was first to file, that it filed with the secretary of state so as to cover itself with respect to personal property, that it filed with the town clerk of Old Saybrook so as to cover itself as to fixtures (if any be involved), and that General Electric, by failing to file with the secretary of state, does not have priority as to the personal property, and by filing when it did with said town clerk, acquired no rights superior to those of First Hartford in any fixtures, if any there were.

The claim of General Electric is that the evidence shows that as of August 15, 1962, when the financing statement of First Hartford was filed, and as of August 16, 1962, when its security agreement was made, the debtor defendant corporation had only possession of the property subsequently bought from Hewitt, the assignor of General Electric; that there is no evidence showing that as of those dates and within the meaning of [UCC] 9-204(1) either a "security interest" had been created or the defendant corporation had acquired any "rights" in the property which defendant debtor bought from Hewitt, rights which defendant attempted as of that time to give to First Hartford. [Footnote omitted.] The proper place for filing in order to perfect a security interest in goods which at the time the security interest attaches "are or are to become fixtures" is in the office where a mortgage on the real estate concerned would be filed or recorded; and in all other cases, in the office of the secretary of state. [UCC] 9-401(1). Thus, the recording or filing with respect to fixtures would be in the town clerk's office of the town where the affected real estate was located, and as to personal property, the filing would be in the office of the secretary of state.

Under [UCC] 9-204(1), a debtor must have "rights in the collateral" before a security interest may be created. The code does not clearly establish the meaning of this phrase, as for instance whether such rights arise when the debtor enters into a contract to buy goods, or only when he has an interest in the goods when identified with a contract under the Uniform Commercial Code, article 2, "Sales" [UCC] 2-101 [and] 2-725.

In the instant case, while it is shown that the personal property bought August 30, 1962, from Hewitt, called here the Hewitt goods for convenience, was in the possession of the defendant debtor by July 26, 1962, and at least before August 19, 1962, and that the conditional sale contract between defendant and Hewitt was executed August 30, 1962, there is no showing as to the circumstances or arrangement whereby the defendant had this possession. No legal authority has come, or been brought, to the notice of this court that such mere possession may constitute such "rights in the collateral." An inference that defendant was an unconditional owner of the Hewitt goods on August 15, 1962, would be speculation. *   *   *

*   *   *   *

The claim of First Hartford that the Hewitt goods came under the coverage of its financing statement as of August 15, 1962, by virtue of [UCC] 9-312(5)(a) and (b) is not sustained. Those provisions deal with the "priorities among conflicting security interests in the same collateral." As of August 15 or 16, 1962, there was not yet any security interest existing respecting Hewitt, and the Hewitt goods had not yet become "collateral." Since there was no security interest favoring Hewitt in the Hewitt goods until August 30, 1962, when the conditional sale contract was executed between the defendant debtor and Hewitt, it follows that as of August 15 or 16, 1962, there was no security interest in the Hewitt goods to conflict with any other respecting them. *   *   *

*   *   *   *

The conditional sale contract of August 30, 1962, between defendant corporation and Hewitt created a security interest in favor of Hewitt which attached to the property thereby sold. [UCC] 9-204(1). To perfect this security interest, a financing statement was required to be filed [UCC] 9-302(1), which, as to goods which at the time the security attached were or were to become fixtures, would be filed in the office where a mortgage on the real estate would be filed, and in all other cases would be filed in the office of the secretary of state. [UCC] 9-401(1).

Hewitt failed to file in the office of the secretary of state; its financing statement was filed only in the office of the town clerk. *   *   * [It] is plain that, Hewitt not having filed at all with the secretary of state and First Hartford having done so August 15, 1962, and perfected its security interest on August 16, 1962, First Hartford has priority over General Electric as to this portion of the personal property of the debtor within the coverage of the security agreement of First Hartford. [UCC] 9-301(1)(a). [UCC] 9-312(5)(a). Included in this priority of First Hartford are such non-Hewitt goods as might be fixtures as of August 16, 1962, as to which First Hartford filed with the town clerk on August 16, 1962, and Hewitt and General Electric not until August 30, 1962.

The secured claim of First Hartford was filed and perfected and hence given priority over any claim of General Electric Credit Corporation.   **JUDGMENT AND REMEDY**

Classification of Collateral Determines Where to File   The classification of collateral is important in many situations. In determining the place of filing, goods must be classified as consumer goods, equipment, farm products, or inventory. The classes of goods are mutually exclusive; *the same property cannot at the same time and to the same person be both equipment and inventory.* Is a physician's car equipment or a consumer good? Is a farmer's jeep equipment or a consumer good? The principal *use* to which the property is put by the debtor determines its classification. If the physician uses the car primarily for personal use, then it is a consumer good; if it is used primarily for medical practice, then it is equipment. If a farmer's jeep is necessary for farming operations and is used primarily for that, then the jeep is classified as farm equipment. But the car and jeep can never be categorized as both equipment and inventory. [UCC 9-109]

Goods can fall into different classes at different times. For example, a CB radio is *inventory* when it is in the hands of a dealer. [UCC 9-109(4)] But when it is purchased by a consumer for use in a private car, it becomes a *consumer good.* [UCC 9-109(1)] When it is bought and then put in a patrol car, it is *equipment.* [UCC 9-109(2)] Under the Code, the classification and filing are based on the primary use being made of the collateral. According to UCC 9-401, once the security agreement is properly filed, any change in the use of that collateral will not endanger the security interest of the secured party. State laws other than the UCC control where filing is done for each category of collateral. Exhibit 30–3 summarizes the methods of perfecting a security interest.

QUESTIONS AND CASE PROBLEMS

1.   Daniel is interested in purchasing a new automobile. He has read West Bank's ad, which states, "Before you make your next purchase on time, consult with us—it may be cheaper." Daniel agrees to purchase a new car for $10,000 from ABC Auto Corp. He goes to West Bank and borrows the money by signing

---

EXHIBIT 30–3   METHODS OF PERFECTING A SECURITY INTEREST

TYPE OF COLLATERAL	PERFECTION METHOD	UCC SECTION WHERE INDICATED
Consumer goods	For purchase money security interest, attachment is sufficient; for boats, motor vehicles, and trailers, there is a requirement of filing or compliance with a certificate of title statute; for other consumer goods, general rules of filing or possession apply	9-302(1)(d); 9-302(3); 9-302(4); 9-305
General intangibles	Filing only	9 302(1)
Accounts receivable	Filing required (with exceptions)	9-302(1)(e); 9-302(1)(g)
Chattel paper	Filing or possession by secured party	9-304(1); 9-305
Instrument	Unless temporary perfection status is granted, by possession only	9-304(1); 9-304(4); 9-304(5)

a note and a security agreement giving West Bank a security interest in the car Daniel has agreed to purchase. Daniel is going to use the car exclusively in his business as a traveling salesperson. From these facts:

    (a) Explain fully whether West Bank has a purchase money security interest.

    (b) Explain fully where West Bank would file its security interest in most states to be perfected.

2. Diane agrees to purchase a new washing machine for her apartment from retailer Ray's Appliance Store. She signs a security agreement to pay $50 down and the balance in twelve equal installments. The security agreement provides that Ray retain a security interest in the purchased washing machine. Ray does not file either the security agreement or a financing statement. Discuss fully whether Ray is a perfected secured party.

3. Discuss how each secured party would properly perfect his or her security interest in the following cases.

    (a) Martin is the manufacturer of refrigerators. Ray, a retailer, buys a number of these refrigerators. Ray signs a security agreement giving Martin a security interest in the refrigerators.

    (b) Mary sells a refrigerator to Carla, to be used in Carla's home. Carla signs a security agreement giving Mary a security interest in the refrigerator.

    (c) Ray sells a refrigerator to Dr. Dodd, to be used in his office to store medicines. Dr. Dodd signs a security agreement giving Ray a security interest in the refrigerator.

    (d) Mary sells a refrigerator to farmer Jones, who needs it to store excess eggs not sold at market. Jones signs a security agreement giving Mary a security interest in the refrigerator.

4. Smith has a prize horse named Thunderbolt. Smith is in need of working capital. To secure it, she borrows $5,000 from Rodriguez, with Rodriguez taking possession of Thunderbolt as security for the loan. No written agreement is signed. Discuss whether, in absence of written agreement, Rodriguez has a security interest in Thunderbolt *and* whether Rodriguez is a perfected secured party without filing a financing statement.

5. Daniel purchases a new television set from appliance retailer Smith on a retail installment contract. The contract calls for twelve monthly payments and gives Smith a security interest in the set until the balance is paid in full. Smith files a financing statement locally on his security interest. Daniel has signed both the security agreement and the financing statement; Smith has signed neither. Explain whether Smith has a security interest and if it is properly perfected by filing even though Smith's signature does not appear in any document.

6. Canna loaned Diodato a sum of money for the purchase of an automobile. Diodato signed a promissory note and procured a title certificate for the automobile. The title certificate included a typed notation designating Canna as a secured party. First County National Bank sued Diodato for money that Diodato owed the bank. The bank obtained a judgment against Diodato and attempted to levy execution upon the automobile. When it did, it became aware of Canna's claim of a prior lien. The bank then attempted to have Canna's lien set aside. Did Diodato and Canna create a valid security interest in the automobile in Canna's favor? [First County Nat'l. Bank and Trust Co. v. Canna, 124 N.J. Super. 154, 305 A.2d 442 (1973)]

7. Henry Reitz obtained a loan from National-Dime Bank in exchange for which he gave a security interest in a tractor and shovel that he owned. National-Dime drew a security agreement describing the collateral as "5/8 yd. shovel, diesel unit, booms, drag bucket." National-Dime then made a copy of the agreement, which both it and Reitz signed, and filed it with the secretary of state. National-Dime then procured Reitz's signature on the original security agreement and put it in its files without an officer of the bank ever signing it. Has National-Dime a security interest in the tractor and shovel attached (that is, is it enforceable)? Is it perfected? [National-Dime Bank v. Cleveland Brothers Equipment Co., 20 D.&C.2d 511 (Pa.1959)]

8. Federal Bank made a loan to Pre-Fab in the amount of $325,000. In return for the loan, Pre-Fab signed a promissory note and entered into a security agreement whereby Federal Bank took a security interest in Pre-Fab's assets, accounts receivable, and monies due. Federal Bank immediately filed a financing statement that described in detail all of the above items. Pre-Fab subsequently acquired two promissory notes for the sale of some stock it owned. It used these notes as security for a second loan from a different bank. Federal Bank claims priority in the notes by virtue of its prior filing. Does Federal Bank have a perfected security interest in the notes and other described items? [Bowles v. City Nat'l Bank and Trust Co., 537 P.2d 1219 (Okl.App.1975)]

9. A security agreement between plaintiff American Restaurant Supply Company and debtor Wilmark, Inc., and various third parties (defendants) described the collateral as "food service equipment and supplies delivered to San Marco Inn at St. Marks, Florida." Wilmark and its other creditors claimed that the description of the property pledged as security was legally insufficient, so the security interest could not be enforced. What was the result? [American Restaurant Supply Co. v. Wilson, 371 So.2d 489 (Fla.App.1979)]

CHAPTER 31

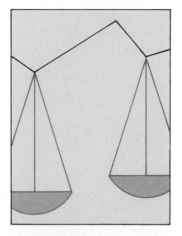

SECURED TRANSACTIONS
Liens and Priorities

In the last chapter, we dealt with definitions pertaining to secured transactions and the perfection of a security interest. Perfection is important because UCC 9-301 makes it clear that an *unperfected* security interest is of little value when challenged by a third party. In this chapter, we will discuss which parties prevail over the unperfected security interest and priorities when two or more secured parties have perfected security interests in the same collateral.

Consider an example. James loans money to Ike, who gives James a written security agreement that gives James a security interest in Ike's antique car collection. James files no financing statement. Before Ike repays James, he files voluntary bankruptcy. The person in charge of Ike's bankruptcy (known as the trustee) claims that the antique cars are part of Ike's estate, free and clear of James's security interest. The trustee is right because James's security interest in the antique cars is unperfected.

PARTIES THAT PREVAIL OVER THE UNPERFECTED SECURITY INTEREST

According to UCC 9-301, certain categories of persons prevail over the unperfected security interest.

1. Persons who have a perfected security interest in the same collateral.
2. Lien creditors—that is, creditors who acquire a lien on property by attachment or **levy** (judicial process), including trustees in bankruptcy.
3. A person who is a transferee in bulk or other buyer not in the ordinary course of business (or who is a buyer of farm products in the ordinary course of business) to the extent that that person gives value and receives delivery of the collateral without knowledge of the security interest and before it is perfected.

4.   A person who is a transferee, to the extent that that, person gives value without knowledge of the security interest and before it is perfected in accounts and general intangibles.

Liens

A *lien* is a claim against property for payment of some debt. Thus, a **lien creditor** is one who acquires a lien on the property involved by attachment, levy, or the like. A lien creditor should be distinguished from a general creditor, who has no such security. [UCC 9-301(3)]

THE RANGE OF PERFECTION AND THE FLOATING LIEN CONCEPT

A security agreement can cover various types of property in addition to collateral already in the debtor's possession—the proceeds of sale, after-acquired property, and future advances.

Proceeds

Proceeds include whatever is received when collateral is sold, exchanged, collected, or disposed of. A secured party has an interest in the proceeds of the sale of collateral. Perfection of the proceeds is available automatically upon perfection of the secured party's security interest and remains perfected for ten days after receipt of the proceeds by the debtor. One way to extend the ten-day automatic period is to provide for such extended coverage in the original security agreement. This is typically done when the collateral is the type that is likely to be sold.

The UCC provides three methods by which the security interest in proceeds remains perfected for longer than ten days after the receipt of the proceeds by the debtor. They are:

1.   When a filed financing statement covers the original collateral, and the proceeds are collateral in which a security interest may be perfected by filing in the office or offices where the financing statement has been filed. Furthermore, if the proceeds are acquired with cash proceeds, the description of collateral in the financing statement must indicate the types of property constituting the proceeds. [UCC 9-306(3)(a)]

2.   Whenever there is a filed financing statement that covers the original collateral and the proceeds are identifiable cash proceeds. [UCC 9-306(3)(b)]

3.   Whenever the security interest in the proceeds is perfected before the expiration of the ten-day period. [UCC 9-306(3)(c)]

After-acquired Property

After-acquired property of the debtor is property acquired after the execution of the security agreement. The security agreement itself may provide for coverage of after-acquired property. [UCC 9-204(1)] This is particularly useful for inventory financing arrangements, because a secured party whose security interest is in existing inventory knows that the debtor will sell that inventory, thereby reducing the collateral subject to the security interest. Generally, the debtor will purchase new inventory to replace the inventory sold. The secured party wants this newly acquired inventory to be subject to the *original* security interest. Thus, the after-acquired property clause continues the secured party's claim onto any inventory acquired thereafter. This is not to say that such original security interest will be superior to the rights of all other creditors with regard to this after-acquired inventory, as will be discussed later.

An after-acquired property clause normally does not allow for attachment of a security interest in consumer goods "unless the debtor acquires rights in them within 10 days after the secured party gives value." [UCC 9-204(2)] Presumably, this protects consumers from encumbering all their present and future property.

Consider a typical example. Anderson buys factory equipment from Blonsky on credit, giving as security an interest in all of her equipment—both what she is buying and what she already owns. The security interest with Blonsky contains an after-acquired property clause. Six months later, Anderson pays cash to another seller for more equipment. Six months after that, Anderson goes out of business before she has paid off her debt to Blonsky. Blonsky claims to have a security interest in *all* of Anderson's equipment, even the equipment bought from the other seller. Blonsky is correct.

Future Advances

Often a debtor will have a continuing *line of credit* under which the debtor can borrow intermittently. This is often done with a *letter of credit*—an agreement in which the issuer of the letter agrees to pay drafts drawn on it by the creditor (as explained earlier). It is an advance arrangement of financing with the maximum amount of advance that the debtor can obtain. A letter of credit, typically issued by a bank, has three parties: the issuer, the customer, and a beneficiary who will draw the drafts under it. Letters of credit typically specify not only a maximum amount but a specified time duration. Letters of credit (sometimes called lines of credit) can be subject to a security interest in certain properly perfected collateral.

The security agreement may provide that any future advances made against that line of credit are also subject to the security interest in the same collateral. For example, Smith is the owner of a small manufacturing plant with equipment valued at $1,000,000. Smith is in immediate need of $50,000 working capital. Smith secures a loan from West Bank, signing a security agreement putting up his entire equipment as security. In the security agreement Smith can borrow up to $500,000 in the future, using the same equipment as collateral (future advances.) In such cases, it is not necessary to execute a new security agreement and perfect a security interest in the collateral each time an advance is made to the debtor. [UCC 9-204(3)]

The Floating Lien Concept

When a security agreement provides for the creation of a security interest in proceeds of the sale of the collateral that was the subject matter of the secured transaction, after-acquired property or future advances, or both, it is referred to as a **floating lien.** Floating liens commonly arise in the financing of inventories, for example. A creditor is not interested in specific pieces of inventory, because they are constantly changing.

Suppose that Ptarmigan Mountaineering, a cross-country ski dealer, has a line of credit with Seattle First National Bank to finance an inventory of cross-country skis. Ptarmigan and Seattle First enter into a security agreement that provides for coverage of proceeds, after-acquired property, inventory, and future advances.

This security interest in inventory is perfected by filing centrally. One day, Ptarmigan sells a new pair of the latest cross-country skis, for which it receives a used pair in trade. That same day, it purchases two new pairs of skis from a local manufacturer with an additional amount of money obtained from Seattle First. Seattle First gets a perfected security interest in the used pair of cross-country skis under the proceeds clause, has a perfected security interest in the two new pairs of skis purchased from the local manufacturer under the after-acquired property clause, and has the new amount of money advanced to Ptarmigan secured by the future-advance clause. All of this is done under the original perfected security agreement. The various items in the inventory have changed, but Seattle First still has a perfected security interest in Ptarmigan's inventory, and hence it has a floating lien on the inventory.

The concept of a floating lien can also apply to a shifting stock of goods. Under Section 9-205, the lien can start with raw materials and follow them as they become finished goods and inventories and as they are sold, turning into accounts receivable, chattel paper, or cash.

Collateral Moved to Another Jurisdiction

Obviously, collateral may be moved by the debtor from one jurisdiction to another. When this occurs, a problem arises in that a secured party's perfection by filing serves as notice only to the third parties who check the records in the county (local filing) or state (central filing) where the perfection properly took place. Frequently, the secured party is not even aware of the collateral being moved out of the jurisdiction.

The Code addresses this problem and at the same time furthers the concept of the floating lien. In general, a properly perfected security interest in collateral moved into a new jurisdiction continues to be perfected in the new jurisdiction for a period of up to four months from the date it was moved, or for the period of time remaining under the perfection in the original jurisdiction, whichever expires first. [UCC-9-103(1)(d) and 9-103(3)(e)]

To illustrate: Suppose that on January 1 Calvin secures a loan from a Kansas bank by putting up all his wheat threshing equipment as security. The Kansas bank files the security interest centrally with the secretary of state. In June, Calvin has an opportunity to harvest wheat crops in South Dakota and moves his equipment into that state on June 15. Applying the above law, the Kansas bank's perfection remains effective in South Dakota for a period of four months from June 15. If the Kansas bank wishes to retain its perfection priority, the bank must perfect properly in South Dakota during this four-month period. Should the bank fail to do so, its perfection is lost after four months, and subsequent perfected security interests in the same collateral in South Dakota would prevail.

In mobile goods, automobiles pose one of the biggest problems. If either the new or the original jurisdiction requires a certificate of title as part of its perfection process in regard to an automobile, perfection does not automatically end after four months. Instead, perfection ends as soon as the automobile is registered again (after the end of the four-month period) and a "clean" certificate of title is obtained. [UCC 9-103(2)]

The Effective Time of Perfection

A filing statement is effective for five years from the date of filing. [UCC 9-403(2)] If a continuation statement is filed *within six months* prior to the expiration date, the effectiveness of the original statement is continued for another five years, starting with the expiration date of the first five-year period. [UCC 9-403(3)] The effectiveness of the statement can be continued in the same manner indefinitely.

PRIORITIES

The consequences of perfection and nonperfec-

tion are important in determining priorities among parties having conflicting interests in the *same* collateral. As a general rule, perfection protects the interest of a secured party against all lien creditors of the debtor, against all unperfected secured parties, and against all *later* perfected, nonpurchase money secured parties of that debtor. [UCC 9-312]

The first question is always whether an *enforceable* security interest has been created (that is, an agreement in writing, with value given, and with the debtor having interest in collateral). The second question is if and when the secured party's interest has been perfected. Assuming a party has an enforceable security interest, his or her priority will depend upon the time when the security interest attached (became enforceable) or the time when it became perfected, or both, according to the following rules:

1. *Conflicting perfected security interests.* When two or more secured parties have perfected security interests in the same collateral, generally the first to perfect (file or take possession of collateral) wins. [UCC 9-312(5)(a)]
2. *Conflicting unperfected security interests.* When two conflicting security interests are unperfected, the first in time to attach has priority. [UCC 9-312(5)(b)]
3. *Conflicting perfected security interests in commingled or processed goods.* When goods, with two or more perfected security interests, are so manufactured or commingled that they lose their identity into a product or mass, the perfected parties' security interests attach to the new product or mass "according to the ratio that the cost of goods to which each interest originally attached bears to the cost of the total product or mass." [UCC 9-315(2)]

EXCEPTIONS TO PERFECTION PRIORITY RULES

Under certain circumstances, the perfection of a security interest will not protect a secured party against certain other third parties having claims to the collateral.

Nonpurchase versus Purchase Money Perfected Security Interests

The general rule, as previously stated, is that the first in time to perfect is first in priority rights to the collateral. This rule is always applicable when the first in time to perfect is a purchase money security interest. However, the Code provides that under certain conditions a purchase money security interest, properly perfected, will prevail over a nonpurchase money security interest in after-acquired collateral, even though the nonpurchase money security interest was perfected first in time.

If the collateral is *inventory*, a perfected purchase money security interest will prevail over a previously perfected nonpurchase security interest, provided (generally) that the purchase money secured party perfects and gives the nonpurchase secured party written notice of his or her interest *before* the debtor takes possession of the newly acquired inventory. [UCC 9-312(3)]

If the collateral is other than inventory, a purchase money security interest will have priority over a previously perfected nonpurchase security interest provided that the purchase money security interest is perfected either before or within ten days *after* the debtor takes possession. No notice is required. [UCC 9-312(4)]

To illustrate: Retailer Mary needs a loan of money to be used as working capital. On May 1, she secures a one-year installment loan from West Bank, signing a security agreement and putting up her present inventory plus any after-acquired inventory as collateral. That same date West Bank perfects by filing a financing statement centrally. On August 1 Mary learns that she can purchase directly from Martin, a manufacturer, $10,000 worth of new inventory, which is a bargain. Since she cannot pay this amount in cash, she signs a security agreement with Martin, giving Martin a security interest in the newly purchased inventory. Delivery of the new inventory is to be on September 1. The new inventory is delivered on September 1 as ordered. On September 7 a fire destroys most of Mary's store and warehouse. There remains only a part of the new inventory, and its value is insufficient to cover both debts. Who has priority on the remaining inventory, West Bank or Martin?

If Martin perfected by filing and gave West Bank notice of its security interest prior to September 1, the date Mary received possession, Martin prevails. If Martin did not meet these conditions, West Bank prevails.

Suppose the collateral is equipment, rather than inventory, and Martin perfected on September 8, after the fire. Since Martin properly perfected his purchase money security interest within ten days after Mary received delivery, Martin prevails over West Bank for the remaining after-acquired equipment.

Buyers in the Ordinary Course of Business

Since buyers should not be required to find out if there is an outstanding security interest on a merchant's inventory, the Code provides that a person who buys "in the ordinary course of business" will take the goods free from any security interest in the merchant's inventory, even if the security interest is perfected and even if the buyer knows of its existence. [UCC 9-307(1)] A *buyer in the ordinary course of business* is defined as any person who in good faith, and without knowledge that the sale is in violation of the ownership rights or security interest of a third party in the goods, buys in ordinary course from a person in the business of selling goods of that kind. [UCC 1-201(9)]

Secondhand Goods: Goods Sold by a Consumer to a Consumer

Carla is a consumer who purchases a refrigerator on credit because she cannot pay the full purchase price. A written security agreement exists in which the seller takes a purchase money security interest in the consumer goods under this type of credit plan. Further, the seller need not file a financing statement because, when a purchase money security interest is taken in consumer goods, perfection occurs automatically. [UCC 9-302(1)(d)] Later, Carla sells the refrigerator to her next door neighbor, Nan, who purchases it for home use without any knowledge of the credit arrangements between Carla and the original seller. Subsequently, Carla defaults on the credit payments to the seller. What are the seller's rights? The seller had a perfected purchase money security interest in the refrigerator when it was held by Carla. However, under UCC 9-307(2), the perfection is not good against the next door neighbor.

UCC 9-307(2) requires that the "next door neighbor" must purchase (give value for) the goods for personal, family, or household use, without knowledge of the original seller's security interest, and the purchase must take place *before* the secured party files a financing state-

ment. In this case, recall that the seller took a purchase money security interest, which is perfected automatically. No filing was required. Hence, the next door neighbor purchased the refrigerator free and clear before the seller had filed a financing statement. The seller could have avoided this possibility simply by filing a financing statement, even though a purchase money security interest had been perfected.

In the following case, the court must determine whether a sale was in the ordinary course of the seller's business.

TANBRO FABRICS CORP. v. DEERING MILLIKEN, INC.
Court of Appeals of New York, 1976.
39 N.Y.2d 632, 385 N.Y.S.2d 260, 350 N.E.2d 590.

BACKGROUND AND FACTS *Tanbro finishes textile fabrics (griege goods) into dyed and patterned fabrics. Tanbro, known in the trade as a "converter," sought damages for the tortious conversion of unfinished textile fabrics from Deering Milliken, a textile manufacturer. The goods in question had been manufactured by Deering and sold to Mill Fabrics. Mill Fabrics resold the goods to Tanbro, while they were still in Deering's warehouse. Deering refused to deliver the goods to Tanbro because, although these goods had been paid for, Mill Fabrics owed Deering on other accounts. Deering claimed a perfected security interest in the goods.*

BREITEL, Chief Judge.

* * * *

* * * [U]nder the terms of the Deering sales agreements with Mill Fabrics, Deering retained a security interest in Mill Fabrics' "property" on a bill and hold basis, whether paid for or not. This security interest was perfected by Deering's continued possession of the goods (Uniform Commercial Code, § 1-201, subd. [37]; § 9-305). Tanbro argued that if it had title by purchase its goods were excluded from the security arrangement which was literally restricted to the "property of the buyer", that is, Mill Fabrics. In any event, unless prevented by other provisions of the code, or the sale was not unauthorized, Tanbro took title subject to Deering's security interest.

Under the code (§ 9-307, subd. [1]) a buyer in the ordinary course of the seller's business takes goods free of even a known security interest so long as the buyer does not know that the purchase violates the terms of the security agreement. As defined in the code (§ 1-201, subd. [9]) "a buyer in ordinary course" is "a person who in good faith and without knowledge that the sale to him is in violation of the ownership rights or security interest of a third party in the goods buys in ordinary course from a person in the business of selling goods of that kind but does not include a pawnbroker. 'Buying' may be for cash or by exchange of other property or on secured or unsecured credit and includes receiving goods or documents of title under a preexisting contract for sale but does not include a transfer in bulk or as security for or in total or partial satisfaction of a money debt." Critical to Tanbro's claim is that it purchased the goods in the ordinary course of Mill

Fabrics' business and that it did not purchase the goods in knowing violation of Deering's security interest.

Under the code whether a purchase was made from a person in the business of selling goods of that kind turns primarily on whether that person holds the goods for sale. Such goods are a person's selling inventory. (Uniform Commercial Code, § 1-201, subd. [9]; § 9-307, subd. [1]; Official Comment, at par. 2.) Note, however, that not all purchases of goods held as inventory qualify as purchases from a person in the business of selling goods of that kind. The purpose of section 9-307 is more limited. As indicated in the Practice Commentary to that section, the purpose is to permit buyers "to buy goods from a dealer in such goods without having to protect himself against a possible security interest on the inventory". Hence, a qualifying purchase is one made from a seller who is a dealer in such goods.

A former Mill Fabrics' employee testified that there were times when Mill Fabrics, like all converters, found itself with excess goods. When it was to their business advantage, they sold the excess fabrics to other converters. Although these sales were relatively infrequent they were nevertheless part of and in the ordinary course of Mill Fabrics' business, even if only incidental to the predominant business purpose. Examples of a nonqualifying sale might be a bulk sale, a sale in distress at an obvious loss price, a sale in liquidation, a sale of a commodity never dealt with before by the seller and wholly unlike its usual inventory, or the like.

All subdivision (1) of section 9-307 requires is that the sale be of the variety reasonably to be expected in the regular course of an on-going business (see *Newton-Waltham Bank & Trust Co. v. Bergen Motors*, 68 Misc.2d 228, 230, 327 N.Y.S.2d 77, 81, affd., 75 Misc.2d 103, 347 N.Y.S.2d 568; cf. *First Nat. Bank, Martinsville v. Crone*, 301 N.E.2d 378, 381 [Ind.App.]). This was such a case.

Tanbro recovered damages from Deering to compensate for the wrongful conversion of the goods.	**JUDGMENT AND REMEDY**

Buyers of Chattel Paper and Instruments

Another purchaser who is not subject to a secured party's interest despite perfection is the purchaser of chattel paper and instruments. This protection is provided by Section 9-308(a). Chattel paper is defined as a writing or writings that evidence both a monetary obligation and a security interest in specific goods. As defined before, *instrument* means a negotiable instrument as defined in UCC 3-104, or a certificated security as defined in UCC 8-102, or basically any other writing that evidences a right to the payment of money and is not itself a security agreement or lease transferred in the ordinary course of business. [UCC 9-105(1)(i)]

Chattel paper is a very important class of collateral used in financing arrangements, especially in automobile financing. When it is sold by a creditor, the creditor can deliver it over to the assignee, who is then responsible for collecting the debt directly from the debtor. This arrangement is known as *notification* or *direct collection*. As an alternative, a creditor can sell chattel paper to an assignee with the understanding that the creditor will retain the chattel paper, make collections from the debtor, and then remit the money to the assignee. This kind of transaction is *nonnotification* or *indirect collec-*

tion. The chattel paper is usually not delivered to the assignee. The widespread use of both methods of dealing with chattel paper is recognized by the Code, and hence the Code permits perfection of a chattel paper security interest either by filing or by taking possession.

Problems arise when perfection is made by filing only. If the chattel paper is thereafter sold to another purchaser who gives *new value* and takes *possession* of the paper in the *ordinary course of business without knowledge* that it is subject to a security interest, the new purchaser usually will have priority over the secured creditor. (Of course, the creditor has rights in the proceeds.)

THE RIGHTS AND DUTIES OF DEBTORS AND CREDITORS UNDER THE UCC

The security agreement itself determines most of the rights and duties of the debtor and the creditor. The UCC, however, imposes some rights and duties that are applicable in the absence of a security agreement to the contrary.

Information Request by Creditors

Under UCC 9-407(1), a creditor has the option, when making the filing, of asking the filing officer to make a note of the file number, the date, and the hour of the original filing on a copy of the financing statement. The filing officer must send this copy to the person making the request. Under UCC 9-407(2), a filing officer must also give information to a person who is contemplating obtaining a security interest from a prospective debtor. The filing officer must give a certificate that provides information on possible perfected financing statements with respect to the named debtor. The filing officer will charge a fee for the certification or information copies provided.

Assignment, Amendment, and Release

Whenever desired, a secured party of record can release part or all of the collateral described in a filed financing statement. This ends his or her security interest in the collateral. [UCC 9-406] A secured party can assign part or all of the security interest to another, called the assignee. That assignee becomes the secured party of record if, for example, he or she either makes a notation of the assignment somewhere on the financing statement or files a written statement of assignment. [UCC 9-405(2)]

It is also possible to amend a financing statement that has already been filed. The amendment must be signed by both parties. The debtor has to sign the security agreement, the original financing statement, and the amendments. [UCC 9-402]

All other secured transaction documents, such as releases, assignments, continuations of perfection, perfections of collateral moved into another jurisdiction, or termination statements, need only be signed by the secured party.

Reasonable Care of Collateral

If a secured party is in possession of the collateral, he or she must use reasonable care in preserving it. Otherwise, the secured party is liable to the debtor. [UCC 9-207 (1) and (3)] If the collateral increases in value, the secured party can hold this increased value or profit as additional security unless it is in the form of money, which must be remitted to the debtor or applied toward reducing the secured debt. [UCC 9-207(2)(c)] Additionally, the collateral must be kept identifiable unless it is fungible. [UCC 9-207(2)(d) Finally, the debtor must pay for all reasonable charges incurred by the secured party in preserving, operating, and taking care of the collateral in possession. [UCC 9-207(2)(a)]

The Status of the Debt

During the time that the secured debt is outstanding, the debtor may wish to know the status of the debt. If so, he or she need only sign a statement that indicates the aggregate amount of the unpaid debt at a specific date (and perhaps a list of the collateral covered by the security agreement). The secured party must then approve or correct this statement in writing. The creditor must comply with the request within two weeks of receipt; otherwise, the creditor is liable for any loss caused to the debtor by the failure to do so. [UCC 9-208(2)] One such request is allowed without charge every six months. For each additional request, the secured party can require a fee not exceeding $10 per request. [UCC 9-208(3)]

DEFAULT

Article 9 defines the rights, duties, and remedies of a secured party and of the debtor upon a debtor's default. Should the secured party fail to comply with its duties, the debtor is afforded particular rights and remedies.

The topic of default is one of great concern to secured lenders and to the lawyers who draft security agreements. What constitutes default is not always very clear. In fact, Article 9 does not define the term. Thus, parties are encouraged in practice and by the Code to include in their security agreements certain standards to be applied in the event that default actually comes about. Consequently, parties can stipulate the conditions that will constitute a default. [UCC 9-501(1)]

Typically, because of the unusual disparity in the bargaining position between a debtor and creditor, these critical terms are shaped with exceeding breadth by the creditor to arrive at some sense of security. The ultimate terms, however, are not allowed to run afoul of the limitations imposed by the good faith requirement of UCC 1-208 and the unconscionability doctrine.

Although any breach of the terms of the security agreement can constitute default, default occurs most commonly when the debtor fails to meet the scheduled payments that the parties have agreed upon or when the debtor becomes bankrupt. However, if the security agreement covers equipment, the debtor may have warranted that he or she is the owner of the equipment or that no liens or other security interests are pending on that equipment. Breach of any of these representations can result in default.

Basic Remedies

According to UCC 9-501, upon default, a secured creditor can reduce a claim to judgment, foreclose, or enforce a security interest by any available judicial process. Where the collateral consists of documents of title, a secured party can proceed against either the documents or the underlying goods.

A secured party's remedies can be divided into two basic categories:

1.   A secured party can relinquish a security interest and proceed to judgment on the underlying debt, followed by execution and levy. [UCC 9-501(1)]
2.   A secured party can take possession of the collateral covered by the security agreement. [UCC 9-503] Upon taking possession, the secured party can retain the collateral covered by the security agreement for satisfaction of the debt [UCC 9-505(2)] or can resell the goods and apply the proceeds toward the debt. [UCC 9-504]

The rights and remedies under UCC 9-501(1) are *cumulative*; therefore, if a creditor is unsuccessful in enforcing rights by one method, another method can be pursued. The UCC does not require election of remedies between an action on the obligation or repossession of the collateral.[1]

When a security agreement covers both real and personal property, the secured party can proceed against the personal property in accordance with the remedies of Article 9. On the other hand, the secured party can proceed against the entire collateral under procedures set down by local real estate law, in which case the Code does not apply. [UCC 9-501(4)]

This situation occurs when the security interest on a corporate loan can apply to the manufacturing plant (real property) and also to the inventory (personal property). Determining whether particular collateral is personal or real property can prove difficult, especially when

---

1.   See White and Summers, *Uniform Commercial Code*, 2nd Ed. (St. Paul: West Publishing Co., 1980), pp. 1093–1094.

dealing with fixtures—things affixed to real property. Under certain circumstances, the Code allows the removal of fixtures upon default; however, such removal is subject to the provisions of Article 9. [UCC 9-313]

The Secured Party's Right to Take Possession

The secured party has the right to take possession of the collateral upon default unless the security agreement states otherwise. As long as there is no breach of the peace, the secured party can use self-help to repossess the collateral. Otherwise the secured party must resort to judicial process. [UCC 9-503]

What constitutes a breach of the peace is of prime importance to both parties, for such an act can open the secured party to tort liability. The Code does not define *breach of the peace*. Therefore, parties must resort to state law to determine it.

Generally, the creditor or the creditor's agent cannot enter a debtor's home, garage, or place of business without permission. Consider a situation where an automobile is collateral. If the repossessing party walks onto the debtor's premises, proceeds up the driveway, enters the vehicle without entering the garage, and drives off, it probably will not amount to a breach of the peace. However, in some states, an action for wrongful trespass could meet the threshold test and start a cause of action for breach of the peace. (Most car repossessions occur when the car is parked on a street or in a parking lot.)

Reasonable Care of the Collateral Required Once the secured party comes into possession of the collateral after breach by repossession, the rights, remedies, and duties provided by Section 9-207, as previously discussed, come into play. The main requirement of that section calls for the secured party to exercise "reasonable care" in the custody and preservation of any collateral in its possession.

This duty cannot be disclaimed, and any exculpatory clause will be unenforceable. [UCC 1-102(3)] Reasonable limitations as to what will be required, however, can be agreed upon by the parties. Where the collateral consists of instruments or chattel paper, reasonable care extends to taking necessary steps to preserve rights against prior parties unless otherwise agreed. Should the secured party fail to meet its obligations as prescribed in UCC 9-207, he or she will be liable for any damages occasioned by such failure. The secured party does not, however, lose the security interest for failure to exercise reasonable care.

Assembling the Collateral UCC 9-503 provides authorization for security agreements to require that, upon default, the debtor assemble the collateral and make it available to the secured party at a location designated by that party. The location must be reasonably convenient to both parties. This provision is important to a creditor when the collateral is located in several locations or when the debtor is in a better position to assemble it.

The Code also recognizes the inherent practical problems involved in removal and disposition of collateral when it is heavy equipment. Removal and storage costs could quickly reach an impractical level. The Code therefore authorizes the secured party to render such equipment "unusable" and to dispose of the collateral on the debtor's premises. [UCC 9-503] This authorization does not permit unreasonable action by the secured party, because every aspect of the repossession and disposition must comply with the standards of commercial reasonableness of Section 9-504.

Disposition of Collateral

Once default has occurred, the secured party is faced with several alternatives to secure payment of the debt. The party can sell, lease, or otherwise dispose of the collateral in any commercially reasonable manner. [UCC 9-504(1)] Any sale is always subject to procedures established by state law.

Retention of Collateral by Secured Party after Default The Code recognizes that parties are sometimes better off if they do not sell the collateral. Therefore, a secured party can retain collateral, but this general right is subject to several conditions. The secured party must send written notice of the proposal to the debtor if the debtor has not signed a statement renouncing or modifying his or her rights after default. With consumer goods, no other notice has to be given. In all other cases, notice must be sent to any other secured party from whom the secured party has received written notice of a claim of interest in the collateral in question. If within twenty-one days after the notice is sent the secured party receives an objection in writing from a person entitled to receive notification, then the secured party must dispose of the collateral under UCC 9-504. If no such written objection is forthcoming, the secured party can retain the collateral in full satisfaction of the debtor's obligation. [UCC 9-505(2)]

Consumer Goods When the collateral is consumer goods with a purchase money security interest, and the debtor has paid more than 60 percent of the cash price, then the secured party must dispose of the collateral under UCC 9-504 within ninety days. Failure to comply opens the secured party to an action for conversion or other liability under UCC 9-507(1) unless the consumer-debtor signed a written statement *after default* renouncing or modifying the right to demand the sale of the goods. [UCC 9-505(1)]

Disposition Procedures A secured party who does not choose to retain the collateral must resort to the disposition procedures prescribed under UCC 9-504. The Code allows a great deal of flexibility with regard to disposition. The only real limitation is that it must be accomplished in a commercially reasonable manner. UCC 9-507(2) supplies some examples of what does or does not meet the standard of commercial reasonableness:

> The fact that a better price could have been obtained by a sale at a different time or in a different method from that selected by the secured party is not of itself sufficient to establish that the sale was not made in a commercially reasonable manner. If the secured party either sells the collateral in the usual manner in any recognized market therefor or if he sells at the price currently in such a market at the time of sale or if he has otherwise sold in conformity with reasonable commercial practices among dealers in the type of property sold, he has sold in a commercially reasonable manner.

To be a sale conducted in a commercially reasonable manner, generally notice of the place, time, and manner of sale is required. The following case illustrates the importance of compliance with such requirement.

BACKGROUND AND FACTS *Glenn Stensel borrowed $35,000 from a bank, pledging sixteen mobile homes that he owned as collateral. Glenn's father, Vernell Stensel, co-signed the notes. Glenn defaulted in payments on the notes, and his father sold the mobile homes at a public auction. Using the proceeds of the sale and his own funds, Vernell satisfied his son's debt. After Vernell's death, his widow sought a deficiency judgment against Glenn. The trial court entered judgment for the widow. Glenn contended he was not liable for the money his father added to the auction proceeds because he was not notified of the sale.*

STENSEL v. STENSEL

Appellate Court of Illinois, Fourth District, 1978.
63 Ill.App.3d 639, 20 Ill.Dec. 548, 380 N.E.2d 526.

WEBBER, Justice.

*   *   *   *

Plaintiff contends that no notice was required because the collateral was in danger of destruction and threatened to decline speedily in value, and in any event, Glenn renounced his right to notice by sending certain written instructions to the bank and to Vernell.

The pertinent provision of the Code relating to the secured party's right to dispose of collateral is section 9-504(3) which reads as follows:

"Disposition of the collateral may be by public or private proceedings and may be made by way of one or more contracts. Sale or other disposition may be as a unit or in parcels and at any time and place and on any terms but every aspect of the disposition including the method, manner, time, place and terms must be commercially reasonable. *Unless collateral is perishable or threatens to decline speedily in value or is of a type customarily sold on a recognized market, reasonable notification of the time and place of any public sale or reasonable notification of the time after which any private sale or other intended disposition is to be made shall be sent by the secured party to the debtor, if he has not signed after default a statement renouncing or modifying his right to notification of sale.* In the case of consumer goods no other notification need be sent. In other cases notification shall be sent to any other secured party from whom the secured party has received (before sending his notification to the debtor or before the debtor's renunciation of his rights) written notice of a claim of an interest in the collateral. The secured party may buy at any public sale and if the collateral is of a type customarily sold in a recognized market or is of a type which is the subject of widely distributed standard price quotations he may buy at private sale."

We are not persuaded that a mobile home is collateral which "threatens to decline speedily in value." * * * In our opinion, that application of this provision to chattel property would be a rarity. Its obvious intent was to apply to securities in a rapidly falling market, or any other item, such as gold bullion, which is subject to price fluctuations on a daily basis.

* * * Plaintiff makes much of some letters in the record from Glenn to the bank and to Vernell. * * *

While the letters *prima facie* authorize a sale, nothing in either of them can be construed as a waiver of notice of the time and place of the sale. This is especially true in view of section 9-501(3) of the Code which reads, in part, as follows:

"To the extent that they give rights to the debtor and impose duties on the secured party, the rules stated in the subsections referred to below *may not be waived or varied* except as provided with respect to compulsory disposition of collateral (subsection (3) of Section 9-504 and Section 9-505 and with respect to redemption of collateral (Section 9-506)) but the parties may by agreement determine the standards by which the fulfillment of these rights and duties is to be measured if such standards are not manifestly unreasonable."

We have already held that the disposition here was not one under compulsion and there is nothing in the record to indicate that the parties made any other agreement regarding these rights. Under the authority just set forth, Glenn could not legally waive his rights to notice and since he received none, the purported sale was void as to him.

* * * *

Since the sale was void as to Glenn, the remaining problem is whether a deficiency judgment could be obtained against him.

The commentary to section 9-504 of the Code indicates that there is a divergence of authority in the United States on this subject. One line holds that any damages recoverable by the debtor must be offset by any deficiency on the sale, but the burden shifts to the secured party to prove that he obtained a commercially reasonable sale, especially in the absence of notice to the debtor.

Another line of cases holds that a failure of the secured party to give notice of sale to the debtor absolutely bars any deficiency judgment.

We are persuaded that the latter line of authority is the better reasoned. The deprivation of the ability to be present at the sale and guard one's interests is serious and allows the secured party too free a hand in making disposition.

The judgment of the trial court was reversed. Vernell's widow could not recover because Glenn was not given proper notice of the sale.	**JUDGMENT AND REMEDY**

A secured party is not compelled to resort to public sale to dispose of the collateral. The party is given the latitude under the Code to seek out the best terms possible in a private sale. Generally, no specific time requirements must be met; however, the time must ultimately meet the standard of commercial reasonableness.

Notice must be sent by the secured party to the debtor if the debtor has not signed a statement renouncing or modifying the right to notification of sale after default. For consumer goods, no other notification need be sent. In all other cases, notification must be sent to any other secured party from whom the secured party has received written notice of claim of an interest in the collateral. [UCC 9-504(3)] Such notice is not necessary, however, when the collateral is perishable or threatens to decline speedily in value, or when it is of a type customarily sold on a recognized market.

Proceeds from Disposition Proceeds from the disposition must be applied in a certain order:

1. Reasonable expenses stemming from the retaking, holding, or preparing for sale are covered first. When authorized by law and if provided for in the agreement, these can include reasonable attorneys' fees and legal expenses.
2. The satisfaction of the debt is covered second.
3. Subordinate security interests whose written demands have been received prior to the completion of distribution of the proceeds are covered third. [UCC 9-504(1)]
4. Any surplus generally goes to the debtor.

Deficiency Judgment Often, after proper disposition of the collateral, the secured party does not collect all that is still owed by the debtor. Unless otherwise agreed, the debtor is liable for any deficiency. On the other hand, if the underlying transaction was a sale of accounts or of chattel paper, the secured party can collect a deficiency judgment only if the security agreement so provides. [UCC 9-504(2)]

Redemption Rights Any time before the secured party disposes of the collateral or enters into a contract for its disposition, or before the debtor's obligation has been discharged through the secured party's retention of the collateral, the debtor or any other secured party can exercise the right of *redemption* of the collateral. The debtor can do this by tendering performance of *all* obligations secured by the collateral, by paying the expenses reasonably incurred by the secured party, and by retaking the collateral and maintaining its care and custody. [UCC 9-506]

TERMINATION

When a debt is paid, the secured party generally must send to the debtor or file a termination statement with the filing officer to whom the original financing statement was given. If the financing statement covers consumer goods, the termination statement must be filed by the secured party within one month after the debt is paid, or if the debtor requests the termination statement in writing, it must be filed within ten days after the debt is paid whichever is earlier.

[UCC 9-404(1)] In all other cases, the termination statement must be filed or furnished to the debtor within ten days after a written request is made by the debtor. If the affected secured party fails to file such a termination statement, as required by UCC 9-404(1), or fails to send the termination statement within ten days after proper demand, the secured party shall be liable to the debtor for $100. Additionally, the secured party will be liable for any loss caused to the debtor.

QUESTIONS AND
CASE PROBLEMS

1. Ray is a seller of electric generators. He purchases a large quantity of generators from manufacturer Martin Corp. by making a down payment and signing a security agreement to make the balance of payments over a period of time. The security agreement gives Martin Corp. a security interest in the generators sold and the proceeds. Martin Corp. files a financing statement on its security interest centrally. Ray receives the generators and immediately sells one of them to Green on an installment contract, with payment to be made in twelve equal installments. At the time of sale, Green knows of Martin's security interest. Two months later Ray goes into default on his payments to Martin. Discuss Martin's rights against purchaser Green in this situation.

2. Martin Corporation is a manufacturer of washing machines. On September 1, in need of working capital, Martin contacts Smith, a loan officer for the First Bank. Martin asks to borrow $200,000, putting up all its equipment as security. Smith agrees to make the loan. In the security agreement signed by Martin's president is a clause stating that this loan is secured not only by the existing equipment presently located at Martin's plant but by any equipment acquired in the future by Martin. The First Bank files a financing statement centrally on *September 5*. On *November 1* Martin has an opportunity to purchase from Daniel Equipment Corporation some newly manufactured Daniel equipment at a bargain price of $50,000. On that same date Martin contracts by a security agreement to purchase the equipment from Daniel, paying $20,000 down and the balance in monthly payments

over a three-year period, with Daniel having a security interest in the purchased equipment. The new equipment is delivered on *December 1*. On *December 7* Daniel perfects its security interest in the newly delivered equipment by filing a financing statement centrally. Later Martin goes into default to both parties. Discuss who has priority over the new equipment, the First Bank or Daniel.

3. Ray is a retail seller of television sets. Ray sells a color television set to Clara for her apartment for $600. Clara cannot pay cash and signs a security agreement, paying $100 down and the balance in twelve equal installments of $50 each. The security agreement gives Ray a security interest in the television set sold. Clara makes six payments on time; then she goes into default because of unexpected financial problems. Ray repossesses the set and wants to keep it in full satisfaction of the debt. Discuss Ray's rights and duties in this matter.

4. Ray is a retailer of stereo equipment and appliances in City Z. On March 1 Jim, a college senior, purchases several items of stereo equipment and appliances on an installment contract for $3,000. He signs a security agreement giving Ray a security interest in the stereo equipment and appliances sold. Ray files a financing statement locally. Jim had intended to get a job in City Z, where he lives. However, he is offered and accepts a job in City X in another state. Without Ray's knowledge, on June 1 Jim moves all his belongings into an apartment near his new job after graduation. Jim continues to make payments to Ray. Jim's living expenses are much higher at his new location, and on August 1 he secures a loan from East Bank, signing a security agreement that puts up all his household possessions, including the stereo equipment and appliances, as collateral for the loan. On August 2 East Bank files a financing statement locally. Jim fails to make the September payment to Ray, and on October 5 Jim is in default to both Ray and East Bank. Ray is now aware of all events and claims priority on the stereo equipment and appliances over East Bank. Assuming Jim's property is insufficient to cover the balance of both debts, discuss who has priority over the stereo equipment and appliances.

5. Denise owns and operates a successful restaurant. One year ago she borrowed money from West Bank to make two purchases, an expensive television set for her home and a piece of restaurant equipment. Denise signed security agreements for both purchases with West Bank, giving West Bank a security interest in all of the collateral. West Bank filed a financing statement locally for perfection of its security interest in the television set and centrally for the restaurant

equipment. Denise has now made the last payments on both. Discuss West Bank's duties and liabilities to Denise for its failure to file termination statements on the security interests.

6. The city of Vermillion brought a declaratory judgment action to have a court determine to whom the city should pay the proceeds of a construction contract between the city and a bankrupt contractor. Shortly after the contract was formed, the contractor assigned its interest in the proceeds from the contract to the National Bank as security for a loan. The bank did not properly file a financing statement. The contract was the contractor's sole account receivable. Subsequently, the IRS filed notice of a tax lien upon all property of the contractor. On January 15, 1970, the contractor filed for bankruptcy. The IRS renewed its tax lien, and the trustee in bankruptcy claimed all the contractor's assets. Does the National Bank's claim to the proceeds from the construction contract have priority over either the IRS tax lien or the trustee in bankruptcy? [City of Vermillion v. Stan Houston Equipment Co., 341 F.Supp. 707 (D.C.S.D.1972)]

7. Chrysler Credit corporation held a perfected security interest in the inventory of Worthey Chrysler Dealer (floor plan). Worthey owed Malone $10,000 and gave Malone a check for $5,000 as part payment. The same day, Malone returned to Worthey and indorsed the check back to Worthey in payment for an automobile in which Chrysler Credit held a security interest. Should Malone take free of Chrysler Credit's security interest? [Chrysler Credit Corp. v. Malone, 502 S.W.2d 910 (Tex.Civ.App.1973)]

8. In 1969 Jones and Percell executed a promissory note and a security agreement covering a converted military aircraft built in the 1950s. Upon default, the Bank of Nevada repossessed the aircraft. After provid-

ing the required notice to Jones and Percell, the bank placed advertisements in several trade journals as well as in major newspapers in several large cities. In addition, the bank sent 2,000 brochures to 240 sales organizations. A sales representative was hired to market the aircraft. The plane was later sold for $71,000 to an aircraft broker, who in turn resold it for $123,000 after spending $33,000 on modifications. Since the price obtained on the sale of the plane was about $75,000 less than the amount Jones and Percell owed the bank, the bank initiated a lawsuit to obtain the amount of the deficiency. Can Jones and Percell object to the bank's manner of resale? [Jones v. Bank of Nevada, 91 Nev. 368, 535 P.2d 1279 (1975)]

9. Mueller bought a 32-foot motor boat for a cash sale price of $29,000. Part of the sale was financed by Chemical Bank. The retail installment contract security agreement was assigned to Chemical on June 15, 1976. Ten days after the assignment, Chemical Bank filed a financing statement. Approximately a year later, Mueller, now representing himself as Lawrence J. Miller, traded the 32-foot boat in on a 36-foot boat at Miller Yacht Sales. Mueller made a down payment of $2,000. He was given a trade-in allowance of $22,500. The balance due was financed with another bank. When Miller Yacht Sales took possession of the 32-foot boat as Mueller's trade-in, it resold it to someone else. Then Mueller defaulted on his payments on the original retail installment contract to Chemical Bank and disappeared. Chemical Bank notified Miller Yacht Sales that it had a security interest. Since Miller Yacht Sales had already resold the boat, Chemical brought suit against Miller Yacht Sales. What was the result? [Chemical Bank v. Miller Yacht Sales, 173 N.J.Super. 90, 413 A.2d 619 (1980)]

FOCUS ON ETHICS

Commercial Transactions and the Uniform Commercial Code

Transactions involving the sale of goods constitute a major portion of business activity in the commercial and manufacturing sectors of this economy. Since the 1960s, the sale of goods has been governed by the Uniform Commercial Code in virtually every state. Many of the Code provisions express our ethical standards. Much of the conduct of businesspersons in the business world has an ethical basis.

THE SALES CONTRACT

It would seem that the requirements for the formation of the sales contract would be detailed and explicit. However, the UCC states that a sales contract will not fail for indefiniteness even if one or more terms are left open, as long as the parties intend to make the contract and there is a reasonably certain basis for the court to grant an appropriate remedy. For example, there can be open price and quantity terms, open delivery terms, and open payment terms and a valid contract will still exist.

The Code attempts to maximize the probability that two willing parties will engage in a mutually beneficial economic transaction.

Underlying this effort is the notion that commercial transactions form the basis of our country's economic well-being. Rather than make such transactions difficult, the UCC attempts to facilitate commercial transactions.

Under such circumstances, businesspersons could try to take advantage of the flexibility of the UCC's requirements for a valid sales contract. Occasionally, one reads of a business scandal in which an unscrupulous seller requires buyers of a product to sign a written sales contract with a number of blanks. The contract's blanks are filled in later in a manner not agreed upon by the two parties prior to signature. The fact is that our shared beliefs reject the notion that businesspersons should be able to take advantage of as many willing customers as possible.

The competitive marketplace limits unethical behavior by businesspersons. Virtually all successful businesses, particularly those dealing in goods, must have "repeat" customers to be successful. Unethical dealings with customers invariably become publicly known, and repeat customers dwindle so that the unethical businessperson will

often eventually go out of business. Unfortunately for the consumer, this process may take time. During that time, some consumers will be harmed.

PERFORMANCE AND OBLIGATION

Two key concepts permeate the Uniform Commercial Code. They are "good faith" and "commercial reasonableness." These are objective standards even though they are subjective words.

With respect to good faith, under previous law, the only time this concept was discussed in any detail was normally in an equitable proceeding where the "ethics" of a situation has always been emphasized more strongly (e.g., "He who seeks equity must do equity."). By making good faith a clear obligation in every contract for the sale of goods, and then defining good faith as *honesty in fact*, the drafters of the UCC are stating a very broad policy principle—one that maintains a high standard. Present UCC law does not require that actions be "fair," only that they be honest in fact.

The concepts of good faith and commercial reasonableness are read into every contract and impose certain duties on all parties. Sec. 2–311(1) indicates that "any such specification must be made in good faith and within limits set by commercial reasonableness." It is implicitly understood that good faith applies to actions and intent. It implies that one party will not take advantage of another party by manipulating contract terms.

All commercial actions, including performance and enforcement of contract terms, must also exhibit commercial reasonableness. The UCC makes it clear that innocent parties *can* be excused from certain types of nonperformance when it is a result of a commercially reasonable intervening phenomenon. Indeed, the doctrine of commercial impracticability relies on a theory of reasonableness. The fact that the word "reasonable" appears about ninety times in Article II of the UCC demonstrates the UCC's opposition to imposing undue hardship on merchants and those with whom they deal. A merchant is expected to act in a reasonable manner according to reasonable commercial customs. Also, throughout the UCC merchants are held to a higher standard than are nonmerchants. This clearly represents an ideal which the drafters of the UCC were seeking.

WARRANTIES

The higher standard to which merchants must conform carries over to warranties. The UCC makes it difficult for merchants to disclaim warranties and requires that disclaimers be conspicuous (they should not be hidden). Certainly the implied warranties of merchantability and fitness for a particular purpose were necessary to help the consumer in

a world of complex products. (Some scholars have argued that nonetheless the UCC sections addressing disclaimer, waiver, and modification, when properly used, have *reduced* the effectiveness of such warranty protection for the consumer.) The creation of the Consumer Product Safety Commission (CPSC) occurred after numerous Congressional studies showed a need for it. The CPSC presumably was created because the marketplace somehow failed to provide products that were safe enough. Also, apparently the warranty provisions of the UCC had failed to provide adequate protection for consumers.

The businessperson has not only a legal obligation to provide safe products, but also an ethical one. When faced with the possibility of providing additional safety at no extra cost, every ethical businessperson will indeed opt for a safer product. At issue, however, is the policy relating to what a producer should do when a safer product requires higher costs and therefore higher consumer prices. The marketplace presumably will determine the optimal level of safety; however, that level has been deemed too low. That is why the Consumer Product Safety Commission was created. Arguably, unsafe products lead to social costs because injured individuals must sometimes receive medical care, often at public expense. Also, dependents of injured individuals may find themselves in financial difficulties and require "welfare" payments from the state.

PRODUCTS LIABILITY

The broader issue of products liability is certainly susceptible to the same analysis. The doctrine of strict liability implies that even if the consumer is careless, the

manufacturer is liable for any resulting damages from a defective product. This leads not only to an ethical question but to an economic efficiency question. As increasing liability is imposed upon manufacturers, consumers have less incentive to be careful when they use products. In the insurance industry, this phenomenon is called moral hazard. An important question therefore arises: To what extent should consumers be responsible for their own actions? No one has ethical qualms about requiring that the manufacturer of an exploding soft drink bottle pay for damages, but what about when the user of a rotary lawn mower leaves it running and sticks his or her hand underneath to remove a rock and is subsequently injured? Should the manufacturer of the lawn mower be held 100 percent liable for such damages? Or should the user of the machinery be completely responsible for his or her negligent action? Or should there be a compromise?

The fact is that whatever rule is decided upon, future activities will be affected. For example, the Consumer Product Safety Commission may require that all lawn mowers be made in such a way that it is impossible for anyone, no matter how negligent, to touch a moving blade. This may sound like a "good" rule except that such a rule will require additional use of resources. After all, the building of safer lawn mowers costs more. These costs will be passed on to the consumer. We then must ask an economic question: What are the costs and what are the benefits? If the anticipated aggregate costs far exceed the anticipated long-run benefits, should the Consumer Product Safety Commission be allowed to pass such a rule? Or do we have an ethical obligation, no matter what the economic cost, to provide maximum safety for every product that is generated in our economic system?

CHECKS AND THE BANKING SYSTEM

Numerous moral and ethical questions face members of the banking community. Banks and other financial institutions offer a variety of services to their customers. Some financial institutions would certainly like to prevent customers from using stop payments. The marketplace, as well as custom and law nonetheless provides for the customer's use of such stop payments. How much should a bank or other financial institution be allowed to charge a customer for the use of a stop payment? If the bank or other financial institution charges too much for this service, is it in fact effectively removing that service by over-pricing it? The same issue applies to return checks (usually for insufficient funds). What is the appropriate bank charge?

DISCUSSION QUESTIONS

1. To what extent does competition in the marketplace obviate the need for ethical business standards?
2. Should the question of product safety be decided according to economic analysis only? Or is product safety simply an ethical consideration? How far removed is economic analysis from ethical considerations here?
3. Can a human life be subjected to a cost-benefit analysis? For example, consider the following situation: A rule is proposed that will require all commercial airlines to use jets that have two additional emergency exit doors. Given the average number of airline crashes per year and the average number of individuals injured or killed in such crashes, it is estimated that the new safety standard will save an additional ten lives per year. Should the standard therefore be instituted? What if it costs $10 million? $50 million? $3 billion?

UNIT V

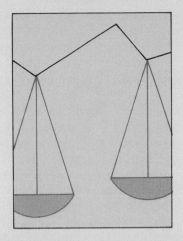

CREDITORS' RIGHTS AND BANKRUPTCY

CHAPTER 32

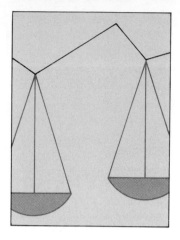

Rights of Debtors and Creditors

The law of debtor-creditor relations has undergone various changes over the years. Throughout history, debtors and their families have been subjected to terrible punishment for their inability to pay debts, including involuntary servitude, imprisonment, and dismemberment. The modern legal system has moved away from a punishment philosophy in dealing with debtors. In fact, many people say that it has moved too far in the other direction, to the detriment of creditors. Today, consumer protection is emphasized, and the legal system is designed to aid and protect the debtor and the debtor's family.

This chapter deals with various rights and remedies available through statutory laws, common law, and contract law to assist the debtor and creditor in resolving their disputes without the debtor having to resort to bankruptcy. The next chapter discusses bankruptcy as a so-called last resort to resolve debtor-creditor problems.

LAWS ASSISTING CREDITORS

Mechanic's Lien on Real Property

When a person contracts for labor, services, or material to be furnished for the purpose of making improvements on real property but does not immediately pay for the improvements, a special type of debtor-creditor relationship called a **mechanic's lien** is created. The real estate itself becomes security for the lien (debt).

For example, a roofer repairs a leaky roof at the request of a homeowner. The homeowner owes the roofer the agreed-upon price for the materials, labor, and services performed. If the homeowner cannot pay or pays only a portion of the charges, a mechanic's lien against the property can be created. The roofer is the lienholder, and the real property is encumbered with a mechanic's lien for the amount owed. If the homeowner does not pay the lien, the property can be sold to satisfy the debt.

The procedures by which a mechanic's lien is created are controlled by state statutory law. Generally, the lienholder must file a written notice of lien against the particular property involved. The notice of lien must be filed within a specific time period, measured from the last date that materials or labor were provided (usually within 60 to 120 days). Failure to pay the debt entitles the lienholder to foreclose on the real estate where the improvements were made and sell it in order to satisfy the amount of the debt. Of course, the lienholder is required by statute to give notice to the owner of the property prior to foreclosure and sale. The sale proceeds are used to pay the debt and the costs of the legal proceedings and the surplus, if any, is paid to the former owner.

Artisan's and Hotelkeeper's Liens on Personal Property

An **artisan's lien** and a **hotelkeeper's lien** are security devices, created at common law, similar to a mechanic's lien but used to charge personal property with the payment of a debt for labor done, for value added, or for caring for the personal property (bailee or warehousing costs).

For example, Ann leaves her watch at the jeweler's to be repaired and to have her initials engraved on the back. In absence of agreement, the jeweler can keep the watch until Ann pays for the repairs and services that the jeweler provides. Should Ann fail to pay, the jeweler has a lien on Ann's watch for the amount of the bill and can sell the watch in satisfaction of the lien.

An artisan's lien is a *possessory lien*. The lienholder ordinarily must have retained possession of the property and have expressly or impliedly agreed to provide the services on a *cash, not a credit, basis.* Usually the lienholder retains possession of the property. When this occurs, the lien remains as long as the lienholder maintains possession and terminates once possession is voluntarily surrendered—unless the surrender is only temporary. If it is a temporary surrender, there must be an agreement that the property will be returned to the lienholder. Even

with such an agreement, if a third party obtains rights in that property while it is out of the possession of the lienholder, the lien is lost. The only way a lienholder can protect a lien and surrender possession at the same time is to record notice of the lien in accordance with state lien and recording statutes.

Modern statutes permit the holder of an artisan's lien to foreclose and sell the property subject to the lien in order to satisfy payment of the debt. As with the mechanic's lien, the lienholder is required to give notice to the owner of the property prior to foreclosure and selling. The sale proceeds are used to pay the debt and the costs of the legal proceedings and the surplus, if any, is paid to the former owner.

A hotelkeeper's lien is given on the baggage of guests for the agreed-upon charges that remain unpaid. If no express agreement was made on those charges, then the lien will be the reasonable value of the accommodations furnished. The hotelkeeper's lien is terminated either by the guest's payment of the hotel's charges or by surrender of the baggage to the guests, unless such surrender is temporary. Also, the lien is terminated by conversion of the guest's baggage by the hotelkeeper. Although state statutes permit such conversion by means of a public sale, there is a trend toward requiring that the guest first be given an impartial judicial hearing.[1]

Writ of Execution

A debt must be past due in order for a creditor to commence legal action against a debtor. If the creditor is successful, the court awards the creditor a judgment against the debtor (usually for the amount of the debt plus any interest and legal costs incurred in obtaining the judgment). Attorneys' fees are not included in this amount unless provided for by statute or contract.

If the debtor does not or cannot pay the judgment, the creditor is entitled to go back to the court and obtain a **writ of execution.** This writ is an order, usually issued by the clerk of the

---

1. *Klim v. Jones*, 315 F.Supp. 109 (D.C.N.D.Cal. 1970).

court, directing the sheriff to seize (levy) and sell any of the debtor's nonexempt real or personal property that is within the court's geographic jurisdiction (usually the county in which the courthouse is located). The proceeds of the sale are used to pay off the judgment and costs of the sale. Any excess is paid to the debtor. The debtor can pay the judgment and redeem the nonexempt property any time before the sale takes place.

Attachment

Attachment is a court-ordered seizure and taking into custody of property that is in controversy over a debt. Attachment rights are created by state statutes. Attachment is normally a *prejudgment* remedy. It occurs either at the time of or immediately after the commencement of a lawsuit but before the entry of a final judgment. By statute, the restrictions and requirements for a creditor to attach before judgment are very specific and limited. The Due Process Clause of the Fourteenth Amendment to the Constitution limits courts' power to authorize seizure of debtors' property without notice to the debtor or a hearing on the facts. In recent years, a number of state attachment laws have been held to be unconstitutional.

In order to use attachment as a remedy, the creditor must follow certain procedures. He or she must file with the court an affidavit stating that the debtor is in default and stating the statutory grounds under which attachment is sought. A bond must be posted by the creditor to cover court costs, value of the loss of use of the good suffered by the debtor, and the value of the property attached. When the court is satisfied that all the requirements have been met, it issues a **writ of attachment.** This writ is similar to a writ of execution in that it directs the sheriff or other officer to seize nonexempt property. If the creditor prevails at trial, the seized property can be sold to satisfy the judgment.

The following case illustrates that strict compliance with every specific procedure established by the state's attachment statute is required before the property is subject to an enforceable writ of attachment because a writ of attachment operates against a debtor's property simply on the strength of the creditor's sworn statement that a debt is owed.

JACK DEVELOPMENT, INC. v. HOWARD EALES, INC.

District of Columbia Court of Appeals, 1978. 388 A.2d 466.

BACKGROUND AND FACTS *Corcoran was the owner of a large building in Washington, D.C. In April 1976 Eales, a creditor of Corcoran, obtained a prejudgment writ of attachment from a Washington, D.C., court against the building. In June 1976 notice of the writ was posted on the building. In October 1976 Corcoran conveyed the building to Jack Development, Inc. Up to this time, Eales had been unable to serve notice on Corcoran as required by Washington, D.C., statute. In the alternative, the statute allowed the notice requirement to be fulfilled by three-week publication of the writ in a local newspaper. Eales first published notice of the writ in February 1977. Jack Development argues that it is the owner since title was transferred to it before the writ "attached"—that is, before the statutory notice requirements had been fulfilled. Eales argues that the writ attached when notice was posted on the building, and therefore Corcoran was unable to transfer clear title.*

PER CURIAM [By the Court—an opinion of the whole court].

The sequence of relevant events therefore was:

April 15, 1976—Writ of attachment before judgment issued by trial court against defendant's realty [real estate].

June 21, 1976—Marshal posts realty with writ.

October 19, 1976—Defendant conveys realty to Jack Development, Inc., by quit-claim deed [a deed passing title, but not professing that the title is valid or not containing any warranty for title].

December 10, 1976—Quitclaim deed to realty recorded by Jack Development, Inc.

February 2, 1977—Marshal signs and files the indorsement on the writ of attachment before judgment which he had posted on the realty the previous June.

February 28, 1977—First date of service of process on defendant by publication.

*   *   *   *

Appellant Jack Development argues that it acquired title to the property at 1718 Corcoran Street, N.W., free of the writ of attachment before judgment which had been issued against the transferor, since the defendant transferred his interest *prior to service upon the transferor of the writ of attachment and the indorsement and notice,* as required by D.C.Code 1973, §§ 16-502, -508. *   *   *

*   *   *   *

Initially, we note that because a writ of attachment before judgment is a harsh and drastic remedy, strict compliance with the procedures established by the statute is required. In this case, the delivery of the writ of attachment before judgment to the marshal did create an inchoate [contingent] lien on the defendant's property. The mere posting of the property did *not* comply, however, with the notice procedures mandated by D.C.Code 1973 §§ 16-502, -508.

[The code in Washington, D.C., provides that if a debtor cannot be found within the district, the creditor must obtain a court order granting permission to inform the debtor by publication (for three consecutive weeks) that said debtor must appear and show cause why the property conditionally attached should not be subject to final attachment and sale.]

The statutory requirements were not completed in this case until three weeks after the first date of publication on February 28, 1977. At that time, the attachment normally would relate back to the date of the delivery of the writ to the marshal, i.e., April 15, 1976. Here, however, the defendant during the intervening period had transferred the property by quitclaim deed to Jack Development and appellant had recorded its deed on December 10, 1976—all such dates being prior to appellee's full compliance with the attachment statute. *   *   *

*   *   *   *

*   *   * Here, a valid transfer occurred before the defendant himself had been given notice of a sufficiently levied writ of attachment in compliance with the statute. D.C.Code 1973, § 16-508. Jack Development therefore took the property free of the writ of attachment which had been sought against the transferor.

The appellate court quashed the writ of attachment. Jack Development kept title to the property free of the writ of attachment. The judgment of the trial court was reversed.

JUDGMENT AND REMEDY

Attachment does not always prevent a subsequent transfer of the attached property. If the attachment has been perfected under statutory requirements, the transferee takes the property subject to the terms and conditions of the attachment and its underlying lien. The buyer, however, would ordinarily be aware of this, since the public records would indicate it.

COMMENTS

Enforceable Right Required Attachment is one way that personal property in the debtor's possession can be taken into custody and held until the creditor's claim is adjudicated in a court of law. Of course, the property must be capable of manual delivery for this to happen. Also, the creditor must not only follow the statutory requirements but must also have an enforceable right to payment of the debt under law. Otherwise, the creditor can be liable for damages for wrongful attachment with malice, as the following case illustrates.

MILLER v. FOX
Supreme Court of Montana,
1977.
174 Mont. 504, 571 P.2d 804.

BACKGROUND AND FACTS *Miller and Fox entered into a contract for the sale of stud horses. The full contract price was not paid at the time of the transaction. Four and a half years later, the plaintiff, Miller, sued the defendant, Fox, for the unpaid balance due on the contract and also obtained a writ of attachment against the defendant's property. The writ was subsequently enforced.*

The court found that the sale of the horses was never completed because of the plaintiff's own failure to perform a condition precedent— that is, to produce stud papers for a particular horse involved in the proposed sale. Miller could not properly seek a writ of attachment before he was entitled to payment, and he was not entitled to payment until he produced the stud papers.

When there has been a wrongful attachment, the property is returned and damages are awarded as compensation for loss of the use of the property.

HATFIELD, Chief Justice.

* * * *

Plaintiff also claims that the district judge erred in finding that plaintiff had wrongfully attached defendant's property. [Montana statute], allows prejudgment attachments only in actions upon contracts for the "direct payment of money." In this case, the trial judge found the contract did not call for direct payment of money, but required further performance (presentation of stud horse registration paper) as a condition to payment. Plaintiff's attachment therefore did not meet the statutory requirements and was wrong.

* * * *

Plaintiff maintains that even if the attachment was wrongful it was not done with the malice necessary * * * to sustain an award of exemplary damages. Malice necessary for an award of exemplary damages need not consist of spite or hatred; it is sufficient proof of malice in a wrongful attachment action that the defendant knew when the attachment was made that it was wrongful. In this case, plaintiff stated in his affidavit for attachment that the action was on a "contract for the direct payment of money now due", and that the payment of the contract obligation "has not been secured by any mortgage or lien upon real or personal property." Plaintiff, however, knew when he filed the affidavit that the money was not "now due" until he showed defendant the stud registration paper and that defendant's contract debt was "secured" by plaintiff's retention of that registration paper.

For the reasons stated, the judgment of the district court as to plaintiff's liability for wrongful attachment is affirmed. The district court's judgment that defendant was not in breach of contract until the time of trial is affirmed, and the case is remanded to determine the amount on the contract price defendant owes plaintiff for a stud horse whose registration papers were not presented until the time of trial, nine years after the contract was made.

* * * *

The trial court's ruling was affirmed, but the case was remanded to the trial court to determine the amount of the contract price that the defendant owed the plaintiff for a stud horse and the money value of the damages that the defendant incurred as a result of the wrongful attachment. The trial court's award of $400 exemplary damages for plaintiff's malicious action in seeking a wrongful attachment was upheld.

JUDGMENT AND REMEDY

The original contract for the sale of the horses was enforced between the parties, although it was left to the trial court to determine a fair amount for the contract price, considering the number of years that had passed since the parties had made their agreement.

The wrongful writ of attachment was punishable in both actual damages and exemplary damages, both of which the plaintiff had to pay to the defendant.

Garnishment

Garnishment is similar to attachment except that it is a collection remedy that is directed not at the debtor but at a third person. The third person, the garnishee, owes a debt to the debtor or has property that belongs to the debtor, such as wages or a bank account. The typical garnishee is an employer. The wages an employer owes to the debtor-employee are subject to garnishment. Both state and federal laws, however, permit only a limited portion of the debtor's wages to be garnished.[2]

Typically, a garnishment judgment will be served on a person's employer so that part of the person's usual paycheck will be paid to the creditor. Federal law provides a minimal framework to protect debtors from losing all their income in order to pay judgment debts.[3] State laws also provide dollar exemptions, and these amounts are often larger than those provided by federal law. State and federal statutes can be applied together to help create a pool of funds sufficient to enable a debtor to continue to provide for family needs while also reducing the amount of the judgment debt in a reasonable way.

Garnishment of an employee's wages cannot be grounds for dismissal of an employee because federal law prohibits any employer from discharging an employee who has been involved in only one garnishment proceeding.

The legal proceeding for a garnishment action is governed by state law. As a result of a garnishment proceeding, the debtor's employer

---

2. Some states (for example, Texas) do not permit garnishment of wages by private parties.

3. For example, the federal Consumer Credit Protection Act, 15 USCA 1601 et seq., provides that a debtor can retain either 75 percent of the disposable earnings per week or the sum equivalent to thirty hours of work paid at federal minimum wage rates, whichever is greater.

is ordered by the court to turn over a portion of the debtor's wages to pay the debt. However, garnishment operates differently from state to state. According to the laws in some states, the judgment creditor needs to obtain only one order of garnishment that will then continuously apply to the judgment debtor's weekly wages until the entire debt is paid. In other states, the judgment creditor must go back to court for a separate order of garnishment for each pay period. In the following case, the Colorado Supreme Court was asked to clarify whether, under its state statute, a writ of garnishment operated continuously or had to be renewed each pay period.

OLSON v. STONE
(IN RE STONE)
Supreme Court of Colorado, 1977.
573 P.2d 98.

BACKGROUND AND FACTS   *The judgment creditor (plaintiff) had obtained a judgment against the debtor (defendant) for $16,168.10. The plaintiff sought to execute on the judgment by garnishing the defendant's wages. The defendant received regular salary payments on the fifteenth and last day of each month. The plaintiff wanted the court to grant a single order allowing a continual garnishment against the defendant's wages until the entire debt was paid. The defendant opposed such an order, saying that the Colorado statute required the plaintiff to undertake a separate garnishment procedure for each regular payment of salary or wages.*

KELLEY, Justice.

*   *   *   *

This case is here for a determination of a question certified to us pursuant to C.A.R. 21.1 by the United States District Court for the District of Colorado. The question reads:

"Under Colorado Rule of Civil Procedure 103, and in particular, subsections (b), (j), (t) and (z) thereof, may the trial court, upon application by the judgment creditor, issue a writ in the nature of a continuing garnishment against an employer of the judgment debtor requiring the employer to pay into the Registry of the Court the appropriate portion of each regular paycheck or wage payment to the judgment debtor, as it becomes due, without the necessity of serving a separate Writ of Garnishment directed to each such wage payment?

"Alternatively stated, the question might be posed as follows: Where a judgment debtor receives payments of salary or wages at regular intervals from his employer, must a judgment creditor, in effecting execution of his judgment, undertake a separate garnishment procedure against each such regular payment of salary or wages, or may a Writ of Continuing Garnishment, containing appropriate instructions and safeguards for the interests of the judgment debtor, issue from the Trial Court in order to obviate the necessity of a series of individual garnishments against the same employer?"

We answer the question in the negative.

On March 24, 1976, the Bankruptcy Court of the United States District Court for the District of Colorado entered a default judgment in the amount of $16,168.10 against the defendant, Joseph R. Stone (hereinafter defendant). The United States District Court for the District of Colorado affirmed on appeal the judgment of the Bankruptcy Court and the denial of the defendant's motion to set aside the default judgment.

*   *   *   *

[The Colorado statute] provides for garnishment if "[t]he answer of the garnishee shows that he has *personal property* of any kind in his possession, or under his control, *belonging to the defendant. . .*" and "[i]f the answer shows that the garnishee *is indebted* to the defendant. * * *" [emphasis added]. It is well settled in this jurisdiction that garnishment is not available to reach debts that are not due and payable since the garnishee's liability is contingent.

Future earnings are contingent because they depend upon future performance. The employee cannot sue his employer for wages due before the employee has fulfilled his employment contract. At that stage, prospective earnings are hypothetical. Thus, future wages cannot be said to be an indebtedness which is due.

The Colorado garnishment statute does not allow continuing writs of garnishment against future wages. The plaintiff (judgment creditor) could not obtain a continuing writ of garnishment against the defendant's wages but had to secure a separate writ on the fifteenth and last days of each month in order to collect the debt owed.   **JUDGMENT AND REMEDY**

Both garnishment and attachment procedures are governed by state law. Both procedures require that the debtor's constitutional right to due process be scrupulously preserved.   **COMMENTS**

Further Garnishment Issues The court must always be sure that it is the debtor's property that is actually being taken in a garnishment or attachment proceeding. The following case illustrates that when garnishment is sought against property not owned by the debtor, the garnishment will be refused by the courts.

BACKGROUND AND FACTS *The plaintiff and the defendant were divorced. The defendant was delinquent in making child support payments, and the plaintiff obtained a judgment against him. The plaintiff then sought a writ of garnishment against funds deposited in a checking account held in the defendant's name. The defendant was successful in having the garnishment writ set aside by establishing in the lower court that the funds in the garnished account were not his but belonged to his second wife.*   **PETERSON v. PETERSON**
Supreme Court of Utah, 1977.
571 P.2d 1360.

WILKINGS, Justice.
*   *   *   *

At the hearing on defendant's motion to set aside the garnishment execution, the evidence demonstrated that the garnished account was held in defendant's name; that only his name was on the bank's signature card and, therefore, only he was authorized to write checks against the account. However, defendant had not worked for over a year, and the funds in the account were almost exclusively derived from the paychecks of defendant's present wife; and these checks were routinely endorsed to the defendant by her and deposited by him. During the course of the year, defendant did deposit some of his funds in the account, but they amounted to less than $1,000. The money in the account was used for defendant's child support payments to plaintiff, totaling $1,200, as well as for the general living expenses of defendant and his wife. The defendant and his wife each considered the money in the account to be the wife's money though the defendant withdrew for his personal obligations more than he contributed to the account. On the basis of these facts, the District Court found that none of the money belonged to the defendant and all of the funds remaining in the account belonged to defendant's wife, and were not subject to garnishment for the defendant's debts.

*   *   *   *

[The plaintiff insisted that her former husband had the burden of proof to show by clear and convincing evidence he had no ownership rights to the money in the checking account.]

Among the classes of cases to which this special standard of persuasion (clear and convincing proof) has been applied are the following: (1) charges of fraud, and undue influence, (2) suits on oral contracts to make a will, and suits to establish the terms of a lost will, (3) suits for the specific performance of an oral contract, (4) proceedings to set aside, reform or modify written transactions or official acts on grounds of fraud, mistake or incompleteness, and (5) miscellaneous types of claims and defenses, varying from state to state, where there is thought to be special danger of deception, or where the court considers that the particular type of claim should be disfavored on policy grounds.

We agree with plaintiff that persuasion by defendant of a clear and convincing nature is required in this matter, believing that there is a "special danger of deception" in cases such as this one but hold that the defendant sustained that burden and the evidence below was sufficient to support the Court's finding, especially in view of the fact that both defendant and his present wife testified that defendant had not been working and earning money for a year because of his medical problems and plaintiff presented no evidence to rebut that testimony.

JUDGMENT AND REMEDY   *The judgment was affirmed. The wrongful garnishment was correctly set aside by the lower court.*

Composition of Creditors' Agreements

As discussed in Chapter 8, creditors may contract with a debtor for discharge of the debtor's liquidated debts upon payment of a sum less than that owed. These agreements are called compositions or creditors' composition agreements and are usually held to be enforceable.

Secured Transactions—Article 9

Chapter 31 discussed in detail a secured party's

rights upon a debtor's default. One such right is the repossession of the collateral upon breach of the security agreement. Upon repossession, the secured party has the right to keep the collateral in full satisfaction of the debt (unless there is a purchase money security interest in consumer goods with 60 percent or more of the price paid or unless proper objection is received). Alternatively, the secured party may sell the collateral and use the proceeds to discharge the debt. If the proceeds are insufficient to cover the balance owed, the secured party is entitled to a deficiency judgment and can proceed with a writ of execution, as previously discussed. Therefore, either way, a debt resolution can be accomplished.

Assignment for Benefit of Creditors

Both common law and statutes may provide for a debtor's assignment of assets to a trustee or assignee for the benefit of the debtor's creditors. In these situations the debtor voluntarily transfers title to assets owned to a trustee or assignee, who in turn sells or liquidates these assets, tendering payment to the debtor's creditors on a pro rata basis.

The creditors have a choice of accepting or rejecting the tender. Those who accept it effectively discharge the debt owed to them. Those who do not accept it can proceed against any remaining nonexempt assets, or they may elect to petition the debtor into involuntary bankruptcy. This differs from a composition of creditors' arrangement in that there is no agreement made between the debtor and creditors as to the amount acceptable to discharge the debt.

Suretyship and Guaranty

When a third person promises to pay a debt owed by another in the event the debtor does not pay, a suretyship or guaranty relationship is created. The third person's credit becomes the security for the debt owed.

Surety　A contract of strict suretyship is a promise made by a third person to be responsible for the debtor's obligation. Suretyship is an express contract between the surety and the creditor. The surety in the strictest sense is *primarily* liable for the debt of the principal. The creditor can demand payment from the surety from the moment that the debt is due. A suretyship is not a form of indemnity; that is, it is not merely a promise to make good any loss that a creditor may incur as a result of the debtor's failure to pay. The creditor need not exhaust all legal remedies against the principal debtor before holding the surety responsible for payment.

A surety agreement does not have to be in writing to be enforceable but usually is.

Guaranty　A guaranty contract is similar to a suretyship in that it includes a promise to answer for the debt or default of another. With suretyship, however, the surety is primarily liable for the debtor's obligation of the principal. With a guaranty arrangement, the guarantor—the third person making the guaranty—is *secondarily liable*. The guarantor can be required to pay the obligation only after the debtor defaults, and then usually only after the creditor has made an attempt to collect from the principal debtor.

A guaranty contract between the guarantor and creditor must be in writing to be enforceable unless the "main purpose" exception applies. Briefly, this exception provides that if the main purpose of the guaranty agreement is to benefit the guarantor, then the contract need not be in writing to be enforceable. (See Chapter 12 for a more detailed discussion.)

The guaranty contract terms determine the extent and time of the guarantor's liability. For example, a guaranty can be *continuing*, designed to cover a series of transactions by the debtor. Also, the guaranty can be *unlimited* or *limited* as to time and amount. In addition, the guaranty can be *absolute*, wherein the guarantor becomes liable immediately upon the debtor's default, or *conditional*, wherein the guarantor becomes liable only upon the happening of a certain event.

The rights and defenses of the surety and guarantor are basically the same. Therefore, the following discussion applies to both.

Defenses of the Surety　A creditor must try to prevent certain actions that will release the surety from the obligation. Any material change made in the terms of the original contract between the principal debtor and the creditor, including the awarding of a binding extension of time for making payment without first obtaining the consent of the surety, will discharge the surety either completely or to the extent that the surety suffers a loss.

When a creditor discharges the principal debtor (or debtors), discharge of any one of them releases the surety from any obligation unless the surety agrees to the discharge. Naturally, if the principal obligation is paid by the debtor or by another person on behalf of the debtor, the surety is discharged from obligation. Similarly, if valid tender of payment is made, and the creditor for some reason rejects it with knowledge of the surety's existence, then the surety is released from any obligation on the debt.

Generally, any defenses available to a principal debtor can be used by the surety to avoid liability on the obligation to the creditor; the defenses that cannot be used are incapacity, bankruptcy, and the statute of limitations. The ability of the surety to assert any defenses the debtor may have against the creditor is the most important concept in suretyship, since most defenses available to the surety are those of the debtor.

Obviously, a surety may have his or her own defenses—for example, incapacity or bankruptcy. Another defense is when the creditor fraudulently induced the surety to guaranty the debt of the debtor. In most states, prior to formation of the suretyship contract, the creditor has a legal duty to inform the surety of material facts known by the creditor that would materially increase the surety's risk. Failure to so inform is fraud and makes the suretyship obligation voidable.

In addition, if a creditor surrenders or impairs the debtor's collateral while knowing of the surety and without the surety's consent, the surety is released to the extent that the surety would suffer a loss from the creditor's actions. The primary reason for this is to protect the surety who agreed to become obligated only because the debtor's collateral was in the possession of the creditor.

Rights of the Surety When the surety pays the debt owed to the creditor, the surety is entitled to certain rights. First, the surety has a legal **right of subrogation.** Simply stated, this means that any right the creditor had against the debtor now becomes the right of the surety. Included are creditor rights in bankruptcy, rights to collateral possessed by the creditor, and rights to judgments secured by the creditor. In short, the surety now stands in the shoes of the creditor.

Next, the surety has a **right of reimbursement** from the debtor. This right either stems from the suretyship contract or from equity. Basically, the surety is entitled to receive from the debtor all outlays the surety has made on behalf of the suretyship arrangement. This can include expenses incurred as well as the actual amount of the debt paid the creditor.

Third, if there are co-sureties (two or more sureties on the same obligation owed by the debtor), a surety who pays more than his or her proportionate share upon a debtor's default is entitled to recover from the co-sureties the amount paid above the surety's obligation. This is referred to as the surety's **right of contribution.** Generally, a co-surety's liability either is determined by agreement or, in absence of agreement, is set at the maximum liability under the suretyship contract.

For example, two co-sureties are obligated under a suretyship contract to guarantee the debt of a debtor. One surety's maximum liability is $15,000, and the other's is $10,000. The debtor owes $10,000 and is in default. The surety with the $15,000 maximum liability pays the creditor the entire $10,000. In the absence of other agreement, this surety can recover $4,000 from the other surety ($10,000/$25,000 $\times$ $10,000 = $4,000, this co-surety's obligation).

Mortgage Foreclosure on Real Property

A real estate mortgage agreement provides that when the **mortgagor** (debtor/borrower) *defaults* in making payment in accordance with the terms of the agreement, the **mortgagee** (creditor/lender) can declare that the entire mortgage debt is due immediately. The mortgagee/creditor can enforce payment in full by a legal action called **foreclosure.**

There are four statutory methods of foreclosure permitted in the United States:

1. Strict foreclosure—permitted in only a few states. Upon default and after a specified period, the mortgagee acquires absolute title to the property.

2. Entry or writ of entry—permitted in only a few states. Upon default, the mortgagee gets a writ entitling him or her to possession; after a specified statutory period, the mortgagee receives absolute title.
3. Power of sale—permitted in most states. Instead of following a statutory judicial sale of the property, the sale provisions are stated in the mortgage agreement.
4. Foreclosure sale—usual method (to be discussed). Statutory procedures must be followed to protect the rights of the mortgagor.

Foreclosure Sales   In this action, the real estate that is covered by the mortgage is sold at a judicial sale.[4] If the proceeds of the sale are sufficient to cover both the costs of the foreclosure and the mortgaged debt, any surplus is received by the debtor. If, on the other hand, the sale proceeds are insufficient to cover the foreclosure costs and the mortgaged debt, the mortgagee can seek to recover the difference from the mortgagor by obtaining a *deficiency judgment*. This type of judgment represents the "deficiency amount"—that is, the difference between the mortgaged debt and the amount actually received from the proceeds of the foreclosure sale. A deficiency judgment is obtained in a separate legal action that is pursued subsequent to the foreclosure action. It entitles the creditor to recover from other property owned by the debtor. However, only nonexempt property can be used to satisfy a deficiency judgment. A number of states (for example, California) do not allow a deficiency judgment for real estate.

From the time of default until the time of foreclosure sale, a mortgagor can redeem the property by paying the full amount of the debt, plus any interest and other costs that have accrued. This mortgagor's right is known as the **equity of redemption.** In some states, the mortgagor may even redeem within a statutory period after the judicial sale. This is called a **statutory period of redemption**, and the deed to the property is usually not delivered to the purchaser until the expiration of this period.

Bulk Sales—Article 6 of the UCC

As discussed in Chapter 19, a creditor may have certain rights when a seller-debtor sells a substantial portion of the assets of the business to a purchaser. This is referred to as a bulk sale or transfer—that is, one not normally made in the seller's ordinary course of business. Because a creditor's recovery against the debtor could be substantially diminished with the sale of bulk assets being transferred to an innocent purchaser, the Code treats such transfer as a potential fraud on creditors.

To avoid any possibility of fraud and protect the rights of the creditors and of the purchaser of the bulk goods, the UCC sets forth certain procedures for bulk transfers. Basically, the bulk seller is required to give the purchaser a sworn list of creditors, and the purchaser is obligated to give the seller's creditors notice of the pending sale at least ten days prior to payment or to the purchaser taking possession. Creditors who receive notice must act within that ten-day period or their claims are cut off by the sale to the purchaser. However, any creditor not receiving notice of the sale can take action against the debtor seller and levy against the goods so transferred to the purchaser for a period of up to six months. In this way, creditors' interests are protected in the bulk transfer of a debtor's business assets.

Fraudulent Conveyances

As also discussed in Chapter 19, any conveyance by a debtor through sale (or gift) to a third person that is expressly or impliedly *fraudulent* allows the creditor to set aside the transfer and proceed against the property (even if the property is in the possession of a third person).

There are two types of fraud: fraud in fact and fraud implied in law. Fraud in fact is the transfer of the property with the *intent* to defraud the creditor. Fraud implied in law occurs when the transfer is made in such a manner that a non-merchant transferor retains *possession* (and

---

4. This is true even if the property is the debtor's homestead. A mortgage is one debt that is *not* subject to the homestead statutory exemption that exempts the homestead from execution of any general debts of a householder or head of a family.

usually use) of the property. In the latter case fraud is presumed, but it can be rebutted.

PROTECTION OF THE DEBTOR

Exemptions

In most states, certain types of real and personal property are exempt from levy of execution or attachment. Probably the most familiar of these exemptions is the **homestead exemption.** Each state permits the debtor to retain the family home, either in its entirety or up to a specified dollar amount, free from unsecured creditors' or trustees' in bankruptcy claims. The purpose is to ensure that the debtor will retain some form of shelter.

For example, Daniels owes Carey $40,000. The debt is the subject of a lawsuit, and the court awards Carey a judgment of $40,000 against Daniels. The homestead of Daniels is valued at $50,000. To satisfy the judgment debt, Daniels's family home is sold at public auction for $45,000. Assume the homestead exemption is $25,000. The proceeds of the sale are distributed as follows:

1. Daniels is paid $25,000 as his homestead exemption.
2. Carey is paid $20,000 toward the judgment debt, leaving a $20,000 deficiency judgment (that is, "leftover debt") that can be satisfied (paid) from any other nonexempt property (personal or real) that Daniels may have, if allowed by state law.

In some states, statutes permit the homestead exemption only if the judgment debtor has a family. The policy behind this type of statute is to protect the family. If a judgment debtor does not have a family, a creditor may be entitled to collect the full amount realized from the sale of the debtor's home.

State exemption statutes usually include both real and personal property. Personal property that is most often exempt from satisfaction of judgment debts includes:

1. Household furniture up to a specified dollar amount.

2. Clothing and certain personal possessions, such as family pictures or a bible.
3. A vehicle (or vehicles) for transportation (at least up to a specified dollar amount).
4. Certain classified animals, usually livestock but including pets.

ADDITIONAL PROTECTION FOR THE CONSUMER DEBTOR

There are numerous *consumer* protection statutes and rules that apply to the debtor-creditor relationship. Most of these are discussed in detail in Chapter 48. A brief listing and discussion here will illustrate the breadth and importance of these consumer-oriented protection laws.

Consumer Credit Protection Act (CCPA)

This federal statute is commonly known as the Truth-in-Lending Act. It is basically a *disclosure law,* administered by the Federal Reserve Board, that requires sellers and lenders to disclose credit terms and loans so that a consumer-debtor can shop around for the best financing arrangements. Generally, the creditor must clearly indicate to the consumer-debtor what charges are being made for the privilege of paying the debt over a period of time, including what the total annual percentage rate is.

Uniform Consumer Credit Code (UCCC)

In an attempt to make consumer credit laws at the state level uniform, the National Conference of Commissioners on Uniform Laws proposed legislation called the Uniform Consumer Credit Code (UCCC).

The essential points of the UCCC are as follows:

1. To place statutory ceilings on interest rates and other charges.
2. To require disclosure similar to that required by the truth-in-lending law.
3. To limit garnishment actions against take-home wages to a certain amount and to prohibit

discharge of an employee solely because of garnishment proceedings.

4. To allow cancellation of a contract solicited by a seller in the consumer-debtor's home within three business days of the solicitation.

5. To limit the holder-in-due-course concept to acceptance of a check, rather than any other type of negotiable instrument, from the consumer-debtor.

6. To prohibit referral sales, which are sales in which a seller offers a rebate or discount to a buyer for furnishing the names of other prospective purchasers.

7. To provide criminal as well as civil penalties for violations.

Only a handful of states have adopted the UCCC even though it has undergone numerous drafts. Some other states have passed laws similar to some of the provisions of the UCCC, such as laws concerning the home solicitation sales.

Federal Trade Commission Rule—Holder in Due Course (HDC)

As part of the consumer protection movement, the FTC promulgated a rule that limited the rights of an HDC where the debtor buyer executes a negotiable promissory note as a part of a consumer transaction. As stated in Chapter 27, the rule provides basically that any personal defenses the buyer could assert against the seller can also be asserted against an HDC. The seller must disclose this rule clearly on the sales agreement.

This rule basically eliminates the use of a buyer's waiver of defense clause in a consumer transaction. These clauses in security agreements, otherwise permitted under UCC 9-206, waive any claim or defense the debtor might have against a good faith assignee for value of a security interest.

For example, a buyer purchases a refrigerator for home use from a seller by a retail installment security agreement and negotiable promissory note. In the agreement and note is a clause that prohibits the buyer from asserting against a good faith assignee for value any defense available against the seller. The seller sells the security interest installment agreement to a financial institution. One month later, the refrigerator stops working because of a defect. The buyer wants to return the refrigerator, rescind the contract and receive a refund. The seller refuses. The buyer stops making payments. Under UCC 9-206, the financial institution could enforce the payment agreement, as the buyer by waiver could not assert the breach of warranty defense against the assignee. Under the FTC Rule, however, which supersedes state law, the financial institution is subject to the same defense the buyer has against the seller.

QUESTIONS AND CASE PROBLEMS

1. Sylvia takes her car to the Crank's Auto Repair Shop. A sign in the window states that all repairs must be paid for in cash unless credit is approved in advance. Sylvia and Crank agree that Crank will repair Sylvia's car engine and put in a new transmission. No mention is made of credit. Because Crank is not sure how much engine repair will be necessary, he refuses to give Sylvia an estimate. He repairs the engine and puts in a new transmission. When Sylvia comes to pick up her car, she learns that the bill is $795. Sylvia is furious, refuses to pay Crank that amount, and demands possession of her car. Crank demands payment. Discuss the rights of the parties in this matter.

2. James is employed by the Cross-Bar Packing Corporation and earns take-home pay of $400 per week. He is $2,000 in debt to the Holiday Department Store for goods purchased on credit over the past eight months. Most of this property is nonexempt and is presently located in James's apartment. James is in default on his payments to Holiday. Holiday learns that James has a girlfriend in another state and that he plans on giving her most of this property for Christmas. Discuss what actions are available and should be taken by Holiday to resolve the debt owed by James.

3. Ann is a student at Slippery Stone University. In need of funds to pay tuition and books, she attempts to secure a short-term loan from West Bank. The bank agrees to make a loan if Ann will have someone financially responsible guarantee the loan payments. Sheila, a well-known businesswoman and a friend of

Ann's family, calls the bank and agrees to pay the loan if Ann cannot. Because of Sheila's reputation, the loan is made. Ann is making the payments, but because of illness she is not able to work for one month. She requests that West Bank extend the loan for three months. West Bank agrees, raising the interest rate for the extended period. Sheila has not been notified of the extension (and therefore has not consented to it). One month later Ann drops out of school. All attempts to collect from Ann have failed. West Bank wants to hold Sheila liable. Discuss West Bank's claim against Sheila.

4. Smith is the owner of a relatively old home valued at $45,000. He notices that the bathtubs and fixtures in both bathrooms are leaking and will need to be replaced. He contracts with Plumber to replace the bathtubs and fixtures. Plumber replaces them, and on June 1 she submits her bill of $4,000 to Smith. Because of financial difficulties, Smith does not pay the bill. Smith's only asset is his home, which, under state law, is exempt up to $40,000 as a homestead. Discuss fully Plumber's remedies in this situation.

5. Kloster-Madsen, Inc., a general contractor, entered into a contract with the owner of a building to do certain remodeling work. About a month later, pursuant to the contract, an electrical subcontractor proceeded to remove several light fixtures from one of the ceilings, cutting four holes in the ceiling and placing the removed light fixtures in the holes. Immediately after this work was begun, a new owner, Tafi's, Inc., purchased the building. Several thousand dollars' worth of material and labor was expended before Tafi's informed the general contractor that it did not wish to have the building remodeled. Can Koster-Madsen impose a mechanic's lien on the building even though the building contract was entered into with a different owner? [Kloster-Madsen, Inc. v. Tafi's, Inc., 303 Minn. 59, 226 N.W.2d 603 (1975)]

6. Jackson, the owner of a trailer with a refrigeration unit, brought the trailer to North Broadway Service Station for repairs. When the service station owner finished the repairs, Jackson was unable to pay. He pleaded with the owner to permit him to use the trailer to enable him to earn the money necessary to pay the repair bill. The owner kindheartedly returned the trailer to Jackson. Shortly thereafter, the trailer was repossessed by the Trailer Refrigeration Company, which held a mortgage on the trailer on which Jackson had defaulted. The service station owner then attempted to enforce an artisan's lien against the trailer, claiming

priority over Trailer Refrigeration Company's mortgage. Will he succeed? What if the owner of the service station had obtained a written memorandum from Jackson at the time he released the trailer to him, stating that he retained an artisan's lien on the trailer and was releasing it only to enable Jackson to earn the money to pay the repair bill? Would the results be different? [Jackson v. Kusmer, 411 S.W.2d 257 (Mo. App.1967)]

7. One of the ways in which a plaintiff can collect a money judgment from a defendant is by garnishing a debt that is due from a garnishee to the defendant. Garnishment is allowed only where the debt due from the garnishee is unconditional. With this in mind, discuss the following situation. Cummings Company sued C & E Excavating Company. C & E had a contract with Volpe Construction Company to do certain excavating work for Volpe. Can Cummings garnish the money owed under this contract? What must be known about the contract in order to answer this question? [Cummings General Tire Co. v. Volpe Constr. Co., 230 A.2d 712 (D.C.App.1967)]

8. Asher entered into a contract with Herman for the sale of land. The contract provided that in the event the vendors were unable to convey title, the vendors' sole liability would be to refund the purchaser's deposit. Subsequently, the contract fell through, but the escrow agent, who was holding the deposit made by the purchaser, embezzled the money. Under rules of escrow, the loss fell on the purchasers since it was their money. Can the purchasers argue that under the provision in the contract mentioned above the vendors could be deemed guarantors of the deposit money? Explain. [Asher v. Herman, 49 Misc.2d 475, 267 N.Y.S.2d 932 (1966)]

9. John Shumate parked his car in a vacant lot where he had left it several times previously. When he returned, he was informed that the car had been towed at the property owner's request. Thomas Younger had a collision with another car. His car was towed from the scene of the accident at the request of the police while Younger was discussing his accident with the police. The towing companies informed both car owners that they must pay towing and storage charges before their autos would be returned. The car owners sued to challenge this claim of a possessory lien asserted by the towing companies. Could the owners be prevented from removing their cars until payment was made? [Younger v. Plunkett, 395 F.Supp. 702 (E.D.Pa.1975)]

CHAPTER 33

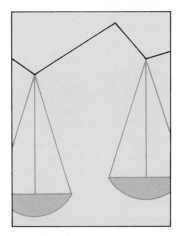

Bankruptcy and Reorganization

The U.S. Constitution, Article I, Section 8, provides that "The Congress shall have the power * * * to establish * * * uniform laws on the subject of bankruptcies throughout the United States." Bankruptcy proceedings are therefore rooted in federal laws; bankruptcy courts are special federal courts; and bankruptcy judges are federally appointed.

The original Bankruptcy Act was enacted in 1898 and was amended by the 1938 Chandler Act. A major overhaul of the federal bankruptcy law occurred in 1978 with the passage of the Bankruptcy Reform Act of 1978. The Bankruptcy Reform Act became effective on October 1, 1979, and governs all bankruptcy proceedings filed after that date.

GOALS OF BANKRUPTCY

Bankruptcy law is designed to accomplish two main goals. The first is to provide relief and protection to debtors who have "gotten in over their heads." The second major goal of bankruptcy is to provide a fair means of distributing a debtor's assets among all creditors.

Although the Bankruptcy Act is a federal law, state laws on secured transactions, liens, judgments, and exemptions also play a role in a federal bankruptcy proceeding.

THE BANKRUPTCY REFORM ACT OF 1978

The Bankruptcy Reform Act of 1978 (hereinafter the Code) is contained in Title 11 of the United States Code and has eight odd-numbered chapters. Chapters 1, 3, and 5 include general definitional provisions and provisions governing case administration, creditors, the debtor,[1] and the

---

1. It is noteworthy that the term *bankrupt* no longer exists under the Code. Those who were formerly *bankrupts* under the old Bankruptcy Act are now merely *debtors* under the Code.

estate. These three chapters apply generally to all kinds of bankruptcies. The next four chapters set forth the different types of bankruptcy relief that debtors or creditors may seek. Chapter 7 provides for liquidations. Chapter 9 governs the adjustment of debts of a municipality. Chapter 11 governs reorganizations and Chapter 13 provides for the adjustment of debts of individuals with regular income. The last chapter, Chapter 15, sets up a pilot United States trustee system.

The following sections deal with Chapter 7 liquidations, Chapter 11 reorganizations and Chapter 13 plans. The latter two chapters have been referred to as "rehabilitation" chapters.

CHAPTER 7
LIQUIDATIONS

This is the most familiar type of bankruptcy proceeding and is often referred to as an ordinary or "straight" bankruptcy. Put simply, a debtor in a straight bankruptcy states his debts and turns his assets over to a trustee. The trustee sells the assets and distributes the proceeds to creditors. With certain exceptions, the balance of the debts is then discharged (extinguished) and the debtor is relieved from his obligation to pay the debts. Any "person"—defined as including individuals, partnerships and corporations[2]—may be a debtor under Chapter 7. Railroads, insurance companies, banks, savings and loan associations, and credit unions cannot be Chapter 7 debtors. Other chapters of the Code, or federal or state statutes, apply to them.

Filing the Petition

A straight bankruptcy may be commenced by the filing of either a voluntary or involuntary petition.

Voluntary Bankruptcy A voluntary petition is brought by the debtor, who files official forms designated for that purpose in the bankruptcy court. Anyone who is liable on a claim held by

a creditor can do this. The debtor does not even have to be insolvent to file a petition. The voluntary petition contains the following schedules:

1. A list of both secured and unsecured creditors, their addresses, and the amount of debt owed to each.
2. A statement of the financial affairs of the debtor.
3. A list of all property owned by the debtor, including property claimed by the debtor to be exempt.

The official forms must be completed accurately, sworn to under oath, and signed by the debtor. To conceal assets or knowingly supply false information on these schedules is a crime under the bankruptcy laws. If the voluntary petition for bankruptcy is found to be proper, the filing of the petition will itself constitute an *order for relief*.

A new feature allows a husband and wife to file jointly for bankruptcy under a single petition. As mentioned previously, debtors do not have to be insolvent (debts exceed fair market value of assets exclusive of exempt property) to file for voluntary bankruptcy.

Involuntary Bankruptcy An involuntary bankruptcy occurs when the debtor's creditors force the debtor into bankruptcy proceedings. An involuntary case cannot be commenced against a farmer[3] or a charitable institution. For an involuntary case to be filed against other debtors, the following requirements must be met. If the debtor has twelve or more creditors, three or more of these creditors having unsecured claims aggregating at least $5,000 must join in the petition. If a debtor has fewer than twelve creditors, one or more creditors having a claim of $5,000 may file.

---

2. The definition of a *corporation* includes unincorporated companies and associations. It also covers labor unions.

3. The definition of *farmer* includes persons who receive more than 80 percent of their gross income from farming operations, such as tilling the soil, dairy farming, ranching, or the production or raising of crops, poultry or livestock. Corporations and partnerships can be *farmers*.

If the debtor challenges the involuntary petition, a trial will be held and the bankruptcy court will enter an *order for relief* if it finds that:

1.   The debtor is generally not paying debts as they become due.[4]

2.   A custodian was appointed or took possession of a portion of the debtor's property within 120 days before the filing of the petition for the purpose of enforcing a lien against such property.

If the court grants an order for relief, the debtor will be required to supply the information in the bankruptcy schedules discussed above.

An involuntary petition should not be used as an everyday debt collection device, and the Code provides penalties for the filing of frivolous petitions against debtors. Judgment may be granted against the petitioning creditors for the costs and attorneys' fees incurred by the debtor in defending against an involuntary petition that is dismissed by the court. If the petition is filed in bad faith, damages can be awarded for injury to the debtor's reputation. Punitive damages may also be awarded.

Automatic Stay

The filing of a petition, either voluntary or involuntary, operates as an automatic stay or suspension of virtually all litigation and other action by creditors against the debtor or the debtor's property. In other words, once a petition is filed, creditors cannot commence or continue most legal actions against the debtor to recover claims they have against him or her. Nor can creditors take any action to repossess property in the hands of the debtor. However, a secured creditor may petition the bankruptcy court for relief from the automatic stay in certain circumstances.

Underlying the Code's automatic stay provision for a secured creditor is a concept known as *adequate protection*. The adequate protection doctrine, among other things, protects secured creditors from losing their security as a result of the automatic stay. The bankruptcy court can provide adequate protection by requiring the debtor to make periodic cash payments (or provide additional collateral or replacement liens) to the extent that the stay causes the value of the property involved to decrease. Or the court may grant other relief that is the "indubitable equivalent" of the secured party's interest in the property, such as a guaranty by a solvent third party to cover losses suffered by the secured party as a result of the stay.

For example, suppose Speedy Express, a delivery service, owns three delivery trucks in which First Bank has a security interest. Speedy Express has failed to make its monthly payments for two months. Speedy Express files a petition in bankruptcy, and the automatic stay prevents First Bank from repossessing the trucks. Meanwhile, the trucks (whose collective value is already less than the balance due) are depreciating at a rate of several hundred dollars a month. First Bank's inability to repossess and immediately resell the delivery trucks is harming First Bank to the extent of several hundred dollars per month. The bankruptcy court may prevent First Bank from being harmed by requiring Speedy Express to at least make cash payments (or provide additional collateral or replacement liens) to the extent that the delivery trucks are depreciating in value. If the debtor is unable to provide adequate protection, the court may vacate the stay and allow First Bank to repossess the trucks.

The Trustee

Promptly after the order for relief has been entered, an interim or provisional trustee is appointed to preside over the debtor's property until the first meeting of creditors. At this first meeting, either a permanent trustee is elected or the interim trustee becomes the permanent trustee. The trustee's principal duty is to collect and reduce to money the "property of the estate"

---

4.   The inability to pay debts as they become due is known as *equitable* insolvency. A *balance sheet* insolvency, which exists when a debtor's liabilities exceed assets, is not the test. Thus, it is possible for debtors to be thrown into involuntary bankruptcy even though their assets far exceed their liabilities. This may occur when a debtor's cash flow problems become severe.

for which he serves, and to close up the estate as expeditiously as is compatible with the best interests of the parties. Trustees are entitled to compensation for services rendered plus reimbursement for expenses.

Creditors' Meeting

Within a reasonable time after the order of relief is granted (currently not less than ten days or more than thirty days) the bankruptcy court must call a meeting of creditors listed in the schedules filed by the debtor. The bankruptcy judge does not attend or preside at this meeting.

Generally, at this meeting a permanent trustee is elected (by 20 percent or more of the unsecured creditors with fixed claims), and the interim trustee's duties are discharged or, more typically, in the absence of election the interim trustee becomes the permanent trustee. The debtor is required to attend this meeting (unless excused by the court) and to submit to examination under oath by the creditors and the trustee. Failure to appear when required or false statements made under oath may result in the debtor being denied a discharge of bankruptcy.

Proof of claims by creditors must normally be filed within six months of this meeting. (The Code merely calls for "timely filing," without specifying the length of time.)

Property of the Estate

Upon commencement of a Chapter 7 proceeding, an *estate in property* is created. The estate consists of all the debtor's legal and equitable interests in property presently held, wherever located, together with community property, property transferred in a transaction voidable by the trustee, proceeds and profits from the property of the estate, and certain after-acquired property. Interests in certain property such as gifts, inheritances, property settlements (divorce), or life insurance death proceeds to which the debtor becomes entitled within 180 days after filing may also become part of the estate. Thus, the filing of a bankruptcy petition generally fixes a dividing line: property acquired prior to the petition becomes property of the estate and property acquired after the filing of the petition, except as just noted, remains the debtor's.

Exemptions

An individual debtor is entitled to exempt certain property from the property of the estate. Prior to the enactment of the Code, state law exclusively governed the extent of the exemptions. See Chapter 32 for discussion. However, the Code establishes a federal exemption scheme. An individual debtor now has the option of choosing between the exemptions provided under the applicable state law and the federal exemptions.[5] The Code exempts the following property:

1.   Up to $7,500 in equity in the debtor's residence and burial plot.
2.   Interest in a motor vehicle up to $1,200.
3.   Interest, up to $200 for *any* particular item, in household goods and furnishings, wearing apparel, appliances, books, animals, crops or musical instruments (unlimited in aggregate amount).
4.   Interest in jewelry up to $500.
5.   Any other property worth up to $400, plus any unused part of the $7,500 homestead exemption.
6.   Up to $750 interest in any tools of the debtor's trade.
7.   Any unmatured life insurance contract owned by the debtor.
8.   Certain interests in accrued dividends or interest under life insurance contracts owned by the debtor.
9.   Professionally prescribed health aids.
10.   Debtor's right to receive social security and certain welfare benefits, alimony and support, and certain pension benefits.
11.   Debtor's right to receive certain personal injury and other awards.

Trustee's Powers

The basic duty of the trustee is to collect the debtor's available estate and reduce it to money

---

5.   Individual states are given the power to pass legislation precluding the use of the federal exemptions by debtors in their states. At least seventeen states have passed such legislation. In these states, only state exemptions are available.

for distribution, preserving the interests of both the debtor and unsecured creditors. This requires that the trustee be accountable for administering the debtor's estate. To enable the trustee to accomplish this duty, the Code gives the trustee certain powers, stated in both general and specific terms.

General powers are vouchsafed by the statement that the trustee occupies a position *equivalent* in rights to that of other parties. For example, the trustee has the same rights as a *lien creditor* on a simple contract who could have obtained a judicial lien on the debtor's property or who could have levied execution on the debtor's property. This means that a trustee has priority over an unperfected secured party to the debtor's property. A trustee also has power equivalent to that of a *bona fide purchaser* of real property from the debtor. Thus, the trustee would prevail in priority over a secured party's *unperfected* fixture security interest.

In addition, the trustee has specific powers of avoidance. These powers include any voidable rights available to the debtor, preferences, certain statutory liens, and fraudulent transfers by the debtor. Each will be discussed in more detail in this chapter.

With these powers, persons holding the debtor's property at the time the petition is filed are required to deliver the property to the trustee.

Voidable Rights   A trustee steps into the shoes of the debtor. Thus, any reason that a debtor can use to obtain return of his or her property can be used by the trustee as well. These grounds include fraud, duress, incapacity, and mutual mistake.

For example, Ben sells his boat to Frank. Frank gives Ben a check, knowing that there are insufficient funds in the bank account to cover the check. Frank has committed fraud. Ben has the right to avoid that transfer and recover the boat from Frank. Once an order for relief has been entered for Ben, the trustee can exercise the same right to recover the boat from Frank.

Preferences   A debtor should not be permitted to transfer property or make a payment that favors one creditor over others. Thus, the trustee is allowed to recover payments made both voluntarily and involuntarily to one creditor in preference to another.

To constitute a preference that can be recovered, an *insolvent* debtor *generally* must have transferred property, for a *preexisting* debt, within *ninety days* of the filing of the petition in bankruptcy. The transfer must give the creditor more than would have been received if the case were a Chapter 7 liquidation proceeding. The trustee does not have to prove insolvency, as the Code provides that the debtor is presumed to be insolvent during this ninety-day period. Sometimes the creditor receiving the preference is an "insider." An insider is an individual, partner, partnership, officer or director of a corporation (or relative of these) who has a close relationship with the debtor. If such is the case, the avoidance power of the trustee is extended to transfer preferences made within *one year* before the petition is filed; however, the *presumption* of insolvency is confined to the ninety-day period. Therefore, the trustee must prove that the debtor was insolvent at the time of earlier transfer.

Not all transfers and conveyances are preferences. To be a preference, the transfer must be made for something other than current consideration. Therefore, it is generally assumed by most courts that payment for services rendered within ten to fifteen days prior to the payment of the current consideration is not a preference. If a creditor receives payment in the ordinary course of business, such as payment of last month's telephone bill, the payment cannot be recovered by the trustee in bankruptcy. To be recoverable, a preference must be a transfer for an antecedent debt, such as a year-old telephone bill.

If a preferred creditor has sold the property to an innocent third party, the property cannot be recovered from the innocent party, but in such circumstances the creditor generally can be held accountable for the value of the property.

Liens on Debtor's Property   The trustee is permitted to avoid the fixing of certain statutory liens, such as a landlord's lien on property of the debtor. Liens that first become effective on the bankruptcy or insolvency of the debtor are voidable by the trustee. Liens that are not perfected or enforceable on the date of the petition against a bona fide purchaser are voidable.

Fraudulent Transfers The trustee may avoid fraudulent transfers or obligations if made within one year of the filing of the petition and/or if made with actual intent to hinder, delay, or defraud a creditor. Transfers made for less than a reasonable equivalent consideration are also vulnerable if the debtor thereby became insolvent, was engaged in business with an unreasonably small capital, or intended to incur debts that would be beyond his or her ability to pay.

The debtor shares most of the trustee's avoiding powers. Thus, if the trustee does not take action to enforce one of his or her rights (for example, to recover a preference), the debtor in a Chapter 7 bankruptcy would nevertheless be able to enforce that right.[6]

Claims of Creditors

Generally, any legal obligation of the debtor is a claim. In the case of disputed or unliquidated claims, the bankruptcy court will estimate the value of the claim. Any creditor holding a debtor's obligation can file a claim against the debtor's estate.

These claims are automatically allowed unless contested by the trustee, debtor, or another creditor. However, the Code does not allow claims for breach of employment contracts or real estate leases for terms longer than one year. Such claims are limited to one year's rent or wages, despite the remaining length of either contract in breach. Therefore, an employee who has a three-year employment contract that is breached during the first year by the employer's bankruptcy would be limited to damages accruing during one year from the filing of the petition, or the date the employment contract was repudiated, whichever is earlier.

Distribution of Property

Creditors are either *secured* or *unsecured*. (The rights of secured creditors were discussed in

Chapter 31.) Basically, a secured creditor has a security interest in collateral that secures the debt. The secured creditor can enforce the security interest either by accepting the property in full satisfaction of the debt or by foreclosing on the collateral and using the proceeds to pay off the debt. In this way, the secured party has priority over unsecured parties to the proceeds from the disposition of the secured collateral. Indeed, the Code provides that if the value of the secured collateral exceeds the secured party's claim, the secured party also has priority to the proceeds in an amount that will cover reasonable fees and costs incurred because of the debtor's default. Any excess over this amount is used by the trustee to satisfy the claims of unsecured creditors. Should the secured collateral be insufficient to cover the secured debt owed, the "secured" creditor becomes an unsecured creditor for the difference.

Bankruptcy law establishes an order or priority for classes of debts owed to *unsecured creditors*, and they are paid in the order of their priority. Each class of debt must be fully paid before the next class is entitled to any of the proceeds—if there are sufficient funds to pay the entire class. If not, the proceeds are distributed *proportionately* to each creditor in a class, and all classes lower in priority on the list receive nothing. The order of priority among classes of unsecured creditors is as follows:

1.   All costs and expenses for preserving and administering the estate, including such items as court costs and trustee and attorney fees and costs incurred by the trustee during the administration of the estate, such as rental fees and appraisal fees.
2.   Unsecured claims in an involuntary proceeding arising in the ordinary course of the debtor's business after commencement of the case but before the appointment of a trustee or issuance of an order for relief.
3.   Claims for wages, salaries and commissions up to an amount of $2,000 per claimant, provided that they were earned within ninety days of the filing of the petition in bankruptcy. Any claims in excess of $2,000 are treated as the "claims of general creditors" (listed as number 7 below).

---

6.   In a rehabilitation proceeding—Chapter 11 or Chapter 13, to be discussed later—where no trustee generally exists, the debtor has the same avoiding powers as a trustee under Chapter 7.

4. Unsecured claims for contributions to employee benefit plans arising under services rendered within 180 days before filing the petition and limited to the number of employees covered by the plan multiplied by $2,000.

5. Unsecured claims for money deposited (up to $900) with the debtor before the filing of the petition in connection with the purchase, lease or rental of property or services that were not delivered or provided.

6. Certain taxes and penalties legally due and owing various governmental units (rules vary depending on type of tax owed).

7. Claims of general creditors. These debts have the lowest priority and are paid on a pro rata basis if, and only if, funds remain after all the debts having priority are paid in full.

8. Any remaining balance is returned to the debtor.

Discharge

From the debtor's point of view, the primary purpose of a Chapter 7 liquidation is to obtain a fresh start through the discharge of debts.[7] How-

---

7. Discharges are granted only to "individuals" who are debtors under Chapter 7, not corporations or partnerships. The latter may use Chapter 11, or they may liquidate under state law.

ever, there are circumstances in which a claim will not be discharged.

Exceptions to Discharge A debt may not be discharged because of the nature of the claim or the conduct of the debtor. Claims that are not dischargeable include:

1. Claims for back taxes accruing within three years prior to bankruptcy.

2. Claims against property or money obtained by the debtor under false pretenses or by false representations.

3. Unscheduled claims.

4. Claims based on fraud or misuse of funds while the debtor was acting in a fiduciary capacity, or claims involving the debtor's embezzlement or larceny.

5. Alimony and child support.

6. Claims based on willful or malicious injury by the debtor to another or to the property of another.

7. Certain fines and penalties payable to governmental units.

8. Certain student loans.

In the following case, the question of a student loan is at issue.

BACKGROUND AND FACTS *The facts of this case are stated by the court.*

BAKER v. UNIVERSITY OF TENNESSEE AT CHATTANOOGA (IN RE BAKER)

United States Bankruptcy Court, E.D. Tennessee, 1981. 10 B.R. 870.

KELLEY, Bankruptcy Judge.

This cause came on to be heard on May 5, 1981 on debtor's complaint to determine dischargeability of certain educational loans. The complaint alleges that debtor is entitled to relief under 11 U.S.C. 523(a)(8) which reads as follows:

Exceptions to discharge.

(a) A discharge under section 727, 1141, or 1328(b) of this title does not discharge an individual debtor from any debt—

* * * *

(8) to a governmental unit, or a nonprofit institution of higher education, for an educational loan, unless—

(B) excepting such debt from discharge under this paragraph will impose an undue hardship on the debtor and the debtor's dependents;

    *   *   *   *

In her trial memorandum the debtor states:

Plaintiff will show that it would be an undue hardship on her to repay the loans. She will show that the student loans would require payments which she will not be able to make. She will show that without consideration of the student loans, her expenses are several hundred dollars in excess of her monthly income. She will show that she has had to get financial aid from her church and from relatives to meet her monthly expenses.

She would further show that her husband has left town and she is not receiving regular financial aid from him. She would further show that she has been unable to locate his whereabouts, even though governmental institutions have also attempted to help find him.

    *   *   *   *

From the record in this cause it appears that debtor has three educational loans in the amounts indicated:

University of Tennessee at Chattanooga	$ 600.00
Cleveland State Community College	2,335.00
Baroness Erlanger School of Nursing	3,700.00
Total	$6,635.00

From the proof the court finds that debtor is employed and has take home pay of less than $650.00 a month. She has monthly expenses of $925.00 for herself and three children. She receives no child support. She receives no public support. She has no other income.

The debtor prepared a list of her monthly expenses:

Expenses

Housenote		$197.00
Utilities		
Electricity	$71.00	
H_2O	25.00	
Heat	70.00	
Telephone	15.00	
Total		$181.00
Food		$225.00
Clothing		$ 30.00
Laundry & Cleaning		$ 15.00
Books . . . folders, paper, school supplies . . .		$ 8.00
Doctor & Rx Expense		$ 20.00

Recreation (Children only)	$ 45.00
Transportation	$150.00
Insurance (Life Ins.)	$ 14.90
Church	$ 40.00
Total	$925.90
Take Home Pay	$650.00

After carefully listening to direct and cross examination the court finds no irregularities regarding the monthly expenses. Debtor could possibly reduce expenses some, but the court finds that debtor's reasonable expenses each month far exceed her income.

In January 1981 debtor's church paid $306.00 to the Chattanooga Gas Company so that debtor and her children could have heat in their home. Debtor has not been well. She has not been able to pay all of her medical bills. Debtor used 200 hours sick leave last year. One child has a reading difficulty. Another requires special shoes which are expensive.

In 1976 the Congress passed the Educational Amendments which restricted a discharge in bankruptcy. The restriction was designed to remedy an abuse by students who, immediately upon graduation, would file bankruptcy to secure a discharge of educational loans. These students often had no other indebtedness and could easily pay their debts from future wages. See: *Discharging Student Loans In Bankruptcy*, 52 Am.Bkcy.L.J. 201.

[2] In the present case the debtor did not file bankruptcy to secure a discharge only from her educational loans. Her petition shows that she had been sued and her wages were subject to garnishment. This situation often triggers bankruptcy. The debtor's present income is not sufficient to maintain her and her three children.

As noted in 3 *Collier on Bankruptcy*, 15th edition, at paragraph 523.18:

> Paragraph (B) of subdivision (a)(8) is the "hardship" provision that permits the court to discharge a student loan otherwise nondischargeable, if excepting the debt from discharge will impose an undue hardship on the debtor or the debtor's dependents. This exemption from the exception to discharge is discretionary with the bankruptcy judge who will have to determine whether payment of the debt will cause undue hardship on the debtor and his dependents thus defeating the "fresh start" concept of the bankruptcy laws. There may well be circumstances that justify failure to repay a student loan such as illness, incapacity or other extenuating circumstances. Where the court finds that such circumstances exist, it may order the debt discharged.

The court concludes that under the circumstances of this case, that requiring the debtor to repay the debts owed to the *three* defendants in the amount of $6,635.00 plus interest would impose upon her and her dependents an undue hardship. In passing the Educational Amendments of 1976 and including these amendments in the Bankruptcy Reform Act of 1978, Congress intended to correct an abuse. It did not intend to deprive those who have truly fallen on hard times of the "fresh start" policy of the new Bankruptcy Code.

The debtor's student loans were discharged.   **JUDGMENT AND REMEDY**

COMMENT   *The Code makes it appear that student loans are not dischargeable. But the preceding case tells us that in hardship situations equity can step in to alter this rule.*

Objections to Discharge   In addition to the exceptions to discharge previously listed, there are other circumstances that will cause a discharge to be denied. When a discharge is denied, the assets of the debtor are still distributed to the creditors, but the debtor remains liable for the unpaid portions of all claims. Some grounds for the denial of discharge include:

1. Debtor's concealment or destruction of property with the intent to hinder or delay or defraud a creditor.
2. Debtor's fraudulent concealment or destruction of records of his financial condition.
3. Debtor's refusal to obey a lawful order of a bankruptcy court.
4. Debtor's failure to satisfactorily explain the loss of assets.
5. Grant of a discharge to debtor within six years of the filing of the petition.[8]
6. Debtor's written waiver of discharge approved by the court.

Effect of Discharge   The primary effect of a discharge is to void any judgment on a discharged debt and enjoin any action to collect a discharged debt. A discharge does not affect the liability of a co-debtor.

Revocation of Discharge   The Code provides that a debtor may lose his or her bankruptcy discharge by revocation. The bankruptcy court may within one year revoke the discharge decree if it is discovered that the debtor was fraudulent or dishonest during the bankruptcy proceedings. The revocation renders the discharge null and void, allowing creditors not satisfied by the dis-

tribution of the debtor's estate to proceed with their claims against the debtor.

Reaffirmation of Debt   A debtor may voluntarily wish to pay off a discharged debt. This is called a reaffirmation of the debt. Prior to the new Code, reaffirmations were binding without consideration, although many states required them to be in writing to be enforceable.

The new Code severely restricts the making of enforceable reaffirmations. Basically, to be enforceable, reaffirmation agreements must be made before a debtor is granted a discharge, and a hearing must be conducted wherein the debtor is informed of the consequences of such action. In addition, if the reaffirmation is for a consumer debt, court approval is generally required. Furthermore, the debtor has a right to rescind the reaffirmation within *thirty* days after it is made.

CHAPTER 11
REORGANIZATIONS

The type of bankruptcy proceeding used most commonly by a corporate debtor is a Chapter 11 reorganization. Essentially, in a reorganization the creditors and the debtor formulate a plan under which the debtor pays a portion of his or her debts and is discharged of the remainder. The debtor is allowed to continue in business. Although this type of bankruptcy is commonly a corporate reorganization, any debtor who is eligible for Chapter 7 relief is eligible for Chapter 11 relief. In addition, railroads are also eligible for Chapter 11 relief.

The same principles that govern the filing of a Chapter 7 petition apply to Chapter 11 proceedings. The case may be brought either voluntarily or involuntarily. The same principles govern the entry of the order for relief. The automatic stay and adequate protection provisions previously discussed are applicable in reorganizations.

---

8.   A discharge under Chapter 13 of the Code within six years of the filing of the petition does not bar a subsequent Chapter 7 discharge where a good faith Chapter 13 plan paid at least 70 percent of all allowed unsecured claims.

Debtor-in-Possession

Upon entry of the order for relief, the debtor generally continues to operate his or her business as a *debtor-in-possession*. However, the court may appoint a trustee to operate the debtor's business if gross mismanagement of the business is shown or if it is in the best interests of the estate. As soon as practicable after entry of the order for relief, a creditors' committee of unsecured creditors is appointed. The committee may consult with the trustee or the debtor-in-possession concerning the administration of the case or the formulation of the plan.

Creditors' Committees

Additional creditors' committees may be appointed to represent special interest creditors. The creditors' committee is, in a sense, a party in interest in the proceedings. Orders affecting the estate generally will not be entered without either the consent of the committee or after a hearing in which the judge hears the position of the creditors' committee.

The Plan

Filing the Plan Only the debtor may file a plan within the first 120 days after the date of the order for relief. However, if the debtor does not meet the 120 day deadline, or if the debtor fails to obtain the required creditor consent within 180 days, any party may propose a plan.

Contents of the Plan A Chapter 11 plan must be "fair and equitable" and must:

1. Designate classes of claims and interests under the plan.
2. Specify the treatment to be afforded the classes. The plan must provide the same treatment for each claim in a particular class.
3. Provide an adequate means for the plan's execution.

Acceptance of the Plan Once the plan has been developed, it is submitted to each class of creditors for acceptance. Acceptance of a plan is re-

quired by each class unless the class is impaired. [11 U.S.C.A. § 1129(8)] A class of claims has accepted the plan when a majority of the number of creditors, representing two-thirds of the amount of the total claim, vote to approve the plan.

Confirmation of the Plan The plan must be "in the best interests of the creditors." Even when all classes of claims accept the plan, the court may refuse to confirm it if it fails to meet this requirement. Also, even if only one class of claims has accepted the plan, the court may still confirm it under the Code's so-called "cram down" provision. The plan is binding upon confirmation. Upon confirmation, the debtor is given a Chapter 11 discharge from all claims not protected under the plan. However, this discharge does not apply to any claims denied discharge under Chapter 7 (as previously discussed).

CHAPTER 13 PLANS

The former Bankruptcy Act provided for the formulation of "wage earner" plans as a means of allowing wage earners to pay off their debts free from the harassment of creditors. Under these plans, the wage earner avoided the stigma of being adjudicated a "bankrupt." Chapter 13 of the Bankruptcy Code provides for "Adjustment of Debts of an Individual with Regular Income."

Individuals (not partnerships or corporations) with *regular income* who owe noncontingent, liquidated, unsecured debts of less than $100,000 or similar secured debts of $350,000 may take advantage of Chapter 13. This includes individual proprietors and individuals on welfare, social security, fixed pensions or investment income.[9] Many small business debtors will have a choice of filing a plan either under Chapter 11 or 13. There are several advantages in filing a Chapter 13 plan when eligible. One of these advantages is that it is less expensive and less complicated than a Chapter 11 proceeding, or even a Chapter 7 liquidation.

---

9. Prior to the new Bankruptcy Act, self-employed persons could not file under Chapter 13.

Filing the Petition

A Chapter 13 case can be initiated only by the filing of a voluntary petition by the debtor. Certain Chapter 7 and 11 cases may be converted to Chapter 13 cases with the consent of the debtor. A trustee must be appointed.

Automatic Stay

Upon the filing of a Chapter 13 petition, the automatic stay previously discussed takes effect. It enjoins creditors from taking action against co-obligors of the debtor. Although it applies to all or part of a consumer debt, it does not apply to any business debt incurred by the debtor. A creditor has the right to seek relief from the automatic stay.

The Plan

Filing the Plan   Only the debtor may file a plan under Chapter 13. This plan may provide either for the payment of all obligations in full or for payment of an amount less than 100 percent.

Contents of the Plan   A Chapter 13 plan must:

1.   Provide for the turnover of such future earnings or income of the debtor to the trustee as is necessary for execution of the plan.
2.   Provide for full payment in deferred cash payments of all claims entitled to priority.
3.   Provide for the same treatment of each claim within a particular class.

The time for payment under the plan may not exceed three years unless the court approves an extension. The term, with extension, may not exceed five years.

Confirmation of the Plan   After the plan is filed, the court holds a confirmation hearing at which interested parties may object to the plan. The court will confirm a plan with respect to each claim of a secured creditor:

1.   If the secured creditors have accepted the plan.
2.   If the plan provides that creditors retain their liens and if the value of the property to be distributed to them under the plan is not less than the secured portion of their claims.
3.   If the debtor surrenders the property securing the claim to the creditors.

Unsecured creditors are protected only by the requirements that the plan be proposed "in good faith" and that they will receive at least as much under the plan as they would under a Chapter 7 liquidation. Unsecured creditors do not have a vote to confirm a Chapter 13 plan.

Discharge

After completion of all payments under a Chapter 13 plan, the court grants a discharge of all debts provided for by the plan. The exemptions to discharge are for certain long-term debts. Except for claims constituting a priority debt and except for alimony and child support, all other debts are dischargeable. Priority debts must be paid because the priority claims are a minimum requirement of what must be included in a plan. That means that the present status of the law allows a Chapter 13 discharge to include fraudulently incurred debt and claims resulting from malicious or willful injury. Therefore, a Chapter 13 discharge is much more beneficial to the debtor than a Chapter 7 discharge.

Even if the debtor does not complete the plan, a "hardship" discharge may be granted if the failure to complete the plan was due to circumstances beyond the debtor's control and if the property distributed with the plan was of greater value than would have been paid in a Chapter 7 liquidation. A discharge can be revoked within one year if it was obtained by fraud.

The following case illustrates a Chapter 13 petition and the problem of confirmation of the debtors' plans which proposed no payment to unsecured creditors.

IN RE IACOVONI
United States Bankruptcy Court,
D.Utah C.D., 1980.
2 B.R. 256.

BACKGROUND AND FACTS   *Various debtors filed petitions under Chapter 13 of the Bankruptcy Code. The debtors proposed to pay nothing to unsecured creditors under their plans. The debtors sought confirmation of their plans.*

MABEY, Bankruptcy Judge.

*   *   *   *

The Chapter 13 Requirement of Payment of Unsecured Claims

The common issue presented by the cases now before the Court and meriting the major focus of this opinion is the payment requirement, if any, of the Chapter 13 plan. Initially, the Court addresses the question of whether a plan which proposes no payments may be confirmed, and if not, what standard must be met in respect to payments required for confirmation.

The requirements for confirmation are set out in 11 U.S.C. § 1325 which states in part:

(a) The court shall confirm a plan if *   *   *

(3) the plan has been proposed in good faith and not by any means forbidden by law;

(4) the value, as of the effective date of the plan, of property to be distributed under the plan on account of each allowed unsecured claim is not less than the amount that would be paid on such claim if the estate of the debtor were liquidated under chapter 7 of this title on such date. . .

(6) the debtor will be able to make all payments under the plan and to comply with the plan.

The so-called "best interest of creditors test," embodied in Section 1325(a)(4), requires only that the unsecured creditors of the debtor receive at least as much as they would have received if the debtor had liquidated under Chapter 7. When all of the debtor's assets are exempt, as is the situation in each of the cases herein, compliance with this requirement would result when no payments were made at all. A careful examination of the legislative history and the other provisions of Chapter 13 demonstrates, however, that a plan without payments leaves much of the chapter without meaning and confirmation of such a plan vitiates the concept of Chapter 13.

For an individual to be entitled to file under Chapter 13, 11 U.S.C. § 109(e) requires that he have "regular income," as defined by 11 U.S.C. § 101(24). The clear expectation underlying this requirement is that the debtor use his future income to make payments to his creditors. Indeed, the legislative history *   *   * shows this to be the *raison d'etre* of Chapter 13—to give debtors who have regular future income, out of which creditors can be paid, an alternative to liquidation by the partial or full payment of claims from future income.[1] If no payments are to be made out of future income, such a limitation on those eligible to file under Chapter 13 appears arbitrary.

11 U.S.C. § 1325(a)(6) requires, as a prerequisite to confirmation, that the debtor be able to make "all *payments* under the plan and to comply with the plan." (Emphasis added.) This section contemplates that some payments be made under a plan. Under the section, the Court is to determine whether the plan is feasible, *i.e.*, in light of the debtor's budget, whether the proposed payments can be made. It anticipates that the debtor live within a proposed budget to make such payments. One may reasonably conclude from this requirement for confirmation that

---

1. Payment of claims may also be made from property of the estate or of the debtor, if the plan so provides. 11 U.S.C. § 1322(a)(8). Nevertheless, the principal thrust of the Chapter 13 provisions is that payments be made from future income, regular income being the main prerequisite of Chapter 13 relief. However, the liquidation by the debtor of some of his assets may supplement future income.

if a debtor cannot feasibly make any payments under a plan, because the debtor has no excess income, then his "plan" cannot be confirmed, and he is left with the remedy of Chapter 7 liquidation. Indeed, an individual with regular income is one whose income is "sufficiently stable and regular to *enable* such individual to *make payments* under a plan ..." 11 U.S.C. § 101(24). (Emphasis added.) It may be argued that one whose income does not enable him to make payments under the plan does not have "regular income" within the statutory meaning. If the debtor has no excess income out of which to make payments, he is in practical effect no different from the debtor without regular income.

11 U.S.C. § 1326, entitled "Payments," contemplates by its terms that at least some payments will be made under the proposed plan. This is also true of 11 U.S.C. § 1325(b), which allows the Court to order after confirmation that the debtor pay "all or any part" of his income over to the trustee for disbursement.

The operation of 11 U.S.C. § 1328(b) and (c), which allow for a narrower, hardship discharge "to a debtor that has not completed payments under the plan," rests upon payments as an integral requirement for a confirmed plan. There is no purpose in allowing a hardship discharge if debtors may file plans proposing no payments, for a debtor need never fail to complete his payments if none are proposed. Further, under Section 1328(b), a hardship discharge, where the debtor is unable to make his payments, is no broader than under a Chapter 7 liquidation. It seems unlikely that Congress intended to grant the Chapter 13 debtor who does not attempt to repay his debts a more generous discharge than the debtor who tries, but fails. In fact, it follows logically from the limited hardship discharge provision that before a debtor may have the advantage of the broader Chapter 13 discharge, he must both attempt repayment of unsecured debts, since the discharge of unpaid secured claims is not at issue, and succeed to some extent. Confirmation of a plan proposing no payments allows the debtor the broader discharge and offends this provision and its obvious intent. In summary, if the integrated provisions of Chapter 13 are to have meaning, payments must be required under a proposed plan.

*   *   *   *

"Good Faith" Effort to Make Meaningful Payments

*   *   *   *

*   *   * The following factors may be considered in determining whether a good faith effort to make meaningful payment to holders of unsecured claims has been made:

1.   The budget of the debtor, *i.e.*, how much the debtor feasibly can pay.

2.   The future income and payment prospects of the debtor.

3.   The dollar amount of debts outstanding, and the proposed percentage of repayment.

4.   The nature of the debts sought to be discharged; specially, to what extent the debtor is invoking the advantage of the broader Chapter 13 discharge which may carry with it concomitant obligations of repayment effort.

As seems intended by the flexible standard of "good faith," discretion is to be left with the court to insure that all parties are treated fairly. The "good faith" requirement must be applied in light of the intent of Congress to increase both the availability of Chapter 13 relief and the repayment received by creditors. A proposal of meaningful repayment must be made, in light of the debtor's particular circumstances, even, when, as in these cases, all of the debtor's assets are exempt.

If no meaningful repayment can be proposed, the debtor is not entitled to Chapter 13 relief. This flexible, equitable standard of Section 1325(a)(3) is not foreign to the bankruptcy law. As aptly stated by Justice Douglas in *Bank of Marin v. England*, 385 U.S. 99, 103, 87 S.Ct. 274, 277 (1966), in a similar context: "Yet we do not read these statutory words with the ease of a computer. There is an overriding consideration that equitable principles govern the exercise of bankruptcy jurisdiction."

Confirmation of the plans was denied.

JUDGMENT AND REMEDY

The plans mentioned in this case are usually called zero plans. They are plans that provide for no payment in excess of what the creditor would receive in liquidation. Some courts have found that there is no statutory requirement suggesting that a Chapter 13 debtor pay more than a creditor would get in a straight liquidating proceeding. Thus, if the creditor would have received nothing in a straight bankruptcy, there is no requirement to pay that creditor anything in order to obtain a Chapter 13 discharge. However, it is anticipated that eventually the United States Supreme Court will be required to resolve the conflict that exists among various jurisdictions on this issue.

COMMENT

QUESTIONS AND CASE PROBLEMS

1. Carlton has been a rancher all his life, raising cattle and crops. His ranch is valued at $500,000, almost all of which is exempt under state law. Carlton has eight creditors and a total indebtedness of $70,000. Two of his largest creditors are Samson ($30,000 owed) and Greed ($25,000 owed). The other six creditors have claims of less than $5,000 each. A drought has ruined all of Carlton's crops and forced him to sell many of his cattle at a loss. He cannot pay off his creditors.

  (a) Under the Code, can Carlton, with a $500,000 ranch, voluntarily petition himself into bankruptcy? Explain.

  (b) Could either Samson or Greed force Carlton into involuntary bankruptcy? Explain.

2. Sam is a retail seller of television sets. He sells Martha a $900 set on a retail installment security agreement in which she pays $100 down and the balance in equal installments. Sam retains a security interest in the set sold, and he perfects that security interest by filing a financing statement locally. Two months later Martha is in default on her payments to Sam and is involuntarily petitioned into bankruptcy by her creditors. Sam wants to repossess the television set as provided in the security agreement, and he wants to have priority over the trustee in bankruptcy to any proceeds from disposal of the set. Discuss fully Sam's right to repossess and whether he has priority over the trustee in bankruptcy to any proceeds from disposal of the set.

3. Green is not known for common business sense. He started a greenhouse and nursery business two years ago and because of his lack of experience, he soon was in debt to a number of creditors. On February 1 Green borrowed $5,000 from his father to pay some of these creditors. On May 1 Green paid back the $5,000, depleting his entire working capital. One creditor, the ABC Nursery Supply Corporation, had extended credit to Green on numerous purchases. ABC has pressured Green for payment, and on July 1 Green pays ABC half the money owed. On September 1 Green voluntarily petitions himself into bankruptcy. The trustee in bankruptcy claims that both Green's father and ABC must turn over to the debtor's estate the amounts Green paid to them. Discuss fully the trustee's claims.

4. Smith petitions himself into voluntary bankruptcy. Smith has three major claims against his estate. One is by Carlton, a friend who holds Smith's negotiable promissory note for $2,500; one is by Elmer, an employee who is owed three months' back wages of $4,500; and one is by United Bank of the Rockies on an unsecured loan of $5,000. In addition, Able, an accountant retained by the trustee, is owed $500, and property taxes of $1,000 are owed to Rock County. If Smith's nonexempt property has been liquidated, with proceeds of $5,000, discuss fully what amount will be received by the United Bank of the Rockies.

5. The East Bank is a secured party on a loan of $5,000 it has made to Sally. Sally later got into financial difficulty, and creditors other than the East Bank petitioned her into involuntary bankruptcy. The value of the secured collateral has substantially decreased in value, and upon sale, the debt to East Bank was reduced to only $2,500. Sally's estate consisted of $100,000 in exempt assets and $2,000 in nonexempt assets. After the bankruptcy costs and back wages to Sally's employees were paid, nothing was left for unsecured creditors. Sally received a discharge in bankruptcy. Later she decided to go back into business. By selling a few exempt assets and getting a small loan, she would be able to buy a small but profitable restaurant. She went to East Bank for the loan. East Bank claimed that the balance of its secured debt was not discharged in bankruptcy. Sally agreed and signed an agreement to pay East Bank the $2,500, as the bank was not a party to the petitioning of Sally into bankruptcy. Because of this, East Bank made the new unsecured loan to Sally.

(a) Discuss East Bank's claim that the balance of its secured debt was not discharged in bankruptcy.

(b) Discuss the legal effect of Sally's agreement to pay East Bank $2,500 after the discharge in bankruptcy.

(c) If one year later Sally went into voluntary bankruptcy, what effect would the bankruptcy proceedings have on the new unsecured loan.

6. Tracey Service Co., Inc., filed a petition for a Chapter 11 reorganization. Acar Supply Co., one of Tracey's creditors, filed a motion to convert the case to a Chapter 7 liquidation. The court found that the debtor corporation had no place of business, no inventory, no equipment, no employees, and no business phone. Should Tracey Service be permitted to reorganize under Chapter 11? [In Re Tracey Service Co., Inc., 17 B.R. 405 (1982)]

7. Donald Lewis filed a voluntary petition for bankruptcy. One of the debts on which he sought discharge was a $1,500 judgment that had been entered against him for assault on Betty Dunson. Lewis testified in the bankruptcy court that he "put both hands around [Dunson's] neck and told her to leave his wife alone or he would break her neck." Will the court grant a discharge of the judgment claim? [In Re Lewis, 17 B.R. 341 (1982)]

8. Mr. and Mrs. Tomeo obtained a loan from HCC Consumer Discount Company and gave HCC a security interest in their household goods, which Mr. Tomeo had valued at $5,000. Four months later the Tomeos filed a voluntary petition in bankruptcy and listed the value of the same household items at $600. HCC objected to the discharge of the debt on the ground that Mr. Tomeo had made materially false representations for the purpose of deceiving HCC. Mr. Tomeo stated that he had valued the items at what he had paid for them ten years previously. Was the debt nondischargeable? [In Re Tomeo, 1 B.R. 673 (1979)]

9. Would a Chapter 13 plan that absorbed the debtor's entire income after expenses, and proposed a 100 percent repayment to secured creditors to the extent of their security, and a 1 percent repayment over a three-and-one-half-year period of general unsecured creditors be approved by the court? [In Re Barnes, 5 B.R. 376 (1980)]

10. Prior to filing for bankruptcy, Bray was making loan payments to his company's credit union through payroll deductions. Bray's employer continued to deduct the loan payments from Bray's paychecks after being notified of the bankruptcy petition. Is this a violation of the Bankruptcy Code? [In Re Bray, 17 B.R. 152 (1982)]

11. Does conversion of nonexempt property to exempt property on the eve of a bankruptcy constitute a fraudulent conveyance? (E.g., purchasing a home could convert $7,500 in cash to $7,500 in exempt property.) [Wudrick v. Clements, 451 F.2d 988 (9th Cir. 1971)].

FOCUS ON ETHICS

Creditors' Rights and Bankruptcy

We are certainly many years away from that period in our history when debtors' prisons existed. Some say, however, that we have proceeded too far in the opposite direction, making it too easy for debtors to avoid what they legally owe.

THE GENERAL QUESTION OF CREDITORS' RIGHTS

When a debtor fails to meet his or her financial obligations, the creditor has numerous remedies, such as a mechanic's lien on real property, an artisan's lien on personal property, foreclosure, attachment, and garnishment. When such rights and remedies are invoked, the creditor is often considered by the general public to employ "unfair" tactics. There is clearly a distinction in the public's mind between the nonrepayment of a loan and the theft of personal property. But from a purely economic point of view, the result is the same—the wealth of the credit-seller is reduced.

An ethical question arises as to whether the creditor or the debtor should be favored when the debtor has not performed. For many, this ethical question revolves around the way in which the debtor has reduced the net worth of the creditor. Also, the

public at large often judges the debtor's action on the basis of the purpose for which the debt was incurred. If the debt was incurred for a "needed" item, such as a refrigerator, then common opinion seems to be that such a debtor should be dealt with in a lenient manner. On the other hand, if the debt was incurred for a trip to the Bahamas, the ethical issue appears to be significantly different.

THE EFFECT OF NONREPAYMENT OF LOANS

Whatever the ethical issue may be when a debtor fails to perform, the economic consequence to those debtors who do perform is clear: the cost of nonperformance is imposed on all of those who do perform. This cost is in the form of higher average interest rates to obtain credit. That is to say, the greater the percentage of loan agreements not consummated as per the agreement, the larger the "risk factor" added to normal interest rates. Creditors deal in a highly competitive market. They expect to earn a normal rate of return for investment in such an industry. If costs increase because of nonperformance by debtors, those costs will have to be recouped somewhere. In general, the only way to recoup them is to

charge all debtors a higher interest rate.

Now let us reconsider the ethical question regarding creditors' rights. The more creditors are able to enforce their rights and thereby obtain greater performance on loan agreements, the lower will be the interest rate paid by debtors as a group. Who, then, has a greater right in this situation—the debtor who has not performed or the group of debtors that has, does, and will perform?

ETHICS VERSUS ECONOMICS: AN EXAMPLE

Consider an example of a court decision and the ethical versus the economic issues involved. To purchase furniture and consumer durable goods, residents in low-income areas are required to sign an agreement which includes a statement that failure to make timely payment can result in the repossession not only of the goods purchased under the instant contract, but also of any prior goods purchased under similar contracts from the same vendor. Suppose that Mrs. Brown, a poor, single mother of three children, makes three separate purchases at a furniture store. First she buys a television, then a stereo, and then a couch. Each one of these items is purchased on credit. Each time

599

she purchases an item, she makes a down payment and signs a contract containing the clause stated above. She duly makes payments on the first two items but fails to make payments on time for the last item. The vendor, invoking its rights under the so-called add-on clause, repossesses not only the couch but also the stereo and television. Mrs. Brown sues.

What should the court decide? For many, the add-on clause offends their sense of justice. After all, why should Mrs. Brown relinquish those items for which she has properly paid according to the sales agreement? Indeed, when similar cases have reached the courts, judgment has favored the plaintiffs on the grounds of public policy.

But now consider the long-run implications of such a court decision. Add-on clauses allowing for the repossession (replevin) of previously purchased items, in addition to the one under contract, give vendors in low-income areas additional security to reduce the costs of nonperformance. The reason, presumably, that one does not find such add-on clauses in similar sales agreements in middle-income areas is because vendors do not find it necessary to seek the additional security. Without this additional security in a low-income area, vendors will reduce the amount of credit offered. How? They will screen applicants more carefully, eliminating those who previously might have been able to obtain credit. The long-term result of Mrs. Brown's successful litigation will be a reduction in the amount of credit given in low-income areas. Those buyers with the lowest credit ratings are the ones who will be hurt.

Now try to determine whether the vendor's business conduct in repossessing the stereo and the television, in addition to the couch, was ethically appropriate.

GARNISHMENT OF WAGES

Ethical considerations are invariably involved in the whole issue of garnishment of wages. There will always be a conflict between creditors' rights and the necessary needs of the debtor, plus those of the employer. Certainly many an employer would like to terminate an individual's employment because of garnishment proceedings. Certainly a creditor would like garnishment to allow for repayment of a debt at the earliest possible date. But the employee must continue working. Also, there must be enough income left over after garnishment for the employee to survive and indeed to have the incentive to continue working.

BANKRUPTCY

The first goal of bankruptcy law is to provide relief and protection to debtors who have "gotten in over their heads." The U.S. Constitution provides that Congress shall have the power to establish uniform laws on the subject of bankruptcies throughout the United States. Our first bankruptcy law was enacted in 1898 and was amended in 1938. In 1978 the Bankruptcy Reform Act was passed and became effective on October 1, 1979. In addition to the general issue of creditors' versus debtors' rights, there is the issue of the rights of those in bankruptcy relative to the rights of the bankrupt party's creditors.

Consider the concept of bankruptcy from the point of view

of the creditor. The creditor has extended a transfer of purchasing power from himself or herself to the debtor. That transfer of purchasing power represents, as it were, a transfer of an asset for an asset. The debtor obtains the asset of money, goods, or services: the creditor obtains the asset called a secured or unsecured legal obligation to pay. Once the debtor is in bankruptcy, voluntarily or involuntarily, the asset that the creditor owns most often has a diminished value. Indeed, in many circumstances that asset will have a zero value. Bankruptcy law attempts to provide a "fair" means of distributing to creditors the assets remaining in the debtor's possession.

Again, as we pointed out in previous sections, the reduction in the wealth of the creditor due to the bankruptcy of the debtor is similar to the reduction in the wealth of the creditor that results from a robbery. It is not surprising that numerous irate creditors have called the bankruptcy laws "legal thievery." But what is the ethical issue here? It is to be fair to all parties concerned. In the absence of bankruptcy laws, debtors would find themselves unable to legally extinguish debts without full repayment or some mutually agreed upon partial repayment. This would prevent numerous individuals and businesses from ever starting over again.

Certainly, our shared beliefs provide that everyone should be given the chance to start over again. Thus, bankruptcy law is a balancing act between providing such a chance and ensuring that creditors are given "a fair shake." But the question of "moral hazard," as it is termed in the insurance industry, arises with bankruptcy law just as it does with products liability law. The easier it becomes for debtors to hide behind bankruptcy laws, the greater will be the incentive for debtors to use such laws to avoid payment of legally owned sums of money. That also means that the more easily a debtor can hide behind bankruptcy laws, the more risk-taking will occur in the business world. Risk-taking is a desired activity by business men and women, but not "too" much risk-taking.

Again, consider the fact that the more lenient bankruptcy laws are, the more bankruptcies there will be, all other things held constant. This is evidence by the fact that the total number of bankruptcies has more than doubled since the enactment of the Bankruptcy Reform Act of 1978. What this means is that creditors will incur higher risks in making loans. In order to compensate for these higher risks, creditors will do one or more of the following: increase interest rates charged everyone, require more security (collateral), or be more selective in the granting of credit. Thus, a trade-off situation exists: the more lenient bankruptcy laws are, the better off will be those debtors who find themselves in bankruptcy; but those debtors who will never be in bankruptcy will be worse off. Ethical concerns here must be matched with the economic concerns of other groups of individuals affected by the law.

DISCUSSION QUESTIONS

1. What inadequacies existed in the private legal system (mostly contract law) and the private market system to prompt so much federal and state legislation concerning debtors' and creditors' rights?

2. Does this legislation accomplish what was intended?

3. What should be the balance between creditors' and debtors' rights?

4. Who gains and who loses from usury laws? What are the ethical issues involved here?

5. How moral-ethical is it for a business to refuse to deal with a customer simply because that person once went into bankruptcy, even though that person is now a good credit risk in every other way?

UNIT VI

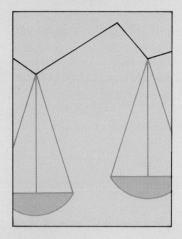

AGENCY AND
EMPLOYMENT

CHAPTER 34

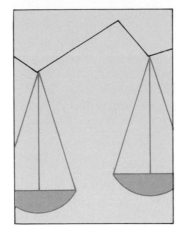

Agency Creation, and Duties and Rights of Agents and Principals

One of the most common, important, and pervasive legal relationships is that of agency. In an **agency** relationship between two parties, one of the parties, called the **agent**, agrees to represent or act for the other, called the **principal**. The principal has the right to control the agent's conduct in matters entrusted to the agent. More formally, the Restatement, Second, Agency, defines *agency* as "the fiduciary relation which results from the manifestation of consent by one person to another that the other shall act in his behalf and subject to his control, and consent by the other so to act."[1] In general, the law of agency is based on the maxim that "one acting by another is acting for himself."

THE NATURE OF AGENCY

Using agents, one individual can conduct multiple business operations simultaneously in various locations. Thus, contracts can be made at different places with different persons at the same time. A familiar example of an agent is a corporate officer who serves in a representative capacity for the owners of the corporation. In this capacity, the officer has the authority to bind the principals to a contract. Indeed, agency law is essential to the existence and operation of a corporate entity, because only through its agents can a corporation function and enter into contracts.

KINDS OF AGENCY RELATIONSHIPS

The first step in analyzing an agency relation-

---

1. Restatement, Second, Agency, Section 1(1). This is an authoritative summary of the law of agency, which is often referred to by jurists in decisions and opinions.

ship is to determine whether or not such a relationship exists. Traditional analysis in the law of agency distinguishes three types of relationships:

1. Principal and agent.
2. Master and servant.
3. Employer and independent contractor.

Principal-Agent

In a principal-agent relationship, the parties have agreed that the agent will act *on behalf of and instead of* the principal in negotiating and transacting business with third persons. This relationship will affect the principal's rights and duties. Thus, an agent is empowered to perform legal acts that are binding on the principal. For example, an agent can bind a principal in a contract with a third person.

An agent has *derivative authority* to use a degree of independent discretion in carrying out the principal's business.[2] For example, Earl is hired as a booking agent for a rock group—Harry and the Rockets. As the group's agent, Earl can negotiate and sign contracts for the rock group to appear at concerts. The contracts will be binding and thus legally enforceable against the group.

Master-Servant

Today's law defines *servant* as an employee—one employed by a master to perform services; the servant's physical conduct is *controlled* or is subject to control by the master. A servant can be a species of agent. However, the term *master-servant relationship* is anachronistic. Accountants and truck drivers are not referred to as servants. For that matter, employers are not called masters. The current terminology for the old master-servant relationship is *employer-employee*.

The term *employee* had no significance for common law rules of agency. However, with the industrial revolution and recent social legislation, the term has come into prominence. An **employee** is an agent (other than an independent

contractor) who has an appointment or contract for hire with authority to represent the employer.

For example, Dana owns a dress shop. She employs Sandy, Sheila, and Sue as salespeople. Dana is the employer (master); the other women are the employees (servants). The key feature of the employer-employee relationship is that the employer controls, or at least has the right to control, the employee in the performance of the tasks involved in the employment. The employees do not have *independent* business discretion. The dress shop salespeople not only can be told to sell the dresses but also can be told how to sell them. And in selling the dresses, they are agents as well as employees.

Independent Contractor

Independent contractors are not employees (servants), because their employers have no control over the details of their physical performance. Restatement, Second, Agency, Section 2, defines an independent contractor as:

> * * * a person who contracts with another to do something for him but who is not controlled by the other nor subject to the other's right to control with respect to his physical conduct in the performance of the undertaking. He may or may not be an agent.

The following factors are relevant in determining the status of independent contractors:

1. What is the extent of control that the employer can exercise over the details of the work?
2. Is the employed person engaged in an occupation or business distinct from that of the employer?
3. Is the work usually done under the employer's direction, or is it done by a specialist without supervision?
4. Does the employer supply the tools at the place of work?
5. How long is the person employed?
6. What is the method of payment—by time or at the completion of the job?
7. What is the degree of skill required by the person employed?

---

2. But usually an agent is not an independent contractor as described here.

Building contractors and subcontractors are independent contractors, and a property owner does not control the acts of either of these professionals. Truck drivers who own their equipment and hire out on an ad hoc basis are independent contractors; however, truck drivers who drive company trucks on a regular basis are usually employees (servants). A collection agency is another example of an independent contractor.

Commingling of the Relationships

It is important to note that the employer-employee (master-servant) relationship may not necessarily involve an agency relationship. The same holds true for the relationship between an employer and an independent contractor. To illustrate: An employer who hires a traveling salesperson as an employee has created not only an employer-employee relationship but one of agency as well. A seller-owner of real estate who hires a real estate broker to negotiate a sale of his or her property has not only contracted with an independent contractor (the real estate broker) but has also established an agency relationship for the specific purpose of assisting in the sale of the property. On the other hand, an employer who hires someone exclusively as a janitor has created only an employer-employee relationship, and the janitor is not an agent.

Statutes Laws governing employment apply only to the employer-employee relationship, not to the employer-independent contractor relationship. The difference between the two relationships can be extremely important. The main significance is that employers are not generally liable for the torts of independent contractors. Consider also the fact that federal law requires employers to deduct monies for withholding, social security, and the like from wages paid to employees. No such taxes need be withheld from payments made to independent contractors.

In the following case, an insurance company paid taxes to the Internal Revenue Service but later attempted to characterize the employees involved as independent contractors and sought to recover the taxes it had paid to the government.

M.F.A. MUTUAL INS. CO. v. UNITED STATES

United States District Court, Western District of Missouri, Central District, 1970. 314 F.Supp. 590.

BACKGROUND AND FACTS *The plaintiff, an insurance company, hired "agents" to sell its insurance policies and to service its clients. The company had a special program for new agents, called an "Agent Financing Agreement," whereby the company guaranteed a monthly salary to each agent in lieu of a commission. The agreement was to last for one year, during which the agents were specially supervised, were fully compensated for expenses incurred, and received instruction and training. The Agent Financing Agreement specifically characterized these agents as "independent contractors."*

From 1962 to 1965, the company paid the employment taxes required under the Social Security Act for all of its employees, including its "financed agents." Later, the company questioned whether it was responsible for paying employment taxes and argued that it should be able to recover the tax money that it had paid to the Internal Revenue Service on the ground that the financed agents were not employees within the the meaning of the Internal Revenue Code definition, but rather were independent contractors. Therefore, the company claimed it had no responsibility to pay federal employment taxes for them. The IRS refused to return the money that the company had paid, claiming that the financed agents were in fact employees and that the company was responsible under the Social Security Act for paying employment taxes for them.

OLIVER, judge.

*   *   *   *

MEMORANDUM OPINION

The parties have stipulated [formally agreed] that the questions of law and fact presented are whether plaintiff's financed agents are:

(a) Employees for purposes of the Federal Insurance Contributions Act *   *   * and the Federal Unemployment Tax Act, *   *   *; and

(b) If they are employees *   *   * then whether they are remunerated solely by way of commission *   *   *.

There is no real dispute about the principles of law to be applied. The parties agree that common law principles (of agency) are applicable[.] *   *   *

*   *   *   *

*   *   * [T]here is no shorthand formula or magic phrase that can be applied to find the answer, but all of the incidents of the relationship must be assessed and weighed with no one factor being decisive. What is important is that the total factual context is assessed in the light of the pertinent common-law agency principles.

*   *   *   *

[The court proceeded to evaluate the factual circumstances involved between the company and the financed agents.]

(a) Plaintiff could and did exercise by way of concrete suggestions and required procedures, a considerable amount of control over the details of the work of its financed agents, particularly as evidenced by its demand for daily reports concerning the full time activities of its financed agents and by the presence of its absolute power of termination.

(b) The financed agents were engaged in the business of selling plaintiff's insurance policies. Such an occupation or business cannot fairly be said to be distinct from that of plaintiff's business; indeed, the sale of insurance policies is but one phase of plaintiff's business.

(c) The work usually done by the financed agents could, in one sense of the word, be done by a "specialist without supervision." But such a view would ignore the fact that the work of a financed agent could just as well be done by a salaried employee under the direction of the employer. A financed agent, *   *   *, was in a process of training which required that much of his work be done under the direction and supervision of plaintiff's district sales manager.

(d) No specialized skill other than of a salesman was required to become a financed agent. An insurance salesman must, of course, as must any other salesman, learn something about the product he is selling. But the occupation of an insurance salesman does not involve *   *   * specialized skill[.] *   *   *

(e) Plaintiff supplied many forms and business "tools," such as forms of policies, and the like, to its financed agents. A financed agent's place of work, as any insurance salesman, was among members of the public wherever he may catch them. The circumstance of whether an insurance salesman's desk, typewriter, filing cabinet, adding machine, and the like, are located in his home or in an office furnished by the insurance company *   *   * is not a particularly weighty factor in the determination of the relationship question because it is obvious that sales of insurance policies infrequently occur at either place.

(f) Plaintiff's financed agents were employed for a year but plaintiff retained complete control over the employment tenure of a financed agent; he could be discharged at any time for any or no reason at all.

(g) A financed agent was, in effect, given a guaranteed draw and the amount of money received was not related to the job performed. The money was paid to obtain the full time services of the financed agent; indeed, the system of reporting was designed to make certain that plaintiff received what it paid for. As long as plaintiff did not elect to terminate, the financed agent was entitled to be paid the amount specified in his agreement. The fact that plaintiff's right to terminate was in no way restricted to how its financed agents performed a specific and particular job (in the sense of selling a particular insurance policy to a particular prospect) is totally inconsistent with the basic concept of an independent contractor relationship.

(h) The sales work performed by the financed agents was a regular part of the general insurance business of the plaintiff. Such work could as well be performed by a salaried employee as by a financed agent.

(i) The contract recited a relationship of independent contractor, but, under all the cases, this single factor is not controlling.

(j) Plaintiff, of course, is in the insurance business, a part of which includes the sale of its policies.

* * * [W]e conclude that plaintiff's financed agents are employed to perform sales services in plaintiff's affairs under circumstances in which the performance of those services is subject to plaintiff's right of control. None of the separate factors are fully supportive of plaintiff's contention that its financed agents are independent contractors. All the facts and circumstances, when considered as a whole, make it clear that plaintiff has retained the requisite right, on a full time basis, to control the details and means by which its financed agents are to conduct their sales activity.

JUDGMENT AND REMEDY   *The court concluded that the company's financed agents were employees rather than independent contractors. Thus, the company's claim for a refund of employment taxes was rejected.*

COMMENTS   *In this case, labeling by the parties did not determine their relationship. In fact, labeling by the parties is never decisive, although it may be a factor considered by the court.*

FORMATION OF THE AGENCY RELATIONSHIP

The following discussions will emphasize the usual form that an agency relationship takes. An agency relationship is a *consensual* relationship; that is, it comes about by voluntary consent and agreement between the parties. The agreement need not be in writing, and consideration is not required.[3] The same basic rights and duties are involved whether it is a gratuitous agency or an agency for hire.

---

3.   There are two main exceptions to oral agency agreements:

a. In many states, the Statute of Frauds makes the following requirement. Whenever agency authority empowers the agent to enter into a contract that the Statute of Frauds requires to be in writing, then the agent's authority from the principal must likewise be in writing. This is known as the "equal dignity rule." It occurs most frequently in contracts for the sale of an interest in land or contracts that cannot be performed within one year. The Statute of Frauds is discussed in Chapter 12.

b. A power of attorney is written authority conferred to an agent. It is conferred in a formal writing, usually acknowledged by a notary public, whose seal is attached to the formal document. A power of attorney can be general, giving the agent broad powers, or it can grant the agent only restricted authority.

Generally, no formalities are required to create an agency. The agency relationship can arise by acts of the parties in one of four ways:

1. By agreement.
2. By ratification.
3. By apparent authority, or estoppel.
4. By operation of law.

To create a power of attorney, a form of writing is required. The following case illustrates the problems in this area.

BACKGROUND AND FACTS *Joseph Weinberg purchased a condominium unit with Rachela Weiser as joint tenants with right of survivorship. Thereafter Weinberg executed a general power of attorney making his son, Arthur Winters, his agent. Winters conveyed Weinberg's one-half interest in the condominium to Weinberg's daughter, Miriam Bloom. After Weinberg's death, Bloom wanted to sell the condominium, but Weiser claimed complete ownership by right of survivorship on the ground that the agent had no authority to transfer the real estate to Bloom.*

BLOOM v. WEISER

District Court of Appeal of Florida, Third District, 1977. 348 So.2d 651.

HAVERFIELD, Judge.

*   *   *   *

The established rule is that a power of attorney must be strictly construed and the instrument will be held to grant only those powers which are specified. We are of the view that for a power of attorney to authorize a conveyance of real estate, the authority of the agent to do so must be plainly stated. Reviewing the power of attorney granted Winters, we find the instrument contains no specific grant of power authorizing him to convey real estate. Therefore, the July 18 deed executed by Winters and purporting to convey Weinberg's one-half interest in the subject condominium unit to Miriam Bloom is void.

It is interesting to note that the instant power of attorney, prepared and executed in New York, contains almost the identical wording of the power of attorney found to be insufficient to authorize the agent to convey or dispose of real estate in *Graham v. State*, Ct.Cl., 51 N.Y.S.2d 437 (1944) where the court at page 441 explained:

> "A power of attorney to convey real estate is an instrument of title. Either expressly or by necessary implication it should state the authority of the agent without leaving it to be established by parol, inferred from coincidences or based on speculation. *   *   * It is not merely a matter between principal and attorney. The deed and the agent's authority are instruments of equal dignity. The language of the so-called power of attorney herein confers no authority on Robert H. Dunnets [the agent]. It lacks an operative clause. It is not a general power of attorney; he is authorized to act only 'in and about the premises.' It is not a special power of attorney; no premises or things to be done appear on the face of the instrument. The document states nothing to which the grant of powers can be related. Drawn, as it would seem, on the usual blank form of special power of attorney, it omits after the words, 'for me and in my name, place and stead,' the usual statement of specific acts authorized."

The deed executed by Winters was void. Title to the condominium belonged to Weiser.

JUDGMENT AND REMEDY

Agency by Agreement

Agency is a consensual relationship, because it must be based on some *affirmative* indication that the agent agrees to act for the principal and the principal agrees to have the agent so act.

An agency agreement can take the form of an express written contract. For example, Paula enters into a sales agreement with Adam, a realtor, to sell Paula's house. An agency relationship exists between Paula and Adam for the sale of the house. Most express agreements can be oral. For example, Paula asks Bob, a gardener, to contract with others for the care of her lawn on a regular basis. Bob agrees. An agency relationship exists between Paula and Bob for the lawn care.

An agency agreement can be implied from conduct. For example, a hotel expressly allows Jack Andrews to park cars, but Andrews has no employment contract there. He can infer from the hotel's conduct that he has authority to act as a valet. It can be implied that he is an agent for the hotel. His purpose is to provide valet parking services for hotel guests.

Agency by Ratification

On occasion, a person who is in fact not an agent, or who is an agent acting outside the scope of his or her authority, may make a contract on behalf of another (a principal). If the principal ratifies that contract by word or by action, an agency relationship is created by **ratification.** Ratification is a question of intent, and intent can be expressed by either words or conduct.

For example, Alfred James is a clerk (employee) of Anne Paul's Chic Fashion Store. Alfred contracts to purchase a tract of land in Paul's name without her authority to do so. Paul learns of James's actions and decides that the land is of great value and that she will go through with the sale. When a principal accepts the benefits or in some way affirms the conduct of one purporting to act on his or her behalf, an agency relationship is created. In this case, Paul has *ratified* James's acts, thereby creating an agency relationship between them. (The creation of the agency "relates back" to the time of James's unauthorized act.) The third party may revoke the offer or rescind the contract if he or she does so before ratification by the principal.

Agency by Estoppel

When a principal *causes* a third person to believe that another person is his or her agent, and the third person deals with the supposed agent, the principal is "estopped to deny" the agency relationship. In these situations, the principal's actions create the *appearance* of an agency that does not in fact exist. For example: Martin accompanies Paul to call on a customer, Sam, the proprietor of the General Store. Martin has done sales work but is not employed by Paul at this time. Paul boasts to Sam that he wishes he had three more assistants "just like Martin." Sam has reason to believe from Paul's statements that Martin is an agent for Paul. Sam then places seed orders with Martin. If Paul does not correct the impression that Martin is an agent, Paul will be bound to fill the orders just as if Martin were really Paul's agent. Paul's representation to Sam created the impression that Martin was Paul's agent and had authority to solicit orders.

Agency by estoppel does not extend to all acts under all circumstances. For example, the acts or declarations of the purported agent in and of themselves do not create an agency by estoppel. It is the deeds or statements of the principal that create an agency. In addition, the third person must prove that he or she *reasonably* believed that an agency relationship existed and the agent had authority. Facts and circumstances must show that an ordinary, prudent person who is familiar with business practice and custom would be justified in concluding that the agent had authority.

Agency by Operation of Law

In some cases, the courts have found it desirable to find an agency relationship in the absence of a formal agreement. This may occur in family relationships. For example, suppose one spouse purchases certain basic necessaries and charges them to the other spouse's charge account. The courts will often rule that the latter is liable for payment of such necessaries either because of a social policy of promoting the general welfare of the other spouse or because of a legal duty to supply necessaries to family members. Sometimes agency by operation of law is created, giving an agent emergency power to act under unusual circumstances that are not covered by the agreement when failure to act would cause a principal substantial loss. If the agent is unable to contact the principal, the courts will often grant this emergency power.

LEGAL CAPACITY

A principal must have legal capacity to enter contracts. The logic is simple. A person who cannot legally enter contracts directly should not be allowed to do it indirectly through an agent. An agent derives the authority to enter contracts from the principal, and a contract made by an agent is legally viewed as a contract of the principal. It is immaterial whether the agent personally has the legal capacity to make that contract. Thus, a minor can be an agent but cannot be a principal appointing an agent (in some states).[4] Where permitted, however, any resulting contracts will be voidable by the minor principal, but not by the adult third party.

Thus, any person can be an agent, regardless of whether he or she has the capacity to contract. Even a person who is legally incompetent can be appointed an agent if that person is capable of performing the required functions.

PURPOSE

An agency relationship can be created for any *legal* purpose. One created for an illegal purpose or contrary to public policy is unenforceable. If X (as principal) contracts with Y (as agent) to sell illegal narcotics, the agency relationship is unenforceable because it is a felony and there-

fore against public policy to sell narcotics illegally. It is also illegal for medical doctors and other licensed professionals to employ unlicensed agents to perform professional actions.

AGENCY POWER COUPLED WITH AN INTEREST

An agency *coupled with an interest* is a relationship created for the benefit of the agent. The agent actually acquires a beneficial interest in the subject matter of the agency. Under these circumstances it is not equitable to permit a principal to terminate at will. Hence, this type of agency is "irrevocable."

For example, Sarah Roberts (principal) owns Blackacre. She needs some immediate cash, so she enters into an agreement with John Hartwell that Hartwell will lend her $10,000, and she agrees to grant Hartwell a one-half interest in Blackacre and "the exclusive right to sell" it for $25,000 if she fails to repay the $10,000. The loan is to be repaid out of the sales proceeds. Hartwell's power to sell Blackacre is coupled with a beneficial interest of one-half ownership in Blackacre created at the time of the loan for the purpose of supporting it and securing its repayment. Hartwell's agency power is irrevocable.

An agency coupled with an interest should not be confused with situations in which the agent merely derives proceeds or profits from the sale of the subject matter. For example, an agent who merely receives a commission from the sale of real property does not have a beneficial interest in the property itself. Likewise, an attorney whose fee is a percentage of the recovery (a contingency fee) merely has an interest in the proceeds. These agency relationships are revocable by the principal, subject to any express contractual arrangements that the principal has with the agent.

Since, in an agency coupled with an interest, the interest is not created for the benefit of the principal, it is not really an agency in the usual sense. Therefore, any attempt by the principal to revoke an agency coupled with an interest normally has no legal force or effect and is not terminated by the death of either the principal or the agent.

---

4. Exceptions have been granted by some courts to allow a minor to appoint an agent for the limited purpose of contracting for the minor's necessities of life. [Casey v. Kastel, 237 N.Y. 305, 142 N.E. 671 (1924)]

DUTIES OF AGENTS AND PRINCIPALS

Once the principal-agent relationship has been created, both parties have duties that govern their conduct. The principal-agent relationship is fiduciary—one of trust. In it, each party owes the other the duty to act with the utmost good faith. Neither party may keep from the other information that has any bearing on their agency relationship.

It is logical to separate the discussion into the agent's duty to the principal and the principal's duty to the agent.

THE AGENT'S DUTY TO THE PRINCIPAL

The duties that an agent owes to a principal are set forth in the agency agreement or arise by operation of law. They are implied from the agency relationship whether or not the identity of the principal is disclosed to a third party.

Duty to Perform

An implied condition in every agency contract is the agent's agreement to use reasonable diligence and skill in performing the work. When an agent fails to perform his or her duties entirely, liability for breach of contract generally will occur.

For example, an insurance agent who fails to obtain the insurance coverage requested by a principal is guilty of breach of contract. When an agent performs carelessly or negligently, the agent can be liable in tort as well.

In many situations, an agent who does not act for money (a gratuitous, or free, agent) can be subject to the same standards of care and duty to perform as other agents. A gratuitous agent cannot, however, be liable for breach of contract, because there is no contract. A gratuitous agent is subject only to tort liability. However, once the agent has begun to act in an agency capacity, he or she has the duty to continue to perform in this capacity in an acceptable manner.

For example, Alex Paul's friend, Amy Foster, is a real estate broker. She (the agent) gratuitously offers to sell Paul's (the principal's) farm, Black Acre. If she never attempts to sell Black Acre, Paul has no legal cause of action to force her to do so. But assume that Foster finds a buyer. She keeps promising the buyer a sales contract but fails to provide one within a reasonable period of time. The buyer becomes disgruntled and seeks another property, and the sale ultimately falls through. Paul has a cause of action in tort for negligence—that is, failure to use the degree of care reasonably expected of real estate brokers.

The degree of skill or care required of an agent is usually that expected of a reasonable person under similar circumstances. Although in most cases this is interpreted to mean ordinary care, an agent may have presented himself or herself as possessing special skills (such as those that an accountant or attorney possesses). In these situations, the agent is expected to exercise the skill claimed. Failure to do so constitutes a breach of the agent's duty.

Duty to Notify

A basic concept of agency law is that the agent is required to notify the principal of all matters that come to his or her attention concerning the subject matter of the agency. This is the duty of notification. Because of this duty, the law imputes all the agent's knowledge to the principal. What the agent actually tells the principal is not relevant; what the agent *should have told* the principal is crucial.

For example, Able is Paula's agent for the purchase of a certain property from Tom. In the course of dealing, Able discovers that many years ago, Green obtained subsurface mineral rights. Thinking that this is unimportant, Able neglects to tell Paula. The purchase of the land takes place subject to Green's right to mine and remove the minerals. Paula does not have recourse against Tom; that is, Paula cannot rescind the sale or use the existence of Green's right to remove minerals as a defense to avoid going through with the sale. Able had the duty to notify Paula. The fact that he failed to do so and breached his fiduciary duty cannot be allowed to prejudice the rights of the innocent third party, Tom. Paula, however, does have recourse against Able.

Duty of Loyalty

Loyalty is one of the most fundamental duties in a fiduciary relationship. Basically stated, the agent has the duty to act solely for the benefit of his or her principal and not in the interest of the agent or a third party.

Numerous principles result from this duty. For example, an agent cannot represent two principals in the same transaction unless both know of the dual capacity and consent to it. Thus, a real estate agent cannot represent both the seller and the buyer in collecting commissions, unless seller and buyer so agree. A salesperson representing Avon cannot sell products of a competing line at the same time unless Avon consents. In addition, an agent who owns property cannot sell the property to the principal without indicating that ownership prior to the sale. Furthermore, an agent employed by a principal to buy cannot buy from himself or herself, and an agent

employed to sell cannot become the purchaser without the principal's consent. In short, the agent's loyalty must be undivided. The agent's actions must be strictly for the benefit of the principal and must not result in any secret profit for the agent.

The duty of loyalty means that any information or knowledge acquired through the agency relationship is considered confidential. It would be a breach of loyalty to disclose such information both during the agency relationship and after its termination. Typical examples of confidential information are trade secrets and customer lists compiled by the principal. Note, however, that an agent has the right to use skills and basic knowledge acquired during the course of agency employment in his or her own behalf (such as using sales techniques learned during the agency relationship), as long as such actions do not violate confidentiality.

The rules on disclosure of confidential information apply to employer-employee relationships. The following case involves customer lists that were clearly confidential.

BACKGROUND AND FACTS   *The corporation (the plaintiff) was involved in freight forwarding, which is a highly competitive business. Salespersons in this kind of business often expend considerable time soliciting prospective clients to ascertain their specialized needs. The corporation hired Robert Agnes as its president, and after a few years the corporation began to operate at a profit. Agnes made increasing salary demands and finally tendered his resignation, but not before copying customer lists and actively recruiting a vice-president, Brownstein, to leave and set up a competing air forwarding company (the defendant). The plaintiff sought an injunction to restrain Agnes's new corporation from soliciting or servicing plaintiff's former customers.*

ABC TRANS, ETC. v. AERONAUTICS FORWARDERS, INC.
Appellate Court of Illinois, 1978.
62 Ill.App.3d 671, 20 Ill.Dec. 160, 379 N.E.2d 1228.

SULLIVAN, Presiding Justice.

*   *   *   *

While acting as an agent or employee of another, one owes the duty of fidelity and loyalty; accordingly, a fiduciary cannot act inconsistently with his agency or trust; *i.e.,* solicit his employer's customers for himself, entice coworkers away from his employer, or appropriate his employer's personal property. However, "[i]t is not necessarily a breach of duty for an agent to form a rival concern and purchase machinery for it while working for his principal, though it would be for an agent to continue to work for his principal after a rival corporation which he also served as agent begins business." Thus, as a means of fostering free enterprise, the employee who gains general skills and knowledge and forms relationships with customers and coworkers during the course of his employment may use such skills, knowledge and relationships to compete with his former employer once the employment is terminated but may not compete while still employed as his employer who, lulled by trust in the employee's fidelity and loyalty, is deprived of the opportunity to compete with that employee.

Turning to the question of relief where a betrayal of confidence and trust has been demonstrated, we note that equity will prevent the continuance of such conduct in a proper case and will compel the former employee to turn over the gains to one equitably entitled thereto. *   *   *

*   *   *   *

During January, 1978, plaintiff's facilities, funds and personal property had been used by its employees under the direction of [defendant] Brownstein to pre-stamp Aeronautics's air bills, to furnish office supplies and airline containers to Aeronautics, and to prepare Aeronautics's daily station report forms. Furthermore, Brownstein continued to meet with plaintiff's customers in order to obtain commitments for Aeronautics on the basis that plaintiff was in financial trouble and would suffer a massive employee walkout. He also had meetings with plaintiff's employees to inform them of the nationwide plan to leave work on a certain Friday, and to devastate plaintiff's ability to compete by simply reporting to Aeronautics on the following Monday morning.

Brownstein admitted securing equipment and supplies for Aeronautics while still employed by plaintiff but denied that plaintiff's funds were used for this purpose. He also admitted that he told plaintiff's staff he would be following Agnes; that he expressed the hope that circumstances would then allow him to ask them to join him; and that he had informed plaintiff's clients of its unhealthy financial prognosis and its management by untrustworthy executives while asking them for the opportunity to solicit their business once he had changed jobs.

JUDGMENT AND REMEDY *The appellate court reversed the trial court's denial of injunctive relief. The case was remanded to the lower court for a hearing on whether the injunction should be issued.*

Duty of Obedience

When an agent is acting on behalf of the principal, a duty is imposed on the agent to follow all lawful and clearly stated instructions of the principal. The agent violates this duty whenever the agent deviates from such instructions. However, during emergency situations, when the principal cannot be consulted, the agent may deviate from such instructions without violating this duty if the circumstances so warrant. Whenever instructions are not clearly stated, the agent can fulfill the duty of obedience by acting in good faith in a reasonable manner under the circumstances.

Duty to Account

Unless an agent and a principal agree otherwise, the agent has the duty to keep and make available to the principal an account of all property and money received and paid out on behalf of the principal. This includes gifts from third persons in connection with the agency. The agent has a duty to maintain separate accounts for the principal's funds and for personal funds, and no intermingling of these accounts is allowed. Whenever a licensed professional violates this duty to account, he or she may be subject to disciplinary proceedings by the appropriate regulatory institution. Such proceedings would be in addition to the agent's liability to the principal for failure to account.

Duties Owed by Subagents

A subagent is any person employed or appointed by an agent to assist the agent in transacting the affairs of the principal. Since the agent has authority to appoint a subagent, the subagent has authority to bind the principal. Consequently, there exists a fiduciary relationship between the subagent and the principal as well as between the subagent and the agent. Generally, the principal's authorization is needed for the hiring of subagents except in emergencies. On the other hand, if the agent is normally expected in his or her line of work to hire subagents, they may be hired without the *explicit* authorization of the principal. For example, agents typically may hire subagents to do mechanical or ministerial duties without the explicit authorization of the principal. Subagents owe the same duties to agents and to principals as agents owe to principals.

Unauthorized Subagents If an agent hires a subagent without the principal's authority, then the subagent has no legal relationship to the principal—expressed, implied, or apparent. Since the subagent and the principal have no agency relationship to one another, no duties arise between them. A principal will not be liable to third parties for that subagent's acts. However, the agent who hires the subagent without authority will be liable to the principal if the subagent acts wrongfully, and the agent will bear the loss.

PRINCIPAL'S DUTIES
TO THE AGENT

The principal also has certain duties to the agent. These involve payment for services, reimburse-

ment for expenditures, and indemnity for losses under certain circumstances. The principal's duties to an agent may be expressed or they may be implied by law.

Compensation and Reimbursement

Except in a gratuitous agency relationship, the principal must pay the agreed-upon value (or reasonable value) for an agent's services. In addition, the principal must reimburse or indemnify the agent for all expenses or losses involved in carrying out the agent's authorized duties. Whenever the amount of compensation is agreed upon by the parties, the principal owes the duty to pay it upon completion of the agent's specified activities. If no amount is expressly agreed upon, then the principal owes the agent the customary compensation for such services. If no amount is established either by custom or by law, the principal owes the agent the reasonable value of his or her services.

In general, when a principal requests certain services from an agent, the agent reasonably expects payment. A duty is therefore implied for the principal to pay the agent for services rendered. For example, when an accountant or an attorney is asked to act as an agent, compensation is implied. The principal has the duty to pay that compensation in a timely manner.

Whenever an agent disburses sums of money at the request of the principal, and whenever the agent disburses sums of money to pay for necessary expenses in the course of a reasonable performance of his or her agency duties, the principal has the duty to reimburse. Agents cannot recover for expenses incurred by their own misconduct or negligence, however.

Duty of Cooperation

A principal has a duty both to cooperate with and to assist an agent in performing his or her duties. The principal must do nothing to prevent such performance. For example, when a principal grants an agent an exclusive territory, the principal cannot compete with the agent or appoint or allow another agent to so compete in violation of the *exclusive agency*. Such competition would expose the principal to liability for the agent's lost sales or profits.

Duty to Provide Safe Working Conditions

The common law requires the principal to provide safe premises, equipment, and conditions for all agents and employees. The principal has a duty to inspect working conditions and to warn agents and employees about any unsafe areas. If the agency is one of employment, the employer's liability is frequently covered by worker's compensation acts, which are the primary remedy for an employee's injury on the job. In addition, regulations promulgated under the Occupational Safety and Health Act of 1970 provide employees with the right to refuse to expose themselves to dangerous conditions without being subjected to subsequent discrimination by the employer as illustrated by the following case.

WHIRLPOOL CORP. v. MARSHALL

Supreme Court of the United States, 1980.
445 U.S. 1, 100 S.Ct. 883.

BACKGROUND AND FACTS   *The Occupational Safety and Health Act of 1970 protects the right of an employee to choose not to perform an assigned task because of a reasonable apprehension of death or serious injury. It also prohibits an employer from discharging or discriminating against any employee who exercises this right. The secretary of labor brought this action against a manufacturer, Whirlpool Corp., for depriving two employees of work and reprimanding them when they refused to perform a dangerous task.*

STEWART, Justice.

*   *   *   *

The petitioner company maintains a manufacturing plant in Marion, Ohio, for the production of household appliances. Overhead conveyors transport appliance components throughout the plant. To protect employees from objects that occasionally fall from these conveyors, the petitioner has installed a horizontal wire-mesh guard screen approximately 20 feet above the plant floor. This mesh screen is welded to angle-iron frames suspended from the building's structural steel skeleton.

*   *   *   *

In 1973, the company began to install heavier wire in the screen because its safety had been drawn into question. Several employees had fallen partly through the old screen, and on one occasion an employee had fallen completely through to the plant floor below but had survived. A number of maintenance employees had reacted to these incidents by bringing the unsafe screen conditions to the attention of their foremen. The petitioner company's contemporaneous safety instructions admonished employees to step only on the angle-iron frames.

*   *   *   *

On July 7, 1974, two of the petitioner's maintenance employees, Virgil Deemer and Thomas Cornwell, met with the plant maintenance superintendent to voice their concern about the safety of the screen. The superintendent disagreed with their view, but permitted the two men to inspect the screen with their foreman and to point out dangerous areas needing repair. Unsatisfied with the petitioner's response to the results of this inspection, Deemer and Cornwell met on July 9 with the plant safety director. At that meeting, they requested the name, address, and telephone number of a representative of the local office of the Occupational Safety and Health Administration (OSHA). Although the safety director told the men that they "had better stop and think about what [they] were doing," he furnished the men with the information they requested. Later that same day, Deemer contacted an official of the regional OSHA office and discussed the guard screen.

The next day, Deemer and Cornwell reported for the night shift at 10:45 p.m. Their foreman, after himself walking on some of the angle-iron frames, directed the two men to perform their usual maintenance duties on a section of the old screen. Claiming that the screen was unsafe, they refused to carry out this directive. The foreman then sent them to the personnel office, where they were ordered to punch out without working or being paid for the remaining six hours of the shift. The two men subsequently received written reprimands, which were placed in their employment files.

*   *   *   *

The Act itself creates an express mechanism for protecting workers from employment conditions believed to pose an emergent threat of death or serious injury. Upon receipt of an employee inspection request stating reasonable grounds to believe that an imminent danger is present in a workplace, OSHA must conduct an inspection. In the event the inspection reveals workplace conditions or practices that "could reasonably be expected to cause death or serious physical harm immediately or before the imminence of such danger can be eliminated through the enforcement procedures otherwise provided by" the Act, the OSHA inspector must inform the affected employees and the employer of the danger and notify them that he is recommending to the Secretary that injunctive relief be sought. At this juncture, the Secretary can petition a federal court to restrain the conditions or practices giving rise to the imminent danger. By means of a temporary restraining order or preliminary injunction, the court may then require the employer to avoid, correct, or remove the danger or to prohibit employees from working in the area.

To ensure that this process functions effectively, the Act expressly accords to every employee several rights, the exercise of which may not subject him to discharge or discrimination. An employee is given the right to inform OSHA of an imminently dangerous workplace condition or practice and request that OSHA inspect that condition or practice. *   *   *

*   *   *   *

Nothing in the Act suggests that those few employees who have to face this dilemma must rely exclusively on the remedies expressly set forth in the Act at the risk of their own safety. But nothing in the Act explicitly provides otherwise. Against this background of legislative silence, the Secretary has exercised his rulemaking power and has determined that, when an employee in good faith finds himself in such a predicament, he may refuse to expose himself to the dangerous condition, without being subjected to "subsequent discrimination" by the employer.

*   *   *   *

The regulation clearly conforms to the fundamental objective of the Act—to prevent occupational deaths and serious injuries. The Act, in its preamble, declares that its purpose and policy is "to assure so far as possible every working man and woman in the Nation safe and healthful working conditions and to preserve our human resources. *   *   *"

JUDGMENT
AND REMEDY

Finding that the employees acted under a valid regulation, the Supreme Court remanded the case to the district court for further consideration. The secretary of labor sought to have the reprimands expunged from the employees' personnel files and to have the two employees compensated for their lost pay.

AGENT'S RIGHTS AND REMEDIES AGAINST PRINCIPAL

Indemnification by Principal

Subject to the terms of the agency agreement, the principal has the duty to indemnify an agent for authorized payments or liabilities incurred because of authorized and lawful acts and transactions and also for losses suffered because of the principal's failure to perform any duties. Additionally, the principal must indemnify the agent for the value of benefits that the agent confers upon the principal unofficially.

The amount of indemnification is usually specified in the agency contract. If it is not, the courts will look to the nature of the business and the type of loss.

Authorized subagents can recover from either the principal or the agent who hires them, since the subagent is in a fiduciary relationship to both. If the authorized subagent gets indemnification from the agent who does the hiring, the agent can then seek indemnification from the principal.

Other Remedies

An agent can:

1. Withhold further performance.
2. Counterclaim if the principal sues.
3. Demand that the principal give an accounting.

These contract remedies are all for damages. Since the principal-agent relationship is deemed to be consensual in nature, an agent has no right to specific performance in an ordinary agency contract. An agent can recover for past services and future damages but cannot force the principal to allow him or her to continue acting as an agent.

PRINCIPAL'S RIGHTS AND REMEDIES AGAINST AGENT

In general, a principal has contract remedies for an agent's breach of fiduciary duties. The principal also has tort remedies for fraud, misrepresentation, negligence, deceit, libel, slander, and trespass committed by the agent. In addition, any breach of a fiduciary duty by an agent may justify the principal's termination of the agency.

Constructive Trust

Anything an agent obtains by virtue of the employment or agency relationship belongs to the principal. It is a breach of an agent's fiduciary duty to secretly retain benefits or profits that, by right, belong to the principal. Courts in this case will imply a **constructive trust.** The agent actually holds the money on behalf of the principal, and the principal can recover it in a lawsuit. For example, Andrews, a purchasing agent, gets cash rebates from a customer. If Andrews keeps the rebates, he violates his fiduciary duty to his principal, Metcalf. Upon finding out about the cash rebates, Metcalf can sue Andrews and recover them.

The rules against self-purchase prohibit an agent from taking advantage of the agency relationship to obtain goods or property that the principal wants to purchase. For example, Peterson (the principal) wants to purchase property in the suburbs. Cox, Peterson's agent, learns that a valuable tract of land has just become available. Cox cannot buy the land for herself. Peterson gets the right of first refusal. If Cox purchases the land for her benefit, the courts will impose a constructive trust on the land; that is, the land will be held for and on behalf of the principal despite the fact that the agent attempted to buy it in her own name.

Avoidance

When an agent breaches the agency agreement or agency duties under contract, the principal has a right to avoid any contract entered into with the agent. This right is voidable at the election of the principal.

In the following case, a real estate agent, supposedly acting on behalf of a landowner, purchased the property for himself without disclosing the rapid appreciation of the value of the land. The right of avoidance is illustrated.

BACKGROUND AND FACTS   *Ramsey, the plaintiff, was a licensed real estate broker and was also in the business of buying and holding land for resale. Gordon, the defendant, was the owner of approximately 181 acres of land. Gordon agreed to sell Ramsey the tract of land for $800 per acre. A contract of sale to convey the property was drawn up; but before the contract was executed, Gordon conveyed the property to a third party for the same price ($800 per acre).*

Meanwhile, Ramsey, acting for himself, began negotiating for the resale of that property to another customer for a price of $1,250 per acre. Naturally, when Ramsey learned that Gordon had conveyed the property to another buyer, he blamed Gordon for his lost profits. Ramsey claimed that he lost over $90,000 in profits on the resale of the property.

RAMSEY v. GORDON
Court of Civil Appeals of Texas,
Waco, 1978.
567 S.W.2d 868.

HALL, Justice.

* * * *

Ramsey [the plaintiff] testified that he operated two businesses, "Ramsey Realty" and "Ramsey Properties," that both are sole proprietorships owned by him, that under Ramsey Realty he acts as a real estate agent selling others' property for a commission, and that under Ramsey Properties he purchases property for himself. Although Ramsey now claims he was only a purchaser in the transaction with Gordon [the defendant], he testified on the trial that he was both agent and purchaser—that he was "a purchasing agent." Specifically, Ramsey testified again and again that under the contract he was Gordon's agent for the sale of the property. The trial court expressly found that he was Gordon's agent. The court also found that Ramsey knew the property was appreciating in value when the contract was made, and "up until and through January, 1974," that Ramsey failed to disclose that fact to Gordon; that he became personally interested in the property transaction by attempting to purchase the property himself, that the appreciation in value of the property from $800.00 per acre to $1,000.00 per acre was a material fact relating to the sale of the property; and that Ramsey failed to find a purchaser for Gordon for the best price available. Upon these findings the court concluded that Ramsey had breached his agency agreement and duties under the contract, and that the contract was therefore voidable at Gordon's election.

Ramsey does not challenge the finding that the property was increasing in value when the contract was being negotiated and made with Gordon, nor the findings that he knew the value was increasing and failed to disclose that fact to Gordon. Indeed, he may not do so because they are amply supported by the evidence and its inferences. His response to the conclusion that he breached his duties as Gordon's agent is to argue that he was only a purchaser and to cite Gordon's testimony that Gordon believed $800.00 per acre was a fair price when he made the contract. The over-all import of the record is that when it served Ramsey's purposes he would claim that under the contract he was Gordon's agent, but that in fact he used the contract to speculate with the property to his personal advantage without disclosure to Gordon. As we have said, the [trial] court found that Ramsey was Gordon's agent. Ramsey's testimony supports that finding.

Whenever an agent breaches his duty to his principal by becoming personally interested in an agency agreement, the contract is voidable at the election of the principal without full knowledge of all the facts surrounding the agent's interest. [Emphasis added.] * * * [It is a] "settled rule" that "an agent in dealing with a principal on his own account owes it to the principal not only to make no misstatements concerning the subject matter of the transaction, but also to disclose to him fully and completely all material facts known to the agent which might affect the principal; and that unless this duty on the part of the agent has been met, the principal cannot be held to have ratified the transaction."

JUDGMENT AND REMEDY   *The judgment of the trial court was affirmed. Ramsey was denied recovery because an agency relationship existed between Ramsey and Gordon, and Ramsey had breached his duties under this relationship.*

Shop Right

An interesting question occurs when an employee invents a product and the employer (or principal as an employer) claims a right to the invention or to the patent. The **shop-right** rule, or doctrine, is involved here. This doctrine says that if the employee's duties do not include conducting research and making inventions, the employer is not entitled to the invention but merely has a shop-right interest in it. This interest allows the employer a nonexclusive right to use the invention without paying any royalties to the employee. The employee retains ownership and, subject to the shop-right interest, full rights to the invention. The employer's right is irrevocable even after the employment relationship ends.

The following well-known case involves an invention created by a sales clerk at Sears, Roebuck & Co. during his off-duty hours. As you will see, the court considered whether the employer had a right to the invention even after the employment relationship had ended.

ROBERTS v. SEARS, ROEBUCK & CO.

Court of Appeals of the United States, Seventh Circuit, 1978. 197 U.S.P.Q. (BNA) 516, 573 F.2d 976, U.S. Cert. Den. in 199 U.S.P.Q. (BNA) 640.

BACKGROUND AND FACTS   *Peter Roberts sued Sears for damages for fraud, breach of a confidential relationship, and negligent misrepresentation. The case arose from Roberts's assignment of a patent to his former employer. The trial court entered a judgment in favor of Roberts, and Sears appealed.*

SPRECHER, Circuit Judge.

*   *   *   *

This case involves the efforts of one of this nation's largest retail companies, Sears, Roebuck & Co. (Sears), to acquire through deceit the monetary benefits of an invention of a new type of socket wrench created by one of its sales clerks during his off-duty hours. That sales clerk, Peter M. Roberts (Plaintiff), initiated the unfortunate events that led to this appeal in 1963, when at the age of 18 he began work on a ratchet or socket wrench that would permit the easy removal of the sockets from the wrench. He, in fact, designed and constructed a prototype tool with a quick-release feature in it that succeeded in permitting its user to change sockets with one hand. Based on that prototype, plaintiff filed an application for a United States patent. In addition, since he was in the employ of Sears, a company that sold over a million wrenches per year, and since he had only a high school education and no business experience, he decided to show his invention to the manager of the Sears store in Gardner, Massachusetts where he worked. Plaintiff was persuaded to submit formally his invention as a suggestion to Sears. In May 1964, the prototype, along with a completed suggestion form, was sent to Sears' main office in Chicago, Illinois. Plaintiff, thereafter, left Sears' employ when his parents moved to Tennessee.

It was from this point on that Sears' conduct became the basis for the jury's determination that Sears appropriated the value of the plaintiff's invention by fraudulent means. Plaintiff's evidence proved that Sears took steps to ascertain the utility of the invention and that based on the information it acquired, Sears became convinced that the invention was in fact valuable. *   *   *

Sears also took pains to ascertain the patentability of the quick-release feature. In April 1965, it received outside patent counsel's advice that there was "some basis for limited patentability" (defendant's Exhibit 9). It had previously learned in February 1965 from plaintiff's lawyer, Charles Fay, that he believed the invention was patentable based on a limited search. In addition, Sears was informed in early May 1965, by plaintiff's lawyer that a patent had been issued to plaintiff.[1]

With all of this information either available or soon to be available, Sears contacted plaintiff in January 1965, and began negotiations regarding the purchase of rights to use plaintiff's invention. During these negotiations, conducted with plaintiff's attorney, Sears' lawyer, Leonard Schram, made various representations to plaintiff that serve as the essential basis for plaintiff's complaint. In April 1965, in a letter seeking merely a license, Schram first told plaintiff that the invention was not new and that the claims in any patent that would be permitted would be "quite limited."

Based on this letter, plaintiff entered into the agreement on July 29, 1965, which provided for a two cent royalty per unit up to a maximum of $10,000 to be paid in return for a complete *assignment* of all of plaintiff's rights. In fact, for no extra charge, plaintiff's attorney gave Sears all of plaintiff's foreign patent rights. A provision was included in the contract regarding what would happen if Sears failed to sell 50,000 wrenches in a given year, thus reinforcing the impression that the wrenches might not sell very well. Also, a provision was inserted dealing with the contingency that a patent might not be issued, notwithstanding that Sears already knew, and plaintiff did not, that the patent had been granted.

---

1. We might note here that Mr. Fay contacted Sears before informing plaintiff that a patent had issued. In addition, it was shown that Sears had contacted Mr. Fay during the period of these negotiations about doing some work for it and that he, in fact, did perform a couple of routine matters for Sears, thus raising some doubt about the independence of his advice to plaintiff.

By July, Sears knew that it planned to sell several hundred thousand wrenches with a cost per item increase of only 20 cents, that a patent had issued and that this product in all likelihood would have tremendous appeal with mechanics. Nonetheless, it entered into this agreement both having failed to disclose vital information about the product's appeal and structural utility and having made representations to plaintiff that were either false at the time they were made or became false without disclosure prior to the time of the signing of the contract.

*   *   * Within *nine months*, Sears had sold over 500,000 wrenches and paid plaintiff his maximum royalty thereby acquiring all of plaintiff's rights. Between 1965 and 1975, Sears sold in excess of 19 million wrenches, many at a premium of one to two dollars profit because no competition was able to market a comparable product for several years. To say the least, plaintiff's invention has been a commercial success.

Plaintiff, a Tennessee resident, filed suit against Sears, an Illinois Corporation, in federal district court in December 1969, based on diversity jurisdiction, seeking alternatively return of the patent and restitution or damages for fraud, breach of a confidential relationship and negligent misrepresentation. A jury trial was held from December 20, 1976, until January 18, 1977. During the trial, plaintiff basically proved the facts as presented above. Sears argued that it did not misrepresent any facts to plaintiff, that he had a lawyer and thus there was no confidential relationship and that the success of the wrenches was a function of advertising and the unforeseeable boom in do-it-yourself repairs, and thus Sears did not misrepresent the salability of plaintiff's wrenches. *   *   * The jury apparently believed the plaintiff's evidence because it found Sears guilty *   *   * and entered judgment for one million dollars.

*   *   *   *

Sears' final argument in its cross-appeal is that plaintiff failed to prove the existence of a confidential relationship between himself and Sears. In assessing that argument, we recognize at the outset that there are no hard and fast rules for determining whether a confidential relationship exists. The trier of fact must examine all of the circumstances surrounding the relationship between the parties and determine whether "one person reposes trust and confidence in another who thereby gains a resulting influence and superiority over the first."

Various factors have been recognized judicially as being of particular relevance to that inquiry. Among them are disparity of age, education and business experience between the parties. Additional factors are the existence of an employment relationship and the exchange of confidential information from one party to the other. All five of those factors are present in this case. In addition, one of Sears' witnesses admitted that the company expected plaintiff to "believe" and to "rely" on various representations that Sears made to him.

JUDGMENT AND REMEDY   *The verdict of $1 million was affirmed.*

COMMENTS   *In April 1982, a jury awarded Roberts an additional $5 million after concluding that Sears was guilty of patent infringement with respect to 15 million wrenches sold after the original trial.*

Principal's Right to Indemnification

A principal can be sued by a third party for an agent's negligent conduct, and in certain situations the principal can sue the agent for an equal amount of damages. This is called **indemnification.** The same holds true if the agent violates the principal's instructions. For example, Lewis (the principal) tells his agent, Moore, who is a used car salesman, to make no warranties for the used cars. Moore is eager to make a sale to Walters, the third party, and makes a warranty for the car's engine. Lewis is not absolved from liability to Walters for engine failure, but if Walters sues Lewis, Lewis can then sue Moore for indemnification for violating his instructions.

Sometimes it is difficult to distinguish between instructions of the principal that limit an agent's authority and those that are mere advice. For example, Willis (the principal) owns an office supply company; Jones (the agent) is the manager. Willis tells Jones, "Don't order any more supplies this month." Willis goes on vacation. A large order comes in from a local business, and the present inventory is insufficient to meet it. What is Jones to do? In this situation, Jones probably has the inherent power to order more supplies despite Willis's statement. It is unlikely that Jones would be required to indemnify Willis in the event that the local business subsequently canceled the order.

In the following case, an insurance company sought indemnification from an insurance broker. The court had to determine whether the broker was the agent of the insurance company or of the insured.

BACKGROUND AND FACTS   *Industrial Fire and Casualty Company denied coverage under a policy it had issued to Lydia Elie. A trial court found there was coverage under the policy, and Industrial sued the insurance broker, AMI Insurance Agency, to recover the benefits paid to Elie. AMI appealed the trial court's finding that it was liable to Industrial.*

AMI INS. AGENCY v. ELIE

District Court of Appeal of Florida, Third District, 1981. 394 So.2d 1061.

MELVIN (Ret.), Associate Judge.

* * * *

We hold that the existence of an agency relationship between AMI and Industrial is a prerequisite to the imposition of the indemnification here complained of. Indemnity is a right which inures to one who discharges a duty owed by him, but which, as between himself and another, should have been discharged by the other and is allowable only where the whole fault is in the one against whom indemnity is sought. *   *   * It is clear that an insurance *agent* who binds a contract of insurance, when he is not so authorized, becomes liable to indemnify the company for losses arising from that contract.

Under the general rule, which is here applicable, an insurance broker is the agent of the insured in matters connected with the procurement of insurance. An insurance *broker* is ordinarily employed by the person seeking insurance, and, when so employed, is to be distinguished from the ordinary insurance *agent*, who is employed by insurance companies to solicit and write insurance. The fact that the insurer furnished the broker an application blank which was given to the person requesting insurance coverage does not make the broker an agent of the insurer issuing the policy.

We thus find that AMI was not the agent of Industrial, but was the agent of Elie. Therefore, because there is no principal-agent relationship between AMI and

Industrial, the lower court erred in ruling that Industrial was entitled to indemnification from AMI.

JUDGMENT AND REMEDY   *AMI was not liable to Industrial.*

QUESTIONS AND CASE PROBLEMS

1. Paul Gett is a well-known, wealthy financier living in the city of Torris. Adam Wade, a friend of Gett, tells Timothy Brown that he is Gett's agent for the purchase of rare coins. Wade even shows Brown a local newspaper clipping mentioning Gett's interest in coin collecting. Brown, knowing of Wade's friendship with Gett, contracts with Wade to sell a rare coin valued at $25,000 to Gett. Wade takes the coin and disappears with it. On the date of contract payment Brown seeks to collect from Gett, claiming Wade's agency made Gett liable. Gett does not deny that Wade was a friend, but he claims that Wade was never his agent. Discuss fully whether an agency was in existence at the time the contract for the rare coin was made.

2. Paula owes Adam $1,000, and the debt is due and payable. Paula does not have the cash to pay the debt, but she has some stereo equipment valued at $1,800. Paula gives Adam authority to sell the stereo equipment to satisfy the debt, with any surplus being paid back to Paula. Later Paula and Adam have a severe disagreement over another matter, and Paula sends a letter to Adam terminating his authority and agency to sell the stereo equipment. Despite receiving the letter, Adam contracts to sell the equipment to Francis for $1,200. Francis pays Adam, but Paula refuses to turn over the stereo equipment to Francis or accept the $200 from Adam. Paula claims that at the time the contract with Francis was made no agency existed. Discuss fully Paula's contention.

3. Adam is hired by Peter as an agent to sell a piece of property owned by Peter. The price to be obtained is to be not less than $30,000. Adam discovers that because a shopping mall is planned for the area of Peter's property, the fair market value of the property will be at least $45,000 and could be higher. Adam forms a real estate partnership with his cousin Carl, and Adam prepares for Peter's signature a contract for $32,000 for sale of the property to Carl. Peter signs the contract. Just before closing and passage of title, Peter learns about the shopping mall and the increased fair market value of his property. Peter refuses to deed the property to Carl. Carl claims that Adam, as agent, solicited a price above that agreed upon in the creation of the agency and that the contract is therefore binding and enforceable. Discuss fully whether Peter is bound to this contract.

4. John Paul Corporation made the following contracts:

(a) A contract with Able Construction to build an addition to the corporate office building.

(b) A contract with a CPA, a recent college graduate, to head the cost accounting section.

(c) A contract with a saleswoman to travel a designated area to solicit orders (contracts) for the corporation.

Able contracts with Apex for materials for the addition; the CPA hires an experienced accountant to advise her on certain accounting procedures; and the saleswoman contracts to sell a large order to Green, agreeing to deliver the goods in person within twenty days. Able refuses to pick up the materials, the CPA is in default in paying the hired consultant, and the saleswoman does not deliver on time. Apex, the accountant and Green claim John Paul Corporation is liable under agency law. Discuss fully whether an agency relationship was created by John Paul with Able, the CPA, or the saleswoman.

5. Able is hired by Peters as a traveling salesman. Able not only solicits orders but delivers the goods and collects payments from his customers. Able places all payments in his private checking account and at the end of each month draws sufficient cash from his bank to cover the payments made. Peters is totally unaware of this procedure. Because of a slowdown in the economy, Peters tells all his salespeople to offer 20 percent discounts on orders. Able solicits orders, but he offers only 15 percent discounts, pocketing the extra 5 percent paid by customers. Able has not lost any orders by this practice, and he is rated one of

Peters's top salespersons. Peters now learns of Able's actions. Discuss fully Peters's rights in this matter.

6. When the Mileses applied for a mortgage loan, the bank president told them a termite inspection was always required and arranged by the bank. The bank president was advised that termites were found on the property and that extermination would be necessary, but he did not advise the Mileses. Do the Mileses have a cause of action against the bank? [Miles v. Perpetual Sav. & Loan Co., 58 Ohio St.2d 93, 388 N.E.2d 1364 (1979)]

7. Miller sold insurance for Massachusetts Mutual Life Insurance Company under a contract that he renewed annually. Miller derived his income almost exclusively from the efforts of agents who worked under him. In connection with his job, Miller borrowed and invested large sums of money to promote sales by his agents. He was free to vary the terms of the contracts he had with them in regard to their rates and commissions. In addition, he could hire and fire them without Massachusetts Mutual's approval. Miller received a commission from Massachusetts Mutual for all the sales that he or his agents made. Is Miller an employee of Massachusetts Mutual or an independent contractor? [Massachusetts Mutual Life Ins. Co. v. Central Penn Nat'l Bank, 372 F.Supp. 1027 (E.D.Penn. 1974)]

8. Roy Haven brought a medical malpractice action against his surgeon, Judson Randolph, M.D., and the hospital where the surgery had been performed. Haven claimed that the doctor's negligence caused him to suffer paralysis as a result of minor surgery. Haven also wished to hold the hospital responsible as Randolph's principal. Randolph was not employed by the hospital, and any services that the hospital provided were at Randolph's direction. Would Randolph be deemed an agent of the hospital? [Haven v. Randolph, 342 F.Supp. 538 (D.C.D.C.1972)]

9. Crittendon took his Chevrolet to a service station operated by Mendenhall and discussed the problem of its faulty wheel bearings. During the conversation, Mendenhall stated that he had previously worked at a Chevrolet garage and was familiar with the repair of Chevrolets. The service station at which Mendenhall worked was owned by State Oil Company and displayed two signs, each containing only the word *State*. Mendenhall leased the service station from State but received neither a salary nor repair tools from State. Crittendon left his car for Mendenhall to repair. After Mendenhall repaired it, he took it out for a test drive, went off the road, and damaged it extensively. Crittendon wished to establish an agency relationship between State and Mendenhall so he could recover from State. Does Crittendon have any grounds to argue for the existence of a principal-agent relationship? [Crittendon v. State Oil Co., 78 Ill.App.2d 112, 222 N.E.2d 561 (1966)]

10. Sam Kademenos was about to sell a $1 million life insurance policy to a prospective customer when he resigned from the company, Equitable Life. Before resigning, however, he had expended substantial company money and had utilized Equitable's medical examiners in order to procure the $1 million sale. After resigning, Kademenos joined a competitor, Jefferson Life Insurance Company, and made the sale through it. Has he breached any duty to Equitable? [Kademenos v. Equitable Life Assur. Soc'y, 513 F.2d 1073 (3d Cir. 1975)]

11. During the course of the administration of the estate of Baldwin M. Baldwin, it became necessary to sell a vast apartment complex owned by the estate, known as "Baldwin Hills Village." Lemby, a real estate broker, doing business as Skyline Realty, was commissioned to make the sale. A number of prospective purchasers were contacted, and they were present at the private sale of Baldwin Hills Village. On a number of prior occasions, Lemby had indicated to the executors of Baldwin's estate that he was interested in purchasing the property. At the private sale, Lemby outbid all others and bought Baldwin Hills Village. Lemby then sought his commission on the sale from the Baldwin estate. Will anything in agency law prevent Lemby from recovering? [In re Estate of Baldwin, 34 Cal.App.3d 596, 110 Cal.Rptr. 189 (1973)]

CHAPTER 35

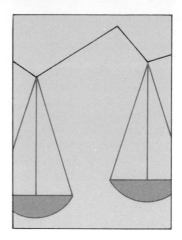

Liability of Principals and Agents to Third Parties and Termination of Agency Relationship

Once the principal-agent relationship is created, attention often focuses on the rights of third persons who deal with the agent. The first part of this chapter is concerned with the rights of these third parties when they *contract* with agents. Such contracts will make an agent's principal liable to the third party only if the agent had authority to make the contract or if the principal ratified or was estopped from denying the agent's acts.

The second part of this chapter examines tort liability and the distinctions among employer-employee, employer-independent contractor, and principal-agent relationships. The chapter concludes by discussing termination of the principal-agent relationship and of the agent's authority to bind the principal.

SCOPE OF AUTHORITY

A principal's liability in a contract with a third party arises from the authority given the agent

to enter legally binding contracts on the principal's behalf. An agent's authority to act stems from three types of sources:

1. Express (or specific).
2. Implied.
3. Apparent (or by estoppel).

If an agent contracts outside the scope of his or her authority, the principal may still be liable by ratifying the contract.

Express Authority

Express authority is embodied in that which the principal has engaged the agent to do. It can be given orally or in writing. For example, giving an agent a power of attorney confers express authority.[1] The power of attorney is a written doc-

_____

1. An agent who holds the power of attorney is called an attorney-in-fact for the principal. The holder does not have to be an attorney-at-law.

626

ument and is usually notarized. Like all agency relationships, a power of attorney can be special—permitting the agent to do specified acts only—or it can be general—permitting the agent to transact all business dealings for the principal. See Exhibit 35–1.

The **equal dignity** rule in most states requires that if the contract being executed is in writing, then the agent's authority must also be in writing.[2] Failure to comply with the equal dignity rule can make a contract voidable *at the option of the principal.* The law regards the contract at that point as a mere offer. If the principal decides to accept the offer, acceptance must be ratified in writing. For example, Palmer (the principal) orally asks Larkins (the agent) to sell a ranch that Palmer owns. Larkins finds a buyer and signs a sales contract on behalf of Palmer to sell the ranch. The buyer cannot enforce the contract unless Palmer subsequently ratifies Larkins's agency status in *writing.* Once the contract is ratified, either party can enforce rights under the contract.

The equal dignity rule does not apply when an agent acts in the presence of a principal or when the agent's act of signing is merely perfunctory. For example, Lucas (the principal) negotiates a contract, but the day it is to be signed, Lucas is called out of town. Lucas authorizes Hilton to sign the contract. In that case, oral authorization is sufficient.

Implied Authority

Implied authority is conferred by custom, can be inferred from the position the agent occupies, or is implied by virtue of being reasonably necessary to carry out express authority.

For example, Adams is employed by Packard Grocery to manage one of its stores. Packard has not specified (expressly stated) Adams's authority to contract with third persons. In this situation, authority to manage a business implies authority to do what is reasonably required (as is customary or can be inferred from a manager's position) to operate the business. This includes contracts for employee help, for buying merchandise and equipment, and even for advertising the products sold in the store.

Because implied authority is conferred on the basis of custom, it is important for the third person to be familiar with the custom of the trade. For example, a traveling salesperson normally may have implied authority to solicit orders for the principal, but may not have implied authority to collect for goods unless the salesperson is in possession of the goods.

The list of basic principles of implied authority based on custom or on the agent's position is extensive. It suffices to state that implied authority is always authority customarily associated with the position occupied by the agent, or authority that can be inferred from the express authority given to the agent to fully perform his or her duties. The test is whether it was reasonable for the agent to believe that he or she had the authority to enter the contract in question.

Mistakes can create unintended agents. For example, Shaffer (the principal) goes to a stockbroker's office looking for Powell. Shaffer leaves a note on McPherson's desk, thinking it is Powell's desk. The note says, "I authorize you to sell my 100 shares of IBM stock at market price. [Signed] Shaffer." Even though Shaffer intended the authorization for Powell, McPherson can act with valid authority to sell the stock. Again, the test is whether it was reasonable for the agent to believe that he or she had the authority to act on behalf of the principal.

Apparent Authority—Estoppel

Apparent authority, or authority by estoppel, exists when the principal, by either word or action, causes a third party to reasonably believe that an agent has authority to act, even though the agent has no express or implied authority.

For example, a traveling salesperson has no express authority to collect for orders solicited from customers. Since the agent neither possesses the goods ordered nor delivers them, the agent also has no implied authority to collect.

---

2. An exception to the equal dignity rule exists in modern business practice. An executive officer of a corporation, when acting for the corporation in an ordinary business situation, is not required to obtain written authority from the corporation.

EXHIBIT 35–1   SAMPLE POWER OF ATTORNEY

POWER OF ATTORNEY

GENERAL

Know All Men by These Presents: That I, _____

_____

the undersigned (jointly and severally, if more than one) hereby make, constitute and appoint _____

_____

any true and lawful Attorney for me and in my name, place and stead and for my use and benefit:

(a) To ask, demand, sue for, recover, collect and receive each and every sum of money, debt, account, legacy, bequest, interest, dividend, annuity and demand (which now is or hereafter shall become due, owing or payable) belonging to or claimed by me, and to use and take any lawful means for the recovery thereof by legal process or otherwise, and to execute and deliver a satisfaction or release therefor, together with the right and power to compromise or compound any claim or demand;

(b) To exercise any or all of the following powers as to real property, any interest therein and/or any building thereon: To contract for, purchase, receive and take possession thereof and of evidence of title thereto; to lease the same for any term or purpose, including leases for business, residence, and oil and/or mineral development; to sell, exchange, grant or convey the same with or without warranty; and to mortgage, transfer in trust, or otherwise encumber or hypothecate the same to secure payment of a negotiable or non-negotiable note or performance of any obligation or agreement;

(c) To exercise any or all of the following powers as to all kinds of personal property and goods, wares and merchandise, choses in action and other property in possession or in action: To contract for, buy, sell, exchange, transfer and in any legal manner deal in and with the same; and to mortgage, transfer in trust, or otherwise encumber or hypothecate the same to secure payment of a negotiable or non-negotiable note or performance of any obligation or agreement;

(d) To borrow money and to execute and deliver negotiable or non-negotiable notes therefor with or without security; and to loan money and receive negotiable or non-negotiable notes therefor with such security as he shall deem proper;

(e) To create, amend, supplement and terminate any trust and to instruct and advise the trustee of any trust wherein I am or may be trustor or beneficiary; to represent and vote stock, exercise stock rights, accept and deal with any dividend, distribution or bonus, join in any corporate financing, reorganization, merger, liquidation, consolidation or other action and the extension, compromise, conversion, adjustment, enforcement or foreclosure, singly or in conjunction with others of any corporate stock, bond, note, debenture or other security; to compound, compromise, adjust, settle and satisfy any obligation, secured or unsecured, owing by or to me and to give or accept any property and/or money whether or not equal to or less in value than the amount owing in payment, settlement or satisfaction thereof;

(f) To transact business of any kind or class and as my act and deed to sign, execute, acknowledge and deliver any deed, lease, assignment of lease, covenant, indenture, indemnity, agreement, mortgage, deed of trust, assignment of mortgage or of the beneficial interest under deed of trust, extension or renewal of any obligation, subordination or waiver of priority, hypothecation, bottomry, charter-party, bill of lading, bill of sale, bill, bond, note, whether negotiable or non-negotiable, receipt, evidence of debt, full or partial release or satisfaction of mortgage, judgment and other debt, request for partial or full reconveyance of deed of trust and such other instruments in writing of any kind or class as may be necessary or proper in the premises.

Giving and Granting unto my said Attorney full power and authority to do and perform all and every act and thing whatsoever requisite, necessary

or appropriate to be done in and about the premises as fully to all intents and purposes as I might or could do if personally present, hereby ratifying all that my said Attorney shall lawfully do or cause to be done by virtue of these presents. The powers and authority hereby conferred upon my said Attorney shall be applicable to all real and personal property or interests therein now owned or hereafter acquired by me and wherever situate.

My said Attorney is empowered hereby to determine in his sole discretion the time when, purpose for and manner in which any power herein conferred upon him shall be exercised, and the conditions, provisions and covenants of any instrument or document which may be executed by him pursuant hereto; and in the acquisition or disposition of real or personal property, my said Attorney shall have exclusive power to fix the terms thereof for cash, credit and/or property, and if on credit with or without security.

The undersigned, if a married woman, hereby further authorizes and empowers my said Attorney, as my duly authorized agent, to join in my behalf, in the execution of any instrument by which any community real property or any interest therein, now owned or hereafter acquired by my spouse and myself, or either of us, is sold, leased, encumbered, or conveyed.

When the contest so requires, the masculine gender includes the feminine and/or neuter, and the singular number includes the plural.

WITNESS my hand this _____ day of _____ , 19_____

_____   _____

_____   _____

State of California,   } SS.
   County of _____

On _____ , before me, the undersigned, a Notary Public in and for said State, personally appeared _____

_____

known to me to be the person _____ whose name _____ subscribed to the within instrument and acknowledged that _____ executed the same.

Witness my hand and official seal.   (Seal) _____
                                              Notary Public in and for said State.

Assume that a customer, Carla, pays an agent, Adam, for a solicited order. Adam then takes the payment to the principal's accounting department. An accountant accepts payment and sends Carla a receipt. This procedure is thereafter followed for other orders solicited and paid for by Carla. Later Adam solicits an order, and Carla pays Adam as before. This time, however, Adam absconds with the money. Can Carla claim that the payment to Adam was authorized and thus, in effect, was a payment to the principal? The answer is yes, because the principal's *repeated* acts of accepting Carla's payment led Carla to reasonably believe that Adam had authority to receive payments for goods solicited. Although Adam did not have express or implied authority,

the principal's *conduct* gave Adam apparent authority to collect. The principal would be estopped from denying the agent's authority to collect in this particular case.

Sometimes it is not reasonable for a third person to rely on the statements made by an agent. In fact, apparent authority can never be created by statements of the agent alone. This is especially true when a contract contains language indicating that it must be approved by the home office. When such information is disclosed, as in the following case, the agent's own statements or assurances will not overcome the express restriction on the agent's authority. (It should be noted, however, that disclaimers of authority are not always enforced.)

BACKGROUND AND FACTS *The plaintiffs signed a written contract for the purchase of a shell house. One of its provisions specifically stated that the terms of purchase were subject to the approval of a particular individual. The plaintiffs were aware of the provision and admitted that approval was never obtained. However, the plaintiffs maintained that the defendant corporation's agent assured them that their request would be approved and that the sale would go through. Thus, the plaintiffs went ahead and made certain repairs and improvements to the house while awaiting approval of the sales contract. Meanwhile, not only did the corporation refuse to convey the property, but the house was destroyed by fire.*

The trial court, sympathetic to the plaintiffs' plight, entered a judgment in their favor. The corporation appealed the judgment, arguing that the plaintiffs had no reason to rely on the apparent authority of the agent, especially in light of the fact that the written contract clearly conditioned the sale upon corporate approval and not upon the agent's approval.

MID-STATE HOMES, INC. v. BERRY
Court of Civil Appeals of Alabama, 1978.
359 So.2d 401.

WRIGHT, Presiding Judge.

* * * *

Plaintiffs learned that [defendant] Mid-State Homes had repossessed an unfinished shell house located in Crenshaw County, Alabama, and was offering it for sale. They contacted the sales representative for Mid-State at his office in Montgomery.

They were informed of the conditions of the sale of the house and signed an instrument entitled an "agreement for deed." They gave the sales representative three hundred dollars as down payment. The instrument which the plaintiffs signed stated on its face that its terms were subject to the approval of Herb Clarkson [principal]. The Mid-State representative told plaintiff that the agreement would have to be forwarded to Tampa, Florida and signed and approved by Clarkson. * * *

According to plaintiffs' testimony, the representative of defendant told them he was sure the sale would go through and approved their request to make repairs and improvements to the house while awaiting the approval of the sale by Clarkson. Acting on such alleged assurance, plaintiffs did make improvements and performed labor on the house. * * *

On March 5, 1977, plaintiffs attempted to make the first scheduled payment on the house. They were informed that the prior owner was trying to pick up his payments and no more money could be accepted until the problem was straightened out. A few days thereafter the house was destroyed by fire. Plaintiffs' down payment was returned to them. * * *

* * * *

We have carefully examined the evidence and discern no authority, apparent or otherwise, shown to have been possessed by the sales representative to enter into such a contract as that claimed by plaintiffs. The record is very clear that the representative expressly was without authority to execute a contract of sale of the property. That authority was expressly reserved to Herb Clarkson of the Tampa office by the written contract signed by plaintiffs. They stated they were aware of that provision in the contract. The evidence is undisputed that the contract to purchase the house * * * was never executed by defendant. The * * * contract stated the sale was subject to the approval of Clarkson. The complaint further says that in spite of the statement in the contract requiring its approval by Clarkson, plaintiffs were assured by defendant's agent that they could make improvements with safety and they did make improvements. The evidence of plaintiffs followed these allegations:

There was alleged only one contract between plaintiffs and defendant. Its existence was then nullified by proof that it required the approval of Clarkson. The assurances of safety to make improvements by the agent was not a contract. If plaintiffs' testimony as to such assurance is true, it amounts only to a representation or opinion by the agent which plaintiffs acted upon to make improvements upon defendant's property. The essence of the assurance was that the agent was sure that the contract would be approved by Clarkson, the sale consummated and the property become that of plaintiffs. There was no real authority in the agent to make such an assurance. It was directly opposed to the subjection stated on the face of the contract. An agent cannot negative by his own representation the express restriction of his authority known to the third party.

The evidence discloses no apparent authority. Apparent authority cannot come from the acts or declarations of the agent but arises from the action or declaration of the principal disclosed to the plaintiff.

JUDGMENT
AND REMEDY

Since there was no evidence to support the existence of a contract between the plaintiffs and the defendant, the plaintiffs could not recover for a breach of contract. The judgment of the trial court was reversed.

Agent's Possession and Apparent Ownership as Apparent Authority   Sometimes a principal will go beyond mere statements or actions that convince a third party that a certain person is the principal's agent. If, for example, the principal has "clothed the agent" with both possession and apparent ownership of the principal's property, the agent will have very broad powers and can deal with the property as if he or she were the true owner.

For example, to deceive certain creditors, Baker (the principal) and Hunter (the agent) agree verbally that Hunter will hold certain stock certificates for Baker. Hunter's possession and apparent ownership of the stock certificates are such strong indications of ownership that a reasonable person would conclude that Hunter was the actual owner. If Hunter negotiates the stock certificates to a third person, Baker will be estopped from denying Hunter's authority to transfer the stock.

Where land is involved, courts have held that possession alone is not a sufficient indication of ownership. Therefore, if an agent has mere possession of realty, a reasonable person should realize that possession alone is not an adequate assurance of ownership. (See Chapter 53 for details.) If, on the other hand, the agent also possesses the deed to the property and sells the property against the principal's wishes to an unsuspecting buyer, the principal cannot cancel the sale or assert a claim to title. Of course, in this event the principal would have the right to recover from the agent for violation of a fiduciary duty. The next case illustrates the operation of apparent authority to bind a principal.

BACKGROUND AND FACTS   *William Kirchberg, a food broker, placed orders for lettuce on behalf of O'Day, the principal. Kirchberg ordered the lettuce from Arakelian Farms, and the bills were sent to and paid by O'Day. In August 1970, Kirchberg terminated his agency relationship with O'Day. Arakelian was not notified that Kirchberg was no longer O'Day's agent. Thereafter Kirchberg placed twenty lettuce orders with Arakelian, all of which were billed to O'Day. O'Day refused to pay for the lettuce ordered after termination of the agency agreement with Kirchberg, and Arakelian sued O'Day to recover for the twenty shipments.*

O'DAY v. GEORGE ARAKELIAN FARMS, INC.

Court of Appeals of Arizona, Division 1, 1975.
24 Ariz.App. 578, 540 P.2d 197.

FROEB, Judge.

*   *   *   *

The trial court ruled in favor of Arakelian and entered judgment against O'Day for $22,089.80 plus costs. In its judgment, the court found and concluded that Kirchberg had apparent authority to act on behalf of O'Day and bind him to the 20 lettuce sales on the basis of their dealings in the previous 55 transactions. It found that evidence of the previous transactions in which Kirchberg had acted as O'Day's agent constituted apparent authority for him to act in the 20 subsequent transactions. The court then found that the lettuce had been shipped by Arakelian to the cooler where delivery to O'Day was complete. It found that bills of lading confirming the shipments were prepared at the cooler and sent to Arakelian and that in due course an invoice for each shipment was prepared and sent to O'Day and not thereafter returned.

*   *   *   *

The evidence pertaining to the formation of the contracts is clear. Telephone orders were received by Arakelian from Kirchberg. Although there is no evidence that Kirchberg had *actual* authority to bind *these* sales to O'Day, circumstances bringing into effect the doctrine of apparent authority are most certainly present. The principle is set forth in Restatement (Second) of Agency, § 8, as follows:

> Apparent authority is the power to affect the legal relations of another person by transactions with third persons, professedly as agent for the other, arising from and in accordance with the other's manifestations to such third persons.

Apparent authority may be derived from a course of dealing, or from the fact that a number of acts similar to the ones in question were assented to by the principal.

The manifestations of O'Day in the prior 55 transactions clearly indicate a willingness by him to have Arakelian deal with Kirchberg until Arakelian had notice of termination of authority or until there had been such a lapse of time after the 55 transactions that Arakelian, in the exercise of ordinary prudence, would realize that the authority might no longer exist. As the facts reveal, Arakelian received no such notice and the period of time over which all of the transactions occurred was not so long as to make Arakelian's reliance thereon beyond the exercise of ordinary prudence. Thus, we hold the acts of Kirchberg in these transactions are binding upon O'Day.

JUDGMENT   *Arakelian recovered the price of the twenty orders from O'Day. Kirchberg*
AND REMEDY   *had apparent authority to act for O'Day.*

Emergency Powers

When an unforeseen emergency demands action by the agent to protect or preserve the property and rights of the principal, but the agent is unable to communicate with the principal, the agent has emergency power.

For example, Fisher is a brakeman on Pacific Railroad. While Fisher is acting within the scope of his employment, he falls under the train many miles from home and is severely injured. Davis, the conductor, directs Thompson, a doctor, to give medical aid to Fisher. Davis has no express authority to bind Pacific Railroad for the services of Thompson. Yet, because of the emergency situation, the law recognizes him as having authority to act appropriately under the circumstances.

Ratification

Ratification is the affirmation of a previously unauthorized contract or act. Ratification can be either express or implied. Generally, only a principal can ratify. The principal must be aware of all material facts; otherwise, the ratification is not effective. Ratification binds the principal to the agent's acts and treats the acts or contracts as if they had been authorized by the principal *from the outset*. If the principal does not ratify, there is no contract binding the principal,

and the third party agreement with the agent is viewed merely as an unaccepted offer. Because the third party's agreement is treated merely as an unaccepted offer, the third party can revoke the offer (rescind the agreement) at any time before the principal ratifies, without liability. The agent, however, may well be liable to the third party for misrepresenting his or her authority.

The principal's acceptance (that is, the ratification) is binding only if the principal knows all the terms of the contract. If not, the principal can thereafter rescind ratification unless, of course, the third party has proceeded to change position in reliance on the contract.

Suppose an agent, without authority, contracts with a third person on behalf of a principal for repair work to the principal's office building. The principal learns of the contract from the agent and agrees to "some repair work," thinking that it will involve only patching and painting the exterior of the building. In fact, the contract includes resurfacing the parking lot, which the principal does not want done. Upon learning of the additional provision, the principal rescinds the contract. If the third party has made no preparations to do the work (such as purchasing materials, hiring additional workers, or renting equipment), then the principal can still rescind. But if the third party has, to his or her detriment, relied on the principal's ratification by making preparations, the principal must reimburse the third party for the cost of the preparations.

Two important points must be stressed. First, it is immaterial whether the principal's lack of knowledge results from the agent's fraud or is simply a mistake on the principal's part. If the third party has not changed position in reliance on the principal, the principal can repudiate the ratification. The unauthorized contract remains an offer, and the principal's acceptance is not valid, because contract law provides that one cannot accept terms one does not know about. Second, the whole transaction must be ratified; a principal cannot affirm the desirable parts of a contract and reject the undesirable parts.

Death or incapacity of the third party *before* ratification will void an unauthorized contract. Most courts will also recognize intervening and extraordinary change of circumstances as a basis for setting aside a principal's ratification to permit a third party to revoke.

Assume that Able, without authority, enters into a contract with a third party who wants to purchase Paula's shopping center. The following night the shopping center is destroyed by fire. Paula's subsequent ratification will not be effective to bind the third party. The courts will reason that it is unjust to hold a third party liable in such a case and will permit the transaction to be avoided despite ratification.

Express Ratification   If a principal's statements or conduct express an intent to be bound, the prior unauthorized act will be ratified, and the principal will become a party to the contract.

For example, Smith (the agent) negotiates the sale of a shipment of oranges to World Markets without the authorization of Samuelson (the principal). Samuelson sees the completed paperwork and tells Smith to go ahead with it. Samuelson thus expressly ratifies the sale and is now bound to the terms of the sales contract.

Implied Ratification   Implied ratification oc-

curs most commonly when a principal decides to accept the benefits of a previously unauthorized transaction. In the preceding example, if Samuelson had known of the unauthorized acts and failed to repudiate or object to them within a reasonable time, the contract would be ratified. In addition, if World Markets had paid for the oranges, and if Samuelson, upon learning that World Markets had paid, did not object or repudiate, Samuelson would have impliedly ratified the contract.

Requirements for Ratification Summarized
The previous discussion can be put in the form of a list of requirements for ratification, as follows:

1.   The presumptive agent must have acted on behalf of a principal who subsequently ratifies, although some states permit ratification by an undisclosed principal.
2.   The principal must know of all material facts involved in the transaction.
3.   The agent's act must be affirmed in its entirety by the principal.
4.   The principal must have the legal capacity to authorize the transaction at the time the agent engages in the act and at the time the principal ratifies.
5.   The principal's affirmance must occur prior to the withdrawal of the third party from the transaction or prior to a changing of the circumstances in such a way that it would be unjust to hold the third party to the transaction.
6.   The principal must observe the same formalities when he or she approves the act purportedly done by the agent on his or her behalf as would have been required to authorize it initially.

The following case illustrates the need of the principal to promptly repudiate unauthorized acts of an agent to avoid ratification.

BACKGROUND AND FACTS   *Charles Theis maintained an investment account with the brokerage firm of duPont, Glore Forgan Inc. Theis discovered that Benjamin, a duPont account executive, was making unauthorized transactions in his account and reprimanded him. Theis finally*

THEIS v. duPONT, GLORE FORGAN INC.
Supreme Court of Kansas, 1973, 212 Kan. 301, 510 P.2d 1212.

closed the account when Benjamin directly contravened Theis's order not to buy on May 24, 1968. Theis filed suit against duPont for all the unauthorized trading by Benjamin from the inception of the Theis account. The trial court allowed recovery on only the May 24 transaction.

FROMME, Justice.

*   *   *   *

Ratification is the adoption or confirmation by a principal of an act performed on his behalf by an agent which act was performed without authority. The ratification by the principal of an unauthorized act of his agent is equivalent to an original grant of authority. On acquiring knowledge of the unauthorized act of an agent, the principal should promptly repudiate the act, otherwise it will be presumed he has ratified and affirmed the act.

The principles governing ratification, including the requirement of prompt repudiation of an unauthorized act of an agent, are applicable in brokerage transactions.

*   *   *   *

The record is clear the trial court correctly applied these principles to this entire period. During this period of time there were 36 transactions in the Theis account. The court determined that by Theis' failure to promptly repudiate unauthorized transactions he had either authorized or ratified the first 35 transactions. However, the court found that Theis promptly repudiated the final transaction of May 24 when he learned it had been made contrary to his express orders. This was evidenced not only by registering a protest with Benjamin but also by closing his commodities account with the broker.

It is pointed out the requirement of prompt repudiation is to prevent an investor from withholding his disapproval until the market has taken a turn for the worse, and then deciding to assert the alleged wrongdoing. In such case if prompt repudiation were not required he might sit back and quietly accept profits resulting from an unauthorized trade when it turned out to be to his advantage.

In the present case Theis had previously absorbed the losses, as well as the gains, resulting from Benjamin's unauthorized transactions. However, on May 24 Theis did not hesitate in closing his account as soon as he learned that Benjamin had bought in his short position contrary to express instructions. The record shows he did so without waiting to see whether the market price would ultimately rise or fall. His actions indicate he was unconcerned with the wisdom of the May 24 purchase. He was irate over the unauthorized purchase by Benjamin. The action of Theis in closing his account with duPont was found by the trial court to be an express repudiation of the May 24 transaction and this finding is supported by substantial evidence. Whether there has been a repudiation within a reasonable time is a question of fact and the ratification of a former unauthorized act is not the ratification of another entirely distinct act.

JUDGMENT AND REMEDY   *Although the court found Theis had ratified Benjamin's earlier actions, duPont, Glore Forgan Inc. was liable for the unauthorized act of its employee on May 24.*

AGENT'S LIABILITY
FOR CONTRACTS

Normally, an agent is not party to a contract that he or she makes with a third party on behalf of a *disclosed* principal, because the contract is between the third person and the principal. A principal is disclosed whenever the third person knows of both the agency relationship and the identity of the principal. When an agent performs within the scope of his or her agency authority without any wrongdoing, the agent has no liability for the non-performance of either the principal or the third party.

An agent becomes personally liable to third parties when he or she:

1. Enters into a contract on behalf of an undisclosed or partially disclosed principal.
2. Acts without authority or exceeds the scope of authority granted by the principal.
3. Personally guarantees performance by the principal.

Whenever the agent lacks authority or exceeds the scope of authority, the agent's liability is based on the theory of breach of implied warranty of authority, not on breach of the contract itself.[3]

The agent's implied warranty of authority can be breached intentionally or by a good faith mistake.[4] The agent's liability remains, as long as the third party has relied on agency status. Conversely, where the third party knows at the time of the contract that the agent is mistaken, or the agent indicates to the third party *uncertainty* about the extent of authority, the agent is not personally liable for breach of warranty.

Agent's Authorized Acts

An agent's acts are *authorized* if they are either within the scope of the agent's authority or sub-

sequently ratified by the disclosed principal. However, the rules of liability differ on the basis of whether the principal's identity is disclosed or undisclosed to the third party.

Undisclosed Principal When neither the fact of agency nor the identity of the principal is disclosed, a third party is deemed to be dealing with the agent personally, and the agent is liable as a party on the contract.

For example, in a contract for the sale of a horse, a third party knows only that Scammon (the agent) wants to purchase the horse. The third party does not know that Scammon is actually negotiating for Johnson (the principal). Scammon signs a written contract in her own name, not indicating any agency relationship. She delivers the horse to Johnson, who is in fact the principal, but Johnson refuses to pay her. Scammon tries to return the horse to the third party, who refuses to take it. The third party is entitled to hold Scammon liable for payment. The agent's subjective intent is not relevant. The third party contracted with the agent on the basis of the *agent's* credit and reputation, not the undisclosed principal's. Therefore, the agent is liable.

If the agent is forced to pay the third party, and if the agent has contracted within the scope of authority granted,[5] the agent is entitled to indemnification by the principal. It was the principal's duty to perform even though his or her identity was undisclosed,[6] and failure to do so will make the principal ultimately liable. Once the undisclosed principal's identity is revealed, the third party has the right to elect to hold either the principal or the agent liable on contract. (In some states no election is necessary.)

In the following case, the undisclosed principal creates a liability problem for the travel agent.

---

3. The agent's liability is not on the contract because the agent was never personally intended as a party to the contract.
4. If the agent intentionally misrepresents his or her authority, then the agent can also be liable in tort for misrepresentation.

5. The agent can never establish apparent authority because the principal has not previously been revealed and cannot, therefore, have informed the third party of an agency relationship.
6. If A is a gratuitous agent, and P accepts the benefits of A's contract with a third party, then P will be liable to A on the theory of quasi-contract.

ROSEN v. DEPORTER-BUTTERWORTH TOURS, INC.

Appellate Court of Illinois,
1978.
62 Ill.App.3d 762, 19 Ill.Dec.
743, 379 N.E.2d 407.

BACKGROUND AND FACTS *The plaintiff purchased a packaged tour for an African safari from a travel bureau, the defendant. The travel bureau failed to disclose that it was in fact a special agent for the tour's sponsor, World Trek. Prior to the purchase of the package, the plaintiff had direct contact with the travel bureau but never with the tour sponsor. Hence, the tour sponsor, World Trek, was an undisclosed principal.*

The plaintiff planned to travel through Europe and then to join the tour in Egypt. Before leaving the United States, the plaintiff informed the travel bureau of where he could be reached in Europe and in Egypt prior to the start of the tour. The tour itinerary had to be changed. The travel bureau failed to contact the plaintiff overseas, leaving the plaintiff stranded in Egypt for a week. The plaintiff sued the travel bureau for damages sustained. The travel bureau claimed that it was not liable because it was merely an agent for World Trek and that World Trek was the proper party to the lawsuit.

BARRY, Presiding Justice.

*   *   *   *

The final issue presented for review is whether the trial court erred in finding defendant [the travel bureau] liable to the plaintiff for the price of the tour. Inherent in a decision of this issue is a determination of the relationship between plaintiff and defendant and defendant and the tour sponsor, World Trek. *   *   * [I]n the normal situation between a travel bureau and its traveler client a special agency relationship arises for the limited object of the one business transaction between the two parties. It is clear in the present case that the plaintiff employed the defendant travel bureau as his special agent for the limited purpose of arranging the African Safari Tour sponsored by World Trek.

Although the sponsor of the tour, World Trek, as advertised in the brochure, was not a party to this lawsuit, their relationship to the defendant is an important factor in deciding liability. The record contains a letter from defendant to World Trek as plaintiff's exhibit No. 4, which admits to defendant's selling of World Trek's tour to the plaintiff and hints of a principal-agency relationship between World Trek and the defendant. The evidence also disclosed that the defendant received a 10% commission from World Trek for selling its tour. *The legal principle that an agent is liable as a principal [to] a third party in the case of an undisclosed agency relationship* is well established and needs no citation for authority. [Emphasis added.] In the instant case the plaintiff was aware that World Trek was sponsoring the tour but was without knowledge as to whether the defendant was truly representing him as his special agent for arranging the tour or whether defendant was acting as an agent for World Trek in selling its tour to plaintiff.

The traditional relationship between a travel bureau, such as defendant, and the tour sponsors of the various tours sold has been categorized as one of agent and principal particularly in the field of tort liability of the travel bureau for injuries that occur to the traveler. No sound reason exists for not finding the same principal-agent relationship between a tour sponsor and a travel bureau in the case of alleged liability for breach of an agreement involving the ultimate sale of the tour to an ordinary member of the traveling public, such as the plaintiff.

   *   *   * *[I]f an agent does not disclose the existence of an agency relationship and the identity of his principal, he binds himself to the third party with whom he acts as if he, himself, were the principal. [Emphasis added.]* *   *   * The fact that the plaintiff knew that World Trek and not defendant was the tour sponsor does not satisfy the necessary disclosure to prevent defendant from becoming liable as principal. *   *   *

The travel bureau is liable to the plaintiff because it did not reveal that it was acting as an agent for World Trek as an undisclosed principal.   **JUDGMENT AND REMEDY**

Negotiable Instruments   The agency rule for negotiable instruments is controlled primarily by the Uniform Commercial Code, not agency law. UCC 3-401(1) provides that only the one whose signature is on negotiable paper can be held liable. Extrinsic evidence to show an agency relationship is not normally admissible. Therefore, if an agent signs the paper using his or her own name and not indicating any agency status, the agent is personally liable. [UCC 3-403(2)(b)] For examples of proper signature form indicating agency, see Chapter 28.

Undisclosed Principal's Rights against the Third Party   The undisclosed principal is entitled to contract rights obtained on his or her behalf by an agent, regardless of whether the third party knows of the agency. The undisclosed principal normally is, in effect, the beneficiary of all contract rights.

Undisclosed Principal's Liability for Agent's Dishonesty   As a general rule, an undisclosed principal is liable for an agent's dishonesty after an authorized contract has been made. If a third person gives money to an agent as provided by the contract and the agent absconds with the money, the principal absorbs the loss. The same is generally true where the agent has made an authorized purchase on credit from the third party and the principal has given the money for payment to the agent. Should the agent abscond with the funds, the principal absorbs the loss.

The Third Party's Right to Rescind a Contract with an Undisclosed Principal   In some cases, nondisclosure of the existence and identity of a principal is a fraud upon the third person. For example, Knight and Jones are neighbors with adjoining property. They have been fighting for years because Jones will not sell Knight his property. Knight hires Short to buy the property. Short *assures* Jones that he is purchasing the land on his own behalf. Upon learning of the fraud, Jones can opt to rescind the sale or to complete it.

The Third Party's Right to an Agent's Personal Performance   In certain instances involving undisclosed principals, the contracted duties are personal to the agent's performance and cannot be delegated under contract law. The third party can refuse to permit the principal's performance and can hold the agent liable for personal performance. Typical examples involve extensions of credit or highly personal service contracts.

PRINCIPAL'S OR EMPLOYER'S LIABILITY FOR TORTS OF AN AGENT OR EMPLOYEE

An agent or employee is liable for his or her own torts and crimes. A principal or employer becomes liable for an agent's torts if the torts are committed within the scope of the agency or scope of employment. A principal or employer is not, however, liable for an agent's or employee's crimes, unless he participates by conspiracy or other action.

A principal or employer is liable if:

1. He directs the agent or employee to do the act.
2. There is a negligent entrustment.
3. The principal or employer fails to properly supervise the subordinate.

Misrepresentation

A principal is exposed to tort liability whenever a third person sustains loss due to the agent's misrepresentation. The key to a principal's liability is whether or not the agent was actually or apparently authorized to make representations, and whether such representations were made within the scope of the agency.

Assume Lewis is a demonstrator for Moore's products. Moore sends Lewis to a home show to demonstrate the products and answer questions from consumers. Moore has given Lewis authority to make statements about the products. If Lewis makes only true representations, all is fine; but if he makes false claims, Moore will be liable for any injuries or damages sustained by third parties in reliance on Lewis's false representations.

An interesting series of cases have arisen on the theory that when a principal has placed an agent in a position to defraud a third party, the principal is liable for the agent's fraudulent acts.

For example, Pratt is a loan officer at First Security Bank. In the ordinary course of the job, Pratt approves and services loans and has access to the credit records of all customers. Pratt falsely represents to a borrower, McMillan, that the bank feels insecure about McMillan's loan and intends to call it in unless McMillan provides additional collateral such as stocks and bonds. McMillan gives Pratt numerous stock certificates that Pratt keeps in her own possession, later using them to make personal investments. The bank is liable to McMillan for losses sustained on the stocks even though the bank had no direct role or knowledge of the fraudulent scheme.

The legal theory used here is that the agent's position conveys to third persons the impression that the agent has the authority to make statements and perform acts that are consistent with the ordinary duties that are within the scope of the position. When an agent appears to be acting within the scope of the authority that the position of agency confers but is actually taking advantage of a third party, the principal who placed the agent in that position is liable. In the example above, if a bank teller or security guard had told McMillan that the bank required additional security for a loan, McMillan would not be justified in relying on either person's authority to make that representation. However, McMillan could reasonably expect that the loan officer was telling the truth.

Innocent Misrepresentation   Tort liability based on fraud requires proof that a material misstatement was made knowingly and with the intent to deceive. An agent's innocent mistakes occurring in a contract transaction or involving a warranty contained in the contract can provide grounds for the third party's rescission of the contract and the award of damages. Moreover, justice dictates that where a principal knows that an agent is not accurately advised of facts but does not correct either the agent's or the third party's impressions, the principal is directly responsible to the third party for resulting damages. The point is that the principal is always directly responsible for an agent's misrepresentation made within the scope of authority.

Negligence: Personal Injury

The principal (employer) is liable for the physical harm by an agent (employee) that occurs in the scope of the principal's authority (scope of employment) and furtherance of the principal's business. The theory of liability used here involves the doctrine of *respondeat superior*.

The Doctrine of Respondeat Superior   The theory of liability based on *respondeat superior*[7] is

---

7.   The theory of *respondeat superior* is similar to the theory of strict liability covered in Chapter 21. This doctrine may not apply if the principal or employer has sovereign or charitable organization immunity. The practice of granting such immunity is diminishing in most states.

that it imposes vicarious liability on the principal or employer (that is, liability without regard to the personal fault of the master for torts committed by a servant in the course of employment).[8]

At early common law, a servant (employee) was viewed as the master's (employer's) property. The master was deemed to have absolute control over the servant's acts and was held strictly liable for them no matter how carefully the master supervised the servant. The rationale for the doctrine of *respondeat superior* is based on the principle of social duty. Every person shall manage his or her own affairs, whether alone or through agents or servants, so as not to injure another. Liability is imposed on employers or principals because they are deemed to be in better financial positions to bear the loss. The superior financial position carries with it the duty to be responsible for damages.

Today the doctrine continues, but employers carry liability insurance and spread the cost of risk over the entire business enterprise. Public policy requires that an injured person be afforded effective relief, and recovery from a business enterprise provides far more effective relief than recovery from an individual employee. Liability rights exist under law and under public policy protections of third parties. Thus, a master (employer) cannot contract with a servant (employee) to disclaim responsibilities for injuries resulting from the servant's acts, because such disclaimers are against public policy.

The Restatement, Second, Agency, Section 229, indicates the general factors that courts will consider in determining whether or not a particular act occurred within the course and scope of employment. They are:

1. Whether the act was authorized by the master.
2. The time, place, and purpose of the act.
3. Whether the act was one commonly performed by employees on behalf of their employers.
4. The extent to which the employer's interest was advanced by the act.
5. The extent to which the private interests of the employee were involved.
6. Whether the employer furnished the means or instrumentality (for example, a truck or a machine) by which the injury was inflicted.
7. Whether the employer had reason to know that the employee would do the act in question and whether the employee had ever done it before.
8. Whether the act involved the commission of a serious crime.

Subagents As stated before, there are three instances in which an agent can hire a subagent (subservant):

1. To perform ministerial or mechanical duties.
2. Whenever it is the business custom.
3. For unforeseen emergencies.

If an agent is authorized to hire subagents for the employer under any one of these three circumstances, then the employer is liable for the acts of the subagents. There is a slight difference in result if the agent hires for an *undisclosed* employer. In that case, the agent is responsible for the subagent in contract law for such things as wages. However, the undisclosed employer is generally held to be liable for tort injuries. The doctrine of *respondeat superior* imposes liability on the true "master". An agent's unauthorized hiring of a subagent generally will not create any legal relationship between the principal and the subagent.

Borrowed Servants Employers can lend the services of their employees to other employers. Suppose that an employer leases ground-moving equipment to another employer and sends along an employee to operate the machinery. Who is liable for injuries caused by the employee's negligent actions on the job site? Liability turns on which employer had the right to control the employee at the time the injuries occurred. Generally, the employer who rents out the equipment is presumed to retain control over his or her em-

---

8. The doctrine of *respondeat superior* applies not only to master-servant relationships but also to principal-agent relationships as long as there is the right of control by the principal over the agent.

ployee. If the rental is for a relatively long period of time, however, control may be deemed to pass to the employer who is renting the equipment and presumably controlling and directing the employee.

Notice of Dangerous Conditions   The employer is charged with knowledge of any dangerous conditions discovered by an employee and pertinent to the employment situation. To illustrate, a maintenance employee in M's apartment notices a lead pipe protruding from the ground. The employee neglects either to fix it or to inform the employer of the danger. X falls on the pipe and is injured. The employer is charged with knowledge of the dangerous condition regardless of whether or not the employee actually informed the employer. That knowledge is imputed to the employer by virtue of the employment relationship.

"Frolic" by an Employee or Agent   The act causing injury must have occurred as part of the employee's regular duties in employment. For example, Sutton (the employee) is a delivery driver for Schwartz (the employer). Schwartz provides Sutton with a vehicle and instructs him to use it for making company deliveries. Nevertheless, one day Sutton drives his own car in-stead of the company vehicle and negligently injures Walker. Even though Sutton's act (driving the car) was unauthorized, the negligence occurred as part of Sutton's regular duties of employment (making deliveries). Hence, Schwartz is still liable to Walker for the injuries caused by Sutton, even though Sutton used his own car contrary to Schwartz's instructions. Only if Sutton's acts exceed the scope of employment duties in a way that the employer would not reasonably expect to happen will Schwartz be relieved of liability.

An employee going to and from work or to and from meals is usually considered outside the scope of employment. All travel time of a traveling salesperson, however, is normally considered within the scope of employment for the duration of the business trip, including the return trip home.

When an employee or agent goes on a frolic of his or her own—that is, departs from the employer's business to take care of personal affairs—is the employer liable? It depends. If the employee's or agent's activity is a substantial departure akin to an utter abandonment of the employer's business, then the employer is not liable.

The following case is a classic in master-servant law. Although it is nearly 150 years old, the legal principle for which it stands is still viable in the law of agency and employment law today.

JOEL v. MORISON

Court of Exchequer, England, 1834.
6 Carrington & Payne Reports 501.

BACKGROUND AND FACTS   *The plaintiff was walking across Bishops-gatestreet when he was knocked down by a cart driven negligently by a servant of the defendant. The plaintiff suffered a fractured leg and multiple injuries. The plaintiff took the position that the defendant was liable for his injuries because the defendant's servant was driving the cart that caused the injuries. The defendant argued that his cart was never driven in the neighborhood in which the plaintiff was injured. Moreover, it was suggested that the defendant's servant had gone out of his way for his own purposes and might have taken the cart at a time when it was not wanted for business purposes to pay a visit to some friends.*

PARKE, Judge.

*   *   *   *

His Lordship afterwards, in summing up, said—This is an action to recover damages for an injury sustained by the plaintiff, in consequence of the negligence of the defendant's servant. There is no doubt that the plaintiff has suffered the injury, and there is no doubt that the driver of the cart was guilty of negligence, and there is no doubt also that the master, if that person was driving the cart on his master's business, is responsible. If the servants, being on their master's business, took a detour to call upon a friend, the master will be responsible. If you think the servants lent the cart to a person who was driving without the defendant's knowledge, he will not be responsible. Or, if you think that the young man who was driving took the cart surreptitiously, and was not at the time employed on his master's business, the defendant will not be liable. The master is only liable where the servant is acting in the course of his employment. If he was going out of his way, against his master's implied commands, when driving on his master's business, he will make his master liable; but if he was going on a frolic of his own, without being at all on his master's business, the master will not be liable. As to the damages, the master *   *   * [although not himself] guilty of any offence, *   *   * is only responsible in law, therefore the amount should be reasonable.

The verdict was for the plaintiff, and he was awarded damages of £30.   **JUDGMENT**
In this case, the master was held liable for the acts of his servant.   **AND REMEDY**

Fellow-Servant Injuries A key exception to *respondeat superior* is the fellow-servant rule: an employer is not liable for injuries inflicted by one employee upon another while both are engaged in the same general enterprise.

Traditionally, employees were expected to assume the risk of injury by fellow employees. An employee was deemed as capable as an employer of protection from such danger on the job. So except in cases where the employer was negligent in hiring responsible personnel or where a supervisor injured a worker, the employer was held blameless.

Today, broad coverage is provided for on-the-job injuries for industrial workers under **worker's compensation statutes.** These statutes broadly define the scope of employment and provide fixed compensation to insured workers who are injured in industrial accidents. Worker's compensation statutes create an absolute liability on the part of the employer at the sacrifice of all common law defenses. The employer can benefit because the employee cannot recover common law damages. Thus, worker's compensation statutes eliminate contributory or comparative negligence, assumption of risk, and the fellow-ser-

vant rule, reducing the common law defenses based on risk taking.

Worker's compensation, however, leaves large numbers of people in the labor force unprotected. For example, domestic workers, laborers, and independent contractors are not protected. Some industrial companies have very few employees who are covered. Finally, worker's compensation will not cover injuries caused by willful misconduct of a fellow employee. In these cases, the fellow-servant rule is still significant.

Independent Contractors The doctrine of *respondeat superior* is limited to master-servant (employer-employee) and principal-agent relationships. Thus, the general rule concerning liability for the acts of an independent contractor is that the employer is not liable for physical harm caused to a third person by the negligent act of an independent contractor in the performance of the contract. An employer who has no legal power to control the details of the physical performance of a contract cannot be held liable. Here again the test is the *right to control*. Since an employer bargains with an independent contractor only for results and retains no control over the manner in which those results are achieved, the employer is generally not expected to bear the responsibility for torts committed by an independent contractor. A collection agency is a typical example of an independent contractor relationship. The creditor is generally not liable for the acts of the collection agency because collection is a distinct business occupation.

An exception to this doctrine prevails when exceptionally hazardous activities are involved. Typical examples of such activities include blasting operations, transportation of highly volatile chemicals, or use of poisonous gases. In these cases an employer cannot be shielded from liability merely by using an independent contractor. Strict liability is imposed upon the employer as a matter of law. Also, in some states, strict liability is imposed by statute.

EMPLOYER'S OR PRINCIPAL'S LIABILITY FOR EMPLOYEE'S OR AGENT'S INTENTIONAL TORTS

Under *respondeat superior*, the employer is liable for intentional torts of the employee within the scope of employment, just as the employer is liable for negligence. For example, an employer is liable for an employee's assault and battery or an employee's false imprisonment while acting within the scope of employment. Also, an employer is liable for permitting an employee to engage in reckless acts that can injure others. For example, an employer observes an employee smoking while filling containerized trucks with highly flammable liquids. Failure to stop the employee will cause the employer to be liable for any injuries that result.

An employee acting at the employer's direction can be liable as a tortfeasor, along with the employer, for committing the tortious act even if the employee was unaware of the wrongfulness of the act. For example, an employer directs an employee to burn out a field of crops. The employee does so, assuming that the field belongs to the employer, which it does not. Both can be found liable to the owner of the field for damages.

Employer Has a Duty of Care in Hiring and Retaining Employees

An employer who knows or should know that an employee has a propensity for committing tortious acts is liable for the employee's acts even if they would not ordinarily be considered within the scope of employment. For example, the Blue Moon employs Joe Green as a bouncer, knowing that he has a history of arrests for assault and battery. While he is working one night within the scope of his employment, he viciously attacks a patron who "looks at him funny." The Blue Moon will bear the responsibility for Green's acts because it knew that he had a propensity for committing tortious acts.

TERMINATION OF AN AGENCY

Agency law is similar to contract law in that both an agency and a contract terminate by an act of the parties or by operation of law. Once the relationship between the principal and agent has ended, the agent no longer has the right to bind the principal. However, third persons may also need to be notified when the agency has been terminated.

Termination by Act of the Parties

Lapse of Time   An agency agreement may specify the time period during which the agency relationship will exist. If so, the agency ends when that time expires. For example, Able signs an agreement of agency with Paula "beginning January 1, 1980, and ending December 31, 1985." The agency is automatically terminated on December 31, 1985. Of course, the parties can agree to continue the relationship, in which case the same terms will apply.

If no definite time is stated, then the agency continues for a reasonable time and can be terminated at will by either party. A "reasonable time" depends upon the circumstances and the nature of the agency relationship. For example, Paula asks Able to sell Paula's car. After two years, if Able has not sold Paula's car and there has been no communication between Paula and

Able, it is safe to assume that the agency relationship has terminated. Able no longer has the authority to sell Paula's car.

Purpose Achieved   An agent can be employed to accomplish a particular objective, such as the purchase of stock for a cattle rancher. In that case, the agency automatically ends after the cattle have been purchased.

If more than one agent is employed to accomplish the same purpose, such as the sale of real estate, the first agent to complete the sale automatically terminates the agency relationship for all the others.

Occurrence of a Specific Event   An agency can be created to terminate upon the happening of a certain event. For example, Paula appoints Able to handle her business affairs while she is away. When Paula returns, the agency automatically terminates.

Sometimes one aspect of the agent's authority terminates on the occurrence of a particular event, but the agency relationship itself does not terminate. For example, Paula, a banker, permits Able, the credit manager, to grant a credit line of $1,000 to certain depositors who maintain $1,000 in a savings account. If any customer's savings account falls below $1,000, Able can no longer continue making the credit line available to that customer. But Able's right to extend credit to the other customers maintaining the minimum balance will continue.

Mutual Agreement   Recall from basic contract law that parties can cancel (rescind) a contract by mutually agreeing to terminate the contractual relationship. The same holds true in agency law regardless of whether the agency contract is in writing or whether it is for a specific duration. For example, Paula no longer wishes Able to be her agent, and Able does not want to work for Paula any more. Either party can communicate to the other the intent to terminate the relationship. Such communication effectively relieves each of the rights, duties, and powers inherent in the relationship.

The agent's act is said to be a renunciation of authority. The principal's act is a revocation of authority.

Termination by One Party   As a general rule, either party can terminate the agency relationship; but although both parties may have the *power* to terminate, they may not each possess the *right*. Wrongful termination can subject the canceling party to a suit for damages.

For example, Able has a one-year employment contract with Paula for $12,000. Paula can discharge Able before the contract period expires (Paula has the *power* to breach the contract); however, Paula will be liable to Able for money damages because Paula has no *right* to breach the contract.

Even in an agency at will, the principal who wishes to terminate must give the agent a reasonable notice, that is, at least long enough to allow the agent to recoup his or her expenses and, in some cases, to make a normal profit.

The next case involves the premature termination of an agency relationship.

BACKGROUND AND FACTS   *The appellant, a real estate broker, had an exclusive listing contract for the sale of the appellees' home. During the time the contract was in force, the McDonalds sold their home to a third party and refused to pay the realtor's commission.*

DOWD MORE CO. REALTORS v. McDONALD

Court of Civil Appeals of Texas, Houston (1st Dist.), 1973. 494 S.W.2d 282.

EVANS, Justice.

* * * *

In this case the appellants Dowd More established the essential facts which entitle them to a recovery for breach of contract. While the appellants were admittedly not the procuring cause of the sale, it is undisputed that appellants had initiated performance under the contract and had advertised the property for sale, had placed their "For Sale" sign in the yard, had listed the property with Multiple Listing Service and had shown the property to prospective customers. The contract was no longer nudum pactum [a voluntary promise for good will only] but on the contrary was a bilateral agreement which appellees could not unilaterally revoke by a sale to a third party.

This principle is, we believe, clearly set forth in McDonald v. Davis, 389 S.W.2d 494, wherein this court speaking through Chief Justice Bell at page 496, said:

* * * *

"The principal may of course revoke an agent's authority where not coupled with an interest, but there is a distinction between his power to revoke and his right to revoke. He at any time before full performance can revoke the authority of an agent so the agent will lose his authority to bring the principal into legal relations with a third party. However, if he has no right to revoke it, he will be liable for damages suffered by the agent by reason of the wrongful revocation. Where, as here, there is a bilateral contract, the principal has no right to revoke to the prejudice of the agent.

Where a principal breaches the contract, he becomes liable in damages. Where, as here, suit is for breach of a contract granting the agent the exclusive right for a definite period of time to sell property, the damages are for breach of contract and not for the commission promised if the agent sold. He is entitled to recover the reasonable profit he would have made. Prima facie that profit is the amount represented by the stipulated commission."

As stated above, appellants' compensation under the exclusive real estate listing contract was stipulated to be 6% of the listed price of $18,500.00, or $1100.00. In the absence of satisfactory evidence that appellants' reasonable profits were in a lesser sum than the stipulated commission the sum specified in the contract is prima facie evidence of their damages. Accordingly, the judgment of the trial court is reversed and judgment is rendered for the appellants in the amount of $1100.00 with interest at 6% per annum from and after September 3, 1971.

JUDGMENT AND REMEDY

The trial court's judgment for the McDonalds was reversed. The McDonalds were liable for the full amount of the real estate commission.

Termination by Operation of Law

Death or Insanity The general rule is that death or insanity of either the principal or the agent automatically and immediately terminates the ordinary agency relationship. Knowledge of the death is not required.[9] For example, Paula sends

Able to the Far East to purchase a rare book. Before Able makes the purchase, Paula dies. Able's agent status is terminated at the moment of death, even though Able does not know that Paula has died. Some states, however, have changed this common law by statute.

Agents' transactions that occur after the death of the principal are not binding on the principal's estate. Assume Able is hired by Paula to collect a debt from Tom (a third party). Paula dies, but Able still collects the money from Tom,

9. An exception to virtually all notice and termination rules occurs in an agency coupled with an interest, which is not automatically terminated by death or incapacity.

not knowing of Paula's death. Tom's payment to Able is no longer legally sufficient to discharge Tom's debt to Paula because Able no longer has Paula's authority to collect the money. If Able absconds with the money, Tom must again pay the debt to Paula's estate.

Unforeseen Circumstances

Impossibility   When the subject matter of an agency is destroyed or lost, the agency terminates. For example, Paula employs Able to sell Paula's house. Prior to any sale, the premises are destroyed by fire. Able's agency and authority to sell Paula's house terminate. When it is impossible for the agent to perform the agency lawfully, because of war or because of a change in the law, the agency terminates.

Changed Circumstances   When an event occurs that has such an unusual effect on the subject matter of the agency that the agent can reasonably infer that the principal will not want the agent to continue, the agency terminates. Paula hires Able to sell a tract of land for $10,000. Subsequently, Able learns that there is oil under the land and that the land is therefore worth $1 million. The agency and Able's authority to sell the land for $10,000 is terminated.

Bankruptcy   Bankruptcy of the principal (or the agent) *usually* terminates the agency relationship.[10] Some situations, such as a serious financial loss, might indicate that future contracts should not be made.

Notice Required for Termination

When an agency terminates by operation of law because of death, insanity, or some other unforeseen circumstance, there is no duty to notify

third persons.[11] However, if the parties themselves have terminated the agency (although notice may be given by others), it is the principal's duty to inform any third parties who know of the existence of the agency that it has been terminated.

An agent's *authority* continues until the agent receives some notice of termination. No particular form of notice is required to be effective. The principal can actually notify the agent, or the agent can learn of the termination through some other means. For example, Marshall bids on a shipment of steel, and Smith is hired as an agent to arrange transportation of the shipment. When Smith learns that Marshall has lost the bid, Smith's authority to make the transportation arrangement terminates.

Notice to third parties, however, follows the general rule that an agent's *apparent authority* continues until the third person is notified (from any source of information) that authority has been terminated.

The principal is expected to notify *directly* any third person whom the principal knows has dealt with the agent. For third persons who have heard about the agency but have not dealt with the agent, *constructive* notice is sufficient.[12]

If the agent's authority is written, it must be revoked in writing, and the writing must be shown to all people who saw the original writing that established the agency relationship. Sometimes a written authorization (like that granting power of attorney) contains an expiration date.

---

10. Insolvency, as distinguished from bankruptcy, will not necessarily terminate the relationship. Most states do not consider the appointment of a receiver grounds for terminating the agency.

11. There is an exception to this rule in banking. UCC 4-405 provides that the bank as the agent can continue to exercise specific types of authority even after the customer's death or insanity unless it has knowledge of the death or insanity. When it has knowledge of the customer's death, it has authority for ten days after the death to pay checks (but not notes or drafts) drawn by the customer unless the bank receives a stop-payment order from someone who has an interest in the account, such as an heir. (This rule does not apply to insanity.)

12. Constructive notice is information or knowledge of a fact imputed by law to a person if he or she could have discovered the fact by proper diligence. Constructive notice is often accomplished pursuant to a statute by newspaper publication.

The passage of the expiration date is sufficient notice of termination for third parties.

Death or incapacity (terminations by operation of law) of the principal automatically and immediately terminates the agent's apparent authority. Under these circumstances, no notice is required to third parties unless the agent's power is coupled with an interest.

QUESTIONS AND CASE PROBLEMS

1. Adam is a traveling salesman for Peter Petri Plumbing Supply Corporation. Adam has express authority to solicit orders from customers and to offer a 5 percent discount if payment is made within thirty days of delivery. Petri has said nothing to Adam about extending credit. Adam calls on a new prospective customer, the Here's Johnny Plumbing Firm. Johnny tells Adam he will place a large order for Petri products if Adam will give him a 10 percent discount with payment in installments on a thirty-sixty-ninety-day basis. Adam says he has authority to make such a contract. Johnny calls Petri and asks if Adam is authorized to make contracts giving a discount. No mention is made of payment terms. Petri replies that Adam has authority to make discounts on purchase orders. On the basis of this information, Johnny orders $10,000 worth of plumbing supplies and fixtures. The goods are delivered and are being sold. One week later Johnny receives a bill for $9,500, if paid in thirty days. Johnny insists he owes only $9,000 and can pay it in three equal installments, at thirty, sixty, and ninety days from delivery. Discuss the liability of Petri and Johnny only.

2. Alice Adams is a purchasing agent-employee for the A & B Coal Supply partnership. Adams has authority to purchase the coal needed by A & B to satisfy the needs of its customers. While Adams is leaving a coal mine from which she just purchased a large quantity of coal, her car breaks down. She walks into a small roadside grocery store for help. While there, she runs into Will Wilson. Wilson owns 360 acres back in the mountains with all mineral rights. Wilson, in need of money, offers to sell Adams the property at $1,500 per acre. Upon inspection, Adams believes the sub-surface contains valuable coal deposits. Adams contracts to purchase the property for A & B Coal Company, signing the contract, "A & B Coal Supply, Alice Adams, agent." The closing date is August 1. Adams takes the contract to the partnership. The managing partner is furious, as A & B is not in the property business. Later, just before closing, both Wilson and the partnership learn that the value of the land is at least $15,000 per acre. Discuss the rights of A & B and Wilson concerning the land contract.

3. Paula Development Enterprises hires Able to act as its agent to purchase a 1,000-acre tract of land from Thompson for $1,000 per acre. Paula Enterprises does not wish Thompson to know that it is the principal or that Able is its agent. Paula wants the land for a new country housing development, and Thompson may not sell the land for that purpose or may demand a premium price. Able makes the contract for the purchase, signing only Able's name as purchaser and not disclosing to Thompson the agency relationship. The closing and transfer of deed is to be September 1.

   (a) If Thompson learns of Paula's identity on August 1, can Thompson legally refuse to deed the property on September 1? Explain.

   (b) Paula gives Able the money for the closing, but Able absconds with the money, causing a breach of Able's contract at the date of closing. Assume Thompson now learns of Paula's identity and wants to enforce the contract. Discuss fully Thompson's rights under these circumstances.

4. Able is hired as a traveling salesperson for the ABC Tire Corporation. Able has a designated geographic area and time schedule within which to solicit orders and service customers. Able is given a company car to be used in covering the territory. One day Able decides to take his personal car to cover part of his territory. It is 11:00 A.M., and Able has just finished calling on all customers in the city of Tarrytown. Able's next appointment is in the city of Austex, twenty miles down the road, at 2:00 P.M. Able starts out for Austex, but halfway there he decides to visit a former college roommate who runs a farm ten miles off the main highway. Able is enjoying his visit with his former roommate when he realizes that it is 1:45 P.M. and that he will be late for the appointment in Austex. Driving at a high speed down the country road to reach the main highway, Able crashes his car into Thomas's tractor, severely injuring Thomas, a farmer. Thomas claims he can hold the ABC Tire Corporation liable for his injuries. Discuss fully ABC's liability in this situation.

5. Adam is an agent for Fish Galore Inc. Adam has

express authority to solicit orders and receive payments in advance of shipment. He is well-known as an agent in the region. One of his customers, Seafood Quality, has been a regular customer for five years, has usually made large orders, and has always paid Adam in advance to get the discount offered by Fish Galore. Fish Galore learns that Adam has incurred large gambling debts and has recently used some of the customers' payments to pay off these debts. When Adam cannot reimburse Fish Galore, he is fired. Fish Galore hires a new agent and publishes in the regional newspapers that the new agent will be covering the territory. Desperately in need of cash, Adam solicits a large order from Seafood Quality and receives payment. Then he calls on a new customer, Catfish Heaven, who also gives Adam an order and payment. Adam absconds with the money. Fish Galore refuses to honor either order. Seafood Quality and Catfish Heaven claim Fish Galore is in breach of contract. Discuss fully their claims.

6. A real estate salesman accepted $7,500 in cash as a contract deposit on the purchase of a home. The salesman kept the money for himself, and the sale was not completed. A state law provided that all real estate salesmen were the agents of the brokers for whom they worked when they were collecting funds in the name of the broker. The contract provided that the deposit would be held by the broker. Although the funds never reached the broker, is he liable to the prospective purchaser for the return of the $7,500? [Bunch v. Althauser Realty, Inc., 55 Ohio App.2d 123, 379 N.E.2d 613 (1977)]

7. Under the Fair Housing Act, racial discrimination in housing practices (including the renting of apartments) is prohibited. Leach owned two apartment complexes in Columbus, Mississippi, and employed Jenkins as office manager of the apartments. For the entire time that she managed the apartments, Jenkins did not rent to any blacks, even though blacks make up about 37 percent of the local population. The United States Attorney General brought suit against Leach for violations of the Fair Housing Act. Leach contended that Jenkins did all the renting and made all the decisions as to whom she rented the apartments. Will the government win its case against Leach? [United States v. Real Estate Development Corp., 347 F.Supp. 776 (N.D.Miss. 1972)]

8. Hohenberg Brothers was a Memphis-based cotton merchandiser, and Killebrew was a Mississippi cotton farmer. Both parties were represented by D. T. Syle, Jr., a cotton agent. In February 1973, Killebrew signed and delivered to Syle a one-page purchase and sales agreement form covering the sale of Killebrew's 1973 cotton crop. All of the blanks in this document were completed, except for the name and signature of the purchaser, who was still unknown. On March 2, Syle secured an oral commitment that Hohenberg would purchase Killebrew's crop at the prices set forth in the one-page contract. Hohenberg immediately sent Syle its standard three-page purchase and sales agreement, the terms of which were identical to Syle's one-page document. Syle signed Killebrew's name and returned it to Hohenberg. Has Syle acted beyond the scope of his agency in signing Killebrew's name? [Hohenberg Brothers Co. v. Killebrew, 505 F.2d 643 (5th Cir. 1974)]

9. Roland "Cookie" Gomez began doing business as Cookie's Auto Sales in 1954 and continued operating as a sole proprietorship until May 29, 1963, at which time Cookie's Auto Sales became Cookie's Auto Sales, Inc. John Prevost did business with Cookie Gomez in a number of different capacities from the mid 1950s through the early 1970s. Prevost began working for University Volkswagen Inc. in January 1968, and in July of the same year Gomez began sending automobiles from his place of business to University Volkswagen for body work. Prevost handled Volkswagen accounts. Because of his longtime friendship with Gomez, Prevost made arrangements so that Gomez would not have to pay for work done by University Volkswagen until thirty days after the work was performed. Several years later, Gomez defaulted on his payments to University Volkswagen. The company wished to hold Gomez personally liable for the money owed by Cookie's Auto Sales, Inc. Gomez pointed out that since his business was incorporated, he could not be held personally liable because he was acting as an agent for "Cookie's Auto Sales Inc." Gomez also argued that Prevost should have realized that Cookie's Auto Sales was incorporated because all Gomez's ads were in the name of "Cookie's Auto Sales, Inc." Should Gomez be held personally liable? [Prevost v. Gomez, 251 So.2d 470 (La.App.1971)]

10. For many years Abell Company, publisher of the Sun newspaper in Baltimore City, ran advertisements for Warner and Company, a long-established and well-known haberdashery located in Baltimore City. Each February two contracts were entered into; they provided that morning, evening, and Sunday editions would advertise the clothing store's merchandise. Skeen, Warner's advertising manager, was responsible for procuring the advertisements, and he always signed the contracts with his name followed by the words "Warner & Co." When Warner and Company went bankrupt, Abell argued that Skeen was personally responsible for the advertising debt owed by the com-

pany. Abell contended that the use of the name "Warner & Co." was not sufficient to indicate the corporate status of Warner, and thus Skeen should be held personally liable. Will Skeen be liable? [Abell Co. v. Skeen, 265 Md. 53, 288 A.2d 596 (1972)]

11.   Pro Golf manufactured and marketed golf equipment both in the United States and abroad. In 1961 Robert Wynn became Pro Golf's sales representative in the Far East. Wynn and Pro Golf did not have a formal contract, but letters exchanged between them indicated the type of relationship they had. In a 1970 letter from Pro Golf to Wynn, Pro Golf stated, "You will continue to have the exclusive right to import and promote the sale of golf equipment in the Far East market. However, this is not an irrevocable right but would remain in effect only so long as you did a satisfactory business in this market." Several years later Pro Golf terminated Wynn's exclusive right, but first it gave Wynn five months' notice of its desire to ter-minate. Was Pro Golf's termination proper? What if Pro Golf had given Wynn no notice? [First Flight Associates, Inc. v. Professional Golf Co., 527 F.2d 931 (6th Cir. 1975)]

12.   On October 11, 1973, John Gray, owner of a 50 percent interest in a government oil and gas lease, assigned 20 percent of the operating rights and working interest to John Tylle in consideration of Tylle's payment of $10,000. The assignment was in writing and stated: "Until further notice assignee hereby appoints and designates assignor as agent and operator of the said lease for the purpose of development and management." A few weeks later, John Gray died unexpectedly. Tylle filed a claim against Gray's estate, seeking to recover the $10,000 he paid Gray. In order for Tylle to be successful, he must show that the agency relationship between him and Gray had been terminated. Will Tylle be successful? [In the matter of the estate of Gray, 37 Colo.App. 47, 541 P.2d 336 (1975)]

FOCUS ON ETHICS

Agency and Employment

Agency law is concerned with the duties, rights, and liabilities of principals and agents. Foremost within the area of agency is the nature of duty.

THE DUTY OF THE AGENT TO THE PRINCIPAL

What is the nature of the duty that an agent owes to a principal in an employment situation? Does the agent have the duty to disclose all favorable information that could be used by the principal to increase the principal's profits? Or does the agent have the right to use some of the information gleaned during the course of normal employment for his or her own benefit? In order to understand the answers to these questions, we must understand the nature of a fiduciary relationship where the word "fiduciary" implies a high standard of loyalty.

The very nature of the principal-agent relationship is one of trust, which we call a fiduciary relationship. Because of this, it is expected that an agent owes certain duties to the principal. These duties include loyalty and obedience informing the principal of important facts concerning the agency, accounting to the principal for property or money received, obeying, and performing with reasonable diligence and skill.

Thus, ethical conduct would prevent an agent from representing two principals in the same transaction, or making a secret profit from the agency, or failing to disclose the interest of the agent in property the principal was purchasing. The expected ethical conduct of the agent soon evolved into rules which, if breached, caused the agent to be held liable.

What about looking beyond the duty of the principal in considering one's duty to society? Those employees of Firestone, who knew of the company's defective tires in the early 1980s, presumably could have divulged that information to the public (at the risk of losing their jobs, of course). Employees aware of deliberate and fraudulent cost overruns on government contracts could make this information public, again at the risk of losing their jobs. Some scholars have argued that many of the greatest "evils" in the past twenty-five years have been accomplished in the name of "duty" to the principal. Duty in this context means placing the well-being of the principal above that of the public.

AGENCY BY ESTOPPEL

Sometimes a third person may be led to believe, either by the agent or the principal, that an individual is acting in the capacity of an agent for a principal. The notion of agency by estoppel certainly involves ethical issues. To the extent that a third person is in fact led to believe that an agency relationship exists, to what extent should that third person be able to rely on the apparent agency relationship? For the most part, agency law seems to follow ethical considerations in such situations: the notion of agency by estoppel is one in which the potential harm caused by the apparent agency relationship to the innocent third party is either prevented altogether or minimized.

THE DUTY OF PRINCIPALS

A principal has the duty to the agent of providing adequate compensation and reimbursement, cooperation, and safe working conditions. Think about the ethical considerations of the latter point. To what extent does a businessperson have an ethical mandate to provide a safe working environment for employees? For example, to what extent should a company use its own resources to eliminate reproductive risks to both men and women from some type of air-borne by-product of production? In general, an ethical consideration involves the quality of the workplace and the quality of the work provided by an employer.

Clearly, there is a trade-off involved here. A businessperson concerned only with the rate of return to investment may feel totally unconstrained by a poor working environment for employees. For example, profitability considerations may dictate a monotonous assembly-line operation. Does the employer have an ethical duty to attempt to reduce monotony in the workplace?

GOVERNMENT REGULATION OF THE WORKPLACE

Government regulation of the workplace has increased dramatically in the last quarter decade. Such government regulation, mostly carried out by the Occupational Safety & Health Administration (OSHA), was a result of presumed inadequate action on the part of employers. Nonetheless, not all scholars agree with OSHA's operating methods. One can argue that there is such a thing as "too" much safety in the workplace. We are then faced with the trade-off between economic and ethical concerns. For many employers, the safer the workplace or the less monotonous the work, the higher the cost related to the labor input in the production process. That higher cost is paid by consumers in the form of

higher prices, by stockholders in the form of lower profits, or by employees in the form of lower wages. Some studies have shown that in the long run, the higher costs for safer working conditions are paid almost entirely by employees in the form of lower wages.

To understand the last point, consider an example that has to do with smog. Smog affects the health and well-being of all residents and employees in a geographical area. Wage rates for the same type of work, holding all other things constant, are generally higher in smoggy environments than they are in cleaner environments. In the long run, workers who care more about higher wages and less about clean air will gravitate toward work environments with more smog. If a law is passed requiring all factories in a smoggy environment to reduce smog output, wage rates in that area will fall. They will fall because workers concerned about air quality will now be able to move into the area to offer their labor services, this increase in the supply of labor will drive down wages to levels comparable to those in other areas where the air is already clean. Those previously working at higher wage rates, but breathing bad air, will now find their wages reduced. This process of long-run economic equilibrium demonstrates that some workers will lose because of the imposition of a higher quality work environment. The ethical issue is, Who should be protected?

DISCUSSION QUESTIONS

1. How much obedience and loyalty does an employee owe an employer?
2. If an agent injures a third party during the course of employment, to what extent should the employer be held liable for the agent's actions? Does the amount of negligence on the part of the agent have any bearing on your answer? Is there any situation under which the agent should be held personally liable for his or her actions that harm third parties?
3. The above question relates to the doctrine of *respondeat superior*. What ethical considerations generated this doctrine?
4. Agency by estoppel occurs when the principal's actions create the appearance of apparent authority by a presumed agent. Do you think that agency by estoppel should be allowed under all circumstances? Or, rather, do you believe that the third person must prove that he or she reasonably believed that the agent had authority?
5. The termination of an agency agreement can occur by operation of law. In particular when unforeseen circumstances, (such as impossibility or bankruptcy) occur, termination by operation of law may obtain. What ethical considerations are involved here?

UNIT VII

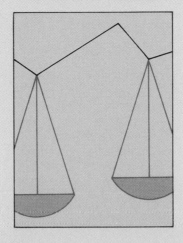

BUSINESS ORGANIZATIONS

CHAPTER 36

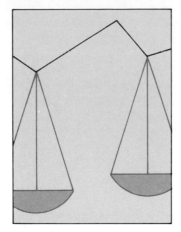

Forms of Business Organization

There are basically three types of business organizations—sole proprietorships, partnerships, and corporations. Additionally, there are two types of partnerships—limited partnerships and general, or unlimited, partnerships—and various classifications of corporations, such as closely held corporations and Subchapter S corporations.

Other types of business organizations also exist—among them joint ventures, syndicates or investment groups, joint stock companies, business trusts, and cooperatives—but these are essentially hybrid forms of partnerships or of corporations.

This chapter will first describe the form of these business organizations. Then it will compare a partnership with a corporation in more detail. A person starting out in business most often chooses between these two forms when deciding how a business should be organized.

SOLE PROPRIETORSHIP

The simplest form of business is a sole proprietorship. The owner is the business. This form is used by anyone who does business without creating an organization. One usually associates a sole proprietorship with small enterprises, although this is not necessarily the case. The owner's personal estate is liable for his or her business debts.

PARTNERSHIP

A partnership arises from an agreement, express or implied, between two or more persons to carry on a business for profit. Partners are co-owners of a business and have joint control over its operation and the right to share in its profits. Both partnerships and sole proprietorships are creatures of common law rather than of statutes. No particular form of partnership agreement is necessary for the creation of a partnership, although it is desirable that the agreement be in writing. The Uniform Partnership Act (UPA), adopted in forty-seven states, governs the operation of partnerships *in the absence* of express agreements. Basically, the partners may agree to almost any terms when establishing the partnership so long as they are not illegal or contrary to public policy. The UPA comes into play only if the partners have neglected to include a necessary term. In a sense, then, the UPA is a gap-filler. It is not a code that must be followed in order to create the legal entity called a partnership.

A partnership is a legal entity for limited purposes, such as the partnership name and title of ownership and property. Otherwise, it is not a legal entity. Rather, the personal net worth of the partners is subject to partnership obligations. The partnership itself is not subject to levy for federal income taxes; only an information return must be filed. However, a partner's profit from the partnership (whether or not distributed) is taxed as individual income to the individual partner.

Chapter 37 will detail the creation and termination of general partnerships. Chapter 38 will deal with the duties, rights, and liabilities of partners to each other and to third persons.

Limited Partnerships

The most popular special form of partnership is the limited partnership, which is comprised of at least one general partner and one or more limited partners. The limited partnership is created by an agreement; but unlike a general partnership, the limited partnership does not come into existence until a certificate of partnership is filed appropriately in a state.

Furthermore, unlike a general partnership, a limited partnership is completely a creature of statute. If the statute is not followed almost to the letter, the courts will hold that a general partnership exists instead. Then those who thought their liability was limited by their investment in a limited partnership will be held generally liable to the full extent of their personal net worth.

Once a limited partnership is created, the law treats the general partner(s) exactly the same as any partner in an ordinary partnership. The limited partner(s) is treated basically as an investor; that is, the limited partner contributes capital but does not participate in the management or control of the partnership. As long as the limited partner's activities are confined to the investor role only, the limited partner will have limited liability. This means that the liability of the limited partner, if he or she refrains from management activities, is limited to his or her capital contribution, and personal assets are not subject to partnership obligations. Limited partnerships are discussed in more detail in Chapter 39. All states permit limited partnerships. Forty-eight states have adopted the Uniform Limited Partnership Act (ULPA) or its revision (see Appendixes C and D), which govern the organization and operation of limited partnerships.

BUSINESS CORPORATIONS

The most important form of business organization is the corporation. A corporation comes into existence by an act of the state, and therefore it is a legal entity. It typically has perpetual existence. One of the key features of a corporation is that the liability of its owners is limited to their investments. Their personal estates are usually not liable for the obligations of the corporation.

Corporations consist of shareholders, who are the owners of the business. A board of directors, elected by the shareholders, manages the business. The board of directors normally employs officers to oversee day-to-day operations.

The law on the formation, management and operation, liability, and termination of corporations will be discussed in detail in Chapters 40 to 44.

OTHER FORMS OF BUSINESS ORGANIZATION

There are a number of other, less common forms of business organization. They include joint ventures, syndicates or investment groups, joint stock companies, business trusts, and cooperatives.

Joint Ventures

When two or more persons or entities combine their interests in a particular business enterprise and agree to share in losses or profits jointly or in proportion to their contributions, they are engaged in a joint venture. The jont venture is treated much like a partnership, but it differs in that its creation is in contemplation of a limited activity or a single transaction.

For example, Able and Cain pool their resources to buy an old boat, remodel it, and sell it, dividing the profits. This creates not a partnership but a joint venture. The same is true if Able, owning a piece of land, and Cain, owning an adjoining piece of land, agree to sell both parcels together as one unit to the highest bidder and then divide the proceeds proportionately to the value of each parcel of land held.

Members of a joint venture usually have limited powers to bind their co-venturers. A joint venture is normally not a legal entity and therefore cannot be sued as such, but its members can be sued individually. Usually joint ventures are taxed like partnerships. They range in size from very small activities to huge, multimillion-dollar joint actions engaged in by some of the world's largest corporations.

Syndicates, or Investment Groups

A group of individuals getting together to finance a particular project like the building of a shopping center or the purchase of a professional basketball franchise is called a syndicate, or an investment group. The form of such groups varies considerably. They may exist as corporations or as general or limited partnerships. In some cases, the members merely own property jointly and have no legally recognized business arrangement.

Joint Stock Companies

A joint stock company or association is a true hybrid between a partnership and a corporation. It has many characteristics of a corporation but is usually treated like a partnership. For example, the joint stock company resembles a corporation in that its ownership is represented by transferable shares of stock, it is usually managed by directors and officers of the company or association, and it can have a perpetual existence.

However, most other features are more characteristic of a partnership. For example, the joint stock company is formed by agreement (not statute); property is usually held in the names of the members; shareholders have personal liability; and generally the company is not treated as a legal entity for purposes of a lawsuit. However, shareholders are not treated as agents of each other, as would be the case if the company were a true partnership.

The joint stock company is not widely used, but a modern example is the American Express Company, which was a joint stock association until 1965.

Business Trusts

A business trust is created by a written trust agreement that sets forth the interests of the beneficiaries and the obligations and powers of the trustees. With a business trust, legal ownership and management of the property of the business stays with one or more of the trustees, and the profits are distributed to the beneficiaries.

The business trust was started in Massachusetts in an attempt to obtain the limited liability advantage of corporate status while avoiding certain restrictions on a corporation's ownership and development of real property.

The business trust resembles a corporation in many aspects. Death or bankruptcy of a beneficiary do not terminate the trust, and beneficiaries are not personally responsible for the debts or obligations of the business trust. In fact, in a number of states business trusts must pay corporate taxes. The business trust was more popular at the turn of the century than it is today. Its decline is a result of antitrust laws (discussed in detail in Chapter 50 and 51).

In a few states only, the beneficiaries are treated as partners and they are personally liable to business creditors; thus the limited liability advantage is eliminated.

Cooperatives

A cooperative is an association, either incorporated or not, that is organized to provide an economic service without profit to its members (or shareholders). An incorporated cooperative is subject to state laws governing nonprofit corporations. It will make distributions of dividends, or profits, to its owners on the basis of their transactions with the cooperative rather than on the basis of the amount of capital they contributed. Cooperatives that are unincorporated are often treated like partnerships. The members have joint liability for the cooperative's acts. Cooperatives are generally formed by groups of individuals who wish to pool their resources in order to gain some advantage in the marketplace. Consumer purchasing co-ops are formed to obtain lower prices through quantity discounts. Seller marketing co-ops are formed to control the market and thereby obtain higher sales prices from consumers. Often cooperatives are exempt from certain federal laws—for example, antitrust statutes—because of their special status.

THE ADVANTAGES AND DISADVANTAGES OF A SOLE PROPRIETORSHIP

Advantages

The proprietor receives all the profits because he or she takes all the risk. In addition, it is often easier and less costly to start a sole proprietorship than to start any other kind of business. Few legal forms must be completed, and since the proprietor makes all the decisions, the problem of reaching agreement among all the people involved is avoided. The sole proprietor is also free from corporate income taxes, paying only personal income taxes on profits. However, these taxes are not necessarily lower than those for a corporation.

Disadvantages

As sole owner, the proprietor alone bears the risk of losses. In addition, the proprietor's opportunity to raise capital is limited to personal funds and the funds of those who are willing to make loans. Additionally, and perhaps more importantly for many potential entrepreneurs, the sole proprietor has unlimited liability, or legal responsibility, for all obligations incurred in doing business.

COMPARING A PARTNERSHIP WITH A CORPORATION

Exhibit 36–1 is an abbreviated comparison between a partnership and a corporation, giving the essential advantages and disadvantages of each.

Other Points of Comparison for Choosing a Form of Business

Liability of Owners The form of the organization does not always in and of itself determine the liability of the owners. Generally, sole proprietorships and general partners have personal liability, and limited partners and shareholders of corporations have liability limited to their investment. Because of this, creditors frequently look to personal liability in extending credit. It simply determines who is liable. For example, a bank may be unwilling to lend money to a corporation that is relatively small and has only a few shareholders. The corporate form for the business does not guarantee that it is a better risk for the bank. Typically, in such situations the relatively few shareholders must personally sign for any loans made to the corporation. That is, the shareholders agree to become personally liable for the loan. In essence, they must be guarantors for the corporation's debt. Hence, the corporate form of business does not prevent them from having personal liability in such a case, because they have assumed the liability voluntarily.

Need for Capital One of the most common reasons for changing from a sole proprietorship to a partnership or a corporation is the need for additional capital to finance expansion. A sole proprietor can seek partners who will bring capital with them. The partnership might be able to secure more funds from potential lenders than could the sole proprietor. But when a firm wants to expand greatly, simply increasing the number

EXHIBIT 36–1   COMPARING A PARTNERSHIP WITH A CORPORATION

CHARACTERISTIC	PARTNERSHIP	CORPORATION
1. Method of Creation	Created by agreement of the parties.	Charter issued by state—created by statutory authorization.
2. Legal Position	Not a separate legal entity in many states.	Always a legal entity separate and distinct from its owners—a legal fiction for the purposes of owning property and being party to litigation.
3. Liability	Unlimited liability (except for limited partners in a limited partnership).	Limited liability of shareholders—shareholders are not liable for the debts of the corporation.
4. Duration	Terminated by agreement of the partners, by the death of one or more of the partners, by withdrawal of a partner, by bankruptcy, etc.	Can have perpetual existence.
5. Transferability of Interest	Although partnership interest can be assigned, assignee does not have full rights of a partner.	Shares of stock can be transferred.
6. Management	Each general partner has a direct and equal voice in management unless expressly agreed otherwise in the partnership agreement. (Limited partner has no rights in management in a limited partnership.)	Shareholders elect directors who set policy and appoint officers.
7. Taxation	Each partner pays pro rata share of income taxes on net profits, whether or not they are distributed.	Double taxation—corporation pays income tax on net profits, with no deduction for dividends, and shareholders pay income tax on disbursed dividends they receive.
8. Organizational Fees, Annual License Fees, and Annual Reports	None.	All required.
9. Transaction of Business in Other States	Generally no limitation.[a]	Normally must qualify to do business and obtain certificate of authority.

[a]A few states have enacted statutes requiring that foreign partnerships qualify to do business there—for example, 3 N.H.Rev.Stat.Ann. Chapter 305-A in New Hampshire.

of partners can lead to too many partners for the firm to operate effectively. Therefore, incorporation might be the best choice for an expanding business organization. There are many possibilities for obtaining more capital by issuing shares of stock. The original owners will find that although their proportion of the company is reduced, they are able to expand much more rapidly by selling shares in the company.

Tax Considerations   Various tax considerations must be taken into account when one compares a partnership with a corporation. These considerations are listed in Exhibit 36–2.

EXHIBIT 36–2   PARTNERSHIP VERSUS CORPORATION—TAX CONSIDERATIONS

TAX ASPECT	PARTNERSHIP	CORPORATION
1. Federal Income Tax	Partner is taxed on proportionate share of partnership income, even if not distributed; the partnership files information returns only.	Income of the corporation is taxed; stockholders are also taxed on distributed dividends. Must file corporate income tax forms.
2. Accumulation	Partners taxed on accumulated as well as distributed earnings.	Corporate stockholders not taxed on accumulated earnings. There is, however, a penalty tax, in some instances, that the corporation must pay for accumulations of income.
3. Capital Gains and Losses	All partners taxed on their proportionate share of capital gains and losses.	Corporation taxed on capital gains and losses. There is no special deduction to reduce taxes for any excess of long-term gains over short-term losses, but there is a special rate.
4. Exempt Interest	Partners are not taxed on exempt interest received from the firm.	Any exempt interest distributed by a corporation is fully taxable income to the stockholders. Exempt interest can come, for example, from municipal bonds.
5. Pension Plan	Partners are not eligible for an exempt pension trust. The firm cannot deduct payments for partners except under what is called a Keogh Plan.	Employees and officers who are also stockholders can be beneficiaries of a pension trust. The corporation can deduct its payments to the trust.
6. Social Security	Partners do not pay social security tax, but often must pay a self-employment tax.	All compensation to officers and employee stockholders subject to social security taxation up to the maximum.
7. Death Benefits (excluding those provided by insurance)	There is no exemption for payments to partners' beneficiaries.	Benefits up to $5,000 can be received tax free by stockholders' and employees' beneficiaries.
8. State Taxes	In many states, the partnership is not subject to state income taxes.	The corporation is subject to state income taxes (although these taxes can be deducted on federal returns).

QUESTIONS AND CASE PROBLEMS

1. Suppose Ann, Betty, and Carla are college graduates, and Ann has come up with an idea for a new product that she believes could make the three of them very rich. Her idea is to manufacture beer dispensers for home use, and her goal is to market them to consumers throughout the Midwest. Ann's personal experience qualifies her to be both first line supervisor and general manager of the new firm. Betty is a born salesperson. Carla has little interest in sales or management but would like to invest a large sum of money that she has inherited from her aunt. What should Ann, Betty, and Carla consider in deciding which form of business organization to operate under?

2. In the situation described in Question 1, assume that Carla is willing to put her inherited money in the business, but she does not want any further liability should the beer dispenser manufacturing business fail. The bank is willing to lend some capital at a 20 percent interest rate, but it will do so only if certain restrictions are placed on management decisons. This is not satisfactory to Ann or Betty and the two decide to bring Carla into the business. Under these circum-

stances, discuss which types of business organizations are best suited to meet the needs of Carla.

3. The limited liability aspect of the corporation is one of the most important reasons that firms choose to organize as corporations rather than as partnerships or sole proprietorships. Limited liability means that if a corporation is not able to meet its obligations with corporate assets, creditors will not be allowed to look to the owners (stockholders) of the corporation to satisfy their claims. Assume that Ann and Betty (from Problem 1) do not have a wealthy friend like Carla who wishes to go into business with them and that therefore they must borrow money to start their business. Ann and Betty decide to incorporate. What do you think a lender will ask them when they seek a loan? What effect does this have on the "advantage" of limited liability under incorporation?

4. Assume that XYZ Corporation is considering entering into two contracts, one with a joint stock company that distributes home products east of the Mississippi River, and the other with a business trust formed by a number of sole proprietors who are sellers of home products on the West Coast. Both contracts involve large capital outlays for the XYZ Corporation in supplying each business with beer dispensers. In both business organizations, at least two shareholders or beneficiaries are personally wealthy, but each business organization has limited financial resources. The owner-managers of XYZ Corporation are not familiar with either form of business organization. Since each form resembles a corporation, they are concerned with the possibility of liability in the event that either business organization breaches the contract by failing to make the deferred payments. Discuss fully XYZ's concern.

5. Assume A and B formed a general partnership. After six months the partnership had assets of $100,000 and debts totaling $150,000. A and B decide to dissolve their partnership. How will the debts that the partnership could not pay be handled?

CHAPTER 37

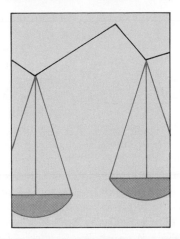

PARTNERSHIPS
Creation and Termination

To a great extent, partnership law derives from agency law. Each partner is considered an agent of every other partner. Thus, the agency concepts of imputing knowledge and responsibility for acts done within the scope of the partnership relationship will apply.

In one important way, however, partnership law is distinct from agency law. A partnership is based on a voluntary contract between two or more competent persons, who agree to place some or all of their money, effects, labor, and skill in a business with the understanding that profits and losses will be proportionately shared. On the other hand, in an agency relationship, one person (the agent) can be compensated from business profits but does not agree to share the ordinary business losses and has no ownership interest in the business.

Partnership law in the United States is codified in the *Uniform Partnership Act* (UPA). The UPA, which has been adopted in most states, replaces the body of common law principles dealing with partnerships.[1] As pointed out in the last chapter, a partnership agreement can include virtually any terms that the partners wish, unless they are illegal or contrary to public policy. Only when certain essential terms are left out does the UPA come into play.

In the past, attempts to formulate a concrete definition of the term *partnership* caused endless controversy among judges, lawyers, and members of the business community. **Partnership** is defined by the UPA as "an association of two or more persons to carry on as co-owners a business for profit."[2] Therefore, three essential elements of a partnership are (1) a common ownership interest in a business, (2) sharing of the profits and losses of the business, and (3) the

---

1. The UPA was first passed in 1914 by Pennsylvania. To date, Louisiana, Georgia, and Mississippi have not adopted it.

2. UPA Section Sec. 6(1).

right to manage the operations of the partnership.

CHARACTERISTICS OF A PARTNERSHIP

A partnership is sometimes called a *firm*, or company, terms that connote an entity separate and apart from its aggregate members. Sometimes the law of partnership recognizes the independent entity, but for certain other purposes, the law treats it as an aggregate of individual partners. At common law, a partnership was never treated as a separate legal entity. Thus, a common law suit could never be brought by or against the firm in its own name; each individual partner had to sue or be sued.

Many states today provide specifically that the partnership can be treated as an entity for certain purposes. This usually includes the capacity to sue or be sued, to collect judgments, and to have all accounting procedures in the name of the partnership. In addition, the UPA recognizes that partnership property may be held in the name of the partnership rather than in the names of the individual partners. Finally, federal procedural laws frequently permit the partnership to be treated as an entity in such matters as suits in federal courts, bankruptcy proceedings, and filing of informational federal tax returns. These will be discussed here in some detail.

Partnership as an Entity

Legal Capacity States vary on how a partnership is viewed as a party in a legal suit. Some permit a partnership to sue and be sued in the firm name; others allow a partnership to be sued as an entity but not to sue others in its firm name (that is, the partnership must use the names of the individual partners). Federal courts recognize the partnership as an entity that can sue or be sued when a federal constitutional question is involved. Otherwise, federal courts follow the practice adopted by the state in which the federal court is located.

Judgments Partnership liability is first paid out of partnership assets when a judgment is rendered *against the firm name*. In a general partnership, the personal assets of the individual members are subject to liability if the partnership's assets are inadequate. Even in limited partnerships, at least one of the partners—called a general partner—subjects his or her personal assets to liability for the partnership's obligations. Good legal practice dictates that where state law permits a firm to be sued, the partners should be joined as parties to the suit. This insures that a wide range of assets will be available for paying the judgment.

The general rule is that a judgment creditor of a partnership can execute the judgment against the partners either jointly or severally. In some states, the judgment creditor must, however, exhaust the remedies against partnership property before proceeding to execute against the individual property of the partners. This is referred to as *the doctrine of marshalling assets*. Marshalling assets is a common law equitable doctrine; it is not statutory.

Marshalling Assets The arrangement or ranking of assets in a certain order toward the payment of debts outstanding is involved in marshalling assets. In particular, when there are two classes of assets, and some creditors can enforce their claims against both whereas others can enforce their claims against only one, then the creditors of the former class are compelled to exhaust the assets against which they alone have a claim before they can have recourse to the other assets. This provides for the settlement of as many claims as possible.

As applied to a partnership, marshalling of assets requires that the partnership's creditors have first priority to the partnership's assets; and personal creditors of the individual partners have priority to the individual assets of a partner. When the partnership's assets are insufficient to satisfy a partnership creditor, that partnership creditor does not have access to the assets of any individual partner until the personal creditors of that partner have been satisfied from such assets.

Consider an example. X, Y, and Z are equal partners. On dissolution, the partnership has assets of $100,000 and liabilities of $70,000. The partners therefore have a net equity of $10,000 each. X, Y, and Z have no personal assets but owe $10,000 each in personal debts. Under the rule of marshalling of assets, the personal creditors of X, Y, and Z cannot reach the partnership assets until the $70,000 of partnership liabilities have been paid off. After that each partner's personal creditors may resort to each partner's $10,000 equity to satisfy their personal claims.

Now assume that in the preceding example the partnership liabilities are $130,000 rather than $70,000. Assume also that partners X and Y are insolvent. Z, on the other hand, has personal assets of $25,000 and personal liabilities of $25,000. The partnership's creditors cannot resort to Z's personal assets because Z's personal creditors come first and will, in this hypothetical example, exhaust them.

Bankruptcy   In federal court, an adjudication of bankruptcy in the firm name applies only to the partnership entity. It does not constitute personal bankruptcy for the partners. Similarly, the personal bankruptcy of an individual partner does not bring the partnership entity or its assets into bankruptcy.

The doctrine of marshalling of assets may be modified when a partnership is granted an order of relief in bankruptcy. In such situations, if there is a deficiency of partnership assets to cover debts owed to partnership creditors, each general partner becomes personally liable to the bankruptcy trustee for the amount of the deficiency.

Conveyance of Property   The title to real or personal property can be held in the firm name. This means that the partnership as an entity can own property apart from that owned by its individual members.[3] As such, the property can be conveyed (transferred) without having each individual partner join in the transaction.

At common law, title to real estate could not be held in a partnership's firm name. Each partner was regarded as a co-owner (known in legal terminology as a *tenant in partnership*).[4] Each partner had to join in all conveyances. Although the modern rule of partnership property ownership disregards the need for aggregate action to convey property, there are some practical difficulties to consider.

Most states do not require public records to keep lists of members of a partnership, although other states have statutes that require the filing of a certificate of co-partnership. Hence, in determining the validity of a conveyance in a partnership name, it may be impossible to tell whether the person executing the deed is actually a partner and has authority to convey. Some states have passed laws requiring firms to file a statement of partnership. This list names members of the firm authorized to execute conveyances on behalf of the firm.

Aggregate Theory of Partnership

When the partnership is not regarded as a separate legal entity, it is treated as an *aggregate* of the individual partners. For example, for federal income tax purposes, a partnership is not a taxpaying entity. The income or losses incurred by it are "passed through" the partnership framework and attributed to the partners on their individual tax returns. The partnership as an entity has no tax identity or liability. It is an entity only for the filing of an informational return with the IRS, indicating the profit and loss that each partner will report on his or her individual tax return.

FORMATION OF A PARTNERSHIP

A partnership is ordinarily formed by an explicit agreement among the parties. The law does recognize another form of partnership —*partnership by estoppel*. This form arises when persons who are not partners represent or hold themselves out as partners when dealing with third

---

3. UPA Section 8(3).

4. UPA Section 25(1).

parties. The liability of partners by estoppel is covered later in the chapter.

This section will describe the requirements for the creation of a true partnership, including references to the liability of "alleged partners." The next section will deal with the process by which partnerships are terminated.

A partnership is a voluntary association of individuals. As such, a *true partnership* is generally based on an agreement among the parties that reflects their intention to create a partnership, contribute capital, share profits and losses, and participate in management. The partnership relationship involves a high degree of trust and reliance. Each partner is an agent for the other partners.

Parties cannot avoid partnership liability, even by *expressly* designating themselves as some other business form, if the evidence establishes the essential elements of a partnership. In the following case, a physician purchased an interest in a medical center along with numerous other doctors. The amount of money each doctor received for practicing at the center was based upon the billing for the services that each performed. The bills were collected in the name of the center. From the total billing, a percentage was deducted to cover expenses and profit sharing. The center's method of allocating expenses to the doctors bore no direct relationship to their actual expenses.

STUART v. OVERLAND MEDICAL CENTER

Missouri Court of Appeals, 1978.
510 S.W.2d 494.

BACKGROUND AND FACTS *The plaintiff, a physician, sued to settle a dispute arising out of his withdrawal from a claimed professional partnership. The trial court concluded that the plaintiff practiced medicine in a partnership with the defendants at the Overland Medical Center. The court further determined that the partnership between the plaintiff and the defendants was dissolved by the plaintiff's lawsuit. The court evaluated the dollar amount of the plaintiff's interest in the partnership; and after deducting certain amounts due the defendants for expenses, the court entered a judgment for the plaintiff.*

The defendants not only challenged the formula used by the lower court in determining the value of the plaintiff's interest in the medical center, but they also challenged the court's conclusion that the relationship between the plaintiff and the defendants was a partnership. In support of their contention, the defendants tried to show that the relationship was one of expense-sharing rather than partnership.

WEIER, Judge.

*   *   *   *

Under the Uniform Partnership Law which was adopted in this state in 1949, a partnership is defined as "an association of two or more persons to carry on as co-owners a business for profit." A partnership is defined judicially as "a contract of two or more competent persons to place their money, effects, labor and skill, or some or all of them, in lawful commerce or business and to divide the profits and bear the loss in certain proportions." The contract creating the partnership need not be written, but may be expressed orally or implied from the acts and conduct of the parties. The primary consideration in determining the existence of a partnership is whether the parties intended to carry on as co-owners a business for profit. With this general background in mind, we proceed to the facts in this case.

*   *   *   *

The amount of money each doctor received for practicing his profession at the Center was based upon billing for services performed by each doctor and collected by and in the name of the Center less a percent of the expenses. By way of illustration, if one doctor collected $1,000.00 and the amount collected by all the doctors was $10,000.00, the doctor who collected $1,000.00 would receive $1,000.00 less 10% of the expenses since the $1,000.00 was ten percent of the total amount collected by all the doctors. The amount of expenses to which each doctor's income was subject was determined by the same method used to allocate collections. Again by way of illustration, if the expenses of all the doctors totaled $2,000.00 for the year in which they collected $10,000.00, the doctor who collected $1,000.00 would be liable for ten percent of the expenses or $200.00. Thus, at the end of this hypothetical year, the doctor who collected $1,000.00 would receive $800.00 as income. Defendants argue that since this method of allocating income is not a profit sharing arrangement but rather an expense sharing arrangement, the relationship between the doctors at the Center cannot be denominated a partnership. We find this argument unconvincing. Each doctor received compensation for the services he performed at the Center. The amount each doctor received as compensation may properly be called income or profit as the two terms are often used interchangeably and, for the most part, have the same meaning. Each doctor shared to some extent in the income or profit of the other doctors although the sharing was not the result of proportionally dividing the total amount of money collected by all the doctors without considering the amount of money each doctor collected individually. Rather, the profit sharing was accomplished by the Center's method of allocating the expenses to be deducted from each doctor's collections. For example, if the doctor referred to in our illustration above had actual expenses of $100.00, $100.00 of the $200.00 he had to pay as expenses was used to pay or help pay another doctor's expenses. It was in this manner that the doctors in the Center actually shared profits. Because the expenses each doctor had to pay bore no relationship to the actual expenses of each doctor, some doctors were receiving profits that otherwise might have been distributed to the doctor or doctors whose actual expenses were slight when compared to the actual expenses of other doctors.

Thus the evidence proved that plaintiff was practicing his profession with the other doctors in the Center as a co-owner of the Center's facilities for a profit. While co-ownership and the sharing of profits by those engaged in business are not factors which conclusively establish the parties' relationship as that of partnership, they are prima facie evidence of partnership. As such, the presumption of partnership prevails unless evidence sufficient to rebut the presumption is brought forward. In this case, defendants presented no evidence which would lead to the conclusion that the relationship between plaintiff and them was anything other than a partnership.

JUDGMENT AND REMEDY

The appellate court affirmed the trial court's judgment that the professional arrangement between the plaintiff and the defendants was a partnership. The plaintiff's interest in the partnership was evaluated by the trial court, and that determination of value was upheld by the appellate court.

COMMENTS   *The rights and liabilities of the partners among themselves, although fixed by law, are subject to agreements between the parties insofar as such agreements—and intentions—can be ascertained. Even an oral agreement can be sufficient to establish a framework for a partnership. If there are sufficient circumstances to indicate the intent to carry on a business for profit as co-owners, and if the court can ascertain a method for determining the value of any partner's interest, then a partnership will be presumed unless sufficient contrary evidence is introduced.*

Formalities

As a general rule, agreements to form a partnership can be oral, written, or implied by contract. Some partnership agreements, however, must be in writing to be legally enforceable within the Statute of Frauds. (See Chapter 12 for details.) For example, a partnership agreement that, by its terms, is to continue for more than one year or one that authorizes the partners to deal in real property transfers must be evidenced by a sufficient writing. A sample partnership agreement is shown in Exhibit 37–1.

Practically speaking, the provisions of any partnership agreement are better put in writing. The terms of an oral agreement are difficult to prove, because a court must evaluate oral testimony given by persons with an interest in the eventual decision. In addition, in the course of drafting a written agreement, the partners may see potential problems that they would not see if they were making an oral agreement.

For instance, Tomkins and Fredericks plan to enter into a partnership agreement to sell tires. Among the provisions to be included is that Tomkins is to provide two-thirds of the capital to start up the business and in return is to receive two-thirds of the profits. The agreement is made orally. Tomkins now sues because Fredericks claims that one-half the profits should be his. Without a writing, Tomkins may have a hard time overcoming the presumption that he is entitled to only one-half the profits of a two-person partnership.[5] A partnership agreement, called *articles of partnership*, usually specifies each partner's share of the profits and is binding regardless of how uneven the distribution appears to be.

Duration of Partnership

The partnership agreement can specify the duration of the partnership in terms of a date or the completion of a particular project. This is called a *partnership for a term*. A dissolution without the consent of all the partners prior to the expiration of the partnership term constitutes a breach of the agreement, and the responsible partner can be liable for any losses resulting from it.

If no fixed duration is specified, the partnership is a *partnership at will*. This type of partnership can be dissolved any time by any partner without violating the agreement or incurring liability for resulting losses to other partners because of the termination.

Capacity

Any person having the capacity to enter a contract can become a partner. A partnership contract entered into with a minor as a partner is voidable and can be disaffirmed by the minor. (See Chapter 9 for details.)

Lack of legal capacity due to insanity at the time of the agreement likewise allows the purported partner either to avoid the agreement or to enforce it. If a partner becomes insane and is adjudicated mentally incompetent during the course of the partnership, the partnership is not automatically dissolved, but dissolution can be decreed by a court upon petition.

---

5. The law assumes that members of a partnership share profits and losses equally unless a partnership agreement provides otherwise [UPA Section 18(a)].

EXHIBIT 37–1   SAMPLE PARTNERSHIP AGREEMENT

PARTNERSHIP AGREEMENT

This agreement, made and entered into as of the _____, by and among _____
_____ (hereinafter collectively sometimes referred to as "Partners").

WITNESSETH:

Whereas, the Parties hereto desire to form a General Partnership (hereinafter referred to as the "Partnership"), for the term and upon the conditions hereinafter set forth;

Now, therefore, in consideration of the mutual covenants hereinafter contained, it is agreed by and among the Parties hereto as follows:

Article I
BASIC STRUCTURE

Form. The Parties hereby form a General Partnership pursuant to the Laws of _____
_____.

Name. The business of the Partnership shall be conducted under the name of _____
_____.

Place of Business. The principal office and place of business of the Partnership shall be located at _____, or such other place as the Partners may from time to time designate.

Term. The Partnership shall commence on _____, and shall continue for _____ years, unless earlier terminated in the following manner: (a) By the completion of the purpose intended, or (b) Pursuant to this Agreement, or (c) By applicable _____ law, or (d) By death, insanity, bankruptcy, retirement, withdrawal, resignation, expulsion, or disability of all of the then Partners.

Purpose—General. The purpose for which the Partnership is organized is _____

Article II
FINANCIAL ARRANGEMENTS

Each Partner has contributed to the initial capital of the Partnership property in the amount and form indicated on Schedule A attached hereto and made a part hereof. Capital contributions to the Partnership shall not earn interest. An individual capital account shall be maintained for each Partner. If at any time during the existence of the Partnership it shall become necessary to increase the capital with which the said Partnership is doing business, then (upon the vote of the Managing Partner(s)): each party to this Agreement shall contribute to the capital of this Partnership within _ days notice of such need in an amount according to his then Percentage Share of Capital as called for by the Managing Partner(s).

The Percentage Share of Profits and Capital of each Partner shall be (unless otherwise modified by the terms of this Agreement) as follows:

Names	Initial Percentage Share of Profits and Capital

No interest shall be paid on any contribution to the capital of the Partnership. No Partner shall have the right to demand the return of his capital contributions except as herein provided. Except as herein provided, the individual Partners shall have no right to any priority over each other as to the return of capital contributions except as herein provided.

Distributions to the Partners of net operating profits of the Partnership, as hereinafter defined, shall be made at _____. Such distributions shall be made to the Partners simultaneously.

For the purpose of this Agreement, net operating profit for any accounting period shall mean the gross receipts of the Partnership for such period, less the sum of all cash expenses of operation of the Partnership, and such sums as may be necessary to establish a reserve for operating expenses. In determining net operating profit, deductions for depreciation, amortization, or other similar charges not requiring actual current expenditures of cash shall *not* be taken into account in accordance with generally accepted accounting principles.

EXHIBIT 37–1 Continued

No Partner shall be entitled to receive any compensation from the Partnership, nor shall any Partner receive any drawing account from the Partnership.

Article III
MANAGEMENT

The Managing Partner(s) shall be _____.

The Managing Partner(s) shall have the right to vote as to the management and conduct of the business of the Partnership as follows:

Names   **Vote**

Article IV
DISSOLUTION

In the event that the Partnership shall hereafter be dissolved for any reason whatsoever, a full and general account of its assets, liabilities and transactions shall at once be taken. Such assets may be sold and turned into cash as soon as possible and all debts and other amounts due the Partnership collected. The proceeds thereof shall thereupon be applied as follows:

(a) To discharge the debts and liabilities of the Partnership and the expenses of liquidation.

(b) To pay each Partner or his legal representative any unpaid salary, drawing account, interest or profits to which he shall then be entitled and in addition, to repay to any Partner his capital contributions in excess of his original capital contribution.

(c) To divide the surplus, if any, among the Partners or their representatives as follows: (1) First (to the extent of each Partner's then capital account) in proportion to their then capital accounts. (2) Then according to each Partner's then Percentage Share of [*Capital/Income*].

No Partner shall have the right to demand and receive property in kind for his distribution.

Article V
MISCELLANEOUS

The Partnership's fiscal year shall commence on January 1st of each year and shall end on December 31st of each year. Full and accurate books of account shall be kept at such place as the Managing Partner(s) may from time to time designate, showing the condition of the business and finances of the Partnership; and each Partner shall have access to such books of account and shall be entitled to examine them at any time during ordinary business hours. At the end of each year, the Managing Partner(s) shall cause the Partnership's accountant to prepare a balance sheet setting forth the financial position of the Partnership as of the end of that year and a statement of operations (income and expenses) for that year. A copy of the balance sheet and statement of operations shall be delivered to each Partner as soon as it is available.

Each Partner shall be deemed to have waived all objections to any transaction or other facts about the operation of the Partnership disclosed in such balance sheet and/or statement of operations unless he shall have notified the Managing Partner(s) in writing of his objectives within thirty (30) days of the date on which such statement is mailed.

The Partnership shall maintain a bank account or bank accounts in the Partnership's name in a national or state bank in the State of _____. Checks and drafts shall be drawn on the Partnership's bank account for Partnership purposes only and shall be signed by the Managing Partner(s) or their designated agent.

Any controversy or claim arising out of or relating to this Agreement shall only be settled by arbitration in accordance with the rules of the American Arbitration Association, one Arbitrator, and shall be enforceable in any court having competent jurisdiction.

Witnesses   **Partners**

_____   _____

_____   _____

Dated: _____

The Corporation as Partner

Disagreement exists on whether a corporation can become a partner. After all, general partners are personally liable for the debts incurred by the partnership. But if one of the general partners is a corporation, then what does personal liability mean?

One view is that a corporation cannot be a partner unless the corporation's articles of incorporation specifically empower it to enter into a partnership as a partner. The opposite view, which prevails today, is contained in the Model Business Corporation Act which allows corporations to generally make contracts and incur liabilities. Basically, then, the capacity of corporations to contract is a question of corporation law. The UPA, on the other hand, specifically permits a corporation to be a partner. By definition, "a partnership is an association of two or more persons," and the UPA defines a person as including corporations.[6]

Many states have restrictions on corporations becoming partners, though such restrictions have become less common over the years. Many decisions in jurisdictions that do not permit corporate partners nevertheless validate the arrangements by characterizing them as joint ventures rather than partnerships.

Mutual Consent

A partnership is a voluntary association of co-owners. It cannot be forced upon anyone. The *intent* to associate is a key element of a partnership, and one cannot join a partnership unless all other partners consent.[7]

Indications of Partnership

Parties commonly find themselves in conflict over whether their business enterprise is a legal partnership, especially in the absence of a formal written contract. To answer this question, the UPA and the courts have developed broad guidelines for interpreting partnership status.

In determining whether a partnership is created, the court usually looks for three factors:

1. A sharing of profits or losses.
2. A joint ownership of the business.
3. An equal right of management of the business.

A problem arises when evidence is insufficient to establish all three factors. The UPA provides a set of guidelines in this event. For example, the sharing of profits and losses from a business is considered *prima facie* evidence that a partnership is created. However, no such inference is made, for example, if the profits were received as payment of:

1. A debt by installments or interest on a loan.
2. Wages of an employee.
3. Rent to a landlord.
4. An annuity to a widow or representative of a deceased partner.
5. A sale of goodwill of a business or property.[8]

To illustrate: A debtor businessperson owes a creditor $5,000 on an unsecured debt. To repay the debt, the debtor agrees to pay (and the creditor to accept) 10 percent of the debtor's monthly profits until the loan with interest is paid. Although the creditor is sharing profits from the business, the debtor and creditor are not presumed to be partners.

Take, for example, a young college graduate who wants to start a retail dress shop. The graduate leases a building from the landlord. Both the landlord and graduate know that it will take time to establish a clientele, and standard equal rental payments could severely restrict the graduate's ability to purchase inventory. Thus, the lease calls for a minimum low rental payment plus a percentage of the monthly profits for the term of the lease. This sort of arrangement does not make the landlord and tenant partners, even though there is a sharing of profits.

Joint ownership of property, obviously, does not in and of itself create a partnership. Therefore, the fact that Able and Baker own real prop-

---

6. UPA Section 2.

7. UPA Section 18(g).

8. UPA Section 7(4).

erty as joint tenants or as tenants-in-common (form of joint ownership) does not establish a partnership. In fact, the sharing of gross returns and even profits from such ownership will usually not be enough to create a partnership.[9] Thus, if Able and Baker jointly own a piece of rural

property and lease the land to a farmer, the sharing of the profits from the farming operation by the farmer in lieu of set rental payments would ordinarily not make Able, Baker, and the farmer partners.

In the following case, a widow attempted to persuade the court that she and her late husband were business partners.

---

9. UPA Section 7(2)(3).

MILLER v. CITY BANK & TRUST CO., N.A.
Court of Appeals of Michigan,
1978.
82 Mich.App. 120, 266 N.W.2d 687.

BACKGROUND AND FACTS   *The plaintiff was a widow who, for tax reasons, attempted to establish that a partnership had existed between herself and her late husband. At the trial, she testified that her deceased husband asked her to marry him and move with him to another city to help run his nursery business. They married, and the plaintiff gave up her well-paying job to move south with her new husband. Although the plaintiff did not make any capital contributions to the partnership, she held a management position in the nursery business, and she did physical labor. In addition, she kept all the books and hired and fired employees. She received periodic payments of $50 or $100. Whenever the plaintiff received a check, her husband also received one for the same amount. Money for household expenses was taken out of the business account.*

Along with the nursery business, her husband had been engaged in making land sales. However, no land had ever been conveyed to the partnership.

The year after the plaintiff married her husband, a business registration certificate was filed for the nursery, indicating that the business was a partnership. Checking accounts, vehicles, and other equipment were acquired and held under the business name. On the other hand, annual tax forms and schedules listed the business as a sole proprietorship and the plaintiff's occupation as housewife. A Michigan business activities form also indicated a sole proprietorship. Finally, in applying for a self-employment and pension and profit-sharing plan, the husband stated in his application that his business was a sole proprietorship.

There was never any formal written partnership agreement. The plaintiff, however, stated that her husband had described the relationship when he asked her to marry him and at all times since as one of partnership. She was under the impression that they were business partners. Furthermore, the plaintiff testified that her husband told her that she was "the best partner he ever had."

DANHOF, Chief Judge.

* * * *

The burden of proof to show a partnership is on the one alleging the partnership, and the burden is stricter when relatives are the alleged partners. Also the fact that the alleged partner is deceased further raises the burden of proof.

* * * The elements of a partnership are generally considered to include a voluntary association of two or more people with legal capacity in order to carry on, via co-ownership, a business for profit. Co-ownership of the business requires more than merely joint ownership of the property and is usually evidenced by joint control and the sharing of profits and losses. With the intentions of the party to form a partnership as our polestar we will review the trial court's finding.

It is not disputed that the parties were involved in a business venture for profit and had the legal capacity to form a partnership. However, the evidence relating to co-ownership does not indicate that a legal partnership was contemplated. Prior to the marriage, Mr. Miller [the plaintiff's husband] operated the business and owned all the property. Mrs. Miller [the plaintiff] made no capital contributions except her services. Even though plaintiff worked long and hard hours, this does not establish that the parties had an agreement to form a partnership. This evidence could also be viewed as consistent with an employee-employer relationship or that of a helpful wife who assisted her husband without them intending a legal partnership.

Co-ownership is also indicated by profit sharing. In fact, profit sharing is prima facie evidence of a partnership. However, the [trial] court did not find an agreement to share profits and we cannot say that this was clearly erroneous. [When an appellate court reviews a trial court's findings of fact, it will not disturb the resulting judgment unless there is absolutely no factual evidence to support the trial court's conclusion. In this case, the appellate court showed that there were many possible interpretations to be made from the fact that Mr. and Mrs. Miller each received monthly payments from the business.] That Mr. and Mrs. Miller each received monthly payments from the nursery checking account does not necessarily establish profit sharing. The payments could also be reasonably viewed as salary or wages. Another possible interpretation would be that Mr. Miller was withdrawing money from his sole proprietorship and was dividing it equally because he felt an obligation to share equally with his wife, as a wife rather than a business partner.

Another indicia of co-ownership is mutual agency and control. That Mrs. Miller kept the books, wrote checks, and hired and fired does not necessarily establish any control other than that which might be given to a trusted employee. However, it is not necessary that this control be exercised as long as it exists. In view of the absence of the exercise of control or mutual agency, evidence of an agreement in respect to the division of control is about the only way to prove mutual agency and control. However, no evidence of an agreement with respect to mutual control was presented.

*   *   *   *

The evidence introduced against these claims indicated that the deceased did not intend to form a legal partnership with his wife. First, there is no written agreement and there is only plaintiff's testimony in support of an oral one. The income tax returns and schedules listed the business as a sole proprietorship, listed Mr. Miller's income as wages and Mrs. Miller's occupation as a housewife. In 1964, Mr. Miller applied for a self-employee retirement deduction plan as a sole proprietorship. Mr. Miller's social security forms listed the business as a sole proprietorship. All the capital contributions came from Mr. Miller and the property remained in his name (or his and his wife's name), and none was transferred to the partnership. Shortly before his death, Mr. Miller deeded his homestead to his wife and himself as tenants by the entirety and this would seem needless if they already owned it as partners. Although none of these facts are conclusive, they are all factors to be weighed in the decision.

JUDGMENT
AND REMEDY

After reviewing the entire trial court record, the appellate court agreed that the presumption of partnership established by the filing of business registration papers was rebutted by other competent evidence, which tended to show that Mr. Miller intended the business to be run as a sole proprietorship. The trial court's judgment that no partnership existed was affirmed.

Partnership by Estoppel

Parties who are not partners can hold themselves out as partners and make representations that third persons rely on in dealing with these alleged partners. The law of partnership imposes liability on the alleged partner or partners, but it does not confer any partnership rights on these persons.

There are two aspects of liability. The person representing himself or herself to be a partner in an actual or alleged partnership is liable to any third person who extends credit in good faith reliance on such representations. Similarly, a person who expressly or impliedly *consents* to such misrepresentation of an alleged partnership relationship is also liable to third persons who extend credit in good faith reliance.[10]

For example, Moore owns a small shop. Knowing that the Midland Bank will not make a loan on his credit alone, Moore represents that Lewis, a financially secure businesswoman, is a partner in Moore's business. Lewis knows of Moore's misrepresentation but fails to correct the bank's information. Midland Bank, relying on the strength of Lewis's reputation and credit, extends a loan to Moore. Moore will be liable to the bank for the loan repayment. In many states, Lewis would also be held liable to the bank in such a loan transaction. Lewis has impliedly consented to such misrepresentation and will normally be estopped from denying that Moore is her partner. She will be regarded as if she were in fact a partner in Moore's business to the extent that this loan is concerned.

When a real partnership exists, and a partner represents that a nonpartner is a member of the firm, the nonpartner is regarded as an agent whose acts are binding on the partner.

For example, Middle Earth Movers has three partners—Johnson, Mathews, and Huntington. Mathews represents to the business community that Thompson is a partner. If Thompson negotiates a contract in Middle Earth Movers' name, the contract will be binding on Mathews, but normally not on Johnson and Huntington (unless, of course, Johnson and Huntington knew and consented to Mathews's representation).

In summary, partnership by estoppel requires that a third person reasonably and detrimentally rely on the representation that a person was part of the partnership.

PARTNERSHIP PROPERTY RIGHTS

For financial and credit reasons, it is frequently necessary to distinguish between property belonging to the firm and property belonging to each individual partner, particularly in bankruptcy proceedings. A partnership can own any real or personal property, unless the partnership agreement contains some prohibition or limitation on what it can acquire. Holding property in the firm name can be merely a convenience, so *title alone is not conclusive* in establishing that a particular asset belongs to the partnership.

Factors Indicating Partnership Property

UPA Section 8(1) provides that "all property originally brought into the partnership's stock or subsequently acquired, by purchase or otherwise, *on account of the partnership,* is partnership property." (Emphasis added.) Indications that the assets were acquired with the intention that it be a partnership asset is the heart of the phrase

---

10.   UPA Section 16.

on *account of the partnership.* Thus, the more closely an asset is associated with the business operations of the partnership, the more likely it is to be a partnership asset. Moreover, when such an asset is purchased with partnership funds, it will belong to the partnership unless a contrary intention is shown.

TERMINATION

Introduction

Any change in the relations of the partners that demonstrates unwillingness or inability to carry on partnership business dissolves the partnership, resulting in termination.[11] If any of the partners wish to continue the business, they are free to reorganize into a *new* partnership.

The termination of a partnership has two stages—dissolution and winding up. Both must take place before termination is complete.

11.　UPA Section 29.

Dissolution occurs when any partner (or partners) indicates an intention to disassociate from the partnership. *Winding up* is the actual process of collecting and distributing the partnership's assets.

Dissolution is the principal remedy of a partner against co-partners. Events causing the dissolution can be grouped into three basic categories:

1.　Acts of partners.[12]
2.　Operation of law.[13]
3.　Judicial decree.[14]

Dissolution terminates the right of a partnership to exist as a going concern, but the partnership continues to exist long enough to wind up its affairs. When winding up is complete, the partnership's *legal existence* is terminated. The concepts of dissolution and winding up are discussed by the Supreme Court of Minnesota in the next case.

12.　UPA Section 31(1)(2).
13.　UPA Section 33(4)(5).
14.　UPA Section 32.

BACKGROUND AND FACTS　*The plaintiff, Mary Stilinovich, brought this appeal to contest the finding of a referee appointed to liquidate the assets of a partnership between herself and the defendant, Nick Maras. The referee ordered the dissolution of the partnership due to irreconcilable differences between the partners. The plaintiff and the defendant were a sister and brother who had formed a partnership by oral agreement with assets left to them by their deceased father. There were accusations of misappropriation on both sides, and the referee was appointed. Maras tendered a written offer to buy out his sister for $65,000. No such offer was submitted by the plaintiff. A hearing was held, and the referee ordered an accounting. After the accounting, he ordered the business to be sold to Maras for the $65,000. The plaintiff contended that the referee erred in his order.*

**MARAS v.
STILINOVICH**
Supreme Court of Minnesota,
1978.
268 N.W.2d 541.

YETKA, Justice.

*　*　*　*

[This] was essentially a partnership dissolution in which the undivided two-thirds interest in the land and building was treated as a partnership asset. *　*　*　[W]hether a sale could be ordered to one partner over the objection of the other [is contested.] The parties stipulated that the assets were partnership assets and not subject to mere partition. We find the stipulation is broad enough to allow sale to one partner where the other fails to tender a timely bid.

*   *   *   *

After dissolution, a partnership continues until liquidated or wound up. Although dissolution of a partnership is usually followed by liquidation, a withdrawing partner may be paid his partnership contribution and share of accumulated profits and no liquidation need occur. Minn. [law] provides, in effect, that the partnership affairs must be wound up after dissolution unless otherwise agreed. Crane and Bromberg, Law of Partnership, § 86, suggests that the most logical buyers of a dissolved partnership are the remaining partners, and in the stipulation the parties agreed to one of the partners carrying on the business. Agreements for continuation of partnership business after dissolution are generally valid and enforceable. Oral agreements 'are generally sufficient to establish a partnership relationship, and we hold that the oral agreement in this case was sufficient to establish the framework for dissolution of a partnership. The referee was clearly acting within the scope of his powers by ordering the sale to Nick Maras.

*   *   *   *

The method of conducting and confirming a judicial sale is within the discretion of the court, and the policy of the law should be to sustain judicial sales where no injustice occurs. Thus, if the parties were treated fairly and the rights of [plaintiff] were not prejudiced by the terms of the sale, then the trial court [judgment] should be affirmed.

JUDGMENT AND REMEDY   *The court examined the proceedings and concluded that dissolution was fair. The trial court's judgment was therefore affirmed.*

Dissolution by Acts of the Partners

By Agreement A partnership can be dissolved if certain events stipulated in the partnership agreement occur. For example, when a partnership agreement expresses a fixed term or a particular business objective to be accomplished, the passing of the date or the accomplishment of the project dissolves the partnership. However, partners do not have to abide by the stipulations in the agreement. They can mutually agree to dissolve the partnership early or to extend it. If they agree to continue in the partnership, they become *partners at will*, with all the rights and duties remaining as originally agreed.

Partner's Power to Withdraw A partnership is a personal legal relationship among co-owners. No person can be compelled either to be a partner or to remain one. Implicit in a partnership is each partner's *power* to disassociate from the partnership at any time. Able and Carla form a partnership with no definite term or particular undertaking specified—that is, a partnership at will. Both Able and Carla have the power and the right to withdraw from the partnership. The partnership continues for three years, until one day Carla announces that she no longer wishes to continue in the partnership. Assuming that Carla's sudden withdrawal will not do irreparable damage to the firm, her act is sufficient to begin the process of dissolution.

Admission of New Partners Any change in the composition of the partnership, whether by withdrawal of a partner or by *admission of a new partner*, results in dissolution. In practice, this result is usually modified by providing that the remaining or new partners continue in the firm's business. Nonetheless, a new partnership arises. The new partnership carries over the debts of the dissolved partnership. Creditors of the prior partnership become creditors of the one that is continuing the business.[15]

Transfer of a Partner's Interest   The UPA provides that voluntary transfer[16] or involuntary sale of a partner's interest for the benefit of creditors does not by itself dissolve the partnership.[17] However, either occurrence can ultimately lead to judicial dissolution of the partnership, as will be discussed.

Dissolution by Operation of Law

Death   A partnership is dissolved upon the death of any partner, even if the partnership agreement provides for carrying on the business with the executor of the decedent's estate. Any change in the composition among partners results in a new partnership. (But there is always the possibility of a reformation of the partnership upon the death of a partner.)

---

15.   UPA Section 41.
16.   A single partner cannot make another person a partner in a firm merely by transferring his or her interest to that person. [UPA Section 27]
17.   UPA Section 28.

Bankruptcy   Because a partner's credit reputation is an intrinsic part of his or her contribution to a partnership, the bankruptcy of a partner will dissolve a partnership. Insolvency alone will not result in dissolution. Naturally, bankruptcy of the firm itself will result in dissolution.

Illegality   Any event that makes it unlawful for the partnership to continue its business or for any partner to carry on in the partnership will result in dissolution. Even if the illegality of the partnership business is a cause for dissolution, the partners can decide to change the nature of their business and continue in the partnership.

For example, Able and Baker enter a partnership agreement to run a tuna fishing business. Subsequently, a maritime law prohibiting tuna fishing by private concerns is passed. Able and Baker do not necessarily have to dissolve their partnership. They can choose to remain partners and fish for something that is not prohibited.

When the illegality applies to an individual partner, then dissolution *must* occur. For example, suppose the state legislature passes a law making it illegal for magistrate judges to engage in the practice of law. If an attorney in a law firm is appointed a magistrate, the partnership must be dissolved. The next case deals with dissolution of a partnership due to illegality.

BACKGROUND AND FACTS   *Williams sued the defendant, Burrus, for an accounting and dissolution of their partnership. Burrus bought the partnership asset, a restaurant, in his name alone because Williams could not secure a liquor license. If disclosure of Williams's interest had been known, the license would have been denied. The only issue to be considered on appeal was whether the trial court erred in refusing to give Williams any relief in the form of his share of partnership assets.*

WILLIAMS v. BURRUS

Court of Appeals of Washington, Division 1, 1978. 20 Wash.App. 494, 581 P.2d 164.

ANDERSEN, Judge.
*   *   *   *

Courts will not assist in the dissolution of an illegal partnership or entertain an action for an accounting or distribution of its assets. The trial court's decision was not erroneous.
*   *   *   *

No state retail liquor license of any kind can be issued to a partnership unless all of the members thereof are qualified to obtain a license, and no licenseholder can allow any other person to use such a license.

Furthermore, a partnership is dissolved by any event which makes it unlawful for the business of the partnership to be carried on or for the members to carry it on in partnership.

The issue of illegality may be raised at any time.

Under the general rule that the courts will not aid either party to an illegal agreement where a partnership is formed to carry out an illegal business or to conduct a lawful business in an illegal manner, the courts will refuse to aid any of the parties thereto in an action against the other. *   *   *

JUDGMENT AND REMEDY   *The appellate court affirmed the trial court's dismissal of Williams's case. Since the partnership was illegal, neither party had any rights that a court would enforce. (They were in pari delicto.)*

Dissolution by Judicial Decree

Dissolution of a partnership can result from judicial decree. For dissolution to occur, an application or petition must be made in an appropriate court. The court then either denies the petition or grants a decree of dissolution. UPA Section 32 cites the following situations in which a court can dissolve a partnership.

Insanity   A partnership can obtain judicial declaration of dissolution when a partner is adjudicated insane or is shown to be of unsound mind. This action often involves a series of complex tests and standards.

Incapacity   When it appears that a partner has become incapable of performing his or her duties under the partnership agreement, a decree of dissolution may be required. It must appear that the incapacity is permanent and will substantially affect the partner's ability to discharge his or her duties to the firm.

Business Impracticality   When it becomes obvious that the firm's business can be operated only at a loss, judicial dissolution may be ordered.

Improper Conduct   A partner's impropriety involving partnership business (for example, fraud perpetrated upon the other partners) or improper behavior reflecting unfavorably upon the firm (for example, habitual drunkenness) will provide grounds for a judicial decree of dissolution.

Dissolution may also be granted when personal dissension between partners becomes so persistent and harmful as to undermine the confidence and cooperation necessary to carry on the firm's business. (In general, courts are reluctant to allow partners to sue each other except for dissolution.)

Notice of Dissolution

Dissolution ends the partnership as a going concern. Thereafter, it remains viable only for the purpose of winding up its affairs. In some circumstances, however, a partnership or a withdrawing partner can become bound to a contract made after dissolution has begun but before winding up is complete.

Notice to Partners   The intent to dissolve or withdraw from a firm must be communicated *clearly*. All partners will share liability for the acts of any partner who continues conducting business for the firm without knowing the partnership has been dissolved. For example, Ann, Baker, and Carl have a partnership. Ann tells Baker of her intent to withdraw. Before Carl learns of Ann's intentions, Carl enters into a contract with a third party. The contract is equally binding on Ann, Baker, and Carl. Unless the other partners have notice, the withdrawing partner will continue to be bound as a partner to all contracts created for the firm.

The following case illustrates the importance of giving notice of the intention to terminate a partnership.

BACKGROUND AND FACTS   *Plaintiff and defendant were partners in a restaurant. At first they operated the restaurant themselves, but in April 1968 they leased the restaurant to Moran. The partners evicted Moran in November 1968. Sjo, the plaintiff, immediately began negotiating a lease to Brown's Chicken, Inc. Sjo's partner, Cooper, signed a twenty-year lease with Brown's Chicken in June 1970. Sjo filed suit for a dissolution of the partnership and an accounting in 1972. Cooper contended that the partnership was dissolved prior to the execution of the lease with Brown's Chicken and that Sjo was not entitled to benefit from the lease.*

SJO v. COOPER
Appellate Court of Illinois, First District, Fifth Division, 1975.
29 Ill.App.3d 1016, 331 N.E.2d 206.

LORENZ, Justice.

*   *   *   *

The partners gave contradictory testimony concerning events in 1969. Defendant testified that on three occasions he requested that plaintiff contribute additional funds to help meet mortgage payments and he offered carbon copies of two requests as proof. Plaintiff testified that additional funds had been requested only once and he had declined because defendant would not give him an accounting as to the money Moran had paid the partnership. Plaintiff further testified that on two other occasions he had requested, but did not receive an accounting. Defendant testified that he had sent an accounting, but offered no proof. Defendant had taken the money as repayment of his loans to the partnership. From December, 1969 to July, 1970 the partners did not communicate and defendant continued to meet all partnership obligations.

In June, 1970 defendant signed a 20-year lease with Brown's Chicken, Inc. In July, 1970, the partnership met and defendant stated that plaintiff's failure to contribute over the preceding 18 months had ended their partnership and plaintiff had no interest in Brown's lease. Plaintiff then filed suit.

Plaintiff contends that the trial court erred in finding that the partnership had been dissolved in 1969. He states that neither party's actions give rise to a dissolution. We concur.

Under the Uniform Partnership Act (Ill.Rev.Stat.1971, ch. 106½, par. 31) a partnership for no fixed term may be dissolved at the express will of either party. The dissolving party need not give any reason for his desire to end the partnership, but he must give *notice* of his intention to do so. (Salter v. Condon, 236 Ill.App. 17.) A search of the record finds that at no time prior to July, 1970, did defendant give any such notice. In fact, defendant testified that he was conducting partnership business in early July, 1970.

Defendant contends that plaintiff's failure to contribute additional funds from April, 1969 to July, 1970, constituted a withdrawal from the partnership resulting in dissolution. While there are no Illinois cases on point, we note that the California courts, which are also guided by the Uniform Partnership Act, have found that a *partner's failure to contribute capital does not in itself constitute a dissolution.*

We, therefore, conclude that the partnership was not dissolved in 1969, but rather defendant's statement caused dissolution in July, 1970.

The court determined that the correct date of dissolution of the partnership was July 1970. The plaintiff would be entitled to an accounting of

JUDGMENT AND REMEDY

all partnership funds through that date. The profits or losses in which a partner must share are determined by the date of dissolution.

Notice to Third Parties Dissolution of a partnership by the act of a partner requires notice to all affected third persons. The manner of giving notice depends upon the third person's relationship to the firm. Any third person who has dealt with the firm must receive *actual notice*. For all others, a newspaper or similar public notice is sufficient. Dissolution resulting from operation of law generally requires *no notice* to third parties.[18]

Winding Up

Once dissolution occurs and partners have been notified, they cannot create new obligations on behalf of the partnership. Their only authority is to complete transactions begun but not finished at the time of dissolution and to wind up the business of the partnership. Winding up includes collecting and preserving partnership assets, discharging liabilities (paying debts), and accounting to each partner for the value of his or her interest in the partnership.

Where dissolution is caused by a partner's act that violates the partnership agreement, the innocent partners may have rights to damages resulting from the dissolution. Also, the innocent partners have the right to buy out the offending partner and continue the business instead of winding up the partnership.

Dissolution resulting from the death of a partner vests all partnership assets in the surviving partners. The surviving partners act as a fiduciary in settling partnership affairs in a quick, practicable manner and in accounting to the estate of the deceased partner for the value of the decedent's interest in the partnership. The surviving partners are entitled to payment for their services in winding up the partnership as well as to reimbursement for any costs incurred in the process.[19]

Distribution of Assets

Both creditors of the partnership and creditors of the individual partners can make claims on the partnership's assets. In general, creditors of the partnership have priority over creditors of individual partners in the distribution of partnership assets; the converse priority is usually followed in the distribution of individual partner assets, except under the new Bankruptcy Act.

The distribution of partnerships' assets is made *after* third-party debts are paid. The priorities, after third-party debts, are as follows:[20]

1. Refund of advances (loans) made to or for the firm by a partner.
2. Return of capital contribution to a partner.
3. Distribution of the balance, if any, to partners in accordance with their respective share in the profits.

QUESTIONS AND CASE PROBLEMS

1. Daniel is the owner of a chain of shoe stores. He hires Martin as a manager of a new store, which is to open in Grand Rapids, Michigan. Daniel, by written contract, agrees to pay Martin a monthly salary. In addition, Daniel and Martin have agreed to an 80–20 percent split in profits. Without Daniel's knowledge, Martin represents himself to Carlton as Daniel's partner, showing Carlton the agreement to share profits. Carlton extends credit to Martin. Martin defaults. Discuss whether Carlton can hold Daniel liable as a partner.

2. Adam wishes to purchase some real property owned by Tropical Gardens. He learns that Tropical Gardens is a partnership comprised of Smith, Jones,

---

18. Childers v. United States, 442 F.2d 1299 (5th Cir. 1971).
19. UPA Section 18(f).

20. UPA Section 40(b).

and Green. He also learns that the partnership needs capital and that is one of the major reasons the partners are selling their real property. Since Tropical Gardens is a partnership, Adam has the following concerns:

(a) Can the partnership convey the land in the name of Tropical Gardens?

(b) If there is a breach of contract, against whom must Adam file a lawsuit?

(c) If he obtains a judgment against Tropical Gardens, against whom can he execute it?

Discuss Adam's concerns.

3. Two individuals, Able and Baker, orally agree to form a partnership to run a television sales and repair business. No specific term of partnership duration is stated. Able is an adult, and Baker is a minor. The oral partnership agreement provides for each partner to contribute capital of $5,000, with Baker's contribution due at the end of the first year's operation. Two months prior to the end of the first year's operation, Able and Baker orally agree to take in Super TV Supply Corporation as a third partner. Two weeks later, both Super TV Supply Corporation and Baker assert that neither of them had the capacity to be a partner and that, in any event, there was no written agreement to form a partnership. Discuss whether Baker and Super TV Supply Corporation can disclaim partnership responsibility to Able.

4. Able, Baker, and Carlton have formed a twenty-year partnership to purchase land, develop it, manage it, and then sell the property. The partnership agreement calls for the partners to devote their full time to the business. Assume the following *separate* events take place:

(a) After two years, Baker and Carlton agree that the working hours of the partnership will be from 8:00 A.M. to 6:00 P.M. rather than the previously established schedule of 9:00 A.M. to 5:00 P.M. Able refuses to come to work before 9:00 A.M. and quits promptly at 5:00 P.M.

(b) After two years, Able quits the partnership and walks out.

(c) After two years, Able becomes insolvent.

(d) After two years, Able dies.

Discuss fully which of the above acts constitutes a dissolution and whether there is any ensuing liability of Able.

5. Able and Baker have formed a partnership. At the time of formation Able's capital contribution was $10,000, and Baker's was $15,000. Later Able made a $10,000 loan to the partnership when it needed working capital. The partnership agreement provides that profits are to be shared, with 40 percent for Able and

60 percent for Baker. The partnership is dissolved by Baker's death. At the end of the dissolution and the winding up of the partnership, the partnership's assets are $50,000, and the partnership's debts are $8,000. Discuss fully how the assets will be distributed.

6. Able, Baker, and Charlie were partners in a partnership at will. Able and Baker excluded Charlie from partnership management affairs and then sought a dissolution of the partnership. A trial court dissolved the partnership and ordered a sale of the partnership asset, a shopping center. Able and Baker were the highest bidders at the court-ordered sale and were therefore able to retain the shopping center. Will the courts protect Charlie from this type of freeze-out? [Prentiss v. Sheffel, 20 Ariz.App. 415, 513 P.2d 953 (1973)]

7. In April 1970 Harber, Pittman, and Calvert entered into an oral agreement to build and sell 235 houses. Following their agreement, Harber withdrew $6,000 in partnership funds and purchased three lots on which houses were to be built. The lots were purchased in his name, and after the homes were constructed, title was also in his name. When Harber sells the houses (at a profit) can he retain the proceeds for himself? [Davis v. Pioneer Bank and Trust Co., 272 So.2d 430 (La.App.1973)]

8. In 1969 Simon, Genia, and Ury Rapoport entered into an agreement with Morton, Gerome, and Burton Parnes to form the partnership known as Perry Company. Each of the families owned 50 percent of the partnership interests. In December 1974 Simon and Genia Rapoport assigned a 10 percent interest of their share in the partnership to their adult children, Daniel and Kalia. An amended partnership certificate was filed in the county clerk's office, as required by law, indicating the addition of Daniel and Kalia as partners. However, when the Rapoports requested the Parneses to execute an amended partnership agreement reflecting this change in the partnership, the Parneses refused. In a court action by the Rapoports to force the Parneses to execute the amended partnership agreement, what will be the result? What interest in the partnership, if any, can Daniel and Kalia Rapoport take without the Parneses' consent? [Rapoport v. 55 Perry Co., 50 A.D.2d 54, 376 N.Y.S.2d 147 (1975)]

9. Lynne, Ernest, and Stanley Timmermann established a partnership in 1965 for the purpose of engaging in farming activities. In January 1969 Lynne stated to the other two partners that he no longer wished to be involved in the partnership. It was not until August 31, 1970, however, that Lynne ceased to participate in the farming activities of the partnership. In January 1972 Lynne attempted to bring about a forced liquidation of the partnership through a lawsuit. In January 1969 the value of the partnership was approximately

$50,000. On August 31, 1970, the value of the partnership was slightly less than $10,000; and in January 1972 the value of the partnership was in excess of $300,000. Assuming Lynne had a one-third interest in the partnership, approximately how much should he receive when he withdraws? Explain your answer. [Timmermann v. Timmermann, 272 Or. 613, 538 P.2d 1254 (1975)]

10. On September 28, 1958, Reid and three others entered into a written partnership agreement for the purpose of leasing for profit certain real property located in Montgomery County, Pennsylvania. Reid was to manage the property, and the others were to perform the physical labor necessary to maintain the premises in good condition. One year later, Reid notified the others that she was dissolving the partnership and requested that the partnership assets be liquidated as soon as possible. Has dissolution occurred? Assuming dissolution has occurred, can the other partners recover damages for breach of partnership agreement on the ground that the partnership was a partnership for a particular undertaking and hence not terminable at will? [Girard Bank v. Haley, 460 Pa. 237, 332 A.2d 443 (1975)]

11. Respass and Sharp were partners who owned and managed a racing stable. In addition, they were engaged in bookmaking. At the time Sharp died, $4,724, representing the undistributed profits of the bookmaking business, was on deposit in Sharp's personal bank account. Respass, arguing that Sharp's death resulted in dissolution of the partnership, sought to recover one-half of the profits from the bookmaking business. What was the result? [Central Trust and Safe Co. v. Respass, 112 Ky. 606, 66 S.W. 421 (1902)]

CHAPTER 38

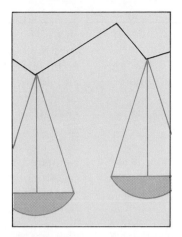

PARTNERSHIPS
Operation and Duties

The rights and duties of partners are governed largely by the specific terms of their partnership agreement. In the absence of provisions to the contrary in the partnership agreement, the law imposes the rights and duties discussed in this chapter. The character and nature of the partnership business generally influence the application of these rights and duties.

RIGHTS AMONG PARTNERS

Management

"All partners have equal rights in the management and conduct of partnership business."[1] Management rights belong to all partners in an ordinary partnership.[2] Each partner has one vote in management matters *regardless of the proportional size of his or her interest in the firm.* Often, in a large partnership, partners will agree to delegate daily management responsibilities to a management committee made up of one or more partners.

The majority rule controls decisions in ordinary matters connected with partnership business, unless specified otherwise in the agreement. However, unanimous consent of the partners is required to bind the firm in any of the following actions:

1. To alter the essential nature of the firm's business as expressed in the partnership agreement or to alter the capital structure of the partnership.[3]
2. To admit new partners or enter a wholly new business.
3. To assign partnership property into a trust for the benefit of creditors.

---

1. UPA Section 18(e).
2. Compare the management rights of general and limited partners in limited partnerships. The absence of management responsibility and the concomitant liability limitations are distinguishing characteristics of such partnerships. See the discussion on limited partnership in Chapter 39.

3. UPA Section 18(h).

4. To dispose of the partnership's goodwill.

5. To confess judgment against the partnership or submit partnership claims to arbitration.

6. To undertake any act that would make further conduct of partnership business impossible.[4]

Each of these matters significantly affects the nature of the partnership.

Interest in the Partnership Each partner is entitled to the proportion of business profits and losses that is designated in the partnership agreement. If the agreement does not apportion profits or losses, the UPA provides that profits shall be shared equally and losses shall be shared in the same ratio as profits.[5]

---

4. UPA Section 9(3) various subsections.
5. UPA Section 18(a).

For example, Able and Baker form a partnership. The partnership agreement provides for capital contributions of $6,000 from Able and $4,000 from Baker, but it is silent as to how Able and Baker will share profits or losses. In this case, Able and Baker would share both profits and losses equally. Had the partnership agreement provided for profits to be shared in the same ratio as capital contributions, the profits would be shared 60 percent for Able and 40 percent for Baker; and had it been silent as to losses, losses would be shared in the same ratio as the profits (60-40 percent).

In the following case, the partners agreed to share profits equally. When the court found that one partner had appropriated more than 50 percent of the profits, the other partner was granted an interest in the assets acquired through the diversion of partnership funds.

CLEMENT v. CLEMENT

Supreme Court of Pennsylvania, 1970.

436 Pa. 466, 260 A.2d 728.

BACKGROUND AND FACTS *Charles Clement and his brother, L. W., formed a partnership and agreed to share the profits equally after payment of debts. Forty years later Charles learned that L. W. had taken more than half the profits and had acquired real estate and life insurance policies, which L. W. owned in his own name. Charles sought a dissolution of the partnership and an accounting. A receiver was appointed, and the chancellor of the equity court awarded Charles an interest in the property L. W. had purchased with partnership funds. Sitting **en banc** [all judges of a court reviewing a case], the equity court reversed the chancellor's decision, and Charles appealed to the Supreme Court of Pennsylvania.*

ROBERTS, Justice.

Charles and L. W. Clement are brothers whose forty year partnership has ended in acrimonious litigation. The essence of the conflict lies in Charles' contention that L. W. has over the years wrongfully taken for himself more than his share of the partnership's profits. Charles discovered these misdeeds during negotiations with L. W. over the sale of Charles' interest in the partnership in 1964. He then filed an action in equity, asking for dissolution of the partnership, appointment of a receiver, and an accounting. Dissolution was ordered and a receiver appointed. After lengthy hearings on the issue of the accounting the chancellor decided that L. W., who was the brighter of the two and who kept the partnership books, had diverted partnership funds. The chancellor awarded Charles a one-half interest in several pieces of property owned by L. W. and in several insurance policies on L. W.'s life on the ground that these had been purchased with partnership assets.

* * * *

*   *   * There was ample evidence of self-dealing and diversion of partnership assets on the part of L. W.—more than enough to sustain the chancellor's conclusion that several substantial investments made by L. W. over the years were bankrolled with funds improperly withdrawn from the partnership. *   *   *
*   *   *   *

In the instant case L. W. dealt loosely with partnership funds. At various times he made substantial investments in his own name. He was totally unable to explain where he got the funds to make these investments. The court en banc held that Charles had no claim on the fruits of these investments because he could not trace the money that was invested therein dollar for dollar from the partnership. Charles should not have had this burden. He did show that his brother diverted substantial sums from the partnership funds under his control. The inference that these funds provided L. W. with the wherewithal to make his investments was a perfectly reasonable one for the chancellor to make and his decision should have been allowed to stand.

Charles was entitled to a one-half interest in the assets that L. W. purchased with partnership funds.   **JUDGMENT AND REMEDY**

The consequences of breach of a fiduciary duty to the other partner are not only damages but also the resulting profit.   **COMMENT**

Compensation

A partner's time, skill, and energy on behalf of partnership business is a duty and generally not a compensable service. Partners can, of course, agree otherwise. For example, the managing partner of a law firm often receives a salary in addition to his share of profits for performing special administrative duties in office and personnel management. UPA Section 18(f) provides that a surviving partner is entitled to compensation for services in winding up partnership affairs (and reimbursement for expenses incurred in the process) above and apart from his or her share in the partnership profits.

Each partner impliedly promises to devote full time and render exclusive service to the partnership. Assume that Hunter, Brooks, and Palmer enter a partnership. Palmer undertakes independent consulting for an outside firm without the consent of Hunter and Brooks. Palmer's compensation from the outside firm is considered partnership income.[6] A partner cannot engage in any independent competitive or even noncompetitive activities that involve the partnership's time.

If Palmer engages in an activity that competes with the partnership, then Palmer has breached the fiduciary duty that he owes it. Even with a noncompetitive activity, Palmer can breach his fiduciary duty if the partnership suffers from the loss of his efforts. Of course, the partnership agreement or unanimous consent of the partners can permit a partner to engage in any activity.

Inspection of Books

Partnership books and records must be kept accessible to all partners. Each partner has the right to receive (and each partner has the corresponding duty to produce) full and complete information concerning the conduct of all aspects of partnership business.[7] Each firm retains books in which to record and secure such information. Partners contribute the information, and a bookkeeper typically has the duty to preserve it. The

---

6. UPA Section 21.

7. UPA Section 20.

books must be kept at the firm's principal business office and cannot be removed without the consent of all the partners.[8] Every partner, whether active or inactive, is entitled to inspect all books and records upon demand and can make copies of the materials. The personal representative of a deceased partner's estate has the same right of access to partnership books and records that the decedent would have had.

Accounting

An accounting of partnership assets or profits is done to determine the value of each partner's proportionate share in the partnership. An accounting can be performed voluntarily, or it can be compelled by order of a court in equity.[9] Formal accounting occurs by right in connection with dissolution proceedings, but, under UPA Section 22, a partner also has the right to a formal accounting in the following situations:

1.   When the partnership agreement provides for a formal accounting.
2.   When a partner is wrongfully excluded from the business, from access to the books, or both.
3.   When any partner is withholding profits or benefits belonging to the partnership in breach of the fiduciary duty.
4.   When circumstances "render it just and reasonable."

Property Rights

A partner has three basic property rights. They are:

1.   A right in specific partnership property.
2.   An interest in the partnership.
3.   A right to participate in the management of the partnership, as previously discussed.[10]

---

8.   UPA Section 19.
9.   The principal remedy of a partner against co-partners is an equity suit for dissolution, an accounting, or both. With minor exceptions, a partner cannot maintain an action against other firm members for damages until partnership affairs are settled and an accounting is done. This rule is necessary because legal disputes between partners invariably involve conflicting claims to shares in the partnership. Logically, the value of each partner's share must first be determined by an accounting.
10.   UPA Section 24.

There is an important legal distinction between a partner's rights in specific property belonging to the firm to be used for business purposes, and a partner's right to share in the firm's earned profits to the extent of his or her interest in the firm. No individual partner has an absolute right to specific property of the firm. A partner is co-owner with his partners of specific partnership property, holding as a tenant in partnership. Chapter 37 discussed the factors that the courts use in determining property rights of partners and the rights of creditors in regard to partnerships. A judgment creditor of an individual partner has no right to execute or attach specific partnership property, but he or she can obtain the partner's share of profits. A creditor of the firm can levy directly upon partnership property (as will be discussed).

Partner's Interest in the Firm   A partner's interest in the firm is a personal asset consisting of a proportionate share of the profits earned [11] and a return of capital after dissolution and winding up.

A partner's interest is susceptible to assignment or to a judgment creditor's lien. Judgment creditors can attach a partner's interest by petitioning the court that entered the judgment to grant the creditors a charging order. This order entitles the creditors to profits of the partner and to any assets available to the partner upon dissolution.[12] Neither an assignment nor a court's charging order entitling a creditor to receive a share of the partner's money will cause dissolution of the firm.[13]

Partnership Property   Partners are *tenants in partnership* of all firm property.[14] Tenancy in partnership has several important effects. If a partner dies, the surviving partners, not the heirs of the deceased partner, have the right of survivorship to the specific property. Although surviving partners are entitled to possession, they have a duty to account to the decedent's estate

---

11.   UPA Section 26.
12.   UPA Section 28.
13.   UPA Section 27.
14.   UPA Section 25(1).

for the *value* of the deceased partner's interest in said property.[15]

A partner has no right to sell, assign, or in any way deal with a particular item of partnership property as an exclusive owner.[16] Nor is a partner's personal credit related to partnership property; creditors cannot use it to satisfy the personal debts of a partner. Partnership property is available only to satisfy partnership debts, to enhance the firm's credit, or to achieve other business purposes.

Every partner is a co-owner with all other partners of specific partnership property such as office equipment, paper supplies, and vehicles. Each partner has equal rights to possess partnership property for business purposes or in satisfaction of firm debts, but not for any other purpose without the consent of all the other partners. These principles are aptly illustrated by the next case.

---

15.   UPA Section 25(2)(d)(e).
16.   UPA Section 25(2)(a)(b).

BACKGROUND AND FACTS   *The plaintiff and the defendant, who were partners in a real estate business, dissolved the partnership by mutual agreement on May 1, 1975. The original agreement called for each partner to share equally in profits and losses. On November 29, 1972, the defendant made a down payment on a piece of property in his own name and reimbursed himself out of the partnership's checking account. The property was carried on the books of the partnership. At dissolution, the plaintiff wanted the defendant to turn over 50 percent of the rents and profits from that property. The trial court ruled for the plaintiff, and the defendant appealed.*

STAUTH v. STAUTH

Court of Appeals of Kansas, 1978.

2 Kan.App.2d 512, 582 P.2d 1160.

SPENCER, Judge.

*   *   *   *

The evidence was conflicting as to whether defendant was to hold the property for the partnership. Defendant testified that sometime after he had signed the real estate purchase contract, but prior to closing, it was agreed between plaintiff and defendant that they would share profits on the sales of houses and lots as long as plaintiff supervised construction on the lots. The lots were then entered as assets on the partnership records as a matter of convenience, and if plaintiff was to share in the profits, the expenses should be paid by the partnership. Plaintiff testified that the agreement prior to closing was that the lots were to be partnership property, but that defendant told him the lots could be held in defendant's name alone as a convenience in making sales. In that way only defendant and his wife would be required to execute conveyances. Plaintiff stated that defendant told him that the attorney for the partnership had indicated that title to the real estate might be held in defendant's name alone as long as there was a written agreement that the lots were indeed partnership property.

In 60 Am.Jur.2d, *Partnership* § 93, pp. 22–23, it is stated:

"*   *   * An agreement that certain real estate should be part of the firm assets may be implied from the acts and conduct of the partners; the agreement need not be express.

"*   *   * [A]mong indicia of partnership ownership are the payment by the partnership of taxes *   *   *.

"Partnership books may also be considered to determine the question, as, for example, how the property was entered and carried on the books of the company. The manner in which the accounts are kept, whether the purchase money is severally charged to the members of the firm, or whether the accounts treat it the same as other firm property, may be controlling circumstances in determining such intention, and from these circumstances the agreement of the parties may be inferred."

From the record, it appears that the purchase of the real estate was entered on the partnership records prior to the closing of that transaction. Thereafter, abstract fees, taxes, and payments on the purchase money mortgage were paid by the partnership. Profits were reported as partnership income.

* * * *

Did the partnership provide the purchase money or some part thereof? Defendant made the down payment from his personal account but was reimbursed from partnership funds on the day of closing the transaction. The purchase money was provided by a 100 percent loan obtained in the names of defendant and his wife and secured by a mortgage on the real estate. This loan was entered as a liability on the partnership records on the day that purchase was finalized. The partnership made all payments on the loan. Even though funds for the purchase of the real estate were provided from another source, it is evident that the liability for repayment of those funds was assumed by the partnership, which thereafter did in fact make all payments that were made on the loan. There was evidence from which the trial court could properly find that the partnership paid the purchase money or some part thereof.

JUDGMENT AND REMEDY   *The appellate court affirmed the trial court's ruling that the defendant had to turn over 50 percent of the profits in rents from the disputed property to the plaintiff.*

DUTIES AND POWERS OF PARTNERS

Fiduciary Duty

Partners stand in a fiduciary relationship to one another the way that principals and agents do. (See Chapter 34.) It is a relationship of extraordinary trust and loyalty. The fiduciary duty imposes a responsibility upon each partner to act in good faith for the benefit of the partnership. It requires that each partner subordinate his or her personal interests in the event of conflict to the mutual welfare of the partners.

This fiduciary duty underlies the entire body of law pertaining to partnership and to agency. From it, certain other duties are commonly implied. Thus, a partner must account to the part-

nership for any personal profits or benefits derived without consent of all of the partners in any partnership transaction.[17] These include transactions among partners or with third parties connected with the formation, conduct, or liquidation of the partnership, or with any use of partnership property.[18]

Upon the death of a partner, the surviving partner is under a fiduciary duty to liquidate partnership assets without delay and to credit the estate of the deceased partner for the value

---

17. In this sense, "to account" to the partnership means not only to divulge the information but also to determine the value of any benefits or profits derived and to hold that money or property in trust on behalf of the partnership.

18. UPA Section 21.

of the decedent's interest in the partnership. The fiduciary duty of good faith owed the deceased partner arises by implication in the personal representative of the deceased partner's estate as well. The principles of fiduciary duty and property rights are illustrated in the next case.

BACKGROUND AND FACTS   *About 45 doctors, including Dr. Witlin, owned and operated a health center as partners. When Dr. Witlin died, the other doctors, in accordance with their partnership agreement, purchased his share of the center, paying his widow $65,228. The partnership agreement provided that on Witlin's death a management committee of the partnership was required to make a good faith determination of the fair market value of Witlin's share. The partnership had the option to offer this amount to Witlin's widow. The $65,228 offer, however, was based only on the book value of the partnership's assets. In addition, although the partnership was in the process of bargaining to sell the health center at a price which would have doubled Dr. Witlin's widow's proportionate share, the partnership did not inform her of that fact. Mrs. Witlin now seeks a greater amount for her husband's share, even though she has accepted the partnership's offer.*

ESTATE OF WITLIN
California Court of Appeal, 1978.
83 Cal.App.3d 167, 147 Cal.Rptr. 723.

COBEY, Associate Justice.

*   *   *   *

Appellants [the forty-five doctors] owed such a [fiduciary] duty to plaintiff as the widow and executrix of their deceased partner in purchasing from her their deceased partner's interest in the partnership. Throughout the transaction they were bound to act toward her "in the highest good faith" and they were forbidden to obtain any advantage over her in the matter by, among other things, the slightest concealment. Yet the management committee never revealed to plaintiff or her representative, King, that the basic value in their formula for determining the fair market value of the partnership was book value alone. Likewise, as already noted, the management committee did not mention to King the possibility that the hospital might be shortly sold.

This possibility of sale was quite real. It appears from plaintiff's improperly rejected offers of proof that the management committee reached in 1969 a tentative agreement with General Health Services to sell the partnership's assets to it for approximately $60,000 a percentage point, that between April and September 28, 1971, the management committee and the American Cyanamid Corporation were discussing a sale of the partnership to it for at least $93,000 a percentage point, and, as already noted from the evidence itself, that the partnership's assets were finally sold in June 1972 to Hospital Corporation of America for about $84,000 a percentage point.

The management committee knew all of this, but they apparently never breathed a word of it to either plaintiff or her attorney. It seems that in discussing the fair market value of the partnership they talked out of both sides of their mouths. They talked to plaintiff and her attorney in terms of $16,000 and $24,600 per percentage point while they were more or less simultaneously talking to conglomerates interested in purchasing the hospital and the other assets of the partnership in terms of selling prices ranging from $60,000 to $93,500 per percentage point.

Given this situation, how could their offer of $24,600 per percentage point to plaintiff have been a good faith determination on their part of the fair market value of the partnership? Obviously the jury's verdict was correct and solidly supported in this respect.

JUDGMENT AND REMEDY   *The judgment was affirmed on appeal. The partners were held to have breached their fiduciary duty to their deceased partner by failing to make a full and fair disclosure.*

General Agency Powers

Each partner is an *agent* of every other partner and acts as both a principal and an agent in any business transaction within the scope of the partnership agreement. Each partner is a general agent of the partnership to carry on the usual business of the firm. Thus, every act of a partner in every contract and in every contract signed in the partnership name, concerning partnership business, binds the firm.[19]

The UPA affirms general principles of agency law that pertain to the authority of a partner to bind a partnership in contract or tort. When a partner is apparently carrying on partnership business with third persons in the usual way, both the partner and the firm share liability. It is only when third persons *know* that the partner has no such authority that the partnership is not liable.

For example, Peter, a partner in Firm X, applies for a loan on behalf of the partnership without authorization from the other partners. The bank manager knows Peter has no authority. If the bank manager grants the loan, Peter will be personally bound, but the firm will not be liable.

Joint Liability   Partners have only joint liability on all partnership debts and contracts. Partners are jointly and severally liable for tort actions and breaches of trust to third persons.[20]

Joint liability means that the group of partners wins or loses as a group. One partner cannot be singled out to be sued. Unless the partnership is treated as an entity, every partner's name must be listed in the suit, and the individual assets of each partner are equally exposed to potential liability (although the actual contribution in the event of a judgment is calculated on each partner's proportionate share of the firm). If the court awards the claimant a judgment, the claimant is barred from further suits against the partners and against the firm, once satisfaction (that is, payment) of the judgment is made.

In states that allow a firm to be sued in its own name, a contract claimant or a creditor claimant can sue the firm as an *entity* without joining each partner. A judgment against the partnership binds only partnership assets. In such states, the better practice is to sue both the firm as an *entity* and all partners *jointly*. Then, judgment is enforceable against the assets of the partnership and the assets of the individual partners. The judgment rendered in such a case must be internally consistent. For example, if Carl sues Firm X and all its partners jointly for breach of contract and the court finds the firm liable, then it must hold the partners liable (and vice versa).

Joint and several liability means that a claimant can sue one partner without joining the others. Moreover, regardless of the outcome of the suit against the first partner, **res judicata** (a matter or thing settled by judgment in the courts) does not protect the other partners in subsequent suits filed against them.

Liability of Incoming Partner   A newly admitted partner to an existing partnership has limited liability for whatever debts and obligations the partnership incurred prior to the new partner's admission. UPA Section 17 provides that the new partner's liability can be satisfied only from partnership assets. This means that the new

---

19.   UPA Section 9(1).
20.   UPA Section 15.

partner has no personal liability for these debts and obligations, but any capital contribution made by him or her is subject to these debts.

Trading versus Non-Trading Partnerships—A Digression   At common law, prior to the UPA, a distinction was drawn between trading and non-trading partnerships. Essentially, any partnership business that had goods in inventory and made profits in buying and selling those goods was considered a trading partnership. All other partnerships were non-trading. The distinction between these two types of partnerships is important in discussing the apparent authority of the partnership and of its individual members. The UPA does not expressly adopt the distinction between these two types of partnerships, but many cases decided under the UPA nonetheless followed the distinction.

Authority of Partners   Agency concepts relating to apparent authority, actual authority, and ratification are also applicable to partnerships. The extent of *implied authority* is generally broader for partners than for ordinary agents. The character and scope of the partnership business and the customary nature of the particular business operation determine the scope of implied powers. For example, the usual course of business in a trading partnership involves buying and selling commodities. Consequently, each partner in a trading partnership has a wide range of implied powers to borrow money in the firm name and to extend the firm's credit in issuing or indorsing negotiable instruments.

In an ordinary partnership, firm members can exercise all implied powers reasonably necessary and customary to carry on that particular business. Some customarily implied powers include the authority to make warranties on goods in the sales business, the power to convey real property in the firm name where such conveyances are part of the ordinary course of partnership business, the power to enter contracts consistent with the firm's regular course of business, and the power to make admissions and representations concerning partnership affairs.[21]

----
21.   UPA Section 11.

If a partner acts within the scope of authority, the partnership is bound to third parties. For example, a partner's authority to sell partnership products carries with it the implied authority to transfer title and make usual warranties. Hence, in a partnership that operates a retail tire store, any partner negotiating a contract with a customer for sale of a set of tires can warrant that "each tire will be warranted for normal wear for 40,000 miles."

However, this same partner would not have authority to sell office equipment, fixtures, or the partnership office building without the consent of all of the other partners. In addition, since partnerships are formed for profit, a partner does not generally have authority to make charitable contributions without consent of the other parties. Any such actions are not binding on the partnership unless ratified by all of the other partners.

As in the law of agency, the law of partnership imputes one partner's knowledge to all other partners because members of a partnership stand in a fiduciary relationship to one another. Such a fiduciary relationship implies that each partner willfully discloses to every other partner all relevant information pertaining to the business of the partnership. The same rule applies to members of a joint venture.

QUESTIONS AND
CASE PROBLEMS

1.   Able, Baker, and Clark form a partnership to operate a window washing service. Able contributes $10,000 to the partnership, and Baker and Clark contribute $1,000 each. The partnership agreement is silent on how profits and losses will be shared. One month after the partnership is in operation, Baker and Clark vote, over Able's objection, to purchase another truck for the firm's operation. Able believes that since he contributed $10,000, a major commitment to purchase by the partnership cannot be made over his objection. In addition, Able claims that, in absence of agreement, profits must be divided in the same ratio

as each partner's capital contribution. Discuss Able's contentions.

2. Able, Betty, and Carla form a partnership to operate a hairstyling salon. After one year's operation, the salon has become very busy and profitable. Most customers prefer one of the partners to perform the various services offered. Able becomes ill, and Betty and Carla start working sixty-hour weeks. It appears that Able will not return to work for at least two months. Betty and Carla want to bring in Dana as a new partner. Able objects to Dana and refuses to consent to Dana's admission into the partnership. Betty and Carla insist that they be paid extra compensation for having to work additional hours because of Able's illness. Discuss whether Betty and Carla are entitled to the compensation claimed and whether Dana can be admitted as a new partner by majority vote.

3. Able and Baker are partners in a law firm. Able has substantial personal assets. Able, driving his own car, is on his way to take a deposition from a witness when he negligently runs into Thomas. The damages and injuries to Thomas amount to $5,000. Unknown to Able, Baker at the same time has contracted to purchase $9,000 worth of word processing equipment from Copycat Inc. Both partners have express partnership authority to purchase office equipment. Able is angry about the purchase and wrongfully cancels the contract with Copycat. Both Copycat and Thomas want to sue. Discuss the nature of the partners' liability in both cases.

4. Able and Baker operate as partners a car dealership. The partnership has existing debts of $300,000 with General Motors. Able and Baker take in a new partner, Carlson. Carlson contributes to the partnership land valued at $100,000 to be used by the partnership as a used car lot. Carlson is new to the car dealership business and in making his first sale warrants to a customer that the partnership will repair the car at no cost for a period of two years regardless of mileage. General Motors sues the partners jointly on the debt and obtains a judgment. Able and Baker insist that Carlson's warranty to the customer is not binding on the partnership.

   (a) Discuss Carlson's liability to General Motors.
   (b) Discuss Able's and Baker's claim that Carlson's warranty is not binding on the partnership.

5. Able, Baker, and Carlson form a television repair partnership. Profits are to be shared equally. Each partner draws a monthly salary of $1,000. Without Able's and Baker's knowledge, Carlson, who has principal authority to purchase supplies and equipment, is receiving a rebate from large orders made with a supplier. Also, Carlson keeps the books and records

at his home and continually denies Able and Baker access to the books. Able and Baker want an accounting. Discuss fully whether they are entitled to it.

6. Two brothers formed a partnership of indefinite duration. The partnership agreement provided that if "any dispute * * * over any matter pertaining to the operation of the partnership" should arise between the parties, the dispute would be subject to arbitration. Lawrence Stone sought a dissolution of the partnership, alleging that his brother had neglected partnership business. Does Lawrence have to submit his differences with his brother to arbitration before the partnership can be dissolved? [Stone v. Stone, 292 So. 2d 686 (La. 1974)]

7. Plaintiff Hodge brought action against a partnership that owned a movie theater. Volar, the managing partner, signed a contract for the sale to Hodge of real estate adjacent to the theater and belonging to the partnership. The agreement reserved an easement for use as a driveway into the premises. At trial, Volar claimed that prior to signing he had told Hodge that Hodge would have to present him with a plat plan of the property and that Volar's other partners would have to approve before the sale of the property. At trial, Hodge denied this. The partners argued that, in any event, Volar did not have authority to sell the property. Did he? [Hodge v. Garrett, 101 Idaho 397, 614 P.2d 420 (1980)]

8. A patient sued a physician for medical malpractice and successfully obtained a money judgment. The patient did not sue the partnership to which the physician belonged and made no allegation against the partnership. Injury to the patient occurred in the course of partnership business. Can the physician now recover from his co-partners for damages that he paid out of his personal funds? [Flynn v. Reaves, 135 Ga. App. 651, 218 S.E.2d 661 (1975)]

9. Harestad and Weitzel entered into an oral agreement in August 1970 to be "partners in a real estate and building business," and each contributed equal amounts to the partnership. In October 1970, Weitzel purchased an apartment project in his own name with his own funds. Over the next two years, he oversaw the development and consummated the sale of the apartment project for a handsome profit. Upon voluntary dissolution of the partnership by both parties, Harestad sought half the profit that Weitzel had made from his apartment project deal. Can she recover? [Harestad v. Weitzel, 272 Or. 199, 536 P.2d 522 (1975)]

10. David Bell and Fred Herzog were partners in a real estate partnership. The partnership operated from August 1968 until August 1969, when Herzog notified Bell that he, Herzog, considered Bell's failure to devote his time and efforts to the real estate business

and his failure to make payments required by the partnership agreement a breach of the agreement and that he was therefore terminating the partnership. Bell in turn wrote to Herzog, stating that he considered Herzog's letter to be the "last straw" and that he, Bell, was therefore terminating the partnership. Bell then sought an accounting of all the partnership's assets and liabilities. Herzog objected on the ground that Bell's failure to contribute to the management of the partnership constituted a breach of fiduciary duty, a breach of the partnership agreement, and a breach of the Uniform Partnership Act. Should Bell's demand for an accounting be denied? [Bell v. Herzog, 39 A.D.2d 813, 332 N.Y.S.2d 501 (1972)]

CHAPTER 39

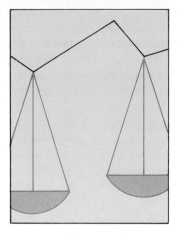

PARTNERSHIPS
Limited
Partnerships

This chapter will look in detail at the management, formation, and termination of limited partnerships. It will also look at a highly specialized form of partnership, the limited partnership association.

DEFINITION OF
LIMITED PARTNERSHIP

Limited partnerships are formed by compliance with statutory requirements. They consist of at least one general partner and one or more limited partners.[1] The general partner (or partners) assumes management responsibility of the partnership and, as such, has full personal liability for all debts of the partnership. The limited partner (or partners) contributes cash (or other property) and owns an interest in the firm but does

not undertake any management responsibilities and is not personally liable for partnership debts beyond the amount of his or her investment. A limited partner can forfeit limited liability by taking part in managing the business. In many respects, limited partnerships are like general partnerships, discussed in Chapters 37 and 38. They are sometimes referred to as special partnerships, in contrast to general partnerships.

HISTORY OF THE
LIMITED PARTNERSHIP

Business employs services and capital. A need therefore exists for a form of organization that permits capital investment without responsibility for management and without liability for losses beyond the initial investment. Such an organization should also allow the right to share in the profits with limited liability for losses.

---

1. ULPA Section 1.

During the Middle Ages, this kind of organization was called a *commenda*.[2] In a commenda, the *commendator* supplied money to the *tractator* and received a major portion of the profits but was not liable for losses. If the tractator lost the capital investment, the commendator was liable only if proven negligent. This particular institution was sanctioned by the French Commercial Code in 1707, Sections 23-28. Over a century later, the first limited partnership acts were adopted in Connecticut and Pennsylvania in 1836 and in New York in 1882.

Limited Partnership Statutes—Early Versions

All states have enacted limited partnership statutes. The earlier interpretations of such acts displayed an obvious hostility toward limited liability that derived from the common law. Courts imposed full liability on limited partners when there were only trivial failures to comply with the law.

The Uniform Limited Partnership Act

The Uniform Limited Partnership Act was promulgated in 1916. It has been adopted by forty-eight states (not Delaware or Louisiana) and by the District of Columbia and the Virgin Islands. Its thirty-one sections are set forth in Appendix E of this book. The great virtue of the ULPA is that it expressly provides protection against technical defects if there has been a substantial compliance in good faith.[3] Under the ULPA, a limited partnership can conduct any business that can be carried on by a general partnership unless there is an exception in the state statutes.[4] The most predominant exceptions are banking and insurance.

The Revised Uniform Limited Partnership Act

On August 5, 1976, the National Conference of

Commissioners on Uniform State Laws approved a Revised Uniform Limited Partnership Act. It contains eleven articles and sixty-four sections (set forth in Appendix F), and it was made available to state legislatures in 1977. The articles are:

1. General Provisions.
2. Formation; Certificate of Limited Partnership.
3. Limited Partners.
4. General Partners.
5. Finance.
6. Distributions and Withdrawal.
7. Assignment of Partnership Interest.
8. Dissolution.
9. Foreign Limited Partnerships.
10. Derivative Actions.
11. Miscellaneous.

For a comparison of the basic characteristics of general partnerships, limited partnerships, and those limited partnerships formed under the Revised Uniform Limited Partnership Act, see Exhibit 39–1.

FORMATION

The creation of a limited partnership is a public and formal proceeding that must follow statutory requirements. Contrast this with the informal, private, and voluntary agreement that usually suffices for a general partnership as described in Chapter 37. For a limited partnership, there must be two or more partners, and they must sign a certificate that sets forth, at a minimum, the following information:[5]

1. Firm name.
2. Character of the business.
3. Location of the principal place of business.
4. Name and place of residence of each member and whether each is a general or a limited partner.
5. Duration of the partnership.

2. W. Holdsworth, *History of English Law*, 195, Methuen and Co. Ltd., London (1956).
3. ULPA Section 2(2).
4. ULPA Section 3.

5. ULPA Section 2(1).

EXHIBIT 39-1   BASIC COMPARISON OF PARTNERSHIPS

CHARACTERISTIC	GENERAL PARTNERSHIP	LIMITED PARTNERSHIP	REVISED LIMITED PARTNERSHIP
Creation	By agreement of two or more persons to carry on a business as co-owners for profit.	By agreement of two or more persons, under the laws of the state, having one or more general partners and one or more limited partners to carry on a business as co-owners for profit. Filing of certificate in appropriate state office is required.	Same as limited partnership, except filing of certificate with Secretary of State is required.
Sharing of profits and losses	By agreement, or in absence thereof, profits are shared equally by partners and losses are shared in same ratio as profits.	Profits are shared as required in certificate agreement, and losses shared likewise, except limited partners share losses only up to their capital contributions.	Same as limited partnership, except in absence of provision in certificate agreement, profits and losses are shared on basis of percentages of capital contributions.
Liability	Unlimited personal liability of all partners.	Unlimited personal liability of all general partners; limited partners only to extent of capital contributions.	Same as limited partnership.
Capital contribution	No minimal or mandatory amount; set by agreement.	Set by agreement; may be cash, property, or any obligation except services.	Same as limited partnership; contribution of services is allowed.
Management	By agreement, or in absence thereof, all partners have an equal voice.	General partners by agreement, or else each has an equal voice. Limited partners have no voice, or else subject to liability as a general partner.	Same as limited partnership, except limited partner involved in partnership management is liable as a general partner *only* if third party has knowledge of such involvement. Limited partner may act as agent or employer of partnership, and vote on amending certificate or sale or dissolution of partnership.
Duration	By agreement, or can be dissolved by action of partner (withdrawal), operation of law (death or bankruptcy), or court decree.	By agreement in certification, or by withdrawal, death, or insanity of general partner in absence of right of other general partners to continue the partnership. Death of a limited partner, unless he or she is only remaining limited partner, does not terminate partnership.	Same as limited partnership, except it enlarges class of activities by general partner that result in termination. (Section 402)
Assignment	Interest can be assigned, although assignee does not have rights of substituted partner, without consent of other partners.	Same as general partnership. If partners consent to assignee becoming a partner, certificate must be amended.	Same as limited partnership. Upon assignment of all interest, partner ceases to be a partner.
Priorities (order) upon liquidation	1. Outside creditors. 2. Partner creditors. 3. Capital contribution of partners.	1. Outside creditors. Limited partner creditors. 2. Profits to limited partners.	1. Outside creditors. Limited partner creditors. 2. Amounts before withdrawal to which partners are entitled.

EXHIBIT 39–1 *Continued*

4. Profits of partners.	3. Limited partner capital contributions.	3. Capital contributions—limited and general partners.
	4. General partner creditors.	4. Profits—limited and general partners.
	5. Profits to general partners.	
	6. Capital contributions of general partners.	

6. Amount of cash and a description and agreed-upon valuation of any other property contributed by each limited partner.

7. Additional contributions (if any) to be made by each limited partner and the times at which they are to be made.

8. Rights for changes in partnership personnel (if any) and subsequent continuance of the business.

9. Share of profits or other compensation that each limited partner is entitled to receive.

In essence, the content of the certificate and the method of filing resemble that for the corporate charter. Often, there are private, informal agreements covering matters that do not have to be stated in the certificate, such as the profit shares of the general partners. See Exhibit 39–2 for a sample certificate of limited partnership.

Where to File Certificates

The certificate must be filed with the designated state official. It is usually open to public inspection. The official is normally in the county where the principal business of the firm will be carried on. Some states require multiple filings if business is carried on in numerous counties. Others require only one filing, usually at the state capital. Constructive notice (by reason of law) does not usually exist for a certificate filed in another state. Thus, if a limited partnership chooses to do business where a certificate is not filed, a court can rule that its failure to file locally makes it a general partnership. This is similar to the qualification rules for foreign corporations. Some states require newspaper publication of certificates, or at least a summary of them, in addition to a filing.

Number of Limited Partners Originally, limited partnerships were conceived to accommodate only a few limited partners. There seems, however, to be no statutory limit to their numbers and, in some cases, very large groups have been assembled. In a 1966 case, the limited partners of a real estate syndicate brought a class action suit against the general partners and some outsiders.[6] The limited partners numbered several hundred.

The Role of the Limited Partner and Liability

General partners, unlike limited partners, are personally liable to the partnership's creditors; thus at least one general partner is necessary in a limited partnership, so that someone has personal liability. This policy can be circumvented in states that allow a corporation to be the general partner in a partnership. Since the corporation has limited liability by virtue of corporate laws, no one in the limited partnership actually has personal liability.

Limited Partners Cannot Participate in Management

The exemptions from personal liability of the limited partners rest on their not participating in management.[7] First, the contribution of a limited partner cannot be in his or her services as manager—it has to be in cash or other property.[8] Second, the surname of a limited partner cannot be included in the partnership name.[9] A viola-

---

6. Lichtyger v. Franchard Corp., 18 N.Y.2d 528, 223 N.E.2d 869 (1966).
7. ULPA Section 7.
8. ULPA Section 4.
9. ULPA Section 5.

EXHIBIT 39–2   SAMPLE CERTIFICATE OF LIMITED PARTNERSHIP

CERTIFICATE OF LIMITED PARTNERSHIP

The undersigned, desiring to form a Limited Partnership under the Uniform Limited Partnership Act of the State of _____ , make this certificate for that purpose.

§ 1.   Name.   The name of the Partnership shall be "_____ _____ ".

§ 2.   Purpose.   The purpose of the Partnership shall be to [*describe*].

§ 3.   Location.   The location of the Partnership's principal place of business is _____County, _____ .

§ 4.   Members and Designation.   The names and places of residence of the members, and their designation as General or Limited Partners are:

_____	[*Address*]	General Partner
_____	[*Address*]	General Partner
_____	[*Address*]	Limited Partner
_____	[*Address*]	Limited Partner

§ 5.   Term.   The term for which the Partnership is to exist is indefinite.

§ 6.   Initial Contributions of Limited Partners.   The amount of cash and a description of the agreed value of the other property contributed by each Limited Partner are:

[*Name*]	[*Describe*]
[*Name*]	[*Describe*]

§ 7.   Subsequent Contributions of Limited Partners.   Each Limited Partner may (but shall not be obliged to) make such additional contributions to the capital of the Partnership as may from time to time be agreed upon by the General Partners.

§ 8.   Profit Shares of Limited Partners.   The share of the profits which each Limited Partner shall receive by reason of his contribution is:

[*Name*]	_____ %
[*Name*]	_____ %

Signed _____ , 19____

_____
_____
_____
_____

Signed and sworn before me, the undersigned authority, this _____ _____ , 19____ .

Notary Public
_____County, _____

tion of either of these provisions renders the limited partner just as liable as a general partner to any creditor who does not know that he or she is a limited partner.

Note that no law expressly bars the participation of limited partners in the management of the partnership. Rather, the threat of personal liability deters their participation.

The revised ULPA does restrict a limited partner's liability. Only if the third party had knowledge of the limited partner's management activities is the limited partner liable as a general partner. How much actual review and advisement a limited partner can engage in before being exposed to liability is an unsettled question.[10]

The issue of the degree of control of the limited partner comes up in the following case.

_____

10. See Plasteel Products Corp. v. Helman, 271 F.2d 354 (1st Cir. 1959) (interpreting Massachusetts law).

BACKGROUND AND FACTS   *Weil, the general partner, sought to have the court declare the limited partners as general partners because of their participation in management activities. The limited partnership was having financial difficulties, and creditors were seeking payment from Weil, who was the sole general partner. He wished to spread the liability to all the limited partners.*

WEIL v. DIVERSIFIED PROPERTIES
U.S. District Court, District of Columbia, 1970.
319 F.Supp. 778.

GESELL, District Judge.

*   *   *   *

Cases relating to whether or not limited partners have taken part in control of the business and are thus to be treated as general partners involve claims by creditors against the partners. No case has been found where a general partner has invoked Section 7 of the Act against his own limited partners. The purpose of Section 7 is to protect creditors:

> The Act proceeds on the assumption that no public policy requires a person who contributes to the capital of a business, acquires an interest in its profits, and some degree of control over the conduct of the business to become bound for the obligations of the business, provided creditors have no reason to believe that when their credits were extended that such persons were so bound.

*   *   *   *

Even if a general partner might hold his limited partners to account as general partners under certain circumstances, Weil cannot do so on the facts of this case. Weil considers himself still a general partner and recognizes that the written partnership agreement by its terms is a bona fide limited partnership under the Code. As between themselves, partners may make any agreement they wish which is not barred by prohibitory provisions of statutes, by common law, or by considerations of public policy. Whatever may be the obligations of the limited partners as against creditors or third parties, Weil may not prevail against them if they have not breached the terms of the agreement. Having entered into the partnership agreement with advice of counsel, an agreement made largely for his own benefit in a field where he was especially experienced, he is bound by its terms. Accordingly, the initial inquiry must be to determine whether the limited partners have in any way violated the terms of the written agreement.

*   *   *   *

Thus it is apparent that the partners contemplated the general partner would receive a substantial salary and have the day-to-day management of the properties. For reasons already suggested, this expectation was altered by events which resulted in the general partner foregoing his salary and turning over immediate day-to-day responsibility to Rubenstein and Tempchin, [outside partners] who were employed on a commission basis. After May 1 1969, the partnership operation became a matter of salvaging what could be salvaged in the enterprise as it then existed. This naturally involved refinancing and sale of properties and other matters not in the normal course of day-to-day business. As to these non-routine matters, the limited partners by the very terms of their agreement had a majority vote, and were certainly authorized to comment upon them. Weil believes he should have had exclusive say as to how and what bills were to be paid with any money available beyond immediate operating needs, but under the prevailing conditions this clearly was not a normal day-to-day business question; it involved the very ability of the enterprise to survive. Moreover, the funds coming in were far from sufficient to meet current obligations, and no partnership account was being accumulated.

*   *   *   *

The foregoing analysis is wholly consistent with the understanding that the partners had back in 1968. Plaintiff's exhibit No. 1, in evidence, is a letter from Steinberg, one of the limited partners, written to Rubenstein and Tempchin under date of October 14, 1968. The letter was composed by Weil and distributed to all of the partners. It will be recalled that Rubenstein and Tempchin were conducting the routine handling of rent collections and expenditures for the garden apartments then being operated by the partnership. As the letter discloses in more detail, Steinberg pointed out that while Rubenstein and Tempchin were expected to continue normal activities in leasing and managing the properties and payment of bills generated by the projects, major decisions involving new obligations, closing phases of the operation, etc., were beyond the scope of their responsibilities as property managers but were to be determined by policies set with the knowledge and consent of all the partners. While Weil points to this letter as demonstrating a taking-over by the limited partners of operating responsibility, it appears rather to emphasize the clear distinction that the partners themselves drew at the time between the normal leasing, managing and bill-paying as it related to the properties and the decisions not normal to the day-to-day operations which, under the agreement, were always the responsibility of all the partners. While, to be sure, the letter suggests that not all partners were being consulted, Weil failed to establish that his views could not be considered. Weil was employed in another business, creditors were harassing him, his affairs were in disarray and he could not always be reached. He was busy developing a proposal for sale of the properties. Steinberg called most of the meetings, which were held at Steinberg's home, and the major problems of the partnership were acted upon at these meetings to which Weil was invited. It appears that while he was invited to partnership meetings he often failed to attend and was not available for consultation.

Weil has not by a preponderance of the evidence established any violation by the limited partners of terms of the agreement with him, which at the very most is all that Weil can complain of in his effort to have the limited partners declared general partners. Since the partnership agreement was not violated by the limited partners, Weil has no cause of action and his request for the appointment of a receiver and an accounting will be denied. The provisions of the Limited Partnership Act were primarily designed to protect creditors. So long as the provisions of the agreement were followed, no partner can complain.

Weil's case was dismissed.

JUDGMENT AND REMEDY

A creditor can seek to have a limited partner declared a general partner because of participation in management, but a general partner can complain of violation of the partnership agreement only if a limited partner interferes with management of the partnership.

COMMENTS

Liability to Creditors A limited partner is liable to creditors to the extent of any contribution that had been promised to the firm or any part of a contribution that was withdrawn from the firm.[11] If the firm is defectively organized, and the limited partner fails to renunciate (withdraw from the partnership) on discovery of the defect, the partner can be held liable to the firm's creditors. Note, though, that the ULPA and the Revised ULPA allow people to remain limited partners regardless of whether they comply with statutory technicalities. Decisions on liability for false statements in a partnership certificate run in favor of persons relying on the false statements and against members who sign the certificate knowing of the falsity.[12] A limited partnership is formed by good faith compliance with requirements for signing and filing the certificate even if it is incomplete or defective. When a limited partner discovers a defect in the formation of the limited partnership, he or she can obtain shelter from future liability by renouncing an interest in the profits of the partnership, thereby avoiding any future reliance by third parties.[13]

Liability of Limited Partners The liability of a limited partner is limited to the capital that he or she contributes or agrees to contribute to the partnership. By contrast, the liability of a general partner for partnership indebtedness is virtually unlimited.

---

11. See Kittredge v. Langley, 252 N.Y. 405, 169 N.E. 626 (1930).

12. See Walraven v. Ramsay, 335 Mich. 331, 55 N.W.2d 853 (1953) and ULPA Section 6.
13. ULPA Section 11.

BACKGROUND AND FACTS *Chemical Bank of Rochester filed suit against the limited partners of a partnership to recover funds advanced on a note. Stanndco Developers was the sole general partner in Meadowbrook Farm Apartments. In exchange for Stanndco's promise to transfer apartment units to the Meadowbrook limited partnership, eighteen limited partners executed promissory notes payable to Meadowbrook for their "shares" in the limited partnership. The notes totaled $101,000. Stanndco later sought a $101,000 bank loan for purposes unrelated to Meadowbrook and used the notes given by the Meadowbrook limited partners as collateral. Stanndco endorsed the notes to itself without the consent or ratification of the limited partners. The bank sought to collect on the notes from the limited partners.*

CHEMICAL BANK OF ROCHESTER v. ASHENBURG
Supreme Court of Monroe County, 1978.
94 Misc.2d 64, 405 N.Y.S.2d 175.

SCHNEPP, Justice.

*   *   *   *

Plaintiff [bank] had knowledge that Stanndco was negotiating the instruments in a transaction for its own benefit, without authority, and in breach of its duty as a fiduciary. Plaintiff knew from the outset of the transaction, when Stanndco first approached it for a corporate loan, that the notes were not being used by Stanndco for a partnership purpose. *   *   * In the face of these facts, plaintiff acted in bad faith. Chemical Bank had actual knowledge or knowledge of facts sufficient to impute notice on the infirmities, defects and defenses to the instrument. In short, plaintiff, having taken the notes with notice and in bad faith, is not entitled to the rights of a holder in due course.

*   *   *   *

It is held that plaintiff takes subject to the defendants' claim that the notes were negotiated for the individual purpose of a general partner in breach of its fiduciary duty. Plaintiff, a non-holder in due course, may not recover on the notes against the defendant makers *   *   *.

*   *   * The defendants, as both makers of the notes and limited partners, had a legitimate expectation that the provisions of the Partnership Law would be followed. They had no cause to anticipate that a general partner would exceed his authority by assigning their rights in specific partnership property without their written consent or ratification and thus effectively terminate their right to have their contribution returned. It was the written consent or ratification of each defendant limited partner that was required for the proper negotiation of the notes—and this is what Stanndco failed to secure. Clearly, each defendant maker is offended and damaged by Stanndco's breach of duty, because each is a limited partner.

*   *   * Plaintiff's conduct permitted the diversion of the partnership assets and it should not profit from its own wrongdoing. Under these circumstances it would be unconscionable not to permit the defendants to assert their claim as a defense against plaintiff. *   *   *

JUDGMENT AND REMEDY   *The court dismissed Chemical Bank's lawsuit against the limited partners. Since Chemical Bank knew that Stanndco was transferring the notes for other than legitimate partnership purposes, it was not permitted to recover any money from the limited partners.*

Restrictions on What the Limited Partner Can Do   As already mentioned, the limited partner cannot take control of the firm, cannot contribute services and cannot allow his or her name to appear in the firm name. Additionally, the limited partner has no authority to bind the firm, even though, in some sense, he or she is a "member" of it.

Rights of the Limited Partner   Subject to these limitations, limited partners have essentially the same rights as general partners: the right of access to partnership books, the right to an accounting of partnership business, and the right to participate in the dissolution if the winding up and distribution of partnership assets is by court decree. They are entitled to a return of their contributions in accordance with the partnership certificate.[14] They can also assign their interests subject to specific clauses in the certificate.[15]

---

14.   ULPA Section 10.

15.   ULPA Section 19.

Limited Partner's Right to Sue   In jurisdictions that have considered the matter, courts seem to recognize fully the limited partner's right to sue, either individually or on behalf of the firm, for economic injury to the firm by the general partners or by outsiders. In addition, investor protection legislation, such as security laws (discussed in Chapter 45) may give some protection to limited partners.

THE USE OF A LIMITED PARTNERSHIP

The limited partnership is a less effective liability shield than the corporation. In many respects, the corporation is more flexible, and its charter does not require the frequent amendments that a limited partnership certificate does.[16] One might conclude that limited partnerships have little utility, except for special reasons.

Before World War II, limited partnerships were used sparingly, but during and after the war, their number increased, largely because of high federal income tax rates, particularly on corporations. A limited partnership allows the limited partners to deduct expenses or losses against other income directly and to be protected from personal liability.

There are three primary uses for limited partnerships today:

1.   To buy, build, and lease commercial property, hold it for a period of five or more years, and then resell it.
2.   To purchase and lease heavy equipment.
3.   To loan money and take back first mortgages.

Limited partnerships are also popular with people who start new Individual Retirement Accounts (IRAs) and are used extensively for oil and gas ventures.

DISSOLUTION

A limited partnership is dissolved in the same way as an ordinary partnership. The retirement,

death, or insanity of a general partner can dissolve the partnership, but not if the business can be continued by one or more of the other general partners in accordance with their certificate or by consent of all members.[17] The death or assignment of interest of a limited partner does not dissolve the limited partnership.[18] With respect to dissolution, limited partnerships resemble corporations more closely than they do general partnerships. Public filings, passive investors, and limited liability are all features of both corporations and limited partnerships.

Causes of Dissolution

A limited partnership is dissolved by the expiration of its term or the completion of its undertaking. When there is no definite term or undertaking, the express will of any general partner will usually dissolve the partnership. Limited partners do not have the power to dissolve unless they have rightfully, but unsuccessfully, demanded return of their contribution.[19] If, however, the general partners dissolve the partnership without the consent of the limited partners before the end of the term fixed by the certificate, this dissolution is considered a breach.

Illegality, expulsion, and bankruptcy of the general partners dissolve a limited partnership. However, bankruptcy of a limited partner does not dissolve the partnership unless it causes the bankruptcy of the firm.

The retirement of a general partner causes a dissolution unless the members consent to a continuation by the remaining general partners or unless this contingency is provided for in the certificate.

Consequences of Dissolution

The consequences of the dissolution of general partnerships apply to limited partnerships (see Chapter 37). Therefore, the firm continues in operation while winding up. The general partners of a limited partnership have the authority to wind up, as in an ordinary partnership. The rep-

---

16.   ULPA Section 24(2).

17.   ULPA Section 20.
18.   ULPA Section 21.
19.   ULPA Section 16.

resentatives of general partners, not the limited partners, succeed the general partners. Limited partners have the right to obtain dissolution and winding up by a court decree.[20]

Assuming that the general partners continue the business, the limited partners generally have the right to be paid the value of their interests at dissolution, plus profits or interest on that value from dissolution until payment.

Priorities in Distribution of Assets   Upon dissolution, creditors' rights to distribution of assets precede partners' rights, and limited partners' rights precede general partners' rights. Limited partners take both their share of profits and of contributed capital before general partners receive anything.[21]

LIMITED PARTNERSHIP ASSOCIATIONS

Certain states allow the formation of limited partnership associations. They are legal hybrids that actually resemble corporations, although they are called partnership associations in some states. They originated in Pennsylvania in 1874, and the capital subscribed to the association was solely responsible for its debts. In 1966, the Pennsylvania Act was repealed except for professions not permitted to incorporate. Three other states have similar laws: Michigan, New Jersey, and Ohio. (Virginia had one from 1874 to 1918.) This type of organization is seldom seen outside Pennsylvania and Michigan.

The organizational document is publicly filed and can be changed by amendment. It fixes the capital of the association, and there is no maximum or minimum amount. Each member contributes a designated part of the capital.

The association's life is restricted—usually to twenty years. There must be at least three members, and Ohio has established a maximum of twenty-five. The word *limited* must be the last word in the association's name, and it must be conspicuously used on advertisements, signs, and stationery. Dissolution of the limited partnership association occurs when the prescribed term expires or by a majority vote of the members.

An important difference between this type of association and corporations involves the transfer of shares. The shares are freely transferable in a limited partnership association, but the new transferee does not become a member of the association unless duly elected by the other members. When membership is refused, however, the transferee can recover the value of his or her shares from the association.

QUESTIONS AND CASE PROBLEMS

1.   Able and Baker form a limited partnership with Able as the general partner and Baker as the limited partner. Baker puts up $15,000, and Able contributes some office equipment that he owns. A certificate of limited partnership is properly filed, and business is begun. One month later Able becomes ill. Instead of hiring someone to manage the business, Baker takes over complete management himself. While Baker is in control, he makes a contract with Thomas involving a large sum of money. Able returns to work. Because of other commitments, the Thomas contract is breached. Thomas contends that he can hold Able and Baker personally liable if his judgment cannot be satisfied out of the assets of the limited partnership. Discuss this contention.

2.   Able, Baker, and Clark want to form a limited partnership. Able and Baker are recent college graduates with no business experience. They are to be the general partners. Clark, an experienced businesswoman, is to be the limited partner. Clark is to put up $10,000 and to manage the business for the first six months, until Able and Baker get experience. For this, the partnership will list her capital contribution as $15,000. Profits are to be divided equally. The limited partnership name has not been determined. For the present the partners plan on simply using their surnames. Discuss what advice an attorney might give Able, Baker, and Clark on forming a limited partnership.

---

20.   Klebanow v. New York Produce Exchange, 344 F.2d 294 (2d Cir. 1965).

21.   ULPA Section 23, and see Exhibit 39–1.

3. Ann, Betty, and Carla form a limited partnership. Ann is a general partner, and Betty and Carla are limited partners. Assume each of the events below takes place separately. Discuss fully which acts constitute a dissolution of the limited partnership.

    (a) Betty assigns her partnership interest to Diana.

    (b) Carla is petitioned into involuntary bankruptcy.

    (c) Ann dies.

4. Able and Baker form a limited partnership to operate a retail jewelry business. Able is the general partner and Baker the limited partner. The certificate of partnership does not specify a definite term for the partnership existence. Able and Baker disagree over the management of the business by Able. Baker demands, in writing, the return of his contribution. Discuss fully the following:

    (a) Can a limited partner dissolve the partnership?

    (b) If the limited partnership is dissolved, who has authority to wind up the affairs of the partnership?

5. Able and Baker form a limited partnership, with Able as the general partner. During the existence of the partnership, Able's contribution of capital is $2,000, and Baker's is $50,000. The limited partnership is dissolved, and the sale of partnership assets in winding up the partnership affairs results in proceeds of $100,000. Partnership creditors have claims totaling $45,000, and the profit accounts of Able and Baker are $5,000 each. Discuss the priority of these liabilities to the remaining $100,000.

6. In a limited partnership having one general partner, the general partner loaned over $1 million to the partnership and executed notes payable to herself. The limited partner knew that these notes were carried as outstanding debts on the partnership books for seven years. When the general partner died, the limited partner maintained that the partnership agreement did not authorize the general partner to borrow money and that the plus $1 million constituted a contribution to capital rather than loans. How did the court treat the money? [Park Cities Corp. v. Byrd, 522 S.W.2d 572 (Tex.Civ.App.1975)]

7. The Ponderosa Land Company was a properly established limited partnership whose members were Harold Brown, Walter Brown, and W. D. Blaster. The Browns were general partners, and Blaster was the sole limited partner. His only contribution to the firm was providing it with start-up capital of $50,000. After a number of years of successful operation, Blaster decided to withdraw from the firm since he was badly in need of cash. He requested that the partnership return his capital contribution. Is the partnership dissolved? [Brown v. Brown, 15 Ariz.App. 333, 488 P.2d 689 (1971)]

8. Fidelity Lease Limited, a limited partnership, had over twenty limited partners and one general partner. The general partner was a corporation, Interlease Corporation, and was managed by Sanders, Kahn, and Crombie, all three of whom happened to be limited partners of Fidelity Lease Limited. Assuming that in Texas, where this partnership was established, corporations are allowed to be partners in a limited partnership, what will the liability of Sanders, Kahn, and Crombie be in a suit against Fidelity Lease Limited? Will their liability be limited? [Delaney v. Fidelity Lease Limited, 517 S.W.2d 420 (Tex.Civ.App.1974)]

CHAPTER 40

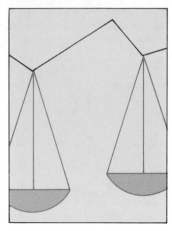

CORPORATIONS
Nature and
Classifications

A BRIEF HISTORY OF THE CORPORATION

The corporation can be owned by a single person, or it can have hundreds, even thousands, of shareholders. The shareholder form of business organization developed in Europe at the end of the seventeenth century. The firms were called joint stock companies, and they frequently collapsed because their organizers absconded with the funds or proved incompetent.

The most famous collapse involved the South Sea Company, which assumed England's national debt in 1711 and obtained in return a monopoly over British trade with the South Sea Islands in South America plus an annual interest payment. The shares of the company were driven up by speculation, fraud was exposed, and a collapse followed. The event came to be known as the South Sea Bubble, and it led to the Bubble Act of 1720, a law that curtailed the use of joint stock companies in England for over a hundred

years. Because of this history of fraud and collapse, organizations resembling corporations were regarded with suspicion in the United States during its early years.

In the eighteenth century, a typical U.S. corporation was a municipality. Although several business corporations were formed after the Revolutionary War, it was not until the nineteenth century that the corporation came into common use for private business. In 1811, New York passed a general incorporation law allowing businesses to incorporate. Incorporation was permissible by five or more persons for the manufacture of textiles, glass, metals, and paint. The corporation could have capital of only $100,000 and a life of twenty years.

The significance of the New York law was that it allowed voluntary incorporation using standard bureaucratic procedures rather than special acts of the legislature, which were usually available only to businesspersons with political influence. By the mid-nineteenth century, railroads predominated among corporations. After the Civil War, manufacturing corporations became numerous.

The Corporation as a Creature of Statute

The corporation is a creature of statute. Its existence depends generally upon state law, although some corporations, especially public organizations, can be created under federal law. Each state has its own body of corporate law, and these laws are not entirely uniform. The Model Business Corporation Act (often called the Model Act) is a codification of modern corporation law. It enunciates principles of corporate law that have been adopted to some degree or another by every state.

The key distinctions among the various organizational forms available to business involve:

1. The relationships among members of the organization.
2. The personal financial liability of members of the organization.
3. The control and continuity of the organization.
4. The establishment of credit and the acquisition of capital for the organization.

5. The tax implications of the chosen organizational form.

THE NATURE OF A CORPORATION

The Corporation as a Legal "Person"

A **corporation** is a legal entity created and recognized by state law. It can consist of one or more *natural* persons identified under a common name. It is recognized under state and federal law as a "person," and it enjoys many, but not all, of the same rights and privileges that U.S. citizens enjoy.

The Bill of Rights guarantees a "person", as a citizen, certain protections, and corporations are considered citizens in most instances. For example, a corporation has the same right as a natural person to equal protection of laws under the Fourteenth Amendment. It has the right of access to the courts as an entity that can sue or be sued. It also has the right of due process before denial of life, liberty, or property as well as the freedom from unreasonable search and seizure and from double jeopardy.

In the following case, the Supreme Court determined that freedom of speech applies to corporations as well as to natural persons.

BACKGROUND AND FACTS *Appellants—national banking associations and business corporations—sought Supreme Court review of a Massachusetts statute that prohibited corporations from making contributions or expenditures that individuals were permitted to make.*

FIRST NAT'L BANK OF BOSTON v. BELLOTTI
United States Supreme Court, 1978.
435 U.S. 765, 98 S.Ct. 1407.

Mr. Justice Powell delivered the opinion of the Court.

In sustaining a state criminal statute that forbids certain expenditures by banks and business corporations for the purpose of influencing the vote on referendum proposals, the Massachusetts Supreme Judicial Court held that the First Amendment rights of a corporation are limited to issues that materially affect its business, property, or assets. The court rejected appellants' claim that the statute abridges freedom of speech in violation of the First and Fourteenth Amendments. The issue presented in this context is one of first impression in this Court. * * *

The statute at issue, Mass.Gen.Laws Ann., ch. 55, § 8 (West Supp. 1977), prohibits appellants, two national banking associations and three business corporations, from making contributions or expenditures "for the purpose of * * * influencing or affecting the vote on any question submitted to the voters, other than one materially affecting any of the property, business or assets of the corporation." The statute further specifies that "[n]o question submitted to the voters solely concerning the taxation of the income, property or transactions of individuals shall be deemed materially to affect the property, business or assets of the corporation." A corporation that violates § 8 may receive a maximum fine of $50,000; a corporate officer, director, or agent who violates the section may receive a maximum fine of $10,000 or imprisonment for up to one year, or both.

Appellants wanted to spend money to publicize their views on a proposed constitutional amendment that was to be submitted to the voters as a ballot question at a general election on November 2, 1976. The amendment would have permitted the legislature to impose a graduated tax on the income of individuals. After appellee, the Attorney General of Massachusetts, informed appellants that he intended to enforce § 8 against them, they brought this action seeking to have the statute declared unconstitutional. *   *   *

*   *   *   *

The court below framed the principal question in this case as whether and to what extent corporations have First Amendment rights. We believe that the court posed the wrong question. The Constitution often protects interests broader than those of the party seeking their vindication. The First Amendment, in particular, serves significant societal interests. The proper question therefore is not whether corporations "have" First Amendment rights and, if so, whether they are coextensive with those of natural persons. Instead, the question must be whether § 8 abridges expression that the First Amendment was meant to protect. We hold that it does.

The speech proposed by appellants is at the heart of the First Amendment's protection.

> "The freedom of speech and of the press guaranteed by the Constitution embraces at the least the liberty to discuss publicly and truthfully all matters of public concern without previous restraint or fear of subsequent punishment. *   *   * Freedom of discussion, if it would fulfill its historic function in this nation, must embrace all issues about which information is needed or appropriate to enable the members of society to cope with the exigencies of their period."

The referendum issue that appellants wish to address falls squarely within this description. In appellants' view, the enactment of a graduated personal income tax, as proposed to be authorized by constitutional amendment, would have a seriously adverse effect on the economy of the State. The importance of the referendum issue to the people and government of Massachusetts is not disputed. Its merits, however, are the subject of sharp disagreement.

As the Court said in *Mills* v. *Alabama*, "there is practically universal agreement that a major purpose of [the First] Amendment was to protect the free discussion of governmental affairs." If the speakers here were not corporations, no one would suggest that the State could silence their proposed speech. It is the type of speech indispensable to decisionmaking in a democracy, and this is no less true because the speech comes from a corporation rather than an individual. The inherent worth of the speech in terms of its capacity for informing the public does not depend upon the identity of its source, whether corporation, association, union, or individual.

The court below nevertheless held that corporate speech is protected by the First Amendment only when it pertains directly to the corporation's business interests. In deciding whether this novel and restrictive gloss on the First Amendment comports with the Constitution and the precedents of this Court, we need not survey the outer boundaries of the Amendment's protection of corporate speech, or address the abstract question whether corporations have the full measure of rights that individuals enjoy under the First Amendment. The question in this case, simply put, is whether the corporate identity of the speaker deprives this proposed speech of what otherwise would be its clear entitlement to protection. We turn now to that question.

*   *   *   *

We *   *   * find no support in the First or Fourteenth Amendment, or in the decisions of this Court, for the proposition that speech that otherwise would be within the protection of the First Amendment loses that protection simply because its source is a corporation that cannot prove, to the satisfaction of a court, a material effect on its business or property. The "materially affecting" requirement is not an identification of the boundaries of corporate speech etched by the Constitution itself. Rather, it amounts to an impermissible legislative prohibition of speech based on the identity of the interests that spokesmen may represent in public debate over controversial issues and a requirement that the speaker have a sufficiently great interest in the subject to justify communication.

Section 8 permits a corporation to communicate to the public its views on certain referendum subjects—those materially affecting its business—but not others. It also singles out one kind of ballot question—individual taxation—as a subject about which corporations may never make their ideas public. The legislature has drawn the line between permissible and impermissible speech according to whether there is a sufficient nexus, as defined by the legislature, between the issue presented to the voters and the business interests of the speaker.

In the realm of protected speech, the legislature is constitutionally disqualified from dictating the subjects about which persons may speak and the speakers who may address a public issue. If a legislature may direct business corporations to "stick to business," it also may limit other corporations—religious, charitable, or civic—to their respective "business" when addressing the public. Such power in government to channel the expression of views is unacceptable under the First Amendment. Especially where, as here, the legislature's suppression of speech suggests an attempt to give one side of a debatable public question an advantage in expressing its views to the people, the First Amendment is plainly offended.

JUDGMENT AND REMEDY

The Supreme Court ruled that the Massachusetts law was unconstitutional. Under the First Amendment, corporations are entitled to freedom of speech.

COMMENTS

A corporation is a legal fiction; that is, it is considered to be a person for most purposes under the law. However, certain constitutional privileges do not apply to a corporate person, although they do apply to a natural person. An unsettled area of corporation law has to do with the criminal acts of a corporation. It is obvious that a corporation cannot be sent to prison even though, under law, it is a person. Most courts hold a cor-

poration that has violated the criminal statutes liable for fines. Where criminal conduct can be attributed to corporate officers or agents, those individuals, as natural persons, are held liable and can be imprisoned for their acts.

Characteristics
of the Corporate Entity

A corporation is an artificial person, with its own corporate name, owned by individual shareholders. It is a legal entity with rights and responsibilities. The corporation substitutes itself for its shareholders in conducting corporate business and in incurring liability. Its authority to act and the liability for its actions are separate and apart from the individuals who own it, although in certain limited situations, the "corporate veil" can be pierced (that is, liability for the corporation's obligations can be extended to shareholders). In some instances, shareholders can voluntarily make themselves personally liable for some or all of the debts of the corporation. This is particularly true with smaller corporations that attempt to obtain financing.

Responsibility for overall management of the corporation is entrusted to the board of directors, which is elected by shareholders. Corporate officers and other employees are hired by the board of directors to run the daily business operations of the corporation.

The following sections briefly discuss the relationships and responsibilities of the shareholders, board of directors, officers, and employees in the management of the corporation. More detail will be found in Chapter 43.

Shareholders   The acquisition of a share of stock makes a person an owner or shareholder in a corporation. Unlike the members in a partnership, the body of shareholders can change constantly without affecting the continued existence of the corporation. Thus, a corporation is not affected by the death of a shareholder, whereas the death of a partner would dissolve a partnership.

As a general rule, a shareholder is not personally liable for the corporation's business debts; nor is the corporation responsible for a shareholder's personal debts. Each shareholder's liability is limited to the amount of the investment (that is, the money actually paid when the stock was acquired).

Thus, if Paul Ginsberg purchases one hundred shares of Ace Manufacturing stock at $1 per share, and Ace Manufacturing goes bankrupt owing creditors millions of dollars, Ginsberg's loss is limited to the $100 purchase price that he originally paid for the shares. The converse is also true. If Ginsberg declares bankruptcy and owes creditors thousands of dollars, the Ace Manufacturing Company is not liable, and the creditors can claim only the one hundred shares of stock.

Shareholders have no legal title to corporate property vested in the corporation, such as buildings and equipment. They have only an *equitable* interest in the corporation.

A shareholder can sue the corporation, and the corporation can sue a shareholder. The shareholder's derivative suit and the special responsibility of majority shareholders of the corporation will be discussed in the next two chapters. Briefly, a **derivative suit** is an action by a shareholder to enforce a corporate cause of action. It occurs when the action is based upon a primary right of a corporation but is asserted on its behalf by the stockholder because of the corporation's failure, deliberate or otherwise, to act upon the primary right.

Shareholders are owners without direct control over the management of the corporation's business. Only through the election of the board of directors can they exercise influence over corporate policy. They are neither managers nor agents of the corporation. In a partnership, on the other hand, general partners have control and responsibility for the management of the business, and each partner is an agent who can bind all other partners in the course of business.

Board of Directors A general rule in corporate law says, "Directors must direct the corporate business affairs." The board of directors is elected by shareholders and is periodically accountable to them for reelection.

The board is responsible for making decisions about overall policy. Directors declare dividends, authorize major corporate contracts, appoint or remove officers and set their salaries, issue authorized shares of stock, and recommend changes in the corporate charter. They delegate the day-to-day operation of corporate affairs to the officers and other employees of the corporation. The board can organize itself into executive committees and delegate these committees particular responsibilities to act on behalf of the entire board or to report back to it. Then, it acts as a unit.

Officers and Other Employees Officers are agents of the corporation. They answer to the board of directors rather than to the shareholders directly, and they can be removed at any time by the board.

Tax Considerations Since a corporation is a separate legal entity, corporate profits are taxed by the state and federal governments. Corporations can do one of two things with corporate profits—retain them or pass them on to shareholders in the form of dividends. The corporation receives no tax deduction for dividends distributed to shareholders.

When dividends are money payments, they are again taxable (except when they represent distributions of capital) as ordinary income to the shareholder receiving them. This double taxation feature of the corporate organization is one of its major disadvantages. On the other hand, retained earnings, if invested properly, will yield higher corporate profits in the future and thus cause the price of the company's stock to rise. Individual shareholders can then reap the benefits of these retained earnings in the gains they receive when they sell their shares. These gains are treated for tax purposes as capital gains. For many individuals, capital gains tax rates are lower than the tax rates applied to ordinary income.

DOMESTIC, FOREIGN, AND ALIEN CORPORATIONS

Except for alien corporations, corporations are incorporated in a particular state. The corporation is referred to as a *domestic corporation* by its home state (the state in which it incorporates). A corporation formed in one state but doing business in another is referred to in that other state as a *foreign corporation*. A corporation formed in another country, say Mexico, doing business within the United States is referred to in the United States as an *alien corporation*.

A foreign corporation does not have an automatic right to do business in a state other than its state of incorporation. It must obtain a *certificate of authority* in the states where it plans to do business. Usually, the process of obtaining a certificate is a mere formality, but often the foreign corporation must comply with standards of financial responsibility before the certificate will be issued.

Should a foreign corporation actually do business without obtaining a certificate, the state can fine it, deny it the privilege of using state courts, and even hold its officers, directors, or agents personally liable for corporate obligations incurred in that state.

Once the certificate has been issued, the powers conferred upon a corporation by its home state generally can be exercised in the other state. Numerous states have specific laws designed to regulate foreign corporations. One such law is the requirement that foreign corporations maintain a registered office or agent (address) in the state. One of the purposes of such a statute is to provide a place to serve process in the event of a suit against the corporation. Frequently, state laws governing corporations apply equally to domestic and foreign corporations. However, when these statutes relate to internal corporate affairs, they normally do not apply to foreign corporations.

Some jurisdictions require a foreign corporation to post a bond before the corporation is permitted to do business. This bond is intended to ensure performance of the foreign corporation's contracts within the state.

Frequently, the biggest issue in dealing with foreign corporations is whether such corporations are actually doing business within the state. A single transaction or mere contact or presence of the corporation's product in the state may not be enough to constitute doing business there.

Before a state court can hear a dispute in which a foreign corporation is the defendant, the state court must have *jurisdiction* over the defendant. A state court only has jurisdiction over foreign corporations which have sufficient *contacts* with the state. A foreign corporation which has its home office within the state or has manufacturing plants in the state meets this "con-tacts" requirement. A foreign corporation whose only contact with the state is that one of its directors resides there does not have sufficient contact with the state for the state court to exercise jurisdiction over it.

In the following case, the defendant was a foreign corporation that manufactured a defective component part for a forklift vehicle that injured the plaintiff. The Florida court had to determine whether or not the foreign corporation had sufficient legal presence in the state of Florida to permit it to be the subject of a lawsuit in Florida.

HARLO PRODUCTS CORP. v. J. I. CASE CO.
District Court of Appeals of Florida, First District, 1978.
360 So.2d 1328.

BACKGROUND AND FACTS *A personal injury action was brought against a forklift owner (Case) when the arm of the forklift fell and injured someone. The accident occurred as a result of an allegedly defective forklift component manufactured by the defendant, Harlo. The forklift owner, Case, was engaged in business in Florida. Harlo was a foreign corporation with its principal place of business in Grandville, Michigan.*

At the trial, Case argued that a component part of the forklift that produced the injury was manufactured by Harlo and that other forklifts in Case's possession in Florida contained similar defective component parts, also manufactured by Harlo. Therefore, Case argued that the Florida courts had jurisdiction over Harlo. In its defense, Harlo argued that it was a Michigan corporation not licensed to do business in Florida and that it did not engage in business in Florida. Its only contact with Florida occurred when the forklifts that contained a component that it had manufactured found their way into the state. Therefore, Harlo moved to dismiss the action pending against it. The trial court refused, and Harlo immediately appealed the denial.

MILLS, Judge.

* * *

Harlo [the defendant] filed an affidavit stating that it was a Michigan corporation not licensed to do business in Florida, that it did not engage in business in Florida, and that it maintained no offices, agents, employees, bank accounts, books, records, telephone listings or other business activities in Florida. Case [plaintiff] filed a counter-affidavit stating that a component of the injury producing forklift was manufactured by Harlo and that other forklifts in its possession in Florida contained the component manufactured by Harlo.

Case contends that the facts alleged in its * * * complaint clearly bring [Harlo] within Florida Statutes Section 48.193(1)(f)2 (1977), which states:

"(1) Any person, whether or not a citizen or resident of this state, who personally or through an agent does any of the acts enumerated in this subsection thereby submits that person and, if he is a natural person, his personal representative to the jurisdiction of the courts of this state for any cause of action arising from the doing of any of the following: *　*　*

(f) Causes injury to persons or property within this state arising out of an act or omission outside of this state by the defendant, provided that at the time of the injury either: *　*　*

2. Products, materials, or things processed, serviced, or manufactured by the defendant anywhere were used or consumed within this state in the ordinary course of commerce, trade, or use, and the use of consumption resulted in the injury."

[The court decided that Harlo came within the scope of the Florida statute because it manufactured a product that injured a person in the state of Florida. However, the mere presence in Florida of Harlo's product was not a sufficient contact for the assertion of personal jurisdiction over it by a Florida court.]

Before a state court can acquire personal jurisdiction over a foreign corporation, the foreign corporation must have certain minimum contacts with the forum state so that the maintenance of the suit does not offend traditional notions of fair play and substantial justice. It is necessary that there be some act by which the foreign corporation purposely avails itself of the privilege of conducting activities within the forum state, thus invoking the benefits and protection of its laws.

In *Dunn v. The Upjohn Co.*, we held that a Georgia pharmacist, who filled and delivered a prescription to a Florida resident in Georgia who was injured after using the prescription in Florida, was not subject to personal jurisdiction in Florida because the pharmacist did not purposely avail himself of the privilege of conducting activities in Florida and did not have minimum contacts with Florida.

In *Jack Pickard Dodge, Inc. v. Yarbrough*, we held that Section 48.193(1)(f)2 was unconstitutional as applied to a North Carolina automobile dealer, who serviced a car owned by Avis who later sold it at auction in Florida to a Florida resident who was injured in Florida *　*　*.

The facts in this case, although not the same, are sufficiently similar to warrant the same result. The only allegation connecting Harlo with Florida is that it manufactured a component of forklifts which are used throughout Florida. The statements in Harlo's affidavit that it was a Michigan corporation not licensed to do business in Florida, that it did not engage in business in Florida and that it maintained no offices, agents, employees, bank accounts, books, records, telephone listings or other business activities in Florida, are unrefuted by Case. There are no allegations showing that Harlo purposely availed itself of the privilege of carrying on business activities in Florida nor that it had minimum contacts with Florida.

The court dismissed the complaint against Harlo because the mere presence in Florida of its product was not a sufficient contact to constitutionally permit the assertion of personal jurisdiction over the foreign corporation by a Florida court.　　**JUDGMENT AND REMEDY**

PUBLIC AND PRIVATE CORPORATIONS

A public corporation is one formed by the government to meet some political or governmental purpose. Cities and towns that incorporate are common examples. In addition, many federal government organizations, such as the U.S. Postal Service, the Tennessee Valley Authority, and Amtrak, are public corporations.

Private corporations are created either wholly or in part for private benefit. Most corporations are private. Private corporations can serve a public purpose, such as a public utility does, but they are nonetheless owned by private persons rather than the government.

NONPROFIT CORPORATIONS

Some corporations are formed without a profit-making purpose. These are called nonprofit, not-for-profit, or eleemosynary corporations. They are usually (although not necessarily) private corporations. They can be used in conjunction with an ordinary corporation to facilitate making contracts with the government. Private hospitals, educational institutions, charities, religious organizations, and the like are frequently organized as nonprofit (not-for-profit) corporations.

Although shares of stock can be issued, dividends are not paid to the members. Formation of nonprofit corporations often follows state statutes that are based on the Model Nonprofit Corporation Act. Eleven states plus the District of Columbia have adopted this act in at least modified form. In any event, the corporation statutes provide for the organization of nonprofit corporations in much the same way that other types of corporations are formed. The nonprofit corporation is a convenient form of organization that allows various groups to own property and to form contracts without the individual members being personally exposed to liability.

CLOSE CORPORATIONS

This section deals with close corporations—sometimes called closed corporations, closely held corporations, family corporations, or privately held corporations. A close corporation is one whose shares are closely held by members of a family or by relatively few persons. Usually, the members of the small group that is involved in a close corporation are personally known to each other. Because there is such a small number of shareholders, there is no trading market for the shares.

In practice, a close corporation is often operated like a partnership. A few states recognize this in the special statutory provisions that cover close corporations. Under these statutes, a number of the formalities and mechanics required of a regular corporation are waived. Under Maryland statute, for example, the close corporation can elect to eliminate the board of directors.

Close Corporation Statutes

In order to be eligible for small corporation status, a corporation has to have a limited number of shareholders, the transfer of corporation stock must be subject to certain restrictions, and the corporation must not make any public offering of its securities.[1] Close corporation statutes provide greater flexibility by expressly permitting electing corporations to vary significantly from traditional corporation law.[2]

Management

The close corporation has a single shareholder or a closely-knit group of shareholders who usually hold the positions of directors and officers. The management of a close corporation resembles that of a sole proprietorship or a partnership. In the eyes of the law, however, it is still a corporation and must meet the same legal requirements as other corporations subject to the special statutes mentioned previously. In states where special statutes have not been enacted, close corporations have sometimes had to circumvent the law.

Consider an example where a state law requires that a corporation have two directors, and a close corporation has only one shareholder. In the articles of incorporation, the number of directors can be set at two, but the corporation can operate with a permanent vacancy on the board

---

1. See, for example, 8 Del. Code Annotated, Section 342. This section provides that electing corporations must have a maximum limitation on the number of shareholders, not exceeding thirty.
2. For example, in some states, the close corporation need not have a board of directors.

of directors. Alternatively, a disinterested person, usually a friend, can be convinced to put his or her name down as director.

Transfer of Shares

Since, by definition, a close corporation has a small number of shareholders, the transfer of shares of one shareholder to someone else can cause serious management problems. In other words, the other shareholders can find themselves required to share control with someone they may not know or like. To avoid this problem, it is usually advisable for the close corporation with several shareholders to specify restrictions on the transferability of stock in its articles of incorporation.

Consider an example. Tom, Dick, and Harry Smith are the only shareholders of Smith Boat Company. Tom and Dick Smith do not want Harry to sell his shares to an unknown third person. The articles of incorporation might therefore restrict the transferability of shares to outside persons. For example, the articles might stipulate that shareholders offer their shares to the corporation or other shareholders before going to an outside purchaser.

Another way that control of a close corporation can be stabilized is through the use of a shareholder agreement. Agreements among shareholders to vote their stock in a particular way are generally upheld. Shareholder agreements can also provide that when one of the original shareholders dies, his or her shares of stock in the corporation will be divided in such a way that the proportionate holdings of the survivors, and thus their proportionate control, will be maintained.

BACKGROUND AND FACTS   *Benjamin and Isadore Galler were brothers and 50 percent shareholders in a wholesale drug business that was incorporated under Illinois law as the Galler Drug Company.*

The corporation prospered, and in July 1955 Benjamin and Isadore and their wives entered into a carefully drafted agreement among themselves and the corporation. The written agreement purported to provide that, in the event of the death of either brother, the corporation would provide income for the support and maintenance of his immediate family. In addition, the family of the deceased brother would have equal control over the corporation.

Benjamin died in 1957. Shortly thereafter, his widow, Emma, requested that Isadore, the surviving brother, comply with the terms of the 1955 agreement. Isadore refused to cooperate. Emma sued, seeking specific performance of the 1955 agreement. The trial court agreed with Emma, holding that the shareholder agreement was valid. The intermediate appellate court subsequently held that the 1955 agreement was void on the ground of public policy. The Illinois Supreme Court reviewed the case.

GALLER v. GALLER

Supreme Court of Illinois, 1965.
32 Ill.2d 16, 203 N.E.2d 577.

UNDERWOOD, Justice.

*   *   *   *

The power to invalidate the agreements on the grounds of public policy is so far reaching and so easily abused that it should be called into action to set aside or annul the solemn engagement of parties dealing on equal terms only in cases where the corrupt or dangerous tendency clearly and unequivocally appears upon the face of the agreement itself or is the necessary inference from the matters which are expressed, and the only apparent exception to this general rule is to be found in those cases where the agreement, though fair and unobjectionable on its face, is a part of a corrupt scheme and is made to disguise the real nature of the transaction.

* * * *

At this juncture it should be emphasized that we deal here with a so-called close corporation. Various attempts at definition of the close corporation have been made. For our purposes, a close corporation is one in which the stock is held in a few hands, or in a few families, and wherein it is not at all, or only rarely, dealt in by buying or selling. Moreover, it should be recognized that shareholder agreements similar to that in question here are often, as a practical consideration, quite necessary for the protection of those financially interested in the close corporation. While the shareholder of a public-issue corporation may readily sell his shares on the open market should management fail to use, in his opinion, sound business judgment, his counterpart of the close corporation often has a large total of his entire capital invested in the business and has no ready market for his shares should he desire to sell. He feels, understandably, that he is more than a mere investor and that his voice should be heard concerning all corporate activity. Without a shareholder agreement, specifically enforceable by the courts, insuring him a modicum of control, a large minority shareholder might find himself at the mercy of an oppressive or unknowledgeable majority. Moreover, as in the case at bar, the shareholders of a close corporation are often also the directors and officers thereof. With substantial shareholding interests abiding in each member of the board of directors, it is often quite impossible to secure, as in the large public-issue corporation, independent board judgment free from personal motivations concerning corporate policy. For these and other reasons too voluminous to enumerate here, often the only sound basis for protection is afforded by a lengthy, detailed shareholder agreement securing the rights and obligations of all concerned.

* * * *

The Appellate Court correctly found many of the contractual provisions free from serious objection, and we need not prolong this opinion with a discussion of them here. That court did, however, find difficulties in the stated purpose of the agreement as it relates to its duration, the election of certain persons to specific offices for a number of years, the requirement for the mandatory declaration of stated dividends (which the Appellate Court held invalid), and the salary continuation agreement.

* * * While limiting voting trusts in 1947 to a maximum duration of 10 years, the [Illinois State] legislature has indicated no similar policy regarding straight voting agreements although these have been common since prior to 1870. In view of the history of decisions of this court generally upholding, in the absence of fraud or prejudice to minority interests or public policy, the right of stockholders to agree among themselves as to the manner in which their stock will be voted, we do not regard the period of time within which this agreement may remain effective as rendering the agreement unenforceable.

The clause that provides for the election of certain persons to specified offices for a period of years likewise does not require invalidation.

We turn next to a consideration of the effect of the stated purpose of the agreement upon its validity. The pertinent provision is: "The said Benjamin A.

Galler and Isadore A. Galler desire to provide income for the support and maintenance of their immediate families." Obviously, there is no evil inherent in a contract entered into for the reason that the persons originating the terms desired to so arrange their property as to provide post-death support for those dependent upon them. Nor does the fact that the subject property is corporate stock alter the situation so long as there exists no detriment to minority stock interests, creditors or other public injury.

The Illinois Supreme Court held that the provisions of the shareholder agreement were enforceable.   **JUDGMENT AND REMEDY**

SUBCHAPTER S CORPORATIONS

Certain corporations can choose to qualify under Subchapter S of the Internal Revenue Code to avoid the imposition of income taxes at the corporate level while retaining all the advantages of a corporation, particularly limited legal liability. A Subchapter S corporation is sometimes known as a *tax option* corporation. Basically, it elects to be taxed in a manner similar to that of a partnership—to file only an informational return that allocates income among the shareholders regardless of dividend distributions. This is the way corporate taxes can be avoided.

While the Subchapter S corporation has the advantages of the corporate form without the double taxation of income (corporate income is not taxed separately), it does have some disadvantages. One of the most important disadvantages relates to the amount of income that can be placed in pension plans that permit corporate shareholders to shelter income from personal federal income taxes.

Requirements for Subchapter S Qualification

There are numerous requirements for Subchapter S qualification. The following are some of the more important:

1. The corporation must be a domestic corporation.
2. The corporation must not be a member of an affiliated group of corporations.

3. The shareholders of the corporation must be either individuals, estates, or certain trusts that are treated as owned by an individual who is a citizen or resident of the United States. Corporations and partnerships cannot be shareholders.
4. The corporation must have thirty-five or fewer shareholders.
5. The corporation can have only one class of stock. Not all shareholders need have the same voting rights.
6. The corporation must not derive more than 25 percent of its gross receipts from passive investment income.
7. No shareholder of the corporation can be a nonresident alien.

Benefits of Electing Subchapter S

At times it is beneficial for a regular corporation to elect Subchapter S status. The following is a checklist of situations where Subchapter S election can be beneficial.

1. When the corporation has losses, the Subchapter S election allows the shareholders to use such to offset other income.
2. Whenever the stockholders are in a lower tax bracket than the corporation, the Subchapter S election causes their entire income to be taxed in the shareholders' bracket, whether or not it is distributed. This is particularly attractive when the corporation wants to accumulate earnings for some future business purpose.
3. Taxable income of a Subchapter S corporation is taxable only to those who are shareholders at the end of the corporate year when that income is distributed.

4. The Subchapter S corporation can choose a fiscal year that will permit it to defer some of its shareholders' taxes. This is important because undistributed earnings are not taxed to the shareholder until after the corporation's (not the shareholder's) year.

5. The shareholder in a Subchapter S corporation can give some of his or her stock to other members of the family who are in a lower tax bracket.

6. A Subchapter S corporation can still offer some tax-free corporate benefits. These fringe benefits can mean federal tax savings to the shareholders.

PROFESSIONAL CORPORATIONS

Professional corporations are relatively new in corporate law. In the past, professional persons such as physicians, lawyers, dentists, and accountants could not incorporate. Today they can, and their corporations are typically called professional service associations or professional corporations. They can be identified by the letters S.C. (service corporation), P.C. (professional corporation), Inc. (incorporated), or P.A. (professional association). In general, a professional corporation is formed like an ordinary business corporation.

Liability of Members

Subject to certain exceptions, the shareholders of a professional corporation have limited liability. There are three basic areas of liability which deserve brief attention:

1. Malpractice of a member,
2. Ordinary tort committed by other members, and
3. Shareholder liability for his or her own torts.

Malpractice of a Member The liability of a shareholder in a professional service association for the malpractice of another member is not clear. In a partnership, dentists Able, Baker and Carl are each unlimitedly liable for whatever malpractice liability is incurred by the others within the scope of the partnership. If the three formed a professional corporation, the orthodox corporate law rule would apply, and none of the dentists would be liable for the malpractice of the others. As far as statutory reference to malpractice liability is concerned, a conservative court might interpret the statutory preservation of malpractice liability, thus causing the individual shareholder in a professional association to be liable for the acts of his or her associates as if the professional corporation were a partnership.

Torts Unrelated to Professional Activities Torts that are not related to malpractice are often treated differently from malpractice. A shareholder in a professional corporation is protected from the liability imposed because of torts committed by other members. If a secretary has been sent from the office to pick up tax forms from the IRS and, in the process, runs into another car, both the corporation and the secretary will be held liable. Ordinarily, the shareholder in a professional corporation will not be personally liable.

Shareholder Liability Any shareholder of a professional corporation who engages in a negligent action and who is guilty of malpractice is *personally* liable for the damage caused. Basically, this is the same rule of law that applies to ordinary business corporations. On the other hand, many professional corporation statutes retain personal liability of professional persons for their acts and the professional acts performed under their supervision.

Tax Benefits

The tax benefits of the professional corporation are basically those that apply to all corporations. One of the major benefits is that pension and profit-sharing plans can be set up. These plans are discussed in the next chapter in the section on benefits of incorporating.

QUESTIONS AND CASE PROBLEMS

1.   Able, Baker, and Carter are active members of a partnership called Swim City. The partnership manufactures, sells, and installs outdoor swimming pools in the states of Texas and Arkansas. The partners want to continue to be active in management and to expand the business into other states as well. They are concerned about rather large recent judgments being entered against swimming pool companies throughout the United States. Based on these facts only, discuss whether the partnership should incorporate.

2.   The Swim City partnership decides to incorporate in the state of Texas under the name of Swim City, Inc. The partners also decide that they want to continue to do business in the state of Arkansas. Later, a man from Oklahoma comes into the corporate office in Texas and purchases an outdoor swimming pool. The swimming pool is shipped to Oklahoma and installed personally by the new owner. Later the owner is injured while swimming in the pool and claims his injury is due entirely to the defective manufacture of the pool. Discuss fully how the corporation can continue to do business in Arkansas. Also discuss the liability the corporation has in a suit filed by the injured man in an Oklahoma state court.

3.   When the partnership of Able, Baker, and Carter decided to form the Texas corporation, Swim City, Inc., it was their desire that the only shareholders be the former partners. Discuss what the partners can and should do to limit the management, ownership, and control to the three of them and still incorporate.

4.   Able, Baker, and Carter, as partners of Swim City, decide that they need to incorporate in order to have limited personal liability. However, they wish to avoid double taxation—that is, the corporation paying corporate income taxes on profits and then the shareholders paying personal income taxes on dividends they receive. Discuss whether, upon incorporation, there is any way the partners can avoid paying corporate income taxes without criminal liability.

5.   Able, Baker, and Clark are doctors who have formed a partnership. Recently they have become concerned about their individual personal liability in the event of a malpractice suit against one of the doctors or even in the event of ordinary negligence on the part of a doctor in the course of driving his or her personal car to make a house call. Discuss how the doctors can avoid personal liability from any of these kinds of torts committed by another doctor in the partnership.

6.   The Internal Revenue Service subpoenaed the books and records of Air Conditioning Supply Company. Albert J. Wild, the president and sole owner of the corporation, refused to produce the records on the ground that they might tend to incriminate him and were thus protected by the Fifth Amendment. Is a corporation entitled to Fifth Amendment protection? [Wild v. Brewer, 329 F.2d 924 (9th Cir. 1964)]

7.   Pacific Development, Inc., was incorporated in the District of Columbia for the purpose of international brokerage consulting. Pacific's founder, president, and sole shareholder was Tongsun Park, a South Korean who was on close terms with South Korea's President Park Chung Hee. The government alleged that Park's main purpose was to influence Congress to give economic and military aid to South Korea. The IRS assessed $4.5 million in back taxes against Park in 1977. It then seized the assets of Pacific Development, Inc., claiming that the company was a mere alter ego of Park. Valley Finance, Inc., was another of Park's wholly owned corporations. It had loaned money to Pacific Valley Finance, and it held a second deed of trust on the real property that the IRS had seized. Both Pacific Development and Valley Finance attempted to obtain the return of Pacific Development's assets that the IRS had seized. The plaintiffs claimed that the IRS had improperly pierced the corporate veil of Pacific. Do you agree? [Valley Finance, Inc. v. United States, 629 F.2d 162 (D.C. Cir. 1980)]

8.   Michigan-Wisconsin Pipeline Company was a Delaware corporation. It operated a natural gas pipeline that extended through more than a dozen states, including Kentucky. In that state, it had a warehouse as well as a compressor station. Twenty-one individuals were employed by Michigan-Wisconsin to carry on its business in Kentucky. No gas was either acquired or marketed in Kentucky. It simply flowed through a pipeline. The pipeline company claimed that it was exempt from Kentucky regulations because it was not doing business there. Do you agree? [Michigan-Wisconsin Pipeline Co. v. Kentucky, 474 S.W.2d 873 (Ky. 1971)]

CHAPTER 41

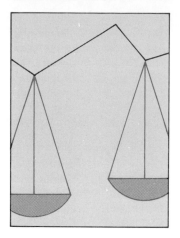

CORPORATIONS
Formation and Corporate Financing

Incorporation refers to the procedural mechanics of forming a corporation. The corporation is entirely a creature of statute. Therefore, it must meet the requirements of the state's statutes. Although state statutes differ, their basic requirements for incorporation are similar. This chapter will not only deal with these basic requirements but will discuss pre-incorporation arrangements and activities.

In addition, since corporations need financing to be formed and to continue to exist, this chapter will briefly discuss the various methods, called securities, used to finance corporations.

PROMOTERS' ACTIVITIES

Before a corporation becomes a reality, people invest in the proposed corporation as subscribers, and contracts are frequently made by **promoters** on behalf of the not-yet-existent corporation. Promoters are those who, for themselves or others, take the preliminary steps for organizing a corporation. They issue the prospectus for the proposed organization and secure a charter.

It is not unusual for a promoter to purchase or lease property with a view to selling it to the corporation to be organized. In addition, the promoter enters into contracts with attorneys, accountants, architects, or other professionals whose services will be needed in planning for the proposed corporation. Finally, a promoter induces people to purchase stock in the corporation.

Some interesting legal questions arise in regard to the promoter's activities. The most important problem centers on whether the promoter is personally liable for contracts made on behalf of a corporation that does not yet have any legal existence. In addition, once the corporation is formed, does it assume liability on these contracts, or is the promoter still personally liable?

As a general rule, a promoter is held personally liable on pre-incorporation contracts. Courts simply hold that promoters are not agents where a corporation has yet to come into existence. However, if the promoter secures the contracting party's agreement to hold only the corporation (not the promoter) liable on the contract, the promoter will not be liable for breach.

Basically, the same rule of personal liability of the promoter continues even after incorporation unless the third party *releases* the promoter. In most states this rule is applied whether or not the promoter made the agreement in the name of or with reference to the proposed corporation.

Once the corporation is formed (the charter issued), the promoter remains personally liable until the corporation assumes the pre-incorporation contract by *novation*. (See Chapter 14.) Novation releases the promoter and makes the corporation personally liable for performing the contractual obligations. In some cases, the corporation *adopts* the promoter's contract by undertaking to perform it. Most courts hold that adoption in and of itself does not discharge the promoter from contractual liability. Obviously, a corporation cannot normally *ratify* a pre-incorporation contract, as there was no principal in existence at the time the contract was made.

Incorporation does not make the corporation automatically liable for pre-incorporation contracts. Until the newly formed corporation consents, the third party cannot enforce the promoter's contract against the corporation.

In the following case, a corporation offered to purchase land. Its offer was signed by the promoter as president before the corporation came into existence. The sellers agreed to accept the offer under the erroneous belief that a corporation existed.

BACKGROUND AND FACTS   *An offer to purchase a forty-eight acre parcel of land from the defendant, Ramey, was signed as follows:*

> *"Macy Corporation*
> *by B. Ruben, Pres.*
> *Macy T. Block."*

Ramey signed an acceptance of the offer to purchase made by Macy Corporation. At the time the offer was made, the corporation had not yet completed the process of incorporation.

Several weeks after the offer had been accepted, the defendant and her husband withdrew their acceptance of the offer and advised the plaintiff that they would not perform their part of the agreement to sell. The withdrawal letter was mailed to "Macy Corporation, c/o Bernard R. Ruben," and copies were mailed to B. Ruben and Macy T. Block, the persons signing the offer. The articles of incorporation for the corporation were not filed until six days after the letter of repudiation had been received.

After receiving the notice, the corporation twice notified the defendant and her husband that it was ready, willing, and able to proceed according to the terms of the contract for sale. The defendant, however, refused to execute and deliver a deed to the premises. The plaintiff sought specific performance.

The defendant's position was that she and her husband, Dr. Ramey (who died before the trial), signed the acceptance believing that they were dealing with a large corporation with plenty of money backing it. After they made their qualified acceptance of the offer, they learned that the corporation had not yet been formed. Thus the defendant argued that

MACY CORP. v. RAMEY
Court of Common Pleas of Ohio,
1957.
144 N.E.2d 698.

since one of the parties to the contract was a nonexistent corporation, the transaction lacked the parties essential to the execution of a contract, and it was not binding.

BARTLETT, Judge.

* * * *

The Court is constrained to believe the testimony of Mrs. Ramey that she was led to believe that she and her husband were dealing with an existing company and this is supported by the signing of the offer of February 4, 1955, as "Macy Corporation, By B. Ruben, Pres." This was a false pretense, since there was no such corporation in existence at the time.

"Mutual consent is essential to every agreement and agreement is essential to every contract. There can be no binding contract where there is no real consent and it is no agreement where one party enters into the contract under a mistake as to the identity of the other party as where one party accepted an offer meant for another." * * *

"In many cases it is said, * * * that the promoter is the agent of the corporation. But this is hardly true, at least until the corporation is actually organized, because until then no principal would be in existence, and the corporation would not be bound by contracts made before its existence."

"Attempt of promoter to bind corporation that is not in existence is contrary to public policy."

* * * *

"The difficulty surrounding the situation is that such a contract could not be made that would be binding upon anybody. How could two men make a contract that would bind a corporation which must have at least five directors in Ohio? Even if the two men owned all the stock except the qualifying shares for the directors, the directors could turn down and refuse to make such a contract, and the attempt to bind a corporation that was not in existence in my judgment is contrary to public policy and ought not be tolerated and, in my view, the courts do not tolerate such contracts."

* * * *

In the instant case there was no valid contract with the so-called "Macy Corporation" prior to its creation, since the transaction lacked the necessity of two parties to the execution of a contract.

There was at no time a contract with B. Ruben and Macy T. Block since they never made any promise that was binding on them, and moreover, the Rameys at all times believed they were making a contract with "Macy Corporation."

* * * *

The Court finds that the Rameys had withdrawn from the arrangement and had so notified Mr. Ruben, Mr. Block and their embryo corporation, at least one week before the corporation came to life and made its attempt to accept the promise of the Rameys to sell their land at a certain price. Consequently, the acceptance was too late to effect a contract between the Rameys and the Macy Corporation.

* * * *

"One who asks specific performance of a contract in the procurement of which he has practised deceit is always an unwelcome suitor in a court of equity and will generally be denied relief. Misrepresentation leading to the execution of a contract is likewise a ground for the refusal of a court of equity to grant specific performance."

The maxim, "He who comes into equity must come with clean hands," as a basis for the refusal of specific performance or other equitable relief, is as old as the equity courts themselves.

This transaction with the Rameys was conceived in deceit and misrepresentation. They were wilfully deceived into believing they were dealing with the "Macy Corporation" when there was no such entity; they were led to believe "B. Ruben was its president," and he never was; there was deceit practised in the adding of the name of "Macy T. Block" to the offer after it was accepted by the Rameys; and finally, on April 20, 1955, the Rameys were notified the Macy Corporation was ready, willing and able to proceed with arrangement to buy the land of the Rameys, when in truth and fact the corporation had not yet come into existence.

*   *   *   *

The deceit and misrepresentations in this case cannot be justified.

The plaintiff's request for a decree of specific performance was denied. The defendant was not required to sell the land to the corporation.

JUDGMENT AND REMEDY

Subscribers and Subscriptions

Prior to the actual formation of the corporation, the promoter can contact potential individual investors and they can agree to purchase capital stock in the future corporation. This agreement is often called a subscription agreement, and the potential investor is called a subscriber. Depending on state law, subscribers become shareholders as soon as the corporation is formed or as soon as the corporation accepts the agreement. Thus, if the XYZ Corporation becomes insolvent, the trustee in bankruptcy can collect the consideration for any unpaid stock from a pre-incorporation subscriber.

Most courts view the pre-incorporation subscriptions as continuing offers to purchase corporate stock. On or after its formation, the corporation can choose to accept the offer to purchase. Most courts also treat a subscription as a contract between the subscribers. It is therefore irrevocable except with the consent of *all* of the subscribers. Under Section 17 of the Model Business Corporation Act, a subscription is irrevocable for a period of six months unless otherwise provided in the subscription agree-

ment or unless all the subscribers agree to the revocation of the subscription.[1]

A minority of courts do not follow the Model Act, and in those jurisdictions the pre-incorporation subscriber can revoke the offer to purchase before acceptance without liability.

There are various ways that a *promoter* can avoid the problem of revocation. One way is to set up a trust with the promoter as trustee and the corporation as beneficiary (under the law of trusts, a beneficiary need not exist at the creation of the trust). The promoter-trustee enters a contract with the subscriber. By the terms of the contract, the subscriber promises to buy the stock. If the subscriber fails to subscribe or fails to pay, he or she is liable to the promoter-trustee for breach of contract.

A typical problem in pre-incorporation subscription agreement cases is that the corporation actually formed differs from the corporation in which the subscriber originally agreed to invest. The rule of thumb is that if the departure is min-

---

1. The Model Business Corporation Act is simply a proposal and not law in many areas of the country.

imal (for example, merely a change in name), the agreement is likely to be upheld. But if the change is material (such as entering a different business entirely), the agreement will not be enforced against an unwilling investor. More important problems arise, however, when the corporation is not formed or it fails after formation.

Incorporation

Exact procedures for incorporation differ among states, but the basic requirements are relatively similar.

State Chartering   Since state incorporation laws differ, individuals have found some advantage in looking for the states that offer the most advantageous tax or incorporation provisions. Delaware has historically had the least restrictive laws. Consequently, a significant number of corporations, including a number of the largest, have incorporated there. Delaware's statutes permit firms to incorporate in Delaware and carry out business and locate operating headquarters elsewhere. (Most other states now permit this.)

On the other hand, closely held corporations, particularly those of a professional nature, generally incorporate in the state where their principal stockholders live and work. In recent years, a number of policymakers have suggested that differences among state corporation statutes have led to some undesirable consequences. This has prompted various proposals, including a proposal for federal chartering with a more standardized and restrictive incorporation process.[2]

Articles of Incorporation   The primary document needed to begin the incorporation process is called the charter, the articles, or the certificate of incorporation (see Exhibit 41–1). The articles include basic information about the corporation and serve as a primary source of authority for its future organizational and business functioning.

---

2.   See, for example, Symposium, Federal Chartering of Corporations, 61 Geo.L.J. 71 (1972); Carey, Federalism and Corporate Law: Reflections upon Delaware, 83 Yale L.J. 663 (1974).

Generally, the following should be included in the articles of incorporation:

1.   Corporate name.
2.   Purpose(s) and nature of business activities.
3.   Duration.
4.   Initial capital structure.
5.   Internal organization.
6.   Incorporators.
7.   Registered or principal office.

Corporate Name   Choice of a corporate name is subject to state approval to insure against duplication or deception. Fictitious name statutes usually require that the secretary of state run a check on the proposed name in the state of incorporation. Once cleared, a name can be reserved for a short time, pending the completion of the articles of incorporation. All corporate statutes require the corporation name to include the word *Corporation, Incorporated, Co., Limited*, or abbreviations.

Some states require that the name of the corporation be expressed in English letters or characters. States usually require that a corporate name not be the same as or deceptively similar to the name of an existing corporation doing business within the state.

For example, if an existing corporation is named General Dynamics, the state will not allow another corporation to be called General Dynamic. Not only would that name be deceptive to third parties, but it impliedly transfers a part of the goodwill established by the first corporate user to the second corporation.

General Nature and Purpose   The intended business activities of the corporation must be specified in the articles, and naturally, they must be lawful. A general statement of corporate purpose is usually sufficient to give rise to all of the powers necessary or convenient to the purpose of the organization. The corporate charter can state, for example, that the corporation is organized "to engage in the production and sale of agricultural products." There is a trend toward allowing corporate charters to state that the corporation is organized for any legal business with no mention of specifics.

EXHIBIT 41–1   ARTICLES OF INCORPORATION (MINIMUM REQUIREMENTS) FOR THE HYPOTHETICAL
STATE OF NEW PACUM

ARTICLE ONE

The name of the corporation is _____ .

ARTICLE TWO

The period of its duration is perpetual (may be a number of years or until a certain date).

ARTICLE THREE

The purpose or purposes for which the corporation is organized are _____

_____

ARTICLE FOUR

The aggregate number of shares that the corporation shall have authority to issue is _____ of the par value of
_____ dollars each (or without par value).

ARTICLE FIVE

The corporation will not commence business until it has received for the issuance of its shares consideration of the value
of $1,000 (can be any sum not less than $1,000).

ARTICLE SIX

The address of the corporation's registered office is _____ , New Pacum and the name of its registered agent at such
address is _____ . (Use the street or building or rural route address of the registered office, not a post office box number.)

ARTICLE SEVEN

The number of initial directors is _____ , and the names and addresses of the directors are _____ .

ARTICLE EIGHT

The name and address of the incorporator is _____

_____ .

(signed) _____
                                      Incorporator

Sworn to on _____ by the above-named incorporator.
           (date)

_____
Notary Public _____County, New Pacum

(Notary Seal)

Some states have prohibitions against the incorporation of certain professionals, such as doctors or lawyers, except pursuant to a professional incorporation statute. In some states, certain industries, such as banks, insurance companies, or public utilities, cannot be operated in the general corporate form and are governed by special incorporation statutes.

Duration   A corporation can have perpetual existence under most state corporate statutes. However, a few states prescribe a maximum duration after which the corporation must formally renew its existence.

Capital Structure   The capital structure of the corporation is generally set forth in the articles.

A few state statutes require a minimum capital investment for ordinary business corporations, while those engaged in insurance or banking can be required to have a greater capital investment. The number of shares of stock authorized for issuance, their par value, the various types or classes of stock authorized for issuance, and other relevant information concerning equity, capital, and credit must be outlined in those provisions of the articles. The range of possibilities is discussed later in this chapter.

Internal Organization Whatever the internal management structure of the corporation, it should be described in the articles, although it can be included in bylaws adopted after the corporation is formed. The articles of incorporation commence the corporation; the bylaws are formed after commencement.

Bylaws are subject to and cannot conflict with the incorporation statute or the corporation's charter. Section 27 of the Model Act, for example, provides that "the power to alter, amend, or repeal the bylaws or adopt new bylaws shall be vested in the board of directors unless reserved to the shareholders by the articles of incorporation." That section further indicates that the bylaws must be consistent with the articles of incorporation. Typical bylaw provisions describe the quorum and voting requirements for shareholders, the election of the board of directors, the methods of replacing directors, and the manner and time of fixing shareholder and board meetings.

Registered Office and Agent The corporation must indicate the location and address of its registered office within the state. Usually the registered office is also the principal office of the corporation. The corporation must give the name and address of a specific person designated as *agent* to receive legal documents on behalf of the corporation.

Incorporators Each incorporator must be listed by name and must indicate an address. An incorporator is a person (or persons) who applies to the state on behalf of the corporation to obtain its corporate charter. The incorporator need not be a subscriber and need not have any interest at all in the corporation. Many states do not impose residency or age requirements for incorporators. States vary on the required number of incorporators; it can be as few as one or as many as three. Incorporators *must* sign the articles of incorporation when they are submitted to the state; often this is their only duty. In some states, they participate at the first organizational meeting of the corporation.

Certificate of Incorporation Once the articles of incorporation have been prepared, signed, and authenticated by the incorporators, they are sent to the appropriate state official, usually the secretary of state, along with the appropriate filing fee. In many states, the secretary of state then issues a *certificate of incorporation* representing the state's authorization for the corporation to conduct business. The certificate and a copy of the articles are returned to the incorporators, who then hold the initial organizational meeting that completes the details of incorporation.

First Organizational Meeting The first organizational meeting is provided for in the articles of incorporation but is held after the charter is actually granted. At this meeting, the incorporators elect the first board of directors and complete the routine business of incorporation (pass bylaws, issue stock, and so forth). Sometimes, the meeting is held after the election of the board of directors, and the business to be transacted depends upon the requirements of the state's incorporation statute, the nature of the business, the provisions made in the articles, and the desires of the promoters.

Adoption of bylaws is probably the most important function of the first organizational meeting. The bylaws are the internal rules of management for the corporation. The shareholders, directors, and officers must abide by them in conducting corporate business. Unless they have knowledge of the bylaws, corporation employees and third persons dealing with the corporation are not bound by them.

Corporate Status

Improper Incorporation   The procedures for incorporation are very specific. If they are not followed precisely, errors can be made that allow others to challenge the existence of the corporation. This can become important when, for example, a third person attempts to enforce a contract or bring suit for a tort injury and fortuitously learns of the defect in the incorporation procedure. The plaintiff could then seek to make the would-be shareholders personally liable.

Also, when the corporation seeks to enforce a contract against a defaulting party, if the defaulting party learns of the defective incorporation, he or she may seek to avoid liability on that ground. Courts have developed three theories to prevent the windfall that would occur in giving a contracting party the benefit of the stockholders' personal liability. The theories are *de jure* corporation, *de facto* corporation, and corporation by estoppel.

De Jure Corporation   If there is at least substantial compliance with all conditions precedent to incorporation, the corporation is said to have *de jure* existence in law. In most states the certificate of incorporation is viewed as evidence that all mandatory statutory provisions have been met. This means that the corporation is properly formed, and neither the state nor a third party can attack its existence.

To illustrate, Brown Motor Company, Inc., a domestic corporation, is being sued by a customer, Fred Muris, for an injury sustained at Brown's headquarters. Muris wants to challenge Brown's corporate status because he knows that the personal assets of the owners, Gary and Edward Brown, far exceed the company's assets. Muris discovers that the address of one of the incorporators is incorrectly listed in the articles and argues that this error means that the corporation was improperly formed. Hence, it is not a duly authorized corporation and Gary and Edward Brown are personally liable. The law regards such inconsequential procedural defects as substantial compliance, and courts will uphold the *de jure* status of Brown Motor Company. Fred Muris can sue only Brown Motor Company as a corporate entity.

De Facto Corporation   In some situations, there is a defect in compliance with statutory mandates—for example, the expiration of the corporation charter. Under these circumstances, the corporation may have a *de facto* status, and its existence cannot be challenged by third persons (except for the State). The following elements are required for *de facto* status:

1.   There must be a state statute under which the corporation can be incorporated validly.
2.   The parties must have made a good faith attempt to comply with the statute.
3.   The enterprise must have already undertaken to do business as a corporation.

Practically speaking, the concept of *de facto* status has limited utility in modern corporate law. The Model Business Corporation Act (Sec. 56) and most state statutes agree that the issuance of a certificate of incorporation (charter) by the secretary of state is *prima facie* evidence of corporate status (that is, *de jure* corporation). However, the right of the state to command a corporation to correct irregularities in corporate formation can be enforced under the *de facto* doctrine.

Corporation by Estoppel   Sometimes a corporation has neither *de jure* nor *de facto* status. When justice requires, the courts treat an alleged corporation as if it were an actual corporation for the purpose of determining the rights and liabilities involved in that particular situation. Corporation by estoppel is thus determined by the situation. It does not extend recognition of corporate status beyond the resolution of the problem at hand.

If an association which is neither an actual corporation nor a *de facto* or *de jure* corporation holds itself out as being a corporation, it will be estopped from denying corporate status in a lawsuit by such a third party. This usually occurs when a third party contracts with an association that claims to be a corporation, but does not hold a certificate of incorporation. When the third party brings suit naming the "corporation" as the defendant, the association may not escape from liability on the ground that no corporation exists.

DISREGARDING THE CORPORATE ENTITY

In some unusual situations, a corporate entity is used by its owners to perpetrate a fraud, circumvent the law, or in some other way accomplish an illegitimate objective. In these cases, the court will ignore the corporate structure by "piercing the corporate veil" and will expose the shareholders to personal liability.

In the next case, the court must determine whether the corporate owner should have been held personally liable for the judgment against his corporation.

GARTNER v. SNYDER
United States Court of Appeals,
Second Circuit, 1979.
607 F.2d 582.

BACKGROUND AND FACTS *Gartner contracted to purchase a home from Snyder-Westerlind Enterprises (referred to as Enterprises by the court). Gartner obtained a judgment against Enterprises for breach of the contract to deliver the home by a certain date. Enterprises was one of three corporations owned by Snyder. Enterprises had no major assets with which to satisfy the judgment, and the trial judge ruled that Snyder was personally liable to Gartner.*

LUMBARD, Circuit Judge.

*　*　*　*

*　*　* Because New York courts disregard corporate form reluctantly, they do so only when the form has been used to achieve fraud, or when the corporation has been so dominated by an individual or another corporation (usually a parent corporation), and its separate identity so disregarded, that it primarily transacted the dominator's business rather than its own and can be called the other's alter ego. The court will also generally consider whether the corporation was adequately capitalized in determining whether to disregard the corporate form.

The district court held that Snyder had inadequately capitalized Enterprises, had disregarded its separate identity, had used it to a fraudulent end, and should therefore be personally liable for its breach. As badly as Snyder conducted the Hunter Highlands project, we cannot say that Gartner has shown by a preponderance of evidence either that Snyder engaged in a fraud to get more than the contract price for Unit C-21, or that he transacted purely personal business through Enterprises to the extent that the corporation became his alter ego.

*　*　*　*

The district court found as a further reason for disregarding Enterprises' corporate form the fact that Snyder himself failed to observe Enterprises' separate identity. To be sure, Snyder does not deny that Enterprises had no books, files, or office distinct from those of the other corporations he controlled, nor that the Hunter Highlands files did not distinguish among the different corporations involved in the project. But we do not think that the district court properly applied New York law to those facts. Snyder's disregard suggests that Enterprises was simply one arm of a larger corporate combine; it does not prove that Snyder used Enterprises, or the larger combine, to conduct his purely personal business. *　*　*

Similarly, the fact that Enterprises conveyed its two parcels of land to another Snyder-controlled corporation, while it suggests that Gartner may have claims against the larger Snyder-controlled corporate combine, does not show that Snyder used Enterprises to conduct purely personal business. * * * Snyder ignored the separate identities of the corporations he controlled, but did not use them to pursue personal business.

Thus, while it may be appropriate to disregard Enterprises' form and hold Snyder's larger corporate combine liable for Enterprises' breach—although we of course make no judgment on that question because the other Snyder-controlled corporations were not parties to this action—we do not find evidence in the record to justify holding Snyder personally liable for Enterprises' breach. Although Enterprises was thinly capitalized, that alone is not a sufficient ground for disregarding the corporate form. We know of no New York authority that disregards corporate form solely because of inadequate capitalization.

The judgment against Snyder was reversed. Snyder's actions were not sufficient to expose him to personal liability.

JUDGMENT AND REMEDY

Inadequate Capitalization

In other typical cases, a corporation may have insufficient capital at the time it is formed to meet its prospective debts or potential liabilities. Such "thin capitalization" is exacerbated when a corporation fails to obtain the amount of insurance that any reasonable business can be expected to have in the interest of public responsibility. Hence, victims who are injured may be able to reach the personal assets of stockholders to satisfy their claims. This is illustrated by the following case.

BACKGROUND AND FACTS *The plaintiff's daughter drowned in a public swimming pool operated by Seminole Hot Springs Corporation (Seminole). The defendant, Cavaney, was a director and the secretary-treasurer of Seminole. Cavaney stated that Seminole had never had any assets and had never functioned as a corporation. No stock was ever issued. The trial court entered a judgment for the plaintiff, Minton.*

MINTON v. CAVANEY
Supreme Court of California, 1961.
56 Cal.2d 576, 15 Cal.Rptr. 641, 364 P.2d 473.

TRAYNOR, Justice.

* * * *

The figurative terminology "alter ego" and "disregard of the corporate entity" is generally used to refer to the various situations that are an abuse of the corporate privilege. The equitable owners of a corporation, for example, are personally liable when they treat the assets of the corporation as their own and add or withdraw capital from the corporation at will, when they hold themselves out as being personally liable for the debts of the corporation or when they provide inadequate capitalization and actively participate in the conduct of corporate affairs.

In the instant case the evidence is undisputed that there was no attempt to provide adequate capitalization. Seminole never had any substantial assets. It leased the pool that it operated, and the lease was forfeited for failure to pay the rent. Its capital was " 'trifling compared with the business to be done and the risks of loss' * * *."

JUDGMENT AND REMEDY   *The Supreme Court of California concluded that defendant Cavaney could be liable as an individual for the debts of the corporation. It held that a new trial would be required to determine whether plaintiffs could pierce the corporate veil to recover from Cavaney, since undercapitalization is only one factor to be considered in such a decision.*

COMMINGLING OF PERSONAL AND CORPORATE INTEREST

Often corporations are formed according to law by a single person or by a few family members. The corporate entity and the sole stockholder (or family member stockholders) must carefully preserve the separate status of the corporation and its owners. Certain practices invite trouble for the one-person or family-owned corporation—the commingling of corporate and personal funds, the failure to hold and record minutes of board of directors' meetings, or the shareholders' continuous, personal use of corporate property (for example, vehicles). When the corporate privilege is abused for personal benefit and the corporate business is treated in such a careless manner that the corporation and the shareholder in control are no longer separate entities, the court will require an owner to assume personal liability to creditors for the corporation's debts.

In short, where the facts show that great injustice would result from use of a corporation to avoid individual responsibility, a court of equity will look behind the corporate structure to the individual stockholder.

General corporation law has no specific prohibition against a stockholder lawfully lending money to his or her corporation. However, when an officer or director lends money and takes back security in the form of corporate assets, the courts will scrutinize the transaction closely. Any such transaction must be made in good faith and for fair value.

In the following case, two shareholders made a lawful loan of money to a corporation (which later became insolvent) and in return took a security interest in certain pieces of corporate property. When the corporation became insolvent, some creditors charged that the shareholders' loan transaction was not made in good faith and therefore that their security interest should be set aside.

INTERTHERM, INC. v. OLYMPIC HOMES SYSTEMS, INC.

Court of Appeals of Tennessee, 1978.
569 S.W.2d 467.

BACKGROUND AND FACTS *The plaintiffs were creditors of the Olympic Homes Systems Corporation (Olympic). Two of its shareholders, Langley and Clayton, the defendants, had made a sizable loan to the corporation. In return, they took a security interest in certain corporate property.*

When the corporation became insolvent, the general creditors attempted to set aside the priority of the defendants' security interest. The defendants argued that the general creditors failed to show either that there was any fraud involved in making the loan or that the loan was not an "arm's length" transaction. Moreover, the general creditors did not establish that the defendants were in a fiduciary capacity with the corporation or that they showed a lack of good faith in the loan transaction. The trial court entered judgment for the general creditors, and the shareholders appealed.

DROWOTA, Judge.

*   *   *   *

This is a suit by general creditors against an insolvent corporation and three of its shareholders. The issue is whether a security interest taken by two of the shareholders in personal property of the corporation is valid, and whether it entitles the two shareholders to priority over the general creditors as to the property covered by it.

*   *   *   *

It is true, in Tennessee as elsewhere, that there is no general prohibition against a good faith transaction between a shareholder and his corporation. Accordingly, a shareholder may lawfully loan money to his corporation and receive security therefor.

It is also generally held that officers and directors may, in good faith, lawfully loan money to the corporation they serve and take security therefor. This rule is clearly followed in Tennessee. The rule further provides, however, that "such transactions will invite the closest investigation by the courts, and must be characterized by the utmost good faith." The burden of proving good faith is on the officer or director.

*   *   * As a fiduciary, the officer or director has a strong influence on how the corporation conducts its affairs, and a correspondingly strong duty not to conduct those affairs to the unfair detriment of others, such as minority shareholders or creditors, who also have legitimate interests in the corporation but lack the power of the fiduciary.

It is also generally held that courts will closely scrutinize the transactions of a majority, dominant, or controlling shareholder with his corporation, and will place the burden of proof upon the shareholder when the good faith and fairness of such a transaction is challenged. *   *   * It is obvious, however, that the reason for applying the rule to a shareholder is the same as the reason for applying it to an officer or director, that is, that he occupies a fiduciary position with regard to the corporation and those interested in it. Unless it is shown that a shareholder owns a majority of the stock or that he otherwise controls or dominates a corporation, however, a shareholder cannot be said to be a fiduciary and the reason for closely scrutinizing his transactions with the corporation disappears. Further, in reviewing the cases in which the courts have closely scrutinized transactions between a corporation and a shareholder and have put the burden of justifying them on the latter, we find that they almost invariably involve a majority, dominant, or controlling shareholder. Accordingly, it is clear that courts should apply the rule of close scrutiny and place the burden on the shareholder to justify a transaction with his corporation only when the shareholder owns a majority of stock, or is shown to dominate or control the corporation to a significant degree in some other way.

In the instant case, defendants contend that their secured loan to Olympic should be upheld under the general rule that shareholders may lawfully contract with their corporation. Plaintiffs, on the other hand, argue that this Court should scrutinize this transaction closely and put the burden of justifying it on defendants who, plaintiffs further argue, have failed to carry that burden. We hold that the instant transaction should not be subjected to close scrutiny, and that the burden of proof should not be on defendant shareholders, because plaintiffs have offered no evidence from which we could conclude that defendants owned a majority of Olympic's stock or otherwise dominated it in such a way as to justify imposing fiduciary responsibilities on them.

There is no evidence in this record that either defendant Langley or defendant Clayton was ever an officer or director of Olympic. The evidence is that each owned 15% of the capital stock of Olympic. It is clear that both were involved in setting up the corporation, but there is nothing to show that they participated in the business afterward. There is evidence that they did not intend to participate in the corporation's everyday affairs. *   *   * In short, there is no evidence of any degree of power or control by defendants over the corporation at any time. As far as we can tell from this record, defendants were simply two 15% shareholders who, although they participated in setting up the corporation, were not even its promoters. It is our conclusion that plaintiffs are required to present at least some evidence that defendant shareholders were also officers or directors, or that they in some significant way dominated the corporation, in order to invoke close scrutiny of the transaction and place the burden of justifying it on defendants. Plaintiffs have failed to do so here.

Plaintiffs, then, by failing to show that defendants Langley and Clayton had any fiduciary capacity with Olympic, have failed to shift from themselves the burden of proving fraud or absence of good faith in the loan transaction. *   *   *
*   *   *   *

On the meager evidence in this record, then, we have no choice but to conclude that defendants were minority shareholders without control[.] *   *   *
*   *   *   *

We hold that defendants Langley and Clayton have a valid security interest in the property of Olympic recited in the security agreement of September 18, 1973, and that no reason appears for subordinating that interest to the claims of Olympic's general creditors.

JUDGMENT   *The Supreme Court of Tennessee reversed the lower court and held that*
AND REMEDY   *the defendants, Langley and Clayton, held a valid security interest and*
were entitled to priority over the general creditors.

COSTS AND BENEFITS OF INCORPORATION

The Costs of Incorporating

Just about anyone in any state can start a corporation. There are, however, numerous expenses associated with starting and running such a venture. Below is a list of the possible expenses:

1. *Lawyers' fees.* Most can range from a minimum of $250 to as much as $5,000.
2. *Accountants' fees.* It can cost several hundred dollars to establish a bookkeeping system for a corporation.
3. *Fees to the state.* The state can require an annual corporate fee ranging from a few dollars to several hundred dollars.

4. *Unemployment insurance taxes.* Even if the corporation has only one employee, and it is clearly set up for tax reasons only, it must still pay unemployment insurance taxes, either to the state in which it is registered or to the federal government.
5. *Employer's contribution to social security.* Even if a person is a salaried employee of some other company, as an employee of his or her own corporation, he or she must pay an employer's "contribution" to social security. This "contribution" is nonrefundable and seems to be on the rise.
6. *Annual legal and accounting fees.* Forms must be filed for corporations. In addition, corporate records and minutes books must be maintained. Typically, an accountant or a lawyer does this. Annual fees for such services can run into many hundreds or thousands of dollars. Numerous

forms must be filled out every year, for retirement funds in particular.

The Benefits of Incorporating

One of the major benefits of incorporating is the tax benefit of starting a pension or profit-sharing plan and the tax-related benefits associated with fringe benefits.

Pension and Profit-Sharing Plans Employee-shareholders of corporations are allowed to participate in pension and profit-sharing plans. For example, the IRS might allow a pension plan that consists of a contribution by the corporation for every qualified employee of 10 percent of that employee's gross salary. A separate profit-sharing plan might be allowed in which 15 percent of each qualified employee's gross salary is contributed by the corporation. These contributions are tax-deductible to the corporation and are not immediately taxed to the individual employee. The major benefit here is that the payment of the employee's income taxes is deferred until some later date. Moreover, the tax-exempt pension and profit-sharing plans do not pay taxes on the interest income earned until the proceeds of the plans are distributed to the individual employee upon retirement. To be sure, one does not have to incorporate to participate in tax-exempt retirement plans. Keogh plans and Individual Retirement Accounts (IRAs) are available. However, for the high-income individual, these two plans do not allow for as much sheltering of income as do corporate pension and profit-sharing plans.

Fringe Benefits

An individual who starts a corporation can take advantage of a number of fringe benefits that provide items that might otherwise have to be bought with after-tax dollars.

Term Life Insurance An individual, through his or her own corporation, can purchase up to $50,000 of term life insurance every year with dollars out of the corporation. Because these dollars are a cost to the corporation, they are not taxable. If the person is in the 50 percent tax bracket, for example, that means that he or she

is buying $50,000 of term insurance for "fifty-cent dollars." In this example, the cost of that insurance is essentially one-half what it would have been if it had been purchased outside the corporate structure.

A Medical Plan An individual can set up a completely comprehensive medical plan to cover virtually all kinds of medical expenses. Thus, the corporation can reimburse the individual with before-tax dollars for any payments made for medical insurance. The corporation can pay for all medicines, dental work, and anything that relates to physical well-being. For someone with a large family, this comprehensive medical plan can mean substantial savings every year.

The benefit of a medical plan is reduced by the availability of medical deductions that the individual could have taken off his or her income before figuring federal income taxes. Part of the person's medical insurance, plus any medical expenses exceeding 7 percent of the adjusted gross income, can be itemized as specific deductions on his or her personal federal income tax return. Essentially, then, a medical plan within the corporation for the individual and his or her dependents provides a method for the corporation to deduct medical expenses that generally are not deductible to the individual.

The Revenue Act of 1978 requires that a medical plan not discriminate among employees. In other words, if it is made available to the president of the corporation, it must also be made available to all employees of the corporation.

Disability Insurance An individual can purchase, with before-tax dollars, long-term disability insurance through the corporation. In other words, a person can buy a salary-continuation policy with before-tax dollars that might otherwise have to be bought with after-tax dollars. Such policies pay a certain amount of money every month if the person becomes disabled and is unable to work.

CORPORATE FINANCING

In order to obtain financing, corporations issue **securities**—evidence of the obligation to pay money or of the right to participate in earnings and the distribution of corporate trusts and other property. The principal method of long-term and initial corporate financing is the issuance of stocks—**equity**—and bonds—**debt**—both of which are sold to investors. Stocks, or **equity securities,** represent the purchase of ownership in the business firm. Bonds (debentures), or **debt securities,** represent the borrowing of money by firms (and governments).[3] Of course, not all debt is in the form of debt securities. Some is in the form of accounts payable, some in the form of notes payable, and still more in the form of leaseholds. Accounts and notes payable are typically short-term debts. Bonds are simply a way for the corporation to split up its long-term debt so that it can market it more easily.

Characteristics of Bonds

Bonds are issued by business firms and by governments at all levels as evidence of the funds they are borrowing from investors. Bonds almost always have a designated maturity date—the date when the principal or face amount of the bond (or loan) is returned to the investor. Bonds are sometimes referred to as *fixed income securities* because their owners receive a fixed dollar interest payment during the period of time until maturity.

In the bond trade, the word *bond* refers specifically to a debenture with a face value of $1,000. Bonds can be sold below their face value at a *discount* or above their face value at a *premium.* Bonds sold at premiums have yields that are less than their coupon, or stated, rates; those sold at a discount have yields that are greater than the face rate.

Corporate Bonds

The characteristics of corporate bonds vary widely, in part because corporations differ in their ability to generate the earnings and cash flow

necessary to make interest payments and to repay the principal amount of the bonds at maturity. Furthermore, corporate bonds are only part of the total debt and overall financial structure of corporate business.

Because debt financing represents a legal obligation on the part of the corporation, various features and terms of a particular bond issue are specified in a lending agreement called a **bond indenture.** A corporate trustee, often a commercial bank trust department, represents the collective well-being of all bondholders in insuring that the terms of the bond issue are met by the corporation.

The bond indenture specifies the maturity date of the bond and the pattern of interest payments until maturity. Most corporate bonds pay semiannually a coupon rate of interest on the $1,000 face amount of the bond.

For example, the owner of a 6 percent corporate bond would receive $30 interest every six months. The indenture indicates whether any portion of the bond is to be retired each year in a series of *sinking fund payments*, and it specifies any collateral for the bond issue, such as buildings or equipment. Additionally, the indenture indicates how the bondholder (and other creditors of the business firm) will fare if the firm gets into serious financial difficulty and is unable to meet all its legal obligations.

Debentures No specific assets of the corporation are pledged as backing for debentures. Rather, they are backed by the general credit rating of the corporation, plus any assets that can be seized if the corporation allows the debentures to go into default.

Mortgage Bonds Mortgage bonds pledge specific property. If the corporation defaults on the bonds, the bondholders can take the mortgage property.

Equipment Trust Bonds The collateral for the equipment trust bond (loan) is a specific piece of equipment. Title to the equipment is vested in a trustee, who holds it for the benefit of the bond owners.

---

3. The term *bonds* is often used to describe both secured and unsecured obligations. Technically, however, bonds are secured by a lien or other security interest, and debentures are unsecured.

Collateral Trust Bonds   Collateral trust bonds are secured by intangibles. They can be shares of stock in another corporation or accounts receivable.

Convertible Bonds   Convertible bonds can be exchanged for a specified number of shares of common stock when and if the bondholder so desires. The rate of conversion is determined when the convertible bond is issued.

Callable Bonds   Callable bonds, which may be debentures or any other kinds of bonds, may be called in and the principal repaid at specified times or under specified conditions. The callable provision is included in the bond when it is issued.

CHARACTERISTICS OF STOCKS

Issuing stocks is another way corporations obtain financing. Stocks represent ownership in a business firm; bonds represent borrowing by the firm.

The most important characteristics of stocks are:

1.   They need not be paid back.
2.   The stockholder receives dividends only when voted by the directors.
3.   Stockholders are the last to be paid off upon dissolution.
4.   Shareholders vote for management and on major issues.

The two major types of stocks are preferred stock and common stock.

Common Stock

Common stock represents the true ownership of a corporation. Ownership of this stock represents a threefold proportionate interest in the corporation with regard to:

1.   Control.
2.   Earning capacity.
3.   Net assets.

A shareholder's interest is generally in proportion to the number of shares owned out of the total number of shares issued.

Voting rights in a corporation apply to election of the firm's board of directors and to any proposed changes in the ownership structure of the firm.[4] For example, a holder of common stock generally has the right to vote in a decision on a proposed merger, since mergers can change the proportion of ownership. Many small investors in giant corporations probably feel that their small number of votes has little impact on the business firm—particularly when incumbent management owns or obtains the right to vote shares by proxy and thus has a significant and often controlling proportion of the total votes. Still, voting rights are an important characteristic of common stock and one that some investors take seriously.

There is no obligation to return a principal amount per share to each common stock shareholder. No firm can ensure that the market price per share of its common stock will not go down over time. Neither does the issuing firm guarantee a dividend; indeed, some business firms never pay dividends. Considering these negative aspects, why would an individual even consider investing in common stock? The answer, of course, is that all owners are entitled to their proportional share of the corporation's after-tax earnings. If Janet Gray owns 100 shares (0.01 percent of 1 million shares outstanding) of a firm that earns $3 million after taxes, she will receive a proportional share of those earnings totaling $300. Earnings are the key to the benefits that an investor receives from common stock.

Either the earnings of a corporation are paid out in the form of cash dividends to shareholders, or they are retained in the business for the express purpose of enhancing future earnings. If the board of directors of Janet Gray's firm (and it is her firm because she owns common stock declares a dividend of $1.20 per share, then $120 of her $300 earnings are received now as a tangible benefit, with the other $180 retained. Her other tangible benefit is the market price per share that she will receive if and when she ultimately

---

4.   State corporation law specifies the types of issues on which shareholder approval must be obtained.

sells part or all of her 100 common shares. Market price depends, among other things, on the recent earnings (and dividends) of the firm and, more importantly, on expectations for future earnings and dividends, as well as on the overall economic well-being of the country.

Holders of common stock, then, are a group of investors who assume the *residual* position in the overall financial structure of a business. In terms of receiving payment for their investment, they are last in line. The earnings to which they are entitled also depend on all the other groups—suppliers, employees, managers, bankers, governments, bondholders, and holders of preferred stock—being paid what is due them first. Once those groups are paid, however, the owners of common stock are entitled to *all* the remaining earnings. (But the board of directors is not normally under any duty to declare the remaining earnings as dividends.) This is the central feature of ownership in any business, be it a corner newsstand, a retail store, an architectural firm, or a giant international oil corporation. In each instance, the common stock owners occupy the riskiest position, but they can expect a correspondingly greater return on their investment. Again, it can be seen why the return and risk pattern holds. As one moves from savings accounts and U.S. government bonds to corporate bonds with different ratings to preferred stock and, finally, to common stock, expected returns increase to compensate for the higher risks that are undertaken. Exhibit 41–2 is a comparison of stocks and bonds.

Authorized, Issued, and Outstanding Shares   A share of stock is the basic unit of ownership of the corporation. **Authorized shares** are those that the corporation is allowed to issue by its articles of incorporation. Under modern law, there generally is no limit on the number of authorized shares. **Issued shares** are those that are actually issued to shareholders. There is no specific percentage of authorized shares that must be issued. The number of issued shares does not always equal the number of outstanding shares because corporations sometimes repurchase some of their shares. **Outstanding shares** are those that are still held by the shareholders. Repurchased shares are known as **treasury shares;** these shares are authorized and issued, but not outstanding.

Par Value and No Par Shares   The specific monetary value assigned to shares in the articles of incorporation is called *par value*. It is the *stated* value of a share. Although of historical interest, par value is no longer of primary importance. Its one lingering effect is that the price per common share initially sold must be greater than or equal to par value. This creates no problem when nominal amounts are used for par value.

The issuance of *no par shares* is permitted in most jurisdictions. As their name implies, these shares are assigned no dollar value. Some statutes provide that the board of directors has the

EXHIBIT 41–2 HOW DO STOCKS AND BONDS DIFFER?	
STOCKS	BONDS
1. Stocks represent ownership.	1. Bonds represent owed debt.
2. Stocks (common) do not have a fixed dividend rate.	2. Interest on bonds must always be paid, whether or not any profit is earned.
3. Stockholders can elect a board of directors, which controls the corporation.	3. Bondholders usually have no voice in or control over management of the corporation.
4. Stocks do not have a maturity date; the corporation does not usually repay the stockholder.	4. Bonds have a maturity date when the bondholder is to be repaid the face value of the bond.
5. All corporations issue or offer to sell stocks. This is the usual definition of a corporation.	5. Corporations do not necessarily issue bonds.
6. Stockholders have a claim against the property and income of a corporation after all creditors' claims have been met.	6. Bondholders have a claim against the property and income of a corporation that must be met before the claims of stockholders.

right to fix the price for no par shares issued, but the articles of incorporation may expressly reserve this right for the shareholders. One of the most attractive features of no par stock is that in most states the entire consideration received constitutes the stated capital. These states even permit the board of directors to allocate this consideration to be split between stated capital and capital surplus.

Stated capital represents the basic capital of the corporation. Generally, it consists of the sum of the par values for all issued shares plus the consideration received for the no par shares. In many jurisdictions, the stated capital amount cannot be delved into unless the corporation is liquidated.

Preferred Stock

Preferred stock is stock with *preferences*. Usually this means that holders of preferred stock have priority over holders of common stock to dividends and to payment on dissolution of the corporation. Preferred stock shareholders may or may not have the right to vote. There are a number of different types of preferred stock, as will be defined.

From an investment standpoint, preferred stock is more like bonds than like common stock. It is not included among the liabilities of a business because it is equity. Like all equity securities, preferred shares have no fixed maturity time when they must be retired by the firm. Occasionally, firms do retire preferred stock, but they are not legally obligated to do so.

Preferred shareholders receive periodic dividend payments, usually established as a fixed percentage of the face amount of each preferred share. A 7 percent preferred stock with a face amount of $100 per share would pay its owner a $7 dividend each year. This is not a legal obligation on the part of the firm, but the interest payments due to bondholders are legal obligations.

Cumulative Preferred Stock Any dividend payment on cumulative preferred stock not made in a given year must be paid in a subsequent year before any dividends can be paid to owners of common stock. In other words, the corporation is liable to the preferred shareholders for past dividends not yet paid (called dividend arrearages). If, for example, a corporation fails to pay dividends for three years on a stock with a $100 par value and a $5 annual dividend preference, then the company must pay the cumulative preferred stock owners $15 per share at the end of the three years before any dividends can be paid to common stock owners. Sometimes there are limits as to how far back dividends have to be paid—for example, there may be three- or five-year cumulative limits.

Participating Preferred Stock With participating preferred stock, the owner can share to some extent in additional dividends that are paid by the firm. Usually, the preferred stock owners are paid their agreed-upon rate of, say, $5 per share (the dividend preference), and then common stock owners are paid an equal percentage rate, after which any additional dividends declared by the board of directors are distributed equally among preferred and common stockholders.

Convertible Preferred Stock The owner of shares of convertible preferred stock has an option of converting each share into a specified number of common shares. Sometimes convertible preferred stock can be exchanged for common stock in another company. In any event, the exchange ratio is determined when the convertible preferred shares of stock are issued. Hence, if there is an increase in the market value of the corporation's common stock, the market value of the convertible preferred stock also rises.

Redeemable, or Callable, Preferred Stock Redeemable or callable preferred stock is issued by a corporation under the express condition that the corporation have the right to buy back the shares of stock from the preferred stock owners at some future time. The terms of such a buy-back arrangement are specified when the preferred stock is issued. Corporations issue callable preferred so that they can call in the higher-cost preferred stock and reissue lower-cost shares if interest rates fall in the the future.

The Cautious Position of the Preferred Stock Owner Holders of preferred stock are investors who have assumed a rather cautious position in their relationship to the corporation. They have a stronger position than common shareholders with respect to dividends and claims on assets, but as a result, they will not share in the full prosperity of the firm if it grows successfully over time.

A preferred stock owner receives fixed dividends periodically, and there may be changes in the market price of the shares. The return and the risk for a share of preferred stock lie somewhere between those of bonds and common stock. As a result, preferred stock is often categorized with corporate bonds as a fixed income security even though the legal status is not the same. Some experts even contend that preferred stock is more similar to a bond than common stock, even though preferred stock appears in the ownership section of the firm's balance sheet (financial statements).

QUESTIONS AND CASE PROBLEMS

1. Able, Baker, and Carter are recent college graduates who want to form a corporation to manufacture and sell personal computers. Peterson tells them he will set in motion the formation of their corporation. First, Peterson makes a contract for the purchase of a piece of land for $20,000 with Owens. Owens does not know of the prospective corporate formation at the time of the signing of the contract. Second, Peterson makes a contract with Beyer to build a small plant on the property being purchased. Beyer's contract is conditional on the corporation's formation. Peterson secures all necessary subscription agreements and capitalization, and he files the articles of incorporation. A charter is issued.

(a) Discuss whether the newly formed corporation or Peterson or both are liable on the contracts with Owens and Beyer.

(b) Discuss whether the corporation is automatically liable to Beyer upon being formed.

2. As a promoter forming a new corporation, Peterson enters into three preincorporation subscription agreements with Mary, Anne, and Harry. The three subscribers each agree to purchase a thousand shares of stock of the future corporation for $2,000. Two months later, just prior to the issuance of the corporate charter, Mary tells Peter she is withdrawing from the agreement. The charter is issued the next week. Just before the first organizational meeting of the corporation, Harry also withdraws from the agreement. Discuss fully whether Mary or Harry or both can withdraw from their subscription agreements without liability.

3. Able, Baker, and Carter form a corporation. The state laws governing incorporation require that the articles of incorporation be signed by three incorporators. A charter is issued, and the corporation begins to do business. Thomas extends credit to the corporation. Because of a national recession, the corporation becomes insolvent. At this time Thomas learns that Able failed to sign the articles of incorporation. Thomas claims that the corporation's formation was improper and that Able, Baker, and Carter are personally liable. Discuss Thomas's claim.

4. Able, Baker, and Carter are brothers who form a corporation to build swimming pools. They are the sole shareholders, members of the board of directors, and officers of the corporation. No meetings are held, and corporate trucks are used on weekends for personal use. In addition, the brothers lend the corporation money, taking a security interest in the corporate property when they cannot get unsecured credit from others because of previous unsecured indebtedness. The corporation becomes insolvent, and the brothers claim they have priority over unsecured creditors on the basis of their security interest. The unsecured creditors claim not only that the security interest can be set aside but that the brothers are personally liable. Discuss these claims.

5. A new corporation is formed. By its articles of incorporation it has 100,000 shares of authorized common stock at a par value of $2 per share. The corporation has limited property assets, since its major function is as a service corporation. The corporation issues 50,000 shares. Soon the corporation needs additional financing. Assume that profits for the first year are relatively low but that the future of the corporation is bright. The corporation needs $90,000 of additional financing, but it wants to plow back next year's profits into the corporation.

(a) Would you recommend funding by issuance of corporate bonds? Discuss.

(b) Would you recommend the issuance of preferred or common stock? Discuss.

6. Pointer formed a corporation with $1,000 capital and later loaned over $400,000 to the corporation. Six

days after he was notified that Tigrett had filed suit against his corporation, Pointer transferred corporate assets amounting to $400,000 to himself as repayment of the loans. Pointer then transferred these assets to another corporation, of which he was the sole shareholder. The second corporation took over all the business and duties of the original corporation. At the time that Pointer undertook these transfers, Tigrett had not obtained a judgment against the corporation and so was not one of its creditors. By the time Tigrett was awarded a judgment against the original corporation, it had no assets. Is there any way for Tigrett to collect the amount of her judgment? [Tigrett v. Pointer, 580 S.W.2d 375 (Tex.Civ.App.1978)]

7. Donald McCallum, John Gray, and Lee Evans entered into a preincorporation agreement that provided: (1) the three named persons would cause a corporation to be organized under the laws of Oregon with an authorized capital of a thousand shares, (2) each would receive one-third of the shares, and (3) no shareholder would sell, transfer, or in any way dispose of his shares unless and until he offered to sell the shares to the other shareholders. Subsequently, Lee Evans wished to withdraw from the corporation and offered his shares to both McCallum and Gray. Gray declined, but McCallum agreed to purchase all the shares. Thereafter, at a stockholders' meeting with McCallum and Gray both present, McCallum voted, over Gray's objections, to amend the bylaws, allowing an additional thousand shares to be issued. Since Gray had no money to invest at the time, the shares would be purchased by outsiders. Gray objected to the dilution of his interest in the company. Does Gray have any legal grounds to object to McCallum's action? [McCallum v. Gray, 273 Or. 617, 542 P.2d 1025 (1975)]

8. Watchie, an entrepreneur, acquired the rights to buy certain property that was later to be developed into a large shopping center. Watchie interested a group of Seattle investors, known as the Seattle Syndicate, in purchasing the land. Over the next two years Watchie was the promoter of a corporation whose investors contributed approximately $1.5 million for the purchase of the land sold to the Seattle Syndicate. Watchie then convinced the Seattle Syndicate to sell the land to the newly formed corporation for $1,458,000 and convinced the investors that this was a good price. The Seattle Syndicate made a handsome profit on the sale, but Watchie shared in none of it. He was, however, paid a commission of $162,000 on the sale by the Seattle Syndicate. He failed to report this amount to the investors of the newly formed corporation. Can he retain it? [Park City Corp. v. Watchie, 249 Or. 493, 439 P.2d 587 (1968)]

9. New Liberty Medical and Hospital Corporation entered into an agreement with New Liberty Hospital District under which the hospital district agreed to purchase the hospital's debentures under the sole condition that the debentures be legally issued. The district then attempted to avoid its obligation under the agreement with the hospital claiming that, even though the hospital held a proper certificate of incorporation issued by the secretary of state of Missouri, it did not properly comply with all of the statutory requirements of nonprofit corporations. In a suit by the hospital against the district to enforce the agreement, can the district raise this defense? Explain. [New Liberty Medical and Hospital Corp. v. E. F. Hutton and Co., 474 S.W.2d 1 (Mo.1971)]

10. Wesley Philpot and his wife engaged the services of Bob Childs Realty Company, Inc., to sell a tract of real estate. Childs Realty sold the property and demanded a commission from the Philpots. The Philpots refused to pay on the ground that Childs Realty had not complied with the Arkansas brokers' law, which required brokers to be incorporated before they could be licensed. Childs Realty argued that it should be deemed a corporation since its president had signed articles of incorporation, and it held itself out as a corporation by use of the designation "Inc." Has Bob Childs Realty Company complied with the Arkansas statute requiring licensed real estate brokers to be incorporated? [Childs v. Philpot, 253 Ark. 589, 487 S.W.2d 637 (1972)]

11. Slowek and Zamparelli are doing business under the assumed name of "New York Office of Consumer Interest" pursuant to a certificate duly filed in the Albany county clerk's office. Their firm is engaged in the business of soliciting advertising from contractors and home repair and improvement businesses for the purpose of publishing a booklet offering the prices of these advertisers. The booklet is called "Consumers' Home Improvement Guide." Should the attorney general for the state of New York take any action against Slowek and Zamparelli? [Lefkowitz v. Slowek, 79 Misc.2d 1098, 362 N.Y.S.2d 110 (1974)]

12. During the early months of 1971, a number of persons began to organize a company later known as Timberjack of Alabama, Inc. On June 8, 1971, a day before the company was formally incorporated, it was assigned certain rights in collateral that was held by Eaton Yale, Ltd. On June 8 Timberjack repossessed the collateral, and on June 9 Timberjack was formally incorporated. Eaton then demanded that Timberjack return the collateral since the right to repossess it was in Timberjack, Inc., and Timberjack, Inc., did not exist on the day repossession took place. Can Eaton reclaim the goods? [In re Wilco Forest Machinery, Inc., 491 F.2d 1041 (5th Cir. 1974)]

CHAPTER 42

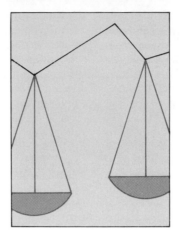

CORPORATIONS
Corporate Powers and Management

CORPORATE POWERS

Express Powers

The express powers of a corporation are found in its articles of incorporation, in the law of the state of incorporation, and in the state and federal constitutions. The order of priority used when conflicts arise among documents involving corporations is:

1. The U.S. Constitution.
2. State constitutions.
3. State statutes.
4. The certificate of incorporation (charter).
5. Bylaws.
6. Resolutions of the board of directors.

It is important to keep in mind that the corporation is a "legal person." Under modern law, except as limited by charters, statutes, or constitutions, a corporation can engage in all acts and enter into any contract available to a natural person *in order to accomplish the purposes for which it was created.*

Implied Powers

Certain inherent powers attach when a corporation is created. Barring express constitutional, statutory, or charter prohibitions, the corporation has the implied power to do all acts reasonably appropriate and necessary to accomplish its corporate purposes. For this reason, a corporation has the implied power to borrow money within certain limits, to lend money or extend credit to those with whom it has a legal or contractual relationship, and to make charitable contributions.[1]

---

1. The right of a corporation to make political contributions in federal elections is prohibited by the Federal Elections Campaign Act. [18 USC Section 321] Early law held that a corporation had no implied authority to make charitable contributions, as such was contrary to the primary purpose of the corporation to make a profit. Modern law, by statutes and court decisions, now holds that a corporation has such implied power.

To borrow money, the corporation acts through its board of directors to authorize the execution of negotiable paper. Most often, the president or chief executive officer of the corporation will execute the necessary papers on behalf of the corporation. In so doing, corporate officers have the implied power to bind the corporation in matters directly connected with the *ordinary* business affairs of the enterprise. This is the issue in the next case.

BACKGROUND AND FACTS   *The plaintiff loaned $5,000 to the defendant corporation. The corporation, through its president, executed a promissory note for $5,000 plus interest. The promissory note became overdue. The plaintiff demanded payment from the defendant many times, but the defendant corporation refused to pay any part of the note.*

The corporation acknowledged that there was a note executed and delivered to the plaintiff by its president, Arne Poulsen, but it alleged that Poulsen had neither the power nor the authority to make or deliver the note on behalf of the corporation or to bind the corporation to the payment of such an obligation. Further, the corporation contended that Poulsen's act was not properly approved by the board of directors.

F.M. BENTALL v. KOENIG BROTHERS, INC.

Supreme Court of Montana, 1962.
140 Mont. 339, 372 P.2d 91.

HARRISON, Justice.

*   *   *   *

It is the defendant corporation's contention that the note in question was executed and delivered by the president, Arne Poulsen, without having been so directed or authorized by any order or resolution of the corporation's board of directors, and hence the authority for the execution and delivery thereof to the plaintiff must rest upon the evidence of the defendant corporation's alleged ratification of those acts by the board of directors or upon such general authority as must be ascribed to the president of the corporation who signed the note.

In the instant case, the defendant corporation's Articles of Incorporation provided for three members to act as directors of the corporation. At the time of the execution of the note in question, R. W. Brenneke, Alvin F. Koenig, and Arne Poulsen were its directors. It is undisputed that Alvin Koenig and Arne Poulsen authorized the execution of the note in question. They constituted a quorum and their action, which was not contrary to law nor contrary to the articles of incorporation or by-laws of the defendant corporation, was binding on the defendant corporation.

The defendant corporation, however, argues that "Arne Poulsen had a conflicting or adverse interest with respect to this loan, and therefore, could not be counted either as part of a quorum of the board of directors, or in any vote by said board, insofar as this loan was concerned."

It is true that a director of a corporation may not cast a vote upon an issue in which he has an adverse interest. However, here, Arne Poulsen, as a director of the defendant corporation, had no interest adverse to that of the defendant corporation.

First of all, *   *   * the $5,000, which is covered by the note in question, was a loan to the defendant corporation and, was not *   *   * [a personal loan to Poulsen].

Secondly, the record discloses that the defendant corporation, at the time the note to the plaintiff was executed, was in debt and in immediate need of money to cover current operating expenses. * * * When he [Poulsen] obtained the $5,000 loan from the plaintiff for the defendant corporation, he was acting as an agent of the defendant corporation. * * *

* * * *

In the case at bar, * * * two of the three directors of the defendant corporation, in the absence of the third director, authorized the execution of a promissory note *to a third party*, the plaintiff. These directors did not execute the note to themselves nor did they stand to profit from its execution.

Arne Poulsen, as president of the defendant corporation, not only had express authority to execute the note in question, but he also had *implied* authority.

In the absence of special authority, the president of a corporation has no power, merely by virtue of his office alone, to execute negotiable paper in the name of the corporation. "Where, however, such power is specially conferred upon him [president] * * * by the corporate charter or by a resolution or by-law of the board of directors, or, *where such power exists, by implication* from the nature of the agency or *by reason of his* * * * being held out by custom or course of dealing as having such authority, or being *intrusted with the conduct and management of the corporate affairs, which requires the use of such instruments in the ordinary course of the business, the president* * * * *may bind the corporation by the execution* * * * *of negotiable paper.*"

The plaintiff's case does not here rest upon the proposition that Poulsen's authority to bind the corporation by promissory notes executed for it or in its name may be implied from the mere fact of his official position. To the proof of the fact that he was president, or chief executive officer of the defendant corporation, is added other evidence that he was also one of its three directors and the *manager* of its business. The entire corporation was made up of Poulsen, Alvin Koenig, and one R. W. Brenneke, who is not shown to have any active hand in the business. The record shows that Poulsen had and exercised "full management and control of the affairs of said corporation." The evidence as to the whole course of conduct of the directors and stockholders of the defendant corporation in allowing Poulsen such "full management and control" was sufficient to justify a finding that he was thereby vested with power to borrow money on the note of the corporation.

The defendant corporation was in debt and Poulsen, as a faithful servant intent on saving his corporation, did what the ordinary prudent business man would do in carrying on the affairs of the corporation (i.e., borrow money in the name of the corporation and bind it by a note evidencing the same) and, in so doing, violated no statute of this state, nor the articles of incorporation or any by-law of the defendant corporation. Poulsen was dealing with a matter directly connected with the ordinary business affairs of the defendant corporation and the promissory note to the plaintiff was such as was usual, proper, and necessary, under the circumstances, in the ordinary prosecution of the corporation's business.

JUDGMENT AND REMEDY *The Supreme Court of Montana affirmed the lower court's decision that the corporation was liable on the $5,000 note.*

Ultra Vires Doctrine

The term *ultra vires* means "beyond the powers." In corporate law, acts of a corporation that are beyond the authority given to it under its charter or under the statutes by which it was incorporated are *ultra vires* acts.

Ultra vires acts can be understood only within the context of the particular purpose for which the corporation was organized. Acts in furtherance of the corporation's expressed purposes are within the corporate power; acts beyond the scope of corporate business as described in the charter are *ultra vires*.

Because *ultra vires* acts frequently stem from a corporation acting beyond its stated purpose, corporations are increasingly aware of the benefit of adopting a very broad statement of purpose in their articles of incorporation to include virtually all conceivable activities. Corporate statutes in many states permit the expression "any lawful purpose" to be a legally sufficient stated purpose in the articles of incorporation.

A majority of cases dealing with *ultra vires* acts have involved contracts made for unauthorized purposes. For example, it is difficult to see how a contract made by a plumbing company for the purchase of six thousand cases of vodka is reasonably related to the conduct and furtherance of the corporation's main purpose of providing plumbing installation and services. Hence, such a contract would probably be held *ultra vires*.

Corporate acts can be *ultra vires* simply in the sense of being beyond corporate powers. Such acts are not necessarily illegal; however, all illegal acts are inherently *ultra vires*.

In certain cases, the law recognizes the right of a shareholder to sue the board of directors for its alleged wrongful exercise of business judgment on behalf of the corporation. A stockholder can bring what is called a *derivative suit* against the corporation by first demanding that the directors correct the wrong. Failing that, the stockholder can ask the court to enforce the corporate right.

Certain acts of the board of directors can be unauthorized at the time they first occur but ratified later by a majority vote of the stockholders. Such ratification of the board of directors' actions by a majority of shareholders will ordinarily cure an otherwise voidable wrong. However, certain acts, such as waste of corporate assets, will usually require unanimous shareholder action for ratifying or condoning the wrong.

The Model Business Corporation Act essentially abolishes the *ultra vires* doctrine. Under Section 7 of the act, the doctrine cannot be asserted by the corporation as a means of avoiding its contractual obligations except in limited circumstances.

BACKGROUND AND FACTS   *In 1966, HFC, Inc. instituted an employee stock option plan as a means of retaining services of valued employees as well as obtaining services of new employees. In April 1974, due to a drop in the market price of HFC stock, HFC's board of directors adopted a resolution cancelling the 1966 plan and replacing it with a more favorable plan (that is, one that allowed employees to purchase HFC stock for a lower price). This was done to ensure that the incentive value of the stock option plan would be maintained. Michelson, a stockholder, brought a derivative suit against the corporation alleging that the board had violated its fiduciary duties to the corporation and its stockholders by the unauthorized modifications in the stock option plan. Prior to trial, the board's action was ratified by a majority of HFC's stockholders. The ratification, however, was not unanimous.*

MICHELSON v.
DUNCAN
Supreme Court of Delaware,
1979.
407 A.2d 211.

HORSEY, Justice.

*   *   *   *

The essential distinction between voidable and void acts is that the former are those which may be found to have been performed in the interest of the corporation but beyond the authority of management, as distinguished from acts which are *ultra vires*, fraudulent or gifts or waste of corporate assets. The practical distinction, for our purposes, is that voidable acts are susceptible to cure by shareholder approval while void acts are not.

*   *   * Plaintiff also contends that even if the ratification were found to be fairly accomplished and to relate back to cure otherwise unauthorized director actions, actions for consequential damages against the directors survive.

It is the law of Delaware, and general corporate law, that a validly accomplished shareholder ratification relates back to cure otherwise unauthorized acts of officers and directors. As stated in 5 Fletcher, *Cyclopedia of Corporations,* § 2139 (perm.ed.rev.1976):

> "Generally, any act of the board of directors or of any of the officers beyond the scope of their authority fixing or increasing compensation may be ratified by the stockholders when the stockholders have originally authorized such act, and this may be done even after suit is filed, provided the ratification is voted by bona fide stockholders *   *   *. [W]here a majority of the stockholders of the corporation at a special meeting ratify a stock option plan for key executives which was authorized by interested directors, such ratification cures any voidable defect in the action by the board of directors."

It is only where a claim of gift or waste of assets, fraud or *ultra vires* is asserted that a less than unanimous shareholder ratification is not a full defense.

*   *   * Furthermore, Michelson's argument that ratification may cure an invalid act of a director but leave open the question of his liability for consequent losses to the corporation must be rejected as inherently inconsistent. If shareholders have approved an otherwise voidable act, their approval extinguishes any claim for losses based on prior lack of authority of the directors to undertake such action.

JUDGMENT AND REMEDY   *The stockholder ratification was upheld.*

COMMENTS   *When officers or directors breach their duty to the corporation, the corporation has a claim against the wrongdoers and can seek damages for breach of duty. Since the corporation can act only through its officers and directors, it is unlikely that the wrongdoers will cause the corporation to bring suit against themselves. In certain instances, a shareholder has the right to bring suit on behalf of the corporation. This suit is called a derivative suit,[2] and any recovery from it goes to the corporation.[3]*

---

2.   A derivative suit is different from a shareholder's individual suit, in which the plaintiff-shareholder claims that the wrongdoing directly injured a group of shareholders.

3.   In the rare instances where recovery to the corporation would result in a windfall to a third party or to the wrongdoers, a court will award minority shareholders individual *pro rata* recovery. See Perlman v. Feldmann, 219 F.2d 173 (2d Cir.), cert denied 349 U.S. 952, 75 S.Ct. 880 (1955).

Before a derivative action can be filed, a stockholder must make a demand to the directors that the corporation bring suit. This gives management a chance to investigate the claim, after which management can have the corporation file suit on its own behalf.[4]

4. In certain limited circumstances, a demand on the board will be excused. For example, if the alleged wrongdoers constituted a majority of the board of directors, a demand would be futile.

Judicial Treatment of *Ultra Vires* Contracts

The courts have treated *ultra vires* contracts in a variety of ways. One treatment is based upon the common law principle of agency, whereby an unauthorized contract made by an agent is void—no rights or duties arise for either party. Early decisions often held that *ultra vires* contracts were void.

The more modern approach is to uphold the validity of contracts that have been performed by all sides. In some states, when a contract is entirely executory, neither party having performed, a defense of *ultra vires* can be used by either party to prevent enforcement of the contract.

Sometimes an *ultra vires* contract is only partially executed at the time of challenge. Courts may still enforce the contract where the circumstances are such that it would be inequitable to allow a party to assert the defense of *ultra vires*.

The current trend in dealing with *ultra vires* contracts is embodied in statutory enactments similar to Section 7 of the Model Act, which upholds the validity and enforceability of an *ultra vires* contract as between the parties involved. However, the right of shareholders on behalf of the corporation, the right of the corporation itself to recover damages from the officers and directors who caused the transaction, and the right of the attorney general of the state to institute an injunction against the transaction or to institute dissolution proceedings against the corporation for *ultra vires* acts have been upheld.

Torts and Criminal Acts

A corporation is liable for the torts committed by its agents or officers within the course and scope of their employment. A corporation can act only through its agents and servants. This principle applies to a corporation exactly as it applies to the ordinary agency relationships discussed in Chapter 35. It follows the doctrine of *respondeat superior*.

At common law, a corporation could not be held liable for a crime, particularly one that required intent. However, under modern criminal law, a corporation can sometimes be held liable for the criminal acts of its agents and employees, provided the punishment can be applied to the corporation.[5]

CORPORATE MANAGEMENT

Shareholders

Shareholder Powers Shareholders must approve fundamental changes affecting the corporation before the changes can be effected. Hence, shareholders are empowered to amend the articles of incorporation (charter) and bylaws, approve merger or dissolution of the corporation, and approve the sale of all or substantially all of the corporation's assets. Some of these powers are subject to prior board approval.

5. Obviously, a corporation cannot be imprisoned; however, it can be fined and possibly dissolved.

Election and removal of the board of directors are accomplished by vote of the shareholders. The first board of directors is either named in the articles of incorporation or chosen by the incorporators to serve until the first shareholders' meeting. From that time on, selection and retention of directors are exclusively a shareholder function.

Directors usually serve their full term. If they are unsatisfactory, they are simply not reelected.

Shareholders have the inherent power to remove a director from office *for cause* (breach of duty or misconduct) by a majority vote.[6] Some state statutes permit removal of directors without cause by the vote of a majority of the holders of outstanding shares entitled to vote.[7] Some corporate charters expressly provide that shareholders, by majority vote or larger than majority vote, can remove a director at any time *without cause.*

---

6. A director can often demand court review of removal for cause.

7. Most states allow cumulative voting for directors. In states in which voting for directors is by cumulative ballot, a director cannot be removed without cause over the negative vote

that would be sufficient to elect that director in the first place. See, for example, California Corporate Code, Section 303A. Also see Section 39 of the Model Code. (Cumulative voting is discussed later in this chapter.)

GRACE v. GRACE
INSTITUTE
Court of Appeals of New York,
1967.
19 N.Y.2d 307, 279 N.Y.S.2d
721, 226 N.E.2d 531.

BACKGROUND AND FACTS   *The Grace Institute was incorporated by an act of the legislature of the state of New York to provide women with instruction in the trades and occupations and in branches of domestic arts and sciences. The corporation was formed under the general corporation law of New York. Three members of the Grace family and their successors were named original life members of the board of trustees. All the powers and privileges of the corporation were to be exercised by these three life members together with such other persons as they might select to be trustees.*

The plaintiff in this action, Michael P. Grace II, was a successor to one of the original life members and, by virtue of that position, became a member of the board of trustees of the institute. During his tenure in office, he brought several lawsuits against the institute, all of which he lost. As a result of these unsuccessful lawsuits, certain charges were drawn up against him, and a hearing was held. Thereafter, he was removed as a trustee and life member of the Grace Institute, despite the fact that no provision in the incorporating statute or the bylaws of the corporation related to the removal of a life member.

KEATING, Judge.

*   *   *   *

The law is settled that a corporation possesses the inherent power to remove a member, officer or director for cause, regardless of the presence of a provision in the charter or by-laws providing for such removal.

The question with which we are presented in this case is whether there exists any triable issues relating to the manner in which this petitioner was removed from his position as a life member and trustee.

It has been the consistent policy of the courts of this State to avoid interference with the internal management and operation of corporations. Although we are dealing here with a charitable corporation over which the Supreme Court is vested with supervisory powers, the Legislature in creating it set up a governing board of trustees and vested in them the power and authority necessary for the management and operation of the Institute. That body, after hearings and deliberation, has decided that the petitioner's conduct was so inimical to the corporate interests as to require his removal. In reaching that conclusion, the trustees had before them evidence of a series of lawsuits commenced by the petitioner against the corporation in each of which he was unsuccessful and in none of which did any of the 13 jurists who took part find even so much as a single triable issue.

After reviewing each of these actions and after studying the entire record in this case, we have reached the conclusion that the evidence clearly supported the finding of the trustees that Michael had embarked on a course of conduct designed to involve the Institute in endless and costly litigation and that the suits were undertaken for the purpose of harassing the Institute and its members. Under these circumstances, courts should not substitute their judgment for the judgment of those charged by the Legislature with the responsibility of running the corporation and seeing to it that it fulfills the purposes for which it was created.

In addition, we have examined the procedure by which the petitioner was removed and we have concluded there is no question but that he was given a reasonable opportunity to be heard and to answer the charges leveled against him. At the hearing during which the charges were aired, he was represented by three attorneys and a law assistant. His attorneys were permitted to cross-examine one of the parties who had been instrumental in preparing the charges against Michael and they could have exercised their right to examine others. Yet despite this opportunity to be heard and to present evidence, Michael never took the stand and never even attempted to answer the charges. The objections of Michael to the hearing we find to be without merit. The things to which he objects in no way detracted from his opportunity to be heard or the validity of his removal.

Michael argues, however, that the position of life member was created by the Legislature and "only the Legislature has the power to change the rights and privileges specifically granted by the act of incorporation." Michael obviously misapprehends the nature of the rights and privileges accorded to him. The Legislature surely could not have intended that a life member retain his position regardless of the manner in which he acted and regardless of the manner in which he abused his trust. The petitioner may not be removed so long as he adheres to what must be regarded as an implied condition of his position—that is so long as he faithfully serves the Institute. Once he breaches that condition and engages in activities that obstruct and interfere with the operation of the corporation and the purposes for which the Legislature created it, he may be removed.

The New York Court of Appeals reached the conclusion that Michael P. Grace II had been rightfully removed from his position as a life member and trustee of the Grace Institute.	**JUDGMENT AND REMEDY**

The Relationship between the Shareholder and the Corporation

As a general rule, shareholders have no responsibility for the daily management of the corporation, but they are ultimately responsible for choosing the board of directors, which does have such control. Ordinarily, corporate officers and other employees owe no direct duty to individual stockholders. Their duty is to the corporation as a whole. However, a director is in a fiduciary relationship to the corporation and therefore serves the interests of the shareholders as a whole.

Generally, there is no legal relationship between shareholders and creditors of the corporation. Shareholders can, in fact, be creditors of the corporation and have the same rights of recovery against the corporation as any other creditor. The rights and liabilities of shareholders are discussed in Chapter 43.

Shareholders' Forum Shareholders' meetings occur annually, but special meetings can be called to take care of urgent matters. Since it is usually not practical for owners of only a few shares of stock of publicly traded corporations to attend the shareholders' meetings, they normally give third persons a written authorization to vote their shares at the meeting. This authorization, called a *proxy*, is often solicited by management.

Shareholders in a corporation enjoy both common law and statutory inspection rights. Shareholders at common law enjoyed qualified rights to inspect corporate books and records, such as the bylaws and minutes of the board of directors' meetings and the shareholders' meetings, as well as documents such as contracts, correspondence, and tax returns. They even had the right to inspect the corporate headquarters.

The shareholders' common law inspection rights exist concurrently with any rights created by statute. However, corporate statutes do not usually deal with the shareholders' right to inspect the minutes of the board of directors' meetings or shareholders' meetings, the bylaws, or other records. The shareholders' common law right of inspection operates in these cases.

Notice of Meetings The notice and time of meetings, including the day and the hour, is announced in writing to each shareholder a reasonable time prior to the date of the shareholders' meeting.[8] Special meeting notices must include a statement of the purpose of the meeting;

business transacted at a special meeting is limited to that purpose.

Shareholder Voting In order for shareholders to act, a minimum number of them (in terms of number of shares held) must be present at a meeting. This minimum number, called a *quorum*, is generally more than 50 percent. Corporate business matters are presented in the form of *resolutions*, which shareholders vote to approve or disapprove. Some state statutes have set forth voting limits, and corporations' articles or bylaws must remain within the statutory limitations. Some states provide that the unanimous written consent of shareholders is a permissible alternative to holding a shareholders' meeting.

Once a quorum is present, a majority vote of the shares represented at the meeting is usually required to pass resolutions. Assume that Midwestern Supply, Inc., has 10,000 outstanding shares of voting stock. Its articles set the quorum at 50 percent of outstanding shares and provide that a majority vote of shares present is necessary to pass on ordinary matters. At the shareholders' meeting, a *quorum* of stockholders representing 5,000 outstanding shares must be present to conduct business, and a *vote* of at least 2,501 of those shares represented at the meeting is needed to pass ordinary resolutions. If more than 5,000 are present, a larger vote will be needed.

At times, a larger than majority vote will be required either by statute or by corporation charter. Extraordinary corporate matters such as merger, consolidation, or dissolution of the corporation will require a higher percentage of the representatives of *all* corporate stock shares entitled to vote, not just a majority of those present at that particular meeting.

Voting Lists Voting lists are prepared by the corporation prior to each shareholders' meeting. Persons whose names appear on the corporation's stockholder records as the record owners of the shares are the persons ordinarily entitled to vote.[9] The voting list contains the name

---

8. The shareholder can waive the requirement of written notice by signing a waiver form. A shareholder who did not receive written notice, but who learned of the meeting and attended without protesting the lack of notice, is said to have waived notice by such conduct. State statutes and the bylaws typically set forth a minimum allowance notice requirement.

9. Where the legal owner is deceased, bankrupt, incompetent, or in some other way under a legal disability, his or her vote can be cast by a person designated by law to control and manage the owner's property.

and address of each shareholder as shown on the corporate records on a given cutoff date (record date). It also includes the number of voting shares held by each owner. The list is usually kept at the corporate headquarters and is available for shareholder inspection.

Voting Techniques   Most states permit or require shareholders to elect directors by *cumulative voting*, a method of voting designed to allow minority representation on the board of directors.[10] Cumulative voting operates as follows: The number of members of the board to be elected is multiplied by the total number of voting shares held. The result equals the number of votes a shareholder has, and this total can be cast for one or more nominees for director. All nominees stand for election at the same time. Where cumulative voting is not required either by statute or under the articles, the entire board can be elected by a majority of shares at a shareholders' meeting.

To illustrate: A corporation has 10,000 shares issued and outstanding. The minority shareholders hold only 3,000 shares. Three members of the board are to be elected. The majority shareholders' nominees are Able, Baker, and Carter. The minority shareholders' nominee is Diamond. Can Diamond be elected by the minority shareholders?

If cumulative voting is allowed, the answer is yes. The minority shareholders have 9,000 votes among them (number of directors to be elected times number of shares equals $3 \times 3,000$, which equals 9,000 votes). All of these votes can be cast to elect Diamond. The majority shareholders have 21,000 votes, but these votes have to be distributed among their three nominees. Thus, mathematically, it is impossible for the majority shareholders to keep Diamond off the board.

Shareholder Agreements   A group of shareholders can agree in writing prior to the meeting to vote their shares together in a specified manner. Voting agreements are usually held valid and enforceable.

Proxy Voting   A shareholder can appoint a voting agent. A proxy is a written authorization to cast the shareholder's vote, and a person can solicit proxies from a number of shareholders in an attempt to concentrate voting power.

Voting Trust   Shareholders can enter an agreement (a trust contract) whereby legal title (record ownership on the corporate books) is transferred to a trustee who is responsible for voting the shares. The agreement can specify how the trustee is to vote, or it can allow the trustee to use his or her discretion. The trustee takes physical possession of the actual stock certificate and in return gives the shareholder a *voting trust certificate*. The shareholder retains all rights of ownership (for example, the right to receive dividend payments) except the power to vote.

A voting trust is not the same thing as a proxy, for the latter can be revoked more easily. The holder of a proxy has neither legal title to the stock nor possession of the certificates, but voting trustees have both.[11]

CORPORATE MANAGEMENT

Directors

Position   Every corporation is governed by directors. Subject to statutory limitations, the number of directors is set forth in the corporation's articles or bylaws. Historically, the minimum number of directors has been three, but today many states permit fewer.

Few qualifications are legally required of directors. Only a handful of states retain minimum age and residency requirements. A director is sometimes a shareholder, but this is not a necessary qualification unless, of course, statutory provisions, corporate articles, or bylaws require ownership.

Compensation for directors is ordinarily specified in the corporate articles or bylaws. Because directors have a *fiduciary* relationship to

---

10.   See, for example, the California Corporate Code, Section 708.

11.   Under Section 34 of the Model Act, the term of a voting trust cannot exceed ten years.

the shareholders and to the corporation, an express agreement or provision for compensation is necessary for them to receive money from the funds they control or for which they have responsibilities.

The first board of directors is normally appointed by the incorporators upon the creation of the corporation, or directors are named by the corporation itself in the articles. The first board serves until the first annual shareholders' meeting. Subsequent directors are elected by majority vote of the shareholders.

The term of office for a director is one year—from annual meeting to annual meeting. Longer and staggered terms are permissible under most state statutes. A board of directors can be divided into categories. A common practice is to have three classes, so that one-third of the board is elected each year for a three-year term. In this way, there is greater management continuity.

A director can be removed *for cause,* either as specified in the articles or bylaws or by shareholder action. Even the board of directors itself may be given power to remove a director for cause, subject to shareholder review. Unless the shareholders have reserved the right at the time of election, a director cannot be removed without cause.

When vacancies occur on the board of directors due to death or resignation, or when a new position is created through amendment of the articles or bylaws, either the shareholders or the board itself can fill the position, depending on state law or the provisions of the bylaws.

Management Responsibilities Directors have responsibility for all policymaking decisions necessary to the management of all corporate affairs. Just as shareholders cannot act individually to bind the corporation, the directors must act as a body in carrying out routine corporate business. One director has one vote, and generally the majority rules.

The general areas of responsibility of the board of directors include:

1. Declaration and payment of corporate dividends to shareholders.
2. Authorization for major corporate policy decisions—for example, the initiation of proceedings for the sale or lease of corporate assets outside the regular course of business, the determination of new product lines, and the overseeing of major contract negotiations and major management-labor negotiations.
3. Appointment, supervision and removal of corporate officers and other managerial employees and the determination of their compensation.
4. Financial decisions involving such things as the issuance of authorized shares or bonds.

Directors' Liability Honest mistakes of judgment and poor business actions on the part of the directors do not make them liable to the corporation for damages sustained. After all, directors are not insurers of the business success of the corporation. Usually, the business judgment rule applies to the actions of directors. In general, this rule sustains corporate transactions and immunizes management (the directors) from liability where the transaction is within the powers of the corporation and within the authority of management, as long as that transaction involves the exercise of due care and compliance with the duties of management.

Of course, directors must be loyal, honest, and reasonably careful at all times. If directors (and their officers) hire employees carefully, they are not personally liable for the willful wrongs and negligent acts of such employees; rather, the corporation is liable.

However, when a director neither attends board meetings nor examines records and books, he or she can be held liable for losses resulting from unsupervised acts of officers and employees. Also, when directors (and officers) allow the assets of the corporation to be diverted to objectives outside the charter or statutory powers, they may be held liable for damages to the corporation, to a trustee appointed for the corporation, or to the shareholders in a derivative suit.

The Board of Directors' Forum The board of directors conducts business by holding formal meetings with recorded minutes.[12] The date upon

---

12. Some states, such as Michigan and Texas (and the Model Code, Section 43), now have a corporate statute authorizing conference phone calls for board of directors' meetings.

which regular meetings are held is usually established in the articles and bylaws or by board resolution, and no further notice is customarily required. Special meetings can be called with notice sent to all directors.

Quorum requirements can vary among jurisdictions. Many states leave the decision to the corporate articles or bylaws. In absence thereof, most states provide that a quorum is a majority of the number of directors authorized in the articles or bylaws. Voting is done *in person* (unlike voting at shareholders' meetings, which can be done by proxy).[13] The rule is one vote per director. Ordinary matters generally require a majority vote; certain extraordinary issues can require a larger than majority vote.

Delegation of Board of Directors' Powers   The board of directors can delegate some of its functions to an executive committee or to corporate officers. In doing so, the board does not avoid its responsibility for directing the affairs of the corporation. Rather, the daily responsibilities of corporate management are given over to corporate officers and managerial personnel, who are empowered to make decisions relating to *ordinary corporate affairs* within *well-defined guidelines.*

Executive Committee   Most states permit the board of directors to elect an executive committee from among the directors to handle the interim management decisions between board of directors' meetings, as provided in the bylaws. The *executive committee* is limited to making management decisions about ordinary business matters.

Corporate Officers   The officers and other executive employees are hired by the board of directors or, in rare instances, by the shareholders. In addition to the duties that are articulated in the bylaws, corporate and managerial officers are agents of the corporation, and the ordinary rules of agency apply or have been applied to their employment (unlike the board of directors, whose powers are conferred by the state).

---

13.   Except in Louisiana, where a director can vote by proxy under certain circumstances.

Qualifications are determined, in the main, at the discretion of the corporation and are included in the articles or bylaws. In most states, a person can hold more than one office and can be both an officer and director of the corporation. Corporate officers can be removed by the board of directors at any time with or without cause and regardless of the terms of the employment contract, although the corporation can still be liable for breach of contract damages.

QUESTIONS AND CASE PROBLEMS

1.   The board of directors of Able, Inc., has to decide whether or not to make the following three transactions, none of which is expressly covered in the articles or bylaws of the corporation: a charitable gift of $100,000 to a private university noted for education of minority students, a secured loan of corporate surplus funds at a high interest rate, and an extension of credit to another corporation that Able owns shares in. Discuss whether Able, Inc., through action by its board, has authority and power to make the above transactions.

2.   Baker, Inc., was formed for the purpose of drilling and servicing water wells. This purpose is specifically stated in its articles of incorporation. One year after formation of the corporation, the board of directors entered into a contract with an independent oil driller, Thomas, to purchase and market all the oil Thomas produced from his wells during a five-year period. The contract has been performed for two years, and Baker has expended corporate funds to set up storage and marketing facilities. Thomas now refuses to sell any more oil to Baker, claiming the corporation contracted outside its powers. Discuss this claim.

3.   Ann owns ten shares of Monmouth Corporation. Monmouth Corporation has 100,000 outstanding issued common shares. Ann believes that many decisions of the board of directors do not consider the preservation of the environment. Two pending proposals approved by the board deal with the purchase of timberland for conversion into condominiums. Both proposals require amending the corporate charter and thus need a two-thirds shareholder vote. Ann knows

other shareholders who she believes would oppose these proposals. Unfortunately, most shareholders live a considerable distance from the site of the shareholders' meeting and will be unable to attend. Discuss any techniques Ann can use to oppose these proposals.

4. Carter Corporation has issued and has outstanding 100,000 shares of common stock. Four stockholders own 60,000 of these shares, and for the past six years they have nominated a slate of people for membership on the board, all of whom get elected. John and twenty other shareholders, owning 20,000 shares, are dissatisfied with corporate management and want a representative on the board who shares their views. Explain under what circumstances John and the minority shareholders can elect their representative to the board.

5. Kathy is elected to the board of directors of a corporation. The board consists of nine members. The articles and bylaws are silent as to what constitutes a quorum. The bylaws do permit the board itself, by majority vote, to elect board members to fill vacancies created by death or resignation. The bylaws also require majority votes for ordinary corporate decisions made at regular corporate board meetings. Just prior to a regular meeting, a board member dies. At the scheduled regular meeting is a proposal that Kathy opposes. She cannot attend the meeting and sends her proxy. The meeting takes place with five members in attendance. By a vote of three to two, John is elected to fill the board vacancy, and the proposal is passed. Kathy's proxy is declared invalid by the chairman of the board. Kathy challenges both votes. Discuss whether her challenges will be successful.

6. A stockholder learned that the corporation had paid over $11 million in kickbacks and bribes. The board of directors investigated the allegations and determined that they were true but decided not to file suit. The directors decided the corporation's actions were excused by the business judgment doctrine (or rule). The stockholder then brought a derivative suit. The directors maintained that the business judgment doctrine was a complete defense to their payment of bribes and sought immediate dismissal of the suit. Is the business judgment doctrine a complete defense to this type of corporate activity? [Auerbach v. Bennett, 64 A.D.2d 98, 408 N.Y.S.2d 83 (1978)]

7. Free For All Missionary Baptist Church, Inc., by and through its pastors (who were also its president and secretary), leased from Southeastern Beverage and Ice Equipment Company, Inc., certain liquor dispensary equipment for use in an establishment known as

Soul On Top of Peachtree. The church made an initial payment of $1,575 and then defaulted on the monthly rental payments. Southeastern brought suit against the church corporation, seeking damages for the balance of the lease. The shareholders of the church corporation defended on the ground that the action by its president and secretary and by the church were all *ultra vires*. Is this a valid defense? [Free For All Missionary Baptist Church, Inc. v. Southeastern Beverage and Ice Equipment Co., Inc., 135 Ga.App. 498, 218 S.E.2d 169 (1975)]

8. The capital stock of G.S.P. Corporation was owned by Plodzik, Ricketts, and Westbury, who were also the sole directors of the corporation. In 1965 Plodzik and Ricketts agreed to sell their company to Star Corporation. Since Plodzik and Ricketts constituted two-thirds of the shareholders of G.S.P. Corporation, as well as a majority of the board of directors, they took this action without consulting Westbury. Have Plodzik and Ricketts exceeded their authority? [Star Corp. v. General Screw Products Co., 501 S.W.2d 374 (Tex.Civ.App.1973)]

9. Harris Lumber Company was a corporation organized under the law of the state of Arkansas. Harris was the president of the corporation; Nelson was its secretary and treasurer; and Jones was its remaining director and shareholder. Several years after its incorporation, Harris Lumber owed Merchants and Farmers Bank $4,500. A promissory note was executed for the amount of the debt, and a mortgage was executed on certain personal property owned by Harris Lumber to secure payment. Nelson, who at the time was general manager of Harris Lumber, signed both the note and the mortgage. Payments amounting to $2,150 were made over the next two-and-one-half years on the promissory note. At that point payment ceased, and Merchants Bank brought this suit to recover the balance of the sum owed. Harris Lumber Company never objected to the execution of the mortgage or the note or to any of the payments under the note until Merchants Bank filed this suit. However, at that point, Harris Lumber claimed that Nelson did not have the authority to sign promissory notes or to execute mortgages on behalf of Harris Lumber. In fact, neither the corporate charter nor any of the board of directors' resolutions vested the general manager with any authority to bind the corporation. Will Merchants Bank be successful in its suit against Harris Lumber Company? [Merchants and Farmers Bank v. Harris Lumber Co., 103 Ark. 283, 146 S.W. 508 (1912)]

<h1 style="text-align:center">CHAPTER 43</h1>

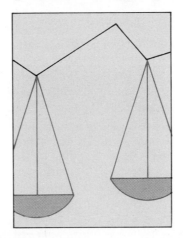

CORPORATIONS
Rights and Duties of Directors, Managers, and Shareholders

A corporation combines the efforts and resources of a large number of individuals to jointly produce greater returns than those individuals could obtain outside the corporation. Sometimes actions that benefit the corporation as a whole do not coincide with the interests of these individuals. This chapter focuses on the rights and duties of directors, managers, and shareholders and the resolution of conflicts among them.

THE ROLE OF OFFICERS AND DIRECTORS

Directors occupy a position of responsibility unlike that of other corporate personnel. Directors are sometimes inappropriately characterized as *agents* because they act for and on behalf of the corporation. However, no individual director can act as an agent to bind the corporation, and, as a group, directors collectively control the corporation in a way no agent can control a principal. Directors are often incorrectly characterized as *trustees* because they occupy positions of trust and control over the corporation. However, unlike trustees, they do not own or hold title to property for the use and benefit of others.

Directors manage the corporation through the officers who are selected by the board; these officers are agents of the corporation. Directors and officers are deemed *fiduciaries* of the corporation. Their relationship with the corporation and its shareholders is one of trust and confidence. The fiduciary duties of the directors and officers include the duty of care and the duty of loyalty.

The Duty of Care

Directors are obligated to be honest and to use prudent business judgment in the conduct of corporate affairs. The so-called business judgment rule does not require directors to ensure the success of every venture that the corporation undertakes. The test is objective—the directors must exercise the same degree of care that reasonably prudent people use in the conduct of their own personal business affairs. Thus, corporate losses resulting merely from poor business judgment or an honest mistake of judgment will not normally result in the imposition of legal liability on directors.

Breach of the Duty of Care Directors can be held answerable to the corporation and to the shareholders for breach of their duty of care. When directors delegate work to corporate officers and employees, they are expected to use a reasonable amount of supervision. Otherwise, they will be held liable for *negligence* or *mismanagement* of corporate personnel.

For example, a corporate bank director failed to attend any board of directors' meetings in five and a half years and never inspected any of the corporate books or records. Meanwhile, the bank president made various improper loans and permitted large overdrafts. The corporate director was held liable to the corporation for losses of nearly $20,000 resulting from the unsupervised actions of the bank president and the loan committee.

The standard of due care has been variously described and codified in many corporation codes.[1] The impact of the standard is to require that directors carry out their responsibilities in an informed, businesslike manner.

Depending on the nature of the business, directors and officers are often expected to act in accordance with their own knowledge and training. However, most states (and Section 35 of the Model Act) allow a director to make decisions in reliance on information furnished by competent officers or employees, professionals such as attorneys and accountants, or even an executive committee of the board, without being ac-

cused of acting in bad faith or failing to exercise due care if such information turns out to be faulty.

Directors are expected to attend board of directors' meetings, and their votes should be entered into the minutes of corporate meetings. Unless a dissent is entered, the director is presumed to have assented. Directors who dissent rarely are held individually liable for mismanagement of the corporation. It is for this reason that a director who is absent from a given meeting sometimes registers with the secretary of the board a dissent to actions taken at the missed meeting with which he or she disagrees.

Directors are expected to be informed on corporate matters and to understand legal and other professional advice rendered to the board. A director who is unable to carry out such responsibilities must resign. Even when the required duty of care has not been exercised, directors and officers are liable only for the damages caused to the corporation by their negligence.

Duty of Loyalty

Perhaps the best way to describe the concept of loyalty is by a definition given by Justice Cardozo:

> Many forms of conduct permissible in a workaday world for those acting at arm's length, are forbidden to those bound by fiduciary ties. Not honesty alone, but the punctilio of an honor the most sensitive, is then the standard of behavior. As to this there has developed a tradition that is unbending and inveterate.[2]

The essence of the fiduciary duty requires subordination of self-interest to the interest of the entity to which the duty is owed. It presumes constant loyalty to the corporation on the part of the directors and officers. In general, the duty of loyalty prohibits directors from using corporate funds or confidential corporate information for personal advantage. It requires officers and directors to fully disclose any corporate opportunity or any possible conflict of interest that

---

1. See, for example, Section 35 of the Model Business Corporation Act, which provides that "a director shall perform his duties as a director, including his duties as a member of any committee of the board upon which he may serve, in good faith, in any manner he reasonably believes to be in the best interest of the corporation, and with such care as an ordinarily prudent person in a like position would use under similar circumstances."

---

2. Meinhard v. Salmon, 249 N.Y. 458, 464, 164 N.E. 545, 546 (1928).

might occur in a transaction involving the directors and the corporation.

Cases dealing with fiduciary duty typically involve one or more of the following:

1. Competing with the corporation.
2. Usurping a corporate opportunity.
3. Having an interest that conflicts with the interest of the corporation.
4. Engaging in insider trading.

5. Authorizing some corporate transaction that is detrimental to minority shareholders.
6. Sale of control of the corporation.

In the following case, the Alabama court reviewed a situation in which officers, directors, and shareholders attempted to secure advantages for themselves at the expense of the corporation.

BACKGROUND AND FACTS   *The defendants, Morad and Thomson, were officers, directors, and shareholders of Bio-Lab, Inc. Bio-Lab had one additional shareholder, the plaintiff, Coupounas. While serving as officers and directors of Bio-Lab, the defendants incorporated and operated a competing business, Med-Lab, Inc. The plaintiff brought a derivative suit on behalf of Bio-Lab against the defendants and Med-Lab, alleging that, in opening the competing business, they had usurped a corporate opportunity of Bio-Lab.*

MORAD v. COUPOUNAS

Supreme Court of Alabama, 1978.
361 So.2d 6.

FAULKNER, Justice.

*   *   *   *

"It is well settled that directors and other governing members of a corporation are so far agents of the corporation that in their dealings respecting corporate interests, they are subject to the rules which apply generally to persons standing in fiduciary relations and which forbid such persons to secure an advantage for themselves which fidelity to the trust reposed in them would carry to others whose interests they ought to represent."

*   *   *   *

"[I]n general the legal restrictions which rest upon such officers in their acquisitions are generally limited to property wherein the corporation has an interest already existing, or in which it has an expectancy growing out of an existing right, or to cases where the officers' interference will in some degree balk the corporation in effecting the purposes of its creation." *   *   *

"[I]f there is presented to a corporate officer or director a business opportunity which the corporation is financially able to undertake, is, from its nature, in the line of the corporation's business and is of practical advantage to it, is one in which the corporation has an interest or a reasonable expectancy, and, by embracing the opportunity, the self-interest of the officer or director will be brought into conflict with that of his corporation, the law will not permit him to seize the opportunity for himself." *   *   *

"[N]umerous factors are to be weighed, including the manner in which the offer was communicated to the officer; the good faith of the officer; the use of corporate assets to acquire the opportunity; the financial ability of the corporation to acquire the opportunity; the degree of disclosure made to the corporation; the action taken by the corporation with reference thereto; and the need or interest of the corporation in the opportunity. These, as well as numerous other factors, are weighed in a given case. The presence or absence of any single factor is not determinative of the issue of corporate opportunity." * * *

Here the trial court specifically found that one of the corporate purposes of Bio-Lab was to expand into specific new areas, including Tuscaloosa. Ample evidence in the record supports this conclusion. Bio-Lab's certificate of incorporation declared that one of the purposes of the business was "to have one or more offices." * * *

* * * *

* * * [T]estimony revealed that $44,000 had been required to establish Med-Lab. At the end of 1974 Bio-Lab had only $24,300 available for this purpose. But, Raburn [a certified public accountant, familiar with the books of both Med-Lab and Bio-Lab] also testified that in 1974 Bio-Lab had paid a "rather high" dividend of $20,000. His testimony indicated that the payment of dividends is often restricted when a corporation wishes to expand. Thus, if the dividend had not been paid, Bio-Lab clearly should have had the financial ability to expand to Tuscaloosa, with or without a loan. In light of this testimony the trial court's finding that defendants improperly formed Med-Lab to the detriment of Bio-Lab is clearly supportable and will not be disturbed by this Court on appeal.

JUDGMENT AND REMEDY   *The Alabama Supreme Court determined that the appropriate remedy for the defendants' breach of duty of loyalty was for the court to impose a "constructive trust," which would require all profits of Med-Lab to be paid to Bio-Lab.*

COMMENTS   *Directors and officers of a corporation are expected to act with undivided loyalty. This rule restricts them from competing with the corporation, and, at the very least, it requires fiduciaries to offer business opportunities to the corporation.*

Conflicts of Interest

Corporate directors often have many business affiliations, and they can even sit on the board of more than one corporation. Of course, they are precluded from entering into or supporting any business that operates in direct competition with the corporation. The fiduciary duty requires them to make full disclosure of any potential *conflicts of interest* that might arise in any corporate transaction.

Contracts between Director and Corporation

Sometimes the corporation will enter into a contract or engage in a transaction in which an officer or director has a material interest. The director

or officer must make full disclosure of that interest and should abstain from voting on the proposed transaction.

For example, Pacific Business Corporation needs office space. Louis Allen, one of its five directors, owns the building adjoining the corporation. He negotiates a lease with Pacific Business for the space, making full disclosure to Pacific Business and the other four board directors. The lease arrangement is fair and reasonable, and it is unanimously approved by the corporation's board of directors. In such a case, the contract is valid. The rule is one of reason; otherwise, directors would be prevented from ever giving financial assistance to the corporations they serve.

The various state statutes contain different standards, but a contract will generally not be voidable if:

1. It was fair and reasonable to the corporation at the time it was entered into.

2. There is full disclosure of the interest of the officers or directors in the transaction.

3. The contract is approved by a majority of the disinterested directors or shareholders.

(See Section 41 of the Model Business Corporation Act.)

Contracts between Corporations Having Common Directors

Often contracts are negotiated between corporations having one or more directors who are members of both boards. Such transactions require great care. They are closely scrutinized by courts.

RIGHTS OF DIRECTORS

Right of Participation

A corporate director must have certain rights in order to function properly in that position. The main right is to be notified of board of directors' meetings, so as to participate in them. As pointed out in Chapter 42, regular board meetings are usually established by the bylaws or board resolution, and no notice of these meetings is required. If special meetings are called, however, notice is required unless waived by the director.

Right of Inspection

A director must have access to all corporate books and records in order to make decisions and exercise the necessary supervision. This right is virtually absolute and cannot be restricted.

Right of Indemnification

It is not unusual for corporate directors to become involved in lawsuits by virtue of their position and their actions as directors. Most states (and the Model Act, Section 5) permit a corporation to indemnify a director for legal costs, fees, and judgments involved in defending corporation-related suits.

At common law, a director had no right to be indemnified; however, there was little objection to indemnification if the director was absolved of liability. Today statutes and court decisions allow indemnification even if the director is not absolved of liability, as long as his or her actions were made in good faith, based on a reasonable belief that such actions were in the best interests of the corporation.

Criminal convictions usually require bad faith, but bad faith is not presumed merely because the director settles the litigation, pleads *nolo contendere* (no contest), or even is found liable civilly. Many states specifically permit a corporation to purchase liability insurance for the directors and officers to cover indemnification. Where the statutes are silent on this matter, the power to purchase such insurance is usually considered to be part of the corporation's implied power.

Right of Compensation

Historically, directors have had no inherent right to compensation for their services as directors. Officers receive compensation, and nominal sums are often paid as honoraria to directors. In many cases, directors are also chief corporate officers and receive compensation in their managerial positions. Most directors, however, gain through indirect benefits, such as business contacts, prestige, and other rewards.

There is a growing trend toward providing more than nominal compensation for directors, especially in large corporations where directorships can be enormous burdens in terms of time, work, effort, and risk. Many states permit the corporate articles or bylaws to authorize compensation for directors, and in some cases the board can set its own compensation unless the articles or bylaws provide otherwise.

DUTIES OF CORPORATE OFFICERS

The duties of corporate officers are the same as the duties of directors because their respective corporate positions involve both of them in decision making and place them in similar control positions. Hence, they are viewed as having the same fiduciary duty of care and loyalty in their conduct of corporate affairs. Officers are subject to the same obligations concerning corporate opportunities and conflicts of interest as are directors.

RIGHTS OF CORPORATE OFFICERS AND OTHER MANAGEMENT EMPLOYEES

Corporate officers and other high-level managers are employees of the company, and their rights are defined by employment contracts.

SHAREHOLDER RIGHTS

Shareholders own the corporation. Their rights are established in the articles of incorporation and under the state's general incorporation law.

The Right to a Stock Certificate

A stock certificate evidences ownership, and shareholders have the right to demand that the corporation issue a certificate and record their names and addresses in the corporate stock record books. Stock is *intangible* personal property—the ownership right exists independently of the certificate itself. A stock certificate may be lost or destroyed, but ownership is not destroyed with it. Corporate records reflect ownership but do not determine it.

A new certificate can be issued to replace one that has been lost or destroyed.[3] Notice of shareholder meetings, dividends, and operational and financial reports are all distributed according to the recorded ownership listed in the corporation's books, not on the basis of possession of the certificate.

Assume that Betty Anderson's corporate stock in Chrysler Corporation is destroyed in a fire on September 1. The corporation declares a dividend on September 5. According to corporate records, Betty Anderson is the "record owner" and receives the dividend even though she no longer has the certificate.

Of course, to sell or otherwise transfer the shares, indorsement and delivery of the actual certificate to the transferee are required.

Preemptive Rights

A **preemptive right** is a common law concept in which a preference is given to a shareholder over all other purchasers to subscribe to or purchase a prorated share of a new issue so the shareholder can maintain his or her portion of control, voting power, or financial interest in the corporation. Most statutes either grant preemptive rights but allow them to be negated in the corporation's articles or deny preemptive rights except to the extent that they are granted in the articles. The result is that the articles of incorporation determine the existence and scope of preemptive rights. Generally, preemptive rights apply only to additional stock sold for cash, not to treasury shares reissued, and generally such rights must be exercised within a specified time period (usually thirty days).

For example, Paula Smith purchases one hundred shares of National Clothing stock. National Clothing had authorized and issued one thousand shares, of which Paula now owns 10 percent. Subsequently, National Clothing, by vote of its shareholders, authorizes the issuance of another one thousand shares (amending the articles of incorporation). This increases its capital stock to a total of two thousand shares.

If preemptive rights have been provided, Smith can purchase one additional share of the new stock being issued for each share currently owned—or one hundred additional shares. Thus she can own two hundred of the two thousand shares outstanding, and her relative position as a shareholder will be maintained. If preemptive rights are not reserved, her proportionate control and voting power will be diluted from that of a 10 percent shareholder to that of a 5 percent shareholder because of the issuance of the additional one thousand shares.

---

3. To have a lost or destroyed certificate reissued, a shareholder is normally required to furnish an indemnity bond to protect the corporation against potential loss should the original certificate reappear at some future time in the hands of a bona fide purchaser. [UCC 8-302 and 8-405(2)]

Preemptive rights are far more significant in a close corporation because of the relatively few number of shares and the substantial interest each shareholder controls.

Stock Warrants

When preemptive rights exist and a corporation is issuing additional shares, each shareholder is usually given *stock warrants*. A **stock warrant** is a transferable option to acquire a given number of shares from the corporation at a stated price (usually below the current market price). Warrants are often publicly traded on securities exchanges. When the warrant option is for a short period of time, the stock warrants are usually referred to as *rights*.

Dividend Rights

A dividend is a distribution of corporate profits or income *ordered by the directors* and paid to the shareholders in proportion to their respective shares in the corporation. Dividends can be paid in cash, property, stock of the corporation that is paying the dividends, or stock of other corporations.[4]

State laws vary, but every state controls the general legal requirements under which dividends are paid. Once declared, a cash dividend becomes a corporate debt enforceable at law like any other debt.[5]

---

4. Technically, dividends paid in stock are not dividends. They maintain each shareholder's proportional interest in the corporation. On one occasion a distillery declared and paid a "dividend" in bonded whiskey.

5. State laws prescribe the circumstances under which dividends can be paid. An insolvent corporation cannot declare a dividend. State laws also control the sources of revenue to be used. Only certain funds are legally available for paying dividends.

Dividends payable from limited funds are prescribed by various state statutes as follows:

1. Current net earnings.
2. Net profits.
3. Surplus.

Dividends can be paid only from the following sources of funds:

1. *Retained earnings.* All states allow dividends to be paid from the undistributed net profits earned by the corporation, including capital gains from the sale of fixed assets. The undistributed net profits are called earned surplus or retained earnings.
2. *Net profits.* A few state statutes allow dividends to be issued from current net profits without regard to deficits in prior years.
3. *Surplus.* A number of state statutes allow dividends to be paid out of any kind of surplus.

When directors fail to declare a dividend, shareholders can ask a court of equity for an injunction to compel the directors to meet and to declare a dividend. It must be shown that the directors have acted so unreasonably in withholding the dividend that their conduct is an abuse of discretion.

Often large money reserves are accumulated for a bona fide purpose such as expansion, research, and other legitimate corporate goals. The mere fact that sufficient corporate earnings or surplus are available to pay a dividend is not enough to compel directors to distribute funds that, in the board's opinion, should not be paid. The courts are circumspect about interfering with corporate operations and will not compel directors to declare dividends unless abuse of discretion is clearly shown. Thus directors are not ordinarily required to declare dividends to shareholders. A striking exception to this rule is exemplified by the following classic case.

BACKGROUND AND FACTS   *Ford Motor Company was formed in 1903. Henry Ford, the president and majority shareholder, attempted to run the corporation as if it were a one-man operation. The business expanded rapidly and, in addition to regular quarterly dividends, often paid special dividends. Sales and profits were:*

DODGE v. FORD MOTOR CO.

Supreme Court of Michigan, 1919.

204 Mich. 459, 170 N.W. 668.

1910   18,664 cars $4,521,509 profit
1911   34,466 cars $6,275,031 profit
1912   68,544 cars $13,057,312 profit, $14,475,095 surplus
1913   168,304 cars $25,046,767 profit, $28,124,173 surplus
1914   248,307 cars $30,338,454 profit, $48,827,032 surplus
1915   264,351 cars $24,641,423 profit, $59,135,770 surplus

By 1916, surplus above capital was $111,960,907.

Originally, the Ford car sold for more than $900. From time to time, the price was reduced, and in 1916 it sold for $440. For the year beginning August 1, 1916, the price was reduced again, to $360. No special dividend was paid after October 1915 for reasons explained in the opinion that follows. The plaintiffs were minority stockholders, who owned one-tenth of the shares of the corporation. They petitioned the court to compel the directors to declare a dividend.

OSTRANDER, Chief Justice.

*   *   *   *

[I]t is charged that notwithstanding the earnings for the fiscal year ending July 31, 1916, the Ford Motor Company has not since that date declared any special dividends:

"And the said Henry Ford, president of the company, has declared it to be the settled policy of the company not to pay in the future any special dividends, but to put back into the business for the future all of the earnings of the company, other than the regular dividend of five per cent. (5%) monthly upon the authorized capital stock of the company—two million dollars ($2,000,000)."

This declaration of the future policy, it is charged in the bill, was published in the public press in the city of Detroit and throughout the United States in substantially the following language:

   " 'My ambition,' declared Mr. Ford, 'is to employ still more men; to spread the benefits of this industrial system to the greatest possible number, to help them build up their lives and their homes. To do this, we are putting the greatest share of our profits back into the business.' "

It is charged further that the said Henry Ford stated to plaintiffs personally, in substance, that as all the stockholders had received back in dividends more than they had invested they were not entitled to receive anything additional to the regular dividend of 5 per cent a month, and that it was not his policy to have larger dividends declared in the future, and that the profits and earnings of the company would be put back into the business for the purpose of extending its operations and increasing the number of its employes, and that, inasmuch as the profits were to be represented by investment in plants and capital investment, the stockholders would have no right to complain. *   *   *

*   *   *   *

"It is a well-recognized principle of law that the directors of a corporation, and they alone, have the power to declare a dividend of the earnings of the corporation, and to determine its amount. Courts of equity will not interfere in the management of the directors unless it is clearly made to appear that they are guilty of fraud or misappropriation of the corporate funds, or refuse to declare a dividend when the corporation has a surplus of net profits which it can, without detriment to its business, divide among its stockholders, and when a refusal to do so would amount to such an abuse of discretion as would constitute a fraud, or breach of that good faith which they are bound to exercise towards the stockholders."

* * * *

There is committed to the discretion of directors, a discretion to be exercised in good faith, the infinite details of business, including the wages which shall be paid to employes, the number of hours they shall work, the conditions under which labor shall be carried on, and the price for which products shall be offered to the public.

* * * [I]t is not within the lawful powers of a board of directors to shape and conduct the affairs of a corporation for the merely incidental benefit of shareholders and for the primary purpose of benefiting others, and no one will contend that, if the avowed purpose of the defendant directors was to sacrifice the interests of shareholders, it would not be the duty of the courts to interfere.

* * * *

Defendants say, and it is true, that a considerable cash balance must be at all times carried by such a concern. But, as has been stated, there was a large daily, weekly, monthly, receipt of cash. The output was practically continuous and was continuously, and within a few days, turned into cash. Moreover, the contemplated expenditures were not to be immediately made. The large sum appropriated for the smelter plant was payable over a considerable period of time. *So that, without going further, it would appear that, accepting and approving the plan of the directors, it was their duty to distribute on or near the 1st of August, 1916, a very large sum of money to stockholders.* [Emphasis added.]

In reaching this conclusion, we do not ignore, but recognize, the validity of the proposition that plaintiffs have from the beginning profited by, if they have not lately, officially, participated in, the general policy of expansion pursued by this corporation. We do not lose sight of the fact that it had been, upon an occasion, agreeable to the plaintiffs to increase the capital stock to $100,000,000 by a stock dividend of $98,000,000. These things go only to answer other contentions now made by plaintiffs, and do not and cannot operate to estop them to demand proper dividends upon the stock they own. It is obvious that an annual dividend of 60 per cent upon $2,000,000, or $1,200,000, is the equivalent of a very small dividend upon $100,000,000, or more.

The defendant, Ford, was ordered by the court to declare a dividend.   **JUDGMENT AND REMEDY**

Right to Vote

Shareholders exercise ownership control through the power of their vote. In the early development of corporate law, each shareholder was entitled to one vote per share. This rule still holds today, but the voting techniques discussed in Chapter 42 (pooling agreements, voting trusts, cumulative voting methods, and so on) all enhance the power of the shareholder's vote.

The articles can exclude or limit voting rights, particularly to certain classes of shares. For example, owners of preferred shares are usually denied the right to vote. Treasury shares, held by the corporation, cannot be voted until they have been reissued by the corporation.

Inspection Rights

Shareholders have the right to inspect and copy

certain corporate books and records for any *proper purpose*, provided they make the request in advance. Either the shareholder can inspect in person, or an attorney, agent, accountant, or other assistant can do so.

The power of inspection is fraught with potential abuses, and the corporation is allowed to protect itself from them. For example, a shareholder can properly be denied access to corporate records to prevent harassment or to protect trade secrets or other confidential corporate information. Section 52 of the Model Act imposes various standard requirements on the shareholder's inspection right:

> Any person who shall have been a holder of record shares * * * at least six months imme-

diately preceding his [or her] demand or [who is] * * * the holder of * * * at least 5 percent of all the outstanding shares of the corporation, upon written demand stating the purpose thereof, shall have the right to examine, in person, or by agent or attorney, at any reasonable time or times, for any purpose its relevant books and records of accounts, minutes, and record of shareholders and to make extracts therefrom.

However, a corporation's improper refusal to allow access to its records can result in severe and costly liability to the corporation. Under Section 52 of the Model Act, the penalty is 10 percent of the value of the shares owned by the shareholder who has been denied access to the books.

SKOURAS v. ADMIRALTY ENTERPRISES, INC.

Court of Chancery
of Delaware,
1978.
386 A.2d 674.

BACKGROUND AND FACTS *The plaintiff, Skouras, was the holder of 2,871 shares (between 4 and 5 percent) of common stock of a closely held family corporation. The plaintiff demanded to inspect the corporate books and records so he could substantiate his fears of mismanagement and his fears that certain corporate acts that were detrimental to the corporation were occurring. Admiralty Enterprises, the defendant corporation, contended that the plaintiff's purpose was merely to harass the corporation and to attempt to force it to offer to buy out the plaintiff's shares at a premium price. The court, however, was persuaded that the plaintiff had acted in good faith and had established a proper purpose for demanding the right of inspection.*

MARVEL, Chancellor.

* * * *

A proper purpose is defined in 8 Del.C. Section 220 as one which is "* * * reasonably related to such person's interest as a stockholder * * *", and it is clearly proper for a stockholder to ask leave to examine corporate books and records to follow up his suspicions of corporate mismanagement, thereby acting not only on his own behalf but on that of the corporation and its other stockholders. * * * [A]lthough the Court cannot, of course, read the thoughts of a stockholder, it must be satisfied that a plaintiff has successfully carried the burden of proving that the purpose behind his demand is proper. Once a proper purpose is established, it becomes irrelevant that the stockholder may have a secondary and perhaps questionable ulterior purpose behind his primary purpose.

A further qualification as to the right of inspection of books and records is that even if a proper purpose for a demand is demonstrated and such demand is shown to be reasonably related to a plaintiff's interest as a stockholder, nonetheless such demand must not be for a purpose adverse to the best interests of the corporation.

Whether or not a plaintiff is entitled to inspection of corporate books and records depends on whether or not a clear indication of wrong-doing on the part of corporate mismanagement [sic] has been established clearly as a result of a trial. Here plaintiff places great emphasis on the fact that Admiralty appears to be in a precarious financial condition, and at trial plaintiff sought to establish the existence of a number of improper transactions on the part of corporate management, including the making of loans by Admiralty not only of money but of stock for the personal benefit of directors, the improper purchase of stock from directors, and the payment of salaries to family members who performed little or no services for Admiralty or its affiliates. *   *   *

Plaintiff concedes that many of the practices complained of have an ostensible business purpose but contends that the apparent precariousness of defendant's financial affairs coupled with its refusal to supply plaintiff with any information relating to the matters as to which he seeks to be informed clearly support the propriety of plaintiff's demand. *   *   *

*   *   *   *

Although it is clear that plaintiff has acted impetuously insofar as the affairs of Admiralty are concerned and could well have been less extravagant in his written complaints about Admiralty, I am satisfied that his basic purpose, in embarking on his present project, has its roots in his concern over the activities of and problems facing Admiralty rather than by a design merely to harass. Thus, letters put in evidence disclose that plaintiff as a minority stockholder was convinced that serious damage is being and has been inflicted upon the corporation by incumbent management. In short, a careful reading of the letters which are the basis of defendant's charge of harassment discloses that plaintiff was in fact seeking to rally support to his battle against what he believed to be corporate acts detrimental to Admiralty and consequently to himself as a minority stockholder of such corporation.

*   *   *   *

Finally, defendant is concerned that plaintiff may use information acquired by him as a result of an inspection of Admiralty's books and records for the purpose of doing harm to Admiralty rather than for his own benefit. However, as stated in 5 Fletcher Cyc. Corporations, Section 2275 (Perm. Ed. 1972) "[i]t is clearly the rule of the cases discussing it that the mere possibility of such abuse or misuse is not grounds for any withholding or restriction of the right [of inspection]."

The present record does not, in my opinion, support defendant's present fears that confidential corporate matters will be divulged as a result of the inspection here granted. Plaintiff assured the Court at trial that he would not use any knowledge he might gain, were inspection to be granted, to defendant's detriment. However, upon a showing that plaintiff has breached his commitment and indeed duty not to harm his corporation by improperly using the knowledge gained from the inspection hereby granted, appropriate relief may be sought.

The chancery court ordered that the plaintiff be granted the right to inspect certain books and records as requested.   **JUDGMENT AND REMEDY**

Right to Transfer Shares

Corporate stock represents an ownership right in intangible personal property. The law generally recognizes the right of an owner to transfer property to another person unless there are valid restrictions on its transferability. Although stock certificates are negotiable instruments and freely transferable by indorsement and delivery, transfer of stock in closely held corporations is generally restricted by contract, the bylaws, or a restriction stamped on the stock certificate. The existence of any restrictions on transferability should always be noted on the face of the stock certificate, and these restrictions must be reasonable.

Right of First Refusal   Sometimes corporations or their shareholders restrict transferability by reserving the option to purchase any shares offered for resale by a shareholder. The option remains with the corporation or the shareholders for only a specified or reasonable time. Variations on the purchase option are possible. For example, a shareholder might be required to offer the shares to other shareholders or to the corporation first.

Corporate Records   When shares are transferred, a new entry is made in the corporate stock book to indicate the new owner. Until the corporation is notified and the entry is complete, voting rights, notice of shareholders' meetings, dividend distribution, and so forth are all held by the current record owner.

Rights upon Dissolution

When a corporation is dissolved and its outstanding debts and the claims of its creditors have been satisfied, the remaining assets are distributed pro rata among the shareholders. Certain classes of preferred stock can be given priority to the extent of their contractual preference. If no preferences to distribution of assets upon liquidation are given to any class of stock, then the stockholders share the remaining assets.

Compelling Receivership   Suppose a minority shareholder knows that the board of directors is mishandling corporate assets or is permitting a deadlock to threaten or irreparably injure the corporation's finances. The minority shareholder is not powerless to intervene. He or she can petition a court to appoint a receiver and to liquidate the business assets of the corporation.

The Model Act, Section 97, permits any shareholder to institute such an action when it appears that:

1.   The directors are deadlocked in the management of corporate affairs, shareholders are unable to break that deadlock, and irreparable injury to the corporation is being suffered or threatened.
2.   The acts of the directors or those in control of the corporation are illegal, oppressive, or fraudulent.
3.   Corporate assets are being misapplied or wasted.

SHAREHOLDER LIABILITIES

One of the hallmarks of the corporate organization is that shareholders are not personally liable for the debts of the corporation. If the corporation fails, shareholders can lose their investment, but that is generally the limit of their liability. In certain instances of fraud, undercapitalization, or careless observance of corporate formalities, a court will pierce the corporate veil (disregard the corporate entity) and hold the shareholders individually liable. But these situations are the exception, not the rule.

Although rare, there are three additional situations in which a shareholder can be personally liable. They are:

1.   Stock subscriptions.
2.   Watered stock issued.
3.   Illegal dividends.

Stock Subscriptions

A preincorporation stock subscription agreement is treated as a continuing offer, and it is usually irrevocable (for up to six months under the Model Act). Once the corporation has been formed, it can sell shares to shareholder investors. In either case, once the subscription agreement or stock offer is accepted, a binding contract is formed. Any refusal to pay constitutes a breach resulting in the personal liability of the shareholder.

Watered Shares

Shares of stock can be paid for by property or by services rendered, instead of cash. The general rule is that for par value shares sold, the corporation must receive a value at least equal to the par value amount. For any no par shares sold, the corporation must receive the value of the shares as determined by the board or shareholders. When shares are issued by the corporation for less than these stated values, the shares are referred to as **watered stock.** In most cases, the shareholder who receives watered stock must pay the difference to the corporation (the shareholder is personally liable). In some states, the shareholder who receives watered stock may be liable to creditors of the corporation for unpaid corporate debts.

Illegal Dividends

Whenever a dividend is paid while the corporation is *insolvent,* it is automatically an illegal dividend, and shareholders can be liable for returning the payment to the corporation or its creditors.

Dividends are generally required by statute to be distributed only from certain authorized corporate accounts representing profits. Sometimes dividends are improperly paid from an unauthorized account, or their payment causes the corporation to become insolvent. Generally, shareholders must return illegal dividends only if they knew that the dividends were illegal when they received them.

In all cases of illegal and improper dividends, the board of directors can be held personally liable for the amount of the payment. However, when directors can show that a shareholder *knew* a dividend was illegal when it was received, the directors are entitled to contribution from the shareholder.

DUTIES AND LIABILITIES OF MAJOR SHAREHOLDERS

In some cases, a majority shareholder is regarded as having a fiduciary duty to the corporation and to the minority shareholders. This occurs when a single shareholder (or a few acting in concert) owns a sufficient number of shares to exercise *de facto* control over the corporation.

QUESTIONS AND CASE PROBLEMS

1. Acme Corporation negotiates with the Jones Construction Company for the renovation of the Acme corporate headquarters. Jones, owner of the Jones Construction Company, is also one of the five members of the board of directors of Acme. The contract terms are standard for this type of contract. Jones had previously informed two of the other directors of his interest in the construction company. The contract was approved by Acme's board on a three-to-two vote, with Jones voting with the majority. Discuss whether this contract is binding on the corporation.

2. Acme, Inc., has a board of directors consisting of three members (Able, Baker, and Carter) and approximately five hundred shareholders. At a regular meeting of the board, the board selects Green as president of the corporation by a two-to-one vote, with Able dissenting. The minutes of the meeting do not register Able's dissenting vote. Later, upon an audit, it is discovered that Green is a former convict and has openly embezzled $500,000 from Acme, Inc. This loss is not covered by insurance. The corporation wants to hold directors Able, Baker, and Carter liable. Able claims no liability. Discuss the personal liability of the directors to the corporation.

3. Ann owns 10,000 shares (10 percent) of Superal Corporation. Superal authorized 100,000 shares and issued all of them during its first six months in operation. Later Superal reacquired 10,000 of these shares. With shareholder approval, Superal amended its articles so as to authorize and issue another 100,000 shares, and, also, by a resolution of the board of directors, to reissue the 10,000 shares of treasury stock. There is no provision in the corporate articles dealing with shareholder preemptive rights. Because of her previous ownership of 10 percent of Superal, Ann claims that she has the preemptive right to purchase 10,000 shares of the new issue and 1,000 shares of the stock being reissued. Discuss her claims.

4. Jane has acquired one share of common stock of a multimillion-dollar corporation with over 500,000 shareholders. Jane's ownership is so small that she is questioning what her rights are as a shareholder. For example, she wants to know whether this one share entitles her to:

(a) Attend and vote at shareholder meetings.

(b) Inspect the corporate books.

(c) Receive yearly dividends.

Discuss Jane's rights in these three matters.

5. Smith has made a preincorporation subscription agreement to purchase 500 shares of a newly formed corporation. The shares have a par value of $100 per share. The corporation is formed, and Smith's subscription is accepted by the corporation. Smith transfers a piece of land he owns to the corporation, and the corporation issues 250 shares for it. One year later, with the corporation in serious financial difficulty, the board declares and pays a $5 per share dividend. It is now learned that the land transferred by Smith had a market value of $18,000. Discuss any liability shareholder Smith has to the corporation or to creditors of the corporation.

6. Grant and Martin were directors of Lincoln Stores, Inc. Both had worked for Lincoln Stores in other capacities—as store manager and as general manager, respectively. Hayley was one of the managers of the very successful Lincoln store that was located in Norwich, Connecticut. The Reid and Hughes Company owned a store several buildings down from the Lincoln store in Norwich. Reid and Hughes presented little competition to Lincoln.

On April 27 Grant, Martin, and Hayley agreed to purchase the Reid and Hughes store, and Hayley resigned from Lincoln's employ to take charge of it. Before he left, however, Hayley obtained certain confidential information that he later used to assist him in setting up operations at the Reid and Hughes store. Grant and Martin, desiring to continue in Lincoln's employ, concealed their ownership of the new store and continued as directors at Lincoln. Thereafter, the Reid and Hughes store became quite successful and competitive with Lincoln. Lincoln Stores then sued Grant, Martin, and Hayley for their breach of loyalty. Should it recover? If so, what should Lincoln be awarded as damages: lost profits? ownership of the competing store? [Lincoln Stores v. Grant, 309 Mass. 417, 34 N.E.2d 704 (1941)]

7. Engdahl was a 10 percent stockholder, a director, and the treasurer of Aero Drapery, Inc. In May of 1967 several Aero employees expressed to Engdahl their dissatisfaction with their employment with Aero. Later that month, at Engdahl's suggestion, Engdahl met with the employees and suggested that they join together and form a new enterprise. In early June, they decided to go into the custom-drapery business in direct competition with Aero. Later that month the new business associates decided upon a location for the new business, contacted suppliers, and secured an advertisement in the Yellow Pages. In July 1967, Engdahl tendered his resignation as director and treasurer of Aero Drapery, Inc. Has Engdahl breached any duty to Aero Drapery, Inc.? Would your answer be different if Engdahl had resigned early in May of 1967? (What additional fact do you need to know to answer the latter question?) [Aero Drapery of Kentucky, Inc. v. Engdahl, 507 S.W.2d 166 (Ky.App.1974)]

8. Hartung, Odle, and Burke were architects. In 1971 they organized as a corporation. Their association, however, was riddled with dissent from the start. As it became apparent that the corporate turmoil would eventually result in reorganization of the corporation, Hartung began conferring with several clients of the firm, informing them that he was willing to continue as their architect after his withdrawal from the corporation. The corporation was later dissolved, and several of its clients continued to do business with Hartung. Do Odle and Burke have any recourse against Hartung for his activities? [Hartung v. Architects Hartung/Odle/Burke, Inc., 157 Ind.App. 546, 301 N.E.2d 240 (1973)]

9. Atlantic Properties, Inc., had only four shareholders, each of whom owned 25 percent of the capital stock. The bylaws required an 80 percent affirmative vote of the shareholders on all actions taken by the corporation. This provision had the effect of giving any of the four original shareholders a veto in corporate decisions. One shareholder refused for seven years to vote for any dividends, although he was warned that his actions might expose the corporation to Internal Revenue penalties for unreasonable accumulation of corporate earnings and profits. The Internal Revenue Service did impose such penalties on the corporation. Can the dissenting shareholder be held personally liable for these penalties? [Smith v. Atlantic Properties, Inc., Mass. App. 1981, 422 N.E.2d 798]

CHAPTER 44

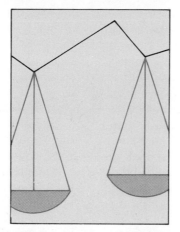

CORPORATIONS
Merger, Consolidation and Termination

Corporations increase their holdings for a number of reasons. They may wish to enlarge their physical plants, increase their property or investment holdings, or acquire the assets, know-how, or goodwill of another corporation. Sometimes acquisition is motivated by a desire to eliminate a competitor, to accomplish diversification, or to ensure adequate resources and markets for the acquiring corporation's product. Whatever the reason, the corporation typically extends its operations by combining with another corporation through:

1. Merger.
2. Consolidation.
3. Purchase of assets.
4. Purchase of a controlling interest of the other corporation.

This chapter will examine the various ways that merger or consolidation alters the fundamental structure of the corporation. The terms *merger* and *consolidation* are often used interchangeably, but they refer to two legally distinct proceedings. Whether a combination is in fact a merger or a consolidation, the rights and liabilities of shareholders, the corporation, and its creditors are the same.

Dissolution and liquidation are the combined processes by which a corporation terminates its existence. The last part of this chapter will discuss the typical reasons and methods for terminating a corporation.

MERGERS AND CONSOLIDATION

Mergers

A **merger** involves the legal combination of two or more corporations. After a merger, only one of the corporations continues to exist. For example, Corporation A and Corporation B decide to merge. It is agreed that A will absorb B, so upon merger, B ceases to exist as a separate entity and A continues as the *surviving corporation.*

A merger can be represented symbolically as A + B = A. After the merger, A is recognized as a single corporation, possessing all the rights, privileges, and powers of itself and B. A automatically acquires all of B's property and assets without the necessity of formal transfer or deed. A becomes liable for all B's debts and obligations. Finally, A's articles of incorporation are deemed *amended* to include any changes that are stated in the *articles of merger.*

Consolidation

In the case of a **consolidation,** two or more corporations combine so that each corporation ceases to exist and a new one emerges. Corporation A and Corporation B consolidate to form an entirely new organization, Corporation C. In the process, A and B both terminate. C comes into existence as an entirely new entity.

A symbolic representation of consolidation, then, is A + B = C. The results of consolidation are essentially the same as the results of merger. C is recognized as a new corporation and a single entity; A and B cease to exist. C accedes to all the rights, privileges, and powers previously held by A and B. Title to any property and assets owned by A and B passes to C without formal transfer. C assumes liability for all debts and obligations owed by A and B. The articles of consolidation *take the place of* A's and B's original corporate articles and are thereafter regarded as C's corporate articles.

When a merger or consolidation takes place, the surviving corporation or newly formed corporation will issue shares or pay some fair consideration to the shareholders of the corporation that ceases to exist.

In a merger, the surviving corporation is vested with the disappearing corporation's preexisting legal rights and obligations. For example, if the disappearing corporation had a right of action against a third party, after the merger, the surviving corporation could then bring suit to recover the disappearing corporation's damages.

The corporation statutes of many states, as illustrated in the following case, provide that a successor (surviving) corporation inherits a *chose in action* (a right to sue for a debt or sum of money) from a merging corporation as a matter of law. So, too, the common law rule recognizes that a chose in action to enforce a property right upon merger will vest with the successor (surviving) corporation, and no right of action will remain with the disappearing corporation.

SUN PIPE LINE CO. v. ALTES

United States Court of Appeals, Eighth Circuit, 1975. 511 F.2d 280.

BACKGROUND AND FACTS *Sun Pipe Line Company (Sun), merged with OMR, Inc., in August 1972. Sun, the plaintiff in this case, was the surviving corporation. As part of the merger agreement, Sun succeeded to all of OMR's rights and liabilities. State law provided that surviving corporations were entitled to maintain legal actions for damages based on the disappearing corporation's rights and liabilities.*

The disappearing corporation, OMR, acquired a right-of-way to lay pipeline across certain property. The property was subsequently sold to the defendant, Altes. At the time he purchased the land in early 1972, Altes knew that there was an easement for the pipeline across it and that the pipeline did in fact exist.

Altes owned and operated a rock quarrying and landfill business which was conducted on the parcel of property in question. The operations consisted of removing rock from below the surface, crushing it, selling it, and then filling the excavation with trash and covering it with soil. Defendant Altes warned his workers not to conduct the quarrying operation in the area where the pipeline was buried. Nonetheless, on March 16, 1972, one of his employees did operate a front end loader in the vicinity of the pipeline and while digging into the soil, he punctured it. A considerable amount of gasoline being pumped at high pressure escaped through the hole, and the pipeline had to be shut down for repairs. There was no question that Altes's employee had been negligent and that this negligence was attributable to Altes.

. At the time of the break in the pipeline, it was owned by OMR, but this litigation was initiated by Sun Pipe Line Company (the plaintiff) after its merger with OMR in August 1972.

The trial court refused to instruct the jury that Sun Pipe Line Company had the right, under state law, to bring this lawsuit. The jury was never instructed as to the law of merger. Instead, the trial judge merely told the members of the jury that it was up to them to determine the effect of the merger.

ROSS, Circuit Judge.

Sun Pipe Line Company (Sun), a Pennsylvania corporation with its principal place of business in Oklahoma, brought this diversity action against Robert Altes, a resident of Arkansas, seeking to recover in excess of $35,000 for damages incurred when one of Altes' employees, while operating an earth moving machine, punctured a pipeline [now] owned by Sun. After a trial in the district court the jury returned a verdict for defendant Altes, and judgment was entered accordingly. Sun appeals, alleging that the court erred in *   *   * refusing to instruct the jury that Sun had the right to bring this action. *   *   *
*   *   *   *

[The] issue which developed at trial was whether Sun had a right to prosecute the action. It was revealed that at the time of the break the pipeline was owned by OMR, Inc., a successor firm to Oklahoma Mississippi River Products, Inc., but that the litigation was initiated by Sun after its merger with OMR in August, 1972, in which Sun was the surviving corporation. Evidence was received on this issue, including the articles of merger.

Since the issue of Sun's right to bring the action had been injected into the trial, Sun requested that the district judge instruct the jury that, in accordance with the merger agreement between Sun and OMR, Sun succeeded to all of OMR's rights and liabilities and was entitled to maintain an action for damages against Altes. The court refused to give this instruction.

During his closing argument Altes' attorney argued to the effect that, since OMR owned the pipeline at the time of the accident, Sun had failed to prove that it had sustained any damages. When Sun objected to this line of argument on the ground that it had the right to bring suit for damages to OMR as a matter of law, the trial judge merely told the jury that it is "for you to determine the effect of the merger." Altes' counsel continued to argue that Sun had sustained no damages.

The instruction requested by Sun was not given and neither was the jury informed as to the law of merger. On the other hand, the jury was told that, before it could award damages to Sun, it must find that Sun had sustained damages. Thus, the jury was left in the position of determining whether Sun could recover for damages to OMR. This was error.

Fed.R.Civ.P. 17(b) states that "[t]he capacity of a corporation to sue or be sued shall be determined by the law under which it was organized." Sun is a Pennsylvania corporation, so the law of that state determines whether it can sue to recover premerger damages to OMR.

Pa.Stat.Ann. tit. 15, § 1907 (1974 Supp.) deals with the effect of a merger or consolidation of corporations and provides:

All the property, real, personal, and mixed and franchises of each of the corporations parties to the plan of merger or consolidation, *and all debts due on whatever account to any of them, including subscriptions to shares and other choses in action belonging to any of them,* shall be taken and deemed to be transferred to and vested in the surviving or new corporation, as the case may be, without further act or deed. (Court's emphasis.)

This statute makes it explicitly clear that Sun, the surviving corporation, was vested with OMR's chose in action against Altes and could bring this lawsuit to recover for OMR's damages. In addition, we note that the merger agreement itself conformed to the Pennsylvania statute by providing that Sun would be vested with "all property, real, personal and mixed, and all debts due to each" of the corporations.

Finally, this Court has stated that statutes, such as Pennsylvania's, which provide that a successor corporation inherits a chose in action from a merging corporation as a matter of law merely serve to codify the common law rule "which recognizes that a chose in action to enforce a property right upon merger vests in the successor corporation and no right of action remains in the merging corporation."

In light of this well settled statutory and common law rule, the trial court should have given Sun's requested instruction. The effect of the court's instructions combined with the argument of Altes' attorney was to leave this question of law to the unfettered and unguided discretion of the jury, and this constituted prejudicial error.

JUDGMENT AND REMEDY   *The circuit court reversed the district court ruling and held that the lower court erred in refusing to instruct the jury that, as a matter of law, Sun had the right to bring the suit. The case was returned to the trial court for further proceedings consistent with the principle of law that the surviving corporation inherits any claims for damages belonging to the disappearing corporation.*

The Procedure

All states have statutes authorizing mergers and consolidations for *domestic* corporations, and most allow the combination of domestic (in-state) and foreign (out-of-state) corporations. Although the procedures vary somewhat among jurisdictions, they all contain the basic requirements outlined below:

1. The board of directors of *each* corporation involved must approve a merger or consolidation plan.

2. The shareholders of *each* corporation must vote approval of the plan at a shareholders' meeting. Most state statutes require approval of two-thirds of the outstanding shares of voting stock, although some states require only a simple majority and others require a four-fifths vote. Frequently, statutes require that each class of stock approve the merger; thus, the holders of non-voting stock must also approve.

3. Once approved by *all* the boards of directors and the shareholders, the plan (articles of merger or consolidation) is filed, usually with the secretary of state.

4. When state formalities are satisfied, the state issues a certificate of merger to the surviving corporation or a certificate of consolidation to the newly consolidated corporation.

Short-Form Merger Statutes (or Parent-Subsidy Mergers)

The Model Act in most states provides a simplified procedure for the merger of a substantially owned subsidiary corporation into its parent corporation. Under these provisions, a **short-form merger** can be accomplished *without approval of the shareholders* of either corporation.

The short-form merger can be utilized only when the parent corporation owns 90 to 95 percent of the outstanding shares of each class of stock of the subsidiary corporation. The simplified procedure requires that a plan for the merger be approved by the board of directors of the parent corporation before it is filed with the state. Minority shareholders (those other than the parent corporation) must be given prior notice of the merger.

Appraisal Rights

What if a shareholder disapproves of the merger or consolidation, but is outvoted by the other shareholders? The law recognizes that a dissenting shareholder should not be forced to become an unwilling shareholder in a corporation that is new or different from the one in which the shareholder originally invested. The shareholder has the right to dissent and may be entitled to be paid fair value for the number of shares held on the date of the merger or consolidation.

This right is referred to as the shareholder's **appraisal right.** An appraisal right is given by state statute. It is available only when the statute specifically provides for it. It may be lost if the elaborate statutory procedures are not precisely followed. Whenever the right is lost, the dissenting shareholder must go along with the objectionable transaction.

The appraisal right is normally extended to regular mergers, short-form mergers, sales of substantially all the corporate assets not in the ordinary course of business, and, in certain states, adverse amendments to the articles of incorporation.

One of the basic procedures usually requires that a written notice of dissent be filed by the dissenting shareholder prior to the vote of the shareholders on the proposed transaction. In addition, after approval the dissenting shareholders must make a written demand for payment.

Valuation of shares is often a point of contention between the dissenting shareholder and the corporation. The Model Act, Section 81, provides that the "fair value of shares" is the value on the day prior to the date on which the vote was taken.[1] The corporation must make a *written* offer to purchase a dissenting shareholder's stock, accompanying the offer with a current balance sheet and income statement for the applicable (appropriate) corporation. If the shareholder and the corporation do not agree on the fair value, a court will determine it.

Shareholder Approval

Shareholders invest in a corporate enterprise with the expectation that the board of directors will manage the enterprise and will approve ordinary business matters. Actions taken on extraordinary matters must be authorized by the board of directors and the shareholders. Often modern statutes will require that certain types of extraordinary matters be approved by a prescribed voter consent of the shareholders. Typically, matters requiring shareholder approval include sale, lease, or exchange of all or substantially all corporate assets outside of the corporation's regular course of business. Other examples include amendments to the articles of incorporation, transactions concerning merger or consolidation, and dissolution.

Hence, when any extraordinary matter arises, the corporation must proceed as authorized by law to obtain shareholder and board of director approval. Sometimes a transaction can be char-

---

1. Section 81 of the Model Act provides for excluding any appreciation or depreciation of the stock in anticipation of the approval.

acterized in such a way as not to require shareholder approval, but a court will use its equity powers to require such approval. In order to determine the nature of the transaction, the courts will look not only to the details of the transaction but also to its consequences. In the following case, a "reorganization agreement" seemed to be a guise for a merger.

FARRIS v. GLEN ALDEN CORP.

Supreme Court of Pennsylvania, 1958.

393 Pa. 427, 143 A.2d 25.

BACKGROUND AND FACTS *The plaintiff, Farris, a shareholder, filed suit to enjoin the corporation and its officers from carrying out a reorganization agreement that would, in effect, transform Glen Alden Corporation, a coal mining company, into a diversified holding company with interests in motion pictures, textile companies, and other industries.*

At a shareholders' meeting, the shareholders approved the reorganization agreement. The plaintiff contended that approval by the shareholders at the annual meeting was invalid because the true intent and purpose of the reorganization was to effect a merger between Glen Alden, the defendant, and another corporation. Had the reorganization been a true merger, the shareholders of both corporations would have been entitled to appraisal rights, and management would have been forced to buy out dissenting shareholders. Instead the agreement provided for a backward reorganization. Glen Alden, the smaller company, purchased the assets of the List Corporation, the larger company, in exchange for a large amount of Glen Alden stock. If Glen Alden had been the selling corporation, Pennsylvania law would have afforded Glen Alden shareholders appraisal rights. Farris, a Glen Alden shareholder, objected and claimed to be entitled to appraisal rights because the transfer was a de facto merger.

COHEN, Justice.

We are required to determine on this appeal whether, as a result of a "Reorganization Agreement" executed by the officers of Glen Alden Corporation and List Industries Corporation, and approved by the shareholders of the former company, the rights and remedies of a dissenting shareholder accrue to the plaintiff.

Glen Alden is a Pennsylvania corporation engaged principally in the mining of anthracite coal and lately in the manufacture of air conditioning units and firefighting equipment. In recent years the company's operating revenue has declined substantially, and in fact, its coal operations have resulted in tax loss carryovers of approximately $14,000,000. In October 1957, List, a Delaware holding company owning interests in motion picture theaters, textile companies and real estate, and to a lesser extent, in oil and gas operations, warehouses and aluminum piston manufacturing, purchased through a wholly owned subsidiary 38.5% of Glen Alden's outstanding stock. This acquisition enabled List to place three of its directors on the Glen Alden board.

* * * *

Two days after the agreement was executed notice of the annual meeting of Glen Alden to be held on April 11, 1958, was mailed to the shareholders together with a proxy statement analyzing the reorganization agreement and recommending its approval as well as approval of certain amendments to Glen Alden's articles of incorporation and bylaws necessary to implement the agreement. At this meeting the holders of a majority of the outstanding shares, (not including those owned by List) voted in favor of a resolution approving the reorganization agreement.

On the day of the shareholders' meeting, plaintiff, a shareholder of Glen Alden, filed a complaint in equity against the corporation and its officers seeking to enjoin them temporarily until final hearing, and perpetually thereafter, from executing and carrying out the agreement.

The gravamen of the complaint was that the notice of the annual shareholders' meeting did not conform to the requirements of the Business Corporation Law, 15 P.S. § 2852-1 et seq., in three respects: (1) It did not give notice to the shareholders that the true intent and purpose of the meeting was to effect a merger or consolidation of Glen Alden and List; (2) It failed to give notice to the shareholders of their right to dissent to the plan of merger or consolidation and claim fair value for their shares, and (3) It did not contain copies of the text of certain sections of the Business Corporation Law as required.

By reason of these omissions, plaintiff contended that the approval of the reorganization agreement by the shareholders at the annual meeting was invalid and unless the carrying out of the plan were enjoined, he would suffer irreparable loss by being deprived of substantial property rights.

*   *   *   *

When use of the corporate form of business organization first became widespread, it was relatively easy for courts to define a "merger" or a "sale of assets" and to label a particular transaction as one or the other. But prompted by the desire to avoid the impact of adverse, and to obtain the benefits of favorable, government regulations, particularly federal tax laws, new accounting and legal techniques were developed by lawyers and accountants which interwove the elements characteristic of each, thereby creating hybrid forms of corporate amalgamation. Thus, it is no longer helpful to consider an individual transaction in the abstract and solely by reference to the various elements therein determine whether it is a "merger" or a "sale". Instead, to determine properly the nature of a corporate transaction, we must refer not only to all the provisions of the agreement, but also the consequences of the transaction and to the purposes of the provisions of the corporation law said to be applicable. We shall apply this principle to the instant case.

*   *   *   *

We hold that the combination contemplated by the reorganization agreement, although consummated by contract rather than in accordance with the statutory procedure, is a merger within the protective purview of the corporation law. The shareholders of Glen Alden should have been notified accordingly and advised of their statutory rights of dissent and appraisal. The failure of the corporate officers to take these steps renders the stockholder approval of the agreement at the 1958 shareholders' meeting invalid. The lower court did not err in enjoining the officers and directors of Glen Alden from carrying out this agreement.

The appellate court held that the shareholders were entitled to appraisal rights.   **JUDGMENT AND REMEDY**

Purchase of Assets

When a corporation acquires all or substantially all of the assets of another corporation by direct purchase, the purchasing or *acquiring* corporation simply extends its ownership and control over more physical assets. Since no change in the legal entity occurs, the *acquiring corporation* is not required to obtain shareholder approval for the purchase.[2]

Although the acquiring corporation may not be required to obtain shareholder approval for such an acquisition, the Department of Justice has issued guidelines that significantly constrain and often prohibit mergers that could result from a purchase of assets, including takeover bids. These guidelines are part of the federal antitrust laws to enforce Section 7 of the Clayton Act (discussed in Chapters 50 and 51).

Note that the corporation that is *selling* all its assets is substantially changing its business position and perhaps its ability to carry out its corporate purposes. For that reason, the corporation whose assets are *acquired* must obtain both board of director and shareholder approval. In some states, a dissenting shareholder of the selling corporation can demand appraisal rights, as discussed in the following case.

---

2. If the acquiring corporation plans to pay for the assets with its own corporate stock and not enough authorized unissued shares are available, the shareholders must vote to approve issuance of additional shares by amendment of the corporate articles. Also, acquiring corporations whose stock is traded in a national stock exchange can be required to obtain their own shareholders' approval if they plan to issue a significant number of shares, such as 20 percent or more of the outstanding shares.

CAMPBELL v. VOSE
United States Court of Appeals,
Tenth Circuit, 1975.
515 F.2d 256.

BACKGROUND AND FACTS   *This lawsuit was brought by a minority stockholder, Campbell, as a stockholder's derivative suit to assert his right as a dissenting shareholder when the defendant corporation sold substantially all its assets to a wholly owned subsidiary. The plaintiff argued that he was entitled to shareholder appraisal rights under the Oklahoma statutes. The trial court entered a judgment adverse to the plaintiff.*

SETH, Circuit Judge.

*   *   *   *

The *   *   * Cause of Action in the complaint is directed to the rights of minority stockholders when the corporation is "reorganized" or when it sells "all" or "substantially all" of its assets. A remedy is provided in such circumstances by [Oklahoma statutes]. The trial court concluded as a matter of law that the creation of a wholly owned subsidiary corporation, and the transfer to it of the land and plant of the Cotton Oil Company without a stockholders' vote, was not an event under Oklahoma law which would give rise to rights in the dissenting stockholders to have their shares redeemed.

This issue of dissenters' rights was advanced by the plaintiff by asserting that the creation of the subsidiary with the transfer of assets to it by the Cotton Oil Company was a "sale, lease, exchange or other disposition of all or substantially all of its assets," as contemplated in [Oklahoma laws]. This [law] requires shareholder approval of such a transaction, and *   *   * creates rights in the minority stockholders who do not consent.

The figures used by the trial court and in the corporate balance sheet at the time of transfer show that about one-third of all corporate assets were transferred to the subsidiary in exchange for stock and for debentures. The record shows that the land, buildings, machinery, inventory, and all tangibles of the company were transferred. The assets retained were bank balances, promissory notes, and the investment portfolio, consisting of common stocks. Thus all the operating property and tangibles that remained of the old Cotton Oil business were transferred. The surpluses and accumulated earnings were retained as represented in the investments and bank accounts. The record shows that the tangibles were instrumental in creating the current income of the corporation which had been a problem to management. This was removed by the transfer and the creation of the debt.

The appellees argue that the transfer was not a "sale" as urged by appellant. Appellees state in their brief that since the transferee was a wholly-owned subsidiary, the parent corporation still had enough "control" over the assets to prevent the transaction from being a sale. Thus the appellees in their brief say:

"In this case, the property which was transferred is still subject to the Company's use, possession and control since Machine Works is a wholly owned subsidiary of the Company."

It is difficult to see how there could be any real corporate entity for the subsidiary for any purpose if the assets transferred are in the present corporation's "possession," and within its control. *   *   * [W]e assume on the basis of the trial court's findings, *   *   * [that] the parent divested itself of possession and title to the assets, and placed them in the possession and control of the subsidiary. Thus it looks more like a sale or "other disposition" under the statute than anything else. An exchange for stock and for evidence of indebtedness was made, and the indicia of ownership were held by the subsidiary. We must hold that the transaction did bring into play the statutory rights of dissenting shareholders, contrary to the trial court's conclusion.

The "all" or "substantially all" of the assets presents another issue, and is also a condition which must exist before the statute comes into play. The statute is in purely quantitive terms, but the appellant urges that other considerations exist because the assets transferred were all the "operating assets," and only money or investments remained. The record shows that the Cotton Oil Company had engaged in dual activities for several years, the plant operations (storage and machine shops) on one hand, and investments of the accumulated earnings on the other hand.

In the corporate resolution relating to the transfer, the recitation is made that the desire was to separate the "operating business activities from its investment activities." About this time, the Cotton Oil Company was changed into a personal holding company for tax purposes. The time that this took place is not clear from the record, but it was apparently related to the need for corporate changes to meet the problems arising from the accumulation of income. Such a change was substantial. Thus the corporate changes surrounding the creation of the subsidiary, the separation of the business activities with the result that the parent corporation has only investments, makes the transfer of assets have much different implications than it would ordinarily have. There is also the accompanying problem that really no values were established relating to the same standard, or related to current conditions. The consequences of the creation of the subsidiary discussed above with the fact all operating assets were transferred to it, together with the debt back makes the transaction a sale and results in a situation where for all practical purposes, "substantially" all of the assets were sold. All the effective operating assets were sold. The investment segment remaining was large in dollars but was the last and a large step in the change in the nature of corporate activity. In these circumstances, more than dollar values must be considered. It was another significant step also in the prevention of current income which was another aspect of the change in corporate purpose. *The transaction was thus one which required consideration by the stockholders, and gives rise to the rights of dissenting shareholders under the Oklahoma statutes.* [Emphasis added.]

JUDGMENT AND REMEDY *The appellate court ruled that this transaction was a sale of corporate assets that required shareholder approval and created appraisal rights in minority stockholders who did not consent.*

Purchase of Stock

An alternative to the purchase of another corporation's assets is the purchase of a substantial number of the voting shares of its stock. This enables the acquiring corporation to control the acquired, or *target*, corporation. The acquiring corporation deals directly with the shareholders in seeking to purchase the shares they hold.

A so-called "take-over bid" is subject to state and federal securities regulations. When the acquiring corporation makes a public offer to all shareholders of the target corporation, it is called a *tender offer* (an offer that is publicly advertised and addressed to all shareholders of the would-be target company). The price of the stock in the tender offer is generally higher than the market price of the target stock prior to the announcement of the tender offer. The higher price induces shareholders to tender their shares to the acquiring firm.

The tender offer can be conditional upon the receipt of a specified number of outstanding shares by a specified date. The offering corporation can make an *exchange* tender offer in which it offers target stockholders its own securities in exchange for their target stock. In a cash tender offer, the offering corporation offers the target stockholders cash in exchange for their target stock.

Federal securities laws strictly control the terms, duration, and circumstances under which most tender offers are made. In addition, over thirty states have passed take-over statutes that impose additional regulations on tender offers.

The use of the tender offer as a method of gaining corporate control began in the mid-1960s. Highly contested legal battles and enormous expenses involved in complying with federal and state regulations have worked in some cases to discourage the use of tender offers as a vehicle for obtaining control of a corporation through stock purchase.

TERMINATION

Termination of a corporate life, like termination of a partnership, has two phases—liquidation and dissolution. **Liquidation** is the process by which corporate assets are converted into cash and distributed among creditors and shareholders according to specific rules of preference.[3] **Dissolution** is the legal death of the artificial "person" of the corporation.

Dissolution can be brought about in any of the following ways:

1. An act of a legislature in the state of incorporation.
2. The expiration of the time provided in the certificate of incorporation.
3. The voluntary approval of the shareholders and the board of directors.
4. Unanimous action by all shareholders.

---

3. Upon dissolution, the liquidated assets are first used to pay creditors. Any remaining assets are distributed to shareholders according to their respective stock rights; preferred stock has priority over common stock, generally by charter.

5. Court decree brought about by the attorney general of the state of incorporation for any of the following reasons: (a) failure to comply with administrative requirements (for example, failure to pay annual franchise taxes or to submit an annual report or to have a designated registered agent), (b) the procurement of a corporate charter through fraud or misrepresentation upon the state, (c) the abuse of corporate powers (*ultra vires* acts), (d) the violation of the state criminal code after the demand to discontinue has been made by the secretary of state, (e) the failure to commence business operations, or (f) the abandonment of operations before starting up.

The following case illustrates a minority shareholders attempt to dissolve a close corporation by court decree.

BACKGROUND AND FACTS   *The plaintiff, Howard Gruenberg, a minority shareholder of a close corporation, instituted this action for involuntary dissolution. The defendant corporation was Goldmine Plantation, Inc. Goldmine's principal asset was a nine-hundred-acre tract of land fronting on the east bank of the Mississippi River. In 1941 the land was acquired for $65,000. In 1975 the property was appraised at $3,000 per acre, giving it a value of $2,700,000.*

The land had been used to grow sugar cane, and the mineral rights had been leased. Between 1966 and the date of the lawsuit, various industrial enterprises had expressed the desire to buy the land. The last price offered was about $3,600 per acre net to vendor.

Although none of the attempts to purchase the land had taken the form of a written or binding offer, evidence presented at the trial court suggested that prospective offers were substantial, and a contract to sell could have materialized had the Goldmine board of directors expressed any interest. However, the board decided not to sell the real estate.

Minority shareholders, frustrated by the board's disinterest in selling the property and by low dividends from the sugar cane operations, petitioned the court for involuntary dissolution under the provisions of the state's corporate statute.

GRUENBERG v. GOLDMINE PLANTATION, INC.
Court of Appeal of Louisiana, Fourth Circuit, 1978.
360 So.2d 884.

STOULIG, Judge.

*   *   *   *

In the light of this situation, we consider whether plaintiffs and intervenors have sustained the proof to support their demands for involuntary dissolution under [any grounds permitted by state law]:

"A.   The court may entertain a proceeding for involuntary dissolution under its supervision when it is made to appear that:

*   *   *   *

(2) The objects of the corporation have wholly failed, or are entirely abandoned, or their accomplishment is impracticable; or

(3) It is beneficial to the interests of the shareholders that the corporation should be liquidated and dissolved; or

*   *   *   *

(7) The corporation has been guilty of gross and persistent ultra vires acts

*   *   *."

First we hold the evidence does not support our concluding the objects of incorporation have "wholly failed" or "been abandoned" or that "their accomplishment is impracticable." [Thus the proof required by (A)(2) is lacking].

*   *   *   *

* * * [Second], [i]t can be urged validly in this case that the low returns of the past have been more than offset by the appreciation of the corporate assets. With the completion of the river bridge at Luling within the next few years, the land value, according to Kuebel, should increase tremendously. Thus the proof required by (A)(3) is lacking.

Finally, we consider the contention that the majority shareholders and the board have been guilty of gross and persistent ultra vires acts. While we question the wisdom of the board's approach in reaching a decision not to sell the real estate, we conclude the action taken is within the scope of the board's authority and therefore legal.

"Unless it clearly appears that the act is an abuse of discretion, intra vires, legal and good faith acts of the board of directors, other corporate officers, or the majority stockholders, i.e., acts pertaining to the internal management, of the corporation, where they are not fraudulent or unfair to minority stockholders, will not be interfered with or remedied at the instance of minority stockholders, regardless of whether such acts are wise or expedient. In other words, to warrant the interposition of a court in favor of the minority shareholders in a corporation, as against the contemplated action of the majority, where such action is within the corporate powers, a case must be made out which plainly shows that such action is so far opposed to the true interests of the corporation itself as to lead to the clear inference that no one thus acting could have been influenced by any honest desire to secure such interests, but that he must have acted with an intent to subserve some outside purpose, regardless of the consequences to the company and in a manner inconsistent with its interests." * * *

We appreciate the frustrations of the minority who are locked into a financial situation in which they have a substantial interest but no control. Appellants suggest the shareholders be equated to partners and be permitted to disengage from the corporation as they could were Goldmine operated as a partnership. Our substantive law provides for involuntary dissolution but offers no remedy for the minority shareholder with substantial holdings who is out of control and trapped in a closed corporation. We will not abrogate the legislative function to provide relief.

JUDGMENT AND REMEDY   *The judgment of the trial court was affirmed. The appellate court concluded that it would not permit the minority shareholder to force involuntary dissolution under the provisions of the statute and that the officers of the corporation had acted within the scope of their delegated authority. The objects of incorporation had not wholly failed, and dissolution was not essential to protect the minority shareholder's interests.*

Process of Liquidation

When dissolution takes place by voluntary action, the members of the board of directors act as trustees of the corporate assets. As trustees, they are responsible for winding up the affairs of the corporation for the benefit of corporate creditors and shareholders. This makes the board members personally liable for any breach of their fiduciary trustee duties.

Liquidation can be accomplished without court supervision unless the members of the board do not wish to act in this capacity, or unless shareholders or creditors can show to the court cause why the board should not be permitted to assume the trustee function. In either case, the court will appoint a receiver to wind up the corporate affairs and liquidate corporate assets. A receiver is always appointed by the court if the dissolution is involuntary.

Involuntary Dissolution

Sometimes an involuntary dissolution of a corporation is necessary. For example, boards of directors may be deadlocked. Courts hesitate to order involuntary dissolution in such circumstances unless there is specific statutory authorization to do so, but if the deadlock cannot be resolved by the shareholders and if it will irreparably injure the corporation, the court will proceed with an involuntary dissolution. Courts can also dissolve a corporation for mismanagement.

QUESTIONS AND
CASE PROBLEMS

1. Smith is chairman of the board of directors of Acme, Inc., and Williams is chairman of the board of directors of Firebrand, Inc. Acme is a manufacturing corporation, and Firebrand is a transportation corporation. Smith and Williams meet to consider the possibility of combining their corporations and activities into a single corporate entity. They consider two alternative courses of action: Acme acquiring all the stock and assets of Firebrand, or both corporations combining to form a new corporation, called Acbrand, Inc. Both chairmen are concerned about the necessity of formal transfer of property, liability for existing debts, and the problem of amending articles of incorporation. Discuss what the two proposed combinations are called and the legal effect each has on the transfer of property, the liabilities of the combined corporations, and the need to amend the articles of incorporation.

2. Ann owns 10,000 shares of Ajax Corporation. Her shares represent a 10 percent ownership in Ajax. Zeta Corporation is interested in acquiring Ajax in a merger, and the board of directors of each corporation has approved the merger. The shareholders of Zeta have already approved the acquisition, and Ajax has called

ready approved the acquisition, and Ajax has called for a shareholder meeting to approve the merger. Ann disapproves of the merger and does not want to accept Zeta shares for the Ajax shares she holds. The market price of Ajax shares is $20 per share the day before the shareholder vote and drops to $16 on the day the shareholders of Ajax approve the merger. Discuss Ann's rights in this matter, beginning with notice of the proposed merger.

3. Green Corporation wants to acquire all the assets of Red Dot Corporation. Green plans to pay for the assets by issuing its own corporate stock. Green's board of directors has already approved the merger. Discuss whether shareholder approval is required for this merger.

4. Acme Corporation is a small midwestern business that owns a valuable patent. Acme has approximately 1,000 shareholders with 100,000 authorized and outstanding shares. Block Corporation would like to have use of the patent, but Acme refuses to give Block a license. Block has tried to acquire Acme by purchasing Acme's assets, but Acme's board of directors has refused to approve the acquisition. Acme's shares are presently selling for $5 per share. Discuss how Block Corporation might proceed in order to gain control and use of Acme's patent.

5. Smith Corporation has been losing money for several years but still has valuable fixed assets. The shareholders see little hope of the corporation ever making a profit. Another corporation, Acme Corporation, has failed to pay state taxes for several years or to file annual reports required by statute. In addition, Acme is accused of being guilty of gross and persistent *ultra vires* acts. Discuss whether these corporations will be terminated and how the assets of each would be handled upon dissolution.

6. Some of the shareholders of the Gulf Company, who were also shareholders of the Warrior Company, wished to have the former sell all its assets to the latter. Both the bylaws and the certificate of incorporation of the Gulf Company were silent on the matter of the sale of company assets, so the shareholders needed to find out how to proceed with the sale of assets. What three steps must they take? [Finch v. Warrior Cement Co., 16 Del.Ch. 44, 141 A. 54 (1928)]

7. For many years, Bellanca Corporation had been in the business of manufacturing airplanes, although in recent years it had engaged in no business operations, had been delisted by the American Stock Exchange, and had in fact become an "empty shell." In 1961, through a series of agreements, the majority shareholder of Bellanca agreed to purchase all the stock of seven California corporations engaged in the egg business and in turn agreed to sell his majority share in Bellanca to Dean and Glen Olson. Orzeck, a minority

shareholder of Bellanca, objected to the entire transaction, but it was carried through in spite of her objections. Orzeck felt that she should have been given dissenting shareholder's appraisal rights, which are available when a minority shareholder objects to a company's merger. Should Orzeck have been granted dissenter's appraisal rights? [Orzeck v. Englehart, 41 Del.Ch. 361, 195 A.2d 375 (1963)]

8. Arthur Gerth owned 53 percent of the XYZ Corporation's common stock and half of its preferred stock. His brother, Harry, owned 1 percent of its common stock, and Kruger owned the remainder of its common and preferred stock. The XYZ Corporation was in the retail lumber business. Of the three shareholders, Gerth was the only employee of the corporation. As its president, he paid himself a combined salary and bonus of approximately $15,000 annually. This left less than $2,000 in profits to be distributed as dividends. Kruger brought suit to have XYZ Corporation dissolved on the ground that Gerth was drawing an excessive salary and bonus and was thus wasting corporate assets and leaving an insufficient amount available for dividends. Under Gerth's leadership, the XYZ Corporation had become quite successful, and Gerth claimed that he deserved the salary and bonus because of his efforts. Should XYZ be dissolved? [Kruger v. Gerth, 22 A.D.2d 916, 255 N.Y.S.2d 498 (1964)]

9. Gabhart was one of five shareholders in a corporation in which all the shareholders were also directors. Gabhart resigned as a director but refused to sell his shares. The other four shareholders formed a new corporation and merged the old one into it. Gabhart was not a stockholder in the new corporation, which was the surviving company. The only reason for the merger was to obtain Gabhart's shares. Could this action by the corporation be viewed as a dissolution? If so, how would this affect Gabhart's rights? [Gabhart v. Gabhart, 267 Ind. 370, 370 N.E.2d 345 (1977)]

CHAPTER 45

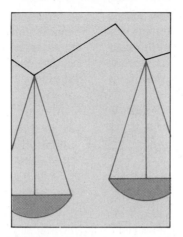

CORPORATIONS
Financial Regulation and Investor Protection

After the great stock market crash of 1929, various studies showed a need for regulation of securities markets. In the main, securities regulation legislation was enacted to provide investors with more information in order to help them to make buying and selling decisions. Furthermore, it was designed to prohibit deceptive, unfair, and manipulative practices. Today, the sale and transfer of securities are heavily regulated by federal and state statutes and by government agencies. This is a complex area of the law. This chapter will outline the nature of federal securities regulations and their effect on the business world.

The most important federal securities regulations are the Securities Act of 1933 and the Securities Exchange Act of 1934. These acts and others are administered by the Securities and Exchange Commission.

THE SECURITIES AND EXCHANGE COMMISSION

Congress has delegated to the Securities and Exchange Commission (SEC) the responsibility of administering all federal securities law. The SEC is an independent regulatory agency established by the Securities and Exchange Act of 1934. Its major responsibilities are:

1. Requiring disclosure of facts concerning offerings of securities listed on national securities exchanges and certain securities traded over the counter.
2. Regulating the trade in securities on the thirteen national and regional securities exchanges and in the over-the-counter markets.
3. Investigating securities frauds.
4. Regulating the activities of securities bro-

kers, dealers, and investment advisers and requiring their registration.

5.   Supervising the activities of mutual funds.

6.   Recommending administrative sanctions, injunctive remedies, and criminal prosecution against those who violate securities laws.

THE SECURITIES ACT OF 1933

The Securities Act of 1933[1] was designed to prohibit various forms of fraud and to stabilize the securities industry by requiring that all essential information concerning the issuing of stocks be made available to the investing public. The 1933 Act is basically a disclosure requirement.

Requirements of the Registration Statement

Section 5 of the Act broadly provides that if a security does not qualify for an exemption, that security must be *registered* before it is offered to the public through the use of either the mails or any facility of interstate commerce, including securities exchanges. Issuing corporations must file a *registration statement* with the SEC. Investors must be provided with a prospectus. In principle, the registration statement and prospectus supply sufficient information to enable unsophisticated investors to evaluate the financial risk involved.

Contents of the Registration Statement   The registration statement must include the following:

1.   A description of the significant provisions of the security offered for sale, including the relationship between that security and the other capital securities of the registrant. Also, the corporation must disclose how it intends to use the proceeds of the sale.

2.   A description of the registrant's properties and business.

3.   A description of the management of the registrant, its security holdings, remuneration, and other benefits, including pensions and stock options. Any interests of directors or officers in any material transactions with the corporation must be disclosed.

4.   A financial statement certified by an independent public accounting firm.

5.   A description of threatened or pending lawsuits.

What the Registering Corporation Can Do Before, During, and After Registration   Before filing the registration statement and prospectus with the SEC, the corporation is allowed to obtain an underwriter who will monitor distribution of the new issue. There is a twenty-day waiting period after registration before the sale can take place. During this period, oral offers between interested investors and the issuing corporation concerning the purchase and sale of the proposed securities may take place; very limited written advertising is allowed. At this time the so-called *red herring* prospectus may be distributed. It gets its name from the red legend printed across it stating that the registration has been filed but has not become effective.

After the waiting period, the registered securities can be legally bought and sold. Written advertising is allowed in the form of a so-called *tombstone ad*, so named because the format resembles a tombstone. Such ads simply tell the investor where and how to obtain a prospectus. Normally, any other type of advertising is prohibited.

Exemptions

A corporation can avoid the high cost and complicated procedures associated with registration by taking advantage of certain exemptions. Transactions are exempt if they do not involve a public offering. Some exempt transactions are private offerings to a limited number of persons, offerings to an institution that has access to the required information,[2] and offerings restricted to residents of the state in which the issuing company is organized and doing business (but these are still subject to state law).[3] The SEC also has the power to exempt small issues under $1,500,000 from the registration requirement.[4]

---

1.   48 Stat. 74, 15 U.S.C. 77a.

2.   Securities Act, Section 4(2), 15 USCA Section 77d(2).

3.   Securities Act, Section 3(a)(11), 15 USCA Section 77c(a)(11).

4.   Securities Act, Section 3(b), 15 USCA Section 77(b). For issues of less than $1,500,000, the commission has adopted a simplified registration process under Regulation A.

Additional Securities That Are Exempt

Other exempt securities are:

1. All bank securities sold prior to July 27, 1933.
2. Commercial paper if the maturity date does not exceed nine months.
3. Securities of charitable organizations.
4. Exchange securities where there has been a corporate reorganization.
5. Stock dividends and stock splits.

6. Securities issued by a common carrier or a contract carrier.
7. Any insurance, endowment, or annuity contract issued by an insurance company.

Registration violations of the 1933 act are not treated lightly. In the following case, the Bar-Chris Construction Corporation was sued by the purchasers of the corporation's debentures under Section 11 of the Securities Act of 1933. Section 11 imposes liability when a registration statement or prospectus contains material false statements or material omissions.

BACKGROUND AND FACTS *This lawsuit was brought by purchasers of BarChris debentures (bonds) under Section 11 of the Securities Act of 1933. The plaintiffs alleged that the registration statement filed with the Securities and Exchange Commission, which became effective on May 16, 1961, contained material false statements and material omissions.*

The defendants fell into three categories: (1) the persons who signed the registration statement, (2) the underwriters (consisting of eight investment banking firms), and (3) BarChris's auditors—Peat, Marwick, Mitchell & Co. Included in the group of defendants who signed the registration statement were: (1) BarChris's nine directors, (2) BarChris's controller, (3) one of BarChris's attorneys, (4) two investment bankers who were later named as directors of the BarChris Corporation, and (5) numerous other persons participating in the preparation of the registration statement.

BarChris grew out of a business started in 1946 as a bowling alley building company. The introduction of automatic pin setting machines in 1952 sparked rapid growth in the bowling industry. BarChris benefited from this increased interest in bowling, and its construction operations expanded rapidly. It was estimated that in 1960 BarChris installed approximately 3 percent of all bowling lanes built in the United States. BarChris's sales increased dramatically between 1956 and 1960, and the company was recognized as a significant factor in the bowling construction industry.

BarChris was in constant need of cash to finance its operations, a need which grew more and more pressing as the operations expanded. In 1959, BarChris sold over a half-million shares of its common stock to the public. By early 1961 it needed additional working capital, and this time it decided to sell debentures.

BarChris filed a registration statement of the debentures with the SEC and received the proceeds of the financing. Nevertheless, it experienced increasing financial difficulties, which in time became insurmountable. By early 1962, it was painfully apparent that BarChris was beginning to fail. In October BarChris filed a petition for an arrangement under the Bankruptcy Act, and it defaulted on the interest due on the debentures in November.

ESCOTT v. BARCHRIS CONSTR. CORP.
United States District Court,
S.D. New York, 1968.
283 F.Supp. 643.

The plaintiffs challenged the accuracy of the registration statement and charged that the text of the prospectus—including many of the figures—was false and that material information had been omitted.

The federal district court reviewed all of the figures and statements included in the prospectus.

McLEAN, District Judge.

*   *   *   *

The action is brought under Section 11 of the Securities Act of 1933. Plaintiffs allege that the registration statement [and the prospectus included in it] with respect to these debentures filed with the Securities and Exchange Commission, which became effective on May 16, 1961, contained material false statements and material omissions.

*   *   *   *

On the main issue of liability, the questions to be decided are (1) did the registration statement contain false statements of fact, or did it omit to state facts which should have been stated in order to prevent it from being misleading; (2) if so, were the facts which were falsely stated or omitted "material" within the meaning of the Act.

*   *   *   *

It is a prerequisite to liability under Section 11 of the Act that the fact which is falsely stated in a registration statement, or the fact that it is omitted when it should have been stated to avoid misleading, be "material." The regulations of the Securities and Exchange Commission pertaining to the registration of securities define the word as follows:

"The term 'material', when used to qualify a requirement for the furnishing of information as to any subject, limits the information required to those matters as to which an average prudent investor ought reasonably to be informed before purchasing the security registered."

What are "matters as to which an average prudent investor ought reasonably to be informed"? It seems obvious that they are matters which such an investor needs to know before he can make an intelligent, informed decision whether or not to buy the security.

Early in the history of the Act, a definition of materiality was given in Matter of Charles A. Howard, which is still valid today. A material fact was there defined as:

"*   *   * a fact which if it had been correctly stated or disclosed would have deterred or tended to deter the average prudent investor from purchasing the securities in question."

The average prudent investor is not concerned with minor inaccuracies or with errors as to matters which are of no interest to him. The facts which tend to deter him from purchasing a security are facts which have an important bearing upon the nature or condition of the issuing corporation or its business.

Judged by this test, there is no doubt that many of the misstatements and omissions in this prospectus were material. This is true of all of them which relate to the state of affairs in 1961, i.e., the overstatement of sales and gross profit for the first quarter, the understatement of contingent liabilities as of April 30, the overstatement of orders on hand and the failure to disclose the true facts with respect to officers' loans, customers' delinquencies, application of proceeds and the prospective operation of several alleys.

BarChris Corporation itself and all the signers of the registration statement for the debentures, the underwriters, and the corporation's auditors were held liable.	**JUDGMENT AND REMEDY**

The Securities Exchange Act of 1934

The Securities Exchange Act provides for the regulation and registration of security exchanges, brokers, dealers, and national securities associations (such as NASD). It regulates the markets in which securities are traded by maintaining a continuous disclosure system for all corporations with securities on the securities exchanges and for those companies that have assets in excess of $1 million and five hundred or more shareholders. These corporations are referred to as Section 12 companies, since they are required to register their securities under Section 12 of the 1934 act. The act regulates proxy solicitation for voting, and it allows the SEC to engage in market surveillance to regulate undesirable market practices such as fraud, market manipulation, misrepresentation, and stabilization. (*Stabilization* is a market manipulating technique whereby securities underwriters bid for securities to stabilize their price during their issuance.)

Insider Trading   One of the most important parts of the 1934 act relates to so-called *insider trading*. Because of their positions, corporate directors and officers often obtain advance inside information that can affect the future market value of the corporate stock. Obviously, their positions can give them a trading advantage over the general public and shareholders. The 1934 Securities Exchange Act defines and extends liability to officers and directors in their personal transactions for taking advantage of such information when they know it is unavailable to the person with whom they are dealing. In addition, in order to deter the use of inside information, the 1934 act requires officers, directors, and certain large shareholders to turn over to the corpora-

tion all short-term profits realized on the purchase and sale of corporate stock.

SEC Rule 10b-5   Section 10(b) of the 1934 act and SEC Rule 10b-5 cover not only corporate officers, directors, and majority shareholders but also any persons having access to or receiving information of a nonpublic nature on which trading is based. Those persons to whom the material information is transmitted are known as *tippees*.

Disclosure under Rule 10b-5   Any material omission or misrepresentation of material facts in connection with the purchase or sale of a security may violate Section 10(b) and Rule 10b-5. The key to liability under this rule is whether the insider's information is "material."

Following are some examples of material facts calling for a disclosure under the rule:

1.   A new ore discovery.
2.   Fraudulent trading in the company stock by a broker-dealer.
3.   A dividend change (whether up or down).
4.   A contract for the sale of corporate assets.
5.   A new discovery (process or product).
6.   A significant change in the firm's financial condition.

When Must Disclosure under Rule 10b-5 Be Made?   Courts have struggled with the problem of when information becomes public knowledge. Clearly, when inside information becomes public knowledge, all insiders should be allowed to trade without disclosure. The courts have suggested that insiders should refrain from trading for a "reasonable waiting period" when the news is not readily translatable into investment action. Presumably, this gives the news time to filter down and to be evaluated by the investing public. What constitutes a reasonable waiting period is not at all clear.

The following is one of the landmark cases interpreting Rule 10b-5. The SEC sued Texas Gulf Sulphur for issuing a misleading press release.

The release underestimated the magnitude and value of a mineral discovery. The SEC also sued several of Texas Gulf Sulphur's directors, officers, and employees under Rule 10b-5 after these persons had purchased large amounts of the corporate stock prior to the announcement of the corporation's rich ore discovery.

SECURITIES AND
EXCHANGE COMM. v.
TEXAS GULF
SULPHUR CO.

United States Court of Appeals,
Second Circuit, 1968.
401 F.2d 833.

BACKGROUND AND FACTS　*Texas Gulf Sulphur Co. (TGS) drilled a hole on November 12, 1963, near Timmins, Ontario. It appeared to yield a core with exceedingly high mineral content. Since TGS did not own the mineral rights in the surrounding regions, it maintained secrecy about the results of the core sample. Evasive tactics were undertaken to camouflage the drill site, and a second hole was drilled. TGS completed an extensive land acquisition program and then began drilling this lucrative site. Rumors began to spread, and by early April 1964, a "tremendous staking rush (was) going on."*

On April 11, 1964, an unauthorized report of the extraordinary mineral find hit the papers. On April 12, TGS announced to the press a strike of at least 25 million tons of ore. Charles Fogarty, executive vice-president of TGS, had already purchased 1,700 shares of stock during the month of November 1963 and an additional 300 shares in December. In March 1964 he bought 400 shares, and in April he bought 300 shares. Other TGS officials also purchased stock. They accepted stock options on February 20, 1964.

The Securities and Exchange Commission filed suit against TGS and several of its officers, directors, and employees to enjoin (prevent) TGS's continued violation of the Securities Exchange Act of 1934 and to compel the individual defendants to rescind the securities transactions they had made. The complaint alleged that, on the basis of material inside information concerning the results of TGS's drilling, the defendants either personally or through agents purchased TGS stock, while the information concerning the drill site remained undisclosed to the investing public. The SEC further charged that certain of the defendants (tippers) had divulged information to certain others (tippees) for their use in purchasing TGS stock before the information was disclosed to the public or to other sellers. In addition, certain defendants had accepted options to purchase TGS stock without disclosing material information about the progress of the drilling to either the stock option committee or the TGS board of directors. Finally, the complaint charged that TGS issued a deceptive press release on April 12, 1964.

The deceptive press release should be the focus in reading the following case. The trial court judge held that the issuance of the press release was lawful because it was not issued for the purpose of benefiting the corporation, and there was no evidence that any insider had used the information in the press release to personal advantage. Thus it was not "misleading or deceptive on the basis of the facts then known." The trial court went on to find that most of the defendants had not violated Rule 10b-5.

WATERMAN, Circuit Judge.

*   *   *   *

This action was commenced in the United States District Court for the Southern District of New York by the Securities and Exchange Commission (the SEC) pursuant to *   *   * the Securities Exchange Act of 1934 (the Act) against Texas Gulf Sulphur Company (TGS) and several of its officers, directors and employees, to enjoin certain conduct by TGS and the individual defendants said to violate Section 10(b) of the Act, *   *   * and Rule 10b-5 *   *   * (the Rule), promulgated thereunder.

*   *   *   *

I. THE INDIVIDUAL DEFENDANTS

A. *Introductory*

Rule 10b-5, 17 CFR 240.10b-5, on which this action is predicated, provides:

It shall be unlawful for any person, directly or indirectly, by the use of any means or instrumentality of interstate commerce, or of the mails, or of any facility of any national securities exchange,

(1) to employ any device, scheme, or artifice to defraud,

(2) to make any untrue statement of a material fact or to omit to state a material fact necessary in order to make the statements made, in the light of the circumstances under which they were made, not misleading, or

(3) to engage in any act, practice, or course of business which operates or would operate as a fraud or deceit upon any person, in connection with the purchase or sale of any security.

Rule 10b-5 was promulgated pursuant to the grant of authority given the SEC by Congress in Section 10(b) of the Securities Exchange Act of 1934 (15 U.S.C. § 78j(b)). By that Act Congress purposed to prevent inequitable and unfair practices and to insure fairness in securities transactions generally, whether conducted face-to-face, over the counter, or on exchanges. The Act and the Rule apply to the transactions here, all of which were consummated on exchanges. [T]he Rule is based in policy on the justifiable expectation of the securities marketplace that all investors trading on impersonal exchanges have relatively equal access to material information. The essence of the Rule is that anyone who, trading for his own account in the securities of a corporation has "access, directly or indirectly, to information intended to be available only for a corporate purpose and not for the personal benefit of anyone" may not take "advantage of such information knowing it is unavailable to those with whom he is dealing," i.e., the investing public. Insiders, as directors or management officers are, of course, by this Rule, precluded from so unfairly dealing, but the Rule is also applicable to one possessing the information who may not be strictly termed an "insider" within the meaning of Sec. 16(b) of the Act. Thus, anyone in possession of material inside information must either disclose it to the investing public, or if he is disabled from disclosing it in order to protect a corporate confidence, or he chooses not to do so, must abstain from trading in or recommending the securities concerned while such inside information remains undisclosed. So, it is here no justification for insider activity that disclosure was forbidden by the legitimate corporate objective of acquiring options to purchase the land surrounding the exploration site; if the information was, as the SEC contends, material, its possessors should have kept out of the market until disclosure was accomplished.

B. *Material Inside Information*

An insider is not, of course, always foreclosed from investing in his own company merely because he may be more familiar with company operations than are outside investors. An insider's duty to disclose information or his duty to abstain from dealing in his company's securities arises only in "those situations which are essentially extraordinary in nature and which are reasonably certain to have a substantial effect on the market price of the security if [the extraordinary situation is] disclosed." Fleischer, Securities Trading and Corporate Information Practices: The Implications of the Texas Gulf Sulphur Proceeding, 51 Va.L.Rev. 1271, 1289.

Nor is an insider obligated to confer upon outside investors the benefit of his superior financial or other expert analysis by disclosing his educated guesses or predictions. The only regulatory objective is that access to material information be enjoyed equally, but this objective requires nothing more than the disclosure of basic facts so that outsiders may draw upon their own evaluative expertise in reaching their own investment decisions with knowledge equal to that of the insiders.

*   *   *   *

In each case, then, whether facts are material within Rule 10b-5 when the facts relate to a particular event and are undisclosed by those persons who are knowledgeable thereof will depend at any given time upon a balancing of both the indicated probability that the event will occur and the anticipated magnitude of the event in light of the totality of the company activity. Here, notwithstanding the trial court's conclusion that the results of the first drill core, * * * were "too 'remote' * * * to have had any significant impact on the market, i.e., to be deemed material," knowledge of the possibility, which surely was more than marginal, of the existence of a mine of the vast magnitude indicated by the remarkably rich drill core located rather close to the surface (suggesting mineability by the less expensive openpit method) within the confines of a large anomaly (suggesting an extensive region of mineralization) might well have affected the price of TGS stock and would certainly have been an important fact to a reasonable, if speculative, investor in deciding whether he should buy, sell, or hold. After all, this first drill core was "unusually good and * * * excited the interest and speculation of those who knew about it."

*   *   *   *

Finally, a major factor in determining whether the * * * discovery was a material fact is the importance attached to the drilling results by those who knew about it. In view of other unrelated recent developments favorably affecting TGS, participation by an informed person in a regular stock-purchase program, or even sporadic trading by an informed person, might lend only nominal support to the inference of the materiality of the * * * discovery; nevertheless, the timing by those who knew of it of their stock purchases and their purchases of *short-term* calls—purchases in some cases by individuals who had never before purchased calls or even TGS stock—virtually compels the inference that the insiders were influenced by the drilling results.

*   *   *   *

We hold, therefore, that all transactions in TGS stock or calls by individuals apprised of the drilling results *   *   * were made in violation of Rule 10b-5.[1] Inasmuch as the visual evaluation of that drill core (a generally reliable estimate though less accurate then a chemical assay) constituted material information, those advised of the results of the visual evaluation as well as those informed of the chemical assay traded in violation of law.

II.   THE CORPORATE DEFENDANT

Introductory

At 3:00 P.M. on April 12, 1964, evidently believing it desirable to comment upon the rumors concerning the Timmins project, TGS issued the press release. *   *   * It read in pertinent part as follows:

*   *   *   *

"Recent drilling on one property near Timmins has led to preliminary indications that more drilling would be required for proper evaluation of this prospect. The drilling done to date has not been conclusive, but the statements made by many outside quarters are unreliable and include information and figures that are not available to TGS.

"The work done to date has not been sufficient to reach definite conclusions and any statement as to size and grade of ore would be premature and possibly misleading. When we have progressed to the point where reasonable and logical conclusions can be made, TGS will issue a definite statement to its stockholders and to the public in order to clarify the Timmins project."

*   *   *   *

It does not appear to be unfair to impose upon corporate management a duty to ascertain the truth of any statements the corporation releases to its shareholders or to the investing public at large. Accordingly, we hold that Rule 10b-5 is violated whenever assertions are made, as here, in a manner reasonably calculated to influence the investing public, e.g., by means of the financial media, Fleischer, supra, 51 Va.L.Rev. at 1294-95, if such assertions are false or misleading or are so incomplete as to mislead irrespective of whether the issuance of the release was motivated by corporate officials for ulterior purposes. It seems clear, however, that if corporate management demonstrates that it was diligent in ascertaining that the information it published was the whole truth and that such diligently obtained information was disseminated in good faith, Rule 10b-5 would not have been violated.

*   *   *   *

We conclude, then, that, having established that the release was issued in a manner reasonably calculated to affect the market price of TGS stock and to influence the investing public, we must remand to the district court to decide whether the release was misleading to the reasonable investor and if found to be misleading, whether the court in its discretion should issue the injunction the SEC seeks.

The appellate court's judgment was favorable to the SEC. The information   JUDGMENT
contained in the press release was material, and the transaction in stock   AND REMEDY

---

1. Even if insiders were in fact ignorant of the broad scope of the Rule and acted pursuant to a mistaken belief as to the applicable law, such an ignorance does not insulate them from the consequences of their acts. Tager v. SEC.

by the insiders who knew of it had violated Rule 10b-5. Thus, the options of the individual defendants were rescinded. However, the questions of whether the press release was misleading and what remedies should be imposed were remanded to the trial court for decision. A trial court is bound to apply the law as enunciated by the court of appeals in making this type of decision.

COMMENTS   *Texas Gulf Sulphur Company was not only sued by the SEC, but numerous civil actions for damages were brought against it by plaintiff-investors who had sold their TGS stock as a result of the deceptively gloomy press release regarding the corporation's mineral exploration. All these suits were settled in 1972.[5] In a federal lawsuit filed against TGS some two years after the initial case, a court of appeals held that investors who had sold stock relying on the representations in the press release could recover damages from the corporation and the officers who drafted the release. The court went on to state that the proper measure of damages was the difference between the selling price and the price at which the investors could have reinvested within a reasonable period of time after they became aware of a curative press release made by TGS.*

After TGS issued its curative press release, the court held that a diligent and reasonable investor would have become informed of it within four days, and investors who sold their stock more than four days after the second press release was issued could not recover under the Securities Exchange Act on the basis of reliance on the earlier, deceptive release.

---

5.   Cannon v. Texas Gulf Sulphur, 55 F.R.D. 308 (S.D.N.Y. 1972).

When Does Rule 10b-5 Apply?   Rule 10b-5 applies in virtually all cases concerning the trading of securities, whether on organized exchanges, in over-the-counter markets, or in private transactions. The rule covers notes, bonds, certificates of interest and participation in any profit-sharing agreement, agreements to form a corporation, and joint venture agreements; in short, it covers just about any form of security. It is immaterial whether a firm has securities registered under the 1933 act for the 1934 act to apply.

Rule 10b-5 is applicable only when the req-uisites of federal jurisdiction, such as the use of the mails, of stock exchange facilities, or of any instrumentality of interstate commerce, are present. However, virtually no commercial transaction can be completed without such contact. In addition, the states have corporate securities laws, many of which include provisions similar to Rule 10b-5.

In the following recent case, the court considers the role of Rule 10b-5 when there is no use of interstate commerce, the mails, or any of the facilities of any national securities exchange.

CHIARELLA v. UNITED STATES
Supreme Court of the United States, 1980. 445 U.S. 222, 100 S.Ct. 1108.

BACKGROUND AND FACTS   *Chiarella was a printer who worked at a New York composing room. He handled announcements of corporate take-over bids. Even though the documents that were delivered to the printer concealed the identity of the target corporations by blank spaces and false names, Chiarella was able to deduce the names of the target* *companies from other information contained in the documents. Without disclosing his knowledge, he purchased stock in the target companies and sold the shares immediately after the take-over attempts were made public. He realized a gain of slightly more than $30,000 in the course of fourteen months. The SEC began an investigation of his trading activities. In May of 1977, Chiarella entered into a consent decree with the SEC in which he agreed to return his profits to the sellers of the shares. In 1978, he was indicted on seventeen counts of violating Section 10b of the Securities Exchange Act of 1934 and SEC Rule 10b-5. The trial court convicted him on all counts. The Court of Appeals affirmed that conviction. The Supreme Court then granted certiorari.*

POWELL, Justice.

*   *   *   *

Section 10(b) of the 1934 Act, 15 U.S.C. § 78j, prohibits the use "in connection with the purchase or sale of any security *   *   * [of] any manipulative or deceptive device or contrivance in contravention of such rules and regulations as the Commission may prescribe." Pursuant to this action, the SEC promulgated Rule 10b-5 which provides in pertinent part that

"It shall be unlawful for any person, directly or indirectly, by the use of any means or instrumentality of interstate commerce, or of the mails or of any facility of any national securities exchange,

"(a) To employ any device, scheme, or artifice to defraud, [or]

*   *   *   *

"(c) To engage in any act, practice, or course of business which operates or would operate as a fraud or a deceit upon any person, in connection with the purchase or sale of any security." 17 CFR § 240.10b-5 (1979).

This case concerns the legal effect of the petitioner's silence. The District Court's charge permitted the jury to convict the petitioner if it found that he willfully failed to inform sellers of target company securities that he knew of a forthcoming takeover bid that would make their shares more valuable.

*   *   *   *

*   *   * [S]ilence in connection with the purchase or sale of securities may operate as a fraud actionable under § 10(b) despite the absence of statutory language or legislative history specifically addressing the legality of nondisclosure. But such liability is premised upon a duty to disclose arising from a relationship of trust and confidence between parties to a transaction. Application of a duty to disclose prior to trading guarantees that corporate insiders, who have an obligation to place the shareholder's welfare before their own, will not benefit personally through fraudulent use of material nonpublic information.

In this case, the petitioner was convicted of violating § 10(b) although he was not a corporate insider and he received no confidential information from the target company. Moreover, the "market information" upon which he relied did not concern the earning power or operations of the target company, but only the plans of the acquiring company. Petitioner's use of that information was not a fraud under § 10(b) unless he was subject to an affirmative duty to disclose it before trading. In this case, the jury instructions failed to specify any such duty. In effect, the trial court instructed the jury that petitioner owed a duty to everyone; to all sellers, indeed, to the market as a whole. The jury simply was told to decide whether petitioner used material, nonpublic information at a time when "he knew other people trading in the securities market did not have access to the same information."

The Court of Appeals affirmed the conviction by holding that "[a]nyone— corporate insider or not—who regularly receives material nonpublic information may not use that information to trade in securities without incurring an affirmative duty to disclose." Although the court said that its test would include only persons who regularly receive material nonpublic information, its rationale for that limitation is unrelated to the existence of a duty to disclose. The Court of Appeals, like the trial court, failed to identify a relationship between petitioner and the sellers that could give rise to a duty. Its decision thus rested solely upon its belief that the federal securities laws have "created a system providing equal access to information necessary for reasoned and intelligent investment decisions." The use by anyone of material information not generally available is fraudulent, this theory suggests, because such information gives certain buyers or sellers an unfair advantage over less informed buyers and sellers.

This reasoning suffers from two defects. First, not every instance of financial unfairness constitutes fraudulent activity under § 10(b). Second, the element required to make silence fraudulent—a duty to disclose—is absent in this case. No duty could arise from petitioner's relationship with the sellers of the target company's securities, for petitioner had no prior dealings with them. He was not their agent, he was not a fiduciary, he was not a person in whom the sellers had placed their trust and confidence. He was, in fact, a complete stranger who dealt with the sellers only through impersonal market transactions.

*   *   *   *

In its brief to this Court, the United States offers an alternative theory to support petitioner's conviction. It argues that petitioner breached a duty to the acquiring corporation when he acted upon information that he obtained by virtue of his position as an employee of a printer employed by the corporation. The breach of this duty is said to support a conviction under § 10(b) for fraud perpetrated upon both the acquiring corporation and the sellers.

We need not decide whether this theory has merit for it was not submitted to the jury. The jury was told, in the language of Rule 10b-5, that it could convict the petitioner if it concluded that he either (i) employed a device, scheme or artifice to defraud or (ii) engaged in an act, practice, or course of business which operated or would operate as a fraud or deceit upon any person. The trial judge stated that a "scheme to defraud" is a plan to obtain money by trick or deceit and that "a failure by Chiarella to disclose material, non-public information in connection with his purchase of stock would constitute deceit." Accordingly, the jury was instructed that the petitioner employed a scheme to defraud if he "did not disclose *   *   * material non-public information in connection with the purchases of the stock."

Alternatively, the jury was instructed that it could convict if "Chiarella's alleged conduct of having purchased securities without disclosing material, non-public information would have or did have the effect of operating as a fraud upon a seller." The judge earlier had stated that fraud "embraces all the means which human ingenuity can devise and which are resorted to by one individual to gain an advantage over another by false misrepresentation, suggestions or by suppression of the truth."

The jury instructions demonstrate that petitioner was convicted merely because of his failure to disclose material, nonpublic information to sellers from whom he bought the stock of target corporations. The jury was not instructed on the nature or elements of a duty owed by petitioner to anyone other than the sellers. Because we cannot affirm a criminal conviction on the basis of a theory not presented to the jury, we will not speculate upon whether such a duty exists, whether it has been breached, or whether such a breach constitutes a violation of § 10(b).

The judgment of the Court of Appeals was reversed. Chiarella could not be convicted for failure to disclose his knowledge to stockholders or to target companies. He was under no duty to disclose his knowledge, because he had had no prior dealings with the stockholders and was not their agent; nor was he a person in whom sellers had placed their trust and confidence. Duty to disclose does not arise from mere possession of nonpublic market information.

JUDGMENT AND REMEDY

Insider Reporting and Trading—Section 16(b)

Officers, directors, and certain large stockholders[6] of Section 12 corporations are required to file reports with the SEC concerning their ownership and trading of the corporation's securities.[7] In order to discourage such insiders from using nonpublic information about their company to their personal benefit in the stock market, Section 16(b) of the 1934 act provides for the recapture by the corporation of all profits realized by the insider on any purchase and sale or sale and purchase of the corporation's stock within any six-month period.[8] It is irrelevant whether the insider actually used inside information; all such short-swing profits must be returned to the corporation.

Section 16(b) applies not only to stock but to warrants, options, and securities convertible into stock. In addition, the courts have fashioned complex rules for determining profits. Corporate insiders are wise to seek competent counsel prior to trading in the corporation's stock. Exhibit 45–1 compares the effects of Rule 10b-5 and Section 16b.

Proxy Statements Section 14(a) of the Securities and Exchange Act of 1934 regulates the solicitation of proxies from shareholders of Section 12 companies. The SEC regulates the content of proxy statements sent to shareholders by corporate managers who are requesting authority to vote on behalf of the shareholders in a particular election on specified issues. Whoever solicits a proxy must fully and accurately disclose all facts that are pertinent to the matter to be voted on. SEC Rule 14a-9 is similar to the antifraud provisions of Rule 10b-5. Remedies for violation are extensive, ranging from injunctions to preventing a vote from being taken, to monetary damages.

Regulation of Investment Companies

Investment companies, and mutual funds in particular, grew rapidly after World War II. Such companies were at that time regulated by the Investment Company Act of 1940.[9] This act provides for SEC regulation of investment company activities. It was expanded by the Investment Company Act Amendments of 1970. Further minor changes were made in the Securities Act Amendments of 1975.

---

6. Those stockholders owning 10 percent of the class of equity securities registered under Section 12 of the 1934 act.
7. 1934 Act, Section 16(a), 15 USCA Section 78.
8. In a declining stock market, one can realize profits by selling at a high price and repurchasing at a later time at a lower price.

---

9. 15 U.S.C. 80a.

EXHIBIT 45–1 COMPARISON OF COVERAGE, APPLICATION, AND LIABILITIES UNDER RULE 10b-5 AND SECTION 16(b)

	RULE 10b-5	SECTION 16(b)
1. Subject matter of transaction.	Any security (does not have to be registered).	Any security (does not have to be registered).
2. Transactions covered.	Purchase or sale.	Short-swing purchase and sale or short-swing sale and purchase.
3. Who is subject to liability?	Virtually anyone with inside information—including officers, directors, controlling stockholders, and tippees.	Officers, directors and certain 10 percent stockholders.
4. Is omission, scheme or misrepresentation necessary for liability?	Yes.	No.
5. Any exempt transactions?	No.	Yes, there are a variety of exemptions.
6. Is direct dealing with the party necessary?	No.	No.
7. Who can bring an action?	A person transacting with an insider or the SEC or a purchaser or a seller damaged by a wrongful act.	Corporation and shareholder by derivative action.

The 1940 Act Coverage

The 1940 act requires that every investment company register with the SEC and imposes restrictions on the activities of such companies and persons connected with them. For the purposes of the act, an investment company is defined as any entity that (a) "is *   *   * engaged primarily *   *   * in the business of investing, reinvesting, or trading in securities" or (b) is engaged in such business and more than 40 percent of the company's assets consist of investment securities. Excluded from coverage of the act are banks, insurance companies, savings and loan associations, finance companies, oil and gas drilling firms, charitable foundations, tax-exempt pension funds, and other special types of institutions, such as closely held corporations.

Regulation of Mutual Fund Activities

All investment companies must register with the SEC by filing a notification of registration. Each year registered companies must file reports with the SEC.

In order to safeguard company assets, all securities must be held in the custody of a bank or stock exchange member, and that bank or stock exchange member must follow strict procedures laid down by the SEC.

No dividends may be paid from any source other than accumulated, undistributed net income. Furthermore, there are restrictions on investment activities. For example, investment companies are not allowed to purchase securities on margin, sell short, or participate in joint trading accounts.

STATE SECURITIES LAWS

Today, all states have their own corporate securities laws that regulate the offer and sale of securities within individual state borders.[10] Often referred to as *blue sky* laws, they are designed to prevent "speculative schemes which have no more basis than so many feet of blue sky."

---

10.   These laws are catalogued and annotated in CCH, *Blue Sky Law Reporter*, a loose-leaf service.

Since the adoption of the 1933 and 1934 federal securities acts, the state and federal governments have regulated securities concurrently. Indeed, both acts specifically preserve state securities laws. Certain features are common to all state blue sky laws. They have antifraud provisions, many of which are patterned after Rule 10b-5. Also, most state corporate securities laws regulate securities brokers and dealers.

Typically, these laws also provide for the registration or qualification of securities offered or issued for sale within the state. Unless an applicable exemption from registration is found, issuers must register or qualify their stock with the appropriate state official, often called a corporations commissioner. There is a difference in philosophy in the state statutes. Many are like the Securities Act of 1933 and mandate certain disclosures before registration is effective and a permit to sell the securities is issued. Others have fairness standards that a corporation must meet in order to offer or sell stock in the state. The Uniform Securities Act, which has been adopted in part by several states, was drafted to be acceptable to states with differing regulatory philosophies.

QUESTIONS AND CASE PROBLEMS

1. Maresh, an experienced geologist, owned certain oil and gas leases covering land in Nebraska. To raise money for the drilling of a test well, he undertook to sell fractional interests in the leases. He approached Garfield, a man with whom he had done business in the past. Garfield had mentioned that he would be interested in investing in some of Maresh's future oil ventures. Garfield had wide business experience in the stock market and in oil stocks. He felt that the investment in Maresh's gas leases could be lucrative. Based on Garfield's promise to wire the money promptly, Maresh began drilling. Soon after, when Maresh realized that the land was dry, Garfield refused to pay his share of the investment. Garfield claimed that he could rescind the agreement to invest since the investment offered by Maresh was a security within the meaning of the Securities Act of 1933, and it had not been registered. Did Maresh offer a security within the meaning of the 1933 act? [Garfield v. Strain, 320 F.2d 116 (10th Cir. 1963)]

2. The Howey Company owned large tracts of citrus acreage in Lake County, Florida. For several years it planted about five hundred acres annually, keeping half of the groves itself and offering the other half to the public to help finance additional development. Howey-in-the-Hills Service, Inc., was a service company engaged in cultivating and developing these groves, including the harvesting and marketing of the crops. Each prospective customer was offered both a land sales contract and a service contract after being told that it was not feasible to invest in a grove unless service arrangements were made. Of the acreage sold by Howey, 85 percent was sold with a service contract with Howey-in-the-Hills Service, Inc. Must Howey register the sales of these parcels of citrus groves with the Securities and Exchange Commission? [Securities and Exchange Comm. v. W. J. Howey Co., 328 U.S. 293, 66 S.Ct. 1100 (1946)]

3. Zabriskie purchased certain notes from Lewis in connection with a real estate venture that Lewis was trying to establish. The notes bore a maturity date of eight months after the date of purchase. The Securities Act of 1933 excludes from its definition of securities any note that has a maturity date not exceeding nine months at the time of issue. Knowing that the Securities Act is an attempt to control the sales of *investment* securities, can a better test be devised than this strict nine-month rule? [Zabriskie v. Lewis, 507 F.2d 546 (10th Cir. 1974)]

4. Children's Hospital offered and sold a number of 8 percent mortgage bonds in order to raise enough money to begin operation. Its promoters solicited purchasers mainly through the mails and through local newspaper advertisements. Children's Hospital was to be a nonprofit medical organization established mainly to serve the needs of children in the local community. The promoters, however, expected to earn large profits from organizing the hospital. Must the promoters of Children's Hospital register the sale of the mortgage bonds with the Securities and Exchange Commission? [Securities and Exchange Comm. v. Children's Hospital, 214 F.Supp. 883 (D.Ariz. 1963)]

5. On September 1, 1971, the Ecological Science Corporation issued a press release stating, in part, that it had renegotiated the terms of approximately $14 million in loans from its prime lender and that, under the renegotiated agreement, $4 million was due upon demand and the remainder on a specified date. The press release, however, failed to mention that, on the same

date as the renegotiated loan agreement, an insurance and annuity association had refused to provide the corporation with the $4 million loan that it had planned to use to repay the demand loan. Moreover, while discussing its European prospects in the press release, Ecological Science Corporation failed to mention the proposed transfer of voting control among its European subsidiaries. Has Ecological Science Corporation violated any of the provisions of the Securities Exchange Act of 1934? [Securities and Exchange Comm. v. Koenig, 469 F.2d 198 (2d Cir. 1972)]

6. Emerson Electric Company owned 13.2 percent of Dodge Manufacturing Company's stock. Within six months of the purchase of this stock, Emerson sold enough shares to a broker to reduce its holding to 9.96 percent. One week later (but still less than six months after Emerson's initial purchase), Emerson sold its remaining shares of Dodge stock. The sole purpose of Emerson's initial sale of just over 3 percent of its Dodge stock was to avoid liability under Section 16 of the Securities Exchange Act of 1934, which prohibits short-swing trading. Assuming Emerson made no profit on the initial sale of stock but made substantial profits when it sold the remaining 9.96 percent of Dodge stock, must it disgorge the profits it made on the sale? [Reliance Electric Co. v. Emerson Electric Co., 404 U.S. 418, 92 S.Ct. 596 (1972)]

7. Leston Nay owned 90 percent of the stock of First Securities Company. Between the years 1942 and 1966, Hochfelder sent large sums of money to Nay to be invested in escrow accounts of First Securities. The whole investment scheme was a fraud, and Nay converted the money sent by Hochfelder to his own use. Hochfelder then sued Ernst & Ernst, First Securities' auditor, for failing to use proper auditing procedures and thus negligently failing to discover the fraudulent scheme. Will Ernst & Ernst be found guilty of violating Section 10(b) and Rule 10b-5 of the 1934 Securities Exchange Act? [Ernst & Ernst v. Hochfelder, 425 U.S. 185, 96 S.Ct. 1375 (1976)]

8. Lakeside Plastics and Engraving Company was a close corporation incorporated in Minnesota. The company suffered losses from the time it was incorporated in 1946. Of its four shareholders, only one was involved in management of the firm. Notwithstanding its earlier difficulties, by 1954, the firm was apparently about to become profitable. Without informing the other shareholders of this fact, the shareholder-manager bought out the remaining shareholders. He accomplished this by making numerous misrepresentations to them. Assuming the shareholder-manager used none of the instrumentalities of interstate commerce, including the mails or the telephone, in making these misrepresentations, can the remaining shareholders bring an action under Section 10(b) of the Securities Exchange Act of 1934? If not, do the remaining shareholders have any legal recourse? [Myzel v. Fields, 386 F.2d 718 (8th Cir. 1967)]

CHAPTER 46

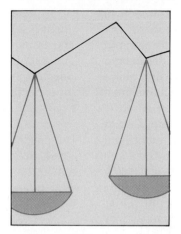

CORPORATIONS
Private Franchises

The Federal Trade Commission has defined *franchise* as "an arrangement in which the owner of a trademark, a trade name, or a copyright licenses others, under specified conditions or limitations, to use the trademark, trade name, or copyright in purveying goods or services." The franchise system has also been described as an organization composed of distributive units established and administered by a supplier as a medium for expanding and controlling the market of its products. Each franchise dealer is a legally independent but economically dependent unit of the integrated business system. The individual *franchisee* (the holder of the franchise) can operate as an independent business; yet it can obtain the advantages of a regional or national organizational affiliation to supply products, advertising, and other services.

The franchise system also provides the consumer public with an opportunity to obtain uniform products at numerous distribution points from small independent contractors. The system

therefore seems good for the businessperson, good for the consumer, and good for the economy.

The use of franchises has expanded rapidly in recent years. It began in the early part of the century. Between 1910 and 1940, franchising was used in the automobile industry, sports, and the soft drink bottling industry. Now franchises account for about 25 percent of all retail sales and more than 13 percent of the gross national product in the United States. The franchise pattern of business development is a particularly appealing form of capitalistic enterprise. It has the advantage of enabling groups of individuals with small amounts of capital to become entrepreneurs.

THE LAW OF FRANCHISING

The growth in franchise operations has outdistanced the law of franchising. There has yet to be developed a solid body of appellate decisions under federal or state laws relating to franchise law. Because of the absence of law precisely addressed to franchising, the courts tend to apply general common law principles and the federal or state statutory definitions where they are appropriate. The franchise relationship has characteristics associated with agency law, employment law, and independent contracting; yet it does not truly fit into any of these traditional classifications.

About fifteen states currently have statutes dealing with franchise law. Although these statutes are not uniform, the following definition was adopted by two states as a basic definition of franchising:

> "Franchise" means a written agreement for a definite or indefinite period, in which a person grants to another person a license to use a trade name, trademark, service mark, or related characteristics, and in which there is a community of interest in the marketing of goods or services at wholesale, retail, by lease, agreement, or otherwise.[1]

TYPES OF FRANCHISES

There are three types of franchises: distributorships, chain-style businesses, and manufacturing or processing plants.

1. A *distributorship* relationship occurs where a manufacturing concern (franchisor) licenses a dealer (franchisee) to sell its product. Often, a distributorship covers an exclusive territory.

2. A *chain-style business* operation occurs when a franchisee operates under a franchisor's trade name and is identified as a member of a select group of dealers that engages in the franchisor's business. The franchisee is generally required to follow standardized or prescribed methods of operations. Often, the franchisor requires that minimum prices and standards of operation be maintained. In addition, sometimes the franchisee is obligated to deal exclusively with the franchisor to obtain materials and supplies.

3. A *manufacturing or processing plant* arrangement is one in which the franchisor transmits to the franchisee the essential ingredients or formula to make a particular product. The franchisee then markets it either at wholesale or at retail in accordance with the franchisor's standards.

THE FRANCHISE AGREEMENT

The franchise relationship is defined by a contract between the franchisor and the franchisee. Each franchise relationship and each industry has its own characteristics, so it is difficult to describe the broad range of details a franchising contract will include. The following sections, however, will define the essential characteristics of the franchise relationship.

Entering the Franchise Relationship

Prospective franchisees must initially decide on the type of business they wish to undertake. Then they must obtain information about the business from the franchisor. Usually, franchisors will have numerous statistics and market studies available for prospective franchisees to examine. Of course, people who acquire franchised businesses vary greatly in their degree of business acumen. Some are experienced business people with a firm grasp of the economic realities of how to operate a franchise. Others have no business experience. The inexperienced franchisee must rely heavily on the franchisor in evaluating and setting up the initial business organization.

Payment for Franchise

The franchisee ordinarily pays an initial fee or lump sum price for the franchise license (the privilege of being granted a franchise). This fee is separate from the various products that the franchisee purchases from or through the franchisor. In some industries, the franchisor relies heavily on the initial sale of the franchise for realizing a profit. In other industries, the continued dealing between the parties brings profit to both.

---

1. N.J. Rev. Stat. Section 56:10-3 (Supp.1972) Wash. Rev. Code Ann. Section 19.100.010 (Supp.1972).

In most situations, the franchisor will receive a stated percentage of the annual sales or annual volume of business done by the franchisee. The franchise agreement may also require the franchisee to pay a percentage of advertising costs and certain administrative expenses incurred throughout the franchise arrangement.

Location and Business Organization

Typically, the franchisor will determine the territory to be served. The franchise agreement can specify whether the premises for the business must be leased or purchased outright. In some cases, construction of a building is necessary to meet the terms of the franchise agreement.

In addition, the agreement will specify whether the franchisor supplies equipment and furnishings for the premises or whether this is the responsibility of the franchisee. When the franchise is a service operation such as a motel, the contract often provides that the franchisor will establish certain standards for the facility and will make inspections to ensure that the standards are being maintained in order to protect the franchise name and reputation.

The business organization of the franchisee is of great concern to the franchisor. Depending on the terms of the franchise agreement, the franchisor may specify particular requirements for the form and capital structure of the business. The franchise agreement can provide that standards of operation, such as sales quotas, quality standards, or record keeping, be conducted by the franchisor. Furthermore, a franchisor may wish to retain stringent control over the training of personnel involved in the operation and over administrative aspects of the business. Although the day-to-day operation of the franchise business is normally left up to the franchisee, the franchise agreement can provide for whatever amount of supervision and control the parties agree upon.

Price and Quality Controls

Franchises provide the franchisor with an outlet for the firm's goods and services. Depending upon the nature of the business, the franchisor may require the franchisee to purchase products from the franchisor at an established price. Of course, a franchisor cannot set the prices at which the franchisee will resell the goods, as this is a violation of state or federal antitrust laws, or both. A franchisor can suggest retail prices but cannot insist on them.

Although a franchisor can require franchisees to purchase supplies from it, requiring a franchisee to purchase *exclusively* from the franchisor may violate federal antitrust laws. The implications of antitrust violations on territorial restrictions, restrictions on products sold, resale price fixing, and price discrimination will be discussed briefly later.

As a general rule, there is no question of the validity of a provision permitting the franchisor to enforce certain quality standards. Since the franchisor has a legitimate interest in maintaining the quality of the product or service in order to protect its name and reputation, it can exercise greater control in this area than would otherwise be tolerated.

Termination of the Franchise Arrangement

The duration of the franchise is a matter to be determined between the parties. Generally, a franchise will start out for a short period, such as a year, so that the franchisee and the franchisor can determine whether they want to stay in business with one another. Usually the franchise agreement will specify that termination must be "for cause" such as death or disability of the franchisee, insolvency of the franchisee, breach of the franchise agreement, or failure to meet specified sales quotas. Most franchise contracts provide that notice of termination must be given. If no set time for termination is given, then a reasonable time with notice will be implied. A franchisee must be given reasonable time to wind up the business—that is, to do the accounting and return the copyright or trademark or any other property of the franchisor.

Much franchise litigation has arisen over termination provisions. Since the franchise agreement is normally a form contract drawn and prepared by the franchisor, and since the bargaining power of the franchisee is rarely equal to that of the franchisor, the termination provisions of contracts are generally more favorable to the franchisor. It is in this area that the lack of statutory law and case law is felt most keenly by the franchisee. In some states, franchisees in automobile dealerships and gasoline stations have some statutory protection, however.

The franchisee normally invests a substantial amount of time and money in the franchise operation to make it successful. Despite this fact, the franchisee may receive little or nothing for the business upon termination. The franchisor owns the trademark and hence the business. The courts have often struggled to offer a terminated franchisee some kind of relief, as is illustrated in the next case.

ATLANTIC RICHFIELD CO. v. RAZUMIC

Supreme Court of Pennsylvania, 1978.
480 Pa., 366, 390 A.2d 736.

BACKGROUND AND FACTS *The plaintiff, Atlantic Richfield Company (Arco), entered into a "dealer lease" with the defendant, Razumic, in 1953. The defendant expended $5,000 for inventory, equipment, and capital. Arco financed the initial supply of gasoline to get the service station on its feet, and the defendant opened for business. Over the years, the parties signed numerous agreements resembling the first dealer lease, as well as various forms concerning the use of Arco's promotional campaign materials, purchase of fuel, and credit card sale arrangements.*

In 1970, Razumic moved into a new service station built by Arco and signed a three-year dealer lease. On June 29, 1973, Arco notified Razumic that the lease would not be renewed and directed Razumic to vacate the premises in thirty days. Razumic refused to leave, and Arco filed suit to force termination of the lease agreement. The trial court found for Arco, holding that the dealership agreement could be terminated at will for any reason.

ROBERTS, Justice.

* * * *

In his pleadings, at trial, and on appeal to this Court, Razumic has urged that he and Arco were parties to a franchise agreement Arco could not terminate at will. Arco, on the other hand, has contended throughout that the dealership agreement could be terminated for any reason. We agree with Razumic.

* * * *

We believe that the 1970 writing and its riders embody a franchise agreement. "In its simplest terms, a franchise is a license from the owner of a trademark or trade name permitting another to sell a product or service under the name or mark. More broadly stated, the franchise has evolved into an elaborate agreement by which the franchisee undertakes to conduct a business or sell a product or service in accordance with methods and procedures prescribed by the franchisor, and the franchisor undertakes to assist the franchisee through advertising, promotion and other advisory services."

"[T]he cornerstone of a franchise system must be the trademark or trade name of a product. It is this uniformity of product and control of its quality and distribution which causes the public to turn to franchise stores for the product."

Given the comprehensive terms of the writing obligating Razumic to operate the Arco service station in a manner Arco determined would reflect favorably upon the public image of the Arco trademark, report and share gross receipts with Arco pursuant to a "FRANCHISE RENT SCHEDULE," and allow Arco to inspect the station to assure Razumic's continued compliance with the many provisions of the form writing, it is clear that Razumic was not pursuing solely his own business interests. Rather, Razumic conducted his business and sold his products in accordance with methods prescribed by Arco.

* * * *

The writing provides Arco the right to terminate the "lease" should Razumic abandon the premises or close them "for a period of seventy-two hours." Razumic's negligence or willful misconduct causing damages to a substantial portion of the premises gives Arco "the right to terminate this lease without liability." Razumic's failure to make timely payment of rent, his death or insolvency, or governmental taking also permit Arco to terminate the "lease." Further, Razumic's "fail[ure] to comply with any of his other obligations" set forth in the writing permits Arco to terminate the agreement if Razumic fails to remedy the situation after fifteen days' notice of non-compliance.

The writing does not, however, contain any provision granting Arco the right to terminate the franchise agreement at will. In view of the provisions authorizing Arco to terminate the parties' franchise agreement for limited, business reasons and an additional provision authorizing Razumic, upon giving "at least sixty days advance written notice," to terminate the agreement without reason upon the anniversary of a term where the stated term exceeds one year, the absence of a similar term authorizing Arco to terminate the agreement without reason is striking.

* * * *

An Arco dealer has his own expectations. He knows that his good service will in many instances produce regular customers. He also realizes, however, that much of his trade will be attracted because his station offers the products, services, and promotions of the well-established and well-displayed name "Arco." Unlike a tenant pursuing his own interests while occupying a landlord's property, a franchisee such as Razumic builds the goodwill of both his own business and Arco.

In exchange, an Arco dealer such as Razumic can justifiably expect that his time, effort, and other investments promoting the goodwill of Arco will not be destroyed as a result of Arco's arbitrary decision to terminate their franchise relationship. Consistent with these reasonable expectations, and Arco's obligation to deal with its franchisees in good faith and in a commercially reasonable manner, Arco cannot arbitrarily sever its franchise relationship with Razumic. A contrary conclusion would allow Arco to reap the benefits of its franchisees' efforts in promoting the goodwill of its name without regard for the franchisees' interests.

* * * *

For the above reasons, the writing's leasehold terminology stating a three year term of occupancy does not govern the duration of the comprehensive contractual business relationship between Razumic and Arco. Rather, the language establishes a right of occupancy which the franchisee Razumic can reasonably expect will not be abruptly halted. Consistent with Razumic's reasonable expectations, principles of good faith and commercial reasonableness, Arco may not arbitrarily recover possession of the service station and thereby summarily terminate the franchise relationship.

JUDGMENT AND REMEDY   *The Supreme Court of Pennsylvania reversed the trial court's decision. Arco was prohibited from terminating the franchise agreement without good cause.*

COMMENTS   *The UCC requirements of good faith in contract dealings are often applied to ongoing franchise relationships when the franchise involves the sale of goods. However, the UCC provisions have ordinarily not been applied to franchise agreements that extend to the leasing of premises.*

Determination of Relief The courts and legal commentators have tried to apply many theories to protect a franchisee's rights upon termination. Some courts have held that every contract contains an implied covenant of good faith and fair dealing. Others have held that if a franchise investment is substantial and the relationship has been established for an indefinite duration, it cannot be terminated until after a reasonable period of time has elapsed. What a reasonable time is will depend upon the circumstances in each case. Some of the circumstances that the courts consider are:

1. The amount of preliminary and promotional expenditures made.
2. The length of time the franchise has been in operation before notice of termination was given.
3. The prospects for forfeiture of profits.
4. Whether or not the franchise has been proven profitable during its actual operation.

If contract provisions allow for termination, even though the provisions may be unfair to the franchisee, it is possible that no cause of action will be found. The Uniform Commercial Code, Section 2-302, has been used by some courts to find that termination provisions dispensing with notification are invalid if their effect is unconscionable. The courts have generally refused to find that franchises terminable by notice at any time or at the end of a specific time are unconscionable *per se.*

Measure of Damages The courts, as illustrated in the *Rea* case following, have also struggled to determine how best to measure damages to pre-

vent injustice or unfairness when misconduct occurs in a franchise relationship. Since franchising is a rather peculiar form of capitalist enterprise, serious franchising problems warrant legislative attention. Congress enacted statutory requirements under the Automobile Dealers' Day in Court Act (15 USCA Section 1221). Thus, in some cases, a franchisee need not rely on common law principles to obtain protection in the courts from franchisor abuses.

Consumer and Franchisee Protection The consumer protection movement and pressures from certain industries (primarily car dealers) have prompted the passage of numerous statutes to protect franchisees from bad faith termination of their franchise contracts. For example, the Automobile Dealers' Day in Court Act allows an auto dealer who contends that the franchisor did not act in good faith in terminating the franchise to take the matter to court for a judicial termination. Moreover, various states have passed laws in recent years that spell out certain conditions and circumstances under which a franchise can be terminated. However, these laws are subject to serious constitutional challenges under the impairment of contracts clause, the due process clause, and the interstate commerce clause of the U.S. Constitution.

The realities of the franchise industry demonstrate a need for uniform regulation. Common law theories and existing statutory remedies have little application to franchising problems. The franchise system is a complex and unique business enterprise. It is growing so fast that it seems almost impossible to design a regulatory scheme that is both comprehensive and flexible enough to meet the needs of franchises.

BACKGROUND AND FACTS *This case involved both an individual and a corporate plaintiff. Both plaintiffs filed the action to recover from the automobile manufacturer (franchisor) for damages based on alleged violations of the Automobile Dealers' Day in Court Act. The suit was under litigation for more than ten years. The basic controversy arose when the manufacturer required the plaintiff to resign his holdings in a competing manufacturer's dealership as a condition for obtaining a Ford franchise.*

In February 1964 the plaintiff, Rea, was given a franchise for a Ford dealership in Pennsylvania. At that time he was already a principal stockholder of an Oldsmobile dealership in Pennsylvania. Rea told Ford that he would acquire the assets needed to operate the Ford dealership by liquidating the Oldsmobile business, and Ford had him sign a letter committing him to taking that step.

Subsequently, Rea suggested to a Ford representative that the Oldsmobile operation might not be closed. The Ford representative then warned Rea that unless he got out of the Oldsmobile business, Ford might not ship him the cars needed to operate the Ford franchise. Shortly thereafter, Rea gave up his interest in the Oldsmobile franchise, kept part of its assets to be used in operating the Ford franchise, and sold the rest.

At the trial, it was established that the manufacturer's requirement was a violation of the Automobile Dealers' Day in Court Act. On appeal, Ford's liability was upheld; the only issue remaining was the measure of damages.

REA AND 22 FORD, INC. v. FORD MOTOR CO.

United States Court of Appeals, Third Circuit, 1977.
560 F.2d 554.

HUNTER, Circuit Judge.

*   *   *   *

At the outset, Ford argues that the trial court erred in refusing to allow Ford to introduce evidence tending to establish that: (1) Ford's acts were not the proximate cause of the sale of Rea's Oldsmobile business; (2) Ford's acts were not the proximate cause of any loss in profits by Rea's corporate entities; and (3) Rea failed to "mitigate" damages and, therefore, Ford had not caused any real harm. These elements of causation, says Ford, go to damages alone and were not foreclosed by this court's affirmance of the finding of liability under the Automobile Dealers' Day in Court Act.

We do not agree. Causation is an element of liability. Our remand left open only the amount of damages, not the fact of damage.

[The court refused to allow Ford to challenge the question of liability. It then went on to discuss the elements of damage and the appropriate calculation.]

Ford also claims that the court below erred in including Rea's projected salary and bonuses at the last Oldsmobile franchise in the damage calculation.

[Ford continued to argue that Rea's compensation should be limited to what he would have received as a principal stockholder.]

Again, we do not agree. The corporate entity that suffered harm was the Oldsmobile franchise, which ceased to exist; the "dealer" for purposes of the action under the Auto Dealers' Act was Edward Rea in his capacity as a Ford dealer. In that capacity, he personally suffered damage not only through loss of income as a shareholder of the Oldsmobile business Ford forced him to close, but also through loss of the salary and bonuses he could have earned in that business. Since Rea was injured in both respects by Ford's action, he can be made whole only by recovering both types of compensation.

Ford's last point of appeal is that the trial court erred in awarding Rea damages covering the period between Ford's successful first appeal and the retrial as to damages. Ford claims to have been "penalized" for taking an appeal.

We do not agree. The court merely exercised its ordinary powers. Lost profits are recoverable in an action for the destruction or interruption of an established business, whenever they are not merely speculative or conjectural. And, in general, a court has the power to award damages occurring up to the date of the ultimate judgment in the case. Ford does not claim that the damages were too speculative; indeed the fact that the injured party—Rea—had survived the intervening period meant precisely that any objection that he might not have lived to suffer "future damages"—those occurring after the first trial—was obviated. As for the supposed "penalty," Ford might likewise claim that it was "penalized" by defending the action at all, since that also prolonged the period for which lost profits might have been recovered.

[The court went on to evaluate certain other calculations. It found that certain deductions were properly made but certain others were improper, so it reversed the latter. After the court assessed the value of all of the assets involved, it arrived at its decision to adjust the award given by the district court.]

JUDGMENT *The court of appeals upheld both the liability and damages award of the*
AND REMEDY *district court. However, the court recalculated the value of the assets and hence the damages suffered by the plaintiff and vacated the district court's judgment, remanding the case with instructions to the district court to add approximately $160,934 to the judgment awarded the plaintiff. In addition, the court of appeals determined that the Oldsmobile dealership as a corporate entity had no right of action. Only the individual plaintiff, Rea, could collect damages.*

REGULATION OF THE FRANCHISING INDUSTRY

Any industry that expands rapidly without a uniform regulatory scheme is likely to engage in certain abusive and destructive practices. The franchising industry is no exception. The Federal Trade Commission has recently begun investigations to determine whether illegal methods have been used to compel restaurant franchises to purchase goods and services at artificially inflated prices. Other abusive practices have been discovered in the form of hidden markups on the capital assets and equipment that must be purchased by a franchisee either from the franchisor or from approved vendors. Cases

of misrepresentation occur in the initial sale of many franchises. More than a few unsuspecting franchisees have learned after entering into the franchise contract that in order to operate the business and meet the established sales quotas, they must work an inordinate number of hours a week.

The franchise relationship grows out of a contract. But because of the nature of the franchise system, the common law remedies that have been applied to contract and sales contract situations do not provide adequate relief. Furthermore, only about fifteen states have enacted statutory laws to govern franchise relationships. Thus, what is permissible in one state may not be permissible in another. Such lack of uniformity places a great hardship on franchise arrangements, especially when they are operated on a national scale.

Within the last ten years, regulation of the franchise industry has finally begun at the federal level. Most federal remedies deal with violations of antitrust laws. Attempts at control using the federal securities laws have been less effective. The courts, the state legislatures, and the Congress are all attempting to develop uniform regulations for the franchising industry.

The Franchise Contract: Disclosure Protection

A franchise purchaser can suffer substantial loss if the franchisor has not provided full and complete information regarding the franchisor-franchisee relationship, as well as the details of the contract under which the business will be operated. When misrepresentation permeates the initial sale of a franchise operation, the common law remedy of fraud in the inducement provides inadequate relief. In most cases, the franchisee has already paid the franchise purchase price and may also have incurred substantial losses in the initial operating phases of the business. The elements of fraud are exceedingly difficult to prove. Even the tort of intentional misstatement or misrepresentation of a material fact upon which the franchisee relied places a great burden on the franchisee to show that the franchisor's original offer was misleading or fraudulent.

Only a few of the states that have enacted legislation concerning franchising have included disclosure provisions. California was the first state to enact a franchise disclosure law, and it has served as a model for other disclosure statutes. The California Franchise Investment Law sets out twenty-two items that must be disclosed in a registration filed with the state. Some of the items of disclosure include:

1. The name and business address of the franchisor.
2. The business experience of any persons affiliated with the franchisor.
3. Whether any person associated with the franchisor has been convicted of a felony.

4. A recent financial statement.
5. A typical franchise agreement.
6. A statement of all fees that the franchisee is required to pay.
7. Other information that the commissioner of corporations may reasonably require.[2]

Some courts have attempted to apply the Securities Act of 1933 and various state blue sky laws to franchise agreements. This has met with limited success. The franchise agreement could possibly be considered an "investment contract" within the meaning of blue sky laws and the 1933 Securities Act. Thus, it would be subject to the registration and disclosure requirements of the securities laws. It has been argued that a franchise arrangement is an investment contract that is a security under the Securities Act.

This theory, however, has not met with much success on the federal level. The United States Supreme Court has defined an investment contract as "a contract, transaction or scheme whereby a person invests his (or her) money in a common enterprise and is led to expect profits solely from the efforts of the promoter or third party."[3] The typical franchise agreement fails this test for determining "investment contracts" because a franchisee must make an effort to make money. Thus, franchise agreements are usually not considered securities under the Securities Act.

Federal law prohibits mail fraud. According to 18 USCA Section 1341, the U.S. mails cannot be used to further a scheme to defraud. Like Section 5 of the FTC Act, the mail fraud provision penalizes misrepresentations made by use of the

---

2. Cal. Corp. Code Section 31001 (West Supp. 1975). The California Franchise Investment Law provides: "California franchisees have suffered substantial losses where the franchisor or his (or her) representative has not provided full and complete information regarding the franchisor-franchisee relationship, the details of the contract between the franchisor and the franchisee, and the prior business experience of the franchisor." It is the intent of this law to provide each prospective franchisee with the information necessary to make an intelligent decision regarding the franchise being offered. Cal. Corp. Code Section 31001 (West Supp. 1975). As cited in 59 Minn.Law Rev. 1027 (1975). Casenote: Franchise Regulation.

3. SEC v. W.J. Howey Co., 328 U.S. 293, 66 S.Ct. 1100 (1946).

mails. This is not a very effective means for preventing fraud or misrepresentation in a franchisor's negotiations with a potential franchisee because it affords only an after-the-fact remedy.

Similarly, the Federal Trade Commission, under Section 5 of the FTC Act, has the power to stop unfair or deceptive practices in commerce and to prohibit deceptive advertising. Both the FTC provisions and the mail fraud provisions lack the affirmative protection that disclosure laws would afford a potential purchaser of a franchise.

The FTC Franchise Rule

The FTC franchise rule was promulgated in response to widespread evidence of deception and unfair practices in connection with the resale of franchises and business opportunity ventures. This rule requires that, within a specified time, franchisors and franchise brokers furnish the information that prospective franchisees need in order to make an informed decision about entering into a franchise relationship. The rule sets forth the circumstances under which a franchisor or broker can make claims about the projected sales income or profits of existing or potential outlets. The rule also imposes requirements that concern the establishment and termination of the franchise relationship.

Franchisee's Relationship to Franchisor: Agent or Independent Contractor?

The mere licensing of a trade name does not create an agency relationship. However, the courts have determined that certain factors in the franchisor-franchisee relationship indicate the existence of an agency relationship:

1. The terms of the agreement create an agency relationship.
2. The franchisor exercises a high degree of control over the franchisee's activities.
3. A third person looking at the relationship between the franchisor and the franchisee would reasonably believe that there is an agency relationship.

4. The franchisor derives an especially great benefit from the franchisee's activities. The greater the benefit, the more likely an agency relationship will be found.[4]

If these factors show a very close relationship between the franchisor and the franchisee, then their relationship will be deemed to be that of an employer-employee or principal-agent. If the factors show a high degree of independence between the franchisee and franchisor, then the franchisee will be deemed an independent contractor.

The characterization of the relationship has tax implications and implications for the regulatory treatment of the business organization. In addition, if an agency relationship is found, the franchisor is liable for the franchisee's improper actions or injuries to third parties both in tort and in contract.

FRANCHISING— ANTITRUST IMPLICATIONS

Two categories of antitrust problems have recently developed. The first involves the distribution of the product. Generally, the franchisor uses the franchise to distribute its goods. Antitrust problems arise when the franchisor attempts to restrict its distributors to selling in only certain areas. Additionally, this action is often accompanied by an attempt by the manufacturers to control or regulate the prices of the goods. Either can be held as a violation of the Sherman Antitrust Act of 1890.

The second major antitrust problem involves trademark licensing arrangements. One of the most notable advantages to a franchisor is the ability to do business under a well-known and respected name. However, the franchise arrangement often produces problems concerning exclusive dealing. In general, the owner of the franchise is required to use only certain products and must buy them from the manufacturer.

---

4. See Kuchta v. Allied Builders Corp., 21 Cal.App.3d 541, 98 Cal.Rptr. 588 (1971).

These two categories of antitrust problems are vast and complex. They can be avoided by proper drafting of the franchise agreement.[5]

QUESTIONS AND
CASE PROBLEMS

1. John Jefferson has a franchise beer distributorship. He has built this distributorship up over ten years to be a very profitable business. Last year Jefferson decided to sell a soft drink and distribute it to the outlet retailers and businesses who purchased the beer. The beer company franchisor was unhappy with the arrangement. There was nothing in the franchise agreement to prohibit Jefferson from distributing a noncompeting product, but there was a provision that required Jefferson to give his full attention to the franchise. The beer company demanded that Jefferson cease distributing the soft drink, and Jefferson refused. The franchisor beer company immediately terminated the franchise agreement. Discuss the franchisee's rights in this matter.

2. Ann has been interested in securing a particular high-quality ice cream franchise. The franchisor is willing to give Ann a franchise. A franchise agreement is made that calls for Ann to sell the ice cream only at a specific location, to buy all the ice cream from the franchisor, to order and sell all the flavors produced by the franchisor, and to refrain from selling any ice cream stored for more than two weeks after delivery by the franchisor, as this ice cream decreases in quality after that period. After two months of operation, Ann believes that she can increase her profits by moving the store to another part of the city. She also refuses to order even a limited quantity of the "fruit delight" flavor because of its higher cost, and she has sold ice cream that has been stored longer than two weeks without customer complaint. Ann claims that the franchisor has no right to restrict her in these practices. Discuss her claims.

3. Smith is approached by Apex Company, a franchisor, to sell Apex products under a franchise ar-

rangement. The franchise contract calls for Smith to pay Apex $20,000, and for Apex to supply Smith with all Apex products on low-interest credit terms. The contract also provides that Apex will advertise its products in the area and furnish Smith, who has had no previous business experience, with bookkeeping and other management services. Smith borrows the money and pays Apex $20,000. Apex is a sole proprietorship on shaky financial ground. Not only does Apex fail to provide the promised management services to Smith, but it also fails to advertise its products in Smith's area. In addition, Apex is often late in filling Smith's orders. Smith wants to hold Apex liable for substantial losses. Discuss under what theories Smith will claim relief.

4. Blake is interested in becoming a service station dealer. He contacts Esco Oil Corporation and obtains a franchise contract in which Esco agrees to furnish Blake all gasoline, oil, and related products to run the service station. In addition, Esco provides Blake with Esco signs and promotional materials. A sign reading "Blake's Esco Service" is provided for the front of the station. In return for supplying all products Blake requires, promotional materials and signs, and other services, Esco is to receive a percentage on all products sold. Esco advertises that it stands behind its dealers. The relationship between Blake and Esco is challenged. Discuss whether the relationship is strictly franchisor-franchisee or whether it is a principal-agent (employer-employee) relationship.

5. Four franchisees of a bicycle manufacturer are located in Clover City. The franchisor-franchisee agreements of each carry the following terms:

   (a) Each franchisee is given a specific territory, and in no case does one territory overlap another. Each franchisee is prohibited from selling a bicycle to any customer who lives in another territory.

   (b) Franchisees must resell bicycles at a price equal to or higher than the suggested retail price furnished by the franchisor.

   (c) Although the franchisee can use any business name wished, the franchisee must represent himself or herself as an authorized dealer of the franchisor and cannot sell or service other brands of bicycles.

Discuss whether this franchise agreement violates antitrust laws.

6. Ger-Ro-Mar, Inc., was a manufacturer and distributor of lingerie and swimwear. Through its multilevel marketing program, Ger-Ro-Mar enlisted the services of men and women throughout the country to sell its products at wholesale and retail. Under the

---

5. For two landmark cases in these areas, see United States v. Arnold, Schwinn & Co., 388 U.S. 365, 87 S.Ct. 1856 (1967); and Fortner Enterprises v. U.S. Steel Corp., 394 U.S. 495, 89 S.Ct. 1252 (1969).

selling arrangement, franchisees were required to buy an inventory before they could participate in the program. A prospective franchisee could enter at any of three levels—key distributor, senior key, or supervisor. Entry at a particular level was based on the amount of inventory initially purchased by the franchisee. To induce individuals to become franchisees, Ger-Ro-Mar distributed various promotional materials that described the marketing system and illustrated how an individual could earn large sums of money by building a large personal group of salespeople through recruitment. The illustration in Ger-Ro-Mar's brochures promised that district managers could earn up to $56,000 and regional managers up to $90,000 yearly. Of the regional manager position, Ger-Ro-Mar's promotional brochure promised, "ANY ONE CAN ACHIEVE THIS LEVEL." An investigation by the FTC revealed that the success promised in the brochure was dependent upon the franchisee's recruitment of salespersons who in turn would recruit salespersons under them. Is there anything wrong with Ger-Ro-Mar's franchising scheme? Why might the FTC wish to order Ger-Ro-Mar to cease and desist distribution of its promotional brochure? [Ger-Ro-Mar, Inc. v. FTC, 518 F.2d 33 (2d Cir. 1975)]

7. A franchise agreement entered into between Shakey's Incorporated, as franchisor, and Charles Martin, as franchisee, included the following provision: "Upon termination of this agreement, for a period of one year thereafter, the franchisee shall not engage in the production or sale of pizza products in a location within a radius of thirty miles from the franchised premises." After operating a Shakey's pizza franchise for several years, Martin ceased doing business as Shakey's, removed all indications of Shakey's trade name from the premises, and proceeded to do business as "Martin's Pizza Parlor." Has Martin violated his agreement not to compete? What protectable business interest does Shakey's have, if any? Is the agreement not to compete a reasonable one? [Shakey's Incorporated v. Martin, 91 Idaho 758, 430 P.2d 504 (1967)]

8. E. T. Runyan and Pacific Air Industries, Inc., entered into a written franchise agreement whereby, in consideration of Runyan's payment of $25,000, he was awarded an exclusive photogrammetric franchise for four southern California counties. Under the agree-

ment, Pacific was obligated to train Runyan in the rudiments of photogrammetry, including twenty-five hours of sales and technical assistance for an initial period. In the meantime, Runyan resigned his position with Tidewater Oil Company. Since Runyan was entering a technical field in which he had no experience, he relied on Pacific's promise. Pacific's training program proved to be entirely inadequate. Runyan nevertheless attempted to operate his franchise, but when he realized that he was unable to do so, he attempted to rescind. Can Runyan rescind the franchise agreement? [Runyan v. Pacific Air Indust., Inc., 2 Cal.3d 304, 85 Cal.Rptr. 138, 466 P.2d 682 (1970)]

9. In June 1963, Econo-Car granted Carl Taute a franchise to operate a rent-a-car business in Billings, Montana. Burko, an Econo-Car agent, told Taute at the time that as a result of a study for Burko, Econo-Car knew the three best locations for a rent-a-car business in Billings, that Burko would send three men to Billings to help Taute during his first few weeks, and that the entire franchise fee paid by Taute would be spent for three pages of newspaper advertisements during the grand opening. In August 1963, while the contract was still in its early stages of performance and very little time or money had been spent by either party, Taute learned that Burko's statements were false. Nevertheless, Taute continued with his preparations to go into business and, in fact, conducted business for about sixteen months. Thereafter, Taute sued Econo-Car to rescind the franchise agreement, claiming that Econo-Car's agent fraudulently induced him into becoming a franchisee. Will Taute be successful in rescinding the franchise agreement? [Taute v. Econo-Car Int'l, Inc., 414 F.2d 828 (9th Cir. 1969)]

10. A fifteen-year-old employee was injured while using a slicing machine at a fast food franchise, the Yankee Doodle Dandy restaurant. Federal law prohibits the operation of meat-slicing machines by persons under eighteen years of age. Under the franchise agreement, the franchisor had the power to terminate the agreement if the franchisee failed to comply with local, state, and federal laws. The franchisor knew that the franchisee was not conforming to the law. Can the franchisor be held liable for the negligent supervision of the franchisee? [Coty v. U.S. Slicing Machine Co., Inc., 58 Ill.App.3d, 15 Ill.Dec. 687, 373 N.E.2d 1371 (1978)]

FOCUS ON ETHICS

Business Organizations

Whenever discussion of business organizations occurs, the central issue is usually the nature of large American business corporations. To be sure, numerous ethical issues are involved in partnership law and in the nature of other specialized forms of business organizations. For example, what should be the treatment of joint ventures—should the individuals involved be treated simply as partners? What about the use of hybrid forms of business organization that are devised to gain either a limitation of liability, e.g., limited partnerships, or tax advantages, e.g., Subchapter S corporations? The ethical questions about these other forms of business organizations are important; however, the issue of big business dominates ethical concerns in both economics and in law in this country. One of the most important considerations is the nature of the control of the large corporation.

WHO CONTROLS THE CORPORATION?

Consider a corporation with literally millions of shareholders. Does any one shareholder affect the way in which the modern corporation governs itself? The answer has to be no. Indeed, the question of the separation of ownership and management is basic. Management of a corporation apparently can do whatever it wants within the scope of the charter of the corporation. The directors and officers seemingly have a duty to perform, but perform for whom? If a director's action cannot be controlled by the owners of the corporation, then by what means is such an action controlled?

There is an ethical question at the heart of all actions of directors and officers. What is the nature of their duty to the entity called the corporation? What is the nature of their duty to society? What is the nature of their duty to the corporation's employees? All of these ethical responsibilities can be considered elements of the question of corporate social responsibility.

CORPORATE SOCIAL RESPONSIBILITY

For a number of years now, numerous speakers have debated the social responsibility of the corporation as an institution. At one end of the spectrum is the notion that the corporation's sole responsibility is to maximize profits within the limits set by the law. In other words, the corporation is simply viewed as an extension of its shareholders. Thus, nonprofit-making activities will diminish the shareholders' wealth and therefore are not considered appropriate corporate conduct. At the other end of the spectrum is the notion that the directors and officers of a corporation have a higher duty. That is to say, they should engage only in those activities that benefit society as a whole. Therefore, if the corporation produces a type of baby food that babies like and that mothers buy, but one that is not "good" for babies because of a high MSG or sugar content, the corporation should not market the baby food.

One of the major problems in discussing corporate social responsibility is our inability to objectively define it. We might have some notion of the nature of socially responsible actions when publicly appointed or elected officials are under study, but we have much less clear-cut notions about socially responsible actions when the directors or officers of a private corporation are concerned. Also, critics of the entire concept of corporate social responsibility argue that they do not want private citizens, in their roles as directors and officers of private

BUSINESS ORGANIZATIONS

UNIT VII

corporations, engaging in activities that those individuals believe are socially responsible. That is the essence of the political process, contend these critics, and the two should be separate.

Despite criticisms of corporate social responsibilities, most major corporations do engage in philanthropic activities. (Note that at early law, the corporation could not give to charity.) Most major corporations usually employ one or more individuals to screen charitable requests and determine which organizations will receive charitable contributions. Corporations routinely donate to hospitals, the arts, universities, and the like. Corporate nonprofit activity is justified for public policy reasons. The argument is that the wealth of the nation is no longer primarily in the hands of private individuals. Much of the nation's wealth is in corporate hands. Additionally, since the share of government has increased dramatically since the 1930s, taxation has increased accordingly. The philanthropic abilities of private individuals have thereby been diminished. For these reasons and others, the law has changed to allow private corporations to give to charity.

THE CORPORATION'S DUTY TO THE CONSUMER

What is the nature of the corporation's duty to the consumer? This is an issue that today often dominates discussions of product quality, pricing, and advertising. The layperson's notion is that he or she has absolutely no effect on the pricing, quality, and nature of the products and services offered by the modern-day giant corporation. Therefore, most consumers believe that corporations must be severely

regulated by the government and the courts in order to maintain the consumer's rights.

But what, really, is at issue here? Can the corporation willfully ignore the well-being of the consumer? The critics of modern-day corporations say yes. The supporters of modern-day corporations do not agree. They contend that the ultimate control of the corporation lies in the hands of the consumer. After all, they argue, it is the consumer who freely chooses to buy or not to buy a corporation's product. Even in the absence of effective competition, the consumer can purchase a smaller quantity of the product being offered. Thus, either through competition or the limited budget of the consumer, the corporation must always attempt to satisfy the consumer. Indeed, in pure economic analysis, the nature of profit-maximization involves a continuous attempt to find ways to reduce costs so that prices can be reduced (thereby increasing quantity demanded) or to improve quality without increasing costs (again, so that quantity demanded will be increased).

Be that as it may, an ethical question remains. The process of competition takes time. Information is costly to obtain and never perfect. If corporate leaders know or suspect that certain of their products may have deleterious long-run effects on the consumer, shouldn't such corporate leaders have an ethical responsibility to inform the consumer? And what about an ethical responsibility to citizens in other countries? If the Food and Drug Administration has prohibited the sale of a particular substance in the United States because it might have long-run carcinogenic effects, should the

producer attempt to sell it in those countries where it is still legal?

THE CORPORATION'S DUTY TO ITS EMPLOYEES

What are the corporation's duties to its employees? The answer to this ethical question is not an easy one because of the necessary trade-offs involved. To the extent that the corporation provides higher than competitive wages, better than "reasonable" working conditions, and the like, its costs per unit of production will be higher. That means that the price of the product will be higher. Who has a greater "right," the employee or the consumer? Also, there is a conflict between the shareholder and the employee. The more employees obtain, presumably the less shareholders will obtain. No easy solution to this conflict is available.

DISCUSSION QUESTIONS

1. If shareholders as individuals own too small a percentage of a corporation to have an effect on its actions, how do shareholders exhibit control over the corporation? Some argue that their control is via the sale of shares in companies with whose actions they are dissatisfied. How would such a sale of shares have any effect on the company's future activities?
2. Should a company act ethically toward its competitors? Toward its suppliers? If so, in what way?
3. Is energy conservation an ethical concern of business?
4. Should conservation of natural resources and other environmental considerations become ethical concerns to which businesses should address themselves?

UNIT VIII

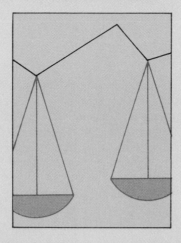

GOVERNMENT REGULATION

CHAPTER 47

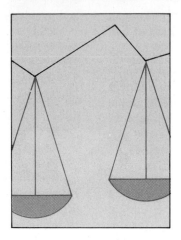

GOVERNMENT REGULATION
Regulation and
Administrative Agencies

In most of the preceding chapters we have concentrated on the rules that constrain business decisions that arise from common law decisions by the courts. Today's business decisions, however, are often more constrained by statutes and rules enforced by administrative agencies. These constraints are called *government regulation.*

Regulation of private business activities has been with us for many years. But it was during the Great Depression that such regulation began to increase. Regulation has always increased during major conflicts, such as World Wars I and II. However, in the last decade or so, business regulations have shifted from rules which primarily evolved from the common law and from judicial interpretation of statutory regulations to more direct controls.

Furthermore, until recently, the functions and authority of many government agencies were primarily ministerial. Their actions were generally limited to carrying out specific activities mandated by legislatures. Thus, social security offices gave information and advice to individ-

uals filing for benefits but possessed relatively few discretionary powers. Starting in the late 1960s, an increasing number of new rules and regulations were established along with new federal regulatory agencies. Probably, the current constraints placed on business transactions by regulatory authorities have more impact on the economy than those that stem from the common law and the courts. For example, seven new regulatory agencies, including the Occupational Safety and Health Administration (OSHA), the Consumer Product Safety Commission (CPSC), and the Environmental Protection Agency (EPA), were created in the early 1970s. The first four years of the 1970s saw a doubling of the number of pages in the Federal Register, the primary document for notification of federal rules and regulations.

REGULATED ACTIVITIES

Virtually every economic activity is subject to some regulation at one stage or another in the process of manufacturing, wholesaling, retailing, or other activity. A few of those activities are discussed here.

Transportation

Most forms of transportation—surface, air, and water—are subject to a multitude of government regulations. The commerce clause of the Constitution gives the federal government the power to regulate commerce and interstate trade. The Interstate Commerce Commission (ICC), created by the Act to Regulate Commerce in 1887, has regulated freight service transportation throughout the United States since that time. The major form of regulation concerns the rates that can be charged for different commodities as well as for distance traveled.[1] In addition to rate regulation, the ICC prohibits carriers from carrying freight on back hauls (return trips) in a number of situations. Such prohibitions decrease the options of shippers, thereby generating higher prices for all shipping.

The ICC also regulates the lease rates on railroad freight cars and other rolling stock. In recent years, the price has not been permitted to rise, so individual firms have found that rail cars have become a cheaper means of storing merchandise. A significant shortage of railroad cars has been the main result of this regulation.

In some cases, the ICC's regulatory powers exceed those of other government agencies. For example, in United States v. Interstate Commerce Comm., the Justice Department unnecessarily attempted to block the commission's approval of the merger of the Great Northern Railway Company and the Northern Pacific Railway Company.[2]

Utilities

Because of the specific monopoly status of utilities, local and state governments have regulated the provision of electrical power and water, gas,

and phone service. Public utility commissions set recoverable revenue on the basis of cost. The cost estimates are crucial in the negotiations between the regulated electric utility and the Public Service Commission. Regulatory commissions also institute requirements to serve new customers or to prohibit individuals from purchasing services. In Santa Barbara, California, for example, the local government placed a moratorium on new construction by prohibiting water and sewer hookups for new homes.

Communications

The most prominent form of regulation of communications is concerned with the right to transmit or broadcast signals in the electromagnetic spectrum. Various regulatory agencies, including the Department of Defense and the Federal Communications Commission, have the right to allocate the air waves. Licenses are generally granted for specific periods of time, and they regulate the mixture of programming that the station can offer its audience. Licenses also specify the station's maximum and minimum wattage power for transmission without interference.

The Federal Communications Commission severely regulated alternative forms of electromagnetic signal transmissions, for example, pay television, cable television and satellite television. After many years of strict regulation, the FCC has in the past few years deregulated much of the cable and pay television industry.

Consumer Products

Ultimately, consumer products are subject to a large number of regulations, since virtually every regulation has its final impact on the price of the commodity in the market. Some regulations, however, are more direct. The Consumer Product Safety Commission (CPSC) has jurisdiction over more than ten thousand products. The agency has been given the authority to establish mandatory safety standards, to require warnings by manufacturers, to require producers to give rebates to consumers and to ban or recall products without a court hearing. In addition, it can impose criminal penalties so that it is possible

---

1. Thomas Gail Moore, "Freight Transportation Regulation: Service Freight and the Interstate Commerce Commission," AEI (1972).

2. 396 U.S. 491, 90 S.Ct. 708 (1970).

for executives in firms with violations to face jail sentences.[3]

Health and Safety

In 1970, Congress passed a comprehensive act to regulate occupational safety and health.[4] In response, the Department of Labor has issued various detailed rules and regulations specifying safety standards for almost every industry. There are standards that apply to fire extinguishers, electrical groundings, exits from buildings, guards for machines, and other resources or activities that affect production in industry. In addition, certain rules apply to particular work activities. For example, regulations can specify the times and locations when construction personnel must wear hard hats. The law imposes numerous recordkeeping requirements concerning accidental injuries and job-related health problems.

Innovation

Many federal regulations indirectly affect investment and innovation. In some industries, however, the regulations are more closely applied to innovative actions and to the research and development process. For example, the 1962 Kefauver-Harris amendments to the Food, Drug and Cosmetic Act of 1938 eliminated the time constraint for the Food and Drug Administration's approval of a new drug application. After 1962, the FDA could withhold a drug from the market indefinitely, until the agency was satisfied that the drug was both safe and effective for its intended use.

Energy

Energy is regulated by a large number of independent agencies, each of which promulgates numerous rules and regulations. More importantly, numerous studies have shown that these organizations have been extremely effective in altering economic activity in energy and related

industries. For example, the Federal Power Commission (FPC) has regulated the price of natural gas for many years. It set initial price ceilings close to market prices so the regulation at that time had little or no effect. Throughout the 1960s, however, in its determination to hold the line against increases in natural gas prices, the FPC failed to increase regional maximum prices to reflect real increases in demand and inflationary pressures. As a consequence, shortages appeared, causing some extreme problems by the 1970s.[5]

Patent and Copyright

The Constitution delegates to Congress the power "to promote the progress of science and useful arts, by securing limited times to authors and inventors concerning the exclusive right to their respective writings and discoveries * * *." As early as 1790, a number of statutes implementing this power were passed. The patent laws exclude others, for a period of seventeen years, from making, using, or selling inventions that are claimed and determined to be patentable. Patent laws are unique in that they permit a number of practices that are considered to be anticompetitive. For example, the owner of a patent can fix prices to at least one licensee—a per se violation of antitrust laws in the absence of a patent. Thus, the patent law deviates from the general policy of preventing monopolies in order to encourage the development and production of goods and services by offering economic protection for a limited time. In a similar manner, authors or their estates hold exclusive rights to the authors' published or unpublished works for life plus fifty years. For works that are anonymous or pseudonymous, protection is given for a minimum of seventy-five years from publication or one hundred years from creation.

Trademarks

At common law, merchants acquire legal rights to the words or symbols they use to distinguish

---

3. Consumer Product Safety Act, Public Law 92-573. 42 USCA Section 3142-1, 29 USCA Section 661.
4. Occupational Safety and Health Act of 1970.

5. Paul MacAvoy, "The Regulated Induced Shortage of Natural Gas," *Journal of Law and Economics* (April 1971): 167–200.

their goods from others by adoption and use. Congress, acting under the commerce clause of the Constitution, enacted legislation long ago to facilitate the acquisition and enforcement of trademark rights. In 1946, the Lanham Act permitted registration of any distinctive mark indicative of its source or origin. (Trademarks include "any word, name, symbol, or device, or any combination thereof adopted and used by the manufacturer [or] merchant to identify its goods and distinguish them from those manufactured or sold by others.") Existing law, however, has determined that if the trademark be-

comes associated as a generic term for the commodity and loses its association with a particular producer, then it is no longer valid. The trademarks *linoleum* and *aspirin*, for example, were lost when they became generally accepted as the generic name of the goods.

TYPES OF REGULATION

Within each regulated sector there are numerous types of regulation. In Exhibit 47–1 we examine some of the more important forms of regulation.

EXHIBIT 47–1   TYPES OF REGULATION

PROFIT REGULATION:	Profit regulation most often arises where the government has granted exclusive rights to produce a commodity. Most electric and water public utilities fall into this category.
PRICE REGULATION:	Price regulation can take the form of maximum, minimum, or uniform prices. New York City, for example, establishes the maximum price that certain apartment owners can charge their tenants. Minimum prices are often established as floors for certain agricultural products, such as wheat.
ADVERTISING:	Restrictions on professional advertising—for lawyers, doctors, and dentists—have survived many constitutional challenges in the past, but they appear to be weakening today. Restrictions on cigarette advertising continue.
QUOTAS AND DUTIES:	Explicit import duties or taxes are often applied to various products. In addition, some products, like petroleum, have been subject to absolute limits or quotas for importation.
LICENSING AND ALLOCATING RIGHTS:	Through their exercise of licensing power, agencies control entry into and operation of given economic activities. No rail, motor, or water carrier, for example can extend its routes without a license from the Interstate Commerce Commission.
STANDARD SETTING:	Government agencies establish many standards for consumers. The U.S. Department of Agriculture, for example, grades beef and issues standards for other meat and poultry products.
DISCLOSURE REQUIREMENTS:	Sellers may be required to disclose certain information prior to the completion of a sale. For example, television ads for automobiles that give specific payment periods must also give the down payment, the amount of monthly payment, and the annual percentage rate of interest.
CONTRACT REVISIONS:	Regulatory agencies may limit the ability of parties to write contracts. For example, in recent years there have been movements to limit the remedies, such as wage attachments, available to creditors for defaults on consumer loans.
MATERIALS AND PROCESS REGULATION:	Regulatory agencies can also specify the type of material or process that can be used in the manufacture of certain goods. The Food and Drug Administration (FDA), for example, has prohibited the use of red dye number 2 in food and cosmetics.
TAXES AND SUBSIDIES:	Taxes and subsidies may be used as a means of changing economic behavior. For example, if taxes are imposed on inputs—factors of production such as raw materials and labor—then firms that use those inputs will be likely to substitute lower-cost alternatives.

ADMINISTRATIVE AGENCIES

Administrative agencies are the primary interpreters and enforcers of many legislative statutes that focus on business regulation. Sometimes these agencies are part of a traditional administrative branch of the government. For example, the Justice Department enforces the Sherman Act, the Clayton Act, and other antitrust laws. The National Highway Traffic Safety Administration and the Department of Transportation enforce regulations regarding safety, emissions, controls, and fuel economy of automobiles. In other cases, Congress has established administrative agencies that are independent of the executive branch. For example, the Interstate Commerce Commission regulates most service transportation within the United States as well as the service transportation of foreign countries that takes place within the boundaries of the United States. Other independent agencies include the Federal Aviation Administration, the Civil Aeronautics Board, the Commodity Futures Trading Commission, the Equal Employment Opportunity Commission, the Export-Import Bank of the United States, the Federal Communications Commission, the Federal Energy Administration, the Federal Home Loan Bank Board, the Federal Maritime Commission, the Federal Power Commission, the Federal Trade Commission, the International Trade Commission, the National Labor Relations Board, the Securities and Exchange Commission, and the Small Business Administration. Exhibit 47-2 lists the most important agencies with rule-making powers.

Regulatory Powers and Procedures

Administrative agencies combine the duties and responsibilities of the judicial, executive, and legislative branches of the government. Heads of administrative agencies are generally appointed by the president with the consent of two-thirds of the Senate. Because Congress has delegated certain powers to agencies, they are able to combine the legislative and judicial powers that are traditionally separated under the Constitution. Thus, agencies are able to promulgate rules, and they have policing powers to ensure compliance. They are also able to render judgments and impose penalties or remedies as prescribed by law if violations have occurred. Administrative decisions can be appealed to the courts, but since the subject matter is generally very specialized or technical in nature (and the agency has been given broad discretionary powers initially), the courts will not generally reverse agency actions unless they are arbitrary and capricious, or unless they are not supported by the record or by legal precedent (or the law).

It is the province and duty of the judiciary to interpret the law, and it is the province of Congress to formulate legislative policy, to mandate programs and projects, and to establish their relative priority for the nation. Once Congress has exercised its legislative power and decided the order of priorities in a given area, the executive branch administers the law, and the courts (the judiciary) interpret and enforce it when enforcement is sought.

Ministerial Powers

The legislative powers of administrators have grown considerably over time. Initially, administrators' actions were more ministerial than legislative and were often explicitly specified by statute. For example, administrators had the power to issue or renew licenses. Sometimes statutes also required them to provide information or give advice to persons eligible for government benefits such as social security or veterans' payments.

Discretionary Powers

Over the years, as society has become more complex, Congress has authorized administrators to formulate rules and guidelines under general authority granted to administrative agencies. Thus the safety and health administrator is authorized to make rules that protect the safety and health of individuals in certain circumstances, such as places of employment. The discretion given administrators effectively transmits legislative power to them. For example, they have been given the power to prohibit unfair methods of competition, to grant licenses "as public interest,

EXHIBIT 47-2   AGENCIES WITH RULE-MAKING POWERS

MAJOR REGULATORY AGENCIES

Consumer Product Safety Commission
Environmental Protection Agency
Equal Employment Opportunity
   Commission
Federal Communications Commission
Federal Deposit Insurance Corporation
Federal Energy Regulatory Commission
Federal Reserve System
Federal Trade Commission
Food and Drug Administration
Interstate Commerce Commission
National Labor Relations Board
Occupational Safety and Health
   Administration
Securities and Exchange Commission

OTHER REGULATORY AGENCIES

Civil Aeronautics Board
Commodity Futures Trading
   Commission
Economic Regulatory Administration
Farm Credit Administration
Federal Election Commission
Federal Home Loan Bank Board
Federal Maritime Commission
National Credit Union Administration
National Mediation Board
National Transportation Safety Board
Nuclear Regulatory Commission
Pension Benefit Guaranty Corporation
Postal Rate Commission
Small Business Administration
U.S. International Trade Commission
U.S. Postal Service
Veterans Administration

AGRICULTURE DEPARTMENT

Agricultural Marketing Service
Agricultural Stabilization and
   Conservation Service
Animal and Plant Health Inspection
   Service
Commodity Credit Corporation
Farmers Home Administration
Federal Grain Inspection Service
Food and Nutrition Service

Food Safety and Quality Service
Foreign Agricultural Service
U.S. Forest Service

COMMERCE DEPARTMENT

Economic Development Administration
Industry and Trade Administration
Maritime Administration
National Bureau of Standards
National Oceanic and Atmospheric
   Administration
Patent and Trademark Office

**HEALTH AND HUMAN SERVICES
   DEPARTMENT**

Office for Civil Rights
Social Security Administration
Public Health Service
Health Care Financing Administration
Office of Human Development Services
Child Support Enforcement
   Administration

**HOUSING AND URBAN
   DEVELOPMENT DEPARTMENT**

Office of Fair Housing and Equal
   Opportunity
Office for Neighborhoods, Voluntary
   Associations and Consumer
   Protection
Office of Community Planning and
   Development
Government National Mortgage
   Association
New Community Development
   Corporation

INTERIOR DEPARTMENT

Bureau of Indian Affairs
Bureau of Land Management
U.S. Fish and Wildlife Service
Geological Survey
Office of Surface Mining Reclamation
   and Enforcement

JUSTICE DEPARTMENT

Antitrust Division
Civil Rights Division
Drug Enforcement Administration
Immigration and Naturalization Service
Office of Justice and Research Statistics

LABOR DEPARTMENT

Employment Standards Administration
Employment and Training
   Administration
Labor-Management Services
   Administration
Mine Safety and Health Administration

TRANSPORTATION DEPARTMENT

Federal Aviation Administration
Federal Highway Administration
Federal Railroad Administration
Materials Transportation Bureau
National Highway Traffic Safety
   Administration
St. Lawrence Seaway Development
   Corporation
U.S. Coast Guard
Urban Mass Transportation
   Administration

TREASURY DEPARTMENT

Bureau of Alcohol, Tobacco and
   Firearms
Comptroller of the Currency
Internal Revenue Service
U.S. Customs Service
Secret Service

**REGULATORY OVERSIGHT AND
   COORDINATION**

Administrative Conference of the
   United States
Consumer Affairs Council
General Accounting Office
Interagency Regulatory Liaison Group
Office of Management and Budget
Task Force on Regulatory Relief

convenience, or necessity requires," and to prevent or promote other generally specified goals.

Investigatory Powers

A number of administrative agencies generally have the power to investigate the records, prac-

tices, or premises of business organizations. For example, OSHA inspectors can obtain a search warrant and enter a place of employment to determine if a violation of safety or health has occurred. In addition, Section 6b of the Federal Trade Commission Act grants the Federal Trade Commission broad investigatory powers to require the inspection of records, the completion of questionnaires, or other assistance to the commission in supplying information prior to a specific rule, complaint, or adjudicative action. Witnesses can also be subpoenaed and examined under oath by the agency.

Complaints

Complaints (or charges) can be initiated by private parties, including individuals and corporations, or by employees of the administrative agency. After a complaint is served on an alleged wrongdoer, the party is given an opportunity to answer. Eventually, the complaint is heard by an administrator appointed by the agency. The administrator makes a final decision and enters an order directing the party to cease (or engage) in certain acts if the party has engaged in misconduct as defined by the agency. Otherwise, the complaint is dismissed. Compliance with the order is usually enforced by a separate division of the administrative agency, and failure to comply can result in fines and other penalties. After the final hearing, the affected party can appeal to the courts. In some cases, the party can engage in an informal settlement process or agree to a **consent decree**—an agreement by the parties that carries the sanction of the court.

Rule-Making Powers

General rule-making powers have been established by statute for a number of administrative agencies. Rule making often derives from evidence or facts obtained from investigatory activities. The process formally begins with *notification*, which can be in the form of a complaint to the party specifying the alleged misconduct. Usually the recipient of the complaint is given an opportunity to file an answer. In the case of general rules, notification is made through public announcement (in the Federal Register if the rule is promulgated by one of the federal administrative agencies). The second stage of rule making involves a hearing. Then the administrator makes a decision and, in the case of an individual complaint, either enters an order or dis-

misses it. In some cases, the administrator has a right to alter actions prior to the hearing, provided certain conditions are met. At any time, of course, there can be an informal settlement with a stipulation, consent decree, or other agreement. Many of these options are shown in Exhibit 47–3.

In some cases, rule making can preempt state law. In 1978, the FTC adopted the final rule on the advertising of ophthalmic goods and services. This rule states that it is an unfair practice for states to enforce restrictions against advertising unless the ads are deceptive.

Adjudicative Powers

Administrative agencies have also been given the power to settle disputes where parties are unable to reach an informal agreement. The process begins with a complaint to one or more businesses that the agency believes have violated a particular rule or standard. The next stage involves a hearing presided over by an administrative law judge in a setting that resembles other courtroom trials. The administrative law judges, however, are employees of the agency; they are not members of the state or federal judiciary. They allow each side to present evidence at the hearing. A major difference between these administrative hearings and the trials in state and federal courts lies in the type of evidence that can be presented for the record. Unlike the formal state and federal courts, which have adopted highly restrictive exclusionary rules of evidence, administrative hearings permit the introduction of evidence that may be less reliable.

In the case of general rules, the administrative hearing can involve extensive presentations of evidence by employees of the administrative agency, by parties who are directly affected, and by the general public. Economic evidence bearing on the potential consequences of the rule can be presented, and testimony can be given about the costs and benefits of the rule. For example, evidence on the prices of eyeglasses in localities with and without restrictions on price advertising was examined in the FTC hearings on ophthalmic goods.

Administrative hearings are also conducted

EXHIBIT 47–3   HOW RULES ARE MADE

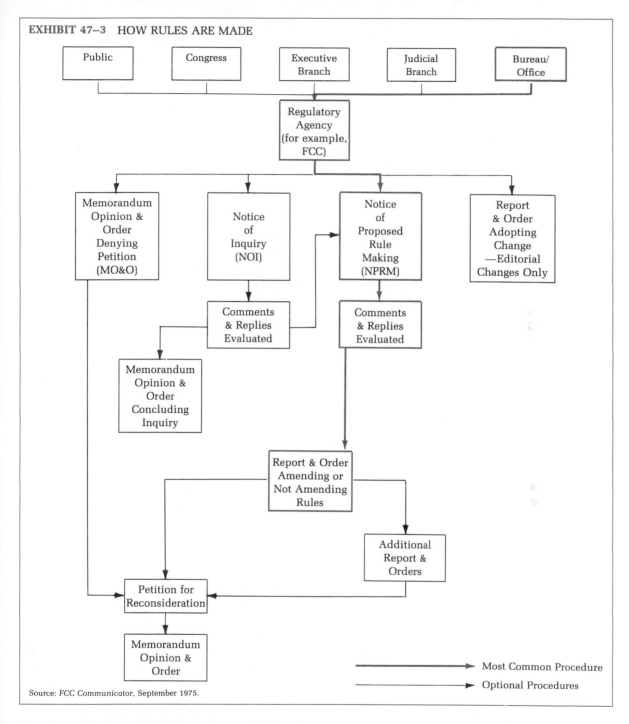

Source: *FCC Communicator*, September 1975.

less formally than the trials in state and federal courts. Once the administrative law judge has considered all the evidence, an opinion is issued. The opinion is usually subject to review by the head of the administrative agency.

Compliance and Enforcement Powers

All final orders carry the weight of statutory law with prescribed penalties for violations unless invalidated by the courts, and failure to comply is treated like any other violation of the law. In most cases, violations are considered civil matters so that money damages must be paid or specific actions taken (such as the installation of pollution control equipment). In recent years, however, there has been a trend toward issuing criminal penalties as well. Thus, violators, including corporate officers, can be subject to jail sentences. For example, the Energy Policy and Conservation Act of 1976 makes the failure of any manufacturer to comply with any average fuel economy standard unlawful conduct. Those deemed guilty of violating final orders can, at some point, obtain a full trial with a right to a jury.

LIMITATIONS ON ADMINISTRATIVE AGENCIES' POWERS

Most limitations on administrative agencies' powers arise from three sources: (1) the Constitution, (2) congressional statutes, and (3) judicial review. Constitutional limitations typically relate to substantive limitations on administrative agency behavior. Any procedural inadequacies are taken care of by judicial review.

Major Constitutional Limitations

Amendments to the Constitution provide the most important limitations on administrative actions. Although most constitutional rights—freedom of speech, of press, and of due process—are regarded primarily as rights of individuals, they nonetheless provide rights to businesses, too.

Commercial Speech The Supreme Court has upheld the right of businesses to make statements about private matters and about public issues. In 1978, the Supreme Court found that speech that otherwise would be protected by the First Amendment would not lose its protection merely because its source was a corporation.[6]

There are, of course, numerous limitations on freedom of speech. Protection is not, for example, granted to persons or firms who attempt to sell illegal materials.

Due Process Both procedural and substantive due process protect businesses against arbitrary, capricious, and unreasonable state actions. Substantive due process arises with issues involving property or other rights affected by government. Procedural due process focuses on proper notice and hearing procedures. Enforcement of due process rights through the Fifth and Fourteenth Amendments, however, follows a dual standard. Whenever state action directly affects economic activity, courts usually find it to be constitutional. On the other hand, when basic human freedoms are involved, courts are generally suspicious of state actions that tend to limit them.

Eminent Domain Federal, state and local governments must give property owners just compensation when property is taken under the power of **eminent domain.** For example, an owner of real property who is forced to give up ownership because the state wishes to build a highway must be given just compensation for the loss of the property.

Unreasonable Searches and Seizures Persons are protected from unwarranted intrusions into their individual privacy by the Constitution. Many of the protections of the Fourth Amendment arise in cases of criminal actions. Also, courts have found that businesses can be protected from unreasonable searches. For example, in the case of Marshall v. Barlow's, Inc.,[7] the Court held that government inspectors must have a warrant before they search work areas. The Fourth Amendment has also been used to prohibit building inspectors from looking for building code violations against the wishes of the owner of the premises if they do not have a warrant.

Judicial Review

Most final actions and orders emanating from administrative agencies can be appealed to the

6. First Nat'l Bank of Boston v. Belliotti, 435 U.S. 765, 98 S.Ct. 1407 (1978).

7. 436 U.S. 307, 98 S.Ct. 1816 (1978).

courts. Judicial review is often provided to interpret the enabling statute or to judge the validity of administrative agency procedures. The Federal Administrative Procedures Act of 1946 provides for such review. At the state level, the Model State Administrative Procedure Act of 1946, revised in 1961, sets forth similar procedures for review of state actions.

Scope of Review   The reviewing court is generally limited to and bound by the findings of fact reached during the original administrative hearing. The courts are guided by the "substantial evidence rule" that prevents trials *de novo*; in other words, appellate courts normally must accept administrative agency findings whenever such findings are based on substantial evidence. Courts generally defer to the conclusions of the administrative agency on questions with which the agency is more familiar.[8] Judicial action is limited to ensuring consistency with statutes and compliance with constitutional safeguards for fair hearings.

Many appeals challenge the validity of the authority of the administrative agency in question to make a particular rule. The courts will investigate first whether that agency has any valid delegated authority for rule making. If so, it will further investigate whether the agency exceeded its properly delegated authority. The first question usually focuses on whether the delegation is definite, although the quality of definiteness is assessed within extremely broad parameters.

Procedural Aspects   Administrative agencies engage in quasi-judicial functions. They develop most of their own rules and procedures. These procedures are far less formal than those of the courts; consequently, the most important aspects of judicial review of administrative agency actions concern (1) access to the administrative process (standing to sue), (2) the exhaustion of available remedies, and (3) primary jurisdiction. The first aspect relates to whether a party in any particular case is able to obtain judicial review. The second relates to the court's practice of re-

fusing to review administrative agency actions until the complaining party has exhausted all available administrative procedures and remedies. The third relates to normal questions of jurisdiction.

Determination of Facts   In the judicial review procedure, courts are generally unwilling to make any independent determination of facts or to reweigh the evidence before them. Moreover, when the agency is one involved with highly technical matters, the courts are less likely than usual to upset the agency's action, unless that action is arbitrary, capricious, or lacking any true supporting evidence.

PUBLIC REVIEW OF REGULATION

In recent years, there has been growing recognition of the broad discretionary powers given to administrative agencies. In response, the federal government has attempted to impose new constraints on agencies as a means of limiting the number of ineffective or potentially harmful rules. For example, in 1978 President Carter issued an order requiring agencies to determine the possible economic impacts of regulations that have substantial economic effects.[9] Agencies that wished to promulgate rules expected to have major economic consequences had to prepare a clear statement of the problem requiring action and an analysis of the economic consequences of the proposed regulation, along with alternative solutions to the problem. Congress has also begun to hold hearings on the costs of complying with regulations. In 1973, for example, Congress held hearings focusing on just the burden of federal paperwork. Furthermore, a 1979 study of forty-eight manufacturing firms by the Business Roundtable found that government regulations account for 10 percent of total capital expenditures.

Finally, the public can seek specific statutory override of administrative powers through the U.S. Congress and other legislative bodies. For

8.   Kesler & Sons Const. Co. v. Utah State Divisions of Health, 30 Utah 2d 90, 513 P.2d 1017 (1973).

9.   Improving Government Regulations, Executive Order #12044.

example, Congress significantly limited the Civil Aeronautics Board's ability to regulate air fares by the Airline Deregulation Act of 1978. And the Depository Institutions Deregulation and Monetary Control Act of 1981 will gradually eliminate interest rate ceilings imposed on financial institutions and restrictions on interstate banking and the like.

QUESTIONS AND CASE PROBLEMS

1. Article III of the Constitution provides that the judicial power shall reside in the Supreme Court of the United States and in such inferior courts as the Congress shall from time to time create. Judicial power is the power to resolve disputes and includes the power to determine whether an individual has committed certain acts and whether the commission of such acts constitutes the breach of a duty owed to another or to society as a whole. Administrative agencies have the power to determine whether a person is guilty or innocent of violating agency rules and regulations. Does this contradict the mandate of Article III?

2. While courts have the power to review all agency decisions, they generally defer to the agency's findings of fact (especially where agency expertise is involved), but they examine carefully the agency's findings of law. This, of course, is because courts deem *themselves* the experts on the law. Even in cases where agency expertise is not important, courts generally defer to the facts as found by the agency. For example, in a patent-related case investigated by the Federal Trade Commission, the commission made a certain finding of fact with respect to the testimony of Lidoff. The commission would not have made the finding if it had not found Lidoff to be a credible witness. Why might the reviewing court be unwilling to question the agency's determination with regard to Lidoff's credibility? [Charles Pfizer and Co. v. Federal Trade Comm., 401 F.2d 574 (6th Cir. 1968)]

3. Administrative agencies act in the capacities of both lawmaker and judge, or fact finder. Under the Constitution, these two roles are distinctly divided between the legislature and the courts. What advantages are there in combining the functions within an administrative agency? What disadvantages are there?

4. All actions taken by an administrative agency, whether legislative or judicial, are subject to review by the courts. The relevant test for review is whether the agency acted in an "arbitrary or capricious" manner in promulgating the rule. This was the question posed in the following case: The Secretary of Commerce issued a flammability standard that required all mattresses, including crib mattresses, to pass a test that involved contact with a burning cigarette. The manufacturers of crib mattresses petitioned the court to excuse crib mattresses from the flammability standard. These manufacturers said that applying such a rule to crib mattresses would not only be unreasonable but arbitrary and capricious since infants do not smoke. How should the court rule? [Bunny Bear, Inc. v. Peterson, 473 F.2d 1002 (5th Cir. 1973)]

5. If an administrative agency acts arbitrarily or capriciously, the reviewing court will strike down its rule. Agencies, however, are given wide latitude or discretion in formulating agency rules. Only when an agency abuses this discretion will a reviewing court reverse it. In Question 4, the administrative agency promulgated a single flammability standard for more than one type of mattress. If the crib mattress manufacturer had clearly demonstrated by proof that a flammability test used on infant mattresses in Europe was equally satisfactory as the "cigarette test" and had been used with good results for years in Europe, would the Secretary of Commerce have abused his discretion in adopting the cigarette test? What if the crib mattress manufacturer proved that the flammability test used in Europe was better than the cigarette test? Would the Secretary of Commerce have abused his discretion?

6. The standard of review that applies to administrative adjudicatory procedures is somewhat higher than the one applied to the rule-making process. When an administrative agency decides whether an agency rule or regulation has been violated, it conducts a hearing somewhat similar to a nonjury trial. Why do courts require stronger support for agencies' adjudicatory decisions than for their rule-making decisions?

7. Reviewing courts readily support rules promulgated by administrative agencies, but they require that the adjudicative findings of an agency be supported by "substantial evidence on the record." When an administrative agency conducts an adjudicative hearing, a record is made of all the evidence and testimony presented at the hearing. If the finding of the hearing is supported by the evidence contained in the record, a reviewing court will uphold the agency's finding. The Adolph Coors Company was accused by the FTC of engaging in certain price-fixing agreements in violation of the Sherman Antitrust Act. After a complete

adjudicative hearing, the commission concluded that Coors had in fact engaged in illegal price fixing. Substantial evidence was presented at the hearing in support of the commission's findings. But Coors also presented substantial evidence that it had never entered into any price-fixing arrangements. Should a reviewing court uphold the FTC's findings? [Adolph Coors Co. v. Federal Trade Comm., 497 F.2d 1178 (10th Cir. 1974)]

CHAPTER 48

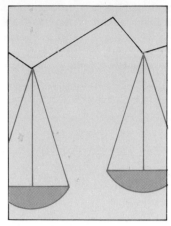

GOVERNMENT REGULATION
Consumer Protection

Consumer grievances about the quality of retail goods and services, the price and terms of credit, repossession practices, warranties and other aspects of the sale, financing, and service of consumer goods represent some of the more important concerns facing individuals in society today. These grievances have prompted ever-growing judicial, legislative, and administrative actions designed to protect the consumer in selecting, purchasing, financing and obtaining service of consumer goods in a seemingly impersonal urbanized marketplace.

Consumer protection arises from three distinct sources—from common law through judicial rulings; from simplification and codification of common law through federal, state, and local statutes, including the Uniform Commercial Code; and from administrative law through rule-making and enforcement activities, such as the Federal Trade Commission's rule allowing con-

sumers to keep unsolicited merchandise received through the mails.

Since parties who make contracts are generally given the right to specify the terms, consumer protection under the common law is sometimes limited. As Chapter 10 and Chapter 12 illustrated, the interests of consumers have often been important in judicial decisions. For example, the unconscionability doctrine (which deals with contracts that would be grossly unfair to enforce) protects consumers from certain pricing techniques for goods that are sold on credit. Consider the example of Williams, who made a series of purchases from Walker-Thomas Furniture Company from 1957 to 1962. Each of the time payment contracts that she signed contained the clause that all payments would be credited pro rata on all outstanding accounts. In 1962 she purchased furniture for $164, bringing her total purchases since 1957 to $1,800. The pro rata claim, however, meant that she still owed money on all items despite the fact that she had paid a total of $1,400 through 1962. A court found this clause to be unconscionable and unenforceable.[1]

CONSUMER PROTECTION SOURCES

A number of federal laws—such as the Consumer Credit Protection Act and the Magnuson-Moss Warranty Act—have been passed to pro-

vide more explicit direction on the duty of sellers and the rights of consumers. In recent years, the pressure on Congress to enact further laws to protect consumers has increased. Exhibit 48-1 lists the major consumer protection statutes by popular name.

State Statutes

Various provisions of the Uniform Commercial Code provide consumer protection in commercial sales transactions.[2] Finally, a number of statutes in California, Florida, New York, and other

---

1. Williams v. Walker-Thomas Furniture Co., 198 A.2d 914 (D.C.App.1964).

2. The UCC is discussed more fully in the sections on sales and commercial transactions.

EXHIBIT 48-1   CONSUMER PROTECTION STATUTES

Popular Name	Purpose	Statute Reference
ADVERTISING		
Federal Trade Commission Act	Prohibits deceptive and unfair trade practices	15 USC 45, 341 *et seq.*
CERTIFICATION AND LABELING		
Child Protection	Requires child-proof devices and special labeling	15 USC 1261 *et seq.*
Smoking Act of 1969	Warns of possible health hazard by surgeon general	15 USC 1331 *et seq.*
Fair Packaging and Labeling Act	Requires accurate names, quantities, weights	15 USC 1451 *et seq.*
Fur Products Labeling Act	Prohibits misbranding of fur products	15 USC 69
Wool Products Labeling Act of 1939	Requires accurate labeling of wool products	15 USC 68
SALES AND WARRANTIES		
Magnuson-Moss Warranty	Provides rules that govern content of warranties	15 USC 2301 *et seq.*
Real Estate Settlement Procedures Act of 1974	Requires disclosure of home buying costs	12 USC 2601 *et seq.*
Uniform Commercial Code (UCC)	Covers unconscionable sales contracts	UCC 2-302 (adopted by all states except Louisiana)
CREDIT		
Consumer Credit Protection Act	Offers comprehensive protection covering all phases of credit transactions	15 USC 1601 *et seq.*
Equal Credit Opportunity Act	Prohibits discrimination in the extending of credit	15 USC 1691 *et seq.*
Fair Credit Collection Practices Act	Prohibits debt collectors' abuses	15 USC 1692
Fair Credit Reporting Act	Protects consumers' credit reputations	15 USC 1681 *et seq.*
Truth-in-Lending Act	Requires full disclosure of credit terms	15 USC 1601 *et seq.*
Uniform Consumer Credit Code	Requires full disclosure of credit terms	Adopted by Colorado, Idaho, Indiana, Kansas, Maine, Oklahoma, Utah, Wyoming

states provide explicit protection to consumers. For example, the California Civil Code permits consumers to keep unsolicited goods. If they are billed for the goods, they can seek an injunction to stop billing, and they can collect reasonable attorneys' fees.[3] In many states, consumers who purchase goods at home must be informed of their right to cancel the transaction prior to midnight of the third business day after the transaction.[4]

Administrative Agencies

Administrative agencies provide an important form of consumer protection. For example, the FTC has been given extensive enforcement responsibilities in a number of statutes, some of which are discussed here. The most important authority, however, is Section 5 of the original Federal Trade Commission Act of 1914 as amended in 1938. It permits the commission to stop "unfair or deceptive acts or practices" that influence, inhibit, or restrict consumers unfairly in their purchasing decisions. Many of these practices are prohibited by industry guidelines or trade regulation rules. Violations are punishable by law and can occur in two circumstances. A company can engage in a practice prohibited by a trade regulation, or it can violate a known cease and desist order issued against *another* party.

If the FTC issues a cease and desist order to Ford Motor Company that prohibits the advertising of fuel economy levels achieved when the automobiles are driven by professional drivers without disclosing that information, the FTC can impose civil penalties against another automobile producer if it advertises mileage tests without the disclosure.[5]

Other agencies of the federal government, such as the Department of Housing and Urban Development, are also engaged in consumer protection activities. HUD, for example, enforces provisions of the National Mobile Home Construction

and Safety Standards Act of 1974, requiring periodic inspections and investigations to enforce federal standards. It also enforces the Interstate Land Sale Full Disclosure Act, which requires that sellers of subdivided lots provide certain statements of record that must include a legal description of the land, who has title to the land, and the present condition of the land.

The Courts

Finally, consumers themselves can use the courts to obtain remedies for their grievances. Since the time, embarrassment, and cost to consumers of private lawsuits can be prohibitive, various mechanisms have been developed to remove these barriers. They include free legal services, small claims courts, and recovery of attorneys' fees in class actions. Attorneys' fees, however, are generally recoverable only when there is an express statutory authorization.[6] Class actions have become a relatively more common form of addressing consumer grievances, but these actions are subject to certain rules and limits that make them difficult to pursue, particularly by individuals.

Private Organizations

Consumers also have access to the Better Business Bureau (BBB) system, a national organization of independent, nonprofit organizations financed by businesses to regulate themselves. The main organization, the Council of Better Business Bureau, Inc., has established the following priority projects:

1. Expanding and improving the services of BBB and seeking standardization and coordination among the parts of the network.
2. Establishing consumer arbitration as a means of achieving consumer justice.
3. Establishing a consumer education program to include the traditional information booklets, audiovisual material, school curriculum material, and programs tailored to meet the needs of minority, low-income, and elderly groups.

---

3. Section 1584.5.
4. N.Y. Business Corporation Law, Section 1101 (McKinney 1964).
5. FTC Improvements Act of 1975.

6. See Alyeska Pipeline Serv. Co. v. The Wilderness Soc'y, 421 U.S. 240, 95 S.Ct. 1612 (1975).

4. Establishing a top-level procedure for voluntary self-regulation of advertising.[7]

A consumer can also contact the local Chamber of Commerce for help in seeking methods of settling a grievance.

ADVERTISING

The increased protection received by consumers during the past two decades against deceptive advertising derives more from statutory and administrative sources than from common law. Common law protection is based on fraud and requires proof of intent to misrepresent facts and other criteria. Statutory law and administrative regulations, on the other hand, focus on whether the advertising is likely to be misleading, regardless of intent. This approach arises from the idea that false advertising should be prohibited in order to protect the consumer rather than to punish the seller or advertiser.

In 1911, in reaction to a number of undesirable advertising claims, an advertising trade

---

7. H. Bruce Palmer, *Association Management Magazine*, November 1970.

journal called *Printers' Inc.* proposed a statute that would make untrue, deceptive, or misleading representations a misdemeanor. Since then, forty-four states have enacted some form of the *Printers' Inc.* model statute. These state statutes, however, have generally not deterred false advertising. Some states have additional statutes that focus on the advertisement of particular products, such as food or drugs. When these statutes are part of a broader regulation for a particular type of good or business activity, they are often actively enforced by the associated regulatory agency.

The Federal Trade Commission Act empowers the FTC to determine what constitutes a deceptive practice within the meaning of Section 5 of the act. The FTC's judgment can be appealed to a court, but it is accorded great weight by the reviewing court. When the commission renders an opinion or issues an order, appeal can be taken through judicial channels. The commission is responsible for enforcing the legislative policy of the act it administers, and the courts will recognize that the administrative agency that deals continually with cases in the area is often in a better position than the courts are to determine when a practice is deceptive within the meaning of the act.

BACKGROUND AND FACTS *The Federal Trade Commission issued a complaint against Colgate-Palmolive Company and Ted Bates & Company, Inc., an advertising agency, for using commercials that misrepresented the characteristics of Colgate's Rapid Shave. Bates had prepared television commercials that showed how Rapid Shave could soften something as tough as sandpaper. In the commercial, Rapid Shave was applied to something that looked like sandpaper, and shortly thereafter a razor shaved it clean. Unknown to the viewers, the "sandpaper" was actually a piece of Plexiglass with sand on it.*

Initially, a hearing examiner thought that Rapid Shave could shave sandpaper, although not as quickly as the advertisement suggested, so the examiner dismissed the complaint, saying that the misrepresentation was not a material one that would mislead the public.

The commission, however, reversed the hearing examiner, finding that, since Rapid Shave could not shave the sandpaper within the time depicted in the commercials, the product's moisturizing power had been misrepresented. In addition, the use of a Plexiglass substitute for sandpaper was material misrepresentation because it misled viewers into be-

FEDERAL TRADE COMM'N v. COLGATE-PALMOLIVE CO.
Supreme Court of the United States, 1965.
380 U.S. 374, 85 S.Ct. 1035.

lieving that *they had seen something which, in fact, they had not. As a result of these findings, the commission entered a cease and desist order against Colgate-Palmolive.*

The court of appeals then set aside the order because it was so broadly written that it forbade all use of undisclosed simulations in television commercials. Five months later, the commission issued a revised order prohibiting Colgate-Palmolive from presenting advertisements depicting a test, an experiment, or a demonstration represented as actual proof of a product claim but not in fact constituting proof because of the use of an undisclosed mock-up.

Once again, the court of appeals set aside the commission's order, so the commission petitioned the Supreme Court to set forth a legal standard of the words, deceptive practice, *within the meaning of Section 5 of the Federal Trade Commission Act.*

WARREN, Chief Justice.

*   *   *   *

The basic question before us is whether it is a deceptive trade practice, prohibited by § 5 of the Federal Trade Commission Act, to represent falsely that a televised test, experiment, or demonstration provides a viewer with visual proof of a product claim regardless of whether the product claim is itself true.

*   *   *   *

In reviewing the substantive issues in the case, it is well to remember the respective roles of the Commission and the courts in the administration of the Federal Trade Commission Act. When the Commission was created by Congress in 1914, it was directed by § 5 to prevent "[u]nfair methods of competition in commerce." Congress amended the Act in 1938 to extend the Commission's jurisdiction to include "unfair or deceptive acts or practices in commerce"—a significant amendment showing Congress' concern for consumers as well as for competitors. *   *   *

This statutory scheme necessarily gives the Commission an influential role in interpreting § 5 and in applying it to the facts of particular cases arising out of unprecedented situations. *   *   *

The Commission's interpretation of what is a deceptive practice seems more in line with the decided cases than that of respondents. This Court said in *Federal Trade Comm'n v. Algoma Lumber Co.*, "[T]he public is entitled to get what it chooses, though the choice may be dictated by caprice or by fashion or perhaps by ignorance." It has long been considered a deceptive practice to state falsely that a product ordinarily sells for an inflated price but that it is being offered at a special reduced price, even if the offered price represents the actual value of the product and the purchaser is receiving his money's worth. Applying respondents' arguments to these cases, it would appear that so long as buyers paid no more than the product was actually worth and the product contained the qualities advertised, the misstatement of an inflated original price was immaterial.

*   *   *[T]he present case is not concerned with a mode of communication, but with a misrepresentation that viewers have objective proof of a seller's product claim over and above the seller's word. Secondly, *   *   * the present case, deal[s] with methods designed to get a consumer to purchase a product, not with whether the product, when purchased, will perform up to expectations. *   *   *

It is generally accepted that it is a deceptive practice to state falsely that a product has received a testimonial from a respected source. *   *   *

*   *   * We find it an immaterial difference that in one case the viewer is told to rely on the word of a celebrity or authority he respects, in another on the word of a testing agency, and in the present case on his own perception of an undisclosed simulation.

*   *   *   *

We agree with the Commission, therefore, that the undisclosed use of plexiglass in the present commercials was a material deceptive practice, independent and separate from the other misrepresentation found. Respondents claim that it will be impractical to inform the viewing public that it is not seeing an actual test, experiment or demonstration, but we think it inconceivable that the ingenious advertising world will be unable, if it so desires, to conform to the Commission's insistence that the public be not misinformed. If, however, it becomes impossible or impractical to show simulated demonstrations on television in a truthful manner, this indicates that television is not a medium that lends itself to this type of commercial, not that the commercial must survive at all costs. *   *   * If the inherent limitations of a method do not permit its use in the way a seller desires, the seller cannot by material misrepresentation compensate for those limitations.

*   *   * [W]hen the commercial not only makes a claim, but also invites the viewer to rely on his own perception for demonstrative proof of the claim, the respondents will be aware that the use of undisclosed props in strategic places might be a material deception. *   *   *

The judgment of the court of appeals was reversed, and the case was remanded for entry of a judgment enforcing the commission's revised cease and desist order prohibiting Colgate-Palmolive from using the commercials.   JUDGMENT AND REMEDY

Defining Deceptive Advertising

As defined by the FTC, deception generally means that the advertisement may be interpreted in more than one way and that one of those interpretations is false or misleading. Deception may involve a false statement or claim about the product's quality, effects, price, origin, or availability. Deception also may occur when an advertisement omits important facts or information about the product. Advertisements may contain "half-truths" if the presented material is true but additional information would be required to prevent consumers from being misled. Finally an advertisement will often be considered decep-

tive if its statements are not supported by adequate scientific evidence. When, however, the claim is incapable of measurement, as in "When you're out of Schlitz, you're out of beer," no problem of deception is perceived by the FTC.

Bait and Switch

In some cases, the Federal Trade Commission has promulgated specific rules to govern advertising. One of its more important rules is called "Guides on Bait Advertising,"[8] and it is de-

---

8.   16 CFR 238 (1968).

signed to prohibit advertisements that specify a very low price for a particular item. The low price is the bait to lure the consumer into the store. Then, the salesperson tries to switch the consumer to some other, more expensive item. According to the FTC guidelines, bait advertising occurs if the seller refuses to show the advertised item, fails to have adequate quantities of it available, fails to promise or deliver the advertised item within a reasonable time, or discourages employees from selling the item.

Numerous techniques fall into the bait and switch category. In the following case, sales personnel not only were directed to engage in certain baiting practices but were rewarded for doing so.

ALL-STATE INDUS. OF NORTH CAROLINA, INC. v. FEDERAL TRADE COMM'N

United States Court of Appeals, Fourth Cir., 1970. 423 F.2d 423.

BACKGROUND AND FACTS *All-State Industries, a producer of residential aluminum siding, storm windows, and other products used a bait and switch sales technique in selling its products. The "ADV" lower-cost grade of aluminum was featured in the company's ads, but salespersons, following the training manual, attempted instead to sell the "PRO" grade after contacting the customers. The Federal Trade Commission found this practice to be an "unfair and deceptive" practice under 5(b) of the FTC Act and issued a cease and desist order. All-State Industries appealed.*

BRYAN, Circuit Judge.

*   *   *   *

From the Hearing Examiner's findings of fact, the following account unfolds of how they vend their products. These are of two grades. The "ADV" is the cheaper. It is extensively advertised, primarily through mailouts to people whose names and addresses are culled from telephone directories. "PRO," the other grade, is of a higher quality and not so widely publicized.

Respondents' sales technique, or "pitch", is devised to create, first, a demand for the "ADV" product. Through inflated promotion it is presented as a "special offer" with "limited time" prices. But the Examiner found the "ADV" is actually priced uniformly and without time limit. He held as untrue All-State's claim that they deal directly from their factory with the output "100% guaranteed."

Inquiries or "leads" are answered by a supposed "sales manager." He attempts to pressure the prospect into signing a contract, a note and a deed, committing him to the purchase of "ADV" articles but leaving blank the monetary obligation. As soon as the contract is executed, the salesperson brings out a sample of the "ADV" and points out deficiencies in it, "whether real or imaginary." The "PRO" is then shown in contrast, to the detriment of the "ADV." Whenever possible the "PRO" is then sold "at the highest price obtainable from the individual customer." The salesmen have incentives to substitute the "PRO"—they receive no commission on "ADV" but only on "PRO" sales.

This "bait and switch" artifice, the Examiner discovered, was fully set forth in the sales force's training manual and was employed generally. He also reported that All-State's agents utilized "gimmicks whereby the original prices quoted for respondents' products can be reduced." For example, the representative would promise a potential buyer a special discount, even below the quoted sale price, if the latter would allow the use of his home for demonstration or display purposes. Rarely, however, would a patron's home be so utilized. It was found as a bare inducement to overcome "sales resistance at a higher price" and provide "some apparently reasonable basis for the reduction in price."

* * * *

The cease and desist order was enforced against All-State Industries as well as against each of All-State's sales agents. **JUDGMENT AND REMEDY**

Labeling and Packaging

A number of federal and state laws that govern labeling and packaging have been passed to provide the consumer with accurate information or warnings about the use or possible misuse of the product. For example, the Fur Products Labeling Act, the Wool Products Labeling Act, the Cigarette Labeling and Advertising Act, the Food, Drug and Cosmetic Act, the Flammable Fabrics Act, the Fair Packaging and Labeling Act, and others have been enacted in part to reduce the amount of incorrect labeling and packaging in consumer products.

In general, labels must be accurate, which means that they must use words as they are ordinarily understood by consumers. For example, a regular size box of cereal cannot be labeled "giant" if that word would exaggerate the amount of cereal. Labels often must specify the raw materials used in the product, such as the percent of cotton, nylon, or other fibers used in a shirt. The Fair Packaging Act requires that consumer goods have labels that identify the product, the manufacturer, the packer or distributor and its place of business, the net quantity of contents, and the quantity of each serving if the number of servings is stated.[9] Additional authority to add requirements governing words that are used to describe packages, terms that are associated with savings claims, information disclosure for ingredients in nonfood products, and standards for partial filling of packages is also included in this statute. The provisions are enforced by the Federal Trade Commission and the Department of Health and Human Services.

SALES

A number of statutes that protect the consumer in sales transactions concern the disclosure of certain terms in sales, rules governing home or door-to-door sales, mail order transactions, and referral sales. For example, the Federal Reserve Board of Governors has issued Regulation Z, which governs credit provisions associated with sales contracts, and numerous states have passed laws governing the remedies available to consumers in home sales. Furthermore, states have adopted a number of provisions as they have incorporated the UCC and the Uniform Consumer Credit Code into their statutory codes.

In 1968, Congress passed the first of a series of statutes regarding the content of information contained in written and oral messages. If, for example, certain credit terms are used in an advertisement, other credit information is also required. Thus, if Prolific Pontiac Sales states in a newspaper advertisement that individuals have thirty-six months to pay, the firm must also include the cash price of the automobiles, the down payment, the amount of each periodic payment, and the annual percentage rate of interest.

Door-to-Door Sales

Door-to-door sales are singled out for special treatment in the laws of most states. The special treatment stems in part from the nature of the sales transaction if the salesperson is able to gain entrance. A door-to-door seller usually has a captive audience because many individuals are actually immobilized at home. Since repeat purchases are not as likely as they are in stores, the seller has little incentive to establish goodwill

---

9. 15 USCA 1451 et seq.

with the purchaser. Furthermore, the seller is unlikely to present alternative products and their prices. Thus, a number of states have passed statutes that permit the buyers of goods sold door-to-door to cancel their contracts within a specified period of time, usually two to three days after the sale.

In addition, a Federal Trade Commission regulation makes it a Section 5 violation for door-to-door sellers to fail to give consumers three days to cancel any sale. This rule applies in addition to state statutes so that consumers are given the most favorable benefits of the FTC rule and their own state statute. In addition, the FTC rule requires that the notification be given in Spanish if the oral negotiation was in that language.

Mail Order Transactions

Consumers buying from mail order houses have typically been given less protection than when they purchase in stores. Many mail order houses are outside the state, and it is more costly to seek redress for grievances in that situation. In addition to the federal statute that prevents the use of mails to defraud individuals, several states have passed statutes governing certain practices by sellers, including insurance companies, that solicit through the mails. The state statutes parallel the federal statutes governing mail fraud.

HEALTH PROTECTION

Health protection laws govern the processing and distribution of such diverse products as meat and poultry, poisonous substances, and drugs and cosmetics. For some products, such as cigarettes, explicit warnings about health hazards are required.

Food

In 1906, Congress passed its first act regulating drugs. Early laws protected consumers against adulteration and misbranding of food and drug products. In subsequent amendments, standards for foods, specification of safe levels of potentially dangerous food additives, and control of classifications of foods and food advertising were established. The most restrictive amendment was passed in 1958, giving the Food and Drug Administration the right to define food additives and to set safe levels. In addition, this amendment forbids the use of any food additive that can be shown to be carcinogenic (cancer-causing) to humans or animals. In general, the law makes manufacturers responsible for ensuring that the food they offer for sale contains no substances that could cause injury to health.[10]

Food Inspection

A number of laws have also been passed to establish standards for meat and poultry shipped interstate. All such meat and poultry used for human consumption is subject to inspection for its wholesomeness and accuracy in labeling. Although federal law does not require grade standards, official grading is offered by the Department of Agriculture to packers, processors, and distributors who are willing to pay a fee. Among the statutes enforced by the Food Safety and Quality Service of the Department of Agriculture are the Agricultural Marketing Act of 1946,[11] Egg Products Inspection Act of 1970,[12] Poultry Products Inspection Act of 1957,[13] and the Wholesome Meat Act of 1967.[14]

Drugs and Cosmetics

Some regulations regarding drugs and cosmetics are set forth in the original Food, Drug and Cosmetic Act of 1938.[15] In addition, a number of amendments, particularly those of 1962, require that all drugs be proven effective as well as safe before they can be marketed.

Food and Drug Administration (FDA)

Most of the statutes involving food and drugs are monitored and enforced by the Food and Drug

---

10.   United States v. Park, 421 U.S. 658, 95 S.Ct. 1903 (1975).
11.   60 Stat. 1087, 7 USC 1621.
12.   84 Stat. 1620, 21 USC 1031.
13.   71 Stat. 441, 21 USC 451.
14.   81 Stat. 584, 21 USC 601.
15.   52 Stat. 1040, 21 USC 301.

Administration, which carries out responsibilities including (but not limited to):

- Inspecting manufacturing facilities for compliance with FDA standards.
- Establishing written and physical standards for biological products.
- Developing policy regarding the safety, effectiveness, and labeling of all drugs for human use.
- Evaluating new drug applications and requests to approve drugs for experimental use.
- Developing standards for the safety and effectiveness of over-the-counter drugs.
- Distributing information on toxicity of household products and medicines.
- Conducting research and developing standards on the composition, quality, nutrition, and safety of food, food additives, colors, and cosmetics.
- Developing regulations for food standards to permit the safe use of color and food additives.

One of the more controversial regulatory actions of the FDA was its attempt to ban the use of saccharin as a noncaloric artificial sweetener. That action brought opposition that forced Congress to enact legislation for a moratorium prohibiting the FDA from removing the food additive from the market. Initial amendments extended the moratorium into 1982 until studies of its potential carcinogenic effect could be completed.

Labeling

Congress has also enacted a number of statutes to protect individuals by providing them with information about products.

Fair Packaging and Labeling Act   In 1976, Congress enacted a law that requires manufacturers to provide consumers with accurate information about the quantity of the contents of products. Moreover, the net quantities must be conspicuously displayed in a uniform location on the package. This law facilitates comparisons among similar products by consumers.

Public Health Cigarette Smoking Act   Congress authorized the Surgeon General to require man-

ufacturers of cigarettes in 1969 to begin warning consumers that smoking is a health hazard. The statement "Warning: The Surgeon General Has Determined That Cigarette Smoking Is Dangerous to Your Health" must, by law, appear on both cigarette and little cigar packages.

Poison Prevention Packaging Act   A 1970 amendment to the Fair Packaging and Labeling Act requires that manufacturers provide so-called childproof devices on all household products that could harm young children if mishandled or ingested by them.

SAFETY PROTECTION

Until the 1960s, manufacturers that developed, designed, produced, or marketed a product in a reasonable manner would generally avoid liability for injury or damage from consumer products. In addition to the changing liability discussed in Chapter 21, manufacturers are now subject to a number of statutes regulating product safety. For example, the Consumer Product Safety Act of 1972 protects consumers from unreasonable risk of injury from hazardous products.[16] In 1953, Congress passed the Flammable Fabrics Act, which prohibits the sale of highly flammable clothing or materials.[17]

THE CONSUMER PRODUCT SAFETY ACT

One of the newest federal agencies designed to protect the consumer is the Consumer Product Safety Commission (CPSC). Established in 1972, it was given sweeping powers to regulate the production and sale of potentially hazardous consumer products.

Consumer product safety legislation began in 1953 with the enactment of the Flammable Fabrics Act. Between 1953 and 1972, Congress enacted legislation regulating specific classes of products or product design or composition, rather

16.   86 Stat. 1207, 15 USC 2051.
17.   67 Stat. 111, 15 USC 1191.

than the overall safety of consumer products. Finally, as a result of 1970 recommendations of the National Commission on Product Safety, the Consumer Product Safety Act was passed in 1972, creating the CPSC to regulate all potentially hazardous consumer products.

Products Subject to the Act

The 1972 Act states that " * * * any article, or component part thereof produced or distributed for sale to a consumer for use in or around a permanent or temporary household or residence, a school, in recreation or otherwise, or for the personal use, consumption or enjoyment of a consumer" shall be subject to regulation by the CPSC. As further evidence of how comprehensive the act is, the authority to administer other acts is transferred to the CPSC. These acts include the Federal Hazardous Substance Act, the Child Protection and Toy Safety Act, the Poison Prevention Packaging Act, the Flammable Fabrics Act, and the Refrigerator Safety Act.

Purposes of the Act

As stated in the act, the Consumer Product Safety Commission was created:

1. To protect the public against unreasonable risk of injury associated with consumer products.
2. To assist consumers in evaluating the comparative safety of consumer products.
3. To develop uniform safety standards for consumer products and to minimize conflicting state and local regulations.
4. To promote research and investigation into causes and prevention of product-related deaths, illnesses, and injuries.

Form and Functions of the CPSC

The CPSC was set up to conduct research on product safety and maintain a clearinghouse to "collect, investigate, analyze, and disseminate injury data, and information, relating to the causes and prevention of death, injury, and illness associated with consumer products * * *"

To this end, the CPSC immediately started gathering data on the two hundred most hazardous consumer products in the nation. The commission required emergency wards in hospitals to indicate the particular cause of any injury, illness, or death related to a consumer product.

The initial CPSC survey found that the most hazardous consumer product was the bicycle. The CPSC hoped that the data obtained and the resulting hazard index for consumer products would move manufacturers to improve their most hazardous products voluntarily and to warn consumers about them.

Powers of the CPSC

Not only can the CPSC set safety standards for consumer products, it can also ban the manufacture and sale of any product deemed hazardous to consumers. The commission has the authority to remove from the market products that are deemed imminently hazardous and can require manufacturers to report information about any products already sold or intended for sale that have proven hazardous.

Impact of the CPSC

Congress sought to create an agency with broad powers to regulate the sale and manufacture of all consumer products. The CPSC could have increasingly profound effects upon the consumer products industry. At the very least, it will give consumers more information about the safety of the products that they buy.

To date, most critics point out that the CPSC's performance has been less than spectacular. There have not been notable reductions in consumer product-related injuries, and where regulations have resulted in safer products, the products are more expensive. Recently, regulations for power mowers were challenged by certain government agencies because they would raise the price of the mowers too much. This involves the thorny problem of weighing the costs of safety against the benefits. In other words, how much safety do people want to pay for?

REAL ESTATE

Various statutes and regulations have been passed at both state and federal levels to either prevent fraud in real estate transactions and/or provide a buyer with information concerning such a transaction. Two such federal acts are the Interstate Sales Full Disclosure act and the Real Estate Settlement Procedures act.

Interstate Sales Full Disclosure Act

The federal government has passed regulations designed to prevent fraudulent sales in real estate transactions. The Interstate Sales Full Disclosure Act (1968) is administered by the Department of Housing and Urban Development (HUD), and its focus is to furnish facts and information to potential buyers so they can make intelligent decisions about whether or not to purchase land.

Land sale abuses have been occurring for years. Everyone has heard about purchasers who invest their life savings in one hundred acres of land for a $10 down payment and $10 a month only to find that the land is under ten feet of water. Federal law does not prohibit land under water from being sold; it merely requires that the seller inform the buyer that it is under water.

Real Estate Settlement Procedures Act

A recent federal law requires that all closing costs be specifically outlined before a person buys a home. The 1976 revisions of the Real Estate Settlement Procedures Act make the following stipulations about buying a house and borrowing money to pay for it:

1. Within three business days after a person applies for a mortgage loan, the lender must send a booklet, prepared by the U.S. Department of Housing and Urban Development, that outlines the applicant's rights and explains settlement procedures and costs.
2. The lender must give an estimate of most of the settlement costs within that three-day period.

3. The lender must clearly identify individuals or firms that the applicant is required to use for legal or other services, including title insurance and search.
4. If the loan is approved, the lender must provide a truth-in-lending statement that shows the annual percentage rate on the mortgage loan.
5. Lenders, title insurers, and others involved in the real estate transaction cannot pay kickbacks for business referred to them.

CREDIT

One of the more important areas of consumer protection concerns the rights of consumers in credit transactions. Credit has become the American way of life; nearly all major purchases are financed by some form of credit.

Consumer Credit Protection Act (CCPA)

The Consumer Credit Protection Act (CCPA) is commonly called the Truth-in-Lending Act. It is basically a "disclosure law," administered by the Federal Reserve Board, that requires sellers and lenders to disclose credit terms or loan terms so that a debtor can shop around for the best financing arrangements.

Disclosure Requirements under the Truth-in-Lending Act The disclosure requirements of the Truth-in-Lending Act apply to any installment sales contract in which payment is to be made in more than four installments. The following is a breakdown of the disclosure requirements as they would apply to the sale of a stereo on such an installment plan:

1. The cash price of the stereo.
2. The down payment or trade-in allowance, if any.
3. The unpaid cash price (cash price minus the down payment).
4. The finance charge, which includes interest, points, service charges, lender's fee, finder's fee, fee for investigation of credit, credit life insurance premium, accident insurance premium, and so on.

5.   Charges not included as part of the finance charge.

6.   The total amount to be financed.

7.   The annual percentage rate of the finance charge.

8.   The date that the finance charge begins to accrue.

9.   The number, amounts, and due dates of payments.

10.   The penalties in case of delinquency or other late payment charges.

11.   A description of the security interest (see Chapters 30 and 31).

12.   A description of the prepayment penalty charge.

13.   Sometimes a comparative index of credit costs to give the purchaser an idea of how much credit will cost on this account. [CCPA Section 127]

Who is Subject to Truth-in-Lending?   Only certain creditors or lenders and only certain types of transactions are subject to the Truth-in-Lending Act. It applies to persons who, in the ordinary course of their businesses, lend money or sell on credit or arrange for the extension of credit. For this reason, sales or loans made between two consumers do not come under the act. Only debtors who are *natural* persons are protected by this law; corporations or other legal entities are not. Transactions involving purchases of property (real or personal) for personal, family, household, or agricultural use come within the terms and provisions of the act if the amount being financed is less than $25,000. Transactions covered by the act typically include retail and installment sales and installment loans, car loans, home improvement loans, and certain real estate loans.

The act distinguishes between the information that must be disclosed in real estate loans and personal property loans. For example, in the latter case, a creditor must provide information about the amount financed, the finance charge (interest rate and all other charges), the annual percentage rate, and the amount and number of payments.

A creditor who fails to comply with the disclosure requirements may be liable to the consumer for twice the amount of the finance charge plus attorneys' fees. In no event will that penalty be less than $100 or more than $1,000 for a violation against an individual consumer. The consumer has one year from the date of the violation to bring suit against a creditor who has failed to provide the disclosure statement or who has failed to discover and correct an error in the disclosure statement provided.

The following case illustrates the need for creditors to comply with all requirements of the Truth-in-Lending Act.

SMITH v. CHAPMAN
United States Court of Appeals,
Fifth Circuit, 1980.
614 F.2d 968.

BACKGROUND AND FACTS   *Mary Smith purchased a car from Don Chapman Motor Sales. Smith brought an action alleging that the sales contract violated the Truth-in-Lending Act and the Texas Consumer Credit Code. Chapman argued that although he had not specifically complied with the terms of the two consumer protection statutes, he was in substantial compliance, and further, that since Smith understood all the terms of the contract, Chapman had achieved the purposes of the statutes and should not be penalized.*

BROWN, Circuit Judge.

*   *   *   *

First, the purpose of TILA is to promote the "informed use of credit *   *   * [and] an awareness of the cost thereof by consumers" by assuring "a meaningful disclosure of credit terms so that the consumer will be able to compare more readily the various credit terms available to him. *   *   *"

It is now well-settled that an objective standard is used in determining violations of TILA. It is not necessary that the plaintiff-consumer actually have been deceived in order for there to be a violation. TILA is primarily enforced through lawsuits filed by consumers acting as "private attorneys general." In fact, consumers who are aware of the true terms of a contract are more able to see that these terms are not clearly and conspicuously disclosed on the installment sales contract form. Thus, the purpose of the Act is more readily served by allowing lawsuits by these consumers who are less easily deceived.

Second, the applicable standard is strict compliance with the technical requirements of the Act. Only adherence to a strict compliance standard will promote the standardization of terms which will permit consumers readily to make meaningful comparisons of available credit alternatives.

*   *   *   *

The "Motor Vehicle Contract" that Smith entered into with Chapman Motors was a one-page document with terms printed on both sides of the page. The front of this document did not mention the security interest that the seller retained in the car; this was set forth as Condition No. 1 on the back of the page. Delinquency charges were stated on the front and as Condition No. 6 on the back of the document as follows:

> The Seller, at its option, shall collect a delinquency charge on each installment in default for a period of more than ten days in an amount not to exceed 5% of each installment or $5.00 whichever is less, or, in lieu thereof, interest after maturity on each such installment, not to exceed the highest lawful contract rate.

The specific interest rate after maturity, imposed by Condition No. 10 on the back of the contract, was ten percent (10%) per annum. At the bottom of both sides of the page was printed: "NOTICE, SEE REVERSE SIDE FOR IMPORTANT INFORMATION, ALL TERMS OF WHICH ARE INCORPORATED BY REFERENCE."

Smith alleged in her complaint that the failure to state these provisions on the front side of the page was a violation of Regulation Z, 12 CFR § 226.8(a)(1) which provides:

*   *   *   *

All of the disclosures shall be made together on either:

(1) The note or other instrument evidencing the obligation on the same side of the page and above the place for the customer's signature; or

(2) One side of a separate statement which identifies the transaction.

(b) *Disclosures in sale and nonsale credit.* In any transaction subject to this section, the following items, as applicable, shall be disclosed:

*   *   *   *

(4) The amount, or method of computing the amount, of any default, delinquency, or similar charges payable in the event of late payments.

(5) A description or identification of the type of any security interest held or to be retained or acquired by the creditor in connection with the extension of credit, and a clear identification of the property to which the security interest relates or, if such property is not identifiable, an explanation of the manner in which the creditor retains or may acquire a security interest in such property which the creditor is unable to identify.

The general rule for disclosures is that they "be made clearly, conspicuously, in meaningful sequence, in accordance with the further requirements of [§ 226], and at the time and in the terminology prescribed in applicable sections."

Chapman first contends that he has complied with the requirements of § 226.8(a)(1) by including the notice of incorporation by reference of terms on both sides of the page. Under a strict compliance standard, incorporating by reference terms on the backside of a page when it is explicitly required that these terms appear on the front side, would be a violation of TILA.

*   *   *   *

Chapman next takes issue with the District Court's holding that the listing of the sales tax on the automobile contract form as an "official fee," and not in the blank labelled "Cash Price (Including Sales Tax)," violated Regulation Z and the TCCC.

*   *   *   *

The District Court inferred from § 226.4(b)(3) that taxes must be included either in the cash price or be listed as a finance charge. We are mindful of the confusion potentially created when taxes, which are imposed regardless of whether or not credit is extended, are listed as finance charges and how, as Chapman urges, this goes against the policy of TILA to make installment sales contracts more easily understood by consumers. Yet, this is what the regulation implies, and this is how we have interpreted it in the past. Any changes in the regulation are not for us, but for the Federal Reserve Board to make. We agree with the District Court's interpretation of § 226.4(b)(3).

*   *   *   *

We reiterate that the purpose of TILA is to "assure a meaningful disclosure of credit terms," and that Regulation Z, § 226.6(a), requires that disclosures be made clearly, conspicuously and in meaningful sequence. To place the tax figure in the wrong space when another space is specifically provided is not a clear disclosure in a meaningful sequence. And when the form states the sales tax is included in the figure stated, but in fact it is not, it is, furthermore, misleading. A misleading disclosure is as much a violation of TILA as a failure to disclose at all.

Because this disclosure is misleading, and because it contradicts the definition of "official fees," which under Texas law do not include sales taxes, it is also in violation of TCCC.

JUDGMENT AND REMEDY   *The judgment of the district court was affirmed. Statutory penalties of twice the amount of the finance charges in connection with the transaction, plus attorneys' fees, were imposed for violation of the federal law and for violation of the state regulations. The entire penalty totaled four times the finance charge.*

Equal Credit Opportunity Act In 1974, Congress enacted the Equal Credit Opportunity Act as part of the CCPA to prohibit discrimination based on race, religion, national origin, color, sex, marital status, age, or whether an individual is receiving certain types of income, such as public assistance benefits. Creditors are permit-

ted to request any information from a credit applicant except that which could be used for the type of discrimination covered in the act and its amendments.

Fair Credit Billing Act (CCPA) In 1974, Congress passed an amendment to the Truth-in-

Lending Act called the Fair Credit Billing Act.[18] Basically, under the rules set up pursuant to this act, a purchaser can withhold payment until a dispute over a faulty product that was purchased and paid for by credit card is resolved. It is up to the credit card issuer to intervene and attempt a settlement between the credit card user and the seller. A purchaser does not have an *unlimited* right to stop payment. A good faith effort to get satisfaction from the seller must first be exercised. If such an effort fails, the purchaser is not legally required to notify the credit card company that payment for the item is being stopped. The purchaser can wait for the issuer to respond to the stopped payment. To minimize settlement difficulties, it is probably a good idea to advise the company.

Other provisions of this act relate to disputes over billing. If the debtor thinks there is an error in a bill, the credit card company must investigate, and the debtor can suspend payments until it does so. The cardholder simply writes to the company within sixty days of receipt of the bill and briefly explains the circumstances and why he or she thinks there is an error. Under the law, the company must acknowledge the letter within thirty days and solve the dispute within ninety days. During that period, the debtor does not have to pay the amount of the dispute or any minimum payment from the amount of dispute. The creditor cannot impose finance charges during that period for unpaid balances in dispute; nor can it close the account. However, if it turns out that there was no error, the creditor can then attempt to collect finance charges for the entire period for which payments were not made.

Credit Card Rules (CCPA)   The Truth-in-Lending Act contains two important provisions regarding credit cardholders. One provision limits the liability of a cardholder to $50 per card when the creditor has been notified that the credit card has been stolen or lost. The second prohibits a credit card company from billing a consumer for unauthorized charges.

Jones loses his MasterCard credit card in the street. Bilas finds it and buys $200 worth of goods with the card. The next day Jones informs MasterCard of his loss. MasterCard later bills Jones for the $200 worth of goods that Bilas bought. Clearly, MasterCard can collect only $50 (or nothing if Jones notified it of the loss before the card was used by Bilas) because that is the maximum liability imposed on the loser of a credit card.

Now consider that MasterCard mails a credit card to Farmer, who has not applied for a card or held one in the past. The envelope is stolen out of Farmer's mailbox, and the thief signs the card and buys $200 worth of goods. MasterCard bills Farmer for the $200. Farmer does not have to pay anything at all, not even $50, because MasterCard performed a prohibited act by sending an unsolicited card.

Credit Reports (CCPA)

A concern over the years has been that government might be monitoring the actions of its citizens too closely.

Investigative reports on consumers' credit status have heightened this concern. One serious objection to this practice is that consumers have no access to the contents of the reports and can in no way control their use. Inaccuracies, once reported, have been almost impossible to uncover, much less to correct.

In 1970, Congress enacted the Fair Credit Reporting Act (Title VI) as a part of the CCPA. This act provides that consumers are entitled, upon request, to be informed of the nature and scope of a credit investigation, the kind of information that is being compiled, and the names of persons who will be receiving the report. They must make the request within specific time limits, however. Consumers have the right to require that any inaccurate or misleading material be reinvestigated and, if not verified, be removed from the file. If there is a dispute about the accuracy of certain parts of the report, consumers have the right to include their own one-hundred-word statement in the file to set forth their position with regard to disputed matters. Such statements become part of the permanent record.

The law also provides for updating information that is obsolete. For example, any bankruptcy adjudication that has occurred more than fourteen years prior to the report can be re-

---

18.   15 USCA 1681.

moved. Lawsuits or judgments that are more than seven years old or for which the statute of limitations has expired (whichever is longer) can be removed. In general, any information unfavorable to consumers that is more than seven years old can also be removed.

Although the law provides that consumers have the right to be informed of the contents of their files, the Truth-in-Lending Act limits that access for others. A person who wishes to obtain information contained in a consumer's credit file must have either a court order or a legitimate business need for the information or must have the permission of the consumer. Consumer reporting agencies must inform the consumer when an investigative report is being compiled and of the right to disclosure. A consumer credit reporting agency that fails to comply with the terms of the act can be held liable not only for actual damages but for punitive damages and attorneys' fees resulting from a lawsuit brought by the consumer.

Fair Debt Collection Practices Act (1977) Many states have passed legislation that prohibits the use of abusive techniques, such as harassment, in bill collection. Bill collectors have been known to telephone consumer-debtors at all hours of the night, making threats about the personal safety of the consumer, and to telephone the consumer's family as well. Another abusive technique is to telephone or appear at the debtor's place of employment and verbally harass the debtor.

States that have enacted collection practice legislation prohibit these kinds of practices but do not prohibit *all* phone calls. Many states provide penalty provisions that include levying a flat penalty fee against the collector and that permit damages for emotional distress. Although debtors have always been able to use traditional tort law to protect themselves from abuse, clearly the trend of the law, at the state and federal levels, is toward limiting abusive action in the debt collection process.[19]

In 1977, Congress enacted the Fair Debt Collection Practices Act (FDCPA). The FDCPA does not apply to all consumer credit collection efforts. Rather, it governs the conduct of debt collectors—persons who regularly collect debts owed to someone else. Those who attempt to collect debts owed to themselves are not covered by this act, except when, in the process of collecting their own debts, such creditors use a name other than their own, leading a debtor to believe that a third person is attempting to collect the debts.

The FDCPA prohibits the following actions on the part of debt collectors:

1.   Contacting the consumer at his or her place of employment if the employer objects.
2.   Contacting the consumer at inconvenient or unusual times, such as 3 o'clock in the morning, or contacting the consumer at any time if he or she is represented by an attorney.
3.   Contacting third parties other than parents, spouses, or financial advisers about the payment of a debt unless the court so authorizes.
4.   Using harassment and intimidation, such as abusive language, or using false or misleading information, such as posing as a policeman.
5.   Communicating with the consumer after receipt of notice that the consumer is refusing to pay the debt, except to advise the consumer of further action to be taken by the collection agency.

The Uniform Consumer Credit Code

In 1968, the National Conference of Commissioners on the Uniform State Laws promulgated the Uniform Consumer Credit Code (UCCC). The UCCC has been controversial, but it has been adopted in approximately 20 percent of the states.[20] The UCCC is an attempt to promulgate a comprehensive body of rules governing the most important aspects of consumer credit. Sections of the UCCC, for example, focus on truth in lend-

---

19.   Federal statutes also ban certain debt collection techniques. See 15 USCA 1692. The Federal Trade Commission prosecutes overly zealous debt collectors under federal regulations for unfair and deceptive trade practices.

20.   By 1974 the UCCC had undergone six redrafts. Furthermore, in those jurisdictions where the law has been adopted, it is not uniform among them. The states that have adopted some form of the UCCC are Colorado, Idaho, Indiana, Iowa, Kansas, Maine, South Carolina, Utah, Wisconsin, and Wyoming.

ing, maximum credit ceilings, door-to-door sales, and referral sales. The UCCC is also concerned with materials contained in fine print clauses and various provisions of creditor remedies, including deficiency judgments (personal judgments for the amount of debt that is not secured by property) and garnishments (proceedings where property, money, or wages controlled by a third person are transferred to the court to satisfy a judgment). (See Chapter 32 for details.) The UCCC applies to most types of sales, including real estate. It also replaces existing state consumer credit laws as well as installment loan, usury, and retail installment sale acts.

QUESTIONS AND CASE PROBLEMS

1. Green receives two new credit cards on May 1. One was *solicited* from the King Department Store and the other was *unsolicited* from the Flyways Airline. During the month of May Green makes numerous credit card purchases from King, but she does not use the Flyways Airline card. On May 31 a burglar breaks into Green's home and, along with other items, steals both credit cards. Green notifies the King Department Store of the theft on June 2, but she fails to notify Flyways Airline. Using the King credit card, the burglar makes a $500 purchase on June 1 and a $200 purchase on June 3. The burglar then charges a vacation flight on the Flyways Airline card for $1,000 on June 5. Green receives the bills for these charges and refuses to pay them. Discuss Green's liability in these situations.

2. Norman's Health Club, Inc., was a chain of recreation centers located in St. Louis, Missouri. The health clubs sold lifetime memberships for $360; the fee could be paid either in full or in twenty-four installments of $15 each. The vast majority of persons joining the health clubs chose the installment plan. Under this plan, Norman's Health Club had prospective members sign installment notes, which in turn were sold to finance companies at discounts of between $85 and $165. Club members who paid cash were charged about 10 percent less than those who paid under the installment plan. Assuming that no disclosures about finance charges were made on the installment notes signed by the prospective club members, has Norman's Health Club violated the disclosure requirements of the Truth-in-Lending Act? Has there been any violation by the finance companies that purchased the notes? [Joseph v. Norman's Health Club, Inc., 532 F.2d 86 (8th Cir. 1976)]

3. In 1969, a door-to-door salesman for Family Publications Services, Inc., sold Leila Mourning a five-year subscription to four magazines. Mourning agreed to pay $3.95 immediately and to remit a similar amount monthly for thirty months. She also signed a form contract that contained a clause stating that the subscriptions could not be cancelled and providing that any default in an installment payment would render the entire balance due. The contract made no reference to service or finance charges. Mourning thereafter defaulted on one of her payments, and Family Publications threatened to bring suit for the balance due. Mourning defended on the ground that Family Publications failed to disclose the nature and amount of the finance charges in its installment contract. Family Publications contended that since no finance charges were involved, no disclosure was necessary. Assuming no finance charges were involved in the installment plan, has Family Publications Services, Inc., violated the Truth-in-Lending Act? [Mourning v. Family Publications Serv. Inc., 411 U.S. 356, 93 S.Ct. 1652 (1973)]

4. On July 16, Polly Ann Barber entered into a retail installment contract with Kimbrell's, Inc., for the purchase of various items of household furniture totaling $592. Barber later sued Kimbrell's for violating the Truth-in-Lending Act because Kimbrell's used the term *total time balance* in its disclosure document rather than *total of payments* as the act required. At the same time, Barber sued Furniture Distributors, Inc., claiming that it too was liable as a creditor under the act. Furniture Distributors, Inc., participated in the development and preparation of the standard contract form and distributed it for use in all the retail stores in the Kimbrell's chain. It was also the parent company of Kimbrell's and had extensive knowledge of the credit terms for all the consumer credit sales that Kimbrell's made. Each time one of the Kimbrell's stores made a consumer credit sale, the installment contract was sent to Furniture Distributors for review. If Kimbrell's is in violation of the Truth-in-Lending Act, can Barber also hold Furniture Distributors liable? [Barber v. Kimbrell's, Inc., 577 F.2d 216 (4th Cir. 1978)]

5. The W. T. Grant Company (Grants), a retailer, sold both on a cash basis and under Grants credit plans. A customer who entered into a credit contract with Grants was offered the opportunity to take out credit

life insurance, health and accident insurance, and property insurance. The election of insurance coverage was purely voluntary and was evidenced by the customer's signature on the contract within the blocked-off "Insurance Agreement" segment. The insurance charges became part of the unpaid balance upon which the finance charge was computed. Must the insurance charges be disclosed as finance charges? [Welmaker v. W. T. Grant Co., 365 F.Supp. 531 (N.D.Ga. 1972)]

6. Under Georgia law, promissory notes signed by consumers must be notarized. Generally, a small fee is charged by notaries for their signatures. American Finance Company was engaged in the business of making consumer loans. The loan contracts complied with all of the requirements of the Truth-in-Lending Act but failed to mention that customers would be charged a fee for notarization. Buford brought suit against American Finance Company. He had signed one of American's promissory notes and claimed in the suit that failure to disclose the notary fee constituted a violation of the Truth-in-Lending Act. Is he correct? American Finance Company argued that Buford was incorrect and further argued that even if Buford was right, American Finance should not be held liable since the charge was a minimal one and was left off inadvertently. Assuming that American Finance did not intentionally omit the charge, is this a valid defense? [Buford v. American Fin. Co., 333 F.Supp. 1243 (N.D.Ga. 1971)]

7. Roseman was employed as a debit agent for the John Hancock Insurance Company. He resigned, following accusations that he had been dishonest with his company expense account. Before his resignation he reimbursed the account. Part of the information concerning Roseman's resignation was contained in a credit report held by the Retail Credit Co. Inc. Subsequently, Roseman was denied a position with another insurance company after it consulted the Retail Credit Co.'s report. Assuming that the information held by Retail Credit was accurate, was its circulation of such information illegal?

Roseman felt that he was unfairly treated by Retail Credit because there were two sides to the story of his resignation, and his side was not included in the company's files. He complained that Retail Credit should have informed him that it had such information, and he claimed further that he had the right to include a statement in the files setting forth his version of the circumstances surrounding his resignation. Is Roseman correct? [Roseman v. Retail Credit Co., Inc., 428 F.Supp. 643 (E.D.Pa. 1977)]

8. Harold Grey signed an installment contract as payment for membership in a European Health Spas

Club. The disclosure documents that accompanied the installment loan contract were printed in regular type, with the exception of the words: "FINANCE CHARGE," "ANNUAL PERCENTAGE RATE," and "MEMBER ACKNOWLEDGES THAT HE HAS READ AND RECEIVED A FILLED-IN SIGNED COPY OF THIS AGREEMENT." In addition, at the top of the disclosure statement, the words "NOTICE TO BUYER" were printed. Under federal truth-in-lending regulations, the words *finance charge* and *annual percentage rate* must be printed conspicuously in the truth-in-lending disclosure statements. Otherwise, the creditor is deemed in violation of the act. Has the requirement of conspicuousness been met? [Grey v. European Health Spas Inc., 428 F.Supp. 841 (D.C.Conn. 1977)]

9. Roger Gonzalez purchased a Ford from Schmerler Ford on credit. The installment credit agreement that Gonzalez signed named Ford Motor Credit Corporation as the payee of the loan. Nowhere on the loan form or the disclosure documents did the name Schmerler Ford appear. Schmerler Ford, however, helped Gonzalez fill out the loan forms and then forwarded them to Ford Motor Credit Corporation. Schmerler lacked the authority to negotiate the interest rate charged on the loan and lacked the ability to approve Gonzalez's loan. Gonzalez's loan was made solely by Ford Motor Credit Corporation. Later it was discovered that the loan forms failed to disclose all of the relevant information that was required under the Truth-in-Lending Act. Who can be held liable as having violated the act—Schmerler Ford, Ford Motor Credit Corporation, or both? [Gonzalez v. Schmerler Ford, 397 F.Supp. 323 (N.D.Ill. 1975)]

10. In the summer of 1972, Robert Martin applied for and was issued an American Express credit card. Approximately three years later, in April 1975, Martin gave his card to E. L. McBride, a business associate, and orally authorized McBride to charge up to $500 on the credit card. He also wrote to American Express requesting that charges on his account be limited to $1,000. However, in June 1975 Martin received a statement from American Express indicating that the amount owed on his credit card account was approximately $5,300. Under the Truth-in-Lending Act, for how much will Martin be liable to American Express? [Martin v. American Exp., Inc., 361 So.2d 597 (Ala. Civ. App. 1978)]

11. GAC Finance Corporation was the holder of a promissory note given by Mr. and Mrs. Burgess. The Burgesses defaulted on the note, and GAC brought suit against them. Mrs. Burgess counterclaimed that the note was in violation of the Truth-in-Lending Act, since delinquent charges were designated in the note as .53

instead of $.53, making the amount of the delinquent charge so unclear that it violated the act. She further complained that general paragraphs on related subjects were separated. She also wanted reimbursement for attorneys' fees regardless of whether she won or lost the case against GAC. Discuss these contentions. [GAC Fin. Corp. v. Burgess, 16 Wash.App. 758, 558 P.2d 1386 (1977)]

CHAPTER 49

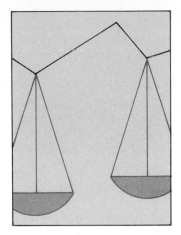

GOVERNMENT REGULATION
Environmental Protection

The traditional belief that air, water, and land will absorb all waste products without being harmed has been refuted by a considerable body of evidence. Furthermore, as society has become more urbanized, concern about future degradation of the environment has been heightened. These forces, plus general economic growth, greater wealth, and the proliferation of synthetic products that resist decomposition, have caused policymakers and some individuals to seek methods to reduce or prevent pollution.

HISTORICAL BACKGROUND

In one sense, concerns about the environment are not new. The English Parliament, for example, passed a number of acts that regulated the burning of soft coal in medieval England. Moreover, through common law nuisance statutes, property owners were given relief from pollu-

tion in situations where the individual could identify a distinct harm separate from that affecting the general public. Thus, if a factory polluted the air and killed a farmer's crops, the farmer could seek an injunction against the factory.

Needless to say, nuisance suits that granted specific relief for individuals were inadequate when the harm from pollution could not be identified with groups separate from the public at large. Under the common law, citizens were denied *standing* (access to the courts) unless specific harm could be shown. Thus, a group of citizens who wished to stop a new development that would cause significant water pollution would be denied access to the courts on the ground that the harm to them did not differ from the harm borne by the general public.[1] A public

---

1. Save the Bay Committee, Inc. v. Mayor, etc., of the City of Savannah, 227 Ga. 436, 181 S.E.2d 351 (1971).

authority, however, could sue for public nuisance.

The common law also limited relief from pollution in situations where the harm was caused by two or more independent sources. For example, if a number of firms were polluting the air, a harmed individual could sue any individual firm; however, until early in the twentieth century, the plaintiff was not able to sue all of the factories simultaneously. Thus, specific proof of damages in individual actions was often impossible. These difficulties in seeking relief in pollution cases, along with the forces creating additional pollution, have been largely responsible for the development of statutory regulations of environmental quality.

REGULATION BY ADMINISTRATIVE AGENCIES

Beginning in 1970, Congress passed a number of federal statutes directing administrative agencies to study the effects of pollution on the environment. On January 1, 1970, the National Environmental Policy Act (NEPA) created the Council of Environmental Quality and mandated that an environmental statement be prepared for every recommendation or report on legislation or major federal action that significantly affects the quality of the environment.[2] Since that time, the government has passed a number of acts that govern air quality, such as the Clean Air Act. In addition, a number of regulations have been promulgated for water quality. They include the Federal Water Pollution Control Act of 1965,[3] the Marine Protection and Research and Sanctuaries Act of 1972,[4] and the Safe Drinking Water Act of 1974.[5] Additional regulations governing the use of pesticides,[6] ra-

diation,[7] solid toxic substances,[8] and noise[9] have also been promulgated.

ENVIRONMENTAL PROTECTION AGENCY

The Environmental Protection Agency (EPA) was created in 1970 to assemble various agencies responsible for environmental protection. It is primarily an administrative organization. It employs approximately ten thousand individuals who carry out the directives of the numerous and complex regulations of federal statutes affecting the environment.

Environmental Impact Statements

One of the important responsibilities of the EPA is to ensure that all proposed federal legislation affecting the environment be analyzed and an environmental impact statement be issued. This statement has become an instrument for private citizens, consumer interests, businesses, and federal agencies to help shape the final outcome of regulatory actions. Even if an agency's analysis concludes that the impact statement is unnecessary, a statement supporting this conclusion must be filed.[10]

PRIVATE LITIGATION

Private parties continue to recover damages or obtain injunctions for environmental harms under a combination of statutory and common law provisions. The Clean Air Act Amendments of 1972, the Water Pollution and Prevention Control Act of 1972, and the Noise Control Act of 1972, for example, authorize private lawsuits for violations of air, water, and noise pollution standards. Furthermore, some courts have held that

---

2. National Environmental Policy Act of 1969, 42 USCA 4321 et seq.

3. Federal Water Pollution Control Act, 33 USCA 1151 (1965).

4. Marine Protection and Research and Sanctuaries Act of 1972, 16 USCA 1431 et seq.; 33 USCA 1407 et seq.

5. Safe Drinking Water Act, 21 USCA 349, 42 USCA 201, 300F et seq. (1974).

6. Federal Insecticide, Fungicide and Rodenticide Act of 1972, 7 USCA 135 et seq. (1947), as amended May 12, 1964.

7. Resource Conservation Recovery Act of 1976, 42 USCA 6901 et seq. (1976).

8. Toxic Substances Control Act of 1976, 15 USCA 2602 (1976).

9. Noise Control Act of 1972, 42 USCA 1604 (1972).

10. Arizona Public Serv. Co. v. Federal Power Comm'n, 483 F.2d 1275 (D.C.Cir.1973).

organizations can have standing in representing members' interests even if there is no direct organizational interest in the dispute.

On the other hand, some federal statutes give the government exclusive rights to lawsuits for violations of environmental protection regulations. For example, the Environmental Protection Agency is given the exclusive right to bring suits involving the violation of the Federal Water Pollution Control Act.

AIR POLLUTION

Federal involvement with air pollution goes back to the 1950s, when Congress authorized funds for air pollution research. In 1963 the federal government passed the Clean Air Act, which focused on multistate air pollution and provided assistance to states. Various amendments, particularly in 1970 and 1977,[11] strengthened the government's authority to regulate the quality of air. In total, these acts provide the regulatory basis for promulgating standards to control pollution, primarily automobile and stationary sources.

Automobile Pollution

Regulations governing air pollution from automobiles and other mobile sources specify pollution standards and time schedules. For example, the 1970 Clean Air Act required a reduction of 90 percent in the amount of carbon monoxide and hydrocarbons emitted from automobiles by 1975.[12] Additional regulations that control air pollution indirectly focus on improved gas mileage for new automobiles and gasoline additives such as lead, as illustrated by the case below. Similar regulations for aircraft are administered by the Federal Aviation Administration. The Environmental Protection Agency also sets national air quality standards for major pollutants throughout the United States.

The 1977 amendments to the Clean Air Act establish multilevel standards. For example, they attempt to prevent the deterioration of air quality even in areas where the existing quality exceeds that required by federal law. These air quality standards cover carbon monoxide, nitrogen dioxide, hydrocarbons, sulfur dioxide, and other harmful materials. They present general guidelines for protecting vegetation, climate, visibility, and certain economic conditions. The Department of Health and Human Services has divided the country into atmospheric areas for the purpose of preparing these controls, and each area is required to institute a plan for meeting the standards.

---

11. Clean Air Act Amendments of 1970, 42 USC 7521, Clean Air Act Amendments of 1977, 42 USC 7521-25, 7541-51.

12. Carbon monoxide, a colorless, odorless gas, can reduce mental performance and result in death if inhaled in sufficient quantities. Hydrocarbons are unburned fuel, one of the principal ingredients that generate smog.

ETHYL CORP. v.
ENVIRONMENTAL
PROTECTION AGENCY
United States Court of Appeals,
District of Columbia Circuit,
1976.
541 F.2d 1.

BACKGROUND AND FACTS *Ethyl Corporation, a leading producer of antiknock compounds for increasing gasoline octane rating, filed for review of the Environmental Protection Agency order that required annual reductions in the lead content of gasoline. The Clean Air Act authorized the agency to regulate gasoline additives that are a danger to public health and welfare. Ethyl Corporation sought judicial review of the agency's order. Review of agency actions under the Clean Air Act is available only in the U.S. Court of Appeals for the District of Columbia Circuit.*

WRIGHT, Circuit Judge.

*   *   *   *

Man's ability to alter his environment has developed far more rapidly than his ability to foresee with certainty the effects of his alterations. It is only recently that we have begun to appreciate the danger posed by unregulated modification of the world around us, and have created watchdog agencies whose task it is to warn us, and protect us, when technological "advances" present dangers unappreciated—or unrevealed—by their supporters. Such agencies, unequipped with crystal balls and unable to read the future, are nonetheless charged with evaluating the effects of unprecedented environmental modifications, often made on a massive scale. Necessarily, they must deal with predictions and uncertainty, with developing evidence, with conflicting evidence, and, sometimes, with little or no evidence at all. Today we address the scope of the power delegated one such watchdog, the Environmental Protection Agency (EPA). We must determine the certainty required by the Clean Air Act before EPA may act to protect the health of our populace from the lead particulate emissions of automobiles.

*   *   *   *

On October 28, 1973, as a result of a motion filed in *Natural Resources Defense Council, Inc. v. EPA*, this court ordered EPA to reach within 30 days a final decision on whether lead additives should be regulated for health reasons. *   *   * [The EPA Document] candidly discusses the various scientific studies, both pro and con, underlying this information, and ultimately concludes that lead from automobile emissions will endanger the public health. *   *   * Under the final regulations, lead in all gasoline would be reduced over a five-year period to an average of 0.5 grams per gallon.

*   *   * Our scope *   *   * requires us to strike "agency action, findings, and conclusions" [only if] we find [them] to be "arbitrary, capricious, an abuse of discretion, or otherwise not in accordance with law." This standard of review is a highly deferential one. It presumes agency action to be valid. Moreover, it forbids the court's substituting its judgment for that of the agency *   *   *.

This is not to say, however, that we must rubber-stamp the agency decision as correct. To do so would render the appellate process a superfluous (although time-consuming) ritual. Rather, the reviewing court must assure itself that the agency decision was "based on a consideration of the relevant factors *   *   *."

Petitioners [Ethyl Corp.] vigorously attack both the sufficiency and the validity of the many scientific studies relied upon by the Administrator, while advancing for consideration various studies allegedly supportive of their position. The record in this case is massive—over 10,000 pages. Not surprisingly, evidence may be isolated that supports virtually any inference one might care to draw. *   *   *

Because of the importance of the issues raised, we have accorded this case the most careful and exhaustive consideration. We find that in this rule-making proceeding the EPA has complied with all the statutory procedural requirements and that its reasons as stated in its opinion provide a rational basis for its action. Since we reject all of petitioners' claims of error the Agency may enforce its low-lead regulations.

JUDGMENT AND REMEDY   *The Environmental Protection Agency regulations were affirmed by the U.S. Court of Appeals. The EPA was permitted to enforce its low lead regulations.*

WATER POLLUTION

Federal regulations governing the pollution of water can be traced back nearly a century to the River and Harbor Act of 1886 as amended in 1899.[13] These regulations required a permit for discharging or depositing refuse in navigable waterways. The courts have even determined that hot water can be considered refuse.[14] In 1965 Congress passed the Federal Water Pollution Control Act, which strengthened the Environmental Protection Agency's enforcement powers.

Clean Water Regulation

Perhaps the most important regulations that govern the quality of water were instituted in 1972 by Congress. These regulations establish goals to (1) make waters safe for swimming, (2) protect fish and wildlife, and (3) eliminate the discharge of pollutants into the water. They set forth specific time schedules, which were extended by amendment in 1977. The 1972 Clean Water Act also specifies a number of regulations with time schedules for controlling industrial water pollution. Regulations for the most part specify that

13.   33 USC 407.
14.   33 USC 1254(t).

the best available technology be installed. Further, the act requires both municipal and industrial dischargers to apply for permits before they discharge wastes into the nation's navigable waters. Finally, the act establishes standing for citizens (or organizations) whose interests have been affected against parties who violate EPA or state standards and orders. Both injunctive relief and damages can be sought through claims under the act.

Other Regulations

In 1972, through the Marine Protection Research and Sanctuaries Act, Congress established a system of permits that regulates the discharge and introduction of materials into coastal waters and continuous marine areas. The Safe Drinking Water Act of 1974 established additional regulations governing drinking water standards. The rules, which are similar to those under the Clean Water Act, provide that states assume the primary responsibility for complying with national standards. The federal government assumes responsibility where states fail to institute or enforce drinking water standards. In most cases, explicit penalties are imposed on parties that pollute the water. The polluting party can also be required to clean up pollution or pay for the cost of doing so, as is illustrated by the following case.

UNITED STATES OF AMERICA v. ATLANTIC RICHFIELD CO.

Eastern District of Pennsylvania
1977.
429 F.Supp. 830.

BACKGROUND AND FACTS   *In this action, a number of oil companies, including Atlantic Richfield Company and Gulf Oil Co., were assessed monetary penalties that included paying for the cost of cleaning up oil discharges. The defendants (Atlantic Richfield) argued that the imposition of such penalties in an accidental oil spill when the reporting and cleaning requirements had been satisfied constituted a criminal action. Therefore, the defendants believed that they had the right to a jury trial. The court had to determine whether these penalties denied due process.*

Two cases were consolidated and heard by the district court simultaneously. In one case, Atlantic Richfield Company (Arco) was the defendant; in the other, Gulf Oil Company was the defendant.

BECKER, District Judge.

*   *   *   *

These cases raise issues concerning the proper construction and the constitutionality of the "civil penalty" provision of the oil and hazardous substance sections of the Federal Water Pollution Control Act Amendments of 1972. *   *   * The constructional issues boil down to whether Congress intended to impose the civil penalty on persons who spill oil accidentally, report such spill to the appropriate authorities, and clean it up at their own expense (hereinafter "accidental, reporting self-cleaners"). *   *   *

Turning now to the operative facts, we note that the stipulations as to the relevant events in each of the cases before us track essentially the same pattern. In each case either Arco or Gulf owned or operated a vessel or facility from which oil was discharged in harmful quantity into the navigable waters of the United States. The discharges were "accidental" or "unintentional," but, perforce, they violated the prohibition on discharge of (b)(3); hence, without more, they subjected the owners (defendants) to liability for the civil penalty under (b)(6). However, the appropriate defendant (or its agent) promptly reported each spill and cleaned it up within the limits of technological feasibility and to the satisfaction of the Coast Guard. Despite defendants' compliance with their reporting and clean up duties, the Coast Guard, following the prescribed administrative procedure, assessed a civil penalty in each case. Upon defendants' refusal to pay, the government sued.

*   *   *   *

The first prong of defendants' argument goes as follows: The stipulated facts would not survive a motion to dismiss for failure to state a claim under the common law of negligence; *i.e.*, although the facts reveal "accidental" spills, they do not reveal a basis for inferring that defendants caused the spills through a lack of due care; but "negligence" is the lowest level of "fault" recognized by our law; *i.e.*, non-negligent conduct is reasonable conduct; therefore, if the spills were not negligent, we can infer that there was no reasonable means for defendants to prevent the spills.

We find that defendants' argument makes most sense when translated into simple economic terms. A rational owner of an oil facility, recognizing his potential liabilities for clean ups *   *   * (and for damages under common law damage remedies which § 1321 [of the act] leaves untouched), will attempt to minimize the costs of spills. To accomplish this he will calculate the marginal costs of preventing spills and of potential liabilities. He will thereupon engage in prevention to the point where the marginal cost of prevention equals his marginal liability for spills. Because that point defines *reasonable* spill prevention, a reasonable person will spend money for just that much prevention and no more. To spend less would be negligent. *   *   * To spend more would be wasteful or inefficient. *   *   *

On this basis we can make some sense of defendants' argument that (b)(6) serves no regulatory purpose when applied to "faultless" spillers. But defendants move from the claim that they were "faultless" to the claim that no regulatory purpose would be served by imposing a (b)(6) penalty, an argument we reject because it proceeds from a faulty premise. While it is true that the stipulated facts about the spills themselves would not be sufficient to support an action in negligence, this is not such an action, but rather an action to enforce a penalty.

The elements of this statutory action are only that defendant violated (b)(3) and that the Coast Guard following the appropriate procedure assessed the (b)(6) penalty. The statute does not make "fault" an element of the cause of action, but rather a factor in the administrative penalty setting procedure. This is proper

because there is no principle of law which requires that civil regulability through imposition of penalty be predicated upon a finding of fault. Moreover, a number of factors support civil regulability here in the absence of fault. First, as we explain more fully in our discussion of the Constitutional issues, *infra*, the principal goal of (b)(6) is to *deter* spills. Second, the Congressional purpose here was to impose a standard of conduct higher than that related just to economic efficiency. Additionally, the Congress obviously believed: (a) that no clean up effort could be complete because, after discharge, it is impossible to guarantee against residual harm from quantities of oil too small or too well dispersed to be detectable; and (b) that even the transitory pollution of waters was deleterious to the environment.
* * * *

In view of the foregoing analysis we must reject defendant's contention that, as applied to accidental, reporting, self-cleaners, (b)(6) is really criminal rather than civil because, (1) the statutory language is not ambiguous; and (2) even where defendants are not at fault, the penalty does not act only as a punishment but serves the ends of civil regulation.

JUDGMENT AND REMEDY   *The district court held that the penalties provided under the Federal Water Pollution Control Act Amendments of 1972 were civil, not criminal, penalties. Therefore, the government could continue to assess and collect them against Atlantic Richfield, Gulf, and other oil companies for accidental oil spills.*

NOISE POLLUTION

In 1972, Congress prescribed standards and regulations for the control of aircraft noise, including sonic booms, and for the control of emissions of railroad and motor vehicles involved in interstate commerce. The Noise Control Acts of 1970 and 1972 established the goal of creating an environment free from noise that is injurious to the health and welfare of the public. The courts have ruled that local control of noise is preempted when state regulations conflict with those established by federal statutes.[15]

Regulations promulgated by the noise control acts are administered by the Federal Aviation Administration, the Environmental Protection Agency, and the Department of Transportation. The EPA, for example, is authorized to establish noise emission levels for equipment, motors, and engines. It also reviews production processes, verifies reports for compliance with the law, conducts audit tests, and makes inspections of manufacturer records.

TOXIC SUBSTANCES

The Toxic Substances Control Act was passed in 1976 to regulate chemicals and chemical compounds that are known to be toxic and to institute investigation of any possible harmful effects from new chemical compounds. The regulations authorize the Environmental Protection Agency to require that manufacturers, processors, and other organizations planning to use chemicals first determine their effect on human health and the environment. The EPA also has the authority to regulate substances that potentially create a hazard or an unreasonable risk of injury.

PESTICIDE CONTROL

The use of chemical pesticides to kill insects and weeds has significantly increased agricultural productivity. On the other hand, there is a grow-

15. Burbank v. Lockheed Air Terminal Inc., 411 U.S. 624, 93 S.Ct. 1854 (1973).

ing body of evidence that residuals from these chemicals have not been absorbed by the environment. In some cases, buildups of residuals have killed animals, and some potential long-term effects detrimental to the public have also been identified. The original regulations governing pesticides were established by the Federal Insecticide, Fungicide and Rodenticide Act of 1947, as amended in 1972.[16] The Environmental Protection Agency has been given the authority to control the introduction of pesticides. Pesticides must be (1) registered before they can be sold, (2) certified and used only for approved applications, and (3) used in amounts that meet established limits when they are applied to crops that provide food for animals or people. The EPA also has the right to inspect manufacturing establishments. In some situations, the supply of pesticides is controlled to keep hazardous chemicals off the market. Those substances that have been identified as harmful are subject to suspension and cancellation of registration.

WASTE DISPOSAL

Waste disposal can occur on land, in the water, or in the air; thus regulations protecting these resources from pollution also apply to waste dis-

---

16. Federal Environmental Pesticide Control Act of 1972.

posal. In 1970 Congress passed the Materials Policy Act, an act designed to reduce solid waste disposal by encouraging the recycling of waste and the reuse of materials by society. The act also provides for pilot waste disposal projects utilizing modern technology. For example, the development and use of technology that converts garbage into useful products have been greatly encouraged by the solid waste programs of the Environmental Protection Agency. The EPA also carries out the provisions of the Resource Conservation and Recovery Act of 1976, which governs EPA studies and recommendations of solid waste disposal, ranging from glass and plastic waste to airport landfill. The EPA is primarily concerned with issuing federal facility permits and reviewing the state permit system for the use of certain equipment. It conducts on-site inspections of hazardous waste generators and cites violators. The Solid Waste Disposal Act gives each state the power to enact its own hazardous waste standards.

Federal statutes also attempt to generate state and local community initiative for solving solid waste disposal problems by providing monies and expert guidance for state and local studies. A number of states have sought to reduce the problem of solid waste disposal by requiring recycling or reuse of various products. One such state is Oregon whose statute was challenged in the following case:

BACKGROUND AND FACTS *The State of Oregon adopted a law prohibiting the use of nonreturnable containers for beer and carbonated beverages. It also prohibited the sale of metal beverage containers that used detachable pull-top opening devices. The American Can Company instituted an action against the Oregon Liquor Control Commission as well as other administrative bodies of the State of Oregon and appealed the initial decision that upheld the law.*

AMERICAN CAN CO. v. OREGON LIQUOR CONTROL COMM'N

Court of Appeals of Oregon, 1974.
15 Or.App. 618, 517 P.2d 691.

TANZER, Judge.

*   *   *   *

The bottle bill, enacted by the Oregon legislature in 1971, became effective on October 1, 1972. The statute's principal provisions are as follows:

1. Every retailer of the covered beverages (beer or carbonated beverages) in Oregon is required to "accept from a consumer any empty beverage containers of the kind, common size and brand sold by the dealer" and to pay the consumer the statutory "refund value" of the container. *   *   *

*   *   *   *

Metal beverage containers, a part of which is wholly detachable in opening without a can opener ("pull top" cans), may not be sold at retail in Oregon.

*   *   *   *

The primary legislative purpose of the bottle bill is to cause bottlers of carbonated soft drinks and brewers to package their products for distribution in Oregon in returnable, multiple-use deposit bottles toward the goals of reducing litter and solid waste in Oregon and reducing the injuries to people and animals due to discarded "pull tops."

As bases for attacking the validity of the statute, plaintiffs [the American Can Company] invoke the Equal Protection and Due Process Clauses of the Fourteenth Amendment to the United States Constitution, and the Commerce Clause, art. 1, § 8, clause 3, of the United States Constitution. In addition, plaintiffs cite various provisions of the Oregon Constitution.

One of the plaintiffs' main objectives at trial was to show that the bottle bill would have an effect not only upon manufacturers of bottles and cans, but also upon an entire distribution chain including brewers, soft drink bottlers and canners, beer wholesalers, retailers and, ultimately, consumers. The evidence in this regard demonstrated that the consumption of malt beverages and soft drinks had increased greatly in the United States in recent years, and that a large part of this increase could be attributed to the use of convenient "one-way" packages, including both cans and non-returnable bottles. Plaintiffs assert that non-returnable containers are essential to the existence of national and regional beer markets, and that non-returnable containers are also essential to the continued existence of soft drink enterprises. The non-returnable containers were shown to have provided economies in the packaging and distribution of soft drinks and beer by eliminating the cost of shipping the containers both ways, thus causing an increase in feasible shipping distances and enlarging the market each manufacturer could cover. Among the effects of the bottle bill, plaintiffs' witnesses predicted, would be a substantial reduction in Oregon sales of soft drinks packaged outside Oregon, and impairment of the ability of distant brewers to compete in the Oregon market. The bottle bill would necessitate substantial changes in the structure of the industries involved in the manufacturing and merchandising of beer and soft drinks.

*   *   *   *

The Oregon legislature was persuaded that the economic benefit to the beverage industry brought with it deleterious consequences to the environment and additional cost to the public. The aggravation of the problems of litter in public places and solid waste disposal and the attendant economic and esthetic burden to the public outweighed the narrower economic benefit to the industry. Thus the legislature enacted the bottle bill over the articulate opposition of the industries represented by plaintiffs.

As with every change of circumstance in the market place, there are gainers and there are losers. Just as there were gainers and losers, with plaintiffs apparently among the gainers, when the industry adapted to the development of non-returnable containers, there will be new gainers and losers as they adapt to the ban. The economic losses complained of by plaintiffs in this case are essentially the consequences of readjustment of the beverage manufacturing and distribution systems to the older technology in order to compete in the Oregon market.

*   *   *   *

*   *   * The introduction of any new circumstance affecting competition will cause economic winners and economic losers throughout the industry as it readjusts to that new circumstance. The evidence is that plaintiffs expect to be among the losers, unless, of course, they are able to make marketing adjustments.

Economic loss restricted to certain elements of the beverage industry must be viewed in relation to the broader loss to the general public of the state of Oregon which the legislature sought, by enactment of the bottle bill, to avoid. The availability of land and revenues for solid waste disposal, the cost of litter collection on our highways and in our public parks, the depletion of mineral and energy resources, the injuries to humans and animals caused by discarded pull tops, and the esthetic blight on our landscape, are all economic, safety and esthetic burdens of great consequence which must be borne by every member of the public. The legislature attached higher significance to the cost to the public than they did to the cost to the beverage industry and we have no cause to disturb that legislative determination.

*   *   *   *

Plaintiffs' and intervenors' constitutional challenges having failed, we hold the bottle bill to be a valid exercise of Oregon's police power. In doing so, we acknowledge having had the benefit of an able analysis by the trial court.

The appellate court affirmed the trial court's ruling that Oregon had legitimately exercised its state police power in passing laws concerning solid waste disposal. The additional cost to the beverage industry was recognized, but the court would not accept it as a justification for overturning a legislative enactment. Hence, the bottle bill was upheld.

**JUDGMENT
AND REMEDY**

JUDICIAL LIMITS

In the first half of the 1970s, federal and state legislators enacted many statutes that regulate environmental quality. Judicial interpretations of these statutes have generally given broad discretionary powers to the administrative agencies that carry out their directives. Beginning in the mid-1970s, however, the courts began to place stricter limits on administrative discretion. Recent court decisions that impose a cost-benefit standard on administrative decisions are likely to limit discretion in the environmental area as well.

In *American Petroleum v. Occupational Safety and Health Adm'n*, an OSHA regulation limiting benzine exposure in the workplace was invalidated by the Fifth Circuit Court of Appeals.[17] In

1977, OSHA promulgated regulations reducing permissible exposure by 90 percent from the 1971 standard. This action was based primarily on the results of three studies that showed an increased risk of leukemia in workers who had been exposed to benzine at levels in excess of one hundred times the 1977 permissible levels. The court interpreted the "reasonably necessary" language of the Occupational Safety and Health Act to require an estimate of the expected benefits of the regulation "in order to determine whether the benefits bear a reasonable relationship to the standard's demonstrably high costs."

The following classic case deals with judicial interpretation of an environmental statute, the Endangered Species Act.

---

17. 581 F.2d 493 (5th Cir. 1978).

BACKGROUND AND FACTS   *The Endangered Species Act of 1973 authorizes the secretary of the interior to declare a species of life "endangered." The secretary listed a small fish popularly known as the snail darter as an endangered species under this act. The snail darter lived in a portion of the Little Tennessee River in which the Tellico Dam was*

**TENNESSEE VALLEY
AUTH. v. HILL**
Supreme Court of the United
States, 1978.
437 U.S. 153, 98 S.Ct. 2279.

under construction. The Secretary ordered all federal agencies to take action to ensure that the critical habitat of the snail darter was not modified or destroyed. An association of scientists, a conservation group, and citizens of the Little Tennessee Valley brought this suit to enjoin completion of the dam, claiming that impoundment of the waters would violate the act by causing the snail darter's extinction.

MR. Chief Justice BURGER delivered the opinion of the court.

*   *   *   *

We begin with the premise that operation of the Tellico Dam will either eradicate the known population of snail darters or destroy their critical habitat. Petitioner does not now seriously dispute this fact. In any event, under § 4(a)(1) of the Act, the Secretary of the Interior is vested with exclusive authority to determine whether a species such as the snail darter is "endangered" or "threatened" and to ascertain the factors which have led to such a precarious existence. By § 4(d) Congress has authorized—indeed commanded—the Secretary to "issue such regulations as he deems necessary and advisable to provide for the conservation of such species." As we have seen, the Secretary promulgated regulations which declared the snail darter an endangered species whose critical habitat would be destroyed by creation of the Tellico Reservoir. Doubtless petitioner would prefer not to have these regulations on the books, but there is no suggestion that the Secretary exceeded his authority or abused his discretion in issuing the regulations. Indeed, no judicial review of the Secretary's determinations has ever been sought and hence the validity of his actions are not open to review in this Court.

Starting from the above premise, two questions are presented: (a) would TVA be in violation of the Act if it completed and operated the Tellico Dam as planned? (b) if TVA's actions would offend the Act, is an injunction the appropriate remedy for the violation? For the reasons stated hereinafter, we hold that both questions must be answered in the affirmative.

It may seem curious to some that the survival of a relatively small number of three-inch fish among all the countless millions of species extant would require the permanent halting of a virtually completed dam for which Congress has expended more than $100 million. The paradox is not minimized by the fact that Congress continued to appropriate large sums of public money for the project, even after congressional Appropriations Committees were apprised of its apparent impact upon the survival of the snail darter. We conclude, however, that the explicit provisions of the Endangered Species Act require precisely that result.

One would be hard pressed to find a statutory provision whose terms were any plainer than those in § 7 of the Endangered Species Act. Its very words affirmatively command all federal agencies "to *insure* that actions *authorized, funded, or carried out* by them do not *jeopardize* the continued existence" of an endangered species or "*result* in the destruction or modification of habitat of such species. *   *   *" 16 U.S.C. § 1536 (1976 ed.). (Emphasis added.) This language admits of no exception. Nonetheless, petitioner urges, as do the dissenters, that the Act cannot reasonably be interpreted as applying to a federal project which was well under way when Congress passed the Endangered Species Act of 1973. To sustain that position, however, we would be forced to ignore the ordinary meaning of plain language. It has not been shown, for example, how TVA can close the gates of the Tellico Dam without "carrying out" an action that has been "authorized" and "funded" by a federal agency. Nor can we understand how such action will *"insure"* that the snail darter's habitat is not disrupted. Accepting the Secretary's determinations, as we must, it is clear that TVA's proposed operation of the dam will have precisely the opposite effect, namely the *eradication* of an endangered species.

Concededly, this view of the Act will produce results requiring the sacrifice of the anticipated benefits of the project and of many millions of dollars in public funds. But examination of the language, history, and structure of the legislation under review here indicates beyond doubt that Congress intended endangered species to be afforded the highest of priorities.

*   *   *   *

Having determined that there is an irreconcilable conflict between operation of the Tellico Dam and the explicit provisions of § 7 of the Endangered Species Act, we must now consider what remedy, if any, is appropriate. It is correct, of course, that a federal judge sitting as a chancellor is not mechanically obligated to grant an injunction for every violation of law. As a general matter it may be said that "[s]ince all or most all equitable remedies are discretionary, the balancing of equities and hardships is appropriate in almost any case as a guide to the chancellor's discretion." D. Dobbs, Remedies 52 (1973). Thus, in *Hecht Co.* the Court refused to grant an injunction when it appeared from the District Court findings that "the issuance of an injunction would have 'no effect by way of insuring better compliance in the future' and would [have been] 'unjust' to [the] petitioner and not 'in the public interest.' "

But these principles take a court only so far. Our system of government is, after all, a tripartite one, with each branch having certain defined functions delegated to it by the Constitution. While "[i]t is emphatically the province and duty of the judicial department to say what the law is," *Marbury v. Madison*, 1 Cranch 137, 177 (1803), it is equally—and emphatically—the exclusive province of the Congress not only to formulate legislative policies and mandate programs and projects, but also to establish their relative priority for the Nation. Once Congress, exercising its delegated powers, has decided the order of priorities in a given area, it is for the Executive to administer the laws and for the courts to enforce them when enforcement is sought.

Here we are urged to view the Endangered Species Act "reasonably," and hence shape a remedy "that accords with some modicum of common sense and the public weal." But is that our function? We have no expert knowledge on the subject of endangered species, much less do we have a mandate from the people to strike a balance of equities on the side of the Tellico Dam. Congress has spoken in the plainest of words, making it abundantly clear that the balance has been struck in favor of affording endangered species the highest of priorities, thereby adopting a policy which it described as "institutionalized caution."

Our individual appraisal of the wisdom or unwisdom of a particular course consciously selected by the Congress is to be put aside in the process of interpreting a statute. Once the meaning of an enactment is discerned and its constitutionality determined, the judicial process comes to an end. We do not sit as a committee of review, nor are we vested with the power of veto. The lines ascribed to Sir Thomas More by Robert Bolt are not without relevance here:

"The law, Roper, the law. I know what's legal, not what's right. And I'll stick to what's legal. *   *   * I'm *not* God. The currents and eddies of right and wrong, which you find such plain-sailing, I can't navigate, I'm no voyager. But in the thickets of the law, oh there I'm a forester. * * * What would you do? Cut a great road through the law to get after the Devil? * * * And when the last law was down, and the Devil turned round on you—where would you hide, Roper, the laws all being flat? * * * This country's planted thick with laws from coast to coast—Man's laws, not God's—and if you cut them down * * * d'you really think you could stand upright in the winds that would blow them? * * * Yes, I'd give the Devil benefit of law, for my own safety's sake." R. Bolt, A Man for All Seasons, Act I, p. 147 (Three Plays, Heinemann ed. 1967).

We agree with the Court of Appeals that in our constitutional system the commitment to the separation of powers is too fundamental for us to pre-empt congressional action by judicially decreeing what accords with "common sense and the public weal." Our Constitution vests such responsibilities in the political branches.

JUDGMENT AND REMEDY   *The Supreme Court enforced the Endangered Species Act by enjoining completion of the Tellico Dam.*

COMMENT   *It was later determined that snail darters could live in another area of the Little Tennessee River that would be unaffected by the dam. The snail darters were moved at government expense, making it possible to complete the Tellico Dam.*

QUESTIONS AND CASE PROBLEMS

1. Citizens Against Toxic Sprays, Inc., was an organization established to challenge the use of toxic sprays in places where they could be harmful to humans, animals, or vegetation. The group sought to enjoin the United States Forest Service from using the herbicide TCDD because of its hazardous effect on people who breathed it. TCDD was used only in national forests, not in any residential areas. Citizens Against Toxic Sprays alleged that some of its members were affected by the use of TCDD in two of the national forests because they lived near them, worked in them, or used them for recreational activities. Does Citizens Against Toxic Sprays have *standing* to sue the United States Forest Service? [Citizens Against Toxic Sprays, Inc. v. Bergland, 428 F.Supp. 908 (D.C.Or.1977)]

2. Virginia Dalsis, the proprietor of a small store in the city of Olean, New York, brought a suit to enjoin

the construction of a mall because of its projected size. Dalsis alleged that the large size of the shopping center would have an adverse environmental effect on the downtown area, causing economic blight and deterioration to the section in which her business was located. Dalsis, however, did not bring the suit until three months after construction of the shopping mall had begun even though she was aware of the mall's potential size almost a year before construction started. Should Dalsis be allowed to enjoin the construction of the shopping mall under the National Environmental Policy Act? [Dalsis v. Hills, 424 F.Supp. 784 (W.D.N.Y.1976)]

3. The Government Services Administration (GSA) entered into an agreement with a private individual under which the individual was to construct a building to GSA's specifications and lease it to the GSA. Under the contemplated lease provision, GSA would have use of the entire building for a five-year (renewable) period. As many as 2,300 government employees would be assigned to the building, and most would commute by automobile. Cost of the lease was approximately $11 million. GSA proceeded with its plans for the building without preparing any environmental impact statement. Was a statement necessary? [S. W. Neighborhood Assembly v. Eckard, 445 F.Supp. 1195 (D.C.D.C.1978)]

CHAPTER 50

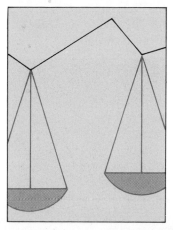

GOVERNMENT REGULATION
Antitrust: Statutes and Exemptions

Competition is the socially desired state of market organization in the United States today. Therefore, antitrust laws have been legislated and enforced to improve business behavior and to keep markets competitive. The next two chapters will look at the important developments in the field of antitrust law and how they affect business today. This chapter will discuss the major antitrust statutes that are enforced by the Department of Justice and the Federal Trade Commission. Particular emphasis will be given to arrangements that create monopolies. Chapter 51 will investigate the enforcement of these statutes, focusing on various contractual and business actions, and will examine current trends in the antitrust law.

COMMON LAW ACTIONS

Today's antitrust laws are direct descendants of common law actions intended to limit restraints of trade. That is not to say, however, that a neat classification of trade restraints can be found in the common law.

Common Law in England

One of the earliest recorded cases about trade restraints in the common law involved a man named John Dyer and has become known as Dyer's Case.[1] Dyer had agreed not to "use his art of a dyer's craft within the town * * * for half a year." The court denied the plaintiff the ability to collect on a bond for Dyer's breach of his agreement. The effect of the agreement was to restrain trade, according to the common law. At that time, restraint of trade was defined as the failure to promote "fair" commercial activity.

The same issue arose on numerous occasions. A celebrated case occurred in 1711 when

---

1. Y. B. Pasch. 2 Hen. 5 f. 5, PL. 26 (1414).

a man named Mitchell leased a baking shop for five years, subject to the condition that the lessor, Reynolds, who was also a baker, would not practice the baking art in the immediate area for the term of the lease. Thus, Mitchell was actually buying the use of a baking shop *and* the trade that went with it. The court rejected Mitchell's argument and ruled in favor of Reynolds.[2]

This case is so celebrated because the court's opinion systematically classified trade restraints into those that were good and those that were bad. Lord Parker, who rendered the opinion, distinguished between general and particular restraints, the former being invalid and the latter valid. *General restraints* were defined as those used for the purpose of limiting competition. On the other hand, certain *particular restraints* that were supported by "good consideration" were acceptable. These *partial*, or *ancillary*, *restraints*, as they became known, were generally upheld if limited in time and place.

Thus, *Mitchell v. Reynolds* provided the basis for the modern formulation of the so-called rule of reason, in which the court determines whether the restraint in question is reasonable. Since the case of *Mitchell v. Reynolds*, the rule of reason has played an important role in antitrust litigation in this country. In order to find out whether a partial restraint is reasonable (that is, legal), the courts inquire into its purpose and its probable effect.

THE BEGINNING OF U.S. ANTITRUST LAW

With the growth of national markets after the Civil War, a number of small companies were combined to form large companies, and they started to engage in practices that were seen as monopolistic. Reported abusive practices by corporate giants in the second half of the nineteenth century finally led to legislation restricting the power of these so-called trusts. The first piece of legislation was the Interstate Commerce Act of 1887, and in 1890 the Sherman Act was passed.

These acts were designed to prevent trusts from acting against the public interest.

The Formation of Trusts

Interestingly, *trusts* were a legal innovation that was made famous by John D. Rockefeller's Standard Oil Company. Standard's attorneys established an arrangement whereby owners of stock in several companies could transfer their stock to a set of trustees. In return, the owners received consideration in the form of certificates entitling them to a specified share in the pooled earnings of the jointly managed companies.

In the late 1800s, the term *trust* was randomly, and sometimes questionably, applied to business combinations of many different types. There were trusts in oil, sugar, cotton, linseed oil, whiskey, and other industries, and the trusts seemed to absorb new enterprises at an expanding rate. Furthermore, some observers felt that the process of consolidation was achieved by *predatory* tactics, that is, tactics that advance the competitive position of one business by threatening to drive another business out of the market. In fact, the activities of the Standard Oil Company are sometimes presented as the prime example of such tactics. Because of its size, Standard Oil was able to sell kerosene at a price below its cost. Standard's lower prices forced many competitors to sell or close down. As total industry output declined, Standard Oil raised the price and presumably obtained monopoly power.[3]

The 1890 Sherman Act was the response, and its purpose was to promote competition within the U.S. economy.[4] The author of the legislation, Senator Sherman, told Congress that the Sherman Act "does not announce a new principle of law, but applies old and well-recognized principles of the common law."[5] However, the common law was never very clear on this point. Certainly it was not very familiar to the legislators

---

2.   1 P. Wms. 181, 24 Eng. Rep 347 (1711).

3.   Not everyone agrees with this rendition of the facts. See, for example, John S. McGee, "Predatory Price Cutting: The Standard Oil (New Jersey) Case," *Journal of Law and Economics* 1 (1958). McGee finds that the facts are consistent with a competitive market with increased supply.

4.   26 Stat 209 (1890) as amended 15 USC 1–7.

5.   21 Congressional Record 2456 (1890).

of the Fifty-first Congress of the United States. Actually, it appears that the Sherman Act was an attempt by Congress to get the federal courts to create a common body of federal antitrust law.

SHERMAN ANTITRUST ACT

Sections 1 and 2 contain the main provisions of the Sherman Act. They are:

§ 1: Every contract, combination in the form of trust or otherwise, or conspiracy, in restraint of trade or commerce among the several States, or with foreign nations, is hereby declared to be illegal [and is a felony punishable by fine and/or imprisonment]. *   *   *

§ 2: Every person who shall monopolize, or attempt to monopolize, or combine or conspire with any other person or persons, to monopolize any part of the trade or commerce among the several States, or with foreign nations, shall be deemed guilty of a felony [and is similarly punishable]. *   *   *

Sections 1 and 2 Compared

The two main sections of the Sherman Act are quite different. Section 1 requires two or more persons, since a person cannot combine or conspire alone. Thus, the essence of the illegal activity is *the act of joining together*. Section 2 applies to both an individual person and several people because it states, "[e]very person who *   *   *." Thus, unilateral conduct can result in a violation of Section 2. The cases brought to court under Section 1 of the Sherman Act differ from those brought under Section 2. Section 1 cases are often concerned with finding an agreement (written or oral) that leads to a restraint of trade. Section 2 cases deal with the structure of a monopoly that exists in the marketplace. Thus, Section 1 focuses on agreements that are restrictive—that is, agreements that have a wrongful purpose. Section 2 looks at the so-called misuse of monopoly power in the marketplace. However, both sections seek to curtail market industrial practices that result in undesired monopoly pricing and output behavior. Any case brought under Section 2, however, must be one in which the "threshold" or "necessary" amount of monopoly power already exists.

The Proscriptive Nature of the Sherman Act

The Sherman Act does not tell businesses how they should act. It tells them how they should *not* act. In this sense, the act is *proscriptive* rather than *prescriptive*. It is the basis for *policing* rather than *regulating* business conduct.

Other Aspects of the Sherman Act

Jurisdiction   The Sherman Act applies only to restraints that have a significant impact on commerce. In principle, only interstate commerce is affected because Congress can regulate only interstate commerce. If, however, a practice has a significant anticompetitive effect on commerce, the courts have construed the meaning of *interstate* more and more broadly. In principle, state regulation of anticompetitive practices covers purely local restraints on competition.

The Sherman Act extends to U.S. nationals abroad who are engaged in activities that will affect U.S. foreign commerce. It was applied, for example, in *Continental Ore Co. v. Union Carbide and Carbon Corp.*[6] In that case, the defendant, Union Carbide, tried to monopolize the Canadian market in Canada by excluding competitors. It did this by having its Canadian subsidiary, Electro-Met, initiate political action that resulted in the Canadian Metals Controller granting it an exclusive market in vanadium products. This effectively prohibited the U.S. plaintiff, Continental Ore Company, from entering Canadian markets.

Standing   The Department of Justice is not the only entity that can file suit under the Sherman Act. Some private parties can also sue for damages or other remedies. The courts have determined that the test of ability to sue depends on the directness of the injury suffered by the purported plaintiff. Thus, a person wishing to sue

---

6.   370 U.S. 690, 82 S.Ct. 1404 (1962).

under the Sherman Act must prove that (1) the antitrust violation either directly caused or was at least a substantial factor in causing the injury that was suffered, and (2) the unlawful actions of the purported defendant affected business activities of the plaintiff that were protected by the antitrust laws.

One of the unique features of the Sherman Antitrust Act is that it allows any person injured as a result of violations of the act to bring a suit for treble damages against the defendants in addition to reasonable attorneys' fees. In the 1960s General Electric Company, along with other major electrical equipment manufacturers, paid over $200 million in treble damage claims. Certain of the corporate officers were fined, and some of them even went to jail.

Remedies and Sanctions Any person found guilty of violating either Section 1 or Section 2 of the Sherman Act is subject to criminal prosecution for a felony. Currently, upon conviction, a person can be fined up to $100,000 or imprisoned for three years, or both. A corporation can be fined $1 million. The Department of Justice can simultaneously institute civil proceedings to restrain the conduct that is in violation of the act.

The various remedies that the Justice Department has asked the court to impose include divestiture, dissolution, and divorcement, or making a company give up one of its operating functions. A group of meat packers, for example, can be forced to divorce itself from controlling or owning butcher shops.

The Courts' Initial Reaction to the Sherman Act

Initially, the Sherman Act was stripped of any effectiveness because the courts interpreted it so narrowly. For example, five years after passage of the act, the Supreme Court refused to apply the Sherman Act to a sugar trust.[7] The Court held that the law did not extend to restraints affecting

just the manufacture of commodities. According to the Court, "commerce secedes to manufacturer, and is not a part of it." In other words, the manufacturer of a commodity does not control commerce and therefore cannot violate the Sherman Act.

Then the Court swung the other way. In essence, it significantly modified antitrust legislation by allowing no opportunity to adjust its decisions to practical necessities. In a series of opinions beginning with *U.S. v. TransMissouri Freight Ass'n*, the Court declared illegal certain price-fixing agreements and territorial divisions because Section 1 of the Sherman Act condemned *every* restraint of trade.[8] This absolute position clearly could not hold for long. The Court then retreated once again. It first condemned direct restraints.[9] It then came to the conclusion that restraints that were lawful at common law might not be prohibited by the Sherman Act.[10]

The Rule of Reason

This change in the Court's view was expressed in its 1911 case against Standard Oil Company of New Jersey, which follows. In this landmark Section 1 decision, the Supreme Court ordered the dissolution of the oil trust into approximately thirty companies. The Court also ruled that only those restraints whose character was *unreasonably* anticompetitive were outlawed by the Sherman Act.

Beginning with this decision, a "standard of reason" would be applied as to the purpose of the arrangement, the powers of the parties, and the effect of their actions in determining restraint of trade. Critics of that decision contended that conservative federal judges would reduce the act to insignificance again. Other critics contended that if the court was to interpret the act as applying only to unreasonable restraints, then businesses should be told in advance which restraints were lawful.

---

7.   United States v. E. C. Knight Co., 156 U.S. 1, 15 S.Ct. 249 (1895).

8.   166 U.S. 290, 17 S.Ct. 540 (1897).
9.   Hopkins v. United States, 171 U.S. 578, 19 S.Ct. 40 (1898).
10.   United States v. Joint Traffic Ass'n, 171 U.S. 505, 19 S.Ct. 25 (1898).

BACKGROUND AND FACTS   *Standard Oil Company of New Jersey and thirty-three other corporations, John D. Rockefeller, William Rockefeller, and five other individual defendants were the appellants in this case. They attempted to reverse a decree holding that they were conspiring "to restrain the trade and commerce in petroleum, commonly called 'crude oil', in refined oil, and in the other products of petroleum, among several States and Territories of the United States and District of Columbia and with foreign nations, and to monopolize the said commerce."*

The government charged that John D. Rockefeller, William Rockefeller, and several other named individuals organized the Standard Oil Corporation of Ohio and soon afterwards became participants in an illegal plan to acquire substantially all of the oil refineries located in Cleveland, Ohio.

In addition, the government charged that there was a trust agreement in which the stock of over forty corporations, including Standard Oil of Ohio, was held for the benefit of the members of the combination. The trust agreement was adjudged void because it was in restraint of trade, and the trust was ordered dissolved.

In the third phase of its case, the government charged that the individual defendants operated a holding company through Standard Oil Company of New Jersey. This company acquired the majority of stock in various other corporations engaging in the purchasing, transporting, refining, shipping, and selling of oil in the United States, the District of Columbia, and foreign nations.

THE STANDARD OIL CO. OF NEW JERSEY v. UNITED STATES
221 U.S. 1, 31 S.Ct. 502 (1911).

WHITE, Chief Justice.

*   *   *   *

It is sufficient to say that, whilst admitting many of the alleged acquisitions of property, the formation of the so-called trust of 1882, its dissolution in 1892, and the acquisition by the Standard Oil Company of New Jersey of the stocks of the various corporations in 1899, *   *   * [the appellants] deny all the allegations respecting combinations or conspiracies to restrain or monopolize the oil trade; and particularly that the so-called trust of 1882, or the acquisition of the shares of the defendant companies by the Standard Oil Company of New Jersey in 1899, was a combination of *independent or competing* concerns or corporations. *   *   *

The [lower] court decided in favor of the United States. In the opinion delivered, all the multitude of acts of wrong-doing charged in the bill were put aside, in so far as they were alleged to have been committed prior to the passage of the Anti-trust Act, "except as evidence of their (the defendants') purpose, of their continuing conduct and of its effect."

*   *   *   *

Giving to the facts just stated, the weight which it was deemed they were entitled to, in the light afforded by the proof of other cognate facts and circumstances, the court below held that the acts and dealings established by the proof operated to destroy the "potentiality of competition" which otherwise would have existed to such an extent as to cause the transfers of stock which were made to the New Jersey corporation and the control which resulted over the many and various subsidiary corporations to be a combination or conspiracy in restraint of trade in violation of the first section of the act, but also to be an attempt to monopolize and a monopolization bringing about a perennial violation of the second section.

We see no cause to doubt the correctness of these conclusions, considering the subject from every aspect, that is, both in view of the facts established by the record and the necessary operation and effect of the law as we have construed it upon the inferences deducible from the facts, for the following reasons:

a. Because the unification of power and control over petroleum and its products which was the inevitable result of the combining in the New Jersey corporation by the increase of its stock and the transfer to it of the stocks of so many other corporations, aggregating so vast a capital, gives rise, in and of itself, *   *   * to the *prima facie* presumption of intent and purpose to maintain the dominancy over the oil industry, not as a result of normal methods of industrial development, but by new means of combination which were resorted to in order that greater power might be added than would otherwise have arisen had normal methods been followed, the whole with the purpose of excluding others from the trade and thus centralizing in the combination a perpetual control of the movements of petroleum and its products in the channels of interstate commerce.

b. Because the *prima facie* presumption of intent to restrain trade, to monopolize and to bring about monopolization resulting from the act of expanding the stock of the New Jersey corporation and vesting it with such vast control of the oil industry, is made conclusive by *   *   * what was done under those agreements and the acts which immediately preceded the vesting of power in the New Jersey corporation as well as by *   *   * the modes in which the power vested in that corporation has been exerted and the results which have arisen from it.

*   *   * [W]e think no disinterested mind can survey the *   *   * question without being irresistibly driven to the conclusion that the very genius for commercial development and organization which it would seem was manifested from the beginning soon begot an intent and purpose to exclude others which was frequently manifested by acts and dealings wholly inconsistent with the theory that they were made with the single conception of advancing the development of business power by usual methods, but which on the contrary necessarily involved the intent to drive others from the field and to exclude them from their right to trade and thus accomplish the mastery which was the end in view. *   *   * The exercise of the power which resulted from that organization fortifies the foregoing conclusions, since the development which came, the acquisition here and there which ensued of every efficient means by which competition could have been asserted, the slow but resistless methods which followed by which means of transportation were absorbed and brought under control, the system of marketing which was adopted by which the country was divided into districts and the trade in each district in oil was turned over to a designated corporation within the combination and all others were excluded, all lead the mind up to a conviction of a purpose and intent which we think is so certain as practically to cause the subject not to be within the domain of reasonable contention.

The inference that no attempt to monopolize could have been intended, and that no monopolization resulted from the acts complained of, since it is established that a very small percentage of the crude oil produced was controlled by the combination, is unwarranted. As substantial power over the crude product was the inevitable result of the absolute control which existed over the refined product, the monopolization of the one carried with it the power to control the other, and if the inferences which this situation suggests were developed, which we deem it unnecessary to do, they might well serve to add additional cogency to the presumption of intent to monopolize which we have found arises from the unquestioned proof on other subjects. *   *   *

The Supreme Court concluded that the decree issued by the lower court was right and should be affirmed. It forbade Standard Oil from engaging in any future combinations in violation of the Sherman Antitrust Act. In addition, it attempted to neutralize the effect of the monopoly that Standard Oil had created by commanding the dissolution of the combination (the trust) and causing the New Jersey corporation to divest itself of the numerous shares of stock that it controlled.

JUDGMENT AND REMEDY

The rule of reason was interpreted and modified many times. For example, it was recently broadened to cover a new situation. In the National Society of Professional Engineers v. United States [435 U.S. 679, 98 S.Ct. 1355 (1978)], the court argued that the rule of reason would be applied to anticompetitive situations that were ancillary to a legitimate transaction such as an employment contract or the sale of an ongoing business.

COMMENTS

The Development of Per Se Violations

According to the rule of reason, only unreasonable restraints were illegal at common law. Clearly, the rule was applied in the *Standard Oil* case. However, no rule of reason is explicitly stated in Section 1 of the Sherman Act. It is irrelevant, according to Section 1, whether the guilty party was *successful* in fixing prices, dividing markets or restraining trade in any other way. Section 1 states very clearly that any *attempt* to restrain trade is illegal. Thus, certain kinds of restrictive contracts will be deemed inherently anticompetitive—that is, in restraint of trade *as a matter of law*. In such *per se violations* of Section 1 there is no need to examine any other facts.

Recall that in *United States v. TransMissouri Freight Ass'n.*, the court held that Section 1 condemned *every* restraint of trade. In 1897 the court recognized no exceptions. The defendants in the case contended that they were exempt from the Sherman Act because they were regulated by the Interstate Commerce Act. Thus,

the fixing of rates was legal because it was reasonable and therefore valid under common law. To the court, the railroads were engaging in a per se violation of Section 1 of the Sherman Act.

In *United States v. Socony Vacuum Oil Co.* [310 U.S. 150, 60 S.Ct. 811 (1940)], the Supreme Court set forth a per se standard, condemning all price-fixing arrangements. Footnote 59 of that opinion has become the most famous footnote in antitrust law. In that footnote Justice Douglas wrote:

[I]t is well established that a person "may be guilty of conspiring, although incapable of committing the objective offense." *   *   * And it is likewise well settled that conspiracies under the Sherman Act are not dependent on any overt act other than the act of conspiring. *   *   * It is the "contract, combination *   *   * or conspiracy, in restraint of trade or commerce" which § 1 of the Act strikes down, whether the concerted activity be wholly nascent or abortive on the one hand, or successful on the other. *   *   * And the amount of interstate or foreign trade involved is not material, since § 1 of the Act brands as illegal the character of the restraint not the amount of com-

merce affected. *   *   * In view of these considerations a conspiracy to fix prices violates § 1 of
the Act though no overt act is shown, though it is
not established that the conspirators had the means
available for accomplishment of their objective, and
though the conspiracy embraced but a part of the
interstate or foreign commerce in the commodity.
Whatever may have been the status of price-fixing
agreements at common law the Sherman Act has
a broader application to them than the common
law prohibitions or sanctions. *   *   * Price-fixing
agreements may or may not be aimed at complete
elimination of price competition. The group making those agreements may or may not have power
to control the market. But the fact that the group
cannot control the market prices does not necessarily mean that the agreement as to prices has no
utility to the members of the combination. The
effectiveness of price-fixing agreements is dependent on many factors, such as competitive tactics,
position in the industry, the formula underlying
price policies. Whatever economic justification
particular price-fixing agreements may be thought
to have, the law does not permit an inquiry into
their reasonableness. They are all banned because
of their actual or potential threat to the central
nervous system of the economy. *   *   *

THE CLAYTON ACT

In 1914 Congress attempted to strengthen federal
antitrust laws by adopting the Clayton Act, which
was aimed at specific monopolistic practices. The
important sections of the Clayton Act are Sections 2, 3, 7, and 8. Briefly these sections prohibit:

> Section 2: [It is illegal to] discriminate in price
> between different purchasers [except in cases where
> the differences are due to differences in selling or
> transportation costs].
> Section 3: [Producers or lessors cannot sell or
> lease] on the condition, agreement or understand-
> ing that the *   *   * purchaser or lessee thereof
> shall not use or deal in the goods *   *   * of a
> competitor or competitors of the seller.
> Section 7: [A person or business organization
> cannot hold stock and/or assets in another busi-
> ness] where the effect *   *   * may be to substan-
> tially lessen competition.

> Section 8: *   *   * no person at the same time
> shall be a director in any two or more competing
> corporations, any one of which has capital, sur-
> plus, and undivided profits aggregating more than
> $1 million, engaged in whole or in part in com-
> merce, other than banks, banking associations, trust
> companies, and common carriers.

Thus, the Clayton Act outlaws price discrimination, exclusive dealing and tying contracts, the
purchase of enough stock in a competing corporation to reduce competition, and interlocking
directorates. Most of these actions are discussed
in the context of current antitrust enforcement
in the next chapter.

THE FEDERAL
TRADE COMMISSION ACT

In 1914 Congress passed the Federal Trade Commission Act, which created a bipartisan, independent administrative agency headed by five
commissioners, no more than three of whom
could be of the same political party.[11] Section 5
of the act gives the FTC broad powers to prevent
"unfair methods of competition in commerce and
unfair or deceptive acts or practices in commerce." Amendments, particularly in 1975, have
broadened the commission's powers.[12] The FTC
also has the authority to conduct investigations
relating to alleged violations of antitrust statutes
and to make reports and recommendations to
Congress regarding legislation. More importantly, the FTC can promulgate interpretive rules
and general statements of policy with respect to
unfair or deceptive acts or practices. It can also
promulgate trade regulation rules, which *define*
particular unfair or deceptive acts or practices,
including requirements for the purpose of preventing such acts or practices. The commission
has issued guidelines defining unfair practices,
but these guidelines are very broad, and many
seemingly unfair practices are allowed.[13]

---

11.   15 USCA 41–51 (1914).

12.   Magnuson-Moss FTC Improvements Act of 1975.

13.   The commission, for example, has indicated that a practice is "unfair" if it offends public policy or is immoral,
unethical, oppressive, unscrupulous, or causes substantial injury to consumers.

The FTC initiates most of its investigations because of oral or written communications from the general public and private business firms. The primary enforcement mechanism of the FTC is **cease and desist orders** (orders to stop certain activities or practices) against violations of the Federal Trade Commission Act. Furthermore, businesses that violate these orders are subject to fines of up to $10,000 per day for each day of continued violation. Cease and desist orders can be appealed to the courts. Unlike the Sherman Act, the FTC Act does not allow for treble damage actions.

Additional Authority

Section 5 of the Federal Trade Commission Act overlaps a number of other antitrust statutes, including the Sherman Act, the Clayton Act, and other laws designed to reduce unfair methods of competition. The FTC initiates investigations and issues cease and desist orders, particularly for violations of Sections 2, 3, 7, and 8 of the Clayton Act as amended by the Celler-Kefauver Act, the Robinson-Patman Act, and other acts.

ROBINSON-PATMAN ACT

One of the more important activities of the Federal Trade Commission has been the detection and prohibition of **price discrimination** (that is, charging different prices to different purchasers for identical goods) when such discrimination lessens competition or tends to create a monopoly.

Subsequent judicial interpretation and responses by businesses effectively circumvented the original intent of Section 2 of the Clayton Act, so in 1936 Congress responded by enacting the Robinson-Patman Act. This act tightened the prohibition against price discrimination. If goods of similar grade and quality were sold at different prices, and these differences could not be justified by differences in production costs, the prac-

tice would violate the Robinson-Patman Act even if the Clayton Act could be circumvented. In addition, the act prohibited sellers from cutting prices to levels substantially below those charged by their competitors.[14]

OTHER ANTITRUST ACTS

Both the Justice Department and the Federal Trade Commission enforce other statutes concerning antitrust. Some of these statutes merely amend the basic Sherman or Clayton Acts,[15] whereas others, such as the Emergency Petroleum Allocation Act, focus on a particular industry.

A number of statutes deal directly with *potential* competition in the economy. For example, the FTC is responsible for registering the articles of association or incorporation for associations that are organized under the Export Trade Act. It is also responsible for receiving and monitoring regulations governing mandatory allocations of crude oil, residual fuel oil, and refined petroleum products under the Emergency Petroleum Act of 1973. And it is responsible for working with the Justice Department in developing voluntary agreements under the International Energy Program. The Energy Policy and Conservation Act also creates responsibilities relating to automobile fuel economy, appliance efficiencies, and recycled oil.

EXEMPTIONS FROM ANTITRUST LAWS

In a sense, Congress's attention to the antitrust laws since the Clayton Act has focused primarily on writing *exceptions* to the coverage of the Sherman Act.

---

14. Robinson-Patman Act, Subsection B.
15. See, for example, the Hart-Scott-Rodino Antitrust Improvement Act, 15 USCA 18 (1976).

The Miller-Tydings Act

The Miller-Tydings Act was passed in 1937 as an amendment to Section 1 of the Sherman Act, and it allows fair-trade agreements. A fair-trade agreement occurs when a manufacturer can specify to all the people who sell its product that they cannot sell it below a listed, or fair-trade, price. This is called resale price maintenance. This type of fair-trade agreement would seem to violate antitrust laws aimed at preventing price-fixing. Nonetheless, the Miller-Tydings Act made this type of price-fixing legal.

On March 13, 1976, Congress repealed the Miller-Tydings Act. It had become clear by then that a major result of this exemption to the Sherman Act was the stifling of price competition among retailers.

Labor and Agriculture

Labor and agricultural organizations are exempted from the Sherman Antitrust Act by Section 6 of the Clayton Act. Agriculture's exemption from antitrust legislation is further extended by the Capper-Volstead Act (1922), the Cooperative Marketing Act (1926), and certain provisions of the Robinson-Patman Act. Labor's exemption was strengthened by the Norris-La Guardia Act of 1932.

The National Labor Relations Act of 1935 protected unions from antitrust legislation. Today, therefore, unions can lawfully engage in actions that are normally prohibited as long as they act in their self-interest and do not conspire or combine with nonlabor groups to accomplish their goals.

Sports

Most commercial activities are subject to the antitrust laws, but there are exceptions. For example, baseball remains untouched by the antitrust laws; it was not thought to be commerce in the Sherman Act's original contemplation and is thus not commerce today. Baseball's exemption is anomalous, especially since no other professional sport receives such treatment.

Professionals

A current controversial topic in antitrust law is the regulation of professionals, such as lawyers and doctors. Professional organizations are no longer exempt from antitrust enforcement. They cannot establish minimum fee schedules or prohibit competitive bidding in any way as illustrated in the following case. The traditional incantations about the maintenance of high quality no longer shield professionals from the antitrust laws.

GOLDFARB v.
VIRGINIA STATE BAR
Supreme Court of the United
States, 1975.
421 U.S. 773, 95 S.Ct. 2004.

BACKGROUND AND FACTS   *When Mr. and Mrs. Goldfarb contracted to purchase a home in Fairfax County, Virginia, they were unable to find a lawyer who would examine the title for less than the fee prescribed in a minimum-fee schedule published by the Fairfax County Bar Association and enforced by the Virginia State Bar. The Goldfarbs brought this action seeking injunctive relief and damages. They alleged that the minimum-fee schedule and its enforcement mechanism, as applied to fees for legal services relating to residential real estate transactions, constituted price-fixing in violation of Section 1 of the Sherman Act.*

BURGER, Chief Justice.
*   *   *   *

Our inquiry can be divided into *   *   * steps: did respondents engage in price fixing? If so, are their activities in interstate commerce or do they affect interstate commerce? If so, are the activities exempt from the Sherman Act because they involve a "learned profession?" *   *   *

The County Bar argues that because the fee schedule is merely advisory, the schedule and its enforcement mechanism do not constitute price fixing. Its purpose, the argument continues, is only to provide legitimate information to aid member lawyers in complying with Virginia professional regulations. Moreover, the County Bar contends that in practice the schedule has not had the effect of producing fixed fees. The facts found by the trier belie these contentions, and nothing in the record suggests these findings lack support.

A purely advisory fee schedule issued to provide guidelines, or an exchange of price information without a showing of an actual restraint on trade, would present us with a different question. The record here, however, reveals a situation quite different from what would occur under a purely advisory fee schedule. Here a fixed, rigid price floor arose from respondents' activities: every lawyer who responded to petitioners' inquiries adhered to the fee schedule, and no lawyer asked for additional information in order to set an individualized fee. The price information disseminated did not concern past standards, but rather minimum fees to be charged in future transactions, and those minimum rates were increased over time. The fee schedule was enforced through the prospect of professional discipline from the State Bar, and the desire of attorneys to comply with announced professional norms, the motivation to conform was reinforced by the assurance that other lawyers would not compete by underbidding. This is not merely a case of an agreement that may be inferred from an exchange of price information, for here a naked agreement was clearly shown, and the effect on prices is plain.

Moreover, in terms of restraining competition and harming consumers like petitioners the price-fixing activities found here are unusually damaging. A title examination is indispensable in the process of financing a real estate purchase, and since only an attorney licensed to practice in Virginia may legally examine a title, consumers could not turn to alternative sources for the necessary service. All attorneys, of course, were practicing under the constraint of the fee schedule. The County Bar makes much of the fact that it is a voluntary organization; however, the ethical opinions issued by the State Bar provide that any lawyer, whether or not a member of his county bar association, may be disciplined for "*habitually* charg[ing] less than the suggested minimum fee schedule adopted by his local bar Association. *   *   *"' These factors coalesced to create a pricing system that consumers could not realistically escape. On this record respondents' activities constitute a classic illustration of price fixing.

The County Bar argues, as the Court of Appeals held, that any effect on interstate commerce caused by the fee schedule's restraint on legal services was incidental and remote. In its view the legal services, which are performed wholly intrastate, are essentially local in nature and therefore a restraint with respect to them can never substantially affect interstate commerce. Further, the County Bar maintains, there was no showing here that the fee schedule and its enforcement mechanism increased fees, and that even if they did there was no showing that such an increase deterred any prospective homeowner from buying in Fairfax County.

These arguments misconceive the nature of the transactions at issue and the place legal services play in those transactions. As the District Court found, "a significant portion of funds furnished for the purchasing of homes in Fairfax County comes from without the State of Virginia," and "significant amounts of loans on Fairfax County real estate are guaranteed by the United States Veterans Administration and Department of Housing and Urban Development, both head-quartered in the District of Columbia." Thus in this class action the transactions which create the need for the particular legal services in question frequently are interstate transactions. * * * Given the substantial volume of commerce involved, and the inseparability of this particular legal service from the interstate aspects of real estate transactions, we conclude that interstate commerce has been sufficiently affected.

* * * *

The County Bar argues that Congress never intended to include the learned professions within the terms "trade or commerce" in § 1 of the Sherman Act, and therefore the sale of professional services is exempt from the Act. No explicit exemption or legislative history is provided to support this contention; rather, the existence of state regulation seems to be its primary basis. Also, the County Bar maintains that competition is inconsistent with the practice of a profession because enhancing profit is not the goal of professional activities; the goal is to provide services necessary to the community. That, indeed, is the classic basis traditionally advanced to distinguish professions from trades, businesses, and other occupations, but it loses some of its force when used to support the fee control activities involved here.

In arguing that learned professions are not "trade or commerce" the County Bar seeks a total exclusion from antitrust regulation. Whether state regulation is active or dormant, real or theoretical, lawyers would be able to adopt anticompetitive practices with impunity. We cannot find support for the proposition that Congress intended any such sweeping exclusion. The nature of an occupation, standing alone, does not provide sanctuary from the Sherman Act, nor is the public-service aspect of professional practice controlling in determining whether § 1 includes professions. Congress intended to strike as broadly as it could in § 1 of the Sherman Act, and to read into it so wide an exemption as that urged on us would be at odds with that purpose.

The language of § 1 of the Sherman Act, of course, contains no exception. "Language more comprehensive is difficult to conceive." And our cases have repeatedly established that there is a heavy presumption against implicit exemptions. Indeed, our cases have specifically included the sale of services within § 1. Whatever else it may be, the examination of a land title is a service; the exchange of such a service for money is "commerce" in the most common usage of that word. It is no disparagement of the practice of law as a profession to acknowledge that it has this business aspect, and § 1 of the Sherman Act

> "[o]n its face * * * shows a carefully studied attempt to bring within the Act every person engaged in business whose activities might restrain or monopolize commercial intercourse among the states."

In the modern world it cannot be denied that the activities of lawyers play an important part in commercial intercourse, and that anticompetitive activities by lawyers may exert a restraint on commerce.

JUDGMENT AND REMEDY *The minimum-fee schedule violated the Sherman Act. The case was remanded to the District Court for issuance of an injunction against the* *legal associations and for determination of the damages suffered by the Goldfarbs.*

Insurance

The McCarran-Ferguson Act exempts from the antitrust laws all activities that are in the "business of insurance." The primary element of the insurance business is the spreading and underwriting of policyholder risk. Thus, any such activity can be exempt from the antitrust laws by the McCarran-Ferguson Act if it is regulated by state law.

Foreign Trade

Sometimes a decision to exempt certain activities from antitrust actions is made in the belief that certain goals can be better achieved through cartelization. For example, the Webb-Pomerene Act exempts acts or agreements made in the course of export trade by associations of producers formed solely for the purpose of engaging in export trade. Cartelization promotes an increased national investment in the covered activities, thereby aiding the nation's balance of payments.

STATE ACTION

In general, actions taken by state, local, and other public jurisdictions are exempt from antitrust laws. In 1978 it was held, however, that the **doc-trine of state action unity** does not exempt all government entities from federal antitrust laws merely because of their status, but that a specific, direct action is required for the antitrust exemption. An example of such a direct state action might be a policy to replace unfettered competition with regulation or to replace unfettered competition with a monopoly public service. Thus, unauthorized anticompetitive practices by state bodies are subject to antitrust laws.[16]

SUMMARY

Overall, the major statutes concerning antitrust activities can be summarized as follows:

1. Those that limit combinations through agreement, merger, or interlocking directorates.
2. Those that limit contractual and business actions, including price-fixing, boycotts, market division, price discrimination, and other such acts.
3. Those that limit controlling prices.

Exhibit 50-1 summarizes the major statutes and their principal amendments in these three categories.

---

16. City of Lafayette, Louisiana v. Louisiana Power and Light Co., 435 U.S. 389, 98 S.Ct. 1123 (1978).

EXHIBIT 50-1   MAJOR ANTITRUST LAWS

Statutes Limiting Combinations	Statutes Limiting Contractual and Business Actions	Statutes Controlling Prices
Sherman Act (1890) Section 2* prohibits monopolies and attempts or conspiracies to monopolize.	**Sherman Act** (1890) Section 1* prohibits combinations and conspiracies in restraint of trade including vertical and horizontal price-fixing, group boycotts, division of markets, and other practices.	**Emergency Price Control Act of 1942** set up the Office of Price Administration to control prices and rents during World War II.
Clayton Act (1914) Section 7 prohibits mergers, when the effect may be to substantially lessen competition or to create a monopoly. Amended (1950)—Celler-Kefauver Act clarified application of Section 7 to acquisition of assets.	**Clayton Act** (1914) Section 2 prohibits price discriminations, substantially lessening sellers' competition (primary violations). Amended (1936)—Robinson-Patman Act prohibits price discriminations, substantially lessening buyers' competition (secondary violation).	**Defense Production Act of 1950** was passed to control prices during the Korean War.
Clayton Act (1914) Section 8 prohibits interlocking directorates.	**Clayton Act** (1914) Section 3 prohibits exclusive dealing and tying arrangements where the effect may be to substantially lessen competition.	**Economic Stabilization Act of 1970** gave the president the power to control prices during a period of high inflation.
	Federal Trade Commission Act (1914) Section 5† prohibits unfair methods of competition; it established and defined powers of FTC. Amended (1938)—Wheeler-Lea Act prohibits unfair trade practices and false advertising. Amended (1976)—Hart-Scott-Rodino Act increases merger-reporting requirements.	

*Amended in 1974 and 1976 to increase penalties and broaden enforcement.
†Amended in 1973 and 1975 to increase penalties and grant industry-wide, rule-making power.

QUESTIONS AND CASE PROBLEMS

1. Meister Brau, Inc., was engaged in the business of brewing beers, malts, and ales. It acquired the Berger Meister Beer Company through a purchase of the latter's common stock. Berger Meister sold the beer it brewed through distributors who operated as individual businesses separate from Berger Meister. Soon after Meister Brau acquired Berger Meister, it terminated some of Berger Meister's distributors. The distributors handled the products of a number of other breweries, but they complained that the reduced sales volume that would result from their being terminated by Meister Brau would drive them out of business. The distributors thus brought suit against Meister Brau, alleging that its agreement with its new subsidiary, Berger Meister, to terminate the distributors constituted a conspiracy in restraint of trade in violation of Section 1 of the Sherman Act. The distributors alleged that the terminations would reduce competition in a market that was already tending toward concentration. Has Meister Brau violated Section 1 of the Sherman Act? [Ricchetti v. Meister Brau, Inc., 431 F.2d 1211 (9th Cir. 1970)]

2. Since 1946 Bay Distributors, Inc., a Florida corporation located in the Tampa Bay area, had been engaged in the wholesale distribution and sale of various brands of wines and distilled spirits in approximately a thirteen-county area of the west coast of Florida. The wines that Bay sold included a line produced by United Vintners, Inc., most of which was marketed under the trade name "Italian Swiss Colony." Bay was the exclusive distributor in the Florida west coast area of United Vintners' wines. Between March 1965 and May 1970, Cal Distributing Company acted as Bay's sub-

distributor in the Sarasota area, which included two of the thirteen counties mentioned above. Cal sold no wine outside the Sarasota area. Although customers in the Sarasota area could have purchased United Vintners' products from either Cal or Bay, neither actually solicited customers from the other. About May 5, 1970, Bay notified Cal that it would no longer sell Cal United Vintners' wines. It would, however, continue to sell Cal all other wines for which Bay was the exclusive distributor. After Bay refused to sell United Vintners' products to Cal as a subdistributor, Bay started selling them directly to the retail businesses to which Cal had been selling them. Considering these facts, along with the other facts given below, answer the following questions. [Cal Distributing Co. v. Bay Distributors, Inc., 337 F.Supp. 1154 (M.D.Fla.1971)]

(a) Which, if any, of the antitrust statutes discussed in this chapter might Bay have violated when it terminated Cal as its subdistributor? Be specific.

(b) In order to establish a claim for relief from monopolization, Bay must be shown to possess *monopoly power* in the relevant market. In determining the relevant market, the court must determine the relevant *geographic* market and the relevant *product* market. Both before and after Bay's termination of Cal, at least six other companies distributed wine at wholesale in the Sarasota area from warehouses located in Tampa. Each of these competitors supplied wine along the entire west coast of Florida, including the Sarasota area, from offices and warehouses located in Tampa. The cost of transporting wine to retailers throughout the Florida west coast area is not such as to prevent wholesale distributors from supplying this area from Tampa. The "relevant geographic market" is the area that Bay would have to monopolize if it were to be deemed in violation of the antitrust laws. Is the relevant geographic market in this case the city of Sarasota, the west coast of Florida, the entire state of Florida, or some other area?

(c) In determining whether Bay's act of discontinuing Cal shows monopoly power, the "relevant product market" must be determined. This involves analyzing the commodities reasonably interchangeable by consumers for the same purposes. For example, in one case, the Supreme Court held that even though the DuPont Company produced approximately 75 percent of the cellophane sold nationwide, the competition between cellophane and other flexible packaging materials was sufficient to prevent cellophane from constituting a separate relevant product market in itself. Using the DuPont case as an analogy, what is the relevant product market in this case—all United Vintners' wines, all wines, all alcoholic beverages, or something else?

(d) Gallo Wines provides the primary competition to United Vintners. However, both Gallo and United Vintners face direct competition from all other wines. This competition prevents Bay from raising its prices without losing business. The competition provided by Gallo was described by Calvin LaHurd, the president of Cal Distributing Company, as "very, very vigorous." In fact, sales of Gallo Wines at wholesale have exceeded Bay's sales of United Vintners continuously for each month since December 1968. In addition, since December 1968, the monthly sales of United Vintners have never exceeded 22 percent of the total volume of wine sold to retailers in the relevant geographic area. In contrast, the monthly sales of Gallo wines by Tampa Wholesale Liquor Company, one of the area distributors, have averaged more than 22 percent of monthly wholesale wine sales in the relevant geographic area during the same period. In order to be deemed in violation of the antitrust laws, Bay Distributors must be shown to possess the power to control prices or exclude competition in the relevant market. In order to establish this, Cal must show that there exists a dangerous probability of monopoly power over prices and competition within the relevant market, coupled with a specific intent to monopolize. On the basis of all the facts given, can Cal establish that Bay possessed the necessary *monopoly power* just described?

3. On August 5, 1969, at a hearing held before the Arizona Corporation Commission, the Arizona Water Company, a private corporation, sought and was granted the right to deliver water in a specified geographic area. Subsequently, the State of Arizona issued the company a "certificate of convenience and necessity," which confirmed the company's exclusive right to sell water in the specified area. In light of antitrust laws that prohibit the exercise of monopoly powers, should Arizona Water Company be granted this exclusive right? Under what conditions should the State of Arizona be allowed to withdraw the "certificate of convenience and necessity" that it awarded Arizona Water Company? [Fernandez v. Arizona Water Co., 21 Ariz.App. 107, 516 P.2d. 49 (1974)]

4. Buckeye and Lamb were competing to be the first to obtain a natural monopoly in the cable television business in Toledo. To be first in obtaining a completed facility was crucial because in the cable television business—like that of the electric, gas, and telephone utilities—it is not feasible to compete house-to-house for customers in the same area. Buckeye arranged construction of its cable television facilities first, whereupon Lamb claimed that this violated the antitrust laws. In order to beat Lamb, Buckeye had to be the first to convince Bell Telephone to assist in the construction of a cable television system along its tele-

phone lines. Lamb objected to the contract between Bell Telephone and Buckeye, claiming that it was "an agreement in restraint of trade." What was the result? [Lamb Enterprises, Inc. v. Toledo Blade Co., 461 F.2d 506 (6th Cir. 1972)]

5. The Professional Golfers Association of America (PGA) was founded in 1916 as a voluntary, unincorporated, nonprofit association. It has some 4,300 members, and it sponsors or cosponsors substantially all of the professional golf tournaments held in the United States. In order to compete in these tournaments, a player must be either a member of the PGA, an approved tournament player, or one of the limited number of participants designated or invited by the local sponsor of the tournament. Because of the increasing popularity of professional tournament golf, some means had to be found to limit the number of golfers who could enter these tournaments. PGA rules limiting entry to the categories of persons named above and defining the qualifications necessary for nonmember entrance were intended to accomplish this purpose. PGA gives official recognition to many tournaments that it neither sponsors nor cosponsors. These "approved tournaments" are free from any PGA control; yet PGA plans its schedule around them and counts them in determining its official standings. Herbert C. Deesen was a professional golfer who competed for several years in PGA-sponsored tournaments. Deesen sued the PGA, alleging that its sheer size and vast control over professional golf tournaments in the United States amounted to monopoly control in violation of Section 2 of the Sherman Antitrust Act. Do the PGA's activities violate the Sherman Act? If so, how? [Deesen v. Professional Golfers Ass'n of America, 358 F.2d 165 (9th Cir. 1966)]

6. American Oil Company was a producer and distributor of oil, gas, and related products. Olson's was engaged in bulk distribution and retail sales of oil products. Early in 1967, American decided to acquire control of Olson's bulk distribution operations, and it purchased substantially all of Olson's assets. Thereafter, American negotiated a contract with Lawrence McMullin under which McMullin was to assume control of the Olson operation. Under the agreement, McMullin was to take charge of the Olson plant and was to be paid on a commission basis for the bulk

petroleum sales that he procured. In addition, the contract between American and McMullin imposed certain territorial limitations and price restrictions on sales by the operations that McMullin was to control. Could the agreement between McMullin and American Oil imposing price restrictions and territorial controls on the operations of which McMullin took charge constitute a violation of Section 1 of the Sherman Antitrust Act? Explain. [American Oil Co. v. McMullin, 508 F.2d 1345 (10th Cir. 1975)]

7. A relatively small number of companies are engaged in the manufacturing of corrugated containers in the United States. Corrugated containers are a fungible product for which demand is relatively inelastic. That is, changes in the price charged for the containers significantly affect demand for them. The dominant sellers in the corrugated container business agreed to give each other, on request, information about their most recent prices charged or quoted. This agreement stabilized corrugated container prices. At no time did the sellers agree to sell at fixed prices. Has a violation of the antitrust laws occurred? [United States v. Container Corp. of America, 393 U.S. 333, 89 S.Ct. 510 (1969)]

8. Klor's was a retail establishment that sold appliances. Broadway-Hale, a retail chain of department stores, operated a store next door that competed with Klor's in the sale of appliances. At Broadway-Hale's request, several manufacturers and distributors of the major brands of appliances agreed to either not sell to Klor's or to sell to it at higher than normal prices. All the participants in this agreement admitted the existence of the agreement. However, they justified their actions by stating that their participation in the agreement was the result of a private quarrel between Broadway-Hale and Klor's. Later, when Klor's sued both Broadway-Hale and these manufacturers and distributors, alleging that they participated in a "group boycott" against Klor's, the manufacturers and distributors asserted that Klor's was "just one small retailer" and therefore their actions could not be deemed in restraint of competition. Have the manufacturers and distributors presented any defense to the charge of group boycott that would stand up in court? [Klor's Inc. v. Broadway-Hale Stores, Inc., 359 U.S. 207, 79 S.Ct. 705 (1959)]

CHAPTER 51

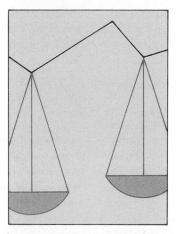

GOVERNMENT REGULATION
Antitrust: Enforcement and Trends

In the last half-century, numerous court decisions and several amendments to the antitrust statutes have modified and narrowed the range of acceptable business behavior. Because such behavior often involves potential violations of more than one statute, and because public enforcement activities have been divided between the Antitrust Division of the Justice Department and the Bureau of Competition of the Federal Trade Commission at the federal level (and various subunits at the state level), antitrust and trade regulation enforcement is generally categorized in one of two ways: as dealing with horizontal activities or as dealing with vertical activities. Horizontal activities are those that involve two or more firms in an industry, whereas vertical activities are those that involve various levels of production, distribution, and marketing within an industry. (A third category, mergers, involves conglomerates in which unrelated and diversified businesses are acquired by a con-

glomerate firm, for example, International Telephone & Telegraph.)

ENFORCEMENT OF PROHIBITIONS ON HORIZONTAL ACTIVITIES

The probability of a costly sentence deters most, if not all, business people from openly entering into agreements or conspiracies to fix prices, boycott competitors, or perform other unlawful activities. However, often the courts must determine whether the parties acted in concert with an implicit agreement to perform such unlawful activities. Such implicit agreement is difficult to detect. The courts must also investigate business behavior suspected of violating the antitrust statutes or associated administrative rules.

Enforcement of prohibitions against certain activities has caused well-defined areas of antitrust action to emerge. These areas include concerted action, certain information exchanges, horizontal market divisions, group boycotts, monopolization, and other horizontal actions.

Defining Concerted Action

Numerous courts have searched for a precise meaning of criminal conspiracy to fix prices under Section 1 of the Sherman Act. Until recently the courts often looked at the effect of such business activities as exchanging price information to see whether the activity raised, fixed, maintained, or stabilized prices. Evidence of such effect of the activity determined guilt as a matter of law. In 1978 the Supreme Court reversed that trend in the following case, holding that a defendant's state of mind or intent is an element that must be considered in determining guilt, and that it must be established by evidence and by inferences from business behavior. The Court held that guilt cannot be proved solely from the effect of the activity upon prices. The Court also held that a party who was once a part of a conspiracy need show only affirmative acts inconsistent with the objective of the conspiracy, not explicit withdrawal from the agreement, in order to be exempt from penalties.

UNITED STATES v.
UNITED STATES
GYPSUM CO.
Supreme Court of the United
States, 1978.
438 U.S. 422, 98 S.Ct. 2864.

BACKGROUND AND FACTS *Several major gypsum board manufacturers and their officers were indicted for violations of Section 1 of the Sherman Act by allegedly engaging in a price-fixing conspiracy. One of the types of actions allegedly taken in the conspiracy was inter-seller price verification, that is, the practice of telephoning a competing manufacturer to determine the price being currently offered on gypsum board to a specific customer. The defendants argued that the price information exchanges were to enable them to take advantage of the meeting-competition defense contained in Section 2(b) of the Clayton Act, as amended by the Robinson-Patman Act (which permits a seller to rebut a prima facie price discrimination charge by showing that a lower price to a purchaser was made in good faith to meet an equally low price of a competitor).*

BURGER, Chief Justice.

*   *   *   *

Beginning in 1966, the Justice Department, as well as the Federal Trade Commission, became involved in investigations into possible antitrust violations in the gypsum board industry. In 1971, a grand jury was empaneled and the investigation continued for an additional 28 months. In late 1973, an indictment was filed in the United States District Court for the Western District of Pennsylvania charging six major manufacturers and various of their corporate officials with violations of § 1 of the Sherman Act.

*   *   * The indictment proceeded to specify some 13 types of actions taken by conspirators "[i]n formulating and effectuating" the combination and conspiracy, the most relevant of which, for our purposes, is specification (h) which alleged that the conspirators

"telephoned or otherwise contacted one another to exchange and discuss current and future published or market prices and published or standard terms and conditions of sale and to ascertain alleged deviations therefrom."

*   *   *   *

*   *   * The jury was instructed that if it found interseller verification had the effect of raising, fixing, maintaining, or stabilizing the price of gypsum board, then such verification could be considered as evidence of an agreement to so affect prices. They were further charged, and it is this point which gives rise to our present concern, that "if the effect of the exchanges of pricing information was to raise, fix, maintain, and stabilize prices, then the parties to them are presumed, *as a matter of law*, to have intended that result."

*　*　*　*

We agree with the Court of Appeals that an effect on prices, without more, will not support a criminal conviction under the Sherman Act, but we do not base that conclusion on the existence of any conflict between the requirements of the Robinson-Patman and the Sherman Acts. Rather, we hold that a defendant's state of mind or intent is an element of a criminal antitrust offense which must be established by evidence and inferences drawn therefrom and cannot be taken from the trier of fact through reliance on a legal presumption of wrongful intent from proof of an effect on prices.

The Supreme Court reversed the trial court's finding that the gypsum board manufacturers were guilty of price conspiracy.

JUDGMENT AND REMEDY

A number of antitrust problems arise in situations where information is exchanged between competing or related businesses, particularly when the data are collected and disseminated through a trade association.

As this case demonstrates, the courts will look for intent, but this is often difficult to define because there are many legitimate reasons for meetings of businesspersons and exchanges of information among them.

COMMENTS

Horizontal Market Divisions

Dividing a territory for the sale of a specific product into two or more divisions allocated by agreement specifically to individual, competing companies is also a per se violation of the Sherman Act. If two cement companies normally sell cement throughout the entire state of California, they cannot enter into an agreement in which one of them sells only in southern California and the other sells only in northern California. As a matter of law, this is illegal, even if it might seem "reasonable."

In some cases the court looks beyond the agreement to a particular effect on prices. In *National Soc'y of Professional Engineers v. United States*,[1] the government found that the Society's Code of Ethics, which prohibited discussion of prices with a potential customer until after the customer had chosen an engineer was a Section 1 violation. The court found that this ban on competitive bidding was "nothing less than a frontal assault on the basic policy of the Sherman Act."

Joint Refusals to Deal, or Group Boycotts

Sellers of goods and services generally have the right to select customers provided that such selection is not based on the customers' religious beliefs, color, sex, or place of natural origin. (Under certain circumstances, a seller may limit sales to persons of a particular religion or sex.)

When two or more sellers act in concert to refuse to sell to a particular buyer or class of buyers, the courts have generally found such acts unlawful under either the Sherman Act or the Clayton Act, or both. In the following classic case, a group of automobile dealers encouraged General Motors to stop further sales to a discount automobile sales outlet.

---

1.   435 U.S. 679, 98 S.Ct. 1355 (1978).

**UNITED STATES v.
GENERAL MOTORS
CORP.**

Supreme Court of the United
States, 1966.
384 U.S. 127, 86 S.Ct. 1321.

BACKGROUND AND FACTS *Beginning in the late 1950s, "discount
houses" and "referral services" began offering to sell new cars to the
public at allegedly bargain prices. By 1960 about eighty-five Chevrolet
dealers, without authorization from General Motors, furnished cars to the
discount houses. As the volume of these sales grew, the nonparticipating
Chevrolet dealers located near one or more of these discount outlets began
to feel the financial pinch.*

*The nonparticipating dealers became increasingly disgruntled. They
began to flood the Chevrolet division of General Motors with letters and
telegrams asking for help.*

*Within a month, General Motors had elicited from each dealer a prom-
ise not to do business with any discounters. But such agreements would
require policing—a fact that had been anticipated. General Motors elicited the help of three of its associations and a number of individual
dealers.*

*The associations made spot checks to assure that no Chevrolet dealer
continued to supply a discounter with cars. They did this by hiring professional investigators to purchase cars from dealers suspected of cooper-
ating with discounters. Each association contributed $5,000 to provide a
fund with which the "professional" shopper would pay for the automobile.*

*Armed with information about violations obtained from the dealers
or their associations, General Motors staff asked the offending dealer to
come in and talk with them. The dealer was then confronted with the car
purchased by the "professional shopper," the documents of the sale, and,
in most cases, a tape recording of the transaction. In every instance, the
embarrassed dealer repurchased the car, sometimes at a substantial loss,
and promised to stop such sales in the future. The checks with which the
cars were repurchased were made payable to an attorney acting jointly
for the three associations.*

*The government charged that these practices were unlawful and that
they constituted a conspiracy to restrain trade in violation of the Sherman
Antitrust Act.*

FORTAS, Justice.

*   *   *   *

Both the Government and the appellees urge the importance, for purposes of
decision, of the "location clause" in the Dealer Selling Agreement which prohibits
a franchised dealer from moving to or establishing "a new or different location,
branch sales office, branch service station, or place of business *   *   * without
the prior written approval of Chevrolet." The appellees contend that this contractual provision is lawful, and that it justifies their actions. They argue that General
Motors acted lawfully to prevent its dealers from violating the "location clause,"
that the described arrangements with discounters constitute the establishment of
additional sales outlets in violation of the clause, and that the individual dealers—
and their associations—have an interest in uniform compliance with the franchise
agreement, which interest they lawfully sought to vindicate.

The Government invites us to join in the assumption, only for purposes of this case, that the "location clause" encompasses sales by dealers through the medium of discounters. But it urges us to hold that, so construed, the provision is unlawful as an unreasonable restraint of trade in violation of the Sherman Act.

* * * We have here a classic conspiracy in restraint of trade: joint, collaborative action by dealers, the appellee associations, and General Motors to eliminate a class of competitors by terminating business dealings between them and a minority of Chevrolet dealers and to deprive franchised dealers of their freedom to deal through discounters if they so choose. Against this fact of unlawful combination, the "location clause" is of no avail. Whatever General Motors might or might not lawfully have done to enforce individual Dealer Selling Agreements by action within the borders of those agreements and the relationship which each defines, is beside the point. And, because the action taken constitutes a combination or conspiracy, it is not necessary to consider what might be the legitimate interest of a dealer in securing compliance by others with the "location clause," or the lawfulness of action a dealer might individually take to vindicate this interest.

* * * Neither individual dealers nor the associations acted independently or separately. The dealers collaborated, through the associations and otherwise, among themselves and with General Motors, both to enlist the aid of General Motors and to enforce dealers' promises to forsake the discounters. The associations explicitly entered into a joint venture to assist General Motors in policing the dealers' promises, and their joint proffer of aid was accepted and utilized by General Motors.

* * * General Motors sought to elicit from all the dealers agreements, substantially interrelated and interdependent, that none of them would do business with the discounters. These agreements were hammered out in meetings between nonconforming dealers and officials of General Motors' Chevrolet Division, and in telephone conversations with other dealers. It was acknowledged from the beginning that substantial unanimity would be essential if the agreements were to be forthcoming. And once the agreements were secured, General Motors both solicited and employed the assistance of its alleged co-conspirators in helping to police them. What resulted was a fabric interwoven by many strands of joint action to eliminate the discounters from participation in the market, to inhibit the free choice of franchised dealers to select their own methods of trade and to provide multilateral surveillance and enforcement. This process for achieving and enforcing the desired objective can by no stretch of the imagination be described as "unilateral" or merely "parallel."

The protection of price competition from conspiratorial restraint is an object of special solicitude under the antitrust laws. We cannot respect that solicitude by closing our eyes to the effect upon price competition of the removal from the market, by combination or conspiracy, of a class of traders. Nor do we propose to construe the Sherman Act to prohibit conspiracies to fix prices at which competitors may sell, but to allow conspiracies or combinations to put competitors out of business entirely.

The Supreme Court found that, beyond question, these activities were a conspiracy to restrain trade in violation of Section 1 of the Sherman Act.   **JUDGMENT AND REMEDY**

Monopolization

Section 2 of the Sherman Act makes practices to "monopolize or attempt to monopolize" unlawful behavior. In practice, this has often been interpreted as actions that aggressively exclude a competitor.

A number of factors are considered. In 1966, the Supreme Court defined two essential elements of monopolization.[2] These elements are:

1. The possession of monopoly power in the relevant market.
2. The willful acquisition or maintenance of that power as distinguished from growth or development as a consequence of a superior product, business acumen, or historic accident.

Monopoly power is usually measured as the size of the market share held by the defendant company. Significant monopoly is associated with a total market share of 75 percent or more, whereas a market share of 25 percent or less is generally considered to be insufficient market power to support most antitrust actions.

Defining the Relevant Market One of the most important questions facing the courts is: What is the relevant market for measuring monopoly power? Over time the courts have narrowed the definition of the relevant market by considering more information about the characteristics of the product, its substitutes, and the geographic area where the product is sold. Because the market share is extremely sensitive to the definition of relevant market, considerable care is taken by both sides in assembling and presenting evidence to determine the market.

The importance of market-sharing was well illustrated in the 1945 Alcoa decision.[3] If the relevant market consisted only of those who bought a virgin ingot, then Alcoa was the sole producer at that time. Another definition of the relevant market included those who bought secondary aluminum, which is an almost perfect substitute

for virgin ingot, and thus significantly broadened the relevant market and lowered the measure of Alcoa's share. And when the market was further broadened to include imported fabricated and secondary aluminum, the measure of Alcoa's share fell to roughly 33 percent of the aluminum production market.

Once relevant market is determined, the court then looks at the extent to which the defendant has exerted pressures on competitors, has prevented potential firms from entering the market, or has engaged in other actions not associated with "natural" growth.

Other Horizontal Restraints

Over the years, the traditional methods for fixing prices by allocating territories or boycotting competitors have been rapidly disappearing. Consequently, the commission has revised its enforcement approach to focus more on the hidden forms of restricting competition. For example, in the early 1970s, the commission began the first of a number of cases attacking shopping center leases that give major tenants a veto over other tenants. For example, in the case of *Tysons Corner*,[4] the three major department stores had been given lease arrangements that permitted them to disapprove prospective tenants who wished to rent space in the shopping center. These clauses were ruled to be *prima facie* evidence of unreasonable restraint of trade. The commission in this case ruled that agreements that create approval rights as broad as those involved in the *Tysons Corner* case are per se illegal and amount to an agreement to fix prices.

ENFORCEMENT OF PROHIBITIONS ON VERTICAL RESTRAINTS

Vertical restraints involve the distribution of goods, the power of suppliers to engage in exclusionary practices, and price discrimination. They include those situations where manufacturers attempt to restrict the prices, locations,

2. United States v. Grinnel Corp., 384 U.S. 563, 86 S.Ct. 1698 (1966).
3. United States v. Aluminum Co. of America, 148 F.2d 416 (2d Cir. 1945).

4. Tysons Corner Regional Shopping Center, 85 FTC 970 (1975).

customers, or retailing methods of goods being sold.

Distribution Restrictions

Restriction on the distribution of goods may come in the form of resale price maintenance, consignment through agents, or territorial or customer restrictions.

Resale Price Maintenance Resale price maintenance, or "fair trade," agreements arise when the manufacturers specify what the retail price to consumers must be. Usually either a minimum or a maximum retail price will be specified in these cases. Early in this century the Supreme Court ruled that a manufacturer that sold medicine to wholesalers was not entitled to restrict resale of the medicine by specifying minimum prices for retailers.[5] Later, this rigid rule against vertical price-fixing was extended to prohibit the specifying of maximum as well as minimum prices.[6] Until 1976, however, Congress permitted states to adopt fair trade laws that allowed resale price maintenance.[7]

Consignment through Agents The antitrust laws are more lenient in permitting manufacturers that continue to retain title and to bear most of the associated risk of ownership, to specify the terms of sale, including limits on resale prices. Until 1974, General Electric sold its light bulbs on consignment with retail outlets. In turn, retailers sold the light bulbs at prices specified by General Electric and received commissions on sales. The court held that this was an agency relationship and upheld General Electric's right to specify the retail price of the light bulbs.[8]

Territorial and Customer Restrictions In arranging for the distribution of a firm's products, manufacturers often wish to insulate dealers from direct competition from other dealers selling the firm's product. In this case, they may institute territorial restrictions. In other cases, manufacturers may attempt to prohibit wholesalers or retailers from reselling the products to certain classes of buyers, such as competing retailers, and therefore they institute consumer restrictions. In *United States v. Arnold, Schwinn & Co.*,[9] such restrictions (of either the territorial or consumer type) in manufacturer contracts with wholesalers or retailers were held to be a Section 1 Sherman Act violation. In 1977 the Supreme Court overruled *Schwinn*, giving the manufacturers significantly more control over the distribution of their products. As the following case shows, territorial and customer restrictions are lawful unless their use unreasonably restricts trade.

---

5. Dr. Miles Medical Co. v. John D. Park & Sons Co., 220 U.S. 373, 31 S.Ct. 376 (1911).
6. Albrecht v. Herald Co., 390 U.S. 145, 88 S.Ct. 869 (1968).
7. See the discussion of the Miller-Tydings Act in Chapter 50.

8. United States v. General Elec. Co., 272 U.S. 476, 47 S.Ct. 192 (1926).
9. 388 U.S. 365, 87 S.Ct. 1856 (1967).

BACKGROUND AND FACTS *Prior to 1962, like most other television manufacturers, Sylvania sold its televisions to independent or company-owned distributors, who in turn resold to a large and diverse group of retailers. In 1962, Sylvania phased out its wholesale distributors and began to sell its televisions directly to a smaller and more select group of franchised retailers. Sylvania limited the number of franchises granted for any given area and required each franchisee to sell the Sylvania products from only the locations of the franchise. A franchise did not constitute an exclusive territory, and Sylvania retained sole discretion to increase the number of retailers in an area, depending on the success or failure of existing retailers in developing their market. Continental T.V., a Sylvania franchisee, withheld all payments due for Sylvania prod-*

CONTINENTAL T.V., INC. v. GTE SYLVANIA, INC.
Supreme Court of the United States, 1977.
433 U.S. 36, 97 S.Ct. 2549.

ucts after a dispute over additional locations sought by Continental. John P. Maguire & Co., the finance company that handled the credit arrangements between Sylvania and its franchisees, sued Continental for payment and for return of secured merchandise. Continental claimed that Sylvania had violated Section 1 of the Sherman Act by entering into and enforcing franchise agreements that permitted the sale of Sylvania products only in specified locations.

POWELL, Justice.

*　*　*　*

In the present case it is undisputed that title to the televisions passed from Sylvania to Continental. Thus, the *Schwinn per se* rule applies unless Sylvania's restriction on locations falls outside Schwinn's prohibition against a manufacturer's attempting to restrict a "retailer's freedom as to where and to whom it will resell the products." As the Court of Appeals conceded, the language of *Schwinn* is clearly broad enough to apply to the present case. Unlike the Court of Appeals, however, we are unable to find a principled basis for distinguishing *Schwinn* from the case now before us.

Both Schwinn and Sylvania sought to reduce but not to eliminate competition among their respective retailers through the adoption of a franchise system. Although it was not one of the issues addressed by the District Court or presented on appeal by the Government, the Schwinn franchise plan included a location restriction similar to the one challenged here. These restrictions allowed Schwinn and Sylvania to regulate the amount of competition among their retailers by preventing a franchisee from selling franchised products from outlets other than the one covered by the franchise agreement. To exactly the same end, the Schwinn franchise plan included a companion restriction, apparently not found in the Sylvania plan, that prohibited franchised retailers from selling Schwinn products to nonfranchised retailers. In *Schwinn* the Court expressly held that this restriction was impermissible under the broad principle stated there. In intent and competitive impact, the retail-customer restriction in *Schwinn* is indistinguishable from the location restriction in the present case. In both cases the restrictions limited the freedom of the retailer to dispose of the purchased products as he desired. The fact that one restriction was addressed to territory and the other to customers is irrelevant to functional antitrust analysis and, indeed, to the language and broad thrust of the opinion in *Schwinn*. As Mr. Chief Justice Hughes stated: "Realities must dominate the judgement.　*　*　* The Anti-Trust Act aims at substance."

*　*　*　*

Vertical restrictions reduce intrabrand competition by limiting the number of sellers of a particular product competing for the business of a given group of buyers. Location restrictions have this effect because of practical constraints on the effective marketing area of retail outlets. Although intrabrand competition may be reduced, the ability of retailers to exploit the resulting market may be limited both by the ability of consumers to travel to other franchised locations and, perhaps more importantly, to purchase the competing products of other manufacturers. None of these key variables, however, is affected by the form of the transaction by which a manufacturer conveys his products to the retailers.

Vertical restrictions promote interbrand competition by allowing the manufacturer to achieve certain efficiencies in the distribution of his products. These "redeeming virtues" are implicit in every decision sustaining vertical restrictions under the rule of reason. Economists have identified a number of ways in which manufacturers can use such restrictions to compete more effectively against other manufacturers. For example, new manufacturers and manufacturers entering new markets can use the restrictions in order to induce competent and aggressive retailers to make the kind of investment of capital and labor that is often required in the distribution of products unknown to the consumer. Established manufacturers can use them to induce retailers to engage in promotional activities or to provide service and repair facilities necessary to the efficient marketing of their products. Service and repair are vital for many products, such as automobiles and major household appliances. The availability and quality of such services affect a manufacturer's goodwill and the competitiveness of his product. Because of market imperfections such as the so-called "free rider" effect, these services might not be provided by retailers in a purely competitive situation, despite the fact that each retailer's benefit would be greater if all provided the services than if none did.

The Supreme Court reversed the trial court's holding that Sylvania had violated Section 1 of the Sherman Act.

JUDGMENT AND REMEDY

In this case, the Supreme Court focused directly on the applications of a strict per se rule. Its rejection of a rigid rule in favor of a "rule of reason" approach has been extended to other important areas of antitrust law. Thus the courts and antitrust enforcers will look at the challenged restraint's impact on competition. In the case of Coors[10], *the Federal Trade Commission found that territorial restrictions on Coors distributors with simultaneous wholesale and retail minimum prices reduced competition in the beer industry.*

COMMENTS

---

10.   83 F.T.C. 32 (1973).

Exclusionary Practices

Exclusionary practices are those involving refusals to deal and so-called tying arrangements wherein firms refuse to sell or lease a good unless the buyer agrees to purchase other goods or articles produced or distributed by the seller. Exclusionary practices also include arrangements wherein the seller requires the purchaser, usually a retailer, not to sell products of competing firms.

Refusals to Deal   Refusals to deal were discussed under the topic of prohibitions on hori-

zontal activities. In vertical arrangements, the Supreme Court has generally given firms the freedom to refuse to sell to individual buyers. In *United States v. Colgate & Co.,*[11] the Court ruled that a manufacturer's advance announcement that it would not sell to price cutters was not a violation of the Sherman Act.

Tying Arrangements   A tying arrangement is one in which the seller of a product conditions the sale of that product upon the buyer's agreement

---

11.   250 U.S. 300, 39 S.Ct. 465 (1919).

to purchase another product produced or distributed by the seller. For example, the seller of a copier machine may tie the sale of a *tying product* (the copier) to the purchase of a *tied product* (paper). The legality of such arrangements depends on many factors, particularly the business purpose or effect of the arrangement.

In 1936, the Supreme Court ruled that International Business Machines' practice of requiring the purchase of cards (the tied product) as a condition of leasing its tabulation machines (the tying product) was unlawful.[12] In enforcing Section 3 of the Clayton Act, however, the Court has not applied a strict rule against tying arrangements. In *United States Steel Corp. v. Fortner Enterprises, Inc.,*[13] the Court ruled in favor of U.S. Steel despite the existence of a tie-in between the purchase of prefabricated homes (the tied product) and credit (the tying product) to purchase the homes. There was no evidence that U.S. Steel had significant economic power in the tying product or credit market, and its arrangement was therefore found to be lawful.

Exclusive Dealings   Section 3 of the Clayton Act as amended prohibits exclusive dealing contracts when the effect of these contracts would be "to substantially lessen competition or tend to create a monopoly."

Exclusive dealing contracts arise when a seller or manufacturer requires that the buyer not purchase the products of competitive sellers. Thus, if a dealer who purchases cars from a manufacturer is required to promote and market only the seller's brand of cars, an exclusive dealing situation would exist. Despite its similarity with a tying contract, an exclusive dealing arrangement is subject to a different judicial standard. In general, the courts apply a modified rule of reason in determining whether the arrangement will substantially lessen competition.

The leading exclusive dealing decision is that of *Standard Oil Co. of California v. United States.*[14] In this case, the largest gasoline seller in the na-

tion made exclusive dealing contracts with independent stations in seven western states. The contracts involved 16 percent of all retail outlets, whose sales were approximately 7 percent of all retail sales in that market. The Supreme Court found that these contracts were a Section 3 violation of the Clayton Act.

Requirements Contracts   Another type of exclusive dealing arrangement requires that the buyer of a particular commodity purchase all that the buyer will use of that commodity for a specified period of time. This is called a requirements contract. Its legality is judged on whether it results in a substantial lessening of competition. In *Tampa Elec. Co. v. Nashville Coal Co.,*[15] the Supreme Court upheld a contract for the Nashville Coal Company to supply all the coal required by Tampa Electric Company for its electricity generation. The contract covered a twenty-year period and specified the per ton price of coal. In this case the Court defined the relevant geographic market as one involving at least seven states, yielding a contract market share of less than 1 percent, an amount judged to be insubstantial.

Price Discrimination

Although price discrimination that potentially lessens competition or creates a monopoly is unlawful, two difficulties arise in enforcing Section 2 of the Clayton Act as amended by the Robinson-Patman Act in vertical activities. First, the various exemptions—such as changing market conditions, meeting price competition from other competitors, and passing on actual cost savings to customers—make proof of a violation difficult. Second, the Federal Trade Commission only sporadically enforces the act.

Other Vertical Restraints

Antitrust enforcers also investigate other vertical restraints, such as *reciprocal buying,* that promote unfair practices or impede competition.

---

12. International Business Machines v. United States, 298 U.S. 131, 56 S.Ct. 701 (1936).
13. 429 U.S. 610, 97 S.Ct. 861 (1977).
14. 337 U.S. 293, 69 S.Ct. 1051 (1949).

15. 365 U.S. 320, 81 S.Ct. 623 (1961).

Reciprocal arrangements exist when the seller of one good is required to purchase one or more goods provided by the buyer of the initial good. Thus, if an automobile manufacturer sells to a leasing company, and the leasing company requires employees of the automobile manufacturer to rent cars from the company, a reciprocal buying arrangement exists; and this is illegal.

BACKGROUND AND FACTS *Consolidated Foods owns a network of food processing plants, wholesale outlets, and retail food stores. It acquired Gentry, a producer of dehydrated onion and garlic products. The FTC maintained that this acquisition violated Section 7 of the Clayton Act because, through reciprocal buying, it gave Consolidated Foods the power to lessen competition in the dehydrated onion and garlic markets. Consolidated appealed the FTC ruling to the United States Court of Appeals, which reversed the FTC judgment. The case then went to the Supreme Court.*

FEDERAL TRADE COMM'N v. CONSOLIDATED FOODS CORP.
Supreme Court of the United States, 1965.
380 U.S. 92, 85 S.Ct. 1220.

DOUGLAS, Justice.
*   *   *   *

Section 7 of the Clayton Act is concerned "with probabilities, not certainties." Reciprocity in trading as a result of an acquisition violates § 7, if the probability of a lessening of competition is shown. We turn then to that, the principal, aspect of the present case.

Consolidated is a substantial purchaser of the products of food processors who in turn purchase dehydrated onion and garlic for use in preparing and packaging their food. Gentry *   *   * principally engaged in the manufacture of dehydrated onion and garlic, had *   *   * immediately prior to its acquisition by Consolidated, about 32% of the total sales of the dehydrated garlic and onion industry.
*   *   *

After the acquisition Consolidated (though later disclaiming adherence to any policy of reciprocity) did undertake to assist Gentry in selling. An official of Consolidated wrote as follows to its distributing divisions:

"Oftentimes, it is a great advantage to know when you are calling on a prospect, whether or not that prospect is a supplier of someone within your own organization. Everyone believes in reciprocity providing all things are equal.

"Attached is a list of prospects for our Gentry products. We would like to have you indicate on the list whether or not you are purchasing any of your supplies from them. If so, indicate whether your purchases are relatively large, small or insignificant.
*   *   *   *

Food processors who sold to Consolidated stated they would give their onion and garlic business to Gentry for reciprocity reasons if it could meet the price and quality of its competitors' products. *   *   *
*   *   *   *

[T]he Commission concluded:

"With two firms accounting for better than 85% of both product lines for eleven successive years, maximum concentration short of monopoly has already been achieved. If it is desirable to prevent a trend toward oligopoly it is *a fortiori* desirable to remove, so far as possible, obstacles to the creation of genuinely competitive conditions in an oligopolistic industry. *   *   *"

*   *   *   *

The Court of Appeals, on the other hand, gave post-acquisition evidence almost conclusive weight. It pointed out that, while Gentry's share of the dehydrated onion market increased by some 7%, its share of the dehydrated garlic market decreased 12%. *   *   *

The Court of Appeals was not in error in considering the post-acquisition evidence in this case. But we think it gave too much weight to it. No group acquiring a company with reciprocal buying opportunities is entitled to a "free trial" period. To give it such would be to distort the scheme of § 7. The "mere *possibility*" of the prohibited restraint is not enough. Probability of the proscribed evil is required, as we have noted. If the post-acquisition evidence were given conclusive weight or allowed to override all probabilities, then acquisitions would go forward willy-nilly, the parties biding their time until reciprocity was allowed fully to bloom. It is, of course, true that post-acquisition conduct may amount to a violation of § 7 even though there is no evidence to establish probability *in limine*. But the force of § 7 is still in probabilities, not in what later transpired. That must necessarily be the case, for once the two companies are united no one knows what the fate of the acquired company and its competitors would have been but for the merger.

Moreover, the post-acquisition evidence here tends to confirm, rather than cast doubt upon, the probable anti-competitive effect which the Commission found the merger would have. The Commission found that Basic's [Gentry's chief competitor] product was superior to Gentry's—as Gentry's president freely and repeatedly admitted. Yet Gentry, in a rapidly expanding market, was able to increase its share of onion sales by 7% and to hold its losses in garlic to a 12% decrease. Thus the Commission was surely on safe ground in reaching the following conclusion:

"If reciprocal buying creates for Gentry a protected market, which others cannot penetrate despite superiority of price, quality, or service, competition is lessened whether or not Gentry can expand its market share. It is for this reason that we reject respondent's argument that the decline in its share of the garlic market proves the ineffectiveness of reciprocity. We do not know that its share would not have fallen still farther, had it not been for the influence of reciprocal buying. This loss of sales fails to refute the likelihood that Consolidated's reciprocity power, which it has shown a willingness to exploit to the full, will not immunize a substantial segment of the garlic market from normal quality, price, and service competition."

*   *   * We do not go so far as to say that any acquisition, no matter how small, violates § 7 if there is a probability of reciprocal buying. Some situations may amount only to *de minimis*. But where, as here, the acquisition is of a company that commands a substantial share of a market, a finding of probability of reciprocal buying by the Commission, whose expertise the Congress trusts, should be honored, if there is substantial evidence to support it.

JUDGMENT AND REMEDY   *The FTC order was upheld by the Supreme Court. Consolidated Foods was required to divest itself of Gentry.*

MERGERS

Horizontal Mergers

The statutory authority for enforcing anticompetitive mergers is Section 7 of the Clayton Act. This section was introduced because it was feared that concentration would potentially facilitate collusion among sellers in the market, and that such collusion would be difficult to detect. In general, the FTC and Artitrust Division of the Justice Department determine the legality of **horizontal mergers** by looking at the degree of concentration or market shares of merging firms, although the Court has indicated that it will look at the likely effects of the merger as well. Thus,

if a merger facilitates horizontal collusion without increasing production or marketing efficiencies, it will be declared unlawful.

Mergers will be permitted when they enhance consumer welfare by increasing efficiency if they do not increase the probability of horizontal collusion. Furthermore, mergers that facilitate and increase efficiency must be evaluated according to the relative magnitude of the two facts. For example, in the case of *Philadelphia National Bank*, the commission held that even in situations with low entry barriers, there may be a loss of actual competition. Thus, mergers can be declared illegal even where entry is relatively easy, as illustrated by the following case.

BACKGROUND AND FACTS *In 1958, Von's Grocery Company ranked third in retail sales in the Los Angeles area. Its largest direct competitor, Shopping Bag Food Stores, ranked sixth in retail sales for the same period. The merger of these two highly successful, expanding, and aggressive competitors created the second largest grocery chain in Los Angeles, with sales of almost $173 million annually. The number of small business owners operating single grocery stores in the Los Angeles retail grocery market had been dropping in the years prior to the merger, and after it, the number dropped still further. The grocery business in the Los Angeles area was being concentrated in the hands of fewer and fewer owners, as small grocery companies were continually being absorbed by the larger firms through mergers.*

On March 25, 1960, the United States brought this action, charging that Von's Grocery Company's acquisitions of its direct competitor, Shopping Bag Food Stores, violated Section 7 of the Clayton Act, which, as amended in 1950 by the Celler-Kefauver Anti-Merger Act, provides in relevant part: "That no corporation engaged in commerce * * * shall acquire the whole or any part of the assets of another corporation engaged also in commerce, where in any line of commerce in any section of the country, the effect of such acquisition may be substantially to lessen competition, or to tend to create a monopoly."

On March 28, 1960, three days later, the district court refused to grant the government's motion for a temporary restraining order. Immediately, Von's took over all of Shopping Bag's capital stock and assets, including its thirty-six grocery stores in Los Angeles. After a hearing, the district court concluded that there was not a reasonable probability that the merger would tend "substantially to lessen competition" or "create a monopoly" in violation of Section 7. The government appealed directly to the Supreme Court of the United States.[1]

UNITED STATES v. VON'S GROCERY CO.
Supreme Court of the United States, 1966.
384 U.S. 270, 86 S.Ct. 1478.

---

1.   Direct appeal is authorized by Section 2 of the expediting act, 15 USC 29.

BLACK, Justice.

*   *   *   *

*   *   * The sole question here is whether the District Court properly concluded on the facts before it that the Government had failed to prove a violation of § 7.

*   *   *   *

From this country's beginning there has been an abiding and widespread fear of the evils which flow from monopoly—that is the concentration of economic power in the hands of a few. On the basis of this fear, Congress in 1890, when many of the Nation's industries were already concentrated into what it deemed too few hands, passed the Sherman Act in an attempt to prevent further concentration and to preserve competition among a large number of sellers. Several years later, in 1897, this Court emphasized this policy of the Sherman Act by calling attention to the tendency of powerful business combinations to restrain competition "by driving out of business the small dealers and worthy men whose lives have been spent therein, and who might be unable to readjust themselves to their altered surroundings." The Sherman Act failed to protect the smaller businessmen from elimination through the monopolistic pressures of large combinations which used mergers to grow ever more powerful. As a result in 1914 Congress, viewing mergers as a continuous, pervasive threat to small business, passed § 7 of the Clayton Act which prohibited corporations under most circumstances from merging by purchasing the stock of their competitors. Ingenious businessmen, however, soon found a way to avoid § 7 and corporations began to merge simply by purchasing their rivals' assets. This Court in 1926, over the dissent of Justice Brandeis, joined by Chief Justice Taft and Justices Holmes and Stone approved this device for avoiding § 7 and mergers continued to concentrate economic power into fewer and fewer hands until 1950 when Congress passed the Celler-Kefauver Anti-Merger Act now before us.

Like the Sherman Act in 1890 and the Clayton Act in 1914, the basic purpose of the 1950 Celler-Kefauver Act was to prevent economic concentration in the American economy by keeping a large number of small competitors. In their bill, both of its sponsors, Representative Celler and Senator Kefauver, emphasized their fear, widely shared by other members of Congress, that this concentration was rapidly driving the small businessman out of the market. *   *   * "The dominant theme pervading congressional consideration of the 1950 amendments was a fear of what was considered to be a rising tide of economic concentration in the American economy." To arrest this "rising tide" toward concentration into too few hands and to halt the gradual demise of the small businessman, Congress decided to clamp down with vigor on mergers. It both revitalized § 7 of the Clayton Act by "plugging its loophole" and broadened its scope so as not only to prohibit mergers between competitors, the effect of which "may be substantially to lessen competition, or to tend to create a monopoly" but to prohibit all mergers having that effect. By using these terms in § 7 which look not merely to the actual present effect of a merger but instead to its effect upon future competition, Congress sought to preserve competition among many small businesses by arresting a trend toward concentration in its incipiency before that trend developed to the point that a market was left in the grip of a few big companies. Thus, where concentration is gaining momentum in a market, we must be alert to carry out Congress' intent to protect competition against ever-increasing concentration through mergers.

The facts of this case present exactly the threatening trend toward concentration which Congress wanted to halt. The number of small grocery companies in the Los Angeles retail grocery market had been declining rapidly before the merger and continued to decline rapidly afterwards. This rapid decline in the number of grocery store owners moved hand in hand with a large number of significant absorptions of the small companies by the larger ones. In the midst of this steadfast trend toward concentration, Von's and Shopping Bag, two of the most successful and largest companies in the area, jointly owning 66 grocery stores merged to become the second largest chain in Los Angeles. This merger cannot be defended on the ground that one of the companies was about to fail or that the two had to merge to save themselves from destruction by some larger and more powerful competitor. What we have on the contrary is simply the case of two already powerful companies merging in a way which makes them even more powerful than they were before. If ever such a merger would not violate § 7, certainly it does when it takes place in a market characterized by a long and continuous trend toward fewer and fewer owner-competitors which is exactly the sort of trend which Congress, with power to do so, declared must be arrested.

The judgment of the district court was reversed and the case was remanded to the district court to order that Von's Grocery Company divest itself of Shopping Bag's capital stock and assets, including the thirty-six grocery stores in the Los Angeles area.   **JUDGMENT AND REMEDY**

Not everyone agreed with this 1966 Supreme Court decision. Currently, the Supreme Court is reexamining its position.   **COMMENT**

Vertical Mergers

Vertical mergers occur when a company at one stage of production acquires a company at a higher or lower stage of production. Thus, the acquisition of a tire plant by an automobile manufacturer would constitute a backward vertical integration, while acquisition of a car-renting agency would constitute a forward vertical integration. The FTC's approach to vertical mergers depends on a number of factors, including the definition of the relevant product in geographic markets as well as the characteristics identified as impeding competition.

For example, the commission will attack any vertical merger that keeps competitors of either party from the segment of the market that otherwise would be open to them.[16] Thus, in *Ashgrove Cement Co. v. Federal Trade Comm.*,[17] the commission found that "foreclosure manifests a particularly anticompetitive character when it occurs as part of a trend toward forward integration in a concentrated market."[18] The potential entrant is faced with the choice of entering at the supply level and competing with a continually shrinking market or entering at both the supply and consumer levels, but incurring increased costs of entry. In such circumstances, the commission clearly has indicated that the potential entrant faces entry barriers.

CONGLOMERATE MERGERS

Conglomerate mergers often extend product lines at the retail level, particularly among products that are complementary, although mergers can also occur among firms using similar suppliers.

---

16. Brown Shoe Co. v. United States, 370 U.S. 294, 82 S.Ct. 1502 (1962).

17. 85 FTC 1123, 519 F.2d 934 (D.C.Cir. 1975).

18. The law's current theory of injury to competition in vertical mergers is contained in the concept of foreclosure. For example, a manufacturer can acquire a retailer and force the new retail subsidiary to sell the parent manufacturer's product. This would "foreclose" rival manufacturers from the market.

A large number of conglomerate mergers, however, occur where the merging firms have no direct functional business link. In such mergers there are no changes in market structure, market shares, or concentration ratios. In many cases, conglomerate mergers serve to reduce overhead costs by spreading them over a larger range of output and reducing advertising and other promotional costs.

FEDERAL TRADE COMM'N v. PROCTER & GAMBLE CO.

Supreme Court of the United States, 1967.
386 U.S. 568, 87 S.Ct. 1224.

BACKGROUND AND FACTS *The Federal Trade Commission argued that Procter & Gamble's acquisition of Clorox Chemical Company violated the Clayton Act and lessened competition in the household liquid bleach market. At the time of the merger, Clorox was the leading manufacturer of household bleach (49 percent of national sales) in a highly concentrated market. The commission found that extensive advertising expenditures could increase Clorox's market share. Purex, the major competitor, did not sell its product in some markets, primarily in the Northeast and Mid-Atlantic states. Procter & Gamble was a large, diversified producer of high-turnover household products primarily sold in grocery stores and drugstores. Through its large advertising budget, Procter & Gamble was able to obtain substantial price reductions. The commission argued that its acquisition of Clorox would discourage entry and competition in this market.*

DOUGLAS, Justice.

*   *   *   *

At the time of the acquisition, Clorox was the leading manufacturer of household liquid bleach, with 48.8% of the national sales—annual sales of slightly less than $40,000,000. Its market share had been steadily increasing for the five years prior to the merger. Its nearest rival was Purex, which manufactures a number of products other than household liquid bleaches, including abrasive cleaners, toilet soap, and detergents. Purex accounted for 15.7% of the household liquid bleach market. The industry is highly concentrated; in 1957, Clorox and Purex accounted for almost 65% of the Nation's household liquid bleach sales, and, together with four other firms, for almost 80%. *   *   *

Since all liquid bleach is chemically identical, advertising and sales promotion are vital. In 1957 Clorox spent almost $3,700,000 on advertising, imprinting the value of its bleach in the mind of the consumer. *   *   * The Commission found that these heavy expenditures went far to explain why Clorox maintained so high a market share despite the fact that its brand, though chemically indistinguishable from rival brands, retailed for a price equal to or, in many instances, higher than its competitors.

Procter is a large, diversified manufacturer of low-price, high-turnover household products sold through grocery, drug, and department stores. Prior to its acquisition of Clorox, it did not produce household liquid bleach. *   *   * Procter has been marked by rapid growth and diversification. It has successfully developed and introduced a number of new products. Its primary activity is in the general area of soaps, detergents, and cleansers; in 1957, of total domestic sales, more than one-half *   *   * were in this field. Procter was the dominant factor in this area.

*   *   *   *

In the marketing of soaps, detergents, and cleansers, as in the marketing of household liquid bleach, advertising and sales promotion are vital. * * * Due to its tremendous volume, Procter receives substantial discounts from the media. As a multi-product producer Procter enjoys substantial advantages in advertising and sales promotion. Thus, it can and does feature several products in its promotions, reducing the printing, mailing, and other costs for each product. It also purchases network programs on behalf of several products, enabling it to give each product network exposure at a fraction of the cost per product that a firm with only one product to advertise would incur.

Prior to the acquisition, Procter was in the course of diversifying into product lines related to its basic detergent-soap-cleanser business. Liquid bleach was a distinct possibility since packaged detergents—Procter's primary product line— and liquid bleach are used complementarily in washing clothes and fabrics, and in general household cleaning. * * *

The decision to acquire Clorox was the result of a study conducted by Procter's promotion department designed to determine the advisability of entering the liquid bleach industry. * * * Since a large investment would be needed to obtain a satisfactory market share, acquisition of the industry's leading firm was attractive. * * *

The final report confirmed the conclusions of the initial report and emphasized that Procter would make more effective use of Clorox's advertising budget and that the merger would facilitate advertising economies. A few months later, Procter acquired the assets of Clorox in the name of a wholly owned subsidiary, the Clorox Company, in exchange for Procter stock.

The Commission * * * found that the substitution of Procter with its huge assets and advertising advantages for the already dominant Clorox would dissuade new entrants and discourage active competition from the firms already in the industry due to fear of retaliation by Procter. * * *

The anticompetitive effects with which this product-extension merger is fraught can easily be seen: (1) the substitution of the powerful acquiring firm for the smaller, but already dominant, firm may substantially reduce the competitive structure of the industry by raising entry barriers and by dissuading the smaller firms from aggressively competing; (2) the acquisition eliminates the potential competition of the acquiring firm.

The liquid bleach industry was already oligopolistic before the acquisition, and price competition was certainly not as vigorous as it would have been if the industry were competitive. Clorox enjoyed a dominant position nationally, and its position approached monopoly proportions in certain areas. The existence of some 200 fringe firms certainly does not belie that fact. * * *

The FTC order that Procter & Gamble divest itself of the Clorox Company was upheld by the Supreme Court of the United States.

JUDGMENT AND REMEDY

OTHER ANTITRUST ENFORCEMENT

The Federal Trade Commission investigates and enforces regulations in the context of industry-wide matters. Industry-wide problems may be indicated by high prices, profits, lack of product innovation, or the absence of entry by new firms. In such cases, the exact cause of reduced performance may not be readily identifiable. Determining the problem and selecting the appropriate remedy require a more extensive analysis than is necessary in other FTC investigations. Industry-wide matters include investigations of the petroleum and automobile industries as well as the breakfast cereal industry as part of the food program investigation. Other matters under FTC investigation in the 1970s involved the household detergent and appliance industries.[19] A typical investigation, such as that concerning the household detergent industry, might involve an initial specification that the industry is highly concentrated, has high profits, lacks price competition, and maintains high entry barriers that are caused by advertising and brand proliferation. In such cases, the commission remedy is likely to be diversification, although neither major violations nor specific remedies have been determined.

QUESTIONS AND CASE PROBLEMS

1. In December 1964, Graflex, Inc., quoted a price to International Film Center, Inc., of $324 apiece for the sale of thirty-two sound projectors. International was to use the quoted price in its bid to supply projectors to the local school board. Graflex knew of International's intention to use its quoted price in its bid to the school board. Graflex also quoted a price of $275 to Rosenfeld for the same projectors. The school board accepted Rosenfeld's low bid to sell it projectors. International Film Center, learning of the difference between the two bids, complained to Graflex and was advised by letter that the difference had been inadvertent. In addition, Graflex apologized for the mistake and assured International that it would never happen again. It did not happen thereafter. International Film Center subsequently charged Graflex with price discrimination and brought a lawsuit against it for damages. Will it succeed? [International Film Center, Inc.

v. Graflex, Inc., 427 F.2d 334 (3rd Cir. 1970)]

2. Febco, Inc., manufactured lawn and turf equipment. The Colorado Pump and Supply Company was a wholesale distributor of such equipment in the Colorado area. An important item that Colorado Pump distributed was a control device for sprinkling systems. Although Febco manufactured one of the better sprinkler controls, a number of other manufacturers competed in the field with competitive and satisfactory substitutes for the Febco controllers. In an agreement between Febco and Colorado Pump under which Colorado Pump was given the right to distribute Febco products, Colorado Pump was required to stock a comlete line of Febco products. Industry data proved that, in this line of goods, it was important for distributors to protect the "goodwill" of manufacturers by carrying a complete line of a manufacturer's goods or none at all. Does the requirement by Febco that Colorado Pump stock an entire line of Febco products constitute an illegal tying arrangement? [Colorado Pump and Supply Co. v. Febco, Inc., 472 F.2d 637 (10th Cir. 1973)]

3. In 1972, the Federal Maritime Commission approved an agreement under which the world's two largest containership operators—Sea Land Service, Inc., and United States Lines, Inc.—would become subsidiaries of the same corporate parent—R. J. Reynolds Tobacco Company. The commission approved the acquisition agreement on condition that the subsidiaries would remain independent companies in competition with each other. The Federal Maritime Commission, however, does not have the power to immunize companies from the antitrust laws. Knowing this, does the agreement violate any of the antitrust statutes discussed in this chapter? [American Mail Line Limited v. Federal Maritime Comm'n, 503 F.2d 157 (D.C.Cir. 1974)]

4. Tampa Electric is a public utility that serves a large area on the west coast of Florida. It entered into a contract with Nashville Coal Company under which it agreed to purchase all of the coal it would require over a twenty-year period for its station in Tampa. In addition, the agreement stated that Tampa Electric would purchase any additional coal it would require for other stations it might build during the term of the contract. Nashville Coal Company competed with approximately seven hundred producers in the "peninsular Florida" area. It was estimated that Tampa Electric would require 2.25 million tons of coal a year from Nashville Coal Company, an amount that would constitute 0.77 percent of the coal sold in peninsular Florida. Nashville Coal Company subsequently notified Tampa Electric that it could not perform as agreed since the contract was in violation of Section 3 of the Clayton Act. Is the contract enforceable? [Tampa Elec.

---

19. In addition, the commission has investigated office copiers, automobile crash parts, title insurance, and automobile rental industries.

v. Nashville Coal Co., 365 U.S. 320, 81 S.Ct. 623 (1961)]

5. The Phillipsburg National Bank and the Second National Bank both conducted business as full-service banks in the town of Phillipsburg. Five other full-service banks operated in the Lehigh Valley area, which encompasses Phillipsburg and a half dozen other cities. Phillipsburg National Bank and the Second National Bank merged, leaving only two banks in Phillipsburg. In determining whether a violation of Section 7 of the Clayton Act had occurred, the key issue is whether the "relevant geographic market" was the town of Phillipsburg or the entire Lehigh Valley. If it can be determined that the merger lessened competition in the "relevant geographic market" then the merger will be held to violate Section 7. What is the "relevant geographic market" in this case? (Consider where people will most likely go to do their banking after the merger). [United States v. Phillipsburg Nat'l Bank, 399 U.S. 350, 90 S.Ct. 2035 (1970)]

CHAPTER 52

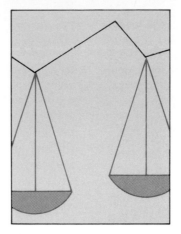

GOVERNMENT REGULATION
Employment and Labor Relations Law

Until the early 1930s, laws at the federal and state levels generally favored management. Collective activities such as unions were discouraged, sometimes forcibly, by employers. Early legislation protecting the rights of employees, such as the National War Labor Board that operated during World War I, was often temporary. Often such legislation was restricted to a particular industry, such as the Railway Labor Act of 1926, which required railroads and their employees to attempt to make employment agreements through representatives chosen by each side. Beginning in 1932, a number of statutes were enacted that greatly increased employees' rights to join unions, to engage in collective bargaining, to receive retirement and income security benefits, to be protected against various discrimination practices, and to have a safe place to work.

UNIONS AND COLLECTIVE BARGAINING

Most of the early legislation to protect employees focused on the rights to join unions and to engage in collective bargaining.

Norris-LaGuardia Act

Congress protected peaceful strikes, picketing, and boycotts in 1932 in the Norris-LaGuardia Act.[1] The statute restricted federal courts in their power to issue injunctions against unions engaged in peaceful strikes. In effect, the act declared a national policy permitting employees to organize.

---

1. 29 USC 101–10, 113–15 (1973).

National Labor Relations Act

The National Labor Relations Act of 1935 (the Wagner Act)[2] established the rights of employees to engage in collective bargaining and to strike. It also created the National Labor Relations Board to oversee elections and to prevent employers and unions from engaging in unfair and illegal union-labor activities and unfair labor practices. The act defined a number of practices as unfair to labor:

1. Interference with the efforts of employees to form, join, or assist labor organizations or to engage in concerted activities for their mutual aid or protection. [Section 8(a)(1)]
2. Employers' domination of a labor organization or contribution of financial or other support to it. [Section 8(a)(2)]
3. Discrimination in the hiring or awarding of tenure to employees for reason of union affiliation. [Section 8(a)(3)]
4. Discrimination against employees for filing charges under the act or giving testimony under the act. [Section 8(a)(4)]
5. Refusal to bargain collectively with the duly designated representative of the employees. [Section 8(a)(5)]

Labor-Managment Relations Act

The Labor-Management Relations Act (Taft-Hartley Act)[3] was signed by President Truman on June 23, 1947, after being passed over his veto. Intended to amend the Wagner Act, it contained provisions protecting employers as well as employees. The act was bitterly opposed by organized labor groups. It did not deny any of the rights that organized labor obtained with the Wagner Act. Rather, it provided a detailed list of unfair labor activities that unions as well as management were now forbidden to practice. Moreover, a "free speech" amendment allowed employers to propagandize against unions prior to any National Labor Relations Board election.

The Closed Shop Made Illegal   A **closed shop** is a company that requires union membership

before employment can be obtained. It was made illegal under the Taft-Hartley Act, which left the union shop legal. A **union shop** does not require membership as a prerequisite for employment but can, and usually does, require that workers join the union after a specified amount of time on the job. Furthermore, the Taft-Hartley Act allowed individual states to pass their own right-to-work laws. A **right-to-work law** makes it illegal for union membership to be required for *continued* employment in any establishment. Thus, union shops are technically illegal in states with right-to-work laws.

The Eighty-Day Cooling Off Period   One of the most controversial aspects of the Taft-Hartley Act was the eighty-day cooling off period. This is a provision in the act that allows federal courts to issue injunctions against strikes that would create a national emergency. The president of the United States can obtain a court injunction that will last for eighty days. Presidents have occasionally used this provision. For example, President Eisenhower applied the eighty-day injunction order to striking steel workers in 1959, President Nixon applied it to striking longshoremen in 1971, and President Carter applied it to striking coal miners in 1978.

Union Conduct That Is Deemed to Contain Unfair Labor Practices   Several union practices were deemed unfair labor practices by the Taft-Hartley Act:

1. Refusing to bargain with the employer if the National Labor Relations Board has designated a representative for the company's employees.
2. Charging new members excessive or discriminatory initiation fees whenever there is a union shop agreement that is not in violation of a right-to-work law.
3. Causing an employer to pay for work not performed (called **featherbedding**).
4. Striking, picketing, and engaging in secondary boycotts for illegal purposes. At the time the act was passed, these illegal purposes included jurisdictional disputes and sympathy strikes. A **jurisdictional dispute** involves two or more unions fighting and striking over which should have control in a particular jurisdiction. A **sym-**

2.   49 Stat. 449, 20 USC 151.
3.   61 Stat. 136, 29 USC 141.

pathy strike occurs when one union strikes in sympathy with another union's problems or another union's strike. A **secondary boycott** is a boycott of a company that is dealing with the struck company. For example, if union workers strike a baking company, then the boycotting of grocery stores that continue to sell that company's products is a secondary boycott.

Labor-Management Reporting and Disclosure Act of 1959

The Labor-Management Reporting and Disclosure Act of 1959 (Landrum-Griffin Act)[4] established an employee bill of rights and reporting requirements for union activities. This act strictly regulated internal union business procedures. A statement in the act points out that Congress found from investigations that there were a number of instances of "breach of trust, corruption, disregard of the rights of individual employees, and other failures to observe high standards of responsibility and ethical conduct which require further and supplementary legislation that will afford necessary protection"[5] of employees and the public.

The act regulates union elections. It requires that regularly scheduled elections of officers occur and that secret ballots be used. Ex-convicts and communists are prohibited from holding union office. Moreover, union officials are made accountable for union property and funds. Members have the right to attend and participate in union meetings, to nominate officers, and to vote in most union proceedings.

Hot Cargo Contracts   In principle, the Taft-Hartley Act made all secondary boycotts illegal. Loopholes, however, appeared. For example, *hot cargo contracts*—wherein employers voluntarily agreed with unions not to handle, use, or deal in the nonunion-produced goods of other employers—became common. This particular type of secondary boycott was not made illegal by the Taft-Hartley Act because the act prevented only unions from inducing employees of an employer

to strike or otherwise act to force the employer not to handle such goods. The Landrum-Griffin Act plugged this loophole and outlawed hot cargo contracts by Section 8(e):

> It shall be unfair and unfair labor practice for any labor organization and any employer to enter into any contract or agreement *   *   * whereby such employer *   *   * agrees to refrain from handling, using, selling, transporting or otherwise dealing in any of the products of any other employer, or to cease doing business with any other person *   *   *.

CIVIL RIGHTS AND EQUAL OPPORTUNITY

At common law, employment was terminable "at will." Any employer could establish the terms and conditions of employment and the rules that the employer wanted the employees to follow. Thus, employers could discriminate for good reasons, bad reasons, or no reason at all. Labor unions were deemed private associations. Therefore, they could determine all membership requirements without oversight of the courts. Common law contract rights of members provided little protection against arbitrary and discriminatory action. In the past several decades, however, as a result of judicial decisions of administrative agency actions, and of legislation, employers and unions have been restricted in their ability to discriminate on the basis of race, religion, creed, age, or sex. The most important statute relating to fair employment practices is Title VII of the Civil Rights Act of 1964.[6] As amended by the Equal Employment Opportunity Act of 1972,[7] the Civil Rights Act is broad in scope, forbidding discrimination in such areas as public accommodation, employment practices, and educational opportunity.

General Provisions of the Civil Rights Act

Title VII of the act applies to employers with fifteen or more employees, to labor unions with

---

4.   73 Stat. 519, 29 USC 401.
5.   Ibid., Section 2b.

6.   78 Stat. 241, 42 USC 2000e et seq.
7.   86 Stat. 103, 42 USC 2000e et seq.

fifteen or more members, to all labor unions that operate hiring halls, and to all employment agencies. The 1972 amendments extend coverage to all state and local governments, government agencies, political subdivisions, and departments. A special section forbids discrimination in most federal government employment. Basically, the act and its amendments eliminate job discrimination against employees, applicants, and union members on the basis of race, color, national origin, religion, and sex.

Race, Color, and National Origin Discrimination   If a company's standards or policies for selecting or promoting employees have the effect of discriminating against blacks or other minorities and do not have a substantial, demonstrable relationship to qualifications for the job in question, they are illegal. Discrimination in employment conditions and benefits is also illegal. Thus, an employer cannot maintain all-white or all-black crews for no demonstrable reason. Nor can an employer grant higher average Christmas bonuses to whites than to blacks.

Religious Discrimination   Employers, except those of religious corporations, associations, or societies, are not allowed to discriminate in their employment practices on the basis of religion. Moreover, employers must make reasonable accommodation to the religious needs of their employees.

Sex Discrimination   Even though states have enacted laws to protect women, they also prohibit by statute the employment of women in certain occupations. Many state statutes have barred women from working during the night or working more than a given number of hours per day or per week. Under the Equal Employment Opportunity Act of 1972, federal courts have struck down many of these laws. For example, states cannot require a separate rest period for women. Furthermore, EEOC guidelines forbid employers from classifying jobs as male or female and from advertising in help-wanted columns that are designated male or female unless sex is a bona fide job qualification. Furthermore, employers cannot have separate male and female seniority lists.

Testing and Educational Requirements   Employers often find it necessary to use interviews and testing procedures in order to choose among a large number of applicants for job openings. Personnel tests are common devices for screening applicants. Minimum educational requirements are also common. In the following case, the Supreme Court of the United States had to grapple with the thorny problem of minimum educational requirements and the use of standardized general intelligence tests as a condition for employment.

BACKGROUND AND FACTS   *The defendant, Duke Power Company, was sued by a number of its black employees for practicing racial discrimination in hiring and assigning employees at its Dan River plant. The plant was organized into five operating departments: (1) labor, (2) coal handling, (3) operation, (4) maintenance, and (5) laboratory testing. Blacks were employed only in the labor department, where the highest paying jobs paid less than the lowest paying jobs in the other four departments (which employed only whites). Promotions were normally made within each deparment on the basis of seniority. Transferees into a department usually began at the lowest position.*

In 1955, the company began to require a high school education for an initial assignment into any department except the labor department. In addition, it required a high school education for any transfer from the coal handling department to any inside department (operations, maintenance, or laboratory). For ten years, this company-wide policy was enforced.

GRIGGS v. DUKE POWER CO.
Supreme Court of the United States, 1971.
401 U.S. 424, 91 S.Ct. 849.

In 1965, when the company abandoned its policy of restricting blacks to the labor department, a high school diploma was nevertheless made a prerequisite to transfer from the labor department into any other department.

From the time the high school requirement was instituted in 1955 to the time the lawsuit was filed, white employees hired before the time of the high school education requirement continued to perform satisfactorily and to achieve promotions in the operating departments.

In 1965, the company added further requirements for any new employees. To qualify for placement in any but the labor department it became necessary to score satisfactorily on two professionally prepared aptitude tests as well as to have a high school education. Completion of high school alone continued to make employees eligible for transfer into the four desirable departments. Of course, blacks who had been employed prior to the time of this new requirement had been ineligible for transfer.

In September 1965, the company began to permit employees who lacked a high school education to qualify for transfer from the labor or coal handling department to an inside job by passing two tests—the Wonderlic Personnel Test, which purported to measure general intelligence, and the Bennett Mechanical Comprehension test. Neither of these tests measured the ability to learn to perform a particular job or category of job. The requisite scores used both for initial hiring and for transfer approximated the national median for high school graduates. Enforcing the median standard screened out approximately half of all high school graduates across the country, not to mention those within the company attempting to pass with a sufficient score. Hence, these two requirements, the diploma and the test, rendered a markedly disproportionate number of blacks ineligible for employment advancement in the company.

The district court hearing the case initially found that while the company had followed a policy of overt racial discrimination prior to the passage of the Civil Rights Act, such conduct had since ceased. Consequently, the impact of prior inequities was beyond the reach of the corrective action authorized by the act. The Court of Appeals found that Duke Power Company had no discriminatory intent in adopting the diploma and test requirements and that the standards had been applied fairly to both whites and blacks. On this basis, it concluded that there was no violation of the Civil Rights Act.

BURGER, Chief Justice.

*   *   *   *

We granted the writ in this case to resolve the question whether an employer is prohibited by the Civil Rights Act of 1964, Title VII, from requiring a high school education or passing of a standardized general intelligence test as a condition of employment in or transfer to jobs when (a) neither standard is shown to be significantly related to successful job performance, (b) both requirements operate to disqualify Negroes at a substantially higher rate than white applicants, and (c) the jobs in question formerly had been filled only by white employees as part of a longstanding practice of giving preference to whites.

* * * *

The objective of Congress in the enactment of Title VII is plain from the language of the statute. It was to achieve equality of employment opportunities and remove barriers that have operated in the past to favor an identifiable group of white employees over other employees. Under the Act, practices, procedures, or tests neutral on their face, and even neutral in terms of intent, cannot be maintained if they operate to "freeze" the status quo of prior discriminatory employment practices.

* * * *

Congress did not intend by Title VII, however, to guarantee a job to every person regardless of qualifications. In short, the Act does not command that any person be hired simply because he was formerly the subject of discrimination, or because he is a member of a minority group. Discriminatory preference for any group, minority or majority, is precisely and only what Congress has proscribed. What is required by Congress is the removal of artificial, arbitrary, and unnecessary barriers to employment when the barriers operate invidiously to discriminate on the basis of racial or other impermissible classification.

* * * *

The Act proscribes not only overt discrimination but also practices that are fair in form, but discriminatory in operation. The touchstone is business necessity. If an employment practice which operates to exclude Negroes cannot be shown to be related to job performance, the practice is prohibited.

On the record before us, neither the high school completion requirement nor the general intelligence test is shown to bear a demonstrable relationship to successful performance of the jobs for which it was used. Both were adopted, as the Court of Appeals noted, without meaningful study of their relationship to job-performance ability. Rather, a vice president of the Company testified, the requirements were instituted on the Company's judgment that they generally would improve the overall quality of the work force.

The evidence, however, shows that employees who have not completed high school or taken the tests have continued to perform satisfactorily and make progress in departments for which the high school and test criteria are now used. The promotion record of present employees who would not be able to meet the new criteria thus suggests the possibility that the requirements may not be needed even for the limited purpose of preserving the avowed policy of advancement within the Company. In the context of this case, it is unnecessary to reach the question whether testing requirements that take into account capability for the next succeeding position or related future promotion might be utilized upon a showing that such long-range requirements fulfill a genuine business need. In the present case the Company has made no such showing.

The U.S. Supreme Court found that the Duke Power Company had in fact violated Title VII of the Civil Rights Act. Accordingly, the company was prohibited from requiring a high school education or the passing of a standardized general intelligence test as a condition of employment or as a prerequisite to transferring from one job to another.   **JUDGMENT AND REMEDY**

INJURY, COMPENSATION, AND SAFETY

Numerous state statutes are designed to protect employees and their families from the risk of accidental injury, death, or disease resulting from their employment. This section covers state workers' compensation acts and the Occupational Safety and Health Act of 1970.

State Workers' Compensation Acts

Workers' compensation laws are usually administered by some administrative agency or board that has quasi-judicial powers. All rulings of such boards are subject to review by the courts, however.

In general, the right to recover under workers' compensation laws is given to the injured employee without regard to the existence of negligence or of fault in the traditional sense. Rather, the right of recovery is predicated on the employment relationship and the fact that the injury *arose out of or was in the course of normal employment*. A simple, two-pronged test for determining whether an employee can receive workers' compensation is:

1. Was the injury accidental?
2. Did the injury arise out of and in the course of employment?

Thus, intentionally inflicted self-injury would not be considered accidental and would not be cov-

ered. In the past, heart attacks or other medical problems arising out of preexisting disease or physical conditions were not covered, but recently they have been.

Basically, employers are under a system of strict liability (see Chapter 3). Few, if any, defenses exist for them. Therefore, the costs of treating workers' injuries are considered a cost of production and are passed on to consumers.

Health and Safety Protection

At the federal level, the main legislation for employee health and safety protection is the Occupational Safety and Health Act of 1970.[8] This act was passed to ensure safe and healthful working conditions for practically every employee in the country. The act created the Occupational Safety and Health Administration (OSHA), the Occupational Safety and Health Review Commission, and the National Institute for Occupational Safety and Health. OSHA promulgates and enforces workers' safety and health standards, as well as conducting inspections and investigations, requires employers to keep detailed records of worker injuries and illnesses, and conducting research.

OSHA inspectors have in the past conducted unannounced inspections. Some employers have deemed this a violation of their constitutional rights, as can be seen in the next case.

---

8. 84 Stat. 1590, 29 USC 553, 651–678.

MARSHALL v. BARLOW'S INC.

Supreme Court of the United States, 1978.
436 U.S. 307, 98 S.Ct. 1816.

BACKGROUND AND FACTS *Prior to 1978, inspectors of the Occupational Safety and Health Administration were not required to obtain permission to enter the work areas of firms subject to OSHA's jurisdiction. In 1975, an OSHA inspector entered the customer service area of Barlow's Inc., an electrical and plumbing installation business. After showing his credentials, the inspector informed the president and general manager, Barlow, that he wished to conduct a search of the working areas of the business.*

Upon inquiry, Barlow learned that no complaint had been received about his company. The inspection was simply the result of a random selection process. On further questioning of the inspector, Barlow learned that he did not have a search warrant. Thereupon, Barlow refused to permit the inspector to enter the working area of his business. He said that he was relying on his rights guaranteed by the Fourth Amendment of the United States Constitution.

OSHA filed suit in the United States District Court and was ultimately successful in having that court issue an order compelling Barlow to admit the inspector for purposes of conducting an occupational safety and health inspection.

Once again, this time with court order in hand, the OSHA inspector presented himself at Barlow's Inc., and Barlow again refused admission. This time Barlow went to court seeking an injunction to prohibit the inspector from making a warrantless search on the ground that it violated the Fourth Amendment of the Constitution.

A court composed of three judges was convened, and it ruled in Barlow's favor, holding that the Fourth Amendment required a warrant for the type of search involved and that the statutory authorization for warrantless inspections under the OSHA statute was unconstitutional. Therefore, a permanent injunction against such searches or inspections was entered. This appeal challenged the validity of that injunction.

WHITE, Justice.

*   *   *   *

The Warrant Clause of the Fourth Amendment protects commercial buildings as well as private homes. To hold otherwise would belie the origin of that Amendment, and the American colonial experience. An important forerunner of the first 10 Amendments to the United States Constitution, the Virginia Bill of Rights, specifically opposed "general warrants, whereby an officer or messenger may be commanded to search suspected places without evidence of a fact committed." The general warrant was a recurring point of contention in the colonies immediately preceding the Revolution. The particular offensiveness it engendered was acutely felt by the merchants and businessmen whose premises and products were inspected for compliance with the several Parliamentary revenue measures that most irritated the colonists. "[T]he Fourth Amendment's commands grew in large measure out of the colonists' experience with the writs of assistance .   .   . [that] granted sweeping power to customs officials and other agents of the King to search at large for smuggled goods."

*   *   *   *

The Secretary urges that an exception from the search warrant requirement has been recognized for "pervasively regulated business[es]."

*   *   *   *

Invoking the Walsh-Healey Act of 1936, the Secretary attempts to support a conclusion that all businesses involved in interstate commerce have long been subjected to close supervision of employee safety and health conditions. But the degree of federal involvement in employee working circumstances has never been of the order of specificity and pervasiveness that OSHA mandates. It is quite unconvincing to argue that the imposition of minimum wages and maximum hours on employers who contracted with the government under the Walsh-Healey Act prepared the entirety of American interstate commerce for regulation of working conditions to the minutest detail. Nor can any but the most fictional sense of voluntary consent to later searches be found in the single fact that one conducts a business affecting interstate commerce; under current practice and law, few businesses can be conducted without having some effect on interstate commerce.

* * * *

We conclude that the concerns expressed by the Secretary do not suffice to justify warrantless inspections under OSHA or vitiate the general constitutional requirement that for a search to be reasonable a warrant must be obtained.

JUDGMENT AND REMEDY *The permanent injunction was upheld. OSHA inspections conducted without warrants were held to be unconstitutional.*

RETIREMENT AND SECURITY INCOME

Social Security

Federal and state governments participate in programs of insurance to cover the financial impact of retirement, disability, death, hospitalization, and unemployment. The key federal law on this subject is the Social Security Act of 1935.[9]

Old Age, Survivors, and Disability Insurance (OASDI)   Both employers and employees must "contribute" under the Federal Insurance Contributions Act (FICA)[10] to help pay for the loss of income benefits on retirement. The basis for the employee's contribution is the employee's annual wage base—the maximum amount of an employee's wages that are subject to the tax. In 1982, for example, the annual wage base was a maximum of $32,400. The employee had to pay 6.7 percent and so, too, did the employer, for a maximum of $4,341.60 per employee.

Benefits are fixed by statute but increase automatically with increases in the cost of living of 3 percent or more between specified periods.

Medicare   A health insurance program, Medicare is administered by the Social Security Administration for people sixty-five years of age and older and for some under sixty-five who are disabled. It has two parts, one pertaining to hospital costs and the other to nonhospital medical costs such as doctors' office visits. People who

have Medicare hospital insurance can obtain additional federal medical insurance if they pay small monthly premiums that increase as the cost of medical care increases.

Private Retirement Plans

There has been significant legislation to regulate retirement plans set up by employers. These plans are used to supplement Social Security benefits. The major piece of this type of legislation is the Employee Retirement Income Security Act of 1974 (ERISA).[11] This act empowers the Labor Management Services Administration of the Department of Labor to enforce its provisions to regulate individuals who operate private pension funds. There are certain fiduciary standards that prohibit activities creating a conflict of interest for individuals entrusted with operating pension plans.

Unemployment Compensation

The United States has a system of unemployment insurance in which employers pay into a fund, the proceeds of which are paid out to qualified unemployed workers. The major piece of federal legislation involved is the Federal Unemployment Tax Act (FUTA),[12] which became law in 1935. This act established a state system that provides unemployment compensation to eligible individuals. The cost of administering the operation of the unemployment insurance program is paid for by the federal government

---

9.   49 Stat. 620, 42 USC 301.
10.   26 USC 3101.

11.   88 Stat. 829, 29 USC 1001.
12.   68A Stat. 439, 26 USC Chapter 23.

out of part of the tax collected. However, the states and the District of Columbia administer programs in their own areas. Employers who are within the provisions of the act are taxed quarterly. Taxes are typically collected by the employers and submitted to the states, which then deposit them with the federal government. The federal government maintains an Unemployment Insurance Fund, in which each state has an account. The tax is based on the percentage of the wage base amount. In 1982, for example, the wage base was $7,000, and the percentage of tax was 3.4.

OTHER EMPLOYMENT LAWS

Among the numerous other employment laws affecting U.S. workers and their employers are the Fair Labor Standards Act, the Davis-Bacon Act, and the Walsh-Healy Public Contracts Act.

Fair Labor Standards Act

The Fair Labor Standards Act (also known as the Wage-Hour Law) was signed by the president on June 25, 1938.[13] It covers child labor, maximum hours, and minimum wages.

Child Labor   The act prohibits oppressive child labor. Children under sixteen years of age cannot be employed full time except by a parent under certain circumstances; nor can children between the ages of sixteen and eighteen be employed in hazardous jobs or those detrimental to their health and well-being. Most states require children under sixteen years of age to obtain work permits.

Maximum Hours   The act provides that any employee who agrees to work more than forty hours must be paid no less than one-and-a-half times his or her regular pay for all hours over forty. Exceptions are made for employees working under the terms of collective bargaining agreements and in some other circumstances.

Minimum Wage   The act provides that minimum hourly wages must be paid to employees in covered industries. Congress periodically revises such minimum wages. The term *wages* is meant to include the reasonable cost of the employer furnishing employees with board, lodging, and other facilities if they are customarily furnished by that employer.

Other Government-Enforced Minimum Wage Laws

In 1931, during the Great Depression, the president signed the Davis-Bacon Act.[14] This act requires the payment of "prevailing wages" to employees of contractors or subcontractors working on government construction projects. In 1936, an act that extended the Davis-Bacon Act was put into effect—the Walsh-Healy Public Contract Act.[15] This act requires a minimum wage as well as overtime pay of time-and-a-half to employees of manufacturers or suppliers entering into contracts with agencies of the federal government.

Recently, these two acts have been attacked as being inflationary and discriminatory.

QUESTIONS AND CASE PROBLEMS

1.   Local 1001 of the Retail Store Employees Union became the certified bargaining representative of some of the employees of Safeco Title Insurance Company in the state of Washington. Contract negotiations between Safeco and the union ended in a deadlock. At this point, the union began picketing the five local independent title companies, as well as the main Safeco office. The picketers carried signs indicating that Safeco was a nonunion employer. Safeco declared that Local 1001 was engaging in a secondary boycott in violation of the National Labor Relations Act. It argued that the union was directing its appeal against Safeco insurance policies. The title companies that were being picketed were not owned by Safeco, and none of the

13.   52 Stat. 1060, 29 USC 201.

14.   46 Stat. 1494, 40 USC 276a.
15.   49 Stat. 2036, 41 USC 35.

daily operations of the title companies was controlled by Safeco. Rather, the title companies simply derived most of their income from the sale of Safeco title insurance policies. Was the Retail Store Employees Union indeed engaging in a secondary boycott? [NLRB v. Retail Store Employees Union, 439 U.S. 819, 99 S.Ct. 81 (S.Ct. 1980)]

2. Donnell was a black General Motors employee in St. Louis who applied for admission into a GM skilled trade apprenticeship program that was established jointly by the company and the United Auto Workers. He was rejected for failure to meet the requirement that all applicants have completed high school. He brought action under Title VII of the Civil Rights Act against both GM and the UAW, claiming that the requirement was discriminatory against blacks as well as unjustified as a business necessity. What was the result? [Donnell v. General Motors Corp., 576 F.2d 1292 (8th Cir. 1978)]

3. Beginning in June 1966, Corning Glass Works started to open up jobs on the night shift to women. The previously separate male and female seniority lists were consolidated, and the women became eligible to exercise their seniority on the same basis as men and to bid for higher-paid night inspection jobs as vacancies occurred. But on January 20, 1969, a new collective bargaining agreement went into effect; it established a new job evaluation system for setting wage rates. This agreement abolished (for the future) separate base wages for night and day shift inspectors and imposed a uniform base wage for inspectors that exceeded the wage rate previously in effect for the night shift. The agreement, however, did allow for a higher "red circle" rate for employees hired prior to January 20, 1969, when working as inspectors on the night shift. This "red circle" wage served essentially to perpetuate the differential in base wages between day and night inspectors. Was Corning in violation of the Civil Rights Act of 1964? [Corning Glass Works v. Brennan, 417 U.S. 188, 94 S.Ct. 839 (S.Ct. 1974)]

4. At an REA shipping terminal, a conveyor belt was inoperative because an electrical circuit had shorted out. The manager called a licensed electrical contractor. When the contractor arrived, REA's maintenance supervisor was in the circuit breaker room. The floor was wet, and the maintenance supervisor was using sawdust to try to soak up the water. While the licensed electrical contractor was attempting to fix the short circuit, standing on the wet floor, he was electrocuted. Simultaneously, REA's maintenance supervisor, who was standing on a wooden platform, was burned and knocked unconscious. OSHA wanted to fine REA Express $1,000 for failure to furnish a place of employment free from recognized hazards. What was the result? [REA Express, Inc. v. Brennan, 495 F.2d 822 (2d Cir. 1974)]

FOCUS ON ETHICS

Government Regulation

Government regulation is all-pervasive in our economic and legal system. It includes consumer protection, environmental protection, antitrust law, employment, and labor relations law. In all areas of government regulation, one can ask the question, "Why does government regulation exist?" Pure capitalist ideology has as its basis a minimum of government intervention in the economic system. Yet today virtually every area of economic activity is regulated by government. Is this increased government regulation due to a change in the capitalist ideology, or is it because the reality has changed? Some say that Adam Smith's "invisible hand" worked well in the absence of large corporations. But today, with the existence of large, impersonal corporations, perhaps the invisible hand cannot work as well as before.

EMPLOYMENT DISCRIMINATION

In the past, traditional concerns in the area of employment discrimination centered on the failure to hire, retain, and promote with equality. Equal opportunity regulations were therefore designed to reduce or eliminate discriminatory practices. Attempts

at "making up" for past patterns of discrimination have resulted in affirmative action programs. Many of these affirmative action programs have upset majority groups. Cases of reverse discrimination have been litigated as a consequence.

An ethical question arises as to the appropriate degree of reverse discrimination in the labor marketplace. How much should the current generation of white male employees pay for past discriminatory practices of employers?

Women, certainly, have come to the forefront in the area of job discrimination. Newer, more subtle arguments state that women have suffered economic discrimination for years and that if comparable-worth evaluations of jobs are made, these patterns of discrimination will be revealed. The doctrine of comparable worth is relatively new in the area of employment law. Equal pay for equal work has already found its place, but comparable-worth evaluations are based on a different premise. How does one measure the comparative worth of different jobs so as to equalize wages? The answers are again not easy. Indeed, is comparable worth an ethical matter with which companies should concern themselves? Or, should companies

wait until they are brought into court and forced to adjust pay scales before eliminating sex-based discrimination in salaries? Here we see a conflict: does a company owe its primary obligation to the shareholder or to the employee? Finally, should a company attempt to redress prior discrimination for which current management was not responsible?

Not all members of minorities believe strongly in affirmative action programs and minority hiring requirements. Even fewer are enamored of comparable-worth doctrines. Why? Because in a competitive economic system, any enforced system of quotas or equal pay will in fact hurt superior members of the protected groups. An analogy might be grades in a business law class. If everyone received an A no matter what type of work he or she did, under normal conditions the potential A student would be harmed. No one on the outside would be able to tell whether that student was actually better than other students since all would have received A's. The same analysis holds for superior members of protected minorities. Under a quota system, for example, the superior member of a protected minority will have a difficult time demonstrating that he or she truly does have superior talents. After all, outsiders could argue that he or she obtained the job simply because of the quota system, and not because of merit.

In any event, society has definitely changed its thinking with respect to employment. At one time, the employer could simply hire and fire at will. Such is no longer the case. Laws affecting employment have revolutionized parts of our economy and their efforts continue.

ENVIRONMENTAL CONCERNS

To what extent is business required to concern itself with the conservation of natural resources? Does a company have to wait until it is besieged by protesters before it acts, such as in the case of Weyerhauser in the northwest? This forest products company found itself severely criticized by protesters who accused it of raping the forest. It ultimately set up an extensive program of replanting trees and became more selective in its cutting, thereafter cutting in a manner to conserve natural resources.

Dow Chemical, as another example, devised and implemented a massive program of pollution control directed toward waste reduction and the conservation of raw materials. Manufacturing processes were closely scrutinized to increase operating efficiency, to recycle raw materials formerly vented to the air or lost to the sewer, and to utilize waste products. While in its press releases Dow touted its good citizenship, as in many of the "ethical" moves of business, the principal emphasis was on profits. Pollution control meant savings that could be transferred directly into higher company profits. The issue, of course, is the extent to which a company should consider as its ethical responsibility the protection of

our environment, particularly if such protection means lower profits.

The fact is that companies typically cannot protect the environment without incurring higher production costs, costs that are ultimately passed on to consumers. If one company among many decides to protect the environment and thereby incur higher costs, that company will have profits lower than all the other companies. Ultimately, if only one company accepts its ethical responsibility to protect the environment, that one company will go out of business. Perhaps here we can see the ultimate dilemma in a competitive economic system. Companies cannot be socially responsible alone. If they try to accept this responsibility alone, it may lead to their ultimate demise. Consequently, we can argue that it is because of our competitive system that we require government regulation, particularly in the environmental protection arena. It is only through government regulation of all competitors that we will achieve a reduction in the amount of environmental destruction due to production processes.

ANTITRUST QUESTIONS

In the last quarter century, antitrust sanctions have been applied to individual corporate officers and directors who have knowingly violated antitrust laws. Jail sentences were given to officers and directors of a corporation due to antitrust violations for the first time in the 1960s when the great electrical conspiracy was discovered. One must ask the question, should a director or officer of a corporation knowingly allow the corporation to engage in activities that are

clearly in violation of antitrust laws? Again we are faced with the problem of where the duty of loyalty lies for a director or officer of a corporation. If the only duty is to the shareholders, then we would not have a difficult time arguing that directors and officers of a corporation should ignore antitrust laws "as long as they can get away with it." On the other hand, if the ethical responsibility of directors and officers of a corporation is to the public at large, then deliberate acts in violation of antitrust laws should never be performed.

But what about antitrust laws that, in fact, seem unreasonable? In particular, the Robinson-Patman Act has been lambasted by lawyers, businesspersons, and economists alike for many years. In principle, this statute was passed to protect the small businessperson from the buying power of chain stores. In practice, however, it has been used on numerous occasions by small stores to effectively extort tribute from large firms. In other words, every time a large operation was able to undercut the price of a smaller operation in the same line of business, the smaller concern entered into antitrust litigation citing violation of the Robinson-Patman Act.

Numerous economic studies have shown that the Robinson-Patman Act has probably resulted in economic inefficiency. But does that mean it should be ignored? Not necessarily, because we may have an ethical responsibility to maintain a large number of small businesses in the United States. After all, the larger the business, presumably the greater the amount of political power. If we wish to maintain a diffuse amount of political power within our system, perhaps we should foster legislation that prevents small firms from being forced out of business by larger businesses, even if the latter are more efficient.

DISCUSSION QUESTIONS

1. Does government regulation work? Why or why not?

2. "The only necessary antitrust legislation we need is that which already exists in the competitive marketplace, and it is called competition." Discuss and analyze this extreme view of antitrust legislation.

3. It is often said that the regulated industries capture the regulators. What does this mean? Is there any way to avoid this "capture" phenomenon?

4. What is a company's ethical responsibility to its workers? How can a company balance its ethical responsibilities to its workers and its legal responsibilities to its shareholders?

UNIT IX

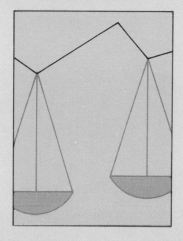

PROTECTION OF PROPERTY AND OTHER INTERESTS

CHAPTER 53

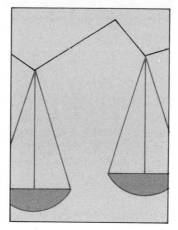

Nature and
Ownership
of Real Property

Real property is land and the buildings and plants and trees that it contains. Real property, also called real estate or realty, is immovable, whereas personal property is movable.

From earliest times, property has provided a means for survival. Primitive peoples lived off the fruits of the land, eating the vegetation and wildlife. Later, as the wildlife was domesticated and the vegetation cultivated, property provided pasturage and farmland. In the twelfth and thirteenth centuries, land was a symbol of the power of feudal lords. The more land they held, the more powerful they were. After the age of feudalism passed, property continued to be an indicator of family wealth and social position.

NATURE OF REAL PROPERTY

Real property usually means land, but other aspects that must be considered are subsurface and air rights, plant life and vegetation, and fixtures.

Land

Land includes the soil on the surface of the earth and natural or artificial structures that are attached to it. Land also includes all the waters contained on or under the surface and all the air space above it. The exterior boundaries of land extend straight down to the center of the earth and straight up to the farthest reaches of the atmosphere (subject to certain qualifications).

Subsurface and Air Rights

The owner of real property has relatively exclusive rights to the air space above the land as well as the soil and minerals underneath it. Until fifty years ago, the right to use air space was not too significant, but today, commercial airlines and high-rise office buildings and apartments use the air space regularly. Early cases involving air rights dealt with matters such as the right to run a telephone wire across a person's property when the wire did not touch any of the property[1] and whether a bullet shot over the person's land constituted trespass.[2]

Today, cases involving air rights present questions such as the right of commercial and private planes to fly over property, and the right of individuals and governments to seed clouds and produce artificial rain. Flights over private land do not normally violate the property owners' rights unless the flights are low and frequent, causing a direct interference with the enjoyment and use of the land.[3] Likewise, if cloud-seeding activities interfere with the enjoyment and use of the land, the property owner may be able to sue to stop them. The owner of land is entitled to use the property without others causing unreasonable noise, pollution, or vibrations.

Property ownership includes all the subsurface of the land. The boundaries of the land extend straight down to the center of the earth. Any oil, minerals, and treasure found under the surface of the land belong to the landowner. Any intrusion into the subsurface of the land violates the rights of its owner.

For example, suppose Homestake Mining Company has a mine directly adjoining Redland Company's land. Homestake digs a shaft several hundred feet deep and hits a rich vein of ore. Homestake begins mining operations and follows the vein up and across into Redland's property. Although Homestake does not intend to mine any of Redland's ore, it is still liable to Redland for trespass. Redland can recover damages for the ore taken from below the surface of its land.

Significant limitations on either air rights or subsurface rights normally have to be indicated on the deed transferring title at the time of purchase. Where no such encumbrances are noted, a purchaser can expect unfettered right to possession of the property. If any preexisting covenant unknown to the purchaser interferes with

these rights, the purchaser can sue for breach of warranty of title. However, most state statutes limit the time period in which the purchaser can sue. An alternative lawsuit is for breach of the covenant of quiet enjoyment. There is a limit on the time for bringing such a suit, but it does not begin to run until after the discovery of the breach.

Separation of Surface and Subsurface Rights   In many states the owner of the surface of a piece of land is not the owner of the subsurface. Thus, the land ownership is separated. Subsurface rights can be extremely valuable, as these rights include the ownership of minerals and, in most states, oil and natural gas. (Water rights are also extremely valuable, especially in the West.)

When the ownership is separated this way (into surface and subsurface rights), each owner can pass title to what he or she owns without consent of the other. Each owner has the right to use the land owned, and in some cases a conflict will arise between a surface owner's use and the subsurface owner's need to extract minerals, oil, and natural gas. States have had to decide which ownership is the *dominant tenement* (to be discussed in Chapter 54), in order to determine the rights and liabilities of the subsurface owner who extracts minerals, oil, and gas from the surface owner's property.

In cases of separated ownership, a conflict arises with regard to the extraction of coal. Coal is sometimes found very near the surface, and surface mining requires the removal of the surface itself. Coal mining companies must therefore deal with both owners (surface and subsurface) before having full rights to mine the coal.

Plant Life and Vegetation

Plant life, both natural and cultivated, is also considered to be real property. Natural vegetation has always been considered a part of the realty. In many instances, the natural vegetation (such as trees) adds greatly to the value of the realty. When a parcel of land is sold and the land has growing crops on it, the sale includes the crops, unless otherwise specified in the sales contract. When crops are sold by themselves, they are considered to be personal property or goods.

---

1. Butler v. Frontier Telephone Co., 186 N.Y. 486, 79 N.E. 716 (1906). Stringing a wire across someone's property violates the air rights of that person. Leaning walls, buildings, projecting eave spouts and roofs also violate the air rights of the property owner.
2. Herrin v. Sutherland, 74 Mont. 587, 241 P. 328 (1925). Shooting over a person's land constitutes trespass.
3. United States v. Causby, 328 U.S. 256, 66 S.Ct. 1062 (1946).

Consequently, the sale of crops (whether they are severed by the buyer or the seller) is a sale of goods, and it is governed by the Uniform Commercial Code rather than by real property law. [UCC 2-107(2)]

Fixtures

Certain personal property can become so closely associated with the real property to which it is attached that the law views it as real property. Such property is known as a **fixture**—a thing affixed to realty. A thing is *affixed* to realty when it is attached to it by roots, embedded in it, or permanently attached by means of cement, plaster, bolts, nails, or screws. The fixture can be physically attached to real property, be attached to another fixture, or even be without any actual physical attachment to the land, as long as the owner *intends* the property to be a fixture.

Fixtures are included in the sale of land if the sales contract does not provide otherwise. The sale of a house includes the land and the house and garage on it as well as the cabinets, plumbing, and windows. Since these are permanently affixed to the property, they are considered a part of it. However, unless otherwise agreed, the curtains and throw rugs are not included. Items such as drapes and window-unit air-conditioners are difficult to classify. Thus, a contract for the sale of a house or commercial realty should indicate which items of this sort are included in the sale.

Intention In order to determine whether or not a certain item is a fixture, the *intention* of the party who placed the fixture must be examined. If the facts indicate that the person intended the item to be a fixture, then it will be a fixture.

When the intent of the party who placed the fixture on the realty is in dispute, the courts usually determine intent based on either or both of the following factors:

1. If the property attached cannot be removed without causing substantial damage to the remaining realty, it is usually deemed a fixture.
2. If the property attached is so adapted to the rest of the realty as to become a part thereof, it is usually deemed a fixture. This can result from the custom in a given community. For example, a built-in stove in an apartment is usually deemed a fixture even if it could be removed without substantial damage to the remaining realty, because it is the custom in most communities to treat it as a fixture.

These rules apply equally to tenants who affix property to the leased premises during the period of their tenancy. The fact that the tenant may be unaware of these rules is irrelevant.

Sometimes the intent of the owner is readily implied by the circumstances. To illustrate: The owner of a house buys a workbench for the garage. The workbench is not bolted to the wall, but it cannot be easily removed. If the owner intended the workbench to become a fixture—part of the garage—then it is a fixture. If the owner plans to remove it after a couple of months, then it is not a fixture. The objective intention of the owner will control.

Certain items can only be attached to property permanently; such items are fixtures. It is assumed that the owner intended them to be fixtures, since they had to be permanently attached to the property. A tile floor, cabinets, and carpeting are examples. Also, when a piece of property is custom-made for installation on real property, such as storm windows, the property is usually classified as a fixture. Again, it is assumed that the owner intended the piece of property to become part of the real property.

The following case illustrates the court's interpretation of whether certain items are considered as fixtures.

PAUL v. FIRST NAT'L BANK OF CINCINNATI

Common Pleas Court of Ohio, Hamilton County, 1976. 52 Ohio Misc. 77, 369 N.E.2d 488.

BACKGROUND AND FACTS *The plaintiff purchased an elegant residence known as Long Acres from the defendant bank, which was the executor of the estate of Augustine Long. When possession was delivered to plaintiff, he found items missing from the property. Long's will left to his children "all household furnishings, appliances, decoration, and equipment." Plaintiff claimed the children had wrongfully removed and* *converted certain fixtures that should have remained with the property.*

BLACK, Judge.

*   *   *   *

The converted items must be considered in two groups, as follows:

(1) 4 Handmade lighting fixtures around swimming pool
     Lighting fixture in living quarters of apartment over stable
     2 Lighting fixtures removed from chapel
     3 Metal cranes
     4 Garden statues.
(2) Oramental housing over well
     Mercury statue
     Walnut organ bench.

In the court's judgment, group (1) are legally, classified as "fixtures," and group (2) are "appurtenances" [articles adapted for use to the property to which they are connected], under the intent and meaning of the purchase contract. This conclusion is based on three considerations: the law of fixtures, the intent and meaning of the purchase contract, and the intent and meaning of the testamentary gift to the children.

*   *   *   *

In *Masheter v. Boehm* (1974), 37 Ohio St.2d 68, 307 N.E.2d 533, the Supreme Court designated, in paragraph two of the syllabus, six "facts" to be considered in determining whether an item is a fixture:

(1) The nature of the property;
(2) The manner in which the property is annexed to the realty;
(3) The purpose for which the annexation is made;
(4) The intention of the annexing party to make the property a part of the realty;
(5) The degree of difficulty and extent of any loss involved in removing the property from the realty; and
(6) The damage to the severed property which such removal would cause.

As the Supreme Court ruled, the expression of "a comprehensive and generally applicable rule of law" about fixtures has bedevilled the courts for years and is complicated by the need for different definitions in those situations where the relationship between the parties is different. That case dealt with eminent domain (what comprises the "real estate" which was appropriated?), while the instant case deals with a buyer and a seller, and the distributees under a will. Nevertheless, the six considerations listed in *Masheter v. Boehm, supra,* are pertinent and applicable in the interpretation of "all fixtures relating to said real estate" in paragraph II of Exhibit "A" of the purchase contract.

Using the Supreme Court's considerations, the light "fixtures" (there is no other available word) from the swimming pool, the stable apartment and the chapel are clearly fixtures in contemplation of law. They are of a type universally recognized as fixtures. This is true even though the pool "fixtures" were hung on brackets and could be unplugged and simply lifted off the brackets. But they were designed and produced solely and only for the swimming pool, from the same design as was used for the light fixture in the porte cochere (which was not removed). Further, the poles from which they were taken are barren and incomplete without them.

The three metal cranes and the four garden statues also meet five of the six criteria, in the judgment of the court. The "nature" of these items is that they were a part of the total elegance of Long Acres. They are not the type of fixture which would be commonly found on other lawns or in other gardens in Hamilton County, but they are an integral part of this sumptuous country estate. The cranes were "annexed" by being bolted or screwed into concrete foundations in a manner similar to the annexation of the marble table in the Great Hall, an item clearly admitted by all defendants to be a fixture passing with the real estate. The 4 garden statues (busts?) were not simply placed on top of their columns, but were held in place by 6-inch pipe protruding from the columns into the bases of the statues. The purpose of fixing these into position was to ensure their presence and preservation as part and parcel of the landscape and approach to Long Acres. These cranes and statues were not items moved about at the whim of the owner or according to the seasons: they were permanent implacements, intended to be part of the continuing visual effect of the estate. While no great difficulty was encountered in removing any of them, their absence is a source of loss. The cranes were prominent in the approach to the front door, and that approach is damaged without them. They are shown in several photographs attached to the appraisal which was prepared by the Cincinnati Real Estate Board and considered by plaintiff before entering into the purchase contract. The removal of the statues leaves the columns on which they stood barren and incomplete; the columns appear to have been vandalized.

Group (2), being the ornamental well housing, the Mercury statue and the organ bench, were not attached in a permanent way. However, interpreting the contract from its four corners, in the light of all the facts and circumstances in evidence, the Court concludes that these items were "appurtenances" to the real estate, both in contemplation of law and in interpretation of this word as used in the purchase contract.

The word "appurtenance" means more than rights of way or other incorporeal rights: it includes an article adapted to the use of the property to which it is connected and which is intended to be a permanent accession to the freehold.

All three items in group (2) form a part of the character of Long Acres and enhance the style of its elegance. They are appurtenant to Long Acres in the sense that they are necessarily connected with the use and enjoyment of this country estate. They are incidental to the total value of this estate. The source of that value is not only the grand design but also all of the details whereby that design is executed: the location of the house on the property, the sweep of the driveway as it approaches the porte cochere, the spread-out location of the barns and other outbuildings, the majesty of the formal gardens, the spaciousness of the lawns on every side, and all the details of the exterior and interior of the mansion itself.

To allow the heirs to walk off with an organ bench, leaving the built-in organ behind would be plainly ridiculous. You cannot play an organ while standing up, and no ordinary bench will do.

The Mercury statue is pictured in two photographs included in the appraisal of Long Acres which was considered by plaintiff before purchase. It may have been moved from the pedestal from time to time by the Long family, and it was not a "sun dial," despite this label in the appraisal. But interpreting the contract in the light of all facts and circumstances in evidence, the Court concludes that these items were appurtenances passing with the real estate.

The stove was not "built-in." It was surrounded by cabinets and an overhead fan and shield. But it could be pulled out from that location, it is a replaceable item, it is an "appliance" under the terms of the will, and it was listed as a chattel in the probate inventory and so disposed of in settling the probate estate.

The term "stair carpeting" is a misnomer. This was a small oriental rug of a size commonly called a "throw rug." It was tacked down to the short set of stairs from the Great Hall to the music room, but that was to keep it from slipping and causing injury. It was a floor rug adapted to this location on what the court considers a temporary basis. It was a "furnishing" which was given to the children by the will; and it was listed as a chattel in the probate inventory and was so disposed of in settling the probate estate.

*   *   *   *

However, the Long children plainly had no right to cut down and remove light fixtures, or to remove and refuse to return the other items comprising group (1). The status of these items is not and was not in doubt, in the judgment of this Court, and the taking was accomplished with knowledge (both actual and constructive) of the legal status of the items, with purpose to deprive the purchaser of them permanently, without a reasonable or lawful excuse, and to the purchaser's injury.

*   *   *   *

The conclusion of the court is that with respect to the conversion of property (Count 1), damages shall be the fair market value of replacement articles (determined as of the day of taking); the principle is to restore plaintiff fairly and reasonably to his position before the wrongful taking of these articles.

The trial court's judgment for the plaintiff was affirmed. The plaintiff recovered the fair market value of the fixtures and appurtenances improperly taken from the estate.   **JUDGMENT AND REMEDY**

Trade Fixtures A **trade fixture** is any article placed in or attached to a rented building by the tenant in order to pursue the trade or business for which the tenant occupies the premises. Trade fixtures are generally removable without material alteration to the premises. Indeed, they are not true fixtures, since the person who installs them intends to remove them eventually. In many cases, the item would be a fixture if the owner had installed it but not if the lessee installed it.

For example, suppose Helen Getty rents a small structure located on a main highway and installs gas pumps and a storage tank. The pumps and tanks are trade fixtures, and Getty can remove them when the lease ends. Naturally, if any damages occur to the property when Getty removes the trade fixtures, she must pay the landlord for the damage.

OWNERSHIP INTEREST IN REAL PROPERTY—ESTATES IN LAND

Ownership of property is an abstract concept that cannot exist independent of the legal system. No one can actually possess or *hold* a piece of land, the air above, the earth below, and all the water contained on it. The legal system therefore recognizes certain rights and duties that constitute the ownership interest in real property.

Freehold Estates

Rights of ownership in real property, called **estates,** are classified according to their nature, interest, and extent. Two major categories of estates are freehold estates, which are held indefinitely, and less than freehold estates, which are held for a predetermined time. There are two kinds of freehold estates—estates in fee, and life estates.

Estates in Fee   There are two kinds of estates in fee: fee simple absolute and fee simple defeasible.

The Fee Simple Absolute   The **fee simple absolute,** or fee simple, is the highest and most complete estate known to the law. It is limited absolutely to a person and his or her heirs and is assigned forever without limitation or condition. In a fee simple, the owner has the greatest aggregation of rights, privileges, and powers possible. The rights that accompany a fee simple include the right to use the land for whatever purpose the owner sees fit, subject to laws that prevent the owner from unreasonably interfering with another person's land, and subject to applicable zoning laws.

A fee simple is potentially infinite in duration and can be disposed of by will or by deed (by selling or giving it away). When the owner of a fee simple dies without a will, the fee simple passes to the owner's legal heirs. The owner of a fee simple absolute also has the rights of *exclusive* possession and waste. *Waste* means that the owner can use the land without replenishing what is used. If Albert Samuelson has fee simple absolute ownership of fifteen acres in the mountains, he can mine any ore on that land without replacing it. The term *waste* refers to injury done to the land by one rightfully in possession of the land.

At early common law, a fee simple absolute could be conveyed only by stating that the conveyance was "to A and his heirs." The words "and his heirs" denoted the fee simple as infinite in duration and distinguished it from other estates such as the *fee simple defeasible* (which is defined below). In the United States today, these so-called words of limitation have been eliminated and a conveyance "to A" as well as "to A and his heirs" will convey a fee simple.

The Fee Simple Defeasible   A **fee simple defeasible** [4] encompasses a number of estates that

almost constitute absolute ownership.[5] Essentially, a fee simple defeasible is a fee simple that can end if a specified condition or event occurs.

For example, a conveyance "to A and his heirs as long as the land is used for charitable purposes" creates a fee simple defeasible. In this type of conveyance the original owner retains a *partial* ownership interest. As long as the condition does not occur, A has full ownership rights, but if the specified condition does occur (for example, if the land ceases to be used for charitable purposes), then the land reverts, or returns, to the original owner.[6] The interest that the original owner retains is called a *future interest* since, if it arises, it will arise in the future.[7] (But a so-called future interest is still a form of present property ownership that has a current market value.)

Consider another example. Simon deeds some land to XYZ Church "for as long as this land is used for church purposes and no longer." For two years, the land is used by the church for a playground for the children going to Sunday School. The church then sells the land to Smith, who intends to build an apartment building on it. As soon as Simon learns of the sale to Smith, he begins a court action to have himself declared the owner of the land.[8] Since Simon deeded a fee simple determinable to XYZ Church, he will succeed in his court action.

The church has absolute ownership of the land as long as it is used for church purposes. XYZ Church can even sell the land or otherwise dispose of it to those who will also use it for church purposes. However, as soon as the land

---

4.   The word *defeasible* refers to an owner's ability to lose ownership of property, whether the loss is voluntary or involuntary.

5.   The term *fee simple defeasible* encompasses the fee simple determinable, the fee simple subject to special limitation, the fee simple subject to condition subsequent, and the fee simple subject to an executory interest.

6.   If the original owner is not living at the time, the land passes to his or her heirs. In other words, once the condition occurs, A is divested of rights regardless of whether the original owner to (or through) whom the land reverts is alive.

7.   In the specific example given in the text, the future interest that the owner holds is known as a *possibility of reverter.* In the conveyance "to A, but if the premises are ever used for the sale of alcoholic beverages then to B," the original owner has conveyed the entire interest. The owner has conveyed a fee simple defeasible to A and future interest to B.

8.   Note that the instant the condition is broken, legal ownership automatically vests in Simon.

stops being used for the specified purpose, the fee simple determinable terminates and ownership reverts to Simon.

The Life Estate A **life estate** is an estate that lasts for the life of some specified individual. A conveyance "to A for his life" creates a life estate.[9] Estates for life can be created by an act of law or by an act of the parties.

In a life estate, the life tenant has fewer rights of ownership than the holder of a fee simple defeasible. The life tenant has the right to use the land provided no waste (injury to the land) is committed. In other words, the life tenant cannot injure the land in a manner that would adversely affect the owner of the future interest in it. The life tenant can use the land to harvest crops or, if mines and oil wells are already on the land, can extract minerals and oil from it. But the life tenant cannot exploit the land by creating new wells or mines.

Consider some examples. Michaelson deeds land to Hitchcock for life. Oil is found under that land. Agents of Mobil Oil Company negotiate an oil and gas lease with Hitchcock, but Mobil never contacts Michaelson. Mobil merely starts drilling an oil well. When Michaelson learns of this, he demands that Mobil stop drilling or negotiate a lease with him. Michaelson can enforce his demand because a life tenant alone cannot make a binding oil and gas lease upon the property if no drilling was taking place at the time the life estate was created. By the same token, Hitchcock cannot sell any of the timber that is on the land without Michaelson's approval, because the removal of standing timber will reduce the value of the land.

However, Hitchcock has the right to possess the land, and if it is farmland, to cultivate it and grow cash crops, retaining the proceeds, or to raise animals for market. Neither activity will reduce the value of the land, and such use is what was intended when the life estate was created.

The life tenant has the right to mortgage the life estate and create liens, easements, and leases;

but none can extend beyond the life of the tenant. In addition, the owner of a life estate has exclusive right of possession during his or her life. Exclusive possession, however, is subject to the rights of the future interest holder to come onto the land and protect the future interest.

Along with these rights, the life tenant also has some *duties*—to keep the property in repair and to pay property taxes. In short, the owner of the life estate has the same rights as a fee simple owner except that the value of the property must be kept intact for the future interest holder, less the decrease in value resulting from normal use of the property allowed by the life tenancy.

Nonfreehold Estates

The **less than freehold estates** are possessory real estate interests treated for some purposes as personal rather than real property. They are covered in this chapter for the sake of convenience because they relate to ownership of an interest in land. These estates include:

1. The tenancy for years.
2. The tenancy from period to period.
3. The tenancy at will.
4. The tenancy by sufferance.

All involve the transfer of the right to possession for *a specified period of time.*

The owner or lessor (landlord) conveys the property to the lessee (tenant) for a certain period of time. In every nonfreehold estate, the tenant has a *qualified* right to exclusive possession (qualified by the right of the landlord to enter upon the premises to assure that no waste is being committed). This is called a **leasehold estate.** The tenant can use the land, for example, by harvesting crops, but cannot injure the land by such activities as cutting down timber for sale or extracting oil.

Tenancy for Years A **tenancy for years** is created by express contract (which can sometimes be oral) by leasing the property for a specified period of time. For example, signing a one-year lease to rent an apartment creates a tenancy for years. At the end of the period specified in the lease, the lease ends (without notice) and possession of the apartment returns to the lessor. If the tenant dies during the period of the lease,

---

9. A less common type of life estate is created by the conveyance "to A for the life of B." This is known as an estate *pur autre vie,* or an estate for the life of another.

the lease passes to the tenant's heirs as personal property. Often, leases include renewal or extension provisions.

Tenancy from Period to Period A **tenancy from period to period** is created by a lease that does not specify how long it is to last but does specify that rent is to be paid at certain intervals. This type of tenancy is automatically renewed for another rental period unless properly terminated. For example, a tenancy from period to period is created by a lease that states, "Rent is due on the tenth day of every month." This is a tenancy from month to month. This type of tenancy can also be from week to week or from year to year. A tenancy from period to period sometimes arises when a landlord allows a tenant under a tenancy for years to hold over and continue paying monthly or weekly rent.

At common law, in order to terminate a tenancy from period to period, the landlord or tenant must give one period's notice to the other party. If the tenancy is month to month, one month's notice must be given. If the tenancy is week to week, one week's notice must be given. State statutes often define the required notice of termination in a tenancy from period to period. Therefore, the particular statute in question should be referred to in order to determine the proper time for notice of termination.

Tenancy at Will Suppose the landlord rents an apartment to a tenant "for as long as both agree." In such a case, the tenant receives a leasehold estate known as a **tenancy at will.** At common law, either party can terminate the tenancy without notice. This type of estate usually arises when a tenant who has been under a tenancy for years retains possession after the termination date of that tenancy with the landlord's consent. Furthermore, nothing is mentioned in the original lease about the effects of what is called a holding over, or holdover. Before the tenancy has been converted into a tenancy from period to period

(by the periodic payment of rent), it is a tenancy at will, terminable by either party without notice. Once the tenancy is treated as a tenancy from period to period, a termination notice must conform to the one already discussed. The death of either party or the voluntary commission of waste by the tenant will terminate a tenancy at will.

Tenancy by Sufferance A **tenancy by sufferance** is not a true tenancy. It is the mere possession of land without right. A tenancy by sufferance is not an estate, since it is created by a tenant *wrongfully* holding over. Whenever a life estate, tenancy for years, tenancy from period to period, or tenancy at will ends, and the tenant continues to retain possession of the premises without the owner's permission, a tenancy by sufferance is created. However, a tenancy by sufferance can be converted into a leasehold if a landlord accepts rent from the tenant. If the landlord does not accept rent and ultimately evicts the tenant, the tenant is liable to the landlord as if he or she were a trespasser.

Termination As long as a tenancy exists, a landlord can collect rent in full, regardless of whether the premises are actually occupied by the tenant. Thus, when a tenant wrongfully abandons the premises and refuses to pay rent, the landlord can permit the premises to remain vacant, refuse to recognize the attempted surrender by the tenant, and bring a lawsuit to collect the rent as it comes due. A tenant who wrongfully abandons the premises and refuses to pay rent cannot require that the landlord find another tenant to pay the rent. In many circumstances, however, the landlord has a duty created by statute or judicial decisions to mitigate his or her damages. As a result, if other tenants are available, the landlord may be unable to collect damages for the tenant's breach of the lease. The issue of termination of tenancy is examined in the following case.

EDWARD BANKERS & CO. v. SPRADLIN

Court of Civil Appeals of Texas, Houston (1st Dist.), 1978. 575 S.W.2d 585.

BACKGROUND AND FACTS *The defendant, Spradlin, leased space, known as Suite 325, in an office building managed by the plaintiff. The lease was for a five-year term. Two years after the lease was signed, Spradlin moved to Suite 1000, a larger and more expensive space in the same building. Both Suite 325 and Suite 1000 were owned and managed* *by the same company. The move to the larger suite was made after an oral agreement between Spradlin and the manager of the building, which was owned by Edward Bankers & Co. After Spradlin moved his offices to Suite 1000, he made no further payments on Suite 325. The plaintiff brought this action against him for recovery of the rental payments on Suite 325.*

EVANS, Justice.

*   *   *   *

The surrender of leased premises by a tenant and the acceptance of possession by the landlord ordinarily releases the tenant from further obligation to pay rentals. An agreement of surrender and release may be express, or it may be implied from the circumstances and acts of the parties. The question of whether there has been an acceptance by the landlord releasing the tenant from further obligations under the lease involves a determination of the intent of the parties, and this may present an issue of fact.

The jury could have concluded from the testimony that Spradlin agreed to vacate his office space in suite 325 and to move his offices to suite 1000, with a substantial increase in his monthly rent, upon the assurance of the plaintiff's building manager that he would not have any further obligation to make rental payments on suite 325. The jury might also have inferred from the testimony that the plaintiff accepted Spradlin's surrender of the office space in suite 325 and that when Spradlin vacated those premises, the plaintiff resumed possession and made use of the space for its own purposes. Thus, from the circumstances presented by the evidence the jury could have concluded that there was a mutual understanding and agreement beween the parties to terminate Spradlin's lease on suite 325 and to enter into a new lease arrangement covering suite 1000. Where the circumstances and acts of the parties are equivalent to an agreement on the part of the tenant to vacate the leased premises and on the part of the landlord to resume possession, a surrender results by operation of law.

The evidence is legally and factually sufficient to support the jury's finding that the plaintiff released Spradlin from liability under the lease covering suite 325.

The jury verdict for the tenant was affirmed. The landlord by his actions had released the tenant from the rental obligation.

JUDGMENT AND REMEDY

RELATIONSHIP OF LANDLORD AND TENANT

Much real property is used by those who do not own it. A **lease** is a contract by which the owner—the landlord—grants the tenant an exclusive right to use and possess the land, usually for an ascertainable period of time. The basic characteristic of this particular estate is that it continues for the ascertainable term and carries with it the obligation by the tenant to pay rent to the landlord. Usually, the creation of the leasehold estate by contract for terms longer than a year (or three years in some jurisdictions) must be in writing.

Duties and Warranties of the Landlord

When a landlord leases premises to a tenant, a *warranty of possession* and a *covenant of quiet enjoyment* are implied by law. Under the warranty of possession, the landlord warrants that the premises have been leased only to one tenant, and that the premises will be available for occupancy at the agreed time. This is particularly important in leasing apartments, offices, and the like in buildings under construction.

Under the covenant of quiet enjoyment, the landlord promises that the tenant or grantee shall enjoy the possession of the premises in peace and without disturbance. Generally, questions regarding a breach of the covenant of quiet enjoyment arise when the landlord's action (or inaction) affects the tenant's use and enjoyment of the premises in such a way that the tenant is constructively evicted. *Constructive eviction* occurs when the landlord fails to perform any of the undertakings required by the lease, if such failure causes a substantial and lasting injury to the tenant's beneficial enjoyment of the premises. This failure is regarded as an eviction of the tenant. Normally, under such circumstances, the courts permit the tenant to abandon the premises and terminate the lease as long as the tenant does so within a reasonable period of time.

For example, suppose Smith, a quiet minister, rents half of a duplex from Lawson. Lawson rents the other half of the duplex to three members of a rock band. The band rehearses in the duplex every night from about 11:00 in the evening to 5:00 in the morning. Smith complains to Lawson that strange people are constantly entering and leaving the premises and that the noise is unbearable. If Lawson fails to take any action, he has breached his covenant of quiet enjoyment to Smith and has *constructively evicted* him from the premises. Smith can probably rescind the rental agreement.

At common law, the landlord was under no duty to repair the premises rented by a tenant or to warrant that the premises were habitable or suitable for the particular purpose for which they were rented. An exception to this common law rule existed for furnished premises that were rented for short periods of time.

Under most state statutes today, and under judicial decisions, a landlord of residential premises impliedly warrants that the premises are habitable and cannot disclaim this warranty unless the landlord and the tenant are of equal bargaining power. Additionally, unless otherwise stated in the lease, a landlord is under an affirmative duty to repair and maintain the structure and all its *common areas* and fixtures. The landlord will be held liable for injuries resulting from negligent failure to maintain the rented premises.

The following case illustrates the development of the doctrine of an implied warranty of habitability in residential leases.

STEELE v. LATIMER
Supreme Court of Kansas, 1974.
214 Kan. 329, 521 P.2d 304.

BACKGROUND AND FACTS *Shirley Steele and her six young children rented a house from Marvin Latimer. When Latimer failed to make repairs to the premises, Steele brought this action to compel the repairs and sought damages from the landlord. The trial court ruled that there was no implied warranty of habitability existing in Kansas but concluded that "if there was such an implied warranty of habitability that in this case plaintiff would be entitled to recover because the conditions of the house are such that it does violate the principle or theory of implied warranty of habitability." The Kansas Supreme Court reviewed the case.*

FONTRON, Justice.

*   *   *   *

It has been said that the development of the common law has been determined largely by the social needs of the society it was designed to serve, and that the capacity for growth and change is one of its most significant features. The most casual student of ages past would agree that the principle of change runs deeply

through human history and like a golden thread weaves new "people requirements" into the fabrics of altered social patterns.
* * * *

In recent years there has been a noticeable trend among courts in this country
to recognize an implied warranty on the part of the lessor of urban residential
property that the premises leased by him are suitable for human habitation and
will be maintained in suitable condition throughout the duration of the tenancy.
* * * *

The feudal concept that a lease is simply the sale or conveyance of an interest
in land has given way to the more realistic view that a lease is essentially a
contract.

The relationship of landlord and tenant being contractual in character, it follows that mutually dependent rights and obligations arise therefrom, binding alike
on lessor and lessee.
* * * *

In discussing the housing problems with which today's urban populations are
confronted, the Wisconsin Supreme Court phrased the situation this way:

"*   *   * To follow the old rule of no implied warranty of habitability in leases
would, in our opinion, be inconsistent with the current legislative policy concerning housing standards. The need and social desirability of adequate housing for people in this era of rapid population increases is too important to be
rebuffed by that obnoxious legal cliché, *caveat emptor*. Permitting landlords
to rent 'tumble-down' houses is at least a contributing cause of such problems
as urban blight, juvenile delinquency, and high property taxes for conscientious landowners."

Building codes are common today in many urban centers throughout the United
States and the modern weight of authority in this country appears to be that the
minimum standards embraced within a housing ordinance, building code or other
municipal regulation are to be read into and will be implied by operation of law
in housing contracts.

[T]he Wichita Housing Code was in full force and effect at all times material
to this action. The Code is broad and comprehensive in its outreach; it sets basic
standards to be met by city housing and requires lessors and lessees to meet the
same as provided therein; it provides for inspections, notices of violations and
procedures for conducting hearings and appeals; and it provides criminal penalties for violating the act. The trial court found that the house at 3138 Ethel did
not meet the standards set by the Wichita Housing Code in that (1) the windows
and front door were not reasonably tight; (2) that there was excess air leakage;
and (3) the cabinet top and bathroom floors were unsanitary and dangerous to
health.

Under familiar legal principles the provisions of the city's housing code relating to minimum housing standards were by implication read into and became
a part of the rental agreement between Shirley Steele and Marvin E. Latimer.

Where a breach of an implied warranty of habitability has occurred traditional
remedies for breach of contract are available to the tenant, including the recovery
of damages.

*The court held that in Kansas a warranty of habitability is implied in all
residential leases. The case was remanded for a new trial on the issue of
damages resulting from the breach of the implied warranty.*   **JUDGMENT
AND REMEDY**

Duties Owed by the Tenant

Tenant's Obligation to Pay The tenant has an implied obligation to pay reasonable rent to the landlord. Most lease contracts contain an express promise, known as a covenant, that indicates that the tenant is to pay a specific amount at specified times. Generally, if the express promise is not in the lease agreement, then the tenant is obliged to pay only rent that is reasonable and only at the end of the term.

Terminating the Tenant's Obligation to Pay Rent

Assignment An assignment of a tenant's lease to another is an agreement to transfer all rights, title, and interest in the lease to the assignee. It is a complete transfer. Many leases require that the assignment have the landlord's written consent, and an assignment that lacks consent can be avoided by the landlord. A landlord who knowingly accepts rent from the assignee, however, will be held to have waived the requirement. Once waived, it cannot later be revised unless new grounds appear.

A tenant does not end his or her liabilities on a lease upon assignment. The tenant may assign rights but not duties. The tenant remains bound on all promises originally made to the landlord, because it is the tenant who remains in privity of contract with the landlord, despite the assignment. Thus, even though the assignee of the lease is required to pay rent, the original tenant is not released from the contractual obligation to pay rent. Whenever the assignee fails to pay, the landlord can look to the original tenant for compensation.

Subleasing Subleasing involves a partial transfer of the original tenant's rights to the lease. Frequently the tenant is prohibited from subleasing the premises without the landlord's consent. By subleasing, the original tenant is not relieved of any obligations to the landlord under the lease.

To illustrate: A student named Ann leases an apartment for a two-year period. Although Ann had planned on attending summer school, she is offered a vacation job in Europe for the summer months and accepts. Ann does not wish to be stuck with three months' rent for an unoccupied apartment. Unless prohibited by a lease requiring landlord permission, she can sublease the apartment to another student (sublessee). The sublessee is bound by the same terms of the lease as the tenant, and should the sublessee violate the lease, Ann can be held liable by the landlord.

Sometimes an assignment can become a sublease. If the assignment permits the original tenant to reenter the premises whenever the assignee fails to pay the rent, most courts treat the right of reentry as a transfer of less than the whole interest in the lease, and thus the agreement is a sublease.

Destruction of the Premises and the Obligation to Pay Rent At common law, destruction by fire or flood of a whole building leased by a tenant did not relieve the tenant of the obligation to pay rent or permit the termination of the lease. The reasoning behind the common law rule was that the tenant's obligation to pay rent was an exchange for the *estate* in the land. At common law, the concept of estate was divorced from any economic benefits that went with it. Presumably, destruction of the leased building destroyed only part of the benefit. The tenant retained a nonfreehold interest in the land on which the building was constructed.

Today, state statutes have altered the common law rule. Thus, if the building burns down, apartment dwellers in most states are not continuously liable to the landlord for the payment of rent. Many leases contain clauses covering destruction of the building. For example, a clause may indicate that the landlord will repair and restore the building, and the tenant's obligation to pay rent will be suspended until the premises are restored, but only if the premises are wholly unsuitable for habitation after the fire or other disaster.

CONCURRENT OWNERSHIP

Property owned by one person is said to be held severally, that is, apart from others. When two or more persons own property, it is said to be held concurrently. There are several types of concurrent estates, including tenancy in common, joint tenancy, tenancy by entirety, and community property.

Tenancy in Common

One type of concurrent estate is a **tenancy in common.** Suppose Henry conveys land "to Able and Baker and Carter." This conveyance creates a tenancy in common among Able, Baker and Carter, whereby each takes a one-third interest. In a tenancy in common, each tenant has the right to convey his or her interest in the property. When one of the tenants dies, that tenant's interest passes to his or her heirs (or, by will, to someone else). Essentially, tenants in a tenancy in common each own an undivided fractional share of the property, an interest that can be conveyed to another.

Joint Tenancy

In a **joint tenancy,** each tenant owns an undivided interest in the property. Thus, when one tenant dies, the others' interests "swallow up" the deceased's share and no property passes to the heirs of the deceased (even by will). Instead, all property of the deceased passes to the other joint tenants. This characteristic, which differs from tenancy in common, is known as *survivorship.*

A joint tenancy is transformed into a tenancy in common when one of the joint tenants transfers his or her interest to another party. A joint tenancy can also be transferred by *partition;* that is, the tenants can physically divide the property in equal parts. Since a joint tenant's interest is capable of being conveyed without the consent of the other joint tenants, it can be levied against by the tenant's creditors. This is also true of the tenancy in common.

Tenancy by the Entirety

Another type of concurrent estate is the **tenancy by the entirety**—a joint tenancy between a husband and wife. At common law, a tenancy by the entirety could be created in a husband and wife only where the conveyance was to, say, "Daniel and Harriet Campbell, husband and wife,

and their heirs and assigns." A tenancy by the entirety differs from a joint tenancy and tenancy in common in that neither spouse can convey his or her interest without the express consent of the other. Since neither can voluntarily convey his or her interest, the creditors of one spouse cannot levy on the property. (However, if the spouses are jointly liable to the creditors, then the creditors can usually levy on the tenancy.)

Divorce terminates a tenancy by the entirety and, in most states, creates a tenancy in common. The tenancy by the entirety is not recognized in many states.[10]

Community Property

Eight states provide for concurrent ownership of property by what is called community property.[11] Generally, any property acquired by a husband and wife during the period of their marriage (except by gift or inheritance) becomes community property, with each owning an undivided half interest. It is immaterial who actually earned or acquired the property.

Some states provide for the right of survivorship upon death of a spouse, treating the ownership much like a tenancy by the entirety. In other states, the surviving spouse's interest is passed by will or laws of descent, much like a tenancy in common.

TRANSFER OF OWNERSHIP

There are a number of ways ownership of real property can pass from one person to another. They include an inheritance, will, eminent domain, adverse possession and deed. Conveyance by deed includes transfer by sale and by gift.

Transfer by Will or Inheritance

Property that is transferred on an owner's death is passed either by *will* or by *inheritance.* If the

---

10. See Dorf v. Tuscarora Pipeline Co., 48 N.J.Super. 26, 136 A.2d 778(1957) and Lindenfelser v. Lindenfelser 396 Pa. 530, 153 A.2d 901 (1959). Some of the states that recognize tenancy by the entirety require express language to create it.
11. Az., Cal., Id., La., N.M., Tex., Wa.

owner of land dies with a will, the land that the owner had prior to death passes according to the terms of the will. If the owner dies without a will, state statutes prescribe how and to whom the property will pass. Ordinarily, when the owner dies without a will, the property passes to the deceased's living heirs. This topic is discussed in Chapter 56.

Eminent Domain

Even where ownership in real property is fee simple absolute, there is a limitation or superior ownership. It is called **eminent domain,** and it is sometimes referred to as the condemnation power of the government to take land for public use. It gives a right to the government to acquire possession of real property in the manner directed by the Constitution and the laws of the state whenever the public interest requires it.

For example, when a new public highway is to be built, the government must decide where to build it and how much land to condemn. The government then starts a condemnation proceeding in which the owner can show why the land should not be appropriated for public use and the government or agency involved can show why the public needs this particular parcel of land. Once the government determines that the land is to be condemned or taken for public use, another proceeding is held to determine the *fair value* of the land, which is usually approximately equal to its market value. The fair value is paid to the property owner as compensation for the taking of the property. Under federal and state constitutions, the government is not allowed to take property without paying just compensation for it.

A condemnation transfers title from the owner to the government. Then the government is considered the true owner and can use the land for whatever purpose was originally contemplated.

Adverse Possession

Adverse possession is a means of obtaining title to land without a deed being delivered. Essentially, when one person possesses the property of another for a certain statutory period of time (three to thirty years, with ten years being most common), that person (called the adverse possessor) acquires title to the land and cannot be removed from the land by the original owner. The adverse possessor is vested with a perfect title just as if there had been a conveyance by deed. Once title to the property has been obtained, if the new owner abandons the premises, in some states title will not pass to the original owner. It will *escheat* to the state according to state law.

In order to hold property adversely, four elements must be satisfied: First, possession must be actual and exclusive; that is, the possessor must take sole physical occupancy of the property. Second, the possession must be open, visible, and notorious, not secret or clandestine. The possessor must occupy the land for all the world to see. Third, possession must be continuous and peaceable for the required period of time. This means that the possessor must not be interrupted in the occupancy by the true owner or by the courts. Being evicted or being served with an eviction notice will stop the statute of limitations from running and likewise stop the adverse possession. Fourth, possession must be hostile and adverse. In other words, the possessor must claim the property as against the whole world. He or she cannot live on the property with the permission of the owner. Thus, a tenant who holds over is not holding adversely to the landlord, since the law presumes that the landlord is permitting the tenant to stay. Until the tenant repudiates the landlord-tenant relationship, he or she is not occupying the premises with hostility and adversity.

Conveyance by Deed

Possession and title to land are passed from person to person by means of a **deed**—the instrument of conveyance of real property. Deeds are writings signed by the owner of property by which title to it is transferred to another. They must meet certain requirements. Exhibit 53–1 shows a deed.

Requirements of a Valid Deed Unlike contracts, a deed does not have to be supported by legally sufficient consideration. Gifts of real

EXHIBIT 53–1   A TYPICAL DEED

RECORDING REQUESTED BY

AND WHEN RECORDED MAIL THIS DEED AND, UNLESS
OTHERWISE SHOWN BELOW, MAIL TAX STATEMENTS TO:

NAME

ADDRESS

CITY &
STATE
ZIP

Title Order No. _____   Escrow No. _____

⎯ SPACE ABOVE THIS LINE FOR RECORDER'S USE ⎯

Warranty Deed

The undersigned declares that the documentary transfer tax is $ _____and is
☐ computed on the full value of the interest or property conveyed, or is
☐ computed on the full value less the value of liens or encumbrances remaining thereon at the time of sale. The land, tenements or realty is
located in
☐ unincorporated area   ☐ city of _____ and

FOR A VALUABLE CONSIDERATION, receipt of which is hereby acknowledged

do   hereby remise, release and forever quitclaim to

the following described real property in the   county of
state of California:

Dated _____

STATE OF CALIFORNIA
COUNTY OF _____⎬ ss.
On _____before me, the under-
signed, a Notary Public in and for said County and State, personally
appeared_____
_____
_____
_____, known to me
to be the person _____ whose name _____ subscribed to the within instrument and acknowledged that _____ executed the same.

_____
        Signature of Notary

FOR NOTARY SEAL OR STAMP

Assessor's Parcel No. _____

MAIL TAX STATEMENTS TO PARTY SHOWN ON FOLLOWING LINE IF NO PARTY SO SHOWN, MAIL AS DIRECTED ABOVE

Name	Street Address	City & State

L-11-A (G.S.) (Rev. 8-75) (8 pt.)

property are common, and they require deeds even though there is no consideration for the gift. The necessary requirements for a valid deed are:

1. The names of the buyer (grantee) and seller (grantor).
2. Words evidencing an intent to convey (for example, "I hereby bargain, sell, grant, or give").
3. A legally sufficient description of the land.
4. The grantor's (and usually the spouse's) signature.
5. Delivery of the deed.

Types of Deeds

General Warranty Deed   General warranty deeds warrant the greatest number of things and thus provide the most extensive protection against defects of title. In most states, special language is required to make a general warranty deed. If the deed states that the seller is providing the "usual covenants," most courts will infer from this language all of the following covenants (warranties) of title:

1. *A covenant of seisin and a covenant of the right to convey* warrant that the seller has title and the power to convey the estate that the deed describes. For example, if Able, the owner of a life estate in Whiteacre, attempts to convey a fee simple to Baker, Able has breached the covenant of seisin. If Baker is damaged by Able's breach, then Baker is entitled to recover from Able.

2. *A covenant against encumbrances* guarantees that the property being sold or conveyed is not subject to any outstanding rights or interests that will diminish the value of the land, except as stated. Examples of common encumbrances include mortgages, liens, profits, easements, and private deed restrictions on the use of land. Unless the deed expressly states that the conveyance is subject to a particular encumbrance, a covenant against encumbrances will be breached if the buyer discovers an undisclosed encumbrance. Again, as in the case of a covenant of seisin, the buyer is entitled to recover for any damage caused by the breach of this covenant.

3. *A covenant for quiet enjoyment* guarantees that the grantee or buyer will not be disturbed in his or her possession of the land by the grantor or any third persons. For example, suppose Janet Parker sells her two-acre lot and office building by general warranty deed. Subsequently, a third person shows better title than Janet had and proceeds to evict the buyer. Here the covenant for quiet enjoyment has been breached, and the buyer can recover the purchase price of the land plus any other damages incurred in being evicted.

The following case illustrates these covenants.

BROWN v. LOBER
Supreme Court of Illinois 1979.
75 Ill.2d 549, 27 Ill.Dec. 780,
389 N.E.2d 1188.

BACKGROUND AND FACTS   *The plaintiff, Brown, purchased real property in 1957 and received a warranty deed. The deed contained no list of encumbrances. In 1974 the plaintiff granted a call option to Consolidated Coal Company, permitting the company rights to subsurface coal. Consolidated agreed to pay the plaintiff $6,000 for these rights. In 1976, it was discovered that the plaintiff did not own the subsurface mineral rights free and clear as indicated by the warranty deed of 1957. Instead, the plaintiff owned only one-third of the rights. The rights to the remaining two-thirds had been deeded away in 1947 by a prior grantor.*

The plaintiff had already been paid $2,000 by the coal company for its one-third interest. The coal company would not pay the remaining $4,000. The plaintiff then filed this lawsuit, seeking the $4,000 in damages against the prior grantor, Lober, the defendant.

Lober asserted that the ten-year statute of limitations for covenant of seisin barred the lawsuit. Brown asserted that a right of action was permitted for breach of the covenant of quiet enjoyment.

The trial court found for Lober, deciding that the ten-year statute of limitations had run from the time the deed was issued in 1957. Brown appealed.

UNDERWOOD, Justice.

* * * *

The deed which plaintiffs received * * * was a general statutory form warranty deed meeting the requirements of section 9 of "An Act concerning conveyances." That section provides:

"Every deed in substance in the above form, when otherwise duly executed, shall be deemed and held a conveyance in fee simple, to the grantee, his heirs or assigns, with covenants on the part of the grantor, (1) that at the time of the making and delivery of such deed he was lawfully seized of an indefeasible estate in fee simple, in and to the premises therein described, and had good right and full power to convey the same; (2) that the same were then free from all incumbrances; and (3) that he warrants to the grantee, his heirs and assigns, the quiet and peaceable possession of such premises, and will defend the title thereto against all persons who may lawfully claim the same. And such covenants shall be obligatory upon any grantor, his heirs and personal representatives, as fully and with like effect as if written at length in such deed."

The effect of this provision is that certain covenants of title are implied in every statutory form warranty deed. Subsection 1 contains the covenant of seisin and the covenant of good right to convey. These covenants, which are considered synonymous, assure the grantee that the grantor is, at the time of the conveyance, lawfully seized and has the power to convey an estate of the quality and quantity which he professes to convey.

* * * *

Subsection 3 sets forth the covenant of quiet enjoyment, which is synonymous with the covenant of warranty in Illinois. By this covenant, "the grantor warrants to the grantee, his heirs and assigns, the possession of the premises and that he will defend the title granted by the terms of the deed against persons who may lawfully claim the same, and that such covenant shall be obligatory upon the grantor, his heirs, personal representatives, and assigns."

* * * *

Since the deed was delivered to the plaintiffs on December 21, 1957, any cause of action for breach of the covenant of seisin would have accrued on that date. The trial court held that this cause of action was barred by the statute of limitations. No question is raised as to the applicability of the 10-year statute of limitations. We conclude, therefore, that the cause of action for breach of the covenant of seisin was properly determined by the trial court to be barred by the statute of limitations since plaintiffs did not file their complaint until May 25, 1976, nearly 20 years after their alleged cause of action accrued.

* * * *

This court has stated on numerous occasions that, in contrast to the covenant of seisin, the covenant of warranty or quiet enjoyment is prospective in nature and is breached only when there is an actual or constructive eviction of the covenantee by the paramount titleholder.

The cases are also replete with statements to the effect that the mere existence of paramount title in one other than the covenantee is not sufficient to constitute a breach of the covenant of warranty or quiet enjoyment: "[T]here must be a union of acts of disturbance and lawful title, to constitute a breach of the covenant for quiet enjoyment, or warranty * * *." '[T]here is a general concurrence that something more than the mere existence of a paramount title is necessary to constitute a breach of the covenant of warranty.' "A mere want of title is no breach of this covenant. There must not only be a want of title, but there must be an ouster under a paramount title."

* * * *

Since no one has, as yet, undertaken to remove the coal or otherwise manifested a clear intent to exclusively "possess" the mineral estate, it must be concluded that the subsurface estate is "vacant." As in *Scott*, plaintiffs "could at any time have taken peaceable possession of it. [They have] in no way been prevented or hindered from the enjoyment of the possession by any one having a better right." Accordingly, until such time as one holding paramount title interferes with plaintiffs' right of possession (e.g., by beginning to mine the coal), there can be no constructive eviction and, therefore, no breach of the covenant of quiet enjoyment.

JUDGMENT   *The judgment of the trial court was affirmed. The statute of limitations*
AND REMEDY   *barred an action for breach of the covenant of seisin. The Browns also could not recover for breach of the covenant of quiet enjoyment because no one had interfered with their right of possession.*

Special Warranty Deed   The general warranty deed gives all the covenants of title listed above, but the special warranty deed (also known as deed with covenant against grantor's acts) warrants only that the grantor or seller has not previously done anything to lessen the value of the real estate. If the special warranty deed discloses all liens or other encumbrances, the seller will not be liable to the buyer if a third person subsequently interferes with the buyer's ownership. However, if the third person's claim arises out of, or is related to, some act of the seller, the seller will be liable to the buyer for damages.

Both the special warranty deed and the general warranty deed warrant that the seller has "marketable" title. Common defects that may render a title unmarketable include variations in the names of grantors and grantees, breaks in the chain of title, outstanding liens, and defectively executed deeds in the chain of title.

Quit Claim Deed   A **quit claim** deed warrants less than any other deed. Essentially, it simply conveys to the grantee whatever interest the

grantor had. In other words, if the grantor had nothing, then the grantee receives nothing. Naturally, if the grantor had a defective title, or no title at all, a conveyance by general warranty deed or special warranty deed will not cure the defects. However, such deeds will give the buyer a cause of action to sue the seller. A quit claim deed gives no cause of action unless the seller had one.

Quit claim deeds are often used to clear up past defects in the title. Suppose husband and wife own a parcel of land as tenants by the entirety.[12] They decide to sell it, and husband makes out a deed in his name only. Baker, the buyer, keeps the property for several years and then wishes to sell it to Carter. Carter's attorney, while examining the title, notices that the deed from husband and wife was signed by husband alone. Therefore, the wife has an outstanding interest in the property that creates a "cloud" over Carter's title. Carter's attorney induces wife to con-

---

12.   An estate held in tenancy by the entirety cannot be conveyed unless both spouses sign the sales contract and deed.

vey any interest she may have by quit claim deed to either Carter or Baker before advising his client to make the purchase. Thus, the quit claim deed removes the cloud over the title, and Carter, after purchasing the land from Baker, becomes the fee simple owner of the land. Quit claims are often used among tenants in common where one tenant "releases" interest to another.

Grant Deed (Bargain and Sale Deed) With a grant deed, the grantor simply states, "I grant the property to you." Or the grantor may state, "I convey, or bargain and sell, the property to you." By state statute, grant deeds carry with them an implied warranty that the grantor either owns the property being transferred or has not previously encumbered it or conveyed it to someone else.

Recording the Deed

Deeds are normally recorded in the presence of a notary public in the county where the property is located. Many state statutes require that the grantor sign the deed in the presence of two attesting witnesses before it can be recorded. Some states require only one witness. In a small number of states, the deed is not eligible for recording unless the grantor signs it in the presence of the required number of witnesses and in these states the deed is considered invalid and will not pass legal title to the real property if this requirement is not met. The majority of states, however, do not require that the grantor's signature be witnessed for the deed to be valid. The purpose of recording the deed is to give notice to the world that a certain person is now the owner of a certain parcel of real estate. Putting everyone on notice as to the true owner is intended to prevent the previous owners from fraudulently conveying the land to a subsequent purchaser.

At common law, priorities as to titles were governed by a *first in time, first in right* rule. Suppose Jane sells Shady Acres to Ann. Ann receives the deed from Jane and is considered the true owner. If Jane subsequently attempts to convey the property to Bob, Bob will receive nothing, since Ann is the true owner.

Today this rule generally governs. However, in the preceding example, if Bob is a bona fide purchaser, he may prevail over Ann unless Ann has recorded the deed. A *bona fide purchaser* is a person who pays valuable consideration for the land, who acts in good faith, and who has no notice of a previous conveyance or sale.

Notice is accomplished by recording, so virtually every state has statutes defining the requirements of recording. Once the deed to Shady Acres is recorded, the records serve as notice to the whole world that Ann is the true owner. Bob cannot then be a bona fide purchaser, since the records give him *constructive* notice of the true owner. Before purchasing real estate, in order to ensure "good" title, one must check the county records to make sure that no one else has recorded the deed to that property.

Warranty of Habitability

At common law the purchaser of a home was entitled to certain warranties with respect to title of the property purchased. However, the common law rule of *caveat emptor* ("let the buyer beware") held that the seller of a home made no warranties with respect to the soundness or fitness of the home unless such a warranty was specifically included in the deed or contract of sale. While *caveat emptor* is still the rule of law in many states, there is currently a strong trend against it and in favor of an implied warranty of habitability. Under this new approach, the courts hold that the seller of a new house warrants that it will be fit for human habitation regardless of whether any such warranty is included in the deed or contract of sale. Essentially, under an implied warranty of habitability, the seller warrants that the house is in reasonable working order and is of reasonably sound construction.

Historically, the protection afforded a new home buyer under the doctrine of *caveat emptor* has not been satisfactory since the buyer of a new home would only recover for defective workmanship if he or she could prove that the seller (builder) of the home was *negligent* in constructing the home. Recall from the chapter on torts that proof of negligence requires a plaintiff to prove the existence of a certain standard of care, and the unreasonable violation of that standard. Such facts are not easily proved in a court of law. Under an implied warranty of habitability, the purchaser is only required to prove that the home he or she has purchased was somehow defective and to prove the damages which the defect caused. Thus, under warranty of habitability theory, the seller of a new home is in efffect a guarantor of the home's fitness.

Sale of Real Estate

Most transfers of ownership interest in real property are accomplished by means of a sale. The sale of real estate is similar to the sale of goods. It involves a transfer of ownership, often with certain warranties. However, in the sale of real estate, certain formalities are observed that are not required in the sale of goods. To meet the requirements of law, a deed must be signed and delivered.[13] In order to illustrate how a transfer of ownership in real property is accomplished, a typical real estate transaction is outlined here.

A Typical Procedure in the Sale of Real Estate

Suppose Janet Parker owns a parcel of real estate—a two-acre lot with an office building. Since her business is expanding to a new location, she has decided to sell the property. The first thing she will do is to attempt to locate a buyer. This can be accomplished in different ways. She can put the property up for sale herself, or she can employ a real estate broker or agent to help her locate a buyer.

Locating a Buyer A broker can put Parker's property on an *open listing*. An open listing contract allows Parker (the landowner) to find a buyer herself and/or to hire brokers with nonexclusive rights to sell the property. In the latter case, the broker who is the first to produce such a buyer is entitled to the commission.

Alternatively, Parker can have an *exclusive agency* with the broker. In this type of arrangement, the broker has the exclusive right as an agent to sell the property, although Parker can employ another broker. If she does, the first broker is still entitled to a commission. However, if Parker sells the property without the assistance of the broker, she need not pay the commission.

Finally, Parker can give the broker an *exclusive right to sell*. In this situation, the broker is normally entitled to a commission no matter who sells the real estate—Parker, this broker, or another broker. An exclusive right to sell usually lasts for a specified period of time; after that time, Parker is free to make arrangements with another broker if the property has not yet been sold.

Contract of Sale Once a buyer is located, a contract for the sale of the land must be negotiated. See Exhibit 53–2 for a typical contract. Here Parker must decide, inter alia (among other things), the cost of title examination and insurance, how to allocate property taxes, and what the actual purchase price will be. Because of the Statute of Frauds, the contract for the sale of real estate must be in writing to be enforceable. The writing need not specify all the details of the transaction, but it should contain the essential terms of the bargain and be signed by the parties. The essential terms are:

1. An identification of the parties.
2. The description of the land to be conveyed.
3. The purchase price.
4. The signatures.

In most cases, after the details of the transaction have been negotiated, an attorney, or an escrow or title company will draw up a long, formal document that will be signed by both the seller and the buyer.

Title Examination After the sales contract has been negotiated, the buyer or buyer's attorney (or the broker, escrow agent, or title insurance company) will begin the *title examination*. Essentially, a title examination is an examination of the history of all past transfers and sales of the piece of property in question. Every county

---

13. The phrase *signed, sealed, and delivered* used to refer to the requirements for transferring title to real property by deed. The seal has fallen from use, but signature and delivery are still required.

EXHIBIT 53–2 A TYPICAL HYPOTHETICAL CONTRACT

Contract for Sale of Real Estate

I, --
seller, have sold and agree to convey to --
--- *(in joint tenancy)*
purchaser, upon the terms hereinafter set forth, the following described real estate, situate in Ramsey County, Minnesota,
namely: --

----

according to the plat thereof, subject, however, to any change in the size of said property caused by the vacating, opening,
widening, narrowing or grading of any street or alley, said property being also known as number -------------------
--- *Saint Paul, Minnesota.*

I, --
have viewed, examined and purchased said real estate and agree to pay therefor the total purchase price of
---*Dollars ($-------------------)*
of which ---*Dollars ($-------------------)*
have been paid at the date hereof, the receipt of which is hereby acknowledged, and the further sum of --------------
--*Dollars ($-------------------)*
is to be paid by said purchaser to said seller as follows: --
--*Dollars ($-------------------)*
in cash on execution and delivery of a -- *Warranty Deed.*
---*Dollars ($-------------------)*
by assuming and agreeing to pay one certain—proposed *mortgage,* now—to become a lien against said property, same
bearing—to bear *interest at* -------------------% *per annum,* interest and principal being payable as follows $------------------
monthly—quarterly—semi-annually with the privilege of multiple payments of $------------------- on any ---------------------------
payment date, *and* $------------------- *in* monthly—quarterly—semi-annual—annual *installments of* $-------------------, or more each;
from the monthly—quarterly—semi-annual—annual *payments shall first be deducted the accumulated interest on deferred
payments at* -------------------% *per annum; and the balance then remaining, shall be applied in reduction of the principal
indebtedness; and in addition thereto, the purchaser shall add to said* ------------------ *payments, beginning* -----------------
------------- 19------, *an amount sufficient to provide payment before penalties accrue of taxes and assessments; fire, windstorm
and other hazard insurance, as estimated by seller* ---

It is understood and agreed that this sale is made subject to the approval within ------------------- days by the owner *of said
premises in writing, and that the undersigned agent is in no manner liable or responsible on account of this agreement, except
to return or account for any of the purchase money paid to him under this contract.*

Said purchaser agrees to pay the purchase price in the manner and at the times aforesaid, and further to pay all taxes
and assessments on said premises, commencing with those assessed thereon for the present year, but not payable until the
first Monday in January next, together with assessments and deferred instalments thereof, if any, heretofore levied against said
land, the payment of which is not yet enforcible.

Said seller shall, within fifteen days inclusive from the date hereof, deliver to said purchaser a properly certified to date
abstract of title or Abstractor's Registered Property Certificate to said land. Said purchaser shall be allowed ten days after
delivery of said Abstract or Certificate for examination of title and report in writing to seller and within which to perform this
contract, provided that, if the title to said real estate, or any part thereof shall be found to be unmarketable, and can be made
marketable in said seller within ninety days after the delivery of said abstract or certificate, said purchaser shall be allowed
ten days after he shall have been notified in writing of the correcting of such title, to perform this contract on his part, and
payments falling due before the time allowed for the correction of such title shall be postponed until such title is corrected, if
corrected within the time specified.

If such title is found to be unmarketable in said seller and cannot be made marketable within ninety days, or said purchaser
does not waive the same, then this contract shall be void, and neither party shall be liable for damages hereunder, and earnest
money shall be refunded forthwith.

Upon the performance of this contract by said purchaser, said seller shall deliver to said purchaser an Abstract of Title
or the owner's duplicate Torrens Certificate of Title, and a duly acknowledged Contract for ---
Warranty Deed entitled to record of said land and all thereof, free from dower or statutory rights, taxes, assessments, mortgages
and all other adverse claims or liens, except as stated above --
----

The purchaser agrees that Abstract of Title or Torrens Certificate of Title and fire, windstorm and other hazard insurance
policies shall remain in possession of mortgagee and or contract seller until all said indebtedness is paid in full.

(OVER)

EXHIBIT 53–2   Continued

If said purchaser agrees in this contract to assume or join in a mortgage, said purchaser and seller and their respective spouses, if any, shall join in executing the necessary papers for renewing said mortgage or placing a new mortgage for any sum not to exceed $_____ so as to keep a mortgage of not to exceed $_____ in effect until the property herein described is conveyed in accordance with terms of this contract and said purchaser agrees to pay all usual and reasonable expenses for the renewing of the present mortgage or the making of a new one.

All storm sheds, sash and doors; screens, awnings, shades and venetian blinds; all porch windows and doors; gas or electric fixtures, oil burners, stokers, air conditioners and motors pertaining to the same; drapes and carpets in public halls; radiators and all other like appliances and betterments, plants and shrubbery (if any) which are now provided for or used in or on said premises; and, except in single residences, stoves, ranges and refrigerator units, plant or system; and, except such as are the property of the tenants, are included in this sale.

All papers shall bear even date herewith, and liability as between the parties hereto to pay taxes and assessments on said property shall be determined as of the date hereof. The policies of insurance shall on final closing of this sale be so written or endorsed as to protect the interests of seller, purchaser and mortgagee, and shall be taken by said purchaser at their pro rata value from the date hereof. Rentals and interest shall be adjusted as follows: _____

_____

_____

Possession of the property herein described shall be given _____ , 19_____ subject however to the rights of the tenants in possession.

All tenders and delivery of papers hereunder shall be made at the office of _____ in Saint Paul, Minn.

Time is of the essence hereof, and if such purchaser shall fail to perform this contract within the time herein limited, said seller or his agent shall retain the earnest money hereof as a part of his just compensation for such failure, and may declare this contract terminated and proceed for damages, or specific performance against such purchaser. Action to enforce this contract shall be commenced within ninety (90) days from the date of forfeiture of this contract.

Dated at Saint Paul, Minnesota, _____ , 19_____

Signed, Sealed and Delivered in Presence of

-- } _____ *Agent (SEAL)*

-- } _____ *Seller (SEAL)*

-- } _____ *(SEAL)*

-- } _____ *Purchaser (SEAL)*

                                                               _____ *(SEAL)*

Adopted by St. Paul Real Estate Board 1943

Contract for Sale of Real Estate

TO

Brady-Margulis Co., St. Paul, Minn.

has a filing system where deeds, plats, and other instruments are recorded.

A skilled examiner can determine from these records whether there are any liens, easements, profits, or other encumbrances on the land. These records, known as the chain of title, go back to the original grant or deed from the United States or the particular state where the land is located.[14] Usually, private abstract companies prepare what is known as an *abstract*. This document lists all of the records relating to a particular parcel of land. This is called a title search. The examiner then gives an opinion as to the validity of the title.

Often, the sales contract requires a buyer to purchase *title insurance*—an insurance that protects the buyer in the event that someone is shown to have a better title. Title insurance companies have their own staffs of attorneys and abstractors who examine titles on a full-time basis. Once a title insurance company's staff approves a title, the company will issue insurance on the property.

Obtaining a Mortgage   Ordinarily, most buyers do not have enough cash to buy real estate outright, so they arrange for a loan. To obtain the loan, the purchaser may put the property up as collateral. *Mortgages* are essentially liens against the property that enable the lender to foreclose and sell the real estate if the borrower fails to make timely payments (see Chapter 32). In most cases, a bank or savings and loan association is contacted for financing. In some cases, the seller may agree to loan the buyer the purchase price in exchange for the buyer's promissory note and mortgage. Either type of mortgage is known as a *(first) purchase money mortgage* because the seller or lender supplies the buyer with the money to purchase the house.

Closing   The final stage of the sale is called the *closing*. In principle, the transaction is closed by the buyer paying the purchase price and the seller delivering the deed to the buyer. Often, however, the buyer's agent delivers the check and the mortgage papers. The seller's agent (broker) turns over the keys and necessary papers to the buyer. Sometimes, when the property is being mortgaged, the lender (for example, a bank) will close the mortgage deal, paying the seller for the property and receiving a lien (mortgage) on the property at the same time. Alternatively, all these matters may be handled by the escrow agent.

QUESTIONS AND CASE PROBLEMS

1.   Anderson contracts to lease an apartment near the campus from landlord Smith for one year, with the monthly rent due and payable on the first of each month. At the end of the year, Anderson does not vacate the apartment, and Smith does not object. Anderson continues to pay the rent on the first of the month, and it is accepted by Smith. Six months later, Smith informs Anderson that the apartment has been leased to Green and that Anderson must vacate the premises by the end of the week. Anderson refuses to leave, and Smith threatens eviction proceedings. Discuss the rights of the parties under these circumstances.

2.   John conveys by warranty deed his summer, lakeside cottage and lot to his three children, Adam, Barbara, and Clara, making them joint tenants with right of survivorship. Sometime later, Barbara sells her interest in the property to Sam. After the transfer, Sam dies, leaving by will all property and interests therein to his wife, Susan. Adam and Clara refuse to acknowledge Susan as a co-owner of the cottage, claiming they did not agree to the sale to Sam by Barbara and that even if the sale was valid, they should acquire Sam's interest upon his death by right of survivorship. Discuss the claims of Adam and Clara.

3.   Adam and Mary are neighbors. Adam's lot is extremely large, and his present and future use of it will not involve the entire area owned. Mary wants to build a single-car garage and driveway along the present lot boundary. Because of ordinances requiring buildings to be set back fifteen feet from an adjoining property

---

14.   Today the title search need not go back all the way to the grant from the government. Nearly every state has a marketable record title act that provides that the roots of title older than thirty or forty years are conclusively presumed to be valid. In other words, if the chain of title can be traced back thirty or forty years with no defects, no further search need be made.

line, and because of the placement of her existing structures, she cannot build the garage. Mary contracts to purchase ten feet of Adam's property along their boundary line for $3,000. Adam is willing to sell but will give Mary only a quit claim deed, whereas Mary wants a general warranty deed. Discuss the differences between these deeds as they affect the rights of the parties in case the title to this ten feet later proves to be defective.

4.   George Benedict bought a newly constructed home from Perfect Construct Home Builders. A warranty deed was given, and George and his family moved into the house. There were no warranties made with respect to the soundness or fitness of the house in either the contract of sale or the warranty deed. One year later, during a wind storm, the roof of the house caves in. George wants to hold Perfect liable, but he cannot prove the builder was negligent in constructing the house. Discuss any possible theory of recovery George may successfully claim against Perfect.

5.   Harold was a wanderer twenty-two years ago. It was at that time that he decided to settle down on a vacant three-acre piece of land, which he did not own. People in the area indicated to him that they had no idea who owned it. Harold built a house on the land, got married, and raised three children while living there. He fenced in the land, placed a gate with a sign, "Harold's Homestead," above it, and had trespassers removed. Harold is now confronted by Joe Moonfeld, who has a deed in his name as owner of the property. Moonfeld orders Harold and family off the property, claiming his title ownership. Discuss who has best "title" to the property.

6.   The owners of the Seven Palms Motor Inn decided that their motel was in need of renovation. Accordingly, they ordered a large quantity of bedspreads, curtain rods, and drapes from Sears, Roebuck and Company. Thereafter, Seven Palms Motor Inn failed to pay its bill, which amounted to approximately $8,000, including installation. Under Missouri law, a supplier of fixtures can establish a lien on the land and building to which the fixtures become attached.

Sears sought to establish such a lien to make it easier to recover the debt that Seven Palms owed it. Which, if any, of the above-named items will Sears be able to argue are fixtures? [Sears, Roebuck & Co. v. Seven Palms Motor Inn, 530 S.W.2d 695 (Mo.1975)]

7.   X conveyed a life estate in certain land to her son, S, with the remainder to T. The deed was properly executed, signed by X, and delivered to S, but it was never recorded. X died one year later, leaving S her sole heir. Eighteen months later, S sold the land to P. The title records showed that the land was owned by X; therefore, P ascertained that S was X's sole heir. After the sale, T, who then occupied the land, refused to relinquish possession to P. Who is entitled to the land? [Earle v. Fiske, 103 Mass. 491 (1870)]

8.   Smyth was the owner of a one-ninth interest in land. The other owners, who were co-tenants, owned a combined eight-ninths interest in the property. Smyth and the other owners were tenants in common. The land was of considerable value, since large quantities of rock asphalt were just below its surface. Smyth mined one-ninth of the rock asphalt, sold it, and personally retained the profits. The other co-tenants of the property sued Smyth, seeking a division of his profits from the mining operations among all the co-tenants. Smyth claimed that since he took only one-ninth of the rock, which was his ownership share, he should not be divested of the profits. What was the result? [White v. Smyth, 147 Tex. 272, 214 S.W.2d 967 (1948)]

9.   A landlord of residential premises leased a building he owned nearby for use as a cocktail lounge. The residential tenants complained to the landlord about the late evening and early morning music and disturbances coming from the lounge. Although the lease for the lounge provided that entertainment had to be conducted so that it could not be heard outside the building and would not disturb residents of the apartments, the landlord was unsuccessful in remedying the problem. The tenants vacated their apartments. Will the landlord be successful in a suit to collect rent from the tenants who vacated? [Blackett v. Olanoff, 371 Mass. 714, 358 N.E.2d 817 (1977)]

CHAPTER 54

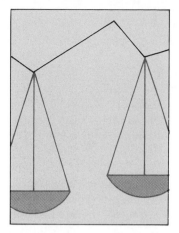

Future Interests, Nonpossessory Interests, and Land Use Control

The last chapter defined real property and then discussed the nature of an estate and how estates are acquired. Generally, the estates discussed were those in which the person having the estate (ownership interest) was also in *present* possession of the land. This chapter discusses estates and other types of interests in land that do not involve present possession by the owner. The last part of the chapter discusses restrictions that affect the way land can be used.

FUTURE INTERESTS

A person can convey an estate that is limited by a specified period of time; the life of the grantor, grantee, or other person; or by an occurrence. The person to whom such an estate is conveyed has a *present possessory interest*. Life estates, terms for years, and fee simple determinable estates are examples of estates that carry present possessory interests, and which include a resid-

uary interest that may or may not have been disposed of by the grantor. This residuary interest is a *future interest*, and it can take several forms. If it remains in the grantor, it is called a *reversion*, a *possibility of reverter*, or a *power of termination*. If the future interest is not retained by the grantor, then it is called either a *remainder* or an *executory interest*. Remainders can be either *vested* or *contingent*, depending upon the terms of the conveyance.

Reversionary Interests and Powers of Termination

When a grantor owns a fee simple estate in land and conveys an estate to another with a duration that is less than the duration of the estate that the grantor owns, there is an undisposed residue remaining in the grantor. That undisposed residue is called a **reversion.**

For example, Owen owns a fee simple estate and conveys a life estate in Blackacre to Ann.

Owen has not disposed of the interest in the land that remains after Ann's life. Therefore, Owen has automatically retained a reversion, and the reversion is a future interest. It is preceded by Ann's life estate, which is an estate in possession. Owen's reversion is created by operation of law. Owen does not have a present possessory interest in Blackacre but has a *vested* future interest—that is, an absolute right to possession of Blackacre at some point in the future, a right that Owen can convey in the present.

If Owen conveys Blackacre "to Ann and her heirs," he conveys a fee simple absolute. There is no future interest in Blackacre, since Owen has conveyed the entire estate to Ann.

However, if Owen conveys a fee simple determinable (which is one of the estates that is less than fee simple), as in "to Ann and her heirs as long as the property is used for educational purposes," Owen has retained a **possibility of reverter**—a future interest in favor of the grantor that is contingent on the happening of the event named in the conveyance. The conveyance of a determinable fee that gives rise to a possibility of reverter usually includes the words "so long as", "until", "while", or "during."

Powers of termination are also future interests retained by a grantor who is conveying an estate subject to a condition. Powers of termination are similar to possibilities of reverter except that future possession by the grantor requires an affirmative act. (That is, it does not occur automatically.) For example, suppose Owen conveys Blackacre "to Ann and her heirs, but if liquor is sold on the premises, the right to enter and terminate the estate is reserved." Owen has retained a power of termination and has the right to repossess the land in the future if liquor is sold on the premises and if Owen acts affirmatively to retake possession of Blackacre.

Remainders and Executory Interests

If the owner of real property conveys an estate that is less than a fee simple absolute and does not retain the residuary interest, then that interest will take the form of either a **remainder** or an **executory interest.** As mentioned previously,

a remainder can be either vested or contingent. Both are future interests, but the holder of a vested remainder has an absolute right to possession at the end of the prior estate. The owner of a contingent remainder has only a conditional right to possession when the prior estate ends. Both are estates in land in favor of persons other than the grantor, and both can be transferred to other persons (that is, purchased and sold, inherited, devised or bequeathed).

Suppose Owen, the owner of Blackacre, transfers it "to Ann for ninety-nine years with remainder to Dan." Ann has a present possessory interest in Blackacre in the form of a ninety-nine-year term. Dan has a future possessory interest in Blackacre, which is presently vested and which takes effect instantly at the end of ninety-nine years. Note the difference between Dan's vested remainder in this example and Ellen's contingent remainder in the following example.

Owen conveys Blackacre "to Carla, my wife, for life, with remainder to my daughter, Ellen, if, and only if, she marries within Carla's lifetime." In this example, Carla has a present possessory interest in the form of a life estate, and Ellen has a contingent remainder—a future possessory interest that is not vested at present. Its vesting is *contingent* upon Ellen's marrying within Carla's lifetime. If Ellen does not marry within Carla's lifetime, then the remainder that Ellen would have taken *reverts* to Owen, who retains a possibility of reverter at the time of the conveyance. If Ellen does marry during Carla's lifetime, then Ellen's future possessory interest *vests* immediately, but Ellen still cannot take possession of Blackacre until the end of Carla's life estate.

Executory interests are future possessory interests in real property that are conveyed to persons other than the grantor at the time of a conveyance. These interests were not recognized at common law but are recognized in all states today. Executory interests are similar to vested and contingent remainders, with one important difference. Executory interests do not occur instantly at the end of a prior estate.

In the examples of vested and contingent remainders above, note that Dan's and Ellen's remainder interests become possessory interests as soon as the preceding estates terminate naturally. Executory interests take effect either before or after the natural termination of a preceding estate. To illustrate: Owen conveys Blackacre "to Ann for twenty years, but if Ann should divorce, then Blackacre is to pass immediately to Carla." Carla has a future interest in Blackacre that will become a present possessory interest if Ann becomes divorced. Carla's future interest is known as a *shifting executory interest,* as the possessory interest would shift from Ann to Carla if Ann should divorce.

If Owen conveys Blackacre "to Barbara for life and one year after Barbara's death to Dan," Barbara has a life estate, and Dan has an executory interest that will not arise until one year after the termination of Barbara's life estate. Such an executory interest is known as a *springing executory interest.* By operation of law, Owen retains a reversion in Blackacre of one year, and Dan's executory interest then *springs* from Owen.

Rule against Perpetuities

The purpose of the rule against perpetuities is to prevent the tying up of property ownership. The rule achieves this purpose by preventing *remoteness in vesting.* In its simplest form, the rule is: No interest is good unless it must vest, if at all, not later than twenty-one years after some life in being at the creation of the interest (excluding periods of gestation). The rule is not a perfect solution to the problem of tying up title, but it is stated in such precise terms that *any* conveyance that ties up title for a long period of time will be voided by the rule.

The student should note that interests in land can be created either by deed while the grantor is alive, or by will (at the grantor's death). This is important in determining the identity of the life in being to which the rule refers. The complexity of the rule will become apparent in the following examples, chosen specifically to demonstrate why the rule is being modified in some jurisdictions. The modifications will be discussed after the examples.

The first example is of a conveyance that is not voided by the rule against perpetuities. Suppose Owen conveys Blackacre by deed "to Barbara for life, then to Carla for life, then to Dan for life, remainder to Dan's children." Barbara, Carla, and Dan all have life estates, and Dan's children have a vested remainder in Blackacre. The rule against perpetuities does not void the vested remainder of Dan's children, since their identity will be known at Dan's death (or within the period of gestation thereafter). Since Owen specifically names Dan in the conveyance, Dan must be alive at the creation of his interest and therefore is a life in being. The interests of Dan's children will vest, if at all, within twenty-one years of Dan's death, since their identities must be alive at the creation of his interest (the gestation period) after Dan's death. If Dan has no children, this will be known at Dan's death, and ownership of Blackacre will revert to Owen or Owen's heirs.

If Owen conveys Blackacre *by will* "to the first of my grandchildren to reach the age of twenty-one," this conveyance does not violate the rule against perpetuities. Since the conveyance was by will, the interest in the first of Owen's grandchildren to reach twenty-one is not created until Owen's death. Owen's *children* will be deemed the "lives in being" under the rule, since Owen can have no more children after death. Within twenty-one years of the death of any of Owen's children (the "lives in being"), the interest in Owen's *grandchildren* must vest, since no grandchild of Owen's can possibly reach the age of twenty-one more than twenty-one years after the death of the last of Owen's children (excluding periods of gestation).

If Owen's will leaves Blackacre "to the first of my grandchildren to reach age thirty," the rule against perpetuities will void any possible interest in Owen's grandchildren unless, at the time of Owen's death, one of the grandchildren is at least thirty years old. Even if at Owen's death, Owen's oldest grandchild is five days short of thirty and in perfect health, he or she cannot obtain ownership of Blackacre under this latter version of Owen's will, since it is possible that he or she might die before age thirty and that none of Owen's other grandchildren will reach age thirty within twenty-one years of the death of Owen's last child. The rule against perpetuities does not take into consideration probabilities of vesting; it considers only possible remoteness of vesting.

Suppose Owen conveys Blackacre *by will* "to the first baby born in Southern Methodist Hospital after my death." Even if two dozen babies are delivered each day at Southern Methodist Hospital, this conveyance by Owen is void, since it violates the rule against perpetuities. Since the conveyance is by will, and the takers under the will are not Owen's descendants, it is impossible to determine a life in being. Owen could not serve as the life in being because Owen will be dead at the time his will takes effect. Since there is a possibility that no baby will be born at Southern Methodist Hospital within twenty-one years after Owen's death, the conveyance violates the rule. Owen could have achieved the desired result and avoided the rule by drafting the provision to read: "To the first baby born at Southern Methodist Hospital; but if none is born within twenty-one years of my death, then to my heirs."

As one can easily see, it is most important to determine who the "life in being" is when deciding whether the rule against perpetuities has been violated. The person whose life serves as the measuring rod need not be mentioned in the document creating the property interest at issue and need not take any interest in the property. Furthermore, the person need not be connected in any way with the property or the persons designated to take it.

Wait and See Doctrine and Cy-Pres Doctrine   The rule against perpetuities is in a state of transition. Because of the sometimes anomalous results obtained by strict application of the rule, some jurisdictions have made slight modifications. The most notable of them are the wait and see doctrine and the cy-pres doctrine. The **wait and see doctrine** is used to determine whether a contingent interest violates the rule against perpetuities. In the states that have enacted it, this doctrine allows the court to look at the circumstances of the contingency and not, as the rule prescribes, only at the creation of the interest. Thus, events occurring after inception of the instruments can be considered if they are relevant to the vesting of a future interest. If the contingency which limits the interest actually

occurs within the period prescribed by the rule, the interest is valid. In some states, this doctrine is called the *second look doctrine.* In the example of Owen conveying Blackacre by will "to the first child born at Southern Methodist Hospital after my death," the interest would likely be saved in a jurisdiction with a wait and see statute, since the child probably would be born at the hospital after Owen's death.

A doctrine with a similar purpose to the wait and see doctrine is the **cy-pres doctrine.** Although this doctrine is often associated with bequests for charitable uses, it is used as a rule for the construction of instruments in equity by which the intention of the party is carried out *as near as may be.* Where a testator attempts, for example, to create a perpetuity, the court, under this doctrine, will endeavor to explain the will in such a way as to carry out the testator's general intentions as far as the rule against perpetuities will allow rather than voiding the testator's bequest. In essence, the court will redraft a conveyance to conform to the intent of the grantor. For example, if Owen conveys Blackacre by will "to the first of my grandchildren to reach twenty-five years of age," the age designated by the grantor will be reduced to twenty-one so that the conveyance will not be voided by the rule against perpetuities.

NONPOSSESSORY INTERESTS

Ownership of land (freehold interests and interests less than freehold) is usually characterized by the owner's *possession* of the land. An owner of an interest in land can have a present right to possession, or, as in the case of future interests, can have a future right to possession. Some interests in land do not include any rights of possession. These interests, known as nonpossessory interests, include easements, profits, and licenses. Because easements and profits are similar, and the same rules apply to both, they will be discussed together.

Easements and Profits

An **easement** is the right of a person to make limited use of another person's property without taking anything from the property. For example, an easement can be the right to walk across another's property. A **profit** is the right to go onto land in possession of another and take away some part of the land itself or some product of the land. For example, Owen, the owner of Sandy View, gives Ann the right to go there and remove all the sand and gravel that Ann needs for her cement business. Ann has a profit. The difference between an easement and a profit is that an easement merely allows a person to use land without taking anything from it, whereas a profit allows a person to take something from the land. Easements and profits can be classified as either *appurtenant* or *in gross*.

Easement (or Profit) Appurtenant   An easement or profit appurtenant arises where the owner of one piece of land has a right to go onto (or remove things from) an adjacent piece of land owned by another. Suppose Owen, the owner of Whiteacre, has a right to drive his car across Green's land, Greenacre, which is adjacent to Whiteacre. This right of way over Greenacre is an easement appurtenant to Whiteacre and can be used only by the owner of Whiteacre. Owen can convey the easement when he conveys Whiteacre.

The outstanding feature of an easement appurtenant is that it involves two neighboring pieces of land owned by two different persons.

The parcels of land and the persons who own them are known respectively as the *dominant tenement*, the *servient tenement*, the *dominant tenant*, and the *servient tenant*. In the example above, Whiteacre is the dominant tenement, since it is benefited by the easement, and Greenacre is the servient tenement, since it is burdened by the easement. In addition, Owen is the dominant tenant, since he is the owner of Whiteacre, and Green is the servient tenant.

Easement (or Profit) in Gross   An easement or profit in gross exists when the right to use or take things from another's land is not dependent upon the owner of the easement or profit also owning an adjacent tract of land. Suppose Owen owns a parcel of land with a marble quarry. Owen conveys to the XYZ Corporation, which owns no land, the right to come onto Owen's land and remove up to five hundred pounds of marble per day. XYZ Corporation owns a profit in gross. An easement or profit in gross requires the existence of only one piece of land that must be owned by someone other than the owner of the easement or profit in gross. Another illustration is that of a utility company granted an easement to run its power lines across another's property.

The following case illustrates a dominant tenant's use of the servient tenant's property in accordance with the purpose of the easement.

BACKGROUND AND FACTS   *Homeowners brought this action to prevent a utility company from installing an aboveground transformer on an easement on the homeowners' lots. The utility company had previously maintained an underground transformer vault on the easement.*

CITY PUBLIC SERV. BD. OF SAN ANTONIO v. KARP
Court of Civil Appeals of Texas, 1979.
585 S.W.2d 838.

MURRAY, Justice.

*   *   *   *

In February 1978 appellant advised appellees that it intended to construct within the easement a pad-mounted transformer to replace the underground transformer. The replacement unit is a box-shaped metal and plastic transformer that would be attached to a three and a half by three and a half feet concrete slab and would extend about forty inches above the level of the presently existing iron grate. Appellees notified appellant that the proposed construction would be in excess of their easement rights and refused to allow this construction. It was agreed between the parties that no construction would proceed and that appellees would commence an action for a declaratory judgment to obtain a judicial determination on the extent and scope of appellant's easement. The trial court, in entering judgment for appellees, held that because the easement was general, vague and indefinite, future use of the easement is restricted to its initial use.

*   *   *   *

In our case, the easement is not general, but is specifically defined in its location (northwest corner of lot 8) and size five by five feet. It is also limited in its purpose to a transformer easement. The trial court's holding that the easement is general, vague, and indefinite is erroneous as a matter of law. Therefore, appellant's easement rights were not fixed by the original construction of the underground transformer.

An easement owner, being the dominant tenant, is entitled to the free and undisturbed use of its property for the purpose of the easement. *Gulf View Courts, Inc. v. Galveston County,* 150 S.W.2d 872 (Tex.Civ.App.—Galveston 1941, writ ref'd). An easement granted for general purposes includes not only the use required at the time of the grant, but also the right to use the easement for any purposes connected with the use to which the property is being put.

The creation of an easement involves looking forward by those participating in its creation, to a future use by the dominant tenant that is not inconsistent with or repugnant to the creating instrument. Restatement of Property § 484, Comment a (1944). Comment "a" goes on to state:

> This use, by necessity, must be made under conditions somewhat different from those existing at the time of the conveyance. In the absence of language specifically negativing it, it will be assumed that the parties contemplated changes in the use of the servient tenement made necessary by the normal development in the use of the dominant tenement.

The grant in this case clearly gives the City Public Service Board the right to use its easement for transformer purposes, which necessarily includes the right to install a pad-mounted transformer within the confines of its easement as a matter of normal development.

JUDGMENT AND REMEDY   *The judgment of the trial court was reversed. A new judgment was entered permitting the utility company to replace the transformer.*

Effect of Sale of Property   Whenever a parcel of land that is benefited by an easement or profit appurtenant is sold, the property carries the easement or profit along with it. Thus, if Owens sells Whiteacre to Thomas and includes the appurtenant right-of-way across Greenacre in the deed to Thomas, Thomas will own both the property and the easement that benefits it.

When a piece of land that has the burden of an easement or profit appurtenant is sold, the new owner must recognize its existence only if he or she knew or should have known of it or if it was recorded in the appropriate office of the county. Thus, if Owen records his easement across Greenacre in the appropriate county office before Green conveys the land, the new owner of Greenacre will have to allow Owen, or any subsequent owner of Whiteacre, to continue to use the path across Greenacre.

Creation of an Easement (or Profit)   Profits and easements can be created by *deed* or *will* or by *implication, necessity,* or *prescription.* Creation by deed or will simply involves delivery of a deed or disposition in a will by the owner of an easement stating that the grantee (the person receiving the profit or easement) is granted the rights in the easement or profit that the grantor had.

An easement or profit is created by *implication* when the circumstances surrounding the division of a piece of property imply its creation. For example, suppose Barrow divides a parcel of land that has only one well for drinking water and conveys the half without a well to Dan. Here, a profit by implication arises, since Dan needs drinking water.

An easement by *necessity* does not require division of property for its existence. A person who rents an apartment, by necessity, has an easement in the private road leading up to it.

Easements and profits by *prescription* arise when one person uses another person's land for a period of time equal to the statute of limitations for recovery of property. If the owner of the land does not object to the use of the land for the required period of time, the person using the land has an easement or profit by prescription.

Suppose Alfred Carin owns a plot of land with an old coal mine on it. Carin's neighbor, Max Beta, goes onto Carin's land every Sunday, Monday, and Tuesday and removes several wheelbarrows of coal for a period of seven years. The applicable statute of limitations for recovery of real property is five years. In this situation, Beta has a profit by prescription since he has openly taken coal for the limitations period without any objection from Carin, and Carin can no longer object. Beta owns the profit and can continue taking the coal as long as he wants. Of course, Beta cannot take substantially more coal than he took in the past. Thus, if he started a regular mining operation, Carin could stop him.

Termination An easement or profit can be terminated or extinguished in several ways. The simplest way is to deed it back to the owner of the land that is burdened by it. Second, the owner of an easement or profit can abandon it and create evidence of his or her intent to relinquish the right to use it. Mere nonuse will not extinguish an easement or profit *unless it is accom-*

panied by an intent to *abandon.* Third, when the owner of an easement or profit becomes the owner of the property burdened by it, then it is merged into the property. Essentially, the individual now owns both the easement or profit and the land, so there is no need for the easement or profit to continue. The individual can simply use the land as owner in fee simple.

Licenses

A license is the revocable right of a person to come onto another person's land. It is a personal privilege that arises from the consent of the owner of the land and that can be revoked by the owner. Therefore, unlike easements or profits, a license cannot arise by prescription, since a prescriptive claim is, by definition, adverse to the rights of the property owner.

An example of a license is a ticket to attend a movie at a theater. A theater owner issues the ticket, which entitles the holder to enter onto the property of the owner. Another example of a license arises when a landowner sells personal property that is located on the land. For example, Ferguson purchases a tractor owned by Wilson that Wilson has left in the middle of his cornfield. Ferguson's purchase gives him the license to enter onto the cornfield to remove the tractor.

A person who has property rights in the nature of a license can also have contractual rights. Since the rights of a licensee are revocable at the will of the licensor, a person should always look to the possible existence of an underlying contract to bolster his or her rights against the licensor.

LAND USE CONTROL

Land use control deals with the *limitations* placed upon property owners that either arise by agreement (covenants running with the land, equitable servitudes) or are imposed by the government (zoning).

Covenants Running with the Land

A **covenant running with the land** is an agreement under which a landowner either acquires certain rights or is under certain obligations merely because he or she owns the land that is bound by the covenant. A covenant running with the land can be classified somewhere between a contract and an easement or profit appurtenant. Instead of binding person to person (as a contract does) or land to land (as an easement does), a covenant running with the land binds a person to land.

Consider an example. Owen is the owner of Grasslands, a twenty-acre estate whose northern half contains a small reservoir. Owen wishes to convey the northern half to Arid City, but before he does, he digs an irrigation ditch connecting the reservoir with the lower ten acres that he uses as farmland. When Owen conveys the northern ten acres to Arid City, he enters into an agreement with the city. The agreement, which is contained in the deed, states, "Arid City, its heirs and assigns, promise not to remove more than five thousand gallons of water per day from the Grasslands reservoir." Owen has created a covenant running with the land under which Arid City and all future owners of the northern ten acres of Grasslands are limited to the amount of water they can draw from its reservoir.

Four requirements must be met for a covenant running with the land to be enforceable. If they are not met, a simple contract is created between the two original parties only.

1. The covenant running with the land must be created in a written agreement (covenant). It is usually contained in the document that conveys the land (deed or will).
2. The parties must intend that the covenant *run with the land*. In other words, the instrument that contains the covenant must state not only that the promisor is bound by the terms of the covenant but that all the promisor's "successors, heirs, or assigns" will be bound.
3. The covenant must *touch and concern* the land. The limitations on the activities of the owner of the burdened land must have some connection with the land. For example, a purchaser of land cannot be bound by a covenant requiring him or her to drive only Ford pickups, since such a restriction has no relation to the land purchased.
4. The original parties to the covenant must be in *privity of estate* at the time the covenant is created. This means that the relationship between them must be landlord-tenant, vendor-purchaser, or testator-devisee, and so forth. Note that this is unlike an easement appurtenant, which can be created by two parties who merely own adjoining land and are not in privity of estate.

The following case illustrates enforcement of a restrictive covenant.

ALLEN v. FORBESS
Court of Appeal of Louisiana,
Second Circuit, 1977.
345 So.2d 950.

BACKGROUND AND FACTS *Plaintiff Allen brought this suit to enforce a restrictive covenant that prohibited commercial establishments within the plantiff's subdivision.*

MARVIN, Judge.

* * * *

Defendant began his worm farm endeavor in 1975. By the time Plaintiff filed suit in 1976, Defendant had erected 35 worm bed structures approximately three feet high, on the rear or easterly portion of his lots. The worm bed structures are of masonry and metal or wood, covered with burlap. Defendant has no customers who come to his lot. He sells for profit and delivers worms to customers who order worms by sometimes telephoning Defendant at his home. Defendant admits that he attempts to raise 1,000 worms per square foot of worm bed and that he has a total of 2,600 square feet of beds in the 35 structures on his subdivision lots.

The subdivision plat and restrictions were recorded in 1953. Plaintiff was residing in the subdivision before Defendant began his worm operation. Plaintiff acknowledged that she knew one person in the subdivision (a Mrs. Long) commercially operated a beauty shop in her home and advertised its operation. Plaintiff was sometimes a customer in this beauty shop, located about 900 yards from Plaintiff's home. Mrs. Long, the shop operator, ceased operating the beauty shop however, some eight years before this litigation arose. Plaintiff also admitted she knew a subdivision resident, about a block away from Plaintiff, was teaching piano lessons in her home.

Plaintiff did not admit being aware that three other persons conducted some type of business in their respective homes in the subdivision. One resident, in his basement hobby shop, has repaired guns and charged therefor since 1966. This resident does not advertise his gun repair services. Another resident calibrates water meters for a charge in the basement of his home. This resident does not advertise this service and his customers do not call at his home. A third resident drew house plans in his home from 1963 until 1969. He advertised his services to a limited degree in the local newspaper and his clients occasionally came to his home.

The restrictions in question are covenants that run with the land for the benefit of the owners of lots in the subdivision. Injunction is a legally proper and available remedy to prevent violation of the restrictions. Civil law principles of interpretation are to be employed in construing restrictive covenants, fairly and faithfully considering the entirety of the instrument and the intent of the subdivider, if interpretation is necessary.

The language of the covenant clearly restricts the use of a lot to residential purposes and prohibits commercial establishments. While the language perhaps could have been more precise and explicit, a fair, but strict conclusion is that the subdividers intended that a family unit structure would be constructed on each lot and that commercial establishments were not to be permitted.

The lower court found the Defendant's worm farm activity to be in contravention of the restriction, but held the restriction to have been abandoned or waived because of the actual use of a significant portion of the developed area of the subdivision. The "actual use" which the trial court found was the five mentioned violations among the 13 families residing in the developed area of the subdivision.

Under the circumstances here, the five violations mentioned were indoor activities, not of similar character to Defendant's erection of 35 worm bed structures visible to Plaintiff and the public. Two of the five violations had been discontinued eight or more years when Defendant began his activity and Plaintiff brought suit. While there are only thirteen family units or residences now in the subdivision, the subdivision is comprised of more than twice that many lots which are subject to the restriction. Under the circumstances shown by the record, a finding of waiver and abandonment of the restriction was not warranted.

An injunction was issued by the appellate court prohibiting Forbess from engaging in the activity of raising and cultivating worms in the subdivision.   **JUDGMENT AND REMEDY**

Equitable Servitudes

Because of the confusion over the meaning and application of the privity of estate requirement, covenants running with the land have not been a very effective device for guiding the development of residential and commercial land. Therefore, courts of equity have created an alternative means of private land use control known as **equitable servitudes.**

Covenants running with the land and equitable servitudes are similar in their application and effect, but the requirements for enforcing an equitable servitude are less stringent. An equitable servitude is created by an instrument that complies with the Statute of Frauds, an intention that the use of land be restricted, and *notice* of the restriction to the person acquiring the burdened land.

For example, Owen owns two adjacent lots, Brownacre and Redacre. Owen conveys Redacre to the city of Pleasantville, stipulating in the deed that it be utilized only as a wildlife sanctuary and that no buildings be built on it. Owen also records the restriction in the county land records office. Thereafter, when the Ace Construction Company purchases Redacre from Pleasantville with the intention of building office buildings on it, it is bound by the restrictions that Owen placed on the land even if the restrictions are not contained in the deed by which it obtains the land from Pleasantville. Because the restrictions are recorded in the appropriate county office, Ace Construction Company is deemed to be on *constructive notice* of the restrictions.

Developers generally utilize equitable servitudes when developing a large parcel of land and subdividing it into residences. The developer will file a **plat** in the county records office that describes the land being developed and the restrictions under which each subdivided lot is sold.[1] Equitable servitudes have been effectively used to retain the integrity and aesthetic value of a neighborhood. Frequently, they involve a so-called architectural committee that must approve any building variations. In this way, the quality of the neighborhood can be protected against a nonconformist landowner.

Equitable servitudes are usually upheld; however, equitable servitudes and covenants running with the land have sometimes been used to perpetuate neighborhood segregation, and in these cases they have usually not been upheld. For example, property owners in entire neighborhoods have joined together and conveyed their homes to a straw man (usually a lawyer) who would write in a restrictive covenant proscribing resale to minority groups. The straw man would then reconvey the property to the initial owners.

In the Supreme Court case of *Shelley v. Kraemer*, such restrictive covenants were declared unconstitutional and could no longer be enforced in a court of law.[2] In addition, the Civil Rights Act of 1968 (also known as the Fair Housing Act) prohibits all discrimination based on race, color, religion, or national origin in the sale and leasing of housing.

Zoning

The government is by far the most potent force in guiding the development and use of land. State and local governments have far greater resources and enforcement powers than private individuals to control land use. Moreover, since ideally the government represents majority interests, it is in the best position to determine what land uses reflect the needs of society as a whole.

The state's power to control the use of land is derived from two sources: eminent domain and police power. Through eminent domain, the government can take land for public use, but it must pay just compensation, so this is an expensive method of land use control.

Under its police power, however, the state can pass laws aimed at protecting public health, safety, morals, and general welfare. These laws can affect owners' rights and uses of land, but the state does not have to compensate the landowner. If the state's legislation restricts the landowner's property rights too much, the state's *regulation* will be deemed a *confiscation* and subject to the eminent domain requirements that just compensation be paid.

For example, suppose Jones owns a large tract of land that she purchased with the intent to subdivide and develop into residential properties. At the time of the purchase, there were no

---

1. A plat, also called a plot, is a map or representation on paper of a piece of land subdivided into lots, with streets, alleys, and so forth usually drawn to scale. When filed with the appropriate records office, the plat contains the restrictions under which the subdivided lots have been sold.

2. 334 U.S. 1, 68 S.Ct. 836 (1948).

zoning regulations restricting use of the land. If the government attempts to zone Jones's entire tract of land as "parkland only" and prohibits her from developing any part of it, the action will be deemed confiscatory, since the government will be denying her the ability to use her property for any purpose for which it is reasonably suited. The government will have to compensate Jones, since it has effectively confiscated her land. However, if the government zones Jones's parcel of land as "three-fourths residential, one-fourth park area" after her purchase, this zoning regulation is not confiscatory since she will be able to use most of the property for building residences.

The state's power to regulate the use of land is limited in two other ways, both of which arise from the Fourteenth Amendment. First, the state cannot regulate the use of land arbitrarily or unreasonably, since this would be a denial of property without due process. There must be a *rational basis* for the classifications that the state imposes on the property. Note, however, that this limitation is not very stringent. Any act that is reasonably related to the health or general welfare of the public is deemed to have a rational basis.

Second, a state's regulation of land use control cannot be discriminatory. The state is prohibited from discriminating against any race, religion, or nationality. The state is also generally prohibited from discriminating against any other group as well. Discrimination on the basis of race, religion, or national origin is never justifiable. However, discrimination based on other factors (for example, low income versus high income groups) may be upheld if there is a rational basis for the discrimination.

Zoning is frequently based on a comprehensive plan (many times associated with a master plan) for the development and use of property within a government jurisdiction, such as a city. The plan divides the government jurisdiction into districts or zones. Zoning then regulates the land use that can be made within the district or zone. Designations such as residential, commercial, and industrial are made, each with its subclassifications. For example, one residential zone may be limited to single family units whereas another residential zone may permit duplexes.

Nonconforming Use

The problems associated with zoning are often the result of normal growing pains experienced by expanding suburban areas that were once rural. John Gordon, a chicken farmer, has lived with his family in Charlesville and has been a chicken farmer all his life. Since Charlesville is located only eighty miles from Megalopolis, a booming sunbelt town, it is being invaded by suburbanites. Charlesville had never heard of zoning until the late 1960s, when its newly elected zoning board decided that the 125 acres surrounding Gordon's two-acre chicken farm were best suited for suburban residents.

Gordon appealed to the zoning board, claiming that his chicken farm, originally owned by his father, was located on the same two-acres for seventy-five years. After hearing Gordon's plea, the zoning board gave him two years to close down and move his business. Gordon's chicken farm, which was in operation long before his area was zoned, is known as a **nonconforming use.**

If the zoning ordinance called for Gordon's immediate removal, this action would be deemed confiscatory, and the government body promulgating the ordinance would have to pay just compensation for taking the farm. But as long as the nonconforming use is permitted to continue for a reasonable period of time, it is not deemed a taking of property, and therefore no compensation is necessary.

Sometimes nonconforming use will be permitted as long as the property owner continues to use the property in the same manner and so long as the property owner does not expand the use of the property. For example, a florist operates and sells flowers from a greenhouse. The zoning in the area is changed to permit only single family living units. The florist could be granted a nonconforming use to continue in business, as this would not substantially affect single family living in the area. However, although the florist could repair the greenhouse, the florist could not build additional greenhouse facilities. Moreover, upon sale of the property the nonconforming use decree would be automatically voided.

Floating Zones

Generally, the state agency charged with the responsibility of land use planning can take one of two approaches. The first is to designate, all at once, use restrictions on each parcel of land located within the entire area to be zoned (usually a city or town). Alternatively, the state agency can use "floating zones," deciding initially how much land should be designated for each of a variety of particular uses (commercial, residential, park, farming) and later assigning such designations at the request of landowners. Under the "floating zone" concept, the amount of land to be used for any one purpose is determined at the outset, but it is not assigned in what otherwise might be an arbitrary manner. This allows for flexibility in zoning.

Variance

A landowner whose land has been limited by a zoning ordinance to a particular use cannot make an alternative use of the land unless he or she first obtains a zoning variance. A landowner must meet three criteria to be entitled to a variance:

1. The landowner must find it impossible to realize a reasonable return on the land as zoned.
2. The adverse effect of the zoning ordinance must be particular to the person seeking the variance and not one that has a similar effect on the other landowners within the same zone.
3. A granting of the variance must not alter the essential character of the zoned area substantially.

By far the most important criterion used in granting a variance is whether it will alter the character of the neighborhood substantially. Courts tend to be rather lenient about the first two requirements. As the following case shows, courts also tend to defer to the discretion of zoning boards unless the board has abused its authority.

CONNER v. HERD
Court of Appeals of Missouri,
1970.
452 S.W.2d 272.

BACKGROUND AND FACTS *The city of Moline planned to build a new firehouse on land that was appropriately zoned for construction of a firehouse. However, the proposed firehouse was slightly larger than the zoning ordinances allowed. Thus, in April 1963 Moline filed with the Board of Zoning Adjustment of St. Louis County for variances from the set-back and building line provisions in the ordinance. Essentially, the city's plans called for construction of a building that would be set back about four feet farther than the zoning allowed. Alfred and Marie Conner, who owned adjacent property that faced the site of the new construction, objected to the variance. The variance was granted, and the Conners appealed the board's ruling to the courts.*

SMITH, Commissioner.

*   *   *   *

The genesis of the litigation was the filing by Moline in April, 1963, of an application to the Board for variances from the set-back and building line provisions.

*   *   *   *

*   *   * [A]ppellants contend the findings of the Board were arbitrary and capricious and not based upon competent and substantial evidence. We take these in order.

*   *   *   *

"JURISDICTION AND POWERS.—The Board of Zoning Adjustment is hereby authorized to: (5) Permit a variation in the yard requirements of any Zoning District or the building and set back lines for Major Highways as provided by law where there are practical difficulties or unnecessary hardships in the carrying out of these provisions due to an irregular shape of the lot, topographical or other conditions, provided such variation will not seriously affect any adjoining property or the general welfare."

This provision, under which the Board acted here, empowers the Board to give variances under specified circumstances where strict enforcement of the regulations would be unjust. It imposes standards for the Board's action and is not a grant of legislative power.

This brings us to the heart of this appeal, appellants' contention that the action of the Board was not based on competent and substantial evidence and was arbitrary and capricious. Neither this court nor the trial court can substitute its judgment on the evidence for that of the Board. We may only determine whether the Board could reach the conclusion it did upon the evidence before it. We hold it could.

*   *   *   *

Having in mind the limited scope of our review of the findings of the Board we turn to the evidence which supports the Board's order. The property in question is on the northwest corner of Chambers Road and Clairmont Drive in an unincorporated portion of St. Louis County. Chambers Road is a major thoroughfare which was widened shortly before the application for variance. The land in question is owned by Moline and has been the site for its fire station since at least 1946. The old fire house complied with the Chambers Road set-back line but not with the Clairmont Drive building line upon which it encroached approximately 4¼ feet as a pre-existing use.

*   *   *   *

The most efficient and satisfactory type of fire station for Moline's purposes is one where returning trucks can enter the back of the station from Clairmont Drive, remove the hoses and other equipment for cleaning, put clean equipment on the truck and move the truck into position for exit through the front onto Chambers Road for the next call. The lot in question is 165 feet in depth (after the widening of Chambers to 80 feet) and 80 feet in width. If the set-back line on Chambers Road, 80 feet, is adhered to there would not be enough room at the rear of the station (39 feet) for the large fire trucks to negotiate the turn from Clairmont Drive into the rear of the station. The entrance from Clairmont would also obviate the need for the trucks to back into the station from Chambers Road. There was also testimony that having the station located nearer the road than the old station would allow greater traffic safety in leaving the station in that both the dispatcher and the driver would have greater visibility along Chambers. This was based upon a difference in elevation of the property from front to rear of 6 feet, the front being higher. In view of testimony that regardless of where the station is located the trucks would have to slow down before entering Chambers Road to be sure the traffic was clear, we doubt that this evidence alone would be enough to establish a hardship based upon topographical conditions.

The width of the lot is such that a 2 foot variance on the building line of Clairmont Drive would be necessary to get the proposed fire station on the property if the regulation of a 6 foot side yard on the west (next to appellants) is met.

The granted variance is less than the previously existing encroachment.

* * * *

The Board could find here that in the absence of a variance Moline would be confronted with substantial additional expense, interruption of fire protection service during the period of construction, and unnecessary inconvenience if not outright danger to the residents of the district. The Board is not required to ignore the source of the funds available to the district (taxpayers) in determining that additional expense constitutes an unnecessary hardship. Under *Rosedale-Skinker*, there exist sufficient "practical difficulties" and "unnecessary hardships" to the district to permit a variance and these arise from the inadequate size of the lot to contain a fire station. This was the essence of the Board's finding "that because of the requirements, the proposed new building and facilities cannot be erected as the eighty foot set back line on Chambers Road and the thirty foot building line on Clairmont Drive are intended."

Appellants contend that there is no evidence to support a conclusion that the variance will not "seriously affect any adjoining property." We do not agree. This contention must be judged only upon the effect of a variance, not upon the effect of a fire house. Appellants' contention is based solely upon the effect upon their property. The fire house to be constructed will be for the front 9 feet, one story in height. The remainder will be two stories. Some air conditioning equipment will be located on the roof of the one story section but the record does not require a conclusion that this will create an undue amount of noise or other disturbance affecting appellants' property, nor that any effect will be the result of the variance. Such equipment would actually be closer to appellants' home if the variance were not granted than if it were. It is also true that the proposed fire house will be 6 feet from appellants' property line and 13 feet from the edge of appellants' home. This, however, is not caused by the variance requested, for Moline could place the building that close without a variance. Appellants contend that the granting of the variance will reduce their view to the east. Appellant husband testified that he had paid $26,500 for his land and house and that "he felt" the proposed new fire house would damage him at least one-third to one-half the value of his property. He offered nothing to support his opinion, and could not state the fair market value of his home before or after the variance. Although such opinion evidence may be competent, its weight is for the trier of fact. Neither the Board, nor the trial court, nor this court is bound to accept such testimony as establishing the effect on appellants' property. The Board had before it pictures of the area involved, taken from several different angles. It could determine from those pictures the degree to which appellants' view is reduced. It could take into account the improvement of traffic safety on Chambers Road, which would inure to appellants' benefit, which had been testified to. We do not doubt that there is some effect on appellants' property. That it is seriously affected we cannot hold as a matter of law on the record before us. Based upon the testimony and evidence before it, we cannot say there was no competent and substantial evidence to support the Board's finding in this regard.

The effect on general welfare finding is supported by the evidence of the need for the new building to render adequate fire protection to the district and by the testimony on the beneficial effect of the proposed construction upon traffic safety on Chambers Road, including the installation of a traffic light on Chambers Road to be controlled by the dispatcher when trucks leave the station.

The court found that the zoning board had enough evidence to grant the variance in accordance with the requirements of the zoning ordinance. The judgment of the circuit court, which had affirmed the action taken by the zoning board, was affirmed by the appellate court.

**JUDGMENT
AND REMEDY**

QUESTIONS AND
CASE PROBLEMS

1. Able is the owner of a lakeside house and lot. He deeds the house and lot to "my wife, Sylvia, for life, with remainder to my son, David, providing he graduates from college with a B or better average during Sylvia's lifetime." Answer the following questions:
   (a) Does Able have any interest in the deeded lakeside house? Explain.
   (b) What is Sylvia's interest called? Explain.
   (c) What is David's interest called? Explain.

2. Green has subdivided a tract of land into two parcels and has sold one to Shaw. The only road that leads to Shaw's property is on the parcel retained by Green. There is nothing in the deed received by Shaw giving Shaw an easement to use this road. However, Shaw uses the road for a number of years without objection from Green. Green now sells his parcel of land to White, who knows of Shaw's use of the road. After taking possession of the land, White denies Shaw further use of the road. Discuss fully Shaw's rights in this matter.

3. Smith owns an apartment building. She contracts with Able for one year to place in laundry rooms in the building complex coin-operated washing machines and dryers. The contract requires Able to service the washers and dryers within twenty-four hours of notice. Some of the apartment leaseholders complain to Smith that Able's service is poor and that Able does not promptly refund money lost in the machines. After an argument, Smith orders Able to remove all machines within one week and not to come on the property again. Able claims that he has a lease of the laundry rooms for one year. Discuss fully the property rights of the parties in this matter.

4. Smith owns 640 acres of rural land. A new highway is being built nearby by Ajax Construction, Inc. Ajax purchases from Smith the rights to build and use a road across Smith's land for construction vehicles to pass over and to remove sand and gravel required to build the highway. A deed is prepared and filed in the county by Ajax. Later, a dispute arises between Smith and Ajax, and Smith refuses Ajax the right to use the road or to remove sand and gravel. Ajax claims its property rights cannot be revoked by Smith. Discuss fully what property rights Ajax has in this matter.

5. Smith owns one hundred acres of land within a city's limits. She contracts to sell and deed fifty acres of this land to developer Gary. The deed states that "Gary, his heirs, and assigns promise never to subdivide the property in less than two-acre tracts." The property is zoned for single residences by the city. Gary subdivides the fifty acres and files a plat that prohibits, after initial construction, certain additions or other buildings to be built without approval of a so-called architectural committee. Gary contracts to sell a two-acre tract to Thompson. The contract contains the prohibition filed in the plat. Thompson builds a single residence home, but she later decides to subdivide the lot and, by modification and addition, build duplexes on each subdivision. Discuss fully by what legal concepts Thompson will be prevented from subdividing the two-acre lot and from building duplexes.

6. Dixie Gardens, Inc., was a developer in Pasco County, Florida. Henry Sloane purchased a lot and residence in a Dixie Gardens development. The deed read in part as follows: "If the developer or the Crestridge Utilities Corporation causes garbage collection service bi-weekly to be made available, the owner of each lot shall pay the developer or its assigns, the sum of $1.75 per month therefor." Sloane wished to employ another contractor for garbage collection, but Dixie Gardens argued that Sloane was bound by the provision quoted above, which amounted to a covenant running with the land. Is Dixie Gardens correct? [Sloane v. Dixie Gardens, Inc., 278 So.2d 309 (Fla.App. 1973)]

7. In 1961, Mary Schaefers divided her real property and conveyed it to her children, William, Elfreda, Julienne, and Rosemary. The deed from Mary Schaefers to her daughter Rosemary contained the following language: "It is further mutually agreed by and between the grantor and the grantee that as part of the consideration set out above, the grantee agrees to provide a permanent home for my daughter, Elfreda, should she desire or request one, and for my son, William Schae-

fers, should he desire or request one. Failure to perform the above will be considered a material breach of the consideration set out herein." In 1974, Rosemary conveyed her portion of her mother's property to Edward and Arthur Apel. Subsequently, William Schaefers attempted to prevent the sale to the Apels from taking place by telling them that the house was encumbered by a covenant running with the land and that if they purchased the house, they would be bound to provide a home for William and Elfreda Schaefers. Is Rosemary's promise to provide a home for William and Elfreda (should they demand one) a covenant running with the land? [Schaefers v. Apel, 295 Ala. 277, 328 So.2d 274 (1976)]

8.   Charles W. Parker died leaving a valid will that placed his property in trust and paid the income from the trust to his wife, Emma, for the remainder of her life. The will provided that at Emma's death the trust assets were to be taken out of trust and given "to William H. Parker [Charles's brother]; but if William H. Parker is not living at the death of my wife, Emma, then his share should vest in the Presbyterian Church of Carlyle." What is the nature of Emma's interest? Of William H. Parker's interest? Of the Presbyterian Church of Carlyle's interest? [Presbyterian Church of Carlyle v. St. Louis Union Trust Co., 18 Ill.App.3d 713, 310 N.E.2d 412 (1974)]

9.   On November 21, 1967, North Clearlake Development Corporation entered into a contract with Clearlake Utilities Co. that provided that "Clearlake Utilities Company shall have and is hereby granted the exclusive right to furnish water and sewer service" to the approximately eighty acres of land that North Clearlake Development Corporation had developed and to "all owners and occupants of any part thereof for and during the entire term of this contract." At the time of the contract, North Clearlake Development Corporation owned a large tract of land that it had just begun developing. Will the contract between Clearlake Utilities and North Clearlake Development constitute a covenant running with the land, binding all persons who thereafter purchase lots and homes in the development? [Clearlake Apartments, Inc. v. Clearlake Utilities Co., 537 S.W.2d 48 (Tex.Civ.App. 1976)]

10.   In his will, Fletcher devised land to his granddaughter for life, then to the heirs of her body, if any, and if not, then to Fletcher's son, his heirs, and assigns. Assuming that at the time Fletcher dies, his only granddaughter is seven years old, what is the nature of her interest? What interest, if any, do the "heirs of her body" have? [Fletcher v. Hurdle, 259 Ark. 640, 536 S.W.2d 109 (1976)]

11.   A corporation, Bewigged by Suzzi, Inc., occupied space in eight stores owned and operated by Atlantic Department Stores, Inc. Bewigged was engaged in the business of selling wigs to retail customers. The agreement between the parties designated specific amounts of space to be utilized for the sale of wigs but did not set aside specific portions of the stores. Was this a license agreement or a lease? [Bewigged by Suzzi, Inc. v. Atlantic Dept. Stores, Inc., 49 Ohio App.2d 65, 359 N.E.2d 721 (1976)]

CHAPTER 55

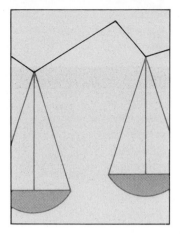

Insurance

THE NATURE OF INSURANCE

Insurance is a contract by which the insurance company (insurer) promises to pay a sum of money or give something of value to another (either the insured or the beneficiary) in the event that the insured is injured or sustains damage as the result of particular stated contingencies. Basically, insurance is an arrangement for *transferring and allocating risk*. In many cases, **risk** can be described as a prediction concerning potential loss, based on known and unknown factors. However, insurance involves much more than a game of chance, and insurers have an interest in seeing that risk is minimized. Many familiar safety devices are now commonplace because of insurer concerns or insurance laws—automobile seat belts, fire escapes, train whistles, railroad crossing lights, reflecting road signs, and break-away highway lightposts, among others.

The Concept of Risk Pooling

All types of insurance use the principle of pooling of risk; that is, they spread the risk among a large number of people—the pool—to make the premiums small compared to the coverage offered. Consider life insurance. For any particular age group, only a small number of individuals will die in any one year. If a large percentage of this age group pays premiums to a life insurance company in exchange for a benefit payment in case of premature death, there will be a sufficient amount of money to pay the beneficiaries of the policyholders who do die. Given a long enough time for correlation of data about the group and the particular disaster—in this case premature death—insurance companies can predict the total number of premature deaths in any one year with great accuracy. Thus, they can estimate the total amount they will have to pay if they insure the group, and they can predict the rates they will have to charge each member of the group in order to make the necessary payments and make a profit for the company.

Classification of Insurance

Insurance is classified according to the nature of the risk involved. For example, fire insurance, casualty insurance, life insurance, and title insurance each apply to a different type of risk. The persons and interests protected under each of these types of insurance policies differ. This is reasonable because, depending upon the nature of the activity, certain types of losses are expected, certain types are foreseeable, and certain others are unforeseeable.

Terminology

An insurance contract is called a **policy**; the consideration paid to the insurer is called a **premium**; and the insurance company is sometimes called an **underwriter**.

Parties The *parties* to an insurance policy are the *insurer* (the insurance company) and the *insured* (the person covered by its provisions). Insurance contracts are usually obtained through an *agent*, who ordinarily works for the insurance company, or a *broker*, who is ordinarily an independent contractor. When a broker deals with an applicant for insurance, the broker is, in effect, the applicant's agent. By contrast, an insurance agent is an agent of the insurance company. Thus, an insurance agent's relationship with the applicant for insurance is controlled by ordinary rules of agency law (see Chapter 35).

As a general rule, the insurance company is bound by the acts of its agents when they act within the agency relationship. On the other hand, a broker has no relationship with the insurance company and is an agent of the applicant for insurance. The status of agent or broker can be extremely important in determining liability. In most situations, state law determines the status of all parties writing or obtaining insurance.

Insurable Interest A person can insure anything in which he or she has an *insurable interest*. Without this insurable interest, there is no enforceable contract, and a transaction to insure would have to be treated as a wager.

In the case of real and personal property, an insurable interest exists when the insured derives pecuniary benefit from the preservation and continued existence of the property. That is, one has an insurable interest in property when one would sustain pecuniary loss from its destruction. In the case of life insurance, one needs to have a reasonable expectation of benefit from the continued life of another in order to have an insurable interest in that person's life. The benefit may be pecuniary or it may be founded upon the relationship between the parties (of blood or affinity).

For example, a person has an insurable interest in his or her own health or life and in the health or life of his or her spouse. But a person cannot obtain fire insurance on the White House or auto insurance on A. J. Foyt's race cars. A mortgagor and a mortgagee would both have an insurable interest in the mortgaged property. So would a landlord and a tenant in leased property, a secured party in the property in which he or she has an interest, a partner in partnership property, and a stockholder in corporate property.

Close family relationships give a person an insurable interest in the life of another. Generally, blood or marital relationships fit this category. A husband can take out an insurance policy on his wife and vice versa, parents can take out life insurance policies on their children, brothers and sisters on each other, and grandparents on grandchildren, as all these are close family relationships.

To further illustrate the concept of insurable interest, assume that James Jones insures his life for $100,000 with Continental Insurance Company, naming Henry Mason as beneficiary of the policy. When Jones dies, Continental Insurance cannot refuse to pay Mason merely because he had no insurable interest in the life of Jones. The *beneficiary* of a life insurance policy need not have an insurable interest in the insured. Jones was actually insuring his own life for the benefit of Mason and is the owner of the policy. Obviously, Jones has an insurable interest in his own life. On the other hand, if Jones bought a policy with Continental Insurance to insure the life of his next door neighbor, Robert Samuel, Continental Insurance could refuse to pay the face value of the policy upon Samuel's death because Jones had no insurable interest in Samuel's life.

The insurable interest in life insurance must exist *at the time the policy is obtained.* This is exactly the opposite of property insurance, where the insurable interest must exist at the time the loss occurs and not necessarily when the policy is purchased. Because of this rule involving life insurance, in most states a divorce will not affect a policy. If the divorced spouse is named as ben-

eficiary, the divorce action will not automatically divest that spouse's right to the proceeds or to an insurable interest.

The existence of an insurable interest is a primary concern when determining liability under an insurance policy. In the following case, the insurance company claimed that the policyholders had lost their insurable interest in certain real property by leasing the premises to a third party. Moreover, since the plaintiffs (the policyholders) had not demonstrated any actual loss, they had no interest in the property and, hence, no insurable interest. The appellate court denied both claims.

BACKGROUND AND FACTS   In 1969, the plaintiffs purchased a $32,000 insurance policy against fire loss effective for three years. The property insured under the policy was a gas station. After they purchased the policy, the plaintiffs leased the service station and the land to Shell Oil Company for an initial term of fifteen years, with a renewal option of three additional five-year terms.

Other parts of the lease provided that Shell could demolish and remove the existing building within one year and build a new ranch-style service station. In addition, Shell was obligated and exclusively entitled to insure any building it constructed during the term of the lease.

In 1971, the station was destroyed by fire. It had been scheduled for demolition but was still being used at the time of the fire. The court first examined the argument that the lease destroyed the plaintiffs' insurable interest in the property.

GENDRON v.
PAWTUCKET MUT. INS.
CO.
Supreme Judicial Court of
Maine, 1978.
384 A.2d 694.

WERNICK, Justice.

*   *   *   *

The existence of an insured's insurable interest in property covered by a contract of insurance is determined by the relationship between the insured and the property insured—more specifically, by whether there is a relationship such that injury to the property will, as a natural consequence, result in a loss to the insured. Since the question of insurable interest thus necessarily involves the insured's relationship to the property insured, we conclude that even if plaintiffs had purported by an executory contract to give a third person exclusive entitlement to place insurance on property already insured by plaintiffs, that fact is not by itself sufficient to terminate plaintiffs' insurable interest in the insured property. Plaintiffs had not, here, made an actual transfer of such of their rights in the insured property as would destroy their insurable interest; the mere leasing of property is not such an alienation of it as destroys insurable interest. This being so, defendant insurance company may not treat the "exclusive right to insure" provisions in the lease with Shell as a waiver or surrender by plaintiffs, capable of redounding to the benefit of defendant insurance company, of plaintiffs' insurable interest in the property they had insured with defendant. The insurer simply cannot thus benefit from collateral contractual relations between the insured and a third person so long as the insured retains legal title to the property.

We turn to the referee's other rationale of decision: that plaintiffs lacked insurable interest because the fire caused them no actual loss.

We take as settled principles of law in Maine that (1) insurable interest signifies such a relationship to property "as will necessarily entail a pecuniary loss in case of its injury [or] destruction" and (2) the term "actual cash value" in the fire insurance policy signifies the fair market value of the insured property, as measured by the usual test of what a willing buyer would offer and a willing seller accept in a cash sale on an open and free market.

Under the plain language of the instant policy (in accordance with Maine's standard form of fire insurance policy), the actual cash value of the insured property is its fair market value *as of the time of its destruction by fire*. True, particular circumstances might render a building utterly worthless by the time fire consumes it; for example, if the process of demolition has been commenced, or if the owner has abandoned the building. If, however, the building has not been "irrevocably committed to demolition or abandoned", the insured retains an insurable interest. And the mere existence of an executory contract for demolition does not destroy the value of the building or deprive the owner of an insurable interest.

These principles have *a fortiori* application, here. Plaintiffs continued to have legal title to the property they had insured with defendant and thus had rights to recover damages in the event Shell should commit a breach of the lease and demolition agreement. Moreover, special circumstances existed here tending to show affirmatively that the building was not worthless at the time of the fire. Plaintiff Dolard Gendron was still operating the gasoline service station as a sublessee, and under a separate contract with Shell plaintiffs had retained rights to the salvage value of the old station, potentially valued at approximately $10,000.00, intending to use the materials to build another garage at another location.

Lastly, that plaintiffs had the benefit of Shell's contractual obligation to build a new service station to replace the old structure cannot support defendant's assertion that thereby plaintiffs lost an insurable interest. An insured's entitlement to be compensated for the value of insured property from sources other than the insurance does not destroy insurable interest of the insured in the insured property.

JUDGMENT AND REMEDY *The decision that the plaintiffs lacked an insurable interest was in error, so the appeal was sustained. The judgment for the defendant was set aside, and the case was remanded to the superior court for further proceedings.*

Key Person Insurance Key person insurance involves an organization insuring the life of a person who is important to that organization. Because the organization expects to receive some pecuniary gain from the fact that the key person's life continues or expects to suffer a financial loss if the key person dies, the organization has an insurable interest.

Typically, a partnership will insure the life of each partner because the death of any one partner will legally dissolve the firm and cause some degree of loss to the partnership. So, too, a corporation has an insurable interest in the life expectancy of a key executive whose death would result in financial loss to the company.

INDEMNITY

In fire insurance policies, insurance coverage is usually an *indemnity*; that is, the insurance pays only for what is actually lost. This is usually the replacement value of the property minus any depreciation. In addition, once payment is made, the insurance company is entitled to "stand in the shoes" of the insured in pursuing any lawsuits arising from the incident. This is called the right of subrogation.

THE INSURANCE CONTRACT

An insurance contract is governed by the general principles of contract law. The application for insurance is usually attached to the policy and made part of the insurance contract. An insurance applicant is bound by any false statements that appear in the application (subject to certain exceptions). Because the insurance company evaluates the risk factors based on the information included in the insurance application, misstatements or misrepresentations can void a policy, especially if the insurance company can show that it would not have extended insurance if it had known the facts.

Timing

When an insurance contract comes into effect is important. In some instances, the insurance applicant is not protected until a formal written policy is issued. In other situations, the applicant is protected between the time the application is received and the time the insurance company either accepts or rejects it. Four facts should be kept in mind:

1.   A broker is merely the agent of an applicant. Therefore, if the broker fails to procure a policy, the customer is not insured. According to general principles of agency law, if the broker fails to obtain policy coverage and the applicant is damaged as a result, then the broker is liable to the damaged applicant/principal for the loss.

2.   A person who seeks insurance from an insurance company's agent will usually be protected from the moment the application is made, provided some form of premium has been paid. Between the time the application is received and either rejected or accepted, the applicant is covered (possibly subject to certain conditions, such as successfully passing a medical examination). Usually the agent will write a memorandum or **binder** indicating that a policy is pending and stating its essential terms.

3.   If the parties agree that the policy will be issued and delivered at a later time, the contract is not effective until the policy is issued and delivered or sent to the applicant, depending upon the agreement. Thus, any loss sustained between the time of application and the delivery of the policy is not covered.

4.   Parties can agree that a life insurance policy will be binding at the time the insured pays the first premium. The policy, however, can be *expressly contingent* upon the applicant's passing a physical examination. If the applicant pays the premium and passes the examination, then the policy coverage is continuously in effect. If the applicant pays the premium but dies before having the physical examination, then the applicant's estate must show that the applicant would have passed the examination had he or she not died.

Coverage on an insurance policy can begin when the policy is issued or, depending upon the terms of the contract, after a certain period of time has elapsed. The following case illustrates some of these factors in determining when an insurance contract comes into effect.

BACKGROUND AND FACTS   *The plaintiff sued both the insurance company and its agent for their negligent failure to process and procure insurance coverage for plaintiff's fishing boat before it was destroyed by fire. The court looked at the type of insurance the plaintiff requested and*

KEDDIE v. BENEFICIAL INS. INC.
Supreme Court of Nevada, 1978.
94 Nev. 418, 580 P.2d 955.

*the type of insurance the defendants would have provided if a policy
had been in effect.*

THOMPSON, Justice.

* * * *

[The plaintiff] Keddie, a resident of Las Vegas, owned a thirty-two-foot, steel
hulled, gas powered vessel moored in or operating from Bristol Bay, Alaska. From
1964 to 1967 he had used the boat for commercial fishing. In the Spring of 1970,
Keddie contacted McDonald about insurance for that boat. *   *   * He did not
request commercial fishing coverage for the Summer of 1970, nor did he advise
McDonald that the vessel was a commercial fishing boat.

McDonald contacted an insurance broker in San Francisco who responded by
letter advising that additional information would be required before the application could be processed. An insurance application was enclosed with the letter.
That application was forwarded to Keddie who filled it out and returned it. The
application was for Yacht Insurance applicable only to vessels not used for commercial purposes. Indeed, the application did not include certain items of equipment which would indicate a commercial use of the vessel.

Upon receipt of the completed application, the San Francisco broker quoted a
yearly rate to McDonald who in turn advised Keddie. Keddie rejected this quotation since he preferred six months coverage to that of a year and asked McDonald
to obtain a six-month quote. McDonald attempted to do so. Meanwhile, Keddie
left Las Vegas for Alaska advising McDonald that any correspondence should be
sent to his, Keddie's, Las Vegas post office box. From there it would be forwarded
by a friend to Keddie in Naknek, Alaska.

By letter of May 25, 1970, the San Francisco broker notified McDonald that it
would not write a six months policy. On June 2, 1970, by letter, McDonald notified
Keddie of that fact. The letter was forwarded to Alaska where it remained unclaimed until it was returned to Las Vegas in August 1970. Beneficial Insurance
never issued a policy to Keddie.

On July 6, 1970, while engaged in commercial fishing off Bristol Bay, Alaska,
the vessel caught fire and was completely destroyed.

Once an agreement to procure insurance has been reached the insurance agent
is obliged to use reasonable diligence to place the insurance and seasonably [within
a reasonable amount of time] to notify the client if he is unable to do so. The
agreement to procure, however, must be one for a policy of insurance which would
have covered the loss incurred. Had an insurance policy been issued pursuant to
Keddie's application for Yacht Insurance, such policy would not have covered
the loss incurred. Consequently, there is no basis for liability of either Beneficial
Insurance or McDonald [the defendants] to Keddie [the plaintiff].

JUDGMENT
AND REMEDY   *The judgment of the trial court was affirmed. The trial court was correct
in ruling for the defendants since the policy applied for by the plaintiff
would not have covered the loss anyway.*

COMMENTS   *Another way to analyze this case is to say that an insurance contract was
never formed because the plaintiff and the defendant did not agree on
all essential terms. For example, the plaintiff wanted six months of cov-*

erage, but the defendant could obtain coverage only for a minimum of a year. If an acceptance modifies any of the essential terms of a contract, it is really a counter-offer and must then be accepted by the other party in order to create an enforceable contract of insurance. Here, the plaintiff applied for a six-month policy, which was, in essence, rejected by a counter-offer for one-year coverage. This counter-offer was never accepted; in fact, the plaintiff's boat was destroyed by fire before the last communication was received. Thus, no insurance contract was ever formed.

Interpreting Provisions of an Insurance Contract

The words used in an insurance contract have their ordinary meaning and are interpreted in light of the nature of the coverage involved. Where there is an ambiguity in the policy, the provision is interpreted against the insurance company. When it is unclear whether an insurance contract actually exists because the written policy has not been delivered, the uncertainty will be determined against the insurance company. The court will presume that the policy is in effect unless the company can show otherwise.

INTERPRETATION

The courts are increasingly cognizant of the fact that most people do not have the special training that is necessary to understand the intricate terminology used in insurance policies. The following case illustrates this problem.

BACKGROUND AND FACTS *The insured (the plaintiff) was covered by an accidental death and dismemberment policy that provided full coverage in the event of "total and irrecoverable loss of entire sight of an eye." The plaintiff was in an accident and had a traumatic cataract surgically removed from his eye. After surgery, the plaintiff was fitted with a contact lens in his right eye. He had some amount of vision with the contact lens but could not tolerate wearing it. In effect, his eye was of little functional value, and there was no medical assurance that his eyesight could ever be regained. The insurance company (defendant) denied coverage under the policy.*

ROY v. ALLSTATE INS. CO.
Superior Court of Connecticut, Appellate Session, 1978.
34 Conn.Sup. 650, 383 A.2d 637.

ARMENTANO, Judge.

*　*　*　*

"[A]n insurance policy is a contract to be interpreted and enforced in accordance with the real intent of the parties. The language used in the policy must be given its ordinary meaning unless some special or technical meaning is intended." In considering the meaning of the phrase "irrecoverable loss of sight," we must ascertain the meaning of the contract which the insured would reasonably expect and consider the intent of the insured in procuring the insurance.

It has been held generally that policies which insure against the total and irrecoverable loss of entire sight protect the insured against the irrecoverable loss of the practical use of sight. *　*　* Recently, the word "irrecoverable," as used in an insurance contract similar to the one in this case, was defined to mean "not able to regain, [put back to a former state, or recapture]." Therefore, we hold that an insured should recover under this kind of insurance contract if, within the [one year] period of time limited by the policy, he has, owing to an accident, lost the practical use of an eye which he will never be able to regain or recapture.

* * * [The Court then applied its definition of irrecoverable to this case.] Two doctors who examined the plaintiff concluded that he had sustained a permanent disability and that his right eye was of little functional value without the use of the contact lens. Without the contact lens which the plaintiff first started to wear in April or May, 1974, he had no vision in his right eye. The longest period of time during which the plaintiff could wear the contact lens in any given day in April or May, 1974, was four hours. Sometime after May 22, 1974, he stopped wearing the contact lens because he was unable to get used to it.

* * * In any event a continuous loss of functional use of the eye came about when the plaintiff concluded some time later, for reasons which are not challenged, that he could no longer wear the contact lens and stopped using it * * *. [T]he plaintiff could not continue to use the lens and * * * his loss of sight, which he previously may have thought could be regained by use of the lens, was never actually recoverable because of his inability to wear the lens. * * *

It is clear that the average man purchasing a policy similar to the one in this case would reasonably expect to be insured for an injury to his eye of the type involved in this case where, within the [one year] period of coverage, vision could be restored only to the limited extent that it was restored here. * * *

JUDGMENT AND REMEDY *The trial court was judged correct in permitting the plaintiff to recover insurance benefits under the policy.*

CANCELLATION OF INSURANCE POLICIES

Under most state laws, once the initial premium on a policy has been paid, the policy does not automatically lapse if the next premium is not paid on the due date. Most policies allow a **grace period** of thirty or thirty-one days.

Moreover, a default in the payment of a life insurance premium may require the insurer to issue a paid-up policy in a smaller amount than originally contracted for, to provide extended insurance for a period of time, or to pay the cash surrender value of the policy. These are alternatives to cancellation. When the insurance contract expressly declares that the insurance company cannot cancel the policy, these alternatives are important.

When the insurance company can cancel the policy, contract provisions or state statutes usually require that the insurer give advance written notice of cancellation. An insurer cannot normally cancel a policy (or refuse to write a renewal policy) because of the national origin or the race of an applicant. Moreover, an insurance company cannot cancel a policy in order to penalize an insured who has just appeared as a witness in a case against the company.

DEFENSES AGAINST PAYMENT TO THE INSURED

An insurance company can raise any of the defenses that would be valid in any ordinary action on a contract and some defenses that do not apply in ordinary contract actions. If the insurance company can show that the policy was procured by fraud, misrepresentation, or violation of warranties, it may have a valid defense for not paying on a claim. (The insurance company may also have the right to disaffirm or rescind an insurance contract.) Improper actions, such as those that are against public policy or are otherwise illegal, can give the insurance company a defense against payment of a claim or allow it to rescind the contract.

The following case involved the issue of liability for fire damage resulting from the actions of one of the insured persons under a contract of insurance. Because the insured individuals were married, the company claimed that the wrongful act of one spouse was attributable to the other, thereby preventing either from recovering fire insurance proceeds.

BACKGROUND AND FACTS *The plaintiffs sued on an insurance policy issued by Insurance Company of North America (INA) for fire damage to their home. The lower court denied the plaintiffs' recovery. The plaintiffs were a husband and wife who owned the property as tenants in the entirety and who were insured under an INA policy. It was undisputed that the husband deliberately set fire to the house, that his actions constituted fraud under the terms of the policy, and that the policy was void and he could not recover under it. It was equally undisputed that the wife was not involved in any way in the act. The wife claimed that she was not barred from recovering under the policy since she was an innocent co-tenant and was entitled to her pro rata share of the fire insurance proceeds.*

STEIGLER v. INS. CO. OF NORTH AMERICA
Supreme Court of Delaware, 1977.
384 A.2d 398.

DUFFY, Justice.

*   *   *   *

As we have noted, the policy contained a standard fraud provision rendering the policy void "in case of any fraud *   *   * by the *insured* relating thereto" (emphasis added); and the policy insured two persons: "Herbert F. Steigler and Arlene R. Steigler."

The [first] critical question, of course, relates to the meaning of the word "insured" in the fraud provision. Does it mean one or both of the Steiglers? The answer is by no means clear because the word "insured" is singular while two persons are named as the "insured," i.e., Herbert F. Steigler and Arlene R. Steigler. Thus, construction of the term is required.

In resolving the ambiguity in the Steigler-INA contract we refer to two rules of construction. First, where ambiguous, the language of an insurance contract is always construed most strongly against the insurance company which has drafted it.

Second, "an insurance contract should be read to accord with the reasonable expectations of the purchaser so far as the language will permit."

Applying these principles, we hold that an "ordinary person owning an undivided interest in property, not versed in the nice distinctions of insurance law, would naturally suppose that his individual interest in the property was covered by a policy which named him without qualification as one of the persons insured."

In our judgment *   *   * Mrs. Steigler had an interest in the property, the policy named her without qualification as one of the persons insured and she should not be barred from recovering under the policy by the fraud of the other co-tenant.

INA contends that because the Steiglers are married the arson of the husband bars recovery by his wife. The theory is that the contract terms govern any claim, the contract is voided by fraud, and that husband and wife are one person, i.e., together and inseparably they hold the entire estate.

We are not persuaded that the "oneness" theory which is, to say the least, somewhat "quaint" in this day and age, should override the other principles at stake here. When two persons own property as tenants in common, it is generally recognized, as INA concedes, that the interests may be separable and, therefore, an innocent tenant in common can recover a *pro rata* [proportionate] share of fire insurance proceeds. Thus, for example, had the Steiglers owned the property and the policy as "co-habitants" rather than as spouses, the general rule would have permitted rather than have barred her recovery. Without pausing to explore the equal protection problems which such a result might raise, we conclude that barring a wife from recovering because she is a wife would be contrary to the public policy clearly mandated by the Married Women's Act.

JUDGMENT AND REMEDY   *The lower court's ruling was reversed. The wife was entitled to half the insurance policy proceeds for the fire damage. The case was remanded to the trial court's jurisdiction under instruction to enter a ruling in the wife's favor and award her half the insurance proceeds.*

REBUTTAL OF THE DEFENSES OF THE INSURANCE COMPANY

There are certain ways in which the insurance company can be prevented from asserting some defenses that are normally available. State statutes and case law provide for such estoppel.

For example, if a company tells an insured that information requested on a form is optional, and the insured provides it anyway, the company cannot use the information to avoid its contractual obligation under the insurance contract. In the life insurance field, certain clauses become incontestable after a stated period of time. For example, statements as to the age of the insured, even though incorrect, normally do not allow the insurance company to escape payment upon the death of the insured. Typically, the time period after which estoppel for such defenses occurs is two years. Incontestable clauses will be discussed later in this chapter.

TYPES OF INSURANCE

Three general types of insurance coverage held by an individual will be covered here:

1. Life insurance.
2. Fire and homeowner's insurance.
3. Automobile insurance.

These will be discussed in detail with special emphasis on life and fire insurance policies in regard to the law.

Different Types of Life Insurance

There are four basic types of life insurance:

1. **Whole life**, sometimes referred to as straight life, ordinary life, or cash value insurance. This type of insurance provides protection with a cumulated cash surrender value that can be used as collateral for a loan. Premiums are paid by the insured during the insured's entire lifetime, with a fixed payment to the beneficiary upon death.
2. **Limited payment life**, such as a twenty-payment life policy. Premiums are paid for a stated number of years, after which the policy is paid up and fully effective during the insured's life. Naturally, premiums are higher than for whole life. This insurance does have a cash surrender value.

3. **Term** insurance, providing for a fixed premium for a specified term. Payment on the policy is due only if death occurs within the term period. Premiums are less expensive than for whole life or limited payment life, and there is usually no cash surrender value. Frequently, this type of insurance can be converted to another type of life insurance.

4. **Endowment** insurance, providing for fixed premium payments for a definite term. At the end of the term a fixed amount is to be paid to the insured or, upon the death of the insured, to a beneficiary. This type of insurance represents both a term insurance and a form of annuity or savings. It has a rapidly increasing cash surrender value, but premiums are high, as payment is required at the end of the term even if the insured is still living.

Because term and whole life insurance are the most common forms of life insurance, each will be discussed further here, though briefly.

Term Insurance   There are three basic types of term insurance:

1. Level.
2. Decreasing.
3. Mortgage.

The premiums vary in cost according to the protection afforded. A person whose current income is low but who expects a higher income in the future can afford a greater amount of term insurance than of whole life insurance by choosing level term insurance, since in level term insurance, premium increases come in later years. Alternatively, the insured can keep the premiums at the same level but receive decreasing protection over the years (decreasing term insurance).

Level Term   Premiums for level term insurance commonly increase at the end of each term, such as every five years, if the insured wishes to keep the same face value on the insurance policy. The increased premium reflects the rising probability of death as age increases.

Decreasing Term   Decreasing term insurance has a level premium but a decreasing face value. It is desirable when a person needs maximum protection early in life, with a relatively low premium, but anticipates that the need for this protection will decrease with changes in family and financial accumulations.

For example, a young person with minor children may want a substantial amount of term insurance to protect these children should he or she die while they are still young. After the children have grown into adulthood and are on their own, however, the need for protection will be substantially decreased. Decreasing term insurance is desirable for a person in this situation.

Mortgage Term   Mortgage term insurance, or home protection insurance, declines in face value by an amount equal to the mortgage left to be paid. The idea is that if the insured dies, the home can be paid off with the proceeds. A mortgage term insurance policy decreases in uneven dollar amounts. (This type of insurance can insure other types of consumer debt also.)

Whole Life Insurance   Whole life insurance premiums generally remain at the same level throughout the life of a policy. As a result, the policyholder pays more than is necessary to cover the insurance company's risk in the early years and less than is necessary to cover the company's risk in later years. Compared with term insurance, whole life is relatively more costly because it is a form of financial investment as well as insurance protection. The investment feature of the policy is known as its cash value.

Living Benefits   Living benefits of a whole life policy include converting it into some sort of lump sum payment or stream of retirement income. When the insured reaches retirement age, premium payments on whole life can be discontinued and one of the following living benefit programs can be started:

1. Protection for the rest of the insured's life but at a lower face value.
2. Full protection but for a definite number of years in the future (extended term insurance).

3. A cash settlement that returns whatever savings and dividends have not been used to pay off the insurance company for excessive costs incurred for the particular age group of the insured (the cash surrender fund).

4. Conversion of a whole life policy into an annuity whereby the insured receives a specified amount of income each year for a certain number of years or for the rest of the insured's life.

Death Benefits   In most life insurance policies, the insured specifies a beneficiary, who receives the death benefits of that policy. If Ken Kerr buys a $10,000 ordinary life policy and does not borrow any money on it, his beneficiary will receive $10,000 plus any paid up accumulations when he dies. However, there are certain options for settling a life insurance policy. The first plan involves a lump sum payment. In the second plan, the face value of the insurance policy is retained by the insurance company, but a small interest payment is made to the beneficiary for a certain number of years or for life. At the end of the specified period, the principal (face value) is then paid according to the terms in the contract. In the third plan, the face value is paid to the beneficiary in the form of annual, semiannual, quarterly, or monthly installments. The company makes regular payments of equal amounts until the fund is depleted. The insurance company guarantees a specific number of payments or payments that will total the face value of the policy. If, however, the beneficiary dies before the guaranteed payments have been made, the remainder goes to the estate of the beneficiary or as otherwise directed in the contract. This is sometimes called an annuity plan.

Special Features and Provisions of Life Insurance

The rights and liabilities of the parties in life insurance are basically dependent upon the insurance contract. There are a few features that deserve additional attention, and they will be discussed below.

Liability   The insurance contract determines not only the extent of the insurer's liability but generally when the insurer is liable upon the death of the insured. Most life insurance contracts exclude liability of the insurer if the death of the insured is caused by one or more of the following: suicide, military action during war, execution by a state or federal government, or even while a passenger in a commercial vehicle. In absence of exclusion, most courts today construe any cause of death to be one of the insurer's risks.

Incontestable Clause   Generally, life insurance contracts contain an incontestable clause which provides that after the expiration of a specified period, the policy cannot be avoided by the insurer due to errors (misstatements) and the like made by the insured. The specified period is usually two years and covers most defenses which would allow the insurer to cancel the policy. The incontestable clause, however, does not include nonpayment of premiums, failure to file proof of death within a required period, lack of insurable interest, and risks expressly excluded by the policy itself.

Adjustment Due to Age Misstated   The insurance policy constitutes the agreement between the parties. The application for insurance is part of the policy and is usually attached to the policy. When the insured misstates his or her age in the application, an error takes place particularly as to the amount of premiums paid. Misstatement of age is not a sufficient material error to allow the insurer to void the policy. Instead, upon discovery of the error the insurer will adjust the premium payments and/or benefits accordingly.

Assignment   Most life insurance policies permit the insured to change beneficiaries. Where this is the case, in absence of prohibition or notice requirement, the insured has a right to assign the life insurance contract without consent of the insurer or beneficiary. If the beneficiary right is vested (insured cannot change), the contract cannot be assigned without the consent of the beneficiary. The vast majority of life insurance contracts permit assignment and only require notice to the insurer to be effective on the insurer.

Creditors' Rights Unless exempt under state law, judgment creditors can resort to the life insured's interest as an asset. These creditors generally can reach insurance proceeds payable to the insured's estate, proceeds payable to anyone if the payment of premiums constituted a fraud on creditors, and any proceeds payable to a named beneficiary if the insured has reserved the right to change beneficiaries. However, creditors cannot compel the insured to make available the cash surrender value of the policy or to change the named beneficiary to that of the creditor. Almost all states exempt at least a part of the proceeds of life insurance from creditors' claims.

Termination Although the insured can cancel and terminate the policy, the insurer cannot do so. Therefore, termination usually takes place only upon the occurrence of the following:
1. Default in premium payments causing policy to lapse (no cash surrender value to purchase paid-up insurance remains).
2. Death and payment of benefits.
3. Expiration of term of policy.
3. Cancellation by insured.

Home, Property, and Liability Insurance Policies

There are basically two types of insurance policies for a home—standard fire insurance policies and homeowner's policies.

Standard Fire Insurance Policy The standard fire insurance policy protects the homeowner against fire and lightning as well as damage from smoke and water caused by the fire or the fire department. Paying slightly more will extend the coverage to damage caused by hail, windstorms, explosions, and so on. Personal theft and a comprehensive liability policy can also be added.

Types of Fire Insurance Policies Most fire insurance policies are classified according to what type of property is covered and to what extent (amount) the issuer is liable. The following are typical.

1. **Blanket policy.** This policy covers a class of property rather than specific property, since the property is anticipated to shift or vary in nature. A policy covering the inventory of a business is an example.

2. **Specific policy.** This policy covers a specific property at a specific location. An example would be a particular painting located in a residence or a piece of machinery located in a factory or business.

3. **Floater policy.** This policy usually supplements a specific policy. It is intended to cover property that may change in either location or quantity. To illustrate, if the painting mentioned in the preceding example were to be exhibited during the year at numerous locations throughout the state, a floater policy would be desirable.

4. **Valued policy.** This policy is one in which, by agreement, a specific value is placed on the subject to be insured to cover the eventuality of its total loss.

5. **Open policy.** This policy is one in which the value of the property insured is not agreed upon. The policy usually provides for a maximum liability of the insurer, but payment for loss is restricted to fair market value of the property at time of loss or to the maximum limit, whichever is less.

Special Features and Provisions of Fire Insurance

As with life insurance, certain features and provisions of fire insurance deserve special mention. In reading the following, it is important to note some basic differences in the treatment of life and fire policies.

Liability As with all forms of insurance, the insurer's liability is determined from the terms of the policy. However, most policies limit recovery only to *hostile* fires and loss resulting therefrom due to smoke, water, and the like. A hostile fire is basically one that breaks out or begins in a place where the fire was not intended to burn. A *friendly* fire is not covered. A friendly fire is one burning in a place where such was intended to burn. Therefore, smoke from a fireplace would not be covered, but smoke due to a fire caused by a defective electrical outlet would. Sometimes an owner will add "extended coverage" to the fire policy to cover losses from friendly fires.

If the policy is a valued policy and the subject matter is completely destroyed, the insurer is liable for the amount specified in the policy. If it is an open policy, then the extent of actual loss must be determined, and the insurer is liable only for the amount of the loss or for the maximum amount specified in the policy, whichever is less. For partial losses, actual loss must always be determined, and the insurer's liability is limited to that amount. Most insurance policies permit the insurer to either restore or replace the property so destroyed, or to monetarily pay for the loss.

Coinsurance Owners of property often insure their property for less than full value. Part of the reason for this is that most fires do not result in a total loss. To encourage owners to insure their property to as close to full value as possible, coinsurance clauses are frequently placed in fire insurance policies. Coinsurance clauses provide that if the owner insures his or her property up to a given percentage (usually 80%) of the property's actual value, the owner can recover up to the full amount provided for in the policy. If the owner insures for less than this percentage, the owner must bear proportionately the loss.

The formula for recovery is thus:

$$\frac{\text{Amount of Insurance (Policy)}}{80\% \text{ of actual value of property at time of loss}}$$
$$\times \text{ Actual loss} = \text{Recovery by owner}$$

To illustrate, Perez has a fire which causes $2,500 damage to the roof of the house. The replacement value or actual value of the house at the time of loss is $50,000, and Perez has fire insurance coverage of $30,000. The recovery for Perez from the insurance coverage is determined as follows:

$$\frac{\$30,000 \text{ (policy)}}{\$40,000 - 80\% \text{ value of house}}$$
$$\times \$2,500 \text{ (actual loss)} = \$1,875 \text{ recovery}$$

Had Perez increased the insurance to $40,000, Perez would receive the full $2,500 loss.

Coinsurance clauses are only applicable to partial losses (not total losses). Coinsurance clauses are found in most homeowners' policies and are implied in marine insurance policies.

Pro Rata Clause On occasion, an owner of property insures the property with more than one insurance carrier. Frequently, a fire insurance policy will include a pro rata clause which requires any loss to be proportionately shared by all carriers. Proportionate means that by percentage, each carrier insures the property to its total amount of coverage.

To illustrate, Jane has two insurance policies covering her home. One policy with Ajax is for $50,000 and another policy with Beta is for $25,000. Jane suffers a $6,000 loss fully covered. If the policies have pro rata clauses, Ajax would be required to pay Jane $4,000 ($50,000/75,000 × $6,000) and Beta $2,000 ($25,000/$75,000 × $6,000).

Proof of Loss Fire insurance policies require the insured to file with the insurer a proof of loss as a condition for recovery within a specified period or immediately (reasonable time). Failure to comply *could* allow the insurance carrier to avoid liability. Courts vary somewhat on the enforcement of such clauses. To avoid this becoming a legal issue, the insured should always report a loss immediately to the insurer and file the proper statements covering the loss.

Occupancy Clause Most standard policies require occupancy of the premises at the time of loss. Therefore, a clause is inserted that if the premises become vacant or unoccupied for a given period, unless consent by insurer is given, the coverage is suspended until the premises are reoccupied. Persons going on extended vacations should check their policies on this matter.

Assignment Fire insurance policies are not assignable without consent of the insurer. The theory is that the fire insurance policy is a personal contract between the insured and the insurer. After a loss has occurred, any recovery entitlement is freely assignable without consent of the insured. The nonassignability of the policy is extremely important in the purchase of a house. The purchaser must procure his or her own insurance, if the purchaser is assuming the remaining insurance coverage period of the seller, consent of the insurer is essential.

To illustrate, Ann is selling her home and lot to Sam. Ann has a one year fire policy with Ajax Insurance Company, with six months remaining at date of closing the sale. Ann agrees to assign the balance of her policy, but Ajax has not given its consent. One day after passage of the deed, a fire totally destroys the house. Can Sam recover from Ajax?

The answer is no, as the policy is actually voided upon the closing of the transaction and deeding the property. The reason the policy is voided is that Ann no longer has an insurable interest at the time of loss, and Sam has no rights in a nonassignable policy.

Cancellation   Generally, either the insured or the insurer can cancel a fire insurance policy by giving the other notice. Notice usually must be given five days (or more) before cancellation is effective.

Homeowner's Policy

The homeowner's policy provides protection against a number of risks under a single policy, allowing the policyholder to save over the cost of buying each protection separately. In addition to a standard fire policy, liability coverage is also available.

There are basically two types of homeowner's policy coverage:

1. *Property coverage* includes garage, house, and other private buildings on the policyholder's lot. It also includes the personal possessions and property of the policyholder at home, in traveling, or at work. It pays additional living expenses for living away from home because of a fire or some other covered peril.
2. *Liability coverage* is for personal liability in case someone is injured on the insured's property, the insured damages someone else's property, or the insured injures someone else who is not in an automobile. It generally does not cover liability for professional malpractice.

Similar to liability coverage is coverage for medical payments for injury to others who are on the policyholder's property and for the property of others that is damaged by a member of the policyholder's family.

Forms of Homeowner's Policies   There are basically five forms of homeowner's and condominium owner's policies. Exhibit 55–1 describes each type. The basic form covers eleven perils, or risks; the broad form covers eighteen, and the comprehensive form covers those eighteen and all others.

Homeowners are not the only ones who take out insurance policies to cover losses. There is also renter's insurance, called "residence contents broad form" (HO-4). It covers personal possessions against the eighteen perils described in Exhibit 55–1. It also includes additional living expenses and liability coverage.

Adding a Personal Articles or Effects Floater Policy   An insured may wish to pay a slightly higher premium to insure specific personal articles—for example, cameras, musical instruments, works of art, jewelry, and other valuables. This is accomplished by adding a personal articles floater to a homeowner's policy. The insured submits a list of the things to be covered and some affidavits giving their current market value. Insuring under a floater provides all risk insurance, and the covered property can therefore be omitted from fire and theft policies.

A personal effects floater policy covers personal items when traveling. In most cases, it is not necessary because a regular homeowner's policy is sufficient coverage. This floater covers the articles only when they are taken off the insured's property. It does not cover theft from an unattended automobile unless there is evidence of forced entry, and even then, the company's liability is generally limited to 10 percent of the amount of insurance and to not more than $250 for all property in any one loss. This restriction in the policy can be removed by paying an additional premium.

Automobile Insurance

There are basically two kinds of automobile insurance: liability insurance and comprehensive and collision insurance.

Property Damage and Bodily Injury Liability   One kind of automobile insurance covers bodily injury and property damage liability. Li-

EXHIBIT 55–1   GUIDE TO PACKAGE POLICIES FOR HOMEOWNERS

These are the principal features of standard types of homeowners' insurance policies.

The amount of insurance provided for specific categories, such as personal property and comprehensive personal liability, can usually be increased by paying an additional premium.

The special limits of liability refer to the maximum amounts the policy will pay for the types of property listed in the notes. Usually, jewelry, furs, boats and other items subject to special limits have to be insured separately to obtain greater coverage. Adapted from New Jersey Insurance Department, *A Shopper's Guide to Homeowners Insurance, 1977.*

	Basic Form Homeowners HO-1	Broad Form Homeowners HO-2	Special Form Homeowners HO-3	Comprehensive Form Homeowners HO-5	HO-6 (For Condominium Owners)
Perils Covered (see key)	Perils 1–11	Perils 1–18	Perils 1–18 on personal property except glass breakage; all risks, except those specifically excluded, on buildings	All risks except those specifically excluded	Perils 1–18 except glass breakage
Standard Amount of Insurance on: House, attached structures	Based on property value; minimum $8,000	Based on property value; minimum $8,000	Based on property value; minimum $8,000	Based on property value; minimum $15,000	$1,000 on owner's additions and alterations to unit
Detached structures	10% of amount of insurance on house	10% of amount of insurance on house	10% of amount of insurance on house	10% of amount of insurance on house	no coverage
Trees, shrubs, and plants	5% of amount of insurance on house; $250 maximum per item	5% of amount of insurance on house; $250 maximum per item	5% of amount of insurance on house; $250 maximum per item	5% of amount of insurance on house; $250 maximum per item	10% of personal property insurance; $250 maximum per item
Personal property on premises	50% of insurance on house	50% of insurance on house	50% of insurance on house	50% of insurance on house	Based on value of property; minimum $4,000
Personal property away from premises	10% of personal property insurance (minimum $1,000)	10% of personal property insurance (minimum $1,000)	10% of personal property insurance (minimum $1,000)	50% of insurance on house	10% of personal property insurance (minimum $1,000)
Additional living expense	10% of insurance on house	20% of insurance on house	20% of insurance on house	20% of insurance on house	40% of personal property insurance
Special Limits of Liability*	Standard	Standard	Standard	Standard	Standard

KEY TO PERILS COVERED:

1. fire, lightning
2. damage to property removed from premises endangered by fire

3. windstorm, hail
4. explosion
5. riots

EXHIBIT 55–1 *continued*

6. damage by aircraft
7. damage by vehicles not owned or operated by people covered by policy
8. damage from smoke
9. vandalism, malicious mischief
10. glass breakage
11. theft
12. falling objects
13. weight of ice, snow, sleet
14. collapse of building or any part of building

15. bursting, cracking, burning, or bulging of a steam or hot water heating system, or of appliances for heating water
16. leakage or overflow of water or steam from a plumbing, heating or air-conditioning system
17. freezing of plumbing, heating and air-conditioning systems and domestic appliances
18. injury to electrical appliances, devices, fixtures and wiring (excluding tubes, transistors and similar electronic components) from short circuits or other accidentally generated currents

*Special limits of liability: Money, bullion, numismatic property, bank notes-$100; securities, bills, deeds, tickets, etc.-$500; manuscripts-$1,000; jewelry, furs-$500 for theft; boats, including trailers and equipment-$500; trailers-$500.

ability limits are usually described by a series of three numbers, such as 25/50/5. This means that the policy will pay a maximum of $25,000 for bodily injury to one person, $50,000 to more than one person, and a maximum of $5,000 for property damage in one accident. Most insurance companies offer liability up to $300,000 and sometimes $500,000.

Individuals who are dissatisfied with the maximum liability limits offered by regular automobile insurance coverage can purchase a separate amount of coverage under an *umbrella* policy. Umbrella limits sometimes go as high as $5 million. They also cover personal liability in excess of homeowner's liability limits.

Physical Damage Coverage Another kind of automobile insurance covers damage to the insured's car in any type of collision. Usually, it is not advisable to purchase full collision coverage (otherwise known as zero deductible). The price per year is quite high because it is likely that small but costly repair jobs will be required each year. Most people prefer to take out $50 or $100 deductible coverage, which costs about one-fourth the price of zero deductible coverage.

Comprehensive Comprehensive insurance covers loss, damage, and destruction by fire, hurricane, hail, vandalism, and theft. It is separate from collision insurance.

Uninsured Motorist Coverage Uninsured motorist coverage insures the driver and passengers against injury caused by any driver without insurance or by a hit-and-run driver. Certain states require that it be included in all insurance policies sold to drivers.

Accidental Death Benefits Sometimes called double indemnity, accidental death benefits provide a lump sum to named beneficiaries if the policyholder dies in an automobile accident. It generally costs very little, but it may not be necessary if the insured has a sufficient amount of life insurance.

Medical Payment Coverage Medical payments provided for in an auto insurance policy cover hospital and other medical bills and sometimes funeral expenses. This insurance protects all the passengers in the insured's car when the insured is driving.

QUESTIONS AND CASE PROBLEMS

1. Ann owns a house and has an elderly third cousin living with her. Ann decides she needs fire insurance on the house and a life insurance policy on her third cousin to cover any funeral and other expenses should her cousin die. Ann takes out a fire insurance

policy from Ajax Insurance Company and a $10,000 life insurance policy from Beta Insurance Company on her third cousin. Six months later, Ann sells the house to John and transfers title to him. Ann and her cousin move into an apartment. With two months remaining on the Ajax policy, a fire totally destroys the house; at the same time, Ann's third cousin dies. Both insurance companies tender back premiums but claim they have no liability under the insurance contracts, as Ann did not have an insurable interest. Discuss their claims.

2. John contracts with an Ajax Insurance Company agent for a $50,000 ordinary life insurance policy. The application form is filled in to show that John's age is thirty-two. In addition, the application form asks whether John has ever had any heart ailments or problems. John answers no, forgetting that as a young child he had been diagnosed as having a slight heart murmur. A policy is issued. Three years later John becomes seriously ill. A review of the policy discloses that John was actually thirty-three at the time of application and issuance of the policy and that he erred in answering the question about a history of heart ailments. Discuss whether Ajax can void the policy and escape liability upon John's death.

3. Ann has an ordinary life insurance policy on her life and a fire insurance policy on her house. Both policies have been in force for a number of years. Ann's life insurance names her son, Rory, as beneficiary. Ann has specifically removed her right to change beneficiaries, and the life policy is silent on right of assignment. Ann is going on a one-year European vacation and borrows money from Leonard to finance the trip. Leonard takes an assignment of the life insurance policy as security for the loan, as the policy has accumulated a substantial cash surrender value. Ann also rents out her house to Leonard and assigns to him her fire insurance policy. Discuss fully whether Ann's assignment of these policies is valid.

4. Frank has an open fire insurance policy on his home for a maximum liability of $60,000. The policy has a number of standard clauses, including the right of the insurer to restore or rebuild the property in lieu of a monetary payment, and it has a standard coinsurance clause. A fire in Frank's house virtually destroys a utility room and part of the kitchen. The fire was caused by an electric water heater overheating. The total damage to the property is $10,000. The property at the time of loss is valued at $100,000. Frank files a proof of loss claim for $10,000. Discuss the insurer's liability in this situation.

5. Lori has a large house. She secures two fire insurance open value policies on the house. Her policy with the Ajax Insurance Company is for a maximum of $100,000, and her policy with Beta Insurance Company is for a maximum of $50,000. Each insurance policy contains a pro rata clause. Lori's house burns to the ground. The value of the house at the time of the loss is $120,000. Discuss the liability of Ajax and Beta to Lori.

6. Thompson contracted with Occidental Life Insurance Company of California for an insurance policy on his life. The beneficiary of the policy was his wife. Before Occidental issued the policy to Thompson, Thompson filled out an application in which he was asked several questions regarding his health. One of the questions was whether Thompson had ever had pressure in his chest. Another was whether he had any disorder with his blood or blood vessels. Thompson entered negative answers to each of these questions since, earlier that morning, one of Occidental's physicians had asked him about these conditions. At that time, he had explained to the physician that two months earlier he had been treated for phlebitis (vein inflammation) and, at about the same time, had experienced minor chest pains. Thompson died in an accident shortly thereafter, and Occidental refused to pay on this life insurance policy, claiming that Thompson misrepresented facts on the application. Under these circumstances, is Thompson's wife entitled to Thompson's life insurance benefits? [Thompson v. Occidental Life Ins. Co., 109 Cal.Rptr. 473, 513 P.2d 353 (1973)]

7. Donald R. Noah was the beneficiary of three life insurance policies that insured the life of William L. Noah, Donald's brother. The insurer was Mutual Savings Life Insurance Company. While the policies were in force, William Noah drowned in Galveston, Texas. Mutual Savings Life refused to pay Donald Noah on the ground that he did not have an insurable interest in his brother's life. Donald Noah sued the company. Is Donald Noah entitled to collect under the policies? Would the answer be the same if William Noah had been Donald's cousin? What if he had been Donald's nephew? [Mutual Sav. Life Ins. Co. v. Noah, 291 Ala. 444, 282 So.2d 271 (1973)]

8. In June 1961, Groban contracted to purchase an inventory of Caterpillar tractor parts from SLDC. Before that purchase was concluded, Groban contracted to resell the inventory to Union. At Union's request, Groban agreed to obtain marine war risk insurance on the shipment at Union's expense. Groban subsequently purchased two contracts of insurance, one naming itself as beneficiary and the second naming Union as beneficiary. The goods were destroyed during shipment. If Groban attempts to recover under the

insurance policy, will it have an insurable interest? If Union attempts to recover, will it have an insurable interest? [Groban v. S. S. Pegu, 331 F.Supp. 883 (S.D.N.Y.1971)]

9. On June 8, 1966, a convent that had been constructed in 1877 burned to the ground. It was insured by Royal Insurance Company. At the time of the fire, the previous residents of the convent, the Sisters of Presentation, had abandoned the old building and moved into a new one. Under an agreement with the bishop, they had obligated themselves to surrender the old convent for demolition. They had already received new land and a new building in exchange for their contractual agreement that the old land would be occupied by an expanding high school. The Sisters of Presentation demanded recovery from Royal Insurance Company, but Royal refused to pay on the ground that the Sisters of Presentation had no insurable interest in the building. The Sisters of Presentation argued that, had their new building been destroyed by fire, they might have been forced to reoccupy the old convent even though it would not be habitable without an expenditure of approximately $120,000. Do the Sisters of Presentation have an insurable interest in the old convent? [Royal Ins. Co. v. Sisters of Presentation, 430 F.2d 759 (9th Cir. 1970)]

10. The insured brought an action to recover losses in excess of $100,000 sustained because of employee theft. The thefts occurred during the terms of two different policies but were not discovered until the second policy had replaced the first. Each policy limited recovery to $50,000 for employee dishonesty and provided that for a loss "which occurs partly during the Effective Period of this endorsement and partly during the period of other policies, the total liability of the Company shall not exceed in the aggregate the amount of this endorsement." The insured maintained that he was entitled to recover $50,000 on each policy. What did the court decide? [Davenport Peters Co. v. Royal Globe Ins. Co., 490 F.Supp. 286 (Mass. 1980)]

CHAPTER 56

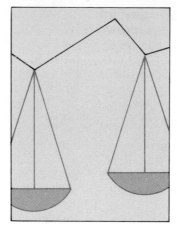

Wills, Trusts, and Estates

The laws of succession of property are a necessary corollary to the concept of private ownership of property. The law requires that upon death, title to the decedent's property must vest (to deliver full possession) somewhere. The decedent can direct the passage of property after death by *will*, subject to certain limitations imposed by the state. If no valid will has been executed, the decedent is said to have died *intestate*, and state law prescribes the distribution of the property among heirs or next of kin. If no heirs or kin can be found, the property escheats (title is transferred) to the state.

In addition, a person can transfer property through a *trust*.[1] The owner (settlor) of the property transfers legal title to a *trustee*, who has a duty imposed by law to hold the property for the use or benefit of another (the beneficiary).

The following sections will describe how testamentary dispositions are made by *will*, by *statutes of descent and distribution*, or with *trusts*.

ORIGINS OF INHERITANCE LAWS

At common law, persons had no power to control the distribution of their property after death. The power of transfer or distribution is derived solely from statutes originating in feudal England, where the transfer of property at death was strictly controlled. The heir (the one who inherited) was required to pay the feudal lord a sum of money[2] for the privilege of succeeding to his or her ancestor's lands. When a tenant died without heirs, the land escheated (title passed) to the feudal lord of the manor.[3]

---

1. A trust can be set up by the property owner *during his or her life* (by a deed accompanied by a trust document) or *at his or her death* (by a will containing or accompanied by a trust document). This chapter discusses both.

2. The sum, called a relief, was usually equivalent to one year's rent.

3. It was not until 1925 that escheat for failure of heirs was abolished. C. J. Moynihan, *Introduction to the Law of Real Property* (St. Paul, Minn. West Publishing, 1962), p. 22.

Sweeping land reforms in England during the 1920s replaced inheritance payments and escheat to the feudal lord with the right of the crown to receive inheritance taxes and to take property of an intestate without heirs. Modern legislation has changed the terminology but not the result. In all states, title to land of persons who die intestate and without heirs vests in the state; the right to make a will and the ways to make one are determined by state law. To be valid, wills normally must follow statutory requirements. Furthermore, taxes are imposed upon the transfer of property at death by state and federal governments.

PURPOSES OF INHERITANCE LAWS

State regulation of inheritance has developed in response to certain desirable social and political goals. Four principles underlie U.S. inheritance and succession laws.[4]

1. *The concept of private property.* Any system of laws to regulate the passage of a decedent's estate must do so in the context of a firmly rooted tradition of private ownership of property.
2. *Effectuating the individual's testamentary intent.* The right to direct the distribution of one's own property to whomever one chooses (subject to the rights of the surviving spouse and children) is often taken as a basic tenet of U.S. jurisprudence. Many formalities surround the court's duty to ensure that when a will is offered for authentication, it is in fact the genuine and final expression of the decedent's wishes. The seriousness of this function is reflected in the highly publicized controversy over the numerous proffers of "authentic" wills belonging to billionaire Howard Hughes. The freedom of an individual to have his or her intentions satisfied after death is subject to limitations imposed by law.

3. *The policy favoring family.* Protection of the family has been a cornerstone of inheritance laws throughout history. As noted earlier, intestate succession is inheritance by heirs of the deceased. In contemporary law, this goal is reinforced by state statutes guaranteeing that an absolute portion of the decedent's estate will be allotted to the surviving spouse and children.
4. *Reflection of societal interests.* State succession laws perpetuate certain social and political goals by: (a) protecting a decedent's family from absolute poverty against creditors' claims (and preventing the family's dependency on the state), (b) obtaining money through escheat (transfer of abandoned property to the state), (c) encouraging educational and scientific research and other civic programs through estate tax exemptions or deductions, and (d) maintaining social stability and confidence in the legal system by adhering to traditional principles of law.

WILLS

Concept of a Will

A **will** is the final declaration of the disposition that a person desires to have made of his or her property after death. A will is referred to as a *testamentary disposition* of property. It is a formal instrument that must follow exactly the requirements of the Statute of Wills in order to be effective. The reasoning behind such a strict requirement is obvious. A will becomes effective only after death. No attempts to modify it after the death of the maker are allowed because the court cannot ask the maker to confirm the attempted modifications. (But sometimes the wording must be "interpreted" by the courts.)

A will can serve other purposes besides the distribution of property. It can appoint a guardian for minor children or incapacitated adults. It can appoint a personal representative to settle the affairs of the deceased.

Vocabulary of Wills Every area of law has its own special vocabulary, and the area of wills is no exception. A man who makes out a will is known as a **testator**, and a woman who makes out a will is called a **testatrix**. The court respon-

---

4. For a discussion of the goals of succession laws and the need for increasing flexibility in applying these laws, see John T. Gaubatz, "Notes toward a Truly Modern Wills Act," 31 *University of Miami Law Review* 497 (Spring 1977).

sible for administering any legal problems sur-rounding a will is called a **probate court**. When a person dies, a *personal representative* settles the affairs of the deceased. An **executor** or **exe-cutrix** is the personal representative named in the will; an **administrator** or **administratrix** is the personal representative appointed by the court for a decedent who dies without a will, who fails to name an executor in the will, who names an executor lacking capacity to serve, or who writes a will that the court refuses to admit to probate. A gift of real estate by will is generally called a **devise**, and a gift of personal property under a will is called a **bequest** or **legacy**.

Types of Gifts   Gifts by will can be *specific, general,* or *residuary*. A *specific* devise or bequest (legacy) describes particular property that can be distinguished from all the rest of the testator's property. For example, Johnson's will provides, "I give my nephew, Tom, my gold pocket watch with initials MTJ." Should the gold watch not be in existence or part of Johnson's property at the time of Johnson's death (if, for example, it has been sold, destroyed, or given away), an ex-tinguishment, or cancellation, of the legacy (*ademption*) exists.

A general devise or bequest (legacy) does not single out any particular item of property to be transferred by will. For example, "I give to my daughter, Dana, $10,000" is a general bequest. Usually, general legacies specify a sum of money.

On occasion, assets are insufficient to pay in full all general bequests provided for in a will. When this happens, an *abatement*, by which the legatees receive reduced benefits, takes place. For example, Johnson's will leaves "$15,000 each to

my children, Mary and Sam." Upon Johnson's death only $10,000 is available to honor these bequests. By abatement, each child will receive $5,000.

A testator or testatrix may wish that a legatee receive a gift whether or not a particular source of assets is available at the time of death. This is accomplished by means of a *demonstrative* bequest. In the will, the testator or testatrix des-ignates a particular source from which the gift is to be made, additionally instructing that if that source is insufficient or no longer existing, the bequest be paid out of the general assets.

If the legatee dies prior to the death of the testator or testatrix or before the legacy is pay-able, a *lapsed legacy* occurs. At common law, the legacy failed. Today, the legacy may not lapse if the legatee is in a certain blood relationship to the testator or testatrix, such as a child, grand-child, brother or sister, if the legatee also left a child or other surviving descendant.

Sometimes a will provides that any assets re-maining after specific gifts are made and debts are paid are to be distributed through a residuary clause. A residuary provision is used because the exact amount to be distributed cannot be de-termined until all other gifts and payouts are made. A residuary estate can pose problems, however, when the will does not specifically name the beneficiaries to receive the residue. In such a case, if the court cannot determine the testator's intent, the remainder of the residuary passes according to state laws of intestacy.

In the following case, the lower court tried to apply a distribution formula that was not spe-cifically provided by the terms of the will's gen-eral residuary clause.

KORTZ v. AMERICAN NAT'L BANK OF CHEYENNE
Supreme Court of Wyoming, 1977.
571 P.2d 985.

BACKGROUND AND FACTS   *The Johnson will contained a residuary clause that provided a general remainder clause:*

"The remainder of my estate shall be divided as follows among the following people.

"FIFTH: I hereby give bequeath and devise one-quarter of the balance of my money and estate of which I may die seised and possessed, both real, personal and mixed, of every kind, character and description whatsoever and wheresoever situate to THE CANCER SOCIETY to be theirs absolutely and forever.

"SIXTH: I hereby give, bequeath and devise one-half (½) of the balance of my money to LILLIAN BUTLER to be hers absolutely and forever."

Only three-quarters of the residuary was disposed of by the terms of the will. One quarter remained. The lower court presumed that Johnson intended one-third of the residuary for the American Cancer Society and two-thirds for Lillian Butler. Johnson's daughter and heir by intestacy objected. She claimed the one-quarter under the laws of intestate succession.

ROSE, Justice.

*   *   *   *

First, in the consideration of a will, the intention of the testator must govern. In ascertaining the testator's intention, it is not for us to read into the will something which the deceased did not place there. We can only glean decedent's intent and purpose from what his testament says. Under Wyoming law, the testator's intention is to be ascertained if at all possible from the meaning of all words used in the context of the entire will. We have declined to supply words for a testator where the will is clear and unambiguous.

*   *   *   *

The residuary clause, in the present case, does not make an express declaration that *all* of the testator's residuary estate was to be distributed to the listed legatees. It says, the remainder "shall be divided *as follows* among the following people," and then goes on to distribute only a portion of the residuary estate. The specific distributive clauses are not, therefore, wholly inconsistent with the general residuary clause and there is no ambiguity created by the plain wording of the instrument which authorizes such interpretation as is contended for by the appellee.

*   *   *   *

We hold that the language of the Johnson will is clear and unambiguous. As a result, the testator intended a portion of his residuary estate to pass by intestacy. The language of residuary paragraphs FIFTH and SIXTH discloses that the Cancer Society is to receive one-quarter of the *property and money* remaining after the payment of debts and specific bequests, or one-sixteenth of the estate. Lillian Butler, in turn, is to receive one-half of the *money,* if any, remaining after payment of debts, specific bequests and the Cancer Society bequest, or three thirty-seconds of the money remaining in the estate. This leaves three thirty-seconds of the money and three-sixteenths of all other property in the estate undistributed. We note a distinction between the assets bequeathed to these residuary legatees, since the bequest to Lillian Butler refers only to money. There is no basis for the trial court to vary these bequests, even though a portion of the testator's residuary estate must thereby pass by intestacy.

The lower court was admonished by the appellate court for attempting to rewrite the testator's will. The case was returned to the trial court for entry of a judgment consistent with the principles of law articulated in this opinion. Johnson's daughter and heir was entitled to one-quarter of the residuary estate. One-quarter went to the American Cancer Society, and one-half to Lillian Butler.

JUDGMENT AND REMEDY

The Uniform Probate Code

Probate laws vary from state to state. In 1969, the American Bar Association and the National Conference of Commissioners on Uniform State Laws approved the Uniform Probate Code (UPC). The UPC codifies general principles and procedures for the resolution of conflicts in settling estates and relaxes some of the requirements for a valid will contained in earlier state laws. References to UPC provisions will be included in the remainder of this chapter where general practice in most states is consistent. However, since succession and inheritance laws vary widely among different states, one should always check the particular laws of the state involved.[5]

Testamentary Capacity

Not everyone who owns property necessarily qualifies to make a valid disposition of that property by will. *Testamentary capacity* requires the testator to be of legal age and sound mind *at the time the will is made*. The legal age for executing a will varies, but in most states and under the UPC, the minimum age is eighteen years. [UPC 2-501] Thus, a will of a twenty-one-year-old decedent written when the person was sixteen is invalid.

The concept of "being of sound mind" refers to the testator's ability to formulate and comprehend a personal plan for the disposition of property. Further, a testator must intend the document to be his or her will.

Courts have grappled with the requirement of *sound mind* for a long time, and their decisions have been inconsistent. Mental incapacity is a highly subjective matter and thus not easily measured. The general test for testamentary capacity has the following provisions:

1. The testator must comprehend and remember the "natural objects of his or her bounty" (usually family members, but including persons for whom the testator has affection).
2. The testator must comprehend the kind and character of the property being distributed.
3. The testator must understand and formulate a plan for disposing of the property to family members and friends.

Less mental ability is required to make a will than to manage one's own business affairs or to enter into a contract. Thus, a testator may be feeble, aged, eccentric, or offensive in behavior and still possess testamentary capacity. Moreover, a person can be judged insane or have insane delusions about certain subjects yet, during lucid moments, still be of *sound mind* to make a valid will.

The problem of determining testamentary mental capacity is illustrated by the following case dealing with a testatrix in a nursing home.

---

5. For example, California law differs *substantially* from the UPC.

IN RE ESTATE OF UNGER

Court of Appeals of Oregon, 1980.
47 Or.App. 951, 615 P.2d 1115.

BACKGROUND AND FACTS *The appellate court examines the testamentary capacity of the testatrix in the following case. She was confined to a nursing home when the will was executed and the staff testified that she was in a state of mental confusion at the time.*

ROBERTS, Judge.

The issue on appeal in this will contest case is whether testatrix, Lena L. Unger, had sufficient testamentary capacity to execute a last will and testament on February 25, 1976. The probate court found that testatrix had sufficient testamentary capacity. We disagree.

The requirements of testamentary capacity were summarized in *Kastner v. Husband*, as follows:

"*   *   * (1) the person must be able to understand the nature of the act in which he is engaged; (2) know the nature and extent of his property; (3) know, without prompting, the claims, if any, of those who are, should or might be, the natural objects of his bounty; and (4) be cognizant of the scope and reach of the provisions of the document. If the foregoing conditions are found to prevail at the time of executing the instrument, the testator is deemed to have sufficient capacity to make a will. *   *   *"

*   *   *   *

The attorney was one of the subscribing witnesses. He testified that he felt testatrix was competent to make the will as he had no data to indicate otherwise. The other subscribing witness, the attorney's secretary, also testified that, in her opinion, testatrix was competent, as she, too, had no reason to believe otherwise. The secretary was present when respondent read aloud the provisions of the will to testatrix in the reception area, but was unable to hear anything said by testatrix although testatrix appeared to the secretary to be asking questions. After respondent's explanation to testatrix and prior to testatrix's execution of the will, testatrix approached the secretary, asking something to the effect of "What is this, what am I doing, what do you want me to do?" The secretary did not recall that an explanation was given to testatrix by anyone. The secretary testified that the attorney then appeared and asked some cursory questions about testatrix's satisfaction with the document. The secretary did not hear testatrix say anything, but she did appear to nod her head. Testatrix then signed the document at the place indicated to her.

The testimony of the subscribing witnesses, aided by the presumption of competency which accompanies a will that has been duly executed, carries great weight in the determination of decedent's testamentary capacity. The reason for this is that the determination of testamentary capacity must focus on the moment the will is executed and subscribing witnesses are in a position to observe the decedent at the time of the execution. Nevertheless, this heavy reliance on the subscribing witnesses' testimony is not always appropriate.

*   *   *   *

Other witnesses who testified were nursing home personnel who had observed testatrix for a period of eight days prior to the signing of the will, and the physician who examined testatrix three days prior to the date the will was executed. These witnesses were disinterested and unanimous in their opinion that at the time the will was executed, testatrix was without testamentary capacity. Those on the nursing staff who were familiar with testatrix until her death, two and one-half years later, also indicated that at no time was she competent.

*   *   *   *

Those individuals who testified that they observed testatrix frequently both prior to and subsequent to the execution of the will were a registered nurse, a licensed practical nurse, the nursing home's activities director, and the home's administrator. They all indicated that testatrix lacked testamentary capacity. Testatrix was described as being very confused; as wandering aimlessly about the nursing home; as being unable to distinguish her room or her possessions from other patients; as being unable to recognize the staff; as being unable to carry on a conversation; and as being able to communicate only on the most basic level and only if a short answer was required. Testimony indicated that her mental confusion left her unable to dress herself appropriately and caused her to have difficulty feeding herself and maintaining personal hygiene.

*   *   *   *

We conclude the evidence of testatrix's mental acuity is not as persuasive as the testimony from the examining physician and the nursing home personnel, who were disinterested and who were dealing with testatrix on a more constant basis than the other witnesses during the period of time surrounding the date of the will's execution.

JUDGMENT AND REMEDY   *The trial court's judgment was reversed. The testatrix was determined to have lacked testamentary capacity; and, therefore, the will executed on February 25, 1976, was invalid.*

COMMENT   *Unger died intestate. The property passed as though there had never been any will.*

FORMAL REQUIREMENTS OF A WILL

A will must comply with statutory formalities designed to ensure that the testator or testatrix understood his or her actions at the time the will was made. These formalities are intended to help prevent fraud. Unless they are followed, the will is declared void and the decedent's property is distributed according to the laws of intestacy of that state. The requirements are not uniform among the jurisdictions. However, most states uphold the following basic requirements for executing a will.

1.   *A will must be in writing.* A written document is generally required, although in some cases oral wills, called nuncupative wills (to be discussed later), are found valid. [UPC 2-502] The writing itself can be informal as long as it substantially complies with the statutory requirements. In some states a will can be handwritten in crayon or ink. It can be written on a sheet or scrap of paper, on a paper bag, or on a piece of cloth. A will that is completely in the handwriting of the testator is called **holographic** (or olographic).

A will also can refer to a written memorandum that itself is not a will but that contains information necessary to carry out the will. For example, Thelma's will provides that a certain sum of money be divided among a group of charities named in a written memorandum that Thelma gave to the trustee *the same day the will was signed*. The written list of charities will be "incorporated by reference" into the will only if it was in existence when the will was executed (signed) and if it is sufficiently described so that it can be identified.

2.   *A formal (nonholographic) will must be signed by the testator.* It is a fundamental requirement in almost all jurisdictions that the testator or testatrix's signature appear, generally at the end of the will. Each jurisdiction dictates by statute and court decision what constitutes a signature. Initials, an "X" or other mark, and words like "Mom" have all been upheld as valid when it was shown that the testator intended them to be a signature.

3.   *A will must be witnessed.* A will must be attested by two and sometimes three witnesses. The number of witnesses, their qualifications, and the manner in which the witnessing must be done are generally set out in a statute.

A witness can be required to be disinterested—that is, not a beneficiary under the will. By contrast, the UPC provides that a will is valid even if it is attested by an interested witness. [UPC 2-505] There are no age requirements for witnesses, but they must be mentally competent.

Witnesses function to verify that the testator actually executed (signed) the will and had the requisite intent and capacity at the time. A witness does not have to read the contents of the will. Usually, the testator and witnesses must all sign in sight or presence of one another, but the UPC deems it sufficient if the testator acknowledges his or her signature to the witnesses. [UPC 2-502] The UPC does not require all parties to sign in the presence of one another.

4. *A will may be required to be "published."* Publication is an oral declaration by the maker to the witnesses that the document they are about to sign is his or her "last will and testament." Publication is becoming an unnecessary formality in most states, and it is not required under the UPC.

In general, strict compliance with the preceding formalities (except for the one relating to witnesses and the one relating to publication) is required before a formal document is accepted as the decedent's will. Holographic wills constitute another exception in some jurisdictions. However, holographic wills must be dated and signed by the decedent in order for them to be probated (validated). [UPC 2-503]

Nuncupative Wills

A nuncupative will is an oral will made before witnesses. Where authorized by statute, such wills are generally permitted only if made during the last illness of the testator or testatrix. They are sometimes referred to as death-bed wills. Only personal property (not real property) can be transferred by a nuncupative will. Statutes frequently permit soldiers and sailors to make nuncupative wills when on active duty.

UNDUE INFLUENCE

A valid will is one that represents the maker's intention to transfer and distribute his or her property. When it can be shown that the decedent's plan of distribution was the result of improper pressure brought by another person, the will is declared invalid.

Undue influence may be inferred by the court if the testator or testatrix ignores blood relatives and names as beneficiary a nonrelative who is in constant close contact and in a position to influence the making of the will. For example,

if a nurse or friend caring for the deceased at the time of death is named as beneficiary to the exclusion of all family members, the validity of the will might well be challenged for undue influence.

REVOCATION OF WILLS

An executed will is revocable by the maker at any time during the maker's lifetime. Wills can also be revoked by operation of law. Revocation can be partial or complete, and it must follow certain strict formalities.

Act of the Maker

Revocation by Physical Act The testator or testatrix may revoke a will by intentionally burning, tearing, canceling, obliterating, or destroying it, or by having someone else do so in the presence of the maker and at the maker's direction.[6] In some states, partial revocation by physical act of the maker is recognized. Thus, those portions of a will lined out or torn away are dropped, and the remaining parts of the will are valid. In no case, however, can a provision be crossed out and an additional or substitute provision written in. Such altered portions require reexecution (resigning) and reattestation (rewitnessing).

To revoke a will by physical act, it is necessary to follow the mandates of a state statute exactly. Where a state statute prescribes the exact methods for revoking a will by physical act, those are the only methods that will revoke the will, as illustrated by the following case.

---

6. The destruction cannot be inadvertent. The maker's intent to revoke must be shown. Where a will has been burned or torn accidentally, it is normally recommended that the maker have a new document created so that it will not falsely appear that the maker intended to revoke the will.

BACKGROUND AND FACTS *The decedent, Lisbeth R. Eglee, was a resident of Charlestown, Rhode Island. She died on November 11, 1973. Subsequently, the defendant, Donald R. Eglee, who was the stepson and an heir of Lisbeth R. Eglee, filed this petition with a local probate court,*

ESTATE OF EGLEE
Supreme Court of Rhode Island, 1978.
119 R.I. 786, 383 A.2d 586.

requesting that a written instrument, executed and dated by the decedent on March 7, 1966, be admitted to probate.

The plaintiff, Milton Haller, successor in interest to Duna Haller, sister of Lisbeth, stipulated that the document offered by the defendant was executed as the decedent's will in compliance with the laws of the state of Connecticut, the place in which the will was executed. The decedent had made lines with a red pencil through every word and signature. In addition, diagonally across each clause of the instrument were the decedent's initials, the word "obliterated," and the date, September 19, 1973. The record indicated, however, that the entire document remained legible despite the defacement. The parties agreed that the will was free of markings, initials, and notation at the time of its execution.

The will was admitted to probate. The trial court found that although the decedent had demonstrated an intention to revoke her will, she had failed to comply with the precise methods of revocation required by state law. Therefore, the will had not been validly revoked and the legible portions did constitute a valid will.

BEVILACQUA, Chief Justice.

*   *   *   *

The issue before us is whether the decedent's actions constituted a sufficient revocation of her will. It is well settled that a will may be validly revoked if the testator, or some third person acting under the testator's direction and in his presence, performs a prescribed physical act with the specified intent of revoking the will. The revocation procedure in Rhode Island is set forth in [the statute] which reads:

"No will or codicil or any part thereof shall be revoked otherwise than as provided in [the statute] or by another will or codicil executed in manner hereinbefore required, or by some writing declaring an intention to revoke the same and executed in the manner in which a will is hereinbefore required to be executed, or by burning, tearing, or otherwise destroying the same by the testator, or by some person in his presence and by his direction, with the intention of revoking the same." (Emphasis added.)

Thus, revocation of a validly executed will under [state statute] requires the intent to revoke coupled with the act of "burning, tearing, or otherwise destroying" the will.

The plaintiff contends that the phrase "otherwise destroying" in [the state statute] should be construed so as to include the acts of cancelling and obliterating. However, in interpreting such provisions our duty is very narrowly described. We must construe statutes, not redraft them. In so doing, we are bound to ascertain the intent of the Legislature and to effectuate that intent when it is lawful and within legislative competence. Specifically, where a statute prescribes the methods and acts by which a will may be revoked, no acts other than those mentioned in the statute can operate as a revocation, because statutes governing revocation are mandatory and must be strictly construed. The rationale for making statutory formalities governing revocation of a will mandatory is to prevent mistake, misrepresentation, and fraud.

Examining the legislative history of [the statute], we find that prior to 1896, our revocation statute omitted the phrase "otherwise destroying" and provided that a will could be revoked by "cancelling" or "obliterating" as well as by other enumerated methods. When the Legislature amended the revocation statute in 1896, it deleted the words "cancelling" and "obliterating" and inserted the phrase "otherwise destroying." Generally, the omission from a revocation statute of one of the modes of revocation previously included renders it impossible to revoke a will by the omitted method. It is obvious that if, as plaintiff argues, the Legislature had intended that the term "otherwise destroying" were to include revocation by cancellation or obliteration, it would have framed the pertinent clause to read "or by burning, tearing, cancelling, obliterating, or otherwise destroying." To adopt plaintiff's construction would contravene both the mandatory method of revocation delineated by [the state statute] and the obvious intent of the Legislature in drafting that statute.

Courts that have considered statutes identical to [the Rhode Island statute] have held that when the Legislature, after mentioning specific acts such as "burning" and "tearing" as sufficient to revoke a will, speaks of "otherwise destroying" a will, it must be understood as intending by the latter some mode of * * * destruction of the same kind or nature as by the methods previously mentioned. Therefore, we believe that the phrase "otherwise destroying" imports a destruction of both the substance and contents of the will. Anything short of a destruction of this degree is entirely ineffectual as a revocation, particularly where the original writing remains legible as in the instant case.

Because [the Rhode Island statute on revocation of a will by physical act] cannot be construed so as to include cancelling and obliterating as appropriate methods of revocation, and because the acts of the testator in this case did not constitute "otherwise destroying" the will, we must agree with the trial justice that despite the testator's obvious intent to revoke, the will was not validly revoked.

The testatrix failed to revoke her validly executed will under the requirements of the state statute. The will continued as a valid testamentary disposition despite the testatrix's obvious intent to revoke. The revocation was incorrectly done, hence invalid.   **JUDGMENT AND REMEDY**

Revocation in Another Writing A **codicil** is a written instrument separate from the will that amends or revokes provisions in the will. It eliminates the necessity of redrafting an entire will merely to add to it or amend it. A codicil can also be used to revoke an entire will. The codicil must be executed with the same formalities required for a will. It must refer expressly to the will. In effect, it updates a will because the will is "incorporated by reference" into the codicil.

A *second will* can be executed that may or may not revoke the first or a prior will, depending upon the language used. The second will must use specific language like, "This will hereby revokes all prior wills." If the second will is otherwise valid and properly executed, it will revoke all prior wills. If the express *declaration of revocation* is missing, then both wills are read together. If any of the dispositions made in the second will are inconsistent with the prior will, the second will controls.

Revocation by Operation of Law

Marriage In general, a will written and executed before marriage will be revoked by the fact of marriage. Public policy provides that a person's new marital obligations change any prior decisions concerning the disposition of property. Under the Uniform Probate Code, a subsequent marriage *does not completely revoke* a will. [UPC 2-508] The new spouse is entitled to whatever share of the estate the state provides to spouses if the testator or testatrix died without a will. The rest of the estate is passed under the will. [UPC 2-301]

Divorce or Annulment   At common law and under the UPC, divorce does not necessarily revoke the entire will. A divorce or an annulment occurring after a will has been executed will revoke those dispositions of property made under the will to the former spouse.

Children Born after a Will is Executed   If a child is born after a will has been executed and if it appears that the testator would have made a provision for the child, then the child is entitled to receive whatever portion of the estate he or she is allowed under state intestate laws. Most state laws allow a child to receive some portion of the estate if no provision is made in a will, unless it appears from the terms of the will that the testator intended to disinherit the child. Under the UPC, the rule is the same. [UPC 2-302]

RIGHTS UNDER A WILL

The law imposes certain limitations on the way a person can dispose of property in a will. For example, a married person who makes a will cannot avoid leaving a certain portion of the estate to the surviving spouse. In most states this is called a "forced share," "widow's share," or "elective share," and it is often one-third.

Beneficiaries under a will have rights as well. A beneficiary can renounce his or her share of the property given under a will.[7] Further, a surviving spouse can renounce the amount given under a will and elect to take the "forced share" if the forced share is larger than the amount of the gift. State statutes provide the methods by

which a surviving spouse accomplishes renunciation. The purpose of these statutes is to allow the spouse to obtain whichever distribution would be most advantageous. The UPC gives the surviving spouse an elective right to take one-third of the total estate. [UPC 2-201]

STATUTES OF DESCENT AND DISTRIBUTION

The rules of descent are statutory. That means each state can regulate how property shall be distributed when a person dies without a will. State laws attempt to carry out the likely intent and wishes of the decedent. These statutes are called **intestacy laws.**

The rules of descent vary widely from state to state. However, there is usually a special statutory provision for the rights of the surviving spouse and children. In addition, the law provides that first the debts of the decedent must be satisfied out of his or her estate, and then the remaining assets can pass to the surviving spouse and to the children.

A surviving spouse usually receives a share of the estate—one-half if there is also a surviving child and one-third if there are two or more children. Only where no children or grandchildren survive the decedent will a surviving spouse succeed to the *entire estate.*

Assume that Able dies intestate and is survived by his wife, Barbara, and his children, Carl and Diane. Able's property passes according to **intestacy laws.** After Able's outstanding debts are paid, Barbara will receive the homestead (either in fee simple or as a life estate) and ordinarily a one-third to one-half interest in all other property. The remaining real and personal property will pass to Carl and Diane in equal portions.

Distribution

State statutes of descent and distribution specify the order in which heirs of an intestate share in the estate. When there is no surviving spouse or child, then grandchildren, brothers and sisters,

---

7.   Usually done for tax reasons or because the recipient would fare better by taking his or her elective share.

and, in some states, parents of the decedent are the next in line to share. These relatives are usually called *lineal descendants*. If there are no lineal descendants, then *collateral heirs* are the next group to share. Collateral heirs include nieces, nephews, aunts, and uncles of the decedent.

If there are still no survivors in any of those groups of people related to the decedent, most statutes provide that the property shall be distributed among the next of kin of any of the collateral heirs. Stepchildren are not considered kin.

However, legally adopted children are recognized as lawful heirs of their adoptive parents.

Whether or not an illegitimate child inherits depends on state statute. In all states, intestate succession between the mother and the child exists. In some states, intestate succession between the father and the child can occur only where the child is "legitimized" by ceremony or the child has been "acknowledged" by the father. The constitutionality of these illegitimacy statutes has recently been upheld by the Supreme Court, and affirmed by the Ohio Supreme Court.

BACKGROUND AND FACTS *An illegitimate child contested the constitutionality of an Ohio statute that prevented her from inheriting from her natural father's estate.*

WHITE v. RANDOLPH
Supreme Court of Ohio, 1979.
59 Ohio St.2d 6, 391 N.E.2d 333.

PER CURIAM [by the Whole Court].

The issue certified for resolution is as follows: "Whether the provisions of R.C. Chapter 2105 denying to one who is illegitimate any right to inherit from the natural father, unless the father has taken certain steps such as *marrying* the mother, *acknowledging* the child, designating the child as an heir-at-law, adoption, or making a provision in a will, are violative of equal protection as guaranteed by the Fourteenth Amendment of the United States Constitution and Article I, Section 2 of the Ohio Constitution."

The unanimous opinion of the Court of Appeals in the cause at bar was written by Judge Robert E. Holmes, now a Justice of this court. In our view, the position taken by Justice Holmes represents the correct one under the instant facts and, therefore, is incorporated at length:

Holmes, P. J.

*   *   *   *

"The facts relevant to this appeal are in brief that Clarence Jackson died testate on January 17, 1975. His will was duly admitted to probate. The will devised all of decedent's property to his wife, but failed to provide for its disposition in the event that she did not survive him. She did not.

"The administrator then brought this action in the Common Pleas Court of Franklin County, Probate Division, for a determination of decedent's heirs-at-law, joining appellant Alice Marie Jackson, who claimed to be decedent's illegitimate daughter, as one of the defendants. Following a hearing on the matter, Judge Metcalf held, as a matter of law, that appellant was not entitled to inherit from the estate of Clarence Jackson because she introduced no evidence tending to show:

" ' *   *   * that the decedent, alleged father, legitimized his illegitimate daughter, or formally acknowledged his daughter in Probate Court, or adopted such

daughter, or provided for her in his will, or designated her as his heir at law
* * *.'

"In Ohio, a child born out of wedlock is capable of inheriting from and through his mother, but may inherit from his father only under certain circumstances. The father may legitimatize an illegitimate child by afterwards marrying the mother of the illegitimate child and acknowledging the child as his. Further, the natural father of an illegitimate child may confer upon such child a right of inheritance from such father by several means: (1) by formal acknowledgement in Probate Court that the child is his with consent of the mother; (2) by designating the illegitimate child as his heir-at-law; (3) by adopting the illegitimate child; and (4) by making a provision for the child in his will.

"Appellant concededly cannot meet any of the above criteria. However, appellant contends that the equal protection clause requires that she be permitted to inherit from decedent if she can establish with sufficient competent evidence that decedent is, in fact, her father. In the cases considering this general issue before us, it has been rather uniformly pointed out that the rationality of the classification must be examined in light of the legitimate state purposes to which it is related.

"It has long been recognized in Ohio that proof of paternity, especially after the death of the alleged father, is difficult, and peculiarly subject to abuse. One of the resultants of such abuse would be the instability of land titles of real estate left by intestate fathers of illegitimate children.
* * * *

"[W]e believe that the Ohio statutory provisions present a reasonable middle ground for the recognition of certain categories of illegitimate children of intestate men. Through these laws inheritance rights may be reasonably recognized without jeopardizing the orderly settlement of estates or the dependability of titles to property passing under intestate laws.

"Clearly, the Ohio classification scheme is rationally related to the legitimate state purpose of assuring efficient disposition of property at death while avoiding spurious claims. Moreover, the Ohio provisions do not discriminate between legitimate and illegitimate children *per se*. All children may inherit from their mothers. Some illegitimate children and all legitimate children may inherit from their fathers. The group 'discriminated against' is that class of illegitimate children whose fathers did not formally acknowledge them or designate them as heirs-at-law."
* * * *

Subsequent to the decision of the Court of Appeals in the instant cause, the United States Supreme Court, in the case of *Lalli v. Lalli* (1978), upheld the constitutionality of a New York statute which allowed illegitimate children to inherit from their father only if a court of competent jurisdiction, during the father's lifetime, entered an order declaring the child's paternity.

Recognizing the difficulty of proving paternity and the possibility of fraudulent assertions of paternity upon the estate of the decedent, the court found that the statutory differences afforded legitimate and illegitimate heirs under intestate succession were justified in furtherance of New York's substantial interest in the just and orderly disposition of property at death. In that regard, we conclude that the Ohio statutes in question in the cause at bar are substantially related to the important state interests discussed by the court in *Lalli, supra*.

The judgments of the probate court and the appellate court were affirmed. The Ohio statute was not unconstitutional. Ohio has a sufficient state interest in the disposition of property at death to justify different laws regarding intestate succession for legitimate and illegitimate children.

JUDGMENT AND REMEDY

Because state statutes differ so widely, few generalizations can be made about the laws of descent and distribution. It is extremely important to refer to the exact terms of the applicable state statutes when addressing any problem of intestacy distribution.

The UPC provides that a surviving spouse, in addition to taking an elective share of one-third of the decedent's estate, is entitled to the following:

1. A homestead allowance of $5,000.
2. A household and personal effects exemption to a value not to exceed $3,500.
3. A family allowance for a period of up to one year after the death occurs to provide for daily expenses before the estate is settled, up to the amount of $6,000. [UPC 2-401, 402, 403, and 404]

The Pattern of Intestacy Distribution for Grandchildren When an intestate is survived by descendants of deceased children, a question arises as to what share the descendants (that is, grandchildren of the intestate) will receive. **Per stirpes** is a method of dividing an intestate share where a class or group of distributees (for example, grandchildren) take the share that their deceased parent *would have been* entitled to inherit had that child lived.

Assume that John, a widower, has three children, Able, Barbara, and Clara. Able has two children (Mark and Sally), Barbara has one child (Greg), and Clara has one child (Peter). At the time of John's death, Able and Barbara have predeceased their father. If John's estate is distributed *per stirpes*, the following distribution would take place:

1. Mark and Sally: one-sixth each, taking Able's one-third.
2. Greg: one-third, taking Barbara's share.
3. Clara: one-third, as surviving child (Peter does not inherit).

Another type of distribution of an estate is on a **per capita** basis. This means that each person takes an equal share of the estate. Assume that John, a widower, has two children, Able and Barbara. Able has two children (Mark and Sally), and Barbara has one child (Greg). At the time of John's death, Able and Barbara have predeceased their father. If John's estate is distributed *per capita*, Mark, Sally, and Greg will each receive a one-third share.

In most states and under the Uniform Probate Code, in-laws do not share in an estate. If a child dies before his or her parents, the child's spouse will not receive an inheritance. Assume that John, a widower, has two married children, Able and Barbara, and no grandchildren. If Able predeceases his father, John's entire estate will go to Barbara. Able's surviving wife will not inherit.

TRUSTS

A trust involves any arrangement whereby property is transferred from one person to be administered by a trustee for a third party's benefit. It can also be defined as a right or property, real or personal, held by one party for the benefit of another. A trust can be created for any purpose that is not illegal or against public policy. The essential elements of a trust are:

1. A designated beneficiary.
2. A designated trustee.
3. A fund sufficiently identified to enable title to pass to the trustee.
4. Actual delivery to the trustee with the intention of passing title.

If Sanford conveys his farm to South Miami First National Bank to be held for the benefit of his daughters, Sanford has created a trust. Sanford is the settlor, South Miami First National Bank is the trustee, and Sanford's daughters are the beneficiaries.

Express Trusts

An express trust is one created or declared in expressed terms, usually in writing. It differs from one that is inferred by the law from the conduct or dealings of the parties (an implied trust, to be discussed later). The two types of express trusts that will be discussed here are *inter vivos* trusts and *testamentary* trusts.

Inter Vivos Trusts An **inter vivos trust** is a trust executed by a grantor during his or her lifetime. The grantor executes a "trust deed," and legal title to the trust property passes to the named trustee. The trustee has a duty to administer the property as directed by the grantor for the benefit and in the interest of the beneficiaries. The trustee must preserve the trust property, make it productive, and, if required by the terms of the trust agreement, pay income to the beneficiaries, all in accordance with the terms of the trust. Once the *inter vivos* trust is created, the grantor has, in effect, given over the property for the benefit of beneficiaries. Often, tax-related benefits exist in setting up an *inter vivos* trust.

Testamentary Trusts A **testamentary trust** is a trust created by will to come into existence upon the settlor's death. Although a testamentary trust has a trustee who maintains legal title to the trust property, actions of the trustee are subject to judicial approval. The trustee of a testamentary trust can be named in the will or be appointed by the court. Unlike the *inter vivos* trust, a testamentary trust will not fail because a trustee has not been named in the will. The legal responsibilities of the trustees are the same in both kinds of trusts. If the will setting up a testamentary trust is invalid, then the trust will also be invalid. The property that was supposed to be in the trust will then pass according to intestacy laws, not according to the terms of the trust.

Implied Trusts

Sometimes a trust will be imposed by law, even in absence of an express trust. Customarily, these implied trusts are divided into **constructive** and **resulting** trusts.

Constructive Trust A constructive trust differs from an express trust in that it arises by operation of law. Whenever a transaction takes place in which the person who takes the legal estate in property cannot also enjoy the beneficial interest without violating some established principle of equity, the court will create a constructive trust. In effect, the legal owner becomes a trustee for the parties who, in equity, are actually entitled to the beneficial enjoyment that flows from the trust. One element of a constructive trust is a wrongful action, whether it be active or constructive.

To illustrate: Able and Baker are partners in buying, developing, and selling real estate. Able learns through the staff of the partnership that a piece of land will soon come on the market that the staff will recommend that the partnership purchase. Able purchases the property secretly in his own name, violating his fiduciary relationship. When these facts are discovered, a court will determine that Able must hold the property in trust for the partnership.

Resulting Trust A resulting trust arises from the conduct of the parties. Here the trust results, or is created from, the *apparent intentions* of the parties. Since the trust is created by law, the conduct of the parties evidencing the intent to create a trust relationship is carefully scrutinized.

To illustrate: Smith purchases one acre of land from Green. Because Smith is going out of the country for a period of two years and will be unable to attend the closing, she asks Green, at the closing, to deed the property to Smith's good friend, Crenshaw. Green does indeed convey the property to Crenshaw. Since the intent of the transaction is not to make Crenshaw a gift of the land, the property will be held in trust (a resulting trust) with Crenshaw as the trustee for the benefit of Smith.

Other Kinds of Trusts

Certain trusts are created for special purposes. Three such trusts that warrant discussion are: charitable, spendthrift, and totten trusts.

Charitable Trust A trust designed for the benefit of a segment of the public or of the public in general is a **charitable trust.** It differs from a private trust in that the identities of the beneficiaries are uncertain. Usually, to be deemed a charitable trust, a trust must be created for charitable, educational, religious, or scientific purposes.

Spendthrift Trust A trust created to provide for the maintenance of a beneficiary by preventing his or her improvidence with the bestowed funds is a **spendthrift trust.** Essentially, the beneficiary is permitted to draw only a certain portion of the total amount to which he or she is entitled at any one time. The majority of states allow spendthrift trust provisions that prohibit creditors from attaching such trusts.

Totten Trust A special type of trust created when one person deposits money in his or her own name as a trustee for another is a **totten trust.** This trust is tentative in that it is revocable at will until the depositor dies or completes the gift in his or her lifetime by some unequivocal act or declaration (for example, delivery of the funds to the intended beneficiary). If the depositor should die before the beneficiary dies and if the depositor has not revoked the trust expressly or impliedly, a presumption arises that an absolute trust has been created for the benefit of the beneficiary. At the death of the depositor, the beneficiary obtains property rights to the balance on hand.

ESTATE ADMINISTRATION

The orderly procedure used to collect assets, settle debts, and distribute the remaining assets when a person dies is the subject matter of estate administration. This section will look at the duties of the personal representative of the deceased.

Principal Duties of the Personal Representative

The rules and procedures for managing the estate of a deceased are controlled by statute. Thus, they vary from state to state. In every state, there is a special court, often called a probate court, which oversees the management of estates of decedents.

The first step after a person dies is usually to determine whether or not the decedent left a will. In most cases the decedent's attorney will have that information. If it is not known for some time whether a valid will exists, the personal papers of the deceased must be reviewed. If a will exists, it probably names a personal representative (executor) to administer the estate. If there is no will, or if the will fails to name a personal representative, then the court must appoint an administrator. Under the UPC, the term *personal representative* includes the executor (person named in the will) and administrator (person appointed by the court). [UPC 1-201(30)]

The first duty of the personal representative is to inventory and collect the assets of the decedent. If necessary, the assets must be appraised to determine their value. Both the rights of creditors and the rights of beneficiaries must be protected during the estate administration proceedings. In addition, the personal representative is responsible for managing the assets of the estate during the administration period and not allowing them to be wasted or unnecessarily depleted.

The personal representative receives and pays valid claims of creditors and arranges for the estate to pay federal and state income taxes and estate taxes (or inheritance taxes, depending on the state). A personal representative is required to post a bond to ensure honest and faithful performance. Usually the bond exceeds the estimated value of the personal estate of the decedent. In some cases, the will can specify that the personal representative need not post a bond.

When the ultimate distribution of assets to the beneficiaries is determined, the personal representative is responsible for distributing the estate pursuant to the court order. Once the assets have been distributed, an accounting is rendered to the court, the estate is closed, and the personal representative is relieved of any further responsibility or liability for the estate. Exhibit 56–1 lists the duties of the personal representative.

EXHIBIT 56–1 THE DUTIES OF THE PERSONAL REPRESENTATIVE

It would be impossible to indicate all the duties the executor must perform, but here are some.

1. Managing the estate until it is settled, including
   a. Collecting debts due the estate.
   b. Managing real estate; arranging for maintenance and repairs.
   c. Registering securities in the name of the estate.
   d. Collecting insurance proceeds.
   e. Running family business, if necessary.
   f. Arranging for the family's support during probate.
   g. Properly insuring assets.

2. Collecting all assets and necessary records, including
   a. Locating the will, insurance policies, real estate papers, car registrations, and birth certificates.
   b. Filing claims for pension, social security, profit sharing and veteran's benefits.
   c. Taking possession of bank accounts, real estate, personal effects, and safe deposit boxes.
   d. Obtaining names, addresses, and social security numbers of all heirs.
   e. Making an inventory of all assets.
   f. Setting up records and books.

3. Determining the estate's obligations, including
   a. Determining which claims are legally due.
   b. Obtaining receipts for all claims paid.
   c. Checking on mortgages and other loans.

4. Computing and then paying all death taxes due, which requires
   a. Selecting the most beneficial tax alternatives.
   b. Deciding which assets to sell to provide necessary funds.
   c. Paying taxes on time to avoid penalties.
   d. Opposing any unfair evaluations of estate property established by governmental taxing authorities.

5. Computing beneficiaries' shares and then distributing the estate, which includes
   a. Determining who gets particular items and settling family disputes.
   b. Transferring title to real estate and other property.
   c. Selling off assets to pay cash legacies.
   d. Paying final estate costs.
   e. Preparing accountings for the court's approval.

Probate versus Nonprobate

To probate a will means to establish its validity and to carry the administration of the estate through a court process. The process of probate is time-consuming and costly, and the court is involved in every step of the proceedings. Attorneys and personal representatives often become involved in probate.

Many states have statutes that allow for the distribution of assets without probate proceedings. Faster and less expensive methods are then used. For example, property can be transferred by affidavit, and problems or questions can be handled during an administrative hearing. In addition, some state statutes provide that title to cars, savings and checking accounts, and certain other property can be passed merely by filling out forms. This is particularly true when most of the property is held in joint tenancy with right of survivorship or when there is only one heir.

Family Settlement Agreements A majority of states provide for *family settlement agreements,* which are private agreements among the beneficiaries. Once a will is admitted to probate, the family members can agree to settle among themselves the distribution of the decedent's assets. Although a family settlement agreement speeds the settlement process, a court order is still needed to protect the estate from future creditors and to clear title to the assets involved.

Summary Procedures The use of summary procedures in estate administration can save time and money. The expense of a personal representative's commission, attorneys' fees, appraisers' fees, and so forth can be eliminated or at least minimized if the parties utilize summary administration procedures. But in some situations—for example, where a guardian for minor children or for an incompetent person must be appointed and a trust has been created to protect the minor or incompetent—probate procedures cannot be avoided. In the ordinary situation, a person can employ various will substitutes to avoid the cost of probate—for example, *inter vivos* trusts, life insurance policies with named beneficiaries, or joint tenancy arrangements. Not all methods are suitable for every estate, but there are alternatives to a complete probate administration.

ESTATE TAXES

The death of an individual may result in tax liabilities at both the federal and state levels.

Federal Estate Tax

At the federal level, there is a tax levied upon the total value of the estate after debts and expenses for administration have been deducted and after various exemptions are allowed. The tax is on the estate itself rather than on the beneficiaries. Therefore, it does not depend on the character of any bequests or on the relationship of the beneficiary to the decedent, unless a gift to charity that is recognized by the IRS as deductible from the total estate for tax purposes is involved. However, bequests to a surviving spouse do affect federal estate taxation.

State Inheritance Taxes

The majority of states impose a death tax in the form of an inheritance tax imposed on the recipient of a bequest rather than on the estate. Some states also have a state estate tax similar to the federal estate tax. In general, inheritance tax rates are graduated according to the type of relationship between the beneficiary and decedent. The lowest rates and largest exemptions are applied to a surviving spouse and children of the decedent.

QUESTIONS AND CASE PROBLEMS

1. John is a widower who has two married children, Frank and Amy. Amy has two children, Phil and Paula. Frank has no children. John dies, leaving a typewritten will that gives all his property equally to his children, Frank and Amy, and provides that should a child predecease him, leaving grandchildren, the grandchildren are to take *per stirpes*. The will was witnessed by Amy and John's lawyer and was signed by John in their presence. Amy has predeceased John. Frank claims the will is invalid.

   (a) Discuss whether the will is valid.
   (b) Discuss the distribution of John's estate if the will is invalid.
   (c) Discuss the distribution of John's estate if the will is valid.

2. James was a bachelor. While single, he made out a will naming his mother, Carol, as the sole beneficiary. Later James married Lisa. Discuss the results of each of the following possible events:

   (a) If James died while married to Lisa without changing his will, would the estate go to his mother, Carol? Explain.
   (b) Assume James made out a new will upon his marriage to Lisa, leaving his entire estate to Lisa. Later he divorces Lisa and marries Sue, but he does not change his will. Discuss the rights of Lisa and Sue to his estate when he dies.
   (c) Assume James divorces Lisa, marries Sue, and changes his will leaving his estate to Sue. Later a daughter, Lori, is born. James dies without having included Lori in his will. Discuss fully whether Lori has any rights in the estate.

3. Ann has drafted and properly executed a will. Assume the following clauses in her will and the following events:

   (a) Her will provides, "I leave my two-carat diamond ring to my sister, Sylvia." At the time of Ann's death, Sylvia had predeceased Ann, leaving one child, Lindsay.

(b) Her will provides, "I leave $5,000 to each of my nieces, Fern and Dorothy." At the time of Ann's death, only $4,000 remains in her estate.

(c) Her will provides, "I leave to my nephew, Donald, my $10,000 Cadillac or equivalent value." Just prior to Ann's death she sold the Cadillac.

Discuss fully each situation, giving its name and describing its effect on the legatees.

4. Sam, an eighty-three-year-old invalid, employs a nurse, Sarah, to care for him. Prior to Sarah's employment, Sam had executed a will leaving his entire estate to his only living relative—his great-grandson Fred. Sarah convinces Sam that Fred is dead and gets Sam to change his will, naming Sarah as his sole beneficiary. After Sam's death, Fred appears and contests the will. Discuss the probable success of Fred's action.

5. The following transfers and events take place:

(a) John lives in Europe. He transfers $20,000 to his good friend, Kate, and orally instructs her to invest and distribute the $20,000 and whatever it accrues so as to finance the MBA education of his daughter, JoAnn.

(b) Fred is on the board of directors of the ABC Corporation and is the chairman of its research policy committee. Through his chairmanship he learns that ABC has come up with a cure for cancer. Fred purchases on the open market 20,000 shares of ABC stock at $10 per share. When the announcement of the cure is made, the market value of ABC's stock increases to $200 per share.

(c) Sue is a successful businesswoman. She is engaged to marry John, a man of modest means who has ambitions to be an inventor. Sue creates a $20,000 joint savings account in the name of "Sue, in trust for John." Sue tells John that the purpose of the account is to encourage him to move forward in his business ventures.

Discuss fully whether a valid trust has been created in each situation, what each trust is called, and, where applicable, what its effect is.

6. Jesse Butterfield Morris died on February 11, 1967. On April 6, 1967, the Security First National Bank offered a document for probate as Morris's holographic will. The document was entirely in Morris's handwriting, but it contained no signatures of witnesses. The document was dated (November 1, 1965), was addressed to the Security First National Bank, and contained the initials J. B. M. at the end. Should Morris's will be probated? [In re Estate of Morris, 268 Cal.App.2d 638, 74 Cal.Rptr. 32(1969)]

7. Harris executed a written instrument in which he named Bishop as trustee of $17,000 in bonds, notes, mortgages, and money. The instrument declared that Harris was hereby transferring these assets to Bishop in trust for the benefit of the public library in Alexandria, Ohio, but Harris never delivered the instrument. Thereafter, Harris received interest on some of the notes and still had access to the money and instruments that were the subject of the trust. Has Harris created a valid trust? Consider the requirements of making a valid gift. [Whitehead v. Bishop, 23 Ohio App. 315, 155 N.E. 565 (1925)]

8. In 1925 Campbell died, leaving a will in which the ninth clause read as follows: "My good friends Clark and Smith I appoint as my trustees. Each of my trustees is competent by reason of familiarity with the property, my wishes and friendships, to wisely distribute some portion at least of said property. I therefore give and bequeath to my trustees all my property in trust to make disposal by the way of a memento from myself, of such articles to such of my friends as they, my trustees, shall select. All of said property, not so disposed of by them, my trustees are directed to sell and the proceeds of such sale or sales to become and be disposed of as a part of the residue of my estate." Is this a valid trust? [Clark v. Campbell, 82 N.H. 281, 133 A. 166 (1926)]

9. H. W. Wolfe died at the age of sixty-seven, leaving personal property worth about $4,000 and more than five hundred acres of land. Just before he died, on July 31, 1911, he properly executed a will that contained the following provision: "I, H. W. Wolfe, will and bequeath to Miss Mary Lilly Luffman, a tract of land near Roaring Gap Post Office, on State Road and South Fork, adjoining the lands of J. M. Royal and others, the land bought by me from H. D. Woodruff. Witness my hand and seal, this thirty-first day of July, 1911." On August 14, 1911, Wolfe wrote another will that provided in part: "I, H. W. Wolfe, do make and declare this to be my last will and testament. I will and bequeath all my effects to my brothers and sisters, to be divided equally among them. Witness my hand and seal, this the fourteenth day of August, 1911." Both wills were properly signed and attested. Who is entitled to what under these wills? [In re Wolfe's Will, 185 N.C. 563, 117 S.E. 804 (1923)]

10. An elderly childless widow had nine nieces and nephews. She devised her entire estate to be divided equally among two nieces and the husband of one of the nieces, who was also the attorney-draftsman of the will and the executor named in the will. The testatrix was definitely of sound mind when the will was executed. If you were one of the seven nieces or nephews omitted from the will, could you think of any way to have the will invalidated? [Estate of Eckert, 93 Misc.2d 677, 403 N.Y.S.2d 633 (1978)]

FOCUS ON ETHICS

Protection of Property and Other Interests

The ethical questions relating to this unit are similar to those of Unit III concerning personal property. The legal structures that support our ideas about property are crucial to the continuation of our economic system. Indeed, private property is at the heart of pure capitalist ideology. Nonetheless, alternative views about private property abound; for example, Marxists have often equated private property with theft. Consider some questions relating to real property that raise ethical issues.

ABSENTEE OWNERSHIP

Nothing brings on the wrath of the public faster than the notion of absentee ownership, particularly of lands that could otherwise be put to "good use." Consider a situation that occurred on the island of Oahu in Hawaii. A beautiful valley had been owned for many, many years by a particular family. Hawaiian families were allowed to live and farm the land at nominal cost. That is to say, the lease payments did not reflect the alternative use value of the land as a housing development for wealthy individuals. After many years, the owners of the land decided to

develop it. They systematically started issuing eviction notices to the tenants. Public outrage ensued. The contention of the public, and particularly the tenants, was that because of continuous use of the land in a meaningful manner—for living and farming—the current tenants had a property right in that land. Certainly the notion of the alienability of private property within the capitalist ideology did not correspond to the attitude of the tenants and the public when the owners decided to change the use of the land. Now for the ethical issue: Do the owners of land have an ethical responsibility to tenants who have been on the land for many years? If so, what is that responsibility?

In answering such an ethical question, one must realize that if such a precedent is established, it will affect the future use of private property. To wit, future owners of private property will be unwilling to lease their land to tenants at low payments for any period of time. Why? Because owners will fear that tenants will establish a property right in their particular use of the land such that the land use will not be allowed to change in the future. If such an event occurs, the net

worth of the private property owner will fall.

THE QUESTION OF LAND USE CONTROL

Land use control legislation and regulation are prevalent throughout the United States. Often such land use control is undertaken in the name of "the public." But, one must realize the consequences of such actions. Consider the effect of legislation altering property owners' rights in coastal sections of the United States. Let's suppose that prior to the legislation, owners of land in coastal areas could use that land in any way they wanted. They could build condominiums, golf courses, or do nothing. After the legislation, a committee is formed which passes judgment on each requested change in the current use of land. Let us suppose that a large amount of unaltered land is desired for coastal areas, even though that land is private property. If the committee routinely does not allow condominiums and housing developments to be built on the land, its market value will fall. Now we are entering into a taking issue, which is part of the Fifth Amendment to the United States

983

Constitution. Government agencies maintain that land use control does not involve a taking because the physical possession of the land remains in the hands of the private owner. From an economic point of view, however, a taking has occurred because the net worth of the property owner subsequently falls when land use controls restrict the way in which the land can be used.

Who has a greater ethical concern in this issue—the private owner of the land and the potential occupants of condominiums and housing developments on the land or the nonowner who would like to see the land remain undeveloped and use the beaches and surrounding lands? No easy answer is available. Whatever decision is made concerning the use of the land, someone will benefit and someone will lose. Whenever there is a trade-off in terms of who benefits and who loses in the use of an economic resource, we can only make value judgments— we cannot provide a cut-and-dried answer as to what is appropriate.

Consider another example. A town is surrounded by numerous citrus groves, owned by individuals who eventually want to develop the land into housing projects. Just when the individual owners are ready to develop the land, a vote is taken. The vote concerns whether the owners will be allowed to divide the citrus groves into individual housing units. When such a vote has been taken in different communities, the outcome is known in advance—the potential developers always lose. Is this good, bad, or indifferent? The only way we can answer the question is to make a predetermination about who should benefit from such an action. Clearly, area residents who prefer open spaces around their

existing homes will benefit. Who will lose (besides the developer)? It can be argued that prospective residents of the community will lose—those individuals who would have liked to move to the community but now cannot do so because of the lack of adequate housing. Those individuals are potential owners of property, but they are not allowed a vote because they do not currently live in the area. From an ethical point of view, who has a greater right?

INSURANCE

In the area of insurance, one of the major ethical concerns involves moral hazard, a topic to which we have referred on several occasions. To repeat, in the insurance industry moral hazard occurs when individuals or companies have an incentive to act negligently or to engage in activities that will result in payment by an insurance company. For example, the businessperson who takes out a large insurance policy on a building has less incentive to take care that the building is protected from potential fire than an individual without an insurance policy. What is the ethical responsibility of the owner of the building when insurance is in effect? Is he or she exempt from taking precautions against a fire?

The same issue arises for insurance policies that cover losses due to theft. The smaller the deductible in such policies, the less incentive the property owner has to prevent loss due to theft. For example, with insurance in effect, the property owner may have less incentive to install alarm systems, to pay for private patrol service, and so on. Of course, the more claims made on such insurance policies, the higher the average insurance rate per dollar

amount insured. Thus, those individuals who are careless about protecting their own property impose costs on all individuals who buy property insurance.

Moral hazard exists with medical insurance also. The smaller the deductible, the greater the incentive for the individual not to practice preventive medicine. What is the ethical responsibility of the individual citizen in terms of providing for his or her own well-being? Because health insurance is available for most individuals in the United States, does that mean that individuals should not be concerned about smoking, being overweight, too much sugar in their diets, and so on? Indeed, it is argued that in the United States, too many resources are devoted to the care of those who are already sick and too few resources to preventive medicine.

Concerning the insurer of property, consider what his or her ethical viewpoint must be. Should the insurer settle when there is a doubt or should he or she require litigation before making payment?

DISCUSSION QUESTIONS

1. What is a property interest?
2. Does one have a property interest in a job, in a welfare payment, in an insurance contract payoff?
3. What should be the limits on the ownership of private property?
4. Whose interests should come first in the question of land use control?
5. Is there any way to eliminate moral hazard in the area of insurance?
6. If an applicant for insurance makes a materially false statement, to what extent is the insurer liable when a subsequent claim is made?

APPENDIX A

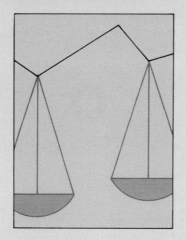

HOW TO BRIEF A CASE

Because you are interested in the law, you should be able to read and understand court decisions. In order to make this task easier, you can use a method of case analysis that is called *briefing*. There is a standard procedure that you can follow when you "brief" a case in this book or in any other book. You must first read the case carefully. When you feel you understand the case, you can prepare a brief of it. Although the format of the brief may vary, it will typically have the following central parts:

1. Full case citation, including the name of the case (sometimes called its style), the date it was decided, and the court that decided it.
2. Plaintiff(s).
3. Defendant(s).
4. Facts.
5. Issue.
6. Lower Court decision.
7. Appellate Court decision (if applicable).
8. Holding.
9. Reasoning.

When you prepare your brief, be sure to incorporate all the important facts. But remember that, by definition, it should be brief. When you state the court's reasoning for the decision, you should either be ready to defend it or to challenge it.

Now consider a typical way to brief the first case in this book, given on page 30 in Chapter 2.

1.	Case Citation	**CANNON v. UNIVERSITY OF CHICAGO** United States Supreme Court, 1979. 441 U.S. 677, 99 S.Ct. 1946.
2.	Plaintiff	Female medical school applicant.
3.	Defendants	Two private universities and officials of the Department of Health, Education, and Welfare.
4.	Facts	Plaintiff alleged she was denied admission to medical school on the basis of her sex and was entitled to damages resulting from the universities' discrimination. Federal law prohibits discrimination on the basis of sex in any educational program receiving federal financial assistance. Both universities received such assistance.
5.	Issue	Whether §901(a) of Title IX of the Education Amendments of 1972 authorizes a private right of action by persons injured by violations of §901.
6.	Lower Court	Dismissed plaintiff's case.
7.	Appellate Court	Held that plaintiff had no right of action against the defendants.
8.	Holding	Title IX authorizes a private right of action for victims of the discrimination prohibited by the statute.
9.	Reasoning	Title IX is patterned after Title VI of the Civil Rights Act of 1964. Private remedies are available for violations of Title VI; therefore, Congress intended that the same remedies would be available under Title IX.

APPENDIX B

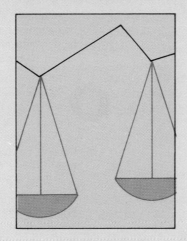

THE CONSTITUTION OF THE UNITED STATES

PREAMBLE

We the People of the United States, in Order to form a more perfect Union, establish Justice, insure domestic Tranquility, provide for the common defence, promote the general Welfare, and secure the Blessings of Liberty to ourselves and our Posterity, do ordain and establish this Constitution for the United States of America.

ARTICLE I

Section 1.   All legislative Powers herein granted shall be vested in a Congress of the United States, which shall consist of a Senate and House of Representatives.

Section 2.   [1] The House of Representatives shall be composed of Members chosen every second Year by the People of the several States, and the Electors in each State shall have the Qualifications requisite for Electors of the most numerous Branch of the State Legislature.

[2] No Person shall be a Representative who shall not have attained to the Age of twenty five Years, and been seven Years a Citizen of the United States, and who shall not, when elected, be an Inhabitant of that State in which he shall be chosen.

[3] Representatives and direct Taxes shall be apportioned among the several States which may be included within this Union, according to their respective Numbers, which shall be determined by adding to the whole Number of free Persons, including those bound to Service for a Term of Years, and excluding Indians not taxed, three fifths of all other Persons. The actual Enumeration shall be made within three Years after the first Meeting of the Congress of the United States, and within every subsequent Term of ten Years, in such Manner as they shall by Law direct. The Number of Representatives shall not exceed one for every thirty Thousand, but each State shall have at Least one Representative; and until such enumeration shall be made, the State of New Hampshire shall be entitled to chuse three, Massachusetts eight, Rhode Island and Providence Plantations one, Connecticut five, New York six, New Jersey four, Pennsylvania eight, Delaware one, Maryland six, Virginia ten, North Carolina five, South Carolina five, and Georgia three.

[4] When vacancies happen in the Representation from any State, the Executive Authority thereof shall issue Writs of Election to fill such Vacancies.

[5] The House of Representatives shall chuse their Speaker and other Officers; and shall have the sole Power of Impeachment.

Section 3.   [1] The Senate of the United States shall be composed of two Senators from each State, chosen by the Legislature thereof, for six Years; and each Senator shall have one Vote.

[2] Immediately after they shall be assembled in Consequence of the first Election, they shall be divided as equally as may be into three Classes. The Seats of the Senators of the first Class shall be vacated at the Expiration of the Second Year, of the second Class at the Expiration of the fourth Year, and of the third Class at the Expiration of the sixth Year, so that one third may be chosen every second Year; and if Vacancies happen by Resignation, or otherwise, during the Recess of the Legislature of any State, the Executive thereof may make temporary Appointments until the next Meeting of the Legislature, which shall then fill such Vacancies.

[3] No Person shall be a Senator who shall not have attained to the Age of thirty Years, and been nine Years a Citizen of the United States, and who shall not, when elected, be an Inhabitant of that State for which he shall be chosen.

[4] The Vice President of the United States shall be President of the Senate, but shall have no Vote, unless they be equally divided.

[5] The Senate shall chuse their other Officers, and also a President pro tempore, in the Absence of the Vice President, or when he shall exercise the Office of President of the United States.

[6] The Senate shall have the sole Power to try all Impeachments. When sitting for that Purpose, they shall be on Oath or Affirmation. When the President of the United States is tried, the Chief Justice shall preside: And no Person shall be convicted without the Concurrence of two thirds of the Members present.

[7] Judgment in Cases of Impeachment shall not extend further than to removal from Office, and disqualification to hold and enjoy any Office of honor, Trust, or Profit under the United States: but the Party convicted shall nevertheless be liable and subject to Indictment, Trial, Judgment, and Punishment, according to Law.

Section 4.   [1] The Times, Places and Manner of holding Elections for Senators and Representatives, shall be prescribed in each State by the Legislature thereof; but the Congress may at any time by Law make or alter such Regulations, except as to the Places of chusing Senators.

[2] The Congress shall assemble at least once in every Year, and such Meeting shall be on the first Monday

in December, unless they shall by Law appoint a different Day.

Section 5. [1] Each House shall be the Judge of the Elections, Returns, and Qualifications of its own Members, and a Majority of each shall constitute a Quorum to do Business; but a smaller Number may adjourn from day to day, and may be authorized to compel the Attendance of absent Members, in such Manner, and under such Penalties as each House may provide.

[2] Each House may determine the Rules of its Proceedings, punish its Members for disorderly Behavior, and, with the Concurrence of two thirds, expel a Member.

[3] Each House shall keep a Journal of its Proceedings, and from time to time publish the same, excepting such Parts as may in their Judgment require Secrecy; and the Yeas and Nays of the Members of either House on any question shall, at the Desire of one fifth of those Present, be entered on the Journal.

[4] Neither House, during the Session of Congress, shall, without the Consent of the other, adjourn for more than three days, nor to any other Place than that in which the two Houses shall be sitting.

Section 6. [1] The Senators and Representatives shall receive a Compensation for their Services, to be ascertained by Law, and paid out of the Treasury of the United States. They shall in all Cases, except Treason, Felony and Breach of the Peace, be privileged from Arrest during their Attendance at the Session of their respective Houses, and in going to and returning from the same; and for any Speech or Debate in either House, they shall not be questioned in any other Place.

[2] No Senator or Representative shall, during the Time for which he was elected, be appointed to any civil Office under the Authority of the United States, which shall have been created, or the Emoluments whereof shall have been increased during such time; and no Person holding any Office under the United States, shall be a Member of either House during his Continuance in Office.

Section 7. [1] All Bills for raising Revenue shall originate in the House of Representatives; but the Senate may propose or concur with Amendments as on other Bills.

[2] Every Bill which shall have passed the House of Representatives and the Senate, shall, before it become a Law, be presented to the President of the United States; If he approve he shall sign it, but if not he shall return it, with his Objections to the House in which it shall have originated, who shall enter the Objections

at large on their Journal, and proceed to reconsider it. If after such Reconsideration two thirds of that House shall agree to pass the Bill, it shall be sent together with the Objections, to the other House, by which it shall likewise be reconsidered, and if approved by two thirds of that House, it shall become a Law. But in all such Cases the Votes of both Houses shall be determined by yeas and Nays, and the Names of the Persons voting for and against the Bill shall be entered on the Journal of each House respectively. If any Bill shall not be returned by the President within ten Days (Sundays excepted) after it shall have been presented to him, the Same shall be a Law, in like Manner as if he had signed it, unless the Congress by their Adjournment prevent its Return in which Case it shall not be a Law.

[3] Every Order, Resolution, or Vote, to Which the Concurrence of the Senate and House of Representatives may be necessary (except on a question of Adjournment) shall be presented to the President of the United States; and before the Same shall take Effect, shall be approved by him, or being disapproved by him, shall be repassed by two thirds of the Senate and House of Representatives, according to the Rules and Limitations prescribed in the Case of a Bill.

Section 8. [1] The Congress shall have Power To lay and collect Taxes, Duties, Imposts and Excises, to pay the Debts and provide for the common Defence and general Welfare of the United States; but all Duties, Imposts and Excises shall be uniform throughout the United States;

[2] To borrow money on the credit of the United States;

[3] To regulate Commerce with foreign Nations, and among the several States, and with the Indian Tribes;

[4] To establish an uniform Rule of Naturalization, and uniform Laws on the subject of Bankruptcies throughout the United States;

[5] To coin Money, regulate the Value thereof, and of foreign Coin, and fix the Standard of Weights and Measures;

[6] To provide for the Punishment of counterfeiting the Securities and current Coin of the United States;

[7] To Establish Post Offices and Post Roads;

[8] To promote the Progress of Science and useful Arts, by securing for limited Times to Authors and Inventors the exclusive Right to their respective Writings and Discoveries;

[9] To constitute Tribunals inferior to the supreme Court;

[10] To define and punish Piracies and Felonies committed on the high Seas, and Offenses against the Law of Nations;

[11] To declare War, grant Letters of Marque and Reprisal, and make Rules concerning Captures on Land and Water;

[12] To raise and support Armies, but no Appropriation of Money to that Use shall be for a longer Term than two Years;

[13] To provide and maintain a Navy;

[14] To make Rules for the Government and Regulation of the land and naval Forces;

[15] To provide for calling forth the Militia to execute the Laws of the Union, suppress Insurrections and repel Invasions;

[16] To provide for organizing, arming, and disciplining, the Militia, and for governing such Part of them as may be employed in the Service of the United States, reserving to the States respectively, the Appointment of the Officers, and the Authority of training the Militia according to the discipline prescribed by Congress;

[17] To exercise exclusive Legislation in all Cases whatsoever, over such District (not exceeding ten Miles square) as may, by Cession of particular States, and the Acceptance of Congress, become the Seat of the Government of the United States, and to exercise like Authority over all Places purchased by the Consent of the Legislature of the State in which the Same shall be, for the Erection of Forts, Magazines, Arsenals, dock-Yards, and other needful Buildings;—And

[18] To make all Laws which shall be necessary and proper for carrying into Execution the foregoing Powers, and all other Powers vested by this Constitution in the Government of the United States, or in any Department or Officer thereof.

Section 9. [1] The Migration or Importation of Such Persons as any of the States now existing shall think proper to admit, shall not be prohibited by the Congress prior to the Year one thousand eight hundred and eight, but a Tax or duty may be imposed on such Importation, not exceeding ten dollars for each Person.

[2] The privilege of the Writ of Habeas Corpus shall not be suspended, unless when in Cases of Rebellion or Invasion the public Safety may require it.

[3] No Bill of Attainder or ex post facto Law shall be passed.

[4] No Capitation, or other direct, Tax shall be laid, unless in Proportion to the Census or Enumeration herein before directed to be taken.

[5] No Tax or Duty shall be laid on Articles exported from any State.

[6] No Preference shall be given by any Regulation of Commerce or Revenue to the Ports of one State over those of another: nor shall Vessels bound to, or from, one State be obliged to enter, clear, or pay Duties in another.

[7] No money shall be drawn from the Treasury, but in Consequence of Appropriations made by Law; and a regular Statement and Account of the Receipts and Expenditures of all public Money shall be published from time to time.

[8] No Title of Nobility shall be granted by the United States: And no Person holding any Office of Profit or Trust under them, shall, without the Consent of the Congress, accept of any present, Emolument, Office, or Title, of any kind whatever, from any King, Prince, or foreign State.

Section 10. [1] No State shall enter into any Treaty, Alliance, or Confederation; grant Letters of Marque and Reprisal; coin Money; emit Bills of Credit; make any Thing but gold and silver Coin a Tender in Payment of Debts; pass any Bill of Attainder, ex post facto Law, or Law impairing the Obligation of Contracts, or grant any Title of Nobility.

[2] No State shall, without the Consent of the Congress, lay any Imposts or Duties on Imports or Exports, except what may be absolutely necessary for executing it's inspection Laws: and the net Produce of all Duties and Imposts, laid by any State on Imports or Exports, shall be for the Use of the Treasury of the United States; and all such Laws shall be subject to the Revision and Controul of the Congress.

[3] No State shall, without the Consent of Congress, lay any Duty of Tonnage, keep Troops, or Ships of War in time of Peace, enter into any Agreement or Compact with another State, or with a foreign Power, or engage in War, unless actually invaded, or in such imminent Danger as will not admit of delay.

ARTICLE II

Section 1. [1] The executive Power shall be vested in a President of the United States of America. He shall hold his Office during the Term of four Years, and, together with the Vice President, chosen for the same Term, be elected, as follows:

[2] Each State shall appoint, in such Manner as the Legislature thereof may direct, a Number of Electors,

equal to the whole Number of Senators and Representatives to which the State may be entitled in the Congress; but no Senator or Representative, or Person holding an Office of Trust or Profit under the United States, shall be appointed an Elector.

[3] The Electors shall meet in their respective States, and vote by Ballot for two Persons, of whom one at least shall not be an Inhabitant of the same State with themselves. And they shall make a List of all the Persons voted for, and of the Number of Votes for each; which List they shall sign and certify, and transmit sealed to the Seat of the Government of the United States, directed to the President of the Senate. The President of the Senate shall, in the Presence of the Senate and House of Representatives, open all the Certificates, and the Votes shall then be counted. The Person having the greatest Number of Votes shall be the President, if such Number be a Majority of the whole Number of Electors appointed; and if there be more than one who have such Majority, and have an equal Number of Votes, then the House of Representatives shall immediately chuse by Ballot one of them for President; and if no Person have a Majority, then from the five highest on the List the said House shall in like Manner chuse the President. But in chusing the President, the Votes shall be taken by States the Representation from each State having one Vote; A quorum for this Purpose shall consist of a Member or Members from two thirds of the States, and a Majority of all the States shall be necessary to a Choice. In every Case, after the Choice of the President, the Person having the greater Number of Votes of the Electors shall be the Vice President. But if there should remain two or more who have equal Votes, the Senate shall chuse from them by Ballot the Vice President.

[4] The Congress may determine the Time of chusing the Electors, and the Day on which they shall give their Votes; which Day shall be the same throughout the United States.

[5] No person except a natural born Citizen, or a Citizen of the United States, at the time of the Adoption of this Constitution, shall be eligible to the Office of President; neither shall any Person be eligible to that Office who shall not have attained to the Age of thirty five Years, and been fourteen Years a Resident within the United States.

[6] In case of the removal of the President from Office, or of his Death, Resignation or Inability to discharge the Powers and Duties of the said Office, the Same shall devolve on the Vice President, and the Congress may by Law provide for the Case of Removal, Death, Resignation or Inability, both of the President

and Vice President, declaring what Officer shall then act as President, and such Officer shall act accordingly, until the Disability be removed, or a President shall be elected.

[7] The President shall, at stated Times, receive for his Services, a Compensation, which shall neither be increased nor diminished during the Period for which he shall have been elected, and he shall not receive within that Period any other Emolument from the United States, or any of them.

[8] Before he enter on the Execution of his Office, he shall take the following Oath or Affirmation: "I do solemnly swear (or affirm) that I will faithfully execute the Office of President of the United States, and will to the best of my Ability, preserve, protect and defend the Constitution of the United States."

Section 2. [1] The President shall be Commander in Chief of the Army and Navy of the United States, and of the militia of the several States, when called into the actual Service of the United States; he may require the Opinion, in writing, of the principal Officer in each of the Executive Departments, upon any Subject relating to the Duties of their respective Offices, and he shall have Power to grant Reprieves and Pardons for Offenses against the United States, except in Cases of Impeachment.

[2] He shall have Power, by and with the Advice and Consent of the Senate to make Treaties, provided two thirds of the Senators present concur; and he shall nominate, and by and with the Advice and Consent of the Senate, shall appoint Ambassadors, other public Ministers and Consuls, Judges of the supreme Court, and all other Officers of the United States, whose Appointments are not herein otherwise provided for, and which shall be established by Law; but the Congress may by Law vest the Appointment of such inferior Officers, as they think proper, in the President alone, in the Courts of Law, or in the Heads of Departments.

[3] The President shall have Power to fill up all Vacancies that may happen during the Recess of the Senate, by granting Commissions which shall expire at the End of their next Session.

Section 3. He shall from time to time give to the Congress Information of the State of the Union, and recommend to their Consideration such Measures as he shall judge necessary and expedient; he may, on extraordinary Occasions, convene both Houses, or either of them, and in Case of Disagreement between them, with Respect to the Time of Adjournment, he may adjourn them to such Time as he shall think proper; he shall receive Ambassadors and other public

Ministers; he shall take Care that the Laws be faithfully executed, and shall Commission all the Officers of the United States.

Section 4. The President, Vice President and all civil Officers of the United States, shall be removed from Office on Impeachment for, and Conviction of, Treason, Bribery, or other high Crimes and Misdemeanors.

ARTICLE III

Section 1. The judicial Power of the United States, shall be vested in one supreme Court, and in such inferior Courts as the Congress may from time to time ordain and establish. The Judges, both of the supreme and inferior Courts, shall hold their Offices during good Behaviour, and shall, at stated Times, receive for their Services a Compensation, which shall not be diminished during their Continuance in Office.

Section 2. [1] The judicial Power shall extend to all Cases, in Law and Equity, arising under this Constitution, the Laws of the United States, and Treaties made, or which shall be made, under their Authority;—to all Cases affecting Ambassadors, other public Ministers and Consuls;—to all Cases of admiralty and maritime Jurisdiction;—to Controversies to which the United States shall be a Party;—to Controversies between two or more States;—between a State and Citizens of another State;—between Citizens of different States;—between Citizens of the same State claiming Lands under the Grants of different States, and between a State, or the Citizens thereof, and foreign States, Citizens or Subjects.

[2] In all Cases affecting Ambassadors, other public Ministers and Consuls, and those in which a State shall be a Party, the supreme Court shall have original Jurisdiction. In all the other Cases before mentioned, the supreme Court shall have appellate Jurisdiction, both as to Law and Fact, with such Exceptions, and under such Regulations as the Congress shall make.

[3] The trial of all Crimes, except in Cases of Impeachment, shall be by Jury; and such Trial shall be held in the State where the said Crimes shall have been committed; but when not committed within any State, the Trial shall be at such Place or Places as the Congress may by Law have directed.

Section 3. [1] Treason against the United States, shall consist only in levying War against them, or, in adhering to their Enemies, giving them Aid and Comfort. No Person shall be convicted of Treason unless on the Testimony of two Witnesses to the same overt Act, or on Confession in open Court.

[2] The Congress shall have Power to declare the Punishment of Treason, but no Attainder of Treason shall work Corruption of Blood, or Forfeiture except during the Life of the Person attainted.

ARTICLE IV

Section 1. Full Faith and Credit shall be given in each State to the public Acts, Records, and judicial Proceedings of every other State. And the Congress may by general Laws prescribe the Manner in which such Acts, Records and Proceedings shall be proved, and the Effect thereof.

Section 2. [1] The Citizens of each State shall be entitled to all Privileges and Immunities of Citizens in the several States.

[2] A Person charged in any State with Treason, Felony, or other Crime, who shall flee from Justice, and be found in another State, shall on demand of the executive Authority of the State from which he fled, be delivered up, to be removed to the State having Jurisdiction of the Crime.

[3] No Person held to Service or Labour in one State, under the Laws thereof, escaping into another, shall, in Consequence of any Law or Regulation therein, be discharged from such Service or Labour, but shall be delivered up on Claim of the Party to whom such Service or Labour may be due.

Section 3. [1] New States may be admitted by the Congress into this Union; but no new State shall be formed or erected within the Jurisdiction of any other State; nor any State be formed by the Junction of two or more States, or Parts of States, without the Consent of the Legislatures of the States concerned as well as of the Congress.

[2] The Congress shall have Power to dispose of and make all needful Rules and Regulations respecting the Territory or other Property belonging to the United States; and nothing in this Constitution shall be so construed as to Prejudice any Claims of the United States, or of any particular State.

Section 4. The United States shall guarantee to every State in this Union a Republican Form of Government, and shall protect each of them against Invasion; and on Application of the Legislature, or of the Executive (when the Legislature cannot be convened) against domestic Violence.

ARTICLE V

The Congress, whenever two thirds of both Houses shall deem it necessary, shall propose Amendments to this Constitution, or, on the Application of the Legislatures of two thirds of the several States, shall call a Convention for proposing Amendments, which, in either Case, shall be valid to all Intents and Purposes, as part of this Constitution, when ratified by the Legislatures of three fourths of the several States, or by Conventions in three fourths thereof, as the one or the other Mode of Ratification may be proposed by the Congress; Provided that no Amendment which may be made prior to the Year One thousand eight hundred and eight shall in any Manner affect the first and fourth Clauses in the Ninth Section of the first Article; and that no State, without its Consent, shall be deprived of its equal Suffrage in the Senate.

ARTICLE VI

[1] All Debts contracted and Engagements entered into, before the Adoption of this Constitution shall be as valid against the United States under this Constitution, as under the Confederation.

[2] This Constitution, and the Laws of the United States which shall be made in Pursuance thereof; and all Treaties made, or which shall be made, under the Authority of the United States, shall be the supreme Law of the Land; and the Judges in every State shall be bound thereby, any Thing in the Constitution or Laws of any State to the Contrary notwithstanding.

[3] The Senators and Representatives before mentioned, and the Members of the several State Legislatures, and all executive and judicial Officers, both of the United States and of the several States, shall be bound by Oath or Affirmation, to support this Constitution; but no religious Test shall ever be required as a Qualification to any Office or public Trust under the United States.

ARTICLE VII

The Ratification of the Conventions of nine States shall be sufficient for the Establishment of this Constitution between the States so ratifying the Same.

AMENDMENT I [1791]

Congress shall make no law respecting an establishment of religion, or prohibiting the free exercise thereof; or abridging the freedom of speech, or of the press; or the right of the people peaceably to assembly, and to petition the Government for a redress of grievances.

AMENDMENT II [1791]

A well regulated Militia, being necessary to the security of a free State, the right of the people to keep and bear Arms, shall not be infringed.

AMENDMENT III [1791]

No Soldier shall, in time of peace be quartered in any house, without the consent of the Owner, nor in time of war, but in a manner to be prescribed by law.

AMENDMENT IV [1791]

The right of the people to be secure in their persons, houses, papers, and effects, against unreasonable searches and seizures, shall not be violated, and no Warrants shall issue, but upon probable cause, supported by Oath or affirmation, and particularly describing the place to be searched, and the persons or things to be seized.

AMENDMENT V [1791]

No person shall be held to answer for a capital, or otherwise infamous crime, unless on a presentment or indictment of a Grand Jury, except in cases arising in the land or naval forces, or in the Militia, when in actual service in time of War or public danger; nor shall any person be subject for the same offence to be twice put in jeopardy of life or limb; nor shall be compelled in any criminal case to be a witness against himself, nor be deprived of life, liberty, or property, without due process of law; nor shall private property be taken for public use, without just compensation.

AMENDMENT VI [1791]

In all criminal prosecutions, the accused shall enjoy the right to a speedy and public trial, by an impartial jury of the State and district wherein the crime shall have been committed, which district shall have been previously ascertained by law, and to be informed of the nature and cause of the accusation; to be confronted with the witnesses against him; to have compulsory process for obtaining witnesses in his favor, and to have the Assistance of Counsel for his defence.

AMENDMENT VII [1791]

In Suits at common law, where the value in controversy shall exceed twenty dollars, the right of trial by jury shall be preserved, and no fact tried by jury, shall be otherwise re-examined in any Court of the United States, than according to the rules of the common law.

AMENDMENT VIII [1791]

Excessive bail shall not be required, nor excessive fines imposed, nor cruel and unusual punishments inflicted.

AMENDMENT IX [1791]

The enumeration in the Constitution, of certain rights, shall not be construed to deny or disparage others retained by the people.

AMENDMENT X [1791]

The powers not delegated to the United States by the Constitution, nor prohibited by it to the States, are reserved to the States respectively, or to the people.

AMENDMENT XI [1798]

The Judicial power of the United States shall not be construed to extend to any suit in law or equity, commenced or prosecuted against one of the United States by Citizens of another State, or by Citizens or Subjects of any Foreign State.

AMENDMENT XII [1804]

The Electors shall meet in their respective states and vote by ballot for President and Vice-President, one of whom, at least, shall not be an inhabitant of the same state with themselves; they shall name in their ballots the person voted for as President, and in distinct ballots the person voted for as Vice-President, and they shall make distinct lists of all persons voted for as President, and of all persons voted for as Vice-President, and of the number of votes for each, which lists they shall sign and certify, and transmit sealed to the seat of the government of the United States, directed to the President of the Senate;—The President of the Senate shall, in the presence of the Senate and House of Representatives, open all the certificates and the votes shall then be counted;—The person having the greatest number of votes for President, shall be the President, if such number be a majority of the whole number of Electors appointed; and if no person have such majority, then from the persons having the highest numbers not exceeding three on the list of those voted for as President, the House of Representatives shall choose immediately, by ballot, the President. But in choosing the President, the votes shall be taken by states, the representation from each state having one vote; a quorum for this purpose shall consist of a member or members from two-thirds of the states, and a majority of all states shall be necessary to a choice. And if the House of Representatives shall not choose a President whenever the right of choice shall devolve upon them before the fourth day of March next following, then the Vice-President shall act as President, as in the case of the death or other constitutional disability of the President.—The person having the greatest number of votes as Vice-President, shall be the Vice-President, if such number be a majority of the whole number of Electors appointed, and if no person have a majority, then from the two highest numbers on the list, the Senate shall choose the Vice-President; a quorum for the purpose shall consist of two-thirds of the whole number of Senators, and a majority of

the whole number shall be necessary to a choice. But no person constitutionally ineligible to the office of President shall be eligible to that of Vice-President of the United States.

AMENDMENT XIII [1865]

Section 1. Neither slavery nor involuntary servitude, except as a punishment for crime whereof the party shall have been duly convicted, shall exist within the United States, or any place subject to their jurisdiction.

Section 2. Congress shall have power to enforce this article by appropriate legislation.

AMENDMENT XIV [1868]

Section 1. All persons born or naturalized in the United States, and subject to the jurisdiction thereof, are citizens of the United States and of the State wherein they reside. No State shall make or enforce any law which shall abridge the privileges or immunities of citizens of the United States; nor shall any State deprive any person of life, liberty, or property, without due process of law; nor deny to any person within its jurisdiction the equal protection of the laws.

Section 2. Representatives shall be apportioned among the several States according to their respective numbers, counting the whole number of persons in each State, excluding Indians not taxed. But when the right to vote at any election for the choice of electors for President and Vice President of the United States, Representatives in Congress, the Executive and Judicial officers of a State, or the members of the Legislature thereof, is denied to any of the male inhabitants of such State, being twenty-one years of age, and citizens of the United States, or in any way abridged, except for participation in rebellion, or other crime, the basis of representation therein shall be reduced in the proportion which the number of such male citizens shall bear to the whole number of male citizens twenty-one years of age in such State.

Section 3. No person shall be a Senator or Representative in Congress, or elector of President and Vice President, or hold any office, civil or military, under the United States, or under any State, who having previously taken an oath, as a member of Congress, or as an officer of the United States, or as a member of any State legislature, or as an executive or judicial officer of any State, to support the Constitution of the United States, shall have engaged in insurrection or rebellion against the same, or given aid or comfort to the enemies thereof. But Congress may by a vote of two-thirds of each House, remove such disability.

Section 4.   The validity of the public debt of the United States, authorized by law, including debts incurred for payment of pensions and bounties for services in suppressing insurrection or rebellion, shall not be questioned. But neither the United States nor any State shall assume or pay any debt or obligation incurred in aid of insurrection or rebellion against the United States, or any claim for the loss or emancipation of any slave; but all such debts, obligations and claims shall be held illegal and void.

Section 5.   The Congress shall have power to enforce, by appropriate legislation, the provisions of this article.

Amendment XV [1870]

Section 1.   The right of citizens of the United States to vote shall not be denied or abridged by the United States or by any State on account of race, color, or previous condition of servitude.

Section 2.   The Congress shall have power to enforce this article by appropriate legislation.

Amendment XVI [1913]

The Congress shall have power to lay and collect taxes on incomes, from whatever source derived, without apportionment among the several States, and without regard to any census or enumeration.

Amendment XVII [1913]

[1] The Senate of the United States shall be composed of two Senators from each State, elected by the people thereof, for six years; and each Senator shall have one vote. The electors in each State shall have the qualifications requisite for electors of the most numerous branch of the State legislatures.

[2] When vacancies happen in the representation of any State in the Senate, the executive authority of such State shall issue writs of election to fill such vacancies: *Provided*, That the legislature of any State may empower the executive thereof to make temporary appointments until the people fill the vacancies by election as the legislature may direct.

[3] This amendment shall not be so construed as to affect the election or term of any Senator chosen before it becomes valid as part of the Constitution.

Amendment XVIII [1919]

Section 1.   After one year from the ratification of this article the manufacture, sale, or transportation of intoxicating liquors within, the importation thereof into, or the exportation thereof from the United States and all territory subject to the jurisdiction thereof for beverage purposes is hereby prohibited.

Section 2.   The Congress and the several States shall have concurrent power to enforce this article by appropriate legislation.

Section 3.   This article shall be inoperative unless it shall have been ratified as an amendment to the Constitution by the legislatures of the several States, as provided in the Constitution, within seven years from the date of the submission hereof to the States by the Congress.

Amendment XIX [1920]

[1] The right of citizens of the United States to vote shall not be denied or abridged by the United States or by any State on account of sex.

[2] Congress shall have power to enforce this article by appropriate legislation.

Amendment XX [1933]

Section 1.   The terms of the President and Vice President shall end at noon on the 20th day of January, and the terms of Senators and Representatives at noon on the 3d day of January, of the years in which such terms would have ended if this article has not been ratified; and the terms of their successors shall then begin.

Section 2.   The Congress shall assemble at least once in every year, and such meeting shall begin at noon on the 3d day of January, unless they shall by law appoint a different day.

Section 3.   If, at the time fixed for the beginning of the term of the President, the President elect shall have died, the Vice President elect shall become President. If the President shall not have been chosen before the time fixed for the beginning of his term, or if the President elect shall have failed to qualify, then the Vice President elect shall act as President until a President shall have qualified; and the Congress may by law provide for the case wherein neither a President elect nor a Vice President elect shall have qualified, declaring who shall then act as President, or the manner in which one who is to act shall be selected, and such person shall act accordingly until a President or Vice President shall have qualified.

Section 4.   The Congress may by law provide for the case of the death of any of the persons from whom the House of Representatives may choose a President whenever the right of choice shall have devolved upon them, and for the case of the death of any of the persons from whom the Senate may choose a Vice President whenever the right of choice shall have devolved upon them.

Section 5.   Sections 1 and 2 shall take effect on the 15th day of October following the ratification of this article.

Section 6.   This article shall be inoperative unless it shall have been ratified as an amendment to the Constitution by the legislatures of three-fourths of the several States within seven years from the date of its submission.

AMENDMENT XXI [1933]

Section 1.   The eighteenth article of amendment to the Constitution of the United States is hereby repealed.

Section 2.   The transportation or importation into any State, Territory, or possession of the United States for delivery or use therein of intoxicating liquors, in violation of the laws thereof, is hereby prohibited.

Section 3.   This article shall be inoperative unless it shall have been ratified as an amendment to the Constitution by conventions in the several States, as provided in the Constitution, within seven years from the date of the submission hereof to the States by the Congress.

AMENDMENT XXII [1951]

Section 1.   No person shall be elected to the office of the President more than twice, and no person who has held the office of President, or acted as President, for more than two years of a term to which some other person was elected President shall be elected to the office of President more than once. But this Article shall not apply to any person holding the office of President when this Article was proposed by the Congress, and shall not prevent any person who may be holding the office of President, or acting as President, during the term within which this Article becomes operative from holding the office of President or acting as President during the remainder of such term.

Section 2.   This article shall be inoperative unless it shall have been ratified as an amendment to the Constitution by the legislatures of three-fourths of the several States within seven years from the date of its submission to the States by the Congress.

AMENDMENT XXIII [1961]

Section 1.   The District constituting the seat of Government of the United States shall appoint in such manner as the Congress may direct:

A number of electors of President and Vice President equal to the whole number of Senators and Representatives in Congress to which the District would be entitled if it were a State, but in no event more than the least populous state; they shall be in addition to those appointed by the states, but they shall be considered, for the purposes of the election of President and Vice President, to be electors appointed by a state; and they shall meet in the District and perform such duties as provided by the twelfth article of amendment.

Section 2.   The Congress shall have power to enforce this article by appropriate legislation.

AMENDMENT XXIV [1964]

Section 1.   The right of citizens of the United States to vote in any primary or other election for President or Vice President, for electors for President or Vice President, or for Senator or Representative in Congress, shall not be denied or abridged by the United States or any State by reason of failure to pay any poll tax or other tax.

Section 2.   The Congress shall have power to enforce this article by appropriate legislation.

AMENDMENT XXV [1967]

Section 1.   In case of the removal of the President from office or of his death or resignation, the Vice President shall become President.

Section 2.   Whenever there is a vacancy in the office of the Vice President, the President shall nominate a Vice President who shall take office upon confirmation by a majority vote of both Houses of Congress.

Section 3.   Whenever the President transmits to the President pro tempore of the Senate and the Speaker of the House of Representatives his written declaration that he is unable to discharge the powers and duties of his office, and until he transmits to them a written declaration to the contrary, such powers and duties shall be discharged by the Vice President as Acting President.

Section 4.   Whenever the Vice President and a majority of either the principal officers of the executive departments or of such other body as Congress may by law provide, transmit to the President pro tempore of the Senate and the Speaker of the House of Representatives their written declaration that the President is unable to discharge the powers and duties of his office, the Vice President shall immediately assume the powers and duties of the office as Acting President.

Thereafter, when the President transmits to the President pro tempore of the Senate and the Speaker of the House of Representatives his written declaration that no inability exists, he shall resume the powers and duties of his office unless the Vice President and a majority of either the principal officers of the executive department or of such other body as Congress may by law provide, transmit within four days to the President pro tempore of the Senate and the Speaker of the House of Representatives their written declaration and the President is unable to discharge the powers and duties of his office. Thereupon Congress shall decide the issue, assembling within forty-eight hours for that purpose if not in session. If the Congress, within twenty-one days after receipt of the latter written declaration, or, if Congress is not in session, within twenty-one days after Congress is required to assemble, determines by two-thirds vote of both Houses that the President is unable to discharge the powers and duties of his office, the Vice President shall continue to discharge the same as Acting President; otherwise, the President shall resume the powers and duties of his office.

Amendment XXVI [1971]

Section 1.   The right of citizens of the United States, who are eighteen years of age or older, to vote shall not be denied or abridged by the United States or by any State on account of age.

Section 2.   The Congress shall have power to enforce this article by appropriate legislation.

APPENDIX C

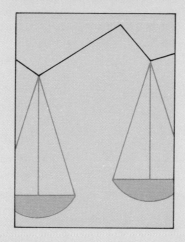

THE UNIFORM COMMERCIAL CODE

(Adopted in 52 jurisdictions; all 50 States, although Louisiana has adopted only Articles 1, 3, 4, and 5; the District of Columbia, and the Virgin Islands.)

The Code consists of 10 Articles as follows:

Art.

1. GENERAL PROVISIONS

2. Sales

3. Commercial Paper

4. Bank Deposits and Collections

5. Letters of Credit

6. Bulk Transfers

7. Warehouse Receipts, Bills of Lading and Other Documents of Title

8. Investment Securities

9. Secured Transactions: Sales of Accounts, Contract Rights and Chattel Paper

10. Effective Date and Repealer

Article 1
GENERAL PROVISIONS

Part 1 Short Title, Construction, Application and Subject Matter of the Act

§ 1—101. **Short Title.**

This Act shall be known and may be cited as Uniform Commercial Code.

§ 1—102. **Purposes; Rules of Construction; Variation by Agreement.**

(1) This Act shall be liberally construed and applied to promote its underlying purposes and policies.

(2) Underlying purposes and policies of this Act are

(a) to simplify, clarify and modernize the law governing commercial transactions;

(b) to permit the continued expansion of commercial practices through custom, usage and agreement of the parties;

(c) to make uniform the law among the various jurisdictions.

(3) The effect of provisions of this Act may be varied by agreement, except as otherwise provided in this Act and except that the obligations of good faith, diligence, reasonableness and care prescribed by this Act may not be disclaimed by agreement but the parties may by agreement determine the standards by which the performance of such obligations is to be measured if such standards are not manifestly unreasonable.

(4) The presence in certain provisions of this Act of the words "unless otherwise agreed" or words of similar import does not imply that the effect of other provisions may not be varied by agreement under subsection (3).

(5) In this Act unless the context otherwise requires

(a) words in the singular number include the plural, and in the plural include the singular;

(b) words of the masculine gender include the feminine and the neuter, and when the sense so indicates words of the neuter gender may refer to any gender.

§ 1—103. **Supplementary General Principles of Law Applicable.**

Unless displaced by the particular provisions of this Act, the principles of law and equity, including the law merchant and the law relative to capacity to contract, principal and agent, estoppel, fraud, misrepresentation, duress, coercion, mistake, bankruptcy, or other validating or invalidating cause shall supplement its provisions.

§ 1—104. **Construction Against Implicit Repeal.**

This Act being a general act intended as a unified coverage of its subject matter, no part of it shall be deemed to be impliedly repealed by subsequent legislation if such construction can reasonably be avoided.

§ 1—105. **Territorial Application of the Act; Parties' Power to Choose Applicable Law.**

(1) Except as provided hereafter in this section, when a transaction bears a reasonable relation to this state and also to another state or nation the parties may agree that the law either of this state or of such other state or nation shall govern their rights and duties. Failing such agreement this Act applies to transactions bearing an appropriate relation to this state.

(2) Where one of the following provisions of this Act specifies the applicable law, that provision governs and a contrary agreement is effective only to the extent permitted by the law (including the conflict of laws rules) so specified:

Rights of creditors against sold goods. Section 2—402.

Applicability of the Article on Bank Deposits and Collections. Section 4—102.

Bulk transfers subject to the Article on Bulk Transfers. Section 6—102.

Applicability of the Article on Investment Securities. Section 8—106.

Perfection provisions of the Article on Secured Transactions. Section 9—103.

§ 1—106. **Remedies to Be Liberally Administered.**

(1) The remedies provided by this Act shall be liberally administered to the end that the aggrieved party may be put in as good a position as if the other party had fully performed but neither consequential or special nor penal damages may be had except as specifically provided in this Act or by other rule of law.

(2) Any right or obligation declared by this Act is enforceable by action unless the provision declaring it specifies a different and limited effect.

§ 1—107. **Waiver or Renunciation of Claim or Right After Breach.**

Any claim or right arising out of an alleged breach can be discharged in whole or in part without consideration by a written waiver or renunciation signed and delivered by the aggrieved party.

§ 1—108. **Severability.**

If any provision or clause of this Act or application thereof to any person or circumstances is held invalid, such invalidity shall not affect other provisions or applications of the Act which can be given effect without the invalid provision or application, and to this end the provisions of this Act are declared to be severable.

§ 1—109. **Section Captions.**

Section captions are parts of this Act.

Part 2 **General Definitions and Principles of Interpretation**

§ 1—201. **General Definitions.**

Subject to additional definitions contained in the subsequent Articles of this Act which are applicable to specific Articles or Parts thereof, and unless the context otherwise requires, in this Act:

(1) "Action" in the sense of a judicial proceeding includes recoupment, counterclaim, set-off, suit in equity and any other proceedings in which rights are determined.

(2) "Aggrieved party" means a party entitled to resort to a remedy.

(3) "Agreement" means the bargain of the parties in fact as found in their language or by implication from other circumstances including course of dealing or usage of trade or course of performance as provided in this Act (Sections 1—205 and 2—208). Whether an agreement has legal consequences is determined by the provisions of this Act, if applicable; otherwise by the law of contracts (Section 1—103). (Compare "Contract".)

(4) "Bank" means any person engaged in the business of banking.

(5) "Bearer" means the person in possession of an instrument, document of title, or certified security payable to bearer or indorsed in blank.

(6) "Bill of lading" means a document evidencing the receipt of goods for shipment issued by a person engaged in the business of transporting or forwarding goods, and includes an airbill. "Airbill" means a document serving for air transportation as a bill of lading does for marine or rail transportation, and includes an air consignment note or air waybill.

(7) "Branch" includes a separately incorporated foreign branch of a bank.

(8) "Burden of establishing" a fact means the burden of persuading the triers of fact that the existence of the fact is more probable than its non-existence.

(9) "Buyer in ordinary course of business" means a person who in good faith and without knowledge that the sale to him is in violation of the ownership rights or security interest of a third party in the goods buys in ordinary course from a person in the business of selling goods of that kind but does not include a pawnbroker. All persons who sell minerals or the like (including oil and gas) at wellhead or minehead shall be deemed to be persons in the business of selling goods of that kind. "Buying" may be for cash or by exchange of other property or on secured or unsecured credit and includes receiving goods or documents of title under a pre-existing contract for sale but does not include a transfer in bulk or as security for or in total or partial satisfaction of a money debt.

(10) "Conspicuous": A term or clause is conspicuous when it is so written that a reasonable person against whom it is to operate ought to have noticed it. A printed heading in capitals (as: NON-NEGOTIABLE BILL OF LADING) is conspicuous. Language in the body of a form is "conspicuous" if it is in larger or other contrasting type or color. But in a telegram any stated term is "conspicuous". Whether a term or clause is "conspicuous" or not is for decision by the court.

(11) "Contract" means the total legal obligation which results from the parties' agreement as affected by this

Act and any other applicable rules of law. (Compare "Agreement".)

(12) "Creditor" includes a general creditor, a secured creditor, a lien creditor and any representative of creditors, including an assignee for the benefit of creditors, a trustee in bankruptcy, a receiver in equity and an executor or administrator of an insolvent debtor's or assignor's estate.

(13) "Defendant" includes a person in the position of defendant in a cross-action or counterclaim.

(14) "Delivery" with respect to instruments, documents of title, chattel paper, or certificated securities means voluntary transfer of possession.

(15) "Document of title" includes bill of lading, dock warrant, dock receipt, warehouse receipt or order for the delivery of goods, and also any other document which in the regular course of business or financing is treated as adequately evidencing that the person in possession of it is entitled to receive, hold and dispose of the document and the goods it covers. To be a document of title a document must purport to be issued by or addressed to a bailee and purport to cover goods in the bailee's possession which are either identified or are fungible portions of an identified mass.

(16) "Fault" means wrongful act, omission or breach.

(17) "Fungible" with respect to goods or securities means goods or securities of which any unit is, by nature or usage of trade, the equivalent of any other like unit. Goods which are not fungible shall be deemed fungible for the purposes of this Act to the extent that under a particular agreement or document unlike units are treated as equivalents.

(18) "Genuine" means free of forgery or counterfeiting.

(19) "Good faith" means honesty in fact in the conduct or transaction concerned.

(20) "Holder" means a person who is in possession of a document of title or an instrument or a certificated investment security drawn, issued, or indorsed to him or his order or to bearer or in blank.

(21) To "honor" is to pay or to accept and pay, or where a credit so engages to purchase or discount a draft complying with the terms of the credit.

(22) "Insolvency proceedings" includes any assignment for the benefit of creditors or other proceedings intended to liquidate or rehabilitate the estate of the person involved.

(23) A person is "insolvent" who either has ceased to pay his debts in the ordinary course of business or cannot pay his debts as they become due or is insolvent within the meaning of the federal bankruptcy law.

(24) "Money" means a medium of exchange authorized or adopted by a domestic or foreign government as a part of its currency.

(25) A person has "notice" of a fact when

(a) he has actual knowledge of it; or

(b) he has received a notice or notification of it; or

(c) from all the facts and circumstances known to him at the time in question he has reason to know that it exists.

A person "knows" or has "knowledge" of a fact when he has actual knowledge of it. "Discover" or "learn" or a word or phrase of similar import refers to knowledge rather than to reason to know. The time and circumstances under which a notice or notification may cease to be effective are not determined by this Act.

(26) A person "notifies" or "gives" a notice or notification to another by taking such steps as may be reasonably required to inform the other in ordinary course whether or not such other actually comes to know of it. A person "receives" a notice or notification when

(a) it comes to his attention; or

(b) it is duly delivered at the place of business through which the contract was made or at any other place held out by him as the place for receipt of such communications.

(27) Notice, knowledge or a notice or notification received by an organization is effective for a particular transaction from the time when it is brought to the attention of the individual conducting that transaction, and in any event from the time when it would have been brought to his attention if the organization had exercised due diligence. An organization exercises due diligence if it maintains reasonable routines for communicating significant information to the person conducting the transaction and there is reasonable compliance with the routines. Due diligence does not require an individual acting for the organization to communicate information unless such communication is part of his regular duties or unless he has reason to know of the transaction and that the transaction would be materially affected by the information.

(28) "Organization" includes a corporation, government or governmental subdivision or agency, business trust, estate, trust, partnership or association, two or more persons having a joint or common interest, or any other legal or commercial entity.

(29) "Party", as distinct from "third party", means a

person who has engaged in a transaction or made an agreement within this Act.

(30) "Person" includes an individual or an organization (See Section 1—102).

(31) "Presumption" or "presumed" means that the trier of fact must find the existence of the fact presumed unless and until evidence is introduced which would support a finding of its non-existence.

(32) "Purchase" includes taking by sale, discount, negotiation, mortgage, pledge, lien, issue or re-issue, gift or any other voluntary transaction creating an interest in property.

(33) "Purchaser" means a person who takes by purchase.

(34) "Remedy" means any remedial right to which an aggrieved party is entitled with or without resort to a tribunal.

(35) "Representative" includes an agent, an officer of a corporation or association, and a trustee, executor or administrator of an estate, or any other person empowered to act for another.

(36) "Rights" includes remedies.

(37) "Security interest" means an interest in personal property or fixtures which secures payment or performance of an obligation. The retention or reservation of title by a seller of goods notwithstanding shipment or delivery to the buyer (Section 2—401) is limited in effect to a reservation of a "security interest". The term also includes any interest of a buyer of accounts or chattel paper which is subject to Article 9. The special property interest of a buyer of goods on identification of such goods to a contract for sale under Section 2—401 is not a "security interest", but a buyer may also acquire a "security interest" by complying with Article 9. Unless a lease or consignment is intended as security, reservation of title thereunder is not a "security interest" but a consignment is in any event subject to the provisions on consignment sales (Section 2—326). Whether a lease is intended as security is to be determined by the facts of each case; however, (a) the inclusion of an option to purchase does not of itself make the lease one intended for security, and (b) an agreement that upon compliance with the terms of the lease the lessee shall become or has the option to become the owner of the property for no additional consideration or for a nominal consideration does make the lease one intended for security.

(38) "Send" in connection with any writing or notice means to deposit in the mail or deliver for transmission by any other usual means of communication with postage or cost of transmission provided for and properly addressed and in the case of an instrument to an address specified thereon or otherwise agreed, or if there be none to any address reasonable under the circumstances. The receipt of any writing or notice within the time at which it would have arrived if properly sent has the effect of a proper sending.

(39) "Signed" includes any symbol executed or adopted by a party with present intention to authenticate a writing.

(40) "Surety" includes guarantor.

(41) "Telegram" includes a message transmitted by radio, teletype, cable, any mechanical method of transmission, or the like.

(42) "Term" means that portion of an agreement which relates to a particular matter.

(43) "Unauthorized" signature or indorsement means one made without actual, implied or apparent authority and includes a forgery.

(44) "Value". Except as otherwise provided with respect to negotiable instruments and bank collections (Sections 3—303, 4—208 and 4—209) a person gives "value" for rights if he acquires them

(a) in return for a binding commitment to extend credit or for the extension of immediately available credit whether or not drawn upon and whether or not a chargeback is provided for in the event of difficulties in collection; or

(b) as security for or in total or partial satisfaction of a pre-existing claim; or

(c) by accepting delivery pursuant to a preexisting contract for purchase; or

(d) generally, in return for any consideration sufficient to support a simple contract.

(45) "Warehouse receipt" means a receipt issued by a person engaged in the business of storing goods for hire.

(46) "Written" or "writing" includes printing, typewriting or any other intentional reduction to tangible form.

Amended in 1962, 1972 and 1977.

§ 1—202. **Prima Facie Evidence by Third Party Documents.**

A document in due form purporting to be a bill of lading, policy or certificate of insurance, official weigher's or inspector's certificate, consular invoice, or any other document authorized or required by the contract to be issued by a third party shall be prima facie evidence of its own authenticity and genuineness and of the facts stated in the document by the third party.

§ 1—203. Obligation of Good Faith.

Every contract or duty within this Act imposes an obligation of good faith in its performance or enforcement.

§ 1—204. Time; Reasonable Time; "Seasonably".

(1) Whenever this Act requires any action to be taken within a reasonable time, any time which is not manifestly unreasonable may be fixed by agreement.

(2) What is a reasonable time for taking any action depends on the nature, purpose and circumstances of such action.

(3) An action is taken "seasonably" when it is taken at or within the time agreed or if no time is agreed at or within a reasonable time.

§ 1—205. Course of Dealing and Usage of Trade.

(1) A course of dealing is a sequence of previous conduct between the parties to a particular transaction which is fairly to be regarded as establishing a common basis of understanding for interpreting their expressions and other conduct.

(2) A usage of trade is any practice or method of dealing having such regularity of observance in a place, vocation or trade as to justify an expectation that it will be observed with respect to the transaction in question. The existence and scope of such a usage are to be proved as facts. If it is established that such a usage is embodied in a written trade code or similar writing the interpretation of the writing is for the court.

(3) A course of dealing between parties and any usage of trade in the vocation or trade in which they are engaged or of which they are or should be aware give particular meaning to and supplement or qualify terms of an agreement.

(4) The express terms of an agreement and an applicable course of dealing or usage of trade shall be construed wherever reasonable as consistent with each other; but when such construction is unreasonable express terms control both course of dealing and usage of trade and course of dealing controls usage trade.

(5) An applicable usage of trade in the place where any part of performance is to occur shall be used in interpreting the agreement as to that part of the performance.

(6) Evidence of a relevant usage of trade offered by one party is not admissible unless and until he has given the other party such notice as the court finds sufficient to prevent unfair surprise to the latter.

§ 1—206. Statute of Frauds for Kinds of Personal Property Not Otherwise Covered.

(1) Except in the cases described in subsection (2) of this section a contract for the sale of personal property is not enforceable by way of action or defense beyond five thousand dollars in amount or value of remedy unless there is some writing which indicates that a contract for sale has been made between the parties at a defined or stated price, reasonably identifies the subject matter, and is signed by the party against whom enforcement is sought or by his authorized agent.

(2) Subsection (1) of this section does not apply to contracts for the sale of goods (Section 2—201) nor of securities (Section 8—319) nor to security agreements (Section 9—203).

§ 1—207. Performance or Acceptance Under Reservation of Rights.

A party who with explicit reservation of rights performs or promises performance or assents to performance in the manner demanded or offered by the other party does not thereby prejudice the rights reserved. Such words as "without prejudice", "under protest" or the like are sufficient.

§ 1—208. Option to Accelerate at Will.

A term providing that one party or his successor in interest may accelerate payment or performance or require collateral or additional collateral "at will" or "when he deems himself insecure" or in words of similar import shall be construed to mean that he shall have power to do so only if he in good faith believes that the prospect of payment or performance is impaired. The burden of establishing lack of good faith is on the party against whom the power has been exercised.

§ 1—209. Subordinated Obligations

An obligation may be issued as subordinated to payment of another obligation of the person obligated, or a creditor may subordinate his right to payment of an obligation by agreement with either the person obligated or another creditor of the person obligated. Such a subordination does not create a security interest as against either the common debtor or a subordinated creditor. This section shall be construed as declaring the law as it existed prior to the enactment of this section and not as modifying it. Added 1966.

Note: *This new section is proposed as an optional provision to make it clear that a subordination agreement does not create a security interest unless so intended.*

Article 2
SALES

Part 1
Short Title, General Construction and Subject Matter

§ 2—101. **Short Title.**

This Article shall be known and may be cited as Uniform Commercial Code—Sales.

§ 2—102. **Scope; Certain Security and Other Transactions Excluded From This Article.**

Unless the context otherwise requires, this Article applies to transactions in goods; it does not apply to any transaction which although in the form of an unconditional contract to sell or present sale is intended to operate only as a security transaction nor does this Article impair or repeal any statute regulating sales to consumers, farmers or other specified classes of buyers.

§ 2—103. **Definitions and Index of Definitions.**

(1) In this Article unless the context otherwise requires

(a) "Buyer" means a person who buys or contracts to buy goods.

(b) "Good faith" in the case of a merchant means honesty in fact and the observance of reasonable commercial standards of fair dealing in the trade.

(c) "Receipt" of goods means taking physical possession of them.

(d) "Seller" means a person who sells or contracts to sell goods.

(2) Other definitions applying to this Article or to specified Parts thereof, and the sections in which they appear are:
"Acceptance". Section 2—606.
"Banker's credit". Section 2—325.
"Between merchants". Section 2—104.
"Cancellation". Section 2—106(4).
"Commercial unit". Section 2—105.
"Confirmed credit". Section 2—325.
"Conforming to contract". Section 2—106.
"Contract for sale". Section 2—106.

"Cover". Section 2—712.
"Entrusting". Section 2—403.
"Financing agency". Section 2—104.
"Future goods". Section 2—105.
"Goods". Section 2—105.
"Identification". Section 2—501.
"Installment contract". Section 2—612.
"Letter of Credit". Section 2—325.
"Lot". Section 2—105.
"Merchant". Section 2—104.
"Overseas". Section 2—323.
"Person in position of seller". Section 2—707.
"Present sale". Section 2—106.
"Sale". Section 2—106.
"Sale on approval". Section 2—326.
"Sale or return". Section 2—326.
"Termination". Section 2—106.

(3) The following definitions in other Articles apply to this Article:
"Check". Section 3—104.
"Consignee". Section 7—102.
"Consignor". Section 7—102.
"Consumer goods". Section 9—109.
"Dishonor". Section 3—507.
"Draft". Section 3—104.

(4) In addition Article 1 contains general definitions and principles of construction and interpretation applicable throughout this Article.

§ 2—104. **Definitions: "Merchant"; "Between Merchants"; "Financing Agency".**

(1) "Merchant" means a person who deals in goods of the kind or otherwise by his occupation holds himself out as having knowledge or skill peculiar to the practices or goods involved in the transaction or to whom such knowledge or skill may be attributed by his employment of an agent or broker or other intermediary who by his occupation holds himself out as having such knowledge or skill.

(2) "Financing agency" means a bank, finance company or other person who in the ordinary course of business makes advances against goods or documents of title or who by arrangement with either the seller or the buyer intervenes in ordinary course to make or collect payment due or claimed under the contract for sale, as by purchasing or paying the seller's draft or making advances against it or by merely taking it for collection whether or not documents of title accompany the draft. "Financing agency" includes also a bank or other person who similarly intervenes between persons who are in the position of seller and buyer in respect to the goods (Section 2—707).

(3) "Between merchants" means in any transaction with respect to which both parties are chargeable with the knowledge or skill of merchants.

§ 2—105. Definitions: Transferability; "Goods"; "Future" Goods; "Lot"; "Commercial Unit".

(1) "Goods" means all things (including specially manufactured goods) which are movable at the time of identification to the contract for sale other than the money in which the price is to be paid, investment securities (Article 8) and things in action. "Goods" also includes the unborn young of animals and growing crops and other identified things attached to realty as described in the section on goods to be severed from realty (Section 2—107).

(2) Goods must be both exiting and identified before any interest in them can pass. Goods which are not both existing and identified are "future" goods. A purported present sale of future goods or of any interest therein operates as a contract to sell.

(3) There may be a sale of a part interest in existing identified goods.

(4) An undivided share in an identified bulk of fungible goods is sufficiently identified to be sold although the quantity of the bulk is not determined. Any agreed proportion of such a bulk or any quantity thereof agreed upon by number, weight or other measure may to the extent of the seller's interest in the bulk be sold to the buyer who then becomes an owner in common.

(5) "Lot" means a parcel or a single article which is the subject matter of a separate sale or delivery, whether or not it is sufficient to perform the contract.

(6) "Commercial unit" means such a unit of goods as by commercial usage is a single whole for purposes of sale and division of which materially impairs its character or value on the market or in use. A commercial unit may be a single article (as a machine) or a set of articles (as a suite of furniture or an assortment of sizes) or a quantity (as a bale, gross, or carload) or any other unit treated in use or in the relevant market as a single whole.

§ 2—106. Definitions: "Contract"; "Agreement"; "Contract for Sale"; "Sale"; "Present Sale"; "Conforming" to Contract; "Termination"; "Cancellation".

(1) In this Article unless the context otherwise requires "contract" and "agreement" are limited to those relating to the present or future sale of goods. "Contract for sale" includes both a present sale of goods and a contract to sell goods at a future time. A "sale" consists in the passing of title from the seller to the buyer for a price (Section 2—401). A "present sale" means a sale which is accomplished by the making of the contract.

(2) Goods or conduct including any part of a performance are "conforming" or conform to the contract when they are in accordance with the obligations under the contract.

(3) "Termination" occurs when either party pursuant to a power created by agreement or law puts an end to the contract otherwise than for its breach. On "termination" all obligations which are still executory on both sides are discharged but any right based on prior breach or performance survives.

(4) "Cancellation" occurs when either party puts an end to the contract for breach by the other and its effect is the same as that of "termination" except that the cancelling party also retains any remedy for breach of the whole contract or any unperformed balance.

§ 2—107. Goods to Be Severed From Realty: Recording.

(1) A contract for the sale of minerals or the like (including oil and gas) or a structure or its materials to be removed from realty is a contract for the sale of goods within this Article if they are to be severed by the seller but until severance a purported present sale thereof which is not effective as a transfer of an interest in land is effective only as a contract to sell.

(2) A contract for the sale apart from the land of growing crops or other things attached to realty and capable of severance without material harm thereto but not described in subsection (1) or of timber to be cut is a contract for the sale of goods within this Article whether the subject matter is to be severed by the buyer or by the seller even though it forms part of the realty at the time of contracting, and the parties can by identification effect a present sale before severance.

(3) The provisions of this section are subject to any third party rights provided by the law relating to realty records, and the contract for sale may be executed and recorded as a document transferring an interest in land and shall then constitute notice to third parties of the buyer's rights under the contract for sale.

Part 2 Form, Formation and Readjustment of Contract

§ 2—201. Formal Requirements; Statute of Frauds.

(1) Except as otherwise provided in this section a contract for the sale of goods for the price of $500 or more

is not enforceable by way of action or defense unless there is some writing sufficient to indicate that a contract for sale has been made between the parties and signed by the party against whom enforcement is sought or by his authorized agent or broker. A writing is not sufficient because it omits or incorrectly states a term agreed upon but the contract is not enforceable under this paragraph beyond the quantity of goods shown in such writing.

(2) Between merchants if within a reasonable time a writing in confirmation of the contract and sufficient against the sender is received and the party receiving it has reason to know its contents, its satisfies the requirements of subsection (1) against such party unless written notice of objection to its contents is given within ten days after it is received.

(3) A contract which does not satisfy the requirements of subsection (1) but which is valid in other respects is enforceable

(a) if the goods are to be specially manufactured for the buyer and are not suitable for sale to others in the ordinary course of the seller's business and the seller, before notice of repudiation is received and under circumstances which reasonably indicate that the goods are for the buyer, has made either a substantial beginning of their manufacture or commitments for their procurement; or

(b) if the party against whom enforcement is sought admits in his pleading, testimony or otherwise in court that a contract for sale was made, but the contract is not enforceable under this provision beyond the quantity of goods admitted; or

(c) with respect to goods for which payment has been made and accepted or which have been received and accepted (Sec. 2—606).

§ 2—202. **Final Written Expression: Parol or Extrinsic Evidence.**

Terms with respect to which the confirmatory memoranda of the parties agree or which are otherwise set forth in a writing intended by the parties as a final expression of their agreement with respect to such terms as are included therein may not be contradicted by evidence of any prior agreement or of a contemporaneous oral agreement but may be explained or supplemented

(a) by course of dealing or usage of trade (Section 1—205) or by course of performance (Section 2—208); and

(b) by evidence of consistent additional terms unless the court finds the writing to have been intended also

as a complete and exclusive statement of the terms of the agreement.

§ 2—203. **Seals Inoperative.**

The affixing of a seal to a writing evidencing a contract for sale or an offer to buy or sell goods does not constitute the writing a sealed instrument and the law with respect to sealed instruments does not apply to such a contract or offer.

§ 2—204. **Formation in General.**

(1) A contract for sale of goods may be made in any manner sufficent to show agreement, including conduct by both parties which recognizes the existence of such a contract.

(2) An agreement sufficient to constitute a contract for sale may be found even though the moment of its making is undetermined.

(3) Even though one or more terms are left open a contract for sale does not fail for indefiniteness if the parties have intended to make a contract and there is a reasonably certain basis for giving an appropriate remedy.

§ 2—205. **Firm Offers.**

An offer by a merchant to buy or sell goods in a signed writing which by its terms gives assurance that it will be held open is not revocable, for lack of consideration, during the time stated or if no time is stated for a reasonable time, but in no event may such period of irrevocability exceed three months; but any such term of assurance on a form supplied by the offeree must be separately signed by the offeror.

§ 2—206. **Offer and Acceptance in Formation of Contract.**

(1) Unless other unambiguously indicated by the language or circumstances

(a) an offer to make a contract shall be construed as inviting acceptance in any manner and by any medium reasonable in the circumstances;

(b) an order or other offer to buy goods for prompt or current shipment shall be construed as inviting acceptance either by a prompt promise to ship or by the prompt or current shipment of conforming or nonconforming goods, but such a shipment of non-conforming goods does not constitute an acceptance if the seller seasonably notifies the buyer that the shipment is offered only as an accommodation to the buyer.

(2) Where the beginning of a requested performance is a reasonable mode of acceptance an offeror who is

not notified of acceptance within a reasonable time may treat the offer as having lapsed before acceptance.

§ 2—207. Additional Terms in Acceptance or Confirmation.

(1) A definite and seasonable expression of acceptance or a written confirmation which is sent within a reasonable time operates as an acceptance even though it states terms additional to or different from those offered or agreed upon, unless acceptance is expressly made conditional on assent to the additional or different terms.

(2) The additional terms are to be construed as proposals for addition to the contract. Between merchants such terms become part of the contract unless:

   (a) the offer expressly limits acceptance to the terms of the offer;

   (b) they materially alter it; or

   (c) notification of objection to them has already been given or is given within a reasonable time after notice of them is received.

(3) Conduct by both parties which recognizes the existence of a contract is sufficient to establish a contract for sale although the writings of the parties do not otherwise establish a contract. In such case the terms of the particular contract consist of those terms on which the writings of the parties agree, together with any supplementary terms incorporated under any other provisions of this Act.

§ 2—208. Course of Performance or Practical Construction.

(1) Where the contract for sale involves repeated occasions for performance by either party with knowledge of the nature of the performance and opportunity for objection to it by the other, any course of performance accepted or acquiesced in without objection shall be relevant to determine the meaning of the agreement.

(2) The express terms of the agreement and any such course of performance, as well as any course of dealing and usage of trade, shall be construed whenever reasonable as consistent with each other; but when such construction is unreasonable, express terms shall control course of performance and course of performance shall control both course of dealing and usage of trade (Section 1—205).

(3) Subject to the provisions of the next section on modification and waiver, such course of performance shall be relevant to show a waiver or modification of any term inconsistent with such course of performance.

§ 2—209. Modification, Rescission and Waiver.

(1) An agreement modifying a contract within this Article needs no consideration to be binding.

(2) A signed agreement which excludes modification or rescission except by a signed writing cannot be otherwise modified or rescinded, but except as between merchants such a requirement on a form supplied by the merchant must be separately signed by the other party.

(3) The requirements of the statute of frauds section of this Article (Section 2—201) must be satisfied if the contract as modified is within its provisions.

(4) Although an attempt at modification or rescission does not satisfy the requirements of subsection (2) or (3) it can operate as a waiver.

(5) A party who has made a waiver affecting an executory portion of the contract may retract the waiver by reasonable notification received by the other party that strict performance will be required of any term waived, unless the retraction would be unjust in view of a material change of position in reliance on the waiver.

§ 2—210. Delegation of Performance; Assignment of Rights.

(1) A party may perform his duty through a delegate unless otherwise agreed or unless the other party has a substantial interest in having his original promisor perform or control the acts required by the contract. No delegation of performance relieves the party delegating of any duty to perform or any liability for breach.

(2) Unless otherwise agreed all rights of either seller or buyer can be assigned except where the assignment would materially change the duty of the other party, or increase materially the burden or risk imposed on him by his contract, or impair materially his chance of obtaining return performance. A right to damages for breach of the whole contract or a right arising out of the assignor's due performance of his entire obligation can be assigned despite agreement otherwise.

(3) Unless the circumstances indicate the contrary a prohibition of assignment of "the contract" is to be construed as barring only the delegation to the assignee of the assignor's performance.

(4) An assignment of "the contract" or of "all my rights under the contract" or an assignment in similar general terms is an assignment of rights and unless the language or the circumstances (as in an assignment for

security) indicate the contrary, it is a delegation of performance of the duties of the assignor and its acceptance by the assignee constitutes a promise by him to perform those duties. This promise is enforceable by either the assignor or the other party to the original contract.

(5) The other party may treat any assignment which delegates performance as creating reasonable grounds for insecurity and may without prejudice to his rights against the assignor demand assurances from the assignee (Section 2—609).

Part 3 General Obligation and Construction of Contract

§ 2—301. General Obligations of Parties.

The obligation of the seller is to transfer and deliver and that of the buyer is to accept and pay in accordance with the contract.

§ 2—302. Unconscionable Contract or Clause.

(1) If the court as a matter of law finds the contract or any clause of the contract to have been unconscionable at the time it was made the court may refuse to enforce the contract, or it may enforce the remainder of the contract without the unconscionable clause, or it may so limit the application of any unconscionable clause as to avoid any unconscionable result.

(2) When it is claimed or appears to the court that the contract or any clause thereof may be unconscionable the parties shall be afforded a reasonable opportunity to present evidence as to its commercial setting, purpose and effect to aid the court in making the determination.

§ 2—303. Allocations or Division of Risks.

Where this Article allocates a risk or a burden as between the parties "unless otherwise agreed", the agreement may not only shift the allocation but may also divide the risk or burden.

§ 2—304. Price Payable in Money, Goods, Realty, or Otherwise.

(1) The price can be made payable in money or otherwise. If it is payable in whole or in part in goods each party is a seller of the goods which he is to transfer.

(2) Even though all or part of the price is payable in an interest in realty the transfer of the goods and the seller's obligations with reference to them are subject to this Article, but not the transfer of the interest in realty or the transferor's obligations in connection therewith.

§ 2—305. Open Price Term.

(1) The parties if they so intend can conclude a contract for sale even though the price is not settled. In such a case the price is a reasonable price at the time for delivery if

(a) nothing is said as to price; or

(b) the price is left to be agreed by the parties and they fail to agree; or

(c) the price is to be fixed in terms of some agreed market or other standard as set or recorded by a third person or agency and it is not so set or recorded.

(2) A price to be fixed by the seller or by the buyer means a price for him to fix in good faith.

(3) When a price left to be fixed otherwise than by agreement of the parties fails to be fixed through fault of one party the other may at his option treat the contract as cancelled or himself fix a reasonable price.

(4) Where, however, the parties intend not to be bound unless the price be fixed or agreed and it is not fixed or agreed there is no contract. In such a case the buyer must return any goods already received or if unable so to do must pay their reasonable value at the time of delivery and the seller must return any portion of the price paid on account.

§ 2—306. Output, Requirements and Exclusive Dealings.

(1) A term which measures the quantity by the output of the seller or the requirements of the buyer means such actual output or requirements as may occur in good faith, except that no quantity unreasonably disproportionate to any stated estimate or in the absence of a stated estimate to any normal or otherwise comparable prior output or requirements may be tendered or demanded.

(2) A lawful agreement by either the seller or the buyer for exclusive dealing in the kind of goods concerned imposes unless otherwise agreed an obligation by the seller to use best efforts to supply the goods and by the buyer to use best efforts to promote their sale.

§ 2—307. Delivery in Single Lot or Several Lots.

Unless otherwise agreed all goods called for by a contract for sale must be tendered in a single delivery and payment is due only on such tender but where the circumstances give either party the right to make or demand delivery in lots the price if it can be apportioned may be demanded for each lot.

§ 2—308. **Absence of Specified Place for Delivery.**

Unless otherwise agreed

(a) the place for delivery of goods is the seller's place of business or if he has none his residence; but

(b) in a contract for sale of identified goods which to the knowledge of the parties at the time of contracting are in some other place, that place is the place for their delivery; and

(c) documents of title may be delivered through customary banking channels.

§ 2—309. **Absence of Specific Time Provisions; Notice of Termination.**

(1) The time for shipment or delivery or any other action under a contract if not provided in this Article or agreed upon shall be a reasonable time.

(2) Where the contract provides for successive performances but is indefinite in duration it is valid for a reasonable time but unless otherwise agreed may be terminated at any time by either party.

(3) Termination of a contract by one party except on the happening of an agreed event requires that reasonable notification be received by the other party and an agreement dispensing with notification is invalid if its operation would be unconscionable.

§ 2—310. **Open Time for Payment or Running of Credit; Authority to Ship Under Reservation.**

Unless otherwise agreed

(a) payment is due at the time and place at which the buyer is to receive the goods even though the place of shipment is the place of delivery; and

(b) if the seller is authorized to send the goods he may ship them under reservation, and may tender the documents of title, but the buyer may inspect the goods after their arrival before payment is due unless such inspection is inconsistent with the terms of the contract (Section 2—513); and

(c) if delivery is authorized and made by way of documents of title otherwise than by subsection (b) then payment is due at the time and place at which the buyer is to receive the documents regardless of where the goods are to be received; and

(d) where the seller is required or authorized to ship the goods on credit the credit period runs from the time of shipment but post-dating the invoice or delaying its dispatch will correspondingly delay the starting of the credit period.

§ 2—311. **Options and Cooperation Respecting Performance.**

(1) An agreement for sale which is otherwise sufficiently definite (subsection (3) of Section 2—204) to be a contract is not made invalid by the fact that it leaves particulars of performance to be specified by one of the parties. Any such specification must be made in good faith and within limits set by commercial reasonableness.

(2) Unless otherwise agreed specifications relating to assortment of the goods are at the buyer's option and except as otherwise provided in subsections (1)(c) and (3) of Section 2—319 specifications or arrangements relating to shipment are at the seller's option.

(3) Where such specification would materially affect the other party's performance but is not seasonably made or where one party's cooperation is necessary to the agreed performance of the other but is not seasonably forthcoming, the other party in addition to all other remedies

(a) is excused for any resulting delay in his own performance; and

(b) may also either proceed to perform in any reasonable manner or after the time for a material part of his own performance treat the failure to specify or to cooperate as a breach by failure to deliver or accept the goods.

§ 2—312. **Warranty of Title and Against Infringement; Buyer's Obligation Against Infringement.**

(1) Subject to subsection (2) there is in a contract for sale a warranty by the seller that

(a) the title conveyed shall be good, and its transfer rightful; and

(b) the goods shall be delivered free from any security interest or other lien or encumbrance of which the buyer at the time of contracting has no knowledge.

(2) A warranty under subsection (1) will be excluded or modified only by specific language or by circumstances which give the buyer reason to know that the person selling does not claim title in himself or that he is purporting to sell only such right or title as he or a third person may have.

(3) Unless otherwise agreed a seller who is a merchant regularly dealing in goods of the kind warrants that the goods shall be delivered free of the rightful claim of any third person by way of infringement or

the like but a buyer who furnishes specifications to the seller must hold the seller harmless against any such claim which arises out of compliance with the specifications.

§ 2—313. Express Warranties by Affirmation, Promise, Description, Sample.

(1) Express warranties by the seller are created as follows:

(a) Any affirmation of fact or promise made by the seller to the buyer which relates to the goods and becomes part of the basis of the bargain creates an express warranty that the goods shall conform to the affirmation or promise.

(b) Any description of the goods which is made part of the basis of the bargain creates an express warranty that the goods shall conform to the description.

(c) Any sample or model which is made part of the basis of the bargain creates an express warranty that the whole of the goods shall conform to the sample or model.

(2) It is not necessary to the creation of an express warranty that the seller use formal words such as "warrant" or "guarantee" or that he have a specific intention to make a warranty, but an affirmation merely of the value of the goods or a statement purporting to be merely the seller's opinion or commendation of the goods does not create a warranty.

§ 2—314. Implied Warranty: Merchantability; Usage of Trade.

(1) Unless excluded or modified (Section 2—316), a warranty that the goods shall be merchantable is implied in a contract for their sale if the seller is a merchant with respect to goods of that kind. Under this section the serving for value of food or drink to be consumed either on the premises or elsewhere is a sale.

(2) Goods to be merchantable must be at least such as

(a) pass without objection in the trade under the contract description; and

(b) in the case of fungible goods, are of fair average quality within the description; and

(c) are fit for the ordinary purposes for which such goods are used; and

(d) run, within the variations permitted by the agreement, of even kind, quality and quantity within each unit and among all units involved; and

(e) are adequately contained, packaged, and labeled as the agreement may require; and

(f) conform to the promises or affirmations of fact made on the container or label if any.

(3) Unless excluded or modified (Section 2—316) other implied warranties may arise from course of dealing or usage of trade.

§ 2—315. Implied Warranty: Fitness for Particular Purpose.

Where the seller at the time of contracting has reason to know any particular purpose for which the goods are required and that the buyer is relying on the seller's skill or judgment to select or furnish suitable goods, there is unless excluded or modified under the next section an implied warranty that the goods shall be fit for such purpose.

§ 2—316. Exclusion or Modification of Warranties.

(1) Words or conduct relevant to the creation of an express warranty and words or conduct tending to negate or limit warranty shall be construed wherever reasonable as consistent with each other; but subject to the provisions of this Article on parol or extrinsic evidence (Section 2—202) negation or limitation is inoperative to the extent that such construction is unreasonable.

(2) Subject to subsection (3), to exclude or modify the implied warranty of merchantability or any part of it the language must mention merchantability and in case of a writing must be conspicuous, and to exclude or modify any implied warranty of fitness the exclusion must be by a writing and conspicuous. Language to exclude all implied warranties of fitness is sufficient if it states, for example, that "There are no warranties which extend beyond the description on the face hereof."

(3) Notwithstanding subsection (2)

(a) unless the circumstances indicate otherwise, all implied warranties are excluded by expressions like "as is", "with all faults" or other language which in common understanding calls the buyer's attention to the exclusion of warranties and makes plain that there is no implied warranty; and

(b) when the buyer before entering into the contract has examined the goods or the sample or model as fully as he desired or has refused to examine the goods there is no implied warranty with regard to defects which an examination ought in the circumstances to have revealed to him; and

(c) an implied warranty can also be excluded or modified by course of dealing or course of performance or usage of trade.

(4) Remedies for breach of warranty can be limited in accordance with the provisions of this Article on liquidation or limitation of damages and on contractual modification of remedy (Sections 2—718 and 2—719).

§ 2—317. Cumulation and Conflict of Warranties Express or Implied.

Warranties whether express or implied shall be construed as consistent with each other and as cumulative, but if such construction is unreasonable the intention of the parties shall determine which warranty is dominant. In ascertaining that intention the following rules apply:

(a) Exact or technical specifications displace an inconsistent sample or model or general language of description.

(b) A sample from an existing bulk displaces inconsistent general language of description.

(c) Express warranties displace inconsistent implied warranties other than an implied warranty of fitness for a particular purpose.

§ 2—318. Third Party Beneficiaries of Warranties Express or Implied.

Note: If this Act is introduced in the Congress of the United States this section should be omitted. (States to select one alternative.)

Alternative A

A seller's warranty whether express or implied extends to any natural person who is in the family or household of his buyer or who is a guest in his home if it is reasonable to expect that such person may use, consume or be affected by the goods and who is injured in person by breach of the warranty. A seller may not exclude or limit the operation of this section.

Alternative B

A seller's warranty whether express or implied extends to any natural person who may reasonably be expected to use, consume or be affected by the goods and who is injured in person by breach of the warranty. A seller may not exclude or limit the operation of this section.

Alternative C

A seller's warranty whether express or implied extends to any person who may reasonably be expected to use, consume or be affected by the goods and who is injured by breach of the warranty. A seller may not

exclude or limit the operation of this section with respect to injury to the person of an individual to whom the warranty extends. As amended 1966.

§ 2   319. F.O.B. and F.A.S. Terms.

(1) Unless otherwise agreed the term F.O.B. (which means "free on board") at a named place, even though used only in connection with the stated price, is a delivery term under which

(a) when the term is F.O.B. the place of shipment, the seller must at that place ship the goods in the manner provided in this Article (Section 2—504) and bear the expense and risk of putting them into the possession of the carrier; or

(b) when the term is F.O.B. the place of destination, the seller must at his own expense and risk transport the goods to that place and there tender delivery of them in the manner provided in this Article (Section 2—503);

(c) when under either (a) or (b) the term is also F.O.B. vessel, car or other vehicle, the seller must in addition at his own expense and risk load the goods on board. If the term is F.O.B. vessel the buyer must name the vessel and in an appropriate case the seller must comply with the provisions of this Article on the form of bill of lading (Section 2—323).

(2) Unless otherwise agreed the term F.A.S. vessel (which means "free alongside") at a named port, even though used only in connection with the stated price, is a delivery term under which the seller must

(a) at his own expense and risk deliver the goods alongside the vessel in the manner usual in that port or on a dock designated and provided by the buyer; and

(b) obtain and tender a receipt for the goods in exchange for which the carrier is under a duty to issue a bill of lading.

(3) Unless otherwise agreed in any case falling within subsection (1)(a) or (c) or subsection (2) the buyer must seasonably give any needed instructions for making delivery, including when the term is F.A.S. or F.O.B. the loading berth of the vessel and in an appropriate case its name and sailing date. The seller may treat the failure of needed instructions as a failure of cooperation under this Article (Section 2—311). He may also at his option move the goods in any reasonable manner preparatory to delivery or shipment.

(4) Under the term F.O.B. vessel or F.A.S. unless otherwise agreed the buyer must make payment against tender of the required documents and the seller may

not tender nor the buyer demand delivery of the goods in substitution for the documents.

§ 2—320. **C.I.F. and C. & F. Terms.**

(1) The term C.I.F. means that the price includes in a lump sum the cost of the goods and the insurance and freight to the named destination. The term C. & F. or C.F. means that the price so includes cost and freight to the named destination.

(2) Unless otherwise agreed and even though used only in connection with the stated price and destination, the term C.I.F. destination or its equivalent requires the seller at his own expense and risk to

(a) put the goods into the possession of a carrier at the port for shipment and obtain a negotiable bill or bills of lading covering the entire transportation to the named destination; and

(b) load the goods and obtain a receipt from the carrier (which may be contained in the bill of lading) showing that the freight has been paid or provided for; and

(c) obtain a policy or certificate of insurance, including any war risk insurance, of a kind and on terms then current at the port of shipment in the usual amount, in the currency of the contract, shown to cover the same goods covered by the bill of lading and providing for payment of loss to the order of the buyer or for the account of whom it may concern; but the seller may add to the price the amount of the premium for any such war risk insurance; and

(d) prepare an invoice of the goods and procure any other documents required to effect shipment or to comply with the contract; and

(e) forward and tender with commercial promptness all the documents in due form and with any indorsement necessary to perfect the buyer's rights.

(3) Unless otherwise agreed the term C. & F. or its equivalent has the same effect and imposes upon the seller the same obligations and risks as a C.I.F. term except the obligation as to insurance.

(4) Under the term C.I.F. or C. & F. unless otherwise agreed the buyer must make payment against tender of the required documents and the seller may not tender nor the buyer demand delivery of the goods in substitution for the documents.

§ 2—321. **C.I.F. or C. & F.: "Net Landed Weights"; "Payment on Arrival"; Warranty of Condition on Arrival.**

Under a contract containing a term C.I.F. or C. & F.

(1) Where the price is based on or is to be adjusted according to "net landed weights", "delivered weights", "out turn" quantity or quality or the like, unless otherwise agreed the seller must reasonably estimate the price. The payment due on tender of the documents called for by the contract is the amount so estimated, but after final adjustment of the price a settlement must be made with commercial promptness.

(2) An agreement described in subsection (1) or any warranty of quality or condition of the goods on arrival places upon the seller the risk of ordinary deterioration, shrinkage and the like in transportation but has no effect on the place or time of identification to the contract for sale or delivery or on the passing of the risk of loss.

(3) Unless otherwise agreed where the contract provides for payment on or after arrival of the goods the seller must before payment allow such preliminary inspection as is feasible; but if the goods are lost delivery of the documents and payment are due when the goods should have arrived.

§ 2—322. **Delivery "Ex-Ship".**

(1) Unless otherwise agreed a term for delivery of goods "ex-ship" (which means from the carrying vessel) or in equivalent language is not restricted to a particular ship and requires delivery from a ship which has reached a place at the named port of destination where goods of the kind are usually discharged.

(2) Under such a term unless otherwise agreed

(a) the seller must discharge all liens arising out of the carriage and furnish the buyer with a direction which puts the carrier under a duty to deliver the goods; and

(b) the risk of loss does not pass to the buyer until the goods leave the ship's tackle or are otherwise properly unloaded.

§ 2—323. **Form of Bill of Lading Required in Overseas Shipment; "Overseas".**

(1) Where the contract contemplates overseas shipment and contains a term C.I.F. or C. & F. or F.O.B. vessel, the seller unless otherwise agreed must obtain a negotiable bill of lading stating that the goods have been loaded on board or, in the case of a term C.I.F. or C. & F., received for shipment.

(2) Where in a case within subsection (1) a bill of lading has been issued in a set of parts, unless otherwise agreed if the documents are not to be sent from abroad the buyer may demand tender of the full set; otherwise only one part of the bill of lading need be

tendered. Even if the agreement expressly requires a full set

(a) due tender of a single part is acceptable within the provisions of this Article on cure of improper delivery (subsection (1) of Section 2—508); and

(b) even though the full set is demanded, if the documents are sent from abroad the person tendering an incomplete set may nevertheless require payment upon furnishing an indemnity which the buyer in good faith deems adequate.

(3) A shipment by water or by air or a contract contemplating such shipment is "overseas" insofar as by usage of trade or agreement it is subject to the commercial, financing or shipping practices characteristic of international deep water commerce.

§ 2—324. **"No Arrival, No Sale" Term.**

Under a term "no arrival, no sale" or terms of like meaning, unless otherwise agreed,

(a) the seller must properly ship conforming goods and if they arrive by any means he must tender them on arrival but he assumes no obligation that the goods will arrive unless he has caused the non-arrival; and

(b) where without fault of the seller the goods are in part lost or have so deteriorated as no longer to conform to the contract or arrive after the contract time, the buyer may proceed as if there had been casualty to identified goods (Section 2—613).

§ 2—325. **"Letter of Credit" Term; "Confirmed Credit".**

(1) Failure of the buyer seasonably to furnish an agreed letter of credit is a breach of the contract for sale.

(2) The delivery to seller of a proper letter of credit suspends the buyer's obligation to pay. If the letter of credit is dishonored, the seller may on seasonable notification to the buyer require payment directly from him.

(3) Unless otherwise agreed the term "letter of credit" or "banker's credit" in a contract for sale means an irrevocable credit issued by a financing agency of good repute and, where the shipment is overseas, of good international repute. The term "confirmed credit" means that the credit must also carry the direct obligation of such an agency which does business in the seller's financial market.

§ 2—326. **Sale on Approval and Sale or Return; Consignment Sales and Rights of Creditors.**

(1) Unless otherwise agreed, if delivered goods may be returned by the buyer even though they conform to the contract, the transaction is

(a) a "sale on approval" if the goods are delivered primarily for use, and

(b) a "sale or return" if the goods are delivered primarily for resale.

(2) Except as provided in subsection (3), goods held on approval are not subject to the claims of the buyer's creditors until acceptance; goods held on sale or return are subject to such claims while in the buyer's possession.

(3) Where goods are delivered to a person for sale and such person maintains a place of business at which he deals in goods of the kind involved, under a name other than the name of the person making delivery, then with respect to claims of creditors of the person conducting the business the goods are deemed to be on sale or return. The provisions of this subsection are applicable even though an agreement purports to reserve title to the person making delivery until payment or resale or uses such words as "on consignment" or "on memorandum". However, this subsection is not applicable if the person making delivery

(a) complies with an applicable law providing for a consignor's interest or the like to be evidenced by a sign, or

(b) establishes that the person conducting the business is generally known by his creditors to be substantially engaged in selling the goods of others, or

(c) complies with the filing provisions of the Article on Secured Transactions (Article 9).

(4) Any "or return" term of a contract for sale is to be treated as a separate contract for sale within the statute of frauds section of this Article (Section 2—201) and as contradicting the sale aspect of the contract within the provisions of this Article on parol or extrinsic evidence (Section 2—202).

§ 2—327. **Special Incidents of Sale on Approval and Sale or Return.**

(1) Under a sale on approval unless otherwise agreed

(a) although the goods are identified to the contract the risk of loss and the title do not pass to the buyer until acceptance; and

(b) use of the goods consistent with the purpose of trial is not acceptance but failure seasonably to notify the seller of election to return the goods is acceptance, and if the goods conform to the contract acceptance of any part is acceptance of the whole; and

(c) after due notification of election to return, the return is at the seller's risk and expense but a merchant buyer must follow any reasonable instructions.

(2) Under a sale or return unless otherwise agreed

(a) the option to return extends to the whole or any commercial unit of the goods while in substantially their original condition, but must be exercised seasonably; and

(b) the return is at the buyer's risk and expense.

§ 2—328. **Sale by Auction.**

(1) In a sale by auction if goods are put up in lots each lot is the subject of a separate sale.

(2) A sale by auction is complete when the auctioneer so announces by the fall of the hammer or in other customary manner. Where a bid is made while the hammer is falling in acceptance of a prior bid the auctioneer may in his discretion reopen the bidding or declare the goods sold under the bid on which the hammer was falling.

(3) Such a sale is with reserve unless the goods are in explicit terms put up without reserve. In an auction with reserve the auctioneer may withdraw the goods at any time until he announces completion of the sale. In an auction without reserve, after the auctioneer calls for bids on an article or lot, that article or lot cannot be withdrawn unless no bid is made within a reasonable time. In either case a bidder may retract his bid until the auctioneer's announcement of completion of the sale, but a bidder's retraction does not revive any previous bid.

(4) If the auctioneer knowingly receives a bid on the seller's behalf or the seller makes or procures such as bid, and notice has not been given that liberty for such bidding is reserved, the buyer may at his option avoid the sale or take the goods at the price of the last good faith bid prior to the completion of the sale. This subsection shall not apply to any bid at a forced sale.

Part 4 Title, Creditors and Good Faith Purchasers

§ 2—401. **Passing of Title; Reservation for Security; Limited Application of This Section.**

Each provision of this Article with regard to the rights, obligations and remedies of the seller, the buyer, purchasers or other third parties applies irrespective of title to the goods except where the provision refers to such title. Insofar as situations are not covered by the other provisions of this Article and matters concerning title became material the following rules apply:

(1) Title to goods cannot pass under a contract for sale prior to their identification to the contract (Section 2—

501), and unless otherwise explicitly agreed the buyer acquires by their identification a special property as limited by this Act. Any retention or reservation by the seller of the title (property) in goods shipped or delivered to the buyer is limited in effect to a reservation of a security interest. Subject to these provisions and to the provisions of the Article on Secured Transactions (Article 9), title to goods passes from the seller to the buyer in any manner and on any conditions explicitly agreed on by the parties.

(2) Unless otherwise explicitly agreed title passes to the buyer at the time and place at which the seller completes his performance with reference to the physical delivery of the goods, despite any reservation of a security interest and even though a document of title is to be delivered at a different time or place; and in particular and despite any reservation of a security interest by the bill of lading.

(a) if the contract requires or authorizes the seller to send the goods to the buyer but does not require him to deliver them at destination, title passes to the buyer at the time and place of shipment; but

(b) if the contract requires delivery at destination, title passes on tender there.

(3) Unless otherwise explicitly agreed where delivery is to be made without moving the goods,

(a) if the seller is to deliver a document of title, title passes at the time when and the place where he delivers such documents; or

(b) if the goods are at the time of contracting already identified and no documents are to be delivered, title passes at the time and place of contracting.

(4) A rejection or other refusal by the buyer to receive or retain the goods, whether or not justified, or a justified revocation of acceptance revests title to the goods in the seller. Such revesting occurs by operation of law and is not a "sale".

§ 2—402. **Rights of Seller's Creditors Against Sold Goods.**

(1) Except as provided in subsections (2) and (3), rights of unsecured creditors of the seller with respect to goods which have been identified to a contract for sale are subject to the buyer's rights to recover the goods under this Article (Sections 2—502 and 2—716).

(2) A creditor of the seller may treat a sale or an identification of goods to a contract for sale as void if as against him a retention of possession by the seller is fraudulent under any rule of law of the state where the goods are situated, except that retention of pos-

session in good faith and current course of trade by a merchant-seller for a commercially reasonable time after a sale or identification is not fraudulent.

(3) Nothing in this Article shall be deemed to impair the rights of creditors of the seller.

(a) under the provisions of the Article on Secured Transactions (Article 9); or

(b) where identification to the contract or delivery is made not in current course of trade but in satisfaction of or as security for a pre-existing claim for money, security or the like and is made under circumstances which under any rule of law of the state where the goods are situated would apart from this Article constitute the transaction a fraudulent transfer or voidable preference.

§ 2—403. **Power to Transfer; Good Faith Purchase of Goods; "Entrusting".**

(1) A purchaser of goods acquires all title which his transferor had or had power to transfer except that a purchaser of a limited interest acquires rights only to the extent of the interest purchased. A person with voidable title has power to transfer a good title to a good faith purchaser for value. When goods have been delivered under a transaction of purchase the purchaser has such power even though

(a) the transferor was deceived as to the identity of the purchaser, or

(b) the delivery was in exchange for a check which is later dishonored, or

(c) it was agreed that the transaction was to be a "cash sale", or

(d) the delivery was procured through fraud punishable as larcenous under the criminal law.

(2) Any entrusting of possession of goods to a merchant who deals in goods of that kind gives him power to transfer all rights of the entruster to a buyer in ordinary course of business.

(3) "Entrusting" includes any delivery and any acquiescence in retention of possession regardless of any condition expressed between the parties to the delivery or acquiescence and regardless of whether the procurement of the entrusting or the possessor's disposition of the goods have been such as to be larcenous under the criminal law.

(4) The rights of other purchasers of goods and of lien creditors are governed by the Articles on Secured Transactions (Article 9), Bulk Transfers (Article 6) and Documents of Title (Article 7).

Part 5 **Performance**

§ 2—501. **Insurable Interest in Goods; Manner of Identification of Goods.**

(1) The buyer obtains a special property and an insurable interest in goods by identification of existing goods as goods to which the contract refers even though the goods so identified are nonconforming and he has an option to return or reject them. Such identification can be made at any time and in any manner explicitly agreed to by the parties. In the absence of explicit agreement identification occurs

(a) when the contract is made if it is for the sale of goods already exiting and identified;

(b) if the contract is for the sale of future goods other than those described in paragraph (c), when goods are shipped, marked or otherwise designated by the seller as goods to which the contract refers;

(c) when the crops are planted or otherwise become growing crops or the young are conceived if the contract is for the sale of unborn young to be born within twelve months after contracting or for the sale of crops to be harvested within twelve months or the next normal harvest season after contracting whichever is longer.

(2) The seller retains an insurable interest in goods so long as title to or any security interest in the goods remains in him and where the identification is by the seller alone he may until default or insolvency or notification to the buyer that the identification is final substitute other goods for those identified.

(3) Nothing in this section impairs any insurable interest recognized under any other statute or rule of law.

§ 2—502. **Buyer's Right to Goods on Seller's Insolvency.**

(1) Subject to subsection (2) and even though the goods have not been shipped a buyer who has paid a part or all of the price of goods in which he has a special property under the provisions of the immediately preceding section may on making and keeping good a tender of any unpaid portion of their price recover them from the seller if the seller becomes insolvent within ten days after receipt of the first installment on their price.

(2) If the identification creating his special property has been made by the buyer he acquires the right to recover the goods only if they conform to the contract for sale.

§ 2—503. **Manner of Seller's Tender of Delivery.**

(1) Tender of delivery requires that the seller put and hold conforming goods at the buyer's disposition and give the buyer any notification reasonably necessary to enable him to take delivery. The manner, time and place for tender are determined by the agreement and this Article, and in particular

(a) tender must be at a reasonable hour, and if it is of goods they must be kept available for the period reasonably necessary to enable the buyer to take possession; but

(b) unless otherwise agreed the buyer must furnish facilities reasonably suited to the receipt of the goods.

(2) Where the case is within the next section respecting shipment tender requires that the seller comply with its provisions.

(3) Where the seller is required to deliver at a particular destination tender requires that he comply with subsection (1) and also in any appropriate case tender documents as described in subsections (4) and (5) of this section.

(4) Where goods are in the possession of a bailee and are to be delivered without being moved

(a) tender requires that the seller either tender a negotiable document of title covering such goods or procure acknowledgment by the bailee of the buyer's right to possession of the goods; but

(b) tender to the buyer of a non-negotiable document of title or of a written direction to the bailee to deliver is sufficient tender unless the buyer seasonably objects, and receipt by the bailee of notification of the buyer's rights fixes those rights as against the bailee and all third persons; but risk of loss of the goods and of any failure by the bailee to honor the non-negotiable document of title or to obey the direction remains on the seller until the buyer has had a reasonable time to present the document or direction, and a refusal by the bailee to honor the document or to obey the direction defeats the tender.

(5) Where the contract requires the seller to deliver documents

(a) he must tender all such documents in correct form, except as provided in this Article with respect to bills of lading in a set (subsection (2) of Section 2—323); and

(b) tender through customary banking channels is sufficient and dishonor of a draft accompanying the documents constitutes non-acceptance or rejection.

§ 2—504. **Shipment by Seller.**

Where the seller is required or authorized to send the goods to the buyer and the contract does not require him to deliver them at a particular destination, then unless otherwise agreed he must

(a) put the goods in the possession of such a carrier and make such a contract for their transportation as may be reasonable having regard to the nature of the goods and other circumstances of the case; and

(b) obtain and promptly deliver or tender in due form any document necessary to enable the buyer to obtain possession of the goods or otherwise required by the agreement or by usage of trade; and

(c) promptly notify the buyer of the shipment.

Failure to notify the buyer under paragraph (c) or to make a proper contract under paragraph (a) is a ground for rejection only if material delay or loss ensues.

§ 2—505. **Seller's Shipment Under Reservation.**

(1) Where the seller has identified goods to the contract by or before shipment:

(a) his procurement of a negotiable bill of lading to his own order or otherwise reserves in him a security interest in the goods. His procurement of the bill to the order of a financing agency or of the buyer indicates in addition only the seller's expectation of transferring that interest to the person named.

(b) a non-negotiable bill of lading to himself or his nominee reserves possesion of the goods as security but except in a case of conditional delivery (subsection (2) of Section 2—507) a non-negotiable bill of lading naming the buyer as consignee reserves no security interest even though the seller retains possession of the bill of lading.

(2) When shipment by the seller with reservation of a security interest is in violation of the contract for sale it constitutes an improper contract for transportation within the preceding section but impairs neither the rights given to the buyer by shipment and identification of the goods to the contract nor the seller's powers as a holder of a negotiable document.

§ 2—506. **Rights of Financing Agency.**

(1) A financing agency by paying or purchasing for value a draft which relates to a shipment of goods acquires to the extent of the payment or purchase and in addition to its own rights under the draft and any

document of title securing it any rights of the shipper in the goods including the right to stop delivery and the shipper's right to have the draft honored by the buyer.

(2) The right to reimbursement of a financing agency which has in good faith honored or purchased the draft under commitment to or authority from the buyer is not impaired by subsequent discovery of defects with reference to any relevant document which was apparently regular on its face.

§ 2—507. Effect of Seller's Tender; Delivery on Condition.

(1) Tender of delivery is a condition to the buyer's duty to accept the goods and, unless otherwise agreed, to his duty to pay for them. Tender entitles the seller to acceptance of the goods and to payment according to the contract.

(2) Where payment is due and demanded on the delivery to the buyer of goods or documents of title, his right as against the seller to retain or dispose of them is conditional upon his making the payment due.

§ 2—508. Cure by Seller of Improper Tender or Delivery; Replacement.

(1) Where any tender or delivery by the seller is rejected because non-conforming and the time for performance has not yet expired, the seller may seasonably notify the buyer of his intention to cure and may then within the contract time make a conforming delivery.

(2) Where the buyer rejects a non-conforming tender which the seller had reasonable grounds to believe would be acceptable with or without money allowance the seller may if he seasonably notifies the buyer have a further reasonable time to substitute a conforming tender.

§ 2—509. Risk of Loss in the Absence of Breach.

(1) Where the contract requires or authorizes the seller to ship the goods by carrier

(a) if it does not require him to deliver them at a particular destination, the risk of loss passes to the buyer when the goods are duly delivered to the carrier even though the shipment is under reservation (Section 2—505); but

(b) if it does require him to deliver them at a particular destination and the goods are there duly tendered while in the possession of the carrier, the risk of loss passes to the buyer when the goods are there duly so tendered as to enable the buyer to take delivery.

(2) Where the goods are held by a bailee to be delivered without being moved, the risk of loss passes to the buyer

(a) on his receipt of a negotiable document of title covering the goods; or

(b) on acknowledgment by the bailee of the buyer's right to possession of the goods; or

(c) after his receipt of a non-negotiable document of title or other written direction to deliver, as provided in subsection (4)(b) of Section 2—503.

(3) In any case not within subsection (1) or (2), the risk of loss passes to the buyer on his receipt of the goods if the seller is a merchant; otherwise, the risk passes to the buyer on tender of delivery.

(4) The provisions of this section are subject to contrary agreement of the parties and to the provisions of this Article on sale on approval (Section 2—327) and on effect of breach on risk of loss (Section 2—510).

§ 2—510. Effect of Breach on Risk of Loss.

(1) Where a tender or delivery of goods so fails to conform to the contract as to give a right of rejection the risk of their loss remains on the seller until cure or acceptance.

(2) Where the buyer rightfully revokes acceptance he may to the extent of any deficiency in his effective insurance coverage treat the risk of loss as having rested on the seller from the beginning.

(3) Where the buyer as to conforming goods already identified to the contract for sale repudiates or is otherwise in breach before risk of their loss has passed to him, the seller may to the extent of any deficiency in his effective insurance coverage treat the risk of loss as resting on the buyer for a commercially reasonable time.

§ 2—511. Tender of Payment by Buyer; Payment by Check.

(1) Unless otherwise agreed tender of payment is a condition to the seller's duty to tender and complete any delivery.

(2) Tender of payment is sufficient when made by any means or in any manner current in the ordinary course of business unless the seller demands payment in legal tender and gives any extension of time reasonably necessary to procure it.

(3) Subject to the provisions of this Act on the effect of an instrument on an obligation (Section 3—802), payment by check is conditional and is defeated as

between the parties by dishonor of the check on due presentment.

§ 2—512. **Payment by Buyer Before Inspection.**

(1) Where the contract requires payment before inspection non-conformity of the goods does not excuse the buyer from so making payment unless

(a) the non-conformity appears without inspection; or

(b) despite tender of the required documents the circumstances would justify injunction against honor under the provisions of this Act (Section 5—114).

(2) Payment pursuant to subsection (1) does not constitute an acceptance of goods or impair the buyer's right to inspect or any of his remedies.

§ 2—513. **Buyer's Right to Inspection of Goods.**

(1) Unless otherwise agreed and subject to subsection (3), where goods are tendered or delivered or identified to the contract for sale, the buyer has a right before payment or acceptance to inspect them at any reasonable place and time and in any reasonable manner. When the seller is required or authorized to send the goods to the buyer, the inspection may be after their arrival.

(2) Expenses of inspection must be borne by the buyer but may be recovered from the seller if the goods do not conform and are rejected.

(3) Unless otherwise agreed and subject to the provisions of this Article on C.I.F. contracts (subsection (3) of Section 2—321), the buyer is not entitled to inspect the goods before payment of the price when the contract provides

(a) for delivery "C.O.D." or on other like terms; or

(b) for payment against documents of title, except where such payment is due only after the goods are to become available for inspection.

(4) A place or method of inspection fixed by the parties is presumed to be exclusive but unless otherwise expressly agreed it does not postpone identification or shift the place for delivery or for passing the risk of loss. If compliance becomes impossible, inspection shall be as provided in this section unless the place or method fixed was clearly intended as an indispensable condition failure of which avoids the contract.

§ 2—514. **When Documents Deliverable on Acceptance; When on Payment.**

Unless otherwise agreed documents against which a draft is drawn are to be delivered to the drawee on

acceptance of the draft if it is payable more than three days after presentment; otherwise, only on payment.

§ 2—515. **Preserving Evidence of Goods in Dispute.**

In furtherance of the adjustment of any claim or dispute

(a) either party on reasonable notification to the other and for the purpose of ascertaining the facts and preserving evidence has the right to inspect, test and sample the goods including such of them as may be in the possession or control of the other; and

(b) the parties may agree to a third party inspection or survey to determine the conformity or condition of the goods and may agree that the findings shall be binding upon them in any subsequent litigation or adjustment.

Part 6 Breach, Repudiation and Excuse

§ 2—601. **Buyer's Rights on Improper Delivery.**

Subject to the provisions of this Article on breach in installment contracts (Section 2—612) and unless otherwise agreed under the sections on contractual limitations of remedy (Sections 2—718 and 2—719), if the goods or the tender of delivery fail in any respect to conform to the contract, the buyer may

(a) reject the whole; or

(b) accept the whole; or

(c) accept any commercial unit or units and reject the rest.

§ 2—602. **Manner and Effect of Rightful Rejection.**

(1) Rejection of goods must be within a reasonable time after their delivery or tender. It is ineffective unless the buyer seasonably notifies the seller.

(2) Subject to the provisions of the two following sections on rejected goods (Sections 2—603 and 2—604),

(a) after rejection any exercise of ownership by the buyer with respect to any commercial unit is wrongful as against the seller; and

(b) if the buyer has before rejection taken physical possession of goods in which he does not have a security interest under the provisions of this Article (subsection (3) of Section 2—711), he is under a duty after rejection to hold them with reasonable care at the seller's disposition for a time sufficient to permit the seller to remove them; but

(c) the buyer has no further obligations with regard to goods rightfully rejected.

(3) The seller's rights with respect to goods wrongfully rejected are governed by the provisions of this Article on seller's remedies in general (Section 2—703).

§ 2—603. Merchant Buyer's Duties as to Rightfully Rejected Goods.

(1) Subject to any security interest in the buyer (subsection (3) of Section 2—711), when the seller has no agent or place of business at the market of rejection a merchant buyer is under a duty after rejection of goods in his possession or control to follow any reasonable instructions received from the seller with respect to the goods and in the absence of such instructions to make reasonable efforts to sell them for the seller's account if they are perishable or threaten to decline in value speedily. Instructions are not reasonable if on demand indemnity for expenses is not forthcoming.

(2) When the buyer sells goods under subsection (1), he is entitled to reimbursement from the seller or out of the proceeds for reasonable expenses of caring for and selling them, and if the expenses include no selling commission then to such commission as is usual in the trade or if there is none to a reasonable sum not exceeding ten per cent on the gross proceeds.

(3) In complying with this section the buyer is held only to good faith and good faith conduct hereunder is neither acceptance nor conversion nor the basis of an action for damages.

§ 2—604. Buyer's Options as to Salvage of Rightfully Rejected Goods.

Subject to the provisions of the immediately preceding section on perishables if the seller gives no instructions within a reasonable time after notification of rejection the buyer may store the rejected goods for the seller's account or reship them to him or resell them for the seller's account with reimbursement as provided in the preceding section. Such action is not acceptance or conversion.

§ 2—605. Waiver of Buyer's Objections by Failure to Particularize.

(1) The buyer's failure to state in connection with rejection a particular defect which is ascertainable by reasonable inspection precludes him from relying on the unstated defect to justify rejection or to establish breach

(a) where the seller could have cured it if stated seasonably; or

(b) between merchants when the seller has after rejection made a request in writing for a full and final written statement of all defects on which the buyer proposes to rely.

(2) Payment against documents made without reservation of rights precludes recovery of the payment for defects apparent on the face of the documents.

§ 2—606. What Constitutes Acceptance of Goods.

(1) Acceptance of goods occurs when the buyer

(a) after a reasonable opportunity to inspect the goods signifies to the seller that the goods are conforming or that he will take or retain them in spite of their nonconformity; or

(b) fails to make an effective rejection (subsection (1) of Section 2—602), but such acceptance does not occur until the buyer has had a reasonable opportunity to inspect them; or

(c) does any act inconsistent with the seller's ownership; but if such act is wrongful as against the seller it is an acceptance only if ratified by him.

(2) Acceptance of a part of any commercial unit is acceptance of that entire unit.

§ 2—607. Effect of Acceptance; Notice of Breach; Burden of Establishing Breach After Acceptance; Notice of Claim or Litigation to Person Answerable Over.

(1) The buyer must pay at the contract rate for any goods accepted.

(2) Acceptance of goods by the buyer precludes rejection of the goods accepted and if made with knowledge of a non-conformity cannot be revoked because of it unless the acceptance was on the reasonable assumption that the non-conformity would be seasonably cured but acceptance does not of itself impair any other remedy provided by this Article for non-conformity.

(3) Where a tender has been accepted

(a) the buyer must within a reasonble time after he discovers or should have discovered any breach notify the seller of breach or be barred from any remedy; and

(b) if the claim is one for infringement or the like (subsection (3) of Section 2—312) and the buyer is sued as a result of such a breach he must so notify the seller within a reasonable time after he receives notice of the litigation or be barred from any remedy over for liability established by the litigation.

(4) The burden is on the buyer to establish any breach with respect to the goods accepted.

(5) Where the buyer is sued for breach of a warranty or other obligation for which his seller is answerable over

(a) he may give his seller written notice of the litigation. If the notice states that the seller may come in and defend and that if the seller does not do so he will be bound in any action against him by his buyer by any determination of fact common to the two litigations, then unless the seller after seasonable receipt of the notice does come in and defend he is so bound.

(b) if the claim is one for infringement or the like (subsection (3) of Section 2—312) the original seller may demand in writing that his buyer turn over to him control of the litigation including settlement or else be barred from any remedy over and if he also agrees to bear all expense and to satisfy any adverse judgment, then unless the buyer after seasonable receipt of the demand does turn over control the buyer is so barred.

(6) The provisions of subsections (3), (4) and (5) apply to any obligation of a buyer to hold the seller harmless against infringement or the like (subsection (3) of Section 2—312).

§ 2—608. **Revocation of Acceptance in Whole or in Part.**

(1) The buyer may revoke his acceptance of a lot or commercial unit whose non-conformity substantially impairs its value to him if he has accepted it

(a) on the reasonable assumption that its non-conformity would be cured and it has not been seasonably cured; or

(b) without discovery of such non-conformity if his acceptance was reasonably induced either by the difficulty of discovery before acceptance or by the seller's assurances.

(2) Revocation of acceptance must occur within a reasonable time after the buyer discovers or should have discovered the ground for it and before any substantial change in condition of the goods which is not caused by their own defects. It is not effective until the buyer notifies the seller of it.

(3) A buyer who so revokes has the same rights and duties with regard to the goods involved as if he had rejected them.

§ 2—609. **Right to Adequate Assurance of Performance.**

(1) A contract for sale imposes an obligation on each party that the other's expectation of receiving due performance will not be impaired. When reasonable grounds for insecurity arise with respect to the performance of either party the other may in writing demand adequate assurance of due performance and until he receives such assurance may if commercially reasonable suspend any performance for which he has not already received the agreed return.

(2) Between merchants the reasonableness of grounds for insecurity and the adequacy of any assurance offered shall be determined according to commercial standards.

(3) Acceptance of any improper delivery or payment does not prejudice the aggrieved party's right to demand adequate assurance of future performance.

(4) After receipt of a justified demand failure to provide within a reasonable time not exceeding thirty days such assurance of due performance as is adequate under the circumstances of the particular case is a repudiation of the contract.

§ 2—610. **Anticipatory Repudiation.**

When either party repudiates the contract with respect to a performance not yet due the loss of which will substantially impair the value of the contract to the other, the aggrieved party may

(a) for a commercially reasonable time await performance by the repudiating party; or

(b) resort to any remedy for breach (Section 2—703 or Section 2—711), even though he has notified the repudiating party that he would await the latter's performance and has urged retraction; and

(c) in either case suspend his own performance or proceed in accordance with the provisions of this Article on the seller's right to identify goods to the contract notwithstanding breach or to salvage unfinished goods (Section 2—704).

§ 2—611. **Retraction of Anticipatory Repudiation.**

(1) Until the repudiating party's next performance is due he can retract his repudiation unless the aggrieved party has since the repudiation cancelled or materially changed his position or otherwise indicated that he considers the repudiation final.

(2) Retraction may be by any method which clearly indicates to the aggrieved party that the repudiating party intends to perform, but must include any assurance justifiably demanded under the provisions of this Article (Section 2—609).

(3) Retraction reinstates the repudiating party's rights under the contract with due excuse and allowance to

the aggrieved party for any delay occasioned by the repudiation.

§ 2—612. "Installment Contract"; Breach.

(1) An "installment contract" is one which requires or authorizes the delivery of goods in separate lots to be separately accepted, even though the contract contains a clause "each delivery is a separate contract" or its equivalent.

(2) The buyer may reject any installment which is non-conforming if the non-conformity substantially impairs the value of that installment and cannot be cured or if the non-conformity is a defect in the required documents; but if the non-conformity does not fall within subsection (3) and the seller gives adequate assurance of its cure the buyer must accept that installment.

(3) Whenever non-conformity or default with respect to one or more installments substantially impairs the value of the whole contract there is a breach of the whole. But the aggrieved party reinstates the contract if he accepts a non-conforming installment without seasonably notifying of cancellation or if he brings an action with respect only to past installments or demands performance as to future installments.

§ 2—613. Casualty to Identified Goods.

Where the contract requires for its performance goods identified when the contract is made, and the goods suffer casualty without fault of either party before the risk of loss passes to the buyer, or in a proper case under a "no arrival, no sale" term (Section 2—324) then

(a) if the loss is total the contract is avoided; and

(b) if the loss is partial or the goods have so deteriorated as no longer to conform to the contract the buyer may nevertheless demand inspection and at his option either treat the contract as voided or accept the goods with due allowance from the contract price for the deterioration or the deficiency in quantity but without further right against the seller.

§ 2—614. Substituted Performance.

(1) Where without fault of either party the agreed berthing, loading, or unloading facilities fail or an agreed type of carrier becomes unavailable or the agreed manner of delivery otherwise becomes commercially impracticable but a commercially reasonable substitute is available, such substitute performance must be tendered and accepted.

(2) If the agreed means or manner of payment fails because of domestic or foreign governmental regula-

tion, the seller may withhold or stop delivery unless the buyer provides a means or manner of payment which is commercially a substantial equivalent. If delivery has already been taken, payment by the means or in the manner provided by the regulation discharges the buyer's obligation unless the regulation is discriminatory, oppressive or predatory.

§ 2—615. Excuse by Failure of Presupposed Conditions.

Except so far as a seller may have assumed a greater obligation and subject to the preceding section on substituted performance:

(a) Delay in delivery or non-delivery in whole or in part by a seller who complies with paragraphs (b) and (c) is not a breach of his duty under a contract for sale if performance as agreed has been made impracticable by the occurrence of a contingency the non-occurrence of which was a basic assumption on which the contract was made or by compliance in good faith with any applicable foreign or domestic governmental regulation or order whether or not it later proves to be invalid.

(b) Where the causes mentioned in paragraph (a) affect only a part of the seller's capacity to perform, he must allocate production and deliveries among his customers but may at his option include regular customers not then under contract as well as his own requirements for further manufacture. He may so allocate in any manner which is fair and reasonable.

(c) The seller must notify the buyer seasonably that there will be delay or non-delivery and, when allocation is required under paragraph (b), of the estimated quota thus made available for the buyer.

§ 2—616. Procedure on Notice Claiming Excuse.

(1) Where the buyer receives notification of a material or indefinite delay or an allocation justified under the preceding section he may by written notification to the seller as to any delivery concerned, and where the prospective deficiency substantially impairs the value of the whole contract under the provisions of this Article relating to breach of installment contracts (Section 2—612), then also as to the whole,

(a) terminate and thereby discharge any unexecuted portion of the contract; or

(b) modify the contract by agreeing to take his available quota in substitution.

(2) If after receipt of such notification from the seller the buyer fails so to modify the contract within a reasonable time not exceeding thirty days the contract lapses with respect to any deliveries affected.

(3) The provisions of this section may not be negated by agreement except in so far as the seller has assumed a greater obligation under the preceding section.

Part 7 Remedies

§ 2—701. **Remedies for Breach of Collateral Contracts Not Impaired.**

Remedies for breach of any obligation or promise collateral or ancillary to a contract for sale are not impaired by the provisions of this Article.

§ 2—702. **Seller's Remedies on Discovery of Buyer's Insolvency.**

(1) Where the seller discovers the buyer to be insolvent he may refuse delivery except for cash including payment for all goods theretofore delivered under the contract, and stop delivery under this Article (Section 2—705).

(2) Where the seller discovers that the buyer has received goods on credit while insolvent he may reclaim the goods upon demand made within ten days after the receipt, but if misrepresentation of solvency has been made to the particular seller in writing within three months before delivery the ten day limitation does not apply. Except as provided in this subsection the seller may not base a right to reclaim goods on the buyer's fraudulent or innocent misrepresentation of solvency or of intent to pay.

(3) The seller's right to reclaim under subsection (2) is subject to the rights of a buyer in ordinary course or other good faith purchaser under this Article (Section 2—403). Successful reclamation of goods excludes all other remedies with respect to them.

§ 2—703. **Seller's Remedies in General.**

Where the buyer wrongfully rejects or revokes acceptance of goods or fails to make a payment due on or before delivery or repudiates with respect to a part or the whole, then with respect to any goods directly affected and, if the breach is of the whole contract (Section 2—612), then also with respect to the whole undelivered balance, the aggrieved seller may

(a) withhold delivery of such goods;

(b) stop delivery by any bailee as hereafter provided (Section 2—705);

(c) proceed under the next section respecting goods still unidentified to the contract;

(d) resell and recover damages as hereafter provided (Section 2—706);

(e) recover damages for non-acceptance (Section 2—708) or in a proper case the price (Section 2—709);

(f) cancel.

§ 2—704. **Seller's Right to Identify Goods to the Contract Notwithstanding Breach or to Salvage Unfinished Goods.**

(1) An aggrieved seller under the preceding section may

(a) identify to the contract conforming goods not already identified if at the time he learned of the breach they are in his possession or control;

(b) treat as the subject of resale goods which have demonstrably been intended for the particular contract even though those goods are unfinished.

(2) Where the goods are unfinished an aggrieved seller may in the exercise of reasonable commercial judgment for the purposes of avoiding loss and of effective realization either complete the manufacture and wholly identify the goods to the contract or cease manufacture and resell for scrap or salvage value or proceed in any other reasonable manner.

§ 2—705. **Seller's Stoppage of Delivery in Transit or Otherwise.**

(1) The seller may stop delivery of goods in the possession of a carrier or other bailee when he discovers the buyer to be insolvent (Section 2—702) and may stop delivery of carload, truckload, planeload or larger shipments of express or freight when the buyer repudiates or fails to make a payment due before delivery or if for any other reason the seller has a right to withhold or reclaim the goods.

(2) As against such buyer the seller may stop delivery until

(a) receipt of the goods by the buyer; or

(b) acknowledgment to the buyer by any bailee of the goods except a carrier that the bailee holds the goods for the buyer; or

(c) such acknowledgment to the buyer by a carrier by reshipment or as warehouseman; or

(d) negotiation to the buyer of any negotiable document of title covering the goods.

(3) (a) To stop delivery the seller must so notify as to enable the bailee by reasonable diligence to prevent delivery of the goods.

(b) After such notification the bailee must hold and deliver the goods according to the directions of the seller but the seller is liable to the bailee for any ensuing charges or damages.

(c) If a negotiable document of title has been issued for goods the bailee is not obliged to obey a notification to stop until surrender of the document.

(d) A carrier who has issued a non-negotiable bill of lading is not obliged to obey a notification to stop received from a person other than the consignor.

§ 2—706. Seller's Resale Including Contract for Resale.

(1) Under the conditions stated in Section 2—703 on seller's remedies, the seller may resell the goods concerned or the undelivered balance thereof. Where the resale is made in good faith and in a commercially reasonable manner the seller may recover the difference between the resale price and the contract price together with any incidental damages allowed under the provisions of this Article (Section 2—710), but less expenses saved in consequence of the buyer's breach.

(2) Except as otherwise provided in subsection (3) or unless otherwise agreed resale may be at public or private sale including sale by way of one or more contracts to sell or of identification to an existing contract of the seller. Sale may be as a unit or in parcels and at any time and place and on any terms but every aspect of the sale including the method, manner, time, place and terms must be commercially reasonable. The resale must be reasonably identified as referring to the broken contract, but it is not necessary that the goods be in existence or that any or all of them have been identified to the contract before the breach.

(3) Where the resale is at private sale the seller must give the buyer reasonable notification of his intention to resell.

(4) Where the resale is at public sale

(a) only identified goods can be sold except where there is a recognized market for a public sale of futures in goods of the kind; and

(b) it must be made at a usual place or market for public sale if one is reasonably available and except in the case of goods which are perishable or threaten to decline in value speedily the seller must give the buyer reasonable notice of the time and place of the resale; and

(c) if the goods are not to be within the view of those attending the sale the notification of sale must state the place where the goods are located and

provide for their reasonable inspection by prospective bidders; and

(d) the seller may buy.

(5) A purchaser who buys in good faith at a resale takes the goods free of any rights of the original buyer even though the seller fails to comply with one or more of the requirements of this section.

(6) The seller is not accountable to the buyer for any profit made on any resale. A person in the position of a seller (Section 2—707) or a buyer who has rightfully rejected or justifiably revoked acceptance must account for any excess over the amount of his security interest, as hereinafter defined (subsection (3) of Section 2—711).

§ 2—707. "Person in the Position of a Seller".

(1) A "person in the position of a seller" includes as against a principal an agent who has paid or become responsible for the price of goods on behalf of his principal or anyone who otherwise holds a security interest or other right in goods similar to that of a seller.

(2) A person in the position of a seller may as provided in this Article withhold or stop delivery (Section 2—705) and resell (Section 2—706) and recover incidental damages (Section 2—710).

§ 2—708. Seller's Damages for Non-Acceptance or Repudiation.

(1) Subject to subsection (2) and to the provisions of this Article with respect to proof of market price (Section 2—723), the measure of damages for non-acceptance or repudiation by the buyer is the difference between the market price at the time and place for tender and the unpaid contract price together with any incidental damages provided in this Article (Section 2—710), but less expenses saved in consequence of the buyer's breach.

(2) If the measure of damages provided in subsection (1) is inadequate to put the seller in as good a position as performance would have done then the measure of damages is the profit (including reasonable overhead) which the seller would have made from full performance by the buyer, together with any incidental damages provided in this Article (Section 2—710), due allowance for costs reasonably incurred and due credit for payments or proceeds of resale.

§ 2—709. Action for the Price.

(1) When the buyer fails to pay the price as it becomes due the seller may recover, together with any incidental damages under the next section, the price

(a) of goods accepted or of conforming goods lost or damaged within a commercially reasonable time after risk of their loss has passed to the buyer; and

(b) of goods identified to the contract if the seller is unable after reasonable effort to resell them at a reasonable price or the circumstances reasonably indicate that such effort will be unavailing.

(2) Where the seller sues for the price he must hold for the buyer any goods which have been identified to the contract and are still in his control except that if resale become possible he may resell them at any time prior to the collection of the judgment. The net proceeds of any such resale must be credited to the buyer and payment of the judgment entitles him to any goods not resold.

(3) After the buyer has wrongfully rejected or revoked acceptance of the goods or has failed to make a payment due or has repudiated (Section 2—610), a seller who is held not entitled to the price under this section shall nevertheless be awarded damages for non-acceptance under the preceding section.

§ 2—710. Seller's Incidental Damages.

Incidental damages to an aggrieved seller include any commercially reasonable charges, expenses or commissions incurred in stopping delivery, in the transportation, care and custody of goods after the buyer's breach, in connection with return or resale of the goods or otherwise resulting from the breach.

§ 2—711. Buyer's Remedies in General; Buyer's Security Interest in Rejected Goods.

(1) Where the seller fails to make delivery or repudiates or the buyer rightfully rejects or justifiably revokes acceptance then with respect to any goods involved, and with respect to the whole if the breach goes to the whole contract (Section 2—612), the buyer may cancel and whether or not he has done so may in addition to recovering so much of the price as has been paid

(a) "cover" and have damages under the next section as to all the goods affected whether or not they have been identified to the contract; or

(b) recover damages for non-delivery as provided in this Article (Section 2—713).

(2) Where the seller fails to deliver or repudiates the buyer may also

(a) if the goods have been identified recover them as provided in this Article (Section 2—502); or

(b) in a proper case obtain specific performance or

replevy the goods as provided in this Article (Section 2—716).

(3) On rightful rejection or justifiable revocation of acceptance a buyer has a security interest in goods in his possession or control for any payments made on their price and any expenses reasonably incurred in their inspection, receipt, transportation, care and custody and may hold such goods and resell them in like manner as an aggrieved seller (Section 2—706).

§ 2—712. "Cover"; Buyer's Procurement of Substitute Goods.

(1) After a breach within the preceding section the buyer may "cover" by making in good faith and without unreasonable delay any reasonable purchase of or contract to purchase goods in substitution for those due from the seller.

(2) The buyer may recover from the seller as damages the difference between the cost of cover and the contract price together with any incidental or consequential damages as hereinafter defined (Section 2—715), but less expenses saved in consequence of the seller's breach.

(3) Failure of the buyer to effect cover within this section does not bar him from any other remedy.

§ 2—713. Buyer's Damages for Non-Delivery or Repudiation.

(1) Subject to the provisions of this Article with respect to proof of market price (Section 2—723), the measure of damages for non-delivery or repudiation by the seller is the difference between the market price at the time when the buyer learned of the breach and the contract price together with any incidental and consequential damages provided in this Article (Section 2—715), but less expenses saved in consequence of the seller's breach.

(2) Market price is to be determined as of the place for tender or, in cases of rejection after arrival or revocation of acceptance, as of the place of arrival.

§ 2—714. Buyer's Damages for Breach in Regard to Accepted Goods.

(1) Where the buyer has accepted goods and given notification (subsection (3) of Section 2—607) he may recover as damages for any non-conformity of tender the loss resulting in the ordinary course of events from the seller's breach as determined in any manner which is reasonable.

(2) The measure of damages for breach of warranty is the difference at the time and place of acceptance be-

tween the value of the goods accepted and the value they would have had if they had been as warranted, unless special circumstances show proximate damages of a different amount.

(3) In a proper case any incidental and consequential damages under the next section may also be recovered.

§ 2—715. Buyer's Incidental and Consequential Damages.

(1) Incidental damages resulting from the seller's breach include expenses reasonably incurred in inspection, receipt, transportation and care and custody of goods rightfully rejected, any commercially reasonable charges, expenses or commissions in connection with effecting cover and any other reasonable expense incident to the delay or other breach.

(2) Consequential damages resulting from the seller's breach include

(a) any loss resulting from general or particular requirements and needs of which the seller at the time of contracting had reason to know and which could not reasonably be prevented by cover or otherwise; and
(b) injury to person or property proximately resulting from any breach of warranty.

§ 2—716. Buyer's Right to Specific Performance or Replevin.

(1) Specific performance may be decreed where the goods are unique or in other proper circumstances.

(2) The decree for specific performance may include such terms and conditions as to payment of the price, damages, or other relief as the court may deem just.

(3) The buyer has a right of replevin for goods identified to the contract if after reasonable effort he is unable to effect cover for such goods or the circumstances reasonably indicate that such effort will be unavailing or if the goods have been shipped under reservation and satisfaction of the security interest in them has been made or tendered.

§ 2—717. Deduction of Damages From the Price.

The buyer on notifying the seller of his intention to do so may deduct all or any part of the damages resulting from any breach of the contract from any part of the price still due under the same contract.

§ 2—718. Liquidation or Limitation of Damages; Deposits.

(1) Damages for breach by either party may be liquidated in the agreement but only at an amount which is reasonable in the light of the anticipated or actual harm caused by the breach, the difficulties of proof of loss, and the inconvenience or nonfeasibility of otherwise obtaining an adequate remedy. A term fixing unreasonably large liquidated damages is void as a penalty.

(2) Where the seller justifiably withholds delivery of goods because of the buyer's breach, the buyer is entitled to restitution of any amount by which the sum of his payments exceeds

(a) the amount to which the seller is entitled by virtue of terms liquidating the seller's damages in accordance with subsection (1), or

(b) in the absence of such terms, twenty per cent of the value of the total performance for which the buyer is obligated under the contract or $500, whichever is smaller.

(3) The buyer's right to restitution under subsection (2) is subject to offset to the extent that the seller establishes

(a) a right to recover damages under the provisions of this Article other than subsection (1), and

(b) the amount or value of any benefits received by the buyer directly or indirectly by reason of the contract.

(4) Where a seller has received payment in goods their reasonable value or the proceeds of their resale shall be treated as payments for the purposes of subsection (2); but if the seller has notice of the buyer's breach before reselling goods received in part performance, his resale is subject to the conditions laid down in this Article on resale by an aggrieved seller (Section 2—706).

§ 2—719. Contractual Modification or Limitation of Remedy.

(1) Subject to the provisions of subsections (2) and (3) of this section and of the preceding section on liquidation and limitation of damages,

(a) the agreement may provide for remedies in addition to or in substitution for those provided in this Article and may limit or alter the measure of damages recoverable under this Article, as by limiting the buyer's remedies to return of the goods and repayment of the price or to repair and replacement of non-conforming goods or parts; and

(b) resort to a remedy as provided is optional unless the remedy is expressly agreed to be exclusive, in which case it is the sole remedy.

(2) Where circumstances cause an exclusive or limited remedy to fail of its essential purpose, remedy may be had as provided in this Act.

(3) Consequential damages may be limited or excluded unless the limitation or exclusion is unconscionable. Limitation of consequential damages for injury to the person in the case of consumer goods is prima facie unconscionable but limitation of damages where the loss is commercial is not.

§ 2—720. Effect of "Cancellation" or "Rescission" on Claims for Antecedent Breach.

Unless the contrary intention clearly appears, expressions of "cancellation" or "rescission" of the contract or the like shall not be construed as a renunciation or discharge of any claim in damages for an antecedent breach.

§ 2—721. Remedies for Fraud.

Remedies for material misrepresentation or fraud include all remedies available under this Article for non-fraudulent breach. Neither rescission or a claim for rescission of the contract for sale nor rejection or return of the goods shall bar or be deemed inconsistent with a claim for damages or other remedy.

§ 2—722. Who Can Sue Third Parties for Injury to Goods.

Where a third party so deals with goods which have been identified to a contract for sale as to cause actionable injury to a party to that contract

(a) a right of action against the third party is in either party to the contract for sale who has title to or a security interest or a special property or an insurable interest in the goods; and if the goods have been destroyed or converted a right of action is also in the party who either bore the risk of loss under the contract for sale or has since the injury assumed that risk as against the other;

(b) if at the time of the injury the party plaintiff did not bear the risk of loss as against the other party to the contract for sale and there is no arrangement between them for disposition of the recovery, his suit or settlement is, subject to his own interest, as a fiduciary for the other party to the contract;

(c) either party may with the consent of the other sue for the benefit of whom it may concern.

§ 2—723. Proof of Market Price: Time and Place.

(1) If an action based on anticipatory repudiation comes to trial before the time for performance with respect to some or all of the goods, any damages based on market price (Section 2—708 or Section 2—713) shall be determined according to the price of such goods prevailing at the time when the aggrieved party learned of the repudiation.

(2) If evidence of a price prevailing at the times or places described in this Article is not readily available the price prevailing within any reasonable time before or after the time described or at any other place which in commercial judgment or under usage of trade would serve as a reasonable substitute for the one described may be used, making any proper allowance for the cost of transporting the goods to or from such other place.

(3) Evidence of a relevant price prevailing at a time or place other than the one described in this Article offered by one party is not admissible unless and until he has given the other party such notice as the court finds sufficient to prevent unfair surprise.

§ 2—724. Admissibility of Market Quotations.

Whenever the prevailing price or value of any goods regularly bought and sold in any established commodity market is in issue, reports in official publications or trade journals or in newspapers or periodicals of general circulation published as the reports of such market shall be admissible in evidence. The circumstances of the preparation of such a report may be shown to affect its weight but not its admissibility.

§ 2—725. Statute of Limitations in Contracts for Sale.

(1) An action for breach of any contract for sale must be commenced within four years after the cause of action has accrued. By the original agreement the parties may reduce the period of limitation to not less than one year but may not extend it.

(2) A cause of action accrues when the breach occurs, regardless of the aggrieved party's lack of knowledge of the breach. A breach of warranty occurs when tender of delivery is made, except that where a warranty explicitly extends to future performance of the goods and discovery of the breach must await the time of such performance the cause of action accrues when the breach is or should have been discovered.

(3) Where an action commenced within the time limited by subsection (1) is so terminated as to leave available a remedy by another action for the same breach such other action may be commenced after the expiration of the time limited and within six months after the termination of the first action unless the termination resulted from voluntary discontinuance or from dismissal for failure or neglect to prosecute.

(4) This section does not alter the law on tolling of the statute of limitations nor does it apply to causes of action which have accrued before this Act becomes effective.

Article 3
COMMERCIAL PAPER

Part 1 Short Title, Form and Interpretation

§ 3—101. **Short Title.**

This Article shall be known and may be cited as Uniform Commercial Code—Commercial Paper.

§ 3—102. **Definitions and Index of Definitions.**

(1) In this Article unless the context otherwise requires

(a) "Issue" means the first delivery of an instrument to a holder or a remitter.

(b) An "order" is a direction to pay and must be more than an authorization or request. It must identify the person to pay with reasonable certainty. It may be addressed to one or more such persons jointly or in the alternative but not in succession.

(c) A "promise" is an undertaking to pay and must be more than an acknowledgment of an obligation.

(d) "Secondary party" means a drawer or endorser.

(e) "Instrument" means a negotiable instrument.

(2) Other definitions applying to this Article and the sections in which they appear are:
"Acceptance". Section 3—410.
"Accommodation party". Section 3—415.
"Alteration". Section 3—407.
"Certificate of deposit". Section 3—104.
"Certification". Section 3—411.
"Check". Section 3—104.
"Definite time". Section 3—109.
"Dishonor". Section 3—507.
"Draft". Section 3—104.
"Holder in due course". Section 3—302.
"Negotiation". Section 3—202.
"Note". Section 3—104.
"Notice of dishonor". Section 3—508.
"On demand". Section 3—108.
"Presentment". Section 3—504.
"Protest". Section 3—509.
"Restrictive Indorsement". Section 3—205.
"Signature". Section 3—401.

(3) The following definitions in other Articles apply to this Article:
"Account". Section 4—104.
"Banking Day". Section 4—104.
"Clearing House". Section 4—104.
"Collecting Bank". Section 4—105.
"Customer". Section 4—104.
"Depositary Bank". Section 4—105.
"Documentary Draft". Section 4—104.
"Intermediary Bank". Section 4—105.
"Item". Section 4—104.
"Midnight deadline". Section 4—104.
"Payor Bank". Section 4—105.

(4) In addition Article 1 contains general definitions and principles of construction and interpretation applicable throughout this Article.

§ 3—103. **Limitations on Scope of Article.**

(1) This Article does not apply to money, documents of title or investment securities.

(2) The provisions of this Article are subject to the provisions of the Article on Bank Deposits and Collections (Article 4) and Secured Transactions (Article 9).

§ 3—104. **Form of Negotiable Instruments; "Draft"; "Check"; "Certificate of Deposit"; "Note".**

(1) Any writing to be a negotiable instrument within this Article must

(a) be signed by the maker or drawer; and

(b) contain an unconditional promise or order to pay a sum certain in money and no other promise, order, obligation or power given by the maker or drawer except as authorized by this Article; and

(c) be payable on demand or at a definite time; and

(d) be payable to order or to bearer.

(2) A writing which complies with the requirements of this section is

(a) a "draft" ("bill of exchange") if it is an order;

(b) a "check" if it is a draft drawn on a bank and payable on demand;

(c) a "certificate of deposit" if it is an acknowledgment by a bank of receipt of money with an engagement to repay it;

(d) a "note" if it is a promise other than a certificate of deposit.

(3) As used in other Articles of this Act, and as the context may require, the terms "draft", "check", "certificate of deposit" and "note" may refer to instru-

ments which are not negotiable within this Article as well as to instruments which are so negotiable.

§ 3—105. **When Promise or Order Unconditional.**

(1) A promise or order otherwise unconditional is not made conditional by the fact that the instrument

    (a) is subject to implied or constructive conditions; or

    (b) states its consideration, whether performed or promised, or the transaction which gave rise to the instrument, or that the promise or order is made or the instrument matures in accordance with or "as per" such transaction; or

    (c) refers to or states that it arises out of a separate agreement or refers to a separate agreement for rights as to prepayment or acceleration; or

    (d) states that it is drawn under a letter of credit; or

    (e) states that it is secured, whether by mortgage, reservation of title or otherwise; or

    (f) indicates a particular account to be debited or any other fund or source from which reimbursement is expected; or

    (g) is limited to payment out of a particular fund or the proceeds of a particular source, if the instrument is issued by a government or governmental agency or unit; or

    (h) is limited to payment out of the entire assets of a partnership, unincorporated association, trust or estate by or on behalf of which the instrument is issued.

(2) A promise or order is not unconditional if the instrument

    (a) states that it is subject to or governed by any other agreement; or

    (b) states that it is to be paid only out of a particular fund or source except as provided in this section.

§ 3—106. **Sum Certain.**

(1) The sum payable is a sum certain even though it is to be paid

    (a) with stated interest or by stated installments; or

    (b) with stated different rates of interest before and after default or a specified date; or

    (c) with a stated discount or addition if paid before or after the date fixed for payment; or

    (d) with exchange or less exchange, whether at a fixed rate or at the current rate; or

    (e) with costs of collection or an attorney's fee or both upon default.

(2) Nothing in this section shall validate any term which is otherwise illegal.

§ 3—107. **Money.**

(1) An instrument is payable in money if the medium of exchange in which it is payable is money at the time the instrument is made. An instrument payable in "currency" or "current funds" is payable in money.

(2) A promise to order to pay a sum stated in a foreign currency is for a sum certain in money and, unless a different medium of payment is specified in the instrument, may be satisfied by payment of that number of dollars which the stated foreign currency will purchase at the buying sight rate for that currency on the day on which the instrument is payable or, if payable on demand, on the day of demand. If such an instrument specifies a foreign currency as the medium of payment the instrument is payable in that currency.

§ 3—108. **Payable on Demand.**

Instruments payable on demand include those payable at sight or on presentation and those in which no time for payment is stated.

§ 3—109. **Definite Time.**

(1) An instrument is payable at a definite time if by its terms it is payable

    (a) on or before a stated date or at a fixed period after a stated date; or

    (b) at a fixed period after sight; or

    (c) at a definite time subject to any acceleration; or

    (d) at a definite time subject to extension at the option of the holder, or to extension to a further definite time at the option of the maker or acceptor or automatically upon or after a specified act or event.

(2) An instrument which by its terms is otherwise payable only upon an act or event uncertain as to time of occurrence is not payable at a definite time even though the act or event has occurred.

§ 3—110. **Payable to Order.**

(1) An instrument is payable to order when by its terms it is payable to the order or assigns of any person therein specified with reasonable certainty, or to him or his

order, or when it is conspicuously designated on its face as "exchange" or the like and names a payee. It may be payable to the order of

(a) the maker or drawer; or

(b) the drawee; or

(c) a payee who is not maker, drawer or drawee; or

(d) two or more payees together or in the alternative; or

(e) an estate, trust or fund, in which case it is payable to the order of the representative of such estate, trust or fund or his successors; or

(f) an office, or an officer by his title as such in which case it is payable to the principal but the incumbent of the office or his successors may act as if he or they were the holder; or

(g) a partnership or unincorporated association, in which case it is payable to the partnership or association and may be indorsed or transferred by any person thereto authorized.

(2) An instrument not payable to order is not made so payable by such words as "payable upon return of this instrument properly indorsed."

(3) An instrument made payable both to order and to bearer is payable to order unless the bearer words are handwritten or typewritten.

§ 3—111. Payable to Bearer.

An instrument is payable to bearer when by its terms it is payable to

(a) bearer or the order of bearer; or

(b) a specified person or bearer; or

(c) "cash" or the order of "cash", or any other indication which does not purport to designate a specific payee.

§ 3—112. Terms and Omissions Not Affecting Negotiability.

(1) The negotiability of an instrument is not affected by

(a) the omission of a statement of any consideration or of the place where the instrument is drawn or payable; or

(b) a statement that collateral has been given to secure obligations either on the instrument or otherwise of an obligor on the instrument or that in case of default on those obligations the holder may realize on or dispose of the collateral; or

(c) a promise or power to maintain or protect collateral or to give additional collateral; or

(d) a term authorizing a confession of judgment on the instrument if it is not paid when due; or

(e) a term purporting to waive the benefit of any law intended for the advantage or protection of any obligor; or

(f) a term in a draft providing that the payee by indorsing or cashing it acknowledges full satisfaction of an obligation of the drawer; or

(g) a statement in a draft drawn in a set of parts (Section 3—801) to the effect that the order is effective only if no other part has been honored.

(2) Nothing in this section shall validate any term which is otherwise illegal.

§ 3—113. Seal.

An instrument otherwise negotiable is within this Article even though it is under a seal.

§ 3—114. Date, Antedating, Postdating.

(1) The negotiability of an instrument is not affected by the fact that it is undated, antedated or postdated.

(2) Where an instrument is antedated or postdated the time when it is payable is determined by the stated date if the instrument is payable on demand or at a fixed period after date.

(3) Where the instrument or any signature thereon is dated, the date is presumed to be correct.

§ 3—115. Incomplete Instruments.

(1) When a paper whose contents at the time of signing show that it is intended to become an instrument is signed while still incomplete in any necessary respect it cannot be enforced until completed, but when it is completed in accordance with authority given it is effective as completed.

(2) If the completion is unauthorized the rules as to material alteration apply (Section 3—407), even though the paper was not delivered by the maker or drawer; but the burden of establishing that any completion is unauthorized is on the party so asserting.

§ 3—116. Instruments Payable to Two or More Persons.

An instrument payable to the order of two or more persons

(a) if in the alternative is payable to any one of them and may be negotiated, discharged or enforced by any of them who has possession of it;

(b) if not in the alternative is payable to all of them and may be negotiated, discharged or enforced only by all of them.

§ 3—117. **Instruments Payable With Words of Description.**

An instrument made payable to a named person with the addition of words describing him

(a) as agent or officer of a specified person is payable to his principal but the agent or officer may act as if he were the holder;

(b) as any other fiduciary for a specified person or purpose is payable to the payee and may be negotiated, discharged or enforced by him;

(c) in any other manner is payable to the payee unconditionally and the additional words are without effect on subsequent parties.

§ 3—118. **Ambiguous Terms and Rules of Construction.**

The following rules apply to every instrument:

(a) Where there is doubt whether the instrument is a draft or a note the holder may treat it as either. A draft drawn on the drawer is effective as a note.

(b) Handwritten terms control typewritten and printed terms, and typewritten control printed.

(c) Words control figures except that if the words are ambiguous figures control.

(d) Unless otherwise specified a provision for interest means interest at the judgment rate at the place of payment from the date of the instrument, or if it is undated from the date of issue.

(e) Unless the instrument otherwise specifies two or more persons who sign as maker, acceptor or drawer or indorser and as a part of the same transaction are jointly and severally liable even though the instrument contains such words as "I promise to pay."

(f) Unless otherwise specified consent to extension authorizes a single extension for not longer than the original period. A consent to extension, expressed in the instrument, is binding on secondary parties and accommodation makers. A holder may not exercise his option to extend an instrument over the objection of a maker or acceptor or other party who in accordance with Section 3—604 tenders full payment when the instrument is due.

§ 3—119. **Other Writings Affecting Instrument.**

(1) As between the obligor and his immediate obligee or any transferee the terms of an instrument may be modified or affected by any other written agreement executed as a part of the same transaction, except that a holder in due course is not affected by any limitation of his rights arising out of the separate written agreement if he had no notice of the limitation when he took the instrument.

(2) A separate agreement does not affect the negotiability of an instrument.

§ 3—120. **Instruments "Payable Through" Bank.**

An instrument which states that it is "payable through" a bank or the like designates that bank as a collecting bank to make presentment but does not of itself authorize the bank to pay the instrument.

§ 3—121. **Instruments Payable at Bank.**

Note: If this Act is introduced in the Congress of the United States this section should be omitted.
(States to select either alternative)

Alternative A—

A note or acceptance which states that it is payable at a bank is the equivalent of a draft drawn on the bank payable when it falls due out of any funds of the maker or acceptor in current account or otherwise available for such payment.

Alternative B—

A note or acceptance which states that it is payable at a bank is not of itself an order or authorization to the bank to pay it.

§ 3—122. **Accrual of Cause of Action.**

(1) A cause of action against a maker or an acceptor accrues

(a) in the case of a time instrument on the day after maturity;

(b) in the case of a demand instrument upon its date or, if no date is stated, on the date of issue.

(2) A cause of action against the obligor of a demand or time certificate of deposit accrues upon demand, but demand on a time certificate may not be made until on or after the date of maturity.

(3) A cause of action against a drawer of a draft or an indorser of any instrument accrues upon demand following dishonor of the instrument. Notice of dishonor is a demand.

(4) Unless an instrument provides otherwise, interest runs at the rate provided by law for a judgment

(a) in the case of a maker, acceptor or other primary obligor of a demand instrument, from the date of demand;

(b) in all other cases from the date of accrual of the cause of action.

Part 2 Transfer and Negotiation

§ 3—201. Transfer: Right to Indorsement.

(1) Transfer of an instrument vests in the transferee such rights as the transferor has therein, except that a transferee who has himself been a party to any fraud or illegality affecting the instrument or who as a prior holder had notice of a defense or claim against it cannot improve his position by taking from a later holder in due course.

(2) A transfer of a security interest in an instrument vets the foregoing rights in the transferee to the extent of the interest transferred.

(3) Unless otherwise agreed any transfer for value of an instrument not then payable to bearer gives the transferee the specifically enforceable right to have the unqualified indorsement of the transferor. Negotiation takes effect only when the indorsement is made and until that time there is no presumption that the transferee is the owner.

§ 3—202. Negotiation.

(1) Negotiation is the transfer of an instrument in such form that the transferee becomes a holder. If the instrument is payable to order it is negotiated by delivery with any necessary indorsement; if payable to bearer it is negotiated by delivery.

(2) An indorsement must be written by or on behalf of the holder and on the instrument or on a paper so firmly affixed thereto as to become a part thereof.

(3) An indorsement is effective for negotiation only when it conveys the entire instrument or any unpaid residue. If it purports to be of less it operates only as a partial assignment.

(4) Words of assignment, condition, waiver, guaranty, limitation or disclaimer of liability and the like accompanying an indorsement do not affect its character as an indorsement.

§ 3—203. Wrong or Misspelled Name.

Where an instrument is made payable to a person under a misspelled name or one other than his own he may indorse in that name or his own or both; but signature in both names may be required by a person paying or giving value for the instrument.

§ 3—204. Special Indorsement; Blank Indorsement.

(1) A special indorsement specifies the person to whom or to whose order it makes the instrument payable.

Any instrument specially indorsed becomes payable to the order of the special indorsee and may be further negotiated only by his indorsement.

(2) An indorsement in blank specifies no particular indorsee and may consist of a mere signature. An instrument payable to order and indorsed in blank becomes payable to bearer and may be negotiated by delivery alone until specially indorsed.

(3) The holder may convert a blank indorsement into a special indorsement by writing over the signature of the indorser in blank any contract consistent with the character of the indorsement.

§ 3—205. Restrictive Indorsements.

An indorsement is restrictive which either

(a) is conditional; or

(b) purports to prohibit further transfer of the instrument; or

(c) includes the words "for collection", "for deposit", "pay any bank", or like terms signifying a purpose of deposit or collection; or

(d) otherwise states that it is for the benefit or use of the indorser or of another person.

§ 3—206. Effect of Restrictive Indorsement.

(1) No restrictive indorsement prevents further transfer or negotiation of the instrument.

(2) An intermediary bank, or a payor bank which is not the depositary bank, is neither given notice nor otherwise affected by a restrictive indorsement of any person except the bank's immediate transferor or the person presenting for payment.

(3) Except for an intermediary bank, any transferee under an indorsement which is conditional or includes the words "for collection", "for deposit", "pay any bank", or like terms (subparagraphs (a) and (c) of Section 3—205) must pay or apply any value given by him for or on the security of the instrument consistently with the indorsement and to the extent that he does so he becomes a holder for value. In addition such transferee is a holder in due course if he otherwise complies with the requirements of Section 3—302 on what constitutes a holder in due course.

(4) The first taker under an indorsement for the benefit of the indorser or another person (subparagraph (d) of Section 3—205) must pay or apply any value given by him for or on the security of the instrument consistently with the indorsement and to the extent that he does so he becomes a holder for value. In addition such taker is a holder in due course if he otherwise complies with the requirements of Section 3—

302 on what constitutes a holder in due course. A later holder for value is neither given notice nor otherwise affected by such restrictive indorsement unless he has knowledge that a fiduciary or other person has negotiated the instrument in any transaction for his own benefit or otherwise in breach of duty (subsection (2) of Section 3—304).

§ 3—207. Negotiation Effective Although It May Be Rescinded.

(1) Negotiation is effective to transfer the instrument although the negotiation is

(a) made by an infant, a corporation exceeding its powers, or any other person without capacity; or

(b) obtained by fraud, duress or mistake of any kind; or

(c) part of an illegal transaction; or

(d) made in breach of duty.

(2) Except as against a subsequent holder in due course such negotiation is in an appropriate case subject to rescission, the declaration of a constructive trust or any other remedy permitted by law.

§ 3—208. Reacquisition.

Where an instrument is returned to or reacquired by a prior party he may cancel any indorsement which is not necessary to his title and reissue or further negotiate the instrument, but any intervening party is discharged as against the reacquiring party and subsequent holders not in due course and if his indorsement has been cancelled is discharged as against subsequent holders in due course as well.

Part 3 Rights of a Holder

§ 3—301. Rights of a Holder.

The holder of an instrument whether or not he is the owner may transfer or negotiate it and, except as otherwise provided in Section 3—603 on payment or satisfaction, discharge it or enforce payment in his own name.

§ 3—302. Holder in Due Course

(1) A holder in due course is a holder who takes the instrument

(a) for value; and

(b) in good faith; and

(c) without notice that it is overdue or has been dishonored or of any defense against or claim to it on the part of any person.

(2) A payee may be a holder in due course.

(3) A holder does not become a holder in due course of an instrument:

(a) by purchase of it at judicial sale or by taking it under legal process; or

(b) by acquiring it in taking over an estate; or

(c) by purchasing it as part of a bulk transaction not in regular course of business of the transferor.

(4) A purchaser of a limited interest can be a holder in due course only to the extent of the interest purchased.

§ 3—303. Taking for Value.

A holder takes the instrument for value

(a) to the extent that the agreed consideration has been performed or that he acquires a security interest in or a lien on the instrument otherwise than by legal process; or

(b) when he takes the instrument in payment of or as security for an antecedent claim against any person whether or not the claim is due; or

(c) when he gives a negotiable instrument for it or makes an irrevocable commitment to a third person.

§ 3—304. Notice to Purchaser.

(1) The purchaser has notice of a claim or defense if

(a) the instrument is so incomplete, bears such visible evidence of forgery or alteration, or is otherwise so irregular as to call into question its validity, terms or ownership or to create an ambiguity as to the party to pay; or

(b) the purchaser has notice that the obligation of any party is voidable in whole or in part, or that all parties have been discharged.

(2) The purchaser has notice of a claim against the instrument when he has knowledge that a fiduciary has negotiated the instrument in payment of or as security for his own debt or in any transaction for his own benefit or otherwise in breach of duty.

(3) The purchaser has notice that an instrument is overdue if he has reason to know

(a) that any part of the principal amount is overdue or that there is an uncured default in payment of another instrument of the same series; or

(b) that acceleration of the instrument has been made; or

(c) that he is taking a demand instrument after demand has been made or more than a reasonable length of time after its issue. A reasonable time for a check drawn and payable within the states and territories of the United States and the District of Columbia is presumed to be thirty days.

(4) Knowledge of the following facts does not of itself give the purchaser notice of a defense or claim

(a) that the instrument is antedated or postdated;

(b) that it was issued or negotiated in return for an executory promise or accompanied by a separate agreement, unless the purchaser has notice that a defense or claim has arisen from the terms thereof;

(c) that any party has signed for accommodation;

(d) that an incomplete instrument has been completed, unless the purchaser has notice of any improper completion;

(e) that any person negotiating the instrument is or was a fiduciary;

(f) that there has been default in payment of interest on the instrument or in payment of any other instrument, except one of the same series.

(5) The filing or recording of a document does not of itself constitute notice within the provisions of this Article to a person who would otherwise be a holder in due course.

(6) To be effective notice must be received at such time and in such manner as to give a reasonable opportunity to act on it.

§ 3—305. **Rights of a Holder in Due Course.**

To the extent that a holder is a holder in due course he takes the instrument free from

(1) all claims to it on the part of any person; and

(2) all defenses of any party to the instrument with whom the holder has not dealt except

(a) infancy, to the extent that it is a defense to a simple contract; and

(b) such other incapacity, or duress, or illegality of the transaction, as renders the obligation of the party a nullity; and

(c) such misrepresentation as has induced the party to sign the instrument with neither knowledge nor reasonable opportunity to obtain knowledge of its character or its essential terms; and

(d) discharge in insolvency proceedings; and

(e) any other discharge of which the holder has notice when he takes the instrument.

§ 3—306. **Rights of One Not Holder in Due Course.**

Unless he has the rights of a holder in due course any person takes the instrument subject to

(a) all valid claims to it on the part of any person; and

(b) all defenses of any party which would be available in an action on a simple contract; and

(c) the defenses of want or failure of consideration, nonperformance of any condition precedent, nondelivery, or delivery for a special purpose (Section 3—408); and

(d) the defense that he or a person through whom he holds the instrument acquired it by theft, or that payment or satisfaction to such holder would be inconsistent with the terms of a restrictive indorsement. The claim of any third person to the instrument is not otherwise available as a defense to any party liable thereon unless the third person himself defends the action for such party.

§ 3—307. **Burden of Establishing Signatures, Defenses and Due Course.**

(1) Unless specifically denied in the pleadings each signature on an instrument is admitted. When the effectiveness of a signature is put in issue

(a) the burden of establishing it is on the party claiming under the signature; but

(b) the signature is presumed to be genuine or authorized except where the action is to enforce the obligation of a purported signer who has died or become incompetent before proof is required.

(2) When signatures are admitted or established, production of the instrument entitles a holder to recover on it unless the defendant establishes a defense.

(3) After it is shown that a defense exists a person claiming the rights of a holder in due course has the burden of establishing that he or some person under whom he claims is in all respects a holder in due course.

Part 4 Liability of Parties

§ 3—401. **Signature.**

(1) No person is liable on an instrument unless his signature appears thereon.

(2) A signature is made by use of any name, including any trade or assumed name, upon an instrument, or by any word or mark used in lieu of a written signature.

§ 3—402. **Signature in Ambiguous Capacity.**

Unless the instrument clearly indicates that a signature is made in some other capacity it is an indorsement.

§ 3—403. **Signature by Authorized Representative.**

(1) A signature may be made by an agent or other representative, and his authority to make it may be established as in other cases of representation. No particular form of appointment is necessary to establish such authority.

(2) An authorized representative who signs his own name to an instrument

(a) is personally obligated if the instrument neither names the person represented nor shows that the representative signed in a representative capacity;

(b) except as otherwise established between the immediate parties, is personally obligated if the instrument names the person represented but does not show that the representative signed in a representative capacity, or if the instrument does not name the person represented but does show that the representative signed in a representative capacity.

(3) Except as otherwise established the name of an organization preceded or followed by the name and office of an authorized individual is a signature made in a representative capacity.

§ 3—404. **Unauthorized Signatures.**

(1) Any unauthorized signature is wholly inoperative as that of the person whose name is signed unless he ratifies it or is precluded from denying it; but it operates as the signature of the unauthorized signer in favor of any person who in good faith pays the instrument or takes it for value.

(2) Any unauthorized signature may be ratified for all purposes of this Article. Such ratification does not of itself affect any rights of the person ratifying against the actual signer.

§ 3—405. **Impostors; Signature in Name of Payee.**

(1) An indorsement by any person in the name of a named payee is effective if

(a) an impostor by use of the mails or otherwise has induced the maker or drawer to issue the instrument to him or his confederate in the name of the payee; or

(b) a person signing as or on behalf of a maker or drawer intends the payee to have no interest in the instrument; or

(c) an agent or employee of the maker or drawer has supplied him with the name of the payee intending the latter to have no such interest.

(2) Nothing in this section shall affect the criminal or civil liability of the person so indorsing.

§ 3—406. **Negligence Contributing to Alteration or Unauthorized Signature.**

Any person who by his negligence substantially contributes to a material alteration of the instrument or to the making of an unauthorized signature is precluded from asserting the alteration or lack of authority against a holder in due course or against a drawee or other payor who pays the instrument in good faith and in accordance with the reasonable commercial standards of the drawee's or payor's business.

§ 3—407. **Alteration.**

(1) Any alteration of an instrument is material which changes the contract of any party thereto in any respect, including any such change in

(a) the number or relations of the parties; or

(b) an incomplete instrument, by completing it otherwise than as authorized; or

(c) the writing as signed, by adding to it or by removing any part of it.

(2) As against any person other than a subsequent holder in due course

(a) alteration by the holder which is both fraudulent and material discharges any party whose contract is thereby changed unless that party assents or is precluded from asserting the defense;

(b) no other alteration discharges any party and the instrument may be enforced according to its original tenor, or as to incomplete instruments according to the authority given.

(3) A subsequent holder in due course may in all cases enforce the instrument according to its original tenor, and when an incomplete instrument has been completed, he may enforce it as completed.

§ 3—408. **Consideration.**

Want or failure of consideration is a defense as against any person not having the rights of a holder in due course (Section 3—305), except that no consideration is necessary for an instrument or obligation thereon given in payment of or as security for an antecedent obligation of any kind. Nothing in this section shall be taken to displace any statute outside this Act under which a promise is enforceable notwithstanding lack or failure of consideration. Partial failure of consideration is a defense pro tanto whether or not the failure is in an ascertained or liquidated amount.

§ 3—409. **Draft Not an Assignment.**

(1) A check or other draft does not of itself operate as an assignment of any funds in the hands of the drawee available for its payment, and the drawee is not liable on the instrument until he accepts it.

(2) Nothing in this section shall affect any liability in contract, tort or otherwise arising from any letter of credit or other obligation or representation which is not an acceptance.

§ 3—410. **Definition and Operation of Acceptance.**

(1) Acceptance is the drawee's signed engagement to honor the draft as presented. It must be written on the draft, and may consist of his signature alone. It becomes operative when completed by delivery or notification.

(2) A draft may be accepted although it has not been signed by the drawer or is otherwise incomplete or is overdue or has been dishonored.

(3) Where the draft is payable at a fixed period after sight and the acceptor fails to date his acceptance the holder may complete it by supplying a date in good faith.

§ 3—411. **Certification of a Check.**

(1) Certification of a check is acceptance. Where a holder procures certification the drawer and all prior indorsers are discharged.

(2) Unless otherwise agreed a bank has no obligation to certify a check.

(3) A bank may certify a check before returning it for lack of proper indorsement. If it does so the drawer is discharged.

§ 3—412. **Acceptance Varying Draft.**

(1) Where the drawee's proffered acceptance in any manner varies the draft as presented the holder may refuse the acceptance and treat the draft as dishonored in which case the drawee is entitled to have his acceptance cancelled.

(2) The terms of the draft are not varied by an acceptance to pay at any particular bank or place in the United States, unless the acceptance states that the draft is to be paid only at such bank or place.

(3) Where the holder assents to an acceptance varying the terms of the draft each drawer and indorser who does not affirmatively assent is discharged.

§ 3—413. **Contract of Maker, Drawer and Acceptor.**

(1) The maker or acceptor engages that he will pay the instrument according to its tenor at the time of his

engagement or as completed pursuant to Section 3—115 on incomplete instruments.

(2) The drawer engages that upon dishonor of the draft and any necessary notice of dishonor or protest he will pay the amount of the draft to the holder or to any indorser who takes it up. The drawer may disclaim this liability by drawing without recourse.

(3) By making, drawing or accepting the party admits as against all subsequent parties including the drawee the existence of the payee and his then capacity to indorse.

§ 3—414. **Contract of Indorser; Order of Liability.**

(1) Unless the indorsement otherwise specifies (as by such words as "without recourse") every indorser engages that upon dishonor and any necessary notice of dishonor and protest he will pay the instrument according to its tenor at the time of his indorsement to the holder or to any subsequent indorser who takes it up, even though the indorser who takes it up was not obligated to do so.

(2) Unless they otherwise agree indorsers are liable to one another in the order in which they indorse, which is presumed to be the order in which their signatures appear on the instrument.

§ 3—415. **Contract of Accommodation Party.**

(1) An accommodation party is one who signs the instrument in any capacity for the purpose of lending his name to another party to it.

(2) When the instrument has been taken for value before it is due the accommodation party is liable in the capacity in which he has signed even though the taker knows of the accommodation.

(3) As against a holder in due course and without notice of the accommodation oral proof of the accommodation is not admissible to give the accommodation party the benefit of discharges dependent on his character as such. In other cases the accommodation character may be shown by oral proof.

(4) An indorsement which shows that it is not in the chain of title is notice of its accommodation character.

(5) An accommodation party is not liable to the party accommodated, and if he pays the instrument has a right of recourse on the instrument against such party.

§ 3—416. **Contract of Guarantor.**

(1) "Payment guaranteed" or equivalent words added to a signature mean that the signer engages that if the instrument is not paid when due he will pay it according to its tenor without resort by the holder to any other party.

(2) "Collection guaranteed" or equivalent words added to a signature mean that the signer engages that if the instrument is not paid when due he will pay it according to its tenor, but only after the holder has reduced his claim against the maker or acceptor to judgment and execution has been returned unsatisfied, or after the maker or acceptor has become insolvent or it is otherwise apparent that it is useless to proceed against him.

(3) Words of guaranty which do not otherwise specify guarantee payment.

(4) No words of guaranty added to the signature of a sole maker or acceptor affect his liability on the instrument. Such words added to the signature of one of two or more makers or acceptors create a presumption that the signature is for the accommodation of the others.

(5) When words of guaranty are used presentment, notice of dishonor and protest are not necessary to charge the user.

(6) Any guaranty written on the instrument is enforcible notwithstanding any statute of frauds.

§ 3—417. **Warranties on Presentment and Transfer.**

(1) Any person who obtains payment or acceptance and any prior transferor warrants to a person who in good faith pays or accepts that

(a) he has a good title to the instrument or is authorized to obtain payment or acceptance on behalf of one who has a good title; and

(b) he has no knowledge that the signature of the maker or drawer is unauthorized, except that this warranty is not given by a holder in due course acting in good faith

(i) to a maker with respect to the maker's own signature; or

(ii) to a drawer with respect to the drawer's own signature, whether or not the drawer is also the drawee; or

(iii) to an acceptor of a draft if the holder in due course took the draft after the acceptance or obtained the acceptance without knowledge that the drawer's signature was unauthorized; and

(c) the instrument has not been materially altered, except that this warranty is not given by a holder in due course acting in good faith

(i) to the maker of a note; or

(ii) to the drawer of a draft whether or not the drawer is also the drawee; or

(iii) to the acceptor of a draft with respect to an alteration made prior to the acceptance if the holder in due course took the draft after the acceptance, even though the acceptance provided "payable as originally drawn" or equivalent terms; or

(iv) to the acceptor of a draft with respect to an alteration made after the acceptance.

(2) Any person who transfers an instrument and receives consideration warrants to his transferee and if the transfer is by indorsement to any subsequent holder who takes the instrument in good faith that

(a) he has a good title to the instrument or is authorized to obtain payment or acceptance on behalf of one who has a good title and the transfer is otherwise rightful; and

(b) all signatures are genuine or authorized; and

(c) the instrument has not been materially altered; and

(d) no defense of any party is good against him; and

(e) he has no knowledge of any insolvency proceeding instituted with respect to the maker or acceptor or the drawer of an unaccepted instrument.

(3) By transferring "without recourse" the transferor limits the obligation stated in subsection (2) (d) to a warranty that he has no knowledge of such a defense.

(4) A selling agent or broker who does not disclose the fact that he is acting only as such gives the warranties provided in this section, but if he makes such disclosure warrants only his good faith and authority.

§ 3—418. **Finality of Payment or Acceptance.**

Except for recovery of bank payments as provided in the Article on Bank Deposits and Collections (Article 4) and except for liability for breach of warranty on presentment under the preceding section, payment or acceptance of any instrument is final in favor of a holder in due course, or a person who has in good faith changed his position in reliance on the payment.

§ 3—419. **Conversion of Instrument; Innocent Representative.**

(1) An instrument is converted when

(a) a drawee to whom it is delivered for acceptance refuses to return it on demand; or

(b) any person to whom it is delivered for payment refuses on demand either to pay or to return it; or

(c) it is paid on a forged indorsement.

(2) In an action against a drawee under subsection (1) the measure of the drawee's liability is the face amount of the instrument. In any other action under subsection (1) the measure of liability is presumed to be the face amount of the instrument.

(3) Subject to the provisions of this Act concerning restrictive indorsements a representative, including a depositary or collecting bank, who has in good faith and in accordance with the reasonable commercial standards applicable to the business of such representative dealt with an instrument or its proceeds on behalf of one who was not the true owner is not liable in conversion or otherwise to the true owner beyond the amount of any proceeds remaining in his hands.

(4) An intermediary bank or payor bank which is not a depositary bank is not liable in conversion solely by reason of the fact that proceeds of an item indorsed restrictively (Sections 3—205 and 3—206) are not paid or applied consistently with the restrictive indorsement of an indorser other than its immediate transferor.

Part 5 Presentment, Notice of Dishonor and Protest

§ 3—501. **When Presentment, Notice of Dishonor, and Protest Necessary or Permissible.**

(1) Unless excused (Section 3—511) presentment is necessary to charge secondary parties as follows:

(a) presentment for acceptance is necessary to charge the drawer and indorsers of a draft where the draft so provides, or is payable elsewhere than at the residence or place of business of the drawee, or its date of payment depends upon such presentment. The holder may at his option present for acceptance any other draft payable at a stated date;

(b) presentment for payment is necessary to charge any indorser;

(c) in the case of any drawer, the acceptor of a draft payable at a bank or the maker of a note payable at a bank, presentment for payment is necessary, but failure to make presentment discharges such drawer, acceptor or maker only as stated in Section 3—502(1)(b).

(2) Unless excused (Section 3—511)

(a) notice of any dishonor is necessary to charge any indorser;

(b) in the case of any drawer, the acceptor of a draft payable at a bank or the maker of a note payable at a bank, notice of any dishonor is necessary,

but failure to give such notice discharges such drawer, acceptor or maker only as stated in Section 3—502(1)(b).

(3) Unless excused (Section 3—511) protest of any dishonor is necessary to charge the drawer and indorsers of any draft which on its face appears to be drawn or payable outside of the states, territories, dependencies, and possessions of the United States, the District of Columbia and the Commonwealth of Puerto Rico. The holder may at his option make protest of any dishonor of any other instrument and in the case of a foreign draft may on insolvency of the acceptor before maturity make protest for better security.

(4) Notwithstanding any provision of this section, neither presentment nor notice of dishonor nor protest is necessary to charge an indorser who has indorsed an instrument after maturity.

§ 3—502. **Unexcused Delay; Discharge.**

(1) Where without excuse any necessary presentment or notice of dishonor is delayed beyond the time when it is due

(a) any indorser is discharged; and

(b) any drawer or the acceptor of a draft payable at a bank or the maker of a note payable at a bank who because the drawee or payor bank becomes insolvent during the delay is deprived of funds maintained with the drawee or payor bank to cover the instrument may discharge his liability by written assignment to the holder of his rights against the drawee or payor bank in respect of such funds, but such drawer, acceptor or maker is not otherwise discharged.

(2) Where without excuse a necessary protest is delayed beyond the time when it is due any drawer or indorser is discharged.

§ 3—503. **Time of Presentment.**

(1) Unless a different time is expressed in the instrument the time for any presentment is determined as follows:

(a) where an instrument is payable at or a fixed period after a stated date any presentment for acceptance must be made on or before the date it is payable;

(b) where an instrument is payable after sight it must either be presented for acceptance or negotiated within a reasonable time after date or issue whichever is later;

(c) where an instrument shows the date on which

it is payable presentment for payment is due on that date;

(d) where an instrument is accelerated presentment for payment is due within a reasonable time after the acceleration;

(e) with respect to the liability of any secondary party presentment for acceptance or payment of any other instrument is due within a reasonable time after such party becomes liable thereon.

(2) A reasonable time for presentment is determined by the nature of the instrument, any usage of banking or trade and the facts of the particular case. In the case of an uncertified check which is drawn and payable within the United States and which is not a draft drawn by a bank the following are presumed to be reasonable periods within which to present for payment or to initiate bank collection:

(a) with respect to the liability of the drawer, thirty days after date or issue whichever is later; and

(b) with respect to the liability of an indorser, seven days after his indorsement.

(3) Where any presentment is due on a day which is not a full business day for either the person making presentment or the party to pay or accept, presentment is due on the next following day which is a full business day for both parties.

(4) Presentment to be sufficient must be made at a reasonable hour, and if at a bank during its banking day.

§ 3—504. **How Presentment Made.**

(1) Presentment is a demand for acceptance or payment made upon the maker, acceptor, drawee or other payor by or on behalf of the holder.

(2) Presentment may be made

(a) by mail, in which event the time of presentment is determined by the time of receipt of the mail; or

(b) through a clearing house; or

(c) at the place of acceptance or payment specified in the instrument or if there be none at the place of business or residence of the party to accept or pay. If neither the party to accept or pay nor anyone authorized to act for him is present or accessible at such place presentment is excused.

(3) It may be made

(a) to any one of two or more makers, acceptors, drawees or other payors; or

(b) to any person who has authority to make or refuse the acceptance or payment.

(4) A draft accepted or a note made payable at a bank in the United States must be presented at such bank.

(5) In the cases described in Section 4—210 presentment may be made in the manner and with the result stated in that section.

§ 3—505. **Rights of Party to Whom Presentment Is Made.**

(1) The party to whom presentment is made may without dishonor require

(a) exhibition of the instrument; and

(b) reasonable identification of the person making presentment and evidence of his authority to make it if made for another; and

(c) that the instrument be produced for acceptance or payment at a place specified in it, or if there be none at any place reasonable in the circumstances; and

(d) a signed receipt on the instrument for any partial or full payment and its surrender upon full payment.

(2) Failure to comply with any such requirement invalidates the presentment but the person presenting has a reasonable time in which to comply and the time for acceptance or payment runs from the time of compliance.

§ 3—506. **Time Allowed for Acceptance or Payment.**

(1) Acceptance may be deferred without dishonor until the close of the next business day following presentment. The holder may also in a good faith effort to obtain acceptance and without either dishonor of the instrument or discharge of secondary parties allow postponement of acceptance for an additional business day.

(2) Except as a longer time is allowed in the case of documentary drafts drawn under a letter of credit, and unless an earlier time is agreed to by the party to pay, payment of an instrument may be deferred without dishonor pending reasonable examination to determine whether it is properly payable, but payment must be made in any event before the close of business on the day of presentment.

§ 3—507. **Dishonor; Holder's Right of Recourse; Term Allowing Re-Presentment.**

(1) An instrument is dishonored when

(a) a necessary or optional presentment is duly made and due acceptance or payment is refused or cannot be obtained within the prescribed time or in case of bank collections the instrument is seasonably returned by the midnight deadline (Section 4—301); or

(b) presentment is excused and the instrument is not duly accepted or paid.

(2) Subject to any necessary notice of dishonor and protest, the holder has upon dishonor an immediate right of recourse against the drawers and indorsers.

(3) Return of an instrument for lack of proper indorsement is not dishonor.

(4) A term in a draft or an indorsement thereof allowing a stated time for re-presentment in the event of any dishonor of the draft by nonacceptance if a time draft or by nonpayment if a sight draft gives the holder as against any secondary party bound by the term an option to waive the dishonor without affecting the liability of the secondary party and he may present again up to the end of the stated time.

§ 3—508. **Notice of Dishonor.**

(1) Notice of dishonor may be given to any person who may be liable on the instrument by or on behalf of the holder or any party who has himself received notice, or any other party who can be compelled to pay the instrument. In addition an agent or bank in whose hands the instrument is dishonored may give notice to his principal or customer or to another agent or bank from which the instrument was received.

(2) Any necessary notice must be given by a bank before its midnight deadline and by any other person before midnight of the third business day after dishonor or receipt of notice of dishonor.

(3) Notice may be given in any reasonable manner. It may be oral or written and in any terms which identify the instrument and state that it has been dishonored. A misdescription which does not mislead the party notified does not vitiate the notice. Sending the instrument bearing a stamp, ticket or writing stating that acceptance or payment has been refused or sending a notice of debit with respect to the instrument is sufficient.

(4) Written notice is given when sent although it is not received.

(5) Notice to one partner is notice to each although the firm has been dissolved.

(6) When any party is in insolvency proceedings instituted after the issue of the instrument notice may be given either to the party or to the representative of his estate.

(7) When any party is dead or incompetent notice may be sent to his last known address or given to his personal representative.

(8) Notice operates for the benefit of all parties who have rights on the instrument against the party notified.

§ 3—509. **Protest; Noting for Protest.**

(1) A protest is a certificate of dishonor made under the hand and seal of a United States consul or vice consul or a notary public or other person authorized to certify dishonor by the law of the place where dishonor occurs. It may be made upon information satisfactory to such person.

(2) The protest must identify the instrument and certify either that due presentment has been made or the reason why it is excused and that the instrument has been dishonored by nonacceptance or nonpayment.

(3) The protest may also certify that notice of dishonor has been given to all parties or to specified parties.

(4) Subject to subsection (5) any necessary protest is due by the time that notice of dishonor is due.

(5) If, before protest is due, an instrument has been noted for protest by the officer to make protest, the protest may be made at any time thereafter as of the date of the noting.

§ 3—510. **Evidence of Dishonor and Notice of Dishonor.**

The following are admissible as evidence and create a presumption of dishonor and of any notice of dishonor therein shown:

(a) a document regular in form as provided in the preceding section which purports to be a protest;

(b) the purported stamp or writing of the drawee, payor bank or presenting bank on the instrument or accompanying it stating that acceptance or payment has been refused for reasons conconsistent with dishonor;

(c) any book or record of the drawee, payor bank, or any collecting bank kept in the usual course of business which shows dishonor, even though there is no evidence of who made the entry.

§ 3—511. **Waived or Excused Presentment, Protest or Notice of Dishonor or Delay Therein.**

(1) Delay in presentment, protest or notice of dishonor is excused when the party is without notice that

it is due or when the delay is caused by circumstances beyond his control and he exercises reasonable diligence after the cause of the delay ceases to operate.

(2) Presentment or notice or protest as the case may be is entirely excused when

(a) the party to be charged has waived it expressly or by implication either before or after it is due; or

(b) such party has himself dishonored the instrument or has countermanded payment or otherwise has no reason to expect or right to require that the instrument be accepted or paid; or

(c) by reasonable diligence the presentment or protest cannot be made or the notice given.

(3) Presentment is also entirely excused when

(a) the maker, acceptor or drawee of any instrument except a documentary draft is dead or in insolvency proceedings instituted after the issue of the instrument; or

(b) acceptance or payment is refused but not for want of proper presentment.

(4) Where a draft has been dishonored by nonacceptance a later presentment for payment and any notice of dishonor and protest for nonpayment are excused unless in the meantime the instrument has been accepted.

(5) A waiver of protest is also a waiver of presentment and of notice of dishonor even though protest is not required.

(6) Where a waiver of presentment or notice or protest is embodied in the instrument itself it is binding upon all parties; but where it is written above the signature of an indorser it binds him only.

Part 6 Discharge

§ 3—601. **Discharge of Parties.**

(1) The extent of the discharge of any party from liability on an instrument is governed by the sections on

(a) payment or satisfaction (Section 3—603); or

(b) tender of payment (Section 3—604); or

(c) cancellation or renunciation (Section 3—605); or

(d) impairment of right of recourse or of collateral (Section 3—606); or

(e) reacquisition of the instrument by a prior party (Section 3—208); or

(f) fraudulent and material alteration (Section 3—407); or

(g) certification of a check (Section 3—411); or

(h) acceptance varying a draft (Section 3—412); or

(i) unexcused delay in presentment or notice of dishonor or protest (Section 3—502).

(2) Any party is also discharged from his liability on an instrument to another party by any other act or agreement with such party which would discharge his simple contract for the payment of money.

(3) The liability of all parties is discharged when any party who has himself no right of action or recourse on the instrument

(a) reacquires the instrument in his own right; or

(b) is discharged under any provision of this Article, except as otherwise provided with respect to discharge for impairment of recourse or of collateral (Section 3—606).

§ 3—602. **Effect of Discharge Against Holder in Due Course.**

No discharge of any party provided by this Article is effective against a subsequent holder in due course unless he has notice thereof when he takes the instrument.

§ 3—603. **Payment or Satisfaction.**

(1) The liability of any party is discharged to the extent of his payment or satisfaction to the holder even though it is made with knowledge of a claim of another person to the instrument unless prior to such payment or satisfaction the person making the claim either supplies indemnity deemed adequate by the party seeking the discharge or enjoins payment or satisfaction by order of a court of competent jurisdiction in an action in which the adverse claimant and the holder are parties. This subsection does not, however, result in the discharge of the liability

(a) of a party who in bad faith pays or satisfies a holder who acquired the instrument by theft or who (unless having the rights of a holder in due course) holds through one who so acquired it; or

(b) of a party (other than an intermediary bank or a payor bank which is not a depositary bank) who pays or satisfies the holder of an instrument which has been restrictively indorsed in a manner not consistent with the terms of such restrictive indorsement.

(2) Payment or satisfaction may be made with the consent of the holder by any person including a stranger to the instrument. Surrender of the instrument to such a person gives him the rights of a transferee (Section 3—201).

§ 3—604. **Tender of Payment.**

(1) Any party making tender of full payment to a holder when or after it is due is discharged to the extent of all subsequent liability for interest, costs and attorney's fees.

(2) The holder's refusal of such tender wholly discharges any party who has a right of recourse against the party making the tender.

(3) Where the maker or acceptor of an instrument payable otherwise than on demand is able and ready to pay at every place of payment specified in the instrument when it is due, it is equivalent to tender.

§ 3—605. **Cancellation and Renunciation.**

(1) The holder of an instrument may even without consideration discharge any party

(a) in any manner apparent on the face of the instrument or the indorsement, as by intentionally cancelling the instrument or the party's signature by destruction or multilation, or by striking out the party's signature; or

(b) by renouncing his rights by a writing signed and delivered or by surrender of the instrument to the party to be discharged.

(2) Neither cancellation nor renunciation without surrender of the instrument affects the title thereto.

§ 3—606. **Impairment of Recourse or of Collateral.**

(1) The holder discharges any party to the instrument to the extent that without such party's consent the holder

(a) without express reservation of rights releases or agrees not to sue any person against whom the party has to the knowledge of the holder a right of recourse or agrees to suspend the right to enforce against such person the instrument or collateral or otherwise discharges such person, except that failure or delay in effecting any required presentment, protest or notice of dishonor with respect to any such person does not discharge any party as to whom presentment, protest or notice of dishonor is effective or unnecessary; or

(b) unjustifiably impairs any collateral for the instrument given by or on behalf of the party or any person against whom he has a right of recourse.

(2) By express reservation of rights against a party with a right of recourse the holder preserves

(a) all his rights against such party as of the time when the instrument was originally due; and

(b) the right of the party to pay the instrument as of that time; and

(c) all rights of such party to recourse against others.

Part 7 Advice of International Sight Draft

§ 3—701. **Letter of Advice of International Sight Draft.**

(1) A "letter of advice" is a drawer's communication to the drawee that a described draft has been drawn.

(2) Unless otherwise agreed when a bank receives from another bank a letter of advice of an international sight draft the drawee bank may immediately debit the drawer's account and stop the running of interest pro tanto. Such a debit and any resulting credit to any account covering outstanding drafts leaves in the drawer full power to stop payment or otherwise dispose of the amount and creates no trust or interest in favor of the holder.

(3) Unless otherwise agreed and except where a draft is drawn under a credit issued by the drawee, the drawee of an international sight draft owes the drawer no duty to pay an unadvised draft but if it does so and the draft is genuine, may appropriately debit the drawer's account.

Part 8 Miscellaneous

§ 3—801. **Drafts in a Set.**

(1) Where a draft is drawn in a set of parts, each of which is numbered and expressed to be an order only if no other part has been honored, the whole of the parts constitutes one draft but a taker of any part may become a holder in due course of the draft.

(2) Any person who negotiates, indorses or accepts a single part of a draft drawn in a set thereby becomes liable to any holder in due course of that part as if it were the whole set, but as between different holders in due course to whom different parts have been negotiated the holder whose title first accrues has all rights to the draft and its proceeds.

(3) As against the drawee the first presented part of a draft drawn in a set is the part entitled to payment, or if a time draft to acceptance and payment. Acceptance of any subsequently presented part renders the drawee liable thereon under subsection (2). With respect both to a holder and to the drawer payment of a subsequently presented part of a draft payable at sight has the same effect as payment of a check notwithstanding an effective stop order (Section 4—407).

(4) Except as otherwise provided in this section, where any part of a draft in a set is discharged by payment or otherwise the whole draft is discharged.

§ 3—802. **Effect of Instrument on Obligation for Which It Is Given.**

(1) Unless otherwise agreed where an instrument is taken for an underlying obligation

(a) the obligation is pro tanto discharged if a bank is drawer, maker or acceptor of the instrument and there is no recourse on the instrument against the underlying obligor; and

(b) in any other case the obligation is suspended pro tanto until the instrument is due or if it is payable on demand until its presentment. If the instrument is dishonored action may be maintained on either the instrument or the obligation; discharge of the underlying obligor on the instrument also discharges him on the obligation.

(2) The taking in good faith of a check which is not postdated does not of itself so extend the time on the original obligation as to discharge a surety.

§ 3—803. **Notice to Third Party.**

Where a defendant is sued for breach of an obligation for which a third person is answerable over under this Article he may give the third person written notice of the litigation, and the person notified may then give similar notice to any other person who is answerable over to him under this Article. If the notice states that the person notified may come in and defend and that if the person notified does not do so he will in any action against him by the person giving the notice be bound by any determination of fact common to the two litigations, then unless after seasonable receipt of the notice the person notified does come in and defend he is so bound.

§ 3—804. **Lost, Destroyed or Stolen Instruments.**

The owner of an instrument which is lost, whether by destruction, theft or otherwise, may maintain an action in his own name and recover from any party liable thereon upon due proof of his ownership, the facts which prevent his production of the instrument and its terms. The court may require security indemnifying the defendant against loss by reason of further claims on the instrument.

§ 3—805. **Instruments Not Payable to Order or to Bearer.**

This Article applies to any instrument whose terms do not preclude transfer and which is otherwise negotiable within this Article but which is not payable to order or to bearer, except that there can be no holder in due course of such an instrument.

Article 4
BANK DEPOSITS AND COLLECTIONS

Part 1 General Provisions and Definitions

§ 4—101. **Short Title.**

This Article shall be known and may be cited as Uniform Commercial Code—Bank Deposits and Collections.

§ 4—102. **Applicability.**

(1) To the extent that items within this Article are also within the scope of Articles 3 and 8, they are subject to the provisions of those Articles. In the event of conflict the provisions of this Article govern those of Article 3 but the provisions of Article 8 govern those of this Article.

(2) The liability of a bank for action or non-action with respect to any item handled by it for purposes of presentment, payment or collection is governed by the law of the place where the bank is located. In the case of action or non-action by or at a branch or separate office of a bank, its liability is governed by the law of the place where the branch or separate office is located.

§ 4—103. **Variation by Agreement; Measure of Damages; Certain Action Constituting Ordinary Care.**

(1) The effect of the provisions of this Article may be varied by agreement except that no agreement can disclaim a bank's responsibility for its own lack of good faith or failure to exercise ordinary care or can limit the measure of damages for such lack or failure; but the parties may by agreement determine the standards by which such responsibility is to be measured if such standards are not manifestly unreasonable.

(2) Federal Reserve regulations and operating letters, clearing house rules, and the like, have the effect of agreements under subsection (1), whether or not specifically assented to by all parties interested in items handled.

(3) Action or non-action approved by this Article or pursuant to Federal Reserve regulations or operating letters constitutes the exercise of ordinary care and, in the absence of special instructions, action or nonac-

tion consistent with clearing house rules and the like or with a general banking usage not disapproved by this Article, prima facie constitutes the exercise of ordinary care.

(4) The specification or approval of certain procedures by this Article does not constitute disapproval of other procedures which may be reasonable under the circumstances.

(5) The measure of damages for failure to exercise ordinary care in handling an item is the amount of the item reduced by an amount which could not have been realized by the use of ordinary care, and where there is bad faith it includes other damages, if any, suffered by the party as a proximate consequence.

§ 4—104. **Definitions and Index of Definitions.**

(1) In this Article unless the context otherwise requires

(a) "Account" means any account with a bank and includes a checking, time, interest or savings account;

(b) "Afternoon" means the period of a day between noon and midnight;

(c) "Banking day" means that part of any day on which a bank is open to the public for carrying on substantially all of its banking functions;

(d) "Clearing house" means any association of banks or other payors regularly clearing items;

(e) "Customer" means any person having an account with a bank or for whom a bank has agreed to collect items and includes a bank carrying an account with another bank;

(f) "Documentary draft" means any negotiable or nonnegotiable draft with accompanying documents, securities or other papers to be delivered against honor of the draft;

(g) "Item" means any instrument for the payment of money even though it is not negotiable but does not include money;

(h) "Midnight deadline" with respect to a bank is midnight on its next banking day following the banking day on which it receives the relevant item or notice or from which the time for taking action commences to run, whichever is later;

(i) "Properly payable" includes the availability of funds for payment at the time of decision to pay or dishonor;

(j) "Settle" means to pay in cash, by clearing house settlement, in a charge or credit or by remittance,

or otherwise as instructed. A settlement may be either provisional or final;

(k) "Suspends payments" with respect to a bank means that it has been closed by order of the supervisory authorities, that a public officer has been appointed to take it over or that it ceases or refuses to make payments in the ordinary course of business.

(2) Other definitions applying to this Article and the sections in which they appear are:
"Collecting bank" Section 4—105.
"Depositary bank" Section 4—105.
"Intermediary bank" Section 4—105.
"Payor bank" Section 4—105.
"Presenting bank" Section 4—105.
"Remitting bank" Section 4—105.

(3) The following definitions in other Articles apply to this Article:
"Acceptance" Section 3—410.
"Certificate of deposit" Section 3—104.
"Certification" Section 3—411.
"Check" Section 3—104.
"Draft" Section 3—104.
"Holder in due course" Section 3—302.
"Notice of dishonor" Section 3—508.
"Presentment" Section 3—504.
"Protest" Section 3—509.
"Secondary party" Section 3—102.

(4) In addition Article 1 contains general definitions and principles of construction and interpretation applicable throughout this Article.

§ 4—105. **"Depositary Bank"; "Intermediary Bank"; "Collecting Bank"; "Payor Bank"; "Presenting Bank"; "Remitting Bank".**

In this Article unless the context otherwise requires:

(a) "Depositary bank" means the first bank to which an item is transferred for collection even though it is also the payor bank;

(b) "Payor bank" means a bank by which an item is payable as drawn or accepted;

(c) "Intermediary bank" means any bank to which an item is transferred in course of collection except the depositary or payor bank;

(d) "Collecting bank" means any bank handling the item for collection except the payor bank;

(e) "Presenting bank" means any bank presenting an item except a payor bank;

(f) "Remitting bank" means any payor or intermediary bank remitting for an item.

§ 4—106. **Separate Office of a Bank.**

A branch or separate office of a bank [maintaining its own deposit ledgers] is a separate bank for the purpose of computing the time within which and determining the place at or to which action may be taken or notices or orders shall be given under this Article and under Article 3.

Note: The brackets are to make it optional with the several states whether to require a branch to maintain its own deposit ledgers in order to be considered to be a separate bank for certain purposes under Article 4. In some states "maintaining its own deposit ledgers" is a satisfactory test. In others branch banking practices are such that this test would not be suitable.

§ 4—107. **Time of Receipt of Items.**

(1) For the purpose of allowing time to process items, prove balances and make the necessary entries on its books to determine its position for the day, a bank may fix an afternoon hour of two P.M. or later as a cut-off hour for the handling of money and items and the making of entries on its books.

(2) Any item or deposit of money received on any day after a cut-off hour so fixed or after the close of the banking day may be treated as being received at the opening of the next banking day.

§ 4—108. **Delays.**

(1) Unless otherwise instructed, a collecting bank in a good faith effort to secure payment may, in the case of specific items and with or without the approval of any person involved, waive, modify or extend time limits imposed or permitted by this Act for a period not in excess of an additional banking day without discharge of secondary parties and without liability to its transferor or any prior party.

(2) Delay by a collecting bank or payor bank beyond time limits prescribed or permitted by this Act or by instructions is excused if caused by interruption of communication facilities, suspension of payments by another bank, war, emergency conditions or other circumstances beyond the control of the bank provided it exercises such diligence as the circumstances require.

§ 4—109. **Process of Posting.**

The "process of posting" means the usual procedure followed by a payor bank in determining to pay an item and in recording the payment including one or more of the following or other steps as determined by the bank:

(a) verification of any signature;

(b) ascertaining that sufficient funds are available;

(c) affixing a "paid" or other stamp;

(d) entering a charge or entry to a customer's account;

(e) correcting or reversing an entry or erroneous action with respect to the item.

Part 2 Collection of Items: Depositary and Collecting Banks

§ 4—201. **Presumption and Duration of Agency Status of Collecting Banks and Provisional Status of Credits; Applicability of Article; Item Indorsed "Pay Any Bank".**

(1) Unless a contrary intent clearly appears and prior to the time that a settlement given by a collecting bank for an item is or becomes final (subsection (3) of Section 4—211 and Sections 4—212 and 4—213) the bank is an agent or sub-agent of the owner of the item and any settlement given for the item is provisional. This provision applies regardless of the form of indorsement or lack of indorsement and even though credit given for the item is subject to immediate withdrawal as of right or is in fact withdrawn; but the continuance of ownership of an item by its owner and any rights of the owner to proceeds of the item are subject to rights of a collecting bank such as those resulting from outstanding advances on the item and valid rights of setoff. When an item is handled by banks for purposes of presentment, payment and collection, the relevant provisions of this Article apply even though action of parties clearly establishes that a particular bank has purchased the item and is the owner of it.

(2) After an item has been indorsed with the words "pay any bank" or the like, only a bank may acquire the rights of a holder

(a) until the item has been returned to the customer initiating collection; or

(b) until the item has been specially indorsed by a bank to a person who is not a bank.

§ 4—202. **Responsibility for Collection; When Action Seasonable.**

(1) A collecting bank must use ordinary care in

(a) presenting an item or sending it for presentment; and

(b) sending notice of dishonor or non-payment or returning an item other than a documentary draft to the bank's transferor [or directly to the depositary bank under subsection (2) of Section 4—212] (see note to Section 4—212) after learning that the item has not been paid or accepted as the case may be; and

(c) settling for an item when the bank receives final settlement; and

(d) making or providing for any necessary protest; and

(e) notifying its transferor of any loss or delay in transit within a reasonable time after discovery thereof.

(2) A collecting bank taking proper action before its midnight deadline following receipt of an item, notice or payment acts seasonably; taking proper action within a reasonably longer time may be seasonable but the bank has the burden of so establishing.

(3) Subject to subsection (1)(a), a bank is not liable for the insolvency, neglect, misconduct, mistake or default of another bank or person or for loss or destruction of an item in transit or in the possession of others.

§ 4—203. Effect of Instructions.

Subject to the provisions of Article 3 concerning conversion of instruments (Section 3—419) and the provisions of both Article 3 and this Article concerning restrictive indorsements only a collecting bank's transferor can give instructions which affect the bank or constitute notice to it and a collecting bank is not liable to prior parties for any action taken pursuant to such instructions or in accordance with any agreement with its transferor.

§ 4—204. Methods of Sending and Presenting; Sending Direct to Payor Bank.

(1) A collecting bank must send items by reasonably prompt method taking into consideration any relevant instructions, the nature of the item, the number of such items on hand, and the cost of collection involved and the method generally used by it or others to present such items.

(2) A collecting bank may send

(a) any item direct to the payor bank;

(b) any item to any non-bank payor if authorized by its transferor; and

(c) any item other than documentary drafts to any non-bank payor, if authorized by Federal Reserve regulation or operating letter, clearing house rule or the like.

(3) Presentment may be made by a presenting bank at a place where the payor bank has requested that presentment be made.

§ 4—205. Supplying Missing Indorsement; No Notice from Prior Indorsement.

(1) A depositary bank which has taken an item for collection may supply any indorsement of the customer which is necessary to title unless the item contains the words "payee's indorsement required" or the like. In the absence of such a requirement a statement placed on the item by the depositary bank to the effect that the item was deposited by a customer or credited to his account is effective as the customer's indorsement.

(2) An intermediary bank, or payor bank which is not a depositary bank, is neither given notice nor otherwise affected by a restrictive indorsement of any person except the bank's immediate transferor.

§ 4—206. Transfer Between Banks.

Any agreed method which identifies the transferor bank is sufficient for the item's further transfer to another bank.

§ 4—207. Warranties of Customer and Collecting Bank on Transfer or Presentment of Items; Time for Claims.

(1) Each customer or collecting bank who obtains payment or acceptance of an item and each prior customer and collecting bank warrants to the payor bank or other payor who in good faith pays or accepts the item that

(a) he has a good title to the item or is authorized to obtain payment or acceptance on behalf of one who has a good title; and

(b) he has no knowledge that the signature of the maker or drawer is unauthorized, except that this warranty is not given by any customer or collecting bank that is a holder in due course and acts in good faith

(i) to a maker with respect to the maker's own signature; or

(ii) to a drawer with respect to the drawer's own signature, whether or not the drawer is also the drawee; or

(iii) to an acceptor of an item if the holder in due course took the item after the acceptance or obtained the acceptance without knowledge that the drawer's signature was unauthorized; and

(c) the item has not been materially altered, except that this warranty is not given by any customer or collecting bank that is a holder in due course and acts in good faith

(i) to the maker of a note; or

(ii) to the drawer of a draft whether or not the drawer is also the drawee; or

(iii) to the acceptor of an item with respect to an alteration made prior to the acceptance if the holder in due course took the item after the acceptance, even though the acceptance provided "payable as originally drawn" or equivalent terms; or

(iv) to the acceptor of an item with respect to an alteration made after the acceptance.

(2) Each customer and collecting bank who transfers an item and receives a settlement or other consideration for it warrants to his transferee and to any subsequent collecting bank who takes the item in good faith that

(a) he has a good title to the item or is authorized to obtain payment or acceptance on behalf of one who has a good title and the transfer is otherwise rightful; and

(b) all signatures are genuine or authorized; and

(c) the item has not been materially altered; and

(d) no defense of any party is good against him; and

(e) he has no knowledge of any insolvency proceeding instituted with respect to the maker or acceptor or the drawer of an unaccepted item.

In addition each customer and collecting bank so transferring an item and receiving a settlement or other consideration engages that upon dishonor and any necessary notice of dishonor and protest he will take up the item.

(3) The warranties and the engagement to honor set forth in the two preceding subsections arise notwithstanding the absence of indorsement or words of guaranty or warranty in the transfer or presentment and a collecting bank remains liable for their breach despite remittance to its transferor. Damages for breach of such warranties or engagement to honor shall not exceed the consideration received by the customer or collecting bank responsible plus finance charges and expenses related to the item, if any.

(4) Unless a claim for breach of warranty under this section is made within a reasonable time after the person claiming learns of the breach, the person liable is discharged to the extent of any loss caused by the delay in making claim.

§ 4—208. Security Interest of Collecting Bank in Items, Accompanying Documents and Proceeds.

(1) A bank has a security interest in an item and any accompanying documents or the proceeds of either

(a) in case of an item deposited in an account to the extent to which credit given for the item has been withdrawn or applied;

(b) in case of an item for which it has given credit available for withdrawal as of right, to the extent of the credit given whether or not the credit is drawn upon and whether or not there is a right of charge-back; or

(c) if it makes an advance on or against the item.

(2) When credit which has been given for several items received at one time or pursuant to a single agreement is withdrawn or applied in part the security interest remains upon all the items, any accompanying documents or the proceeds of either. For the purpose of this section, credits first given are first withdrawn.

(3) Receipt by a collecting bank of a final settlement for an item is a realization on its security interest in the item, accompanying documents and proceeds. To the extent and so long as the bank does not receive final settlement for the item or give up possession of the item or accompanying documents for purposes other than collection, the security interest continues and is subject to the provisions of Article 9 except that

(a) no security agreement is necessary to make the security interest enforceable (subsection (1)(b) of Section 9—203); and

(b) no filing is required to perfect the security interest; and

(c) the security interest has priority over conflicting perfected security interests in the item, accompanying documents or proceeds.

§ 4—209. When Bank Gives Value for Purposes of Holder in Due Course.

For purposes of determining its status as a holder in due course, the bank has given value to the extent that it has a security interest in an item provided that the bank otherwise complies with the requirements of Section 3—302 on what constitutes a holder in due course.

§ 4—210. Presentment by Notice of Item Not Payable by, Through or at a Bank; Liability of Secondary Parties.

(1) Unless otherwise instructed, a collecting bank may present an item not payable by, through or at a bank

by sending to the party to accept or pay a written notice that the bank holds the item for acceptance or payment. The notice must be sent in time to be received on or before the day when presentment is due and the bank must meet any requirement of the party to accept or pay under Section 3—505 by the close of the bank's next banking day after it knows of the requirement.

(2) Where presentment is made by notice and neither honor nor request for compliance with a requirement under Section 3—505 is received by the close of business on the day after maturity or in the case of demand items by the close of business on the third banking day after notice was sent, the presenting bank may treat the item as dishonored and charge any secondary party by sending him notice of the facts.

§ 4—211. **Media of Remittance; Provisional and Final Settlement in Remittance Cases.**

(1) A collecting bank may take in settlement of an item

(a) a check of the remitting bank or of another bank on any bank except the remitting bank; or

(b) a cashier's check or similar primary obligation of a remitting bank which is a member of or clears through a member of the same clearing house or group as the collecting bank; or

(c) appropriate authority to charge an account of the remitting bank or of another bank with the collecting bank; or

(d) if the item is drawn upon or payable by a person other than a bank, a cashier's check, certified check or other bank check or obligation.

(2) If before its midnight deadline the collecting bank properly dishonors a remittance check or authorization to charge on itself or presents or forwards for collection a remittance instrument of or on another bank which is of a kind approved by subsection (1) or has not been authorized by it, the collecting bank is not liable to prior parties in the event of the dishonor of such check, instrument or authorization.

(3) A settlement for an item by means of a remittance instrument or authorization to charge is or becomes a final settlement as to both the person making and the person receiving the settlement

(a) if the remittance instrument or authorization to charge is of a kind approved by subsection (1) or has not been authorized by the person receiving the settlement and in either case the person receiving the settlement acts seasonably before its

midnight deadline in presenting, forwarding for collection or paying the instrument or authorization,—at the time the remittance instrument or authorization is finally paid by the payor by which it is payable;

(b) if the person receiving the settlement has authorized remittance by a non-bank check or obligation or by a cashier's check or similar primary obligation of or a check upon the payor or other remitting bank which is not of a kind approved by subsection (1)(b),—at the time of the receipt of such remittance check or obligation; or

(c) if in a case not covered by sub-paragraphs (a) or (b) the person receiving the settlement fails to seasonably present, forward for collection, pay or return a remittance instrument or authorization to it to charge before its midnight deadline,—at such midnight deadline.

§ 4—212. **Right of Charge-Back or Refund.**

(1) If a collecting bank has made provisional settlement with its customer for an item and itself fails by reason of dishonor, suspension of payments by a bank or otherwise to receive a settlement for the item which is or becomes final, the bank may revoke the settlement given by it, charge back the amount of any credit given for the item to its customer's account or obtain refund from its customer whether or not it is able to return the items if by its midnight deadline or within a longer reasonable time after it learns the facts it returns the item or sends notification of the facts. These rights to revoke, charge-back and obtain refund terminate if and when a settlement for the item received by the bank is or becomes final (subsection (3) of Section 4—211 and subsections (2) and (3) of Section 4—213).

[(2) Within the time and manner prescribed by this section and Section 4—301, an intermediary or payor bank, as the case may be, may return an unpaid item directly to the depositary bank and may send for collection a draft on the depositary bank and obtain reimbursement. In such case, if the depositary bank has received provisional settlement for the item, it must reimburse the bank drawing the draft and any provisional credits for the item between banks shall become and remain final.]

Note: Direct returns is recognized as an innovation that is not yet established bank practice, and therefore, Paragraph 2 has been bracketed. Some lawyers have doubts whether it should be included in legislation or left to development by agreement.

(3) A depositary bank which is also the payor may

charge-back the amount of an item to its customer's account or obtain refund in accordance with the section governing return of an item received by a payor bank for credit on its books (Section 4—301).

(4) The right to charge-back is not affected by

(a) prior use of the credit given for the item; or

(b) failure by any bank to exercise ordinary care with respect to the item but any bank so failing remains liable.

(5) A failure to charge-back or claim refund does not affect other rights of the bank against the customer or any other party.

(6) If credit is given in dollars as the equivalent of the value of an item payable in a foreign currency the dollar amount of any charge-back or refund shall be calculated on the basis of the buying sight rate for the foreign currency prevailing on the day when the person entitled to the charge-back or refund learns that it will not receive payment in ordinary course.

§ 4—213. Final Payment of Item by Payor Bank; When Provisional Debits and Credits Become Final; When Certain Credits Become Available for Withdrawal.

(1) An item is finally paid by a payor bank when the bank has done any of the following, whichever happens first:

(a) paid the item in cash; or

(b) settled for the item without reserving a right to revoke the settlement and without having such right under statute, clearing house rule or agreement; or

(c) completed the process of posting the item to the indicated account of the drawer, maker or other person to be charged therewith; or

(d) made a provisional settlement for the item and failed to revoke the settlement in the time and manner permitted by statute, clearing house rule or agreement.

Upon a final payment under subparagraphs (b), (c) or (d) the payor bank shall be accountable for the amount of the item.

(2) If provisional settlement for an item between the presenting and payor banks is made through a clearing house or by debits or credits in an account between them, then to the extent that provisional debits or credits for the item are entered in accounts between the presenting and payor banks or between the presenting and successive prior collecting banks seriatim,

they become final upon final payment of the item by the payor bank.

(3) If a collecting bank receives a settlement for an item which is or becomes final (subsection (3) of Section 4—211, subsection (2) of Section 4—213) the bank is accountable to its customer for the amount of the item and any provisional credit given for the item in an account with its customer becomes final.

(4) Subject to any right of the bank to apply the credit to an obligation of the customer, credit given by a bank for an item in an account with its customer becomes available for withdrawal as of right

(a) in any case where the bank has received a provisional settlement for the item,—when such settlement becomes final and the bank has had a reasonable time to learn that the settlement is final;

(b) in any case where the bank is both a depositary bank and a payor bank and the item is finally paid,— at the opening of the bank's second banking day following receipt of the item.

(5) A deposit of money in a bank is final when made but, subject to any right of the bank to apply the deposit to an obligation of the customer, the deposit becomes available for withdrawal as of right at the opening of the bank's next banking day following receipt of the deposit.

§ 4—214. Insolvency and Preference.

(1) Any item in or coming into the possession of a payor or collecting bank which suspends payment and which item is not finally paid shall be returned by the receiver, trustee or agent in charge of the closed bank to the presenting bank or the closed bank's customer.

(2) If a payor bank finally pays an item and suspends payments without making a settlement for the item with its customer or the presenting bank which settlement is or becomes final, the owner of the item has a preferred claim against the payor bank.

(3) If a payor bank gives or a collecting bank gives or receives a provisional settlement for an item and thereafter suspends payments, the suspension does not prevent or interfere with the settlement becoming final if such finality occurs automatically upon the lapse of certain time or the happening of certain events (subsection (3) of Section 4—211, subsections (1)(d), (2) and (3) of Section 4—213).

(4) If a collecting bank receives from subsequent parties settlement for an item which settlement is or becomes final and suspends payments without making a settlement for the item with its customer which is

or becomes final, the owner of the item has a preferred claim against such collecting bank.

Part 3 Collection of Items: Payor Banks

§ 4—301. **Deferred Posting; Recovery of Payment by Return of Items; Time of Dishonor.**

(1) Where an authorized settlement for a demand item (other than a documentary draft) received by a payor bank otherwise than for immediate payment over the counter has been made before midnight of the banking day of receipt the payor bank may revoke the settlement and recover any payment if before it has made final payment (subsection (1) of Section 4—213) and before its midnight deadline it

(a) returns the item; or

(b) sends written notice of dishonor or nonpayment if the item is held for protest or is otherwise unavailable for return.

(2) If a demand item is received by a payor bank for credit on its books it may return such item or send notice of dishonor and may revoke any credit given or recover the amount thereof withdrawn by its customer, if it acts within the time limit and in the manner specified in the preceding subsection.

(3) Unless previous notice of dishonor has been sent an item is dishonored at the time when for purposes of dishonor it is returned or notice sent in accordance with this section.

(4) An item is returned:

(a) as to an item received through a clearing house, when it is delivered to the presenting or last collecting bank or to the clearing house or is sent or delivered in accordance with its rules; or

(b) in all other cases, when it is sent or delivered to the bank's customer or transferor or pursuant to his instructions.

§ 4—302. **Payor Bank's Responsibility for Late Return of Item.**

In the absence of a valid defense such as breach of a presentment warranty (subsection (1) of Section 4—207), settlement effected or the like, if an item is presented on and received by a payor bank the bank is accountable for the amount of

(a) a demand item other than a documentary draft whether properly payable or not if the bank, in any case where it is not also the depositary bank, retains the item beyond midnight of the banking day of receipt without settling for it or, regardless of whether

it is also the depositary bank, does not pay or return the item or send notice of dishonor until after its midnight deadline; or

(b) any other properly payable item unless within the time allowed for acceptance or payment of that item the bank either accepts or pays the item or returns it and accompanying documents.

§ 4—303. **When Items Subject to Notice, Stop-Order, Legal Process or Setoff; Order in Which Items May Be Charged or Certified.**

(1) Any knowledge, notice or stop-order received by, legal process served upon or setoff exercised by a payor bank, whether or not effective under other rules of law to terminate, suspend or modify the bank's right or duty to pay an item or to charge its customer's account for the item, comes too late to so terminate, suspend or modify such right or duty if the knowledge, notice, stop-order or legal process is received or served and a reasonable time for the bank to act thereon expires or the setoff is exercised after the bank has done any of the following:

(a) accepted or certified the item;

(b) paid the item in cash;

(c) settled for the item without reserving a right to revoke the settlement and without having such right under statute, clearing house rule or agreement;

(d) completed the process of posting the item to the indicated account of the drawer, maker or other person to be charged therewith or otherwise has evidenced by examination of such indicated account and by action its decision to pay the item; or

(e) become accountable for the amount of the item under subsection (1)(d) of Section 4—213 and Section 4—302 dealing with the payor bank's responsibility for late return of items.

(2) Subject to the provisions of subsection (1) items may be accepted, paid, certified or charged to the indicated account of its customer in any order convenient to the bank.

Part 4 Relationship Between Payor Bank and Its Customer

§ 4—401. **When Bank May Charge Customer's Account.**

(1) As against its customer, a bank may charge against his account any item which is otherwise properly payable from that account even though the charge creates an overdraft.

(2) A bank which in good faith makes payment to a holder may charge the indicated account of its customer according to

(a) the original tenor of his altered item; or

(b) the tenor of his completed item, even though the bank knows the item has been completed unless the bank has notice that the completion was improper.

§ 4—402. Bank's Liability to Customer for Wrongful Dishonor.

A payor bank is liable to its customer for damages proximately caused by the wrongful dishonor of an item. When the dishonor occurs through mistake liability is limited to actual damages proved. If so proximately caused and proved damages may include damages for an arrest or prosecution of the customer or other consequential damages. Whether any consequential damages are proximately caused by the wrongful dishonor is a question of fact to be determined in each case.

§ 4—403. Customer's Right to Stop Payment; Burden of Proof of Loss.

(1) A customer may by order to his bank stop payment of any item payable for his account but the order must be received at such time and in such manner as to afford the bank a reasonable opportunity to act on it prior to any action by the bank with respect to the item described in Section 4—303.

(2) An oral order is binding upon the bank only for fourteen calendar days unless confirmed in writing within that period. A written order is effective for only six months unless renewed in writing.

(3) The burden of establishing the fact and amount of loss resulting from the payment of an item contrary to a binding stop payment order is on the customer.

§ 4—404. Bank Not Obligated to Pay Check More Than Six Months Old.

A bank is under no obligation to a customer having a checking account to pay a check, other than a certified check, which is presented more than six months after its date, but it may charge its customer's account for a payment made thereafter in good faith.

§ 4—405. Death or Incompetence of Customer.

(1) A payor or collecting bank's authority to accept, pay or collect an item or to account for proceeds of its collection if otherwise effective is not rendered ineffective by incompetence of a customer of either bank existing at the time the item is issued or its col-

lection is undertaken if the bank does not know of an adjudication of incompetence. Neither death nor incompetence of a customer revokes such authority to accept, pay, collect or account until the bank knows of the fact of death or of an adjudication of incompetence and has reasonable opportunity to act on it.

(2) Even with knowledge a bank may for ten days after the date of death pay or certify checks drawn on or prior to that date unless ordered to stop payment by a person claiming an interest in the account.

§ 4—406. Customer's Duty to Discover and Report Unauthorized Signature or Alteration.

(1) When a bank sends to its customer a statement of account accompanied by items paid in good faith in support of the debit entries or holds the statement and items pursuant to a request or instructions of its customer or otherwise in a reasonable manner makes the statement and items available to the customer, the customer must exercise reasonable care and promptness to examine the statement and items to discover his unauthorized signature or any alteration on an item and must notify the bank promptly after discovery thereof.

(2) If the bank establishes that the customer failed with respect to an item to comply with the duties imposed on the customer by subsection (1) the customer is precluded from asserting against the bank

(a) his unauthorized signature or any alteration on the item if the bank also establishes that it suffered a loss by reason of such failure; and

(b) an unauthorized signature or alteration by the same wrongdoer on any other item paid in good faith by the bank after the first item and statement was available to the customer for a reasonable period not exceeding fourteen calendar days and before the bank receives notification from the customer of any such unauthorized signature or alteration.

(3) The preclusion under subsection (2) does not apply if the customer establishes lack of ordinary care on the part of the bank in paying the item(s).

(4) Without regard to care or lack of care of either the customer or the bank a customer who does not within one year from the time the statement and items are made available to the customer (subsection (1)) discover and report his unauthorized signature or any alteration on the face or back of the item or does not within three years from that time discover and report any unauthorized indorsement is precluded from asserting against the bank such unauthorized signature or indorsement or such alteration.

(5) If under this section a payor bank has a valid defense against a claim of a customer upon or resulting from payment of an item and waives or fails upon request to assert the defense the bank may not assert against any collecting bank or other prior party presenting or transferring the item a claim based upon the unauthorized signature or alteration giving rise to the customer's claim.

§ 4—407. **Payor Bank's Right to Subrogation on Improper Payment.**

If a payor bank has paid an item over the stop payment order of the drawer or maker or otherwise under circumstances giving a basis for objection by the drawer or maker, to prevent unjust enrichment and only to the extent necessary to prevent loss to the bank by reason of its payment of the item, the payor bank shall be subrogated to the rights

(a) of any holder in due course on the item against the drawer or maker; and

(b) of the payee or any other holder of the item against the drawer or maker either on the item or under the transaction out of which the item arose; and

(c) of the drawer or maker against the payee or any other holder of the item with respect to the transaction out of which the item arose.

Part 5 **Collection of Documentary Drafts**

§ 4—501. **Handling of Documentary Drafts; Duty to Send for Presentment and to Notify Customer of Dishonor.**

A bank which takes a documentary draft for collection must present or send the draft and accompanying documents for presentment and upon learning that the draft has not been paid or accepted in due course must seasonably notify its customer of such fact even though it may have discounted or bought the draft or extended credit available for withdrawal as of right.

§ 4—502. **Presentment of "On Arrival" Drafts.**

When a draft or the relevant instructions require presentment "on arrival", "when goods arrive" or the like, the collecting bank need not present until in its judgment a reasonable time for arrival of the goods has expired. Refusal to pay or accept because the goods have not arrived is not dishonor; the bank must notify its transferor of such refusal but need not present the draft again until it is instructed to do so or learns of the arrival of the goods.

§ 4—503. **Responsibility of Presenting Bank for Documents and Goods; Report of Reasons for Dishonor; Referee in Case of Need.**

Unless otherwise instructed and except as provided in Article 5 a bank presenting a documentary draft

(a) must deliver the documents to the drawee on acceptance of the draft if it is payable more than three days after presentment; otherwise, only on payment; and

(b) upon dishonor, either in the case of presentment for acceptance or presentment for payment, may seek and follow instructions from any referee in case of need designated in the draft or if the presenting bank does not choose to utilize his services it must use diligence and good faith to ascertain the reason for dishonor, must notify its transferor of the dishonor and of the results of its effort to ascertain the reasons therefor and must request instructions.

But the presenting bank is under no obligation with respect to goods represented by the documents except to follow any reasonable instructions seasonably received; it has a right to reimbursement for any expense incurred in following instructions and to prepayment of or indemnity for such expenses.

§ 4—504. **Privilege of Presenting Bank to Deal With Goods; Security Interest for Expenses.**

(1) A presenting bank which, following the dishonor of a documentary draft, has seasonably requested instructions but does not receive them within a reasonable time may store, sell, or otherwise deal with the goods in any reasonable manner.

(2) For its reasonable expenses incurred by action under subsection (1) the presenting bank has a lien upon the goods or their proceeds, which may be foreclosed in the same manner as an unpaid seller's lien.

Article 5
LETTERS OF CREDIT

§ 5—101. **Short Title.**

This Article shall be known and may be cited as Uniform Commercial Code—Letters of Credit.

§ 5—102. **Scope.**

(1) This Article applies

(a) to a credit issued by a bank if the credit requires a documentary draft or a documentary demand for payment; and

(b) to a credit issued by a person other than a bank if the credit requires that the draft or demand for payment be accompanied by a document of title; and

(c) to a credit issued by a bank or other person if the credit is not within subparagraphs (a) or (b) but conspicuously states that it is a letter of credit or is conspicuously so entitled.

(2) Unless the engagement meets the requirements of subsection (1), this Article does not apply to engagements to make advances or to honor drafts or demands for payment, to authorities to pay or purchase, to guarantees or to general agreements.

(3) This Article deals with some but not all of the rules and concepts of letters of credit as such rules or concepts have developed prior to this act or may hereafter develop. The fact that this Article states a rule does not by itself require, imply or negate application of the same or a converse rule to a situation not provided for or to a person not specified by this Article.

§ 5—103. **Definitions.**

(1) In this Article unless the context otherwise requires

(a) "Credit" or "letter of credit" means an engagement by a bank or other person made at the request of a customer and of a kind within the scope of this Article (Section 5—102) that the issuer will honor drafts or other demands for payment upon compliance with the conditions specified in the credit. A credit may be either revocable or irrevocable. The engagement may be either an agreement to honor or a statement that the bank or other person is authorized to honor.

(b) A "documentary draft" or a "documentary demand for payment" is one honor of which is conditioned upon the presentation of a document or documents. "Document" means any paper including document of title, security, invoice, certificate, notice of default and the like.

(c) An "issuer" is a bank or other person issuing a credit.

(d) A "beneficiary" of a credit is a person who is entitled under its terms to draw or demand payment.

(e) An "advising bank" is a bank which gives notification of the issuance of a credit by another bank.

(f) A "confirming bank" is a bank which engages either that it will itself honor a credit already is-

sued by another bank or that such a credit will be honored by the issuer or a third bank.

(g) A "customer" is a buyer or other person who causes an issuer to issue a credit. The term also includes a bank which procures issuance or confirmation on behalf of that bank's customer.

(2) Other definitions applying to this Article and the sections in which they appear are:
"Notation of Credit". Section 5—108.
"Presenter". Section 5—112(3).

(3) Definitions in other Articles applying to this Article and the sections in which they appear are:
"Accept" or "Acceptance". Section 3—410.
"Contract for sale". Section 2—106.
"Draft". Section 3—104.
"Holder in due course". Section 3—302.
"Midnight deadline". Section 4—104.
"Security". Section 8—102.

(4) In addition, Article 1 contains general definitions and principles of construction and interpretation applicable throughout this Article.

§ 5—104. **Formal Requirements; Signing.**

(1) Except as otherwise required in subsection (1)(c) of Section 5—102 on scope, no particular form of phrasing is required for a credit. A credit must be in writing and signed by the issuer and a confirmation must be in writing and signed by the confirming bank. A modification of the terms of a credit or confirmation must be signed by the issuer or confirming bank.

(2) A telegram may be a sufficient signed writing if it identifies its sender by an authorized authentication. The authentication may be in code and the authorized naming of the issuer in an advice of credit is a sufficient signing.

§ 5—105. **Consideration.**

No consideration is necessary to establish a credit or to enlarge or otherwise modify its terms.

§ 5—106. **Time and Effect of Establishment of Credit.**

(1) Unless otherwise agreed a credit is established

(a) as regards the customer as soon as a letter of credit is sent to him or the letter of credit or an authorized written advice of its issuance is sent to the beneficiary; and

(b) as regards the beneficiary when he receives a letter of credit or an authorized written advice of its issuance.

(2) Unless otherwise agreed once an irrevocable credit is established as regards the customer it can be modified or revoked only with the consent of the customer and once it is established as regards the beneficiary it can be modified or revoked only with his consent.

(3) Unless otherwise agreed after a revocable credit is established it may be modified or revoked by the issuer without notice to or consent from the customer or beneficiary.

(4) Notwithstanding any modification or revocation of a revocable credit any person authorized to honor or negotiate under the terms of the original credit is entitled to reimbursement for or honor of any draft or demand for payment duly honored or negotiated before receipt of notice of the modification or revocation and the issuer in turn is entitled to reimbursement from its customer.

§ 5—107. **Advice of Credit; Confirmation; Error in Statement of Terms.**

(1) Unless otherwise specified an advising bank by advising a credit issued by another bank does not assume any obligation to honor drafts drawn or demands for payment made under the credit but it does assume obligation for the accuracy of its own statement.

(2) A confirming bank by confirming a credit becomes directly obligated on the credit to the extent of its confirmation as though it were its issuer and acquires the rights of an issuer.

(3) Even though an advising bank incorrectly advises the terms of a credit it has been authorized to advise the credit is established as against the issuer to the extent of its original terms.

(4) Unless otherwise specified the customer bears as against the issuer all risks of transmission and reasonable translation or interpretation of any message relating to a credit.

§ 5—108. **"Notation Credit"; Exhaustion of Credit.**

(1) A credit which specifies that any person purchasing or paying drafts drawn or demands for payment made under it must note the amount of the draft or demand on the letter or advice of credit is a "notation credit".

(2) Under a notation credit

(a) a person paying the beneficiary or purchasing a draft or demand for payment from him acquires a right to honor only if the appropriate notation is made and by transferring or forwarding for honor the documents under the credit such a person warrants to the issuer that the notation has been made; and

(b) unless the credit or a signed statement that an appropriate notation has been made accompanies the draft or demand for payment the issuer may delay honor until evidence of notation has been procured which is satisfactory to it but its obligation and that of its customer continue for a reasonable time not exceeding thirty days to obtain such evidence.

(3) If the credit is not a notation credit

(a) the issuer may honor complying drafts or demands for payment presented to it in the order in which they are presented and is discharged pro tanto by honor of any such draft or demand;

(b) as between competing good faith purchasers of complying drafts or demands the person first purchasing his priority over a subsequent purchaser even though the later purchased draft or demand has been first honored.

§ 5—109. **Issuer's Obligation to Its Customer.**

(1) An issuer's obligation to its customer includes good faith and observance of any general banking usage but unless otherwise agreed does not include liability or responsibility

(a) for performance of the underlying contract for sale or other transaction between the customer and the beneficiary; or

(b) for any act or omission of any person other than itself or its own branch or for loss or destruction of a draft, demand or document in transit or in the possession of others; or

(c) based on knowledge or lack of knowledge of any usage of any particular trade.

(2) An issuer must examine documents with care so as to ascertain that on their face they appear to comply with the terms of the credit but unless otherwise agreed assumes no liability or responsibility for the genuineness, falsification or effect of any document which appears on such examination to be regular on its face.

(3) A non-bank issuer is not bound by any banking usage of which it has no knowledge.

§ 5—110. **Availability of Credit in Portions; Presenter's Reservation of Lien or Claim.**

(1) Unless otherwise specified a credit may be used in portions in the discretion of the beneficiary.

(2) Unless otherwise specified a person by presenting a documentary draft or demand for payment under a

credit relinquishes upon its honor all claims to the documents and a person by transferring such draft or demand or causing such presentment authorizes such relinquishment. An explicit reservation of claim makes the draft or demand non-complying.

§ 5—111. **Warranties on Transfer and Presentment.**

(1) Unless otherwise agreed the beneficiary by transferring or presenting a documentary draft or demand for payment warrants to all interested parties that the necessary conditions of the credit have been complied with. This is in addition to any warranties arising under Articles 3, 4, 7 and 8.

(2) Unless otherwise agreed a negotiating, advising, confirming, collecting or issuing bank presenting or transferring a draft or demand for payment under a credit warrants only the matters warranted by a collecting bank under Article 4 and any such bank transferring a document warrants only the matters warranted by an intermediary under Articles 7 and 8.

§ 5—112. **Time Allowed for Honor or Rejection; Withholding Honor or Rejection by Consent; "Presenter".**

(1) A bank to which a documentary draft or demand for payment is presented under a credit may without dishonor of the draft, demand or credit

(a) defer honor until the close of the third banking day following receipt of the documents; and

(b) further defer honor if the presenter has expressly or impliedly consented thereto.

Failure to honor within the time here specified constitutes dishonor of the draft or demand and of the credit [except as otherwise provided in subsection (4) of Section 5—114 on conditional payment].

Note: *The bracketed language in the last sentence of subsection (1) should be included only if the optional provisions of Section 5—114(4) and (5) are included.*

(2) Upon dishonor the bank may unless otherwise instructed fulfill its duty to return the draft or demand and the documents by holding them at the disposal of the presenter and sending him an advice to that effect.

(3) "Presenter" means any person presenting a draft or demand for payment for honor under a credit even though that person is a confirming bank or other correspondent which is acting under an issuer's authorization.

§ 5—113. **Indemnities.**

(1) A bank seeking to obtain (whether for itself or another) honor, negotiation or reimbursement under a credit may give an indemnity to induce such honor, negotiation or reimbursement.

(2) An indemnity agreement inducing honor, negotiation or reimbursement

(a) unless otherwise explicitly agreed applies to defects in the documents but not in the goods; and

(b) unless a longer time is explicitly agreed expires at the end of ten business days following receipt of the documents by, the ultimate customer unless notice of objection is sent before such expiration date. The ultimate customer may send notice of objection to the person from whom he received the documents and any bank receiving such notice is under a duty to send notice to its transferor before its midnight deadline.

§ 5—114. **Issuer's Duty and Privilege to Honor; Right to Reimbursement.**

(1) An issuer must honor a draft or demand for payment which complies with the terms of the relevant credit regardless of whether the goods or documents conform to the underlying contract for sale or other contract between the customer and the beneficiary. The issuer is not excused from honor of such a draft or demand by reason of an additional general term that all documents must be satisfactory to the issuer, but an issuer may require that specified documents must be satisfactory to it.

(2) Unless otherwise agreed when documents appear on their face to comply with the terms of a credit but a required document does not in fact conform to the warranties made on negotiation or transfer of a document of title (Section 7—507) or of a certificated security (Section 8—306) or is forged or fraudulent or there is fraud in the transaction:

(a) the issuer must honor the draft or demand for payment if honor is demanded by a negotiating bank or other holder of the draft or demand which has taken the draft or demand under the credit and under circumstances which would make it a holder in due course (Section 3—302) and in an appropriate case would make it a person to whom a document of title has been duly negotiated (Section 7—502) or a bona fide purchaser of a certificated security (Section 8—302); and

(b) in all other cases as against its customer, an issuer acting in good faith may honor the draft or demand for payment despite notification from the customer of fraud, forgery or other defect not apparent on the face of the documents but a court of appropriate jurisdiction may enjoin such honor.

(3) Unless otherwise agreed an issuer which has duly honored a draft or demand for payment is entitled to immediate reimbursement of any payment made under the credit and to be put in effectively available funds not later than the day before maturity of any acceptance made under the credit.

[(4) When a credit provides for payment by the issuer on receipt of notice that the required documents are in the possession of a correspondent or other agent of the issuer

(a) any payment made on receipt of such notice is conditional; and

(b) the issuer may reject documents which do not comply with the credit if it does so within three banking days following its receipt of the documents; and

(c) in the event of such rejection, the issuer is entitled by charge back or otherwise to return of the payment made.]

[(5) In the case covered by subsection (4) failure to reject documents within the time specified in subparagraph (b) constitutes acceptance of the documents and makes the payment final in favor of the beneficiary.]

Amended in 1977.

Note: *Subsections (4) and (5) are bracketed as optional. If they are included the bracketed language in the last sentence of Section 5—112(1) should also be included.*

§ 5—115. **Remedy for Improper Dishonor or Anticipatory Repudiation.**

(1) When an issuer wrongfully dishonors a draft or demand for payment presented under a credit the person entitled to honor has with respect to any documents the rights of a person in the position of a seller (Section 2—707) and may recover from the issuer the face amount of the draft or demand together with incidental damages under Section 2—710 on seller's incidental damages and interest but less any amount realized by resale or other use or disposition of the subject matter of the transaction. In the event no resale or other utilization is made the documents, goods or other subject matter involved in the transaction must be turned over to the issuer on payment of judgment.

(2) When an issuer wrongfully cancels or otherwise repudiates a credit before presentment of a draft or demand for payment drawn under it the beneficiary has the rights of a seller after anticipatory repudiation by the buyer under Section 2—610 if he learns of the repudiation in time reasonably to avoid procurement of the required documents. Otherwise the beneficiary

has an immediate right of action for wrongful dishonor.

§ 5—116. **Transfer and Assignment.**

(1) The right to draw under a credit can be transferred or assigned only when the credit is expressly designated as transferable or assignable.

(2) Even through the credit specifically states that it is nontransferable or nonassignable the beneficiary may before performance of the conditions of the credit assign his right to proceeds. Such an assignment is an assignment of an account under Article 9 on Secured Transactions and is governed by that Article except that

(a) the assignment is ineffective until the letter of credit or advice of credit is delivered to the assignee which delivery constitutes perfection of the security interest under Article 9; and

(b) the issuer may honor drafts or demands for payment drawn under the credit until it receives a notification of the assignment signed by the beneficiary which reasonably identifies the credit involved in the assignment and contains a request to pay the assignee; and

(c) after what reasonably appears to be such a notification has been received the issuer may without dishonor refuse to accept or pay even to a person otherwise entitled to honor until the letter of credit or advice of credit is exhibited to the issuer.

(3) Except where the beneficiary has effectively assigned his right to draw or his right to proceeds, nothing in this section limits his right to transfer or negotiate drafts or demands drawn under the credit.

§ 5—117. **Insolvency of Bank Holding Funds for Documentary Credit.**

(1) Where an issuer or an advising or confirming bank or a bank which has for a customer procured issuance of a credit by another bank becomes insolvent before final payment under the credit and the credit is one to which this Article is made applicable by paragraphs (a) or (b) of Section 5—102(1) on scope, the receipt or allocation of funds or collateral to secure or meet obligations under the credit shall have the following results:

(a) to the extent of any funds or collateral turned over after or before the insolvency as indemnity against or specifically for the purpose of payment of drafts or demands for payment drawn under the designated credit, the drafts or demands are entitled to payment in preference over depositors or other general creditors of the issuer or bank; and

(b) on expiration of the credit or surrender of the beneficiary's rights under it unused any person who has given such funds or collateral is similarly entitled to return thereof; and

(c) a charge to a general or current account with a bank if specifically consented to for the purpose of indemnity against or payment of drafts or demands for payment drawn under the designated credit falls under the same rules as if the funds had been drawn out in cash and then turned over with specific instructions.

(2) After honor or reimbursement under this section the customer or other person for whose account the insolvent bank has acted is entitled to receive the documents involved.

Article 6
BULK TRANSFERS

§ 6—101. Short Title.

This Article shall be known and may be cited as Uniform Commercial Code—Bulk Transfers.

§ 6—102. "Bulk Transfer"; Transfers of Equipment; Enterprises Subject to This Article; Bulk Transfers Subject to This Article.

(1) A "bulk transfer" is any transfer in bulk and not in the ordinary course of the transferor's business of a major part of the materials, supplies, merchandise or other inventory (Section 9—109) of an enterprise subject to this Article.

(2) A transfer of a substantial part of the equipment (Section 9—109) of such an enterprise is a bulk transfer it if is made in connection with a bulk transfer of inventory, but not otherwise.

(3) The enterprises subject to this Article are all those whose principal business is the sale of merchandise from stock, including those who manufacture what they sell.

(4) Except as limited by the following section all bulk transfers of goods located within this state are subject to this Article.

§ 6—103. Transfers Excepted From This Article.

The following transfers are not subject to this Article:

(1) Those made to give security for the performance of an obligation;

(2) General assignments for the benefit of all the cred-

itors of the transferor, and subsequent transfers by the assignee thereunder;

(3) Transfers in settlement or realization of a lien or other security interest;

(4) Sales by executors, administrators, receivers, trustees in bankruptcy, or any public officer under judicial process;

(5) Sales made in the course of judicial or administrative proceedings for the dissolution or reorganization of a corporation and of which notice is sent to the creditors of the corporation pursuant to order of the court or administrative agency;

(6) Transfers to a person maintaining a known place of business in this State who becomes bound to pay the debts of the transferor in full and gives public notice of that fact, and who is solvent after becoming so bound;

(7) A transfer to a new business enterprise organized to take over and continue the business, if public notice of the transaction is given and the new enterprise assumes the debts of the transferor and he receives nothing from the transaction except an interest in the new enterprise junior to the claims of creditors;

(8) Transfers of property which is exempt from execution.

Public notice under subsection (6) or subsection (7) may be given by publishing once a week for two consecutive weeks in a newspaper of general circulation where the transferor had its principal place of business in this state an advertisement including the names and addresses of the transferor and transferee and the effective date of the transfer.

§ 6—104. Schedule of Property, List of Creditors.

(1) Except as provided with respect to auction sales (Section 6—108), a bulk transfer subject to this Article is ineffective against any creditor of the transferor unless:

(a) The transferee requires the transferor to furnish a list of his existing creditors prepared as stated in this section; and

(b) The parties prepare a schedule of the property transferred sufficient to identify it; and

(c) The transferee preserves the list and schedule for six months next following the transfer and permits inspection of either or both and copying therefrom at all reasonable hours by any creditor of the transferor, or files the list and schedule in (*a public office to be here identified*).

(2) The list of creditors must be signed and sworn to or affirmed by the transferor or his agent. It must contain the names and business addresses of all creditors of the transferor, with the amounts when known, and also the names of all persons who are known to the transferor to assert claims against him even though such claims are disputed. If the transferor is the obligor of an outstanding issue of bonds, debentures or the like as to which there is an indenture trustee, the list of creditors need include only the name and address of the indenture trustee and the aggregate outstanding principal amount of the issue.

(3) Responsibility for the completeness and accuracy of the list of creditors rests on the transferor, and the transfer is not rendered ineffective by errors or omissions therein unless the transferee is shown to have had knowledge.

§ 6—105. **Notice to Creditors.**

In addition to the requirements of the preceding section, any bulk transfer subject to this Article except one made by auction sale (Section 6—108) is ineffective against any creditor of the transferor unless at least ten days before he takes possession of the goods or pays for them, whichever happens first, the transferee gives notice of the transfer in the manner and to the persons hereafter provided (Section 6—107).

[§ 6—106. **Application of the Proceeds.**

In addition to the requirements of the two preceding sections:

(1) Upon every bulk transfer subject to this Article for which new consideration becomes payable except those made by sale at auction it is the duty of the transferee to assure that such consideration is applied so far as necessary to pay those debts of the transferor which are either shown on the list furnished by the transferor (Section 6—104) or filed in writing in the place stated in the notice (Section 6—107) within thirty days after the mailing of such notice. This duty of the transferee runs to all the holders of such debts, and may be enforced by any of them for the benefit of all.

(2) If any of said debts are in dispute the necessary sum may be withheld from distribution until the dispute is settled or adjudicated.

(3) If the consideration payable is not enough to pay all of the said debts in full distribution shall be made pro rata.]

Note: *This section is bracketed to indicate division of opinion as to whether or not it is a wise provision, and to suggest that this is a point on which State enactments may differ without serious damage to the principle of uniformity. In any State*

where this section is omitted, the following parts of sections, also bracketed in the text, should also be omitted, namely:
Section 6—107(2)(c).
    6—108(3)(c).
    6—109(2).
In any State where this section is enacted, these other provisions should be also.

Optional Subsection (4)

[(4) The transferee may within ten days after he takes possession of the goods pay the consideration into the (specify court) in the county where the transferor had its principal place of business in this state and thereafter may discharge his duty under this section by giving notice by registered or certified mail to all the persons to whom the duty runs that the consideration has been paid into that court and that they should file their claims there. On motion of any interested party, the court may order the distribution of the consideration to the persons entitled to it.]

Note: *Optional subsection (4) is recommended for those states which do not have a general statute providing for payment of money into court.*

§ 6—107. **The Notice.**

(1) The notice to creditors (Section 6—105) shall state:

    (a) that a bulk transfer is about to be made; and

    (b) the names and business addresses of the transferor and transferee, and all other business names and addresses used by the transferor within three years last past so far as known to the transferee; and

    (c) whether or not all the debts of the transferor are to be paid in full as they fall due as a result of the transaction, and if so, the address to which creditors should send their bills.

(2) If the debts of the transferor are not to be paid in full as they fall due or if the transferee is in doubt on that point then the notice shall state further:

    (a) the location and general description of the property to be transferred and the estimated total of the transferor's debts;

    (b) the address where the schedule of property and list of creditors (Section 6—104) may be inspected;

    (c) whether the transfer is to pay existing debts and if so the amount of such debts and to whom owing;

    (d) whether the transfer is for new consideration and if so the amount of such consideration and the time and place of payment; [and]

[(e) if for new consideration the time and place where creditors of the transferor are to file their claims.]

(3) The notice in any case shall be delivered personally or sent by registered or certified mail to all the persons shown on the list of creditors furnished by the transferor (Section 6—104) and to all other persons who are known to the transferee to hold or assert claims against the transferor.

§ 6—108. **Auction Sales; "Auctioneer".**

(1) A bulk transfer is subject to this Article even though it is by sale at auction, but only in the manner and with the results stated in this section.

(2) The transferor shall furnish a list of his creditors and assist in the preparation of a schedule of the property to be sold, both prepared as before stated (Section 6—104).

(3) The person or persons other than the transferor who direct, control or are responsible for the auction are collectively called the "auctioneer". The auctioneer shall:

(a) receive and retain the list of creditors and prepare and retain the schedule of property for the period stated in this Article (Section 6—104);

(b) give notice of the auction personally or by registered or certified mail at least ten days before it occurs to all persons shown on the list of creditors and to all other persons who are known to him to hold or assert claims against the transferor; [and]

[(c) assure that the net proceeds of the auction are applied as provided in this Article (Section 6—106).]

(4) Failure of the auctioneer to perform any of these duties does not affect the validity of the sale or the title of the purchasers, but if the auctioneer knows that the auction constitutes a bulk transfer such failure renders the auctioneer liable to the creditors of the transferor as a class for the sums owing to them from the transferor up to but not exceeding the net proceeds of the auction. If the auctioneer consists of several persons their liability is joint and several.

§ 6—109. **What Creditors Protected; [Credit for Payment to Particular Creditors].**

(1) The creditors of the transferor mentioned in this Article are those holding claims based on transactions or events occurring before the bulk transfer, but creditors who become such after notice to creditors is given (Sections 6—105 and 6—107) are not entitled to notice.

[(2) Against the aggregate obligation imposed by the provisions of this Article concerning the application of the proceeds (Section 6—106 and subsection (3)(c) of 6—108) the transferee or auctioneer is entitled to credit for sums paid to particular creditors of the transferor, not exceeding the sums believed in good faith at the time of the payment to be properly payable to such creditors.]

§ 6—110. **Subsequent Transfers.**

When the title of a transferee to property is subject to a defect by reason of his non-compliance with the requirements of this Article, then:

(1) a purchaser of any of such property from such transferee who pays no value or who takes with notice of such non-compliance takes subject to such defect, but

(2) a purchaser for value in good faith and without such notice takes free of such defect.

§ 6—111. **Limitation of Actions and Levies.**

No action under this Article shall be brought nor levy made more than six months after the date on which the transferee took possession of the goods unless the transfer has been concealed. If the transfer has been concealed, actions may be brought or levies made within six months after its discovery.

Note to Article 6: *Section 6—106 is bracketed to indicate division of opinion as to whether or not it is a wise provision, and to suggest that this is a point on which State enactments may differ without serious damage to the principle of uniformity.*

In any State where Section 6—106 is not enacted, the following parts of sections, also bracketed in the text, should also be omitted, namely:

Sec. 6—107(2)(e).
6—108(3)(c).
6—109(2).

In any State where Section 6—106 is enacted, these other provisions should be also.

Article 7
Warehouse Receipts, Bills of Lading and Other Documents of Title

Part 1 General

§ 7—101. **Short Title.**

This Article shall be known and may be cited as Uniform Commercial Code—Documents of Title.

§ 7—102. Definitions and Index of Definitions.

(1) In this Article, unless the context otherwise requires:

(a) "Bailee" means the person who by a warehouse receipt, bill of lading or other document of title acknowledges possession of goods and contracts to deliver them.

(b) "Consignee" means the person named in a bill to whom or to whose order the bill promises delivery.

(c) "Consignor" means the person named in a bill as the person from whom the goods have been received for shipment.

(d) "Delivery order" means a written order to deliver goods directed to a warehouseman, carrier or other person who in the ordinary course of business issues warehouse receipts or bills of lading.

(e) "Document" means document of title as defined in the general definitions in Article 1 (Section 1—201).

(f) "Goods" means all things which are treated as movable for the purposes of a contract of storage or transportation.

(g) "Issuer" means a bailee who issues a document except that in relation to an unaccepted delivery order it means the person who orders the possessor of goods to deliver. Issuer includes any person for whom an agent or employee purports to act in issuing a document if the agent or employee has real or apparent authority to issue documents, notwithstanding that the issuer received no goods or that the goods were misdescribed or that in any other respect the agent or employee violated his instructions.

(h) "Warehouseman" is a person engaged in the business of storing goods for hire.

(2) Other definitions applying to this Article or to specified Parts thereof, and the sections in which they appear are:
"Duly negotiate". Section 7—501.
"Person entitled under the document". Section 7—403(4).

(3) Definitions in other Articles applying to this Article and the sections in which they appear are:
"Contract for sale". Section 2—106.
"Overseas". Section 2—323.
"Receipt" of goods. Section 2—103.

(4) In addition Article 1 contains general definitions and principles of construction and interpretation applicable throughout this Article.

§ 7—103. Relation of Article to Treaty, Statute, Tariff, Classification or Regulation.

To the extent that any treaty or statute of the United States, regulatory statute of this State or tariff, classification or regulation filed or issued pursuant thereto is applicable, the provisions of this Article are subject thereto.

§ 7—104. Negotiable and Non-Negotiable Warehouse Receipt, Bill of Lading or Other Document of Title.

(1) A warehouse receipt, bill of lading or other document of title is negotiable

(a) if by its terms the goods are to be delivered to bearer or to the order of a named person; or

(b) where recognized in overseas trade, if it runs to a named person or assigns.

(2) Any other document is non-negotiable. A bill of lading in which it is stated that the goods are consigned to a named person is not made negotiable by a provision that the goods are to be delivered only against a written order signed by the same or another named person.

§ 7—105. Construction Against Negative Implication.

The omission from either Part 2 or Part 3 of this Article of a provision corresponding to a provision made in the other Part does not imply that a corresponding rule of law is not applicable.

Part 2 Warehouse Receipts: Special Provisions

§ 7—201. Who May Issue a Warehouse Receipt; Storage Under Government Bond.

(1) A warehouse receipt may be issued by any warehouseman.

(2) Where goods including distilled spirits and agricultural commodities are stored under a statute requiring a bond against withdrawal or a license for the issuance of receipts in the nature of warehouse receipts, a receipt issued for the goods has like effect as a warehouse receipt even though issued by a person who is the owner of the goods and is not a warehouseman.

§ 7—202. Form of Warehouse Receipt; Essential Terms; Optional Terms.

(1) A warehouse receipt need not be in any particular form.

(2) Unless a warehouse receipt embodies within its written or printed terms each of the following, the

warehouseman is liable for damages caused by the omission to a person injured thereby:

(a) the location of the warehouse where the goods are stored;

(b) the date of issue of the receipt;

(c) the consecutive number of the receipt;

(d) a statement whether the goods received will be delivered to the bearer, to a specified person, or to a specified person or his order;

(e) the rate of storage and handling charges, except that where goods are stored under a field warehousing arrangement a statement of that fact is sufficient on a non-negotiable receipt;

(f) a description of the goods or of the packages containing them;

(g) the signature of the warehouseman, which may be made by his authorized agent;

(h) if the receipt is issued for goods of which the warehouseman is owner, either solely or jointly or in common with others, the fact of such ownership; and

(i) a statement of the amount of advances made and of liabilities incurred for which the warehouseman claims a lien or security interest (Section 7—209). If the precise amount of such advances made or of such liabilities incurred is, at the time of the issue of the receipt, unknown to the warehouseman or to his agent who issues it, a statement of the fact that advances have been made or liabilities incurred and the purpose thereof is sufficient.

(3) A warehouseman may insert in his receipt any other terms which are not contrary to the provisions of this Act and do not impair his obligation of delivery (Section 7—403) or his duty of care (Section 7—204). Any contrary provisions shall be ineffective.

§ 7—203. **Liability for Non-Receipt or Misdescription.**

A party to or purchaser for value in good faith of a document of title other than a bill of lading relying in either case upon the description therein of the goods may recover from the issuer damages caused by the non-receipt or misdescription of the goods, except to the extent that the document conspicuously indicates that the issuer does not know whether any part or all of the goods in fact were received or conform to the description, as where the description is in terms of marks or labels or kind, quantity or condition, or the receipt or description is qualified by "contents, con-

dition and quality unknown", "said to contain" or the like, if such indication be true, or the party or purchaser otherwise has notice.

§ 7—204. **Duty of Care; Contractual Limitation of Warehouseman's Liability.**

(1) A warehouseman is liable for damages for loss of or injury to the goods caused by his failure to exercise such care in regard to them as a reasonably careful man would exercise under like circumstances but unless otherwise agreed he is not liable for damages which could not have been avoided by the exercise of such care.

(2) Damages may be limited by a term in the warehouse receipt or storage agreement limiting the amount of liability in case of loss or damage, and setting forth a specific liability per article or item, or value per unit of weight, beyond which the warehouseman shall not be liable; provided, however, that such liability may on written request of the bailor at the time of signing such storage agreement or within a reasonable time after receipt of the warehouse receipt be increased on part or all of the goods thereunder, in which event increased rates may be charged based on such increased valuation, but that no such increase shall be permitted contrary to a lawful limitation of liability contained in the warehouseman's tariff, if any. No such limitation is effective with respect to the warehouseman's liability for conversion to his own use.

(3) Reasonable provisions as to the time and manner of presenting claims and instituting actions based on the bailment may be included in the warehouse receipt or tariff.

(4) This section does not impair or repeal . . .

Note: Insert in subsection (4) a reference to any statute which imposes a higher responsibility upon the warehouseman or invalidates contractual limitations which would be permissible under this Article.

§ 7—205. **Title Under Warehouse Receipt Defeated in Certain Cases.**

A buyer in the ordinary course of business of fungible goods sold and delivered by a warehouseman who is also in the business of buying and selling such goods takes free of any claim under a warehouse receipt even though it has been duly negotiated.

§ 7—206. **Termination of Storage at Warehouseman's Option.**

(1) A warehouseman may on notifying the person on whose account the goods are held and any other person known to claim an interest in the goods require payment of any charges and removal of the goods from

the warehouse at the termination of the period of storage fixed by the document, or, if no period is fixed, within a stated period not less than thirty days after the notification. If the goods are not removed before the date specified in the notification, the warehouseman may sell them in accordance with the provisions of the section on enforcement of a warehouseman's lien (Section 7—210).

(2) If a warehouseman in good faith believes that the goods are about to deteriorate or decline in value to less than the amount of his lien within the time prescribed in subsection (1) for notification, advertisement and sale, the warehouseman may specify in the notification any reasonable shorter time for removal of the goods and in case the goods are not removed, may sell them at public sale held not less than one week after a single advertisement or posting.

(3) If as a result of a quality or condition of the goods of which the warehouseman had no notice at the time of deposit the goods are a hazard to other property or to the warehouse or to persons, the warehouseman may sell the goods at public or private sale without advertisement on reasonable notification to all persons known to claim an interest in the goods. If the warehouseman after a reasonable effort is unable to sell the goods he may dispose of them in any lawful manner and shall incur no liability by reason of such disposition.

(4) The warehouseman must deliver the goods to any person entitled to them under this Article upon due demand made at any time prior to sale or other disposition under this section.

(5) The warehouseman may satisfy his lien from the proceeds of any sale or disposition under this section but must hold the balance for delivery on the demand of any person to whom he would have been bound to deliver the goods.

§ 7—207. **Goods Must Be Kept Separate; Fungible Goods.**

(1) Unless the warehouse receipt otherwise provides, a warehouseman must keep separate the goods covered by each receipt so as to permit at all times identification and delivery of those goods except that different lots of fungible goods may be commingled.

(2) Fungible goods so commingled are owned in common by the persons entitled thereto and the warehouseman is severally liable to each owner for that owner's share. Where because of overissue a mass of fungible goods is insufficient to meet all the receipts which the warehouseman has issued against it, the persons entitled include all holders to whom overissued receipts have been duly negotiated.

§ 7—208. **Altered Warehouse Receipts.**

Where a blank in a negotiable warehouse receipt has been filled in without authority, a purchaser for value and without notice of the want of authority may treat the insertion as authorized. Any other unauthorized alteration leaves any receipt enforceable against the issuer according to its original tenor.

§ 7—209. **Lien of Warehouseman.**

(1) A warehouseman has a lien against the bailor on the goods covered by a warehouse receipt or on the proceeds thereof in his possession for charges for storage or transportation (including demurrage and terminal charges), insurance, labor, or charges present or future in relation to the goods, and for expenses necessary for preservation of the goods or reasonably incurred in their sale pursuant to law. If the person on whose account the goods are held is liable for like charges or expenses in relation to other goods whenever deposited and it is stated in the receipt that a lien is claimed for charges and expenses in relation to other goods, the warehouseman also has a lien against him for such charges and expenses whether or not the other goods have been delivered by the warehouseman. But against a person to whom a negotiable warehouse receipt is duly negotiated a warehouseman's lien is limited to charges in an amount or at a rate specified on the receipt or if no charges are so specified then to a reasonable charge for storage of the goods covered by the receipt subsequent to the date of the receipt.

(2) The warehouseman may also reserve a security interest against the bailor for a maximum amount specified on the receipt for charges other than those specified in subsection (1), such as for money advanced and interest. Such a security interest is governed by the Article on Secured Transactions (Article 9).

(3) (a) A warehouseman's lien for charges and expenses under subsection (1) or a security interest under subsection (2) is also effective against any person who so entrusted the bailor with possession of the goods that a pledge of them by him to a good faith purchaser for value would have been valid but is not effective against a person as to whom the document confers no right in the goods covered by it under Section 7—503.

(b) A warehouseman's lien on household goods for charges and expenses in relation to the goods under subsection (1) is also effective against all persons if the depositor was the legal possessor of the goods at the time of deposit. "Household goods" means furniture, furnishings and personal effects used by the depositor in a dwelling.

(4) A warehouseman loses his lien on any goods which he voluntarily delivers or which he unjustifiably refuses to deliver.

§ 7—210. Enforcement of Warehouseman's Lien.

(1) Except as provided in subsection (2), a warehouseman's lien may be enforced by public or private sale of the goods in bloc or in parcels, at any time or place and on any terms which are commercially reasonable, after notifying all persons known to claim an interest in the goods. Such notification must include a statement of the amount due, the nature of the proposed sale and the time and place of any public sale. The fact that a better price could have been obtained by a sale at a different time or in a different method from that selected by the warehouseman is not of itself sufficient to establish that the sale was not made in a commercially reasonable manner. If the warehouseman either sells the goods in the usual manner in any recognized market therefor, or if he sells at the price current in such market at the time of his sale, or if he has otherwise sold in conformity with commercially reasonable practices among dealers in the type of goods sold, he has sold in a commercially reasonable manner. A sale of more goods than apparently necessary to be offered to insure satisfaction of the obligation is not commercially reasonable except in cases covered by the preceding sentence.

(2) A warehouseman's lien on goods other than goods stored by a merchant in the course of his business may be enforced only as follows:

(a) All persons known to claim an interest in the goods must be notified.

(b) The notification must be delivered in person or sent by registered or certified letter to the last known address of any person to be notified.

(c) The notification must include an itemized statement of the claim, a description of the goods subject to the lien, a demand for payment within a specified time not less than ten days after receipt of the notification, and a conspicuous statement that unless the claim is paid within the time the goods will be advertised for sale and sold by auction at a specified time and place.

(d) The sale must conform to the terms of the notification.

(e) The sale must be held at the nearest suitable place to that where the goods are held or stored.

(f) After the expiration of the time given in the notification, an advertisement of the sale must be published once a week for two weeks consecutively in a newspaper of general circulation where the sale is to be held. The advertisement must include a description of the goods, the name of the person on whose account they are being held, and the time and place of the sale. The sale must take place at least fifteen days after the first publication. If there is no newspaper of general circulation where the sale is to be held, the advertisement must be posted at least ten days before the sale in not less than six conspicuous places in the neighborhood of the proposed sale.

(3) Before any sale pursuant to this section any person claiming a right in the goods may pay the amount necessary to satisfy the lien and the reasonable expenses incurred under this section. In that event the goods must not be sold, but must be retained by the warehouseman subject to the terms of the receipt and this Article.

(4) The warehouseman may buy at any public sale pursuant to this section.

(5) A purchaser in good faith of goods sold to enforce a warehouseman's lien takes the goods free of any rights of persons against whom the lien was valid, despite noncompliance by the warehouseman with the requirements of this section.

(6) The warehouseman may satisfy his lien from the proceeds of any sale pursuant to this section but must hold the balance, if any, for delivery on demand to any person to whom he would have been bound to deliver the goods.

(7) The rights provided by this section shall be in addition to all other rights allowed by law to a creditor against his debtor.

(8) Where a lien is on goods stored by a merchant in the course of his business the lien may be enforced in accordance with either subsection (1) or (2).

(9) The warehouseman is liable for damages caused by failure to comply with the requirements for sale under this section and in case of willful violation is liable for conversion.

Part 3 Bills of Lading: Special Provisions

§ 7—301. Liability for Non-Receipt or Misdescription; "Said to Contain"; "Shipper's Load and Count"; Improper Handling.

(1) A consignee of a non-negotiable bill who has given value in good faith or a holder to whom a negotiable

bill has been duly negotiated relying in either case upon the description therein of the goods, or upon the date therein shown, may recover from the issuer damages caused by the misdating of the bill or the non-receipt or misdescription of the goods, except to the extent that the document indicates that the issuer does not know whether any part of all of the goods in fact were received or conform to the description, as where the description is in terms of marks or labels or kind, quantity, or condition or the receipt or description is qualified by "contents or condition of contents of packages unknown", "said to contain", "shipper's weight, load and count" or the like, if such indication be true.

(2) When goods are loaded by an issuer who is a common carrier, the issuer must count the packages of goods if package freight and ascertain the kind and quantity if bulk freight. In such cases "shipper's weight, load and count" or other words indicating that the description was made by the shipper are ineffective except as to freight concealed by packages.

(3) When bulk freight is loaded by a shipper who makes available to the issuer adequate facilities for weighing such freight, an issuer who is a common carrier must ascertain the kind and quantity within a reasonable time after receiving the written request of the shipper to do so. In such cases "shipper's weight" or other words of like purport are ineffective.

(4) The issuer may by inserting in the bill the words "shipper's weight, load and count" or other words of like purport indicate that the goods were loaded by the shipper; and if such statement be true the issuer shall not be liable for damages caused by the improper loading. But their omission does not imply liability for such damages.

(5) The shipper shall be deemed to have guaranteed to the issuer the accuracy at the time of shipment of the description, marks, labels, number, kind, quantity, condition and weight, as furnished by him; and the shipper shall indemnify the issuer against damage caused by inaccuracies in such particulars. The right of the issuer to such indemnity shall in no way limit his responsibility and liability under the contract of carriage to any person other than the shipper.

§ 7—302. **Through Bills of Lading and Similar Documents.**

(1) The issuer of a through bill of lading or other document embodying an undertaking to be performed in part by persons acting as its agents or by connecting carriers is liable to anyone entitled to recover on the document for any breach by such other persons or by

a connecting carrier of its obligation under the document but to the extent that the bill covers an undertaking to be performed overseas or in territory not contiguous to the continental United States or an undertaking including matters other than transportation this liability may be varied by agreement of the parties.

(2) Where goods covered by a through bill of lading or other document embodying an undertaking to be performed in part by persons other than the issuer are received by any such person, he is subject with respect to his own performance while the goods are in his possession to the obligation of the issuer. His obligation is discharged by delivery of the goods to another such person pursuant to the document, and does not include liability for breach by any other such persons or by the issuer.

(3) The issuer of such through bill of lading or other document shall be entitled to recover from the connecting carrier or such other person in possession of the goods when the breach of the obligation under the document occurred, the amount it may be required to pay to anyone entitled to recover on the document therefor, as may be evidenced by any receipt, judgment, or transcript thereof, and the amount of any expense reasonably incurred by it in defending any action brought by anyone entitled to recover on the document therefor.

§ 7—303. **Diversion; Reconsignment; Change of Instructions.**

(1) Unless the bill of lading otherwise provides, the carrier may deliver the goods to a person or destination other than that stated in the bill or may otherwise dispose of the goods on instructions from

(a) the holder of a negotiable bill; or

(b) the consignor on a non-negotiable bill notwithstanding contrary instructions from the consignee; or

(c) the consignee on a non-negotiable bill in the absence of contrary instructions from the consignor, if the goods have arrived at the billed destination or if the consignee is in possession of the bill; or

(d) the consignee on a non-negotiable bill if he is entitled as against the consignor to dispose of them.

(2) Unless such instructions are noted on a negotiable bill of lading, a person to whom the bill is duly negotiated can hold the bailee according to the original terms.

§ 7—304. **Bills of Lading in a Set.**

(1) Except where customary in overseas transportation, a bill of lading must not be issued in a set of parts. The issuer is liable for damages caused by violation of this subsection.

(2) Where a bill of lading is lawfully drawn in a set of parts, each of which is numbered and expressed to be valid only if the goods have not been delivered against any other part, the whole of the parts constitute one bill.

(3) Where a bill of lading is lawfully issued in a set of parts and different parts are negotiated to different persons, the title of the holder to whom the first due negotiation is made prevails as to both the document and the goods even though any later holder may have received the goods from the carrier in good faith and discharged the carrier's obligation by surrender of his part.

(4) Any person who negotiates or transfers a single part of a bill of lading drawn in a set is liable to holders of that part as if it were the whole set.

(5) The bailee is obliged to deliver in accordance with Part 4 of this Article against the first presented part of a bill of lading lawfully drawn in a set. Such delivery discharges the bailee's obligation on the whole bill.

§ 7—305. **Destination Bills.**

(1) Instead of issuing a bill of lading to the consignor at the place of shipment a carrier may at the request of the consignor procure the bill to be issued at destination or at any other place designated in the request.

(2) Upon request of anyone entitled as against the carrier to control the goods while in transit and on surrender of any outstanding bill of lading or other receipt covering such goods, the issuer may procure a substitute bill to be issued at any place designated in the request.

§ 7—306. **Altered Bills of Lading.**

An unauthorized alteration or filling in of a blank in a bill of lading leaves the bill enforceable according to its original tenor.

§ 7—307. **Lien of Carrier.**

(1) A carrier has a lien on the goods covered by a bill of lading for charges subsequent to the date of its receipt of the goods for storage or transportation (including demurrage and terminal charges) and for expenses necessary for preservation of the goods incident to their transportation or reasonably incurred in their

sale pursuant to law. But against a purchaser for value of a negotiable bill of lading a carrier's lien is limited to charges stated in the bill or the applicable tariffs, or if no charges are stated then to a reasonable charge.

(2) A lien for charges and expenses under subsection (1) on goods which the carrier was required by law to receive for transportation is effective against the consignor or any person entitled to the goods unless the carrier had notice that the consignor lacked authority to subject the goods to such charges and expenses. Any other lien under subsection (1) is effective against the consignor and any person who permitted the bailor to have control or possession of the goods unless the carrier had notice that the bailor lacked such authority.

(3) A carrier loses his lien on any goods which he voluntarily delivers or which he unjustifiably refuses to deliver.

§ 7—308. **Enforcement of Carrier's Lien.**

(1) A carrier's lien may be enforced by public or private sale of the goods, in bloc or in parcels, at any time or place and on any terms which are commercially reasonable, after notifying all persons known to claim an interest in the goods. Such notification must include a statement of the amount due, the nature of the proposed sale and the time and place of any public sale. The fact that a better price could have been obtained by a sale at a different time or in a different method from that selected by the carrier is not of itself sufficient to establish that the sale was not made in a commercially reasonable manner. If the carrier either sells the goods in the usual manner in any recognized market therefor or if he sells at the price current in such market at the time of his sale or if he has otherwise sold in conformity with commercially reasonable practices among dealers in the type of goods sold he has sold in a commercially reasonable manner. A sale of more goods than apparently necessary to be offered to ensure satisfaction of the obligation is not commercially reasonable except in cases covered by the preceding sentence.

(2) Before any sale pursuant to this section any person claiming a right in the goods may pay the amount necessary to satisfy the lien and the reasonable expenses incurred under this section. In that event the goods must not be sold, but must be retained by the carrier subject to the terms of the bill and this Article.

(3) The carrier may buy at any public sale pursuant to this section.

(4) A purchaser in good faith of goods sold to enforce

a carrier's lien takes the goods free of any rights of persons against whom the lien was valid, despite non-compliance by the carrier with the requirements of this section.

(5) The carrier may satisfy his lien from the proceeds of any sale pursuant to this section but must hold the balance, if any, for delivery on demand to any person to whom he would have been bound to deliver the goods.

(6) The rights provided by this section shall be in addition to all other rights allowed by law to a creditor against his debtor.

(7) A carrier's lien may be enforced in accordance with either subsection (1) or the procedure set forth in subsection (2) of Section 7—210.

(8) The carrier is liable for damages caused by failure to comply with the requirements for sale under this section and in case of willful violation is liable for conversion.

§ 7—309. **Duty of Care; Contractual Limitation of Carrier's Liability.**

(1) A carrier who issues a bill of lading whether negotiable or non-negotiable must exercise the degree of care in relation to the goods which a reasonably careful man would exercise under like circumstances. This subsection does not repeal or change any law or rule of law which imposes liability upon a common carrier for damages not caused by its negligence.

(2) Damages may be limited by a provision that the carrier's liability shall not exceed a value stated in the document if the carrier's rates are dependent upon value and the consignor by the carrier's tariff is afforded an opportunity to declare a higher value or a value as lawfully provided in the tariff, or where no tariff is filed he is otherwise advised of such opportunity; but no such limitation is effective with respect to the carrier's liability for conversion to its own use.

(3) Reasonable provisions as to the time and manner of presenting claims and instituting actions based on the shipment may be included in a bill of lading or tariff.

Part 4 Warehouse Receipts and Bills of Lading: General Obligations

§ 7—401. **Irregularities in Issue of Receipt or Bill or Conduct of Issuer.**

The obligations imposed by this Article on an issuer apply to a document of title regardless of the fact that

(a) the document may not comply with the requirements of this Article or of any other law or regulation regarding its issue, form or content; or

(b) the issuer may have violated laws regulating the conduct of his business; or

(c) the goods covered by the document were owned by the bailee at the time the document was issued; or

(d) the person issuing the document does not come within the definition of warehouseman if it purports to be a warehouse receipt.

§ 7—402. **Duplicate Receipt or Bill; Overissue.**

Neither a duplicate nor any other document of title purporting to cover goods already represented by an outstanding document of the same issuer confers any right in the goods, except as provided in the case of bills in a set, overissue of documents for fungible goods and substitutes for lost, stolen or destroyed documents. But the issuer is liable for damages caused by his overissue or failure to identify a duplicate document as such by conspicuous notation on its face.

§ 7—403. **Obligation of Warehouseman or Carrier to Deliver; Excuse.**

(1) The bailee must deliver the goods to a person entitled under the document who complies with subsections (2) and (3), unless and to the extent that the bailee establishes any of the following:

(a) delivery of the goods to a person whose receipt was rightful as against the claimant;

(b) damage to or delay, loss or destruction of the goods for which the bailee is not liable [, but the burden of establishing negligence in such cases is on the person entitled under the document];

Note: *The brackets in (1)(b) indicate that State enactments may differ on this point without serious damage to the principle of uniformity.*

(c) previous sale or other disposition of the goods in lawful enforcement of a lien or on warehouseman's lawful termination of storage;

(d) the exercise by a seller of his right to stop delivery pursuant to the provisions of the Article on Sales (Section 2—705);

(e) a diversion, reconsignment or other disposition pursuant to the provisions of this Article (Section 7—303) or tariff regulating such right;

(f) release, satisfaction or any other fact affording a personal defense against the claimant;

(g) any other lawful excuse.

(2) A person claiming goods covered by a document of title must satisfy the bailee's lien where the bailee so requests or where the bailee is prohibited by law from delivering the goods until the charges are paid.

(3) Unless the person claiming is one against whom the document confers no right under Sec. 7—503(1), he must surrender for cancellation or notation of partial deliveries any outstanding negotiable document covering the goods, and the bailee must cancel the document or conspicuously note the partial delivery thereon or be liable to any person to whom the document is duly negotiated.

(4) "Person entitled under the document" means holder in the case of a negotiable document, or the person to whom delivery is to be made by the terms of or pursuant to written instructions under a non-negotiable document.

§ 7—404. **No Liability for Good Faith Delivery Pursuant to Receipt or Bill.**

A bailee who in good faith including observance of reasonable commercial standards has received goods and delivered or otherwise disposed of them according to the terms of the document of title or pursuant to this Article is not liable therefor. This rule applies even though the person from whom he received the goods had no authority to procure the document or to dispose of the goods and even though the person to whom he delivered the goods had no authority to receive them.

Part 5 Warehouse Receipts and Bills of Lading: Negotiation and Transfer

§ 7—501. **Form of Negotiation and Requirements of "Due Negotiation".**

(1) A negotiable document of title running to the order of a named person is negotiated by his indorsement and delivery. After his indorsement in blank or to bearer any person can negotiate it by delivery alone.

(2) (a) A negotiable document of title is also negotiated by delivery alone when by its original terms it runs to bearer.

(b) When a document running to the order of a named person is delivered to him the effect is the same as if the document had been negotiated.

(3) Negotiation of a negotiable document of title after it has been indorsed to a specified person requires indorsement by the special indorsee as well as delivery.

(4) A negotiable document of title is "duly negoti-ated" when it is negotiated in the manner stated in this section to a holder who purchases it in good faith without notice of any defense against or claim to it on the part of any person and for value, unless it is established that the negotiation is not in the regular course of business or financing or involves receiving the document in settlement or payment of a money obligation.

(5) Indorsement of a non-negotiable document neither makes it negotiable nor adds to the transferee's rights.

(6) The naming in a negotiable bill of a person to be notified of the arrival of the goods does not limit the negotiability of the bill nor constitute notice to a purchaser thereof of any interest of such person in the goods.

§ 7—502. **Rights Acquired by Due Negotiation.**

(1) Subject to the following section and to the provisions of Section 7—205 on fungible goods, a holder to whom a negotiable document of title has been duly negotiated acquires thereby:

(a) title to the document;

(b) title to the goods;

(c) all rights accruing under the law of agency or estoppel, including rights to goods delivered to the bailee after the document was issued; and

(d) the direct obligation of the issuer to hold or deliver the goods according to the terms of the document free of any defense or claim by him except those arising under the terms of the document or under this Article. In the case of a delivery order the bailee's obligation accrues only upon acceptance and the obligation acquired by the holder is that the issuer and any indorser will procure the acceptance of the bailee.

(2) Subject to the following section, title and rights so acquired are not defeated by any stoppage of the goods represented by the document or by surrender of such goods by the bailee, and are not impaired even though the negotiation or any prior negotiation constituted a breach of duty or even though any person has been deprived of possession of the document by misrepresentation, fraud, accident, mistake, duress, loss, theft or conversion, or even though a previous sale or other transfer of the goods or document has been made to a third person.

§ 7—503. **Document of Title to Goods Defeated in Certain Cases.**

(1) A document of title confers no right in goods against

a person who before issuance of the document had a legal interest or a perfected security interest in them and who neither

(a) delivered or entrusted them or any document of title covering them to the bailor or his nominee with actual or apparent authority to ship, store or sell or with power to obtain delivery under this Article (Section 7—403) or with power of disposition under this Act (Sections 2—403 and 9—307) or other statute or rule of law; nor

(b) acquiesced in the procurement by the bailor or his nominee of any document of title.

(2) Title to goods based upon an unaccepted delivery order is subject to the rights of anyone to whom a negotiable warehouse receipt or bill of lading covering the goods has been duly negotiated. Such a title may be defeated under the next section to the same extent as the rights of the issuer or a transferee from the issuer.

(3) Title to goods based upon a bill of lading issued to a freight forwarder is subject to the rights of anyone to whom a bill issued by the freight forwarder is duly negotiated; but delivery by the carrier in accordance with Part 4 of this Article pursuant to its own bill of lading discharges the carrier's obligation to deliver.

§ 7—504. Rights Acquired in the Absence of Due Negotiation; Effect of Diversion; Seller's Stoppage of Delivery.

(1) A transferee of a document, whether negotiable or non-negotiable, to whom the document has been delivered but not duly negotiated, acquires the title and rights which his transferor had or had actual authority to convey.

(2) In the case of a non-negotiable document, until but not after the bailee receives notification of the transfer, the rights of the transferee may be defeated

(a) by those creditors of the transferor who could treat the sale as void under Section 2—402; or

(b) by a buyer from the transferor in ordinary course of business if the bailee has delivered the goods to the buyer or received notification of his rights; or

(c) as against the bailee by good faith dealings of the bailee with the transferor.

(3) A diversion or other change of shipping instructions by the consignor in a non-negotiable bill of lading which causes the bailee not to deliver to the consignee defeats the consignee's title to the goods if they have been delivered to a buyer in ordinary course of business and in any event defeats the consignee's rights against the bailee.

(4) Delivery pursuant to a non-negotiable document may be stopped by a seller under Section 2—705, and subject to the requirement of due notification there provided. A bailee honoring the seller's instructions is entitled to be indemnified by the seller against any resulting loss or expense.

§ 7—505. Indorser Not a Guarantor for Other Parties.

The indorsement of a document of title issued by a bailee does not make the indorser liable for any default by the bailee or by previous indorsers.

§ 7—506. Delivery Without Indorsement: Right to Compel Indorsement.

The transferee of a negotiable document of title has a specifically enforceable right to have his transferor supply any necessary indorsement but the transfer becomes a negotiation only as of the time the indorsement is supplied.

§ 7—507. Warranties on Negotiation or Transfer of Receipt or Bill.

Where a person negotiates or transfers a document of title for value otherwise than as a mere intermediary under the next following section, then unless otherwise agreed he warrants to his immediate purchaser only in addition to any warranty made in selling the goods

(a) that the document is genuine; and

(b) that he has no knowledge of any fact which would impair its validity or worth; and

(c) that his negotiation or transfer is rightful and fully effective with respect to the title to the document and the goods it represents.

§ 7—508. Warranties of Collecting Bank as to Documents.

A collecting bank or other intermediary known to be entrusted with documents on behalf of another or with collection of a draft or other claim against delivery of documents warrants by such delivery of the documents only its own good faith and authority. This rule applies even though the intermediary has purchased or made advances against the claim or draft to be collected.

§ 7—509. Receipt or Bill: When Adequate Compliance With Commercial Contract.

The question whether a document is adequate to fulfill the obligations of a contract for sale or the conditions of a credit is governed by the Articles on Sales (Article 2) and on Letters of Credit (Article 5).

Part 6 Warehouse Receipts and Bills of Lading: Miscellaneous Provisions

§ 7—601. **Lost and Missing Documents.**

(1) If a document has been lost, stolen or destroyed, a court may order delivery of the goods or issuance of a substitute document and the bailee may without liability to any person comply with such order. If the document was negotiable the claimant must post security approved by the court to indemnify any person who may suffer loss as a result of non-surrender of the document. If the document was not negotiable, such security may be required at the discretion of the court. The court may also in its discretion order payment of the bailee's reasonable costs and counsel fees.

(2) A bailee who without court order delivers goods to a person claiming under a missing negotiable document is liable to any person injured thereby, and if the delivery is not in good faith becomes liable for conversion. Delivery in good faith is not conversion if made in accordance with a filed classification or tariff or, where no classification or tariff is filed, if the claimant posts security with the bailee in an amount at least double the value of the goods at the time of posting to indemnify any person injured by the delivery who files a notice of claim within one year after the delivery.

§ 7—602. **Attachment of Goods Covered by a Negotiable Document.**

Except where the document was originally issued upon delivery of the goods by a person who had no power to dispose of them, no lien attaches by virtue of any judicial process to goods in the possession of a bailee for which a negotiable document of title is outstanding unless the document be first surrendered to the bailee or its negotiation enjoined, and the bailee shall not be compelled to deliver the goods pursuant to process until the document is surrendered to him or impounded by the court. One who purchases the document for value without notice of the process or injunction takes free of the lien imposed by judicial process.

§ 7—603. **Conflicting Claims; Interpleader.**

If more than one person claims title or possession of the goods, the bailee is excused from delivery until he has had a reasonable time to ascertain the validity of the adverse claims or to bring an action to compel all claimants to interplead and may compel such interpleader, either in defending an action for non-delivery of the goods, or by original action, whichever is appropriate.

Article 8
INVESTMENT SECURITIES

Part 1 Short Title and General Matters

§ 8—101. **Short Title.**

This Article shall be known and may be cited as Uniform Commercial Code—Investment Securities.

§ 8—102. **Definitions and Index of Definitions.**

(1) In this Article, unless the context otherwise requires:

(a) A "certificated security" is a share, participation, or other interest in property of or an enterprise of the issuer or an obligation of the issuer which is

(i) represented by an instrument issued in bearer or registered form;

(ii) of a type commonly dealt in on securities exchanges or markets or commonly recognized in any area in which it is issued or dealt in as a medium for investment; and

(iii) either one of a class or series or by its terms divisible into a class or series of shares, participations, interests, or obligations.

(b) An "uncertificated security" is a share, participation, or other interest in property or an enterprise of the issuer or an obligation of the issuer which is

(i) not represented by an instrument and the transfer of which is registered upon books maintained for that purpose by or on behalf of the issuer;

(ii) of a type commonly dealt in on securities exchanges or markets; and

(iii) either one of a class or series or by its terms divisible into a class or series of shares, participations, interests, or obligations.

(c) A "security" is either a certificated or an uncertificated security. If a security is certificated, the terms "security" and "certificated security" may mean either the intangible interest, the instrument representing that interest, or both, as the context requires. A writing that is a certificated security is governed by this Article and not by Article 3, even though it also meets the requirements of that Article. This Article does not apply to money. If a certificated security has been retained by or surrendered to the issuer or its transfer agent for reasons other than registration of transfer, other temporary purpose, payment, exchange, or acquisition by the issuer, that security shall be treated as an uncertificated security for purposes of this Article.

(d) A certificated security is in "registered form" if

(i) it specifies a person entitled to the security or the rights it represents; and

(ii) its transfer may be registered upon books maintained for that purpose by or on behalf of the issuer, or the security so states.

(e) A certificated security is in "bearer form" if it runs to bearer according to its terms and not by reason of any indorsement.

(2) A "subsequent purchaser" is a person who takes other than by original issue.

(3) A "clearing corporation" is a corporation registered as a "clearing agency" under the federal securities laws or a corporation:

(a) at least 90 percent of whose capital stock is held by or for one or more organizations, none of which, other than a national securities exchange or association, holds in excess of 20 percent of the capital stock of the corporation, and each of which is

(i) subject to supervision or regulation pursuant to the provisions of federal or state banking laws or state insurance laws,

(ii) a broker or dealer or investment company registered under the federal securities laws, or

(iii) a national securities exchange or association registered under the federal securities laws; and

(b) any remaining capital stock of which is held by individuals who have purchased it at or prior to the time of their taking office as directors of the corporation and who have purchased only so much of the capital stock as is necessary to permit them to qualify as directors.

(4) A "custodian bank" is a bank or trust company that is supervised and examined by state or federal authority having supervision over banks and is acting as custodian for a clearing corporation.

(5) Other definitions applying to this Article or to specified Parts thereof and the sections in which they appear are:

"Adverse claim". Section 8—302.
"Bona fide purchaser". Section 8—302.
"Broker". Section 8—303.

"Debtor". Section 9—105.
"Financial intermediary". Section 8—313.
"Guarantee of the signature". Section 8—402.
"Initial transaction statement". Section 8—408.
"Instruction". Section 8—308.
"Intermediary bank". Section 4—105.
"Issuer". Section 8—201.
"Overissue". Section 8—104.
"Secured Party". Section 9—105.
"Security Agreement". Section 9—105.

(6) In addition, Article 1 contains general definitions and principles of construction and interpretation applicable throughout this Article.

Amended in 1962, 1973 and 1977.

§ 8—103. **Issuer's Lien.**

A lien upon a security in favor of an issuer thereof is valid against a purchaser only if:

(a) the security is certificated and the right of the issuer to the lien is noted conspicuously thereon; or

(b) the security is uncertificated and a notation of the right of the issuer to the lien is contained in the initial transaction statement sent to the purchaser or, if his interest is transferred to him other than by registration of transfer, pledge, or release, the initial transaction statement sent to the registered owner or the registered pledgee.
Amended in 1977.

§ 8—104. **Effect of Overissue; "Overissue".**

(1) The provisions of this Article which validate a security or compel its issue or reissue do not apply to the extent that validation, issue, or reissue would result in overissue; but if:

(a) an identical security which does not constitute an overissue is reasonably available for purchase, the person entitled to issue or validation may compel the issuer to purchase the security for him and either to deliver a certificated security or to register the transfer of an uncertificated security to him, against surrender of any certificated security he holds; or

(b) a security is not so available for purchase, the person entitled to issue or validation may recover from the issuer the price he or the last purchaser for value paid for it with interest from the date of his demand.

(2) "Overissue" means the issue of securities in excess of the amount the issuer has corporate power to issue.
Amended in 1977.

§ 8—105. Certificated Securities Negotiable; Statements and Instructions Not Negotiable; Presumptions.

(1) Certificated securities governed by this Article are negotiable instruments.

(2) Statements (Section 8—408), notices, or the like, sent by the issuer of uncertificated securities and instructions (Section 8—308) are neither negotiable instruments nor certificated securities.

(3) In any action on a security:

(a) unless specifically denied in the pleadings, each signature on a certificated security, in a necessary indorsement, on an initial transaction statement, or on an instruction, is admitted;

(b) if the effectiveness of a signature is put in issue, the burden of establishing it is on the party claiming under the signature, but the signature is presumed to be genuine or authorized;

(c) if signatures on a certificated security are admitted or established, production of the security entitles a holder to recover on it unless the defendant establishes a defense or a defect going to the validity of the security;

(d) if signatures on an initial transaction statement are admitted or established, the facts stated in the statement are presumed to be true as of the time of its issuance; and

(e) after it is shown that a defense or defect exists, the plaintiff has the burden of establishing that he or some person under whom he claims is a person against whom the defense or defect is ineffective (Section 8—202).

Amended in 1977.

§ 8—106. Applicability.

The law (including the conflict of laws rules) of the jurisdiction of organization of the issuer governs the validity of a security, the effectiveness of registration by the issuer, and the rights and duties of the issuer with respect to:

(a) registration of transfer of a certificated security;

(b) registration of transfer, pledge, or release of an uncertificated security; and

(c) sending of statements of uncertificated securities.

Amended in 1977.

§ 8—107. Securities Transferable; Action for Price.

(1) Unless otherwise agreed and subject to any applicable law or regulation respecting short sales, a person obligated to transfer securities may transfer any certificated security of the specified issue in bearer form or registered in the name of the transferee, or indorsed to him or in blank, or he may transfer an equivalent uncertificated security to the transferee or a person designated by the transferee.

(2) If the buyer fails to pay the price as it comes due under a contract of sale, the seller may recover the price of:

(a) certificated securities accepted by the buyer;

(b) uncertificated securities that have been transferred to the buyer or a person designated by the buyer; and

(c) other securities if efforts at their resale would be unduly burdensome or if there is no readily available market for their resale.

Amended in 1977.

§ 8—108. Registration of Pledge and Release of Uncertificated Securities.

A security interest in an uncertificated security may be evidenced by the registration of pledge to the secured party or a person designated by him. There can be no more than one registered pledge of an uncertificated security at any time. The registered owner of an uncertificated security is the person in whose name the security is registered, even if the security is subject to a registered pledge. The rights of a registered pledgee of an uncertificated security under this Article are terminated by the registration of release.

Added in 1977.

Part 2 Issue—Issuer

§ 8—201. "Issuer"

(1) With respect to obligations on or defenses to a security, "issuer" includes a person who:

(a) places or authorizes the placing of his name on a certificated security (otherwise than as authenticating trustee, registrar, transfer agent, or the like) to evidence that it represents a share, participation, or other interest in his property or in an enterprise, or to evidence his duty to perform an obligation represented by the certificated security;

(b) creates shares, participations, or other interests in his property or in an enterprise or undertakes obligations, which shares, participations, interests, or obligations are uncertificated securities;

(c) directly or indirectly creates fractional interests in his rights or property, which fractional interests are represented by certificated securities; or

(d) becomes responsible for or in place of any other person described as an issuer in this section.

(2) With respect to obligations on or defenses to a security, a guarantor is an issuer to the extent of his guaranty, whether or not his obligation is noted on a certificated security or on statements of uncertificated securities sent pursuant to Section 8—408.

(3) With respect to registration of transfer, pledge, or release (Part 4 of this Article), "issuer" means a person on whose behalf transfer books are maintained.

Amended in 1977.

§ 8—202. Issuer's Responsibility and Defenses; Notice of Defect or Defense.

(1) Even against a purchaser for value and without notice, the terms of a security include:

(a) if the security is certificated, those stated on the security;

(b) if the security is uncertificated, those contained in the initial transaction statement sent to such purchaser or, if his interest is transferred to him other than by registration of transfer, pledge, or release, the initial transaction statement sent to the registered owner or registered pledgee; and

(c) those made part of the security by reference, on the certificated security or in the initial transaction statement, to another instrument, indenture, or document or to a constitution, statute, ordinance, rule, regulation, order or the like, to the extent that the terms referred to do not conflict with the terms stated on the certificated security or contained in the statement. A reference under this paragraph does not of itself charge a purchaser for value with notice of a defect going to the validity of the security, even though the certificated security or statement expressly states that a person accepting it admits notice.

(2) A certificated security in the hands of a purchaser for value or an uncertificated security as to which an initial transaction statement has been sent to a purchaser for value, other than a security issued by a government or governmental agency or unit, even though issued with a defect going to its validity, is valid with respect to the purchaser if he is without notice of the particular defect unless the defect involves a violation of constitutional provisions, in which case the security is valid with respect to a subsequent purchaser for value and without notice of the defect. This subsection applies to an issuer that is a government or

governmental agency or unit only if either there has been substantial compliance with the legal requirements governing the issue or the issuer has received a substantial consideration for the issue as a whole or for the particular security and a stated purpose of the issue is one for which the issuer has power to borrow money or issue the security.

(3) Except as provided in the case of certain unauthorized signatures (Section 8—205), lack of genuineness of a certificated security or an initial transaction statement is a complete defense, even against a purchaser for value and without notice.

(4) All other defenses of the issuer of a certificated or uncertificated security, including nondelivery and conditional delivery of a certificated security, are ineffective against a purchaser for value who has taken without notice of the particular defense.

(5) Nothing in this section shall be construed to affect the right of a party to a "when, as and if issued" or a "when distributed" contract to cancel the contract in the event of a material change in the character of the security that is the subject of the contract or in the plan or arrangement pursuant to which the security is to be issued or distributed.

Amended in 1977.

§ 8—203. Staleness as Notice of Defects or Defenses.

(1) After an act or event creating a right to immediate performance of the principal obligation represented by a certificated security or that sets a date on or after which the security is to be presented or surrendered for redemption or exchange, a purchaser is charged with notice of any defect in its issue or defense of the issuer if:

(a) the act or event is one requiring the payment of money, the delivery of certificated securities, the registration of transfer of uncertificated securities, or any of these on presentation or surrender of the certificated security, the funds or securities are available on the date set for payment or exchange, and he takes the security more than one year after that date; and

(b) the act or event is not covered by paragraph (a) and he takes the security more than 2 years after the date set for surrender or presentation or the date on which performance became due.

(2) A call that has been revoked is not within subsection (1).

Amended in 1977.

§ 8—204. **Effect of Issuer's Restrictions on Transfer.**

A restriction on transfer of a security imposed by the issuer, even if otherwise lawful, is ineffective against any person without actual knowledge of it unless:

(a) the security is certificated and the restriction is noted conspicuously thereon; or

(b) the security is uncertificated and a notation of the restriction is contained in the initial transaction statement sent to the person or, if his interest is transferred to him other than by registration of transfer, pledge, or release, the initial transaction statement sent to the registered owner or the registered pledgee.

Amended in 1977.

§ 8—205. **Effect of Unauthorized Signature on Certificated Security or Initial Transaction Statement.**

An unauthorized signature placed on a certificated security prior to or in the course of issue or placed on an initial transaction statement is ineffective, but the signature is effective in favor of a purchaser for value of the certificated security or a purchaser for value of an uncertificated security to whom the initial transaction statement has been sent, if the purchaser is without notice of the lack of authority and the signing has been done by:

(a) an authenticating trustee, registrar, transfer agent, or other person entrusted by the issuer with the signing of the security, of similar securities, or of initial transaction statements or the immediate preparation for signing of any of them; or

(b) an employee of the issuer, or of any of the foregoing, entrusted with responsible handling of the security or initial transaction statement.

Amended in 1977.

§ 8—206. **Completion or Alteration of Certificated Security or Initial Transaction Statement.**

(1) If a certificated security contains the signatures necessary to its issue or transfer but is incomplete in any other respect:

(a) any person may complete it by filling in the blanks as authorized; and

(b) even though the blanks are incorrectly filled in, the security as completed is enforceable by a purchaser who took it for value and without notice of the incorrectness.

(2) A complete certificated security that has been improperly altered, even though fraudulently, remains enforceable, but only according to its original terms.

(3) If an initial transaction statement contains the signatures necessary to its validity, but is incomplete in any other respect:

(a) any person may complete it by filling in the blanks as authorized; and

(b) even though the blanks are incorrectly filled in, the statement as completed is effective in favor of the person to whom it is sent if he purchased the security referred to therein for value and without notice of the incorrectness.

(4) A complete initial transaction statement that has been improperly altered, even though fraudulently, is effective in favor of a purchaser to whom it has been sent, but only according to its original terms.

Amended in 1977.

§ 8—207. **Rights and Duties of Issuer With Respect to Registered Owners and Registered Pledgees.**

(1) Prior to due presentment for registration of transfer of a certificated security in registered form, the issuer or indenture trustee may treat the registered owner as the person exclusively entitled to vote, to receive notifications, and otherwise to exercise all the rights and powers of an owner.

(2) Subject to the provisions of subsections (3), (4), and (6), the issuer or indenture trustee may treat the registered owner of an uncertificated security as the person exclusively entitled to vote, to receive notifications, and otherwise to exercise all the rights and powers of an owner.

(3) The registered owner of an uncertificated security that is subject to a registered pledge is not entitled to registration of transfer prior to the due presentment to the issuer of a release instruction. The exercise of conversion rights with respect to a convertible uncertificated security is a transfer within the meaning of this section.

(4) Upon due presentment of a transfer instruction from the registered pledgee of an uncertificated security, the issuer shall:

(a) register the transfer of the security to the new owner free of pledge, if the instruction specifies a new owner (who may be the registered pledgee) and does not specify a pledgee;

(b) register the transfer of the security to the new owner subject to the interest of the existing pledgee, if the instruction specifies a new owner and the existing pledgee; or

(c) register the release of the security from the existing pledge and register the pledge of the security to the other pledgee, if the instruction specifies the existing owner and another pledgee.

(5) Continuity of perfection of a security interest is not broken by registration of transfer under subsection (4)(b) or by registration of release and pledge under subsection (4)(c), if the security interest is assigned.

(6) If an uncertificated security is subject to a registered pledge:

(a) any uncertificated securities issued in exchange for or distributed with respect to the pledged security shall be registered subject to the pledge;

(b) any certificated securities issued in exchange for or distributed with respect to the pledged security shall be delivered to the registered pledgee; and

(c) any money paid in exchange for or in redemption of part or all of the security shall be paid to the registered pledgee.

(7) Nothing in this Article shall be construed to affect the liability of the registered owner of a security for calls, assessments, or the like.

Amended in 1977.

§ 8—208. **Effect of Signature of Authenticating Trustee, Registrar, or Transfer Agent.**

(1) A person placing his signature upon a certificated security or an initial transaction statement as authenticating trustee, registrar, transfer agent, or the like, warrants to a purchaser for value of the certificated security or a purchaser for value of an uncertificated security to whom the initial transaction statement has been sent, if the purchaser is without notice of the particular defect, that:

(a) the certificated security or initial transaction statement is genuine;

(b) his own participation in the issue or registration of the transfer, pledge, or release of the security is within his capacity and within the scope of the authority received by him from the issuer; and

(c) he has reasonable grounds to believe the security is in the form and within the amount the issuer is authorized to issue.

(2) Unless otherwise agreed, a person by so placing his signature does not assume responsibility for the validity of the security in other respects.

Amended in 1962 and 1977.

Part 3 Transfer

§ 8—301. **Rights Acquired by Purchaser.**

(1) Upon transfer of a security to a purchaser (Section 8—313), the purchaser acquires the rights in the security which his transferor had or had actual authority to convey unless the purchaser's rights are limited by Section 8—302(4).

(2) A transferee of a limited interest acquires rights only to the extent of the interest transferred. The creation or release of a security interest in a security is the transfer of a limited interest in that security.

Amended in 1977.

§ 8—302. **"Bona Fide Purchaser"; "Adverse Claim"; Title Acquired by Bona Fide Purchaser.**

(1) A "bona fide purchaser" is a purchaser for value in good faith and without notice of any adverse claim:

(a) who takes delivery of a certificated security in bearer form or in registered form, issued or indorsed to him or in blank;

(b) to whom the transfer, pledge, or release of an uncertificated security is registered on the books of the issuer; or

(c) to whom a security is transferred under the provisions of paragraph (c), (d)(i), or (g) of Section 8—313(1).

(2) "Adverse claim" includes a claim that a transfer was or would be wrongful or that a particular adverse person is the owner of or has an interest in the security.

(3) A bona fide purchaser in addition to acquiring the rights of a purchaser (Section 8—301) also acquires his interest in the security free of any adverse claim.

(4) Notwithstanding Section 8—301(1), the transferee of a particular certificated security who has been a party to any fraud or illegality affecting the security, or who as a prior holder of that certificated security had notice of an adverse claim, cannot improve his position by taking from a bona fide purchaser.

Amended in 1977.

§ 8—303. **"Broker".**

"Broker" means a person engaged for all or part of his time in the business of buying and selling securities, who in the transaction concerned acts for, buys a security from, or sells a security to, a customer. Nothing in this Article determines the capacity in which a person acts for purposes of any other statute or rule to which the person is subject.

§ 8—304. **Notice to Purchaser of Adverse Claims.**

(1) A purchaser (including a broker for the seller or buyer, but excluding an intermediary bank) of a certificated security is charged with notice of adverse claims if:

   (a) the security, whether in bearer or registered form, has been indorsed "for collection" or "for surrender" or for some other purpose not involving transfer; or

   (b) the security is in bearer form and has on it an unambiguous statement that it is the property of a person other than the transferor. The mere writing of a name on a security is not such a statement.

(2) A purchaser (including a broker for the seller or buyer, but excluding an intermediary bank) to whom the transfer, pledge, or release of an uncertificated security is registered is charged with notice of adverse claims as to which the issuer has a duty under Section 8—403(4) at the time of registration and which are noted in the initial transaction statement sent to the purchaser or, if his interest is transferred to him other than by registration of transfer, pledge, or release, the initial transaction statement sent to the registered owner or the registered pledgee.

(3) The fact that the purchaser (including a broker for the seller or buyer) of a certificated or uncertificated security has notice that the security is held for a third person or is registered in the name of or indorsed by a fiduciary does not create a duty of inquiry into the rightfulness of the transfer or constitute constructive notice of adverse claims. However, if the purchaser (excluding an intermediary bank) has knowledge that the proceeds are being used or the transaction is for the individual benefit of the fiduciary or otherwise in breach of duty, the purchaser is charged with notice of adverse claims.

Amended in 1977.

§ 8—305. **Staleness as Notice of Adverse Claims.**

An act or event that creates a right to immediate performance of the principal obligation represented by a certificated security or sets a date on or after which a certificated security is to be presented or surrendered for redemption or exchange does not itself constitute any notice of adverse claims except in the case of a transfer:

(a) after one year from any date set for presentment or surrender for redemption or exchange; or

(b) after 6 months from any date set for payment of money against presentation or surrender of the security if funds are available for payment on that date. Amended in 1977.

§ 8—306. **Warranties on Presentment and Transfer of Certificated Securities; Warranties of Originators of Instructions.**

(1) A person who presents a certificated security for registration of transfer or for payment or exchange warrants to the issuer that he is entitled to the registration, payment, or exchange. But, a purchaser for value and without notice of adverse claims who receives a new, reissued, or re-registered certificated security on registration of transfer or receives an initial transaction statement confirming the registration of transfer of an equivalent uncertificated security to him warrants only that he has no knowledge of any unauthorized signature (Section 8—311) in a necessary indorsement.

(2) A person by transferring a certificated security to a purchaser for value warrants only that:

   (a) his transfer is effective and rightful;

   (b) the security is genuine and has not been materially altered; and

   (c) he knows of no fact which might impair the validity of the security.

(3) If a certificated security is delivered by an intermediary known to be entrusted with delivery of the security on behalf of another or with collection of a draft or other claim against delivery, the intermediary by delivery warrants only his own good faith and authority, even though he has purchased or made advances against the claim to be collected against the delivery.

(4) A pledgee or other holder for security who redelivers a certificated security received, or after payment and on order of the debtor delivers that security to a third person, makes only the warranties of an intermediary under subsection (3).

(5) A person who originates an instruction warrants to the issuer that:

   (a) he is an appropriate person to originate the instruction; and

   (b) at the time the instruction is presented to the issuer he will be entitled to the registration of transfer, pledge, or release.

(6) A person who originates an instruction warrants to any person specially guaranteeing his signature (subsection 8—312(3)) that:

(a) he is an appropriate person to originate the instruction; and

(b) at the time the instruction is presented to the issuer

(i) he will be entitled to the registration of transfer, pledge, or release; and

(ii) the transfer, pledge, or release requested in the instruction will be registered by the issuer free from all liens, security interests, restrictions, and claims other than those specified in the instruction.

(7) A person who originates an instruction warrants to a purchaser for value and to any person guaranteeing the instruction (Section 8—312(6)) that:

(a) he is an appropriate person to originate the instruction;

(b) the uncertificated security referred to therein is valid; and

(c) at the time the instruction is presented to the issuer

(i) the transferor will be entitled to the registration of transfer, pledge, or release;

(ii) the transfer, pledge, or release requested in the instruction will be registered by the issuer free from all liens, security interests, restrictions, and claims other than those specified in the instruction; and

(iii) the requested transfer, pledge, or release will be rightful.

(8) If a secured party is the registered pledgee or the registered owner of an uncertificated security, a person who originates an instruction of release or transfer to the debtor or, after payment and on order of the debtor, a transfer instruction to a third person, warrants to the debtor or the third person only that he is an appropriate person to originate the instruction and, at the time the instruction is presented to the issuer, the transferor will be entitled to the registration of release or transfer. If a transfer instruction to a third person who is a purchaser for value is originated on order of the debtor, the debtor makes to the purchaser the warranties of paragraphs (b), (c)(ii) and (c)(iii) of subsection (7).

(9) A person who transfers an uncertificated security to a purchaser for value and does not originate an instruction in connection with the transfer warrants only that:

(a) his transfer is effective and rightful; and

(b) the uncertificated security is valid.

(10) A broker gives to his customer and to the issuer and a purchaser the applicable warranties provided in this section and has the rights and privileges of a purchaser under this section. The warranties of and in favor of the broker, acting as an agent are in addition to applicable warranties given by and in favor of his customer.

Amended in 1962 and 1977.

§ 8—307. **Effect of Delivery Without Indorsement; Right to Compel Indorsement.**

If a certificated security in registered form has been delivered to a purchaser without a necessary indorsement he may become a bona fide purchaser only as of the time the indorsement is supplied; but against the transferor, the transfer is complete upon delivery and the purchaser has a specifically enforceable right to have any necessary indorsement supplied.

Amended in 1977.

§ 8—308. **Indorsements; Instructions.**

(1) An indorsement of a certificated security in registered form is made when an appropriate person signs on it or on a separate document an assignment or transfer of the security or a power to assign or transfer it or his signature is written without more upon the back of the security.

(2) An indorsement may be in blank or special. An indorsement in blank includes an indorsement to bearer. A special indorsement specifies to whom the security is to be transferred, or who has power to transfer it. A holder may convert a blank indorsement into a special indorsement.

(3) An indorsement purporting to be only of part of a certificated security representing units intended by the issuer to be separately transferable is effective to the extent of the indorsement.

(4) An "instruction" is an order to the issuer of an uncertificated security requesting that the transfer, pledge, or release from pledge of the uncertificated security specified therein be registered.

(5) An instruction originated by an appropriate person is:

(a) a writing signed by an appropriate person; or

(b) a communication to the issuer in any form agreed upon in a writing signed by the issuer and an appropriate person.

If an instruction has been originated by an appropriate person but is incomplete in any other respect, any person may complete it as authorized and the issuer may rely on it as completed even though it has been completed incorrectly.

(6) "An appropriate person" in subsection (1) means the person specified by the certificated security or by special indorsement to be entitled to the security.

(7) "An appropriate person" in subsection (5) means:

(a) for an instruction to transfer or pledge an uncertificated security which is then not subject to a registered pledge, the registered owner; or

(b) for an instruction to transfer or release an uncertificated security which is then subject to a registered pledge, the registered pledgee.

(8) In addition to the persons designated in subsections (6) and (7), "an appropriate person" in subsections (1) and (5) includes:

(a) if the person designated is described as a fiduciary but is no longer serving in the described capacity, either that person or his successor;

(b) if the persons designated are described as more than one person as fiduciaries and one or more are no longer serving in the described capacity, the remaining fiduciary or fiduciaries, whether or not a successor has been appointed or qualified;

(c) if the person designated is an individual and is without capacity to act by virtue of death, incompetence, infancy, or otherwise, his executor, administrator, guardian, or like fiduciary;

(d) if the persons designated are described as more than one person as tenants by the entirety or with right of survivorship and by reason of death all cannot sign, the survivor or survivors;

(e) a person having power to sign under applicable law or controlling instrument; and

(f) to the extent that the person designated or any of the foregoing persons may act through an agent, his authorized agent.

(9) Unless otherwise agreed, the indorser of a certificated security by his indorsement or the originator of an instruction by his origination assumes no obligation that the security will be honored by the issuer but only the obligations provided in Section 8—306.

(10) Whether the person signing is appropriate is determined as of the date of signing and an indorsement made by or an instruction originated by him does not become unauthorized for the purposes of this Article by virtue of any subsequent change of circumstances.

(11) Failure of a fiduciary to comply with a controlling instrument or with the law of the state having jurisdiction of the fiduciary relationship, including any law requiring the fiduciary to obtain court approval of the transfer, pledge, or release, does not render his indorsement or an instruction originated by him unauthorized for the purposes of this Article.

Amended in 1962 and 1977.

§ 8—309. **Effect of Indorsement Without Delivery.**

An indorsement of a certificated security, whether special or in blank, does not constitute a transfer until delivery of the certificated security on which it appears or, if the indorsement is on a separate document, until delivery of both the document and the certificated security.

Amended in 1977.

§ 8—310. **Indorsement of Certificated Security in Bearer Form.**

An indorsement of a certificated security in bearer form may give notice of adverse claims (Section 8—304) but does not otherwise affect any right to registration the holder possesses.

Amended in 1977.

§ 8—311. **Effect of Unauthorized Indorsement or Instruction.**

Unless the owner or pledgee has ratified an unauthorized indorsement or instruction or is otherwise precluded from asserting its ineffectiveness:

(a) he may assert its ineffectiveness against the issuer or any purchaser, other than a purchaser for value and without notice of adverse claims, who has in good faith received a new, reissued, or re-registered certificated security on registration of transfer or received an initial transaction statement confirming the registration of transfer, pledge, or release of an equivalent uncertificated security to him; and

(b) an issuer who registers the transfer of a certificated security upon the unauthorized indorsement or who registers the transfer, pledge, or release of an uncertificated security upon the unauthorized instruction is subject to liability for improper registration (Section 8—404).

Amended in 1977.

§ 8—312. **Effect of Guaranteeing Signature, Indorsement or Instruction.**

(1) Any person guaranteeing a signature of an indorser of a certificated security warrants that at the time of signing:

(a) the signature was genuine;

(b) the signer was an appropriate person to indorse (Section 8—308); and

(c) the signer had legal capacity to sign.

(2) Any person guaranteeing a signature of the originator of an instruction warrants that at the time of signing:

(a) the signature was genuine;

(b) the signer was an appropriate person to originate the instruction (Section 8—308) if the person specified in the instruction as the registered owner or registered pledgee of the uncertificated security was, in fact, the registered owner or registered pledgee of the security, as to which fact the signature guarantor makes no warranty;

(c) the signer had legal capacity to sign; and

(d) the taxpayer identification number, if any, appearing on the instruction as that of the registered owner or registered pledgee was the taxpayer identification number of the signer or of the owner or pledgee for whom the signer was acting.

(3) Any person specially guaranteeing the signature of the originator of an instruction makes not only the warranties of a signature guarantor (subsection (2)) but also warrants that at the time the instruction is presented to the issuer:

(a) the person specified in the instruction as the registered owner or registered pledgee of the uncertificated security will be the registered owner or registered pledgee; and

(b) the transfer, pledge, or release of the uncertificated security requested in the instruction will be registered by the issuer free from all liens, security interests, restrictions, and claims other than those specified in the instruction.

(4) The guarantor under subsections (1) and (2) or the special guarantor under subsection (3) does not otherwise warrant the rightfulness of the particular transfer, pledge, or release.

(5) Any person guaranteeing an indorsement of a certificated security makes not only the warranties of a signature guarantor under subsection (1) but also warrants the rightfulness of the particular transfer in all respects.

(6) Any person guaranteeing an instruction requesting the transfer, pledge, or release of an uncertificated security makes not only the warranties of a special signature guarantor under subsection (3) but also warrants the rightfulness of the particular transfer, pledge, or release in all respects.

(7) No issuer may require a special guarantee of signature (subsection (3)), a guarantee of indorsement (subsection (5)), or a guarantee of instruction (subsection (6)) as a condition to registration of transfer, pledge, or release.

(8) The foregoing warranties are made to any person taking or dealing with the security in reliance on the guarantee, and the guarantor is liable to the person for any loss resulting from breach of the warranties.

Amended in 1977.

§ 8—313. **When Transfer to Purchaser Occurs; Financial Intermediary as Bona Fide Purchaser; "Financial Intermediary".**

(1) Transfer of a security or a limited interest (including a security interest) therein to a purchaser occurs only:

(a) at the time he or a person designated by him acquires possession of a certificated security;

(b) at the time the transfer, pledge, or release of an uncertificated security is registered to him or a person designated by him;

(c) at the time his financial intermediary acquires possession of a certificated security specially indorsed to or issued in the name of the purchaser;

(d) at the time a financial intermediary, not a clearing corporation, sends him confirmation of the purchase and also by book entry or otherwise identifies as belonging to the purchaser

(i) a specific certificated security in the financial intermediary's possession;

(ii) a quantity of securities that constitute or are part of a fungible bulk of certificated securities in the financial intermediary's possession or of uncertificated securities registered in the name of the financial intermediary; or

(iii) a quantity of securities that constitute or are part of a fungible bulk of securities shown on the account of the financial intermediary on the books of another financial intermediary;

(e) with respect to an identified certificated security to be delivered while still in the possession of a third person, not a financial intermediary, at the time that person acknowledges that he holds for the purchaser;

(f) with respect to a specific uncertificated security the pledge or transfer of which has been registered to a third person, not a financial intermediary, at the time that person acknowledges that he holds for the purchaser;

(g) at the time appropriate entries to the account of the purchaser or a person designated by him on the books of a clearing corporation are made under Section 8—320;

(h) with respect to the transfer of a security interest where the debtor has signed a security agreement containing a description of the security, at the time a written notification, which, in the case of the creation of the security interest, is signed by the debtor (which may be a copy of the security agreement) or which, in the case of the release or assignment of the security interest created pursuant to this paragraph, is signed by the secured party, is received by

(i) a financial intermediary on whose books the interest of the transferor in the security appears;

(ii) a third person, not a financial intermediary, in possession of the security, if it is certificated;

(iii) a third person, not a financial intermediary, who is the registered owner of the security, if it is uncertificated and not subject to a registered pledge; or

(iv) a third person, not a financial intermediary, who is the registered pledgee of the security, if it is uncertificated and subject to a registered pledge;

(i) with respect to the transfer of a security interest where the transferor has signed a security agreement containing a description of the security, at the time new value is given by the secured party; or

(j) with respect to the transfer of a security interest where the secured party is a financial intermediary and the security has already been transferred to the financial intermediary under paragraphs (a), (b), (c), (d), or (g), at the time the transferor has signed a security agreement containing a description of the security and value is given by the secured party.

(2) The purchaser is the owner of a security held for him by a financial intermediary, but cannot be a bona fide purchaser of a security so held except in the circumstances specified in paragraphs (c), (d)(i), and (g) of subsection (1). If a security so held is part of a fungible bulk, as in the circumstances specified in paragraphs (d)(ii) and (d)(iii) of subsection (1), the purchaser is the owner of a proportionate property interest in the fungible bulk.

(3) Notice of an adverse claim received by the financial intermediary or by the purchaser after the finan-

cial intermediary takes delivery of a certificated security as a holder for value or after the transfer, pledge, or release of an uncertificated security has been registered free of the claim to a financial intermediary who has given value is not effective either as to the financial intermediary or as to the purchaser. However, as between the financial intermediary and the purchaser the purchaser may demand transfer of an equivalent security as to which no notice of adverse claim has been received.

(4) A "financial intermediary" is a bank, broker, clearing corporation, or other person (or the nominee of any of them) which in the ordinary course of its business maintains security accounts for its customers and is acting in that capacity. A financial intermediary may have a security interest in securities held in account for its customer.
Amended in 1962 and 1977.

§ 8—314. **Duty to Transfer, When Completed**

(1) Unless otherwise agreed, if a sale of a security is made on an exchange or otherwise through brokers:

(a) the selling customer fulfills his duty to transfer at the time he:

(i) places a certificated security in the possession of the selling broker or a person designated by the broker;

(ii) causes an uncertificated security to be registered in the name of the selling broker or a person designated by the broker;

(iii) if requested, causes an acknowledgment to be made to the selling broker that a certificated or uncertificated security is held for the broker; or

(iv) places in the possession of the selling broker or of a person designated by the broker a transfer instruction for an uncertificated security, providing the issuer does not refuse to register the requested transfer if the instruction is presented to the issuer for registration within 30 days thereafter; and

(b) the selling broker, including a correspondent broker acting for a selling customer, fulfills his duty to transfer at the time he:

(i) places a certificated security in the possession of the buying broker or a person designated by the buying broker;

(ii) causes an uncertificated security to be registered in the name of the buying broker or a person designated by the buying broker;

(iii) places in the possession of the buying broker or of a person designated by the buying broker a transfer instruction for an uncertificated security, providing the issuer does not refuse to register the requested transfer if the instruction is presented to the issuer for registration within 30 days thereafter; or

(iv) effects clearance of the sale in accordance with the rules of the exchange on which the transaction took place.

(2) Except as provided in this section or unless otherwise agreed, a transferor's duty to transfer a security under a contract of purchase is not fulfilled until he:

(a) places a certificated security in form to be negotiated by the purchaser in the possession of the purchaser or of a person designated by the purchaser;

(b) causes an uncertificated security to be registered in the name of the purchaser or a person designated by the purchaser; or

(c) if the purchaser requests, causes an acknowledgment to be made to the purchaser that a certificated or uncertificated security is held for the purchaser.

(3) Unless made on an exchange, a sale to a broker purchasing for his own account is within subsection (2) and not within subsection (1).

Amended in 1977.

§ 8—315. **Action Against Transferee Based Upon Wrongful Transfer**

(1) Any person against whom the transfer of a security is wrongful for any reason, including his incapacity, as against anyone except a bona fide purchaser, may:

(a) reclaim possession of the certificated security wrongfully transferred;

(b) obtain possession of any new certificated security representing all or part of the same rights;

(c) compel the origination of an instruction to transfer to him or a person designated by him an uncertificated security constituting all or part of the same rights; or

(d) have damages.

(2) If the transfer is wrongful because of an unauthorized indorsement of a certificated security, the owner may also reclaim or obtain possession of the security or a new certificated security, even from a bona fide purchaser, if the ineffectiveness of the purported indorsement can be asserted against him under the provisions of this Article on unauthorized indorsements (Section 8—311).

(3) The right to obtain or reclaim possession of a certificated security or to compel the origination of a transfer instruction may be specifically enforced and the transfer of a certificated or uncertificated security enjoined and a certificated security impounded pending the litigation.

Amended in 1977.

§ 8—316. **Purchaser's Right to Requisites for Registration of Transfer, Pledge, or Release on Books**

Unless otherwise agreed, the transferor of a certificated security or the transferor, pledgor, or pledgee of an uncertificated security on due demand must supply his purchaser with any proof of his authority to transfer, pledge, or release or with any other requisite necessary to obtain registration of the transfer, pledge, or release of the security; but if the transfer, pledge, or release is not for value, a transferor, pledgor, or pledgee need not do so unless the purchaser furnishes the necessary expenses. Failure within a reasonable time to comply with a demand made gives the purchaser the right to reject or rescind the transfer, pledge, or release.

Amended in 1977.

§ 8—317. **Creditors' Rights**

(1) Subject to the exceptions in subsections (3) and (4), no attachment or levy upon a certificated security or any share or other interest represented thereby which is outstanding is valid until the security is actually seized by the officer making the attachment or levy, but a certificated security which has been surrendered to the issuer may be reached by a creditor by legal process at the issuer's chief executive office in the United States.

(2) An uncertificated security registered in the name of the debtor may not be reached by a creditor except by legal process at the issuer's chief executive office in the United States.

(3) The interest of a debtor in a certificated security that is in the possession of a secured party not a financial intermediary or in an uncertificated security registered in the name of a secured party not a financial intermediary (or in the name of a nominee of the secured party) may be reached by a creditor by legal process upon the secured party.

(4) The interest of a debtor in a certificated security

that is in the possession of or registered in the name of a financial intermediary or in an uncertificated security registered in the name of a financial intermediary may be reached by a creditor by legal process upon the financial intermediary on whose books the interest of the debtor appears.

(5) Unless otherwise provided by law, a creditor's lien upon the interest of a debtor in a security obtained pursuant to subsection (3) or (4) is not a restraint on the transfer of the security, free of the lien, to a third party for new value; but in the event of a transfer, the lien applies to the proceeds of the transfer in the hands of the secured party or financial intermediary, subject to any claims having priority.

(6) A creditor whose debtor is the owner of a security is entitled to aid from courts of appropriate jurisdiction, by injunction or otherwise, in reaching the security or in satisfying the claim by means allowed at law or in equity in regard to property that cannot readily be reached by ordinary legal process.

Amended in 1977.

§ 8—318. **No Conversion by Good Faith Conduct**

An agent or bailee who in good faith (including observance of reasonable commercial standards if he is in the business of buying, selling, or otherwise dealing with securities) has received certificated securities and sold, pledged, or delivered them or has sold or caused the transfer or pledge of uncertificated securities over which he had control according to the instructions of his principal, is not liable for conversion or for participation in breach of fiduciary duty although the principal had no right so to deal with the securities.

Amended in 1977.

§ 8—319. **Statute of Frauds**

A contract for the sale of securities is not enforceable by way of action or defense unless:

(a) there is some writing signed by the party against whom enforcement is sought or by his authorized agent or broker, sufficient to indicate that a contract has been made for sale of a stated quantity of described securities at a defined or stated price;

(b) delivery of a certificated security or transfer instruction has been accepted, or transfer of an uncertificated security has been registered and the transferee has failed to send written objection to the issuer within 10 days after receipt of the initial transaction statement confirming the registration, or payment has been made, but the contract is enforceable under this provision only to the extent of the delivery, registration, or payment;

(c) within a reasonable time a writing in confirmation of the sale or purchase and sufficient against the sender under paragraph (a) has been received by the party against whom enforcement is sought and he has failed to send written objection to its contents within 10 days after its receipt; or

(d) the party against whom enforcement is sought admits in his pleading, testimony, or otherwise in court that a contract was made for the sale of a stated quantity of described securities at a defined or stated price.

Amended in 1977.

§ 8—320. **Transfer or Pledge Within Central Depository System**

(1) In addition to other methods, a transfer, pledge, or release of a security or any interest therein may be effected by the making of appropriate entries on the books of a clearing corporation reducing the account of the transferor, pledgor, or pledgee and increasing the account of the transferee, pledgee, or pledgor by the amount of the obligation or the number of shares or rights transferred, pledged, or released, if the security is shown on the account of a transferor, pledgor, or pledgee on the books of the clearing corporation; is subject to the control of the clearing corporation; and

(a) if certificated,

(i) is in the custody of the clearing corporation, another clearing corporation, a custodian bank, or a nominee of any of them; and

(ii) is in bearer form or indorsed in blank by an appropriate person or registered in the name of the clearing corporation, a custodian bank, or a nominee of any of them; or

(b) if uncertificated, is registered in the name of the clearing corporation, another clearing corporation, a custodian bank, or a nominee of any of them.

(2) Under this section entries may be made with respect to like securities or interests therein as a part of a fungible bulk and may refer merely to a quantity of a particular security without reference to the name of the registered owner, certificate or bond number, or the like, and, in appropriate cases, may be on a net basis taking into account other transfers, pledges, or releases of the same security.

(3) A transfer under this section is effective (Section 8—313) and the purchaser acquires the rights of the transferor (Section 8—301). A pledge or release under this section is the transfer of a limited interest. If a pledge or the creation of a security interest is in-

tended, the security interest is perfected at the time when both value is given by the pledgee and the appropriate entries are made (Section 8—321). A transferee or pledgee under this section may be a bona fide purchaser (Section 8—302).

(4) A transfer or pledge under this section is not a registration of transfer under Part 4.

(5) That entries made on the books of the clearing corporation as provided in subsection (1) are not appropriate does not affect the validity or effect of the entries or the liabilities or obligations of the clearing corporation to any person adversely affected thereby.

Added in 1962; amended in 1977.

§ 8—321. Enforceability, Attachment, Perfection and Termination of Security Interests

(1) A security interest in a security is enforceable and can attach only if it is transferred to the secured party or a person designated by him pursuant to a provision of Section 8—313(1).

(2) A security interest so transferred pursuant to agreement by a transferor who has rights in the security to a transferee who has given value is a perfected security interest, but a security interest that has been transferred solely under paragraph (i) of Section 8—313(1) becomes unperfected after 21 days unless, within that time, the requirements for transfer under any other provision of Section 8—313(1) are satisfied.

(3) A security interest in a security is subject to the provisions of Article 9, but:

(a) no filing is required to perfect the security interest; and

(b) no written security agreement signed by the debtor is necessary to make the security interest enforceable, except as provided in paragraph (h), (i), or (j) of Section 8—313(1). The secured party has the rights and duties provided under Section 9—207, to the extent they are applicable, whether or not the security is certificated, and, if certificated, whether or not it is in his possession.

(4) Unless otherwise agreed, a security interest in a security is terminated by transfer to the debtor or a person designated by him pursuant to a provision of Section 8—313(1). If a security is thus transferred, the security interest, if not terminated, becomes unperfected unless the security is certificated and is delivered to the debtor for the purpose of ultimate sale or exchange or presentation, collection, renewal, or registration of transfer. In that case, the security interest becomes unperfected after 21 days unless, within that

time, the security (or securities for which it has been exchanged) is transferred to the secured party or a person designated by him pursuant to a provision of Section 8—313(1).

Added in 1977.

Part 4 Registration

§ 8—401. Duty of Issuer to Register Transfer, Pledge, or Release

(1) If a certificated security in registered form is presented to the issuer with a request to register transfer or an instruction is presented to the issuer with a request to register transfer, pledge, or release, the issuer shall register the transfer, pledge, or release as requested if:

(a) the security is indorsed or the instruction was originated by the appropriate person or persons (Section 8—308);

(b) reasonable assurance is given that those indorsements or instructions are genuine and effective (Section 8—402);

(c) the issuer has no duty as to adverse claims or has discharged the duty (Section 8—403);

(d) any applicable law relating to the collection of taxes has been complied with; and

(e) the transfer, pledge, or release is in fact rightful or is to a bona fide purchaser.

(2) If an issuer is under a duty to register a transfer, pledge, or release of a security, the issuer is also liable to the person presenting a certificated security or an instruction for registration or his principal for loss resulting from any unreasonable delay in registration or from failure or refusal to register the transfer, pledge, or release.

Amended in 1977.

§ 8—402. Assurance that Indorsements and Instructions Are Effective

(1) The issuer may require the following assurance that each necessary indorsement of a certificated security or each instruction (Section 8—308) is genuine and effective:

(a) in all cases, a guarantee of the signature (Section 8—312(1) or (2)) of the person indorsing a certificated security or originating an instruction including, in the case of an instruction, a warranty of the taxpayer identification number or, in the absence thereof, other reasonable assurance of identity;

(b) if the indorsement is made or the instruction is originated by an agent, appropriate assurance of authority to sign;

(c) if the indorsement is made or the instruction is originated by a fiduciary, appropriate evidence of appointment or incumbency;

(d) if there is more than one fiduciary, reasonable assurance that all who are required to sign have done so; and

(e) if the indorsement is made or the instruction is originated by a person not covered by any of the foregoing, assurance appropriate to the case corresponding as nearly as may be to the foregoing.

(2) A "guarantee of the signature" in subsection (1) means a guarantee signed by or on behalf of a person reasonably believed by the issuer to be responsible. The issuer may adopt standards with respect to responsibility if they are not manifestly unreasonable.

(3) "Appropriate evidence of appointment or incumbency" in subsection (1) means:

(a) in the case of a fiduciary appointed or qualified by a court, a certificate issued by or under the direction or supervision of that court or an officer thereof and dated within 60 days before the date of presentation for transfer, pledge, or release; or

(b) in any other case, a copy of a document showing the appointment or a certificate issued by or on behalf of a person reasonably believed by the issuer to be responsible or, in the absence of that document or certificate, other evidence reasonably deemed by the issuer to be appropriate. The issuer may adopt standards with respect to the evidence if they are not manifestly unreasonable. The issuer is not charged with notice of the contents of any document obtained pursuant to this paragraph (b) except to the extent that the contents relate directly to the appointment or incumbency.

(4) The issuer may elect to require reasonable assurance beyond that specified in this section, but if it does so and, for a purpose other than that specified in subsection (3)(b), both requires and obtains a copy of a will, trust, indenture, articles of co-partnership, by-laws, or other controlling instrument, it is charged with notice of all matters contained therein affecting the transfer, pledge, or release.
Amended in 1977.

§ 8—403. Issuer's Duty as to Adverse Claims

(1) An issuer to whom a certificated security is presented for registration shall inquire into adverse claims if:

(a) a written notification of an adverse claim is received at a time and in a manner affording the issuer a reasonable opportunity to act on it prior to the issuance of a new, reissued, or re-registered certificated security, and the notification identifies the claimant, the registered owner, and the issue of which the security is a part, and provides an address for communications directed to the claimant; or

(b) the issuer is charged with notice of an adverse claim from a controlling instrument it has elected to require under Section 8—402(4).

(2) The issuer may discharge any duty of inquiry by any reasonable means, including notifying an adverse claimant by registered or certified mail at the address furnished by him or, if there be no such address, at his residence or regular place of business that the certificated security has been presented for registration of transfer by a named person, and that the transfer will be registered unless within 30 days from the date of mailing the notification, either:

(a) an appropriate restraining order, injunction, or other process issues from a court of competent jurisdiction; or

(b) there is filed with the issuer an indemnity bond, sufficient in the issuer's judgment to protect the issuer and any transfer agent, registrar, or other agent of the issuer involved from any loss it or they may suffer by complying with the adverse claim.

(3) Unless an issuer is charged with notice of an adverse claim from a controlling instrument which it has elected to require under Section 8—402(4) or receives notification of an adverse claim under subsection (1), if a certificated security presented for registration is indorsed by the appropriate person or persons the issuer is under no duty to inquire into adverse claims. In particular:

(a) an issuer registering a certificated security in the name of a person who is a fiduciary or who is described as a fiduciary is not bound to inquire into the existence, extent, or correct description of the fiduciary relationship; and thereafter the issuer may assume without inquiry that the newly registered owner continues to be the fiduciary until the issuer receives written notice that the fiduciary is no longer acting as such with respect to the particular security;

(b) an issuer registering transfer on an indorsement by a fiduciary is not bound to inquire whether the transfer is made in compliance with a controlling instrument or with the law of the state having jurisdiction of the fiduciary relationship, including any law requiring the fiduciary to obtain court approval of the transfer; and

(c) the issuer is not charged with notice of the contents of any court record or file or other recorded or unrecorded document even though the document is in its possession and even though the transfer is made on the indorsement of a fiduciary to the fiduciary himself or to his nominee.

(4) An issuer is under no duty as to adverse claims with respect to an uncertificated security except:

(a) claims embodied in a restraining order, injunction, or other legal process served upon the issuer if the process was served at a time and in a manner affording the issuer a reasonable opportunity to act on it in accordance with the requirements of subsection (5);

(b) claims of which the issuer has received a written notification from the registered owner or the registered pledgee if the notification was received at a time and in a manner affording the issuer a reasonable opportunity to act on it in accordance with the requirements of subsection (5);

(c) claims (including restrictions on transfer not imposed by the issuer) to which the registration of transfer to the present registered owner was subject and were so noted in the initial transaction statement sent to him; and

(d) claims as to which an issuer is charged with notice from a controlling instrument it has elected to require under Section 8—402(4).

(5) If the issuer of an uncertificated security is under a duty as to an adverse claim, he discharges that duty by:

(a) including a notation of the claim in any statements sent with respect to the security under Sections 8—408(3), (6), and (7); and

(b) refusing to register the transfer or pledge of the security unless the nature of the claim does not preclude transfer or pledge subject thereto.

(6) If the transfer or pledge of the security is registered subject to an adverse claim, a notation of the claim must be included in the initial transaction statement and all subsequent statements sent to the transferee and pledgee under Section 8—408.

(7) Notwithstanding subsections (4) and (5), if an uncertificated security was subject to a registered pledge at the time the issuer first came under a duty as to a particular adverse claim, the issuer has no duty as to that claim if transfer of the security is requested by the registered pledgee or an appropriate person acting for the registered pledgee unless:

(a) the claim was embodied in legal process which expressly provides otherwise;

(b) the claim was asserted in a written notification from the registered pledgee;

(c) the claim was one as to which the issuer was charged with notice from a controlling instrument it required under Section 8—402(4) in connection with the pledgee's request for transfer; or

(d) the transfer requested is to the registered owner.

Amended in 1977.

§ 8—404. Liability and Non-Liability for Registration

(1) Except as provided in any law relating to the collection of taxes, the issuer is not liable to the owner, pledgee, or any other person suffering loss as a result of the registration of a transfer, pledge, or release of a security if:

(a) there were on or with a certificated security the necessary indorsements or the issuer had received an instruction originated by an appropriate person (Section 8—308); and

(b) the issuer had no duty as to adverse claims or has discharged the duty (Section 8—403).

(2) If an issuer has registered a transfer of a certificated security to a person not entitled to it, the issuer on demand shall deliver a like security to the true owner unless:

(a) the registration was pursuant to subsection (1);

(b) the owner is precluded from asserting any claim for registering the transfer under Section 8—405(1); or

(c) the delivery would result in overissue, in which case the issuer's liability is governed by Section 8—104.

(3) If an issuer has improperly registered a transfer, pledge, or release of an uncertificated security, the issuer on demand from the injured party shall restore the records as to the injured party to the condition that would have obtained if the improper registration had not been made unless:

(a) the registration was pursuant to subsection (1); or

(b) the registration would result in overissue, in which case the issuer's liability is governed by Section 8—104.

Amended in 1977.

§ 8—405. Lost, Destroyed, and Stolen Certificated Securities

(1) If a certificated security has been lost, apparently destroyed, or wrongfully taken, and the owner fails to notify the issuer of that fact within a reasonable time after he has notice of it and the issuer registers a transfer of the security before receiving notification, the owner is precluded from asserting against the issuer any claim for registering the transfer under Section 8—404 or any claim to a new security under this section.

(2) If the owner of a certificated security claims that the security has been lost, destroyed, or wrongfully taken, the issuer shall issue a new certificated security or, at the option of the issuer, an equivalent uncertificated security in place of the original security if the owner:

(a) so requests before the issuer has notice that the security has been acquired by a bona fide purchaser;

(b) files with the issuer a sufficient indemnity bond; and

(c) satisfies any other reasonable requirements imposed by the issuer.

(3) If, after the issue of a new certificated or uncertificated security, a bona fide purchaser of the original certificated security presents it for registration of transfer, the issuer shall register the transfer unless registration would result in overissue, in which event the issuer's liability is governed by Section 8—104. In addition to any rights on the indemnity bond, the issuer may recover the new certificated security from the person to whom it was issued or any person taking under him except a bona fide purchaser or may cancel the uncertificated security unless a bona fide purchaser or any person taking under a bona fide purchaser is then the registered owner or registered pledgee thereof.

Amended in 1977.

§ 8—406. Duty of Authenticating Trustee, Transfer Agent, or Registrar

(1) If a person acts as authenticating trustee, transfer agent, registrar, or other agent for an issuer in the registration of transfers of its certificated securities or in the registration of transfers, pledges, and releases of its uncertificated securities, in the issue of new securities, or in the cancellation of surrendered securities:

(a) he is under a duty to the issuer to exercise good faith and due diligence in performing his functions; and

(b) with regard to the particular functions he performs, he has the same obligation to the holder or owner of a certificated security or to the owner or pledgee of an uncertificated security and has the same rights and privileges as the issuer has in regard to those functions.

(2) Notice to an authenticating trustee, transfer agent, registrar or other agent is notice to the issuer with respect to the functions performed by the agent.

Amended in 1977.

§ 8—407. Exchangeability of Securities

(1) No issuer is subject to the requirements of this section unless it regularly maintains a system for issuing the class of securities involved under which both certificated and uncertificated securities are regularly issued to the category of owners, which includes the person in whose name the new security is to be registered.

(2) Upon surrender of a certificated security with all necessary indorsements and presentation of a written request by the person surrendering the security, the issuer, if he has no duty as to adverse claims or has discharged the duty (Section 8—403), shall issue to the person or a person designated by him an equivalent uncertificated security subject to all liens, restrictions, and claims that were noted on the certificated security.

(3) Upon receipt of a transfer instruction originated by an appropriate person who so requests, the issuer of an uncertificated security shall cancel the uncertificated security and issue an equivalent certificated security on which must be noted conspicuously any liens and restrictions of the issuer and any adverse claims (as to which the issuer has a duty under Section 8—403(4)) to which the uncertificated security was subject. The certificated security shall be registered in the name of and delivered to:

(a) the registered owner, if the uncertificated security was not subject to a registered pledge; or

(b) the registered pledgee, if the uncertificated security was subject to a registered pledge.

Added in 1977.

§ 8—408. Statements of Uncertificated Securities

(1) Within 2 business days after the transfer of an uncertificated security has been registered, the issuer shall send to the new registered owner and, if the security has been transferred subject to a registered pledge, to the registered pledgee a written statement containing:

(a) a description of the issue of which the uncertificated security is a part;

(b) the number of shares or units transferred;

(c) the name and address and any taxpayer identification number of the new registered owner and, if the security has been transferred subject to a registered pledge, the name and address and any taxpayer identification number of the registered pledgee;

(d) a notation of any liens and restrictions of the issuer and any adverse claims (as to which the issuer has a duty under Section 8—403(4)) to which the uncertificated security is or may be subject at the time of registration or a statement that there are none of those liens, restrictions, or adverse claims; and

(e) the date the transfer was registered.

(2) Within 2 business days after the pledge of an uncertificated security has been registered, the issuer shall send to the registered owner and the registered pledgee a written statement containing:

(a) a description of the issue of which the uncertificated security is a part;

(b) the number of shares or units pledged;

(c) the name and address and any taxpayer identification number of the registered owner and the registered pledgee;

(d) a notation of any liens and restrictions of the issuer and any adverse claims (as to which the issuer has a duty under Section 8—403(4)) to which the uncertificated security is or may be subject at the time of registration or a statement that there are none of those liens, restrictions, or adverse claims; and

(e) the date the pledge was registered.

(3) Within 2 business days after the release from pledge of an uncertificated security has been registered, the issuer shall send to the registered owner and the pledgee whose interest was released a written statement containing:

(a) a description of the issue of which the uncertificated security is a part;

(b) the number of shares or units released from pledge;

(c) the name and address and any taxpayer identification number of the registered owner and the pledgee whose interest was released;

(d) a notation of any liens and restrictions of the issuer and any adverse claims (as to which the is-

suer has a duty under Section 8—403(4)) to which the uncertificated security is or may be subject at the time of registration or a statement that there are none of those liens, restrictions, or adverse claims; and

(e) the date the release was registered.

(4) An "initial transaction statement" is the statement sent to:

(a) the new registered owner and, if applicable, to the registered pledgee pursuant to subsection (1);

(b) the registered pledgee pursuant to subsection (2); or

(c) the registered owner pursuant to subsection (3).

Each initial transaction statement shall be signed by or on behalf of the issuer and must be identified as "Initial Transaction Statement".

(5) Within 2 business days after the transfer of an uncertificated security has been registered, the issuer shall send to the former registered owner and the former registered pledgee, if any, a written statement containing:

(a) a description of the issue of which the uncertificated security is a part;

(b) the number of shares or units transferred;

(c) the name and address and any taxpayer identification number of the former registered owner and of any former registered pledgee; and

(d) the date the transfer was registered.

(6) At periodic intervals no less frequent than annually and at any time upon the reasonable written request of the registered owner, the issuer shall send to the registered owner of each uncertificated security a dated written statement containing:

(a) a description of the issue of which the uncertificated security is a part;

(b) the name and address and any taxpayer identification number of the registered owner;

(c) the number of shares or units of the uncertificated security registered in the name of the registered owner on the date of the statement;

(d) the name and address and any taxpayer identification number of any registered pledgee and the number of shares or units subject to the pledge; and

(e) a notation of any liens and restrictions of the issuer and any adverse claims (as to which the issuer has a duty under Section 8—403(4)) to which the uncertificated security is or may be subject or a statement that there are none of those liens, restrictions, or adverse claims.

(7) At periodic intervals no less frequent than annually and at any time upon the reasonable written request of the registered pledgee, the issuer shall send to the registered pledgee of each uncertificated security a dated written statement containing:

(a) a description of the issue of which the uncertificated security is a part;

(b) the name and address and any taxpayer identification number of the registered owner;

(c) the name and address and any taxpayer identification number of the registered pledgee;

(d) the number of shares or units subject to the pledge; and

(e) a notation of any liens and restrictions of the issuer and any adverse claims (as to which the issuer has a duty under Section 8—403(4)) to which the uncertificated security is or may be subject or a statement that there are none of those liens, restrictions, or adverse claims.

(8) If the issuer sends the statements described in subsections (6) and (7) at periodic intervals no less frequent than quarterly, the issuer is not obliged to send additional statements upon request unless the owner or pledgee requesting them pays to the issuer the reasonable cost of furnishing them.

(9) Each statement sent pursuant to this section must bear a conspicuous legend reading substantially as follows: "This statement is merely a record of the rights of the addressee as of the time of its issuance. Delivery of this statement, of itself, confers no rights on the recipient. This statement is neither a negotiable instrument nor a security."

Added in 1977.

Article 9
Secured Transactions; Sales of Accounts and Chattel Paper

Note: *The adoption of this Article should be accompanied by the repeal of existing statutes dealing with conditional sales, trust receipts, factor's liens where the factor is given a non-possessory lien, chattel mortgages, crop mortgages, mortgages on railroad equipment, assignment of accounts and generally statutes regulating security interests in personal property.*

Where the state has a retail installment selling act or small loan act, that legislation should be carefully examined to determine what changes in those acts are needed to conform them to this Article. This Article primarily sets out rules de- *fining rights of a secured party against persons dealing with the debtor; it does not prescribe regulations and controls which may be necessary to curb abuses arising in the small loan business or in the financing of consumer purchases on credit. Accordingly there is no intention to repeal existing regulatory acts in those fields by enactment or re-enactment of Article 9. See Section 9—203(4) and the Note thereto.*

Part 1 Short Title, Applicability and Definitions

§ 9—101. **Short Title.**

This Article shall be known and may be cited as Uniform Commercial Code—Secured Transactions.

§ 9—102. **Policy and Subject Matter of Article.**

(1) Except as otherwise provided in Section 9—104 on excluded transactions, this Article applies

(a) to any transaction (regardless of its form) which is intended to create a security interest in personal property or fixtures including goods, documents, instruments, general intangibles, chattel paper or accounts; and also

(b) to any sale of accounts or chattel paper.

(2) This Article applies to security interests created by contract including pledge, assignment, chattel mortgage, chattel trust, trust deed, factor's lien, equipment trust, conditional sale, trust receipt, other lien or title retention contract and lease or consignment intended as security. This Article does not apply to statutory liens except as provided in Section 9—310.

(3) The application of this Article to a security interest in a secured obligation is not affected by the fact that the obligation is itself secured by a transaction or interest to which this Article does not apply. Amended in 1972.

§ 9—103. **Perfection of Security Interest in Multiple State Transactions**

(1) Documents, instruments and ordinary goods.

(a) This subsection applies to documents and instruments and to goods other than those covered by a certificate of title described in subsection (2), mobile goods described in subsection (3), and minerals described in subsection (5).

(b) Except as otherwise provided in this subsection, perfection and the effect of perfection or non-perfection of a security interest in collateral are governed by the law of the jurisdiction where the collateral is when the last event occurs on which is based the assertion that the security interest is perfected or unperfected.

(c) If the parties to a transaction creating a purchase money security interest in goods in one jurisdiction understand at the time that the security interest attaches that the goods will be kept in another jurisdiction, then the law of the other jurisdiction governs the perfection and the effect of perfection or non-perfection of the security interest from the time it attaches until thirty days after the debtor receives possession of the goods and thereafter if the goods are taken to the other jurisdiction before the end of the thirty-day period.

(d) When collateral is brought into and kept in this state while subject to a security interest perfected under the law of the jurisdiction from which the collateral was removed, the security interest remains perfected, but if action is required by Part 3 of this Article to perfect the security interest,

> (i) if the action is not taken before the expiration of the period of perfection in the other jurisdiction or the end of four months after the collateral is brought into this state, whichever period first expires, the security interest becomes unperfected at the end of that period and is thereafter deemed to have been unperfected as against a person who became a purchaser after removal;

> (ii) if the action is taken before the expiration of the period specified in subparagraph (i), the security interest continues perfected thereafter;

> (iii) for the purpose of priority over a buyer of consumer goods (subsection (2) of Section 9—307), the period of the effectiveness of a filing in the jurisdiction from which the collateral is removed is governed by the rules with respect to perfection in subparagraphs (i) and (ii).

(2) Certificate of title.

(a) This subsection applies to goods covered by a certificate of title issued under a statute of this state or of another jurisdiction under the law of which indication of a security interest on the certificate is required as a condition of perfection.

(b) Except as otherwise provided in this subsection, perfection and the effect of perfection or non-perfection of the security interest are governed by the law (including the conflict of laws rules) of the jurisdiction issuing the certificate until four months after the goods are removed from that jurisdiction and thereafter until the goods are registered in another jurisdiction, but in any event not beyond surrender of the certificate. After the expiration of that period, the goods are not covered by the certificate of title within the meaning of this section.

(c) Except with respect to the rights of a buyer described in the next paragraph, a security interest, perfected in another jurisdiction otherwise than by notation on a certificate of title, in goods brought into this state and thereafter covered by a certificate of title issued by this state is subject to the rules stated in paragraph (d) of subsection (1).

(d) If goods are brought into this state while a security interest therein is perfected in any manner under the law of the jurisdiction from which the goods are removed and a certificate of title is issued by this state and the certificate does not show that the goods are subject to the security interest or that they may be subject to security interests not shown on the certificate, the security interest is subordinate to the rights of a buyer of the goods who is not in the business of selling goods of that kind to the extent that he gives value and receives delivery of the goods after issuance of the certificate and without knowledge of the security interest.

(3) Accounts, general intangibles and mobile goods.

(a) This subsection applies to accounts (other than an account described in subsection (5) on minerals) and general intangibles (other than uncertificated securities) and to goods which are mobile and which are of a type normally used in more than one jurisdiction, such as motor vehicles, trailers, rolling stock, airplanes, shipping containers, road building and construction machinery and commercial harvesting machinery and the like, if the goods are equipment or are inventory leased or held for lease by the debtor to others, and are not covered by a certificate of title described in subsection (2).

(b) The law (including the conflict of laws rules) of the jurisdiction in which the debtor is located governs the perfection and the effect of perfection or non-perfection of the security interest.

(c) If, however, the debtor is located in a jurisdiction which is not a part of the United States, and which does not provide for perfection of the security interest by filing or recording in that jurisdiction, the law of the jurisdiction in the United States in which the debtor has its major executive office in the United States governs the perfection and the effect of perfection or non-perfection of the security interest through filing. In the alternative, if the debtor is located in a jurisdiction which is not a part of the United States or Canada and the collateral is accounts or general intangibles for money due or to become due, the security interest may be perfected by notification to the account debtor. As used in this paragraph, "United States" includes its territories and possessions and the Commonwealth of Puerto Rico.

(d) A debtor shall be deemed located at his place of business if he has one, at his chief executive office if he has more than one place of business, otherwise at his residence. If, however, the debtor is a foreign air carrier under the Federal Aviation Act of 1958, as amended, it shall be deemed located at the designated office of the agent upon whom service of process may be made on behalf of the foreign air carrier.

(e) A security interest perfected under the law of the jurisdiction of the location of the debtor is perfected until the expiration of four months after a change of the debtor's location to another jurisdiction, or until perfection would have ceased by the law of the first jurisdiction, whichever period first expires. Unless perfected in the new jurisdiction before the end of that period, it becomes unperfected thereafter and is deemed to have been unperfected as against a person who became a purchaser after the change.

(4) Chattel paper.

The rules stated for goods in subsection (1) apply to a possessory security interest in chattel paper. The rules stated for accounts in subsection (3) apply to a non-possessory security interest in chattel paper, but the security interest may not be perfected by notification to the account debtor.

(5) Minerals.

Perfection and the effect of perfection or non-perfection of a security interest which is created by a debtor who has an interest in minerals or the like (including oil and gas) before extraction and which attaches thereto as extracted, or which attaches to an account resulting from the sale thereof at the wellhead or minehead are governed by the law (including the conflict of laws rules) of the jurisdiction wherein the wellhead or minehead is located.

(6) Uncertificated securities.

The law (including the conflict of laws rules) of the jurisdiction of organization of the issuer governs the perfection and the effect of perfection or non-perfection of a security interest in uncertificated securities.

Amended in 1972 and 1977.

§ 9—104. **Transactions Excluded From Article.**

This Article does not apply

(a) to a security interest subject to any statute of the United States, to the extent that such statute governs the rights of parties to and third parties affected by transactions in particular types of property; or

(b) to a landlord's lien; or

(c) to a lien given by statute or other rule of law for services or materials except as provided in Section 9—310 on priority of such liens; or

(d) to a transfer of a claim for wages, salary or other compensation of an employee; or

(e) to a transfer by a government or governmental subdivision or agency; or

(f) to a sale of accounts or chattel paper as part of a sale of the business out of which they arose, or an assignment of accounts or chattel paper which is for the purpose of collection only, or a transfer of a right to payment under a contract to an assignee who is also to do the performance under the contract or a transfer of a single account to an assignee in whole or partial satisfaction of a preexisting indebtedness; or

(g) to a transfer of an interest in or claim in or under any policy of insurance, except as provided with respect to proceeds (Section 9—306) and priorities in proceeds (Section 9—312); or

(h) to a right represented by a judgment (other than a judgment taken on a right to payment which was collateral); or

(i) to any right of set-off; or

(j) except to the extent that provision is made for fixtures in Section 9—313, to the creation or transfer of an interest in or lien on real estate, including a lease or rents thereunder; or

(k) to a transfer in whole or in part of any claim arising out of tort; or

(l) to a transfer of an interest in any deposit account (subsection (1) of Section 9—105), except as provided with respect to proceeds (Section 9—306) and priorities in proceeds (Section 9—312).

Amended in 1972.

§ 9—105. **Definitions and Index of Definitions**

(1) In this Article unless the context otherwise requires:

(a) "Account debtor" means the person who is obligated on an account, chattel paper or general intangible;

(b) "Chattel paper" means a writing or writings which evidence both a monetary obligation and a security interest in or a lease of specific goods, but a charter or other contract involving the use or hire of a vessel is not chattel paper. When a transaction is evidenced both by such a security agreement or a lease and by an instrument or a series of instruments, the group of writings taken together constitutes chattel paper;

(c) "Collateral" means the property subject to a security interest, and includes accounts and chattel paper which have been sold;

(d) "Debtor" means the person who owes payment or other performance of the obligation secured, whether or not he owns or has rights in the collateral, and includes the seller of accounts or chattel paper. Where the debtor and the owner of the collateral are not the same person, the term "debtor" means the owner of the collateral in any provision of the Article dealing with the collateral, the obligor in any provision dealing with the obligation, and may include both where the context so requires;

(e) "Deposit account" means a demand, time, savings, passbook or like account maintained with a bank, savings and loan association, credit union or like organization, other than an account evidenced by a certificate of deposit;

(f) "Document" means document of title as defined in the general definitions of Article 1 (Section 1—201), and a receipt of the kind described in subsection (2) of Section 7—201;

(g) "Encumbrance" includes real estate mortgages and other liens on real estate and all other rights in real estate that are not ownership interests;

(h) "Goods" includes all things which are movable at the time the security interest attaches or which are fixtures (Section 9—313), but does not include money, documents, instruments, accounts, chattel paper, general intangibles, or minerals or the like (including oil and gas) before extraction. "Goods" also includes standing timber which is to be cut and removed under a conveyance or contract for sale, the unborn young of animals, and growing crops;

(i) "Instrument" means a negotiable instrument (defined in Section 3—104), or a certificated security (defined in Section 8—102) or any other writing which evidences a right to the payment of money and is not itself a security agreement or lease and is of a type which is in ordinary course of business transferred by delivery with any necessary indorsement or assignment;

(j) "Mortgage" means a consensual interest cre-

ated by a real estate mortgage, a trust deed on real estate, or the like;

(k) An advance is made "pursuant to commitment" if the secured party has bound himself to make it, whether or not a subsequent event of default or other event not within his control has relieved or may relieve him from his obligation;

(l) "Security agreement" means an agreement which creates or provides for a security interest;

(m) "Secured party" means a lender, seller or other person in whose favor there is a security interest, including a person to whom accounts or chattel paper have been sold. When the holders of obligations issued under an indenture of trust, equipment trust agreement or the like are represented by a trustee or other person, the representative is the secured party;

(n) "Transmitting utility" means any person primarily engaged in the railroad, street railway or trolley bus business, the electric or electronics communications transmission business, the transmission of goods by pipeline, or the transmission or the production and transmission of electricity, steam, gas or water, or the provision of sewer service.

(2) Other definitions applying to this Article and the sections in which they appear are:
"Account". Section 9—106.
"Attach". Section 9—203.
"Construction mortgage". Section 9—313(1).
"Consumer goods". Section 9—109(1).
"Equipment". Section 9—109(2).
"Farm products". Section 9—109(3).
"Fixture". Section 9—313(1).
"Fixture filing". Section 9—313(1).
"General intangibles". Section 9—106.
"Inventory". Section 9—109(4).
"Lien creditor". Section 9—301(3).
"Proceeds". Section 9—306(1).
"Purchase money security interest". Section 9—107.
"United States". Section 9—103.

(3) The following definitions in other Articles apply to this Article:
"Check". Section 3—104.
"Contract for sale". Section 2—106.
"Holder in due course". Section 3—302.
"Note". Section 3—104.
"Sale". Section 2—106.

(4) In addition Article 1 contains general definitions and principles of construction and interpretation ap-

plicable throughout this Article.

Amended in 1966, 1972 and 1977.

§ 9—106. Definitions: "Account"; "General Intangibles".

"Account" means any right to payment for goods sold or leased or for services rendered which is not evidenced by an instrument or chattel paper, whether or not it has been earned by performance. "General intangibles" means any personal property (including things in action) other than goods, accounts, chattel paper, documents, instruments, and money. All rights to payment earned or unearned under a charter or other contract involving the use or hire of a vessel and all rights incident to the charter or contract are accounts. Amended in 1966, 1972.

§ 9—107. Definitions: "Purchase Money Security Interest".

A security interest is a "purchase money security interest" to the extent that it is

(a) taken or retained by the seller of the collateral to secure all or part of its price; or

(b) taken by a person who by making advances or incurring an obligation gives value to enable the debtor to acquire rights in or the use of collateral if such value is in fact so used.

§ 9—108. When After-Acquired Collateral Not Security for Antecedent Debt.

Where a secured party makes an advance, incurs an obligation, releases a perfected security interest, or otherwise gives new value which is to be secured in whole or in part by after-acquired property his security interest in the after-acquired collateral shall be deemed to be taken for new value and not as security for an antecedent debt if the debtor acquires his rights in such collateral either in the ordinary course of his business or under a contract of purchase made pursuant to the security agreement within a reasonable time after new value is given.

§ 9—109. Classification of Goods; "Consumer Goods"; "Equipment"; "Farm Products"; "Inventory".

Goods are

(1) "consumer goods" if they are used or bought for use primarily for personal, family or household purposes;

(2) "equipment" if they are used or bought for use primarily in business (including farming or a profession) or by a debtor who is a non-profit organization or a governmental subdivision or agency or if the goods are not included in the definitions of inventory, farm products or consumer goods;

(3) "farm products" if they are crops or livestock or supplies used or produced in farming operations or if they are products of crops or livestock in their unmanufactured states (such as ginned cotton, woolclip, maple syrup, milk and eggs), and if they are in the possession of a debtor engaged in raising, fattening, grazing or other farming operations. If goods are farm products they are neither equipment nor inventory;

(4) "inventory" if they are held by a person who holds them for sale or lease or to be furnished under contracts of service or if he has so furnished them, or if they are raw materials, work in process or materials used or consumed in a business. Inventory of a person is not to be classified as his equipment.

§ 9—110. Sufficiency of Description.

For purposes of this Article any description of personal property or real estate is sufficient whether or not it is specific if it reasonably identifies what is described.

§ 9—111. Applicability of Bulk Transfer Laws.

The creation of a security interest is not a bulk transfer under Article 6 (see Section 6—103).

§ 9—112. Where Collateral Is Not Owned by Debtor.

Unless otherwise agreed, when a secured party knows that collateral is owned by a person who is not the debtor, the owner of the collateral is entitled to receive from the secured party any surplus under Section 9—502(2) or under Section 9—504(1), and is not liable for the debt or for any deficiency after resale, and he has the same right as the debtor

(a) to receive statements under Section 9—208;

(b) to receive notice of and to object to a secured party's proposal to retain the collateral in satisfaction of the indebtedness under Section 9—505;

(c) to redeem the collateral under Section 9—506;

(d) to obtain injunctive or other relief under Section 9—507(1); and

(e) to recover losses caused to him under Section 9—208(2).

§ 9—113. Security Interests Arising Under Article on Sales.

A security interest arising solely under the Article on Sales (Article 2) is subject to the provisions of this

Article except that to the extent that and so long as the debtor does not have or does not lawfully obtain possession of the goods

(a) no security agreement is necessary to make the security interest enforceable; and

(b) no filing is required to perfect the security interest; and

(c) the rights of the secured party on default by the debtor are governed by the Article on Sales (Article 2).

§ 9—114. **Consignment.**

(1) A person who delivers goods under a consignment which is not a security interest and who would be required to file under this Article by paragraph (3)(c) of Section 2—326 has priority over a secured party who is or becomes a creditor of the consignee and who would have a perfected security interest in the goods if they were the property of the consignee, and also has priority with respect to identifiable cash proceeds received on or before delivery of the goods to a buyer, if

>   (a) the consignor complies with the filing provision of the Article on Sales with respect to consignments (paragraph (3)(c) of Section 2—326) before the consignee receives possession of the goods; and

>   (b) the consignor gives notification in writing to the holder of the security interest if the holder has filed a financing statement covering the same types of goods before the date of the filing made by the consignor; and

>   (c) the holder of the security interest receives the notification within five years before the consignee receives possession of the goods; and

>   (d) the notification states that the consignor expects to deliver goods on consignment to the consignee, describing the goods by item or type.

(2) In the case of a consignment which is not a security interest and in which the requirements of the preceding subsection have not been met, a person who delivers goods to another is subordinate to a person who would have a perfected security interest in the goods if they were the property of the debtor.

Added in 1972.

Part 2 Validity of Security Agreement and Rights of Parties Thereto

§ 9—201. **General Validity of Security Agreement.**

Except as otherwise provided by this Act a security agreement is effective according to its terms between the parties, against purchasers of the collateral and against creditors. Nothing in this Article validates any charge or practice illegal under any statute or regulation thereunder governing usury, small loans, retail installment sales, or the like, or extends the application of any such statute or regulation to any transaction not otherwise subject thereto.

§ 9—202. **Title to Collateral Immaterial.**

Each provision of this Article with regard to rights, obligations and remedies applies whether title to collateral is in the secured party or in the debtor.

§ 9—203. **Attachment and Enforceability of Security Interest; Proceeds; Formal Requisites**

(1) Subject to the provisions of Section 4—208 on the security interest of a collecting bank, Section 8—321 on security interests in securities and Section 9—113 on a security interest arising under the Article on Sales, a security interest is not enforceable against the debtor or third parties with respect to the collateral and does not attach unless:

>   (a) the collateral is in the possession of the secured party pursuant to agreement, or the debtor has signed a security agreement which contains a description of the collateral and in addition, when the security interest covers crops growing or to be grown or timber to be cut, a description of the land concerned;

>   (b) value has been given; and

>   (c) the debtor has rights in the collateral.

(2) A security interest attaches when it becomes enforceable against the debtor with respect to the collateral. Attachment occurs as soon as all of the events specified in subsection (1) have taken place unless explicit agreement postpones the time of attaching.

(3) Unless otherwise agreed a security agreement gives the secured party the rights to proceeds provided by Section 9—306.

(4) A transaction, although subject to this Article, is also subject to . . . .*, and in the case of conflict between the provisions of this Article and any such statute, the provisions of such statute control. Failure to comply with any applicable statute has only the effect which is specified therein.

Amended in 1972 and 1977.

Note: At * in subsection (4) insert reference to any local statute regulating small loans, retail installment sales and the like.

The foregoing subsection (4) is designed to make it clear that certain transactions, although subject to this Article, must also comply with other applicable legislation.

This Article is designed to regulate all the "security" aspects of transactions within its scope. There is, however, much regulatory legislation, particularly in the consumer field, which supplements this Article and should not be repealed by its enactment. Examples are small loan acts, retail installment selling acts and the like. Such acts may provide for licensing and rate regulation and may prescribe particular forms of contract. Such provisions should remain in force despite the enactment of this Article. On the other hand if a retail installment selling act contains provisions on filing, rights on default, etc., such provisions should be repealed as inconsistent with this Article except that inconsistent provisions as to deficiencies, penalties, etc., in the Uniform Consumer Credit Code and other recent related legislation should remain because those statutes were drafted after the substantial enactment of the Article and with the intention of modifying certain provisions of this Article as to consumer credit.

§ 9—204. After-Acquired Property; Future Advances.

(1) Except as provided in subsection (2), a security agreement may provide that any or all obligations covered by the security agreement are to be secured by after-acquired collateral.

(2) No security interest attaches under an after-acquired property clause to consumer goods other than accessions (Section 9—314) when given as additional security unless the debtor acquires rights in them within ten days after the secured party gives value.

(3) Obligations covered by a security agreement may include future advances or other value whether or not the advances or value are given pursuant to commitment (subsection (1) of Section 9—105).

Amended in 1972.

§ 9—205. Use or Disposition of Collateral Without Accounting Permissible.

A security interest is not invalid or fraudulent against creditors by reason of liberty in the debtor to use, commingle or dispose of all or part of the collateral (including returned or repossessed goods) or to collect or compromise accounts or chattel paper, or to accept the return of goods or make repossessions, or to use, commingle or dispose of proceeds, or by reason of the failure of the secured party to require the debtor to account for proceeds or replace collateral. This section does not relax the requirements of possession where perfection of a security interest depends upon possession of the collateral by the secured party or by a bailee.

Amended in 1972.

§ 9—206. Agreement Not to Assert Defenses Against Assignee; Modification of Sales Warranties Where Security Agreement Exists.

(1) Subject to any statute or decision which establishes a different rule for buyers or lessees of consumer goods, an agreement by a buyer or lessee that he will not assert against an assignee any claim or defense which he may have against the seller or lessor is enforceable by an assignee who takes his assignment for value, in good faith and without notice of a claim or defense, except as to defenses of a type which may be asserted against a holder in due course of a negotiable instrument under the Article on Commercial Paper (Article 3). A buyer who as part of one transaction signs both a negotiable instrument and a security agreement makes such an agreement.

(2) When a seller retains a purchase money security interest in goods the Article on Sales (Article 2) governs the sale and any disclaimer, limitation or modification of the seller's warranties.

Amended in 1962.

§ 9—207. Rights and Duties When Collateral is in Secured Party's Possession.

(1) A secured party must use reasonable care in the custody and preservation of collateral in his possession. In the case of an instrument or chattel paper reasonable care includes taking necessary steps to preserve rights against prior parties unless otherwise agreed.

(2) Unless otherwise agreed, when collateral is in the secured party's possession

    (a) reasonable expenses (including the cost of any insurance and payment of taxes or other charges) incurred in the custody, preservation, use or operation of the collateral are chargeable to the debtor and are secured by the collateral;

    (b) the risk of accidental loss or damage is on the debtor to the extent of any deficiency in any effective insurance coverage;

    (c) the secured party may hold as additional security any increase or profits (except money) received from the collateral, but money so received, unless remitted to the debtor, shall be applied in reduction of the secured obligation;

    (d) the secured party must keep the collateral identifiable but fungible collateral may be commingled;

    (e) the secured party may repledge the collateral

upon terms which do not impair the debtor's right to redeem it.

(3) A secured party is liable for any loss caused by his failure to meet any obligation imposed by the preceding subsections but does not lose his security interest.

(4) A secured party may use or operate the collateral for the purpose of preserving the collateral or its value or pursuant to the order of a court of appropriate jurisdiction or, except in the case of consumer goods, in the manner and to the extent provided in the security agreement.

§ 9—208. Request for Statement of Account or List of Collateral.

(1) A debtor may sign a statement indicating what he believes to be the aggregate amount of unpaid indebtedness as of a specified date and may send it to the secured party with a request that the statement be approved or corrected and returned to the debtor. When the security agreement or any other record kept by the secured party identifies the collateral a debtor may similarly request the secured party to approve or correct a list of the collateral.

(2) The secured party must comply with such a request within two weeks after receipt by sending a written correction or approval. If the secured party claims a security interest in all of a particular type of collateral owned by the debtor he may indicate that fact in his reply and need not approve or correct an itemized list of such collateral. If the secured party without reasonable excuse fails to comply he is liable for any loss caused to the debtor thereby; and if the debtor has properly included in his request a good faith statement of the obligation or a list of the collateral or both the secured party may claim a security interest only as shown in the statement against persons misled by his failure to comply. If he no longer has an interest in the obligation or collateral at the time the request is received he must disclose the name and address of any successor in interest known to him and he is liable for any loss caused to the debtor as a result of failure to disclose. A successor in interest is not subject to this section until a request is received by him.

(3) A debtor is entitled to such a statement once every six months without charge. The secured party may require payment of a charge not exceeding $10 for each additional statement furnished.

Part 3 Rights of Third Parties; Perfected and Unperfected Security Interests; Rules of Priority

§ 9—301. Persons Who Take Priority Over Unperfected Security Interests; Rights of "Lien Creditor".

(1) Except as otherwise provided in subsection (2), an unperfected security interest is subordinate to the rights of

(a) persons entitled to priority under Section 9—312;

(b) a person who becomes a lien creditor before the security interest is perfected;

(c) in the case of goods, instruments, documents, and chattel paper, a person who is not a secured party and who is a transferee in bulk or other buyer not in ordinary course of business or is a buyer of farm products in ordinary course of business, to the extent that he gives value and receives delivery of the collateral without knowledge of the security interest and before it is perfected;

(d) in the case of accounts and general intangibles, a person who is not a secured party and who is a transferee to the extent that he gives value without knowledge of the security interest and before it is perfected.

(2) If the secured party files with respect to a purchase money security interest before or within ten days after the debtor receives possession of the collateral, he takes priority over the rights of a transferee in bulk or of a lien creditor which arise between the time the security interest attaches and the time of filing.

(3) A "lien creditor" means a creditor who has acquired a lien on the property involved by attachment, levy or the like and includes an assignee for benefit of creditors from the time of assignment, and a trustee in bankruptcy from the date of the filing of the petition or a receiver in equity from the time of appointment.

(4) A person who becomes a lien creditor while a security interest is perfected takes subject to the security interest only to the extent that it secures advances made before he becomes a lien creditor or within 45 days thereafter or made without knowledge of the lien or pursuant to a commitment entered into without knowledge of the lien.

Amended in 1972.

§ 9—302. **When Filing Is Required to Perfect Security Interest; Security Interests to Which Filing Provisions of This Article Do Not Apply**

(1) A financing statement must be filed to perfect all security interests except the following:

(a) a security interest in collateral in possession of the secured party under Section 9—305;

(b) a security interest temporarily perfected in instruments or documents without delivery under Section 9—304 or in proceeds for a 10 day period under Section 9—306;

(c) a security interest created by an assignment of a beneficial interest in a trust or a decedent's estate;

(d) a purchase money security interest in consumer goods; but filing is required for a motor vehicle required to be registered; and fixture filing is required for priority over conflicting interests in fixtures to the extent provided in Section 9—313;

(e) an assignment of accounts which does not alone or in conjunction with other assignments to the same assignee transfer a significant part of the outstanding accounts of the assignor;

(f) a security interest of a collecting bank (Section 4—208) or in securities (Section 8—321) or arising under the Article on Sales (see Section 9—113) or covered in subsection (3) of this section;

(g) an assignment for the benefit of all the creditors of the transferor, and subsequent transfers by the assignee thereunder.

(2) If a secured party assigns a perfected security interest, no filing under this Article is required in order to continue the perfected status of the security interest against creditors of and transferees from the original debtor.

(3) The filing of a financing statement otherwise required by this Article is not necessary or effective to perfect a security interest in property subject to

(a) a statute or treaty of the United States which provides for a national or international registration or a national or international certificate of title or which specifies a place of filing different from that specified in this Article for filing of the security interest; or

(b) the following statutes of this state; [list any certificate of title statute covering automobiles, trailers, mobile homes, boats, farm tractors, or the like, and any central filing statute.]; but during any period in which collateral is inventory held for sale

by a person who is in the business of selling goods of that kind, the filing provisions of this Article (Part 4) apply to a security interest in that collateral created by him as debtor; or

(c) a certificate of title statute of another jurisdiction under the law of which indication of a security interest on the certificate is required as a condition of perfection (subsection (2) of Section 9—103).

(4) Compliance with a statute or treaty described in subsection (3) is equivalent to the filing of a financing statement under this Article, and a security interest in property subject to the statute or treaty can be perfected only by compliance therewith except as provided in Section 9—103 on multiple state transactions. Duration and renewal of perfection of a security interest perfected by compliance with the statute or treaty are governed by the provisions of the statute or treaty; in other respects the security interest is subject to this Article.

Amended in 1972 and 1977.

§ 9—303. **When Security Interest Is Perfected; Continuity of Perfection.**

(1) A security interest is perfected when it has attached and when all of the applicable steps required for perfection have been taken. Such steps are specified in Sections 9—302, 9—304, 9—305 and 9—306. If such steps are taken before the security interest attaches, it is perfected at the time when it attaches.

(2) If a security interest is originally perfected in any way permitted under this Article and is subsequently perfected in some other way under this Article, without an intermediate period when it was unperfected, the security interest shall be deemed to be perfected continuously for the purposes of this Article.

§ 9—304. **Perfection of Security Interest in Instruments, Documents, and Goods Covered by Documents; Perfection by Permissive Filing; Temporary Perfection Without Filing or Transfer of Possession**

(1) A security interest in chattel paper or negotiable documents may be perfected by filing. A security interest in money or instruments (other than certificated securities or instruments which constitute part of chattel paper) can be perfected only by the secured party's taking possession, except as provided in subsections (4) and (5) of this section and subsections (2) and (3) of Section 9—306 on proceeds.

(2) During the period that goods are in the possession of the issuer of a negotiable document therefor, a security interest in the goods is perfected by perfecting a security interest in the document, and any security interest in the goods otherwise perfected during such period is subject thereto.

(3) A security interest in goods in the possession of a bailee other than one who has issued a negotiable document therefor is perfected by issuance of a document in the name of the secured party or by the bailee's receipt of notification of the secured party's interest or by filing as to the goods.

(4) A security interest in instruments (other than certificated securities) or negotiable documents is perfected without filing or the taking of possession for a period of 21 days from the time it attaches to the extent that it arises for new value given under a written security agreement.

(5) A security interest remains perfected for a period of 21 days without filing where a secured party having a perfected security interest in an instrument (other than a certificated security), a negotiable document or goods in possession of a bailee other than one who has issued a negotiable document therefor

> (a) makes available to the debtor the goods or documents representing the goods for the purpose of ultimate sale or exchange or for the purpose of loading, unloading, storing, shipping, transshipping, manufacturing, processing or otherwise dealing with them in a manner preliminary to their sale or exchange, but priority between conflicting security interests in the goods is subject to subsection (3) of Section 9—312; or

> (b) delivers the instrument to the debtor for the purpose of ultimate sale or exchange or of presentation, collection, renewal or registration of transfer.

(6) After the 21 day period in subsections (4) and (5) perfection depends upon compliance with applicable provisions of this Article.

Amended in 1972 and 1977.

§ 9—305. **When Possession by Secured Party Perfects Security Interest Without Filing**

A security interest in letters of credit and advices of credit (subsection (2)(a) of Section 5—116), goods, instruments (other than certificated securities), money, negotiable documents, or chattel paper may be perfected by the secured party's taking possession of the collateral. If such collateral other than goods covered by a negotiable document is held by a bailee, the secured party is deemed to have possession from the time the bailee receives notification of the secured party's interest. A security interest is perfected by possession from the time possession is taken without a relation back and continues only so long as possession is retained, unless otherwise specified in this Article. The security interest may be otherwise perfected as provided in this Article before or after the period of possession by the secured party.

Amended in 1972 and 1977.

§ 9—306. **"Proceeds"; Secured Party's Rights on Disposition of Collateral.**

(1) "Proceeds" includes whatever is received upon the sale, exchange, collection or other disposition of collateral or proceeds. Insurance payable by reason of loss or damage to the collateral is proceeds, except to the extent that it is payable to a person other than a party to the security agreement. Money, checks, deposit accounts, and the like are "cash proceeds". All other proceeds are "non-cash proceeds".

(2) Except where this Article otherwise provides, a security interest continues in collateral notwithstanding sale, exchange or other disposition thereof unless the disposition was authorized by the secured party in the security agreement or otherwise, and also continues in any identifiable proceeds including collections received by the debtor.

(3) The security interest in proceeds is a continuously perfected security interest if the interest in the original collateral was perfected but it ceases to be a perfected security interest and becomes unperfected ten days after receipt of the proceeds by the debtor unless

> (a) a filed financing statement covers the original collateral and the proceeds are collateral in which a security interest may be perfected by filing in the office or offices where the financing statement has been filed and, if the proceeds are acquired with cash proceeds, the description of collateral in the financing statement indicates the types of property constituting the proceeds; or

> (b) a filed financing statement covers the original collateral and the proceeds are identifiable cash proceeds; or

> (c) the security interest in the proceeds is perfected before the expiration of the ten day period.

Except as provided in this section, a security interest in proceeds can be perfected only by the methods or under the circumstances permitted in this Article for original collateral of the same type.

(4) In the event of insolvency proceedings instituted by or against a debtor, a secured party with a perfected security interest in proceeds has a perfected security interest only in the following proceeds:

(a) in identifiable non-cash proceeds and in separate deposit accounts containing only proceeds;

(b) in identifiable cash proceeds in the form of money which is neither commingled with other money nor deposited in a deposit account prior to the insolvency proceedings;

(c) in identifiable cash proceeds in the form of checks and the like which are not deposited in a deposit account prior to the insolvency proceedings; and

(d) in all cash and deposit accounts of the debtor in which proceeds have been commingled with other funds, but the perfected security interest under this paragraph (d) is

(i) subject to any right to set-off; and

(ii) limited to an amount not greater than the amount of any cash proceeds received by the debtor within ten days before the institution of the insolvency proceedings less the sum of (I) the payments to the secured party on account of cash proceeds received by the debtor during such period and (II) the cash proceeds received by the debtor during such period to which the secured party is entitled under paragraphs (a) through (c) of this subsection (4).

(5) If a sale of goods results in an account or chattel paper which is transferred by the seller to a secured party, and if the goods are returned to or are repossessed by the seller or the secured party, the following rules determine priorities:

(a) If the goods were collateral at the time of sale, for an indebtedness of the seller which is still unpaid, the original security interest attaches again to the goods and continues as a perfected security interest if it was perfected at the time when the goods were sold. If the security interest was originally perfected by a filing which is still effective, nothing further is required to continue the perfected status; in any other case, the secured party must take possession of the returned or repossessed goods or must file.

(b) An unpaid transferee of the chattel paper has a security interest in the goods against the transferor. Such security interest is prior to a security interest asserted under paragraph (a) to the extent

that the transferee of the chattel paper was entitled to priority under Section 9—308.

(c) An unpaid transferee of the account has a security interest in the goods against the transferor. Such security interest is subordinate to a security interest asserted under paragraph (a).

(d) A security interest of an unpaid transferee asserted under paragraph (b) or (c) must be perfected for protection against creditors of the transferor and purchasers of the returned or repossessed goods.

Amended in 1972.

§ 9—307. **Protection of Buyers of Goods.**

(1) A buyer in ordinary course of business (subsection (9) of Section 1—201) other than a person buying farm products from a person engaged in farming operations takes free of a security interest created by his seller even though the security interest is perfected and even though the buyer knows of its existence.

(2) In the case of consumer goods, a buyer takes free of a security interest even though perfected if he buys without knowledge of the security interest, for value and for his own personal, family or household purposes unless prior to the purchase the secured party has filed a financing statement covering such goods.

(3) A buyer other than a buyer in ordinary course of business (subsection (1) of this section) takes free of a security interest to the extent that it secures future advances made after the secured party acquires knowledge of the purchase, or more than 45 days after the purchase, whichever first occurs, unless made pursuant to a commitment entered into without knowledge of the purchase and before the expiration of the 45 day period. Amended in 1972.

§ 9—308. **Purchase of Chattel Paper and Instruments.**

A purchaser of chattel paper or an instrument who gives new value and takes possession of it in the ordinary course of his business has priority over a security interest in the chattel paper or instrument

(a) which is perfected under Section 9—304 (permissive filing and temporary perfection) or under Section 9—306 (perfection as to proceeds) if he acts without knowledge that the specific paper or instrument is subject to a security interest; or

(b) which is claimed merely as proceeds of inventory subject to a security interest (Section 9—306) even though he knows that the specific paper or instrument is subject to the security interest.

Amended in 1972.

§ 9—309. Protection of Purchasers of Instruments, Documents and Securities

Nothing in this Article limits the rights of a holder in due course of a negotiable instrument (Section 3—302) or a holder to whom a negotiable document of title has been duly negotiated (Section 7—501) or a bona fide purchaser of a security (Section 8—302) and the holders or purchasers take priority over an earlier security interest even though perfected. Filing under this Article does not constitute notice of the security interest to such holders or purchasers.

Amended in 1977.

§ 9—310. Priority of Certain Liens Arising by Operation of Law.

When a person in the ordinary course of his business furnishes services or materials with respect to goods subject to a security interest, a lien upon goods in the possession of such person given by statute or rule of law for such materials or services takes priority over a perfected security interest unless the lien is statutory and the statute expressly provides otherwise.

§ 9—311. Alienability of Debtor's Rights: Judicial Process.

The debtor's rights in collateral may be voluntarily or involuntarily transferred (by way of sale, creation of a security interest, attachment, levy, garnishment or other judicial process) notwithstanding a provision in the security agreement prohibiting any transfer or making the transfer constitute a default.

§ 9—312. Priorities Among Conflicting Security Interests in the Same Collateral

(1) The rules of priority stated in other sections of this Part and in the following sections shall govern when applicable: Section 4—208 with respect to the security interests of collecting banks in items being collected, accompanying documents and proceeds; Section 9—103 on security interests related to other jurisdictions; Section 9—114 on consignments.

(2) A perfected security interest in crops for new value given to enable the debtor to produce the crops during the production season and given not more than three months before the crops become growing crops by planting or otherwise takes priority over an earlier perfected security interest to the extent that such earlier interest secures obligations due more than six months before the crops become growing crops by planting or otherwise, even though the person giving new value had knowledge of the earlier security interest.

(3) A perfected purchase money security interest in inventory has priority over a conflicting security interest in the same inventory and also has priority in identifiable cash proceeds received on or before the delivery of the inventory to a buyer if

(a) the purchase money security interest is perfected at the time the debtor receives possession of the inventory; and

(b) the purchase money secured party gives notification in writing to the holder of the conflicting security interest if the holder had filed a financing statement covering the same types of inventory (i) before the date of the filing made by the purchase money secured party, or (ii) before the beginning of the 21 day period where the purchase money security interest is temporarily perfected without filing or possession (subsection (5) of Section 9—304); and

(c) the holder of the conflicting security interest receives the notification within five years before the debtor receives possession of the inventory; and

(d) the notification states that the person giving the notice has or expects to acquire a purchase money security interest in inventory of the debtor, describing such inventory by item or type.

(4) A purchase money security interest in collateral other than inventory has priority over a conflicting security interest in the same collateral or its proceeds if the purchase money security interest is perfected at the time the debtor receives possession of the collateral or within ten days thereafter.

(5) In all cases not governed by other rules stated in this section (including cases of purchase money security interests which do not qualify for the special priorities set forth in subsections (3) and (4) of this section), priority between conflicting security interests in the same collateral shall be determined according to the following rules:

(a) Conflicting security interests rank according to priority in time of filing or perfection. Priority dates from the time a filing is first made covering the collateral or the time the security interest is first perfected, whichever is earlier, provided that there is no period thereafter when there is neither filing nor perfection.

(b) So long as conflicting security interests are unperfected, the first to attach has priority.

(6) For the purposes of subsection (5) a date of filing or perfection as to collateral is also a date of filing or perfection as to proceeds.

(7) If future advances are made while a security interest is perfected by filing, the taking of possession, or under Section 8—321 on securities, the security interest has the same priority for the purposes of subsection (5) with respect to the future advances as it does with respect to the first advance. If a commitment is made before or while the security interest is so perfected, the security interest has the same priority with respect to advances made pursuant thereto. In other cases a perfected security interest has priority from the date the advance is made.

Amended in 1972 and 1977.

§ 9—313. **Priority of Security Interests in Fixtures.**

(1) In this section and in the provisions of Part 4 of this Article referring to fixture filing, unless the context otherwise requires

(a) goods are "fixtures" when they become so related to particular real estate that an interest in them arises under real estate law

(b) a "fixture filing" is the filing in the office where a mortgage on the real estate would be filed or recorded of a financing statement covering goods which are or are to become fixtures and conforming to the requirements of subsection (5) of Section 9—402

(c) a mortgage is a "construction mortgage" to the extent that it secures an obligation incurred for the construction of an improvement on land including the acquisition cost of the land, if the recorded writing so indicates.

(2) A security interest under this Article may be created in goods which are fixtures or may continue in goods which become fixtures, but no security interest exists under this Article in ordinary building materials incorporated into an improvement on land.

(3) This Article does not prevent creation of an encumbrance upon fixtures pursuant to real estate law.

(4) A perfected security interest in fixtures has priority over the conflicting interest of an encumbrancer or owner of the real estate where

(a) the security interest is a purchase money security interest, the interest of the encumbrancer or owner arises before the goods become fixtures, the security interest is perfected by a fixture filing before the goods become fixtures or within ten days thereafter, and the debtor has an interest of record in the real estate or is in possession of the real estate; or

(b) the security interest is perfected by a fixture

filing before the interest of the encumbrancer or owner is of record, the security interest has priority over any conflicting interest of a predecessor in title of the encumbrancer or owner, and the debtor has an interest of record in the real estate or is in possession of the real estate; or

(c) the fixtures are readily removable factory or office machines or readily removable replacements of domestic appliances which are consumer goods, and before the goods become fixtures the security interest is perfected by any method permitted by this Article; or

(d) the conflicting interest is a lien on the real estate obtained by legal or equitable proceedings after the security interest was perfected by any method permitted by this Article.

(5) A security interest in fixtures, whether or not perfected, has priority over the conflicting interest of an encumbrancer or owner of the real estate where

(a) the encumbrancer or owner has consented in writing to the security interest or has disclaimed an interest in the goods as fixtures; or

(b) the debtor has a right to remove the goods as against the encumbrancer or owner. If the debtor's right terminates, the priority of the security interest continues for a reasonable time.

(6) Notwithstanding paragraph (a) of subsection (4) but otherwise subject to subsections (4) and (5), a security interest in fixtures is subordinate to a construction mortgage recorded before the goods become fixtures if the goods become fixtures before the completion of the construction. To the extent that it is given to refinance a construction mortgage, a mortgage has this priority to the same extent as the construction mortgage.

(7) In cases not within the preceding subsections, a security interest in fixtures is subordinate to the conflicting interest of an encumbrancer or owner of the related real estate who is not the debtor.

(8) When the secured party has priority over all owners and encumbrancers of the real estate, he may, on default, subject to the provisions of Part 5, remove his collateral from the real estate but he must reimburse any encumbrancer or owner of the real estate who is not the debtor and who has not otherwise agreed for the cost of repair of any physical injury, but not for any diminution in value of the real estate caused by the absence of the goods removed or by any necessity of replacing them. A person entitled to reimbursement may refuse permission to remove until the secured

party gives adequate security for the performance of this obligation. Amended in 1972.

§ 9—314. **Accessions.**

(1) A security interest in goods which attaches before they are installed in or affixed to other goods takes priority as to the goods installed or affixed (called in this section "accessions") over the claims of all persons to the whole except as stated in subsection (3) and subject to Section 9—315(1).

(2) A security interest which attaches to goods after they become part of a whole is valid against all persons subsequently acquiring interests in the whole except as stated in subsection (3) but is invalid against any person with an interest in the whole at the time the security interest attaches to the goods who has not in writing consented to the security interest or disclaimed an interest in the goods as part of the whole.

(3) The security interests described in subsections (1) and (2) do not take priority over

(a) a subsequent purchaser for value of any interest in the whole; or

(b) a creditor with a lien on the whole subsequently obtained by judicial proceedings; or

(c) a creditor with a prior perfected security interest in the whole to the extent that he makes subsequent advances

if the subsequent purchase is made, the lien by judicial proceedings obtained or the subsequent advance under the prior perfected security interest is made or contracted for without knowledge of the security interest and before it is perfected. A purchaser of the whole at a foreclosure sale other than the holder of a perfected security interest purchasing at his own foreclosure sale is a subsequent purchaser within this section.

(4) When under subsections (1) or (2) and (3) a secured party has an interest in accessions which has priority over the claims of all persons who have interests in the whole, he may on default subject to the provisions of Part 5 remove his collateral from the whole but he must reimburse any encumbrancer or owner of the whole who is not the debtor and who has not otherwise agreed for the cost of repair of any physical injury but not for any diminution in value of the whole caused by the absence of the goods removed or by any necessity for replacing them. A person entitled to reimbursement may refuse permission to remove until the secured party gives adequate security for the performance of this obligation.

§ 9—315. **Priority When Goods Are Commingled or Processed.**

(1) If a security interest in goods was perfected and subsequently the goods or a part thereof have become part of a product or mass, the security interest continues in the product or mass if

(a) the goods are so manufactured, processed, assembled or commingled that their identity is lost in the product or mass; or

(b) a financing statement covering the original goods also covers the product into which the goods have been manufactured, processed or assembled.

In a case to which paragraph (b) applies, no separate security interest in that part of the original goods which has been manufactured, processed or assembled into the product may be claimed under Section 9—314.

(2) When under subsection (1) more than one security interest attaches to the product or mass, they rank equally according to the ratio that the cost of the goods to which each interest originally attached bears to the cost of the total product or mass.

§ 9—316. **Priority Subject to Subordination.**

Nothing in this Article prevents subordination by agreement by any person entitled to priority.

§ 9—317. **Secured Party Not Obligated on Contract of Debtor.**

The mere existence of a security interest or authority given to the debtor to dispose of or use collateral does not impose contract or tort liability upon the secured party for the debtor's acts or omissions.

§ 9—318. **Defenses Against Assignee; Modification of Contract After Notification of Assignment; Term Prohibiting Assignment Ineffective; Identification and Proof of Assignment.**

(1) Unless an account debtor has made an enforceable agreement not to assert defenses or claims arising out of a sale as provided in Section 9—206 the rights of an assignee are subject to

(a) all the terms of the contract between the account debtor and assignor and any defense or claim arising therefrom; and

(b) any other defense or claim of the account debtor against the assignor which accrues before the account debtor receives notification of the assignment.

(2) So far as the right to payment or a part thereof under an assigned contract has not been fully earned

by performance, and notwithstanding notification of the assignment, any modification of or substitution for the contract made in good faith and in accordance with reasonable commercial standards is effective against an assignee unless the account debtor has otherwise agreed but the assignee acquires corresponding rights under the modified or substituted contract. The assignment may provide that such modification or substitution is a breach by the assignor.

(3) The account debtor is authorized to pay the assignor until the account debtor receives notification that the amount due or to become due has been assigned and that payment is to be made to the assignee. A notification which does not reasonably identify the rights assigned is ineffective. If requested by the account debtor, the assignee must seasonably furnish reasonable proof that the assignment has been made and unless he does so the account debtor may pay the assignor.

(4) A term in any contract between an account debtor and an assignor is ineffective if it prohibits assignment of an account or prohibits creation of a security interest in a general intangible for money due or to become due or requires the account debtor's consent to such assignment or security interest.

Amended in 1972.

Part 4 Filing

§ 9—401. **Place of Filing; Erroneous Filing; Removal of Collateral.**

First Alternative Subsection (1)

(1) The proper place to file in order to perfect a security interest is as follows:

(a) when the collateral is timber to be cut or is minerals or the like (including oil and gas) or accounts subject to subsection (5) of Section 9—103, or when the financing statement is filed as a fixture filing (Section 9—313) and the collateral is goods which are or are to become fixtures, then in the office where a mortgage on the real estate would be filed or recorded;

(b) in all other cases, in the office of the [Secretary of State].

Second Alternative Subsection (1)

(1) The proper place to file in order to perfect a security interest is as follows:

(a) when the collateral is equipment used in farming operations, or farm products, or accounts or general intangibles arising from or relating to the sale of farm products by a farmer, or consumer goods, then in the office of the .... in the county of the debtor's residence or if the debtor is not a resident of this state then in the office of the .... in the county where the goods are kept, and in addition when the collateral is crops growing or to be grown in the office of the .... in the county where the land is located;

(b) when the collateral is timber to be cut or is minerals or the like (including oil and gas) or accounts subject to subsection (5) of Section 9—103, or when the financing statement is filed as a fixture filing (Section 9—313) and the collateral is goods which are or are to become fixtures, then in the office where a mortgage on the real estate would be filed or recorded;

(c) in all other cases, in the office of the [Secretary of State].

Third Alternative Subsection (1)

(1) The proper place to file in order to perfect a security interest is as follows:

(a) when the collateral is equipment used in farming operations, or farm products, or accounts or general intangibles arising from or relating to the sale of farm products by a farmer, or consumer goods, then in the office of the .... in the county of the debtor's residence or if the debtor is not a resident of this state then in the office of the .... in the county where the goods are kept, and in addition when the collateral is crops growing or to be grown in the office of the .... in the county where the land is located;

(b) when the collateral is timber to be cut or is minerals or the like (including oil and gas) or accounts subject to subsection (5) of Section 9—103, or when the financing statement is filed as a fixture filing (Section 9—313) and the collateral is goods which are or are to become fixtures, then in the office where a mortgage on the real estate would be filed or recorded;

(c) in all other cases, in the office of the [Secretary of State] and in addition, if the debtor has a place of business in only one county of this state, also in the office of .... of such county, or, if the debtor has no place of business in this state, but resides in the state, also in the office of .... of the county in which he resides.

Note: *One of the three alternatives should be selected as subsection (1).*

(2) A filing which is made in good faith in an im-

proper place or not in all of the places required by this section is nevertheless effective with regard to any collateral as to which the filing complied with the requirements of this Article and is also effective with regard to collateral covered by the financing statement against any person who has knowledge of the contents of such financing statement.

(3) A filing which is made in the proper place in this state continues effective even though the debtor's residence or place of business or the location of the collateral or its use, whichever controlled the original filing, is thereafter changed.

Alternative Subsection (3)

[(3) A filing which is made in the proper county continues effective for four months after a change to another county of the debtor's residence or place of business or the location of the collateral, whichever controlled the original filing. It becomes ineffective thereafter unless a copy of the financing statement signed by the secured party is filed in the new county within said period. The security interest may also be perfected in the new county after the expiration of the four-month period; in such case perfection dates from the time of perfection in the new county. A change in the use of the collateral does not impair the effectiveness of the original filing.]

(4) The rules stated in Section 9—103 determine whether filing is necessary in this state.

(5) Notwithstanding the preceding subsections, and subject to subsection (3) of Section 9—302, the proper place to file in order to perfect a security interest in collateral, including fixtures, of a transmitting utility is the office of the [Secretary of State]. This filing constitutes a fixture filing (Section 9—313) as to the collateral described therein which is or is to become fixtures.

(6) For the purposes of this section, the residence of an organization is its place of business if it has one or its chief executive office if it has more than one place of business.

Amended in 1962 and 1972.

Note: *Subsection (6) should be used only if the state chooses the Second or Third Alternative Subsection (1).*

§ 9—402. Formal Requisites of Financing Statement; Amendments; Mortgage as Financing Statement.

(1) A financing statement is sufficient if it gives the names of the debtor and the secured party, is signed by the debtor, gives an address of the secured party

from which information concerning the security interest may be obtained, gives a mailing address of the debtor and contains a statement indicating the types, or describing the items, of collateral. A financing statement may be filed before a security agreement is made or a security interest otherwise attaches. When the financing statement covers crops growing or to be grown, the statement must also contain a description of the real estate concerned. When the financing statement covers timber to be cut or covers minerals or the like (including oil and gas) or accounts subject to subsection (5) of Section 9—103, or when the financing statement is filed as a fixture filing (Section 9—313) and the collateral is goods which are or are to become fixtures, the statement must also comply with subsection (5). A copy of the security agreement is sufficient as a financing statement if it contains the above information and is signed by the debtor. A carbon, photographic or other reproduction of a security agreement or a financing statement is sufficient as a financing statement if the security agreement so provides or if the original has been filed in this state.

(2) A financing statement which otherwise complies with subsection (1) is sufficient when it is signed by the secured party instead of the debtor if it is filed to perfect a security interest in

(a) collateral already subject to a security interest in another jurisdiction when it is brought into this state, or when the debtor's location is changed to this state. Such a financing statement must state that the collateral was brought into this state or that the debtor's location was changed to this state under such circumstances; or

(b) proceeds under Section 9—306 if the security interest in the original collateral was perfected. Such a financing statement must describe the original collateral; or

(c) collateral as to which the filing has lapsed; or

(d) collateral acquired after a change of name, identity or corporate structure of the debtor (subsection (7)).

(3) A form substantially as follows is sufficient to comply with subsection (1):

Name of debtor (or assignor) ....
Address ....
Name of secured party (or assignee) ....
Address ....
1. This financing statement covers the following types (or items) of property:
    (Describe) ....

2. (If collateral is crops) The above described crops are growing or are to be grown on:

(Describe Real Estate) ....

3. (If applicable) The above goods are to become fixtures on *

*Where appropriate substitute either "The above timber is standing on . . . ." or "The above minerals or the like (including oil and gas) or accounts will be financed at the wellhead or minehead of the well or mine located on . . . ."

(Describe Real Estate) ....

and this financing statement is to be filed [for record] in the real estate records. (If the debtor does not have an interest of record) The name of a record owner is ....

4. (If products of collateral are claimed) Products of the collateral are also covered.

(use	....
whichever	Signature of Debtor (or Assignor)
is	....
applicable)	Signature of Secured Party
	(or Assignee)

(4) A financing statement may be amended by filing a writing signed by both the debtor and the secured party. An amendment does not extend the period of effectiveness of a financing statement. If any amendment adds collateral, it is effective as to the added collateral only from the filing date of the amendment. In this Article, unless the context otherwise requires, the term "financing statement" means the original financing statement and any amendments.

(5) A financing statement covering timber to be cut or covering minerals or the like (including oil and gas) or accounts subject to subsection (5) of Section 9—103, or a financing statement filed as a future filing (Section 9—313) where the debtor is not a transmitting utility, must show that it covers this type of collateral, must recite that it is to be filed [for record] in the real estate records, and the financing statement must contain a description of the real estate [sufficient if it were contained in a mortgage of the real estate to give constructive notice of the mortgage under the law of this state]. If the debtor does not have an interest of record in the real estate, the financing statement must show the name of a record owner.

(6) A mortgage is effective as a financing statement filed as a fixture filing from the date of its recording if

(a) the goods are described in the mortgage by item or type; and

(b) the goods are or are to become fixtures related to the real estate described in the mortgage; and

(c) the mortgage complies with the requirements for a financing statement in this section other than a recital that it is to be filed in the real estate records; and

(d) the mortgage is duly recorded.

No fee with reference to the financing statement is required other than the regular recording and satisfaction fees with respect to the mortgage.

(7) A financing statement sufficiently shows the name of the debtor if it gives the individual, partnership or corporate name of the debtor, whether or not it adds other trade names or names of partners. Where the debtor so changes his name or in the case of an organization its name, identity or corporate structure that a filed financing statement becomes seriously misleading, the filing is not effective to perfect a security interest in collateral acquired by the debtor more than four months after the change, unless a new appropriate financing statement is filed before the expiration of that time. A filed financing statement remains effective with respect to collateral transferred by the debtor even though the secured party knows of or consents to the transfer.

(8) A financing statement substantially complying with the requirements of this section is effective even though it contains minor errors which are not seriously misleading. Amended in 1972.

Note: *Language in brackets is optional.*

Note: *Where the state has any special recording system for real estate other than the usual grantor-grantee index (as, for instance, a tract system or a title registration or Torrens system) local adaptations of subsection (5) and Section 9—403(7) may be necessary. See Mass.Gen.Laws Chapter 106, Section 9—409.*

§ 9—403. **What Constitutes Filing; Duration of Filing; Effect of Lapsed Filing; Duties of Filing Officer.**

(1) Presentation for filing of a financing statement and tender of the filing fee or acceptance of the statement by the filing officer constitutes filing under this Article.

(2) Except as provided in subsection (6) a filed financing statement is effective for a period of five years from the date of filing. The effectiveness of a filed financing statement lapses on the expiration of the five

year period unless a continuation statement is filed prior to the lapse. If a security interest perfected by filing exists at the time insolvency proceedings are commenced by or against the debtor, the security interest remains perfected until termination of the insolvency proceedings and thereafter for a period of sixty days or until expiration of the five year period, whichever occurs later. Upon lapse the security interest becomes unperfected, unless it is perfected without filing. If the security interest becomes unperfected upon lapse, it is deemed to have been unperfected as against a person who became a purchaser or lien creditor before lapse.

(3) A continuation statement may be filed by the secured party within six months prior to the expiration of the five year period specified in subsection (2). Any such continuation statement must be signed by the secured party, identify the original statement by file number and state that the original statement is still effective. A continuation statement signed by a person other than the secured party of record must be accompanied by a separate written statement of assignment signed by the secured party of record and complying with subsection (2) of Section 9—405, including payment of the required fee. Upon timely filing of the continuation statement, the effectiveness of the original statement is continued for five years after the last date to which the filing was effective whereupon it lapses in the same manner as provided in subsection (2) unless another continuation statement is filed prior to such lapse. Succeeding continuation statements may be filed in the same manner to continue the effectiveness of the original statement. Unless a statute on disposition of public records provides otherwise, the filing officer may remove a lapsed statement from the files and destroy it immediately if he has retained a microfilm or other photographic record, or in other cases after one year after the lapse. The filing officer shall so arrange matters by physical annexation of financing statements to continuation statements or other related filings, or by other means, that if he physically destroys the financing statements of a period more than five years past, those which have been continued by a continuation statement or which are still effective under subsection (6) shall be retained.

(4) Except as provided in subsection (7) a filing officer shall mark each statement with a file number and with the date and hour of filing and shall hold the statement or a microfilm or other photographic copy thereof for public inspection. In addition the filing officer shall index the statement according to the name of the debtor and shall note in the index the file number and the address of the debtor given in the statement.

(5) The uniform fee for filing and indexing and for stamping a copy furnished by the secured party to show the date and place of filing for an original financing statement or for a continuation statement shall be $. . . . . . . if the statement is in the standard form prescribed by the [Secretary of State] and otherwise shall be $. . . . . . ., plus in each case, if the financing statement is subject to subsection (5) of Section 9—402, $. . . . . . . The uniform fee for each name more than one required to be indexed shall be $. . . . . . . The secured party may at his option show a trade name for any person and an extra uniform indexing fee of $. . . . . . . shall be paid with respect thereto.

(6) If the debtor is a transmitting utility (subsection (5) of Section 9—401) and a filed financing statement so states, it is effective until a termination statement is filed. A real estate mortgage which is effective as a fixture filing under subsection (6) of Section 9—402 remains effective as a fixture filing until the mortgage is released or satisfied of record or its effectiveness otherwise terminates as to the real estate.

(7) When a financing statement covers timber to be cut or covers minerals or the like (including oil and gas) or accounts subject to subsection (5) of Section 9—103, or is filed as a fixture filing, [it shall be filed for record and] the filing officer shall index it under the names of the debtor and any owner of record shown on the financing statement in the same fashion as if they were the mortgagors in a mortgage of the real estate described, and, to the extent that the law of this state provides for indexing of mortgages under the name of the mortgagee, under the name of the secured party as if he were the mortgagee thereunder, or where indexing is by description in the same fashion as if the financing statement were a mortgage of the real estate described. Amended in 1972.

Note: *In states in which writings will not appear in the real estate records and indices unless actually recorded the bracketed language in subsection (7) should be used.*

§ 9—404. **Termination Statement.**

(1) If a financing statement covering consumer goods is filed on or after . . . ., then within one month or within ten days following written demand by the debtor after there is no outstanding secured obligation and no commitment to make advances, incur obligations or otherwise give value, the secured party must file with each filing officer with whom the financing statement was filed, a termination statement to the effect that he no longer claims a security interest under the financing statement, which shall be identified by file

number. In other cases whenever there is no outstanding secured obligation and no commitment to make advances, incur obligations or otherwise give value, the secured party must on written demand by the debtor send the debtor, for each filing officer with whom the financing statement was filed, a termination statement to the effect that he no longer claims a security interest under the financing statement, which shall be identified by file number. A termination statement signed by a person other than the secured party of record must be accompanied by a separate written statement of assignment signed by the secured party of record complying with subsection (2) of Section 9—405, including payment of the required fee. If the affected secured party fails to file such a termination statement as required by this subsection, or to send such a termination statement within ten days after proper demand therefor, he shall be liable to the debtor for one hundred dollars, and in addition for any loss caused to the debtor by such failure.

(2) On presentation to the filing officer of such a termination statement he must note it in the index. If he has received the termination statement in duplicate, he shall return one copy of the termination statement to the secured party stamped to show the time of receipt thereof. If the filing officer has a microfilm or other photographic record of the financing statement, and of any related continuation statement, statement of assignment and statement of release, he may remove the originals from the files at any time after receipt of the termination statement, or if he has no such record, he may remove them from the files at any time after one year after receipt of the termination statement.

(3) If the termination statement is in the standard form prescribed by the [Secretary of State], the uniform fee for filing and indexing the termination statement shall be $. . . . ., and otherwise shall be $. . . . ., plus in each case an additional fee of $. . . . . . . for each name more than one against which the termination statement is required to be indexed. Amended in 1972.

Note: *The date to be inserted should be the effective date of the revised Article 9.*

§ 9—405. **Assignment of Security Interest; Duties of Filing Officer; Fees.**

(1) A financing statement may disclose an assignment of a security interest in the collateral described in the financing statement by indication in the financing statement of the name and address of the assignee or by an assignment itself or a copy thereof on the face or back of the statement. On presentation to the filing officer of such a financing statement the filing officer shall mark the same as provided in Section 9—403(4). The uniform fee for filing, indexing and furnishing filing data for a financing statement so indicating an assignment shall be $. . . . . if the statement is in the standard form prescribed by the [Secretary of State] and otherwise shall be $. . . . ., plus in each case an additional fee of $. . . . . . . for each name more than one against which the financing statement is required to be indexed.

(2) A secured party may assign of record all or part of his rights under a financing statement by the filing in the place where the original financing statement was filed of a separate written statement of assignment signed by the secured party of record and setting forth the name of the secured party of record and the debtor, the file number and the date of filing of the financing statement and the name and address of the assignee and containing a description of the collateral assigned. A copy of the assignment is sufficient as a separate statement if it complies with the preceding sentence. On presentation to the filing officer of such a separate statement, the filing officer shall mark such separate statement with the date and hour of the filing. He shall note the assignment on the index of the financing statement, or in the case of a fixture filing, or a filing covering timber to be cut, or covering minerals or the like (including oil and gas) or accounts subject to subsection (5) of Section 9—103, he shall index the assignment under the name of the assignor as grantor and, to the extent that the law of this state provides for indexing the assignment of a mortgage under the name of the assignee, he shall index the assignment of the financing statement under the name of the assignee. The uniform fee for filing, indexing and furnishing filing data about such a separate statement of assignment shall be $. . . . . . if the statement is in the standard form prescribed by the [Secretary of State] and otherwise shall be $. . . . . . ., plus in each case an additional fee of $. . . . . . for each name more than one against which the statement of assignment is required to be indexed. Notwithstanding the provisions of this subsection, an assignment of record of a security interest in a fixture contained in a mortgage effective as a fixture filing (subsection (6) of Section 9—402) may be made only by an assignment of the mortgage in the manner provided by the law of this state other than this Act.

(3) After the disclosure or filing of an assignment under this section, the assignee is the secured party of record. Amended in 1972.

§ 9—406. **Release of Collateral; Duties of Filing Officer; Fees.**

A secured party of record may by his signed statement release all or a part of any collateral described in a filed financing statement. The statement of release is sufficient if it contains a description of the collateral being released, the name and address of the debtor, the name and address of the secured party, and the file number of the financing statement. A statement of release signed by a person other than the secured party of record must be accompanied by a separate written statement of assignment signed by the secured party of record and complying with subsection (2) of Section 9—405, including payment of the required fee. Upon presentation of such a statement of release to the filing officer he shall mark the statement with the hour and date of filing and shall note the same upon the margin of the index of the filing of the financing statement. The uniform fee for filing and noting such a statement of release shall be $...... if the statement is in the standard form prescribed by the [Secretary of State] and otherwise shall be $......, plus in each case an additional fee of $...... for each name more than one against which the statement of release is required to be indexed. Amended in 1972.

[§ 9—407. **Information From Filing Officer**].

[(1) If the person filing any financing statement, termination statement, statement of assignment, or statement of release, furnishes the filing officer a copy thereof, the filing officer shall upon request note upon the copy the file number and date and hour of the filing of the original and deliver or send the copy to such person.]

[(2) Upon request of any person, the filing officer shall issue his certificate showing whether there is on file on the date and hour stated therein, any presently effective financing statement naming a particular debtor and any statement of assignment thereof and if there is, giving the date and hour of filing of each such statement and the names and addresses of each secured party therein. The uniform fee for such a certificate shall be $...... if the request for the certificate is in the standard form prescribed by the [Secretary of State] and otherwise shall be $....... Upon request the filing officer shall furnish a copy of any filed financing statement or statement of assignment for a uniform fee of $...... per page.] Amended in 1972.

Note: *This section is proposed as an optional provision to require filing officers to furnish certificates. Local law and practices should be consulted with regard to the advisability of adoption.*

§ 9—408. **Financing Statements Covering Consigned or Leased Goods.**

A consignor or lessor of goods may file a financing statement using the terms "consignor," "consignee," "lessor," "lessee" or the like instead of the terms specified in Section 9—402. The provisions of this Part shall apply as appropriate to such a financing statement but its filing shall not of itself be a factor in determining whether or not the consignment or lease is intended as security (Section 1—201(37)). However, if it is determined for other reasons that the consignment or lease is so intended, a security interest of the consignor or lessor which attaches to the consigned or leased goods is perfected by such filing. Added in 1972.

Part 5 Default

§ 9—501. **Default; Procedure When Security Agreement Covers Both Real and Personal Property.**

(1) When a debtor is in default under a security agreement, a secured party has the rights and remedies provided in this Part and except as limited by subsection (3) those provided in the security agreement. He may reduce his claim to judgment, foreclose or otherwise enforce the security interest by any available judicial procedure. If the collateral is documents the secured party may proceed either as to the documents or as to the goods covered thereby. A secured party in possession has the rights, remedies and duties provided in Section 9—207. The rights and remedies referred to in this subsection are cumulative.

(2) After default, the debtor has the rights and remedies provided in this Part, those provided in the security agreement and those provided in Section 9—207.

(3) To the extent that they give rights to the debtor and impose duties on the secured party, the rules stated in the subsections referred to below may not be waived or varied except as provided with respect to compulsory disposition of collateral (subsection (3) of Section 9—504 and Section 9—505) and with respect to redemption of collateral (Section 9—506) but the parties may by agreement determine the standards by which the fulfillment of these rights and duties is to be measured if such standards are not manifestly unreasonable:

(a) subsection (2) of Section 9—502 and subsection (2) of Section 9—504 insofar as they require accounting for surplus proceeds of collateral;

(b) subsection (3) of Section 9—504 and subsection (1) of Section 9—505 which deal with disposition of collateral;

(c) subsection (2) of Section 9—505 which deals with acceptance of collateral as discharge of obligation;

(d) Section 9—506 which deals with redemption of collateral; and

(e) subsection (1) of Section 9—507 which deals with the secured party's liability for failure to comply with this Part.

(4) If the security agreement covers both real and personal property, the secured party may proceed under this Part as to the personal property or he may proceed as to both the real and the personal property in accordance with his rights and remedies in respect of the real property in which case the provisions of this Part do not apply.

(5) When a secured party has reduced his claim to judgment the lien of any levy which may be made upon his collateral by virture of any execution based upon the judgment shall relate back to the date of the perfection of the security interest in such collateral. A judicial sale, pursuant to such execution, is a foreclosure of the security interest by judicial procedure within the meaning of this section, and the secured party may purchase at the sale and thereafter hold the collateral free of any other requirements of this Article. Amended in 1972.

§ 9—502. Collection Rights of Secured Party.

(1) When so agreed and in any event on default the secured party is entitled to notify an account debtor or the obligor on an instrument to make payment to him whether or not the assignor was theretofore making collections on the collateral, and also to take control of any proceeds to which he is entitled under Section 9—306.

(2) A secured party who by agreement is entitled to charge back uncollected collateral or otherwise to full or limited recourse against the debtor and who undertakes to collect from the account debtors or obligors must proceed in a commercially reasonable manner and may deduct his reasonable expenses of realization from the collections. If the security agreement secures an indebtedness, the secured party must account to the debtor for any surplus, and unless otherwise agreed, the debtor is liable for any deficiency. But, if the underlying transaction was a sale of accounts or chattel paper, the debtor is entitled to any surplus or is liable for any deficiency only if the security agreement so provides. Amended in 1972.

§ 9—503. Secured Party's Right to Take Possession After Default.

Unless otherwise agreed a secured party has on default the right to take possession of the collateral. In taking possession a secured party may proceed without judicial process if this can be done without breach of the peace or may proceed by action. If the security agreement so provides the secured party may require the debtor to assemble the collateral and make it available to the secured party at a place to be designated by the secured party which is reasonably convenient to both parties. Without removal a secured party may render equipment unusable, and may dispose of collateral on the debtor's premises under Section 9—504.

§ 9—504. Secured Party's Right to Dispose of Collateral After Default; Effect of Disposition.

(1) A secured party after default may sell, lease or otherwise dispose of any or all of the collateral in its then condition or following any commercially reasonable preparation or processing. Any sale of goods is subject to the Article on Sales (Article 2). The proceeds of disposition shall be applied in the order following to

(a) the reasonable expenses of retaking, holding, preparing for sale or lease, selling, leasing and the like and, to the extent provided for in the agreement and not prohibited by law, the reasonable attorneys' fees and legal expenses incurred by the secured party;

(b) the satisfaction of indebtedness secured by the security interest under which the disposition is made;

(c) the satisfaction of indebtedness secured by any subordinate security interest in the collateral if written notification of demand therefor is received before distribution of the proceeds is completed. If requested by the secured party, the holder of a subordinate security interest must seasonably furnish reasonable proof of his interest, and unless he does so, the secured party need not comply with his demand.

(2) If the security interest secures an indebtedness, the secured party must account to the debtor for any surplus, and, unless otherwise agreed, the debtor is liable for any deficiency. But if the underlying transaction was a sale of accounts or chattel paper, the debtor is entitled to any surplus or is liable for any deficiency only if the security agreement so provides.

(3) Disposition of the collateral may be by public or private proceedings and may be made by way of one

or more contracts. Sale or other disposition may be as
a unit or in parcels and at any time and place and on
any terms but every aspect of the disposition including the method, manner, time, place and terms must
be commercially reasonable. Unless collateral is perishable or threatens to decline speedily in value or is
of a type customarily sold on a recognized market,
reasonable notification of the time and place of any
public sale or reasonable notification of the time after
which any private sale or other intended disposition
is to be made shall be sent by the secured party to the
debtor, if he has not signed after default a statement
renouncing or modifying his right to notification of
sale. In the case of consumer goods no other notification need be sent. In other cases notification shall
be sent to any other secured party from whom the
secured party has received (before sending his notification to the debtor or before the debtor's renunciation
of his rights) written notice of a claim of an interest
in the collateral. The secured party may buy at any
public sale and if the collateral is of a type customarily
sold in a recognized market or is of a type which is
the subject of widely distributed standard price quotations he may buy at private sale.

(4) When collateral is disposed of by a secured party
after default, the disposition transfers to a purchaser
for value all of the debtor's rights therein, discharges
the security interest under which it is made and any
security interest or lien subordinate thereto. The purchaser takes free of all such rights and interests even
though the secured party fails to comply with the requirements of this Part or of any judicial proceedings

  (a) in the case of a public sale, if the purchaser has
  no knowledge of any defects in the sale and if he
  does not buy in collusion with the secured party,
  other bidders or the person conducting the sale; or

  (b) in any other case, if the purchaser acts in good
  faith.

(5) A person who is liable to a secured party under a
guaranty, indorsement, repurchase agreement or the
like and who receives a transfer of collateral from the
secured party or is subrogated to his rights has thereafter the rights and duties of the secured party. Such
a transfer of collateral is not a sale or disposition of
the collateral under this Article. Amended in 1972.

§ 9—505. Compulsory Disposition of Collateral; Acceptance of the Collateral as Discharge of Obligation.

(1) If the debtor has paid sixty per cent of the cash
price in the case of a purchase money security interest
in consumer goods or sixty per cent of the loan in the

case of another security interest in consumer goods,
and has not signed after default a statement renouncing or modifying his rights under this Part a secured
party who has taken possession of collateral must dispose of it under Section 9—504 and if he fails to do
so within ninety days after he takes possession the
debtor at his option may recover in conversion or under Section 9—507(1) on secured party's liability.

(2) In any other case involving consumer goods or any
other collateral a secured party in possession may, after
default, propose to retain the collateral in satisfaction
of the obligation. Written notice of such proposal shall
be sent to the debtor if he has not signed after default
a statement renouncing or modifying his rights under
this subsection. In the case of consumer goods no other
notice need be given. In other cases notice shall be
sent to any other secured party from whom the secured party has received (before sending his notice to
the debtor or before the debtor's renunciation of his
rights) written notice of a claim of an interest in the
collateral. If the secured party receives objection in
writing from a person entitled to receive notification
within twenty-one days after the notice was sent, the
secured party must dispose of the collateral under
Section 9—504. In the absence of such written objection the secured party may retain the collateral in satisfaction of the debtor's obligation. Amended in 1972.

§ 9—506. Debtor's Right to Redeem Collateral.

At any time before the secured party has disposed of
collateral or entered into a contract for its disposition
under Section 9—504 or before the obligation has been
discharged under Section 9—505(2) the debtor or any
other secured party may unless otherwise agreed in
writing after default redeem the collateral by tendering fulfillment of all obligations secured by the collateral as well as the expenses reasonably incurred by
the secured party in retaking, holding and preparing
the collateral for disposition, in arranging for the sale,
and to the extent provided in the agreement and not
prohibited by law, his reasonable attorneys' fees and
legal expenses.

§ 9—507. Secured Party's Liability for Failure to Comply With This Part.

(1) If it is established that the secured party is not
proceeding in accordance with the provisions of this
Part disposition may be ordered or restrained on appropriate terms and conditions. If the disposition has
occurred the debtor or any person entitled to notification or whose security interest has been made known
to the secured party prior to the disposition has a right
to recover from the secured party any loss caused by

a failure to comply with the provisions of this Part. If the collateral is consumer goods, the debtor has a right to recover in any event an amount not less than the credit service charge plus ten per cent of the principal amount of the debt or the time price differential plus 10 per cent of the cash price.

(2) The fact that a better price could have been obtained by a sale at a different time or in a different method from that selected by the secured party is not of itself sufficient to establish that the sale was not made in a commercially reasonable manner. If the secured party either sells the collateral in the usual manner in any recognized market therefor or if he sells at the price current in such market at the time of his sale or if he has otherwise sold in conformity with reasonable commercial practices among dealers in the type of property sold he has sold in a commercially reasonable manner. The principles stated in the two preceding sentences with respect to sales also apply as may be appropriate to other types of disposition. A disposition which has been approved in any judicial proceeding or by any bona fide creditors' committee or representative of creditors shall conclusively be deemed to be commercially reasonable, but this sentence does not indicate that any such approval must be obtained in any case nor does it indicate that any disposition not so approved is not commercially reasonable.

Article 10
EFFECTIVE DATE AND REPEALER

10—101. **Effective Date.**

This Act shall become effective at midnight on December 31st following its enactment. It applies to transactions entered into and events occurring after that date.

§ 10—102. **Specific Repealer; Provision for Transition.**

(1) The following acts and all other acts and parts of acts inconsistent herewith are hereby repealed:
(Here should follow the acts to be specifically repealed including the following:
    Uniform Negotiable Instruments Act
    Uniform Warehouse Receipts Act
    Uniform Sales Act
    Uniform Bills of Lading Act
    Uniform Stock Transfer Act
    Uniform Conditional Sales Act

    Uniform Trust Receipts Act
      Alsc any acts regulating:
    Bank collections
    Bulk sales
    Chattel mortgages
    Conditional sales
    Factor's lien acts
    Farm storage of grain and similar acts
    Assignment of accounts receivable)

(2) Transactions validly entered into before the effective date specified in Section 10—101 and the rights, duties and interests flowing from them remain valid thereafter and may be terminated, completed, consummated or enforced as required or permitted by any statute or other law amended or repealed by this Act as though such repeal or amendment had not occurred.
Note: *Subsection (1) should be separately prepared for each state. The foregoing is a list of statutes to be checked.*

§ 10—103. **General Repealer.**

Except as provided in the following section, all acts and parts of acts inconsistent with this Act are hereby repealed.

§ 10—104. **Laws Not Repealed.**

(1) The Article on Documents of Title (Article 7) does not repeal or modify any laws prescribing the form or contents of documents of title or the services or facilities to be afforded by bailees, or otherwise regulating bailees' businesses in respects not specifically dealt with herein; but the fact that such laws are violated does not affect the status of a document of title which otherwise complies with the definition of a document of title (Section 1—201).

[(2) This Act does not repeal . . . .*, cited as the Uniform Act for the Simplification of Fiduciary Security Transfers, and if in any respect there is any inconsistency between that Act and the Article of this Act on investment securities (Article 8) the provisions of the former Act shall control.]
Note: *At * in subsection (2) insert the statutory reference to the Uniform Act for the Simplification of Fiduciary Security Transfers if such Act has previously been enacted. If it has not been enacted, omit subsection (2).*

Article 11
(REPORTERS' DRAFT) EFFECTIVE DATE AND TRANSITION PROVISIONS

This material has been numbered Article 11 to distinguish it from Article 10, the transition provision of the 1962 Code, which may still remain in effect in some states to cover transition problems from pre-Code law to the original Uniform Commercial Code. Adaptation may be necessary in particular states. The terms "[old Code]" and "[new Code]" and "[old U.C.C.]" and "[new U.C.C.]" are used herein, and should be suitably changed in each state.

Note: *This draft was prepared by the Reporters and has not been passed upon by the Review Committee, the Permanent Editorial Board, the American Law Institute, or the National Conference of Commissioners on Uniform State Laws. It is submitted as a working draft which may be adapted as appropriate in each state.*

§ 11—101. **Effective Date.**

This Act shall become effective at 12:01 A.M. on _____, 19__.

§ 11—102. **Preservation of Old Transition Provision.**

The provisions of [here insert reference to the original transition provision in the particular state] shall continue to apply to [the new U.C.C.] and for this purpose the [old U.C.C. and new U.C.C.] shall be considered one continuous statute.

§ 11—103. **Transition to [New Code]—General Rule.**

Transactions validly entered into after [effective date of old U.C.C.] and before [effective date of new U.C.C.], and which were subject to the provisions of [old U.C.C.] and which would be subject to this Act as amended if they had been entered into after the effective date of [new U.C.C.] and the rights, duties and interests flowing from such transactions remain valid after the latter date and may be terminated, completed, consummated or enforced as required or permitted by the [new U.C.C.]. Security interests arising out of such transactions which are perfected when [new U.C.C.] becomes effective shall remain perfected until they lapse as provided in [new U.C.C.], and may be continued as permitted by [new U.C.C.], except as stated in Section 11—105.

§ 11—104. **Transition Provision on Change of Requirement of Filing.**

A security interest for the perfection of which filing or the taking of possession was required under [old U.C.C.] and which attached prior to the effective date of [new U.C.C.] but was not perfected shall be deemed perfected on the effective date of [new U.C.C.] if [new U.C.C.] permits perfection without filing or authorizes filing in the office or offices where a prior ineffective filing was made.

§ 11—105. **Transition Provision on Change of Place of Filing.**

(1) A financing statement or continuation statement filed prior to [effective date of new U.C.C.] which shall not have lapsed prior to [the effective date of new U.C.C.] shall remain effective for the period provided in the [old Code], but not less than five years after the filing.

(2) With respect to any collateral acquired by the debtor subsequent to the effective date of [new U.C.C.], any effective financing statement or continuation statement described in this section shall apply only if the filing or filings are in the office or offices that would be appropriate to perfect the security interests in the new collateral under [new U.C.C.].

(3) The effectiveness of any financing statement or continuation statement filed prior to [effective date of new U.C.C.] may be continued by a continuation statement as permitted by [new U.C.C.], except that if [new U.C.C.] requires a filing in an office where there was no previous financing statement, a new financing statement conforming to Section 11—106 shall be filed in that office.

(4) If the record of a mortgage of real estate would have been effective as a fixture filing of goods described therein if [new U.C.C.] had been in effect on the date of recording the mortgage, the mortgage shall be deemed effective as a fixture filing as to such goods under subsection (6) of Section 9—402 of the [new U.C.C.] on the effective date of [new U.C.C.].

§ 11—106. **Required Refilings.**

(1) If a security interest is perfected or has priority when this Act takes effect as to all persons or as to certain persons without any filing or recording, and if the filing of a financing statement would be required for the perfection or priority of the security interest against those persons under [new U.C.C.], the perfection and priority rights of the security interest continue until 3 years after the effective date of [new U.C.C.]. The perfection will then lapse unless a financing statement is filed as provided in subsection (4) or unless the security interest is perfected otherwise than by filing.

(2) If a security interest is perfected when [new U.C.C.] takes effect under a law other than [U.C.C.] which requires no further filing, refiling or recording to continue its perfection, perfection continues until and will lapse 3 years after [new U.C.C.] takes effect, unless a

financing statement is filed as provided in subsection (4) or unless the security interest is perfected otherwise than by filing, or unless under subsection (3) of Section 9—302 the other law continues to govern filing.

(3) If a security interest is perfected by a filing, refiling or recording under a law repealed by this Act which required further filing, refiling or recording to continue its perfection, perfection continues and will lapse on the date provided by the law so repealed for such further filing, refiling or recording unless a financing statement is filed as provided in subsection (4) or unless the security interest is perfected otherwise than by filing.

(4) A financing statement may be filed within six months before the perfection of a security interest would otherwise lapse. Any such financing statement may be signed by either the debtor or the secured party. It must identify the security agreement, statement or notice (however denominated in any statute or other law repealed or modified by this Act), state the office where and the date when the last filing, refiling or recording, if any, was made with respect thereto, and the filing number, if any, or book and page, if any, of recording and further state that the security agreement, statement or notice, however denominated, in another filing office under the [U.C.C.] or under any statute or other law repealed or modified by this Act is still effective. Section 9—401 and Section 9—103 determine the proper place to file such a financing statement. Except as specified in this subsection, the provisions of Section 9—403(3) for continuation statements apply to such a financing statement.

§ 11—107. **Transition Provisions as to Priorities.**

Except as otherwise provided in [Article 11], [old U.C.C.] shall apply to any questions of priority if the positions of the parties were fixed prior to the effective date of [new U.C.C.]. In other cases questions of priority shall be determined by [new U.C.C.].

§ 11—108. **Presumption that Rule of Law Continues Unchanged.**

Unless a change in law has clearly been made, the provisions of [new U.C.C.] shall be deemed declaratory of the meaning of the [old U.C.C.].

APPENDIX D

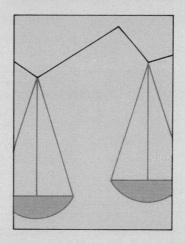

THE UNIFORM PARTNERSHIP ACT

(Adopted in 48 States, all except Georgia and Louisiana; the District of Columbia, the Virgin Islands, and Guam. The adoptions by Alabama and Nebraska do not follow the official text in every respect, but are substantially similar, with local variations.)

The Act consists of 7 Parts as follows:

I. Preliminary Provisions

II. Nature of Partnership

III. Relations of Partners to Persons Dealing with the Partnership

IV. Relations of Partners to One Another

V. Property Rights of a Partner

VI. Dissolution and Winding Up

VII. Miscellaneous Provisions

An Act to make uniform the Law of Partnerships

Be it enacted, etc.:

Part I Preliminary Provisions

Sec. 1. **Name of Act**

This act may be cited as Uniform Partnership Act.

Sec. 2. **Definition of Terms**

In this act, "Court" includes every court and judge having jurisdiction in the case.

"Business" includes every trade, occupation, or profession.

"Person" includes individuals, partnerships, corporations, and other associations.

"Bankrupt" includes bankrupt under the Federal Bankruptcy Act or insolvent under any state insolvent act.

"Conveyance" includes every assignment, lease, mortgage, or encumbrance.

"Real property" includes land and any interest or estate in land.

Sec. 3. **Interpretation of Knowledge and Notice**

(1) A person has "knowledge" of a fact within the meaning of this act not only when he has actual knowledge thereof, but also when he has knowledge of such other facts as in the circumstances shows bad faith.

(2) A person has "notice" of a fact within the meaning of this act when the person who claims the benefit of the notice:

(a) States the fact to such person, or

(b) Delivers through the mail, or by other means of communication, a written statement of the fact to such person or to a proper person at his place of business or residence.

Sec. 4. **Rules of Construction**

(1) The rule that statutes in derogation of the common law are to be strictly construed shall have no application to this act.

(2) The law of estoppel shall apply under this act.

(3) The law of agency shall apply under this act.

(4) This act shall be so interpreted and construed as to effect its general purpose to make uniform the law of those states which enact it.

(5) This act shall not be construed so as to impair the obligations of any contract existing when the act goes into effect, nor to affect any action or proceedings begun or right accrued before this act takes effect.

Sec. 5. **Rules for Cases Not Provided for in this Act.**

In any case not provided for in this act the rules of law and equity, including the law merchant, shall govern.

Part II Nature of Partnership

Sec. 6. **Partnership Defined**

(1) A partnership is an association of two or more persons to carry on as co-owners a business for profit.

(2) But any association formed under any other statute of this state, or any statute adopted by authority, other than the authority of this state, is not a partnership under this act, unless such association would have been a partnership in this state prior to the adoption of this act; but this act shall apply to limited partnerships except in so far as the statutes relating to such partnerships are inconsistent herewith.

Sec. 7. **Rules for Determining the Existence of a Partnership**

In determining whether a partnership exists, these rules shall apply:

(1) Except as provided by Section 16 persons who are not partners as to each other are not partners as to third persons.

(2) Joint tenancy, tenancy in common, tenancy by the entireties, joint property, common property, or part ownership does not of itself establish a partnership,

whether such co-owners do or do not share any profits made by the use of the property.

(3) The sharing of gross returns does not of itself establish a partnership, whether or not the persons sharing them have a joint or common right or interest in any property from which the returns are derived.

(4) The receipt by a person of a share of the profits of a business is prima facie evidence that he is a partner in the business, but no such inference shall be drawn if such profits were received in payment:

(a) As a debt by installments or otherwise,

(b) As wages of an employee or rent to a landlord,

(c) As an annuity to a widow or representative of a deceased partner,

(d) As interest on a loan, though the amount of payment vary with the profits of the business.

(e) As the consideration for the sale of a good-will of a business or other property by installments or otherwise.

Sec. 8. **Partnership Property**

(1) All property originally brought into the partnership stock or subsequently acquired by purchase or otherwise, on account of the partnership, is partnership property.

(2) Unless the contrary intention appears, property acquired with partnership funds is partnership property.

(3) Any estate in real property may be acquired in the partnership name. Title so acquired can be conveyed only in the partnership name.

(4) A conveyance to a partnership in the partnership name, though without words of inheritance, passes the entire estate of the grantor unless a contrary intent appears.

Part III Relations of Partners to Persons Dealing with the Partnership

Sec. 9. **Partner Agent of Partnership as to Partnership Business**

(1) Every partner is an agent of the partnership for the purpose of its business, and the act of every partner, including the execution in the partnership name of any instrument, for apparently carrying on in the usual way the business of the partnership of which he is a member binds the partnership, unless the partner so acting has in fact no authority to act for the partnership in the particular matter, and the person with whom

he is dealing has knowledge of the fact that he has no such authority.

(2) An act of a partner which is not apparently for the carrying on of the business of the partnership in the usual way does not bind the partnership unless authorized by the other partners.

(3) Unless authorized by the other partners or unless they have abandoned the business, one or more but less than all the partners have no authority to:

(a) Assign the partnership property in trust for creditors or on the assignee's promise to pay the debts of the partnership,

(b) Dispose of the good-will of the business,

(c) Do any other act which would make it impossible to carry on the ordinary business of a partnership,

(d) Confess a judgment,

(e) Submit a partnership claim or liability to arbitration or reference.

(4) No act of a partner in contravention of a restriction on authority shall bind the partnership to persons having knowledge of the restriction.

Sec. 10. **Conveyance of Real Property of the Partnership**

(1) Where title to real property is in the partnership name, any partner may convey title to such property by a conveyance executed in the partnership name; but the partnership may recover such property unless the partner's act binds the partnership under the provisions of paragraph (1) of section 9 or unless such property has been conveyed by the grantee or a person claiming through such grantee to a holder for value without knowledge that the partner, in making the conveyance, has exceeded his authority.

(2) Where title to real property is in the name of the partnership, a conveyance executed by a partner, in his own name, passes the equitable interest of the partnership, provided the act is one within the authority of the partner under the provisions of paragraph (1) of section 9.

(3) Where title to real property is in the name of one or more but not all the partners, and the record does not disclose the right of the partnership, the partners in whose name the title stands may convey title to such property, but the partnership may recover such property if the partners' act does not bind the partnership under the provisions of paragraph (1) of section 9, unless the purchaser or his assignee, is a holder for value, without knowledge.

(4) Where the title to real property is in the name of one or more or all the partners, or in a third person in trust for the partnership, a conveyance executed by a partner in the partnership name, or in his own name, passes the equitable interest of the partnership, provided the act is one within the authority of the partner under the provisions of paragraph (1) of section 9.

(5) Where the title to real property is in the names of all the partners a conveyance executed by all the partners passes all their rights in such property.

Sec. 11. Partnership Bound by Admission of Partner

An admission or representation made by any partner concerning partnership affairs within the scope of his authority as conferred by this act is evidence against the partnership.

Sec. 12. Partnership Charged with Knowledge of or Notice to Partner

Notice to any partner of any matter relating to partnership affairs, and the knowledge of the partner acting in the particular matter, acquired while a partner or then present to his mind, and the knowledge of any other partner who reasonably could and should have communicated it to the acting partner, operate as notice to or knowledge of the partnership, except in the case of a fraud on the partnership committed by or with the consent of that partner.

Sec. 13. Partnership Bound by Partner's Wrongful Act

Where, by any wrongful act or omission of any partner acting in the ordinary course of the business of the partnership or with the authority of his co-partners, loss or injury is caused to any person, not being a partner in the partnership, or any penalty is incurred, the partnership is liable therefor to the same extent as the partner so acting or omitting to act.

Sec. 14. Partnership Bound by Partner's Breach of Trust

The partnership is bound to make good the loss:

(a) Where one partner acting within the scope of his apparent authority receives money or property of a third person and misapplies it; and

(b) Where the partnership in the course of its business receives money or property of a third person and the money or property so received is misapplied by any partner while it is in the custody of the partnership.

Sec. 15. Nature of Partner's Liability

All partners are liable

(a) Jointly and severally for everything chargeable to the partnership under sections 13 and 14.

(b) Jointly for all other debts and obligations of the partnership; but any partner may enter into a separate obligation to perform a partnership contract.

Sec. 16. Partner by Estoppel

(1) When a person, by words spoken or written or by conduct, represents himself, or consents to another representing him to any one, as a partner in an existing partnership or with one or more persons not actual partners, he is liable to any such person to whom such representation has been made, who has, on the faith of such representation, given credit to the actual or apparent partnership, and if he has made such representation or consented to its being made in a public manner he is liable to such person, whether the representation has or has not been made or communicated to such person so giving credit by or with the knowledge of the apparent partner making the representation or consenting to its being made.

> (a) When a partnership liability results, he is liable as though he were an actual member of the partnership.

> (b) When no partnership liability results, he is liable jointly with the other persons, if any, so consenting to the contract or representation as to incur liability, otherwise separately.

(2) When a person has been thus represented to be a partner in an existing partnership, or with one or more persons not actual partners, he is an agent of the persons consenting to such representation to bind them to the same extent and in the same manner as though he were a partner in fact, with respect to persons who rely upon the representation. Where all the members of the existing partnership consent to the representation, a partnership act or obligation results; but in all other cases it is the joint act or obligation of the person acting and the persons consenting to the representation.

Sec. 17. Liability of Incoming Partner

A person admitted as a partner into an existing partnership is liable for all the obligations of the partnership arising before his admission as though he had been a partner when such obligations were incurred, except that this liability shall be satisfied only out of partnership property.

Part IV Relations of Partners to One Another

Sec. 18. Rules Determining Rights and Duties of Partners

The rights and duties of the partners in relation to the partnership shall be determined, subject to any agreement between them, by the following rules:

(a) Each partner shall be repaid his contributions, whether by way of capital or advances to the partnership property and share equally in the profits and surplus remaining after all liabilities, including those to partners, are satisfied; and must contribute towards the losses, whether of capital or otherwise, sustained by the partnership according to his share in the profits.

(b) The partnership must indemnify every partner in respect of payments made and personal liabilities reasonably incurred by him in the ordinary and proper conduct of its business, or for the preservation of its business or property.

(c) A partner, who in aid of the partnership makes any payment or advance beyond the amount of capital which he agreed to contribute, shall be paid interest from the date of the payment or advance.

(d) A partner shall receive interest on the capital contributed by him only from the date when repayment should be made.

(e) All partners have equal rights in the management and conduct of the partnership business.

(f) No partner is entitled to remuneration for acting in the partnership business, except that a surviving partner is entitled to reasonable compensation for his services in winding up the partnership affairs.

(g) No person can become a member of a partnership without the consent of all the partners.

(h) Any difference arising as to ordinary matters connected with the partnership business may be decided by a majority of the partners; but no act in contravention of any agreement between the partners may be done rightfully without the consent of all the partners.

Sec. 19. Partnership Books

The partnership books shall be kept, subject to any agreement between the partners, at the principal place of business of the partnership, and every partner shall at all times have access to and may inspect and copy any of them.

Sec. 20. Duty of Partners to Render Information

Partners shall render on demand true and full information of all things affecting the partnership to any partner or the legal representative of any deceased partner or partner under legal disability.

Sec. 21. Partner Accountable as a Fiduciary

(1) Every partner must account to the partnership for any benefit, and hold as trustee for it any profits derived by him without the consent of the other partners from any transaction connected with the formation, conduct, or liquidation of the partnership or from any use by him of its property.

(2) This section applies also to the representatives of a deceased partner engaged in the liquidation of the affairs of the partnership as the personal representatives of the last surviving partner.

Sec. 22. Right to an Account

Any partner shall have the right to a formal account as to partnership affairs:

(a) If he is wrongfully excluded from the partnership business or possession of its property by his co-partners,

(b) If the right exists under the terms of any agreement,

(c) As provided by section 21,

(d) Whenever other circumstances render it just and reasonable.

Sec. 23. Continuation of Partnership Beyond Fixed Term

(1) When a partnership for a fixed term or particular undertaking is continued after the termination of such term or particular undertaking without any express agreement, the rights and duties of the partners remain the same as they were at such termination, so far as is consistent with a partnership at will.

(2) A continuation of the business by the partners or such of them as habitually acted therein during the term, without any settlement or liquidation of the partnership affairs, is prima facie evidence of a continuation of the partnership.

Part V Property Rights of a Partner

Sec. 24. Extent of Property Rights of a Partner

The property rights of a partner are (1) his rights in specific partnership property, (2) his interest in the partnership, and (3) his right to participate in the management.

Sec. 25. **Nature of a Partner's Right in Specific Partnership Property**

(1) A partner is co-owner with his partners of specific partnership property holding as a tenant in partnership.

(2) The incidents of this tenancy are such that:

(a) A partner, subject to the provisions of this act and to any agreement between the partners, has an equal right with his partners to possess specific partnership property for partnership purposes; but he has no right to possess such property for any other purpose without the consent of his partners.

(b) A partner's right in specific partnership property is not assignable except in connection with the assignment of rights of all the partners in the same property.

(c) A partner's right in specific partnership property is not subject to attachment or execution, except on a claim against the partnership. When partnership property is attached for a partnership debt the partners, or any of them, or the representatives of a deceased partner, cannot claim any right under the homestead or exemption laws.

(d) On the death of a partner his right in specific partnership property vests in the surviving partner or partners, except where the deceased was the last surviving partner, when his right in such property vests in his legal representative. Such surviving partner or partners, or the legal representative of the last surviving partner, has no right to possess the partnership property for any but a partnership purpose.

(e) A partner's right in specific partnership property is not subject to dower, curtesy, or allowances to widows, heirs, or next of kin.

Sec. 26. **Nature of Partner's Interest in the Partnership**

A partner's interest in the partnership is his share of the profits and surplus, and the same is personal property.

Sec. 27. **Assignment of Partner's Interest**

(1) A conveyance by a partner of his interest in the partnership does not of itself dissolve the partnership, nor, as against the other partners in the absence of agreement, entitle the assignee, during the continuance of the partnership, to interfere in the management or administration of the partnership business or affairs, or to require any information or account of partnership transactions, or to inspect the partnership books; but it merely entitles the assignee to receive in accordance with his contract the profits to which the assigning partner would otherwise be entitled.

(2) In case of a dissolution of the partnership, the assignee is entitled to receive his assignor's interest and may require an account from the date only of the last account agreed to by all the partners.

Sec. 28. **Partner's Interest Subject to Charging Order**

(1) On due application to a competent court by any judgment creditor of a partner, the court which entered the judgment, order, or decree, or any other court, may charge the interest of the debtor partner with payment of the unsatisfied amount of such judgment debt with interest thereon; and may then or later appoint a receiver of his share of the profits, and of any other money due or to fall due to him in respect of the partnership, and make all other orders, directions, accounts and inquiries which the debtor partner might have made, or which the circumstances of the case may require.

(2) The interest charged may be redeemed at any time before foreclosure, or in case of a sale being directed by the court may be purchased without thereby causing a dissolution:

(a) With separate property, by any one or more of the partners, or

(b) With partnership property, by any one or more of the partners with the consent of all the partners whose interests are not so charged or sold.

(3) Nothing in this act shall be held to deprive a partner of his right, if any, under the exemption laws, as regards his interest in the partnership.

Part VI Dissolution and Winding up

Sec. 29. **Dissolution Defined**

The dissolution of a partnership is the change in the relation of the partners caused by any partner ceasing to be associated in the carrying on as distinguished from the winding up of the business.

Sec. 30. **Partnership not Terminated by Dissolution**

On dissolution the partnership is not terminated, but continues until the winding up of partnership affairs is completed.

Sec. 31. **Causes of Dissolution**

Dissolution is caused:

(1) Without violation of the agreement between the partners,